THE HENRY L. STIMSON LECTURES SERIES

OTHER BOOKS BY THE AUTHOR

Dealing with the Devil: East Germany, Détente, and Ostpolitik, 1969–1973

German Military Reform and European Security

1989: The Struggle to Create Post–Cold War Europe

The Collapse: The Accidental Opening of the Berlin Wall

German Reunification: A Multinational History, with Frédéric Bozo
    and Andreas Rödder

NOT ONE INCH

America, Russia, and the Making of
Post–Cold War Stalemate

M. E. SAROTTE

Yale

UNIVERSITY PRESS

New Haven & London

The Henry L. Stimson Lectures at the Whitney and Betty
MacMillan Center for International and Area Studies at Yale

Published with assistance from the Kingsley
Trust Association Publication Fund established
by the Scroll and Key Society of Yale College.

Yale University Press books may be purchased in quantity for
educational, business, or promotional use. For information,
please e-mail sales.press@yale.edu (U.S. office) or sales@yaleup
.co.uk (U.K. office).

Set in Janson by Westchester Publishing Services.
Printed in the United States of America.

Library of Congress Control Number: 2021938889

ISBN 978-0-300-25993-3 (hardcover: alk. paper)

A catalogue record for this book is available from the
British Library.

ἔννους τὰ καινὰ τοῖς πάλαι τεκμαίρεται

a man of sense judges the new events by the past

—SOPHOCLES, *Oedipus Rex*, 916

Contents

Note on Names and Places

THIS BOOK'S RELIANCE ON EVIDENCE in languages other than English creates challenges in spelling proper nouns in the main text. In the interest of producing a clearly written English-language account, I have adopted anglicized versions of frequently cited place names, such as *Pristina* for *Prishtinë* or *Priština*, and *Visegrad* for *Visegrád*. I also refer to *East Germany* and *West Germany*, although these exact names are relatively infrequent in the original German-language sources from the Cold War. Those sources generally refer to the eastern half of the divided country by its formal name, the German Democratic Republic or GDR, and to the western half as the Federal Republic of Germany or FRG. I also use *East Berlin* for the capital of East Germany, although the ruling regime generally called its half of the divided city *Berlin*. A further complication arises from the fact that, after unification on October 3, 1990, newly reunited Germany kept the former West German name, so references to the FRG after that date describe the united country. With regard to individuals, I have tried to provide names in the original spelling where feasible (that is, if there are no common English equivalents and the original is not in a different alphabet).

Contests over borders create further complications. After Ukraine's December 1, 1991 vote to break away from the Soviet Union, this book switches the spelling of the capital city from *Kiev* to the version preferred by the newly independent state, *Kyiv*. Another contested issue was the status of the three Baltic countries during the Soviet era; neither they nor the United States (among other countries) recognized their incorporation into the USSR. Moscow dominated the Baltics nonetheless, and they were commonly shown as part of the Soviet Union on maps. Bearing the non-recognition in mind, this book follows the convention of showing the Baltics as part of the USSR after their incorporation. Finally, due to the scale of the maps as printed and the resulting small size of some locations—such as Andorra, the Vatican, and some islands—markings on some of the smallest places and borders may vary slightly or be omitted; such minor variations are for visual clarity of the map as a whole and do not carry geopolitical implications.

Abbreviations

ABM	Anti-Ballistic Missile (Treaty)
ACTORDs	Activation Orders
BALTBAT	Baltic Battalion
CDU	Christian Democratic Union (German political party)
CEE	Central and Eastern Europe (also, Central and Eastern European)
CFE	Conventional Forces in Europe (Treaty)
CIA	Central Intelligence Agency (US)
CIS	Commonwealth of Independent States (association of post-Soviet states)
CJTF	Combined Joint Task Force
CNN	Cable News Network
CSCE	Conference on Security and Cooperation in Europe
CTBT	Comprehensive Test Ban Treaty
CTR	Cooperative Threat Reduction (Program, US)
DC	District of Columbia
DM	Deutsche mark, the former currency of Germany
DoD	Department of Defense (US)
EAPC	Euro-Atlantic Partnership Council
EC	European Community
EU	European Union
FDP	Free Democratic Party (German party, also known as the Liberals)
FOTL	Follow-On to Lance (Missiles)

FRG	Federal Republic of Germany, also known as West Germany before October 3, 1990
FSB	Federal Security Service (Russian domestic intelligence service, partial successor to KGB)
FSU	Former Soviet Union
FYROM	Former Yugoslav Republic of Macedonia
G7	Group of 7
G8	Group of 8
GDR	German Democratic Republic, also known as East Germany
GRU	Main Intelligence Directorate (Russian, military intelligence agency of the General Staff of the Armed Forces)
IAEA	International Atomic Energy Association
ICBM	Intercontinental ballistic missile
IFOR	Implementation Force
IGC	Intergovernmental Conference (EC)
IMF	International Monetary Fund
INF	Intermediate-Range Nuclear Forces (Treaty)
JCS	Joint Chiefs of Staff (US)
KFOR	Kosovo Force
KGB	Committee for State Security, Russian initials for (Soviet Union)
MAP	Membership Action Plan (NATO)
MIRVs	Multiple independent reentry vehicle(s)
NAC	North Atlantic Council (NATO)
NACC	North Atlantic Cooperation Council (NATO)
NATO	North Atlantic Treaty Organization
NIC	National Intelligence Council (US)
NIS	Newly Independent States (US designation for post-Soviet states other than the Baltics)
NPT	Treaty on the Non-Proliferation of Nuclear Weapons
NRA	National Rifle Association
NSC	National Security Council (US)
OECD	Organisation for Economic Co-operation and Development
OSCE	Organization for Security and Co-operation in Europe

OSD	Office of the Secretary of Defense (US)
PfP	Partnership for Peace
PJC	Permanent Joint Council (NATO)
RAND	US think tank
SACEUR	Supreme Allied Commander Europe (NATO)
SED	Socialist Unity Party, German initials for (East German)
SFOR	Stabilization Force
SHAPE	Supreme Headquarters Allied Powers Europe
SNF	Short-Range Nuclear Forces
SNOG	Senate NATO Observer Group (US)
SPD	Social Democratic Party of Germany, German initials for
START	Strategic Arms Reduction Treaty
SVR	Foreign Intelligence Service (Russian, partial successor to KGB)
TASS	Soviet news agency, Russian initials for
THAAD	Theater High Altitude Area Defense (also Terminal High Altitude Area Defense)
UK	United Kingdom of Great Britain and Northern Ireland
UN	United Nations
UNPROFOR	UN Protection Force
UNSC	UN Security Council
US	United States
USG	United States government
USSR	Union of Soviet Socialist Republics, also known as the Soviet Union
WEU	Western European Union
WTO	World Trade Organization

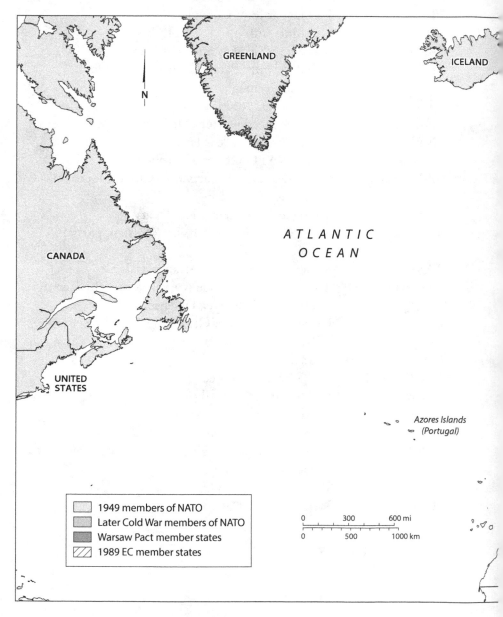

NATO and the Warsaw Pact in 1989.

SWEDEN

FINLAND

Faroe Islands
(Denmark)

NORWAY

Helsinki

Leningrad

UNITED
KINGDOM

DENMARK

BALTIC
SEA

Moscow

NETHERLANDS

BELGIUM

SOVIET UNION

East
Berlin

London

POLAND

IRELAND

EAST
GERMANY

Warsaw

Bonn

Kiev

LUXEMBOURG

Paris

WEST
GERMANY

Prague

CZECHOSLOVAKIA

SWITZERLAND

AUSTRIA

Budapest

Stavropol

FRANCE

HUNGARY

ITALY

ROMANIA

Arkhyz

YUGOSLAVIA

BULGARIA

BLACK SEA

PORTUGAL

SPAIN

ALBANIA

GREECE

TURKEY

MOROCCO

TUNISIA

MEDITERRANEAN SEA

SYRIA

IRAQ

ALGERIA

LIBYA

EGYPT

Introduction

Foreclosing Options

It is the hallmark of any deep truth that its negation is also a
deep truth.

—MAX DELBRÜCK

NOT ONE INCH. THE FIGHT over Europe's future beyond the Cold War
entered its decisive phase with these words, spoken in February 1990 by
the American secretary of state, James Baker, to the leader of the Soviet
Union, Mikhail Gorbachev. The Berlin Wall's collapse on November 9,
1989 had by then gravely weakened Moscow's grip on Central Europe.
But thanks to the Soviet victory over the Nazis in World War II, decades later Moscow still had hundreds of thousands of troops in East
Germany and the legal right to keep them there. To convince Gorbachev
to relinquish this military and legal might, Baker uttered the words as a
hypothetical bargain: what if you let your part of Germany go, and we
agree that NATO will "not shift one inch eastward from its present
position?"[1]

A controversy erupted over this exchange almost immediately, at first
behind closed doors and then publicly; but more important was the decade to follow, when these three words took on far-reaching new meanings. Gorbachev did let his part of Germany go, but along the way
Washington rethought its options, not least after the Soviet Union's collapse in December 1991. The United States realized it could not only win

I

big, but win bigger. Not one inch of territory need be off-limits to NATO. Washington could lead the alliance in opening a path for large numbers of eager new members to join. In the 1990s it did just that, resulting by March 12, 1999 in enlargement across Central and Eastern Europe and to the Polish-Russian border. But on December 31 of that year, Vladimir Putin rose to the top in Moscow. As NATO kept expanding, he ultimately decided to use violence in an effort to ensure that not one inch more of territory would join. The game of moving by inches resulted in a stalemate.

Between the fall of the Wall and the rise of Putin, animosity between Moscow and Washington over NATO's future became central to the making of a post–Cold War political order that looked much like its Cold War predecessor—and to the unmaking of hopes for cooperation from Vancouver to Vladivostok. To show how and why, this book examines the conflict between Russia and America against the backdrop of the sprawling, unpredictable landscape of the 1990s. That decade witnessed the astonishing overnight collapse of an empire, yielding a host of new Eurasian states; produced visionary leaders, some rising from prisons to presidencies, earning Nobel Prizes and global admiration; and redefined the realm of the possible for democratization, disarmament, market economies, and the tenets of liberal international order—but it also opened the door to new expressions of authoritarianism, de-democratization, and ethnic cleansing.[2]

Telling the unruly history of the nineties as a narrative is hard but necessary. Without a story to follow, the odds of getting from the beginning to the end of the list of actors, concepts, and locales approaches zero. This book uses the fight over NATO expansion as its through line. It tells the story not of the alliance itself but of the strategic choices that American and Russian leaders made during their decade-long conflict over the start of its enlargement to Central and Eastern Europe, and of the cumulative weight of those choices on today's world. The book begins with a focus on the 1989 contest over the future of divided Germany—which, for Washington, swiftly turned into a struggle to preserve the Atlantic Alliance. Then, widening its field of view, the book examines how American success produced opportunities for the courageous leaders of new European democracies, but also challenges for the West's relationship with former Soviet republics—most notably for Western efforts to cure, as one American defense secretary memorably put it, their nuclear hangover. Widening still more, the book shows how the way expansion was implemented brought a loss of options for twenty-first-century transatlantic relations.[3]

Throughout, the book asks how and why US presidents George H. W. Bush and Bill Clinton—together with their European contemporaries Tony Blair, Jacques Chirac, Václav Havel, Helmut Kohl, John Major, François Mitterrand, Gerhard Schröder, Margaret Thatcher, and Lech Wałęsa, plus Baltic leaders and NATO secretaries general Manfred Wörner and Javier Solana—launched the enlargement that eventually took the alliance to thirty nations. This accomplishment represented a major success for American strategists. It saved many (though not all) of the new post–Cold War democracies from life in a security gray zone between East and West. With Washington's help, over 100 million Central and Eastern Europeans enjoyed well-deserved success in their efforts to become NATO allies. And, as it enlarged, the alliance helped to quell bloody conflicts in the Balkans.

Today, NATO stretches from North America, Iceland, and Greenland to the United Kingdom, Europe, and the Baltics, covering nearly a billion people. Its members all possess the so-called Article 5 guarantee, a promise rooted in the alliance's founding treaty: "an armed attack against one or more of them . . . shall be considered an attack against them all." Since gaining that guarantee, the new members of the alliance have indeed remained free from large-scale armed attacks, even as fighting began across some former Soviet borders. American military might and its deterrent power remain the cornerstone of the alliance's strength.[4]

Yet success came at a price. It is no small thing to guarantee the security of a billion people. In the 1990s, two American presidents were so focused on achieving the eastward extension of Article 5 that they did not sufficiently consider the consequences of how they achieved that goal. As President Bush said in response to the idea that Washington might compromise with Moscow over NATO's future, "to hell with that." President Clinton was certain that Russia could be "bought off." Along the way, a promising alternative mode of enlargement, in the form of a partnership that would have avoided drawing a new line across Europe, fell to hard-line opposition.[5] This tougher attitude achieved results, but it obscured options that might have sustained cooperation, decreased chances of US-Russian conflict reoccurring, and served Washington's interests better in the longer term.

Put differently, the expansion of NATO was a justifiable response to the challenges of the 1990s and to the entreaties of new Central and Eastern European democracies. The problem was *how* it happened. The fall of the Wall in 1989 had briefly created the potential for a newly cooperative post–Cold War order. But a decade later, the border between NATO and non-NATO Europe remained a clearly demarcated front line, Ukraine and other post-Soviet states languished in a gray zone, nuclear competition was renewing, and early hopes for cooperation had waned—and the manner of enlargement had contributed to that outcome.

Perhaps it was not surprising that the outcome would be contentious, given that, throughout the 1990s, American leaders had to struggle with the tension between two priorities. Either they could enable the region of Central and Eastern Europe writ large—including post-Soviet states such as the Baltics and Ukraine—to choose its own destiny at long last, regardless of the impact on Moscow; or they could promote cooperation with Russia's fragile new democracy, particularly in the interest of nuclear disarmament.[6] The question for Washington was figuring out which of these goals should take precedence. The correct answer was both.

As the Nobel Prize–winning scientist Max Delbrück writes, the negation of any simple, correct statement is a false statement. But "it is the hallmark of any deep truth that its negation is also a deep truth": light is a particle; light is a wave. Translated into geopolitical terms, this insight illuminates the tension between the two compelling truths, or strategic imperatives, facing the United States after the end of the Cold War: Washington's highest priority should be the peoples formerly dominated by Moscow; Washington's highest priority should be Moscow.[7]

When the choice is between two such profoundly significant imperatives, the smart move is to avoid rushing a decision—and the best way to do that is to avoid calling the question too soon. It is the job of those engaged in top-level statecraft to figure out the smart move and the best timing. In Washington in the early 1990s, some did.

Strategists inside the Bush administration's State Department and, more significantly, inside the Clinton administration's Pentagon produced policies that gave both strategic imperatives their due and allowed Washington leeway on the timing of irrevocable decisions. They implemented a strategy of incremental security partnership, open to European and post-Soviet states alike, ultimately embodied in the Partnership for Peace (PfP). Through this Partnership, potential NATO members could gain experience in working with the West and acquire the full weight of the Article 5 guarantee over time. Such a widely applicable, incremental approach did not require Washington either to draw a new line through post–Cold War Europe or to leave Ukraine and most other post-Soviet republics to their own devices. It might also have helped to entrench a new democratic order in Central and Eastern Europe, since subsequent events demonstrated that the prospect of incrementally gaining membership in desirable institutions—not membership itself—most effectively solidifies reforms.[8]

But having figured out the smart move, Washington called the question too soon anyway—and the American decision to do so ultimately combined with Russia's own tragic choices in fateful ways. Once President Boris Yeltsin made decisions in late 1993 and 1994 to shed the blood of his opponents in Moscow and Chechnya, and Russian voters decided to give antireform extremists a victory in the December 1993 parliamentary elections, the survival of a vision of partnership that included both Moscow and the peoples it once dominated became much more challenging. Rampant inflation in Russia as part of the transition to a market economy only intensified the sense of disintegrating hopes. Bloodshed in the Balkans added urgency to all questions of European security and created new frictions between Washington and Moscow over how to handle the violence. Domestic developments in the United States—most notably the stunning victory of the Republican Party in the 1994 midterm congressional elections—similarly influenced foreign policy, tilting Clinton toward a different, more confrontational strategy of alliance enlargement.

Savvy members of the US National Security Council and State Department seized upon these events, and on Central and Eastern Europeans' urgent appeals for full Article 5 guarantees, to best the Pentagon in constructing the post–Cold War geopolitical order. Military planners had played a surprisingly small role in policy formulation in the years immediately after the fall of the Wall—the Pentagon under Bush complained that, while consulted, it had no real "input"—and were eventually relegated to the backseat again under Clinton.[9] American advocates of more assertive expansion, emphasizing that Central and Eastern Europe had suffered too many historical wrongs and waited too long to join the West, switched the mode of NATO enlargement. Instead of incremental accession by a large number of states, they had the alliance extend the full weight of the Article 5 guarantee to a small number of states. While their motives had merit, their mode of expansion accelerated the timing and drew a new line between the former Soviet Bloc states that had managed to secure Article 5 and those that had not. One consequence was that American options for managing post–Cold War contingency—namely, through the creation of a variety of relationships with such states, most notably with Georgia and Ukraine—became dramatically more limited just as Putin was rising within the ranks in Russia.

Some commentators recognized, at the time, the cost of calling the question too soon. George Kennan, the former US ambassador to Moscow who in the 1940s had conceived of the American strategy of containment, argued that post–Cold War NATO expansion tipped the balance too far away from protecting newfound cooperation with Moscow.[10] Even Baker later recognized in his memoirs that "every achievement contains within its success the seeds of a future problem."[11] Those seeds took root in the relationship between what remain the globe's two nuclear superpowers, the United States and Russia.

Despite the passing of the Cold War, these two nations still possess more than 90 percent of the world's nuclear warheads and the ability to kill nearly every living creature on earth. That threat makes understanding the decay in their relationship in the 1990s an essential story of our time, because it eroded the best chance for establishing lasting cooperation between them. Cold wars are not short-lived affairs, so thaws are precious.[12] Neither country made the best possible use of the thaw in the nineties. After unexpectedly being delivered from the threat of a nuclear confrontation with each other, they let deliverance slip.

The effects of American and Russian decisions during that crucial decade have been far-reaching. The window of opportunity for comprehensive strategic nuclear disarmament—the most significant opening since the dawn of the atomic age—closed relatively quickly. By the end of the 1990s, as this book will show, intelligence agencies reported on the beginnings of renewed nuclear competition. Other forms of competition emerged soon thereafter, not least in the shredding of hard-won arms control accords. Today's permissive environment of a world almost wholly lacking such accords means both sides are reassessing the roles of not just nuclear but also conventional capabilities. In Europe in recent years, both the post–Cold War American drawdown of forces and the Russian shift of troops eastward have reversed.[13] Increasing tensions have also raised questions about not just physical but also economic security. As the historian Adam Tooze has shown, renewed Russian aggression reveals that the post–Cold War "disavowal of the obvious connection between trade and security policy" was a grievous error, one fully exposed by "the resurgence of Putin's Russia." Despite having a GDP not that much larger than Spain's, once the cooperative spirit died, Russia began leveraging "its military assets to upend the geopolitical balance in Western Asia and the Middle East," and its cyber capabilities to wound governments and businesses around the globe.[14]

Given the profound consequences, it is crucial to understand the root cause: why relations between Moscow and Washington deteriorated so badly after a period of so much promise. This deterioration was all the more startling because of how close Russia and the United States briefly were in the 1990s. One measure of this rapport was Yeltsin's reaction to Baker's request in 1991 for the most closely held secret of state: details of how Moscow would launch nuclear attacks. The Russian leader provided them willingly, partly to curry favor with Baker and to win American help in his power struggle with Gorbachev, but partly out of trust. Moscow and Washington began a brief but extraordinary collaboration in countering nuclear proliferation. Another measure came in 1997, when Yeltsin had his own request for Clinton: "What if we were to give up having to have our finger next to the button all the time?" The American president responded, "well, if we do the right thing in the next four years, maybe we won't have to think as much about this problem."

By the end of the 1990s, however, trust had largely vanished. Putin divulged little in his grudging conversations with Clinton and the American president's top Russia advisor, Strobe Talbott. Instead of sharing nuclear secrets, he gave the Americans his account of the grim consequences of reduced Russian power: in former Soviet regions, terrorists now played soccer with the decapitated heads of their hostages. The idea that Putin would reveal launch protocols to Clinton was laughable.

What happened? To break that enormous question down into more manageable components: Why did the United States decide to enlarge NATO after the Cold War, how did the American decision interact with contemporary Russian choices, and did that interaction yield the fateful decline in relations between the two countries? Were there feasible alternatives to the decisions that they made? What was the cost of expansion as it occurred, and how did it help to shape the era between the Cold War and COVID? Finally, recognizing from the Italian philosopher Benedetto Croce that all history is ultimately contemporary history, written with an eye on today's concerns: If we widen the time horizon, how can knowledge of this history guide efforts to create a better future?[15]

These questions receive detailed answers over the course of the narrative and in the conclusion, but it is worth previewing the argument here. NATO enlargement did not, by itself, cause the deterioration of US-Russian relations. Major events happen for multiple reasons; history is rarely, if ever, monocausal. American and Russian choices interacted with each other, cumulatively over time, and with each country's domestic politics, to produce the decay. Misunderstanding played a role as well; as the former US ambassadors Alexander Vershbow and Daniel Fried have written, "both the Bush and Clinton administrations were mistaken in some basic assumptions about post-Soviet Russia." Both failed to understand the extent to which the liberation of Central and Eastern Europe, when viewed from Moscow, looked more like imperial collapse.[16]

But it is hard to avoid the reality that alliance expansion added to the burdens on Russia's fragile young democracy when it was most in need of friends. As Talbott told Chirac in 1997, "the Russian side is all screwed up." The American added, "I don't say that disrespectfully" but in recognition of the way that Russians "have gone through one of the greatest traumas in history, with more sudden change in their internal order, external relations, and ideology" than any other country "which has not lost a major war." The result was that, as the historian Margaret MacMillan has written, after the collapse of both the Berlin Wall and the Soviet Union "the world stood at a crossroads . . . with competing visions of how the future should unfold," not just in economic but also in security terms. The alliance's expansion became a major factor in the subsequent competition among various visions of the future.[17] The stories of NATO expansion and of Moscow's modern time of troubles became intertwined while the best chance for lasting cooperation between the nuclear superpowers dwindled, unmaking the precious post–Cold War moment of optimism.

I experienced some of that optimism firsthand as a young American studying abroad in West Berlin in 1989. Ever since then, I have been trying to understand the political legacy of events that I witnessed as a bystander. But how can I, or indeed anyone not directly involved in top-level political decisions, claim to know the NATO expansion story? The answer is that interactions between leaders of governments and states, and then with their own advisors, comrades, congresses, parliaments, and peoples, generate mountains of paperwork that are generally kept secret. Once the Berlin Wall collapsed, however, so too did the Warsaw Pact states' ability to keep their documents and secrets hidden. I began researching in such sources in the 1990s, most notably in the files of the East German secret police, the Stasi. I also started conducting interviews and writing the first of what eventually became a series of books and articles on the Cold War and its legacy for today, including *The Collapse: The Accidental Opening of the Berlin Wall,* and *1989: The Struggle to Create Post–Cold War Europe.*[18]

In the opening decade of this century, I began a sustained effort to see if I could get the corresponding Western documents—most of which were still under lock and key—declassified and released. In a sense, I created my own archive based on declassifications from six countries, even as I took advantage of regular archival openings and sources that other researchers had declassified.[19] This process took many years, partly because there were numerous locations, and partly because I had to persuade many people and institutions to grant me access. If simple requests failed, appeals became necessary, adding more years to the process. My research in this evidence produced the analysis that follows. Readers interested only in the narrative, if they wish, can read the entire text without ever looking at the references to these sources in the notes at the end; but those seeking to dive deeply into the evidence can use the citations to do so.

Some research breakthroughs and publications are worth noting here. In 2007, James Baker generously allowed me to access the collection of his papers that he had donated to Princeton University, including documents from crucial meetings in Moscow in 1990.[20] In 2008, hardworking staff at the George H. W. Bush Presidential Library helped me to file many hundreds of hard-copy requests, opening up new avenues not just for me but for other researchers as well.[21] In 2009, I was able to reverse a denial of my 2005 request to see German foreign ministry records after former German foreign minister Joschka Fischer and others were kind enough to prompt the ministry to reconsider.[22] In 2014, NATO decided to implement its so-called Directive on the Public Disclosure of NATO Information, giving me a wedge with which to pry open alliance archives with the help of staff in Brussels.[23] Perhaps the biggest challenge, however, was declassifying transcripts of Clinton's conversations with Yeltsin, which required three years of appeals after my initial requests in 2015 and 2016 failed. With the help of archivists and others dedicated to transparency, however, my appeals to the William J. Clinton Presidential Library ultimately succeeded in 2018, yielding a collection so rich (including in references to Putin) that Russian presidential spokesman Dmitry Peskov protested the library's declassification of "documents concerning current politicians"—meaning above all his boss.[24]

But not everything is written down. I benefited enormously from the willingness of more than a hundred participants in events to share their memories in interviews; their names appear in the bibliography and they have my gratitude. Given the limits of human memory—it is understandably hard to remember exact words used decades ago—I also compared those interviews to the archival evidence whenever possible. When inconsistencies arose, I stuck with the written record from the historical time period. In other words, I followed a hierarchy of evidence for this book.

Sources produced as events were happening, and held securely since then—what historians call primary sources—represent a higher caliber of evidence than comments made or interviews conducted years or decades later. In a further effort to provide the most accurate possible record of remarks on the controversial topic of NATO expansion, the quotations in this book come exclusively from printed or recorded matter, not from my memory of interviews or of evidence. I have further differentiated quotations into ones I found in primary sources, indicated by double quotation marks in the main text, and ones I quote from others (that is, quotes of quotes), indicated by double then single quotation marks. The sources for all quotations appear in the endnotes.

Taken together, these sources offer a rich picture of the past. As the historian John Lewis Gaddis has written, "the direct experience of events isn't necessarily the best path toward understanding them, because your field of vision extends no further than your own immediate senses." Participants in events are, by definition, on the ground, in a crowd with many others, amid the pressures of the day. Although I lived through some of the events as a bystander, only after completing my training in the PhD program in history at Yale University did I realize how much I had missed. Historians are the equivalent of onlookers from a great distance: the detail is less, but the perspective is greater. As Gaddis put it, "the historian of the past is *much better off* than the participant in the present, from the simple fact of having an expanded horizon."[25]

The way personal involvement can even become problematic for later historical assessments is apparent in comments by and about the two men who kicked off the fight over NATO expansion: Gorbachev and Baker. The former Soviet leader made headlines in 2014 with passionate remarks on whether Baker had promised him the alliance would never expand. Gorbachev's views matter because, by refraining from the use of force to shore up crumbling Soviet power in 1989, he opened the door to all that followed. That self-restraint justly earned Gorbachev the Nobel Peace Prize—but it also contributed to his fall from power after the Atlantic Alliance started enlarging eastward across the Cold War line.

Asked about expansion in 2014, the former Soviet leader became defensive. He told an interviewer that the alliance's enlargement was not his fault because the issue never came up on his watch: "the topic of 'NATO expansion' was not discussed at all, and it wasn't brought up in those years." Referring to himself in the third person and assigning blame to his successors, he instructed the interviewer what to write: "don't portray Gorbachev and the then-Soviet authorities as naïve people who were wrapped around the West's finger. If there was naïveté, it was later, when the issue arose." For good measure, he repeated that "not a single Eastern European country raised the issue, not even after the Warsaw Pact ceased to exist in 1991," and "Western leaders didn't bring it up, either."[26] Numerous commentators have uncritically repeated Gorbachev's claims, often verbatim, that NATO expansion arose only after his fall from power—or that, if it did come up on his watch, it did so only with regard to eastern German territory, not Central and Eastern Europe.[27] Yet the Soviet leader's claims do not accord with his own written records, such as this one from May 1990: "I told Baker: we are aware of your favorable attitude toward the intention expressed by a number of representatives of East European countries to withdraw from the Warsaw Pact in order to join NATO later."[28]

Records from other world leaders tell a similar story—even before 1990. By November 24, 1989, just two weeks after the fall of the Wall, President Bush was already thinking strategically about the future of all of Europe. As he told British prime minister Thatcher that day, "leave out East Germany. What if East European countries want to leave Warsaw Pact. NATO must stay." In other words, if those countries were considering an exit from the pact, their involuntary military alliance with Moscow, then the obvious question—which Bush sensed intuitively—was what they would do after leaving. Thatcher thought that "keeping . . . the Warsaw Pact"—which she later described as a "fig leaf for Gorbachev"—made the most sense, but Bush was not convinced.[29]

Instead, by February 2–4, 1990, there were communications between the State Department, its West German counterpart, and the chancellery speculating on whether the question of "territorial coverage" from NATO for "Eastern Europe" might arise—a development Moscow would obviously oppose. On February 6, the West German and British foreign ministers discussed whether Gorbachev would specifically insist that "Hungary should not become part" of the alliance. On February 8, the day before meeting with Gorbachev, Baker informed Bush that he had discussed NATO with Czechoslovak leaders, and that "managing the unification of Germany within NATO could be very important for these Central Europeans." From February 20 to 27, the US deputy secretary of state visited Hungary and Poland (among other countries in the region) and discussed with the Hungarian foreign minister how "a new NATO could provide a political umbrella for Central and Eastern Europe." On March 3, the Czechoslovak foreign minister visited NATO headquarters in Brussels. On March 12, Baker's subordinates produced an early assessment of the alliance's potential role in Central and Eastern Europe. By March 17, Czechoslovakia, Hungary, and Poland were openly criticizing Moscow for its opposition to NATO moving eastward across the Cold War line. On March 21, the Polish foreign minister also visited alliance headquarters. During the summer and fall, many of his fellow Central and Eastern European leaders either made similar visits themselves or hosted NATO's secretary general.[30] In 1991, Bush even speculated with Wörner on ways for NATO to create connections to the Baltics.

Moreover, these signs of interest in the alliance paralleled similar signs of interest in the European Community (EC), such as Hungary's formal request for membership, submitted on November 16, 1989—just one week after the fall of the Berlin Wall. Hungary and other reform-minded Warsaw Pact members also signaled to West Germany in 1989 that the main reason they were not yet trying to exit the pact (as well as join the EC) was tactical. Because they knew the survival of the pact was an "existential question" for Gorbachev, they did not want to undermine it, or him, too soon. Doing so might lead to his ouster by Soviet reactionaries, who would end "the reform process in all of Central and Eastern Europe" and reassert Moscow's control over the region. But the end of the pact was nonetheless in sight, and the exploration of future options was underway.[31] In short, contrary to Gorbachev's oft-cited statement, the fight over Central and Eastern Europe's future in Western institutions such as the EC and NATO began with the fall of the Wall.

Like Gorbachev, Baker was also forced to leave office, and he also put a great deal of subsequent effort into shaping the narrative of what he had done while in power. After Bush's loss in the 1992 election returned the secretary to private life, Baker hired a team of researchers and writers to help him produce his memoirs. One of them was Andrew Carpendale, an admirer of Baker's who had worked with the secretary in the State Department, become his chief speechwriter, and taken part personally in the dramatic events of those years. But when Baker excised or rewrote numerous passages of the book manuscript his team had drafted, particularly concerning the history of the years 1990–91, Carpendale felt compelled to assail his boss in writing on January 23, 1995: "I want to register my vehement disagreement with several of the substantive changes you made." He warned Baker, "you alone will have to bear the burden when the lead review in *The New York Times Book Review* begins something like this: 'In a colorful and readable memoir, James A. Baker, III, manages to do as an author what he did so well in over twelve years in power in Washington: glorify his own successes, avoid any hint of failure, and skirt the truth.'"[32]

Carpendale's prediction was accurate. Nine months later, the reviewer for the *Times* concluded that "the man famous for spinning the message of the week is now spinning his own image for history."[33] As British prime minister Winston Churchill once confessed, his personal prescription for ensuring a favorable image in history was "to write that history myself," and Gorbachev and Baker appear to have embraced the sentiment.[34] Political actors understandably want to tell their story, but history needs to be more than autobiography, especially when the consequences of their actions are so far-reaching. Seizing instead on all possible sources to take a dispassionate look at the start of NATO's post–Cold War expansion yields a large payoff: we see how both its successes and its failures set up the Atlantic world's time of troubles today—and we gain wisdom on how to prepare for an uncertain future.

While this history may be complicated, the narrative setup of this book is simple. It investigates NATO's decade of change in three parts. Each one blends the most relevant historical events into an analytical narrative.

Part I, covering the years 1989–92, opens with a wall falling and new democracies rising, to the joy of most of the world but to the horror of Putin and Soviet leaders who believe their victory in World War II earned them the lasting right to dominate Central and Eastern Europe. Kohl, the West German chancellor at the time, consistently uses one metaphor to advise his fellow Western leaders how to respond: get their harvest in before the coming storm. He means that the West must rush in 1990 to secure the gains of its Cold War success before hard-liners in Moscow mount a resistance to Gorbachev. Acting accordingly, Bush and Kohl pull off both unification and the enlargement of NATO beyond its Cold War border to eastern Germany in a mere 329 days. Soon thereafter, a battle for power in Moscow indeed breaks out, just as Kohl predicted; but the storm is stronger than even he expected. The attempted coup and its consequences sweep away not just Gorbachev but the entire Soviet state by the end of 1991, creating opportunities for the Atlantic Alliance to expand farther eastward—but introducing dramatic new risks as the old Soviet nuclear arsenal falls into multiple untested hands. And even as Washington is attempting to master these challenges, US voters send the Bush administration packing in 1992, putting a young Arkansas governor in the geopolitical hot seat.

Part II, 1993–94, explores the clearing in US-Russian relations after this storm and the potential that it reveals. Despite the upheaval in Moscow, reactionaries do not regain control as Kohl had feared. Instead, remarkably, there's a precious second chance at cooperation. Power falls to another leader willing to implement reforms and cooperate with the West—Yeltsin, who in 1993 swiftly establishes a rapport with Clinton. "Boris and Bill," as they become known, develop the closest relationship ever to exist between a Russian and an American leader, with Clinton eventually visiting Moscow more times than any US president before or since. Trying to protect that rapport, but also trying to respond to both Central and Eastern European appeals for NATO membership and Balkan bloodshed, Clinton seizes on the incremental partnership plan for all of Europe, authored largely by his Polish-born chairman of the Joint Chiefs of Staff (JCS), General John Shalikashvili. But the events of late 1993 and 1994—Yeltsin's tragic use of force against opponents in Moscow and Chechnya, the resurgence of the Republican Party, and skilled maneuvering by insiders in Washington—combine to convince Clinton to abandon the partnership solution.

Part III, 1995–99, chronicles Clinton taking a more aggressive stance on NATO expansion as the "Boris and Bill" relationship disintegrates into alcohol-fueled tirades by Yeltsin and stonewalling by the US president over military action in Kosovo. Meanwhile, Central and Eastern Europeans are justifiably thrilled as the countdown to their NATO membership commences. Western Europeans decide privately that Russia will never join the EU. And a frost settles over US-Russian relations as Clinton suddenly faces the question of whether he will survive in office, thanks to the revelation of his sexual relationship with White House intern Monica Lewinsky—which bursts into the headlines just as Putin is climbing the ladder of power in Russia. With both Moscow and Washington having failed to create lasting cooperation in the thaw after the Cold War, the Russian forces of reaction that Kohl had feared back in 1990 win out after all.

The conclusion steps back from the narrative and examines how, as described in each of these three parts, the sitting US president makes irreversible decisions about NATO's future—and how those decisions interact with Russian choices. In essence, the American leader turns the policymaking equivalent of a ratchet—a tool that allows motion in one direction only—and Russia responds. Each turn forecloses other possibilities, making it impossible to reverse course and choose a different direction. The consequences become cumulative as the sequence of decisions unfolds. First, as part of the larger goal of German unification, Bush forecloses all options for post–Cold War transatlantic security other than an Atlantic Alliance capable of extending Article 5 beyond the Cold War line.

Next, Clinton forecloses his own administration's option of incremental partnership as a means of achieving that expansion. Finally, Clinton forecloses options to limit either the location or number of new allies, or the pace at which they are added, or the membership benefits they can enjoy. These presidential ratchet turns matter greatly to the Atlantic Alliance. Although NATO contains many countries, each with its own opinions, American military dominance means it is ultimately American views that matter when NATO's Article 5 guarantee is at issue. This was as true in the 1990s as it is today. And these ratchet turns have a lasting impact—not least in the way they constrain subsequent US policymakers, who no longer have a full array of options either for structuring transatlantic security or for dealing with post-Soviet states when their tour of duty commences.

Finally, the book looks at the legacy of these events for today. Central and Eastern Europeans become NATO allies, only to discover that alliance membership does not automatically lock in their hard-won democratic gains. Washington wins its struggle with Moscow over NATO in the 1990s, but the way the United States goes about enlargement means it loses options with regard to Russia in the longer term. The big play in Europe would have been to create a dynamic that established lasting cooperation, rather than confrontation, between Russia and the West. After World War II, America worked with former adversaries to turn them into long-term allies, so there was a precedent for such an achievement. The challenge after the joyous, peaceful ending to the Cold War was to repeat that performance.[35] Instead, leaders in Washington and Moscow snatch stalemate from the jaws of victory.

American choices combine with the tragic failures of both Gorbachev and Yeltsin to undercut the potential for post–Cold War cooperation and to push the US-Russian relationship into a period of uneven decline. Although there are notable episodes reprising the spirit of cooperation— such as the expressions of sympathy from Moscow to the United States after the September 11, 2001 attacks, or the signing of a nuclear accord in 2010—the overall trend is downward. It reaches a frightening new low with the 2014 invasion of Ukraine and hits bottom (so far) in the years 2016–21, when Putin conducts massive cyber infiltration of US businesses, institutions, and elections.[36]

If this history ends with Putin, it also begins with him. In 1989, he is a bit player in divided Germany, watching in horror as the Wall opens and the

West moves east. In 1999, he becomes Yeltsin's handpicked heir. In the decade between, he largely disappears—fitting behavior for a member of the secret police—from the international stage as he struggles to find his footing back home. But his grievance at Russia's loss of empire and international standing endures throughout, and is widely shared among other displaced servants of the Soviet state. If it is surprising that he eventually reemerges from among them as the country's leader, it is not surprising that someone with his views becomes a serious contender for power once Russian reforms yield economic chaos. And when it becomes clear that it is indeed Putin who has ended up on top, his personal preferences swiftly assume an outsized role. He chooses to vent his grievances by using a re-purposed history of the 1990s, citing NATO's decision in those years to deploy "military infrastructure at our borders" as justification for renewed bloodshed and competition with the West.[37]

Given the significance of these events for today's world, it is time to take a serious look, using all available historical evidence, at what unfolded during the 1990s. At the start of that decade, a better future seemed not only possible but likely. To understand how we got to where we are today, we must judge the new times by the past.

PART I

Harvest and Storm, 1989–92

CHAPTER ONE

Two Dresden Nights

L IEUTENANT COLONEL VLADIMIR PUTIN decided, on a December night in Dresden in 1989, to do whatever it took to defend
Soviet authority, his colleagues, and himself. No one else was
coming to do it.[1] The Berlin Wall was open, and the East German regime was collapsing. A crowd of peaceful protesters had just flooded
the nearby headquarters of his secret police allies, the Stasi, overwhelming the guards as they had overwhelmed the regime: through conviction
and sheer numbers rather than through violence. Now some two dozen
protesters were drifting around the corner to the deceptively modest outpost of Soviet State Security, or the KGB, on Angelika Street, where on
December 5 he was the senior officer on site.

Putin worried about more than himself and the handful of men on
duty. As he later admitted, "we had documents in our building." Those
documents reportedly contained information on front companies holding
billions of deutsche marks for the KGB and its partners; on espionage
against Western high-tech industries to benefit their inept Eastern rivals;
and on contacts with the violent Red Army Faction, taking advantage of
Dresden's backwater status as a place to plan assassinations. Putin also safe-
guarded his own work against the "main opponent," NATO.[2]

Seeking armed support, he called a colleague with the Soviet military
forces in Dresden. The person who answered the phone, however, refused
to grant Putin's request without explicit permission from Moscow—and

then added, "Moscow is silent." Putin decided to act on his own. He walked toward the small crowd at the front gate in what a witness later described as a slow and calm manner.[3] For a while he simply stared. Then, after a brief conversation during which the protesters were surprised to hear his fluent German, he informed them that if they entered, they would be shot.

The two dozen protesters paused, murmured, and decided to go back to the Stasi headquarters. Putin returned to the house, where he and his crew "destroyed everything," burning "papers night and day" until "the furnace burst." According to his own account, the phrase "Moscow is silent" haunted him for years. His country should have defended itself, he later remarked, instead of offering silence: "we would have avoided a lot of problems if the Soviets had not made such a hasty exit from Eastern Europe." Putin formed a lasting conviction on the need to avoid what he called a paralysis of power. As he put it in the year he became president of Russia, "only one thing works in such circumstances—to go on the offensive. You must hit first, and hit so hard that your opponent will not rise to his feet."[4]

As the young KGB officer was coming to this realization, the heavyweights who ran their respective countries readied themselves for combat as well. A high-stakes game to fill the vacuum left by retreating Soviet power was beginning; it soon moved from the streets of East Germany to the grandest halls of power. If the venues became more refined, the struggles were no less fierce. The opening of the Berlin Wall had signaled the end of the Cold War order and the beginning of another, as yet unknown; everything, including NATO's future, was on the table. Moscow could demand that Germany pull out of NATO in exchange for Soviet approval of its reunification, a presumably fatal development for an alliance that had been a prominent landmark of the transatlantic world for forty years.

The Fight over NATO's Creation

The alliance's longevity belied how big the fight had been over whether to create it in the first place. NATO had come into being with the signing of the Washington Treaty on April 4, 1949, in a grand neoclassical ballroom on Constitution Avenue near the White House. President Harry Truman made brief remarks, calling on the new alliance to become "'a shield against aggression and fear of aggression.'" Afterward, some of the attendees shared bourbons in the bar of the nearby Willard Hotel, but in London, a British diplomat was not celebrating. Hugh Dalton noted in his diary with bitter satisfaction that "'it is a final entanglement of US

(& Canada) in Europe.'" The alliance was "'the best we can do—&, of its kind, very good—in this miserable situation.'"[5]

The misery arose from the destroyed hopes of harmony after World War II. Although the conflict had ended, Europe lay in ruins, hunger and disease were everywhere, and tensions with Moscow over the division of postwar authority created fresh threats. President Franklin D. Roosevelt, who had led the United States to a victory he did not live to see, had died hoping to create lasting peace both in Europe and with the Soviet Union. He sought to construct a durable postwar order by offering Moscow a prominent place in it.[6] Knowledge of Roosevelt's strategy for accomplishing this goal had, however, largely disappeared on April 12, 1945, when he died without having taken Vice President Truman into his confidence. Stunned by the swiftness with which he had become the leader of a country in the throes of reshaping world order, Truman urgently grilled Roosevelt's advisors, trying to figure out what his predecessor had intended. With some advisors promoting cooperative action with Moscow and others urging less cooperation, Truman increasingly found himself drawn to the latter group. Its members seized on his inexperience to promote a harder line than Roosevelt likely would have pursued.[7] Increasingly aggressive Soviet moves to crush independence in Central and Eastern Europe reinforced Washington's growing sense that even though one conflict had barely ended, another had begun: the Cold War. As Moscow began drawing what Winston Churchill famously termed an iron curtain across Europe, the ostensibly temporary dividing line within occupied Germany became increasingly permanent. A new state also emerged on that front, namely, the Federal Republic of Germany (FRG) or West Germany.[8]

Rising tension with Moscow also helped persuade a reluctant Congress, in 1948, to approve a generous plan of economic aid to Europe, originally proposed by Secretary of State George Marshall in June 1947. British foreign minister Ernest Bevin felt, however, that economic assistance was not enough; there needed to be military muscle as well. Bevin had already called for a new Western union consisting of Britain, France, and the Benelux countries (Belgium, the Netherlands, and Luxembourg) as a first step. It came into being with the Brussels Treaty of March 17, 1948, in the wake of the de facto Soviet takeover of the Czechoslovak government.[9] His larger hope, however, was for a transatlantic organization.

The US Congress responded to the Brussels Treaty in a cautiously favorable way with the Vandenberg Resolution, named for its sponsor, Michigan senator Arthur Vandenberg. He was, in the words of the soon-to-be secretary of state, Dean Acheson, a "hurricane" of a man, capable of producing impressively "'heavy word-fall.'" Vandenberg also enjoyed a "'rare capacity for instant indignation, often before he understood an issue, or even that there was an issue.'" This talent proved useful for bulldozing opposition, as Vandenberg and like-minded politicians struggled to bring the skeptical majority around to the idea of US membership in an expanded version of the Brussels alliance. They convinced the Senate to pass his resolution on June 11, 1948, opening the door to American "association" with "regional and other collective arrangements," though without specific details—and with an understanding that nothing would happen until after that year's election.[10]

Soviet miscalculations soon helped advance Bevin and Vandenberg's cause. Moscow began blockading Berlin two weeks after the resolution's passage, leading to the Berlin Airlift of 1948–49. The Soviet blockade was a major strategic blunder: it profoundly shifted the trajectory of the early Cold War by diminishing US opposition to remilitarizing the American commitment to Europe.[11]

As the alliance took shape, however, supporters still had to fight off doubters at home and abroad. George Kennan, the US diplomat who had proposed the strategy of containing rather than actively combating Moscow, was aghast; he preferred the economic approach embodied in the Marshall Plan. To be sure, Kennan sympathized with the pleas of devastated European states seeking cover. Washington could hardly tell wartorn countries to stop "'looking down into the chasm of their own military helplessness'" as tensions with the Soviet Union rose.[12] But he opposed a permanent alliance because he felt the long-term cost was too high. Such an alliance, he felt, would undermine the ultimate goals of his patient-but-firm containment policy: to induce, by economic and political means, a change in Moscow's thinking that would eventually enable a negotiated settlement of differences while avoiding the twin dangers of domestic authoritarianism and global war. A standing alliance against Moscow would hinder, not help, the achievement of those goals—especially since NATO would have no obvious stopping point in Europe if it started taking on members beyond those directly on the Atlantic seaboard. In Kennan's view, such an alliance—while understandably desirable in the short run—would ultimately increase tensions and reduce US options for peaceful resolution of any conflict with the Soviet Union. French diplomats had their own concerns; they made clear that they wanted the alliance's membership strictly limited. But the United States insisted on reaching out widely, to add both "stepping stones" across the Atlantic—the Azores, Greenland, and Iceland—and Scandinavian countries. While interested in membership, such countries knew they had to avoid provoking their Soviet neighbors and had been considering some kind of Scandinavian defense union among themselves.

A compromise resulted: Denmark, Iceland, and Norway became NATO allies—after negotiations over such a defense union collapsed—but restricted or refused nuclear warheads, bases, and certain military activities on their territory.[13] In April 1949, the fight over NATO's creation ended in success for its supporters. The Senate voted 82 to 13 to ratify the Washington Treaty.

On paper, the accord's guarantees were impressively strong—with Article 5, the strongest of all, requiring each member to consider an attack on any other state's territory as an attack on its own.[14] A North Atlantic Council (NAC), composed of member states' leaders or their representatives, presided over by a secretary general, came into being as the top policymaking body. But the alliance remained a paper tiger for roughly the first fourteen months of its existence. Neither NATO's civilian nor its military components evolved much at first. Armies in Western Europe had demobilized significantly since the war's end, in contrast with 175 Soviet divisions in the East, which despite the cessation of hostilities had remained in varying states of readiness.[15]

It took three startling developments to make NATO begin serious military preparations: the unexpectedly early detonation of a Soviet nuclear device in August 1949, the success of the Communists in China in October 1949, and, most important, the North Korean invasion of South Korea in June 1950.[16] The first two developments signaled rising Communist power, and the third set a dangerous precedent. If Communists were detonating nuclear weapons, seizing China, and invading South Korea, the logic went, they would certainly try to take West Germany.

The resulting panic had far-reaching consequences. In Europe, it helped advocates of multilateral organizations such as a European economic community. In Washington, it meant victory for supporters of a hard-line policy document that called for extensive militarization and nuclearization of containment. And in the new transatlantic alliance, the panic helped put the *O* in *NATO*.[17]

Truman announced on September 9, 1950 that he was sending substantial ground forces back to Europe. Those forces would serve under an integrated NATO command structure, but with a US general—the first Supreme Allied Commander Europe, or SACEUR, Dwight D. Eisenhower—at the top. The most prominent remaining opponent of entangling alliances, Ohio senator Robert Taft, tried to fight these developments but failed. A Senate resolution in April 1951 cleared the legal path.[18]

At this point NATO started taking on structure. It established a military headquarters, known as Supreme Headquarters Allied Powers Europe, or SHAPE. A permanent civilian secretariat emerged to support the first secretary general, Lord Ismay of Great Britain. The alliance's structures became even more defined at a meeting in Lisbon in February 1952; among other topics, this conference set the "Lisbon Goals" on burden sharing, setting off decades of debate.[19]

The alliance also began expanding, reaching out to Greece and Turkey, which became members in 1952.[20] The big question, however, was what to do about West Germany. With NATO getting serious about preparing for a Soviet invasion, the value of both strengthening and including the western half of that divided country became glaringly apparent. But the sensitivities of the FRG's neighboring states, all seared by memories of the Nazis, made it anything but straightforward to hand guns back to Germans.

Here, too, Korea had a decisive impact. The war there made Germany's occupiers and neighbors worry less about past enemies than about future ones. They reluctantly agreed to take West Germany as an ally, but how to do it proved complicated. In October 1950, French prime minister René Pleven proposed to the National Assembly a European Defense Community, calling for the creation of a European army under supranational authority and funded by a common budget. Although the plan had support from both American and European leaders and would have enabled German units to become part of such an army, the National Assembly ultimately rejected the idea.[21]

Recalibrating, in 1954 NATO members decided on a different strategy. The allies allowed West Germany (along with Italy) to accede to the original five-member Brussels pact and to what was now called the Western European Union (WEU). They also invited the FRG to join NATO, but the occupying powers in West Germany insisted on a "Convention on the Presence of Foreign Forces." The main thrust of this October 23, 1954 convention was that the Western powers preserved their right to keep troops stationed in their former occupation zones for an unlimited time. West Germany also had to renounce the production of any "ABC"—atomic, biological, or chemical—weapons on its territory.[22]

Moreover, the divided city of Berlin had to remain in a separate category. There, despite all of the confrontation since 1945, America, Britain, and France still shared occupation authority with the Soviet Union. That shared authority had persisted even after 1949, when Moscow had turned the Soviet occupation zone—which encompassed divided Berlin—into the German Democratic Republic (GDR, or East Germany). Despite the new official name, however, the GDR was thoroughly undemocratic and firmly under Soviet control.

These deals brought West Germany into NATO in 1955.[23] In response, Moscow compelled the countries of Central and Eastern Europe that year to join an opposing military alliance known as the Warsaw Pact. The division of Europe came to seem permanent.

As year after year of Cold War confrontation passed, divided Europeans, particularly divided Germans, increasingly became enemies to themselves. Fortifications on the borders and plans for combat grew in complexity and lethality. The US Strategic Air Command produced a nuclear target list in the 1950s with ninety-one designated ground zeros, meaning sites slated for obliteration by atomic weapons, in the eastern half of Berlin. It is unclear whether the Strategic Air Command carried out a corollary study of the consequences for West Berlin of nearly a hundred atomic fireballs bursting just down the street.[24] Perhaps there was a quiet sense that the command would never hit those targets, or perhaps the consequences seemed regrettable but necessary. The lines of division running through Berlin, Germany, and Europe were now the front lines in the Cold War, and the command had to strategize accordingly.

Meanwhile, Eastern European regimes did all they could to prevent their populace from fleeing west, fortifying borders with weapons facing not only outward but also inward. The East German regime produced the most iconic symbol of a government repressing its own people. In 1961, it encased the western part of Berlin in a hundred-mile-long concrete wall to stop the huge numbers of its citizens trying to get there, and then onward to the West, in search of political freedom and a better life. The division of Germany and Berlin seemed to have become permanent—until 1989, when it suddenly became temporary again.

Once Soviet power started crumbling, certain aspects of the way NATO had developed during the earlier decades took on new significance. By then, West Germany hosted so many Western troops and weapons—especially Americans and nuclear ones—that any West German attempt to shed either would seriously undermine not only US military standing

Divided Germany during the Cold War.

in Europe but the entire alliance. For that reason, Washington had already become worried, earlier in the 1980s, about the massive antinuclear protests in West Germany.[25] But the idea that Germany might suddenly unify, announce neutrality, and demand withdrawal of all foreign troops and forces was a problem orders of magnitude more challenging.

Abandoning the Warsaw Pact

How did Soviet power in Europe unravel in the course of 1989, raising the specter of German unification and possibly neutrality? One of the first critical steps happened not in Germany but in Hungary, where reformist leaders showed open willingness to cooperate with the West in the teeth of opposition from their more hard-line Warsaw Pact allies. Budapest would not, however, have dared to jump ship without several major precursors—most notably the rise to power of a reform-minded Soviet leader, Mikhail Gorbachev, in 1985.

Gorbachev, born in 1931, had painful childhood memories not just of World War II but of his family's suffering in the purges of the Stalinist era. One grandfather was tortured and the other was executed. The new Soviet leader hoped for a better future, partly inspired by the détente of the 1970s and partly by the success of Socialist and Communist parties in places like Italy. As he wrote in his memoirs, "people deserve a better life—that was always on my mind." His optimism and call for new thinking inspired reformers all across the Warsaw Pact, particularly the long-suppressed Solidarity movement in Poland, which achieved a power-sharing regime in Warsaw.[26]

The courage of Polish dissident leaders such as Lech Wałęsa, who had won the Nobel Peace Prize in 1983, inspired other activists. He had received that award for leading the independent trade union called Solidarity through dark years of repression, despite frequently being under house arrest or detention; eventually he would rise to the presidency in Poland. In the 1980s, his example inspired other activists, including in Hungary. One of them was Viktor Orbán, who first came to world attention on June 16, 1989 with a passionate speech in Budapest's Heroes Square. The occasion was memorable: in an undeniably powerful display, hundreds of thousands converged to witness the ceremonial reburial of former prime minister Imre Nagy, who decades earlier had been hanged and thrown into a mass grave for supporting the Hungarian revolt against the Soviet invasion of 1956. Orbán, the spokesman for a group called the

Federation of Young Democrats, capitalized on the emotional reburial to call for the Soviets to remove their still-present forces entirely. Although he was only in his twenties, the speech catapulted him to fame, putting him on a trajectory toward the office of prime minster.[27]

The Hungarian who held that office at the time, Miklós Németh, had also seized the moment, but behind closed doors. On March 3, 1989, he had informed Gorbachev, "we made a decision—to remove completely the electronic and technological protection from the Western and Southern borders of Hungary." In other words, he was punching a hole in the Iron Curtain.[28]

Németh's East German counterpart, Erich Honecker, was profoundly worried by Hungary's action. Unless something changed, Honecker was certain Hungary would "drift father into the camp of the bourgeoisie." But Hungary was hardly alone in its desire to burst out of Cold War strictures, as became apparent at the Warsaw Pact's July 7–8, 1989 summit in Bucharest. As one of Gorbachev's subordinates noted, the summit "had all the characteristics of a burial service." By then, East German citizens had swarmed into Hungary, hoping Németh's open-border policy applied to them too. Technically it did not, because Hungary had signed an accord obliging it to prevent East German citizens from exiting the Soviet Bloc.[29] If Budapest opened its borders in defiance of this agreement, it effectively would be abandoning the pact and changing sides in the Cold War.

With every passing day in late summer 1989, both the number of East Germans on the Hungarian border and the pressure on Németh to break the agreement increased. He was smart enough to know that if he was going to play his big card, he should get Western help for his country in exchange—but also smart enough to know it would not come from Washington. The new US president, George H. W. Bush, preferred caution to risky geopolitical card playing.

Bush viewed that summer's developments with mixed emotions. On the one hand, discord within the enemy alliance was obviously welcome; on the other, he preferred a more restrained response than his predecessor, Ronald Reagan, had shown to Gorbachev's dramatic changes. Although Bush, a successful Texas businessman, had a competitive streak, he had originally been raised in New England, the Andover- and Yale-schooled son of a former senator from Connecticut. He chose to draw on this background as the scion of a center-right political family once becoming a statesman, inclining toward a more cautious approach to foreign policy than Reagan had adopted.

Even though he followed a president from the same party, one of Bush's first acts in office had been to institute a review and rethinking of previous national security strategy.[30] He had also asked James Baker—his old friend, former tennis doubles partner at the Houston Country Club, and subsequently Reagan's chief of staff and Treasury secretary—to be his secretary of state. Brent Scowcroft, a retired US Air Force general and former advisor to Richard Nixon and Henry Kissinger, was Bush's pick for national security advisor.[31] The two men balanced each other temperamentally, with Baker inclined to push for action and Scowcroft inclined to consider all consequences carefully. But both advisors agreed on the need to keep the group of those in the know small and tight. Truly significant decisions in the Bush era happened—in the words of Scowcroft's deputy, Robert Gates—among "Bush, Baker, Scowcroft and their respective inner circles working in harness together."[32] Bush was particularly solicitous toward Scowcroft, whose wife's extended illness left the national security advisor with a day job in the White House and a night job as caregiver.[33]

Unsurprisingly, Baker, Scowcroft, and their teams agreed with Bush that, as the president put it, Poland and Hungary should not "expect a blank check" from the West but instead "must help themselves."[34] Baker also told his Soviet counterpart, Eduard Shevardnadze, on September 21, 1989 that "we do not desire to stir up things up or ferment [*sic*] unrest." Instead, Washington would "try to assist Poland and Hungary in moving their economies towards more of a free market system." The Bush administration sought a slower pace of change, one that would not trigger reversals. The Soviet foreign minister appreciated the assurance, aware the United States could choose to exploit the situation more aggressively, and replied with what he termed a "reasonable proposal": "Let's disband both NATO and the Warsaw Pact. Let's release your allies and ours. While NATO exists, the Warsaw Pact also exists." Baker did not encourage him to continue in this vein and nothing came of the remark, but it was a warning that serious questions were surfacing about NATO's future.[35]

This cautious American attitude, welcome in Moscow, was unwelcome in Budapest, as the Hungarian ambassador to West Germany complained. Prime Minister Németh decided to try his luck directly with the chancellor of West Germany, Helmut Kohl. Like Bush, Kohl was the leader of his country's center-right party, namely the Christian Democratic Union (CDU); but unlike Bush, he was the leader of half of a divided nation on the front line of the Cold War, which gave him different priorities. Another difference was that the chancellor had by 1989 spent seven years in the top office. Even though critics both outside and inside his own party were gaining ground, this experience gave him the assertiveness to take risks after the dramatic developments of that year unexpectedly created the potential for change. By August 18, 1989, the situation had become so fluid that the West German Foreign Office was even gaming out the consequences of Hungary's quitting the Warsaw Pact. Its departure would "exceed Moscow's pain threshold" and produce a dramatic reaction that could have unpredictable consequences—even in the seemingly permissive age of Gorbachev. Not only Hungary but all of Europe "found itself in a precarious position."[36]

Németh signaled to Kohl that he was willing to jump anyway, if someone in the West would hold out a net. Sensing an opportunity, the chancellor arranged a secret conversation between himself, Németh, and his foreign minister, Hans-Dietrich Genscher, for August 25, 1989. Kohl invited the Hungarian not to Bonn, the capital of West Germany, but to Gymnich Castle, a government-owned historic property far away from prying eyes. There, Németh complained to the two Germans about the lukewarm support from Washington. As far as he could tell, Bush's highest priority was to avoid "hasty developments," not to support revolutionary change.[37]

The Hungarian, in contrast, wanted haste—and a deal. What he could offer was his country's border, and the enormous number of East Germans imprisoned behind it. What he needed was money and support. He described his country's economic crisis and its extensive debt, which one historian later estimated was the highest per capita in Eastern Europe. Németh was also willing to give East Germans what they clearly wanted, which was the freedom to go west. They enjoyed automatic citizenship under West German law, so all they needed was someone to let them out, and Németh was willing to become that person. Kohl later recalled that, upon learning this, he felt tears welling up in his eyes.[38] Reuniting divided Germans had long seemed an impossible dream, but now it was becoming possible. Taking this all in, the chancellor indicated his willingness to help, among other ways by contacting German bankers.

It was the safety net Németh needed. On August 31, he had his foreign minister inform the rulers of East Germany that unless they allowed travel and emigration freedom—which they were not willing to do—Hungary would break its written obligations and open its border to everyone wanting to depart.[39] He delayed implementation of the opening until September 11 and then threw the gates open at midnight—without Moscow's approval.[40] That delay was apparently a favor to Kohl. The chancellor was, in the words of British prime minister Margaret Thatcher, "a politician to his fingertips" and had realized that news of the opening would burst as a welcome bombshell during the mid-September CDU party conference, where he was facing a leadership challenge.[41] By contrast, the Soviet leader was apparently not consulted. As far as French diplomats could tell, Gorbachev had not given the opening "a green light."[42]

The televised images of joyous, tearful East Germans flooding across the Austro-Hungarian border made the rift in the Warsaw Pact obvious for all to see. The West German Foreign Office estimated that in the two months following the opening, nearly 50,000 refugees fled west via Hungary.[43] Kohl's advisors noted privately that they had "not reckoned with such a large stream of refugees."[44] The West German Foreign Office later called the dramatic surge a major "catalytic factor" for all that followed, with "political and psychological consequences."[45]

Kohl wrote warmly to Németh, thanking him for "this big-hearted act of humanity" that "we will never forget. You have, in an overwhelming way, kept your word." The chancellor smoothed the way for Hungary to access a credit line of 500 million DM. He also welcomed Németh to his home, a rare honor, to discuss how to respond to breakdowns in the Soviet transport of energy to Hungary.[46]

By November 16, 1989, Hungary was so emboldened that it formally requested entry into the European Community (EC), and leaders of Poland and Yugoslavia indicated that they would soon follow suit as well. Delivering the official membership request personally to resounding applause at a meeting in Strasbourg, the Hungarian foreign minister asked that his country's Warsaw Pact membership not be held against it.[47] The reason Hungary did not simply announce it was leaving the pact outright, according to a confidential West German assessment, was that such a rupture might endanger Gorbachev. With matters going so well, Budapest did not want to risk reactionaries toppling the Soviet leader.[48]

Hungary's behavior prompted Soviet analysts to begin speculating what would happen if Warsaw Pact states with Soviet troops on their territory demanded those troops leave—or, even worse, if the Baltics demanded to leave the Soviet Union. The West German ambassador in Moscow reported home that "the search for a substitute for the Warsaw Pact" was already on. One idea was to merge the pact and NATO into a larger, pan-European system. Perhaps as part of that thinking, on December 19, 1989, Shevardnadze paid the first-ever visit by a Soviet foreign minister to the NATO secretary general in Brussels. To his happy surprise, alliance staffers gathered at the building's entrance and, as Shevardnadze walked in, showered him with applause.[49]

Hungary thus burst out of the Warsaw Pact even before the Berlin Wall opened. The hole Németh created in the Iron Curtain was a hole below the pact's waterline. Hard-line regimes scrambled to seal off the breach, usually by blocking their citizens' ability to travel to Hungary. But closing off Hungary as a place to which disgruntled Eastern Europeans could flee only led to intensified protests within their own borders, most notably in East Germany. By November, waves of demonstrations were bringing the East German government to its knees, though it clung to the Berlin Wall to the last. Scowcroft had his subordinates carry out "GDR contingency planning" for outcomes to the chaos. As his subordinate Robert Blackwill wrote on November 7, "the future of the GDR means the future of divided Germany, which in turn means the future of divided Europe. Nothing save the US-Soviet strategic relationship is more central to our national security."[50]

Facing this existential threat, the dictators in East Germany understood that an intact Wall was their most valuable property. It not only kept East Germany from bleeding out but also offered a financial lifeline. They hoped to secure desperately needed financial support from the West in exchange for doling out "generous" opportunities for "tourist and visitor traffic" across the Wall.[51] In other words, they would sell periodic, limited openings for regular infusions of cash. The GDR's ruling regime planned to retain firm control of such openings, which would remain tightly limited for "national security" reasons—the same spurious reasons the country's leaders had long used to prevent most East Germans from ever leaving. But in an epic, irreversible display of incompetence, the regime botched its attempt to hint at greater travel opportunities to come. The unlucky Politburo member charged with announcing the proposed new policy on November 9, 1989 made it sound as if the regime had instead declared the Wall open.

In the heady atmosphere of that tumultuous year, this mistake was the catalytic spark for an explosion that brought down the Wall. Thousands, then tens of thousands, then hundreds of thousands massed on the border that night and flooded over it, with or without crossing points. For those crowds, it became a night of jubilation as, one by one, border guards without instructions decided to give way to the massive surge.[52]

Once he learned what had happened, Gorbachev sent alarmist messages to Washington, London, Paris, and Bonn, saying he feared "a chaotic situation with unpredictable consequences." This panicky message made Scowcroft realize that the Wall's opening had shattered Gorbachev's confidence. In the national security advisor's view, the Soviet leader had "looked benignly, or at least indifferently," at "what was happening inside Eastern Europe until the Wall fell. Then he got scared."[53] Gorbachev also backed off the tentative feeler Shevardnadze had extended to Baker about dissolving both military blocs; now he felt it would be unwise "to raise the question of liquidating the Warsaw Pact and NATO."[54]

Meanwhile, in London, Soviet diplomats did not even pause to proof-read the English translation of Gorbachev's garbled plea before hand-delivering it to Thatcher: "I have just conveyed to chansellor Kohl an oral message, the content of which I consider necessary to disclose to You." Gorbachev had "appealed to chansellor G. Kohl to take necessary and most urgent measures in order to prevent deterioration of the situation, with its destabilization." The upshot seemed to be that Gorbachev was demanding consultation among the four powers "without delay" to put pressure on Kohl not to do anything dramatic.[55] Commenting from Moscow, the British ambassador to the USSR, Sir Rodric Braithwaite, took this anxious plea as a sign that Gorbachev's "problem now is to control the forces he has unleashed," adding, "I do not think the Russians know how" to regain such control.[56] Like Scowcroft, Braithwaite worried that the Soviet leader's "panicked" message "signaled his effective impotence."[57]

Thatcher, meanwhile, had her own worries, namely what she was seeing on television from Bonn. She was, in the words of her staff, "frankly horrified by the sight of the *Bundestag* [the West German parliament] rising to sing *Deutschland über alles* when the news of the developments on the Berlin Wall came in."[58] She was apparently unaware of, or uninterested in, the fact that the lyrics to the German national anthem had changed since World War II. The Bundestag members had not, contrary to her belief, revived lyrics last used in the Nazi era. In Thatcher's mind, with Hungary abandoning the pact, the Wall coming down, and West Germans singing *Deutschland über alles*—on television, no less—the unthinkable had begun.[59]

No NATO and No Nukes

To defend their interests, all of the big players realized they needed to discern not just the best opening moves following the fall of the Wall, but where to make those moves and with whom. Their choice of forum, and of participants in it, would decisively affect the outcome. Baker, known as a remorseless competitor and hunter, understood this point better than anyone. As his wife remarked to a journalist, her husband did not "'waste a lot of time on guilt. . . . In fact, he doesn't waste any time on it.'" As Baker later said of himself, "I used to like to kill." In his memoirs, he included a detailed list of animals he particularly enjoyed killing: "kudu, impala, lechwe, sable antelope, and sitatunga."[60]

The secretary knew intuitively that in the coming big game for Germany, getting the first step right was crucial. "Any complex negotiation was actually a series of discrete problems," he later wrote, and how one solved the "first problem had ramifications far beyond that single issue." His first challenge was blocking the rise "of the host of ill-advised fora" and securing the right one for Washington. His ideal negotiating situation was one-on-one, but with so many players, that would be hard to pull off.

Bush and Baker sought a forum that could quickly constrain debate on the more explosive consequences of the fall of the Wall. The longer uncertainty lasted, the more the seemingly permanent fundamentals of European order would come into question. Europe was about to test whether its borders were truly as fixed as a host of Cold War accords attested. West Germany's neighbors were about to learn whether Germans were as happy to subsume their national identity into a European collective as they had long professed to be, or whether they wished to return to their old nationalist path, thereby endangering the EC. And the future of not just the Warsaw Pact but of NATO was in question. Having lost its main enemy, the alliance would have a harder time justifying its existence; would NATO need "re-founding" to survive?

As they set about determining a forum and a strategy, Bush decided he would not publicly exacerbate Gorbachev's anxieties by "posturing on the Berlin Wall." Instead, he would make his move behind closed doors.[61] But behind which doors, exactly—perhaps those to a large hall containing the peace conference for World War II? Decades after the war's end, no such treaty had been negotiated; it had long ago fallen victim to the hostility between the Soviets and their former allies. Scowcroft thought Moscow would almost certainly "propose a Peace Treaty" conference "in order to slow things down," which could become a major obstacle to progress. By 1945, Nazi Germany had been at war with no fewer than 110 countries.[62] While it was unlikely that all of them would gather in the wake of the events of 1989, the process of negotiating which states to exclude, and which might receive a hearing for demands for reparations, would be long and contentious, thus winning Gorbachev time.

Foreign Minister Genscher openly opposed a peace conference for an additional reason. Even if West Germans could somehow avoid being cast as latter-day Nazis, they would not sit at a children's table while the big powers decided Germany's fate.[63] Internal communications back at the foreign ministry were even blunter. Fearing Germans might come under pressure to participate in a peace-treaty conference, legal experts generated a long list of reasons why such a treaty was unnecessary.[64] As one of Genscher's subordinates noted in dismissing the idea, "even the USA will have to get used to the fact that Yalta is now in the past!"[65] The superpowers could no longer dictate Europe's future as they had done at that summit.

Bush sought advice, as he often did, from his NATO ally and friend, Prime Minister Brian Mulroney of Canada. Bush was due to meet Gorbachev in Malta in early December, and since Mulroney had recently visited Gorbachev in the USSR, Bush asked for a full report.[66] The Canadian recounted that he and his traveling party had "found nothing in the stores . . . not even any fur hats in Leningrad." There were "no carpets in carpet stores and no shoes. Even Gorbachev said that times are tough and pressures are building." Mulroney also said he had raised the topic of "neutrality for Poland and Hungary and their withdrawal from the Warsaw Pact." The prime minister sensed that the idea "was clearly 'not on.'"[67] Instead, Gorbachev said that "there should be no changes in the alliances." Robert Hutchings, one of Bush's National Security Council (NSC) advisors, recalled that Mulroney's account led him and his colleagues to reduce their expectations for what the US-Russian summit might achieve.[68] If Gorbachev was not yet willing to answer questions about NATO's and Germany's future in the way the United States wanted, it was best not to ask hard questions in the first place.

Meanwhile, Kohl was facing questions that were suddenly shot across a secret back channel he and Gorbachev had set up. Kohl's equivalent of a national security advisor, Horst Teltschik, personally managed the channel's West German end.[69] At the Moscow end was Valentin Falin, the powerful head of the International Department within the Central Committee of the Communist Party.[70] His department controlled immense amounts of funding for the party's foreign operations; after the Soviet Union collapsed, according to a journalistic account, a receipt surfaced for a $22 million transfer to Falin on December 5, 1989, ostensibly for party work—most likely just one of many transfers.[71]

On November 21, Falin's deputy, Nikolai Portugalov, appeared in Teltschik's office bearing a two-part handwritten document—with the cryptic explanation that the first part was official and the second part was not.[72] The former, which Portugalov led Teltschik to believe came straight from Gorbachev, contained general statements to the effect that Moscow worried events were moving in an "undesirable and dangerous direction."[73] The unofficial text was more surprising: "asking purely hypothetically," it inquired whether Bonn was "intending to introduce the question of unification or reunification as a matter of practical politics." If so, then it was necessary to consider "the future alliance memberships of the German states" and consult the "clause on exit" provided in the "Paris treaties and the Rome treaty."[74]

These treaty references made Teltschik's hair stand on end. The Rome Treaty was the founding document of the EC. The Paris Agreements were the legal means by which West Germany had joined NATO. The "clause of exit" was an allusion to the fact that any NATO member wishing to depart the alliance could do so after twenty years of membership.[75] Having joined in 1955, the FRG had long since qualified for exit. All told, the cryptic document was a Soviet ultimatum masquerading as a hypothetical: if you want German unity, you must leave both the EC and NATO.

The unofficial text demanded a price even if West Germany wanted something less than full unification. A looser "German confederation" would be acceptable to Moscow only if Germans agreed to "no foreign nuclear presence at all on German soil," either East or West. That was a "Conditio sine qua non"—a condition without which the Soviet Union would oppose even a confederation.

Someone high up in the Moscow hierarchy knew enough to apply pressure where it hurt. Polling showed that 84 percent of West Germans wanted to denuclearize their country entirely—not least because all of the nuclear weapons in the country were controlled by foreigners—so a majority would be not only willing but happy to trade those weapons for unity.[76] Both Teltschik and Kohl knew, the chancellor later recalled, that if Moscow offered "quick reunification in exchange for an exit from NATO and neutrality," it would find "widespread support among the members of the public in both East and West Germany."[77] This was such an obvious card to play that, even without access to the ultimatum, London guessed that something like it must be in the offing. As the Foreign Office advised Thatcher, "if the Russians made clear that the de-nuclearisation of Germany is really the bottom line of their demands in respect of German unification, then the bulk of German public opinion is likely to be sympathetic."[78]

The unofficial note concluded that it would be "wise to consider the matter confidentially together."[79] The import was clear: deal with us, not with them. The note was an attempt to cleave West Germany from its allies and make bilateral relations between Bonn and Moscow into the forum for deciding the future of Germany. The ghosts of the signers of the Rapallo Treaty, a 1922 accord between Russia and Germany that had shocked the Western powers, stood in the room.

Stunned, Teltschik rapidly tried to calculate whether the unofficial document was truly a top-level communication—since it had come through a bona fide back channel—or a ploy executed without Gorbachev's knowledge by someone lower down, possibly Falin himself.[80] Falin reportedly made a secret visit to the Soviet embassy in East Berlin three days later, to make the same demand: that a united Germany exit NATO.[81] Teltschik concluded that, regardless of authorship, he had to take the threat seriously. As a result, although the authorship of the unofficial note remained unclear, its impact did not.[82] Teltschik immediately informed Kohl, on whom the news also had a profound effect: like Thatcher, he felt "the unbelievable was starting to happen."[83]

The next time Kohl saw Baker, he confidentially informed the secretary about Moscow's desire for Germany to "pull back out of NATO" if it wanted to unify. The demand had the chancellor deeply worried that he might "wake up one day and discover that Gorbachev had tabled such a proposal" to the world at large. Baker replied that "Gorbachev had in fact raised similar considerations with the USA," suggesting that the ultimatum did have top-level approval. After learning of these developments, Blackwill later recalled, he woke up every morning dreading that might be the day Gorbachev went public with the deal of no NATO and no nukes in exchange for unification.[84]

The chancellor decided to spring his own plan first. He could not prevent the Soviets from making their demands public, but he hoped to create as many facts on the ground as possible before they did so. He was already scheduled to address the West German parliament on November 28, 1989, and he decided to use the event to call for a German confederation.[85] Because achieving that confederation would, he thought, take many years, it was essential to start as soon as possible.

Bush was one of the few people who received a short-notice warning of this surprise. The rest of the world learned of the chancellor's "ten-point plan" on television, which caused enormous resentment among allies, enemies, and neighbors alike. Gorbachev and Shevardnadze were livid and likened the chancellor to Adolf Hitler.[86] Kohl was unrepentant, confiding afterward to Baker that "if *he* had not produced his ten-point plan," he would have been caught flat-footed by a Soviet ultimatum. Now at least he was off and running.

But his rush to the microphone had a price. The experience of hearing about the ten-point plan on the news, rather than directly from Bonn beforehand, wounded French President François Mitterrand, who commiserated with Gorbachev afterward about how Kohl had blindsided them both.[87] To repair the damage, the chancellor became more accommodating toward Mitterrand in the following weeks. Those weeks were a critical time in the history of the EC: they included hugely significant decision-making on a common European currency and other next steps for integration, to be approved by an EC summit on December 8–9, 1989 in Strasbourg.[88]

The upheaval in Eastern Europe had also put on the agenda questions about the EC's role beyond the Iron Curtain—a daunting prospect. The EC did not want, as one later analyst put it, "to be the vehicle for political consolidation because [it] was serious business." EC membership "involved money!" Poland might even want agricultural or other support. "For a long time it was more politically difficult to let Poland sell tomatoes in France than [for NATO] to give Warsaw a pledge to fight and die to save it."[89]

But however much the EC might wish to slow the process down, it could not stop questions about the future from bubbling up. By December 1989, Austrians were already worried about what the aspirations of Eastern European states might mean for Austria's own potential membership in the EC. The Austrian foreign minister, Alois Mock, warned his British counterpart, Douglas Hurd, against putting Austria "into one category with the East European states" because Austrians should not be "handled any better or worse than other candidates for membership." Hurd reassured Mock "that Austria could not be mentioned in the same breath as Hungary and Poland."[90] During a visit in early 1990, the US deputy secretary of state, Lawrence Eagleburger, found Austrians "so fixated on the prospect of EC membership that they were unwilling to consider a larger role in what one described as the 'swamp' of Eastern Europe."[91]

Washington was also less than thrilled about the consequences of Kohl's ten-point plan, despite having at least received advance warning. Baker pointedly announced that the continued membership of a united Germany in NATO was one of the four conditions—diplomatically described as "principles"—that the United States expected to be observed.[92] There was much resentment inside Bonn as well; as the US embassy in

Bonn put it, Kohl did not even "clear his speech with Genscher or with the leaders of the other major parties."[93]

That Kohl had kept his own foreign minister in the dark at this decisive moment was a sign of the complicated relationship between the two titans of German politics. The chancellor was stuck with Genscher because Kohl's parliamentary majority rested on an alliance between the CDU, its smaller Bavarian sister party, and Genscher's Liberals (formally known as the Free Democratic Party, or FDP). Genscher was thus not only foreign minister but also kingmaker. He, however, was not stuck with Kohl. He and his fellow liberals could switch coalitions at will and join the center-left party instead, as they had done previously.[94] Because the chancellor could not dismiss his foreign minister but did not quite trust him either, Kohl preferred to manage the most crucial aspects of foreign policy through his trusted aide Teltschik. Genscher as a result resented Teltschik, which created other problems—but Kohl felt the cost was worth it.[95]

As Kohl and Teltschik were hustling in Bonn to fend off the potential Soviet ultimatum, Bush was readying himself for a summit with Gorbachev in Malta. In theory, Washington could seize the opportunity to turn the summit into the key decision-making forum on what was happening. Any effort by Washington and Moscow to decide the fate of Europe and its military alliances over the heads of the Europeans, however, would immediately awaken memories of the way the Yalta summit had done much the same at the end of World War II. Bush's advisors also stuck to their recommendation that, given Gorbachev's evident bitterness and weakness, now was not the time to forge major new initiatives with him. The Malta meeting, they decided, should have more limited goals.[96] National Security Council staffers spelled out a realistic, lower-key aim: "to get something from the Soviets for the defense budget cuts we probably will be making in any event."[97]

The Malta summit itself, held on December 2–3, 1989, was a curious mix of spectacle and anticlimax. Visually, it had all kinds of dramatic elements: the sight of majestic US and Soviet warships anchored near each other in a foreign harbor, with the delegations motoring back and forth on smaller boats for meetings; throngs of journalists; and an epic storm as the backdrop. It also produced the first face-to-face conversation between an American and a Soviet leader since the Wall had come down, obviously an event of no small importance.

The events behind closed doors were less noteworthy. As Scowcroft summarized the Malta summit afterward, "it was simply a chance for the two leaders to sit down and talk in a relaxed atmosphere, take the measure of each other. . . . That's about all it was."[98] The president made it abundantly clear to Gorbachev that he did not see Malta as the decision-making forum, saying, "I do not propose that we negotiate here." Instead, they should simply "move through various topics of interest."[99] Gorbachev tried to make the discussion more substantive. Echoing an offer he had once made to Reagan, he proposed the elimination of all tactical nuclear weapons, along with the elimination, according to Baker's notes, of "all nuclear on ships." Bush listened to these offers but stuck to his cautious approach.[100]

The opportunity for a breakthrough dwindled even further when the disastrous weather and high seas made it impossible to transfer safely between the two leaders' warships. Gorbachev became irate when Bush insisted on returning for a break on his ship, the USS *Belknap*. The Soviet leader predicted that the storm would intensify and eliminate any chance of Bush's return, and he was right. Another consequence was that a gourmet meal, brought along for a scheduled dinner on the *Belknap* with the Soviet delegation, ended up feeding just the US delegation and sailors instead.[101]

After leaving Malta, Bush went on to Brussels to have dinner with the West German chancellor, Kohl, before a NATO summit the next day. It was also their first face-to-face meeting since the fall of the Wall. In contrast to the meeting at Malta, here the two leaders spoke freely and at length about the challenges facing Germany. The flood of humanity through the holes in the Berlin Wall, Kohl believed, had two long-term causes. The first was NATO's resolve. Because of the alliance's unified front in the contest with the Warsaw Pact, "Gorbachev realized that he was losing the arms race and that his economic situation was getting worse and worse." The second was European integration: "it was unbearable for Eastern Europe to remain standing outside the door."[102]

Years later, Scowcroft remembered that dinner, rather than the larger NATO summit that followed, as the key moment in the development of US strategy after the fall of the Wall.[103] The German chancellor "outlined his hopes for Germany [*sic*] unification," the national security advisor recalled, and the president responded, "'go ahead. I'm with you completely.'" Scowcroft recalled his jaw dropping as Bush "gave him a *carte blanche*. To me that was the decisive step on German unification." In their joint memoir Bush and Scowcroft pointed to that dinner as the moment the president gave Kohl "a green light."[104] It was a smart move. Bush correctly sensed that German unification was coming, so he should be on the right side of that issue, and poised to catch any sign the chancellor might become willing to weaken or abandon NATO to accommodate Moscow.

Kohl thought creating the confederation he envisaged would require many years. By contrast, Henry Kissinger had suggested in a TV interview on November 29, 1989 that Germany might unify within just two, but the chancellor criticized Kissinger's timeline as far too rushed and risky. He believed a "calm period of development" was necessary, and he did not feel "under pressure" to rush matters. By signaling a close partnership, Bush positioned himself to protect US interests over the years or decades it would take Germany to unify.[105]

Having temporarily headed off a Soviet ultimatum, Kohl was weary of the tumult and yearning for a holiday break. But 1989 held one more crucial development in store. The chancellor finally took time to go to East Germany, which he had not yet done since the opening of the Wall—and was overwhelmed by what he found.

Kohl agreed to give a public speech in Dresden on the night of December 19, just two weeks after the protesters there had backed away from Putin. It is possible, indeed probable, that the young KGB officer stopped throwing files in the furnace long enough to listen to a broadcast of Kohl's remarks, or even attend in person. Later in life, Putin admitted to another time during the East German revolution when he simply "stood in the crowd and watched it happen," so perhaps he did the same with Kohl's speech; it was given outdoors, not far from his outpost.

If Putin did attend, he witnessed a transformative event in Kohl's life. The chancellor could scarcely believe the extent of desire for unification. The chanting Dresden crowd was a sea of West German flags, many improvised by cutting the hammer-and-sickle out of the center of the East German version of the same colors. Filled with emotion, Kohl told his overjoyed Dresden audience that his goal was "the unity of our nation."[106] The crowd, as the British ambassador to East Germany cabled home, hailed him as "their saviour."[107] Out of all the many unexpected, dramatic events that he experienced on the road to German unification, Kohl later recalled that evening as "my crucial moment."[108]

Two men—one seeking to unify 80 million Germans, the other a minor servant of the failing Soviet state and its secret police—had both experienced transformative nights in Dresden in December 1989. Their subsequent actions would have far-reaching consequences, although the younger man would have to wait another decade to begin his starring role on the world stage. Kohl, in contrast, had realized that he did not have to wait after all. Unification need not take years, or require power sharing in some clumsy interim confederation; he could reap a political harvest right away. The East German regime was collapsing and the crowds were cheering. The moment for unity was now. Having just told the US president he was not in a hurry, suddenly he was.

CHAPTER TWO

To Hell with That

WITH UNIFICATION ON THE HORIZON, the Cold War dividing line between the two Germanies was going to disappear. It was an open question whether the Atlantic Alliance would as well. Moscow could make a compelling case that, with border fortifications coming down, Bonn no longer needed NATO—so why not trade a superfluous alliance for national unity and a new relationship with eastern neighbors? Even before the Wall had fallen, Soviet leader Mikhail Gorbachev had spoken of building a common European home. Although the details remained vague, he seemed to have in mind a pan-European organization stretching from the Atlantic to the Ural Mountains or even the Pacific Ocean. President George H. W. Bush, in contrast, had a clear goal: to maintain NATO and secure its future in a united Germany by extending Article 5 to that country's new eastern territory. His response to the idea that Moscow might decide Germany's relationship with NATO was unequivocal: "to hell with that."

What mattered most, however, were the desires not of Bush or Gorbachev but of Chancellor Helmut Kohl. It was clear that the German wanted to unify his country; the question was what he would be willing to give up in exchange. Depending on the answer to that question, the German would tip the balance between America and Russia. The source of Kohl's leverage was the significance of his country to NATO. Given the number of troops and atomic weapons on German soil—by 1990, divided Germany had the highest concentration of nuclear arms per square mile anywhere on the planet—a decision by Kohl to demand removal of those forces from some or all of his territory in exchange for unity would have profound consequences for the viability of not just of NATO but Western defense and transatlantic relations writ large.[1]

The ugly truth for Washington was that Kohl's goal of unifying his country and Bush's goal of preserving the alliance were separable. There existed realistic scenarios under which the chancellor could cut a deal with Moscow to achieve German unification at the cost of NATO expansion beyond the Cold War line, or even of NATO membership altogether. Kohl and Gorbachev could reshape political order in Europe without having any Americans in the room. As the national security advisor, Brent Scowcroft, later admitted, "my nightmare" was "Gorbachev making an offer to Kohl" that the German "couldn't refuse"—"that is, an offer for German reunification in exchange for neutrality." The consequences of such a deal were clear to the Americans in advance; as Robert Zoellick, Secretary of State James Baker's top aide, bluntly put it, "'if the Germans work out unification with the Soviets,'" then "'NATO will be dumped.'"[2]

This reality meant that Moscow, thanks to its legal and military hold over Germany since World War II, still possessed—despite its declining power in 1990—the ability to undermine the established order of West European security and transatlantic relations. Combined with the public disapproval of the foreign-controlled nuclear arsenal in divided Germany, it meant Gorbachev had leverage—not least because 1990 was a West German national election year, so Kohl was particularly attuned to public sentiment. If Kohl became willing to pay any price to achieve unity in advance of that election, the consequences would be profound.[3] Bush and his team were, as a result, aghast to hear belatedly and indirectly at the start of February 1990 that Kohl had agreed to go to Moscow for bilateral negotiations—without telling Washington. It was game on.

Lost in Translation

One of Scowcroft's most trusted advisors at the NSC, Robert Blackwill, spoke nearly every morning in 1990 with Zoellick. Baker had chosen Zoellick to be his "gatekeeper" and "'second brain,'" since Baker thought his subordinate's only weakness was that he was "too smart." Blackwill and Zoellick's morning conversations always began with words to the effect of, how can we achieve Bush's goal? What can we do today to advance a unified Germany in NATO, with as few restrictions on the alliance's future as possible?[4]

It was clear to both men, and to their bosses, that they needed as a practical matter to keep the number of people with a say as small as possible. As Baker explained to the British foreign secretary, Douglas Hurd, they planned to make strategy among "a very small circle of people."[5] The challenge would be reconciling that exclusivity with the need to involve players possessing undeniable rights to be heard—namely, the British, the French, and the East Germans—all while accomplishing what the president wanted: ensuring that "NATO must stay."[6]

As a first step, it was crucial to ascertain what Gorbachev would want in exchange for letting all regions of a unified Germany either remain or become part of NATO. The problem was that Gorbachev himself apparently did not yet know what he wanted, and both Bonn and Washington noticed this indecisiveness.[7] He tried for a while simply to promote the idea of more four-power events as the means of deciding on the future of Germany. Neither the Germans nor the Americans agreed to that approach, however, even though London was sympathetic.[8]

Gorbachev also had to deal with a rising rebellion among his own allies, particularly in Eastern Europe. Already on January 12, 1990, West German foreign ministry experts found it necessary to analyze how the Soviet leader would handle the current major "changes (collapse?) of the Warsaw Pact." They concluded Moscow wanted "to move quickly beyond the 'break-up phase' of the old Warsaw Pact regime" but lacked a "fully-formed concept" as to how.[9]

Meanwhile, the US National Intelligence Council (NIC), independently exploring the same issue, concluded that the pact was already de facto impotent, as Moscow could no longer rely on its allies to carry out its wishes or even to tolerate the presence of Soviet forces.[10] The NIC's private suspicions soon received public confirmation. Gorbachev, as part of earlier reforms, had classified the Soviet invasions of Hungary and Czechoslovakia in 1956 and 1968 as errors. Because the Soviet troop presence begun with those invasions had persisted, that new classification effectively called the basis on which the troops were still there into question. Budapest and Prague pressed Soviet forces to leave as a result, and on January 23, 1990, Prime Minister Miklós Németh of Hungary announced Moscow's pullback of all troops in his country. The Czechoslovaks succeeded as well. Soon, planning for the removal of all Soviet forces in both countries was underway. The Warsaw Pact was breaking up in deed, if not yet in word.[11]

Even worse, the Soviet ambassador in West Germany, Yuli Kvitzinsky, suspected that the timing of the pact's final collapse might not be under Moscow's control but Bonn's. Kvitzinsky reportedly advised Moscow that, given the obvious warmth in relations between Kohl and his eastern neighbors, the chancellor could, without any special "exertion," enlist "the help of Hungary, Poland, and Czechoslovakia" in order "to bring about the collapse of the Warsaw Pact in the shortest possible time" whenever he wished it.[12]

Matters were going so badly for Moscow that Gorbachev's advisors began complaining they were wasting precious time as the Soviet-led order disintegrated abroad—and at home. Economic woes created widespread misery in the USSR in the winter of 1990; at the end of 1989, Western banks had stopped providing short-term loans to the Soviet Union, which was increasingly unable to afford imported goods. The Soviet foreign minister, Eduard Shevardnadze, raised the question of a loan with Baker and sent a humiliating request for food to Kohl.[13] In reply, the chancellor approved a subsidized sale of foodstuffs worth 220 million DM.[14] Despite such support, however, discontent and strike threats became so severe that Gorbachev announced he was canceling all foreign commitments to focus on domestic problems.[15]

With so much going wrong, Gorbachev huddled with his closest advisors at the end of January to formulate a strategy. Like Bush, he preferred to keep true decision-making circles small. He consulted only a handful of trusted aides, bypassing the usual military, institutional, and party hierarchies. Valentin Falin, the party's Germany expert who would increasingly find himself among the excluded as the year went on, later sarcastically referred to issues addressed by the inner circle as "Gorbachev's holy zone."[16]

Gorbachev's security advisor, Anatoly Chernyaev, made messy, scrawling notes just after the January brainstorming session. According to his notes, the head of the KGB, Vladimir Kryuchkov, pointed to the writing on the wall, saying "it is necessary to train our people gradually to accept the reunification of Germany." Gorbachev insisted in reply that they had not yet run out of leverage. The USSR still had its legal rights as one of the four occupying powers, as well as troops and weapons in Germany, so it could not be ignored. "The most important thing," Gorbachev pronounced, "is that no one should count on the united Germany joining NATO," and the good news was that "the presence of our troops will not allow that."[17]

The question, he went on, was how to move forward, given that his efforts at reinstating four-power decision-making had failed. Chernyaev suggested considering six-power talks that would include the two Germanies. For his part, Gorbachev felt it was time to invite Kohl to Moscow. Despite all that had happened since November 1989, he had not yet spoken face-to-face with the German leader. Now, dealing with him had become unavoidable because "there are no real powers in the GDR" anymore. Although the Soviet leader would continue to deal publicly with the latest East German leader, Hans Modrow—even inviting him to Moscow to provide an appearance of balance for the Kohl visit—Gorbachev made clear that "we can influence the process only through the FRG."

Nikolai Ryzhkov, a Politburo member and chair of the council of ministers, seconded the Soviet leader, saying that "it is impossible to preserve the GDR," so "everything now is a matter of tactics." With the Wall gone, the East German economy was crumbling, and "all the state institutions are falling apart too." He agreed that focusing solely on the FRG made sense.[18] They had some time to play with, Gorbachev argued, because "economically it will take a few years for Germany to eat the GDR up," so he and his advisors at least had "these years to make our moves." The challenge was to figure out those moves.[19] The conversation failed to yield much in the way of strategy. Instead, the best the Soviet leader could come up with was delay. As of now, he concluded, "the most important thing now is to prolong this process."[20]

This desultory holy-zone session had an unexpected impact. Gorbachev's grudging recognition of unification, twinned with hope of separating a united Germany from NATO and delaying the process as long as possible, turned in translation into much more. When Modrow dutifully showed up in Moscow on January 30, Gorbachev made remarks to journalists covering the visit that were consistent with the sense of the holy zone: the "unity of the Germans" was "no longer in doubt."[21] The next day, one of the West German foreign ministry's Soviet experts, Klaus Neubert, sent an exultant note to his boss. He happily advised Foreign Minister Hans-Dietrich Genscher that Gorbachev had issued "a clear and unconditional commitment to German unity." Neubert added that the Soviet "vote" for unity was "surprising precisely because of its clarity"— even though no vote had occurred, let alone one with a clear result.[22] It was one of many times that a divergence of perceptions on the results of key meetings had significant policy consequences.

Neubert's exaggerated account had an immediate impact on Genscher. The foreign minister had already, in December 1989, started telling NATO colleagues that he saw the idea of a "peaceful order from the

Atlantic to the Urals" as a "winning concept."[23] He had also hinted to party colleagues in January 1990 that he regarded limits on NATO's future role in united Germany, or even integration of the alliance into some kind of European collective security system, as reasonable concessions to Moscow.[24] Genscher was partly motivated by his personal history. Born in 1927 in Halle, which had ended up behind the Iron Curtain, he had promised never to "forget where I come from and what responsibility I have" to make "a new beginning" possible for all who lived in East Germany.[25]

On the day Neubert advised him about Gorbachev's "vote" for unity, the foreign minister apparently decided it was time to go public with how he would make good on that promise. In a January 31, 1990 speech in Tutzing—the site of previous historic speeches by West German leaders in the 1960s on the need for outreach to the Soviet Bloc—he advised Germany's allies to adopt an accommodating attitude to Moscow in the interest of making unification happen. He wanted NATO to "state unequivocally that whatever happens in the Warsaw Pact, there will be no expansion of NATO territory eastward, that is to say, closer to the borders of the Soviet Union."[26]

Upon hearing about this speech, Zoellick was relieved Genscher had not gone even further and openly questioned German membership in NATO altogether. The foreign minister's words nonetheless prompted irate reactions from the top in Washington. Bush and Scowcroft found the foreign minister's "obvious detour around a Four Power role in reunification" to be particularly "troubling."[27] Scowcroft's subordinates, Blackwill and Robert Hutchings, had warned their boss in advance that such public remarks might be coming, having heard about Genscher's similar private comments earlier in the month. Their takeaway was that Germans were suddenly in a "rush to fill the vacuum of ideas for the future of Germany and of Europe." Blackwill and Hutchings advised that immediate US action was needed because "our ability to manage the process is slipping quickly." To add insult to injury, Németh had recently gone even further and appealed for *all* of a unified Germany, not just its eastern part, to become fully demilitarized. The motive behind this appeal, Bush and his advisors guessed, was Németh's desire to deny "any legitimacy" to a continuing Soviet role in Eastern Europe; if the Americans left, then Moscow would have no justification for staying.[28]

Németh was presumably worried about what Soviet forces were doing on his territory. Although Moscow had by then promised to withdraw its troops from both Hungary and Czechoslovakia, the actual pullback was hesitant and violent; one US diplomat described it as "nasty." Soviet forces smashed barracks, ripped out telephone lines, set off unannounced explosions, and left an "environmental 'mess' including leaking oil barrels."[29] They also started selling their weaponry, "including tanks," on the black market.[30] The Hungarian leader appeared to be grasping at extreme measures to get them out, but neither Bush nor his advisors were sympathetic to the concept of a Germany that was not just denuclearized but demilitarized entirely.

Genscher, sensing his ideas might be getting lost in translation, made time for a lightning trip to the United States on February 2, 1990 to explain them in person. In his memoirs, he called the journey the shortest but most important visit he ever paid to Washington.[31] Once there, he not only repeated his inclination to bar NATO from eastern Germany in exchange for unification, but also brought up the question of Central and Eastern Europe. He told Baker there was a "need to assure the Soviets that NATO would not extend its territorial coverage to the area of the GDR nor anywhere else in Eastern Europe for that matter," and repeated the point at their joint press conference afterward.[32]

The two men also addressed the need to deal with the British, French, East German, and Soviet concerns.[33] Genscher said that he would support an idea that Baker's advisors had already started discussing with the West Germans, similar to that debated by Gorbachev's holy zone: negotiations involving all six states, but only if they were called "two-plus-four" talks—in other words, with the two Germanies headlining to show their significance.[34] Neither Genscher nor Kohl wanted four occupying powers obviously talking down to them.

Baker's advisors believed that such talks would have the advantage of giving all six states their required seats at the table while simultaneously preventing any of them, particularly the West Germans, from cutting separate deals.[35] It was an unavoidable fact that the West needed some mechanism both to close out Soviet rights from 1945 and to address the lasting legal rights of the British and French as well—not to mention keeping on top of the daily diplomatic activity rendered essential by fast-paced events—so the two-plus-four forum seemed like a way to tick all relevant boxes. Genscher added that the thirty-five-member Conference on Security and Cooperation in Europe (CSCE) could be strengthened and intensified to give other states besides the six a venue for expressing their views. When the foreign minister had an opportunity to summarize these ideas to the president personally, Bush reportedly "blessed" them.[36]

Despite this sense of agreement, after Genscher's departure Baker covered all his bases just in case. He instructed Vernon Walters, the US ambassador in Bonn, to convey personally to Horst Teltschik, Kohl's security advisor and close confidant, the content of the discussions during the lightning visit. Baker wanted to make certain someone told the chancellor what had been said—and the secretary was not certain Genscher himself would do that.[37] As instructed, Walters briefed Teltschik on February 4, 1990.[38] Taken together, the lightning visit and the subsequent chain of communications represented the crossing of a conceptual watershed. They meant that, by February 4 at the latest, the small circle of top players in Washington and Bonn knew Genscher was sketching the contours of NATO's future relationship not just with the eastern part of his own country but also with Central and Eastern Europe.

Teltschik was grateful for the heads-up. Genscher, ever resentful of the way the chancellery essentially tried to run its own separate foreign policy, did not routinely inform Kohl of what he said abroad. Teltschik would at times contact the foreign ministry directly and request transcripts of the foreign minister's conversations abroad, only to be rebuffed. This omission was apparent not just to Baker but also to the NSC, which reacted by ensuring that significant communications with Bonn went in duplicate to both the chancellery and the foreign ministry—even though, as Hutchings later recalled, "it was tedious always to have to reach agreement with Kohl and Genscher separately."

This two-track approach generated tension between the Department of State and the NSC at times, because the latter hoped to outmaneuver Genscher by going through Teltschik. By contrast, the State Department viewed circumventing a duly appointed foreign minister, particularly one with domestic political might, as unwise. But for Washington there was a compensatory upside to the problem. As Hutchings later recalled, "we occasionally knew more about where Kohl or Genscher stood on an issue than either of them knew of the other."[39] As a shorthand for this odd situation and its complexities, the term *Genscherism* became more popular. Previously in use in Washington as a shorthand for an overly complacent policy toward Moscow (in the view of Americans), it seemed newly relevant.[40]

That accommodating stance was on display yet again when Genscher, now back in Bonn, spoke to his visiting British counterpart. Genscher unambiguously told Hurd that when he "talked about not wanting to extend NATO, that applied to other states besides the GDR." The foreign minister felt that "the Russians must have some assurance that, for example, if the Polish Government left the Warsaw Pact one day, they would not join NATO the next."[41] As a result, it was utterly essential for the Atlantic Alliance to make clear that "NATO does not intend to expand its territory to the East." Genscher even wanted some kind of public statement to that effect and felt it "must refer not just to East Germany but rather be of a general nature. For example, the Soviet Union needs the security of knowing that Hungary, if it has a change of government, will not become part of the Western Alliance."[42]

Hurd expressed agreement and said the topic should be discussed as soon as possible within the alliance itself. One of Britain's biggest grievances was that the Germans were forging ahead with too little notice given to anyone about anything, so London would welcome a chance to consult.[43] Genscher indicated that such discussions should begin "now" and should take into account "developments in Poland, Czechoslovakia, Hungary and East Germany." He summarized the problem that he was facing: "we do not want to extend NATO territory, but we do not want to leave NATO." The solution, he thought, was that "both alliances must become part of the common European security structure."[44]

"Not Shift One Inch Eastward"

Genscher had shared his thinking with Baker and Hurd not just to convince them but also in preparation for a German-Soviet summit in Moscow. As Gorbachev had indicated he would do in the holy-zone session, he had invited the German chancellor to Moscow. Kohl and Genscher were both due there on Saturday, February 10.[45]

Bush and his advisors could not believe when Soviet contacts, apparently assuming the West Germans had cleared the visit with Washington, let the date slip. Kohl had promised to show his cards to Washington, and this was a significant card that he had not shown. Had something else gotten lost in translation too? Was the lack of notice to Washington a sign Kohl was reconsidering his commitment to NATO?[46]

Scowcroft cornered Teltschik at a conference in Munich on February 3 for a private talk, "embarrassed" him with news that Washington had learned of Kohl's travel plans, and questioned him for "Kohl's purpose in going to the Soviet Union." Teltschik responded that the chancellor wanted to accelerate unification and added that Bonn had heard "Gorbachev might be willing to accept a unified Germany within NATO if all ground-based nuclear weapons (Lance and nuclear artillery) are removed from German soil." In Teltschik's view "this would not be a bad deal for the West." He added that Bonn knew Baker was making plans of his own for an extended visit to Moscow starting on February 7. Teltschik asked whether Scowcroft could "find a way to brief the Chancellor on Jim's conversations with the Soviets before Kohl sees Gorbachev." That would give West Germans a secret heads-up regarding what to expect, and Washington would have a chance to learn Bonn's thinking just before the bilateral talks with Moscow.[47]

Scowcroft agreed that his trusted NSC deputy, Bob Gates—who would be on the trip with Baker—should find a way to brief Kohl just before the chancellor saw Gorbachev. Upon learning of this, Baker reportedly added Zoellick to the briefing team. The secretary disliked having an NSC figure such as Gates conduct diplomatic contacts solo. Baker frequently reminded Scowcroft that, under President Ronald Reagan, NSC overzealousness in becoming operational had ended in the disaster of the botched Iran-Contra arms-for-hostages deal.[48]

Reporting on all of these developments to President Bush on February 4, Scowcroft decided to give the Germans an out: he suggested to the president that the extreme stress under which Kohl and Teltschik were operating might have caused their lapse in communications. Although both Germans were glad to see the inner-German border disappear, the massive flow of Easterners to the West was causing overwhelming problems. With the East German regime collapsing, the state-centered economy was collapsing as well; hospitals and other state institutions were ceasing to function; and possibilities for friction with the still-present Soviet forces were rising. The national security advisor's main impression from his brief visit to Munich was that divided Germany "is like a pressure cooker." In Scowcroft's view, it "will take our best efforts, and those of Kohl, to keep the lid from blowing off in the months ahead."[49]

Meanwhile, Genscher, still on a campaign to rally all possible support for his post–Cold War vision before going to Moscow, laid down one final public marker before departing for the Soviet Union. Speaking at a conference on February 9, he repeated yet again that "whatever happens in the Warsaw Pact, an extension of NATO's territory to the east, that is, nearer to the borders of the Soviet Union, will not happen."[50] He had his subordinates in the West German foreign ministry flesh out alternatives to the two-bloc structure of European security. One analyst argued that "at a moment in which the collapse of the Warsaw Pact is foreseeable," the West must move beyond outdated bloc thinking. A better option for the future of European security, the ministry suggested, would be to institutionalize and expand the CSCE.[51]

Not all of Genscher's subordinates agreed with this view, however, and one of them decided to do something about it. Joachim von Arnim, a West German diplomat in Moscow, disagreed strongly with his boss's willingness to call NATO's future into question—and, worse, believed that the foreign minister was doing so far too soon.[52] Contradicting his colleague Neubert, who mistakenly reported there had been a clear Soviet vote for German unification, von Arnim cabled Bonn on February 7 that rather than being a settled matter, "the German question" remained "a significant field of contention" in Moscow. In other words, the time for the kind of concessions Genscher was airing had not yet come.[53]

Von Arnim was so upset that he even took the dramatic step of going behind Genscher's back to his archenemy, Teltschik, in order to fight "Genscher's dangerous conceptions." The diplomat told Kohl's top advisor that it was not necessary to consider constraining NATO and that Genscher should be made to stop doing so. From his vantage point stationed in a disintegrating Soviet Union, von Arnim saw an easier way to achieve unification: "we can purchase unity for ourselves, and by that I mean with money; concessions in the field of security policy will probably not be necessary."[54]

Teltschik reportedly thanked von Arnim for this welcome news and shared it with Kohl.[55] The advice addressed the very conundrum that, according to internal documents, the chancellery was actively considering: whether and to what extent unification would have to come at the cost of separating Germany from its previous security commitments.[56] Given that, ever since Kohl's visit to Dresden in December 1989, it was clear Bonn would (in the words of the British) go "full blast" and "get the outline of a unification treaty into the international arena before the end of the year," the question of what it would cost had become urgent.[57] Teltschik was grateful to hear directly from a German diplomat in Moscow that unification might not sacrifice NATO's future freedom or its nuclear weapons. As Teltschik advised Kohl at the start of February, "the military presence of the US in Europe and in particular the protection provided by their nuclear forces remain for the foreseeable future indispensable."[58]

Back in Washington, Bush and Scowcroft—in the unaccustomed role of distant spectators to a major geopolitical event—could only speculate on what would happen when Kohl visited Moscow. Every aspect of the visit was crucial, down to the exact moment of his arrival. The chancellor

decided to delay landing in Moscow on February 10 until after Baker and
his traveling party had departed. While this ruled out the briefing that
Teltschik had requested, Baker nonetheless agreed to leave Kohl a written summary of his visit—but put together by his own trusted subordinates, Zoellick and Dennis Ross.[59]

Blackwill dubbed the Baker and Kohl trips to Moscow "the Beginning of the Big Game." He guessed, presciently, that "there is a good
chance that Gorbachev will give Kohl his bottom line on German unification." The question was whether that bottom line meant NATO would
have to remain behind the alliance's Cold War border—or, worse, retreat
west if all of Germany became neutral. Blackwill thought Gorbachev
would not demand outright neutrality and withdrawal from NATO. A better play would be to allow a unified Germany to stay in NATO in name,
but demand that it shed all foreign forces and nuclear weapons, using as a
precedent the kind of membership terms Norway and Iceland had been
able to impose at NATO's founding forty years earlier.[60] If Gorbachev
were to request this bespoke status for all of Germany in exchange for unification, Blackwill guessed "many Germans and some of our Congress
would find such a deal all too tempting." For Washington, however, this
outcome was completely unacceptable because it "would forfeit the prime
assets"—the troops and weapons—"that have made the United States a
postwar European power."[61]

As this weighing of options was going on, NATO's secretary general,
former West German CDU politician Manfred Wörner, gave his own vision for the alliance in a speech in Hamburg. Wörner's career in German
politics had stalled when he had been minister of defense because of a
scandal involving alleged homosexual activity by a general, considered a
security risk at the time. Now politically reborn as the secretary general
of NATO, he had earned the respect and trust of Washington, particularly of Bush and Scowcroft. When he called for "a special military status
for the territory of the GDR" as NATO moved eastward after unification, they listened and recognized a potential winning strategy in the big
game.[62] The problem was that neither Bush nor Scowcroft was going to
Moscow, and it soon emerged that Baker got on the plane with a different
concept of US strategy.

The secretary landed in a country going through violent agonies.[63]
By early 1990, a quarter of a million people were protesting in Moscow
for greater democracy and more regional autonomy. The Soviet Union appeared to be tearing itself apart at the seams.[64] Against this backdrop,

Baker began by holding lengthy sessions with his counterpart, Shevard-nadze. They discussed the two-plus-four framework as a better idea for managing German unification than four-power control, which the "Ger-mans won't buy." They also talked about the possibility that NATO might become more a political than a military organization. Baker decided to pose a hypothetical concession, asking whether there "might be an out-come that would guarantee that there would be no NATO forces in the eastern part of Germany. In fact there could be an absolute ban on that."[65] In his handwritten notes from this discussion, Baker put stars and an ex-clamation point next to his summary of these points: "End result: Uni-fied Ger. anchored in a ★ changed (polit.) NATO—★ whose juris. would not move ★ eastward!"[66]

Baker subsequently spoke directly to Gorbachev on February 9.[67] The American swiftly addressed the elephant in the room, a united Germa-ny's relations with NATO. He argued against neutrality, warning Ger-many might decide to "create its own nuclear potential" if NATO were forced to pull its arsenal out. Baker presumably mentioned the prospect because he knew it would raise Moscow's hackles.

Baker then repeated the key concept from his talks with Shevardnadze in the form of a question, unwittingly touching off a controversy that would last decades: "Would you prefer to see a unified Germany outside of NATO, independent and with no US forces, or would you prefer a uni-fied Germany to be tied to NATO, with assurances that NATO's juris-diction would not shift one inch eastward from its present position?" The Soviet leader replied that any expansion of the "zone of NATO" was not acceptable. And, according to Gorbachev, Baker answered, "we agree with that."[68]

For decades after, various leaders in Moscow would point to this ex-change as an agreement barring NATO from expanding beyond its east-ern Cold War border.[69] Baker and his aides and supporters, in contrast, would point to the hypothetical phrasing and lack of any written agree-ment afterward as a sign that the secretary had only been test-driving one potential option of many. Baker's press conference just after finishing with Gorbachev helped to confuse matters further. The rebellious West Ger-man diplomat von Arnim rushed to attend it, only to become "horrified" by what he heard Baker say: NATO's "'jurisdiction' would not be moved eastward."[70]

Von Arnim was not the only one hearing things he did not like. Baker's travel companion, Gates, had a similarly unpleasant experience listening to KGB head Kryuchkov.[71] In their meeting, Gates echoed much of what Baker was saying, asking the KGB leader what he thought of the idea that "NATO troops would move no further east than they now were? It seems to us to be a sound proposal." Kryuchkov replied that the Soviet Union had "'no enthusiasm' about a unified Germany in NATO" and wanted more time for consideration, indicating, "we need not hurry so much."[72]

The KGB chief then proceeded, much to Gates's surprise, to disparage Gorbachev. As Gates later recalled, "Kryuchkov seemed to have written off Gorbachev and concluded that perestroika had been a terrible mistake." This new stance represented "an important and even dangerous turn." The deputy national security advisor was particularly amazed that the head of the KGB was "openly opposing Gorbachev in a meeting with a senior American official." As Gates later recalled, "I decided I would not meet with him again."[73]

As the American delegation prepared to depart, Baker did as agreed and had subordinates draw up a secret summary for Kohl of everything crucial that had been said.[74] The summary repeated the question that he had asked Gorbachev, namely, whether Moscow would accept a unified Germany if NATO did not move one inch east. According to Baker, Gorbachev answered that "'any extension of the zone of NATO would be unacceptable.'" But Baker thought that Gorbachev was "not locked-in," and he looked forward "to comparing notes" once Kohl spoke to him as well.[75]

Kohl had made a number of smart moves to soften up his Soviet negotiating partners just before his arrival. In a briefing for journalists, Teltschik had strategically let slip that East Germany was on the brink of insolvency. In just days it would be unable to pay creditors. This caused an enormous splash in the media and undermined the weakened Modrow government even more. The headlines about economic doomsday in the GDR that accompanied Kohl to Moscow strengthened his case that drastic measures were needed.[76] On top of that, Kohl engineered official approval of emergency food aid, requested by Moscow back in January, on February 8, 1990. The promise of foodstuffs effectively greased the way for Kohl's arrival in the Soviet Union.[77]

But Bush and Scowcroft did not want Kohl, clearly in a generous mood, to give even more to Moscow. They also grew worried when word of Baker's hypothetical question made it back to the White House. Concern immediately arose within the NSC that Baker had leaned much too far forward. Like von Arnim, the NSC saw no need to make concessions on NATO's future in advance of express requests from Moscow. The NSC worried that Baker had not yet "internalized" the preferred White House line and wanted to make sure that Kohl, at least, got the message before speaking to Gorbachev.[78] White House staff drafted, and Bush signed and sent, an urgent message to this effect to Kohl—meaning the chancellor received, just before his time with Gorbachev, not one but two top-level US communications: Baker's secret summary and Bush's discordant message. In contrast to Baker, Bush endorsed a "special military status for what is now the territory of the GDR"—in other words, Wörner's idea.

Although the difference in wording between Baker and the NSC message was slight, the difference in effect was significant. Baker spoke of an alliance that would not shift one inch eastward; Bush spoke of making a minor concession as the alliance shifted many inches eastward beyond its Cold War border.[79] If the president could achieve that, it would form a major precedent. Contemplating these contradictory letters, Kohl had to decide which one to cite to Gorbachev. He made a fateful choice: he used the language most conducive to achieving his goal of German unity.

Greenlighting

As Kohl and his traveling party made their way from the airport to downtown Moscow, the staff of the West German embassy, including von Arnim, assembled to watch Gorbachev welcome them at the Grand Kremlin Palace. It was a sumptuous former imperial residence, originally built on the orders of Czar Nicholas I. Standing in the crowd, von Arnim watched Gorbachev descend and greet the visiting Germans against the backdrop of a magnificent staircase decorated with a large picture of Lenin. Despite the grandeur of his welcome, however, von Arnim sensed that Gorbachev was uncertain: "He clearly had a cold, and did not beam self-confidence and charisma" in the way that he usually did. Kohl and Gorbachev then disappeared for a confidential session with only Chernyaev, Teltschik, and their translators. Meanwhile, Genscher and Shevardnadze headed off to their own small session, leaving von Arnim and the rest of their subordinates to mill around, awaiting a larger session with all delegation members later.[80]

Once alone with the people who mattered, Kohl behaved in a manner consistent with what he had told his fellow party members before departing Bonn: "whatever happens, we want the unity of our nation." He had promised his colleagues to do everything in his power to bring that about, and now he followed through, even though doing so involved setting aside the letter sent directly by the president of the United States.[81] With Gorbachev, the chancellor instead used the phrasing about NATO's future most conducive to getting the Soviet leader to agree, namely, words similar to those of Baker: "naturally, NATO could not expand its territory to the current territory of the GDR."[82] Kohl did not raise Wörner's idea—now endorsed by Bush—that NATO would expand its territory eastward by creating a special status for East German territory within the alliance.

Technically, it was not within either Kohl's or Gorbachev's authority to map out the future of the Atlantic Alliance. The chancellor nonetheless spoke in a manner suggesting that his country's influence would prevail, the need to deal with allies notwithstanding. Even as Kohl uttered these words to Gorbachev, his foreign minister was telling Shevardnadze the same thing. As Genscher put it to the Soviet foreign minister in their parallel session: "For us, it is clear: NATO will not extend itself to the East."[83]

To Gorbachev, Kohl added that he wanted to unify the two Germanies as soon as possible, by taking steps to create economic and monetary union even before an East German election—the first free one—scheduled for March 18, 1990. Gorbachev initially resisted, saying that just a few months earlier, Kohl had been talking in terms of years. To explain his change of heart, Kohl described his transformative experience in Dresden. Given the clear desires of the East Germans, he now had to move more swiftly.[84]

The Soviet leader remained unreceptive, asking instead if Germany could become a nonaligned state.[85] Trying to figure out how to sway Gorbachev, Kohl suddenly had a brilliant negotiating insight. Earlier, Gorbachev had said in passing that "the Germans in the Federal Republic and in the DDR must themselves decide" how to proceed in the future. Kohl realized that this statement could become the opening he needed. Recalling that comment, the chancellor asked Gorbachev if the following paraphrase of the Soviet leader's words was accurate: were they "in agreement that the decision about the unification of Germany is a question that the Germans themselves must now decide"? Gorbachev hedged, uncertain where this line of questioning was going, but he conceded that "everything the chancellor said was very close" to his own statements.[86]

It was close enough for Kohl. He had realized that those words— "Germans themselves must now decide"—could be portrayed as a green light shining on unification, and without conditions.[87] Sensing it was time to offer something in return, he made clear that Gorbachev could count on him for financial help. The German economy, Kohl pointed out, was in a very healthy state: "the last eight years were the best since the war." It was therefore "natural" that West Germany and the Soviet Union "could do much together."[88]

The session ended soon thereafter, without any attempt by Gorbachev to clarify this exchange or any sign that he realized its significance. Those lapses did not change the outcome: Gorbachev had conceded that the question of unity should be decided by the Germans alone, but he had not secured any major concessions in exchange, either orally or in writing, on NATO or any other topic.[89] Perhaps the Soviet leader doubted whether Kohl had the authority to pronounce on NATO's future on his own and assumed it would be decided in more significant talks to come. Gorbachev also apparently did not anticipate that Kohl would immediately operationalize the Soviet leader's remarks. The chancellor had already received an American green light; now, he rushed to portray his talks in Moscow as the Soviet greenlighting of German unification.

Kohl and Gorbachev rejoined their other delegation members, including von Arnim, for a larger joint session. As soon as it began, Kohl repeated what he had just agreed with Gorbachev, expressing gratitude for "the conviction of the general secretary" that the question of whether Germans wanted to "to live in the unity of one state was a question for Germans, a question that they must decide themselves."[90] It was the start of a prolonged effort to point out what sufficiently resembled a green light to as many people as possible before it changed color.

When the session ended, von Arnim found himself briefly next to Kohl and Genscher in a departing crowd. He overheard them talking about how the next German national election would take place *after* unification. As he later wrote in his diary, he "could hardly believe it." He realized that something significant must have happened and was "astonished by the cold-bloodedness with which they immediately turned to the domestic political consequences of their talks." There were more surprises. Von Arnim was further amazed that Kohl had gotten permission to depart the Kremlin by having his chauffeur use a Kremlin gate normally reserved for top Soviet officials. He realized the genius of Kohl's move when the chancellor had the car stop so he could climb out in full view of Western journalists and photographers, apparently tipped off in advance as to where to await Kohl's appearance: "There could not be a better picture than the one of the smiling giant in the blowing snow on Red Square, in front of a giant, open Kremlin gate."[91]

Kohl showed further political genius by calling for a swift press conference. One had been scheduled for the next day, but suddenly that was not soon enough. He needed to televise the green light right away. As Kohl and Genscher settled themselves for the start of the event, an open microphone caught the two rivals speaking quietly to each other with unaccustomed joviality. In a sign of respect, Genscher asked if he could shake Kohl's hand. With a broad smile, Kohl obliged, adding, "now we really should get drunk." Television viewers then saw Kohl proclaim that it was "a good day for Germany" because Gorbachev had acknowledged the "sole right of the German people" to decide whether they wanted to live together in one state.[92] In his memoirs, written years later, Genscher recounted how he could still see "disbelief in the faces of the journalists," who seemed not to comprehend what had happened.[93]

Some viewers did comprehend the announcement, however, and they included Bush and Scowcroft. They followed the press conference closely, presumably wondering, when they heard the words "sole right," whether Kohl had forgotten the ongoing legal status of the four powers in Germany.[94] And if the Americans were concerned, back in Moscow Falin was aghast. "On February 10," he wrote in his memoirs, "the unification of Germany was announced as, de facto, an already completed task," and, even worse, "without any conditions, without clearing up the connection to the foreign aspects." He guessed to his horror that Gorbachev had not realized Kohl would move so quickly, and thereby missed the window of opportunity to spell out conditions for unification, such as a German exit from NATO. Falin concluded that "this carelessness will take its revenge on us."[95]

Shevardnadze was similarly shocked that Gorbachev had made such a far-reaching concession without telling him. Among the many reasons the shock was problematic was the Soviet foreign minister's imminent departure for a high-profile conference in Ottawa on a proposed "Open Skies" accord. Under the terms of this agreement, NATO and the Warsaw Pact states would allow planes to fly over each other's territories for inspectional purposes. Since all of the leading foreign ministers involved in German unification would be in attendance at the Canadian event, the concession seemed like something Shevardnadze would have to explain to his colleagues while there. Upset, the foreign minister speculated to an aide that Kohl might be instrumentalizing some hastily made remark of Gorbachev's.[96] Whatever had transpired, February 10 put Shevardnadze, according to his British colleague whom he saw soon after, into "a melancholy and fatalistic mood," which was presumably made worse when Genscher also began referring to events in Moscow as the "green light" for unification.[97]

The Germans, in contrast, could not have been happier as February 10 drew to a close and the drinking began. Genscher headed off with the staff of West Germany's Moscow embassy in search of whiskey. The exultant foreign minister even had kind words for von Arnim, his rebellious subordinate. Peering over his whiskey glass, he reportedly told von Arnim, "you were right"; it had not been necessary to make major security concessions in order to get a green light for unification. In fact, Genscher could still scarcely believe that "Gorbachev had agreed to unity practically without any conditions." He spoke as if German unity were a done deal, and now it was time to consider the practical consequences.[98]

Kohl and his advisors, meanwhile, were drinking beer.[99] The chancellor felt he had work to do afterward. A door to the future had opened, and he needed to figure out the best way to get through it while it was still open. In his memoirs, he recalled being so excited that, even though it was the middle of the night in February in Moscow, he went for a long walk through Red Square to think and try to calm down enough to sleep.[100]

He was not the only one having a sleepless night. Despite the good mood over whiskeys, the West German embassy staff worried that the Soviet side might wake up the next morning and try to deny what had happened. Von Arnim rushed to check how the Soviet news agency TASS covered the summit early the next day. He felt a huge wave of relief, even "euphoria," when he read a TASS report that stated, "the question of the unity of the German nation should be decided upon by only the Germans themselves."[101] The West German foreign ministry would later quote that press release to their skeptical Soviet negotiating partners when they tried to rein Bonn in.[102]

Von Arnim would have been less euphoric, however, if he could have heard the conversation the next day between Gorbachev and Modrow, the soon-to-be ex-leader of East Germany. Even as Kohl and Genscher were crowing about the green light, Gorbachev was repeating that "a unified Germany staying in NATO" was "unacceptable for us." The Soviet leader was disappointed at what Kohl had done the day before, complaining to Modrow that "overall I had the impression that Kohl behaved arrogantly."[103] And in contrast to the initial TASS announcement, the subsequent coverage of Kohl's visit in other Soviet media—still largely dictated by party leaders, and so a rough barometer of their feelings—downplayed Kohl's visit as "notably unspectacular." The West German embassy wondered whether such statements were meant to undermine Kohl, meant purely for domestic consumption, or both. They guessed that the Soviet leadership, "for domestic political reasons, would prefer that the populace not become aware too quickly of the impact made by the breakthrough during Kohl's visit."[104]

But the effort to switch the green light to red was coming too late. Kohl had gotten the word out, and now everyone was recalibrating. In London, Prime Minister Margaret Thatcher had already begun speculating about what might come next. On February 10, she predicted a deal whereby Germany would unify and remain in NATO, but that NATO would "forswear the deployment of non-German forces in the former GDR." Following unification, the capital of Germany would move to a united Berlin, meaning that the seat of a major NATO ally would be "in an area where NATO would not be militarily present," thus giving a hostage to fortune.[105] But there was little London could do about it. As Hurd later recalled, "Genscher and Kohl were the key. They made the weather, really. . . . And they weren't absolutely in each other's confidence. But they made the weather and we, we acclimatized."[106] Gorbachev had just endured such weather making. As Scowcroft's subordinates Condoleezza Rice and Philip Zelikow later put it, "the mask had slipped. Gorbachev had allowed both the Americans and the Germans to leave Moscow believing that he was not willing—or perhaps not able—to offer decisive opposition to their plans. In fact that was true."[107]

The Lightning Round

Fresh from this triumph in Moscow, Kohl soon had to face the consequences. He had not called Bush right after his conversation with Gorbachev, but he would have to talk to him soon. And having seen the mask slip, Scowcroft and his subordinates were growing convinced they could push Gorbachev harder than previously thought. The national security advisor was now not even sure the much-mooted two-plus-four forum was necessary—indeed, he thought it might cause harm.

Scowcroft had a hard time communicating this to Baker in early February, however, because the secretary was continually on the road. Even by the high standard of a secretary of state, Baker's travel schedule was impressive. On the same journey that included three days of top-level negotiating in Moscow, he also paid groundbreaking visits to three Warsaw Pact countries (Czechoslovakia, Bulgaria, and Romania), then went directly to Ottawa, Canada, for the Open Skies assembly of all twenty-three NATO and Warsaw Pact foreign ministers—without a pit stop in Washington. Although the aviation accord was supposed to be the main topic, as Baker put it in his memoirs, "it became apparent that German unification was the main game in town—and everyone wanted in on the action."[108]

He and his counterparts engaged in frenetic activity on the margin of the conference, conducting a lightning round of diplomacy. In one day, Baker and Shevardnadze held five separate talks; for his part, Shevardnadze also had three with Genscher and cornered Hurd, French foreign minister Roland Dumas, and Polish foreign minister Krzysztof Skubiszewski as well.[109] Baker wanted to turn the two-plus-four idea into reality as quickly as possible, since he now saw establishing the forum as an essential goal. Gorbachev had not definitively agreed to it in Moscow, but he had not vetoed it either, and Baker thought the good fortune of having all six key players in one place at the same time was too good to pass up.

His efforts inspired considerable irritation, however, among the excluded diplomats in Ottawa. At one point Genscher poured fuel on a fire when he snapped at the inquisitive Italian foreign minister, Gianni De Michelis, in front of their assembled colleagues, "You are not part of the game."[110] The diplomats most furious at being excluded from planning Germany's reunification in Ottawa, however, were the Poles. Given their experience with the last incarnation of a unified Germany, their distress was understandable; but the West German ambassador in Warsaw dismissed it as "hysteria."[111]

Baker, a disciplined and relentless negotiator, remained undeterred. He worked hard to corral the relevant countries—and only those countries—into agreeing to two-plus-four talks while all in one place. The secretary wore down Shevardnadze, who confided to an aide in Ottawa that he was "in a stupid situation." His Western colleagues were "talking about the unification of Germany as if it was a fact," and there seemed little he could do about it.[112] Despondent, Shevardnadze gave in to peer pressure and agreed not only to the two-plus-four but also to a US desideratum on arms control. In his State of the Union address on January 31, 1990, President Bush had called for both Washington and Moscow to reduce the enormous number of their troops in the center of Europe to an equal level of 195,000 each. Now, Shevardnadze indicated that Gorbachev was willing to do so. Baker could hardly believe it; the announcement meant that "for the first time since World War II, Moscow was going to have fewer troops in Europe than the United States."

Realizing that Shevardnadze's assent to both the two-plus-four and the troop cuts might fade, Baker and his aides decided "we should move to lock it in" immediately, while still in Ottawa. The secretary knew that "any delay would allow opposition to form in Moscow, London, Paris, and other capitals"—not to mention among those countries excluded in Ottawa, such as Italy and Poland.[113] Baker's efforts almost broke down, however, not because of opposition growing in Moscow but because of the mistrust between Kohl and Genscher. Not once but twice, Bush told Baker to wait while he checked directly whether the chancellor approved of what was going on.

Baker suspected something else was in play as well. Scowcroft reportedly tried to intervene to slow down progress in Ottawa, saying the secretary was "'moving too fast'" to finalize the two-plus-four. Baker refused to change course, however, telling Scowcroft "it's too late for that . . . everybody has agreed to this."[114] Having fended off the national security advisor, however, Baker was suddenly hearing from the president himself to hold up, and he sensed that Scowcroft was ultimately behind it.

The president applying the brakes in this abrupt manner threatened to derail the breakneck negotiations, but Bush persisted, twice calling Kohl, who made clear that what mattered most was making the forum a fait accompli as soon as possible, before Moscow's green light changed color.[115] Finally, Bush told Baker to go ahead. The secretary then sprung the two-plus-four on the world through a hurried press conference with all six foreign ministers.[116]

The Canadian hosts were stunned to see this major announcement in their capital but without their participation.[117] Prime Minister Brian Mulroney complained extensively to his friend Bush about how his conference had been hijacked. He was particularly upset about how "Genscher arrived in Ottawa with the most cavalier attitude." The West German foreign minister had rolled into town saying, "'the big boys will settle this,'" and making clear the big boys did not include Canada. Mulroney was furious at the arrogance: "Jesus Christ, with all those Canadian boys buried in Europe," just who did Genscher think he was?[118]

Mulroney was not the only one who was livid. At the end of a long day in Ottawa, Baker requested yet another call with the White House. This time he ensured that only he and Bush were on the line, and let his old friend George know what he thought about the attempt to apply the brakes: "We had a good day here. In fact, this was a historic achievement.

But, frankly, you almost made it impossible. If you put me in this position again, you'll have to get yourself a new Secretary of State."[119]

Scowcroft's deputy, Gates, later remarked that "Baker was a real piece of work." In Gates's view, what the secretary did not know about "dealing with—and manipulating" the press and negotiating partners "was hardly worth knowing." Gates was "always glad he was on our side." There was serious friction between Baker and Gates at times, with the deputy complaining that Baker "demanded more loyalty of the President than he gave in return" and "had a rarely displayed but formidable temper." These attributes had been on display in Ottawa and had brought together the two-plus-four. Now Scowcroft and his aides resolved to undo as much of it as they could.[120]

They forwarded the president a lengthy set of complaints about the two-plus-four, compiled by Blackwill and Rice. The unnecessary forum would give the Soviets a "dramatic platform" to grandstand against unification. It would allow "the British and the French . . . to slow down or alter the shape of German unity." The upcoming East German elections of March 18, 1990 might bring to power a pacifist, left-wing government, which could then use its perch in the two-plus-four forum to denounce both the Warsaw Pact and NATO and call for a united Germany to be neutral. And the White House would have a hard time defending its interests in the face of these challenges because it was "largely unprepared" for the forum, not having realized that it was about to start work.[121]

Last but not least, Rice pointed out that Dick Cheney, the secretary of defense, and Colin Powell, the chairman of the Joint Chiefs of Staff, were both "distressed by the negotiation of the Six Power agreement without DoD [Department of Defense] input—rightly pointing out that these discussions on Germany's external security arrangements will cut to the heart of NATO and ultimately US defense strategy."[122] Cheney and Powell had fallen prey to Bush, Baker, and Scowcroft's desire to keep decision-making to a very small circle, and had not been consulted. One consequence of events unfolding without Pentagon input was that the impact of military planners and staffs on early decisions about post–Cold War NATO enlargement was surprisingly scant. As Cheney later described his department's limited role in policymaking on German unification, "Defense was supportive but not deeply engaged."[123]

Once Baker and his advisors finally got back to Washington after the long trip and lightning round, they found themselves confronted by all of these grievances. The secretary apparently decided that at least some were justified—or the president told him to decide that—because he changed his behavior. Most important, he ceased using the phrase "not shift one inch eastward." Instead, he followed the president's preference for making clear the alliance would expand eastward beyond its Cold War border, with a special status for East Germany as a face-saving concession in exchange. It took Moscow a while to notice.

Baker and his aides stood their ground on the two-plus-four, however, as his preparatory notes for a summons to the White House on February 16 showed. His opponents were misjudging the two-plus-four, Baker argued, and had failed to realize it offered only "discussions, not decisions." Put differently, the venue addressed other stakeholders' unavoidable concerns without giving them a veto. Since neither the "2, 4, 16, or 35 would work," meaning that neither the two Germanies, nor the four powers, nor NATO, nor the CSCE could manage unification any better, the two-plus-four was the least bad alternative. It was "probably the bare minimum process the Soviets will need to express their interests and justify the result at home."[124] Zoellick backed up his boss by countering the complaint that the two-plus-four would enable Moscow to obstruct German unification. As he pointed out, "the presence of 380,000 Soviet troops in the GDR was means enough for obstruction," against which one more debating club paled in significance.[125] And there was yet one more benefit: "it prevents separate German-Soviet deals that could be prejudicial to our interests." In an effort to prevent such deals, Zoellick believed "Kohl should hear from the President that we do not expect to hear again about upcoming German–Soviet meetings from Moscow," but rather from the Germans themselves.[126] Baker believed the two-plus-four would ultimately contribute to Washington's overall goals, noting in a list of its advantages, "You haven't seen a leveraged buy-out until you see this one! (Not just the economic buy-out of the GDR—but of USSR as well.)"[127]

The NSC grudgingly accepted these arguments, not least because many of its members saw that doing so could prevent a secret bargain between Kohl and Gorbachev. As Rice put it, Washington needed to encase Kohl in a "cocoon of Alliance contacts" so "Bonn would have to engage in outright duplicity—saying one thing to the Allies and another to the Soviets—in order to strike the deal with Moscow."[128] Above all else, the White House should avoid "the day of reckoning" when "Gorbachev looks squarely at Kohl and says, 'Here is the deal—a weaker form of German association in NATO or the USSR will do everything possible to prevent unification.'"

Camp David

In the end, both the NSC and the Department of State could claim victory. The NSC got what it wanted with regard to discussions about NATO's future—use of the phrase "special military status" as the alliance moved eastward—and State got the two-plus-four. Now they had a common goal: ensuring that the two-plus-four did not turn into a true decision-making forum. In the service of that goal, agreed-upon goals were circulated in writing between the NSC and State, with essential ones underlined. "In general, Two-Plus-Four can exchange views on many topics, but it can decide very few," and certain topics must never come up at all. The "issues that we do not discuss in a Two-Plus-Four setting" included the terms under which US forces were stationed in Germany, "NATO's nuclear posture, and the status of SNF negotiations," meaning the short-range nuclear forces. Those topics must only arise in more appropriate settings, including and "especially US-FRG" bilaterals.[129] In dealing with Bonn, "our key objective will be to have Kohl reaffirm Bonn's commitment to having a united Germany retain its membership in NATO," because "maintaining a credible nuclear deterrent in Europe will require Germany's continued membership and agreement to some form of US nuclear basing."[130]

Still, suspicions lingered between State and the NSC. Blackwill advised Scowcroft that Baker, Ross, and Zoellick might be tempted to play heroes. By that he apparently meant they might start soloing again as they had done in Ottawa. As Blackwill put it, "I think Secretary Baker and his close colleagues find the prospect of negotiating the future security structure of Europe in the Two Plus Four Ministerial context irresistible." The NSC needed to keep a sharp eye on them to prevent that from happening.[131]

Baker was not the only one fending off suspicions. Just as he had returned home from an exhausting week of tense, top-level negotiations in both Moscow and Ottawa only to find conflict at home, so too did Genscher—first with cabinet colleagues, then with European colleagues. At a cabinet meeting in Bonn on February 14, 1990, the foreign minister found himself in a pitched battle with the West German defense minister, Gerhard Stoltenberg, who disliked the idea of making concessions about NATO's future just as much as the NSC did. Genscher, perhaps aware that Moscow was trying to switch the green light to yellow or red, still worried that the Soviets might balk in the end if Bonn made no concessions at all. That did not stop the defense minister from airing his objections to a major newspaper, which promptly published them on February 17, 1990. The article forced Genscher to go public as well in response.[132] An ugly public spat developed to the point where Kohl felt it necessary to enforce a cease-fire on February 19.

Kohl announced, in keeping with what he had told Gorbachev, that NATO would move "no units or structures" onto what he hoped would soon be former East German territory. To emphasize the point, the chancellor insisted that both Genscher and Stoltenberg state publicly that they agreed with this view, which they did.[133] Genscher then doubled down at a conference with fellow European leaders on February 21. He repeated yet again that there would be "no expansion of NATO beyond its previous region." And yet again he clarified afterward that both the GDR and Central and Eastern Europe were included in that prohibition. This issue, he said, "was not just of significance with regard to the territory of the GDR. The comments yesterday by the Hungarian foreign minister, [Gyula] Horn, showed that."[134] Horn, to Genscher's intense dismay, had speculated publicly about Hungarian integration into NATO. Even worse, he had raised the idea directly with the US deputy secretary of state, Lawrence Eagleburger, who was on an extended visit to Eastern Europe. Eagleburger had immediately told Baker that his Eastern European hosts were speculating on "the collapse of the Warsaw Pact" and that Horn hoped "a new NATO could provide a political umbrella for Central Europe."[135]

Since Genscher's battles, unlike Baker's, played out largely in public, Washington was able to see them unfold in real time—and did not like what it saw. Bush decided he needed to inform Kohl personally that such views were no longer acceptable. Since Kohl was a foreign head of government, however, Bush could not simply issue an order to him. Instead, he wisely settled on a strategy of flattery and persuasion. He decided to invite Kohl for a cozy winter weekend visit to Camp David on February 24–25, an honor never previously bestowed on a German chancellor.[136] Even by Bush's standards, it would be an impressively small circle. The leaders invited the only aides they truly trusted—Baker, Blackwill, Scowcroft, and Teltschik, plus trustworthy notetakers—because it was clear that this session would be for all the marbles.

It was probably best that Genscher was not invited, as he would not have liked what was on the political menu. As Scowcroft advised the president in a bold-letter briefing, Kohl's spine needed stiffening against the kind of concessions Genscher was proposing. While it was clear that Kohl's "heart is in the right place," it was also clear that "he wants to be the Chancellor who united Germany. All else will become for him secondary and negotiable." If he "opts for a weaker form of NATO association, perhaps withdrawing from the integrated military command as the French did under [President Charles] De Gaulle, NATO will be finished as a viable security institution." As a result, **the time has come for an honest and unadorned talk with Kohl**" about the "**bottom-line on security issues.**"

Bush needed to accomplish several goals at Camp David with Kohl. First, he and Kohl had to agree on how to choreograph the two-plus-four talks "**to minimize Soviet ability to weaken Germany's membership in NATO.**" Next, because "Germany is NATO's fulcrum," Washington needed a pledge from Kohl "that he will not allow Germany's indispensable role in NATO to be weakened in any way." This pledge was utterly essential, given that Genscher and some "Chancellery advisors are also actively considering . . . the dissolution of both NATO and the Warsaw Pact and replacing the Alliances with ill-defined, and toothless, all-European security guarantees." Even measures short of dissolution could be devastating; if NATO had to pull back its nuclear deterrent from German soil, members of Congress would rightly ask why the president was taking nuclear cover away from the hundreds of thousands of US service personnel who were their constituents. To prevent that, Bush had to get "the fundamental commitment of the FRG to full membership in NATO, including its military structures," and "the continued presence of American nuclear weapons on German soil."[137]

As Kohl was inbound on the morning of Saturday, February 24, 1990, Bush used the time to give his fellow leaders, including Thatcher, a chance to share their input. He called her at 8:01 a.m. and, at the start of a lengthy chat, explained that Kohl would arrive without Genscher, since the issues that the president wanted to raise were "delicate to discuss."[138] Bush complained that the Czechoslovak president, Václav Havel, was trying to get "all Soviet and US troops out of Europe." Havel was, like the Polish dissident Lech Wałęsa, a figure of enormous moral stature. The Czech leader had been imprisoned for his beliefs before becoming president in the wake of the 1989 revolution in his country. He had spoken to a joint session of the US Congress two days previously and received seventeen standing ovations. Bush was concerned that Havel's popularity might inspire others to share his stance. Thatcher agreed that Havel was "quite wrong" and was drawing a false equivalency, and she agreed with Bush that US troops had a different, defensive status.[139]

They next discussed Poland, with Bush confessing his surprise that Tadeusz Mazowiecki, the Polish prime minister, "wants the Soviets to stay." Thatcher confirmed that Mazowiecki was indeed "quite prepared for the Soviets to stay," precisely because the Poles "are worried about the Oder-Neisse line," specifically its inviolability if Germany reunified. Unhappy to hear this, Bush responded that he was "not comfortable with Soviet troops staying there." The US president now felt free to express a preference about the continued presence of Soviet troops not just in divided Germany but also in Poland. He told Thatcher that Mazowiecki's view would not remain "popular for long with the Polish people, in spite of worries about the border." Soviet troops should leave even as US forces stayed, he felt; he was also "for keeping our nuclear weapons in Europe."

The president segued to the two-plus-four, saying he wanted to limit its role, to avoid giving "Moscow a forum . . . that it will use to exploit German domestic politics to pressure Kohl to somehow accept a loose arrangement between Germany and NATO that would spell the end of the Alliance."[140] Thatcher pushed back, arguing that the two-plus-four should "deal with the big issues."[141] Her reply was not surprising, given that the forum was the one place where Britain had at least a seat at the table if not a veto, but Bush was unconvinced.[142]

That same day, the president sent Baker to Dulles Airport to greet Kohl's party and escort them by helicopter to Camp David—which Baker did in cowboy boots and a red flannel shirt, in keeping with Camp David's casual dress code. Bush and Scowcroft headed separately to Maryland.[143] At some point the president managed to squeeze in a conversation with NATO secretary general Wörner, another strong opponent of Genscher's accommodating attitude toward Moscow.[144]

Wörner argued there was "only one critical question," namely, "will Germany be neutral," or will it belong to NATO? "The answer to this question," he believed, "will decide future decades of European history."[145] He believed that, if a united Germany were not in NATO, it would become a neutral, dangerous giant sitting in the middle of Europe: "It will not have nuclear weapons for a time, but a neutral Germany may want nuclear weapons." He added, "I am frightened by such a vision"—even though he was speaking of his own country. To avoid a united Germany doing what Nazi Germany had failed to do—become a nuclear power on its own—"we must avoid the classical German temptation: to float freely and bargain with both East and West."[146]

In reply, the president asked about what states east of Germany were thinking. The secretary general replied that "the countries of Eastern Europe are wondering about where they fit in; whether they will be untied either to the rest of Europe or to the West." He added that to "demilitarize part of Germany is a silly idea." Bush, processing the implications, agreed that "we have a selling job to do with Gorbachev." Wörner was not worried: "Gorbachev has no strong cards. He cannot prevent German unification on Western terms."[147]

Before long, Baker and the German party arrived. Bush used one of the camp's golf carts to drive the Kohls to their guest house personally. He tried to lend the chancellor a parka as protection from the cold, but because Kohl's waistline substantially exceeded Bush's, there was no hope of zipping it up. Teltschik was impressed by the extent of the retreat, which was a fifty-eight-acre compound that included tennis courts, a heated swimming pool, a bowling alley, and numerous visitors' residences. Although an icy wind shook the trees of the camp so forcefully that the noise could be heard indoors, Teltschik nonetheless remembered a warm and friendly atmosphere developing as the group assembled in front of a roaring fire on a midwinter Saturday afternoon.[148]

All of the visitors received a photo of themselves with the president standing in front of the fireplace. Bush personally instructed Teltschik that he should take off his tie. Barbara Bush took even more dramatic action: using a big pair of scissors, she cut Blackwill's tie in half. That particular tie had been a running joke between Mrs. Bush and Blackwill. He knew that she hated it, so would purposely wear it whenever she was in attendance to provoke her. Knowing that, Mrs. Bush came prepared with scissors—and the gift of a much nicer tie for Blackwill to wear instead.

The discussion soon turned serious. The chancellor anticipated that "the states of Eastern Europe will probably become members of the EC during the 1990s." Germany would then be geographically in the center of Europe, instead of on its eastern fringe, and "economically, we will be number one." Given its future position and weight, "others must see that Germans are the most European Europeans." East Germany was collapsing; "it looked like a giant, but it was hollow." His own ten-point plan for confederation has already been "swept away." Dramatic action was needed, including rapid monetary union, even though the famous economist "Marty Feldstein says we are crazy." But "textbooks don't help; they don't have answers for problems like this." Kohl also asked about Bush's plans to update the short-range nuclear missiles so detested by Germans, and Bush reassured him that the plans were "dead as a doornail."[149]

The president then asked whether Poland was showing an interest in Soviet forces staying because Kohl would not publicly guarantee the permanence of the current East German–Polish border after unification. In other words, were Poles so afraid of a united Germany trying to reclaim territory given to Poland at the end of World War II that they wanted Moscow's troops to stay as a means of preventing that? The chancellor responded that they should not be; the border was indeed permanent; the problem was the political impact of saying so clearly. It was a sensitive is-sue among older German voters who had fled, or been forced to leave, such territory during and after World War II.[150] Many were CDU voters for whom the opening of the Wall had represented the chance to regain former family property in the East, and Kohl did not wish to alienate them in an election year. The foreign ministry in Bonn had already received hundreds of angry letters from Germans asking why the government was not trying to recover what they saw as their rightful territory. One letter-writer suggested that the East German–Polish border be renamed the "Hans-Dietrich-Genscher-Line" so that "future generations will always be reminded who got rid of our homeland like a sack of potatoes."[151]

Bush decided to move on, noting in passing his dismay about Gen-scher's insult to the Italians in Ottawa. Kohl agreed that the crack had been "totally unnecessary" and that, thanks to Genscher, he would have to do a "master resuscitation" of relations with Italy and others in Europe. But he drew the line at mollifying Thatcher: "I can't do anything about her. I can't understand her. The [British] Empire declined fighting Germany—she thinks the UK paid this enormous price, and here comes Germany again." Bush replied that it was important to keep Thatcher in the loop nonetheless, and that "I called Margaret today just to listen to her, which I did for an hour." It was to no avail; Kohl would not agree to take Thatcher into his confidence.

The chancellor could not escape the need to talk about NATO, how-ever. Bush broached the subject by sharing with Kohl the NSC's thinking on minimizing the scope of the two-plus-four. "I would hate to see the Two Plus Four get involved in the issue of Germany's full membership in NATO," the president said, not least because "full German membership is linked to our ability to sustain troops in Europe. You must understand that." Kohl said he not only understood but was happy about it: "I want America in Europe, and not only its military presence. I want to eradicate the concept of Fortress Europe. Hundreds of steps are required, but we must make Fortress Europe an impossibility." Pleased by the reply, the president seized the moment and moved to the bottom line: "the Soviets are not in a position to dictate Germany's relationship with NATO. What worries me is talk that Germany must not stay in NATO. To hell with that."[152]

A hard line, he went on, was necessary because "we prevailed and they didn't. We can't let the Soviets clutch victory from the jaws of defeat." The chancellor responded that Soviet demands for Germany to leave NATO might be only "poker" tactics to improve the Soviets' position in talks. The game might "end up as a matter of cash. They need money." The question was one of price. Bush noted pointedly, "you've got deep pockets."[153] Bush continued to press his case with the Germans over a dinner of roast beef, followed by a movie afterward.

The hospitality did not stop Kohl from reportedly floating some unwelcome trial balloons, however: the idea of uniting Germany in NATO along French lines, perhaps with a prohibition on troops or military structures ever moving on to eastern German territory—precisely what Scowcroft had feared. As the national security advisor knew all too well, although France was a founding member of the alliance, in the 1960s de Gaulle had pulled it out of NATO's integrated military command after repeated conflicts with Washington. The practical result was that, while still a member in name, France had essentially stopped participating in NATO's day-to-day military activities.[154] Although there remained an expectation that French troops would join the rest of the alliance in case of war, Paris neither took part in major planning processes nor made forces available on a routine basis—and insisted that decision-making about nuclear weapons had to stay in national hands.[155] Even worse, Paris had long since made American troops leave French territory. This was not a model Bush would accept for Germany.

Kohl had to agree to remain fully in NATO, and the president wanted a clear commitment to that effect.[156] Kohl did not immediately respond, asking instead if he could think about it overnight. Blackwill recalled the entire US side being surprised and worried by this delay, but Bush agreed to let Kohl sleep on it and answer on Sunday morning. Before long, most of the jet-lagged Germans disappeared to their beds. Only a lone German notetaker stayed up to watch Charlton Heston and Christian Bale in *Treasure Island* all the way to the end.[157]

Early the next day, the two delegations were scheduled to attend a church service together. Blackwill, who by this point had formed a close relationship with Teltschik, approached the West German just before the service to ask whether Kohl was now in agreement with Bush. Yes, he was, Teltschik replied. Relieved, Blackwill rushed to inform Bush just before the service began. The president thanked him, saying Blackwill had made the church service much less anxious.[158]

Teltschik had a request of his own to pass along: "We should not use the word 'jurisdiction' when referring to NATO and former GDR territory." This wording gave the Soviets (not to mention Genscher) leverage by suggesting that Article 5 might not apply to eastern German territory after unification. Baker responded, "Right. I agree completely. I used the term 'jurisdiction' before I realized that it would impact" Article 5. He also wrote to Genscher on February 28 to confirm that "the term NATO 'jurisdiction' was creating some confusion, and we agreed therefore that it should probably be avoided in the future in describing our common position on Germany's NATO relationship."[159]

The Camp David summit ended with a late-morning press conference. In front of journalists, Bush emphasized "the importance of the North Atlantic Treaty Organization and full German membership in it," explicitly dismissing the idea that "Germany might follow the French pattern, belonging to the organization but not integrating its troops into the NATO command structure." He added for good measure that "American troops could remain in Germany even if all Soviet troops left."[160] Privately, the president and his team knew the weekend had been a huge success. As Blackwill put it, Bush "was able at Camp David to advance Kohl's position significantly and explicitly to support full NATO membership for a united Germany." There were no two ways about it: "that is bad news for Gorbachev."[161]

It was. Gorbachev had lost the big game. Kohl had tipped the balance in favor of Bush's objectives. He did so because he had come to realize he could achieve what he wanted—the unity of his country—without having to make major concessions over NATO's stationing of foreign troops, nuclear weapons, or even its future options for extending Article 5 eastward. Instead, Bush and Kohl would work closely together to keep alliance troops and weapons in the West and to expand NATO across all of Germany as soon as possible. Using Kohl's "deep pockets," they would take advantage of the Soviets' economic weakness and make financial and economic incentives, not security concessions, the core of their strategy.

But justifying and implementing this strategy in the coming months would be profoundly challenging. Bush and Kohl needed to persuade

Gorbachev to give up his legal right to keep troops in divided Germany. While doing so, they needed to avoid undermining Gorbachev so much that it might hasten the storm that Kohl feared: a coup that would topple the Soviet leader before he blessed reunification. As Baker put it, "ensuring a unified Germany in NATO" would "require every ounce of our skills in the months to come."[162] He was more right than he knew.

CHAPTER THREE

Crossing the Line

I N HIS MEMOIRS, ROBERT GATES WROTE of the strategy after Camp
David that "we were trying on two levels to bribe the Soviets out of
Germany." First, "knowing of their desperate economic circumstances, West Germany was offering them a pile of money to agree
to unification in NATO"—and given that "the Soviets approached us for
loans" as well, Washington gained even more leverage by "leaving open
the possibility" of providing them. Second, the United States advanced
"a number of proposals" on the alliance's future, all designed to render
"unification in NATO acceptable" to Soviet leader Mikhail Gorbachev.
The idea was to give him something "he could use at home" with domestic critics.[1] Gates thought it best to present both bribes in as face-saving a
manner as possible—he felt "'inducements' and 'incentives' were nice
diplomatic words" to use instead—but the strategy was clear, and the
remainder of 1990 turned into a mad rush to implement it.

As the West German chancellor, Helmut Kohl, explained to British
foreign minister Douglas Hurd on May 15, 1990, "foreign policy was like
mowing grass for hay. You had to gather what you had cut in case of a
thunderstorm." The chancellor fully expected "that in 12 months' time
we would wake up and read that there had been a major turn for the worse
in the Kremlin."[2] It was crucial to gather the harvest before that storm.
The harvest's key components had been agreed on at Camp David: a
unified Germany fully in NATO, meaning the extension of Article 5 to
its eastern region—that is, across the Cold War front line. Because of

President George H. W. Bush's success in getting Kohl to link unification with expansion in this way, the fight for German unity and the fight for NATO's future beyond the old inner-German dividing line became one and the same.

This contest played out over several locations in 1990, with crucial encounters in Washington in May and June; in the Soviet village of Arkhyz in July; and in Moscow in September. As these encounters unfolded, the European political context shifted. Central and Eastern European leaders began to realize that, despite the upheaval of 1989–90, the structure of post–Cold War European security would largely remain unchanged, with the continent divided between NATO and non-NATO states. They scrambled to obtain berths on their preferred side of the divide, expressing interest in joining the alliance not only to its Brussels headquarters but also to the US National Security Council. These expressions of interest made it even more desirable to keep the alliance's eastern options open. When West Germany unexpectedly showed last-minute willingness to limit the range of NATO forces after all, it yielded a bitter struggle at the eleventh hour.[3] Germany's Western allies signaled that crossing the line was so important, they were willing to risk derailing unification just hours before it was due to be finalized.

"A Mighty Game of Poker"

As part of its preparation to implement the strategy Gates outlined, the NSC prepared a list of "bedrock issues on which we cannot compromise." The number one item and absolute top priority was "<u>Germany in NATO</u>." Number two was "<u>no tradeoff between unification and denuclearization of Germany</u>."[4] In other words, even though certain changes were coming—most notably the end of the division of Germany—the extent of that change needed to be curtailed in ways conducive to America's advantage in the post–Cold War order. NATO's ability to extend Article 5 across all of Germany must not come at the cost of having to move nuclear weapons out of the country.

This strategy of curtailment mandated that top priorities should never come up in the two-plus-four forum, which was to have a strictly limited mandate. As the president personally told his NATO ally, visiting Italian prime minister Giulio Andreotti, the two-plus-four "will not decide the future of NATO or of European security."[5] In the service of that preference, Bush's aides worked hard to keep control over a complicated, multilayered process.

Since other venues besides the two-plus-four had to be involved as well—given the wide array of issues affected by the process of unification—they needed to make sure that NATO's future never came up in any unapproved context. National Security Advisor Brent Scowcroft's subordinates put together a matrix, listing issues on one axis and venues on the other. Tracing over and down to the relevant box on the matrix, a staffer could quickly check whether a topic was allowable or off-limits in any particular forum. If any participant protested, the matrix came with suggested responses on how to deflect pressure for a more inclusive agenda.[6]

These tips were needed for keeping not only Moscow but also Washington's NATO allies in their appropriate boxes.[7] For a meeting with Thatcher in spring 1990, Secretary of State James Baker had a simplified matrix prepared, which insisted that in the two-plus-four forum there should be "no discussion of substance" on "nuclear weapons." If "alliance membership" came up, the two-plus-four should only "discuss why good"—the goal presumably being to avoid any mention of alternatives.[8] The British prime minister, Margaret Thatcher, was not amused. She had by then instructed her Foreign Office to push back against this US effort to marginalize the two-plus-four, which she felt "should negotiate on wider issues."[9] London's dismay prompted NSC staffer Robert Blackwill to ask the British embassy in Washington whether Thatcher might "dust off memories of the war-time coalition," meaning apparently make common cause with Moscow against Germany in the two-plus-four.[10]

The French ambassador to London cabled home his agreement with the British stance, which he thought wise, since "Kohl is capable of anything."[11] Senior civil servants at the Quai d'Orsay, the French ministry of foreign affairs, expressed similar dismay directly to the Germans, complaining that a token role was "obviously inadequate."[12] Undeterred, Bush repeated his red lines directly to French president François Mitterrand, with whom he had a good relationship and felt free to speak openly: the two-plus-four "should not negotiate over Germany's right to remain a full member of NATO," nor should it "decide the fate of allied conventional or nuclear forces on the territory of the current FRG."[13] No entity should weaken or replace NATO—especially not the kind of pan-European organization Hans-Dietrich Genscher, the West German foreign minister, would not stop touting.[14] Bush could not "visualize how a European collective security arrangement including Eastern Europe, and perhaps even the Soviet Union, would have the capability to deter threats to Western Europe." He repeated for emphasis that the Western allies should "in no event . . . allow Moscow to manipulate the two plus four mechanism in ways that could fracture Western defense and Germany's irreplaceable part in it."[15] A clash was clearly coming, because that outcome was precisely what Gorbachev still wanted. On March 7, 1990, speaking to an interviewer for the Soviet newspaper *Pravda*, he declared that membership for a united Germany in NATO "was absolutely ruled out."[16]

But even as Gorbachev was ruling out the possibility, the State Department was beginning to put NATO into its thinking on Central and Eastern Europe. While on a trip to Europe, Deputy Secretary of State Lawrence Eagleburger had cabled on March 1, 1990 that the Hungarian foreign minister had asked how NATO could "provide a political umbrella for Central Europe."[17] A member of the State Department's policy planning staff, Harvey Sicherman, considered the same idea as part of a March 12 report that caught Baker's attention.

In contrast to his NSC colleagues, Sicherman thought that the two-plus-four was an absolutely terrific idea. He preferred to call it "the 'two-by-four'" because he saw it as "a lever to insert a united Germany in NATO whether the Soviets like it or not." Looking east, Sicherman argued that Central and Eastern Europeans—the peoples who had suffered the most from living between Germany and the Soviet Union—were realizing that closer cooperation with NATO offered "the best way out of the German-Russian security dilemma." The "Hungarians and the Poles already see it."[18] Admittedly, Václav Havel, the widely admired Czech leader, was advocating a bloc-free, demilitarized Central Europe, but Sicherman expected Havel would eventually see reason too, and he was right. The waning of Havel's interest in alternatives to NATO membership, such as the potential pan-European confederation that he and Mitterrand had initially promoted, would increasingly undermine such alternatives.[19]

Central and Eastern European interest in NATO made sense, Sicherman thought; with the end of the Warsaw Pact in sight, it was reasonable for pact members to start thinking about other options. He also saw a number of problems, however, not least being Polish fear of German irredentism. As Bush had disapprovingly noted, many Poles felt that Soviet troops should stay to ensure that West Germans who coveted former family lands in Poland did not get them back. Polish leaders were also, as

Kohl let Bush know in March 1990, calling for "billions in reparations" for World War II.[20] Given all of these controversies, Sicherman advised his superiors that Washington needed to ensure that "(1) taking on the burden of 'organizing' this region is really a vital interest [and] (2) we have the means to do so. My answer tentatively is that we alone do not have the means but that NATO and the EC surely do."[21]

Upon reading this analysis, Sicherman's boss at policy planning, Dennis Ross, realized his subordinate was right. As Ross later recalled, the memo made him see that Central and Eastern Europeans would not feel secure until they were in NATO.[22] Ross decided to advise his boss, Baker, that "many Poles and other East Europeans would back NATO as the core security organization if they could eventually be part of it."[23]

Thinking along the same lines, a number of Central and Eastern European foreign ministers took part in a special EC ministerial in Lisbon on March 23–24, 1990 to see what other forms of Western affiliation might be possible.[24] As Mitterrand remarked to Bush, "Eastern Europe is all alone, poor and humiliated." The West needed to avoid treating the residents of the region "like beggars." This concern was one of his motivations in proposing some kind of pan-European confederation where they could find a home. Scowcroft understood that French interest in such a confederation was not a simplistic statement of "resentment" at US power; rather, it was an awareness that "sooner or later, the Congress or the American people would say, 'why do we have troops over there? Why are we spending money to defend Europe?'" Since there was (in Mitterrand's view) a risk of US withdrawal, the French president felt that "Europe had to organize itself to handle its own defense capabilities."

Mitterrand was less enthusiastic about letting Central and Eastern European states into the EC proper, however. Because of this reluctance—which Mitterrand was far from alone in holding—Easterners were realizing that their interest in Western political institutions was not universally welcomed. A young Polish leader, Radoslaw Sikorski, later remembered the US ambassador to Poland, Thomas Simons, wagging his finger at Poles who were expressing too much interest in NATO and telling them to quiet down.[25]

Undeterred, Krzysztof Skubiszewski, the Polish foreign minister, paid a visit to NATO headquarters on March 21, 1990, talking pointedly of NATO's "'stabilizing effect.'"[26] That visit proved to be the start of a sequence of contacts between the alliance leaders and Central and Eastern European representatives. The Czechoslovak foreign minister arrived in

Brussels in March; his Hungarian colleague followed in June, with the Hungarian prime minister hard on his heels; and Romanian, Bulgarian, and more Hungarian visitors soon made their way to Brussels.[27] Perhaps to deflect attention from how Soviet allies were consorting with the enemy, or perhaps to beat them to the punch, the courier on the Soviet–West German back channel, Nikolai Portugalov, popped up again on March 28 with a truly novel suggestion: "a kind of NATO membership for the Soviet Union."[28]

In light of these developments, Gorbachev's disgruntled Germany expert, Valentin Falin, began privately saying good riddance to the Central and Eastern European allies. Falin and his aides, the West German embassy in Moscow reported in April 1990, felt that "the collapse of the Warsaw Pact was not a decisive issue for the Soviet Union. . . . It made no difference to them what Hungary, the Czechs, and possibly even the Poles did."[29]

East Germany, by contrast, mattered. It represented half of a divided nation on the verge of reuniting—and not just any nation, but the one responsible for millions of wartime deaths of Soviet citizens. Moscow did not want to let that reunited entity reemerge without getting as much as possible in return. Reunification was getting closer, however, with the arrival of the March 18, 1990 election in East Germany.

In an effort to promote his East German allies and their plans for rapid unification, Kohl campaigned personally in that election—despite being neither on the ballot nor even a citizen. It was a deeply controversial move, but he felt it essential to pull out all the stops to help the Alliance for Germany, the eastern affiliates of his right-of-center party. While East Germany's ruling Socialist Unity Party was unlikely to have much chance in a free vote after years of detested dictatorial rule, the chancellor worried that voters raised in a socialist state might prefer their version of the left-of-center Social Democratic Party (SPD) to the CDU, not least because former SPD chancellor and Nobel laureate Willy Brandt enjoyed extensive popularity for his policy of outreach to the East, known as Ostpolitik.

Kohl succeeded nonetheless. The chancellor's six rallies in East Germany were jaw-dropping successes, with attendance in the many hundreds of thousands. By the day of the election, the chancellor estimated to Bush that, adding together the crowd totals from all of the rallies, he had literally faced a million people.[30] Those people and many more like them gave Kohl's center-right allies a resounding victory. With more than 93 percent voter participation overall, the Alliance for Germany secured 48 percent of the vote, far more than any other party and more than enough to form a ruling coalition, which it chose to do with the eastern version of the SPD.[31]

The election was a game changer. Kohl's drive for swift unification now had clear electoral legitimacy. One Soviet negotiator noted ruefully that, as a result, the two-plus-four suddenly became one-plus-four, since Moscow's German ally would now be run by Kohl's colleagues.[32] According to the West German ambassador in Moscow, the voting results made painfully obvious what the Soviets already suspected: "the political system of the GDR, which they had built up over decades, enjoyed no democratic legitimacy."[33] Meanwhile, Kohl happily stated the obvious to his fellow party leaders: "this is a very good day today." But he cautioned that there were still challenges ahead. "Probably the worst mistake that the Germans could make," he advised, "would be to forget that the future of Germany, the reunification of Germany, will take place in Europe." Soon thereafter, he made clear that he would move forward with work on European monetary union as well as with national unification, starting to talk of the date of December 31, 1992 for the introduction of a common currency. As he put it, "a mighty game of poker has begun."[34]

The chancellor also decided to move more aggressively with Moscow, summoning Yuli Kvitzinsky, the Soviet ambassador in Bonn. Kohl instructed the ambassador to deliver a message directly to Gorbachev, bypassing "the usual bureaucracy and people with concrete for brains." In the message, Kohl spelled out what he would now make happen. There would be a lot of negotiating on details, and Germany would have to pay, but unity would come. While huge practical problems loomed—including figuring out how to transform existing treaties into post-unification accords, and conducting the withdrawal of Soviet troops—with enough staff work and money, both of which Germany was willing to provide, they could all be solved. Meanwhile, Moscow's forces could stay temporarily, and while they were there, "no German troops" would move into the East, but the Soviet troops would ultimately leave. Western troops and Germany's NATO membership, in contrast, would remain permanent fixtures. When Kvitzinsky protested against this vision, Kohl replied with another one of his favorite metaphors, telling the ambassador that resisting this fate would be like trying to keep the Rhine River from flowing to the sea.[35]

Kohl also felt his hand was strong enough to challenge, in a way that he rarely dared, another major player in the geopolitical poker game: his kingmaker, Genscher. The chancellor demanded, unequivocally and in writing, that Genscher stop calling NATO's future into question. The foreign minister had recently given yet another revealing speech in Luxembourg, calling evocatively for NATO and the Warsaw Pact to come together in a single "composite of common, collective security" for Europe, within which the two alliances "could both finally dissipate."[36] Kohl sent his foreign minister a cease-and-desist letter, saying, "I do not know if the reports are true to your text," but if so, "I do not share and do not support" these ideas. The chancellor added, "I am not prepared to accept" the way in which Genscher was simply announcing policy "without any consultation" by stating his view as if it were the position of the government.[37] The import of Kohl's letter was consistent with the strategy he had agreed upon with Washington: rather than make security concessions, West Germans would take advantage of Soviet economic weakness to gain unification.[38] Moscow's need for economic support from Bonn, Kohl told a British diplomat that April, "was a major lever in getting Soviet agreement to satisfactory security arrangements concerning Germany."[39]

Meanwhile, separatist movements were putting additional pressure on Soviet leadership, with a Lithuanian push for independence particularly undermining Gorbachev. Among the many problems that Lithuanian separatism created for Gorbachev was a geographic one. Lithuania bordered a region known as Kaliningrad, which before World War I had been a major German port called Königsberg. After World War II, the area had become part of what was de facto contiguous Soviet territory, but, thanks to Lithuania, Kaliningrad was now becoming the political equivalent of an island between the Baltics and Poland.

Despite both Kohl's new electoral legitimacy and Baltic separatism, Gorbachev nonetheless retained his various forms of leverage. As one British analyst put it, Moscow's "real weapon" remained "the possibility that they can convince German public opinion to accept denuclearisation . . . as the price of Soviet consent." The Soviet Union could also drag out the surrender of its legal rights emanating from World War II, leaving its troops in place as it did so. It could threaten to slow down or block arms control agreements as well, for instance in multilateral talks limiting the types and amount of conventional forces in Europe. Soviet military leaders would love to throw sand in those gears, as they had long been upset at Gorbachev's penchant for dramatic arms control deals and yearned to take a harder stance.[40]

Another person yearning to throw sand in the gears was Falin. He had not gotten over how Gorbachev had carelessly shown Kohl a green light in February 1990. Now, in April, the savvy Soviet foreign policy expert tried to convince Gorbachev to play the public opinion card. Falin called for a public referendum on whether German unification should take place in NATO. Since Gorbachev's appearances in Western cities routinely caused gridlock as excited residents flocked to see him, and the Nobel Committee would award him the Peace Prize later in 1990, he clearly enjoyed a deep reservoir of goodwill in the West. Falin thought the Soviet leader should capitalize on his public standing abroad by demanding that the German public have a say in the momentous decision of how to unify. Germans should have a voice in whether they wanted unification twinned with NATO membership—or with some kind of all-European alliance instead.

It was an impressively counterintuitive idea. As a Cold War Communist Party leader, Falin was hardly a longtime advocate of asking Soviet citizens their opinion of the Warsaw Pact, but now he apparently saw the proposal as a winning one. If Kohl in fact held such a referendum, there was a reasonable chance it would not go his way, and that Germans would declare themselves willing to give up NATO for unity; and if the chancellor did not call a vote, then Gorbachev could say unification in NATO had no popular legitimacy.[41] Another option would be to capitalize in some way on the enormous unpopularity of the nuclear weapons already in divided Germany by asking whether the united country needed them at all.[42] Particularly unpopular with West Germans were short-range nuclear missiles. They had been installed to deter Soviet tanks—given how difficult it would have been for NATO's conventional forces alone to stop a massive advance—but since their use would also render the heart of Europe uninhabitable, they offered NATO only a tragically Pyrrhic victory.[43] Foreign conventional forces also caused resentment. Although West Germany was, at its narrowest point, only as wide as New York's Long Island was long, there were 900,000 soldiers stationed within its borders.[44] On the other side of the barbed wire, the smaller East German state still managed to field an army of about 180,000, along with 400,000 Soviet troops and an array of nuclear weapons, including yet more short-range missiles.[45] The shared, bitter joke in divided Germany was that the shorter the missile range, the "deader" the Germans. Falin thought that such resentment could provide leverage.

Gorbachev needed to use this leverage as soon as possible, however, because the Western position was, in Falin's words, hardening "from week to week." Falin had noticed by April 18, 1990 that Baker's earlier rhetoric about no expansion of NATO's jurisdiction to the GDR had disappeared. Instead, the West was now working "with all its strength on preparing the ground for NATO's plans with regard to the GDR and the Warsaw Pact." If Moscow did not apply the brakes to unification very soon, Falin worried that there would be nothing to stop NATO from looking for real estate east of Germany. As he euphemistically put it, there might be "'sales'" of Germany's "'earlier' territories" outside its current borders "by Poles, and maybe not just the Poles."[46]

Falin, in other words, was trying to tell his boss it was time to take the gloves off because more than Germany was at stake. Whether his ideas would have stopped the hemorrhage of Soviet power in 1990 will forever remain unknown, however, because Gorbachev decided not to act upon his advice. It appears that the Soviet leader was more enticed by promises of financial and economic support from West Germany than by his own advisor's hardball strategy. Gorbachev chose instead to marginalize the increasingly bitter Falin and rely instead on his closest aide, Anatoly Chernyaev.[47]

Unlike the combative Falin, Chernyaev was resigned to German unification. He advised his boss on May 4 that it was probably no longer possible to prevent Germany from unifying within the Atlantic Alliance—even though the next step might be "possible entry of the Poles into NATO." Chernyaev was not panicked about that possibility, however, because the main threat to Moscow was not "armored personnel carriers and howitzers"—that is, conventional weapons—on the "Oder-Neisse line or the Elbe or somewhere else." The poker game that mattered was over "the nuclear balance between the USSR and USA." Since the Germanies and Poland did not control atomic arsenals, they did not truly matter.[48]

The Washington Summit and the Helsinki Principle

The Soviet leader would soon have a chance to address all of these issues with Bush personally at the US-Soviet summit starting in Washington on May 31, 1990. The US president also invited Gorbachev to go onward, after the main session in the capital, to Camp David by helicopter. That invitation meant, as Bush and Scowcroft noted, that the American and Soviet leaders would be sitting in one helicopter, "accompanied by the military aides carrying the nuclear codes that allowed each of us to destroy the other's country." That was seen as acceptable given the larger goals.[49]

In preparation for this summit, Bush and Kohl worked closely with each other and with the secretary general of NATO, Manfred Wörner. The West Germans were in the process of providing the first of Gates's two bribes—a pile of money—so it was now up to Washington, in consultation with Wörner, to provide the second: proposed reforms to NATO that Gorbachev could "use at home" to win over hard-liners.

Bush felt a NATO summit should take place in summer 1990 in order to publicize a more appealing face to the alliance.[50] A summit was planned for July 5–6, 1990, right in the middle of the Congress of the Communist Party of the Soviet Union, scheduled for July 2–14. To start publicizing NATO's new face even before then, however, Wörner gave a speech on May 17 about how the alliance would adapt to "changed circumstances." He noted that "the newly-democratizing nations of Central and Eastern Europe recognize that without NATO they would not have regained their independence and freedom—and indeed could not retain them." Turning to divided Germany, he unwisely gave a hostage to fortune in his efforts to help Gorbachev make the sale to Soviet hard-liners at the party congress. Instead of repeating the intentionally vague wording about a "special status" for eastern Germany, Wörner used an incautious turn of phrase—which Moscow would use to castigate the West for decades afterward. He said that "the very fact" that the alliance was willing "not to deploy NATO troops beyond the territory of the Federal Republic gives the Soviet Union firm security guarantees."[51]

Kohl visited Washington to help with strategizing for Gorbachev's arrival.[52] By now, the chancellor had become a welcome and frequent visitor to the States; at one point he appeared twice in three weeks. Nevertheless, he and Bush still had differences, mostly over how much economic assistance the United States would provide to the Soviet Union. Although the White House was, as Gates had advised, "leaving open the possibility," it remained fundamentally unwilling to make large loans to Moscow. Given this reluctance, one Baker subordinate worried that "Kohl is likely to come with over-optimistic expectations as to how much progress we are likely to make with Gorbachev on German and European issues during the upcoming Summit."[53]

Bush and Kohl did agree, however, that the trickiest problem would be the removal of Soviet troops from East Germany without parallel requests for the removal of NATO troops from West Germany. The two men needed to find a way for Gorbachev to save face as that happened because, as Kohl told the president on May 17, 1990, "he has big problems. His East European allies say they want to be in NATO."[54] The German chancellor actively welcomed the idea that Central and Eastern European countries might become part of the alliance. As he told his fellow party leaders on June 11, "the best thing that could happen to us would be for Poland to demand NATO membership." If the Poles made such a demand, "we should praise it loudly" because it would both take Germany off the front line and ease Polish anxieties. The alternative—Germans opposing NATO's expansion—would "destroy" the alliance, "with catastrophic consequences," up to and including "the possession of nuclear weapons by Germans."[55]

Gorbachev was indeed complaining about his Warsaw Pact allies wanting to join NATO, including in a meeting with Baker on May 18, 1990. The secretary of state, as he told Bush, found the Soviet leader upset by "indications that we are seeking to wean the East Europeans away." Gorbachev had added, "'if they want to move away on their own, okay,'" but Washington "shouldn't be promoting this." Baker denied making any effort to "wean the East Europeans away," but Gorbachev remained skeptical.[56] The Soviet leader contacted the Czech president, Alexander Dubček, saying on May 21 that "a great game is underway. Naturally you are being pulled in, just like the Hungarians and the Poles." He then asked "if the whole of united Germany is going into NATO, then maybe we should go into this alliance as well?"[57]

The Soviet leader raised the issue yet again with the French president on May 25, saying, "I told Baker: we are aware of your favorable attitude toward the intention expressed by a number of representatives of East European countries to withdraw from the Warsaw Pact and subsequently join NATO." If that happened, Gorbachev said, he would demand entry for the Soviet Union as well, and then what would Washington do? Mitterrand listened accommodatingly to Gorbachev's complaints, but indicated that there was strong momentum toward all of unified Germany becoming a full member in NATO—meaning the alliance would not simply stay behind its old Cold War border—and that he did not want to "become isolated from my Western partners" by opposing that momentum. The French president's comments signaled to Gorbachev that there was little he could do to block a unified Germany in NATO.[58] The Soviet leader nonetheless continued complaining at a meeting of Warsaw Pact leaders, where he lamented Western talk of "bringing the countries of Eastern Europe, or at least part of them, into NATO." The "ulterior motive and goal" of such talk was clear: "to extend the function of NATO in Europe and beyond."[59]

The unhappy Gorbachev also kept questioning Germany's need to be in NATO, or the need for NATO at all. While with Baker on May 18, 1990, he had accused Washington of not taking his ideas about a pan-European security solution seriously, insisting to Baker that a precious opportunity was slipping away. If Germany simply joined one of the old Cold War blocs instead, soon the moment would be lost and it would become impossible to create a new pan-European alliance; instead, as Gorbachev lamented, "it will be too late to build a credible security structure in Europe." Privately, Baker let Bush know afterward that he had interpreted that remark to mean the Soviets "would have lost our leverage and Germany would be a big, dangerous power."[60]

The secretary said aloud to Gorbachev what he thought about Gorbachev's idea of a pan-European security institution: "an excellent dream, but only a dream." Almost exactly one year earlier, in a speech in Mainz on May 31, 1989, Bush had called for "a Europe whole and free," but Baker dismissed the prospect that the whole of Europe might enter into a security alliance as a fantasy. NATO was a reality, and a Germany solidly implanted in it would be in the Soviet Union's interest.[61] Gorbachev asked whether the Soviet Union should join the transatlantic alliance. "I will propose to the President, and will say publicly, that we want to enter NATO," Gorbachev informed Baker. This, he emphasized, was "not some absurdity" but rather a serious consideration. When Baker avoided responding directly, Gorbachev repeated that "our membership in NATO is not such a wild fantasy." The United States and the Soviet Union had once been allies, why not again? In reply, Baker shifted the conversation back to the two-plus-four.[62]

Since Gorbachev was personally raising the subject of German, Central and Eastern European, and Soviet membership in NATO, it would clearly be a contentious issue at the summit. Western leaders decided to use a riposte that Mitterrand had already raised with Gorbachev: the so-called Helsinki principle, the right granted to all signatories of the Helsinki Final Act of 1975 to choose their own military alliances.[63] During the Cold War it had been a hollow promise, as Central and Eastern Europeans knew they were not free to choose anything but the Warsaw Pact. But on paper, at least, the Soviet Union had committed to this principle.

Now, in the changed circumstances of 1990, Bush and Kohl realized that the principle could be useful. Because West Germany was a signatory to the act, a united Germany as its legal successor would have the right to choose its alliance, and it would of course choose NATO. Therefore, it would be unproblematic for the troops of its NATO allies to remain—unlike the Soviet forces, which would enjoy no such justification.[64]

To sweeten this bitter pill, the Bush administration decided to inform Gorbachev at the summit that a united Germany would renounce "ABC" (atomic, biological, and chemical) weapons as West Germany had already done. Bonn would also concede that Soviet troops could remain for a transition period. But Washington would offer no massive financial aid. Because that aid was Gorbachev's immediate main interest, Bush told Kohl not to expect much from the summit. Rather, the US goal was limited: for Gorbachev to "come out feeling he has had a good summit, even though there are no major breakthroughs."[65] The internal briefing papers for the summit concluded that, as a result, expectations should be kept low.[66]

As Bush expected, the Washington summit did not finalize German unification, but there was a significant development: Bush and his advisors succeeded in getting Gorbachev to confirm that the future of European security would indeed follow the Helsinki principle.[67] Few concessions were as important for the future of NATO expansion. Falin, still enough in favor with Gorbachev to be brought to the summit, recalled with no small degree of anguish how he and others were blindsided by Gorbachev's agreement on this point. The Soviet leader's concession, according to Falin, came after a minor "rhetorical flourish" by Bush.[68] Gorbachev had been trying to convince the US president of the desirability of a joint membership for united Germany in both NATO and the Warsaw Pact, suggesting that the alliances would act as "two anchors" to secure the country more firmly. The US side disagreed, with Baker objecting that such an arrangement would smack of schizophrenia. Bush interjected that, thanks to the Helsinki principle, the choice was ultimately up to the Germans themselves: "if Germany does not want to stay in NATO, it has a right to choose a different path."[69]

The Soviet leader grabbed at that comment, Falin later recounted, like a drowning man clutching at a straw. Gorbachev apparently believed that Germany might actually choose something other than NATO.[70] Mistakenly seeing that line as a benefit for his side, the Soviet leader suggested publicly announcing that Germany "would decide on its own which alliance she would be a member of," seemingly unaware how much that remark helped the US side. Sensing a win, Bush agreed, suggesting a slightly different formulation: while the United States wanted Germany in

NATO, if Germany were to make "a different choice, we would not contest it, we will respect it."[71] Gorbachev unwisely agreed.

Soviet delegation members, aware of the concession their leader was making even if he was not, could no longer contain themselves. Bush and Scowcroft later recalled that both Falin and Marshal Sergey Akhromeyev, a Soviet war hero and Gorbachev's security advisor, became visibly angry. The two Soviet advisors suddenly "snapped back and forth in loud stage whispers in an agitated debate as Gorbachev spoke. It was an unbelievable scene, the likes of which none of us had ever seen before—virtually open rebellion against a Soviet leader." Falin even succeeded in claiming the floor for himself. He tried to undo the damage by making a long statement about the desirability of a pan-European security system. Scowcroft later recalled wondering if he were watching an insurrection in real time.[72] But Falin's comments came too late. Plowing ahead despite the obvious dissension in his ranks, "Gorbachev lamely continued the discussion," Bush and Scowcroft remembered, "trying to back away but never completely repudiating his earlier statements."[73]

A press conference that evening publicized the formulation as agreed, driving Falin to despair. He began to ask himself "what was the sense" of advising Gorbachev on this matter anymore.[74] Akhromeyev's despair was even deeper. He increasingly began to oppose Gorbachev, offering his support to the leaders of the coup attempt that would take place a little over a year later. When it failed, he took his own life.

By contrast, the US side could not believe its good fortune at the summit. When Bush shared the news with Kohl, they concluded that the Soviet side, riven by disagreements, did not know what it wanted. Gorbachev and his advisors were reduced to improvising.[75]

Gorbachev faced yet more opposition when he returned home after the summit. Boris Yeltsin, a regional Communist leader from Sverdlovsk whom the Soviet leader had brought to Moscow, was rising in prominence. Although Gorbachev and Yeltsin had both been born in 1931 and shared the searing experience of growing up in a country at war, the two men could not have been more different. Gorbachev had earned a law degree at the oldest and most prestigious university in Russia, Moscow State, had entered the party as a young man, and was married to a Marxist philosopher. Yeltsin, born near the frigid Urals, had studied at a provincial polytechnic, married another engineer, and entered the party late.[76] He had made a name for himself when then–Soviet leader Leonid Brezhnev ordered the demolition of the house where the last czar and his family had been executed, and Yeltsin brought it down less than twenty-four hours later, earning a series of promotions.[77] Once he was in Moscow, however, he clashed increasingly with Gorbachev, and they became enemies.[78]

Instead of continuing to fight Gorbachev for influence within the Communist Party, Yeltsin abruptly announced in July 1990 that he was leaving the party to seek success in the new world of semi-free electoral politics. Gorbachev's reforms had made such politics possible, but since the Soviet leader had unwisely avoided putting himself in front of the electorate even when he might have won, Yeltsin would be the ultimate beneficiary.[79] Scowcroft reportedly thought Yeltsin's sudden conversion to democracy was a smokescreen and that he "'was a pure opportunist'" who became "'a democrat because that was the way to get out'" from under the Soviet leader's thumb. In the end, he "'was fundamentally after power.'" Unlike Gorbachev, however, Yeltsin was "'a populist and knew what appealed and loved that part and did it very well.'"[80]

Yeltsin had made himself popular in Moscow by personally criticizing store managers for empty shelves and bus drivers who turned up late at stops.[81] In May 1990, he became the elected leader of the Russian republic, to the dismay of the Soviet leader. As Gates told Bush that July, "we may have underestimated Yeltsin." The deputy national security advisor noted the significance of Yeltsin's electoral victory, which undercut "Gorbachev's precarious domestic position." Despite a "serious drinking problem"—perhaps self-medication after a plane accident and spinal surgery that left him in ongoing pain—in Gates's view Yeltsin was "going to be a major player," not least because he "has boldly saddled a number of horses that look unbeatable." For example, Yeltsin's "emphasis on the 'sovereignty' of the Russian Republic" and his "plan to renegotiate its relations with other constituent republics of the Soviet Union cuts through the Gordian knot of the nationalities problem which Gorbachev has been unable to cope with."[82] Gorbachev's reforms, by contrast, were becoming an "incoherent mishmash," and the Soviet leader appeared to have not "the faintest idea of a way out" of the morass in which his country found itself. Gates concluded that "Gorbachev has earned his place in history but now history seems to be moving beyond him." He advised Bush that "it would be a pity for you, Mr. President, as you boldly and confidently lead the West into the future, to be seen in the Soviet Union as wagering everything on a man whose vision at the end of the day does not reach far enough."[83]

"Crosswise on Train Tracks"

On top of the threat from Yeltsin, Gorbachev also had to deal with the Soviet economic situation, which kept going from bad to worse. Kohl began to wonder whether the entire country was collapsing.[84] While an enemy's collapse would in theory be good news, the chancellor did not want it to happen before he secured from Moscow the two key concessions necessary for unity: the withdrawal of Soviet troops and the surrender of the country's four-power legal rights.[85]

As a result, Kohl's team worked even more urgently to find what Gates had diplomatically termed "inducements," such as an agreement by the West Germans to cover many of the costs of keeping Soviet troops in East Germany. Those forces had arrived as victorious occupiers, but at the end of the Cold War they were demoralized, housed in deteriorating barracks, and underfed. East Germans living near Soviet bases complained that the troops seemed desperate, hungry, and perhaps dangerous. A particularly worrisome development was that, like their comrades in Hungary, they were apparently selling army property and weapons for personal gain.

If the troops' woes were not bad enough already, German economic and monetary unification was due to occur on July 1, 1990, well in advance of political unification. The event threatened to immiserate Soviet forces by introducing a hard currency those soldiers could scarcely afford at market exchange rates. On top of everything else, there were rumors that Soviet troops withdrawing from Czechoslovakia and Hungary might head to East Germany rather than the Soviet Union because they faced such shortages back home.[86] In light of all these issues, Moscow sought Bonn's help in paying its forces, and Bonn agreed to provide it. On June 25, 1990, West Germany committed to pay 1.25 billion DM in "stationing costs" for Soviet troops in the second half of 1990. The irony of this was heavy. West Germany would pay to continue to be occupied by the USSR after the collapse of the Berlin Wall. Soviet soldiers and their dependents would also be allowed to exchange their so-called field bank savings into deutsche marks at a very favorable rate. As the historian Vladislav Zubok noted, "Moscow still held the keys to German sovereignty," and Bonn held "the keys to the savings of the Soviet military in East Germany." It was "only logical and pragmatic to exchange these keys."[87]

West German bankers and government leaders thus committed a substantial amount of funding to Moscow. The other inducement—a NATO relaunch—was still being assembled. Although the alliance consisted of sixteen states, it was only the close confidants of US and West German leaders—Baker, Scowcroft, Horst Teltschik, and their subordinates—who wrote the crucial NATO communiqué of July 1990. They did so through a secretive exchange of drafts in late June, thrashing out the most sensitive issues among themselves.[88] As Baker put it, "we resisted sending" the draft through the "NATO bureaucracy."[89] Among other reasons, they wanted to retain control over such subjects as how NATO should deal with nuclear issues. According to handwritten notes from a discussion with the president, Baker felt it "critical we not get into debate" on tactical air-to-surface missiles "or other air-launched nucl[ear] weapons—must duck that issue stay general, avoid debate."[90]

Another major question was whether the alliance should try to deal with the Warsaw Pact as a whole or with its individual members. Scowcroft felt that since the pact was crumbling, talking to individual members made more sense. The idea of liaison offices to Central and Eastern European countries resulted. The national security advisor also thought it was too soon for Germany to make concessions on its overall troop numbers. That should be saved for the talks about a potential Conventional Forces in Europe (CFE) Treaty.[91] What mattered more than any details, according to Baker, was to "get Ger. unified in NATO soon."[92]

Once the final draft was complete, Bush specified that only Wörner and the British, French, and Italian leaders should edit it, not the NATO bureaucracy.[93] Although Wörner initially had some "worry" about this procedure, he was so enthusiastic about the final draft of the communiqué that, as he told Bush, he almost offered the messenger who came bearing it "champagne" instead of coffee.[94] He particularly liked the idea of liaison missions opening a door to Central and Eastern Europe. That cause was helped by a joint declaration of the West German Bundestag and its East German equivalent in late June, confirming the existing GDR-Polish border as permanent even after unity. This declaration helped to diminish the Poles' anxiety and made them less willing to let Soviet troops stay.[95]

In London, at the NATO summit itself, the United States and West Germany succeeded in getting their press release through the alliance bureaucracy with hardly any changes (although not without resistance; at one point Baker had to spend six straight hours defending the US position).[96] To ensure that Gorbachev knew about this communiqué and could use it against his opponents at home, Bush highlighted for him on July 6, 1990 "a few of the steps that we have taken to transform NATO" and "to extend the hand of friendship to countries who were our adversaries during the Cold War."[97]

The Soviet leader was glad to hear it, because he was coming under bitter attack from opponents who wanted to oust him at the Communist Party Congress. Foreign Minister Eduard Shevardnadze was pleased that the press release had been approved during the congress, saying later that it had helped his cause greatly. Always a glass-half-full optimist, Gorbachev emerged from the congress feeling confident, despite the vicious attacks he had endured and his loss of favor even among former supporters.[98]

He also proposed ways to make a unified Germany fully in NATO acceptable to the USSR. He began emphasizing the obvious fact that there were many models of alliance membership: French, with nonintegration into the military command; Danish-Norwegian, with prohibitions on the stationing of foreign troops and nuclear weapons; British, with nuclear weapons under domestic control; and West German, with extensive integration of forces. Gorbachev argued that NATO membership for all of Germany should be negotiated à la carte, using these models as options.[99]

To push back against such talk, Kohl sought an invitation to go to the Soviet Union so that he could make the final sale in person, and Gorbachev invited him for July 15 and 16, 1990. Significantly, the Soviet leader invited the chancellor not just to Moscow but also to join him and his wife, Raisa, at their favorite summer vacation spot, the village of Arkhyz near Gorbachev's hometown of Stavropol.[100] Kohl, thinking Gorbachev would hardly do such a thing if he expected a contentious summit, took it as a good sign. Even better, just before leaving for Moscow, he received word that Gorbachev had already exhausted loans from German banks that Teltschik had helped to organize in May 1990 and needed more; that would be to Kohl's advantage too.[101]

Falin hoped to prevent a repeat of the disaster he had witnessed in Washington from taking place in Arkhyz. According to his own later account, he sent Gorbachev written advice on July 9, 1990 on how to avoid one. He also demanded a phone call with Gorbachev to emphasize his points personally. The Soviet leader, presumably annoyed at the demand and still smarting from the way Falin had embarrassed him in front of Bush, kept Falin waiting for a call until the midnight just before the Germans' arrival. Trying to undo the Helsinki principle, Falin insisted Gorbachev tell Kohl that Germany could not enter NATO—or, "minimum minimorum," could not have nuclear weapons of any kind anywhere on its territory. Once again, he pointed out that a majority of Germans supported the idea of denuclearizing their country.[102] But it was too late to change Gorbachev's mind. Saying, "I fear that the train may have already left the station," the Soviet leader got off the phone quickly.[103] Gorbachev also made clear Falin had fallen out of favor by excluding him from the party traveling to Arkhyz.

On July 15, the chancellor and Teltschik touched down in Moscow, where they spent two hours alone with Gorbachev and Chernyaev. In his diary, Chernyaev noted afterward that Kohl was "determined and energetic" in playing an "honest but hard game." Gorbachev and Kohl, according to Chernyaev's overall summary of their talks, discussed how the "bait" of financial inducements was no longer the only, or even the primary, reason Gorbachev was at this point accepting a united Germany's participation in NATO. Rather, the two agreed it was "senseless" to try to "swim against the stream of events."[104] In other words, the Germans had succeeded in creating an overwhelming sense of inevitability.

Kohl asked to begin planning both for Soviet troop withdrawal and for NATO to expand throughout united Germany. He also expressed his willingness to talk about future limits on the size of German armed forces and went through details of past and future economic cooperation between West Germany and the USSR. Gorbachev responded that there were "howls" from Soviet military that he was "selling the Soviet victory in World War II for deutsche marks." Despite their complaints, he was willing to say that the Soviet forces would stay only three to four more years and to concede that "the united Germany will be a member of NATO" provided "the territory of the GDR does not come under NATO jurisdiction as long as Soviet troops are there."[105]

As had happened during his February 1990 visit, the German chancellor was once again thrilled to see enough of a green light to proceed. When the larger delegations, including the staff of the West German embassy in Moscow, joined them afterward, Kohl told the assembled group that "at the end of the year, according to everything that we know now, and plan to do, Germany will reunify."[106] Privately, Teltschik also told the West German diplomat Joachim Von Arnim, still at the Moscow embassy, that their strategy "is working."[107] When Gorbachev later changed his mind and asked if Soviet troops could stay for up to ten years, Kohl would not allow it.[108]

Gorbachev had now plunged not just Falin but also Chernyaev into despair. In his misery, Chernyaev found an excuse to avoid getting on the flight to Arkhyz afterward, even though he was on the guest list and the Germans asked about his absence. He confessed to his diary that he felt "completely destroyed" and considered resigning.[109]

Without either Chernyaev or Falin, the Soviet and West German delegations then flew to a brief intermediate visit to Stavropol. Nazi Germany had occupied the city and, as a gesture of reconciliation, Kohl agreed to the stop in order to lay a wreath at a war memorial. The senior members of both delegations then went on to Arkhyz, with more talks the next day, July 16, 1990, to sort out details.

Once there, Gorbachev made clear that he expected copious funding to cover the Soviet troops' withdrawal, resettlement, and retraining. Kohl would not go into details, saying that such matters were better left for expert subordinates to work out over the summer. The two leaders, he said, should focus on East German territory after the Soviet troops' withdrawal and, by extension, what NATO could do there. Gorbachev declared flatly that "NATO's military structures" could not extend eastward, without saying specifically what that included. The West Germans resisted, pointing out that according to the Helsinki principle, a united Germany had the right to select its own alliance. Whatever structures such an alliance required on German territory would be wholly up to the German government.[110]

Eventually Gorbachev yielded and offered a compromise: he would allow unity if NATO agreed that no nuclear weapons, and only German troops, could be stationed in eastern Germany after the Soviet withdrawal. Both restrictions were limits that Washington had hoped to avoid but were not the deal breakers that complete German denuclearization would have been—and anyway, no Americans were present. Kohl and Genscher found the concessions reasonable. They also agreed to a future ceiling of 370,000 troops for the Bundeswehr.[111]

Kohl held a press conference as soon as possible, and television stations rushed to broadcast the story.[112] Later, the chancellor filled Bush in, confirming that the strategy they had mapped out back in February was now coming to fruition. "I used your formula from Camp David," Kohl recounted, saying that as a sovereign country, Germany "can decide for itself its alliances. And I explained that the Germans would vote unequivocally for NATO." Kohl saw Gorbachev as having "burned all his bridges behind him." Kohl believed Gorbachev could not "go back" and thus needed his Western partners to help him go forward. Some of Bush's advisors were less than thrilled about Kohl's concessions, which evoked memories of an earlier German-Russian deal—one journalist spoke of the "Stavrapallo" summit—but for the Americans too, there was no going back.[113]

In the wake of these events, the Soviet media, still largely controlled by the party, seemed uncertain about how or even whether to publicize the leader's concessions to the domestic audience. Soviet newspapers appearing on July 17, 1990 carried no reports on the Gorbachev–Kohl talks of the preceding two days.[114] Perhaps the most bitter Soviet reaction came, unsurprisingly, from Falin, who described his reaction to the news from Arkhyz as "rage." He complained that not only he but all institutions of the Soviet Union had been kept in the dark during this critical hand of the poker game. He felt that Gorbachev should "'sell'" unification only for a much "higher price," but it was too late.[115] By then Falin had already concluded that his best course of action would be to "lay himself down crosswise on train tracks."[116]

September Struggle

The lower-level Soviet experts who had to finalize matters in a two-plus-four treaty and various associated accords shared Falin's horror. Kohl and Gorbachev had sketched the broad outlines, but plenty of details still needed written clarification, and Moscow's negotiators made those details as devilish as possible.[117] Their West German counterparts quickly realized that Soviet experts saw Gorbachev's concessions in Arkhyz as a "failure" that had "humiliated" their side and were "therefore all the more demanding on the financial conditions of the retreat of Soviet forces."[118] Negotiations dragged on through August, spilling over into September.[119]

As the talks progressed, Soviet hard-liners realized that they had gained a late-breaking advantage. Kohl wanted to complete unification and add East German voters, solidly in his camp, to an expanded electorate during the campaign for the upcoming national election, scheduled for December 2, 1990. To make that happen, he ideally wanted to unite his country no later than early October. That meant all foreign obstacles to unity had to be out of the way in September—a deadline that required Soviet cooperation and thus gave Moscow leverage.[120] Military reactionaries repeatedly made demands not only of the West Germans but also of their own detested foreign minister, Shevardnadze.[121] Long-simmering tensions had now boiled over; the despondent Shevardnadze was openly at war with his own military and on the verge of resigning.[122]

The Soviet side had another new advantage: Washington's distraction. While the Bush Administration still cared about, and kept tabs on, the final talks on German unification, they were no longer the Bush administration's highest priority. Since August 2, when Saddam Hussein had sent 2,000 tanks and 150,000 Iraqi troops into Kuwait, the Persian Gulf had increasingly become Washington's main focus.[123] Hussein's surprise attack and Bush's response resulted in the First Gulf War in 1991 and decades of US fixation on the region.[124] As academic-turned-policymaker Angela Stent pointed out, if the Wall "had fallen six months later and negotiations had begun in the fall of 1990, then Gorbachev would have been far more beholden to his hardline critics and the United States and its allies would have been diverted by the Gulf War." Reunification would have likely become far more difficult, even impossible. She concluded that "timing, in this case, was of the essence."[125]

During the endgame, a new consideration arose. The Czechoslovaks had quietly put out a feeler to the Americans directly about joining NATO. As the biographer of the Czech president put it, "Havel and America were a love story at first sight." The former dissident and political prisoner admired the "unfettered freedom and individuality of the country," and Americans "responded massively to his unquestioned bravery, to his visible modesty, and to his perceived cool."[126] Now one of his aides attempted to capitalize on that love affair. Havel's security advisor asked (as the NSC expert on Eastern Europe, Robert Hutchings, reported to Scowcroft on August 16, 1990), "how NATO would respond if Czechoslovakia applied for membership." Hutchings understood why they were asking. If the "East Europeans want out of the Warsaw Pact but cannot join NATO," he asked, "where do they find their security in the Europe of the future?"[127] Genscher and Mitterrand had previously tried to answer that question by proposing that some kind of pan-European entity replace both military pacts, but the American preference for NATO had prevailed.[128] Hutchings, seeing no easy answer, suggested that "priority attention should be devoted to Poland. Czechoslovakia is next, followed by Hungary. These three, in that order, matter strategically to the West (and Moscow)."[129]

A threat loomed, however. Hutchings also shared with Scowcroft the alarming news that the Soviet side was succeeding, with West German help and despite Washington's best efforts, in restricting NATO's future as part of the final two-plus-four treaty, "leaving us with a Germany that is half in and half out of NATO and undermining the basis for a continued US presence."[130] Thatcher was similarly alarmed.[131] The threat included three lines of attack, each one technical and hidden in the details of what would follow the final Soviet troop withdrawal of 1994. Taken together, however, their overall import was huge.

First, all sides at the negotiating table had agreed that before the 1994 departure, only German territorial defense units (that is, units not integrated into NATO) could deploy to eastern German territory alongside Moscow's forces; after that, German forces integrated into NATO could be present as well. The Soviet military was cannily seizing on the opening provided by this discussion of deployments, however, to add a permanent prohibition on the deployment of *any* non-German troops across the alliance's Cold War eastern border. Worse, the West Germans, in the interest of getting the deal done, had apparently agreed and were now inserting language to that effect into the current draft of the final treaty. The fundamental basis of strategic trust between Bonn and Washington— that German unification and NATO's ability to extend eastward were inseparably fused—suddenly seemed to be disintegrating. Horrified, Hutchings alerted Scowcroft that this prohibition would mean "non-German NATO forces could not 'cross the line' for the purpose of exercises or to meet some future threat to German security"—ever.[132]

Second, Soviet hard-liners were also doing their best belatedly to circumscribe NATO's nuclear presence by the means left available to them. In Arkhyz, Kohl had conceded that there would be no Western nuclear weapons on former East German territory, and Washington had respected that limitation. The Soviets were now demanding, however, that "dual-use" equipment—devices that could carry either conventional or nuclear warheads—had to be excluded too. This prohibition was so broad that, in practice, it would prohibit a huge range of military equipment and vehicles. Most artillery could fire nuclear-armed shells, and nearly all modern military attack aircraft could carry nuclear weapons. They would all potentially fall under such a prohibition.[133]

Third, Bonn's foreign ministry was calling into question the future extent and validity of a number of Cold War accords, which could potentially affect foreign troops not just in the East but also in the West. Among the accords were the 1954 Convention on the Presence of Foreign Forces and its associated status-of-forces agreements, which had been open-ended. Germany's NATO allies thought they should simply continue and expand to eastern German territory, not least because West Germany had indicated that, in general, it intended to maintain its existing treaties after adding eastern territory and becoming a new, unified Germany. But Bonn claimed new agreements on the continued presence of both Soviet troops and Western ones were needed as Germany unified. This claim created, in the words of the US ambassador to Germany, an unnecessary and uncomfortable "moral equivalency between our presence at the request of the Germans and the Soviet presence." Even worse, when Baker wrote to the West German foreign minister about the issue on August 16, Genscher was initially nonresponsive. Taken aback, Western powers indicated they were willing to negotiate some of the terms, but they essentially wanted the Convention and associated accords to stay in effect—not least to avoid a potentially damaging debate over privileges accorded foreign troops from becoming public.[134]

Western allies began to wonder whose side the Germans were on. As a scheduled September 12 signing date for the two-plus-four accord neared, Baker kept communicating his displeasure to Genscher, leading Bonn to show some flexibility on the third issue, concerning the status of foreign forces.[135] Genscher came up with a complicated formulation under which, as he explained to Baker, the most significant provisions of the foreign-forces accords would continue to apply in the West as well as to any troops who moved into eastern Germany—but only to them as individuals, rather than to the eastern territory, as a concession to Moscow. In other words, existing foreign-forces treaties would not simply extend as a blanket policy across all of eastern Germany as the country unified; instead, Bonn would extend the provisions in an ad hoc way to cover any relevant troops there—but it also had the option to decline to do so.[136]

Baker and the NSC grudgingly went along, but the first and second controversies—the permanent prohibition of NATO's foreign troops crossing the inner-German line and the dual-use issue—remained elusive. Hutchings considered the consequences so significant that, despite the pressures of the Kuwait crisis, they required immediate presidential attention. Scowcroft agreed. On September 5, 1990, the national security advisor informed Bush that "a major problem has arisen in the negotiations for a final settlement document on German unification," one that now required Bush's personal attention because "repeated demarches up to and including a letter from Jim Baker to Genscher" had "failed to shift the German position." In the NSC's view, the new Soviet prohibitions went well beyond the Arkhyz agreement. Scowcroft concluded that the current state of play was "incompatible with Germany's full NATO membership" and that "we may lose on this vital point" without top-level intervention. He also advised the president against accepting any invitation to the upcoming German unity celebration, set for October 3, 1990.[137]

The president made time to call Kohl at 8:06 a.m. on Thursday, September 6, and persuaded the German leader to consult with Baker personally about the remaining areas of contention. Bush himself was busy with preparations to meet Gorbachev for a brief summit in Helsinki that Sunday, September 9, to discuss the crisis in the Gulf, and he presumably wanted as many other issues as possible resolved first. As expected, the chancellor seized the opportunity provided by the phone call to petition Bush to attend the unity celebration on October 3: "of course, we would like to see the President of the United States in Berlin, if only for a few hours, if possible." Kohl twisted the president's arm, arguing that a photo "of you, Gorbachev, Thatcher and Mitterrand in Berlin would be a very impressive image," sending a powerful signal of unity and cooperation. The arm-twisting failed. Bush stuck with Scowcroft's advice, replying that he was "not optimistic" about attending.[138]

Kohl, in turn, called Gorbachev the next day, Friday, September 7. With the final signing of the two-plus-four now just days away, the Soviet side had recently demanded 36 billion DM in exchange—eight times what the West Germans had expected. Kohl had already advised Bush of this development in their phone call, letting the president know that Moscow had "unrealistic expectations concerning financing."[139] The West German foreign ministry had similarly reacted to "the size of the Soviet demand with astonishment."[140] Kohl had thought in Arkhyz that the financing could be sorted out by lower-level subordinates, but his finance and treasury experts now balked at the numbers their Soviet counterparts were proposing. The German finance minister, Theo Waigel, mindful of the impact unification-related spending was already having on West Germany, strongly advised Kohl against offering anything above 6 billion DM.[141] Ignoring Waigel's advice, the chancellor began the call with Gorbachev by offering 8 billion DM instead. The Soviet leader dismissed that as a "dead end" and complained that he felt "like he had fallen into a trap."[142] Kohl urged him to calm down, said he would rethink the matter, and offered to phone again on Monday, September 10. The chancellor apparently, despite Bush's request, did not push the dual-use or crossing-the-line controversies with Gorbachev.

Upon hearing that those matters were still not resolved, the US president found himself in the demeaning position of having to ask for the same thing twice. He contacted Kohl yet again on the weekend of the Helsinki summit, saying that he remained "especially concerned that the Soviets not come to expect any further limitations" on the "the stationing of foreign troops."[143] The same day, Bush also told Gorbachev that he intended to decline Kohl's request to attend the October 3 unification ceremony in Germany.[144] Meanwhile, Kohl's own worried advisors told the chancellor over the weekend to hold firm on the total sum.

Disregarding these warnings again in the pursuit of his goal of unity, on Monday Kohl offered the Soviet leader 12 billion DM toward the costs of relocating and rehousing Soviet troops, plus an extra 3 billion DM of interest-free credits.[145] Gorbachev agreed to that amount—but the two men still had not resolved the military issues.[146]

On September 11, the day before the scheduled signing in Moscow, the text of the final two-plus-four treaty remained unfinished. Representatives of Western countries assembled "in the whited sepulchre of the Octyabrskaya Hotel," as the British negotiator P. J. Weston described it, only to discover that "the FRG delegation had already been holding bilaterals with the Russians in an attempt to sew up a deal on the final points, misrepresenting US views (at least to us) into the bargain."[147] Once all six countries' representatives were finally there—with Baker and many other Americans coming directly from Helsinki—they were at least able to resolve the dual-use issue, by allowing such systems in eastern Germany if they were equipped only for conventional weapons while there.[148] With that agreement, the treaty turned the area of the East German state into the only guaranteed nuclear weapons–free zone in Europe.[149]

But the crossing-the-line issue still defied resolution. Genscher was beside himself that his allies were holding out on that point. He felt his own allies were wrecking not only the two-plus-four signing but the entire timetable for unification, and perhaps unification itself. The issue of NATO's future freedom of movement was so significant, however, that the Western allies were willing to risk all of that. Britain and the United States in particular would not accept a permanent prohibition on crossing the inner-German Cold War line, both out of concern for what that would mean for Germany and because of its longer-term implications.[150] Central and Eastern Europeans were already knocking on a number of doors, including those of the NSC, which thought that their concerns merited "priority attention."[151] As a result, the Western powers were not willing to accept a treaty that would, in Weston's words, "indefinitely foreclose options extending far beyond the foreseeable circumstances."[152]

On the evening of September 11, Genscher kept disappearing for private talks with Shevardnadze. Robert Zoellick, Baker's top aide, found it "'tacky'" that the West German indulged in such "private German/Russian bilateral activity elsewhere" in the final hours, leaving his allies to cool their heels and wait for his reappearance.[153] They waited as, from about 7:00 p.m. to 9:00 p.m., Genscher and Shevardnadze spoke one-on-one and agreed on a compromise. After the Soviet departure, while foreign NATO troops could not be permanently stationed or deployed in eastern Germany, they could nonetheless, at the discretion of the German government, cross the Cold War line. Shevardnadze asked whether this agreement should become a formal part of the protocol of negotiations, but Genscher replied no; he would instead simply state this agreement orally to the other foreign ministers and repeat it at the press conference for the signing if asked.[154]

That was not enough. As the irate British put it, "oral assurances would not do." Since the Soviets now, in Weston's words, had 12 billion DM from Kohl "in their kitty and the world expecting signatures in little more than twelve hours, we did not need to offer the Russians any more concessions." Westerners insisted on something in writing on this crucial matter. In reply, Genscher and his staff lashed out at their allies, saying that this "was all totally unrealistic since peace had broken out in Europe." The German foreign minister was beside himself that his dream of reuniting his hometown with the West might be slipping away in the final hours. Sensing discord, later that night the Soviet side threatened to delay or cancel the signing altogether.[155] The Soviet diplomat charged with communicating that threat, Kvitzinsky, recalled years later how much he enjoyed delivering it.[156]

Genscher feared that, if the signing got delayed, the two-plus-four might collapse altogether.[157] Even though by now it was after midnight, he phoned the Hotel International, where the US secretary of state and members of the American delegation had retreated for the night, to demand to speak to Baker in person. He reached Zoellick, who tried to deter Genscher, saying the secretary had already retired after both a sleeping pill and a stiff drink. The foreign minister insisted, saying, "for heaven's sake, we cannot run any more risks," with the treaty and the future of Germany in the balance.[158]

Baker's staff relented and roused the secretary. Once Genscher arrived, shortly after 1:00 a.m., the American delegation received him wearing jogging clothes and bathrobes. Despite the combination of a sleeping pill and alcohol, Baker's negotiation savvy did not desert him. The secretary and Genscher were able to break the impasse by using an idea Zoellick had floated earlier in the day: a written addendum to the treaty.[159] Put more precisely, the formal treaty would continue to state, as Moscow wanted, that foreign troops would be neither stationed nor deployed east of the 1989 inner-German dividing line. However, *deployed* would be defined—per the new addendum, or "agreed minute"—solely at the discretion of the government of a united Germany. That minute served as written confirmation that foreign NATO troops could cross the Cold War line after all.[160] As Zoellick explained afterward, "we needed to secure that possibility because, if Poland were eventually to join NATO in a second step, we wanted American forces to be able to cross East Germany on their way to be stationed in Poland."[161]

The idea satisfied the other signatories as well. All parties consented to add the "agreed minute" to the treaty just in time for the signing to go ahead after all. Some later reproductions of the treaty mistakenly dropped the minute altogether, mistakenly assuming it was trivial.[162] It was not. The Western allies even insisted that all parties sign under the minute as well as under the treaty, so the final, official document bore two full, identical sets of typed titles and handwritten signatures.[163] Shevardnadze signed both of the relevant pages, thereby surrendering Soviet legal rights, setting the slow withdrawal of Soviet troops in motion, and allowing, after completion of that withdrawal, NATO's foreign forces to cross the Cold War line at the discretion of the German government.[164]

During the ceremony, Genscher solemnly promised Gorbachev that the Soviet people would never be disappointed by what they had done.[165] The Soviet leader treated the assembled to what Hurd called a "lavish lunch" in a banquet hall after the signing, and he spoke with optimism about the future. He could not, however, conceal what he had lost—or his weakness. As Hurd wrote in his memoirs, even though the Russian was "so self-confident that he persuades within the four walls" of the hall, "outside all is slipping." The next day, September 13, Gorbachev asked Baker for a no-interest credit of $1 to $1.2 billion. Baker demurred, suggesting they see if a "third country" might help the Soviet leader instead. The American added a request that Gorbachev not ask Israel for such help, however, "because their money is ultimately our money." Meanwhile, that same day, Hurd "called on the man into whose hands the power is slipping," namely "Yeltsin—a dictator in waiting."[166]

On October 3, 1990, Germany was able to unify as planned. NATO's full legal jurisdiction, including the Article 5 guarantee, extended immediately upon unification to cover all of eastern German territory. The alliance had started its post–Cold War expansion to the east.

In December 1990, both Kohl and Gorbachev enjoyed public accolades; Kohl won a resounding victory in the all-German election, and the Soviet leader accepted the Nobel Peace Prize. In Russia, however, the bitterness ran deep. Gorbachev received many sarcastic letters of "congratulation" from Soviet citizens, saying how impressive it was to win a prize for reducing the USSR to a beggar state. Military hard-liners conducted a nuclear test, apparently as a deliberate counterpoint to the peace prize.[167]

Western leaders also bore scars from the September struggle with the West Germans. The British especially resented how Genscher's close aide Frank Elbe, "being particularly disagreeable," had kept saying "all kinds of nonsense about how close 'some people' had come 'to screwing it all up,'" and he did not mean the Soviets.[168] There were no photos of Kohl with Bush, Gorbachev, Mitterrand, and Thatcher on October 3 for the history books, because none of them were willing to attend the public celebration in the heart of Berlin.[169] For Bush, the events of 1989–90 were apparently more about NATO than about Germany, since he did not think it worth the time to witness unification in person—even though Kohl ultimately upheld his end of the bargain by keeping German unity fused to NATO expansion. Instead, the chancellor of newly united Germany had to settle for the political equivalent of mailing Bush and the others thank-you notes.[170]

Once unification was official, Moscow demanded instant payment from Bonn, contrary to an earlier understanding on a longer disbursement schedule. Soviet military leaders also dragged their heels on the physical withdrawal of their roughly 600,000 troops plus dependents. They kept their forces in East Germany at a high state of defense readiness and, according to the American Central Intelligence Agency (CIA), decided to maintain "at least some nuclear weapons in eastern Germany until the last Soviet troops leave" in 1994.[171] The two-plus-four accord had specified that no Western nuclear weapons could go into eastern Germany, but it failed to address Soviet weapons already there, allowing Soviet military leaders to make another last-ditch effort to take advantage of a useful opening. Gorbachev also wrote pointedly to Kohl to note that while the Soviet Union had signed the two-plus-four, it still had not ratified it, implying that it might not yet be valid.[172]

That last threat, at least, proved hollow, as there was no way around the USSR's need for Bonn's financial aid. In light of that, Soviet ratification would take place in March 1991, and the treaty governing Soviet troop withdrawal would be ratified the next month.[173] But there were ominous signs following the September struggle. A bitter Shevardnadze gave up altogether, blindsiding Gorbachev on December 20, 1990 by abruptly resigning as foreign minister.[174] Arms control talks in the wake of the September signing stalled significantly, as both US and Soviet negotiators complained to their superiors that progress was becoming impossible.[175] And the "12 billion in the kitty" that had enabled the two-plus-four signing went missing, presumably into corrupt hands, almost as soon as it crossed Soviet borders. When Baker visited Moscow again in 1991, Gorbachev complained, "'we got a lot of money for German unification, and when I called our people, I was told they didn't know where it was.'" All his advisors could say was that "'it's just gone.'" Learning that those funds had disappeared "without a trace" confirmed Scowcroft's suspicion that any American contributions would "go the same way." The Bush administration, as a result, gave "little thought about serious assistance to the Soviet Union."[176]

In a detailed after-action summary, the British Foreign Office noted that September 1990 had revealed how a united "Germany will not be simply the Federal Republic plus, but a different entity." To achieve unification as quickly as possible, German leaders had been willing to show "general obtuseness" when faced "with the assertion that an important Alliance interest might be at stake."[177] West Germans had seriously considered a permanent prohibition on foreign NATO forces crossing the old Cold War line. Bush had to intervene personally at the last minute as part of the American effort to block that significant precedent and force Bonn to defend NATO's options in the post–Cold War world. German unification and NATO enlargement eastward had become, at last, inseparably fused.

Yet, if the Soviet Union had lost that round, Moscow still retained ways to make trouble. Until Soviet forces and their nuclear weapons left, Bonn would have to remain attentive to Moscow's desires and politics—a process made all the more perilous when the storm Kohl had predicted finally broke over the Soviet Union in 1991. Even the chancellor had not expected it to be so severe. It would sweep away not just Gorbachev but all centralized Soviet authority, fragmenting the country's massive nuclear arsenal into multiple potentially hostile hands. Sicherman, the prescient State Department analyst, had already warned in early 1990 that missteps by the West could turn the post–Cold War era into a copy of the 1920s: seemingly "a rosy time for democracy and capitalism, which within a decade turned into a dictatorship, depression, and then war not long thereafter."[178] Now the cost of missteps was about to become even higher, with not just the Berlin Wall but a nuclear-armed empire collapsing.

CHAPTER FOUR

Oblivion and Opportunity

“GREAT EMPIRES DO NOT go gracefully into oblivion.” Robert Strauss, the new US ambassador to Moscow—who arrived in the middle of a coup in August 1991—used these words to warn Washington about the storm that would destroy the Soviet Union by the end of that year. President George H. W. Bush had picked his old friend Strauss, a colorful and gregarious Texas lawyer, for the post despite the fact that he was a Democrat with “‘no real knowledge about Russia,’” as Strauss himself admitted. The lawyer had also protested that at age seventy-two he was too old, but Bush had insisted; so now Strauss was in the hot seat in Moscow—and his evocative cables home did not disappoint.[1] “The capsize of the Bolshevik party,” Strauss wrote Washington, “is dragging down in its undertow even larger vessels,” including “the Soviet state and the continent-wide great power fashioned by generations of Russian empire builders.” The ambassador could not fathom why Mikhail Gorbachev seemed so blind to the secessionist threat posed by the Soviet republics: “for whatever reason—Russian chauvinism or his Marxist training—Gorbachev has consistently failed to comprehend the power of nationalism as a motivating force.”

Nationalism and secessionism were indeed fueling the storm, as were personal ambitions and animosities, along with the specter of economic collapse. The result would be oblivion for the Soviet Union—after Russia, Ukraine, and Belarus banded together to demand, successfully, the union’s dissolution in December 1991—and opportunity for the West and

NATO. The Atlantic Alliance, in the process of consolidating its role in postunification Germany and exploring possibilities for relations with Central and Eastern European states, could contemplate bolder moves, possibly encompassing post-Soviet regions as well.

The new opportunities developing in 1991 were so great that US defense secretary Dick Cheney advised seizing upon them in the most dramatic way possible. According to National Security Advisor Brent Scowcroft, Cheney "thought we ought to do everything we could to break up the Soviet Union." Secretary of State James Baker disagreed, arguing, "it was important that we try to keep the Soviet Union together—primarily because of command and control over the nuclear forces." In Baker's view, the fragmentation of Moscow's atomic arsenal into the hands of multiple successor states would dangerously increase threats to American security.[2]

The disagreement between Cheney and Baker revealed how the potential disintegration of the USSR posed a profound dilemma for Washington. On the one hand, Soviet collapse would yield a much more permissive environment for structuring post–Cold War order to America's liking, without having to take Soviet wishes into account any longer. But on the other hand, the risk of such disintegration would paradoxically increase incentives for Western leaders to sustain the Soviet Union, or at least to ensure that Russia became the only nuclear successor state, in order to counter the threat of proliferation chaos. And dramatic moves toward NATO expansion could thwart such efforts if a bitter Moscow responded to alliance enlargement by refusing to cooperate on nuclear issues. As if that dilemma were not enough, Bush also had to consider the potential domestic political impact of nuclear chaos abroad as the 1992 presidential election commenced at home. Baker was certain that a Soviet disintegration scenario involving "30,000 nuclear weapons presents an incredible danger to the American people—and they know it and will hold us accountable if we don't respond." Torn between Cheney's and Baker's views, the Bush administration became, in Scowcroft's words, "split, badly split" over what to do.[3]

Dispatching with Hussein—and Gorbachev?

Those events were still to come as the legal process of uniting the two Germanies concluded at the end of 1990 (although practical implementation of unity in all aspects would take many years). Though Chancellor

Helmut Kohl was still privately anticipating trouble, publicly Germans, Europeans, and Americans displayed a sense of closure. Kohl wrapped up the various unity celebrations, albeit without the top-level foreign guests he craved, and began the hard work of making political unification a reality. And Bush directed his energy toward a new foreign policy priority: the American response to the invasion of Kuwait by Iraq.

As Washington turned its focus toward the Gulf in late 1990 and early 1991, queries by Central and Eastern European countries about closer relations with NATO received a measured response, such as the one Bush gave Czechoslovak president Václav Havel on November 18. Havel felt that "as all the old links cease to exist" for Central and Eastern Europe, it was the obligation of the Atlantic Alliance to open its arms. The Czech asked whether Bush "might consider an association agreement" between his country and NATO. Bush replied, "I assure you we don't want Poland, Hungary, or Czechoslovakia in a European no man's land," but for now he suggested concentrating on a Czechoslovak mission to the alliance instead.[4] This tepid response did not dissuade Warsaw or Budapest from making similar remarks. Polish president Lech Wałęsa confessed to Bush that Poles "are in a state of embarrassment" because "we keep begging" for help. They would not stop, however, because "we resolutely desire to join Western Europe and the United States in political, economic, and military terms."[5] The Hungarians similarly remained keen on options for any kind of institutional membership in the West.[6] Back on June 7, 1990, Hungarian prime minister József Antall had called for "immediate liquidation" of the Warsaw Pact's military organization, and that summer both he and the foreign minister, Géza Jeszenszky, had paid cordial calls to NATO's headquarters in Brussels.[7]

Such feelers prompted the State Department to produce, on October 22, 1990, an analysis of "Eastern Europe and NATO," authored in part by the acting head of its European bureau, James Dobbins. His main conclusion was that "it is not in the best interest of NATO or the US that these states be granted full NATO membership and its security guarantees." In fact, the United States should expressly refrain from organizing "an anti-Soviet coalition whose frontier is the Soviet border." If Washington assembled such a coalition, it would not only look predatory but could even "lead to a reversal of current positive trends in Eastern Europe and the USSR." The alliance should, as the president had told Havel, focus instead on building up liaison offices.[8] The European Strategy Steering Group, which Deputy National Security Advisor Bob Gates later recalled as an assemblage of "the closest and most trusted advisors" of Baker, Cheney, Scowcroft, and the chairman of the JCS, Colin Powell, came as a group to a similar conclusion.[9] The question at hand was, "should the US and NATO now signal to the new democracies of Eastern Europe NATO's readiness to contemplate their future membership?" According to analysis prepared for one of the group's sessions in October 1990, the answer was as follows: "all agencies agree that East European governments should not be invited to join NATO anytime in the immediate future."[10]

Over at the Pentagon, Cheney and his staff held a different opinion. As reported to the NSC, the "OSD [Office of the Secretary of Defense] wishes to leave the door ajar," preferring to couch talk of NATO expansion in "caveats such as no discussion at this time."[11] This preference was consistent with some of Cheney's earlier remarks on the matter. He had previously suggested, on July 3, 1990, that NATO needed to "rethink out-of-area" limits that it had imposed on itself. He had also reportedly spoken about some kind of observer or "*'associate status'*" for former Warsaw Pact countries.[12]

Like Cheney, Central and Eastern European countries begged to differ as well. In the wake of German unification, it was becoming ever more obvious that European institutions would not look much different from before. None of the proposals to create demilitarized zones in the middle of Europe had succeeded, nor had an effective pan-European security system arisen; the French were still promoting some kind of confederation, but its prospects were uncertain.[13] In contrast, NATO and the EC endured, although with their eastern flank slightly extended to encompass former East Germany.[14] If post–Cold War order was going to look like that of the Cold War, divided between NATO/EC and non-NATO/non-EC territory, then Germany's newly free neighbors wanted, at long last, to get on the correct side of the persistent divide.

Unsurprisingly, Moscow was not enthused about such entreaties to the West by countries that were still nominally its allies; they added to its long litany of woes. Economic conditions within the USSR remained terrible, and discontent was running high. On November 7, 1990, shots were fired at Gorbachev during the October Revolution Day Parade in Red Square.[15] Soviet foreign policy was reduced to minimizing trouble abroad, and this was the focus of efforts by Yuli Kvitzinsky, the Soviet Union's new deputy foreign minister. Knowing that the Warsaw Pact was crumbling—it would, as Hungarians had demanded, declare an end to its military activities in February 1991—he tried a diplomatic maneuver to limit the future options available to Central and Eastern European countries. He supported the idea of bilateral "security clauses" with other pact members that, in the words of one analyst, "prohibited either side from joining any organization considered by the other party as being against its own interests." The upshot was that the clause would prevent disloyal pact members from joining NATO.[16]

In a united front, Czechoslovakia, Hungary, and Poland all refused to sign the bilateral accords.[17] Instead, they established the so-called Visegrad cooperation in February 1991, a three-way partnership meant to harmonize their appeals to the EC and NATO.[18] All they got in the short run, however, was a somewhat vague NATO declaration, issued in June 1991.[19] NATO secretary general Manfred Wörner informed American vice president Dan Quayle soon thereafter that, while "the Central and East European countries are satisfied" with this declaration temporarily, "if given an opportunity they would all join NATO now."[20]

Immediate NATO or EC membership was still not in the cards, thanks not only to Soviet objections but also to Western hesitations. French president François Mitterrand told Bush when the two met in Martinique in March 1991 that "Europe doesn't need 20 more states."[21] One reason for Mitterrand's reluctance was that Germany, distracted by unification issues, was less able to shoulder the cost of EC expansion. Bush agreed that "Kohl has financial problems because of the monumental task of East Germany," which was turning out "to be a bigger problem than anyone thought." One expert would later estimate that eastern Germany ultimately absorbed $1.9 trillion in German investment and subsidies.[22] Rather than a swift expansion of the EC, Mitterrand was still promoting the creation of a looser European confederation and would subsequently host a large conference centered on that proposal with Havel in Prague on June 12, 1991.[23]

Mitterrand had brought his foreign minister, Roland Dumas, to the Martinique meeting. Dumas told Bush that in terms of European security it was NATO, rather than the EC, that was best suited "to deal with the former Warsaw Pact countries." Both French leaders preferred to avoid a swift extension of the EC to Central and Eastern Europe, so were interested in ways NATO could conduct compensatory outreach to the region. Dumas emphasized that "they want to join NATO. Poland especially wants in," now that the border issue with Germany had been resolved. They "realize that the only firm ground in Europe is the Atlantic Alliance."

Mitterrand seconded Dumas, saying that while "we don't want to convey the impression that we are trying to block European integration," nonetheless "we view NATO as the prime security guarantor."[24] Europeans needed to save their energy to deal with the rising violence in Yugoslavia; in June 1991, Slovenia and Croatia declared independence, prompting an attack by Serbian leader Slobodan Milošević and sending the region spiraling into war.[25] The French president then added: "in the 21st century my wish is that Europe will be able to defend itself but if I have to pay for that hope at the price of a crisis with the United States, the price is too high." Instead, "we have to find a way so that NATO and the embryo of European defense can co-exist." At present, however, "Europe is not ready to have a force adequate to provide its own security. . . . NATO is the only real force."[26]

For his part, Kohl was greatly worried by the possible precedent set by the shots fired at Gorbachev in November 1990. A violent, chaotic Soviet disintegration would have grave consequences, not least for the country's remaining troops in Germany, and Kohl hoped to keep the change as controlled and consensual as possible. As part of that strategy, the chancellor, having just freed eastern Germany from Moscow, counseled Lithuania not to try to free itself. He advised the republic's leader at the start of 1991 that calling for the Soviet Union's dissolution was dangerous because it would entail dismantling "a massive empire" with "nuclear weapons that are widely scattered over its regions."[27]

This unsolicited advice did little to stop the drive of some Soviet republics to become, initially, "sovereign entities" within the USSR, and then, subsequently, independent states. Chernyaev noted in his diary that, as early as August 1990, Gorbachev was raising the possibility that the Soviet Union might dissolve.[28] By the start of 1991, the Soviet leader was panicked enough about separatist movements that he gave permission to the head of the KGB, Vladimir Kryuchkov, and other reactionaries to proceed violently. Gorbachev had held off using force against the Baltic separatists partly because he needed aid from Western countries, which would have balked at such brutal treatment, and partly due to the spirit of perestroika.[29] As Eduard Shevardnadze had once told Baker, "in the Baltics, no one intends to use force," because such violence "would mean an end to perestroika."[30] Now, thanks to Kryuchkov and others, the Lithuanian capital of Vilnius experienced a "bloody Sunday" on January 13, 1991. Tanks attacked protesters, leaving fifteen dead and several hundred wounded. The intervention achieved little, however, other than to damage Gorbachev's image even more.[31]

When Bush sent a message of disapproval about the sudden switch to violence, the Soviet leader replied that if he seemed "to zig and zag at times," it was only because he wanted "to prevent a bloodbath" and "to avoid a civil war."[32]

Failing at home, Gorbachev did what he could to improve his country's standing abroad. He signed, among other accords, a new treaty of friendship and cooperation with Germany.[33] He also continued to emphasize the importance of the Conference on Security and Cooperation in Europe, the only forum other than the UN Security Council (UNSC), where Moscow had equal status with the United States and its allies.[34] Still hoping the CSCE would become the heart of a pan-European security system involving both Western and Eastern states, he did what he could to promote that organization, most notably at its summit in Paris on November 19, 1990.[35] There he also signed the Conventional Forces in Europe Treaty, despite its many downsides for the Soviet Union—most notably, as a pair of arms control experts put it, the elimination of "the Soviet Union's overwhelming quantitative advantage in conventional weapons in Europe." Specifically, the treaty limited the number of armored combat vehicles, attack helicopters, combat aircraft, heavy artillery, and tanks that NATO and the Warsaw Pact could deploy between the Atlantic Ocean and the Ural Mountains. The idea behind the accord was "to prevent either alliance from amassing forces for a blitzkrieg-type offensive, which could have triggered the use of nuclear weapons in response."[36] It was the most comprehensive, legally binding conventional arms control agreement ever produced.[37]

Journalists quickly noted, however, that recalcitrant Soviet military leaders tried to undercut the new CFE accord by relocating equipment behind the Urals, where the treaty's limits did not apply. As the *Financial Times* discovered, to carry out this massive relocation, the Soviet military had, among other measures "severely disrupted collection of the country's record harvest last summer by commandeering thousands of railway wagons."[38] The scale of the effort revealed that it had been planned, and begun, long in advance of the signing—a clear sign of Soviet defense leaders' disagreement with what Gorbachev was doing.

Trying to achieve another foreign policy win to impress such critics at home and abroad, Gorbachev attempted to use his moral authority, still strong in the eyes of the West, to intervene in the Kuwaiti crisis. He sent his advisor Yevgeny Primakov to negotiate with Iraqi leader Saddam Hussein. Bush intervened, however, writing to Gorbachev that he disagreed with such diplomatic efforts. If Moscow succeeded in producing a negotiated settlement, then Hussein "would likely acquire a standing of heroic proportions in the Arab world."[39]

Bush's willingness to use force to prevent that from happening was a bracing introduction to the realities of the post–Cold War order. After 1989, hardly a year passed in which the United States was not involved in a conventional war.[40] Bush's biographer, Jeffrey Engel, later concluded that what the president had meant by a "new world order" was the idea of "great powers fulfilling international will against lesser intransigent states that violated sovereignty and international borders."[41] In keeping with that view, Bush set a January 15, 1991 deadline for Hussein to comply with UN resolutions for a withdrawal from Kuwait. Gorbachev tried to extend that deadline for forty-eight hours for one more round of negotiating with Hussein, but Bush refused.[42]

The thunder of war was beginning to sound in the Gulf.[43] As expected, Hussein did not comply by January 15. A US-led coalition began an air attack the next day, followed by a ground offensive the following month.[44] As Secretary Cheney later remarked, "thank God for the reunification of Germany and the heavy equipment transporters the Russians had bought for East German forces," which turned out to be ideal for carrying US tanks. The transporters had become German equipment as part of unification, and Bonn let Washington use them in the Gulf War. As a result, Washington could easily, in Cheney's words, "move all the Abrams and all the Bradleys out to the desert and launch that flanking maneuver that 7th Corps ran against Saddam Hussein."[45]

With the Gulf War and its consequences to worry about abroad and a recession and backlash against Bush's 1990 tax increase at home, the president remained cautious about providing financial support to the Soviet Union. Speaking at the meeting of the Group of 7 (G7) in London on July 15, 1991, the president said he did not think it right to provide such funding to a country that had "long-range missiles . . . aimed at the United States." He also expressed concerns less publicly about the ongoing Soviet biological weapons program. Canadian prime minister Brian Mulroney shared his doubts as well. If, back in 1985, Gorbachev had said, "I will free Eastern Europe, I will dismantle the Warsaw Pact, a united Germany will be in NATO, the UNSC will take action in the Persian Gulf, we will sign CFE and . . . there will be elections and democracy," then Mulroney "would have hurried in with a check" for him. But now, "here's my dilemma: I find myself saying, what have you done for me lately."[46] And many Westerners worried about the cautionary example of how German financial support at the time of unification had disappeared.

When Gorbachev, who was invited to attend only the latter part of the G7 summit, arrived and asked why Washington could "find $100 billion for a regional war" in the Gulf, "but none to make a [*sic*] Soviet Union a new country," Bush gave Moscow's nuclear arsenal as the reason: "we feel the missiles aimed at New York."[47] Gorbachev's foreign policy advisor Anatoly Chernyaev, who had decided not to resign after all, struggled anew with hopelessness watching his boss fail to get more aid from the G7.[48] Chernyaev had already decided that Gorbachev "will remain in history as a messiah" but was "lost as a politician."[49]

Thinking along similar lines, the NSC had by then sent a "request for an analysis of the Gorbachev succession" to the CIA, asking that only a very limited number of people know about the request. The CIA reported on April 29, 1991 that "all the ingredients are now present" for a rapid change in regime that could "quickly sweep away the current political system."[50] Bush administration officials also heard a similarly pessimistic assessment of Gorbachev's chances from Secretary General Wörner, who had begun calling him the "drowning man." Wörner guessed that "the people hate Gorbachev and in a poll he would only get, at best, 20 percent and probably more like 12 percent support." The secretary general was actively advising "Central and East European countries not to provoke the Soviet military" by showing too much interest in the West at present, given how precarious the situation was.[51]

The US president speculated about the consequences of diminishing Soviet power with Hungarian president Árpád Göncz in May 1991. Bush asked, "if the Soviet Union someday permits Baltic independence and perhaps shrinks some more, would that be beneficial to you?" The Hungarian replied, "I think so," but even a shrunken Soviet Union "will be a great power, and in one or two generations will try again to establish influence." He hoped nonetheless that two generations would give "us some breathing space" to do what he thought needed to be done: to "integrate the Soviet Union into Europe, so that we don't once again become the border lands of Europe."[52]

The Soviet Union was fading more quickly than either of them expected, however; alarm bells about an impending putsch started ringing in Washington in June 1991. The White House received reports of an impending coup that were sufficiently credible for the US embassy in Moscow to warn Gorbachev.[53] Bush also decided to hedge his bets by receiving Gorbachev's rival, Boris Yeltsin, in Washington. Russia had held its own election on June 12, even though it was still part of the USSR, and Yeltsin, thanks to his victory in that election, now sported the title of Russian

president-elect.[54] Gorbachev had allowed the Soviet republics some freedom in framing their own leaders' roles, which he had apparently hoped
would be roughly akin to governors in the United States. Some of those
leaders took the title of president instead and began acting accordingly—
especially Yeltsin.

Even before becoming president-elect, Yeltsin had already made a televised call for Gorbachev's resignation.[55] He also appointed a "Russian
foreign minister"—an idealistic young diplomat named Andrei Kozyrev—
even though foreign relations were notionally still the responsibility of
the Soviet Union as a whole. Kozyrev had been deeply influenced by his
years in the Soviet mission to the UN in New York, starting in 1975. In
his memoirs, he recalled how he once bought a copy of the novel *Doctor
Zhivago*, banned in his home country, and read as much of it as he could
on a bench in Central Park, leaving it there at the end of the day for fear
it would be found in his room at the Soviet mission.[56] Now Kozyrev was
helping to open doors for his new boss. Bush decided to receive the
president-elect in Washington on June 20, 1991; as Bush told his guest,
the fact that Gorbachev was still in charge of the Soviet Union "does not
mean that we cannot do business with you."[57]

Yeltsin explained to Bush that he had "divorced" himself entirely from
the Communist Party and its thinking on state control of enterprise, and
was considering moving to a market economy.[58] During a visit to Texas
in September 1989, Yeltsin had been shocked at the everyday abundance
on offer at a Houston grocery store and wanted the same for his people.[59]
Bush asked whether all of this meant Western oil companies seeking to
do business should now "deal with Russia" rather than the Soviet Union.
Yeltsin responded in the affirmative and added, "we no longer need services from the center. We do not want the command system. We want to
destroy it." He also implied that he would run defense issues as well, stating wrongly that "we have all the nuclear weapons."[60] It was obvious that
Yeltsin now saw himself as the big man in Moscow and planned to dispatch Gorbachev one way or another.

"Who Is Controlling the Nuclear Weapons?"

Yeltsin got his chance to rid himself of the Soviet leader two months later.
The Bush administration had been right to warn Gorbachev that a reac-
tionary coup was coming, but wrong about the timing. It did not happen
in June but on August 19–21, 1991, while Gorbachev was on vacation in

Crimea. Ambassador Strauss reported afterward that the catalyst for the coup had been a desire to stop the scheduled August 20 signing of "a new union treaty" that would lead to "a greatly reduced role for the central Soviet government and to greatly enlarged powers for the republics."[61] The reason publicly given by the coup plotters, however, was that the Soviet leader was ill. Bush wondered aloud whether that was a euphemism for being tortured, and "maybe that means that Gorbachev's fingernails wouldn't come out."[62]

Putschists succeeded in putting Gorbachev under house arrest in his vacation residence. Back in Moscow, Yeltsin and his entourage made their way to the Russian parliament building, where in a show of resistance they climbed onto a tank sent to menace the parliament and waved a Russian flag. Televised around the world, it made for a powerful image.[63] As Yeltsin's biographer Timothy Colton later noted, the sight reminded Russians of "a totemic image from another revolution, tattooed in their heads by the history primers they had read as children," namely, of Lenin inspiring the proletariat "from an armored car in April 1917."[64] Bush, discussing events with Mulroney, admitted how amazed he was to see Yeltsin "on top of a tank saying this coup must be reversed," adding, "you have to give him credit for enormous guts."[65]

The president, who had previously run the CIA, was upset at the lack of intelligence on these dramatic August events. As he complained to Mulroney, "our embassy didn't know a damn thing. We were surprised like everyone else." Scarcely three weeks earlier, thinking the coup danger of June was over, the president had visited the USSR and allowed Soviet vice president Gennady Yanayev to serve as "my host when I was in Moscow." Now, as one of the leaders of the coup, Yanayev was claiming the title of acting president.[66]

While the putsch was unfolding, Bush was unable to get any information from Gorbachev, who was held incommunicado. But he did manage to speak repeatedly to Yeltsin, who explained that he was trying to negotiate with Kryuchkov, the rest of the KGB, and the military to bring an end to the violence.[67] Kryuchkov, who Gates had suspected in 1990 of turning against Gorbachev, appeared to be the main organizer of the coup. In the words of the former US ambassador to Moscow, Jack Matlock, "no credible attempt to overthrow Gorbachev could have been mounted without the support of the KGB chief."[68] According to Kozyrev, Yeltsin at one point stopped protesters from taking over KGB headquarters, perhaps as part of his negotiations with Kryuchkov.[69]

The KGB's special forces, the *spetsnaz*, had reportedly received a spoken command to attack the parliament—but according to a journalist, since nobody was prepared to give a written order, those forces balked and did not attack right away.[70] Yeltsin warned Bush on the morning of August 21, 1991 (US eastern time), that *spetsnaz* forces were "not following my orders and capable of attack," and that the situation remained fluid. There had been deaths in the fighting in Moscow, and Yeltsin told Bush that "30 *Spetznaz* [sic] aircraft are being sent out" in order "to take over a number of sites and locations," apparently in the Baltics.[71] There were also no fewer than three different aircraft racing to Gorbachev in the Crimea. Yeltsin hoped the one piloted by his allies would arrive first.[72]

One person who had by then already successfully completed a flight was the young Russian foreign minister, Kozyrev. Fearful that the coup might succeed, Yeltsin had dispatched him to Paris, to declare a Russian government-in-exile if necessary. Welcoming him, his French hosts did their best to shield him from other Soviet diplomats in France loyal to the coup plotters, but they could not prevent a menacing KGB call to his room at the Hôtel de Crillon, threatening his family back in Moscow. And despite his hosts' solicitousness, Kozyrev noted that French diplomats remained "consistently evasive." He allowed himself "no illusions: the West, however sympathetic to the democrats in Russia, would be careful not to anger the rulers in the Kremlin. . . . The fate of Russia would be decided in Moscow, not in Washington or Paris."[73] He nonetheless allowed himself a sense of hope, feeling that, in the popular resistance to the coup, he saw the signs of the potential triumph of the Russian people.[74]

Back in Moscow, Yeltsin was gradually gaining the upper hand. He conveyed to Bush that he had successfully ordered some forces and tanks to retreat to "the periphery of Moscow," in order to decrease the chance that they would be used.[75] Scowcroft recalled gradually realizing, to his relief, that the putsch leaders were "inept," but "had the coup been more carefully planned" or started sooner, "the results could have been quite different, quite different."[76] Late on August 21 eastern time, Yeltsin shared yet more good news with Washington: the aircraft bearing his allies had succeeded in rescuing Gorbachev and was now bringing the Soviet leader "back to Moscow unharmed and in good health." Even better, the coup attempt was collapsing; Kryuchkov, the defense minister, and other plotters "have been taken into custody." Marshal Sergei Akhromeyev, his long downward slide since the Washington summit of 1990 now complete, would soon thereafter commit suicide.[77] He left behind a note, addressed to no one, saying, "'I cannot live when my fatherland is perishing and everything that I believe to be the meaning of life is being destroyed.'"[78]

The putsch ended, and soon Gorbachev was back in Moscow—but it was far from clear whether he was back in charge.[79] On August 23, Yeltsin dramatically upstaged the Soviet president during a televised speech, making Gorbachev look weak.[80] Yeltsin also suspended the Russian Communist Party, capitalizing on his newly charismatic image as the leader of resistance to the coup.[81] He in effect launched a countercoup of his own.[82]

Shock waves from the failed putsch rippled across the region. They fatally undermined Mitterrand's attempt to create some kind of a pan-European confederation; Moscow now seemed less like a desirable partner and more like an unstable danger.[83] The coup also accelerated secessionist movements throughout the Soviet Union. Prior to August 1991, only Lithuania and Georgia had announced their independence; afterward, nine more republics followed suit, including Ukraine.[84] In a show of nuclear independence, the leader of Kazakhstan, Nursultan Nazarbayev, simply decreed that he was closing a Soviet nuclear test facility on Kazakh territory, the Semipalatinsk Nuclear Test Site, on August 29, 1991, forty-two years to the day after the first Soviet nuclear test had been conducted there.[85]

Speaking to Bush about the coup, Prime Minister Mulroney worried that they were both coming under fire for having done so little to help Gorbachev financially at the G7 meeting in London on July 15–17, 1991. Critics were saying, "if you people had been more generous in London, maybe this wouldn't have happened."[86] Russia expert and journalist Strobe Talbott had already argued as much in *Time* magazine, writing that "'the USSR has conceded so much and the US reciprocated so little for a simple reason: The Gorbachev revolution is history's greatest fire sale. In such transactions, the prices are always very low.'"[87] Regardless, Bush and his advisors continued to oppose large amounts of aid to Moscow; this view increasingly diverged from that of Bonn, Paris, and London. When the British prime minister, John Major, suggested that the G7 consider an aid package to help Gorbachev get back on his feet, the NSC still advised against it, saying, "we will not be stampeded into far-reaching decisions."[88]

Instead, Bush's most urgent question during the coup, as he told Mulroney, was "who is controlling the nuclear weapons?"[89] It was a question of existential interest. The Soviet Union possessed 27,000 nuclear weapons by the end of 1991, according to testimony of Harvard expert Ashton Carter at the time—plus the production facilities and fissile material to make many more.[90]

Bush was not alone in his concern. As Kohl put it to party colleagues, the future of the Soviet nuclear arsenal, specifically of arms control talks, was of "elemental interest." He worried about civilian nuclear plants as well. Living much closer to Moscow than Bush, the chancellor wanted to ensure Europe did not live through "a second Chernobyl," the April 1986 disaster that had exposed millions of Soviet and European residents to plumes of radioactive material.[91] The West also needed to watch out for something else, if the behavior of Soviet forces in Central and Eastern Europe was an accurate guide: the theft and black-market sale of components of the Soviet nuclear arsenal amid the chaos. A 1991 study at Harvard noted the worrisome prevalence of a new saying: "'everything is for sale.'"[92] A *New York Times* article reported that Soviet middlemen were seeking "to sell weapons-grade materials to the highest bidders."[93]

Bush and his aides were coming to realize how threatened not just Gorbachev but all Soviet central authority was. Embassy staff cabled, "we urgently need high-level guidance" because, coup or no coup, the Soviet Union "remains the only country in the world capable of destroying the US in 30 minutes." It was essential to ascertain the status of "command/control and security of nuclear weapons."[94] The American secretary of state rushed to Moscow in September 1991. Ambassador Strauss, who was not just President Bush's friend but also Baker's goose-hunting buddy, accompanied the secretary as they drove around town during his visit, trying to figure out who had the power to kill nearly every American. At one point, Baker reportedly looked out the car window and remarked, "'shithole of a town you got here, Bob.'" Strauss responded, "'fuck you, Jim.'"[95]

The two men faced an embattled Gorbachev, and Baker told him that "control of all types of nuclear weapons" must be maintained. The Soviet leader reassured him, unconvincingly, "that in this respect everything will be as it was before. The Center and the President remain the supreme commander-in-chief."[96] Baker decided nonetheless to take part in a dinner with the heads of a number of Soviet republics, since he suspected that he would need them.[97] The secretary had begun to echo Wörner's assessment of Gorbachev as a man going under; as Baker later recalled in his memoirs, it "was hard not to feel sorry for" him.[98] On top of the coup and the nuclear issue, it was becoming apparent that, once winter arrived, the Soviet Union would face even worse food supply problems than in the past.

Without Western assistance, there would be real hardship.[99] The food problem raised yet another issue; the Bush administration insisted that there be a connection between Western assistance—even emergency food and medicine—and the fulfillment of previous Soviet debt obligations. Moscow had to maintain creditworthiness, be transparent about its gold reserve holdings, and take responsibility for debts incurred by the Soviet Union if it wanted help.[100]

Returning to Washington, the secretary went to the White House for a breakfast with Bush, Cheney, and Scowcroft to share the news from his trip. His underlined notes from the breakfast show that although he had met with various republic leaders, he considered it unwise to court them too soon. In his words, "if we push too rapidly to launch a campaign where we have the team going out to the republics, we're likely to undercut our objective of preserving some cohesion . . . on nuclear weapons." In his opinion, the ultimate goal should be "centralized control of nukes." The United States should do what it could to "preserve center."[101]

Some tentative follow-up with the republics resulted, but mostly at a lower level than talks with the secretary of state. Baker tasked his undersecretary, Reginald Bartholomew, with arranging meetings in the republics possessing parts of the Soviet strategic weapons, namely, Russia, Ukraine, Belorussia, and Kazakhstan. Bartholomew emphasized to all of them that Washington would oppose "efforts by republics to exploit or take exclusive control of nuclear powers on their territory."[102] As Kozyrev later recalled, it was clear that Bush and Baker were, because of their concerns about the atomic arsenal, reluctant about Yeltsin's desire to end Soviet central authority.[103]

Bush and Baker were not alone; concern about the Soviet coup and its effect on nuclear safety was bipartisan. Senator Samuel Nunn, a Georgia Democrat, visited Moscow to ask whether Gorbachev had maintained continuous control over the Soviet nuclear arsenal during the coup. When the senator could not get a straight answer, he became deeply alarmed.[104] Gorbachev did not want to admit that he had temporarily lost control of his nuclear briefcase, one of three necessary to order a launch. For a time, the ministry of defense had apparently become the sole master of the Soviet nuclear forces, because it already possessed two duplicate briefcases and had reportedly taken Gorbachev's for a while.[105] As a result of this troubling development, Nunn initiated a sustained effort with the help of Representative Les Aspin, the Democratic chair of the House Armed Services Committee, to increase the security of Soviet weapons. On November 27, 1991, largely as a result of Nunn's efforts, the Senate passed the Soviet Nuclear Threat Reduction Act by a vote of 86 to 8.[106]

This vote only reinforced Bush's focus, in September 1991, on the status of Soviet nuclear weapons.[107] A particular worry were tactical nuclear arms, both Soviet and American, intentionally designed to have small yields and shorter ranges. As Scowcroft later noted, they "were increasingly troubling politically and—to me—increasingly meaningless militarily." In addition, such weapons would be devastating in the hands of terrorists, so the White House wanted to account for as many of the Soviet ones as possible. There were an estimated 22,000 such weapons in the disintegrating USSR, some tiny enough to fit in a duffel bag. An idea arose to inspire Gorbachev to remove such weapons from deployment by announcing that the United States would do so. The national security advisor had some difficulty convincing Cheney of the desirability of removing them—the Secretary of Defense's initial reaction was "'absolutely not'"—but Scowcroft succeeded in the end.[108]

The larger strategic weapons systems, spread over four of the Soviet republics, obviously remained a worry as well, although the national security advisor was ambivalent as to whether action was needed on that matter. Scowcroft thought four diminished arsenals, divided among weak post-Soviet republics ill-prepared to manage them, might be less threatening to the United States than the original combined Soviet force under centralized control. Scowcroft admitted, though, that "loss of physical control of the country's weapons of mass destruction" was dangerous. And yet again he found himself in conflict with Cheney, who argued for a more "'aggressive'" approach to the Soviet meltdown, such as immediately establishing US diplomatic consulates in all republics. Bush and Scowcroft later criticized Cheney's recommendations as a "thinly disguised effort to encourage the breakup of the USSR."[109]

Undeterred, Cheney pushed in particular for bolstering relations with Ukraine.[110] If it succeeded in its efforts to peel away from the Soviet Union, Ukraine would instantly have the third-largest nuclear arsenal in the world.[111] Cheney thought it desirable to get in on the "'ground floor'" with Kiev.[112] Bush had visited there on August 1, 1991 as part of his recent pre-coup trip to the Soviet Union, during which he had signed the Strategic Arms Reduction Treaty (START).[113] At that time, his primary interest was in shoring up Gorbachev and maintaining central authority, and he dis-

appointed the Ukrainian democratic opposition with lukewarm public remarks on their dream of full independence in an address that was swiftly
nicknamed the "Chicken Kiev" speech.[114]

Now, in the immediate wake of the coup, he was willing to listen to
Cheney—and to Ukrainian leader Leonid Kravchuk, visiting Washington
on September 25, 1991. By then the Ukrainian parliament, or Rada, had
both passed a declaration of independence and scheduled a public referendum on that declaration, to be held on December 1 as part of that day's
presidential election.[115] Kravchuk was blunt in his remarks to Bush, making clear his view that central Soviet authority was "disintegrating" and
that the USSR had no future.[116]

The president decided that the time had come for dramatic measures
on limiting nuclear weapons. He realized that he needed to accomplish as
much arms control as possible while there was still a central Soviet authority to deal with. The best way to do that, he decided, was to call for unilateral cuts—not just for tactical but for other weapons as well—and to hope
that Moscow would copy his moves. Cheney remained skeptical of this approach, but Scowcroft prevailed again.[117] The national security advisor and
his aides felt this dramatic gambit was the fastest way to get Gorbachev to
follow suit while he still could. When informed by phone of these developments, Secretary General Wörner also declared that he would support such
an initiative—as long as it was clear that there would continue to be "air-
based nuclear systems in Europe." Scowcroft responded, "absolutely."[118]

The president decided to make a televised announcement, letting
Americans know he was acting unilaterally to avoid, in Baker's words, getting "bogged down in another protracted, set-piece negotiation," since
events were simply moving too quickly for that. Baker briefed NATO allies in advance, telling them the United States would "withdraw and destroy all of its nuclear artillery shells and nuclear warheads for short-range
ballistic missiles." Bush also planned to "remove all nuclear weapons from
surface ships and attack submarines, and withdraw nuclear weapons for
land-based naval aircraft." Strategic bombers were to come off of their
"alert posture," which meant "bombs loaded and ready to take off on a few
minutes' notice." Bush would also take off alert status "all ICBMs [inter-
continental ballistic missiles]" scheduled for reduction under START. But,
Baker reassured his allies, "we do not intend to de-nuclearize Europe."
Bush and his advisors saw "an indispensable role for air-delivered theater
nuclear weapons into the indefinite future, and remain committed to keeping

NATO's nuclear deterrent modern." In return, Bush hoped to inspire "the Soviets to take comparable steps."[119]

The US president called Gorbachev on the morning of September 27, 1991, the day he planned to make this televised announcement.[120] Bush emphasized that, while these moves were one-sided, the White House hoped the Soviet Union would take parallel steps. A surprised Gorbachev said he could only respond in principle, but that his "answer is a positive one." He asked if Bush would cut back on testing as well, but Bush responded that "we're reluctant on testing" and not yet ready to talk about it.[121] Despite that issue, Gorbachev declared Bush's initiative historic, and comparable to what he and the previous US president, Ronald Reagan, had considered at Reykjavik. Once the White House staff tracked down Yeltsin, the Russian president also approved, telling Bush that his initiative was "a beautiful concept."[122] The dramatic move worked. On October 5, Gorbachev announced that he would follow suit.[123] The Soviet Union would destroy all nuclear artillery ammunition and warheads for tactical missiles, remove all naval nonstrategic weapons from surface ships and submarines, and implement a host of other arms reductions.[124]

Yeltsin Makes the Soviet Union Obsolete

By autumn 1991, the NSC had concluded that the chances of "a long-term role for Gorbachev" were "nil."[125] Scowcroft started referring to "the collapse of the Soviet Union" in October 1991 as if it were an accomplished fact. Looking back on that time from the year 2000, he explained, "what became clear to me was that Yeltsin was maneuvering so that the Ukraine would be the proximate cause of the breakup of the Soviet Union." But the real reason was the Russian leader's cunning in using that country's desire for independence as an excuse for what he wanted to do anyway. Put differently, "the Soviet Union was disintegrating," Scowcroft believed, "almost completely because it was the way Yeltsin could get rid of Gorbachev"—by making the latter man into the leader "of a political entity that no longer existed." The national security advisor realized that "the forces of disintegration were pretty strong," but speculated that "if there had not been that enmity" between Yeltsin and Gorbachev, "I think there still could have been some kind of a Soviet Union today."

That enmity was very real, however, and so in October 1991 Scowcroft began assessing what Soviet disintegration meant for NATO's future, not least because Central and Eastern European leaders were now openly trying to flee into the alliance's arms.[126] Havel renewed his request to Bush for "some form of associate membership" in NATO.[127] That request, Scowcroft thought, confirmed that "the failed coup brought NATO's role vis-à-vis the East front and center." He reminded Bush that "both within the Alliance and within your Administration we have been debating the merits of expanding NATO membership." Now the pros and cons were becoming clearer. Pro was that NATO needed to grow or else risk becoming "increasingly irrelevant to a changing Europe"; con was that expansion risked "diluting NATO's structures and patterns of cooperation on common defense." Another factor was the thinking in Paris: "The French are reluctant to see the EC expand eastward and have opposed a NATO expansion eastward as well." After considering the matter carefully, Scowcroft felt con was more convincing. He advised informing Secretary General Wörner, visiting in October, that "we did not feel the time ripe to extend NATO's security guarantees eastward."[128]

Wörner, by contrast, felt there was a need "to upgrade NATO's relations with the nations of Central and Eastern Europe" in some way.[129] Aides to Baker and the German foreign minister, Hans-Dietrich Genscher, jointly proposed an upgrade short of expansion, namely, some kind of NATO-affiliated organization that Central and Eastern European states could join.[130] The idea was to give those states a new, NATO-adjacent opportunity while avoiding the tricky question of membership in the alliance itself; Mitterrand had hoped his proposed confederation could do the same for the EC. The NSC agreed with this idea, adding that the new Baker-Genscher organization "should leave open the possibility of membership in NATO" so as not to appear to be "a permanent second class waiting room." In the meantime, US policy would calibrate expanded ties to the actual degree of "democratization" in each country.[131]

Discussing the Baker-Genscher upgrade with Wörner on October 11, 1991, Bush asked if its set of potential members should "include the Baltics." The United States had never recognized de jure Soviet takeover of Estonia, Latvia, and Lithuania. But those three states had de facto come under Moscow's domination, so admitting them would be a dramatic slap in the face of the still-extant Soviet Union.[132] Wörner replied, "yes, if the Baltics apply they should be welcomed." In fact he was already in contact with them; the president of Lithuania, Vytautas Landsbergis, "wanted to come see me at NATO, but because I am here today the Vice President of Lithuania" was in Brussels with subordinates instead.[133] It was a sign of just how dramatically the Soviet collapse was expanding NATO's opportunities.

With Bush's support, Wörner returned to Brussels to turn the Baker-Genscher initiative into an organization. The July 1990 NATO summit had rhetorically offered a "hand of friendship" to former enemies. Now, a new North Atlantic Cooperation Council (NACC) was to turn that rhetoric into a reality by becoming a forum for dialogue and cooperation. To achieve this goal, the secretary general worked closely with the US Mission to NATO; all agreed the new organization should focus on the former Warsaw Pact states "plus the Baltics."

The policy made good sense. It began to open doors to Central and Eastern Europe, but not in a way that obviously antagonized Moscow. How exactly joining the NACC would affect the prospect of any given state joining the alliance itself was left open, and that ambiguity was an asset. As the US Mission to NATO noted, it "was not practicable or desirable to define precisely an exact division of labor among NATO, the EC, and CSCE at this point." Furthering the ambiguity, Wörner got the allies to agree on a so-called nondifferentiated approach for processing NACC applications—meaning that applications from Soviet republics would receive the same treatment as those from former Warsaw Pact countries.[134] While obviously not welcome news in Central and Eastern Europe, such an approach helped avoid drawing a new line across Europe between more eligible and less eligible regions. Finally, a plan emerged to announce the new council at a NATO summit in November 1991, with the NACC convening its first full session in December.

There was a rub, however. Would Ukraine be welcome in the NACC as well? What if it asked for a NATO liaison office in Kiev? A shift of Ukraine's loyalties away from Moscow and toward the West during such a tumultuous period as 1991, even in such seemingly minor ways as expressing interest in the NACC, would have far-reaching impacts.

With roughly 52 million inhabitants at the time, Ukraine was, in population terms, both the second-largest Soviet republic and the size of a major European state; the British and French populations were 57 and 58 million, respectively.[135] Ukraine's history as an East Slavic and predominantly Orthodox state had long been deeply intertwined with Russia's. There were millions of ethnic Russians living among, and married to, Ukrainians.[136] If Ukraine decided in its referendum of December 1, 1991 to become fully independent, it would at once commence a painful economic and political divorce from its fellow Slavs and also become a greater nuclear power than either Britain or France. Ukraine's choices would clearly have such far-reaching effects. From Moscow, Ambassador Strauss advised Washington that "the most revolutionary event of 1991 for Russia may not be the collapse of Communism, but the loss of something Russians of all political stripes think of as part of their own body politic, and near to the heart at that: Ukraine."[137]

In short, the question of what to do about potential Ukrainian interest in NATO was fraught with significance; it was, in a way, a question about where Europe ended in the East. There was also an enormous practical problem: Gorbachev was furiously trying to stop Bush from dealing directly with Kiev. As a descendant of both Russians and Ukrainians, he was doing his utmost to prevent his ancestral lands from parting ways.[138] The Soviet leader claimed, as part of that effort, that Ukraine in its current borders would be an unstable construct if it broke away. He told Bush that it had come into existence only because local Bolsheviks had at one point gerrymandered it that way to ensure their own power. They had "added Kharkov and Donbass," and Khrushchev later "passed the Crimea from Russia to the Ukraine as a fraternal gesture."[139] Now, however, Kiev's talk about independence was causing resistance in just those heavily pro-Russian regions, which Gorbachev intimated would rebel against any attempt at independence. Because of all of these concerns, an internal Bush administration "Draft Options Paper" on policy toward the region recommended exploring "the possibility of Ukraine joining the NATO liaison program at a later time."[140]

But the issue would not rest. The future of Ukraine caused controversy when Bush received Gorbachev's advisor, Alexander Yakovlev, on November 19, 1991. Focused as ever on nuclear weapons, Bush asked about plans for the estimated 25 percent of the Soviet nuclear arsenal that was outside of Russia, particularly the weapons in Ukraine.[141] Yakovlev replied, "of course, we won't give up our weapons. They're guarded by central authorities." When Baker pointed out that guards might not remain loyal to Moscow, noting "some troops have moved over to the republics," Yakovlev dismissed the concern: "I know some of the colonels may talk very demonstratively," but "this doesn't mean they actually will act as they talk." Baker pressed the point again, wondering if there would be open conflict between Russia and Ukraine once they separated. Yakovlev, skeptical, responded that there were 12 million Russians in Ukraine, with "many in mixed marriages," so "what sort of war could that be?" Baker answered simply: "a normal war."[142]

The future of the Soviet Union was clearly becoming ever more unpredictable. The coup plotters of August who had hoped to restore Moscow's central authority had instead hastened its disintegration. As Ambassador Strauss wrote that month, "the Russians have never faced a reversal quite like the one they do now: the loss, without a contest of arms, of territories and populations which have been under Russian suzerainty since the early years of the Romanov dynasty."[143] In particular, if Ukraine fell away, the survival of the entire remaining union would be in doubt.

The driving factor remained Yeltsin. He continued to build upon his triumphant role in stopping the August coup. On November 26, 1991, Yeltsin had his foreign minister, Kozyrev, hand-deliver a letter to Bush containing the Russian president's vision for the future. In it, Yeltsin announced that "Russia is breaking with the Communist past." He planned to implement "price de-control even before the end of the year, a stringent monetary-financial and credit policy, a tax reform, and strengthening of the ruble."[144] He welcomed the idea of the NACC and made clear that Russians "intend to get involved in the work of this body" as part of his "support of the NATO efforts to build a new system of security from Vancouver to Vladivostok," thereby echoing a turn of phrase already used by Baker and Genscher.[145] The Russian president also confided to Bush that he was considering a reshaped "political union" with "the Ukraine and other sovereign republics," presumably cutting the detested Gorbachev out of the picture entirely.[146]

To Bush, Yeltsin portrayed his interest in any form of union, whether a continuation of the Soviet Union or a wholly new entity, as entirely conditional upon Ukraine's willingness to participate. As the Russian leader explained to the US president in a follow-up call on November 30, 1991, if Ukraine were absent, "that would dramatically change the balance in the Union between slavic and islamic [*sic*] nations," which would be unacceptable. He would not, for ethnic reasons, tolerate "a situation where Russia and Byelorussia have two votes as slavic states against five for the Islamic nations" in some future union.[147] Yeltsin had also realized that if he were left alone without Ukraine in a political union with much smaller republics, Russia might get stuck with their debts. Since Russians could not afford to subsidize the other republics, their president decided he needed some kind of political ark to keep his people above water as the rest of the union went down in the storm. "Yeltsin and his aides faced the choice of either continuing the imperial burden on their own or quitting the empire," in the words of historian Serhii Plokhy, and they leaned toward the latter: "the Russian ark was leaving the Soviet dock." The scheduled Ukrainian vote on independence, taking place just two days later on December 1, was assuming a new significance: Yeltsin had decided to seize upon it as the moment to decide the future of the entire Soviet Union. The bottom line was that, as Yeltsin told Bush, if Ukrainians voted for independence by a margin of greater than 70 percent, he would immediately recognize Ukraine as a separate state.

Surprised, Bush asked why Russia would take the dramatic step of recognizing the independence of the second-most-populous republic in the Soviet Union so quickly. Yeltsin replied that he wanted to make clear where he stood right away because he needed to work with the new president of Ukraine "in the beginning of December" on urgent next steps, meaning the final destruction of Gorbachev's authority. The Russian president and his advisors also worried that the local armed forces had already started swearing allegiance to the new capital in Kiev (now increasingly known by its Ukrainian name, Kyiv), so if Russia tried to resist independence, there might be fighting. He was additionally concerned about "central control of strategic nuclear weapons" on Ukrainian soil, not least because Ukraine had "very modern installations—large silos." Yeltsin intended to pursue "the removal of nuclear weapons from Ukrainian territory," even though it would be costly and would take "several years." In closing, he implored Bush to keep all of this confidential, and Bush promised that he would.

In the December 1 vote, with a turnout of 84 percent, a jaw-dropping 90 percent of Ukrainians chose independence.[148] Bush called to congratulate Kravchuk, who won the presidential race the same day. The president-elect reported proudly that "not even a single district in Ukraine came in below 50% support for Ukrainian independence"—including the parts of the country that Gorbachev had wrongly predicted would resist independence. Bush asked whether Kravchuk would be willing to receive State Department emissaries to discuss issues such as disarmament, and Kravchuk indicated that he would.[149]

After hearing this news, Bush decided to follow Yeltsin's example and made it known that he would recognize Ukraine "'expeditiously,'" a move that a *Wall Street Journal* editorial on December 4 by the arms-control expert William Potter criticized as unwise. Potter found the president's "unconditional recognition of Ukrainian independence" to be "short-sighted" because Bush should impose a condition: Ukrainian accession to the Treaty on the Non-Proliferation of Nuclear Weapons, or NPT, as the price of that recognition.[150] The NPT had entered into force in 1970 and, in cooperation with the International Atomic Energy Agency, had developed a complex system of institutions and agreements for preventing violations and verifying compliance.[151] Potter advised Bush to "clarify the terms for US diplomatic recognition of Ukraine" and make the country abide by those rules before granting it the high-value gift of full US recognition. The president went ahead with full legal recognition by the end of the month without such a binding condition, presumably hoping that a previously declared Ukrainian intent to forsake nuclear weapons would hold.[152]

If the shocking December referendum result had caused Bush to miss a step, however, it caused Gorbachev to miss many more. The Soviet leader had been trying to resume discussions for the new "Union Treaty" that had been knocked sideways by the coup.[153] Now Kravchuk was no longer willing to sign, and Yeltsin had no interest in belonging to a rump union without Ukraine.[154] Gorbachev was losing the last vestiges of control, and it was not clear what would come next. If the union was disappearing, what would replace it?

To find an answer, Yeltsin decided he needed to get far away from Moscow and Gorbachev. He, Kravchuk, and Belarusian leader Stanislav Shushkevich—that is, the three Slavic leaders with nuclear weapons on their territories—took advantage of a previously scheduled visit by Yeltsin to Belarus to retreat to Viskuli, a hunting estate in the Belavezha forest near the Polish border. Yeltsin had decided to map out the future only with them, excluding other republics and the Soviet leader.[155]

After two days of arm-twisting, brainstorming, and drinking, Yeltsin called a surprised Bush out of the blue on December 8, 1991, with news of what they had decided to do. The option of sticking with the current "system in place and the Union Treaty everyone is pushing us to sign does not satisfy us."[156] As heads of the three republics still in existence among those that had, on paper at least, founded the Soviet Union in 1922, they felt entitled to dissolve that union.[157] They had decided to replace it with a new commonwealth of independent states (CIS) by having a signing ceremony for an accord to that effect in an ornate room at the Viskuli government estate. The amazed US president could respond with little more than "I see" and "uh huh."

Yeltsin promised Bush that the CIS states would "work out, develop, and codify unitary command over the military." They would "provide for single control of nuclear weapons." A stunned Bush could only thank Yeltsin for the news and promise to get back to him after consulting his aides. The Russian president concluded by saying that "this is really, really hot off the press—this is the latest information. To be frank, even Gorbachev doesn't know."[158] Yeltsin did not mention to Bush that he had intentionally gotten out of informing Gorbachev by making Shushkevich phone Moscow.

Upon hearing the news, a livid Gorbachev apparently demanded that Kravchuk come to Moscow, but Kravchuk refused. Yeltsin, however, had to go home to Moscow, but he took precautions. When he finally confronted Gorbachev in person, he brought armed bodyguards because he reportedly was worried that Gorbachev might arrest him. The Soviet leader did not attempt to do so, however, presumably because he could not be sure of the popular consequences.

Thereafter, Yeltsin moved swiftly to implement the Belavezha accords, as the deals struck in the hunting lodge became known. The Ukrainian and Belarusian parliaments ratified them on December 10, 1991, and the Russian parliament followed suit on December 12.[159] Yeltsin also continued his extraordinary openness with Bush, telling him in advance of all the moves he hoped to make. He asked Bush "not to be concerned about nuclear arms" because there would be "a unified strategic military command." There was no place for Gorbachev in the new CIS, but the Russian president promised he would treat Gorbachev "with great respect. Everything will be gradual with no radical measures." Washington should get ready because very soon, possibly by the end of that month, "the structures of the center will cease to exist."[160]

Baker's assessment of these developments was stark. As he put it to the president on December 10, "strategically there is no other foreign issue more deserving of your attention or time" than the future of the Soviet nuclear arsenal in the wake of the country's breakup. Scowcroft still disagreed; as he later put it, "I was pretty relaxed" about the issue because he felt it better to face a nuclear arsenal fractured into parts than a coordinated whole, and because he did not believe Ukraine or Kazakhstan would target the United States. In stark contrast, Baker argued that there was no value for Washington in nuclear rivalries among former Soviet states and that only one nuclear power must emerge: Russia.[161]

Taking Baker's advice to heart, Bush signed into law the Soviet Nuclear Threat Reduction Act, originally promoted by Senator Nunn, which was meant to facilitate the transportation, storage, safeguarding, and elimination of Soviet weapons.[162] Speaking at Princeton University on December 12, 1991, Baker also called for an international aid conference to help the "'disoriented and confused' Soviet people."[163] He also declared there would be an airlift of food to Moscow, St. Petersburg, and other cities.[164] This was not purely charitable. The Defense and State Departments worked with the JCS to find ways to combine the air drops with a closer look at parts of the Soviet Union that had long been of interest to US strategic planners.[165]

After his Princeton speech, Baker flew to the dying Soviet Union for meetings between December 12 and 15 with the leaders of the four republics possessing components of the nuclear arsenal.[166] He had decided that the issue merited his personal attention, given what was at stake. Once he landed, the practical consequences of the Soviet disintegration were immediately visible. As he later recalled in his memoirs, "most of Aeroflot was grounded, and our embassy was having problems finding gasoline for its cars—all this in a country with the largest proven oil reserves in the world!"[167]

Baker's handwritten notes from the trip show that he pressed most of his hosts on the same nuclear questions: "from whom will you take your directions—your polit. guidance? your orders?"[168] He also stressed that soon-to-be-independent states must "begin the process of accession to the NPT" and to accept visits by outside experts starting in January.[169] His goals were clear: to get the nuclear-armed republics to renounce independent command authority and to commit either to disabling weapons or transferring them to Russia for destruction.[170] In Moscow, he additionally stressed to his negotiating partners that "you have agreed to end the biological weapons program and to agree to a deadline for dismantling of these facilities."[171]

On the most dramatic day of his trip—December 16, 1991—Baker met with both Gorbachev and Yeltsin, but not together.[172] Yeltsin was now by far the more important. Feeling confident of victory over his hated political rival, he was in an expansive mood and willing to reveal in detail the inner workings of Moscow's nuclear launch procedures, a conversation that would have been unthinkable a few years earlier.[173]

Welcoming Baker, the Russian president let the American know that he now held the fate of the Soviet Union in his hands. At one point, he said, he had inclined toward preserving the union—but "in the end, the decisive factor . . . was the Ukrainian referendum, since no union without Ukraine made any sense."[174] Turning to defense matters, Yeltsin let the secretary know that he wanted the CIS to have "united strategic military forces, including nuclear deterrence forces," but he rejected the notion that Gorbachev "might be made commander-in-chief of this force." He hoped instead that "'our' Defense Minister Yevgeny Shaposhnikov"—who had opposed the hard-liners' coup in August 1991 even though he was the Soviet defense minister—might potentially fill that role. Yeltsin also hoped that "the military body to be formed as part of CIS" would "form a close association with NATO." Yeltsin even reportedly sent a letter to this effect to NATO headquarters as well, saying that Russia hoped to join the alliance.[175]

Baker had in the past avoided discussing in detail Gorbachev's suggestions that the Soviet Union should join NATO, and he likewise responded in a general way to Yeltsin: "there may be some way in which NATO can relate to the CIS."[176] The secretary maneuvered the conversation to the issues he cared about: command and control of nuclear weapons. He conveyed his strong desire that the CIS place all nuclear weapons under a single authority and that the United States and Russia cooperate to ensure the safety of those weapons as well as the implementation of START. Yeltsin, in reply, tried repeating his earlier sentiment. While it "would be a long-term process," he expressly hoped that "'the defense union of the CIS could merge with NATO.'" The transcript of the meeting showed no recorded reaction from Baker to Yeltsin's hope of far-reaching cooperation with the alliance.

Baker had previously indicated that he needed to address a topic so sensitive that most of their aides would have to leave the room before he could speak, and now the time had come for them to depart.[177] Once the bulk of their delegations cleared the room, he asked Yeltsin to explain how the Soviet Union would launch nuclear weapons in combat. Remarkably, Yeltsin answered the question. Baker took handwritten, underlined notes as Yeltsin spoke, noting that command relied on the three briefcases and a "System of <u>Conference Telephones</u>." The telephone "system is only <u>to decide</u>," Yeltsin explained; the briefcases were necessary to order a launch. These briefcases were in the possession "of 3 people—Gorby, Yeltsin, Shaposh," meaning the president of the USSR, the president of Russia, and the defense minister. According to Yeltsin, "all have to agree to launch unless one is lost, missing," in which case the "other 2 can launch or if 2 missing, etc, 1 can launch." The Russian president told Baker that he would remove the "briefcase from Gorby before end of Dec." so the "result will be <u>only</u> Pres of Russia and Shaposh," the latter presumably in the new post of CIS defense minister, will have "a BRIEFCASE TO PRESS BUT-TON." Yeltsin added that he wanted to establish a system under which Shaposhnikov "won't be able to alone" order a launch.[178]

Finally, Yeltsin gave Baker the welcome news that the "majority of tactical nukes have already been removed from Ukraine" through an earlier agreement. The strategic arsenal was a different matter. While their aides were still present, Yeltsin had explained that "it was 'no secret' that the USSR had some of its most modern MIRVed strategic systems in Ukraine."[179] MIRVs, or multiple independently targetable reentry vehicles, essentially enabled one missile to hit multiple targets with separate warheads, and thus made the systems particularly dangerous. To allay Baker's fears in their one-on-one session, Yeltsin confided that the Ukrainians, like other republics with Soviet nuclear weapons on their territories, "don't know how things work," adding, "that's why I tell only you." In the end, he felt certain that they would be satisfied with only "having telephones," not launch briefcases, and once the "nukes are off their soil—even the telephones will be removed."[180]

Grateful for this information, Baker nonetheless made time to visit Kyiv as well, telling Kravchuk that there was no more important issue "to the American people than avoiding the danger of the use" of nuclear weapons.[181] The secretary also spoke with the leaders of Belarus and Kazakhstan before heading to Brussels to advise his NATO allies of what he had learned. Once there, he told a British colleague that the "deteriorating economic situation could lead to a social explosion," so there was a need for a "concerted and massive international effort to provide humanitarian aid."[182]

Baker could not rest even on the flight home from Brussels on December 21. While he was in the air, Kazakh president Nazarbayev called with a confidential update.[183] Yeltsin, determined to kill off the Soviet Union as swiftly as possible, had organized a CIS summit that day in the Kazakh capital of Alma-Ata.[184] At that summit, the CIS added eight more Soviet republics into the new entity, for a total of eleven so-called co-founders.[185] Nazarbayev had been the host, but now he was acting as confidential informant.

Baker and Nazarbayev had by then realized they could do business with each other, particularly with regard to the oil industry. During a previous stop in Alma-Ata, the secretary had apparently won Nazarbayev over by hinting that the US oil giant Chevron might invest in developing oil fields in Kazakhstan.[186] That visit had gone so well that Secretary Baker and Ambassador Strauss had even accepted the president's offer to share a sauna, complete with the traditional flapping of eucalyptus branches against the backs of all guests. Emerging from the sauna afterward, Strauss informed Baker's security detail that the "'Secretary of State is buck naked, and he's being beaten by the President of Kazakhstan!'"[187]

Now, in the chaos of December 1991, that friendly relationship was paying dividends. Nazarbayev had become angry after Yeltsin decided the fate of the Soviet Union with only the other Slavic nuclear republics. Even worse, Yeltsin had requested that Nazarbayev fly to Moscow at the same time—but only after the Kazakh landed did he learn, while still at the airport, that Yeltsin was instead "'way out in the woods'" in Viskuli with his fellow Slavs. The Russian president held the summit in the Kazakh capital in an apparent effort to mollify Nazarbayev, but it did not entirely work. The Kazakh leader's comments on the December 21 in-flight phone call hinted that he remained bitter—and that he and Baker had colluded to shape the outcome of that summit.[188]

"Mr. Secretary, I did all in my power to carry out what you and I had discussed," Nazarbayev told Baker, even though "it wasn't easy." The summit had resolved that there would be, in the long term, only "one single head in charge of strategic weapons." Baker was glad to hear it, but less happy to learn that, in the near term, there would remain four nuclear republics, and should the decision, "God forbid, ever be made to have to use these weapons," that decision "would be made by these four states." This situation, however, was temporary: "Ukraine and Belarus will transfer their nuclear weapons by 1998 to Russia." Nazarbayev himself was still holding out but would eventually agree to give up his weapons as well.[189]

Apparently unaware of the intelligence already passed along by the Kazakh, Yeltsin also called Bush on December 23 to explain the state of play. He repeated what Nazabayev had told Baker, namely that the four nuclear-armed republics would be the only ones with a say in their deployment. As Yeltsin phrased it, "the Russian President will control the nuclear button after consultations with the three others"—although he had reportedly issued a secret decree allowing the Russian president, that is, himself, to launch weapons without consultation in an emergency. As for the chain of command, Yeltsin expected that Gorbachev would surrender control of his nuclear briefcase and resign from office in about forty-eight hours, on December 25, meaning that Yeltsin and Shaposhnikov would have the three briefcases to themselves. The government of Russia would provide Gorbachev with "money, medical insurance and treatment, a country house, guards and transportation."[190]

The Soviet leader was not the only one about to lose his office. All over Moscow, corner-suite keys were swiftly changing hands. On December 24, Kozyrev began receiving diplomatic visitors in his new office, the hastily vacated suite of the Soviet foreign minister. The British ambassador, Rodric Braithwaite, paid his respects in person and reported home that Kozyrev had "sacked all the old deputy foreign ministers, and looks well installed."[191] Soviet controllers of various media organizations also made way for their Russian successors.

The most dramatic departure, however, was Gorbachev's. He made a series of melancholy phone calls as the minutes counted down to his resignation on December 25, 1991. His tendency to see his Western partners as his crucial allies against domestic reactionaries had by now grown to the point where, in his last moments as leader, he sought comfort from foreigners whom he viewed, perhaps unwisely, as not just peers but friends.[192] Shortly before being forced to vacate his Kremlin suite, he phoned Bush to say, less than believably, "everything is under strict control." He would resign that day and "transfer authority to use nuclear weapons" to Yeltsin, so "you can have a very quiet Christmas evening."[193]

Gorbachev was due on air soon for a nationally televised resignation address, but thirty minutes before it was to begin, he phoned Genscher. The German foreign minister had, throughout the process of his country's unification, consistently pushed for greater concessions to Gorbachev than his Western peers and even Kohl would accept. Now, at the very end, Gorbachev wanted to hear his voice. Their conversation was suffused with an unspoken sense of lost hope.

In his final words to the leader of the Soviet Union, Genscher chose to recall a private word he had shared in Arkhyz in 1990 with Gorbachev's beloved wife, Raisa. She had pulled the foreign minister aside in the midst of the talks, which had ended with the Soviet leader allowing a united Germany to enter NATO. Protective as ever of her husband, she wanted to make sure that the Germans would share their wealth and expertise to help the Soviet Union make the transition to a successful future. Genscher had taken her hand and promised Raisa, "we have learned the lessons of history in every aspect. I know very well what your husband is doing here. Everything will work out fine."[194] Now, as Gorbachev departed history's stage, Genscher recalled that promise. Left unsaid was the obvious: for Gorbachev and the Soviet Union, everything had not worked out fine.[195]

States emerging from the former Soviet Union in 1991.

Gorbachev then gave his televised, twelve-minute resignation address starting at about 7:00 p.m., with Western broadcasters in attendance. The Soviet leader belatedly realized he needed a new pen to sign his resignation papers, since his was not working. The president of CNN, Tom Johnson, a friend of Ambassador Strauss who had accompanied the camera crew to the Kremlin for the historic event, handed over his Mont Blanc.[196] As the ink flowed out of Johnson's pen, Russia became the successor state to the USSR in the UN and a host of other organizations.[197] Afterward, Braithwaite sent a eulogy for Gorbachev back to London. Ultimately, Braithwaite concluded, "exasperation at his endless talk, and his absolute failure to act, in the end destroyed what popular support he had left."[198]

Yeltsin, watching on television, became enraged because he felt Gorbachev's speech did not show sufficient deference to himself. The Russian president showed his displeasure by ordering the Soviet flag, still flying over the Kremlin, to come down as quickly as possible.[199] Only thirty-eight minutes after Gorbachev began his broadcast, a Russian flag replaced the Soviet one in a dramatic visual confirmation of the transition.[200]

It was not Yeltsin's only insult to his defeated enemy that day, in defiance of his promise to Bush that he would show respect for the Soviet leader. The Gorbachevs had thought they would have the Christmas and New Year holiday period to vacate their state residence, but Yeltsin decided instead to evict them right away. A panicky Raisa, still recovering from a stroke she had suffered during the August coup, had to track her husband down by phone on December 25 to tell him men had unexpectedly shown up to throw them out of their home.[201]

"The Pain Is Severe"

Bush too would soon feel the pain of departure from office, although that was not yet clear in December 1991. For now, it was another moment of triumph. For decades, US policymakers had scarcely been able to imagine that the Cold War could end any way other than in nuclear conflict. Instead, with relatively little violence, the Soviet Union had suddenly vanished.[202]

Russia continued consolidating and destroying large portions of the former Soviet arsenal. In the first half of 1992, Moscow was able to secure and dismantle most remaining Soviet tactical nuclear weapons—in some cases simply by taking them from the territory of what were now independent countries. Yeltsin did, however, negotiate bilateral accords with the leaders of Belarus and Kazakhstan about the fate of the strategic weapons on their territory. Following agreements between Baker and the former Soviet republics, Washington sent delegations to help with the numerous technical issues involved.[203] The secretary also convened the hoped-for aid conference in Washington on January 23, 1992.[204]

But, for once, Baker lost a major internal battle in the Bush administration: he did not believe enforcing repayment of Soviet debt at this challenging moment should take priority. Treasury Secretary Nicholas Brady disagreed, however, and got Bush on his side. As Scowcroft later recalled, there was no love lost between Baker and Brady. "They didn't work particularly well [together] because, of course, the Secretary of State had been the Secretary of the Treasury before," which created "underlying tensions" in addition to the ongoing problem that "Treasury is a unique culture inside the government" and its secretary and staff "do not know what coordination and cooperation is—except if they're doing it." On the issue of Soviet debt, it was Brady's subordinates, not Baker's, who took control of economic policy toward the new state of Russia, insisting Moscow was responsible for all Soviet debt—estimated at $65 billion in 1991—and saddling the new democracy with an additional burden. The Treasury secretary and his advisors remembered that, after the Bolshevik Revolution of 1917, the new regime had renounced all responsibility for the debt of the czars, and it did not want a repetition.

This attitude proved controversial. Even prominent Republicans such as Richard Perle argued that "'we should find a way to wipe the books clear and give Yeltsin a fighting chance. The least we can do is cancel the IOU's of his undemocratic predecessors.'" Moscow worried that Washington might cut off grain shipments, however, if it did not service old Soviet debt, and so it did—and even took on some responsibility for czarist-era debt as well.[205]

To mark these dramatic transitions, the UN Security Council held its first-ever meeting at summit level on January 31, 1992, meaning with all heads of government and of state in attendance. That year was a high-water mark of international cooperation.[206] The Russian president announced that he would no longer target the United States with nuclear weapons (although experts noted that it would not be hard to switch the targeting back to US sites).[207] Yeltsin received an invitation to Camp David, where he and Bush declared on February 1, 1992, that the United States and Russia were no longer adversaries and that the Cold War was over.[208] Later that year, Yeltsin and Bush even speculated about marking the fiftieth anniversary of the first manned moon landing with a joint mission to Mars in 2019. As Yeltsin put it, "we should not compete to get there first. We should cooperate."[209]

As Russia expert Anders Åslund later wrote, "Western countries had one big chance to make a difference, at the beginning of 1992. The West, especially the United States, enjoyed enormous goodwill and influence in Russia."[210] Russia received both bilateral assistance from the United States and an International Monetary Fund (IMF) aid package.[211] But the question of whether some form of debt forgiveness—particularly of the $2.8 billion of Soviet debt held by the United States—could have helped Russia during the critical year of 1992 remained open, as none was forthcoming.[212]

The year 1992 saw another significant transition in Europe: the signing on February 7 of the Maastricht Treaty, which subsequently turned the EC into the European Union (EU) in 1993. Yet Kohl's drive for a United States of Europe had fallen short. As the US embassy in Paris reported, he was forced to accept a compromise "between intergovernmental cooperation and total political integration."[213] Kohl was nonetheless resigned to the compromises he had made. He told Bush in March that Central and Eastern Europeans would have to wait until after the end of the decade to join the EU because the organization saw other states— Sweden, Finland, Austria, possibly Norway—as higher priorities.[214] The chancellor also indicated it was unlikely that former Soviet republics would ever join, saying that they should form their own economic zone as a "'bridge from Europe to Asia.'"[215] The EU also needed to address the continuing violence in Yugoslavia. In May 1992, sixteen people died and dozens were injured when a mortar shell landed on a Sarajevo market. That year the UN had created a protection force, known by the acronym UNPROFOR, and tried to establish safe enclaves, but those remained dangerously vulnerable.[216]

With the EU busy with its own transformation and with Bosnia, Central and Eastern Europe turned yet again to NATO with questions about joining, but still found only disappointment. The alliance preferred to put its efforts into building up the NACC instead. On March 10, 1992, that body admitted all of the former Soviet republics except Georgia, which was admitted a month later. They thereby joined the Baltic and Central and Eastern European states, which had already become part of the NACC in December 1991.[217] While a victory for inclusivity—the main motivation was to bring the states covered by the conventional forces accord together in one place—this sweeping move diluted the NACC's importance in the eyes of the Czechs, Hungarians, and Poles; as a member of the US Congress later put it, the NACC now "seemed like a slow train to an unknown destination." At a time when the Visegrad states "and Ukraine were *already* cooperating with their NATO 'partners' in Croatia and Bosnia in real-world activity," the NACC simply did not provide the recognition that they sought. Meeting in Prague on May 6, 1992, the Visegrad leaders declared their goal was full-fledged NATO membership.[218]

This contretemps prompted the Bush State Department to debate yet again the pros and cons of extending NATO to Central and Eastern Europe.[219] The biggest problem, in the words of Assistant Secretary of State Thomas Niles, was that "expansion of NATO would force a choice between being open to all comers—including Russia—or drawing a new line in Europe to replace the old Cold War line." The hard truth was that there was "no politically acceptable way to draw a line." If the line excluded Russia, it "would in effect tell Moscow that the end result of internal revolution and forsaking its Soviet/Warsaw Pact empire is the expansion of NATO to its border."[220] Given the fragility of Russia's new democracy—with inflation topping 2,000 percent in December 1992, the Yeltsin government seemed as if it might fall—it was not the time to put more stress on Moscow. Yet another issue was that "we see no politically sustainable way to stop it [enlargement] once we start" other than to draw a new line across Europe. Niles advised "holding the line on NATO membership" at sixteen for the time being.[221]

These views sparked vehement opposition within the State Department. Stephen Flanagan, a member of the policy planning staff, thought such caution was completely wrong: "now is the time" for enlarging the alliance. He disagreed in particular with the notion that any discussion of NATO expansion "would immediately open the floodgates." Flanagan was convinced that new members could join "sequentially"—meaning both new members from among the current neutral states and the new post-Soviet Bloc states. His recommended sequence was as follows: "first, the interested former neutrals, then the Trokjat [*sic*, presumably Czechoslovakia, Hungary, and Poland] and Bulgarians, followed by the Russians, Ukranians, Byelorussians, Romanians, and other early post-communist states." Flanagan even thought that "the initial entry" by some Central and Eastern European states into the alliance could serve as "an example" to Kyiv "and Moscow of what is possible once one transforms one's economy and social system." An enlarged alliance could also help to contain the fallout from the violence in Yugoslavia. And given that the "Germans are unlikely to host 95% of our military presence in Europe for much longer," the truth was that "we need other real estate." In fact, "old Soviet caserns in Poland would be a bargain and we would be local heroes" by acquiring them and helping the economy of the areas around them. In short, if he were "asked to bet whether a given US Army brigade would be more welcome in Germany or Poland in 1995," he would "put money on the latter." Flanagan concluded that the Bush administration should develop "an agreed set of criteria and a roadmap for new members."[222]

Flanagan was not alone in that opinion. A leak to the *New York Times* in March 1992 suggested that Cheney and his advisors remained sympathetic to a more aggressive approach as well. In what the *Times* called "the clearest rejection to date of collective internationalism," an internal Pentagon strategy paper asserted bluntly that the US post–Cold War mission was not to cooperate with Russia but "to insure that no rival superpower is allowed to emerge."[223] And a Ukrainian minister later asserted that, in 1992, an undersecretary at the State Department reached out to Kyiv's ambassador in Washington to urge Ukraine to seek NATO membership.[224]

Meanwhile, a small group of analysts at the think tank RAND were also trying to make the case for NATO expansion.[225] One of the analysts, former Air Force officer Richard Kugler, found inspiration in conversations with Polish colleagues. They told him that if they did not get membership in NATO, they would get nuclear weapons; then they would use those weapons to defend themselves from the Russians; then the Germans would come to their aid. As a result, Kugler "'had a vision of a nuclear-armed Poland being fortified by German troops facing off with the Russians—I don't think anyone wanted that!'"[226]

Bush, however, stayed on the side of those advising caution.[227] He was scheduled to give a major speech in Warsaw on July 5, 1992, where he could have indicated support for putting Poland and other countries in NATO. The deputy secretary of state, Lawrence Eagleburger, had already hinted at this idea on June 4 at a NATO ministerial, suggesting that "the very composition of the alliance may need to expand."[228] Early drafts of the presidential speech reportedly included language about NATO enlargement, but it disappeared by the time Bush delivered the address.[229] In contrast, concern about Russia and its ability to corral the Soviet nuclear arsenal remained a consistent priority in spring and summer 1992. Baker persuaded all four Soviet nuclear successor states to meet in Lisbon on

May 23, with the smaller three signing an accord stating that they would become non–nuclear weapons states and NPT members in the shortest possible time.[230]

The upcoming US presidential election of that year forced Bush to turn to domestic issues, although treatment of Russia played a role in the campaign. As expected, Bush's Democratic opponent, Governor Bill Clinton of Arkansas, criticized him for having been too cautious with aid to the Soviet Union. Twenty minutes before Clinton was to give a major speech to this effect, Bush announced that the G7 would make $24 billion available to Moscow.[231]

What mattered more than foreign policy in the election, however, was the combination of a slow economy and the actions of Bush's fellow Texas businessman Ross Perot, who entered the race to capitalize on voters' anger at Bush for raising taxes. Not a serious contender for the presidency, the erratic Perot nonetheless diminished Bush's chances of beating Clinton. In his hour of need, Bush turned once again to his old friend Baker, asking the secretary to trade his nonproliferation efforts for political campaigning. As Baker explained to a British colleague on July 25, 1992, he was not eager "to stop being Secretary of State." But the president was "continuing a daily routine which took little account of the fact that he was so far behind in the polls." Bush should instead, in Baker's view, "be addressing the big issues and the long term," since "Clinton was vulnerable as a bad governor of Arkansas." And then there was the problem that Quayle, the vice president, was "'a four percent drag on the ticket.'"[232] There had even been speculation on whether Bush might remove Quayle, an idea Baker supported, and replace him with Cheney, Powell, or Baker himself. Instead, Baker ended up merely joining the 1992 campaign, not the ticket.[233]

It was not enough. The combination of the American public's concern about the economic direction of the country, Perot's challenge, and Clinton's campaigning skills gave the Arkansas governor the win on November 3. Speaking to Prime Minister Major three days afterward, Bush complained that Perot, "'that awful, nutty little man,'" had hurt him "in a number of states" by spending "something like $80 million of his own money." Now Bush was "starting to shift gear and think what to do with the rest of his life."[234] His administration's last foreign policy accomplishments took place in January 1993, with the lame-duck president going to Moscow to conclude the START II accord and sign a chemical weapons convention.[235]

Major also extended condolences to Scowcroft about his impending departure from office. The national security advisor, normally stoic, replied on November 8, 1992 with an unusual display of emotion. As he told Major, "knowing what we could have accomplished together occasions a sense of great loss," and "the pain is severe."[236]

It fell instead to the Clinton administration to deal with the legacy of the Soviet collapse. Ambassador Strauss believed that it would be a challenge on the same level as the one after 1945. As the child of Jews who had fled Nazi Germany for Texas, he grew up with a strong interest in that conflict. He had always respected the way that, at the end of World War II, the United States had "decided to transform former adversaries into allies, friends, and peaceful competitors." Now he hoped that "in the aftermath of the Cold War, we can do so again."[237]

Finding ways to advance that goal would prove enormously challenging, however, and the risks of failure were high. George Kennan, Strauss's predecessor as ambassador to Moscow, had his own take on the challenge posed by a great triumph. Of all the errors a victorious country could make, "'history will rate as the most grievous'" the folly of exploiting defeated enemies.[238]

Western leaders had achieved great triumphs in the tumultuous years between 1989 and 1992. Seizing the opportunity provided by the peaceful revolution in Central and Eastern Europe and by Gorbachev, they had secured their harvest before Kohl's predicted storm broke with unexpected fury. Germany was united, and Europe was on its way to a common currency. NATO had crossed the old Cold War line. The US president and the German chancellor had jointly driven the process by controlling the venues in which it had come about, and by fusing Germany's and NATO's fates—although not without Bush's having to quash some German strategic alternatives along the way. To accomplish these momentous tasks, the president and the chancellor played a "hard game." They bribed the Soviets out through a combination of financial inducements and NATO reforms, only to pull back and belatedly try to shore up Moscow when they realized they were losing not only Gorbachev but centralized control over the Soviet nuclear arsenal altogether.

Neither could be saved. Gorbachev, an idealistic visionary, was undone by the overwhelming failures of the Soviet system and his own ineptitude as a leader and negotiator. He could not weather the political storm of 1991. Yet the West was lucky; the storm that Kohl had foreseen, while more severe than expected, did not return reactionaries to power in Moscow. Instead, Yeltsin obliterated Soviet central authority while also signaling that he would democratize Russia and open up its economy to world markets. The challenge of dealing with the consequences now fell to Clinton. Could the young American president fulfill the expectations of Central and Eastern Europe to join NATO, without angering or abandoning new democracies in post-Soviet states, some armed with nuclear weapons? It was a tall order.

PART II

Clearing, 1993–94

CHAPTER FIVE

Squaring the Triangle

A N AMERICAN PRESIDENTIAL INAUGURATION represents a breath-taking juxtaposition. The risks and opportunities facing the nation remain the same as a few minutes before, yet with the exchange of a few words in front of the Capitol, the cast of characters responding to them abruptly changes. As the weight of the world passes to different, untested shoulders before the audience's eyes, the new incumbent suddenly becomes responsible for answering the strategic questions that faced all of his predecessors. What are our interests, and what threatens them? How can we best respond to the threats, and best justify that response?[1]

It was now Bill Clinton's turn to find answers adapted to the conditions of his watch, which included strong elements of continuity despite the collapse of his country's main enemy. The Soviet Union was no more, but vast numbers of its nuclear missiles were still aimed at American soil. Protecting the newfound cooperation with Russia in destroying them seemed an obvious strategic imperative. But with the former Warsaw Pact countries collectively known as Visegrad—Poland, Hungary, and what were now the Czech Republic and Slovakia—clamoring for NATO membership, and with the violence in former Yugoslavia demanding some response, enlarging both the alliance and its mission seemed imperative as well, even if doing so alienated Russia. There were also the challenges posed by the new democracies inside former Soviet borders—particularly Ukraine, which boasted at least 1,200 strategic nuclear warheads, if not more, many of them with US cities as their preset targets.[2]

Clinton needed to find policy responses that could square the circle of these competing strategic imperatives—or, more precisely, square the triangle with Russia, Visegrad, and Ukraine as its corners. The challenge was great because, in different ways, these competing claims all deserved recognition, but there was reason for hope: unlike circles, triangles can be squared. Put differently, America and the three regions could, working together, find a viable solution. That solution rested in an expansion of the alliance beyond eastern Germany as Visegrad wanted, but in a measured way that did not draw a new line across Europe, did not foreclose future options for Ukraine and other former Soviet states, and did not alienate Russia at a time of extensive collaboration in eliminating nuclear weapons. Keeping a free hand as long as possible and avoiding an overly hasty choice among the three triangle corners were the keys to success.[3] By the end of 1993, Clinton and his advisors—ridiculed in their early months in office as amateurs and hicks, staggering from one disaster to the next—would come tantalizingly close to achieving that solution and keeping the post–Cold War cooperative momentum going.

Advising the Hillbilly

When Clinton took the reins on January 20, 1993, it marked a change of generations as well as of parties in the White House. At forty-five, the Democrat was the same age as his Republican predecessor's eldest son, George W. Bush. The old and new presidents also came from widely disparate backgrounds. President George H. W. Bush was the son of a wealthy New England family with extensive political connections; Clinton had been born to an Arkansas woman of few means, whose husband had died while she was pregnant with the future president. Bush and Clinton's disparate paths through life had joined, however, once the latter man entered a presidential race that seemed unwinnable, given the incumbent's enormous popularity during the Gulf War of 1991. That popularity had scared off more prominent Democrats and left the field open to the young governor of Arkansas. Being junior enough that a failed presidential run seemed excusable and brave rather than career-ending and foolish, he decided to take the risk. His campaign staff quickly developed a winning mantra—"It's the economy, stupid"—that successfully tapped voter anxiety over the lingering effects of a recession and high unemployment. With the independent candidate Ross Perot siphoning votes away from Bush,

Clinton and his "war room" were able to triumph. Now that they were in Washington, the world wondered what to expect.[4]

A moonshine-swigging, jailbait-groping hick leading his fellow "Capitol Hillbillies" in the takeover of the country: that was comedian Jim Carrey's take on the new administration in a popular 1993 TV skit.[5] Many found the portrayal broad but accurate. Critics wondered loudly whether the hillbillies were up to the challenge. How would they fare in the treacherous currents of the capital?[6] And how would they deal with the rest of the world? On the other side of the globe, Russian foreign minister Andrei Kozyrev felt that Clinton's election created a "terrifying reality": Clinton and his inexperienced advisors "had no understanding of the reform efforts under way in Russia."[7] Kozyrev's sinking hopes for Washington mirrored a general decline in Russian regard for the United States.

Like much else, that regard was perishing under the hammer blows of economic corruption and chaos in Russia. According to the US Treasury, in early 1993 inflation there was "running at 40% a month."[8] Having pursued radical reforms on the advice of American experts, Moscow was now having deep regrets. The Russian belief that "intellectual salvation" flowed from the United States was, as German chancellor Helmut Kohl dryly commented, "starting to fade." Leaders in Moscow who had thought they could get all the advice they needed "from Harvard" now felt that "they had been deceived."[9] Since Russia was attempting three major transitions simultaneously—a political one, from an authoritarian system to a democracy; an economic one, from a command to a market-based economy; and an imperial one, from a multiethnic empire to something much smaller—the chancellor saw that deception as a tragedy. He believed the new administration, and the West generally, "should now do everything humanly possible" to help the country, which he called "a piece of Europe."[10]

Much the same advice came to the new Clinton team from the British ambassador to Moscow, Sir Rodric Braithwaite.[11] In his view, the big prize of the post–Cold War era was the creation of a stable, democratized Russia, at ease with its shrunken postimperial frontier and at peace with its neighbors.[12] The question he thought should dominate all others, therefore, was as follows: "what can we do" to ensure Russia democratizes fully?[13] Braithwaite's boss, British prime minister John Major, discussed with Clinton how they "must give maximum support to Russian president

Boris Yeltsin—the only elected leader in a thousand years of Russian history."[14]

Clinton's foreign policy experience might have been limited, but he intuitively got the point: Yeltsin was "'up to his ass in alligators'" and "'needs friends abroad because he's got so many enemies at home.'" The policy prescription was "'to try to keep Yeltsin going.'"[15] An obstacle loomed, however: the bloodshed in former Yugoslavia. By January 1993, the fighting in Bosnia had revealed what Kohl described as "a return to a kind of barbarity that very few of us would have thought possible."[16] It also posed a number of dilemmas for Clinton, because having NATO move aggressively to quell the violence risked resistance from Russia.

There was an emotional complication as well. Many of the policymakers joining the new administration bore the scars of younger years as diplomats, journalists, or soldiers in the Vietnam War. Clinton's avoidance of service had caused scarring of a different sort, when opponents ridiculed him for it during the campaign. As one NSC staff member later recalled, that ridicule made him more inclined to prove his military chops as president, endorsing assertive new roles for NATO in Central and Eastern Europe and in the Balkans. Haunted by that past, he and his advisors collectively wanted to avoid failure in the present, particularly in Bosnia. Even though Vietnam had almost nothing in common with the disintegration of Yugoslavia, the lingering trauma colored the advice Clinton received, with some advisors wanting to avoid involvement altogether and others hoping to use it to prove they could do war right. After one particularly "explosive White House meeting," James Steinberg, the director of policy planning at the State Department, reportedly asked, "'what the hell *happened* to those guys in Vietnam?'"[17]

One of "those guys" was fifty-eight-year-old William Anthony Lake, known as Tony, who had spent time in Vietnam as a young diplomat. Lake, a Harvard graduate, was from a politically well-connected family; his grandfather had advised President Herbert Hoover and his mother had briefly been engaged to George Kennan.[18] Now, as Clinton's national security advisor, he complained to his British colleagues that the anguish over Bosnia was "taking all the attention in the press and a great deal of the time of the American foreign policy machine." Lake was unconvinced that this should be the new president's highest priority. He "wanted the Administration to have time to concentrate on other, in some cases more fundamentally important, items."[19]

Lake, however, did not get to pick priorities by himself. He had to coordinate policy with Clinton's secretary of state, the Carter-era foreign policy veteran Warren Christopher, and with the secretary of defense, former Wisconsin Democratic congressman Les Aspin.[20] Assessing this new team, the British foreign secretary, Douglas Hurd, reported to Major on March 26, 1993 that "the personalities are bedding down. Christopher is the tortoise and Aspin the hare, and if there is a race the result might be as in the fable."[21] Hurd's prediction was prescient. Aspin, smart but overwhelmed, threw himself into the job with such zeal that he ended up in a hospital after a few weeks. To a get-well-soon note from Major, Aspin replied, "your letter was immensely cheering. I am feeling much better now and have promised the doctors not to yell at Republicans anymore."[22]

Despite the promise, the yelling continued. Infighting between Aspin and his senior military officers, plus a tragedy in Somalia, would topple the hare in late 1993, to be replaced by his deputy, the sixty-six-year-old engineer, defense contractor, and Stanford professor Bill Perry.[23] Hurd also predicted correctly that the vice president, Al Gore, would be a player as well, because he had a real "passion" for "the formation of policy." But Lake remained the one to watch, Hurd thought, because "he seeks no publicity" and "is shrewd."[24] Although even his supporters conceded that he was volatile—Clinton reportedly described him as "'mean and nasty'"—Lake showed how effective he could be when he won an important early bureaucratic battle, ensuring that the NSC would chair all principals' meetings, Washington-speak for a session involving all relevant senior advisors on a particular issue.[25]

One major issue, however, eluded Lake's grasp: for the role of his most important advisor on all matters relating to Russia, Clinton tapped Strobe Talbott, an old friend. Talbott had started gaining expertise in Russian language and literature as an undergraduate at Yale, where his grandfather had once captained the football team. After winning a Rhodes Scholarship, he moved to Oxford University in 1968 and became fast friends with another Rhodes Scholar: Clinton. Once they graduated, Clinton went to Yale Law School and Talbott went on to become a foreign correspondent, but they remained in contact.[26] Talbott's interest in Russia only grew with the years he spent in the country, gaining lifelong friends and even, at one point, translating Nikita Khrushchev's memoirs.[27] Because of this background, the president appointed Talbott "Ambassador to the Newly Independent States of the former Soviet Union." Ambassador was not one of the highest-ranking titles available, but Clinton explained to Yeltsin that he wanted to keep Talbott unencumbered by other responsibilities, allowing him to focus solely on policy toward the region. Promising Yeltsin that this arrangement will be "good for both you and me," Clinton added that he intended to "maintain a high level of personal involvement" in US-Russian relations as well.[28]

Clinton's ambassador to the UN, Madeleine Albright, later recalled that it swiftly became apparent Talbott had the president's ear on all issues related to Russia. Assigning this major foreign-policy responsibility to someone other than the secretary of state might in theory have caused problems, but Christopher was willing to accept it. The president wanted it that way; dealing with Russia would be time-consuming and a distraction from other issues; and the prospect of subordinates competing with him was of little concern to the sixty-eight-year-old Christopher, who knew that this would be the last big job of his career. His relaxed attitude was a blessing because it soon became apparent—in the words of the secretary's chief of staff, Thomas Donilon—that "there's only one person in this building the President calls Sunday night to see how he's doing, and that person isn't Warren Christopher."[29]

As the incoming team was showered with solicited and unsolicited advice from all quarters, the input on at least one topic was suboptimal: the NATO enlargement state-of-play. The secretary general of NATO, Manfred Wörner, complained to the Clinton team in March 1993 that alliance issues had been on the back burner for too long; waiting around for "'US leadership'" for "the last six months had not been very agreeable."[30] And, while lower-level civil servants and their filing cabinets stayed in place during the presidential transition, the "very small circle" of those truly in the know about what had happened had all left to find jobs elsewhere. The transition from one party to another had not helped either. As former national security advisor Brent Scowcroft later recalled, when he tried to pass along information to his successors, "I got a fairly cold response." The upshot was that Clinton policymakers found themselves forced to pick up a lot of slack quickly, often on the basis of incomplete knowledge.[31] The extent of that problem would soon become apparent when Yeltsin started citing the two-plus-four treaty as a prohibition on NATO expansion, forcing the new administration to scramble to figure out whether his claims had any validity.

The Russian and Ukrainian Corners

Understanding what Yeltsin wanted remained a strategic priority for many reasons, not least because in 1993, according to US estimates, post-Soviet Russia still commanded between 25,000 and 35,000 nuclear weapons and an army of 2.8 million.[32] Perry, then still deputy secretary, had a succinct summary for what he thought should be the new administration's highest priority: to help Moscow manage its nuclear hangover.[33] To that end, Clinton told Yeltsin in one of their earliest conversations that he wanted to implement two outstanding nuclear weapons agreements, START I and START II.[34] Although Bush had signed both, neither had yet received ratification by the Russian parliament. It was a priority for Clinton that both move forward—particularly START II, which would eliminate some two-thirds of the US and Russian nuclear arsenals.[35]

Meanwhile, Perry initiated regular contacts between the Pentagon and Russian Ministry of Defense officials. He also worked hard to forge a personal bond with the man who was now defense minister in Moscow, the Afghan war veteran Pavel Grachev, some twenty years his junior.[36] As a favor to Grachev, the Defense Department even organized an introduction the Russian greatly desired: to his movie star idol, Arnold Schwarzenegger. Getting the defense minister in a room with the star had diplomatic benefits that made it worth the hassle of dealing with Schwarzenegger's huge number of representatives, intermediaries, and hangers-on—a number that impressed even the men running the Pentagon bureaucracy.[37]

A bigger challenge was to get the new US president in a room with his Russian counterpart. The two leaders decided to have their first of what would become eighteen face-to-face encounters in Vancouver on April 3–4, 1993.[38] Just before it, Clinton received advice from Kohl, who urged the new US president to err on the side of support for Moscow. Kohl suggested viewing Russia the way a former president, Harry Truman, had viewed Germany after World War II: as a defeated adversary in need of essential help. To illustrate the success of that policy, Kohl, who was born in 1930, offered the story of how he had met his wife. When they first laid eyes on each other, at a school dancing class in the late 1940s, he was "wearing a suit donated by American Quaker aid and his future wife was wearing a dress donated by another American organization." The Kohls "had never forgotten that," and neither had "a whole generation of Germans." Such generosity to a defeated foe had, in Kohl's opinion, paid long-term dividends in US-German relations. The chancellor further explained how, at his first meeting with President Ronald Reagan, the German had suggested playing a little game: they should both write who they thought was the greatest American president of the twentieth century on a sheet of paper, and then exchange their notes. They found that each had written "Harry Truman." In Kohl's case, it was because of the Marshall Plan.[39]

Kohl advised that Clinton use the Vancouver summit to extend the same hand of friendship to a struggling Russia, while admitting that there were enormous differences between Germany after 1945 and Russia after 1991. Most important were without question the "crimes of the Nazis" and their legacy for Germany. Another difference was that before the Nazi era, Germany had been a democracy. After his hometown "was captured by the Americans," the chancellor recalled how US occupying forces had drawn up a list of everyone who had won office in the last free election and, if they were still alive, simply "put the survivors back in place a week after taking over the town." In Russia, he said, "we can't do that." The two leaders had to do something, however, because "if we do not assist Yeltsin then he has no chance." To avoid that failure, Kohl suggested working together on big-ticket aid items for Russia because "Germany has reached the maximum of what it can do" on its own. To date "53% of the assistance to Russia so far has come from Germany," mainly "to get former Soviet troops out of eastern Germany." That could not continue. Another question that Moscow had raised was of increasing access for Russian goods to EC markets; improved trade opportunities could help Russia to help itself. On all of these issues, Clinton agreed that it was "far better to try and fail" than to do too little.[40]

Their March 26 prep session for Vancouver concluded with a growing realization: it was the beginning of a beautiful friendship. Kohl told colleagues afterward that he found Clinton's openness about his poor upbringing to be disarming, and he respected the president's ability to synthesize vast amounts of information.[41] Clinton noted in his memoirs simply, "I liked Helmut Kohl a lot."[42]

The president headed for Vancouver not long after. Once the summit began, it quickly developed traits that would characterize the many encounters to follow. The first was a justified sense of satisfaction that, after the long decades of the Cold War, the two former superpower enemies could meet on friendly terms. As the State Department put it, "there was a feeling that after decades of confrontation and several years of uncertainty and probing, the two countries had now crossed a threshold."[43] The sense of clearing, after years of hostility followed by uncertainty, was palpable. The Cold War was over, and Moscow and Washington both had leaders with ample runway ahead of them.

Then there was the personal connection. In his memoirs, Yeltsin recalled, "I was completely amazed by this young, eternally smiling man who was powerful, energetic, handsome."[44] The two presidents agreed to call each other Bill and Boris, and their rapport quickly developed into another summit trait: shows of boisterous bonhomie. In part because of such showmanship, Talbott thought of Yeltsin as at once a very big man and a very bad boy. Since that description could apply to Clinton as well, it was not surprising they got along.[45]

The new US president also showed a surprising tolerance for Yeltsin's drunkenness, which would also become a staple of their encounters. A summit tradition established in Vancouver was the private running tally kept by Clinton staffers of how many drinks Yeltsin consumed. Peak intake at this particular summit occurred when, upon boarding a boat with a bar for a tour around Vancouver Island, Yeltsin downed three scotches before it left the dock. He then went on to drink large quantities of wine while barely eating anything.[46]

Clinton was unfazed. He had grown up with an alcoholic stepfather and, as he said to Talbott afterward, had seen worse. As a boy, Clinton had witnessed his drunken stepfather fire a gun at his mother. When he was fourteen, and could no longer bear listening to his inebriated stepfather beat his mother yet again, he menaced the older man off her with a golf club.[47] Talbott recalled the president shrugging off the Russian president's inebriation by saying, "'at least Yeltsin's not a mean drunk.'"[48]

Clinton also covered for Yeltsin's drinking with other world leaders. Trying to convince Major that they should be tolerant, the president told a story from the time of the US Civil War: "when General [Ulysses S.] Grant started winning battles, President [Abraham] Lincoln's advisors told him that Grant was a crude drunk. Lincoln replied, 'Find out what he drinks and give it to the rest of them.'"[49]

The gist was that Clinton valued Yeltsin for being on the right side of two big substantive issues: democracy versus dictatorship in Russia, and cooperation versus competition with the West.[50] Clinton sensed that Yeltsin drunk was better for the United States than most other Russian leaders sober. As the American president told Major, "perhaps I am biased because I like him. But it is hard to imagine getting someone better" in the position of Russian president.[51]

Proving Clinton's point, in Vancouver Yeltsin proposed mutual "detargeting" of their nuclear weapons, currently preprogrammed to destroy major sites in their two countries.[52] Clinton welcomed that and similar initiatives. At one point, Talbott worried that Yeltsin might even be dominating the summit with such proposals and sent a note to his boss to that effect, but Clinton wrote back not to worry, "'he needs us.'"[53] The US president may have been from Arkansas, but he could figure out what was going on in relations with Russia. In exchange for de-targeting and other offers, Clinton "announced a bilateral package of about $1.6 billion," as he recounted to Kohl in a phone call afterward.[54] He also prompted the IMF and the World Bank to follow suit. Kohl would subsequently help Clinton to argue for a "privatization fund" at the Tokyo meeting of the G7, where the group pledged $3 billion for such a fund.[55]

The Vancouver summit thus put the essential elements of the coming US-Russian relationship in place: outward cooperation paired with darker undercurrents of national and personal weakness and need. These themes were ever-present throughout Clinton's dealings with Russia, as well as with Ukraine.[56] He made clear early in his first term that eliminating the former Soviet nuclear weapons on Ukrainian soil was another top priority, as was preventing black-market trade in so-called loose nukes.

As an expression of that priority, the new US president had made time during his first week in office to call Ukraine's leader, Leonid Kravchuk, and impress upon him the need to denuclearize as soon as possible. In return, Clinton said that the United States was "prepared to provide at least $175 million" under the legislation advanced by Senator Nunn, along with security assurances.[57] These carrots were necessary because Ukraine was backing away from its earlier willingness to relinquish the weapons on its territory to Russia, despite widespread Ukrainian revulsion at all things nuclear since the April 1986 accident at Chernobyl.[58] Fallout from that terrible accident had contaminated about 23 percent of Belarusian and 5 percent of Ukrainian territory.[59] Cows in the affected areas would produce contaminated milk for years afterward.[60] Soviet authorities, unwilling to reveal the full extent of that disaster, had made matters worse by insisting that residents proceed with outdoor holiday parades on May 1, 1986, even though the marchers were parading through radioactive dust.[61] Such actions contributed to growing resentment of central power in Moscow, intensified when cancer among Ukrainian children rose more than 90 percent in the five years after the incident.

Given that history and the ongoing collapse of the Ukrainian economy—it would contract annually between 9.7 percent and 22.7 percent from 1991 to 1996—a bombs-for-butter bargain seemed sensible.[62] But by the time of Clinton's inauguration, members of the parliament, or Rada, had started questioning "the wisdom of Ukraine's previously made commitments to denuclearize."[63] Kravchuk told the prime minister of Spain that he simply "would not comply with nuclear arms agreements" while holding out for "a US nuclear umbrella."[64]

As part of this Ukrainian shift in thinking, on February 2, 1993 the Foreign Ministry in Kyiv produced an internal study analyzing the pros and cons of three options: becoming a fully nonnuclear state, remaining nuclear, or splitting the difference. In the latter case, the country would preserve "a portion of ICBMs" as a minimal deterrent force.[65] The Foreign Ministry conceded that, on the one hand, retention, maintenance, and development of any nuclear arsenal would be costly and difficult. Operational command and control had been set up for Moscow, not Kyiv, even though the weapons were on Ukrainian soil.[66] One of the ministers in Kyiv responsible for managing the weapons later admitted that "Ukraine did not really know the specific characteristics of the nuclear stockpile (the world's third largest) it had inherited."[67] Moreover, retargeting weapons designed for intercontinental combat to hit Moscow or St. Petersburg—Russia being the power Ukraine wanted to deter—would be a "technically daunting task," in the words of another expert.[68] And last but not least, maintaining the arsenal would inevitably produce a "sharp deterioration of relations with the West" and a "sharp escalation" of tensions with Russia.

On the other hand, such weapons would give Ukraine the status of a "great power in the international community" and "a 'strong' position in negotiations both with Western countries and the countries of Central and Eastern Europe," as well as with the Commonwealth of Independent States set up in 1991.[69] Deteriorating relations among members of that commonwealth were another reason for the Ukrainians to rethink denuclearization. The crumbling of any pretense of shared defense among commonwealth states—Yevgeny Shaposhnikov, on paper the military commander of the CIS, had in reality become little more than a figurehead and abandoned that job in June 1993 to become Yeltsin's top security advisor instead—fueled the search for alternatives. Ukrainians informed a visiting Talbott in spring 1993 that they wanted a "Central and Eastern Europe Zone of Security" and asked for US support of that goal.[70] Matters went from bad to worse that July when, as Yeltsin explained to Clinton, "our Supreme Soviet" resolved that the Crimean city of Sevastopol—still home port to major portions of the Russian navy, despite being in what was now an independent Ukraine—"was a Russian city." Yeltsin tried to make light of the development, adding, "thank God no one takes the Supreme Soviet seriously!" But it was hard to deny

Talbott's takeaway from these developments: Ukrainians were "paranoids with real enemies."[71]

Aspin and his advisors pushed their Ukrainian counterparts to detarget missiles aimed at the United States while they sorted matters out.[72] But in the long run, US strategy was clear: as Lake's subordinates advised, "under no circumstance should Ukraine be encouraged to think" that the Clinton Administration "would accept a nuclear Ukraine," because "that outcome would deal a potentially catastrophic blow to stability in the region and the entire arms control regime negotiated over the past 25 years."[73] The US Arms Control and Disarmament Agency classified it as a "vital US interest that Ukraine not gain positive control over the nuclear weapons on its territory."[74] Clinton informed Kravchuk in a letter "directly and personally from me that I attach the highest political importance to this issue."[75]

The carrots and sticks were clear: If Ukraine fulfilled its promise to denuclearize, Washington would in return provide aid and integrate the country into a host of useful bilateral and multilateral relationships. If it did not, the act of keeping the weapons would make Ukraine the enemy of both Russia and the United States, a heavy burden for a young country, and it would be on its own in any future nuclear disaster. Managing relations between these two Slavic states was clearly going to be among the greatest challenges facing the new administration. Lake, a strong supporter of enlarging the Atlantic Alliance, proposed a jaw-droppingly radical solution to British colleagues in May 1993: "if we admitted Ukraine to NATO, the nuclear question would of course resolve itself." His interlocutors wondered afterward if it was a "serious proposal," given that the idea of expanding NATO to include Ukraine would cross the very reddest of Russian red lines. But Lake presumably meant what he said. The national security advisor was rapidly distinguishing himself as one of the strongest proponents of alliance expansion anywhere in the world—and he had the president's ear.[76]

The Visegrad Corner

The third corner of the triangle, Central and Eastern Europe, also saw admission to NATO as the answer. Because of the democratic courage the region's leaders had shown in shedding Soviet control, they justifiably felt that European and transatlantic organizations should welcome them.

Determined that their concerns not suffer from Washington's fixation on the former Soviet nuclear arsenal, they continued their Bush-era efforts, coordinated since the Visegrad conference of 1991, to pry open the doors of Western institutions that were acting less than hospitably.[77]

To date, those efforts with NATO had yielded only NACC memberships, which they felt were not enough—and Talbott agreed. Although the ambassador found the NACC visually "inspiring" because it brought together "38 countries that used to be squared off against each other on either side of the Iron Curtain," he considered it useless in practical terms. Talbott thought of NACC summits as "two days of tedium" bequeathed to him by the Bush team, not as useful decision-making events, and he began thinking about alternatives. Visegrad countries felt the same frustration, amplified by the sense that EC expansion remained on a slow track as well.[78] There was a growing sense of a need to move beyond NACC. The bottom line for Visegrad in 1993 was that, as a diplomat from Hungary put it, he and his colleagues needed "'accelerators.'"[79]

The opening of the United States Holocaust Memorial Museum in April 1993 provided an opening for the leaders of the three countries to press their case. Václav Havel, now president of the Czech Republic after its split from Slovakia on January 1 of that year, managed to secure an extended one-on-one conversation with Clinton on April 20 as part of his visit to the United States for the event.[80] Drawing on his moral stature, Havel expressed his sadness that "we are living in a vacuum," saying, "that is why we want to join NATO." Exceeding what Prague had previously requested from Bush—some kind of associate membership—the Czech president stressed how much his country now merited "association, followed by full membership."[81] On top of that, he also thought that Central and Eastern European countries should collectively have a "nonpermanent seat on the Security Council" and proposed working with Albright to establish such a seat.[82]

Lech Wałęsa, the Polish-dissident-turned-president, echoed Havel's words in his own bilateral meeting with the US president on the same occasion. Wałęsa warned that "we are all afraid of Russia" and that "if Russia again adopts an aggressive foreign policy, that aggression will be directed toward Ukraine and Poland." He felt strongly that "Poland cannot be left defenseless; we need to have the protection of U.S. muscle." Unfortunately, "Western Europe has not yet accepted us" and was, unfathomably, "not capitalizing" on "the biggest victory in history," namely, the defeat of Communism.[83] The president of Estonia, Lennart

Meri, made similar remarks when speaking later with a visiting Talbott. Meri complained that "there is a security vacuum in this part of the world" and hoped "Talbott had come to town to sign Estonia's accession to NATO."[84]

Clinton would afterward remark that such pleas affected him deeply. They fueled his belief that "NATO remains key" to stability in Europe.[85] His advisors, however, were reluctant to give in to such pressures from new democracies too quickly. They felt two major issues needed priority attention: a domestic scandal and Bosnia.

The domestic scandal had its origins in Clinton's troubled first hundred days in office. The British Foreign Office, in its own assessment of those days, observed that Clinton was "working himself to the point of exhaustion" to compensate for the fact that his staff were "young, inexperienced, and overwhelmed."[86] The US president had scored major early successes, including a family leave law and a "motor voter" law that made it possible to register to vote at the same time as applying for a driver's license. But as he himself later admitted, he should have devoted more time, and care, to picking his staff.[87] The practical arrangements for the Holocaust Museum opening, for example, had been a fiasco; "scenes of indescribable chaos" had, in the opinion of the British, marred the event and the standing of the new administration in foreign visitors' eyes.[88] There was also a scandal in the White House travel office. The issues involved were minor, but they gained urgency when the president's lifelong friend Vince Foster, who had moved from Little Rock to the White House only to suffer withering criticism for his handling of the scandal, shot himself.

Foster's violent, unexpected death became conflated with an investigation into presidential financial dealings with other Little Rock acquaintances, including the joint development of a property known as Whitewater. Although the travel office scandal was not related to Whitewater, the shocking suicide allowed the Clintons' opponents to merge the two issues and sensationalize them. The growing attacks on the president and his wife eventually prompted him, in an effort to show he had nothing to hide, to agree to the start of a special counsel investigation.[89]

Newspapers owned by Clinton foe Richard Mellon Scaife nonetheless stayed on the offensive. Among other items, they ran articles by Christopher Ruddy, later owner of the right-wing Newsmax, claiming that Foster's death was murder, not suicide.[90] One of Ruddy's greatest admirers was a White House staffer named Linda Tripp, who had become Foster's assistant after being retained in her job from the Bush era.[91] One of the last people to see Foster alive on July 20, 1993, the day of his suicide, Tripp became convinced there was a cover-up of something sinister, even though she had no independent evidence. As a result, she developed an abiding hatred of the new president.[92]

On top of these domestic worries was the worsening violence in Bosnia.[93] In 1992, Clinton had criticized what he saw as Bush's passivity in the face of Bosnian bloodshed, but now matters were getting uglier on his watch.[94] The fighting there seemed to call not only Clinton's but also NATO's credibility into question: how could they provide leadership in European security writ large if they could not handle the conflict in former Yugoslavia? In an effort to stem some of the bloodshed, NATO in April 1993 launched an operation called "Deny Flight," meant to enforce a UN no-fly zone over Bosnia-Herzegovina. The operation was a watershed moment for NATO, which found itself going "out-of-area," meaning flying outside of its geographic area of defensive responsibility, for the first time ever.[95] But it left many Americans wondering whether Clinton had forgotten to focus on the domestic economy and whether he could master the chaos in his own White House. As James Steinberg, later the deputy national security director, recalled, "there were costs from that very rocky first year" even well into the second term.[96]

Because of these domestic and foreign worries, senior Clinton advisors felt there were higher priorities than enlarging NATO to the Visegrad countries. The chairman of the Joint Chiefs of Staff, General Colin Powell, let it be known "he was personally reluctant to cross the bridge of Eastern European membership of NATO" given that "he was not sure what NATO would mean in such circumstances." Powell also "worried about Ukraine," fearing that if they felt ignored, "the Ukrainians would use the nuclear issue to extract [the] greatest possible concessions" from the West.[97] General John Shalikashvili, who served as SACEUR before succeeding Powell as chairman, feared Russia was "not mature enough to understand expanded membership."[98] Secretary of State Christopher expressed similar concerns at a meeting of NATO foreign ministers in June 1993, saying that at "an appropriate time, we may choose to enlarge NATO membership. But that is not now on the agenda."[99] He also saw Ukraine as the problem. If NATO expanded, it was "hard to see how Ukraine can accept being the buffer between NATO, Europe and Russia. This will militate against our efforts to get rid of Ukraine's nuclear weapons."[100]

Thus, despite Visegrad's best collective efforts, the issue of NATO membership remained on the back burner in summer 1993. When Clinton saw Yeltsin at the G7 Tokyo summit in July, they instead prioritized Ukraine. The Russian president emphasized to Clinton that "it is always difficult to deal with Ukraine" because "today they agree, tomorrow they backtrack." Clinton replied, "it's the same case with us."[101] The question was how to persuade Ukraine to give up its nuclear weapons, and eventual NATO enlargement seemed like an answer. A State Department memo suggested using alliance expansion as "the ultimate 'carrot' in our efforts to promote democracy and reform in the East," and specifically to "ensure Ukrainian denuclearization."[102]

Robert Hunter, the US ambassador to NATO, did not think that expansion should happen eventually; he felt that the time to move was now. Hunter advised Washington on August 3, 1993 that "we are fast approaching the 'fish or cut bait' time in the East."[103] Back in Washington, senior State Department official Lynn Davis was of the same opinion. She thought it would not be possible "to defer a debate on expansion" much longer, "nor would it be in our interest to do so."[104]

Wałęsa liked NATO sitting on the back burner even less. Tired of waiting for his peers' "accelerators" to work, he savvily decided to force matters. Showing the political flair that had made him famous, he took a dramatic gamble that would fail in the short run but would ultimately expedite enlargement to his country and its neighbors.[105] As reported by the US embassy in Warsaw, "over dinner and drinks on August 24, Walesa fairly easily persuaded Yeltsin to go along with a statement indicating that Russia had no objection to Poland joining NATO." Yeltsin agreed to issue a remarkable declaration that Polish membership in NATO was "'not contrary to the interest of any state, also including Russia.'"[106]

Yeltsin regretted his words the next morning, and, under pressure from his advisors, tried to retract them.[107] The Polish president had a flash of insight: he asked if Yeltsin believed that "Poland was a sovereign country." The Russian president replied "yes."[108] Wałęsa then announced that, "'as a sovereign country,'" Poland would join NATO. Getting Yeltsin's public statement of "'concurrence now'" would prevent conflict in the future. Yeltsin, conceding the point, grudgingly affirmed his words about Polish membership in NATO—but not without reportedly getting something that he wanted in exchange. The US embassy in Warsaw learned that Wałęsa and Yeltsin had apparently reached a side deal: "an implicit understanding that the Poles would not intervene in the Ukraine in any dispute involving Russia except in the event of a military attack." This "quid pro quo on Ukraine is widely rumored and plausible, but unconfirmed."[109]

Hints of this thinking had already become apparent to the NSC in Washington, which knew that "many of the East European states have expressed reservations about being too closely associated with Ukraine until serious efforts at economic and political reform are evident." The Central and Eastern Europeans felt "that Ukraine in its present condition would be a drag on their own development" because the country had "not made the same qualitative break with the Soviet past as they have." In other words, Visegrad thought Ukraine was wasting time during this rare window of opportunity and did not want to wait around for it.[110] Clinton, advised of this attitude, found it had larger implications: as Poland looked west, Ukraine would feel increasingly isolated and desperate.[111]

Whatever the true extent of the Wałęsa-Yeltsin deal, it left Yeltsin in a mood to accede to Polish wishes for a while thereafter. Soon after his visit to Warsaw, he confirmed that former Soviet troops would finally leave Poland. It was a welcome announcement. Although the withdrawals had long been promised, locals had been wondering whether they would ever be completed. Germans had similar doubts. As Lake reminded Clinton, the motivation behind Germany's copious aid to Russia, which the State Department estimated to be "some two-thirds of the G7 total $75 billion pledged since 1990," was "largely related" to ensuring that the "scheduled August 31 [1994] departure of Russian forces from eastern Germany" happened as planned.[112]

In the midst of these developments, a September 1993 *Foreign Affairs* article by RAND senior analysts Ronald Asmus, Richard Kugler, and Stephen Larrabee attracted a great deal of attention. The three RAND experts argued forcefully for extending "NATO's collective defense and security arrangements" farther south and east.[113] The same month, Lake gave a much-noticed speech on transatlantic relations in which he stated his strong conviction that "the successor to a doctrine of containment must be a strategy of enlargement."[114]

These developments together produced, as Kozyrev later recalled it, a crucial watershed in the history of NATO expansion. Visegrad gained the initiative, and Moscow "lost the ability to address the matter calmly." The sequence of events poured fuel on the fire of "NATO-fear-mongering hardliners in Russia," creating new tensions at home for Yeltsin. Kozyrev had been trying to promote a policy slogan of "'no hasty enlargement—

yes partnership!'" But Wałęsa's gamble shocked Moscow's hard-liners and undermined the foreign minister's ability to convince them that NATO expansion would be a slow, consensual process. By the autumn of 1993, Kozyrev's main rival, head of foreign intelligence Yevgeny Primakov, could convincingly argue that Kozyrev was deceiving both himself and his nation about the truth of expansion.[115]

Secretary General Wörner agreed that Wałęsa had successfully "changed the landscape concerning NATO expansion," which he saw as a positive development. Thanks to the savvy move by the Polish president, "there is currently an historic moment of opportunity regarding NATO's engagement in the East," and "if the moment is lost, who knows when it will occur again?" Wörner argued that the alliance "must seize the moment" and immediately begin to "admit all the former Warsaw Pact states of Central and Eastern Europe, from north to south" on a staggered time scale. On top of that, "the alliance could not ignore the FSU [former Soviet Union] states," even though "the Russians would view the FSU states differently."[116] Sensing an opportunity, the Hungarians also began pushing Washington for a "forward-leaning" message on NATO enlargement, including an explicit statement that Visegrad countries were first in line.

A Pentagon official, heading a traveling delegation, tried to hold off the Visegrad states, complaining that "key decisions had yet to be made," both within the Clinton administration and the alliance, and that "NATO should not be seen as a charitable organization" because "it was no 'rich uncle from America' that would hand out goodies to local military establishments."[117] As ever, Ukraine remained a worry. Since, in Talbott's words, "the pace of deliberations on NATO expansion has picked up considerably," Washington "must be very careful not to pull this off in a way that makes Ukraine feel it is being left out in the cold with its furry neighbor to the north." If it did, "we could inadvertently—and disastrously—give hardliners in Kiev new arguments for their case that Ukraine needs a nuclear deterrent."[118] Talbott had learned that the Ukrainian deputy foreign minister, Borys Tarasyuk, was pronouncing it "unacceptable for NATO to expand without Ukraine becoming a full member."[119] These words made the dilemma between two strategic imperatives, inherited by Clinton from Bush, ever more apparent: enlarging NATO to Central and Eastern Europe writ large—meaning all the way to Ukraine—thereby solving the Ukrainian nuclear issue but alienating Russia; or stopping enlargement west of Ukraine, but leaving a populous state with nuclear arms in limbo.

The tension between Central and Eastern European, Russia, and Ukraine was coming to a head.

Bloodshed in Moscow

In fall 1993, Russia's hardening position combined with bloodshed in the streets of Moscow to tip the balance toward moving forward with enlargement. The US ambassador in Moscow, Thomas Pickering, had warned Washington to expect such a hardening; Pickering had been convinced that reactionaries in Moscow would almost certainly make Yeltsin walk back his August statement approving Polish NATO membership. In fact, he was surprised that Yeltsin did not retract his comments immediately afterward because "the one constant in what we have heard from all Russian interlocutors has been extreme sensitivity about the role of NATO" among their former allies.[120] When the ambassador prodded Kozyrev for his thoughts on the Warsaw visit, the Russian foreign minister snapped, "if NATO expands, Russia should be first."[121]

Pickering was right about a retraction, but it took longer than expected. On September 7, there was in the first instance more encouraging news out of Moscow: Yeltsin advised Clinton that Ukraine's miserable economic situation was forcing it to make concessions. Kravchuk had agreed, at least on paper, to "the total removal in 24 months of nuclear warheads to Russia for their elimination." In exchange, "we will give Ukraine Low Enriched Uranium for use at nuclear power plants," Yeltsin confirmed. Even better, "we also resolved the Black Sea Fleet matter, finally." Because, in Yeltsin's view, "Ukraine owes $2.5 billion to Russia, we will get their part of the fleet as payment," with the end result that "the fleet will belong to Russia and we will keep the base at Sevastopol." Clinton was pleased to hear it and hoped implementation would happen as agreed, given Ukraine's record of backtracking. The US president also congratulated Yeltsin on withdrawing former Soviet forces from Lithuania—but wanted to know when he would do the same for Estonia and Latvia. Yeltsin, reminding Clinton that "next week we will pull out all our troops in Poland" too, added, "in Latvia and Estonia it is more difficult because of their failure to comply with the human rights of the ethnic Russians living there." They left the issue unresolved, with Clinton adding that he was "working hard on passing the $2.5 billion assistance package for Russia."[122]

Despite these positive signs, by September 15, 1993 Pickering's expected retraction had surfaced; approving NATO membership for Poland was a bridge too far after all.[123] A letter to Clinton, issued that day by the Kremlin over Yeltsin's signature, said that although Moscow was "sympathetic to the by no means nostalgic sentiments of the East Europeans toward past 'cooperation' within the framework of the Warsaw Pact," NATO expansion was not the answer. "A truly pan-European security system" was.

Furthermore, Yeltsin's letter complained that enlargement to Poland was unacceptable because it violated "the spirit" of the two-plus-four treaty of September 12, 1990. Since the terms of that treaty "prohibit the deployment of foreign troops within the eastern lands of the Federal Republic of Germany," by implication the treaty also "precludes the option of expanding the NATO zone into the East." Yeltsin was thereby starting a line of attack that would continue for years: insisting on the relevance of the 1990 discussions and treaty to Central and Eastern Europe, thereby reviving the fight over crossing the Cold War line.[124]

Alarmed, the State Department scrambled to assess this claim. Christopher and Wörner arranged a lunch with the German foreign minister, Klaus Kinkel—who, as a protégé of former foreign minister Hans-Dietrich Genscher, was still in regular contact with his retired predecessor—and Kinkel's top aide Dieter Kastrup to figure out whether the complaint had any merit.[125] Kastrup informed them on October 5, 1993 that the "Yeltsin letter's reference to the 'two-plus-four' treaty was 'formally' wrong" because "Germany had been able to commit only itself in that treaty." But the Russian claim nonetheless had "political and psychological substance that we had to take seriously." Reviving the view that Genscher had tried but failed to turn into policy, Kastrup argued that "the 'basic philosophy' of the agreement had been that NATO would not expand to the east." Kastrup could understand why "Yeltsin thought the West had committed itself not to extend NATO beyond its 1990 limits."

In reply, Wörner expressed his strong disagreement with his fellow German's view, saying all allies should "strongly reject the idea that the two-plus-four agreement had anything to do with NATO expansion." It was indeed accurate, as they sat there that day, that the agreement allowed only united Germany's territorial defense forces—that is, units roughly equivalent to the US National Guard, not assigned to NATO's integrated military command—to be stationed in eastern Germany before the scheduled Soviet withdrawal in the second half of 1994. But German forces integrated into NATO could thereafter move east as well because they were excluded from former East German territory "only as long as Russian troops" remained." There was also the related language in the agreed minute stating that, while foreign forces should be neither stationed nor deployed in eastern Germany after the final Soviet withdrawal, they could nonetheless be present in the region at the discretion of the German government. The upshot was that Moscow had signed—not once but twice, as the Westerners had gotten a separate set of signatures under the agreed minute to leave no doubt about its efficacy—a legally binding treaty permitting NATO forces to cross the old Cold War line as long as the German government approved.[126]

Pushing even harder, Wörner added that they currently had "a rare historical opportunity" provided by Wałęsa "'to anchor some of these nations once and for all to the West.'" Kinkel asked Christopher whether the Clinton administration had made up its mind on enlargement. The secretary of state responded, "the US had yet to reach a decision on NATO expansion." The administration was "looking positively at the possibility of expansion, but would not favor precipitate" actions. In his view, it was "very important that Russia and Ukraine be involved in this process. The criteria should give them a prospect of NATO membership in the future, although not now or in the next five years." He added that "NATO's approach to expansion should not exclude the Baltics, but something less than Article 5 security guarantees was needed" and suggested "Article 4 commitments to consultation" instead, since "the Balts needed reassurance they could not be overrun without NATO being somehow involved."[127]

Washington remaining in such a state of indecision on expansion was proving difficult, however, not least because of the NATO summit scheduled for January 1994. Clinton was inclined to take part personally—but any presidential appearance there essentially required the announcement of some policy on enlargement. He could hardly show up and have nothing to say about it. Eric Edelman, a senior foreign service officer about to begin service in the US embassy in Prague, suggested to Talbott a way to resolve these issues: the United States should begin NATO expansion, but over a decade and in four phases.

In phase one, potential members would be expected to take part in the NACC, if they were not doing so already, and to fulfill all expectations for acceptable performance in that body. This step would "strain out Uzbekistan, Kazakhstan, etc." Phase two would see individual agreements negotiated with would-be NATO members, lasting a couple more years.

High-performing states could then attain associate status in phase three, lasting another three to five years. Finally, in roughly seven to ten years, the last phase would be full membership with Article 5 guarantees—but only as a reward for states that had done well, not as a guaranteed result. Edelman added that "it might be useful to establish some groups" or cohorts for preferential promotion through the phases. "Group A might be the Visegrad countries. Group B would include Russia/Belarus/Ukraine. Group C would be the Balkans/Baltics." He also proposed, as a side arrangement, "a separate NATO-Russian Charter . . . which would help Yeltsin and Co. disarm critics at home."[128]

Edelman's ideas were seconded by Davis at the State Department, who also favored enlargement with Article 5 guarantees coming only in the last phase. Her thinking, she noted, was informed by the views of Germany's defense minister, Volker Rühe. He had established himself as a strong proponent of expansion and even provided funding to the research group at RAND that produced the influential pro-expansion *Foreign Affairs* article of August 1993; it was the first time RAND had ever taken a foreign commission.[129] Following Rühe, Davis expressed worry that "Germany is on the front-line of Central European instability and has neither the resources nor political inclination to handle these problems unilaterally."[130]

Germany's eastern flank was also vulnerable because Kohl had agreed in Arkhyz to a permanent ban on nuclear weapons in the former German Democratic Republic—and as Margaret Thatcher had predicted, the Germans had chosen to return their seat of national government to a city right in the middle of that vulnerability: Berlin. It created a German weakness, yet one more reason to be attentive to Moscow's postunification wishes. Germany's security would be much improved if Poland replaced it on the front line of NATO.[131] As one of Rühe's senior advisors, Vice Admiral Ulrich Weisser, put it, better "'to defend Germany in Poland than in Germany.'"[132]

Kohl was also aware of this consideration and even remarked on it to Clinton. The chancellor did not like being exposed on the easternmost line of the alliance while his country was still dealing with the many challenges of unification. But his government also felt a strong need to add new members in a way that (as summarized by the US State Department) "does not seem to 'draw new lines' in Europe."[133] The chancellor was particularly sensitive to anything that might make Yeltsin's life more difficult because civil strife was continuing in Moscow—and was about to turn bloody.

With inflation and unemployment soaring, Yeltsin and Russian parliamentarians were blaming each other.[134] On September 21, 1993, the Russian president proclaimed that he had disbanded parliament—even though he had no constitutional powers to do so.[135] In response, parliamentarians declared that the country had a new acting president: Aleksandr Rutskoi. Yeltsin complained to Clinton that parliament "has gone totally out of control," no longer supported "the reform process," and had once again "become communist." He had no choice, he said, but to call new elections in December, and in the interim to govern "by Presidential decree."[136]

Kohl and Clinton tried to make sense of these alarming developments, with the American noting hopefully that Yeltsin had promised to "proceed peacefully." The German chancellor was skeptical, saying that "nobody on our side can really tell what is happening," but "out of all the people that play a role there, I trust him [Yeltsin] the most." Whatever Yeltsin's flaws, Kohl added, "if he's removed, it will be much worse."[137]

As October began, Clinton's attention was distracted by an unexpected tragedy in Somalia that had serious political consequences for his administration. A Somali general, Mohamed Farrah Aidid, and his followers were killing UN peacekeepers. American forces deployed to Mogadishu on October 3–4, 1993 in an effort to subdue Aidid's loyalists. Instead, US troops became victims themselves, not least because insurgents shot down two Black Hawk helicopters with rocket-propelled grenades.[138] The spectacle of eighteen American soldiers dying in another distant war of choice was deeply uncomfortable to a generation for whom Vietnam remained a painful living memory. The public demanded to know who should be blamed for the fiasco widely called "Black Hawk Down." US diplomat Richard Holbrooke recorded a response in his audio diary: Defense Secretary Aspin's "'constant losses of self-control, temper tantrums, and childish behavior'" had "'made it easy for Tony Lake and Warren Christopher to agree that he should be the sacrificial lamb to push over the side of the ship to save themselves'" in the wake of the bloodshed. By the end of the year, they would persuade Clinton to fire Aspin, who reportedly wept, begged the president unsuccessfully not to let him go, and soon thereafter died of a stroke.[139]

With US attention focused on this tragedy, Yeltsin reneged on his pledge to proceed peacefully. On October 4, after days of tension and sporadic violence between the opposing camps, Yeltsin had Grachev bring in army tanks. Grachev ordered the tanks' crews to fire on the parliament building, known as the White House; obeying, they killed an estimated 145 of their fellow citizens and wounded 800 more. Rutskoi was imprisoned.[140] Some military leaders resented Grachev for shedding blood in this way, but as Perry noted, Grachev "clearly had Yeltsin's ear and support" and was obviously following orders from the top.[141] Yeltsin began to rule by decree, organize parliamentary elections for December 12, 1993, and seek support for a new constitution that gave him powers well in excess of those held by his French and American peers.[142]

While successful in the short run domestically, his use of violence was a Pyrrhic victory abroad. It sent chills throughout Europe, particularly Germany. As Kohl pointedly advised his fellow party members, they should never forget that "until the summer of next year, we will still have Russian soldiers, formerly Soviet soldiers, on the territory of the Federal Republic."[143] Those troops were, as a *New York Times* reporter put it, "dismembered and demoralized" and had become "the most unwieldy and troublesome legacy of the Soviet empire."[144] Organized crime had taken root among them. In 1994, a reporter investigating their black-market activities died when a bomb in his briefcase exploded.[145]

Given that a CIA report from the time of German unification in 1990 had claimed that Moscow planned to maintain nuclear weapons in Germany until the very last of the Soviet troops left in 1994, Kohl was right to worry about the consequences of instability in Moscow for his own country.[146] The continued presence of those forces and their arsenal represented a risk even in the best of times. Having armed Russian soldiers still inside Germany grew even more worrisome, however, as Yeltsin showed an unexpected willingness to use violence to achieve political ends—and extreme nationalists began doing well in campaigning for the December elections. It was hardly surprising that Kohl not only was generous in giving aid but also increasingly made it a habit to call Yeltsin every other week.[147] And, until the Russians left, Germany could not be too aggressive in supporting NATO expansion. As Kohl advised his party colleagues during the October crisis, "we should not forget that we are still involved."[148]

Yeltsin's use of force and the popularity of extremists also caused nightmares in Budapest. The prime minister of Hungary, József Antall, sent a blunt letter to Clinton, saying that "in the hours of the Moscow clashes," it was clear to Hungarians that Russian instability was "seriously threatening our region during the transition period." The prime minister felt strongly that NATO "cannot avoid the task of investigating the means to improve our region's security," and the best way to achieve that goal would be "to extend the alliance to the democratically most mature states of the region." Before the October violence, it might have been possible to dismiss worries like Antall's as alarmist, but now they seemed apt. Westerners increasingly began to doubt that Russia could reform peacefully (or at all) and to think that there might be something to Central and Eastern European pleas for protection from Moscow. Those doubts only grew when the result of the December 12 election was, as historian Sergey Radchenko memorably phrased it, the triumph of the "Liberal Democratic Party of Russia, which was infamously neither liberal nor democratic, but by all appearances fascist." The party's leader, Vladimir Zhirinovsky, had published a manifesto that was a "mumbo-jumbo of fascist, racist, nationalist, and imperialist snippets" shortly before the election, causing the sense of alarm among Russia's neighbors to grow even more.[149]

Given that, in the meantime, the EC had made it increasingly clear that membership would be a long-term process for Central and Eastern Europeans—a Copenhagen summit on June 21–22, 1993, had instead prioritized adding Austria, Finland, Sweden, and possibly Norway as well—getting into NATO became even more important for Visegrad.[150] They increasingly understood that EC expansion in the 1990s would not include them, not least because of the attitudes of states that hoped to join before they did. In early 1994, the Austrian chancellor, Franz Vranitsky, repeated to Clinton concerns that Austria had previously expressed to the Bush administration: "we have no explicit desire to be in the same box as the former members of the Warsaw Pact."[151]

Partnership for Peace

As the issue of NATO expansion assumed a new intensity, a principals' meeting generated a conceptual breakthrough on October 18, 1993. That breakthrough came in response to the main question up for debate, which (as put by the US State Department) was "whether NATO would commit at the January NATO Summit to expansion, or simply hold out the vague possibility."[152] Even though Lake was rising in influence and Aspin was barely clinging to office, the Pentagon's ideas would prevail.

Aspin and General Shalikashvili had already, on September 13, 1993, made clear through intermediaries to the State Department their concern about the way the NATO enlargement debate "focused on the interests of the Central and East Europeans, rather than on USG [United States government] interests." This was a strategic blunder in their view.[153] The office of the secretary of defense saw "no requirement or advantage in offering membership at this time."[154] The Pentagon also argued against admitting new members until they could be contributors to, rather than consumers of, the security provided by the alliance.[155] Instead, it offered an inspired alternative, building on the idea of phased expansion: a new Partnership for Peace.[156]

Aspin's deputy and soon-to-be successor, Perry, later described this proposal as "a simple, brilliant, and measured idea."[157] It was largely the brainchild of Shalikashvili, who developed it together with civilian Pentagon strategists such as Joseph Kruzel, deputy assistant secretary for Europe; NSC staffers; and diplomats in the US Mission to NATO. In developing this idea, Shalikashvili built on the thinking of the Bush administration's State Department. He was deeply knowledgeable about that thinking, as he had traveled extensively with former secretary James Baker in 1991–92, during the latter man's efforts to deal with the disintegration of centralized control over the Soviet nuclear arsenal and military.[158]

Shalikashvili and like-minded policymakers had as their goal the creation of a peacekeeping organization that simultaneously offered a contingent form of affiliation with NATO.[159] The general was a strong supporter of military-to-military cooperation as a practical way to build bridges among former enemies. He saw PfP as enabling just those kinds of contacts, by letting former Warsaw Pact countries get some NATO mud on their boots before they received the alliance's all-important Article 5 guarantee.[160] The Pentagon noted that PfP "need not carry any" guaranteed link to NATO membership; instead, it could provide useful ambiguity by establishing "such a link in general terms." That would leave open the option for high performers in the Partnership to earn full Article 5 guarantees at a later date. But the smart move was not to rush: as the US Mission to NATO put it, "it is critical that timing on identifying potential NATO members not get out ahead of creating a basic geostrategic structure that effectively accounts for Russia and Ukraine."[161]

This proposal solved five major problems. First, it addressed complaints by civilian and military leaders in the Defense Department that far too much of the discussion treated NATO as merely a club to join. NATO was a military alliance, which required members to standardize equipment, train troops, and contribute to each other's security. Giving unprepared new members Article 5 coverage too soon would weaken the transatlantic alliance—something that the Pentagon understandably wanted to avoid. The Partnership would provide time and flexibility to sort out practical matters, as each new partner could determine the pace and intensity of its evolving partnership with NATO.[162]

Second, PfP could serve as a response to the ongoing, tragic disintegration of Yugoslavia. There was a natural fit: the Balkans crisis was crying out for a solution, and a NATO-affiliated peacekeeping partnership was a solution in search of a problem. The Partnership could thus address Bosnian violence by enlarging the alliance both geographically (to former Warsaw Pact and Soviet republics) and functionally (to include peacekeeping).[163] In the best-case scenario, it could make the NATO military structure more flexible, by providing a means for dealing with non–Article 5 contingencies—perhaps creating new opportunities for Europeans to take leading roles in such events.

Third, PfP deepened relations with Central and Eastern Europe while still avoiding a new front line. Instead, it "would be open to the neutral and non-aligned nations as well as the nations of Central and Eastern Europe, including Russia and Ukraine." Partners would join based on desire and ability rather than location. Europe would "be defined not by geographical boundaries" but by shared principles and "active participation in NATO's Partnership for Peace."[164] In other words, PfP would build on the best aspect of the NACC, namely, its inclusivity, but take cooperation among countries to another level, one involving "'actual military contacts'"—as opposed to NACC events, which Shalikashvili (like Talbott) saw as having become "'just talk.'"[165] While not identical to the kind of pan-European security organization Mitterrand had once promoted—it was too US-centric for that—PfP nonetheless had the potential to take on aspects of such a far-reaching, inclusive organization.[166]

Fourth, the Partnership defined a place for Ukraine in a European security system in a way that did not alienate Russia. Ukraine could have partnership as soon as any other country, whereas its chances of joining NATO were much slimmer. And last but definitely not least, PfP averted the worst Russian reactions, since it did not involve adding new, full members to the alliance anytime soon. This last trait was particularly desirable since, as the US embassy in Moscow advised, "now is not the time to move forward on questions of expanded alliance membership for any of the former Warsaw Pact states (including Russia)" because Russian democracy "remains a fragile entity; we and our NATO allies should not do anything which jeopardizes" its chances.[167]

As an added bonus, PfP enabled Washington to put potential NATO membership at the end, rather than the beginning, of a long-term process.[168] Enlarging the alliance created a great deal of complexity, and the partnership provided a venue in which to address unexpected problems and stagger entry into the alliance if needed. As Albright asked Clinton, Gore, Christopher, and Lake on January 26, 1994, "have we dealt with the realistic possibility that Moscow will qualify before the others do" for NATO membership? By implication, PfP could help to manage that contingency as well, by providing a berth for Russia for an extended period.

The Partnership had its drawbacks, of course. One of the biggest was that NATO had become popular; everyone wanted in. In contrast to full-guarantee membership, PfP seemed like the geopolitical equivalent of an unattractive waiting room. Former Secretary of State Henry Kissinger also criticized it for an aspect that its supporters saw as its biggest advantage: the way PfP provided a berth for all post–Soviet Bloc states. He felt that this feature unnecessarily forced "'victims of Soviet and Russian imperialism'" to coexist with "'perpetrators'" in Moscow. Because of these objections, selling PfP would be a heavy lift, and it was not clear that all key stakeholders would commit to the effort necessary to make that lift work.

But for all its drawbacks and lack of glamour, PfP achieved the near impossible: it reconciled competing political imperatives and provided a strategy for the United States to address the challenges and opportunities in the Visegrad states, Russia, and Ukraine. For that reason, Albright praised it extensively in early 1994 (and still recalled it as an inspired idea years later). The Czech-born diplomat had, at the president's request, taken trips to Albania, Bulgaria, Romania, Slovenia, and the Visegrad states to gauge reactions to the partnership. She reported that "PfP turned out to be considerably more effective than most critics predicted." One reason the policy received support on her trip, despite falling short of full NATO membership, was that "all were concerned about how Ukraine fits into the picture and understood the danger of leaving it out." Despite denigrating PfP as a waiting room, "ultimately, all said they understood the need to avoid, in the near term, 'new artificial dividing lines in Europe.'" In her view, the partnership succeeded at fulfilling "three seemingly competing objectives: to revitalize NATO, to avoid antagonizing Russia by feeding nationalist tendencies, and to calm growing fears in Central and Eastern Europe."[169]

The Partnership also won over Talbott. Talbott thought the State Department should make PfP "rather than expanded NATO membership (which is at least implicitly exclusive) the centerpiece of our NATO position."[170] He particularly counseled against making "happy hints" in private to Central and Eastern European states about getting into NATO because such hints might undermine "our support for reform further East—especially in Russia—which, after all, the President keeps saying is our No. 1 priority." In addition, "the coming six to nine months are just as critical for our relations with Ukraine and, more specifically, our attempt to get them to give up the nukes, which is the single most important and dangerous non-proliferation challenge we face." Talbott had been dismayed that "Kravchuk's ministers have been trying to trade the nukes for membership in NATO"; now PfP would give Washington an out.[171]

With State's support, the Pentagon's view carried the day at the October 18, 1993 principals' meeting.[172] Clinton quickly approved the plan, enabling the secretaries of state and defense to hit the road and begin selling it. The idea was to convince allies that the 1994 NATO summit should issue a "statement of principle that NATO's membership will grow to include new democracies in Europe's east" but "without setting criteria . . . or a timetable." While that would disappoint the Visegrad countries, the vagueness was a strategic necessity because "doing anything at this stage to indicate that NATO's border will move closer to Russia and Ukraine without at the same time including those two states would have major negative consequences within both," ultimately making "the Central Europeans less secure."[173] The resulting policy recommendation for the upcoming 1994 NATO summit was essentially to launch PfP but remain vague on its connection to, and the timetable for, future expansion.[174]

Meanwhile, Lake was reportedly angry at being on the losing end of the debate—even more so when, later that year, Zbigniew Brzezinski, President Carter's former national security advisor, complained that Bush had gotten Germany into NATO, so Clinton had to do the same for Poland.[175] Brzezinski would soon thereafter write a *Foreign Affairs* article condemning PfP as "dangerous in its likely geopolitical consequences." In his view, "insurance is needed against the possibility—one might even argue the probability—that the weight of history will not soon permit Russia to stabilize as a democracy." Only NATO expansion could provide that insurance.[176]

Undeterred, Christopher presented the idea of PfP to Yeltsin and
Kozyrev in Russia on October 22, 1993.[177] In the presidential dacha in
Zavidovo, formerly Brezhnev's hunting lodge, the secretary explained
the partnership in an overheated solarium filled with stuffed game. A
skeptical Kozyrev asked, would NATO add "two or three new members
now?"[178] Christopher replied no, the United States was now "emphasizing
a Partnership for Peace" in order to "develop a habit of interoperability
and cooperation" before adding members.[179] Yeltsin asked him to clarify
that "all countries in CEE [Central and Eastern Europe] and the NIS
[newly independent states of the former Soviet Union] would, therefore,
be on an equal footing." Christopher replied, "'Yes, that is the case, there
would not even be an associate status.'"

Hearing that, the Russian president announced, "'this is a brilliant
idea, it is a stroke of genius.'" He added that "this served to dissipate all of
the tension which we now have in Russia regarding East European states
and their aspirations with regard to NATO." In case Christopher missed
the point, Yeltsin repeated that "'it really is a great idea, really great.'" He
was also thrilled to hear that Clinton was accepting an invitation to visit
Moscow right after the NATO summit. With the fight against parliament
behind him, rapid NATO expansion off the table, and a good relationship with Clinton developing, Yeltsin mused that "'the only thing left for
me to bury is Lenin.'" He repeated that the secretary of state should tell
"'Bill I am thrilled by this brilliant stroke.'"[180]

Toward the end of their conversation, Christopher mentioned briefly
that "we will in due course be looking at the question of membership as a
longer term eventuality," but that caveat seems not to have registered with
Yeltsin. Kozyrev remarked later, however, that he did not miss it and was
deeply concerned about what it might mean. The foreign minister decided
in hindsight that the Americans' performance in front of Yeltsin was "little
more than a smokescreen" and intentionally "deceptive," even though
the secretary's account represented an accurate depiction of US policy at
the time.[181]

The episode nonetheless produced a hardening in Kozyrev's attitude
toward Washington, one that did not go unnoticed. Talbott confided to
Clinton afterward that the Russian foreign minister had "become part of
the problem rather than part of the solution. . . . Kozyrev seems to have
concluded that both his own interests and Russia's require a tougher, more
nationalistic tone." Since Kozyrev had previously been a promoter of US-
Russian cooperation, Talbott felt that this "puzzling, disturbing development" had a dimension of "tragedy to it."[182]

Yeltsin, however, came away satisfied from the conversation. He even spoke afterward with Wörner about the prospects for Moscow's own eventual membership in NATO, suggesting they "get together to prepare for and discuss Russian membership in the alliance."[183] The main worry, as expressed by Kozyrev, was that "Russia as a great country will have trouble seeing itself in the waiting room with all the other supplicants competing for membership."[184] But Yeltsin remained optimistic that these matters could be resolved. His main "worry on this subject is the Chinese aspect" because Russian membership would mean China was sharing a border—the longest in the world—with a massive pan-European security organization. Yeltsin was "ready to engage regardless."[185]

With PfP, Clinton and his advisors had produced a workable solution to the strategic problems they had inherited on Inauguration Day. The main challenge had been clear since that first cold, sunny afternoon in January: how to promote US foreign policy interests, particularly in eliminating the former Soviet nuclear arsenal, by balancing demands from Russia with those from the major states and regions it had formerly dominated. Clinton's team had stumbled over a number of domestic and foreign issues, at times tragically, but it had figured out the smart move in the end: partnership for the many. Rather than calling the question of whether Russia, Ukraine, or Visegrad mattered most, the United States would instead lead the alliance's expansion with a phased process that kept its options open.

While this process was much less dramatic than extending Article 5, in practice PfP worked surprisingly well. As Christopher recalled, in its early days "the Partnership exceeded even our most hopeful expectations." It created "links between NATO and non-member nations" and gave participants "an incentive to modernize their armed forces and pursue democratic reforms."[186] The Partnership even attracted Western and Nordic neutral countries that had shied away from NATO, such as Austria, Finland, Sweden, and Switzerland. The concept also proved acceptable— in places minimally, but sufficiently—to Central and Eastern Europe, Ukraine, and Russia. Most unhappy were the Visegrad countries, but they were willing to accept PfP through gritted teeth as long as it eventually led to membership.

Opponents of PfP inside the United States, however, were not willing to live with the compromise. Clinton administration policymakers who wanted to extend Article 5 to Visegrad, thereby calling the question of which region mattered most, immediately challenged the nascent partnership. Meanwhile, the Republican Party recognized a useful way to attract Polish-Americans and others of Eastern European descent in crucial midwestern states during the US congressional midterm election of 1994.[187] And Yeltsin would unintentionally help the enemies of PfP with a series of major and bloody errors. The combination of these events would cause the partnership to fall as swiftly as it rose.

CHAPTER SIX

Rise and Fall

LTHOUGH THE STRATEGY of a loose partnership for the many
had gained presidential blessing, American and foreign proponents of full membership for the few immediately sought to
overturn it. They felt that Central and Eastern Europeans, having suffered so much in the wars of the twentieth century and the decades behind the Iron Curtain, had a historical and moral right to the full
weight of the Article 5 guarantee as soon as possible. Issues like Russian
resistance and new members' military readiness could be sorted out later;
what mattered now was righting the past. Advocates of such full-guarantee
expansion generally acted out of either an optimistic or a pessimistic
motive—sometimes both. Optimists believed enlargement would promote so much cooperation that borders would cease to matter, so there was
no need to worry about drawing a new dividing line through Europe; the
alliance, and the continent, would simply move beyond past policies of
division and containment. Pessimists regarded a new front line across
Europe as an advantage rather than a curse, since they still saw Russia as a
threat; they sought swift enlargement precisely because it offered containment beyond the Cold War.[1] The strategy in both cases was the same: stran-
gle the Partnership for Peace in the cradle and give Article 5 to a select group
of states instead.

That strategy succeeded: the year 1994 saw the swift rise and fall of
PfP. After President Bill Clinton launched it in January, skilled bureaucratic in-fighters like National Security Advisor Tony Lake and Assistant

Secretary of State Richard Holbrooke immediately mounted an extended
attack. With the fervent support of foreign leaders like German defense
minister Volker Rühe and Polish president Lech Wałęsa, they took advantage of disagreements between Moscow and Washington to undermine
the Partnership. The Democrats' dramatic loss in the US midterm congressional elections of November 1994 to the pro-expansion Republican
Party tipped a wavering Clinton fully toward Lake and his colleagues.
Soon after the election, it was clear that the cumulative weight of the year's
events—capped in December by Russian president Boris Yeltsin's tragic
decision to invade the breakaway region of Chechnya and Defense Secretary Bill Perry's failed last-minute effort to defend PfP—had prompted
Clinton to abandon the Partnership. The president would afterward recall that 1994, which also included his beloved mother's death, was "one
of the hardest" years of his life.[2]

The Importance of Not Drawing a Line

All of those developments were still in the future as the president made
plans to go to Europe in January 1994. The Partnership was the policy,
and the goal was to prepare the ground in advance of Clinton's formal announcement at the January summit. As part of that process, on October 25, 1993, Secretary of State Warren Christopher visited the Ukrainian
president, Leonid Kravchuk.[3] It was worth Christopher's time to make
sure Kravchuk understood that PfP had edged out full-guarantee expansion in large part because of Ukraine, and that Ukraine should respond
by denuclearizing.

It helped Christopher's case that Kyiv had little choice but to comply
with US wishes. Ukraine still had nuclear weapons, but the need to bar-
ter them in exchange for support for its disintegrating economy was increasing.[4] American diplomats were reporting home that heart-wrenching
scenes of desperation and hunger had become common throughout the
country, including "elderly lining the sides of streets selling their used
household goods" and "children abandoned under the seats" in the capital's main train station. One embassy officer observed that, at the cafete-
ria outside Kyiv State University, pensioners were hovered "around trash
bins, fighting for the food that students throw out." Another American
diplomat was grabbed in a grocery store by a sobbing woman, who begged
for help after realizing that she could no longer afford even a container of
sour cream. Workers at the embassy had trouble getting to work, as buses

and trams were ceasing to operate. Pollution from decrepit industries also poisoned the air and the land. For most Ukrainians, US diplomats concluded, life had "lost any margin of comfort."[5]

If Kyiv increasingly felt it had no other options, the Visegrad states felt the opposite: they could and should do better. The US embassy in Budapest reported to Washington on October 29 that the Hungarians felt "strong disappointment" because of the Partnership's "lack of differentiation between the Visegrad group and what they perceive to be the less advanced states to the east," meaning Ukraine and other post-Soviet republics.[6] Wałęsa let journalists know he viewed PfP as "'blackmail,'" and Polish diplomats amplified that message.[7]

Internally, the State Department recorded its disappointment at such pushback, saying the "vehemence" did Central and Eastern Europeans' cause little good.[8] Christopher responded to Polish complaints on December 14, 1993 by pointing out that "to extend the security perimeter of the alliance is as important a foreign policy decision as the US can take."[9] But to soften the blow, he let all Visegrad states know that while PfP "will not guarantee admission to NATO," the alliance nonetheless "expects and would welcome new members in the future, as part of an evolutionary process."[10]

The Clinton administration felt this pressure not just from the Visegrad countries themselves but also from members of Congress whose constituents had family backgrounds in the region. Why should their voters' ancestral countries not be able to choose their own military alliance and receive help from the United States? American muscle should be there for Poles and others if they wanted it, members of Congress felt, because the United States had won the Cold War and had muscle to spare. In 1994 there were still roughly 325,000 US military personnel permanently stationed overseas, and another 60,000 temporarily afloat or abroad.[11]

In the House, Republican Benjamin Gilman of New York sponsored a pro-expansion resolution with the vocal support of Zbigniew Brzezinski; his colleague Representative Henry Hyde, a Republican from Illinois, did something similar. In summer 1994, their staff members began combining some of the wording for use in the Republican Party's "Contract with America," a collection of initiatives circulated as part of the party's campaign for the November midterm elections.[12] Also later that year, Senator Richard Lugar, a strong opponent of the Partnership, took to saying that PfP stood for "'policy for postponement.'"[13]

Realizing he had a selling job to do with PfP, both at home and abroad, Clinton sent General John Shalikashvili, the chairman of the JCS, to convince Central and Eastern European countries that supporting PfP was in their interest.[14] Madeleine Albright, the Czech-born US ambassador to the UN, and Charles Gati, a Hungarian-born US diplomat, went on yet more trips, at times joining the chairman. Together or separately, they spoke with all of the Visegrad leaders as well as those of Bulgaria, Romania, Albania, and Slovenia.[15]

The Poles in particular wisely tried to turn Shalikashvili's visits to their advantage. His father, Dmitri Shalikashvili, had emigrated from Soviet Georgia to Poland and served in the Polish Army at the time John was born. Later, the family moved to the United States. In preparation for one of the general's visits, his Polish hosts searched the military archives and discovered paperwork that the elder Shalikashvili had filed with superior officers upon the birth of his son in 1936. They presented copies to the JCS chairman, who was moved by the gift.[16]

General Shalikashvili nonetheless tried to flatter Wałęsa into accepting PfP during a trip on January 7, 1994, urging the Polish leader "to display the political courage and savvy that made him famous." Wałęsa responded that "the West is losing an important historic opportunity to 'cage the bear.'" He thought "NATO had already missed two easy opportunities to expand NATO to the East"—one right after the collapse of the Soviet Union, and the other in "'the half hour after Yeltsin signed'" his drunken declaration in August 1993. While it was "already too late to stop Russia's full control over the Commonwealth of Independent states," there might be time to save the states that were beyond "the old Soviet frontier."

When the Americans defended their actions by saying that enlargement would anger Moscow, Wałęsa growled, "'let the Russian generals get upset . . . they won't launch a nuclear war.'"[17] Poland was disappointed that after everything Solidarity had done to overthrow Soviet control, only East Germany had been given an entry ticket to the West. Shalikashvili, trying to mollify Wałęsa, pointed out that "PfP would establish unprecedented patterns and levels of military cooperation that would promote enhanced interoperability with NATO forces." In an attempt to mollify his host, he added that the debate in NATO "lately is less about whether to expand to the east, but when and how."

The concession made Wałęsa reconsider, and the US ambassador to Poland bet that Wałęsa would eventually give in.[18] He was right. The Poles grudgingly came around. After an extraordinary Polish cabinet meeting in which PfP was criticized as "an insufficient measure," the Polish government nonetheless agreed to support it.[19]

In the wake of such efforts, Clinton traveled to Belgium for the NATO summit. After arriving on January 9, 1994, he told the prime minister of Belgium, Jean-Luc Dehaene, that the attacks on the Partnership were misguided. As Clinton put it, "why should we draw the line in Europe just a little further east than before? Why should we alienate Ukraine?" PfP was preferable because it avoided both problems. The president then suggested that the United States should "continue to take the lead with Russia," while "Europe should take most of the initiative vis-à-vis Eastern Europe."

Dehaene pushed back, saying, "to take them in now quickly would weaken the EU."[20] Becoming an EU member was an exhaustive, exacting process, which in his view would be unwise to rush. He was hardly alone in this view. A "sizable portion of the members of the European Union in reality do not want enlargement," German chancellor Helmut Kohl complained to Washington; he knew his personal push for early accession for Central and Eastern Europe was unpopular among his fellow leaders of member states. The reasons were varied. The reluctance was partly due to the decision to focus on membership for Western and Scandinavian states first. Southern member states also feared losing advantages if too many new members appeared.[21] And Europeans felt overwhelmed by the Bosnian crisis.[22] The United States and NATO would have to open doors to Eastern countries, because the EU was not going to do so any time soon.

In his formal address to fellow NATO leaders on January 10, 1994, Clinton emphasized again the importance of not drawing "a new line through Europe just a little further east" that would leave a "democratic Ukraine" sitting on the wrong side. The Partnership was the best answer, he explained, because it opened a door but also gave "us time to reach out to Russia and to these other nations of the former Soviet Union, which have been almost ignored through this entire debate."[23] He persuaded his allies to adopt PfP formally and to begin implementing its practical aspects.[24] The alliance opened a "Partnership Coordination Cell" to plan exercises and training.[25] Almost immediately, several states expressed interest in joining; within weeks of the January NATO summit, the Lithuanian president traveled to Brussels and signed up his country.[26]

Meeting Wałęsa and Czech president Václav Havel in Prague immediately after the summit, Clinton yet again used the same arguments he had used with his allies. As he told them on January 11, PfP "lets us begin right now joint training and exercising and the introduction of NATO troops" into Central and Eastern Europe but does not "draw another line dividing Europe a few hundred miles east." He also repeated that "Ukraine especially does not want to be pushed back into Russia's orbit" or find itself left alone on the wrong side of a front line. "Of all countries in the world," he added, the Visegrad states "should understand the damage of dividing lines, of pushing former Soviet republics into Russia's orbit."[27]

Christopher and Ambassador Strobe Talbott, accompanying the president along with Albright, were even blunter. Talbott in particular argued that "one of the best things" about PfP "was that it could go in either direction: it could lean forward to accept Russia if the 'good bear' emerges, but could also lead to a post–Cold War variant of containment" if needed.[28] Havel and his peers still kept pushing back. Wałęsa informed Clinton that whenever Russians signed an agreement, "one hand held a pen; the other a grenade." The Visegrad countries "kept their word" because "they had a Western culture. Russia did not."[29] Havel argued that Clinton must make clear "PfP is a first step leading to full NATO membership" before they would accept it.[30]

Clinton had stuck to the script until now, but the resistance was fierce. Saying no to leaders with the moral standing of Wałęsa and Havel was not easy. The latter man had developed particularly warm relations with the American president, wining and dining Clinton generously as the local host, and making abundantly clear not only to Clinton but also to his fellow Prague native Albright how much the Czechs wanted to be part of the West.[31] The Czech and Polish leaders were hard to resist, and their concerns apparently inspired Clinton to try to find the maximum possible amount of agreement. Always the optimist, he was inclined not to see foreign policy challenges as zero-sum games; instead, in any situation where persuasion was required, he tried to bring everybody along to a mutually agreeable conclusion.[32] He also felt, based on an avid reading of biographies of former Democratic presidents Franklin Roosevelt and Harry Truman, that "neither had grand strategies for how to exert American leadership." Rather, his predecessors had possessed "'powerful instincts about what had to be done'" and followed those, pragmatically tacking when events demanded. This seemed to be one of those times.[33] Since he sympathized with the arguments on all sides, this instinct to promote the greatest possible cooperation led him to complicate the launch of PfP.

Given how dramatic the stage in Prague was, any public comment was sure to receive ample notice. Clinton had even hired the Hollywood producer Mort Engelberg to stage a dramatic walk against the backdrop of Prague's stunning architecture.[34] Photographers snapped Albright, Clinton, and Havel as the convivial party admired the Charles Bridge's statues and stunning views, providing a powerful visual symbol of US support for the Czechs and, by extension, other countries in the region. Albright later recalled that Clinton was greatly moved by this remarkable visit to Prague, among other reasons because it provided distraction from his beloved mother's death just five days earlier.[35]

At the press conference for the summit on January 12, Clinton decided to repeat publicly what Shalikashvili had told Wałęsa privately five days earlier. "While the Partnership is not NATO membership," he announced, "neither is it a permanent holding room. It changes the entire NATO dialogue so that now the question is no longer whether NATO will take on new members but when and how."[36] These words—"no longer whether . . . but when and how"—created new complexity at a stroke, as listeners took away different lessons from them.

On the one hand, supporters of PfP heard them as an endorsement of what had already been decided: the Partnership provided the "how." European allies, as one NSC staff member later recalled, felt that the results of the NATO summit had clearly laid out a path for slow enlargement over the next decade via PfP. But on the other hand, opponents of PfP realized that if they dropped the words "and how," then "not whether but when" was a hugely useful slogan to rally their own partisans. As Lake remarked after the press conference in Prague: "'Finally . . . we've got a Presidential marker.'"[37] Similarly, German defense minister Rühe, a strong supporter of rapid enlargement, started using the slogan at every opportunity, dropping the "how" that Clinton himself always added when he repeated the line.[38]

These words also made Clinton's next stop, in Moscow, more difficult.[39] Russian foreign minister Andrei Kozyrev felt that his worst fears had been confirmed. As Clinton "careened from position to position in connection with NATO enlargement," Kozyrev became increasingly certain PfP was a fraud designed solely to hide hasty enlargement from Moscow.[40] Anticipating his resistance, Clinton's staffers prepared a thick briefing book of arguments why PfP was the right policy, and why it remained advantageous to Russia. As their talking points put it, the partnership's main value lay "in advancing Russia's integration into the new European security architecture." It was "a door to the future and not only for Russia." It provided "security underpinnings for countries—Ukraine, Kazakhstan—that otherwise might not be willing to give up nuclear weapons."[41] As Clinton explained to Yeltsin when they met, "a lot of people in the US and some in Europe . . . felt I should have given early membership for the Visegrad countries." But he did not want to give up on "something that has never been done since the rise of the nation state itself—and that is have a Europe that is truly integrated and not divided."[42]

Yeltsin was more forgiving than Kozyrev. He grasped the significance of sticking with a phased approach but stressed that "Russia has to be the first country to join NATO. Then the others from Central and Eastern Europe can come in." Yeltsin noted, however, that "'Russia is not yet ready to join NATO,'" in part because he was still worried about the "potential Chinese reaction."[43] Clinton deflected criticism by shifting to a shared success: Ukrainian denuclearization.[44]

Kravchuk's desperate economic situation had led him to agree to a trilateral setup.[45] In exchange for transferring weapons to Russia by mid-1996 and joining the NPT as a nonnuclear state, Ukraine would receive financial and other forms of American "assistance to help with the disposal of ICBMs, ICBM silos, bombers, and other infrastructure on Ukrainian territory."[46] The United States, Russia, and Britain, in their formal roles as NPT depository states, also promised that they would assure—not guarantee—Ukrainian territorial integrity.[47] The difference between the words *assure* and *guarantee* might seem slight, but mattered in security terms. A *guarantee* meant the odds that the US Eighty-Second Airborne Division would show up in response to a crisis in Ukraine were high, and an *assurance* meant they were low. Kravchuk had finally assented nonetheless, having little other choice. He told the US ambassador in Kyiv that he was willing to "'confront'" Ukrainian parliamentarians and convince them to back this deal despite its drawbacks.[48] The three signed the resulting Trilateral Accord on January 14, 1994, during the US president's visit to Moscow.

Back in Washington, Clinton reviewed his European trip with a visiting Kohl over a hearty lunch at Filomena Ristorante. The president asked his visitor what he thought about developments in Ukraine. The chancellor responded, "'I told Yeltsin that even any suspicion that Russia wanted to annex Ukraine would be catastrophic.'" Clinton agreed, saying that "'if Ukraine collapses, because of Russian influence or because of militant nationalists within Ukraine or any other reason, it would undermine the whole theory of NATO's Partnership for Peace. Ukraine is the linchpin of the whole idea.'" Indeed, "'one reason why all the former Warsaw Pact states were willing to support [PfP] was because they understood what we were saying about Ukraine'" and the importance of not drawing new dividing lines across Europe.

Kohl agreed on the significance of avoiding new fronts in Europe, adding that he remained frustrated by his inability to get the EU to expand more quickly. He was disappointed in his fellow EU leaders but knew that he could push the topic only so far. Germany was stretched financially: by that point, it was committed to giving roughly $75 billion to Russia, the NIS, and Central and Eastern Europe, and he would have a hard time bankrolling the costly addition of needy members to the EU. His country simply could not afford the additional EU agricultural subsidies, structural adjustment transfers, or cohesion funds that would be due to potential new members.[49] Kohl was therefore all the happier that Clinton had, by contrast, found a workable strategy for slowly starting enlargement of the Atlantic Alliance.[50] Clinton's first trip to Europe as president, he said, had been "a big success."[51]

Strangling the Partnership in the Cradle

In the wake of that success, in March 1994 Perry traveled to Ukraine, where he inspected hardened nuclear launch sites. The first one he visited, controlling 700 nuclear warheads, had a wall covered by maps of the warheads' targets. He watched the officers on duty perform a simulated launch and was "overwhelmed with the absurdity of the situation" as he observed the obliteration of Chicago, Los Angeles, New York, San Francisco, and Washington. As Perry put it, "never has the surrealistic horror of the Cold War been more vivid to me than at that moment."[52] He was happy that former Soviet states were dismantling such weapons—and cooperating in PfP.

The success of early 1994, however, proved to be all too brief. The Partnership was doomed by a combination of missteps by Yeltsin and aggressive maneuvering by PfP's opponents during its implementation. Moscow, to Washington's intense dismay, began aggressively insisting on a special status for Russia within PfP.[53] Yeltsin and his advisors felt—not unreasonably—that as a nuclear power and member of the UN Security Council, Russia deserved some kind of premier partnership.[54] It was galling to them that Estonia was among the first countries to join PfP while Moscow was still far back in line—not least because Russia and Estonia were still negotiating the withdrawal of former Soviet troops.[55] As Yeltsin confided to Kohl, he needed "a statement or 'protocol' that makes it clear that Russia is different from all other countries joining the PfP" because it was a "'great country with a great army and nuclear weapons.'"[56] By June, there were nineteen members in PfP, but Russia had not received any offer of premier membership.[57]

As a result, Yeltsin's advisors turned instead to trying to dilute and weaken PfP; one means of downgrading it was to upgrade the CSCE.[58] Kozyrev thought Russia needed more clarity about the "roles of NATO and CSCE" relative to each other, to avoid the sense that the alliance was "making a 'victorious march eastward.'"[59] He had grown even more disillusioned with his US counterparts, describing them to at least one colleague as "Western thugs."[60]

NATO's increasing role in Bosnia also became, paradoxically, a factor in marginalizing PfP. Even though part of the justification for the Partnership was to have a NATO-adjacent entity to deal with Bosnia, the alliance assumed that role itself. On February 28, 1994, US F-16 fighter jets in the service of NATO shot down four Serbian aircraft carrying out a bombing mission in violation of a UN no-fly zone—NATO's first combat action since its founding in 1949.[61] In a contentious meeting after that, the secretary general, Manfred Wörner—who was now suffering from advanced cancer and needed a physician present just to get through meetings—convinced allies to agree to expand the alliance's role in Bosnia even further. (Wörner would pass away that August, to be followed in office by Willy Claes, the Belgian foreign minister, who continued his predecessor's policies.)[62] And, although unrelated, the 1994 massacre in Rwanda increased the sense that timely intervention was needed to prevent such tragedies elsewhere.

Clinton called Yeltsin about Bosnia on April 10, 1994, since the Russian was dismayed by what he viewed as overly aggressive behavior by NATO, to clarify that "I have no interest in NATO air power changing the course of the war on the ground or changing the balance of the war." He wanted to work with Yeltsin to get all parties "to negotiate some cessation of hostilities."[63] Yeltsin remained unconvinced.

Assessing Moscow's hardening stance, Christopher found that he, British foreign secretary Douglas Hurd, and Hurd's political director, Pauline Neville-Jones, all agreed that it did not bode well. Neville-Jones noted disapprovingly that Moscow "appeared to envisage CSCE as an overriding framework, embracing both NATO" and the former Soviet space. In part because the Russians "felt burned by NATO's decisions on Bosnia," they "wanted to get a grip on our institutions, and equal standing for theirs."[64] These Russian demands were particularly unwelcome in

Washington as the 1994 election campaign heated up.[65] Republicans made clear that they would urge swifter expansion of NATO. Moscow's actions thus came at an unwelcome time, particularly as tensions flared over the 1994 arrest of Aldrich Ames, a CIA officer turned Russian mole.

Visegrad leaders seized on Moscow's missteps to push for full membership; an unrelated nuclear crisis with North Korea that spring also helped them indirectly, by increasing the general sense of threat. The new Polish ambassador to the United States, Jerzy Koźmiński, met with Talbott, now deputy secretary of state, on June 10, 1994 to complain that Poles would only get into NATO "if Russia 'goes bad.'" Talbott contradicted the Polish ambassador, and in doing so revealed his personal take on PfP. Unlike the Pentagon, he saw it the way Kozyrev did: as a placeholder. He explained that PfP was simply one part of a larger plan, based on the handling of eastern Germany in 1990. "The Soviets initially refused to accept that the former East Germany would become part of the alliance," Talbott told Koźmiński, "but over time and with effective reassurances were able to bring themselves to agree." Now he was using the same strategy for the rest of former Warsaw Pact.[66]

Others within the administration also saw PfP as a placeholder, but an unnecessary one. Alexander Vershbow, the NSC senior director for Europe and a strong proponent of full-guarantee expansion, decided to seize on Russian missteps and on a speech the president had recently given in Poland. Visiting there on July 7, 1994, Clinton had repeated that bringing "new members into NATO, as I have said many times, is no longer a question of whether, but when and how."[67] In the wake of that speech, Vershbow, with backing from his NSC colleagues Nicholas Burns and Daniel Fried—known collectively as the pro-expansion troika—made a compelling case for jettisoning PfP.[68] He advised his boss on July 15, 1994 that, while not overtly devaluing the Partnership "in the eyes" of European and post-Soviet countries, Washington should privately inform certain states they had a future with the alliance while Moscow did not. Since "at the end of the day, Russia is not going to qualify for NATO membership," the goal should be a separate "'alliance with the Alliance' for Moscow." This comment represented one of the first written internal statements that Russia was never going to join NATO, providing an answer to the question Albright had asked in January 1994 as to whether anyone had truly thought through the question of Moscow's potential membership.[69]

One consequence of a special alliance-with-the-Alliance would be marginalization of the new PfP and magnification of the eternal question of what to do about Ukraine, which was becoming a renewed source of worry. In summer 1994, Kravchuk lost the Ukrainian presidential election to Leonid Kuchma, a rocket engineer and manager of a missile factory, who showed a fresh willingness to challenge Washington. Soon after taking office, he asked President Clinton pointedly why "no practical steps" had been taken to deliver $350 million promised earlier that year.[70] (Clinton promised to investigate, and on October 13 informed Kuchma that $130 million would be made available by the end of the year.)[71] The new Ukrainian president also made clear that, despite what his predecessor had accepted, denuclearization and Ukraine's accession to the NPT would "not be an overriding priority for him."[72] Ukraine thus rose back up Clinton's priority list, leading the president to try to "make friends" with Kuchma.[73]

The chance that Vershbow's approach to expansion—one without a berth for Ukraine—would succeed despite pressure from Kuchma increased when, at long last, former Soviet forces finally exited Germany. Berlin marked the final withdrawal with a ceremony on August 31, 1994. The departure had originally been scheduled for December, but Kohl had offered an additional $550 million if the troops left a few months sooner, and Yeltsin took it.[74] The numbers were enormous: since German unification on October 3, 1990, a staggering 338,800 Soviet soldiers, 163,700 dependents, and 44,700 civilian employees had all left Germany.[75]

The farewell ceremony marked a humiliating low point in Russian foreign policy. The victory over the Nazis had been a central component of Soviet and Russian identity, politics, and life for decades. Now Moscow was having to beat what felt to Russians like an unworthy retreat. As Russia expert Angela Stent put it, "homeless, unemployed officers symbolized the dramatic humiliation of the once great Soviet armed forces and were potentially a major source of support for right-wing groups."[76] Chancellor Kohl made somber remarks, noting how ten or even six years earlier the withdrawal would have been unthinkable. He spoke movingly of the tragedy of World War II and the millions who had died tragically "in the name of Germany."[77] Unfortunately, Yeltsin had begun drinking heavily the night before, and he continued throughout the morning of the ceremony. As a military band started playing, he unsteadily seized the baton and started conducting. He then tried to prompt the audience to join him in singing the folk song "Kalinka Malinka." Some of his aides were so horrified that they later wrote Yeltsin a joint plea that he address his dependency on "'the well-known Russian vice.'"[78]

Perhaps Yeltsin had felt the need to drink more than usual because he understood the Soviet pullout had more than symbolic significance. It ended the temporary prohibition, granted in the two-plus-four treaty, on NATO forces entering eastern German territory. German alliance forces now had full access to the area, and foreign NATO troops could be there as well with the German government's permission.[79] None of those troops could have nuclear weapons or carriers outfitted for transporting such weapons, or be permanently stationed, but NATO forces could now be active east of the Cold War front line. Yeltsin was a savvy politician and understood intuitively that it was a significant precedent.

Americans also conducted their own withdrawal from Berlin that summer—although, in contrast to Russian troops, some of their forces were remaining in Germany. Those forces would be keeping up a decades-long relationship between US troops and German communities. Between 1945 and 1990, an astounding 15 million US soldiers and family members lived in divided Germany, reshaping the country not only militarily but also culturally and politically. Even in 1990, the United States still had 227,586 soldiers, 254,710 dependents, and 32,203 civilian employees in West Germany and West Berlin.[80] Some of the US bases had long since become sizeable towns in their own right, with American post offices, police forces, schools, and the US dollar as legal tender, even though they were on German soil. By the end of 1995, Washington would reduce those numbers to 83,000 troops and support personnel in uniform in united Germany, as part of a contingent of 109,000 forces in Europe overall.[81]

As part of a series of events to mark the withdrawal of Western allied troops from Berlin, the Germans hosted a ceremony on September 9, 1994 to celebrate "New Traditions" in Germany's relations with the United States. The moving force behind this event was Holbrooke, who was then the outgoing US ambassador to Germany. One of the most vehement opponents of PfP, he was already in transition to his next job as assistant secretary of state for European and Eurasian affairs. Talbott had hired him for that position because Holbrooke was well-known in Democratic foreign policy circles as the policymaking equivalent of a bulldozer, which was what the deputy secretary wanted. As Talbott reportedly remarked when offering Holbrooke the job, "'we assume you will be aggressive.'" Holbrooke also knew Lake from their time as young foreign service officers in Vietnam. Although their friendship had unraveled—Holbrooke was rumored to have had an affair with Lake's wife—professionally they shared the same goal: to move forward aggressively with NATO expansion. Holbrooke's main focus in his new job was former Yugoslavia (as he said in his memoirs, "there was rarely a day when

Bosnia did not overwhelm every other issue"), but he found time to oppose PfP nonetheless. The "New Traditions" ceremony marked the beginning of his sustained assault.[82]

Holbrooke conspired in that effort with Rühe. The two men shared a conviction that Poland must be added to NATO as swiftly as possible.[83] They decided to use the speeches at the ceremony to gain an edge over members of their respective governments opposed to enlargement. Vice President Al Gore had agreed to be the keynote speaker, but he had to deliver his address by video because of a leg injury. Holbrooke won an internal wrestling match and gained the right to author most of Gore's speech.[84] He had the vice president emphasize that the "collapse of the Soviet Union did not in and of itself present us with a benign new world order ripe for the taking." Rather, "it created a period of profound transition from which might emerge either the world we have struggled so hard to secure, or a world submerged in new nightmares." The best way to avoid such nightmares was by working with "the states of Central and Eastern Europe," which "regard NATO as the best hope for military stability and security."[85]

Rühe, who spoke next, reinforced Gore's words. "Not all countries in Central and Eastern Europe," he declared, "are candidates for integration." Hungary, Poland, and the Czech and Slovak Republics were worthy of consideration, but Russia "cannot be integrated, neither into the European Union nor into NATO." The German defense minister next attacked the vague relationship of PfP to future membership: it was "wrong to pursue a policy that is determined by the highest possible degree of ambiguity."[86] In short, while PfP was still in its nascent stage—the first multilateral exercises were scheduled for later that month in Poland—Holbrooke and Rühe were already undermining it.[87]

For Perry, seated onstage at the event, these attacks came as a surprise. During the clearance process for the speech, the Pentagon had reportedly crossed out Holbrooke's provocative phrases, but Holbrooke blindsided the secretary by reinserting them.[88] Perry, in his remarks just afterward, tried to walk back what had just been said.[89] The secretary and his aides still believed strongly in PfP; for them it was neither a placeholder nor a fraud but a way to integrate Russia. Of course, PfP had teething problems. One of the first visits, by an Albanian contingent to Louisiana, had gone wrong when the visitors reportedly disappeared into nearby woods, apparently in an attempt to avoid having to return to their home country.[90] Perry and US military leaders nonetheless saw such incidents as minor and far outweighed by PfP's benefits.

Holbrooke's stunt upset both Perry and his Defense Department colleagues—and they were hardly alone in this view. After witnessing Perry's upstaging, the British emphasized to Washington that "in deference to Russian sensitivities," they strongly preferred the "quiet approach of gradually absorbing the Visegrad into NATO via PfP." But Perry was not able to focus on pushing back against Holbrooke afterward because the Pentagon was engaged in Operation Uphold Democracy, a UN-approved and US-led move to reverse a coup against the democratically elected president of Haiti.[91] The operation even forced Perry to miss the first-ever joint peacekeeping exercise between American and Russian soldiers, which produced lasting bitterness on the part of Russian defense minister Pavel Grachev. The latter man had stuck his neck out to get the exercises running and felt abandoned when his US counterpart was a no-show.[92]

Holbrooke's campaign for rapid NATO expansion continued unchecked. He maneuvered himself into the chairmanship of a crucial interagency process on enlargement, an appointment for which he reportedly had Talbott to thank as well.[93] It was becoming obvious to insiders that the deputy secretary of state was not, as it had first seemed, opposed to NATO enlargement. Rather, Talbott had decided to get Moscow used to the idea of full-guarantee expansion in steps. Both the NACC and PfP had been useful precursors, providing visual symbolism as "genuinely inclusive post–Cold War security arrangements." Now he felt it was time to advance enlargement, but he did not want to telegraph this thinking too widely. Otherwise it might become a little too obvious, as he confided to Secretary Christopher on September 12, 1994, "that NATO expansion will, when it occurs, by definition be punishment, or 'neo-containment,' of the bad Bear."[94]

In the service of those goals, Holbrooke got his interagency process off to an aggressive start. The preparatory papers for the first session, on September 22, displayed a new bluntness. Discussions of phased-in, partial associations disappeared. The briefing papers stated bluntly that "the goal is to achieve NATO expansion." Just as George H. W. Bush had done with German unification, the United States needed to develop "a sense of inevitability" about this policy. The trick was to make opponents think that "the costs of obstructing the inevitable will be too high" and to concentrate on making "the objectionable palatable." All talk of "'compensation'" was to be avoided; rather, the United States should make others think enlargement "is in their interest."

As ever, Ukraine remained a major issue. "Expansion," Holbrooke's briefing admitted, "will leave it wedged between an Alliance it can probably never enter, and Russia." Once Ukrainian denuclearization was concluded satisfactorily, however, Kyiv's uncomfortable situation would be of less concern. Even Russian objections were of secondary importance: "We should not be deterred by whether a rationale for expansion can be sold to the Russians or others. They won't buy it now under any circumstances, and will try to block or delay." Hence, the "goal is to give them something we can use, and which they can work with, when the time comes."[95]

This blunt language caused immediate conflict. According to the accounts from the thirty-odd participants—some of whom leaked to the *Washington Post* immediately afterward—Holbrooke asserted that he had a mandate from the president to enlarge NATO. When Pentagon participants asked why the president had not informed anyone else of that mandate, Holbrooke reportedly cited the "not whether but when" slogan, presidential comments in Europe in July, and Gore's "New Traditions" speech (which Holbrooke had largely written) as proof.[96] General Wesley Clark of the JCS still objected, and Holbrooke shot back that his stance "'sounds like insubordination to me. We need to settle this right now. Either you are on the president's program, or you are not.'" Clark answered that he had never before been accused of insubordination. Participants worried (or hoped) that the two might come to blows. They did not, but the Defense Department fought back in other ways later, by showing the enormous cost and amount of work needed to integrate former Warsaw Pact states into the alliance. Pentagon representatives at one point dumped a four-foot stack of paper on the table in front of Holbrooke and his colleagues. The stack contained the NATO standards potential members would have to meet, covering everything from "helicopter launching pads to the circumference of gasoline nozzles."[97]

Neo-Containment

The same week that Holbrooke was barreling ahead with ways to outmaneuver Russia, Clinton and Yeltsin continued to make progress on reducing strategic weapons. Meeting in Washington on September 27, 1994, they listened to Perry provide an overview of his plans. "First," Perry began, "we will cooperate in ratifying START I and II and bringing them into force." Once that was achieved, "we will accelerate the pace of reductions, to go even faster by informal agreement, using Nunn-Lugar funds to do so." Third, "we will start discussing what reductions will be possible" under a new accord, START III.[98]

Clinton was also pressing Yeltsin on Russian biological weapons development, which the former Soviet leader, Mikhail Gorbachev, had claimed to have discontinued.[99] Yeltsin later admitted that "Gorbachev lied—or his military lied to him. Things were not stopped in 1988." After he came to power, Yeltsin had "ordered that all activity be stopped . . . [and] all the doors . . . locked and sealed." But "we had trouble finding jobs for people in the program. . . . These were people who are devoted to killing people with germs. Dealing with these people is not easy." Yet even though NATO expansion would decrease Yeltsin's willingness to move ahead with arms control, Clinton told him at the September summit that there "will be an expansion of NATO . . . we're going to move forward on this."[100] Trying, as ever, to bring everyone along, he reportedly softened the blow by reassuring Yeltsin that there were three "nos" in place: no surprises, no hurry, and no exclusion of any state from the expanded alliance.[101]

Yeltsin did not erupt in response, perhaps because he was in a stronger position domestically than he had been during previous meetings with Clinton. Inflation at home was down, and he had survived several challenges to his authority. He had even withdrawn all former Soviet troops from the Baltics a few weeks earlier, although it meant abandoning, in his words, the "'several tens of millions of Russians left marooned by the Soviet breakup.'" Yeltsin pointed out that those people thought they "'lived at home'" in the Baltics, but suddenly realized "'they are guests and not always welcomed.'"[102] Tensions between Moscow and the Baltics remained high even after the troops departed. General Clark later remembered that on a visit to Russia in 1994, one of the first questions he got asked was, roughly, how long until NATO ships show up in our port of Riga? Clark recalled replying with words to the effect of the following: it was not Russia's port, it was Latvia's, and leading questions like that one would only hasten the ships' arrival.[103]

Wrapping up, Yeltsin remained optimistic that all problems could be solved, and exclaimed that this was "'the best visit he ever had' to the US."[104] His hosts could not share the sentiment because the erratic drunken behavior on display in Berlin had gotten worse. On the first night of his visit, Yeltsin had reportedly prompted a major predawn alert after Secret Service agents found him walking on Pennsylvania Avenue dressed only in his underwear, drunk and waving for a taxi. When the agents tried to escort him back to his guest residence in Blair House, Yeltsin loudly insisted that he needed a pizza. He grudgingly went back to his bedroom— only to sneak out of it again the next night. This time, as he was still

wandering the halls of Blair House, a guard spotted him—but mistook
him for an intruder. Agents once again showed up to clarify who Yeltsin
was before he was detained—or worse. White House staff were understandably relieved when he left the country without further incident.[105]

Despite his professions of happiness, Yeltsin was clearly struggling
with both the reality of the final withdrawal from Europe and his own
demons. The French tried to make the case that it was time to go easier
on him as a result. In particular, Jacques Chirac, the mayor of Paris who
would become president of France in 1995, had developed a keen interest
in Russia, having studied the language as a younger man and developed a
close relationship with Yeltsin. When he visited the White House on
September 24, 1994, shortly before Yeltsin himself, he tried to make the
case for more understanding. Chirac pointed out that Yeltsin had "taken
his troops out of the Baltic countries" and was "cooperating with us on
the denuclearization of the other republics" as well as "working pretty well
with us in Bosnia." It was all that could reasonably be expected, and it was
hardly surprising that "he does not want us to expand NATO."[106]

Reaction inside the NSC was the opposite of Chirac's. Yeltsin's mild
response to Clinton's comments in September 1994 provided more fuel
for those who felt it safe to push aside PfP. Vershbow and his fellow troika
members, Burns and Fried, gave their boss Lake a road map for what
should happen next, entitled "Moving toward NATO Expansion." Even
Holbrooke, they argued, was not moving quickly enough; his "much heralded" involvement in the matter was "off to a slow and acrimonious start."
The alliance should simply expand, and new members should "acquire all
the rights and responsibilities of current members (full Article 5 guarantee)." At most, there could be "flexibility on operational issues such as stationing of foreign forces." Although NATO should coordinate with the
EU, it should not wait for EU expansion. This "'insurance policy'/ 'strategic hedge' rationale (i.e., neo-containment of Russia) will be kept in the
background only, rarely articulated." The troika was, in essence, making
a confidential case that a new Article 5 front line in Europe would be a
benefit, not a curse. The "possibility of membership" for "a democratic
Russia should not be ruled out explicitly," but it could only happen "in the
long term."[107]

This troika had to contend with fierce opposition inside the NSC from
their colleague Richard Schifter. A successful lawyer and refugee whose
Austrian-Polish parents had perished in the Holocaust—but not before
managing to send him to the States alone at age fifteen—Schifter was a
strong moral voice within the NSC. He sent a dissent to Lake, opposing

this push for rapid full-guarantee enlargement and regretting that the troika's advice emerged from "political rather than military factors." The expansion policy, he wrote, was mainly driven by "domestic pressures,"
particularly "from the Polish American Congress, from Henry Kissinger,
from other critics who argued that what they called 'another Yalta' was in
the making."[108]

Schifter's opposition to swift NATO expansion, like Shalikashvili's,
could not be dismissed as anti-Polish sentiment given his family background. Both men, having personally experienced upheaval and emigration as a result of twentieth-century conflicts, were clearly seeking to do
all they could to avoid conflict in the twenty-first. In their eyes that meant
avoiding a rush to create a new front in Europe. The administration should
stick with PfP's gradual approach even if it was not what the country of
their families' origins wanted. "Not pressed by a 1997 or 1998 deadline,"
Schifter wrote, the Partnership and NATO could undertake "a comprehensive program to integrate the entire CEE region into a European
Zone of Peace." He felt strongly that aggressive expansion would "do
more harm than good in Russia's domestic politics." Even worse, Washington did not need to inflict that damage because what Central and Eastern Europeans wanted more urgently was "membership in the EU." The
United States should not incur such costs only to offer them an institutional consolation prize. Although his opponents had dismissed PfP as
"little more than a charade," in Schifter's view it was not only a "reality"
but also a cost-effective way to help new democracies "achieve interoperability." The correct conclusion was undeniable: "our domestic critics
should be answered with sound policy arguments, which call for the deferring of a decision on NATO membership."[109]

Lake was not persuaded. The national security advisor felt that Central and Eastern European countries had a compelling claim to NATO
membership, and the best time to give it to them was precisely when relations with Russia were good. If Moscow became belligerent again, the alliance would face the unappealing choice of either abandoning states
threatened by its aggression or intensifying hostilities by adding them to
NATO.

On October 13, 1994, Lake did not just forward the troika's neo-
containment proposal to the president without any recorded mention of
Schifter's objections, he upped the ante. The national security advisor put
in front of Clinton his own more pointed version of the working paper,
with wording added in multiple places on the "possibility of NATO membership for Ukraine and Baltic States."[110] The latter group of states had

already, in September, set up a "Baltic Battalion" (BALTBAT), with help from their Nordic neighbors. Its express goal was increasing their suitability for NATO membership, and the boldness of the initiative impressed Westerners and made their membership seem more feasible. Clinton marked up this proposal personally, drawing two thick lines next to Lake's newly added recommendation to "keep the membership door open for Ukraine, Baltic States, Romania, and Bulgaria (countering Alliance inclinations to 'tilt' in favor of Visegrad countries)." As the national security advisor put it, Washington should not "consign them to a gray zone or Russian sphere of influence."[111]

Lake also added a statement that "standardization with NATO forces should be longer-term objective, but need not be attained at the time of accession." Since the potential new members all had old Warsaw Pact equipment, which was unlikely to be operable with NATO gear, standardization with alliance regulations would dramatically slow expansion; so the national security advisor was downplaying the need for it. Instead, he advised the president to use the upcoming December 1994 NATO ministerial to "kick off a formal process within the Alliance." The goal was to have that ministerial issue a "declaration on NATO expansion." Clinton drew a large check mark on the top page of the package of recommendations and wrote, "looks good."[112]

It was the green light Lake needed, and presumably not unrelated to the final weeks of the American 1994 election campaign. It could hardly be otherwise, given that the president of course hoped to be reelected in 1996, and so had to keep an eye on what voters in 1994 were saying they wanted. Clinton had also decided to take electoral risks in areas such as gun control. In the teeth of fierce resistance from the National Rifle Association, he had worked with moderate Republicans to pass a ten-year assault weapons ban that August. One Republican who voted for it, Representative Fred Upton of Michigan, needed police protection for six months afterward because of the threats he received as a consequence. The association fought hard in November 1994 to defeat Democrats who had voted for the ban.[113] Although not directly related to expansion, such opposition constrained the president by threatening to decrease his base of support in Congress. It also lessened his ability to take risks in other ways that might inspire voters to turn against him. Given that public opinion polls showed that a majority of Americans disapproved of the Clinton administration's handling of foreign policy, he had to consider the consequences of his actions in electoral terms.[114]

Meanwhile, staffers working for Gilman and Hyde completed the process of recycling language from their draft legislation on NATO expansion into the Contract with America, calling for swift membership for Visegrad countries. This contract made its intended contribution to the fall election. On November 8, 1994, Republicans won control of both houses of Congress for the first time since the Eisenhower era.[115] Clinton and his advisors were devastated. Christopher considered resigning.[116] Clinton later disclosed that when he learned the results, "I felt like I had just died."[117]

Blow-Ups in Brussels and Budapest

Lake, on the other hand, felt vindicated, and he set in motion a series of events that would have dramatic consequences. As planned, he turned the December 1994 NAC session into a venue for ramping up to full-guarantee expansion. Such sessions were usually "routine affairs," in Perry's words, with anything controversial sorted out well in advance by Washington and key members. All the meeting itself had to do, with "fictional spontaneity," was issue a prewritten, US-approved communiqué.[118] But this NAC meeting was not routine, as fierce preliminary debating dragged on in Brussels itself. Ultimately, the ministerial agreed to do what Lake had advised Clinton: issue a communiqué that formally opened the door to expansion. Issued on December 1, 1994, it read, "we expect and would welcome NATO enlargement that would reach to democratic states to our East."[119]

This success turned the ministerial into "a major turning point in our effort to expand the Alliance," as Christopher later recalled, and the world noticed.[120] The Baltic states and Ukraine both became deeply alarmed. While PfP had been clearly open to all of them, full NATO membership was less likely, given how challenging it would be to fulfill Article 5 commitments to territories on Russia's borders. The Baltics swiftly contacted the State Department to express their worry about "exclusion from rapid, selective NATO expansion."[121] They "objected to suggestions by some European states that the Baltic states were indefensible," pointing out that the West had committed to defending its half of divided Berlin even though it was buried deep inside East Germany.[122]

And if those countries were alarmed, Russia was furious. As the ministers debated the controversial communiqué, Kozyrev waited at the Russian embassy in Brussels. He had come to sign further documents alongside

NATO leaders to bring Russia fully into PfP. His country had already signed a general PfP framework document on June 22, 1994, but there were details still to be formalized. Kozyrev was kept in the dark as the internal debate unfolded. Bored with waiting around, he and the Russian ambassador began playing tennis on the embassy grounds to pass the time. Instead of a NATO leader, however, it was Yeltsin who interrupted their game. He had heard reports on world news media of the alliance announcing expansion and demanded to know what was going on. Kozyrev and the ambassador were caught flat-footed.[123]

Back in Moscow, Kozyrev's enemies smelled blood. The foreign minister was locked in a struggle for influence with Yevgeny Primakov, head of Russia's foreign intelligence service (SVR), who apparently realized he could use the fiasco to undermine Kozyrev.[124] Primakov had previously, on November 25, 1993, taken the unusual step of releasing an SVR report on how NATO, despite Americans claims, still presented just as much of "a danger to Russia . . . as it had to the Soviet Union." Publicized at a press conference, the report represented an attack on Kozyrev's cooperative stance toward the United States.[125] Now these events in Brussels a year later seemed to show that Primakov had been right to be suspicious and Kozyrev had been wrong.

Primakov knew that the Russian president hoped to be reelected in 1996 and did not want NATO expansion mentioned in any meaningful way before then. Reelection would be difficult enough even without it. Although Yeltsin had gotten through a new constitution, it had done little to stop life expectancy from declining, alcoholism and street crime from rising, and the health system from collapsing.[126] Yeltsin now felt angry and cheated.[127] Despite Clinton's promise of three "nos"—no surprises, no hurry, and no exclusion—he now faced all of them. He decided Russia would not sign the detailed PfP accords after all.[128]

That this was more than just a minor diplomatic fracas would become apparent at the Budapest summit on December 5, 1994. The goal of that summit was to rechristen the CSCE the Organization for Security and Co-operation in Europe (OSCE), to signal that it would have a more prominent future as an organization rather than as merely a conference.[129] It was another way of mollifying Russia, since Moscow had long promoted the organization; the OSCE was one of the venues where Russia had an equal footing with the United States.

To lend weight to the rechristening, Christopher had argued back in October that Clinton should personally attend, given that more than fifty heads of state and of government would be present. There was a chance that Kuchma, who would also be in Budapest, might agree to a final resolution on Ukrainian denuclearization if he got long-promised security assurances in some kind of written memorandum.[130] Christopher felt such an agreement "alone, if it were to take place, would justify the trip."[131] Ukraine's atomic arsenal remained dangerous in multiple ways. The US embassy in Moscow had reported on November 16, 1994, on "seizures in Russia, Germany and elsewhere of nuclear materials" most likely pilfered from former Soviet holdings. Such seizures were a chilling reminder of the need to secure nuclear stockpiles, including those in Ukraine, "against theft or diversion."[132] There were even rumors of Ukrainian involvement in weapons trade with North Korea and Iran.[133]

Clinton was initially reluctant to plan a foreign trip so soon after the disastrous November 1994 midterm elections. To convince him to go, the secretary enlisted Talbott, who added "a blunt but pertinent word about our domestic politics: we get this right," he told Clinton, "and at the right time, which means very soon—we can seize control over this issue in a way that essentially takes it away from the Republicans in '96."[134] Swayed by this argument, Clinton gave in. No one on the US side appears to have realized that they were setting him up for a confrontation.

Once Clinton agreed to the trip, a plan coalesced to complete a number of accords on the margins of the OSCE summit: the so-called Budapest Memorandum, under which the United States, the United Kingdom, and Russia would finally give Ukraine long-promised security assurances of its territorial integrity; the NPT accession documents for Ukraine as a nonnuclear state; and the exchange of START I ratification instruments with all post-Soviet nuclear republics, so it could finally enter into force.[135] But pulling all these accords together was a challenge.

The Ukrainians still worried that the memorandum contained weak assurances, not guarantees. A member of the US delegation in Budapest even allegedly went so far as to call "the assurances a worthless piece of paper," and the Ukrainian deputy foreign minister, Borys Tarasyuk, let the US embassy in Kyiv know of his concern about this remark.[136] Unmoved, the signatories agreed only to "consult in the event a situation arises that raises a question concerning these commitments."[137] Even that weak statement was in doubt. Ukrainian diplomats told US officials that they had "no illusions that the Russians would live up to the agreements they signed." Rather, the government of Ukraine was simply hoping for some basis on which to "appeal for assistance in international fora when the Russians violate the agreements."[138] For their part, the Russians, still aghast at their humiliation in Brussels, worried that Clinton would upstage the event by making clear that NATO, not the new OSCE, would be (in Kozyrev's words) "the centerpiece of the European security system."[139]

All of these anxieties collided to produce a contentiousness not seen since the Cold War. Clinton, in his address, emphasized to Kozyrev's horror that "NATO remains the bedrock of security in Europe," thereby sidelining OSCE. The president added for emphasis that no country outside the alliance would be allowed "to veto expansion."[140] The Russian delegation felt that, with those words, Clinton was intentionally adding injury to the insult from Brussels.[141] Yeltsin vented his frustrations publicly in response. The Russian president caustically accused Clinton, in the interest of NATO expansion, of risking a "'cold peace.'"[142]

The plan to sign the Budapest Memorandum almost fell apart. Talbott later disclosed that "it took our President's full personal engagement with Yeltsin to save the Ukrainian trilateral deal at the last minute."[143] Clinton's salvage efforts brought the memorandum and ratification process just barely across the finish line, with the result that START I, which eliminated strategic bombers and missile launchers carrying more than 9,000 warheads, finally entered into force. All sides indicated an interest in making progress on ratification of START II as well, which would retire another 5,000 warheads. If both treaties came into force, they would reduce the arsenals of the United States and former USSR by more than 60 percent from their Cold War peaks.[144]

But cooperation between the United States and Russia had broken down. There was no progress on completing the Russian process of joining PfP. During the summit itself, Kohl confided in Clinton that "this is a highly depressing event," not least because "we aren't doing anything about Bosnia."[145] An anguished appeal from Bosnian president Alija Izetbegović made little difference.[146] The Russian delegates refused to issue a declaration on Bosnia because they felt it unfairly singled out Serbs as aggressors. Grachev felt that the Serbs were holding back "'Muslim extremists and terrorists,'" a threat that he felt he knew well from his deployment to Afghanistan in the 1980s.[147] Meanwhile, Kohl urged Clinton to pull back on "the NATO issue," not least because "we can't allow ourselves to topple Yeltsin. There will be nothing to gain from that." He feared that "at the end we risk only having only rubber and debris."[148]

The bitterness lingered after the event. On the flight back from Budapest to Washington, Talbott recalled, the president "was furious at his foreign-policy team for dragging him across the Atlantic to serve as a punching bag for Yeltsin."[149] Clinton subsequently confided to Kohl that Yeltsin "really hurt me" with what he said in Budapest.[150] The US embassy in Moscow described Yeltsin's anger after the meeting as that "of a businessman who has just learned that his partner has taken out a new insurance policy in case their venture fails."[151]

For Kozyrev, the Budapest summit effectively ended his ability to advocate for NATO expansion in any way. Previously he had tried to counsel Yeltsin that Russia could live with gradual enlargement. After Budapest, however, he felt himself becoming "the sole voice in Moscow speaking against a hasty expansion of NATO" because "all others, including the president, had dropped the word 'hasty'" and simply become opposed to enlargement, full stop.[152]

Trying to assess what had gone so badly wrong, Talbott blamed Kozyrev. The Russian foreign minister, he thought, had goaded Yeltsin into an outburst as payback for his own humiliation in Brussels. And Talbott suspected Kozyrev had been encouraged by West Europeans, who "were doing quite a bit of bad-mouthing of our position, saying to the Russians, 'Your problem is not with us—it's with the Americans; they're the ones pushing expansion.'" Talbott surmised that Yeltsin's angry "cold peace" speech was prompted by Kozyrev intentionally stoking the Russian president's anger.[153]

Yeltsin was not done. Shortly after Budapest, he took a series of tragic steps that would result, among other damage, in self-inflicted wounds. The Russian president had already signed a decree on November 30, 1994 approving measures to counter breakaway rebels in the Chechnya region of Russia. With Kozyrev's support, Yeltsin now initiated what he thought would be a "high-precision police action" against those separatists.[154] But the movement of troops into Chechnya on December 11 instead started a protracted, bloody conflict that horrified leaders of countries near Russia.[155] Rühe was particularly disgusted when he learned that the Russian army sent recently drafted, poorly trained, "half-drunk soldiers into Grozny," who committed unspeakable acts of brutality.[156] The gruesome start to what became the First Chechen War revealed, in the words of the US embassy in Moscow, "the weaknesses of the Russian state and the tragic flaws of its first democratically-elected president."[157]

The bloodshed had far-reaching consequences. Despite the military's mistakes in Chechnya, Yeltsin nonetheless came increasingly to rely on the "power ministries," meaning the military and the heirs to the KGB,

all of whom opposed cooperation with the West.[158] Friends of Russian reformers abroad—such as Gati, the Hungarian-born American diplomat
who also knew Kozyrev from their shared time in New York—despaired
at the First Chechen War. Gati later recalled that war as a watershed moment, when he and other Westerners who had been optimistic about
Russia's future instead became convinced that the country could never
develop in the way Kozyrev hoped it would.[159] A *New York Times* journalist called the invasion of Chechnya "the end of Russia's liberal dream."[160]

The conflict also reduced Russia's ability to oppose NATO expansion
because it seemed to prove that the states insisting Russia remained a military threat were right. Seeking allies to defend themselves against that
threat suddenly seemed reasonable rather than paranoid. In his memoirs,
Kozyrev concluded with regret that the Chechen War strained "relations
with our Western partners for years."[161]

The sense that matters had taken a dark turn in the wake of Budapest and the Chechen invasion prompted Vice President Gore to try to
repair the damage. Visiting Moscow, he sought to assure an ailing Yeltsin, in his hospital room, that no enlargement would happen in 1995—
that is, during the lead-up to Yeltsin's 1996 reelection campaign. Gore
suggested "they shake hands to seal the deal that NATO will not expand
in 1995," and they did. Clinton also wrote to Yeltsin to reinforce Gore's
words: "NATO will not expand in 1995." There would be only internal
study, which would "proceed in parallel" with the development of relations
with Russia.[162]

Gore had armed himself with a metaphor that he hoped would appeal
to his hosts' pride: the idea that simultaneously moving both the US-
Russian relationship and the NATO expansion process forward resembled the docking procedures used to align spacecraft with a space
station.[163] This metaphor and Clinton's efforts succeeded in patching up
relations somewhat. They managed to convince Yeltsin that he had "mistakenly interpreted the NAC communiqué to mean that NATO would
make a decision in 1995 on the timetable of expansion."[164] Somewhat
mollified, Yeltsin resumed the process to join PfP, but it was clear that the
NAC communiqué and the Budapest debacle had significantly set back
US-Russian relations.

Back in Washington, Perry could not understand why the White
House had provoked a confrontation in both Brussels and Budapest when,
as far as he could tell, the president "had not yet made a final decision on
NATO expansion." Where was the gain in exchange for all of that damage? The secretary of defense was also angry that, as he complained to

Talbott, "literally no one in the Pentagon knew anything about" the key passage of "the NAC communiqué" of December 1, 1994 until it was released. He felt strongly that it was not yet time to commence the enlargement of Article 5 territory—especially when he was making so much progress in strategic arms control, even more important in the wake of the recent North Korean nuclear crisis, during which Clinton had nearly authorized destroying key components of the Yongbyon reactor site by military attack.

While the deputy secretary of state thought Perry's view was a "defensible position intellectually," Talbott argued it was too late to go back, since in his view "it's not our Administration's policy—and hasn't been for just over a year now."[165] He believed that the Visegrad countries, after all they had suffered in the twentieth century, had too strong a moral claim to NATO membership to be denied. Talbott also thought Perry was willfully blind to the postelection reality that, under pressure from victorious Republicans in Congress waving their copies of the Contract with America, the push for expansion had to become more aggressive.

Perry sought an opportunity to hear directly from the president what US policy was, and Clinton provided one. On December 21, 1994, the secretary joined Gore, Christopher, Talbott, Lake, and Lake's deputy Samuel "Sandy" Berger in the president's personal study at the White House, with Burns taking notes by hand, for what proved to be a critical assessment of Gore's trip to Moscow.[166] According to Burns's notes, the vice president told the group that one cause of the Budapest debacle was that the "Euros spun up Russians" about US moves, increasing Yeltsin's anxiety.

Gore then voiced what he saw as the heart of the problem. Just for the ears of the people in the room, he said the "truth is: we have conflicting impulses" with regard to the Central and Eastern European states and the Russians.[167] Washington had to choose between the two, he argued. After more debate, Clinton and Gore—in the words of Perry—"felt that right was on the side of the Eastern European countries that wanted to enter NATO soon, that deferring expansion until later in the decade was not feasible, and that the Russians could be convinced that expansion was not directed against them."[168]

The group then discussed a timetable for how to proceed.[169] Clinton and his advisors settled on a four-to-five-year time frame, although, as Christopher noted, "I can't see any of us saying this in public."[170] The decision was, in essence, to shift priority away from Russia and Ukraine, especially now that the latter was truly denuclearizing, and toward Central and Eastern Europe.[171]

Afterward, Perry considered resigning.[172] What should remain "'front and center,'" he thought, was negotiation with Russia to diminish its still-vast nuclear arsenal.[173] The progress on arms control in the early 1990s had been nothing short of astounding. A nuclear superpower had fallen apart, but only one nuclear state had resulted. All other successor states were joining the NPT. There had been only minor leakage of nuclear materials away from controlled sites. No weapons had detonated for any reason. There were even new agreements on safeguards, on transparency about amounts and locations of warhead and fissile materials, and test bans. These were matters of existential importance on which the United States had made historic progress, and now Perry's opponents in the Clinton administration were throwing a spanner into the works by pursuing a policy Russia would find far more threatening than PfP.

After wavering, Perry decided in favor of staying in office. If NATO enlargement had to occur, he would at least do his best to impose realistic conditions—known as the Perry Principles—on the enlargement process, such as the need to keep consensus within the alliance over what was happening.[174] In his memoirs, however, Perry lamented not having taken more dramatic action at the time. "When I look back at this critical decision," he wrote, he regretted that "I didn't fight more effectively for a delay of the NATO decision." If he had resigned, "it is possible that the rupture in relations with Russia would have occurred anyway. But I am not willing to concede that."[175]

Instead, he left the president's study that December day and returned to his office, informing his team that NATO expansion "would go forward on a brisk schedule" and that it would be an "uphill struggle" to keep US-Russian cooperation on track. He found this sequence of events "tragic," particularly for someone like himself who, as he said later, genuinely believed "that we had the opportunity in the 1990s to build a long-lasting cooperative relationship with Russia."[176]

Word of what had happened soon became public. By Christmas Day 1994, a leaked cable from the German ambassador to NATO alerted the world that the United States was abandoning its Russia-first strategy.[177] On January 13, 1995, Clinton gave a speech at a conference in Cleveland on trade and investment in Central and Eastern Europe, during which he described NATO expansion as "inevitable."[178] This represented a significant shift in public tone.[179] That same month, the State Department sent the US Mission to NATO a text "which the US believes should emerge from the alliance's internal deliberations on enlargement," declaring that there "will be no second-tier security guarantees." With that, PfP's descent was complete.[180]

By the end of 1994, partnership for the many had lost out to membership for the few. Roughly a year prior, Clinton had decided that the best way to serve American interests was to promote widespread cooperation with post-Soviet states, not least in order to decrease nuclear threats from them. That thinking, along with the need for peacekeeping in the Balkans, had contributed to the creation of PfP—which also represented the start of alliance expansion into Central and Eastern Europe, a step Moscow had fought hard to prevent. If that process was initially slower than the Visegrad leaders had hoped, however, the decision to pursue PfP nonetheless made clear that the alliance was irrevocably extending itself beyond Germany.

The creation of the Partnership as a means of slow enlargement initially helped to mitigate the cost of that extension with regard to Russia. But the Partnership was undermined by the efforts of enlargement activists and by Moscow's own missteps and aggression, most notably in Chechnya. These missteps came at a time when the belated Soviet departure from Germany created newly permissive conditions for those who wanted a tougher line. Ukraine also was no longer as strategically significant to Washington, given its denuclearization; that and the beginning of weapons reductions under START I created even more permissive conditions. Finally, there had been a widespread assumption that peace in Europe would be the natural post–Cold War condition, but the violence in Bosnia made that idea look naive; hedging against future violence now seemed smart rather than paranoid. The upshot was that, for Americans, Russian and Ukrainian concerns grew less significant. Central and Eastern Europeans wisely took advantage of this shift. The overwhelming Republican victory in the midterm elections gave the opponents of PfP the additional boost they needed to bring the president over to their side.

This outcome caused anguish not just for Perry but for his subordinate and eventual successor, Ashton Carter. Carter later recalled that of the many disagreements he had during his career, on no other issue did he have as much trouble understanding his opponents' position as this one.[181] Nonetheless, by the end of 1994 those opponents had won, pushing the Partnership from center stage to the margins.[182] The arguments for PfP made by a wide array of policymakers—Albright, Les Aspin, Christopher, Perry, Schifter, Shalikashvili, and even Clinton himself—all fell by the wayside. Now the burden was on supporters of full-guarantee expansion to implement their policy without damaging US-Russian relations. As Albright put it, "the key issue was how to manage the devolution of Russia from an imperial to a normal nation."[183] The Clinton administration would have to deal with Russians increasingly inclined to resist such management by Washington.

PART III

Frost, 1995–99

CHAPTER SEVEN

A Terrible Responsibility

WITH FULL-GUARANTEE EXPANSION now the Clinton administration's preferred answer to the question of how to enlarge NATO, the next question was one of timing. The scheduling of the Russian presidential election in summer 1996—the same year that Bill Clinton would seek reelection—made it tricky to answer. Clinton had assured his counterpart, Boris Yeltsin, that there would be no expansion before then as part of the effort to undo the damage in Budapest. Following that assurance, the NSC implemented what it called a "go-slow-and-quiet strategy" in the year 1995, with all "significant steps after the Russian elections."[1] As Clinton told British prime minister John Major, the real strategy was to delay "decisions until after the Russian elections," but "it is imperative that it not be leaked"; otherwise, it would look as if the Russians had a veto.[2] A curious dichotomy arose in 1995 as a result. On the one hand, there was the inactivity caused by the intentional delay. On the other, there was significant development in US thinking. Belief in the rightness of extending Article 5 territory as soon as feasible—particularly to Poland—increased significantly.

That belief was part of the Clinton administration's growing conviction that it had a chance to reshape Europe's future completely. Polish president Lech Wałęsa would come to the same conviction in 1995 and call this chance a "'terrible responsibility'" because it was so far-reaching.[3] But Clinton phrased the challenge in more positive terms: "here we have the first chance ever since the rise of the nation state to have the entire

continent of Europe live in peace."[4] He and his advisors increasingly believed that full-guarantee expansion was the way to achieve that goal, despite Moscow's protests. Deploring this development, Russian foreign
minister Andrei Kozyrev complained in 1995 that although "'nobody has
actually entered NATO yet,'" there was so much chatter about, and praise
for, "'the acceleration of . . . expansion that it is like an echo in a valley in
the mountains that causes an avalanche.'" As a result, "'stones are falling
on our heads before anything really happens.'"[5]

Spectrum of Satisfaction

As awareness of this new reality—a hold followed by a rapid move to full-
guarantee expansion—spread among interested parties on both sides of
the Atlantic, a spectrum of reactions became apparent, ranging from satisfied to horrified. At the most positive end of the spectrum was, unsurprisingly, Poland. Secretary of State Warren Christopher met with the
Polish prime minister, Waldemar Pawlak, to explain that "Poles should
not be alarmed" if their progress in gaining entry to the NATO club
seemed slow at first. Pawlak indicated that he understood.[6] Even Wałęsa,
now increasingly confident of achieving his dream of adding Poland to
NATO, began showing unusual flexibility. Speaking with Assistant Secretary of State Richard Holbrooke on January 27, 1995, at a moving event
in Kraków for the fiftieth anniversary of the liberation of Auschwitz,
Wałęsa indicated that "Poland would accept NATO membership even
without a nuclear guarantee if that would make expansion easier." He and
Holbrooke also discussed an idea from the former secretary of state, Henry
Kissinger, who had proposed softening Article 5 and creating "a class of
political membership in NATO with less than full security guarantees."
Kissinger was apparently implying that part of the two-plus-four treaty—
the prohibition on permanently stationing foreign forces in eastern
Germany—could be a model for Poland and elsewhere.[7]

Wałęsa's unusual flexibility may have arisen from the waning of his
political popularity. In the words of NSC expert Daniel Fried, Wałęsa was
"fighting for political survival as . . . presidential elections approach." The
two-round contest was due to start in late 1995. Despite his standing as a
national hero, voters were showing signs of wanting a change, so he was
perhaps hoping for a shortcut to bring about Polish membership in time
to help his own reelection.[8] (He would ultimately lose nonetheless.) There
was also, in the view of the US Congressional Research Service, a prob-

lem in that Poland was not fully ready for NATO membership, among other reasons because it lacked a "'legal basis for civilian control'" of the military. The subsequent leak of this criticism shamed Polish officials, contributed to the ouster of the chief of the Polish General Staff, and created a push for greater civilian authority over the military.[9] Wałęsa presumably wanted to get Poland in while he was still in charge, and before any more such issues undermined the country's chances.

Holbrooke, as fierce an advocate of full-guarantee expansion as ever, completely dismissed all talk of varying conditions for member states. He stated flatly in reply that "NATO does not allow different classes of membership"—thereby ignoring the reality that Denmark, France, Norway, and Spain (among others), while all enjoying the same Article 5 guarantee, nonetheless had bespoke membership conditions.[10] The alliance's recent extension to eastern Germany had also created, in addition to these Cold War examples, a post–Cold War precedent of contingent enlargement.[11] But by 1995 expansion had become too much of a US domestic and foreign policy priority, and the international context too permissive, to require any more such concessions—particularly for Poles. As Holbrooke put it, "'the process of NATO expansion, after all, is really about Poland.'"[12]

It was now clear that Poland was, finally, on its way to becoming a full member in the alliance. What was unclear was how many other states were as well. Next on the spectrum of satisfaction were, as a result, countries that were pleased to hear full-guarantee expansion was a possibility, but anxious about whether it was a possibility for them. An awkward beauty contest ensued, made all the more contentious by the realization that the contest could not end before the requisite number of calendar pages to 1996 had flipped. The Czech foreign minister, Josef Zieleniec, informed NATO headquarters that his country had the best record of any postcommunist state and so would be a "'natural.'"[13] Romanians also sought to make a good impression, seeking advice from Holbrooke, who told them to resolve their disputes with Hungary over minorities' rights.[14] For their part, the Hungarians raised their chances by enabling NATO flights over their airspace for strikes in Bosnia, for which Washington was grateful.[15]

A consequence of this contest was that there no longer appeared to be any point in competing within PfP. As long as the Partnership had been a gatekeeper to NATO membership, it was worth making an effort, but not now. Vice President Al Gore nonetheless felt it essential, on behalf of the excluded countries, to keep the funding for the Partnership going, because "the more we can enhance the PfP, the better they will feel when

States invited to join NATO in 1997.

they don't get into NATO at the start."[16] With regard to one of those ex-cluded, namely Ukraine, the US Mission to NATO noted around this time that Kyiv was "falling behind" in its activities in the PfP in what appeared to be an act of "self-differentiation."[17] Ukraine's dismay was under-standable: why put money and effort into PfP participation—particularly in the midst of an economic crisis—if the road to alliance membership no longer ran through the Partnership? Kyiv could at least comfort itself that Washington had, in economic terms, hardly forgotten about Ukraine. The country had become the fourth-largest recipient of US aid and technical assistance, with more than $900 million pledged for 1994 and 1995.[18] There was also an international effort to enable Kyiv to shut down Cher-nobyl entirely, which had not yet happened despite the horrific accident of 1986. In December 1995, the G7 countries and the EU agreed that Ukraine would receive Western aid for the closure, which eventually took place in December 2000.[19]

But if Ukraine was no longer as important as when it had been the world's third-largest nuclear power, in one aspect it still commanded pres-idential attention: tensions with Russia, particularly over the former So-viet fleet in Crimea.[20] Clinton worried personally about this issue because, as he said to Kuchma on May 11, 1995, "we came to appreciate earlier than the Europeans the strategic importance of Ukraine to all of Europe in the 21st century." He was convinced "that peace in a broad area depends on what happens to Ukraine and Turkey." And, Clinton added, there were "a large number of Ukrainian-Americans." Although the president did not explicitly say so, it was clear that many of those Americans lived in states electorally significant to Clinton's reelection chances.[21]

These realities notwithstanding, NATO membership for Ukraine could not possibly happen as quickly as it would for Central and Eastern Europe. Even the most ardent advocates of enlargement had to blanch at the thought of giving Article 5 guarantees to the second-most-populous former Soviet republic, still sharing an enormous land border and exten-sive cultural and historical connections to Russia.[22] It was telling that Holbrooke refrained from his usual role of bulldozing away all opposition to enlargement when it came to this particular country. As he put it, "Ukraine is the most delicate issue." In his eyes it had only "three choices or models for the future: Poland, Belarus, or Finland during the Cold War." Because it was, in Holbrooke's opinion, not yet clear which of those three outcomes was most likely, Ukraine still had "a lot of sorting out to do."[23]

Also because of Kyiv's sensitivities, Deputy Secretary Strobe Talbott advised Christopher that they both needed to avoid "any overplaying of the hedge rationale for expansion"—meaning the rationale that NATO should serve as a hedge, or form of neo-containment, against a resurgent Russia. Revealing such a motive "could be counterproductive not just with the Russians" but with other former Soviet states, "especially Ukraine and perhaps the Baltics," because they might feel locked outside of NATO's gates with an increasingly unpredictable bear. The odds of success for Russian reform seemed to be declining by the day; it was becoming thinkable and even probable that Moscow's trajectory could end in renewed aggression. Talbott seemed to be suggesting that they should not advertise the way Russia's immediate neighbors might end up outside those gates.[24]

Ukrainian leaders maintained some level of hope that their country had a role in the Atlantic Alliance's future nonetheless. Deputy Foreign Minister Borys Tarasyuk did what he could to keep that hope alive. "'No matter what we say publicly,'" Tarasyuk made clear to the Americans, "'I can tell you that we absolutely want to join NATO.'"[25] Presumably he meant Ukraine's public expressions of interest in the alliance would be limited, in an effort to avoid antagonizing Russia, but Kyiv's real desire was clear. And the Ukrainians were not alone in that desire; the Baltics shared it. The leader of Estonia, Lennart Meri, wrote to Clinton on June 9, 1995, recalling that "the zone between Berlin and Moscow has twice this century been witness to war and violence" after "Western powers initially refused to become involved."[26] Given the tragic history of their region, Estonians understandably wanted to join as well.

NATO's popularity was rising, and not just with former Soviet republics. At the end of the Cold War, public opinion polls in Europe had shown approval for NATO sinking as low as 27 percent. But now, in 1995, polls showed a striking rebound: even an estimated 65 percent of voters supporting the German environmentalist Green Party approved of their country's NATO membership.[27] That rebound was, however, creating a need to define the relationship between the NATO enlargement process and the European Union enlargement process.

For its part, the EU also fell somewhere in the middle of the spectrum of responses to the change in the Atlantic Alliance's expansion strategy.[28] On the one hand, the union was relieved NATO was taking the lead in expanding to the east, as the EU saw its own potential enlargement to former Warsaw Pact states as a more complicated, exacting, and costly process than alliance expansion. And it had completely ruled out Russia. As Alain Juppé—the French foreign minister who also spoke for the EU while his country held its rotating presidency in the first half of 1995—confided in the US secretary of state on March 22, 1995, "the EU has already decided: Russia cannot join the EU." He also inquired why "the Partnership for Peace had been hastily relegated to the back burner" when it had been "working well."[29]

On the other hand, now that NATO had taken the lead, the EU had to face uncomfortable questions about why the Atlantic Alliance was expanding quickly while the Union was not. Looking back years later, one historian asked why the EU had let NATO "try to reintegrate and stabilise Europe as a whole, which is roughly comparable to using a monkey wrench to repair a computer." The answer, he guessed, was that the EU's "single-minded push to achieve a single currency among its existing members" was taking priority over enlargement.[30] A more charitable view came from the US diplomat Thomas Simons, who argued that it was simply harder to expand the EU.[31]

Strong American advocates of expansion were more than happy to decouple NATO and EU enlargement, however. Peter Tarnoff, undersecretary of state for political affairs, argued on February 28, 1995 that "NATO expansion should not be delayed by the artificial constraint" of the EU's lack of progress on its own enlargement.[32] Going even further, Holbrooke emphasized that NATO should not only expand soon but also ensure "that the first expansion is clearly not the last."[33]

On the unhappiest end of the spectrum of responses to expansion was Moscow. Kozyrev began describing 1995 as the end of the "US-Russian 'honeymoon.'"[34] The dismay came right from the top since, as Talbott advised Clinton in the spring of 1995, "Yeltsin has taken over this issue personally."[35] The Russian president's personal attention to this issue stood in sharp contrast to his policy of leaving most foreign issues to subordinates such as Kozyrev, thus showing how much NATO mattered to him.[36]

"I Think Russia Can Be Bought Off"

Kozyrev was smart enough to realize the honeymoon had not ended solely because of Washington. Yeltsin's decision to move aggressively into Chechnya had left scars as well.[37] Although the Clinton administration adopted the public stance that Chechnya was part of Russia—even at one point unwisely likening Yeltsin's battle with secessionists to that of Abraham Lincoln—the private commentary between Washington and its NATO allies was very different.[38]

The US secretary of state felt that the Chechen invasion of 1994 "cast a dark shadow over our relationship with Russia" and was "inconsistent with pretensions of democracy."[39] He soon learned that the French premier, Juppé, held the same view; the Frenchman thought the invasion was "'a bungled amateur operation, carried out with great violence,'" which had displaced 400,000 people and killed 20,000 needlessly. Christopher replied that "Chechnya had increased his conviction that the current approach on NATO enlargement was the right one."[40] The invasion was thereby becoming a self-inflicted Russian wound, among other reasons because it made expansion more likely. In Christopher's words, Chechnya served as "an alarm bell for all of Central Europe," which could now "visualize the tanks entering their capitals" and make a better case for the need to be in the Atlantic Alliance as a result.[41] Major saw the same dynamic from his vantage point: Chechnya was "stoking the fears of those countries who want to be members of NATO."[42]

Even Kozyrev admitted to the British foreign minister, Douglas Hurd, in February 1995 that the Chechnya decision had been a "'bad mistake.'" Yeltsin, according to Kozyrev, had originally "thought he could conduct a surgical operation" but belatedly realized that the army leaders were incapable of doing so, and now blamed them for the sloppiness and heavy casualties. Kozyrev reassured Hurd that "there was absolutely no question" of "anything similar happening outside of Russia, in the Baltics for example." Hurd was unwilling to accept such explanations and forget the matter, however, pointing out that, while it would have been no surprise to the West "if the 'old Russia' had invaded Chechnya. But we had not expected this of the 'new Russia.'"[43]

In addition to the damage that the Chechen invasion did to US-Russian relations—to say nothing of the damage to Chechnya itself—the fiasco created a new problem: it made compliance with the conventional forces treaty that Gorbachev had signed on November 19, 1990 much harder for Moscow. With the treaty, the West had sought to eliminate the Soviet Union's advantage in conventional weapons by limiting the amount of equipment between the Atlantic Ocean and the Ural Mountains. To prevent flanking maneuvers by one side against the other, there were additional limits on specific geographic areas designated as flanks. The collapse of the Soviet Union had, however, immensely complicated full implementation of the treaty. Russian military leaders also resented (among other aspects) the way that the treaty restricted where they could locate their own equipment in their own country.[44] And with compliance to the treaty's terms coming due in late 1995, the new problem of Russian military equipment involved in the Chechen war—which was in a flank area—now threatened, in Talbott's words, to cause "a train wreck over CFE."[45]

The CIA reported at this time that there was another unusual piece of equipment being moved, even though it was neither a conventional weapon nor in a flank: an "unexploded nuclear device emplaced at an underground site in Kazakhstan in 1991." Instead of leaving it buried, Moscow was spending an estimated 1.5 billion rubles to unearth and relocate it. The CIA noted that "the recovery of an emplaced nuclear device after several years is unprecedented."[46] While this recovery could in theory be a positive development—part of the effort to ensure that any "loose nukes" left over from the Soviet period should be found and secured—there was another curious development on the nuclear front in early 1996 that clearly did not bode well: the CIA reported that Moscow may have conducted a test at the Novaya Zemlya nuclear site. Russian officials issued a denial but added pointedly that adherence to a moratorium on nuclear testing was solely "the prerogative of the Russian president."[47]

The bottom was also falling out of Russian economic reforms, further exacerbating worries. A small tier of oligarchs had enriched themselves impressively while the average Russian was struggling with unemployment, poverty, and pensions of vanishing value. In the course of 1995, it became clear to Talbott that Yeltsin had engaged in a series of Faustian bargains with those oligarchs. In exchange for siphoning their wealth into the Russian president's "campaign war chest," the Kremlin "paid the oligarchs back with vast opportunities for insider trading," including the infamous loans-for-shares deal, which was essentially a corrupt auction of state assets.[48] In addition, organized crime became "the most explosive force to emerge from the wreckage of Soviet communism," in the words of one *Foreign Affairs* author. Such crime was all the more menacing for "its connection to key sections of the government bureaucracy" because "no criminal enterprise of this complexity could have succeeded without the support and encouragement of officials at every level."[49]

As US diplomat Bill Burns recalled in his memoirs, this connection gave Moscow "its own unique charms in the mid-1990s" as a place to do business. He remembered visiting the Moscow mayor's office one day for an appointment and seeing "Russians in suits lying spread-eagled in snow, with men with black ski masks" holding guns over them. The masked men, he later discovered, were "part of Yeltsin's presidential guards," led by Kremlin head of security Aleksandr Korzhakov. They were "paying a courtesy call on executives of the Most Group, run by one of Russia's wealthiest oligarchs, Vladimir Gusinsky, whose offices were a few floors below the mayor's." Gusinsky had run afoul of Korzhakov, and this was how "gentle reminders" not to upset people in power were delivered in Russia at the time.[50]

Meanwhile, a stark contrast had arisen. As Russia was descending into a new "time of troubles"—a common reference to a historical period of upheaval in the early seventeenth century—the United States embarked on the longest economic expansion in its history.[51] The divergence in experience of the 1990s could not have been wider. Americans enjoyed prosperity at home and the luxury of choice as to the nation's engagements abroad. As Clinton advisor James Steinberg later said of NATO expansion, "there were no action-forcing things" other than "the sense that there were countries who now wanted to get in, but you didn't have to do it." It was a heady feeling, he recalled, to be able to ponder not just how but whether to shape the world: to do something because you felt like it, rather than had to do it. He found expansion compelling for precisely that reason: "you're particularly attracted to things that you don't have to do but that you want to do because you think it's shaping."[52] The choice to flex American muscles at leisure, rather than under pressure, felt like a luxury.

One practical manifestation of this view was declining US willingness to provide Moscow with face-saving political options as NATO expanded. According to Steinberg, Christopher initially made the mistake of endorsing a "deferential and solicitous" approach toward the Russians; the result was that they became "even more demanding," and the secretary grew skeptical.[53] By 1995 at the latest, Christopher's attitude had changed. Washington "must be very careful not to be seen as running after the Russians, offering them concessions," because "over the long term, we can get that relationship right without concessions."[54] Instead, the United States would use its economic might in bilateral relations with Russia to achieve strategic political goals.

As Steinberg later put it, "we succeeded in something that had been tried ever since the early '70s, which was bringing the economics into the heart of national security decision-making."[55] Between 1993 and 1996,

Clinton would come up with $4.5 billion in bilateral assistance to Russia to facilitate economic reform, curb inflation, and stabilize the ruble.[56] On his watch, the United States would become Russia's largest foreign investor, and he would inspire a host of entities, such as the Export-Import Bank, the Overseas Private Investment Corporation, and the Trade and Development Agency, to support commercial transactions with Moscow valued at more than $4 billion.

In short, Moscow's economic weakness gave the US president the leverage he needed. Clinton explained this approach to the visiting Dutch prime minister, Willem Kok, in March 1995, saying that "as we expand NATO," his administration needed to find a way to provide "parallel enhancement of relations between NATO and Russia" in order to keep US-Russian relations on an even keel. Clinton concluded: "It will be difficult, but at least in principle I think Russia can be bought off."[57]

There was, as a result, little need to consider such Russian preferences on the details of expansion. According to British foreign minister Hurd, what Moscow truly wanted was something it "cannot get," namely "partial membership in NATO along the lines of France or Spain."[58] Much to the annoyance of US proponents of full-guarantee enlargement, however, the idea of offering just such a partial membership to countries in Central and Eastern Europe had French support. As the secretary general of NATO, Willy Claes, explained to Clinton on March 7, 1995, Paris desired that "new members be given a choice for different formulas" of membership: "the French model, the Spanish model," or "full integration."[59]

The British disagreed strongly. As the Ministry of Defence advised Washington, "there should be no more Frances, Spains, or Norways with special status."[60] Paris lost that debate in the end because its influence was waning. The end of President François Mitterrand's long tenure in office was in sight, due both to the upcoming presidential election of April 1995 and to advanced cancer. French preferences could be presumed temporary until the post-Mitterrand era began and disregarded until then.[61]

The Russian foreign minister nonetheless kept trying to come up with practical ways to make expansion acceptable to his home country. Kozyrev requested that if expansion had to occur, Moscow at least be given opportunities for defense industry collaborations. The industrial collaboration idea found sympathy in Germany in particular, which promoted the idea of creating a giant transport aircraft, built by engineers from both the United States and post-Soviet states, together with electronics experts from the EU.[62] Even better, the contract could provide employment for the Antonov aircraft works in Ukraine as well, given that Antonov had already built the biggest aircraft ever to enter service successfully, the An-225, and so had proven expertise. The idea would potentially have brought jobs and benefits to a wide array of countries, including the economically struggling post-Soviet states.[63]

Asked about opportunities for defense industry collaboration by Kozyrev on February 14, 1995, Hurd was cool, saying that it was only "conceivable."[64] A lobbying alliance of US and EU aircraft industry executives opposed the idea, preferring to secure for themselves contracts to produce the Boeing C-17 and the Airbus A400M aircraft. Russians also undermined themselves. Western defense experts, some initially excited by the novelty of working with rather than in opposition to Moscow, invited delegations from Russia to visit and explore opportunities for cooperation. The US Department of Defense in particular sponsored numerous trips to the United States for Russians. But as one civilian Pentagon official later recalled, the guests would at times appear to be inebriated at meetings—and when hotel bills arrived afterward, some included astronomical minibar and phone charges. A policy of giving Russian visitors hotel rooms with empty minibars and phones routed through a Pentagon switchboard had to be developed. Hopes for large-scale collaboration dissipated in part because of such negative small-scale interactions.

Kozyrev also tried to negotiate compromises related to the two-plus-four accord, meaning legally binding prohibitions on nuclear weapons and the stationing of foreign troops, but with a similar lack of success. The State Department and the US Mission to NATO pushed back. Potential new member states should have neither an "obstacle to nor a priori requirement for permanent basing of forward deployed units." And there would, of course, be a "nuclear guarantee extended to new members." The State Department's one hesitation was that it would be important for new members to remove "KGB/GRU affiliated leaders from new allies' intelligence structures," presumably before significant Western troops or weapons showed up.[65]

In short, the Russian foreign minister made little headway with these suggestions for compromise. But Russian leaders were not entirely lacking in ways to push back. Washington had recently announced the testing of a rapidly deployable, truck-mounted system capable of intercepting short- and medium-range ballistic missiles just outside of the atmosphere, known as the Theater (or Terminal) High Altitude Area Defense (THAAD). The system created controversy at the time because there was disagreement between Moscow and Washington over whether it was subject to the terms of the 1972 Anti-Ballistic Missile (ABM) Treaty.[66] The Clinton administration had initially concluded that THAAD violated the ABM Treaty and had refrained from testing. But as Secretary Christopher informed his Russian counterparts on April 26, 1995, "with the new Republican majority surprisingly intense about the ABM issue," the administration had reconsidered under pressure and decided on reflection that some THAAD testing would, in fact, be permissible.[67] Moscow complained—and also informed the US ambassador there that START II ratification would have to go on the back burner.[68] Just as the US secretary of defense, Bill Perry, had feared, US-Russian progress on arms control was beginning to suffer.[69]

Both Washington and the alliance clearly needed to find a way to keep Moscow and anxious allies occupied during the delay. The answer was the usual one given by any large organization seeking to stall: commission a study, largely prewritten in Washington. In keeping with what Perry called the "fictional spontaneity" of NATO issuing texts drafted in advance by Washington, the State Department circulated the plan that "should emerge from the alliance's internal deliberations on enlargement" later in 1995. Given that there were a number of practicalities needing consideration, such as how to carry out the "basing of foreign troops and of nuclear weapons on the territory of new members, and the possibility of new members trying to block subsequent enlargement," a study of such issues would have the merits of both passing the time and being useful.[70] In short, in the words of Secretary General Claes to Clinton, there was "enough work to do . . . even with respect to candidate number one," that is, Poland, to fill the time.[71]

There would be one topic, however, that would be off-limits to any study. As the State Department advised the US Mission to NATO, "security must be equal for all allies." In other words, the study should not yield any arguments in favor of associate, phased, or tiered membership: "there will be no-second-tier [*sic*] security guarantees."[72] The US Mission to NATO made clear that it understood these instructions, as well as its role more broadly during the 1995 delay. It would "view the work this year" not so much as a "robust NATO decision" but rather as an extended confidence-building exercise. The goal was simply "to get allies used to the idea of having new allies, comfortable with the fact that the alliance which emerges afterward will not" be weakened.[73] Satisfied with how this was developing, by the spring of 1995 Secretary Christopher could inform

Talbott that, during the extended hold, contacts with NATO allies could be "done at lower level" for the time being because "we need to keep main players in Washington more."[74]

Despite such delays to actual enlargement, Kozyrev sensed correctly that a hardening of opinions was underway in Washington. He and his foreign ministry colleagues felt it when they tried to convince Talbott to transform NATO into "a collective security organization rather than a vehicle for containment."[75] Talbott declined, saying, "we're not in the business of having to 'compensate' Russia or buy it off." Although Clinton had spoken of doing precisely that, Talbott saw such concessions as unnecessary. The deputy secretary believed the time for a harder line had come because, as he confidentially told his boss, "Russia is not doing us a favor by allowing NATO to expand."[76] Talbott's private view mimicked that of President George H. W. Bush, who had said in 1990 that "the Soviets are not in a position to dictate" what the alliance could and could not do.[77] The deputy secretary felt the same way, explaining his view of the end of the Cold War to Christopher as follows: "Fact is, we and the Soviet Union didn't meet each other halfway, and we and Russia aren't going to do so either."

Instead, Talbott felt Moscow should see the United States as a lighthouse, showing the way toward "democratic elections, free press, pluralism, open markets, civil society, rule of law, independent judiciary, checks and balances, respect for minority rights, civilian control of the military." As a result, US strategy should be "intended to make sure that the rickety, leaky, oversized, cannon-laden Good Ship Russia, with its stinking bilge, its erratic, autocratic captain, and its semi-mutinous crew (including plenty with peg legs and black eyepatches), has a clearly visible point on the horizon to steer by." Talbott concluded that, whatever Christopher thought of this extended metaphor, "it's at least better" than Kozyrev's "cliché about the end of a honeymoon. Whatever US-Russian relations are like, it ain't love and marriage."[78]

Such pointed remarks showed that Talbott's role in the decision-making process on enlargement had changed considerably since he had supported the Partnership in October 1993. At that time, supporters of PfP had understandably but wrongly assumed that he was on their side. It was becoming clear that Talbott was, however, on the side of Lake and others who sought full-guarantee expansion. Where the deputy secretary differed was in his concern for sequencing; he admired how Bush had gotten Moscow used to Germany in NATO over time. In this regard, Talbott shared a view with the vice president. Gore felt it made "little sense for us to say that, for all time, we rule out even the theoretical possibility of Russia joining NATO." Although there was little "likelihood" of Russia joining, it was still useful to keep the possibility alive as a way of dealing with "what Gorbachev called the 'enemy image'" that many Russians still had of the West.[79] The vice president's comments were a further sign that internal administration thinking, which initially had contained openness to Russian membership, was now moving farther away from that view.

As these debates were unfolding, it became apparent that there was a major new participant in them: the Republican-controlled House and Senate, which had little interest in what Russians thought.[80] Upon swearing their oaths of office in January 1995, members of the House did what they could to accelerate enlargement. They swiftly proposed a "National Security Revitalization Act" in support of expansion. Democratic members, such as Lee Hamilton of Indiana, tried to push back. Hamilton pointed out that it made no sense to take on costly new security commitments in Europe when US force levels had declined by two-thirds since 1990 and defense spending was set to shrink further. Then there was the larger question looming behind expansion: "why is it in the US interest to provide a nuclear guarantee and a pledge to go to war to defend Slovakia?" In short, Hamilton was "not sure the American people are ready for these commitments."[81] The Senate failed to take action, and the legislation died.[82] The House also passed a NATO Expansion Act in 1995, thus formalizing that body's support for enlargement.[83]

One of the president's political advisors, Dick Morris, conducted a poll on NATO enlargement, which showed the public opposed to postponing it.[84] Even though, in Morris's words, Clinton's foreign policy experts "'honked like geese on a pond'" when he came anywhere near them—warning they should not be subject to domestic pressures—the president personally remained reliant on Morris and attentive to public opinion.[85] Clinton was too good a politician to forget that 20 million Americans of Eastern European descent lived in fourteen states that accounted for close to 40 percent of the Electoral College.[86]

Anniversary and Tragedy

Talbott may not have liked the honeymoon metaphor, but he had to admit that anniversary metaphors were powerful ones, and May 1995 provided a big one: fifty years since the end of World War II. Although the anniversary might have been a moment for a renewed focus on what Washington and Moscow could accomplish together, in reality it did not slow the hardening of opinions against cooperation on either side.

The complexities inherent in the anniversary became apparent early, when the visiting German chancellor, Helmut Kohl, sought a chance to discuss them at length with Clinton on February 9, 1995. Kohl wanted to avoid the awkwardness of June 6, 1994, when Germans had not been invited to the fiftieth anniversary of the main D-Day commemoration in France.[87] The chancellor's personal inclination was to hold smaller events to mark the 1995 anniversary, but he had learned that Mitterrand felt otherwise. As Kohl explained to Clinton, Mitterrand hoped to use the occasion not just as his "farewell from office but from life," since his cancer was untreatable (and would cause his death in January 1996). Because the French president was the last major leader "who actually experienced the war, as a POW and member of the resistance," Mitterrand wanted, despite his physical frailty, to appear with Kohl in Germany as a signal of long-lasting reconciliation between enemies fifty years after the war. Kohl believed it would be a fitting tribute if Clinton were there as well for Mitterrand's final bow and his plea on behalf of a united Europe.

Clinton was noncommittal, noting that if he came to Europe for the fiftieth anniversary of the end of the war, he would have to go to Moscow as well, "or else it would be a terrible slap to Yeltsin." A Moscow visit would create a huge problem, however, because if Yeltsin organized a big military parade for the anniversary, "it will not look good after Chechnya."[88] There was also the worrisome chance that Yeltsin might, as he had done in Budapest, spring unpleasant demands about NATO enlargement on a visiting Clinton, such as insisting that there be no forward deployments or nuclear weapons on new NATO members' territories.

Kohl understood Clinton's hesitations. The chancellor confided in the president how much he disliked "calling him [Yeltsin] every week and spelling out for him how Russia's image is going downhill" because of Chechnya.[89] It was becoming tragically apparent to Kohl that Yeltsin "has a military who cheated him." At one point, the German convinced Yeltsin to stop the Chechen bombardment; but twenty-four hours later, as far as Kohl could tell without Yeltsin's knowledge or permission, the violence had resumed. The chancellor was "100 percent certain that Yeltsin didn't lie" when he said the bombing would cease, so Kohl suspected instead that Yeltsin's military officers were no longer obeying him, "perhaps to topple him."[90] Kohl still wanted maximum consideration shown toward Russia, however, not least because "we need Yeltsin with us on Bosnia. Without him we can forget about all of our plans."[91] The UN peacekeeping forces were failing to keep peace in the region, or even to prevent hostage-taking. NATO had approved a plan for the potential deployment of 20,000 US troops to Bosnia.[92] The Serbian leader, Slobodan Milošević, had supporters among the nationalists in the Russian Duma, so the West needed Yeltsin to run interference with those nationalists. Whether the Russian president would do so was an open question, however.[93]

Considering all of the pros and cons of going to Moscow, Clinton noted that the Republican-controlled Congress had "not put big pressure on me over Chechnya," but that could change. What was happening instead was that "a number of Congressmen are pushing for the immediate expansion of NATO." Clinton felt that the enforced delay until after Russian elections was still the right step and that the current timetable was "just right."[94] Kohl agreed, which Clinton was glad to hear, because "the Central and East Europeans and the Russians will be reading what we say with a magnifying glass to see if there is even a millimeter of difference."[95]

Under pressure from Yeltsin, Clinton ultimately decided that, while he needed to mark at least part of the anniversary in the United States, he would thereafter bypass Western Europe altogether and go directly to Moscow for its commemoration of the anniversary—but only after receiving assurances that the Russian event would "not have a heavily military flavor" and there would be no Chechen-associated units in the scheduled parade.[96] As Russian forces had just carried out a massacre in the village of Samashki in April 1995, the latter assurance was particularly important.[97] The president had realized that, despite the various problems with such a visit, he could instrumentalize the anniversary. He could use his visit to inspire Moscow, belatedly, to join PfP fully, which would serve as a kind of tacit acceptance that Russia would continue to work with the alliance during the process of enlargement.[98] And once Russia was in the Partnership, the United States could then offer it a special relationship with NATO. Clinton felt this move was worth braving the downsides of a visit.[99] He decided to add a subsequent stop in Ukraine as well, so it would not look as if he were focusing solely on Russia, but Moscow was clearly the main event.

Once Clinton made this decision, a deputies' committee received the task of defining US objectives for the trip. Showing how harder views had taken over in the White House, they made clear that Clinton should feel no hesitation in twisting Russian arms during the visit, even though it would be a time of tragic emotional significance for Yeltsin, who had nearly starved as a child during the war, and for all Russians. Despite the fact that the country would be looking back on its conflict with the Nazis and feeling triumph mixed with vulnerability and sorrow, Clinton should nonetheless plow ahead and "make explicit" at the event "that NATO expansion is inevitable." His advisors also felt he should make clear "nuclear stationing policy cannot be the subject of NATO negotiations with—or commitments to—non-members."[100] Perry made a plug that the president at least hold an event to promote denuclearization while he was there, trying as ever to keep that priority alive.[101] As threatened, the Russian government had not submitted START II to the parliament for ratification—and it was beginning to look unlikely that parliamentarians would ratify it even if it was submitted. Even worse, Moscow had created a new proliferation worry. As Clinton's briefing book for the event advised him, Russia had announced that it would "provide Tehran with several light-water nuclear reactors and associated technology."[102]

Management of summit strategy overall was ultimately given to Talbott, who described the event to Clinton as a "moment of truth," because it promised "to test your determination to keep on track two strategies that are crucial to your vision of post–Cold War Europe: admitting new members to NATO, and developing a parallel security relationship between the Alliance and Russia."[103] For his part, the president's main concern was avoiding a repetition of the Budapest breakdown. If that happened, in Clinton's words, it would be "'worse than Budapest. That was just comic relief: I flew eighteen hours to spend six hours getting the shit kicked out of me.'" But a "'bad meeting'" in Moscow on the fiftieth anniversary of the end of World War II would be orders of magnitude worse. It would be "'bad for me politically'" and "'turn up the heat on expansion.'" The chances of an adverse outcome were high, in Clinton's view, with the Russians "'madder than hell at us over Bosnia, and NATO expansion,'" and the "'worry that I'm being driven by the Polish-American vote in '96. The Republicans just aggravate this calculus.'"[104]

Once he arrived in Moscow for the anniversary, the president employed his extensive persuasive skills to avoid that outcome. He sensed they might work when the visit started off well. Yeltsin kept his promise to downplay the military invasion of Chechnya. Once behind closed doors with Clinton, Yeltsin also acknowledged the significance of US-Russian cooperation on arms control and the risks that enlargement posed to it. The Russian president pointed out that "we've destroyed all tactical weapons; we've started to destroy strategic weapons," and, last but not least, "we've removed the strategic weapons from Ukraine and Kazakhstan." But "what causes us concern here" is the need for "a common view of pan-European security and NATO. This is a complicated issue. We need to discuss it today in a very frank way."[105]

In Yeltsin's eyes, NATO and an all-European security system were essentially antonyms.[106] He warned, "I see nothing but humiliation for Russia if you proceed." As he pointed out, "how do you think it looks to us if one bloc continues to exist while the Warsaw Pact has been abolished?" He repeated that Europe needed "a new structure for pan-European security, not old ones!" The Russian president suggested taking until the year 2000 to assess the issue overall, adding that in the meantime, Russia would give "every state that wants to join NATO a guarantee that we won't infringe on its security. That way they'll have nothing to fear from the East."[107]

Clinton, bringing his impressive skills for rhetorical persuasion to bear, countered by arguing they should look at the big picture. With the Cold War over, it was indeed fair for Russia to ask whether the United States still needed "a security relationship with Europe, along with a political and economic relationship." But to Clinton's mind, the fiftieth anniversary of the end of World War II revealed unmistakably that it did, because it showed that the United States and Europe were strongest when they worked together. The question now was how to maintain that relationship and expand the alliance in a "way that makes sure Russia is integrated into Europe and plays its rightful role." The president made clear that Washington would open doors for Russia to various international organizations but added that "you have to walk through the doors that we open for you."[108] He emphasized that Russians were "paying a tremendous price in lost opportunities to advance relations with the rest of Europe so long as the debacle" in Chechnya continued.[109]

Yeltsin replied that his room to maneuver was limited because "my position heading into the 1996 election is not exactly brilliant." Clinton sympathized, saying, "I am mindful of the political pressures on you," but that he had his own electoral issues to consider. Pro-expansion Republicans had done extremely well in "Wisconsin, Illinois, and Ohio . . . they represented a big part of my majority last time—states where I won by a narrow margin" and would need to win again. The US president also pointed out to Yeltsin that the Central and Eastern European states themselves strongly desired membership, saying, "they trust you, Boris," but "they are not so sure what's going to happen in Russia if you're not around."[110] He was also able to get Moscow belatedly to agree to sign the remaining paperwork related to PfP. The summit did not end on a resounding high note, but Clinton had at least managed to instrumentalize it sufficiently for the purposes of the extended hold.

One part of Europe not on hold was, tragically, Bosnia. Serb-perpetrated brutality there in 1995 solidified a sense that some further intervention was desperately needed. Sarajevo, a Bosnian city that had played host to the Winter Olympics in 1984, became the site of shelling that killed nearly a dozen people in May 1995. The alliance launched limited airstrikes later that month in response.[111] In 1993 the UN Security Council had tried to establish a safe zone in another Bosnian city, namely Srebrenica; but it tragically became the site of a massacre of an estimated 8,000 people in July 1995. Cables to the US secretary of state lamented that "the surrender of Srebrenica to Bosnian Serbs has resulted in both a humanitarian and human rights tragedy." There were "credible reports of summary executions and the kidnapping and rape of Bosnian women," along with accounts of people "taking their own lives rather than risk falling into Serb hands." These "outrageous and illegal acts" were contributing to what was already "the greatest refugee crisis in Europe since World War II."[112] Germany subsequently estimated that it alone had received more than 400,000 refugees.[113]

There was also a tragic personal coda for US policymakers when three American officials dispatched with Holbrooke to the area—Robert Frasure and Joseph Kruzel, deputy assistant secretaries of state and defense, respectively, along with Colonel Nelson Drew of the NSC—died in a car accident on the treacherous Mt. Igman Road near Sarajevo.[114] The sight of coffins coming back to the United States—another bitter memory from the Vietnam era—only increased the desire of their friends and colleagues in the Clinton administration to take action. Talbott, who met the plane carrying the bodies on the tarmac, agreed with the Bosnian foreign minister, Muhamed Sacirbey, that there should be "'no more fucking around with the UN!'"[115] There was a strong sense that the United States—which, in 1995, was spending four times as much as any other country on defense, and almost twice as much as the other fifteen NATO nations combined—should be able to take care of Bosnia. As Sacirbey told Talbott, "'you people have to bring in NATO air strikes *now!*'"[116]

Former Yugoslavia in the mid-1990s.

Steinberg later recalled the sense of resolve in the air when he, Lake, and others planned the response to the massacre in Srebrenica. The clear feeling was "'we have to grab this'" and "'we have to solve it.'" The result was, in Steinberg's view, an appropriately "aggressive strategy, that included pressing and ultimately being prepared to break with the UN." Demonstrating that the alliance could respond to a "real-time challenge" would prove to be a "turning point."[117]

NATO's Operation Deliberate Force began on August 30, 1995. Nearly 300 aircraft from eight NATO countries flew more than 3,500 sorties over roughly two weeks.[118] Perry called his Russian counterpart, Pavel Grachev, regularly but did not provide the defense minister with advance word of strikes, which deepened Moscow's resentment.[119] Washington also compelled all sides to hold talks coordinated by Holbrooke

in Dayton, Ohio, in November. They ultimately yielded an accord, signed
in Paris on December 14, 1995. To help implement that accord, the UN
gave NATO a mandate, which cleared the way for what was at the time
the largest military operation in NATO's history: an Implementation
Force (IFOR) of approximately 60,000 troops from both member and
partner states.[120] It also showed the success of another concept that had
emerged from General John Shalikashvili's office: combined joint task
forces (CJTFs), which allowed both NATO and non-NATO members to
cooperate beyond the alliance's geographic area. (There was even consideration that Europeans could use the CJTF format for other operations,
ones in which NATO as a whole chose not to cooperate, although that
idea generated resistance from the alliance's top military commander, a
US general.)[121]

Privately, on July 25, 1995, Clinton and Kohl had also discussed the
option of a ground campaign. Kohl was strongly against it, finding the
idea "totally wrong" and saying flatly, "Don't put anyone on the ground."
In the chancellor's view, it was "out of the question to think that we could
conduct a war there and win" because "we would need several hundreds of
thousands of troops and no one wants to make that kind of commitment."
The bottom line, as Kohl saw it, was that "there is no domestic support
for it in the West."[122]

Ironically, even as they increased NATO's importance, these developments showed the merits of PfP. As Robert Hunter of the US Mission
to NATO put it, "Partnership for Peace is moving along smartly." PfP had
brought together the relevant militaries in precisely the kinds of exercises
and training events that enabled them to carry out the Bosnian operations.[123] Thanks to them, Central and Eastern Europeans and Ukrainians could all work successfully with each other and with NATO nations
in Bosnia.[124] And for the first time in alliance history, despite various disagreements, NATO ground forces would deploy with Russians as side-
by-side partners, not enemies, showing that all was not lost in Western
relations with Moscow.[125]

Illness and Scandal

In the midst of this crisis, Talbott decided to go public in early August 1995
with a widely circulated *New York Review of Books* article titled "Why
NATO Should Grow." The fact that his public response to Srebrenica was
a strong statement in favor of NATO expansion signaled that he saw the

alliance, and not any other organization or entity, as "the heart of the European security system."[126] Presumably writing for Russian consumption, Talbott emphasized that "enlargement is going to happen" and that "describing NATO enlargement to your own people in alarmist terms" would be counterproductive. Saying it remained an "open question" as to whether Russia would join the alliance, he added that "among the contingencies for which NATO must be prepared is that Russia will abandon democracy."[127]

Talbott's article was intended to signal that the internal decision-making was done and to convey the result to a wider public. Private citizens such as Michael McFaul, the future US ambassador to Russia, got the message. He saw the appearance of that article as the point of no return. NATO was enlarging eastward; there was no going back.[128] Others got the message as well, and were not happy about it.[129]

A former US ambassador to Poland, Richard T. Davies, sent a sharply worded response to the publication, complaining that Talbott had ignored a host of prominent policymakers who had already pointed out the risks of the strategy that the deputy secretary was now endorsing. Davies emphasized the problem of proliferation in particular: "confronted by the eastward movement of NATO, a militarily and economically weak Russia that is unable, as it now is, to recruit and equip massive conventional forces, would presumably have to rely heavily on nuclear-armed missilery." The results for "the delicate web of East-West and US-Russian arms-control agreements, much of which deals with this category of weapon," could be irreversible. As he put it, "NATO expansion into the Visegrad area and Russian fears that it might only be the first in a series could cause that web to fray and shrivel away."[130]

It was not just past agreements that were at risk. By August 1995, Clinton and his advisors were seeking a "zero yield" limit, meaning a ban on "any nuclear weapon test explosion or any other nuclear explosion with any nuclear yield."[131] The idea was to build on the momentum from the recent success of getting more than 170 nations to agree to extend the 1970 Treaty on the Non-Proliferation of Nuclear Weapons (NPT) indefinitely.[132] Another effort at risk was the ongoing effort, now called the Cooperative Threat Reduction (CTR) program, to help Russia denuclearize. By October 1995 it had, among other accomplishments, relocated over 2,000 strategic warheads from Belarus, Kazakhstan, and Ukraine to Russia; found employment for roughly 8,000 former Soviet nuclear engineers and scientists; and purchased and transferred to the United States about 600 kilograms of poorly secured weapons-grade uranium from Kazakhstan.[133] Arms control experts would later see the period between the Intermediate-Range Nuclear Forces (INF) Treaty of 1987 and negotiations on the Comprehensive Test Ban Treaty (CTBT) roughly a decade later as the "apogee of nuclear arms control."[134] In Davies's view, Talbott's article seemed to endanger many of these arms control desiderata.

Such warnings were not effective in convincing the Clinton administration and NATO officials already committed to enlargement. Peace had broken out, and armed forces were shrinking in countries across NATO, so it was a hard sell to convince policymakers to worry about nuclear weapons and the Russians again. Instead, NATO went public on September 3, 1995—shortly after the release of Talbott's *New York Review of Books* article—with its own study on enlargement. The final report made unambiguously clear that "new members will enjoy all the rights and assume all the obligations of membership under the Washington Treaty."[135]

The response of Vitaly Churkin, the Russian ambassador to Belgium who was invited to take part in a discussion of the newly released study at NATO headquarters, was telling. He did not speak at the event itself; at a press conference afterward, however, he indicated that "'what we have seen so far is not enough for us to change our minds about the prospects of NATO enlargement. Feelings are very strong about this in Russia.'"[136] It did not bode well for Kozyrev's fading attempts to reconcile Washington's hopes for NATO with Moscow's anxieties. Yeltsin began hinting at press conferences in autumn 1995 that he no longer trusted his foreign minister.[137] And when Clinton spoke to Yeltsin by phone on September 27, 1995, to ask what he wanted to talk about at their next summit—to be held at a former Roosevelt family residence in Hyde Park, New York, to inspire thoughts of wartime cooperation under President Franklin Roosevelt—Yeltsin's response was clear: "NATO, NATO, NATO, NATO."[138] The leverage that its potential expansion was giving to his domestic political opponents as an election year approached was apparently never far from his mind.

At the summit itself on October 23, however, it became apparent that it would be difficult to conduct "serious business of any kind," as Talbott put it, because of Yeltsin's physical weakness—and drinking. As ever, the US side kept tabs on his alcohol intake. There was some opportunity for discussion in the morning, but when Yeltsin downed three quick glasses of Californian Russian River wine before lunch was even served, and then proceeded to drink several more glasses over the course of the meal itself, prospects for progress went downhill. At a press event, Talbott recalled that Clinton tried "to cover for Yeltsin" by making it appear as if he were "clowning around" rather than ill and drunk, by laughing ostentatiously at the Russian's behavior. Clinton's view remained unchanged from the earliest days of his presidency: never forget that "'Yeltsin drunk is better than most of the alternatives sober.'"[139] Doing what he could to advance substantive matters, Clinton sought a way to combine the issues of Bosnia and NATO expansion. He hoped to increase Russian comfort with expansion through cooperation with NATO in Bosnia. A by-product would be to make the sickly Yeltsin seem like an engaged world leader to his electorate as he tried to retain office. It was also in Washington's interest, Kohl had advised Clinton, because peace in the Balkans would only endure "if the Russians are brought into the equation."[140]

Following this line of argument, Clinton told the Russian president that, "at a minimum," Russia would "undertake auxiliary operations to help in Bosnia's reconstruction."[141] Yeltsin replied that the tasks should be called special operations, rather than auxiliary, and that Russia wanted to do far more than that. Clinton suggested that Perry and Grachev, who was becoming a leading opponent of NATO expansion, work together on the issue.[142] Their successful collaboration briefly gave rise to optimism within the State Department about the way that recent contacts with Russians, "especially Bill Perry's sessions with Grachev, suggest a new willingness to work constructively with NATO"—or, as Talbott reportedly confided in Holbrooke, that working together in the Balkans could help "'lubricate the NATO-Russia track.'"[143]

Three days after the October 1995 Hyde Park summit, the Russian president suffered a heart attack.[144] Now the delay had a second aspect: waiting for Yeltsin to get through both reelection and his most recent serious illness. Although no one knew it at the time, it would take until spring 1997 for him to overcome the latter. In the meantime, two scandals—one public, one private—created new political realities that would shape not only future expansion but also US politics writ large.

In October 1995, the lower house of the Belgian parliament voted to strip Claes of immunity to permit his indictment in a forgery and fraud scandal. He had to step down as secretary general.[145] The leading candidate to replace him was the former Dutch prime minister, Ruud Lubbers.[146] Steinberg recalled that, right before "the expected coronation was going to take place," Lubbers had a "horrible" lunch with Christopher, revealing that the Dutch leader did not share any of the US priorities for the future of NATO.[147]

For Kohl, it was a case of déjà vu; the German had successfully prevented Lubbers from becoming president of the European commission as revenge for what Kohl saw as unforgiveable opposition to German unification.[148] Now another such "very delicate" situation arose, whereby Steinberg recalled that "we decided afterward that we weren't going to let" Lubbers have the job, but had to conceal the fact that the United States was singlehandedly torpedoing what was theoretically a choice for all allies to make together. As he put it, "you don't want to look like you're a bull in a china shop."[149]

They decided to exacerbate insecurities in Paris about the fact that Lubbers did not speak French, one of NATO's two official languages, by dangling as an alternate "a fluent French speaker, who was from a Latin country," namely Javier Solana, the Spanish foreign minister. More important for Washington than Solana's linguistic skills, however, were his shared priorities with Washington for NATO. The plan worked.[150] Lubbers withdrew in November 1995, sensing his candidacy could not withstand American opposition.[151] Instead, Solana became the secretary general who would lead the alliance as it established IFOR, which Christopher called the alliance's "largest and most significant operation ever," and began expansion.[152] Solana made plain early on that his approach to NATO enlargement "would track with the American" view.[153] Washington had gained a smart and effective partner in Brussels.

Claes's resignation was not the only scandal of autumn 1995; it was just the one that became public. On November 14, 1995, the Republican-led Congress decided to shut down the US government as part of its confrontation with Clinton. It thereby furloughed paid staff members, including those who usually surrounded and protected the president, and left unpaid interns scrambling to do the work of the absent employees. One of the interns was a new graduate of Lewis & Clark College named Monica Lewinsky. Through her well-connected parents—her father was a leading breast cancer specialist in Beverly Hills—the twenty-two-year-old had secured one of the coveted but unpaid positions doing relatively minor tasks for White House staff.[154] Now, thanks to the shutdown, she interacted directly with the president. Lewinsky later testified that on the shutdown's second day, November 15—when she was alone with the president for the first time—they commenced their two-year relationship. Although secret at first, it would have a dramatic impact once revealed during investigations into allegations of harassment leveled at Clinton by Paula Jones and others.[155]

That impact was still in the future, however, as all sixteen NATO foreign and defense ministers gathered in early December 1995 for a show of unity in the face of the Bosnian challenge.[156] Under his new leadership, and with most of the enforced delay now past, the alliance was finally ready to do more than debate. It readied itself for action: making a success of IFOR in Bosnia and making enlargement a reality. The ministerial approved "intensive consultations" with countries wishing to pursue membership.[157] The US Mission to NATO reported that "the time of action is here."[158] Reporting on these events privately to Clinton, the secretary of state noted that "there was a palpable feeling of relief that impotence had been replaced by determination."

Even France under its new president, Jacques Chirac, had realized it needed to reengage with NATO's military structures in the new era.[159] He was willing to reintegrate into NATO's military command if certain reforms could be undertaken. This renewed French interest in NATO was, in Hunter's eyes, a recognition that the EU "has proved incapable of developing a security and defense identity and is not likely to do so for some time to come." Hunter added that the "WEU has proved to be vacuous as an alternative either to NATO or to the American role in Europe." In short, "the NATO train has left the station, and France wants to be on board, with a hand on the (shared) controls." France would seek to use those controls to slow enlargement while reform—or, as France liked to call it, adaptation—took place; given that a slowing pace was also in German interests, it hoped it could succeed.[160]

It was while hosting Holbrooke at the fiftieth-anniversary commemoration of the liberation of Auschwitz in January 1995 that Wałęsa had shared with the American diplomat his feeling that the United States faced a "'terrible responsibility.'"[161] For too many years in the past, Europe had suffered from war and from the genocide carried out at Auschwitz and elsewhere. Later in 1995, the Srebrenica tragedy confirmed that the potential for large-scale killings in Europe had not simply vanished along with the Berlin Wall. Now there was also a precious opportunity to establish a lasting peace. The Polish Nobel laureate understood there were "only relatively rare moments in history when that sort of opportunity comes up," so it was for that reason an enormous, daunting responsibility.[162] Clinton had recognized the challenge as well; as he remarked a month after the Auschwitz commemoration, "we now have a chance to write a new chapter in the history of the world."[163] With the extended delay scheduled to come to an end in 1996, it was time to see whether he and Yeltsin together could be the ones to write that new chapter—and what it would cost to try.

CHAPTER EIGHT

Cost per Inch

I F RUSSIA HAD BEEN IN A POSITION to obstruct the enlargement of NATO in 1996, it would have done so. But Moscow remained too weak to block its former satellites from seeking a permanent connection to the Western alliance. And yet, President Bill Clinton and his advisors did not simply implement expansion that year, although they could have. Despite repeatedly saying Moscow had no veto over enlargement, they nonetheless felt it necessary to secure some form of de facto Russian acceptance beforehand, for two reasons. First, they still found it essential to avoid endangering President Boris Yeltsin's chances of re-election that summer; with an approval rating of 3 percent, Yeltsin remained vulnerable to competitors whom the United States found much less appealing.[1] Second, they wanted to limit enlargement's overall cost, measured partly in dollars but mostly in damage to US-Russian relations.

The question dominating 1996 and early 1997 was what Yeltsin would want in exchange for his consent in some form or another. To estimate whether they could get his agreement for a tolerable price, the Clinton administration needed to decide how many countries to add, because the more countries, the greater the cost. That deceptively simple math, however, hid a deeper complication. Given Russian sensitivities, expansion to particular countries (such as the Baltics and Ukraine) or expansion with particular features (such as the ability to move substantial foreign forces and nuclear weapons to the territory of new allies) would yield a much higher cost per inch.

Clinton's advisors, among whom Deputy Secretary of State Strobe
Talbott remained dominant on this issue, concluded they could lower both
the overall price and the cost per inch by keeping the number of new members small and having NATO as a whole negotiate some special charter
with Moscow in parallel. They faced vociferous criticism from all sides,
however. Central and Eastern European leaders, along with Republicans
in Congress, criticized Clinton for stalling yet more. Moscow, meanwhile,
felt Clinton was moving at breakneck speed, as its new foreign minister,
Yevgeny Primakov, made clear. Primakov, who had successfully shep-
herded much of the KGB unscathed into the post–Cold War era, replaced
Andrei Kozyrev as the Russian foreign minister on January 9, 1996, and
immediately put up new forms of resistance to expansion.[2] A year-and-a-
half struggle to establish the price of enlargement resulted. This fight
encompassed both the Russian and American presidential elections of summer and autumn 1996, respectively, and revived the not-one-inch controversy from German unification before culminating in a bargain in Paris
in May 1997.

"Who Kills/Beats/Screws Whom?"

At the outset of this struggle, one fact was clear: there was much demand
to join NATO. If the feelers put out to the secretary general, Javier Solana, and to diplomats at the US Mission to NATO were to be believed,
the number of states hoping for membership was large.[3] Among the aspirants, the big three—Poland, Hungary, and the Czech Republic—had as
ever the best chances of success. They recognized that a happy conver-
gence in the United States was tilting the balance ever more in their favor.
Proponents of full-guarantee expansion were ascendant just as another US
election year arrived, causing both Democrats and Republicans to court
Polish Americans and other voters of Central and Eastern European ex-
traction. To win reelection, Clinton needed to win the states of the industrial Northeast and upper Midwest, where such voters were particularly
well represented.

If it was agreed that everyone wanted in, nearly every other issue in
the struggle was open to question. One of the trickiest questions for the
Clinton administration was whether to maintain its interest in potentially
adding the Baltic nations and Ukraine to the alliance. There were obvious costs: Moscow warned Talbott that not "'one square inch' of former
Soviet territory" should join. But the United States had long supported

the Baltics' sovereign rights to make their own choices (most notably, of course, by refraining from recognition of the region's forcible incorporation into the Soviet Union during World War II), and the administration believed that the Ukrainians had a right to have their wishes respected as well, even if they were no longer a nuclear power. This conundrum prompted Solana to seek guidance repeatedly in the course of 1996 from his many US contacts: Talbott and his boss, the Secretary of State Warren Christopher; James Steinberg, the head of policy planning at the State Department; John Kornblum, Richard Holbrooke's successor as assistant secretary of state for European and Canadian affairs; and a host of other State Department, NSC, and Defense Department officials.[4] In Solana's view, Baltic and Ukrainian membership represented "'the most difficult part of enlargement.'"[5]

Kornblum favored aggressive expansion. He felt that "if the Baltics and Ukraine were not in the first tranche of new NATO members," they at least "needed to be reassured with a more tangible sense of broader security relations" with Western states.[6] Secretary Christopher found it "unrealistic" that they could join in the short term, but he agreed on the "need to be 'protective'" of the Baltics in particular. The way to express that, he thought, was to "reiterate to them their eligibility" for NATO membership early and often.[7] Steinberg let Solana know on March 16, 1996, that he was also "working on ideas about how to help the Baltics with their own defense."[8]

These conversations showed that, with the big three increasingly certain to become NATO members, the geographic area of contention was shifting eastward. The onus was on the Baltic nations to do what Poland and its neighbors had nearly finished doing: seal the deal with NATO. Baltic leaders intensified their efforts to convince Westerners to let them in the alliance, using every tool at their disposal, including literary ones. In a meeting with Christopher, the foreign minister of Latvia, Valdis Birkavs, quoted the Czech novelist Milan Kundera's definition of a small country: "one which knew it could disappear at any moment."[9] Christopher took the point. Other Baltic diplomats impressed their US counterparts with their eagerness and seriousness, slowly gaining an edge over Ukrainian representatives. Even President Clinton, a strong supporter of Ukraine, was frustrated by Kyiv's tendency toward backsliding on agreements; the Baltic nations, in contrast, displayed a reliability that made them more appealing as partners.[10]

Although it worked with the Americans, the unbridled Baltic campaign to join NATO unsettled Nordic leaders, who encouraged their

The Baltic states.

smaller neighbors to learn instead from their experience, gained through decades spent living in an area that was Soviet-adjacent but not Soviet-controlled. As a Swedish diplomat, Jan Eliasson, confided to his US counterparts, his country "constantly hammered the Baltics with the message that they must work out a *modus vivendi* with the Russians and normalize relations." The Swedes felt it was essential to "avoid giving the Russians legitimate excuses for complaints," particularly on "the sensitive issue of the rights of Russian speakers in Estonia and Latvia."[11]

The president of Finland, Martti Ahtisaari, made similar remarks in confidence both to Christopher and to the US ambassador in Helsinki, Derek Shearer, who was also Talbott's brother-in-law and former Yale classmate. In the president's view, the Baltics needed to avoid rash actions or unilateral declarations. He worried about unnamed "individuals who have encouraged the Balts to take positions not in their long-term interest," particularly with regard to territorial borders. For example, "the Estonians had considered issuing a unilateral declaration on their border dispute with the Russians, hoping the EU and US would support their stand." This, he indicated, "won't do: you can't choose your neighbors." Rather, "all of us (in the region) must establish businesslike relations with the Russians." Ahtisaari, a future Nobel Peace Prize winner, also went out of his way to pay pointed compliments to the (by then increasingly marginalized) Partnership for Peace, saying "it was a brilliant invention."[12] His implication seemed to be that PfP could have promoted such businesslike relations by increasing security in the region without creating a new Article 5 border with Russia. Alternatively, revival of a Nordic defense association concept, with the Baltics joining such an association and the entire group of countries subsequently linking to NATO, might presumably have addressed Ahtisaari's concern about borders as well. Such thinking was out of step with that of the ambassador's brother-in-law, however.

Another enormous, thorny question was how to manage NATO's evolving relationship not just with Eastern states but also with a Western one, namely, with France. The French were of course already members of the alliance, but they had not been part of its integrated military command since 1966, thanks to a partial pullout by President Charles de Gaulle. Now the detailed aspects of adaptations sought by France as part of its potential reintegration were becoming clearer.[13] As President Jacques Chirac told Clinton on February 1, 1996, the alliance needed "to find a system—a single system—that can work in the event that the US does send troops and also if the US does not send troops, because you think it's not worth it."[14]

In other words, he was restating a long-standing French desire for options for action below the level of all-out NATO intervention, allowing the alliance to duck some of the broader questions and frictions with Russia that a full alliance intervention might imply. Chirac hoped in particular that the still-extant Western European Union of 1954 could be reshaped to fill this role.[15] In theory, Chirac's idea of a separable though not entirely separate force could have given Washington greater ability to manage, or delegate, contingency. It would allow a subset of NATO to intervene in a small conflict without the associated costs.[16] For a presidential administration whose top officials were shaped by the trauma of the failed war of choice in Vietnam, it might have been a useful out. Clinton, however, was skeptical. While the United States had "never opposed the development of a greater European security identity," he felt that such matters could be addressed within the existing "framework of the Alliance."[17] American doubts about the WEU further undermined Chirac's chances; as one State Department official put it, that "no one has ever mistaken the WEU for a serious security organization."[18]

Alongside these substantive questions, a major risk was surfacing at home. Although not related to NATO expansion, it threatened Clinton's ability to enact any of his policies, foreign or domestic—or even stay in office. At first that risk was apparent only to a handful of observers immediately around the president. Clinton's relationship with Monica Lewinsky, begun on November 15, 1995, entered its most intense phase in spring 1996—just as the US election got seriously underway, when the damage from exposure would be greatest. He nevertheless continued the relationship, even though a lawsuit brought by Paula Jones, accusing the president of sexual harassment in May 1991, was headed for the Supreme Court. There could be catastrophic damage to his candidacy and presidency if Jones's lawyers learned about Lewinsky and could procure her testimony, which could serve to establish a pattern of improper conduct. Rumors of that misconduct even made it to Russian intelligence, if Yeltsin's memoirs are accurate: he wrote that "Russian intelligence sent me a coded report" for potential use in dealing with the American president, indicating that Republicans intended to make use of Clinton's "predilection for beautiful young women" and specifically "a young provocateur in his entourage" to bring him down.[19]

Lower-level White House employees, presumably aware of the risks, began remarking pointedly to each other about how often Lewinsky was in Clinton's company. Over the 1996 Easter holiday, the deputy chief of staff abruptly transferred her to the White House liaison office in the Pentagon, reportedly the place where the administration parked its problem children. Shocked, Lewinsky complained to Clinton. He mollified her by promising to call her regularly, which he did, and to reemploy her in the White House—after the election.[20]

So the 1996 campaign season began with the president juggling a number of risks and open questions. With regard to Russia, Clinton and his advisors needed, as a *New York Times* article put it, "'to balance policies that don't go together very well: partnership and containment.'"[21] Achieving that balance was tricky. They needed to support Yeltsin but also get his acceptance of an expanded NATO. Worse, it seemed to the secretary of state that "no matter what we do" with Moscow, whether it be "billions of dollars in bilateral support, officer-housing construction," or intervention on its behalf with international financial institutions, "it's not enough."[22]

The president, trying as always to find a way to bring everyone along, kept seeking win-win outcomes in his contacts with the Russian president. As he told Yeltsin, "we cannot allow a split to happen." Both men hoped the positive trends in their relations could be sustained; in particular, Russian and US troops "have been working well together in Bosnia," and they both hoped that cooperation would continue. Yeltsin replied that "deployment of nuclear weapons on the territory of the new NATO countries" would unravel such cooperation.[23] But his ability to resist that deployment was limited by his country's weakness and need for help. Just after officially announcing his run for reelection on February 15, 1996, he pleaded with Clinton to "add a little, from nine to 13 billion dollars," to a package the IMF was considering, to permit him "to deal with social problems in this very important pre-election situation" and help pay overdue salaries, among other things.[24] The Clinton administration succeeded in convincing the IMF to give Russia a $10.2 billion loan. Even better, the loan did not commit Moscow to the IMF's usual onerous requirements for economic reform. Instead, as one analyst put it later, "the political purpose of this IMF credit was obvious to everybody: helping re-elect President Yeltsin in the face of a potent Communist threat. The IMF lost its credibility."[25]

The easy money allowed Yeltsin, when he traveled to Russian cities for campaign events, to open rallies by saying "'my pockets are full.'" He dispensed generous favors to local groups: to a cultural center here, a convent there, and even telephone installations to individual voters.[26] His campaign staff held nighttime planning sessions that they nicknamed "what-shall-we-hand-out-tomorrow" meetings.[27] His approval rating began to tick upward.

German chancellor Helmut Kohl supported this effort to bolster Yeltsin, preferring partnership to containment. As he told US defense secretary Bill Perry on February 3, 1996, "if we could produce 'two years of calm,'" then "'progress in relations' with Russia" would be possible with less risk.[28] The chancellor had a sympathetic listener. Perry had of course long considered relations with Moscow more crucial than NATO expansion, and he had recently visited Ukraine yet again to witness the destruction of empty missile silos. "Seeing the cloud of smoke arising from the silo," he later wrote, was one "of the most memorable moments of my term as secretary."[29] He would later take part in planting "a beautiful and lucrative crop of sunflowers" in a field that formerly contained a weapon that could have killed millions of Americans.[30]

Kohl did not stop with Perry.[31] The German raised the issue with Clinton as well; the US president made special efforts to stay in touch with Kohl by phone on a regular basis, despite the pressures of campaigning. Once, stuck on an icy runway on February 17 while waiting to fly to New Hampshire, the president used the delay to call the chancellor from Air Force One to discuss strategy toward Moscow. Kohl felt that if Yeltsin "does as promised and pays the overdue salaries, he will be fine." Meanwhile, the only sensible course for the West was "to support him without being too obvious or too pushy." Clinton agreed, saying, "it's important that we do it in a way that doesn't hurt him" because "if we do too much, if we're too obvious about it, it could be used against him." Kohl replied, "exactly."[32]

They also addressed the tricky issue of Yeltsin's desire to join the G7 as indirect compensation for NATO enlargement.[33] Clinton and Kohl both worried that if Russia joined and Yeltsin subsequently lost the election, the tight-knit circle of the world's most developed countries would be stuck with the Communist candidate for the presidency, Gennady Zyuganov. Not admitting Russia, however, could delay alliance expansion, which Clinton thought inadvisable, since "the furor will be overwhelming . . . both here and in the Central and East European countries." The idea of NATO enlargement—particularly to countries with widely admired leaders such as Lech Wałęsa and Václav Havel—had become so popular that delays could have political costs. Kohl fully agreed that "the Poles have the right to want to join NATO," but he felt that "we have to go about it in a clever way."[34] In later conversations with the German, the president added that the challenge was to accede to Poland's understandable interest in the alliance while protecting Yeltsin: "if the Russian people knew how much I wanted him re-elected, it might actually hurt his chances."[35] Clinton also expressed optimism about dealing with Yeltsin in general: "Boris is not unreasonable, he just gets misinformed every now and then." Kohl agreed, saying, "Boris listens to us."[36]

Privately, Kohl confided to party colleagues just how risky he found the behavior of American supporters of expansion, particularly "certain groups of Republicans," who he felt were behaving unwisely during the Russian election season. Residents of Siberia, Kohl told his colleagues, were asking their elected representatives how best to prepare for NATO air attacks. Clearly sentiments on the issue were verging on the irrational. The chancellor thought the Germans needed to do their best to promote sensible dialogue among all sides, but that it would be hard because, in his view, expansion was "above all about Poland" and the Republican Party was trying to "reactivate" Polish Americans to punish the president in November 1996 if he did not expand the alliance quickly enough. Even though he ran a center-right party himself, and in theory should have been sympathetic to the Republican effort to unseat a left-of-center leader, Kohl found these developments distressing because Yeltsin had "never left us in the lurch." Instead, at every critical juncture, the Russian president had been "an absolutely reliable partner" to Germany. That reliability had yielded "the withdrawal of Russian soldiers happening exactly as agreed to the last detail," for which Kohl remained deeply grateful.[37]

Foreign Minister Primakov also made clear that he wanted better treatment for his country; as he put it, the United States should treat "Russia as an equal."[38] As Primakov took office in early 1996, Talbott's take on what the Russian would do out of the gate was simple: show "how different he is" from his despised predecessor. Kozyrev had, in Talbott's words, been "guilty of the charge his worst enemies leveled at him: he's pro-Western." He had genuinely believed that "Russia's best hope" was "to take advantage of the opportunity we, above all, are offering it of integration with the West."

Primakov, thought Talbott, was the exact opposite: he "enjoys tangling with us, scoring points off us," and "exposing our 'true' motives" (which he "delights in identifying as every bit as cynical and competitive as what he thinks are quite properly the motives underlying Russian policy and strategy)." As a result, Primakov had a clear view of his mission as foreign minister: "mask Russian weakness while rebuilding Russian power." He would do everything in his power to extract the maximum price for expansion, assuming the worst on the part of Washington. The deputy secretary found Primakov to be a true believer in "Lenin's maxim that all history can be explained" by answering one question, imaginatively translated by Talbott as "who kills/beats/screws whom?"[39]

A Broken Promise and a Poison Pill?

With "'no more Mr. Nice Guy'" in the foreign minister's office, Talbott suggested that Christopher be on guard when he and Primakov commenced battle in early February 1996.[40] Ahtisaari agreed to host both men in Helsinki but wondered aloud why Christopher was unwilling to invite the Russian to the United States: "'is this a step back to Cold War days?'" Christopher replied that it was not; he only wanted to use Helsinki as a way for the two to meet without the pressures of a full-fledged formal visit in either country.[41]

When he began speaking to Primakov, Christopher realized (as he later told Clinton) that the Russian's "considerable talents have a single objective": Yeltsin's reelection in June.[42] Primakov was hardly alone in prioritizing that objective. Russian oligarchs had apparently held a side meeting at the January 1996 Davos conference on making Yeltsin win, since their fortunes were tied so closely to his.[43] Western experts on Russia reported that the president's election campaign was "dirty" as a result of such deals "for political support with the oligarchs," who were "manipulating politics and fighting among themselves over the purchase of former state assets."[44]

In the course of talks on February 9–10, 1996 in Helsinki, however, Christopher's and Primakov's focus stayed on foreign policy. Primakov was at least willing to take "a positive line on Russian cooperation" with the United States and NATO in Bosnia. But the foreign minister "repeatedly returned to the theme that treatment of Russia as an 'equal'— something he insisted has not occurred in the past—will guide his conduct of Russian foreign policy."[45] For his part, the secretary of state highlighted the issue of Ukraine. That country's president, Leonid Kuchma, had recently complained to Clinton that "while declaring in public their friendship and love, the Russians are doing everything possible to suppress us and drive us to our knees." In addition to nonpayment of what Kuchma felt he was owed from deals to denuclearize, Moscow was also promoting labor unrest. It had "provoked the strikes by Ukraine's coal miners" by sending "representatives to virtually all Ukraine's mines." Then "the Russians disconnected us from our joint electrical system, forcing us to use more natural gas." The result was that Ukraine "had to shut down one-half of our enterprises." In Kuchma's view, this was happening because Russia wanted Ukraine back "within the Russian control structure."[46] To Primakov, Christopher insisted that "Russia needs to fulfill its obligation to compensate Ukraine for the tactical nuclear weapons transferred in 1991–92."

Primakov, however, was not forthcoming on Ukraine—or on NATO expansion. Instead, he launched four lines of attack on enlargement. The first was to claim that "the movement of NATO's infrastructure into Central Europe, by bringing missiles closer to Russia, would be tantamount to an abrogation of the INF Treaty" and so was inadmissible. In other words, since short-range missiles moved to new eastern sites "could threaten targets" previously reachable only by INF-restricted weapons, they were prohibited.[47] The second line took advantage of US interest in a comprehensive nuclear test ban as a bargaining chip. Like so many other things, the White House understood that (in the words of an internal summary) "CTBT monitoring and verification" could only succeed if there were "positive United States–Russian relations."[48] Clinton had already tried to flatter Yeltsin into helping with the test ban initiative, saying "you may be the only one who can sell the zero-yield CTB to China."[49] A third line of attack was to link enlargement to proliferation, saying, "'if NATO is to be enlarged, then the cheapest way for us to counter it" would be to "expand our nuclear capability in the region.'"[50] As a corollary to that line of attack, Moscow also called arms control accords into question. Primakov approvingly recounted a remark by a member of the Duma, advising that "'we renounce both START II and the INF Treaty if NATO expands.'" The US Senate had ratified START II in January 1996, but the Russians were letting it languish. Perry feared that the treaty had become "'a casualty of NATO expansion.'"[51]

By far Moscow's most tenacious line of attack, however, was the fourth: using the two-plus-four treaty of 1990 as a weapon. Russian diplomats claimed that the "'spirit'" of the accord and contemporary "side assurances prohibit nations to the east of Germany from joining the alliance."[52] Inspiration for this attack came in part, ironically, from Yeltsin's nemesis Mikhail Gorbachev. The last Soviet leader had given an influential interview in the September 22–28, 1995, issue of the *Moscow News*, entitled

"Russia Will Not Play Second Fiddle," lamenting that the West had been taking advantage of Russia.[53] He was also in the process of writing and publishing memoirs, expressing this lament in multiple languages and countries. Gorbachev's book brought renewed attention to the February 1990 comment by the former secretary of state, James Baker, that NATO would not shift one inch eastward.[54] The signal boosting of this controversy caused by Gorbachev's book was a timely gift to Yeltsin and Primakov, who now faced a West pushing to see just how many inches eastward it could move.

No Russian argument infuriated Western leaders more than this one.[55] Current and former policymakers competed to denounce it fervently. The US embassy in Bonn circulated comments by Baker, who had gone back to private life as an attorney, dismissing the claim: "'this treaty of course deals only with Germany and doesn't pretend to deal with anything else.'"[56] German defense minister Volker Rühe called it "'absurd' to suggest that a treaty on the political unity of Germany could influence the right of the independent nations of Central and Eastern Europe to form alliances of their choosing."[57]

Apparently uncertain that it was so absurd, Baker's successor commissioned a detailed internal investigation of the Russian claim. Christopher chose John Herbst, his acting coordinator for former Soviet states, and Kornblum to carry out the investigation. He distributed their final report widely, providing ammunition for US diplomats and press spokesmen to shoot down Primakov and his team. As a result of both the official imprimatur and the broad distribution, the Herbst and Kornblum account came to be seen as canonical, and for years their views helped shape American attitudes toward the controversy of what, exactly, had been said in 1990.

In their investigation, the two men focused on the discrepancy between spoken negotiations in 1990 and their more limited written results. First, they admitted West German foreign minister Hans-Dietrich Genscher made a spoken "unilateral statement" that NATO's "offensive forces would not be moved eastward.'" He had of course said this in various forms more than once, but the general point was accurate. Genscher's statement had no legal force, however, because "the treaty makes no mention of NATO deployments beyond the boundaries of Germany," and only the written treaty truly mattered. American diplomats should "pointedly remind the Russians of this basic fact."[58]

Second, American envoys should also remind Russians that the Helsinki Final Act of 1975 and the Charter of Paris of 1990—both signed by Moscow—confirmed that every sovereign-state signatory could choose its military alliance freely.[59] The only reason that right had been spelled out separately with regard to Germany in a special two-plus-four treaty was because of "the unique nature of the post-war settlement" over that divided country. As a result of Germany's unconditional surrender to the four allies in 1945, "Moscow had a legal role in German unification," and hence "Germany had a compelling reason to pursue a deal with the Russians." But "the situation vis-à-vis the Central and Eastern Europeans is vastly different." Any suggestion that the United States was "prepared to countenance such deal-making 'about them, but without them'"—a common Polish phrase for other countries deciding their future over their heads—"would be devastating to our political position and credibility there."[60]

Finally and most tellingly, the combination of the two-plus-four treaty and the agreed minute added in the wee hours just before the treaty's signature explicitly allowed NATO forces to cross the old Cold War dividing line after the departure of Soviet troops—meaning Moscow had signed an accord permitting the opposite of what it now claimed. Primakov would later concede this point in his memoirs. He regretted that Gorbachev had neglected to get nonexpansion assurances codified in some way. The Soviet leader's failure to have such assurances "put into a treaty or legal form" meant that Primakov inherited a serious problem: Herbst and Kornblum's 1996 claims were, in terms of the formal written record, accurate.[61]

The two Americans had a problem as well, however, which they did not acknowledge at the time. In their zeal to fight their corner, they were unwilling to acknowledge the significance of NATO's contingent enlargement in 1990. Recognition of that precedent might have helped to arrest the decay in the US-Russian dialogue. Instead, the two men ridiculed Moscow's claim as a "specious argument which we should refute definitively." Although the two-plus-four was a formal treaty, they argued that it "did not set any legal or political precedents." They considered Moscow's ideas so laughable in legal terms that they suspected something else was going on: "the Russians may be groping towards a somewhat more subtle outcome." Primakov, in other words, was preparing the ground for a compromise. Since NATO had accepted legally binding prohibitions on "the stationing or deployment of foreign forces or nuclear weapons" on the "sovereign territory of an ally" (i.e., Germany), "Russia might hope eventually to extract a similar limitation from NATO itself with regard to an enlarged alliance." Primakov was most likely "positioning Russia to pursue a deal in which new allies would have to accept limitations on their membership equivalent to the two-plus-four restrictions on Germany."[62] It was essentially the compromise that Lech Wałęsa had signaled to Richard Holbrooke in January 1995 that he might be willing to accept.

Talbott and Christopher were so alarmed at this prospect that they told Clinton it represented "a poison pill of the most extreme toxicity." In their view, the prospect of applying the two-plus-four to more of Central and Eastern Europe threatened not only the heart of NATO deterrence but NATO itself, which ultimately rested on the forward-deployment of American nuclear weapons.[63] The State Department's bottom line was clear: "we should forcefully remind Moscow that we are not prepared to cut any deals over the heads of the Central and Eastern Europeans."[64]

Leaders from those countries confirmed Herbst and Kornblum's suspicions in March 13, 1996, by reporting that Russia was indeed hinting at two-plus-four-style restrictions on them, meaning "no nukes/no stationed forces." Primakov was apparently worried that without such limits, "'boundless' extension of NATO to Russia's borders" would lead to "membership for the Baltic states or Ukraine."[65] Herbst concluded that Primakov was "simply trolling for an authoritative admission from any of the Central Europeans or any of the Allies that they would settle for something less than full-fledged enlargement."[66] Christopher advised the would-be new allies that given "Primakov's sophistication relative to that of Kozyrev in seeking to disrupt NATO enlargement," they should "reject Primakov's efforts to drive wedges between potential members of the alliance."[67] The NSC also opposed "a 'Norway' status for new NATO members," a reference to Norway's insistence that no troops be stationed on its territory except during a war, no atomic weapons be deployed there, and all exercises be held a certain distance away from the Soviet (later Russian) border.[68]

Sensing victory, the Czech Republic, Hungary, and Poland resisted the poison pill as Washington requested.[69] The only partial exception was Slovakia, where the leaders of a prominent workers' association, Ján Slota and Ján Ľupták, publicly questioned the need to deploy NATO's nuclear arsenal on Slovakian soil, given how little difference it would make to the strategic balance and how much it would damage relations with Russia.[70] It was part of the longer history of Europeans questioning the need for shorter-range nuclear weapons, and the reaction showed that the issue was still sensitive despite the passing of the Cold War. This hint that Slovakians might take the poison pill combined with doubts about Slovakia's uneven progress in democratizing threatened to sink the country's chances of early membership. American diplomats informed Bratislava that summer that "it was not clear to the USG whether Slovakia shared our values."[71]

With campaigning in Russia entering its endgame, contention over these issues could clearly cause trouble—which made it all the more problematic that a regular NATO ministerial, or NAC, was due to take place in Berlin on June 3–4, 1996, shortly before the first round of the Russian election on June 16. A lid had to be kept on stray remarks; loose lips must not sink the ship of enlargement just as it got underway. Solana conferred with the US Mission to NATO about how to keep allies busy talking about something other than expansion; they decided to spend time "'educating' the French on how the NATO military structure actually works."[72]

Clinton weighed in personally, telling Solana that when enlargement did come up at the ministerial, all present were to act in a way that was "methodical, plodding, even bureaucratic." It was essential "to take away the emotional energy from the NATO enlargement issue," not only in "Russia and Central and Eastern Europe" but also "among constituencies that support enlargement in the US and Europe." As he said to Talbott, he wanted to give Yeltsin time to accept enlargement as "'one of those things in life you can't avoid—you just have to get used'" to it. The bottom line: "we should smile and plod ahead." The NATO allies, he added, should also emphasize the success of PfP, which persisted despite the blows to its importance. Despite being marginalized, the Partnership remained, as the president noted, a site of substantive cooperation between multiple countries.[73]

Clinton's advisors also recommended playing up the success of the IFOR mission in Bosnia. An NSC assessment on June 21, 1996 found that it "continues to progress smoothly as it consolidates its successful accomplishments of the first six months and prepares to support elections in September."[74] The Partnership had proved to be a durable framework for bringing the Atlantic Alliance together with a diverse set of partners, with one in six IFOR troops deployed in early 1996 coming from non-NATO countries.[75] Just a few years after the breakup of the Soviet Union, Russian troops were successfully working shoulder to shoulder with NATO forces in Bosnia, and Russian forces were functioning well within a US-led command structure.[76] IFOR showed that real cooperation at the military level was possible under the right conditions.[77]

Political cooperation that summer was extensive as well. Clinton continued to believe that Yeltsin was better than all alternatives (from the American viewpoint) and likely to give Washington the best deal on

NATO. That belief had motivated his arm-twisting of the IMF earlier in the year. It now reportedly motivated him to get the election consultant Richard Dresner, who had worked with Clinton in the past, to advise Yeltsin's campaign.[78] Dresner kept in close touch with Clinton's current political advisor, Dick Morris, providing a conduit of information directly to the White House.[79] Meanwhile, Talbott took weekly advice on the Russian election from John Deutch, the director of the Central Intelligence Agency, who was also keeping a close eye on developments.[80]

Yeltsin knew that Washington needed him to win and took full advantage of it. A month before the first-round vote, he called Clinton and said bluntly, "Bill, for my election campaign, I urgently need for Russia a loan of $2.5 billion." He wanted, as ever, "money to pay pensions and wages," but IMF conditions meant that he would not receive the promised funds in time. Clinton, surprised, said, "I had understood you would get about $1 billion from the IMF before the election." Yeltsin answered, "no, no, only $300 million." Clinton said he would do all he could to get the appropriate wheels turning, which he did.[81]

The US president helped further with an array of announcements. He trumpeted the good news that Russia had, as of June 1, 1996, at long last taken possession of all nuclear weapons stranded in Ukraine after the collapse of the Soviet Union. In a public statement, Clinton rejoiced that "in 1991, there were more than 4000 strategic and tactical nuclear warheads" in Ukraine, and "today there are none."[82] He also announced a compromise on the CFE flank controversy sparked in part by the war in Chechnya, which fell within a flank. Despite the misgivings of Russia's smaller neighbors, Moscow gained the ability to station more weaponry in that flank and an extension until 1999 of the deadline to come into compliance with that new level.[83] It seemed possible that the Chechen war might be winding down; on May 27, 1996, Yeltsin signed an accord with a rebel leader agreeing to the cessation of combat operations.[84] Finally, on top of all of these developments, Russia received an extension of the deadline for completing the reductions required by START II.[85]

Wałęsa, visiting the United States on June 3, 1996 as a private citizen, sought and received an invitation to see Clinton. Once inside the White House, he sounded a warning about this all-out effort to support Yeltsin. Wałęsa reminded the president that "Yeltsin really can be dangerous" and that "he has already shot at his people and at parliament." Those actions crossed a significant threshold and signaled that Yeltsin might authorize violence in the future as well: "he has the will and the structures to carry out such action." While "in a peaceful situation, of course, Yeltsin is preferable because he is a known quantity . . . the situation is not necessarily peaceful in Russia."[86]

Wałęsa's pleas changed little. The push to protect Yeltsin continued and proved successful. On June 16, the Russian president finished first among ten candidates, earning 35 percent of the vote and making it into the second round.[87] Then, exhausted, he suffered another heart attack. His campaign team managed, however, to avoid a disaster by concealing the seriousness of his illness. Despite virtually disappearing from public view, Yeltsin defeated his communist opponent, Zyuganov, on July 3 by thirteen percentage points.[88]

Although the reelected Russian president was barely strong enough to attend his own second inauguration, the cries of relief from the West at Yeltsin's survival in office drowned out all questions, both about his fitness for office and about the election's more dubious aspects.[89] One such aspect was the report by Russian election authorities that despite the years of brutality in Chechnya ordered by Yeltsin—not to mention international observers' estimates that fewer than 500,000 adults remained in the region—more than a million Chechens had cast votes, and 70 percent were for the incumbent. Later, a member of the OSCE election-observation team claimed that he was pressured not to reveal the "widespread voter fraud" he had witnessed. A US diplomat serving in the Moscow embassy at the time of the election, Thomas Graham, asserted that the Clinton administration knew the election was not truly fair, but it was a case of "'the ends justifying the means.'"[90]

Redefining "Not One Inch," Gaining New Leases on Life

As the Russian election was still unfolding, the NSC felt confident enough—despite Yeltsin's physical and political weakness—to finalize its "NATO Enlargement Game Plan: June 96 to June 97."[91] Conscious of the link between the number of new members and the cost in terms of damage to US-Russian relations, the NSC advised starting expansion at the earliest possible date but inviting only the most obvious candidates. As the plan noted, recent "Russian suggestions that partial or limited CEE membership (e.g. no nuclear stationing, no extension of NATO military infrastructure, no Baltic membership at all) could indicate a softening

Russian stance." In light of decreasing French and German support for enlargement, the implication was that the United States should seize the moment and move ahead—even at the risk of having to leave out the Baltic states, which "lack the votes for now" among current NATO members.

The founding treaty of the alliance stated that invitations to new members required "unanimous agreement" among allies. The combination of American military dominance and arm-twisting in the alliance could most likely achieve that result for some states, but not necessarily the Baltics, or the Romanians, who despite strong French support were simply "not ready." There was, however, a silver lining: by inviting only a small group at first, the alliance made clear that other invitations would follow. This strategy enabled the Clinton team to keep "runners-up and also-rans engaged," lest they worry "they are being left in a gray area."[92] In Germany, Defense Minister Rühe supported this strategy. As he later remarked, "if we wanted to bring in the Baltic states and others later, it was just the right thing to bring three in first."[93]

The NSC added that, in the meantime, the United States should find ways to reinforce Baltic sovereignty and that "similar measures should be devised for Ukraine." Clinton put some of the NSC's advice into action even before the second round of the Russian elections. On June 25, 1996, he welcomed Baltic leaders to the White House. He repeated words that Talbott had already said to them a year earlier: "the first new members to join the alliance shall not be the last." The deputy secretary reinforced the president by adding that "the first, second, and third enlargements will not be the last." The alliance had to be cautious, however, about revealing the depth of its support for eventual Baltic membership. As the NSC put it, creating "the impression that the Baltics will be given special consideration in the next tranche could be seen as so provocative as to sour, perhaps for good, prospects for a meaningful NATO-Russia relationship."

To prevent that, the NSC suggested a smart maneuver: to endorse rhetorically Primakov's efforts to enforce as many two-plus-four treaty terms as possible on new NATO members. The alliance could say that, "in the present security environment, NATO has no intention of stationing nuclear weapons or significant forward-based multinational conventional forces on the territories of new members." This would be less confrontational than the Herbst and Kornblum scorched-earth approach of ridiculing Russian claims as specious—but it would not bind Washington to anything. NATO could offer, as previously considered, some new charter or "framework document" between the United States and Russia.[94] As

UN ambassador Madeleine Albright later summarized it, the charter was meant to "give Moscow a voice but not a veto in European security discussions."[95]

The object of all of these arguments was to get Russia to name its price and get moving. As Talbott put it to Christopher, "I need hardly emphasize how tricky this is—diplomatically, strategically, politically and bureaucratically." At this critical moment, it was essential to keep the circle of those in the know tight and small. The deputy secretary saw Steinberg as "the co-captain (with Kornblum) of our Euro-security/NATO expansion team," along with a few others.[96] Talbott was clear: he did "*not* want to broaden the circle any further." If he did, "we'd get leaks, back-biting and God knows what else." But if the deputy secretary kept his team tiny, then one of the biggest problems would be avoiding a new Yalta-style agreement about the future of Europe arising without the direct participation of Central and Eastern European negotiators. Christopher phrased this as avoiding a US-Russian "condominium" over their heads.[97]

Another hard decision was what to say about Russian eligibility for NATO. According to Talbott, "several top Brits and the German Defense Minister," Rühe, had told him "we should stop kidding ourselves and simply say flat out, no way will Russia ever get into NATO." Talbott disagreed, preferring to keep the matter open. As he advised Christopher in bold face, **"never say never about anyone**. No PfP state, including Russia, is precluded from someday entering NATO." In other words, "if Russia knocks on the door, we should not throw a bolt of some kind and shout through the peep-hole, 'Go away! You'll never get in!'" But he added in italics, *"that said, Russia, if it did knock, would have to understand that it would not be entering any time soon—and others would be passing it on the threshold."*

The potential "others" included former Soviet republics. Talbott reported that State Department staff had already done "excellent work" on the "possibility of the Balts' eventually coming in" and that there was "a similar paper in the works on Ukraine, at an earlier stage of development."[98] By October 1996, the NSC would also begin studying "how to build NATO links with the emerging Ukraine-Georgia-Azerbaijan-Uzbekistan group, so as to increase their freedom of maneuver vis-à-vis the CIS," meaning the commonwealth of former Soviet republics de facto led by Russia.[99] Talbott had to be prepared for Primakov's complaints about NATO's interest in all of these regions. The best counterattack would be to say that all countries, including Russia, had equal opportunities to become NATO members, so Talbott wanted to keep that option open publicly. Primakov might call his bluff by saying we want to join now, but Talbott could respond, "take a number and a seat in the garden."[100]

Thus equipped for battle, Talbott flew to Moscow shortly after Yeltsin's reelection. As expected, Primakov waved the two-plus-four treaty at him again on July 15, 1996, saying that he had "been looking at the material in our archives from 1990 and 1991." It was clear, the Russian argued, that Baker, Kohl, and the British and French leaders John Major and François Mitterrand had "all told Gorbachev that not one country leaving the Warsaw Pact would enter NATO—that NATO wouldn't move one inch closer to Russia."[101] Moscow felt in 1996 that because Western spoken promises from 1990 had been worthless, there was little reason to trust current US promises either.[102]

Primakov laid out a "real red line for us: if the infrastructure of NATO moves toward Russia, that will be unacceptable." Talbott tried to deflect this complaint by saying that "there can be only one class of membership in NATO." Primakov countered by pointing out that there were "already different classes of members of NATO." On the issue of greatest importance to Primakov, "nuclear weapons," it was already the case, for example, that "Germany has one set of limits" while "Norway has another." Why should the alliance ignore those precedents? Even Ukraine disliked the prospect of its neighbors gaining nuclear arms when it had given up its own. Talbott refused to answer directly, suggesting instead that they focus on "European security as a whole." Primakov countered that they might find some creative compromise, such as renaming the expanded version of the alliance, because "the very name NATO is a problem" for Russians; "it's a kind of four-letter-word for us." Talbott replied, "maybe after Poland comes in we could rename NATO the Warsaw Pact."[103]

Talbott sensed that Primakov was finding "weak spots on the NATO front" and was hoping to "exploit" divergences of opinions between the United States and some European allies, particularly the French, to "slow down or even stop enlargement." Chirac was in fact becoming increasingly vocal in his complaints about the US treatment of Russians. He advised National Security Advisor Tony Lake on November 1, 1996, that "we have humiliated them too much," that "the situation in Russia is very dangerous," and that "one day there will be dangerous nationalist backlash." Talbott even suspected various European leaders of colluding with Russian foreign ministry officials to develop an alternative plan for European security. As part of Moscow's "tactic of exploiting Euro-squishiness," Moscow had presented a proposal "loaded with showstoppers" such as "nuclear-weapons free zones and 'common security' areas hither and yon." The latter were meant to create "a giant buffer, roughly equivalent to the old Warsaw Pact, between Russia and the West." This alternative plan would also "rule out forever Baltic or Ukrainian eligibility for NATO."[104] Trying to figure out why the French would collude with Moscow in this way, Talbott reported that he got his answer after "cross-examination" of French diplomat Jacques Blot. As Talbott explained to Christopher, the EU had ruled out expansion to "Russia (and all other FSU states)." If Washington kept talking about NATO enlargement in a way that could potentially include former Soviet republics, *it would put the EU under pressure to change its stance.*[105]

Presumably aware of this discord between Western allies, Primakov made clear that he understood that more was at stake than Visegrad. Russian red lines, he told Talbott, included "such issues as the Baltics and Ukraine." Talbott snapped that if Primakov was ruling out their membership in NATO, then "we'll be at an impasse if not in a train wreck," because Washington refused to rule out any country.[106] Clinton backed up Talbott, writing Yeltsin that he saw "no reason to foreclose in advance membership for any of Europe's new democracies."[107] Although the US president did not say so explicitly, "not one inch" was gaining a new meaning: not one inch was off-limits to the alliance.

Meanwhile, to Chancellor Kohl's dismay, the pressure to get enlargement moving kept mounting. Clinton's Republican presidential challenger, Senator Robert Dole, appeared to have forgotten, as Kohl put it, that "Russia is a large and important country." In the midst of Yeltsin's reelection campaign and illness, Dole's party—with the support of some Democrats—had promoted a NATO Enlargement Facilitation Act. This act, once passed and signed into law by Clinton, gave $60 million to Poland, Hungary, and the Czech Republic to improve their chances of joining NATO. Christopher also gave a speech in Stuttgart on September 6, saying after "the first new members pass through NATO's open door, that door will stay open." Kohl understood why expansion supporters wanted to use Russia's, and Yeltsin's, current "condition of weakness" to enlarge the alliance, but he worried about the long-term reaction.[108]

The German saw that weakness for himself when he visited Russia on September 7, 1996, just before Yeltsin was scheduled to have heart surgery. Receiving Kohl at his country home in a forest roughly a hundred miles outside Moscow, the ailing Russian president insisted on having only Kohl's interpreter at their conversation. The chancellor later asked

Clinton, "do you understand the importance of that?" Clinton replied simply, "yes."[109] It meant that even in the woods a hundred miles from Moscow, Yeltsin did not feel safe. He did not want his closest aides and translators hearing him talk about his health and future. The chance that Yeltsin would not survive his surgery had touched off a succession struggle among subordinates and rivals such as Anatoly Chubais, Alexander Lebed, and Viktor Chernomyrdin; Yeltsin, as a consequence, had to be wary of everyone.[110]

The Russian president showed that he trusted Kohl, however, by being "very open about his physical troubles" and his upcoming medical procedure, which he knew "will not be a cakewalk." He emphasized that the West must not launch any surprises while he was in the hospital. He even admitted he had "considered having the surgery done in Germany or the United States" but realized "it would be too difficult to sell to the Russian public."[111] After this visit, Kohl impressed on Clinton the need not to push the Russians too hard, or to send out invitations for NATO membership in 1996 after all. Clinton agreed. He subsequently wrote to Chirac, letting the French president know that they should not "create any impression of taking advantage of Russia during the period of Yeltsin's surgery and convalescence."[112] They would not wait much longer, however; invitations would go out in 1997. At a campaign event in an area near Detroit that had a large Polish American population, Clinton allowed himself to celebrate his expectation that "by 1999, NATO's fiftieth anniversary and ten years after the fall of the Berlin Wall," Central and Eastern European countries would "be full-fledged members of NATO."[113]

A further complication arose, however, when it became apparent that Yeltsin was too frail to undergo surgery at all in September 1996. His physicians abruptly put off the procedure until November.[114] Since Yeltsin would require at least two full months to recover from the operation, he would be out of action until early 1997. In the interim, there would clearly be more infighting and worsening corruption, with little check on the influence of wealthy oligarchs and mafia figures. Talbott decided that his team should "run silent and deep" but keep working. Despite Yeltsin's illness, he was now focused on producing the much-discussed charter between Russia and NATO.[115]

Unfortunately for Washington, with Yeltsin (in Talbott's words) "out of the picture," Primakov was running Russian foreign policy and saying what he really thought.[116] He was sick of hearing that Russia could not veto expansion. As he snapped to the secretary of state during a meeting on September 23, 1996, in New York, "we realize we have no veto power," but Washington still kept talking to him, so clearly he had some leverage.[117] The fact that American diplomats were sitting in front of him, rather than simply out expanding the alliance, spoke volumes. One of Primakov's colleagues also warned Talbott in January 1997 against pushing expansion at a time when a "steel claw of anti-westernism" in Russia was itching to strike out.[118]

Primakov also informed Talbott that he was tired of dealing with Solana. As the Russian bluntly told Talbott, "we know you give the orders. We are not so naive as to think that you don't call the shots." Primakov remained willing to speak with Solana for appearances' sake, but the bottom line was that "if we (US and Russia) come to a conclusion, then we will have a deal." Talbott did not disagree. He replied, "I won't say to you that we are not proud of our leadership position in NATO," but he thought it would be better if Primakov dealt directly with the alliance too.[119] Solana himself later expressed dismay to Washington at Primakov's efforts to "belittle his role."[120] But the secretary general also knew who was ultimately in charge. Later, during a particularly critical round of negotiations in Moscow, NSC senior director Alexander Vershbow met Primakov first. As Solana was arriving in a motorcade for his own session with the Russian foreign minister, Vershbow "snuck out by a side exit and called Solana in his car to give him a readout" of what he and Primakov had just negotiated.[121]

Between his September session with Christopher and his private complaints in March 1997 to Talbott, however, Primakov had to recalibrate what he could say publicly. On November 5, 1996, his boss got a new lease on life on the same day that Clinton got a new lease on office. Yeltsin survived a "seven-hour, multiple-bypass heart operation," with doctors saying afterward, according to the *New York Times*, that he would eventually be able to resume a "full workload."[122] Assessing the implications, US diplomat Toby Gati concluded that Lebed, a former general who had displayed a particularly keen interest in Yeltsin's job during the president's illness, had "badly miscalculated," and that "Yeltsin will not soon forget Lebed's insubordination and arrogance."[123] The US embassy in Moscow concluded that Lebed and other hopefuls were now shifting their "horizons to the year 2000, when Yeltsin's current term ends."[124] As the Russian president gradually resumed his involvement in foreign policy, he also insisted that Primakov return to the more accommodating attitude toward the West that Yeltsin preferred.

That same day, Clinton won states accounting for a total of 370 out of 538 electoral votes and a second term.[125] Soon afterward the president reconfigured his set of advisors for his second term. Perry was succeeded in office by Bill Cohen, a Republican senator from Maine, as a gesture to Republicans.[126] Christopher was replaced by Madeleine Albright. She thereby became the first woman to serve as secretary of state, in no small part thanks to a fervent campaign on her behalf. When advocates of her rivals tried to persuade journalists "that a female secretary of state would be unable to work effectively with conservative Arab leaders," Albright's supporters swung into action and directed those reporters "to Arab diplomats at the UN, who said the allegation was an insult."[127] Albright also had the support of Hillary Clinton, who liked the idea of a chief diplomat to make "'every girl proud.'" President Clinton also reportedly doubted that Holbrooke, the main alternative, was "'sufficiently self-aware'" either to manage confirmation or to cooperate with cabinet colleagues.[128]

Once the president decided to go with Albright, Kissinger complained that she had taken away his status as the only secretary of foreign birth. Albright noted that Kissinger had something going for him still. He was "the only secretary who spoke with an accent." If she was not popular with her rivals, however, Albright's strong relationships with a number of senators, including Jesse Helms of North Carolina, propelled her to a 99–0 Senate confirmation vote.[129]

Albright asked Talbott to stay on as her deputy even though he had reportedly supported Holbrooke. She was wise enough to recognize that firing the president's close friend was not the best way to begin her tenure. Her partner at the NSC, however, would no longer be Lake. Talbott had reportedly persuaded Clinton to move Lake to the CIA, since the national security advisor had been a poor fit for the "'consensus-building, team-managing side'" of the NSC.[130] (Lake ultimately withdrew his name from consideration when it began to look like opposition from Republicans such as Haley Barbour and William Kristol would derail his nomination.)[131] The president promoted Sandy Berger, Lake's former deputy and an old friend of Albright's from their many years on Democratic presidential campaigns, to the top NSC job.[132] A lawyer trained at Cornell and Harvard, Berger had long been the cool-as-a-cucumber counterbalance to Lake's passion and volatility. While his promotion made for a stark transition in personality at the top, it nonetheless provided continuity in policy.

One of the first events the new team had to deal with was the NAC ministerial of December 10, 1996, which fell roughly one year into IFOR's Bosnia mission. In the run-up to it, Solana praised IFOR, saying it had prevented "the recurrence of violence and helped stabilize the country." He felt that "our cooperation with Russia in IFOR has been a real breakthrough." Solana additionally let allies know that "with the help of the Ukrainian Government," he was about to set up "a NATO information office in Kyiv, the first one of its kind," and expressed hope that the alliance could move forward there without unduly burdening relations with Russia.[133] Once assembled, NATO foreign and defense ministers collectively decided to create a successor to IFOR, the Stabilization Force (SFOR), to begin eighteen months of work on December 20, 1996.[134]

Most important, the final NAC communiqué announced an alliance summit in Madrid in July 1997. It was clear to all that this was where and when the formal accession process for new members would commence.[135] The end date of Central and Eastern Europe's wait was now in sight, provided Washington could get Russia's acceptance.

On January 4–5, 1997, Kohl went back to Moscow to check on Yeltsin—and promptly called Clinton on January 6 to let the American know that reports of Yeltsin's new lease on life were misleading. Even though he had survived surgery, "there is virtually nothing left of his vitality." In Kohl's view, he "seems to be very rigid, his face is very mask-like." The chancellor was right to be worried; the Russian leader would soon return to the hospital with pneumonia. Seeing how little difference the surgery had made to Yeltsin's health, Kohl felt it necessary to tell Clinton they needed to get moving on expansion. Although "this may seem blunt or brutal," he said, Yeltsin might not be around much longer.[136] As the German confided in party colleagues, in his view Washington and Moscow should compromise because it was an unnecessary and "absurd process" to hold out for the right to station "atomic weapons in Poland on the Russian-Polish border."[137] The chancellor felt there was a way to cut to the chase with Moscow, but not if they went through "normal, official channels." Instead, the issue must be managed by direct, bilateral diplomacy at the top. Kohl asked Clinton, "who's in charge of this—Strobe Talbott?"[138] When Clinton replied that the deputy secretary was still his top man on this issue, Kohl made time for a long, frank talk with Talbott.

Speaking with the president's old friend in person, Kohl recalled Yeltsin's visit to an EC Council meeting in December 1992. The Russian president felt that European leaders treated him as if he were a student taking an entrance exam. "Under the table," Kohl recalled, Yeltsin "took my hand and said: 'Helmut, they don't like me, they don't like *us*.'" In Kohl's view, the EU member states did not truly like Central and Eastern European states either; as he confided to Talbott, "many are hypocritical about things such as support for Central Europe and expansion of the EU. If there were a truly secret vote among my EU colleagues, I am not sure we would have a majority for expansion." The chancellor, who wanted to be known as the father not just of German unification but of European unification as well, regretted such prejudices and felt that "we can't tell the Poles and the Czechs that they are not welcome after what they did to survive communism." But "despite differences," he added, the common currency will come and "the common European house will be built."[139]

As part of that push, Kohl continued, the moment to expand NATO had now arrived because "I don't think Yeltsin will last out his term." The Russian president's new lease on life was a mirage. They should find a way to move ahead rapidly; Kohl was "absolutely against postponing" anymore. Talbott responded that "the conversation we have just had is one of the more useful I or any other American official has had on this subject," and it contained "exactly the message I hoped you would give me to take back to President Clinton."[140]

"Nothing about This . . . Is in Any Way a Bribe"

Talbott was also able to advise his boss that, with Yeltsin at least successfully past his surgery and able to have some input in foreign policy, his subordinates showed willingness to adopt "our concept of a solution": some kind of charter between NATO and Russia. An additional "cluster of understandings" on more practical matters such as "arms control and economic cooperation" could address details.[141] One sticking point, however, was whether the main charter would be a full treaty or some other kind of accord. The NSC strongly preferred "a politically, *not* legally, binding document."[142] Another was the persistent Russian desire to enforce something like two-plus-four conditions on new members, meaning roughly no stationed foreign forces or nuclear weapons.[143] As Moscow's diplomats put it, they expected NATO "to eschew development of new facilities— bases, arsenals, or airfields—or improvement to existing facilities in new member states. In their view, this would be a legitimate price for Russian acceptance of enlargement." In response, Talbott told Primakov on March 6, 1997 that Russians should simply "stop trying, in both what you're saying and what you're doing, to nullify the military dimension of membership for the countries that will be coming in as new NATO members."[144]

This view followed what had become the overall strategy on the NATO-Russia charter: no real compromises. As Talbott explained to Albright on March 14, he was making sure that accord "commits us to very little up front." In fact, "as one of the lawyers who reviewed the charter noted, 'all we're really promising them is monthly meetings.'"[145] As part of that plan, the NSC also suggested creating a so-called NATO-Russia Joint Council "as a basic mechanism for consultation and decision-making"—but following the caveat from the new secretary of defense, Cohen, that the chair of the council be the NATO secretary general with no "Russian co-chair."[146]

The bottom line was that it all sounded good but amounted to little, given that Moscow had few other options.[147] Upon being briefed of these developments, Clinton reportedly replied, "'so let me get this straight'": All the Russians get out of "'this great deal we're offering them'" is an assurance "'that we're not going to put our military stuff into their former allies who are now going to be our allies, unless we happen to wake up one morning and decide to change our mind.'" Russians would get "a chance to sit in the same room with NATO" but would not have "'any ability to stop us from doing something that they don't agree with'" and could only "'register their disapproval by walking out of the room.'"[148]

It was an accurate summary. Whereas during the reunification of Germany, Western leaders had needed Russia both to surrender its legal rights and to remove its troops before they could move NATO onto eastern German territory, now they needed much less from Moscow in order to move NATO onto Central and Eastern European territory. At a White House news conference, Albright and Berger both made clear that NATO enlargement would happen whether Russia liked it or not.[149] Speaking privately with Primakov, Albright was just as blunt. When Primakov told her that if the United States would not meet Russia halfway, then no deal or charter was possible, Albright reportedly answered, "fine, we don't need one."[150]

The White House was so confident of success that already in February 1997, before NATO and Russia had even reached agreement on the charter, staffers began working on managing the future Senate ratification process. Jeremy Rosner, a former NSC staffer turned private political consultant, began working with Albright, Berger, and others to shape the process of formally adding future alliance members. His goal was to set up "a 'good' win" in the Senate, ideally drawing many more votes than the required two-thirds. They needed to plan ahead, he thought, to avoid duplicating the Senate's refusal to approve the Treaty of Versailles after World War I. Such a defeat would have "grim consequences for NATO and the ability of the US to pursue its goals abroad."[151] In addition, they should resist pressure to add allies the United States did not truly want, in order to avoid having to say to the Senate later, as another Albright advisor put it, "we didn't want Romania but had to acquiesce because of the French."[152]

As these events unfolded in DC, Yeltsin was showing some improvement in his health. He decided, as National Security Advisor Berger put it, to make March 1997 "his comeback month, showing he has recovered from his bypass and bout with pneumonia and resumed full charge at Russia's helm." Yeltsin overhauled his cabinet, installing the most reformist government since 1992. The NSC also noted a "stark change in attitude" on the part of Primakov, who had presumably been put in his place now that Yeltsin was showing renewed "desire for success" in US-Russian relations.[153]

The Russian president had the wind at his back for once, because 1997 was shaping up to be a good year economically. The Russian stock market would surge, enormous numbers of Russians would be able to afford foreign holidays, and the number of cars in Moscow would triple from the 1989 level.[154] Yeltsin would also sign a decree on November 4, 1997 lifting restrictions on foreign investors in oil companies' shareholdings.[155]

Yeltsin agreed to meet Clinton in Helsinki on March 20–21, 1997 to finalize the US-Russia charter and thus the de facto price for Russian acceptance of NATO expansion. In her contribution to the presidential briefing book for this summit, Secretary of State Albright predicted that when the president saw Yeltsin, "you will meet a man reborn politically and physically, furiously engaged in taking back his presidency."[156] Clinton hoped he could use that spirit, his persuasive wiles, and financial inducements to seal the deal—although quietly, because as Primakov told Talbott, "people shouldn't be able to say that the United States used its money to buy off Russia and bribe it into accepting NATO enlargement."[157]

Once in Helsinki, assembled in the living room of the Finnish presidential residence and enjoying a spectacular view of the Baltic Sea, Clinton began to doubt Yeltsin's rebirth, just as Kohl had done after seeing him in person.[158] Recounting the summit afterward to his friend Taylor Branch, who was taping the remarks for him as an audio diary, Clinton called himself and Yeltsin "'pathetic creatures.'" The Russian had lost a great deal of weight and was still weak from his surgery; he would never truly recover. Spring and summer 1997 were the peak months of Yeltsin's second-term health, and once it began going downhill toward the year's end, it never returned. Even at his best, Yeltsin's staff kept him on a limited schedule, with a team of physicians close by, and never let him climb stairs in front of cameras.[159] Meanwhile, the much younger Clinton was in a wheelchair due to a knee injury. Albright later called it the "Summit of the Invalids."

Perhaps irritable because of their physical discomfort, Clinton told Branch, he and Yeltsin "snarled" at each other more than once, "saying, 'that's bullshit, and you know it'" repeatedly.[160] The Russian president tried to block Baltic membership, stating bluntly that "enlargement should not embrace former Soviet republics."[161] The US president rebuffed him, pointing out that even if he were to agree to that request, Congress would invalidate it.[162] Yeltsin also complained to Clinton, "you are conducting naval maneuvers near Crimea," which he thought was unnecessary and provocative. As the Russian remarked in some exasperation, "we are not going out to seize Sevastopol."

The two sides got down to brass tacks over lunch, where Clinton had the deputy secretary of the Treasury, Lawrence Summers, make plain what was on offer. Clinton had signaled in advance to Summers and his boss, Secretary Robert Rubin, that despite their doubts it was essential to offer Russia G7 membership in exchange for NATO expansion. As Clinton reportedly put it, "'as we push Ol' Boris to do the right but hard thing on NATO, I want him to feel the warm, beckoning glow of doors that are opening to other institutions where he's welcome. Got it, people?'"

Now, in Helsinki, Clinton let Summers try to seal the deal. Taking the president's cue, Summers explained how, if Yeltsin agreed to a NATO-Russia charter, Washington would help Moscow "attract capital, both from foreign investors and from Russians who have placed their money overseas." Clinton added that he was "prepared to instruct my government to make available in 1997 funds to support $4 billion in investment, the same amount as the total from 1992–1996." He would not "use the figure" in their joint statement afterward, he added, "but investors should know it." These funds would come in the form of a new aid package for former Soviet republics as well as expanded cooperation on criminal and tax reform and bilateral exchange programs.[163] Clinton also promised to "accelerate Russia's merger into the WTO [World Trade Organization], Paris Club, and OECD [Organisation for Economic Co-operation and Development]," along with the G7 (and, in 1997–98, Russia did join the Paris

Club and the G7).[164] After mulling these words over, later that day Yeltsin expressed a worry that "this economic package you've proposed" could be portrayed as "sort of a bribe to get Russia to accept NATO enlargement." Clinton responded, "there is nothing about this that is in any way a bribe."[165]

That response was not entirely accurate, but it worked. Yeltsin agreed, both to the financial package and to what Washington wanted to put into the NATO-Russia accord. He dropped his insistence on a guarantee against Baltic membership.[166] Clinton told Branch that he "marveled that Yeltsin did all this into the teeth of ferocious opposition from Russian authoritarians back home." While "old Boris may be dying," it was clear that "oxygen was getting to his brain."[167]

At the press conference afterward, the two leaders made clear that they expected a successful conclusion to negotiations between the alliance and Moscow on what was now being called not the charter but the NATO-Russia Founding Act. Yeltsin claimed that the resulting document would be "binding for all," which sidestepped the fact that it would not be legally binding, only politically, as the NSC preferred. He also stated, wrongly and to the surprise of the American delegation, that he and Clinton had "agreed on non-use of the military infrastructure which remained in place after the Warsaw Pact in these countries of Central and Eastern Europe."[168] Talbott later pointed out this error to a member of the Russian delegation, who simply acknowledged "that there had not been such an agreement."[169] In an effort to make the potential Founding Act look better than it was, Yeltsin was taking liberties in his public presentation—and that to repel any suggestion that he had been bought off, he would presumably continue to do so.

The rest was details—contentious ones to be sure, but ultimately manageable. Despite Talbott's worry that Moscow might "nickel-and-dime us down to the wire," he and his subordinates managed to finalize the Founding Act in time for the Madrid NATO summit on July 8–9, 1997.[170] To allow Yeltsin the public image of an important event dedicated to Russia, it was agreed that there would be a formal signing ceremony of the Founding Act before the summit, in Paris on May 27.

With both that ceremony and the subsequent NATO summit in Madrid now on track, the question became one of how to manage the "runners-up strategy."[171] As ever, Ukraine was in a special category; Kuchma was, in Clinton's words, "obsessed with getting his own agreement with NATO"—the president added, "not without reason"—so he would receive a NATO-Ukraine charter, to console him for not getting more.[172] The old Bush-era NACC, which had launched the idea of an organization open to all states from Vancouver to Vladivostok but had become moribund after NATO expansion got underway, got upgraded to a new Euro-Atlantic Partnership Council (EAPC) that could work with the PfP to provide activities for runners-up.[173]

Clinton planned to take part personally in the Paris signing ceremony on May 27, to show respect for Yeltsin. Just before departing, he received an overview of the most important terms in what was now formally the Founding Act on Mutual Relations, Cooperation and Security between NATO and the Russian Federation. The NSC praised the act internally for creating "a permanent NATO-Russia forum" while preserving "in full NATO's capacity for independent decisions and actions." The act stated that "in the current and foreseeable security environment," NATO had "no intention, no plan, and no reason to deploy nuclear weapons" or substantial combat forces on new members' territory. The NSC assured Clinton that with these words, the United States had avoided making "an absolute commitment, in case future circumstances change."[174] The definition of terms such as "substantial" was intentionally left vague, and Western negotiators would successfully resist all efforts to define it.[175]

Meanwhile, Yeltsin made his own preparations. The US embassy reported that he was engaged in an all-out "effort to sell the Russia/NATO Founding Act and answer his domestic critics."[176] As part of that effort, the NSC fully expected that Yeltsin would exaggerate what he had received and drop all "caveats" in an attempt to make "the best possible case" for what he had negotiated. So as not to undermine him, US diplomats should intervene publicly only to correct "egregious" public errors. They must be careful not "to make Yeltsin's political task at home more difficult" in the endgame of this process by embarrassing him with public fact-checking.[177]

There was one issue, however, for which no one was prepared. Just as he was about to see Yeltsin in France, Clinton learned that the US Supreme Court had ruled a sitting president did not have temporary immunity from civil litigation. The decision meant the Jones case could go forward while Clinton was in office, and Jones's lawyers would immediately begin looking for a pattern of inappropriate behavior with women. Talbott noticed that "from the moment he got the news," Clinton seemed to be "sleepwalking" through the rest of the Paris summit.[178]

The decision disrupted the president's ability to conduct the summit even though he likely suspected it was coming. On Saturday, May 24, 1997, shortly before departing for Paris, he had summoned Lewinsky to the White House. She had appeared wearing a pin he had given her; it was part of her habit of displaying, and keeping close track of, all physical objects associated with their relationship. Clinton informed her that their intimate relationship was over. According to Lewinsky's later account, she left weeping and hoping he would change his mind, which he had done after previous breakups.[179] What the president did not know was that she had also kept a blue dress, stained from their intimacies, in an unwashed state. Nor did he know that she had started confiding about their relationship to a new friend at the Pentagon, Vince Foster's former assistant Linda Tripp. The White House had exiled Lewinsky to the same liaison office where it had previously relocated Tripp, after the older woman's angry rejection of evidence that Foster's death had been a suicide. Despising Clinton and seeking opportunities for revenge, Tripp quickly recognized that Lewinsky was a godsend and began actively looking for ways to use her new friend's confidences against the president.[180]

Had the president known all this in Paris, he might have had even more trouble concentrating than he did. To make matters worse, on top of Clinton's sleepwalking at the summit, Yeltsin behaved unpredictably as well. At one moment he would be beaming broadly in his starring role at the big, celebratory public event he had craved; at the next, he would screw up his face in showy concentration as if the weight of the world were on his shoulders. And his spoken exaggerations exceeded even the NSC's expectations. Yeltsin suddenly announced, as part of his main address to the assembled, that "'everything that is aimed at countries present here—all of those weapons—are going to have their warheads removed.'"[181] As a result, it was his aides, rather than US diplomats, who bore the burden of fact-checking him. It became apparent from their remarks afterward that his subordinates knew nothing about, and did not intend to follow up on, Yeltsin's statement.[182]

Speaking together at the end of a day filled with private and public dramas, Clinton thanked Yeltsin for what he cautiously classified as remarks "regarding detargeting weapons aimed at Europe." The US president added, "it has been a good day," in foreign policy terms at least. Yeltsin responded, "yes, I can say that my soul is at rest."[183] Kozyrev, now a private citizen watching from afar, had a different take: the Founding Act would soon be "added to the pile of goodwill declarations implemented as halfheartedly as they were signed."[184]

Yeltsin's actions in the week after the Paris signing suggest that he was making an additional attempt to turn May 1997 into a watershed moment in Russia's foreign relations. He reached a major agreement with Ukraine: an accord allowing Russia to keep its portion of the former Soviet fleet in the Sevastopol port for twenty years. Thanks to this breakthrough, Yeltsin went to Ukraine for his first visit as president, a highly symbolic move that the two countries had previously postponed six times because of various frictions.[185] In Kyiv on May 31, the Russian president signed a treaty of friendship with his Ukrainian counterpart, pledging "mutual respect" for "territorial integrity" and the "inviolability of borders."[186]

Talbott, in his memoirs, had a different take on the month's events. The Paris signing had "an air of artificial triumphalism and even anticlimax, tinged, as so often, with some embarrassment over the performance of the star," by which, being unaware at that point of Clinton's actions with Lewinsky, he meant the Russian president. The deputy secretary was the American policymaker most responsible for making the Founding Act less rather than more substantial, and so was partly the author of that anticlimax. He found it remarkable that an oblivious Yeltsin had "burbled on about the day as though it had been the consummation of all his dreams for Russia's position at the head table of the new transatlantic order."[187]

Clinton, talking with fellow European leaders on May 28, 1997, the day after the Paris summit, spontaneously remarked that "Yeltsin is a great politician." Yet the Russian president, he thought, also had a great weakness: "the problem with Yeltsin is that all the steps in the middle get lost."[188] In his rush to seem in charge again and relaunch reform at home and cooperation abroad, Yeltsin had overlooked a great many middle steps. Washington had not. Seizing on Yeltsin's desire for a win, Clinton and his team had steadily negotiated and then closed the deal for adding a small group of new members to the alliance for what seemed, at first glance, to be a very low cost per inch.

They accomplished that goal through two key moves. First, rather than add the Baltics or other controversial states right away, Washington set up an iterative, continuous process of enlargement that would enable such states to join later, less dramatically, and at lower political cost. Second, rather than forgo foreign forces, nuclear weapons, or both on new territory, Washington managed to persuade Moscow to accept monthly meetings instead. As a consequence, not one inch of territory was off-limits to the alliance, and not one inch had any prohibition on forces or weapons. Central and Eastern Europeans could finally exercise their sovereign right to become NATO allies. It was a major success. But the hidden costs of that success would begin to reveal themselves just as Clinton's relationship with Lewinsky was also becoming public.

CHAPTER NINE

Only the Beginning

O N FEBRUARY 5, 1997, George Kennan, the US diplomat who
first proposed the policy of containment, published a widely
read *New York Times* op-ed in which he called NATO expansion "the most fateful error of American policy in the entire
post-cold-war era."[1] His reason for opposing it mirrored the reason he had
opposed NATO's creation: Kennan thought that the alliance brought
excessive militarization to what should be, in his view, an economic and
political process of negotiating a settlement with Moscow.[2] A cautionary
example of the harm of such over-militarization had arisen, he believed,
in 1986 when US president Ronald Reagan had met Soviet leader Mikhail
Gorbachev in Reykjavik. Gorbachev made a jaw-dropping offer to Reagan: mutual elimination of their nuclear arsenals, on the condition that
Washington restrict its proposed "Star Wars" missile defense system to
laboratory research.[3] Since that system was speculative (and indeed would
never be built), limiting it to the lab seemed reasonable to Kennan—even
if Gorbachev was promising too much, and something less than full elimination might result in exchange. But, to his incredulity, the US president
immediately declined the offer.[4] The diplomat was beside himself at the
opportunity that Reagan had let slip. According to Kennan's biographer,
in private remarks that year the diplomat implied that "Gorbachev in his
dealings with Reagan was facing an American Stalin," because of the leaders' similar levels of intransigence and suspicion.[5] Now, in 1997, Kennan
went public with his disapproval of the way that another US president was,

in his view, making yet another major error with Moscow out of similarly misplaced priorities.

The elder statesman particularly feared the consequences if President Bill Clinton sought "to expand NATO up to Russia's borders," and that worry was not unfounded.[6] With Moscow's public acceptance in the form of the NATO-Russia Founding Act now in hand, the Clinton administration spent the year between May 1997 and May 1998 working with allies, members of the public, and members of Congress in order to launch what outwardly appeared to be sequential rounds of enlargement but was, in reality, a single strategic push across Europe. The goal was to start adding initial new members in time for the fiftieth anniversary of NATO's founding in April 1999, with the door open to more in the future. Clinton's top advisors argued that the alliance should then, after enlarging to the short Russian border between Poland and the Kaliningrad region, continue expanding at least until it encompassed the three Baltic states—even though doing so would mean reaching inside what Moscow considered to be former Soviet territory, a politically sensitive act. Given that America had never recognized the three states' forcible incorporation into the Soviet Union, Strobe Talbott, still Clinton's point man on this issue, argued strongly for Baltic membership in NATO. He was so insistent on this point that his staff christened it the "Talbott Principle." But Moscow had long considered the region an integral part of the Soviet Union and large numbers of ethnic Russians lived there, so the prospect of the Baltics becoming NATO allies remained a tricky one. In light of this contentious history, the Baltics would not be included in the initial group of invitees; but that exclusion meant that Clinton had to ensure a start to enlargement that would give them another chance.

To achieve these goals, the Clinton administration had as a practical matter to clear two major hurdles. First, enlargement's rollout at NATO's Madrid summit on July 8–9, 1997 had to be clearly open-ended. Rising tensions in Europe would help that cause. As Deputy National Security Advisor James Steinberg put it, "there was a sense that probably the adverse events in the Balkans" and "instability in Russia" would, taken together, offer "a further argument for going forward."[7] Second, Clinton had to sell this strategy to the US Senate in early 1998, as he needed its ratification to proceed. That meant fighting off senators who disagreed entirely, or who wanted to put certain Central and Eastern European states into NATO but not others, and so were trying to limit or halt the alliance's stretch across more of the continent. In short, the administration's overarching goal both in Madrid and in the Senate was to launch enlargement in a way that signaled it was only the beginning. But the public revelation of Clinton's relationship with Monica Lewinsky in January 1998 interrupted all this maneuvering, by unexpectedly raising the much bigger question of whether he could stay in office at all.

Preparing for Madrid

With the NATO-Russia Founding Act signed and the Madrid summit approaching quickly, various national leaders tried to assess how best to maneuver in the coming months. German chancellor Helmut Kohl hoped that the Founding Act would help him complete what had become his life's mission: uniting Europe as he had united Germany. Thanks in no small part to his efforts, the launch of a single currency was now scheduled for January 1, 1999. The euro was coming about not least because, as Italian prime minister Romano Prodi explained to Clinton, the chancellor had both the vision and the ability to prevail "over the tendency of the Germans to want to stand alone."[8]

Now Kohl hoped that the Founding Act could further tear down "psychological barriers" between Russia and its neighbors. Ideally, the act would also "remove the feeling that Europeans had written off Central and Eastern Europe"—a feeling that had led, among other consequences, to fresh claims for World War II reparations lodged against Germany. The chancellor found these claims enormously frustrating, partly because he did not want to pay and partly because they indicated that even a half century after the war, the claimants did not feel reconciled.[9] Rather than refight the past, he wanted NATO to expand so Central and Eastern Europe would see that the West had opened a door for them. The longer-term plan was for NATO and EU expansion to complement each other, and Kohl predicted that if they did, Germans would be the greatest beneficiaries.[10] If the plan failed and the German border with Poland remained the "dividing line between East and West," then his country would forever "be vulnerable to the pathologies of racism and the temptations of militarism that can come with living on an embattled frontier."[11] To continue his efforts on all these issues, the chancellor announced in May 1997 that he would run for reelection, despite having been in office since 1982—and despite inspiring widespread protests for having imposed budget cuts to meet the criteria for the new monetary union.[12] Clinton called to congratulate the chancellor on his decision to run again, saying, "now that you've gone by [former German chancellor Konrad] Adenauer, you're going to blow by [Otto von] Bismarck!"[13]

Despite friendly relations at the top, however, Kohl's subordinates began sensing in late 1997 that their view of implementation diverged from that of their American counterparts. The Germans worried about the way that, with a kind of de facto Russian assent to enlargement in hand, Washington's attention to Moscow had diminished. The Russians did not fail to notice this as well. As Foreign Minister Yevgeny Primakov complained to the US secretary of state, Madeleine Albright, Moscow wanted among other things clarification of some CFE treaty terms, but could not get clear answers about them from "your guys."

Primakov hoped to stick with CFE limits negotiated before the collapse of the USSR because he had realized that, in the post–Cold War competition over NATO's future, they could be useful to Moscow in a new way. Because the sixteen current Atlantic Alliance members had, after the end of the Cold War, reduced their equipment holdings below CFE's original 1990 equipment limits, Primakov argued (in contrast to Washington) that there was no need for new, higher limits in light of new members potentially joining.[14] Rather than making room for those new members' equipment by raising the old cap, in the Russians' view NATO should retain the old limits and allow new joiners to have only as much equipment as would fit into the gap between the overall 1990 alliance limits and the current, lowered equipment holdings of the sixteen existing members. Primakov hoped as well that he could persuade Central and Eastern Europe to remain a nuclear-free zone. Thanks to the withdrawal of the Soviet arsenal, by the mid-1990s those states finally had no known nuclear weapons of any kind. Not just Russia but also Belarus and Ukraine argued that the region should stay that way, instead of becoming renuclearized through NATO.[15]

American negotiators saw Primakov's efforts as "one last effort to limit any extension of the Alliance's military reach eastward."[16] Talbott pushed back hard. Retention of the 1990 limits was inadmissible, given that, according to the Talbott Principle, the Clinton team hoped to expand eventually to the Baltics. But turning the old CFE cap from "just before the collapse of the Warsaw Pact and the USSR" into a permanent "single limit or ceiling for the alliance as a whole" would mean "limiting enlargement to one wave, since a second wave, to say nothing of a third, could cause NATO's head to bang up against" that ceiling."[17] As NSC staff member Daniel Fried put it, "at least as important" as the first round of enlargement would be "NATO's relationship to those states not included in the first group to join." It was essential, therefore, to handle the launch of expansion "carefully in light of the continuing NATO relationship with Ukraine, Romania, the Baltics, etc."[18] A permanent cap on forces at 1990 levels would unduly constrain options for those states.

In response to this rejection of their CFE requests, President Boris Yeltsin and Primakov refused Washington's request that they bless NATO expansion further by attending the alliance's Madrid summit. They apparently felt they were being treated like poor relatives, invited to big events for appearance's sake but otherwise ignored. Dismayed by this development, Clinton encouraged the Russians at least to "send someone of a high enough level that people didn't draw the conclusion that Yeltsin wasn't serious about what we did in Paris." They did not.[19]

The Russians were not the only ones with misgivings about the Madrid summit. A fight was brewing over the emerging US preference for the smallest possible first round. Albright and the national security advisor, Sandy Berger, agreed that the best way to accomplish US goals in Madrid was to admit only their three favorites—the Czech Republic, Hungary, and Poland—while also producing a "strong open-door package." By that they meant "making clear that the first new members will not be the last and that there definitely will be a second enlargement decision." But achieving that goal would require convincing skeptical NATO allies. Some remained reluctant about expanding at all; some resisted having more than one round; some wanted to go big and add Romania and Slovenia right away. Albright advised the president that they would have to "withstand grandstanding and grumbles, and insist that big-picture considerations prevail over parochialism."[20]

She seized upon a prominent invitation to make her point publicly. Harvard University decided to mark the fiftieth anniversary of the Marshall Plan, which George Marshall, then the secretary of state, had announced at the school's graduation in 1947, by inviting Albright to speak at its commencement ceremony on June 5, 1997. She used the event to argue that the best way to "fulfill the vision Marshall proclaimed but the Cold War prevented," namely, "the vision of a Europe, whole and free," was to enlarge NATO. Back in Washington, she had previously butted heads with General Colin Powell over the merits of using the US military for political and humanitarian purposes; when he began listing the many conditions that had to be met, she responded, "Colin, what are you saving this incredible military for?" Now, speaking at Harvard, she made clear her view that the United States, NATO, and their incredible militaries would be used to promote security across most of Europe. Hinting at the administration's expansive view of enlargement, she argued that it would demonstrate "from Ukraine to the United States" that "the quest for European security is no longer a zero-sum game."[21]

On this, as on all issues, Clinton's senior foreign policy advisors continued to enjoy strong backing from the NATO secretary general, Javier Solana. Talbott was ever more impressed by how Solana, a former physics professor who had switched to politics, had mastered the "cumbersome, leaky" NATO bureaucracy in the service of their common goals at this critical time. The two men became friends, formulating policy over Talbott's kitchen table.[22] Albright felt similarly; as she put it, "although he was a physicist, our relationship had chemistry."[23] As one measure of that chemistry, Solana sent Albright a note in June 1997 marveling that he had seen her "on both sides of the Atlantic, in three different cities, at one Summit, four ministerials and one birthday party," all in the last fourteen days.[24] Solana's biggest fan, however, was Clinton. One of the president's audio-diary entries from summer 1997 reportedly noted that while Europeans "still smarted over his imposition" of Solana as secretary, it had become clear that the Spaniard was "an indispensable near-genius."[25]

At the same time, Talbott was becoming unexpectedly frustrated with the Baltics. He was putting a great deal of effort into ensuring their long-term future in NATO, telling them expansion would not be "finished or successful unless or until the aspirations of the Baltic states have been fulfilled." He had even hired a deputy assistant secretary, Ronald Asmus, who understood his job to be keeping expansion going "until we have included the Balts."[26] Albright confirmed this understanding by telling Asmus on his first day on the job that she was looking to him to "'come up with a strategy for the Baltic States.'"[27] She and Talbott had hired the right man: Asmus had already published an article in summer 1996 arguing that "NATO is unlikely to be able to implement enlargement successfully without a credible and coherent strategy for dealing with the Baltic states."[28] Given all of this, Talbott could scarcely believe how ungrateful the region's leaders were, particularly Lennart Meri.[29]

The Estonian president was the son of a diplomat and had grown up partly in Paris and Berlin, but his entire family was back in Estonia when Stalin annexed it in 1940. They were all deported to Siberia, and his father was sent to the gulag. The young Meri and his mother peeled potatoes in a Red Army factory to survive; as a child the Russian guards let him get away with pocketing extra for the two of them to eat.[30] Since becoming president, Meri had attempted to reunite Estonia with the West he knew and loved as a child. By spring 1997, however, he was frustrated by his lack of progress. Plans for downsizing a July military exercise in the Baltics with US involvement put him over the edge. He told Talbott on May 28 that his people were fed up; they "'had expected more and got less.'"[31] Talbott responded that he was "deeply disappointed in the level of distrust" shown by such remarks, which were "inaccurate, unfair, and unhelpful." The downgrading of the July 1997 military exercise was an insignificant tactical retreat, necessitated by the scheduling of the Madrid summit at the same time. It should have been unnecessary to explain why it would be inadvisable to have, as previously planned, 2,500 US Marines launching expeditions in the Baltics while sixteen NATO allies launched expansion in Madrid.

Talbott could not fathom why the Baltic nations were belittling, even endangering with their rhetoric, a plan crafted expressly for their benefit. The United States had supported them throughout the long years of World War II and the Cold War by never recognizing their annexation into the Soviet Union. Now, he continued, if not "for the commitment of this administration and especially this president," NATO enlargement "would not be taking place." Even more to the point, "if it were not for the United States, enlargement would most surely be limited to a single round," and that round would not include Meri's country.[32] The Baltic leaders should not be throwing sand in the gears in the run-up to Madrid by behaving inappropriately.

Another potential risk before Madrid was congressional pushback against the price tag of expansion. Clinton asked National Security Advisor Berger to come up with a realistic estimate. Responding on May 30, 1997, the NSC based its calculations on Pentagon estimates that new member states would need thirteen years to develop a "mature collective defense capability." Working from an assumption of four rather than three new members to allow some wiggle room, the NSC estimated the overall cost to be roughly $2.1 to $2.7 billion per year for each of those thirteen years. Of that, new members should pay about $800 million to $1 billion a year, and NATO allies should divide the rest among themselves, with the US share coming to $150 million to $200 million per year.[33]

The Poles, however, had different numbers. The man who was now Poland's president, Aleksander Kwaśniewski, advised Clinton that he expected military modernization in Poland alone to cost $200 million a year—and for fifteen rather than thirteen years. He also needed "credits from the United States" to cover that amount, since it was beyond Polish capabilities. Fried, attending the meeting as the soon-to-be ambassador to Poland, counseled the Polish president that it was important to avoid creating "the impression that Poland is incapable of assuming the responsibilities of NATO membership" on its own. Clinton interjected "sure, though I think Dan could arrange for loans of a few hundred million dollars."[34]

Using the NSC's ballpark figures, Clinton met on the evening of June 11, 1997 with the Senate NATO Observer Group (SNOG), which consisted of about two dozen senators with a keen interest in NATO expansion. (Upon learning the group's name, British diplomats reportedly dissolved in gales of laughter, given that in British slang *to snog* meant to display keen interest in something else entirely.)[35] The president also invited Vice President Al Gore, along with Albright, Berger, Talbott, Steinberg, JCS chairman Joseph Ralston, and the senior presidential advisor on ratification, Jeremy Rosner, who took notes by hand. The SNOG session turned into what Talbott later called an "'intense encounter.'"[36] Some senators were strongly in favor of expansion, while others were much more wary. As Clinton recounted to British prime minister Tony Blair six days later, many had a "fear of provoking a nationalist response in Russia," which the president viewed as "a silly argument."[37]

According to Rosner's handwritten notes, Clinton tried to keep the focus on the issue at hand: how far to expand and how many new states to add. The president clearly wanted to sell the senators on the idea of three.[38] He understood the allure of the Article 5 security guarantee and why so many countries wanted in: "no N[ATO] member has ever been attacked."[39] But not everyone could join immediately, and there was a need to "keep people from going nuts in Baltics—need certain amt. of ambiguity." His solution: "if we go w/3," that would make clear to others "there will be a second round, you will be in it."

There was, however, still resistance to the idea of expansion altogether, regardless of how far. Senator Patrick Leahy, Democrat of Vermont, pointed out that while "I'm a strong supporter of NATO," he nonetheless worried "some in [the Russian] Duma will use it to kill START II." Clinton responded that, "I think they'll come around," and that it was important under any circumstances to have the "broadest, deepest alliance w/democracies of Euro[pe]." Another tense moment came when Senator John Warner, Republican of Virginia, reportedly accused Clinton of trying to ruin the best military alliance in history.[40] Senator Daniel Inouye, Democrat of Hawaii, indicated that he wanted the opinion of the JCS. Ralston anticipated it "will take lots of effort to integrate" new members, so "we prefer 3, do it well, & then bring in others."[41]

Senator Joseph Biden, Democrat of Delaware and future president, was supportive but concerned about the price tag. He pointed out that Poles "expect to be paid $100m for use of airfields," even though most "Americans don't give a damn—don't think any of the V[isegrad]-3 will add to security." His concerns about costs were echoed by a number of senators. Clinton agreed on the need to be transparent on that issue, saying, "we have to be honest about providing what we need to fund defense." By way of reply, he laid out his overall vision: "if we could get good deal w/Russia, strengthen P4P & N[ATO], then could remove possibility of a major upheaval in Euro & if things happen in edges of Euro—like Bosnia—would have mechanism & burdensharing to do it—would free up resources for Asia." According to Rosner, the pivotal moment came when Strom Thurmond, Republican of South Carolina, succinctly summed up the sense of the room: "I'd start w/3, do it quickly, to lend hope to others." Clinton joked in response, "if I could say that much so briefly, I could repeal 22nd amendment," which limits a president to two terms.

The next day, June 12, Clinton decided to announce publicly that "the United States will support inviting three countries—Poland, Hungary and the Czech Republic—to begin accession talks to join NATO when we meet in Madrid next month," even though, as Clinton privately told Blair, "the Republican caucus actually favors letting in more countries" right away.[42] Given that there was no procedure to expel an ally once inside NATO, however, it was worth erring on the side of caution.[43] Most important, Clinton understood that if the first round added five new members, "no one will believe in a second round."[44]

State Department officials sent word of the president's announcement to ambassadors in NATO countries as well as would-be member nations. The diplomats were instructed to inform their host countries that "NATO enlargement is a process, not a one-time event."[45] Talbott briefed unhappy Baltic ambassadors personally, reassuring them yet again that the Clinton administration "'will not regard the process of NATO enlargement as finished or successful unless or until the aspirations of the Baltic states have been fulfilled.'"[46]

Pushback and Success

If Clinton's press release was meant to make three new members the default ahead of Madrid, the French were not having it. Hubert Védrine, the new French foreign minister, informed the US embassy in Paris that "'you cannot just tell everyone to take it or leave it.'" There would have to be a genuine debate about the number of new members once they were all in Spain.[47] Védrine's views were a new complication. He had unexpectedly come to office after Jacques Chirac decided to call an early legislative election. Instead of strengthening Chirac as he expected, voters elevated Védrine's opposing Socialist Party and its allies. The result was "cohabitation," a right-of-center president working with left-of-center ministers, each of whom opposed US plans from a different point of view. Chirac insisted on adding Romania to the initial group, while Védrine was convinced that any expansion was an American plot to keep Europe subservient.[48]

The French foreign minister was hardly alone in pushing back at Clinton's preemptive strike. As Asmus later recalled, "we paid a heavy price politically for what was widely characterized in the European press as American arrogance."[49] Despite the risks on the road to Madrid, however, Washington possessed several forms of persuasion to use on allies before, during, and after the summit. The US secretary of defense, Bill Cohen, communicating with his German counterpart about a NATO surveillance program, noted that European nations should expect "significant industrial participation." In particular, "German industry stands to profit handsomely" while NATO "adapts and modernizes."[50] Unsurprisingly, the defense industry in the United States also liked enlargement because it hoped to equip new countries as they became members.[51] The Aerospace Industries Association estimated a "$10 billion market in fighter jets" alone, to say nothing of other kinds of aircraft.[52] (The US ambassador to the Czech Republic later complained that "two major American defense contractors" were "each trying to persuade the Czechs that US Senate ratification of their NATO membership depended on their buying its supersonic fighter airplane.") A group of private citizens formed the US Committee to Expand NATO to help push for ratification; the head was Bruce Jackson, a vice president at Lockheed Martin. A Raytheon spokesman said that the greater the need for new members to bring their equipment and infrastructure in compliance with NATO standards, the more it "'would benefit US military contractors.'"[53] More generally, the alliance had long functioned as a de facto American subsidy of European defense, freeing European governments to spend state budgets on other needs.[54] This subsidy was a strong inducement that Washington could use against the risk of allied revolt.

A more troublesome risk was domestic: the growing chorus of voices, including Kennan's, that were becoming the biggest form of pushback against expansion. The result was a curious dichotomy. Within the Clinton administration, there was a strong sense that decision-making was done and it was time to execute; among pundits, there was a strong sense that decision-making was flawed and it was time to rethink.[55] An informal poll of members of the Council on Foreign Relations showed that experts opposed expansion by two to one.[56]

One expert opposed was Ronald Steel, who called for more discussion of the fateful question "to expand, or not to expand." He noted that the "great NATO debate" did not follow any clear party lines but instead cut "across both extremes and through the middle, forming a post-ideological crazy quilt." In one corner, Henry Kissinger was making common cause with "Wilsonian liberals like Anthony Lake" and so-called freedom Democrats; in another, similarly strange bedfellows muttered about the effect on Russia. Steel guessed NATO was enlarging out of a sense of self-preservation and felt that a better idea would be for the United States to set itself up not as post–Cold War Europe's "overseer but as a global balancer." He suggested a number of changes in the expansion process, such as deleting Article 5 or making Europeans assume more military responsibility.[57]

The critical voices also included current and former policymakers, who organized a number of open letters. One of the most notable was sent on June 26, 1997, bearing the signatures of fifty former senators, cabinet secretaries, ambassadors, and others, demanding that "the NATO expansion process be suspended." The group of signers—known as the Eisenhower group thanks to the organizing efforts of presidential granddaughter Susan Eisenhower—was bipartisan and included former ambassador Paul Nitze, former secretary of defense Robert McNamara, former ambassador Jack Matlock, and former senator Samuel Nunn, whom Clinton had unsuccessfully courted to be his defense secretary in the first term. The signers' reasoning echoed Kennan's: enlargement was "a policy error of historic proportions," and the fact that Clinton was setting up enlargement as "open-ended" created unnecessary risks. Expansion without end would inevitably "degrade NATO's ability to carry out its primary mission," require giving "US security guarantees to countries with serious

border and national minority problems," and increase risks of confrontation, perhaps of a nuclear kind.[58] While this letter was public, a classified
CIA report written around this time reported that there was "strong evidence that nuclear-weapons related experiments" were underway on Russia's Novaya Zemlya archipelago in the Arctic Ocean. The agency's Office
of Russian and European Analysis concluded that the motivation for these
experiments was what the letter writers feared: the "widespread perceptions" in Russia "of a heightened threat from NATO."[59]

Other opponents echoed the hope of keeping Central and Eastern
Europe nuclear-free. Expansion could enable new alliance members to re-
nuclearize, so the issue of proliferation needed much more attention in the
great NATO debate. Enlargement also endangered arms control efforts
in another way. The START II treaty, awaiting ratification in Moscow,
was falling victim to the alliance's enlargement plans. One critic lamented
that the Russian Duma was expressly linking ratification and NATO expansion, saying START II should be sunk in retaliation for the West's
"reneging on assurances given to Gorbachev and [Eduard] Shevardnadze
at the time Russian consent was obtained" for German reunification in
1990.[60]

Because of Moscow's continued references to German reunification,
both US and NATO officials kept in close touch with their German colleagues on how to respond.[61] On June 13, 1997, Solana advised the German foreign minister, Klaus Kinkel, exactly what he had told Primakov
about the question of the two-plus-four treaty's relevance to current disputes: the secretary general had made abundantly clear that its terms did
not in any way apply.[62] The Spaniard also shared useful information with
the Clinton administration. He had quietly polled NATO members on
how many new states to take in, and a majority accepted the US position
of inviting only three new members at first. Clinton spoke to Kohl about
this US preference on July 3 and received the chancellor's general agreement on the issue.[63]

Despite this emerging consensus for three, however, there was also
bad news: the British were objecting strongly to any more enlargement
after this round. They felt that the Article 5 guarantee was so strong that
it was risky to offer it too widely. As British foreign secretary Malcolm
Rifkind later put it, "one should not enter into solemn treaty obligations,
involving a potential declaration of war, based simply on an assumption
that one would never be called upon to honor such obligations."[64] Nor was
London alone in its hesitation. Asmus later recalled that "several allies"

expressed such sentiments privately to their Washington contacts.[65] And Chirac presented yet another problem because he was insisting on including Romania (and possibly Slovenia too) as he was rethinking France's return to NATO's integrated command.[66] The July 8–9, 1997, gathering was clearly going to be contentious.

Once again, Clinton's relationship with Lewinsky produced a last-minute crisis right before a major NATO event. As Lewinsky had told her Pentagon coworker Linda Tripp, her separation from Clinton was agonizing: "if I ever want to have an affair with a married man again, especially if he's President, please shoot me." She did not know that Tripp was listening to her complaints not out of friendship but out of a desire to undermine Clinton. In service of that cause, Tripp steered Lewinsky to do some pushback of her own at the start of July, just before Madrid: she encouraged her to send the president an ultimatum.[67] In it, Lewinsky reminded Clinton that she had "'left the White House like a good girl in April of '96'" and not revealed anything during the campaign season. He had, in return, made a promise to find her a job in his office once the campaign was over; now she wanted him to fulfill it.[68] In response, Clinton asked her to the White House on Friday, July 4, before his departure for Spain later that day.[69] According to Lewinsky's later testimony, he accused her of threatening him, but when she began weeping, he comforted her. She recalled later that it was "'the most affectionate with me he had ever been'" and she left convinced that "'he was in love with me.'"[70]

Hearing about this and other such interactions inspired Tripp to search for ways to turn Lewinsky's confidences into political trouble for the president. She quickly found someone to help her: the literary agent Lucianne Goldberg. Tripp had been in contact with Goldberg previously about a possible book on the supposed murder of her old boss Vince Foster, but the project had run aground for lack of evidence.[71] Now, in 1997, Tripp let Goldberg know she had a new idea for a best seller: Lewinsky's confessions. Goldberg was thrilled by the idea but wanted more proof so that this project, unlike the one on Foster, would succeed. She instructed Tripp to "go down to the Radio Shack and buy a tape recorder," then "plug it into your phone" and start taping Lewinsky without her knowledge.[72] Although such recording was illegal in Maryland, where Tripp lived, she did it anyway—and the resulting tapes would later form part of the evidence against Clinton during his impeachment trial.[73]

Thus there were, as Air Force One crossed the Atlantic bound for Spain, several risks to Clinton mounting offstage. Following a brief holiday on a Spanish beach, the president gathered Albright, Berger, Solana, and Talbott in Madrid on Monday, July 7, 1997, for last-minute strategizing the night before the summit. The biggest problem was that the British were still not budging. In the words of the president, they "really prefer three and no one else." Berger suggested that London might be able to support a general policy of openness toward future expansion, but "without names or dates." In other words, Washington could have the fight with the British over a future round sometime later, or perhaps enlargement would take on so much momentum that it would be moot. On the subject of dates, Solana emphasized that it was desirable to keep the alliance on track to add the first group of countries in time for the fiftieth anniversary in 1999, which was too good an opportunity to miss. That compelling event had become a motivating force in its own right.[74]

At the summit itself, the expected skirmish over how many countries to admit proved surprisingly short. The decisive moment came when Kohl made public what he had already told Clinton in private: that he supported Washington's preference for only three new allies in the first instance.[75] As Albright put it, "the battle lines were drawn," until Kohl "persuaded everyone to put the heavy artillery away."[76] While late-night negotiations, particularly between Berger and his French and German colleagues, were still required to translate that victory into the final summit communiqué, the United States got what it wanted.

That communiqué stated explicitly that the alliance would "continue to welcome new members," and no democratic country in Europe would be excluded.[77] It indicated that the first new allies would join in time for the fiftieth-anniversary summit and the expansion process as a whole would be revisited there as well, which was a hint that more invitations were forthcoming. Future applicants were advised in the meantime to engage in "active participation" with the EAPC, the updated version of the NACC. The communiqué trod delicately, however, on the exact identities of future members; it got no more specific than a vague reference to "the Baltic region" as containing "aspiring members." The idea of talking about aspiring members in the region without naming individual states originated with Germany and seemed like an acceptable nod to Russian concerns; Clinton told Steinberg that he should use the German idea in the final press release, which he did.[78]

Another nod to Moscow's concerns was the press release's praise for the Founding Act in the very first paragraph and, farther down, for Russia's cooperation in Bosnia.[79] Later that year, Clinton would also announce his decision to keep US troops involved in that shared peacekeeping mission. Albright had been skeptical from the start when IFOR was given only one year, and then "the administration abandoned one premature deadline and immediately established another" for what was called the Stabilization Force (SFOR).[80] Now it was made clear that SFOR would continue indefinitely beyond its original deadline of June 1998.[81]

The upshot was invitations for the Czechs, Hungarians, and Poles to join NATO, and an open door for the Baltics and other countries, but without being too obvious about it. Ukraine, however, seemed a bridge too far for membership, and it was thought best to leave it in a separate category for the time being.[82] Accordingly, Solana mailed formal letters of invitation to Budapest, Prague, and Warsaw. He asked the three to work on individual details of accession through the fall, sign so-called accession protocols by December 1997, and help the sixteen allies achieve ratification of those protocols in 1998, all to complete the process before April 1999. The move eastward was in motion.[83]

Managing Reactions

Before returning to Washington, US leaders took a quick victory lap through the soon-to-be member states. Secretary Cohen went to Hungary, and Secretary Albright went to her native Prague, where she "walked along the streets, tears in my eyes, waving at little old Czech ladies with tears in their eyes, seeing in each the reflection of my mother." Meanwhile, President Clinton went to Poland. The White House worked with the Polish government to organize, on July 10, 1997, an American-style campaign event for him.[84] A jubilant, flag-waving crowd of approximately 30,000 people filled Castle Square to hear Clinton announce that "Poland is coming home."[85] He also met with the former Polish president, Lech Wałęsa, who expressed his profound thanks for the "great deed at Madrid" and then added, "life does not like a vacuum, and Russia really does not."

Clinton, in reply, reminded Wałęsa that "we are not through yet," noting, "we're still arguing with the Russians over CFE because we won't give the new NATO members any kind of second-class status." The US president wanted a clean win; all new members should come in as full partners, with no two-plus-four-style limits on forces or weapons on their soil. He added his hope that "the next three or four countries in NATO will make Russia give up its attempts to block NATO enlargement" because in his view, "enlargement really eliminates threats to all countries."

The greater the number of countries joined into a Europe whole and free, he thought, the greater the overall sense of peace in the region, which would yield a reduction in tensions with Russia. It was not a logic to which the Russians yet subscribed, but the president hoped they would. In reply, Wałęsa promised that he, his fellow countrymen, and all Czechs and Hungarians would do their best to "make Russia peacefully accept NATO and NATO enlargement."[86]

After leaving the Czech Republic, Albright went on to Russia and then the Baltics, to manage reactions in both places. It was essential to keep public responses there within acceptable limits so as not to endanger ratification of NATO enlargement by the congresses and parliaments of member states—especially by the US Senate. If Russia were too hostile or the Baltics too bitter, senators might get spooked. Meeting Primakov in St. Petersburg on July 13, 1997, the secretary repeated one of Talbott's favorite lines, that NATO membership was open "to the Baltics as with any other aspiring European democracy including Russia." She added that "neither the US nor NATO has taken any position on which country or countries will be in the second tranche."[87]

Primakov was dubious. When Albright visited the Baltic states shortly thereafter, he asked her to avoid referring to NATO, but she would not agree. Instead she confirmed yet again to the Lithuanian president, Algirdas Brazauskas, that "the first enlargement will not be the last." When Brazauskas asked about Russian objections, she emphasized as ever that Moscow did not have a veto and that "other NATO countries have agreed to this position, as reflected in the Madrid communiqué."[88] The Lithuanians then asked Albright to use her influence with the EU to make the case for their membership in that club as well.[89] The Latvian foreign minister concluded by saying poignantly that, until they joined NATO, "'we can't sleep.'"[90]

To keep the number of sleepless nights in Latvia to a minimum, within weeks of the Madrid summit Talbott and Asmus began work on an "active strategy" to "bring the Baltics into NATO."[91] The incoming US ambassador to the post-Soviet states, Stephen Sestanovich, recalled being amazed as he came on board in fall 1997 by how quick a pace they were setting for those states' membership. Before the first round of enlargement had even been ratified, they were already calling consultative meetings about the next. Sestanovich did not understand why things had to move so fast, but he sensed that decision had been made before he was on the scene.[92] The "$64,000 question" was how to pull it off.

There was also the problem that some allies considered the Baltics militarily "indefensible." Asmus suggested shrugging off such concerns the way the Nordics had long done. The chief of staff of the Finnish armed forces, for example, joked to Asmus that "the Nordic countries should form their own 'Indefensibility Club.'" Asmus thought the alliance could learn a lot from Nordic military leaders because "these guys think about deterrence in a more subtle way than we do." As he advised Talbott on July 20, 1997, they spent a great deal of "time looking at Russian capabilities in Northern Europe" and understood that they were "not always as overwhelming as some people assume." Even better, if the alliance could get Finland and Sweden to join, that would "mitigate the problem of strategic depth [and] force NATO to think about a defense perimeter that would *de facto* include the Baltics anyway." As a first step in bringing the Baltic nations into NATO, Asmus suggested upgrading BALTBAT, the existing battalion of Baltic forces, into a "brigade-equivalent force as evidence that they can be producers as well as consumers of security."[93] But Asmus thought that, by itself, such a step would be insufficient; they needed other tangible results to prevent "Baltic panic."[94]

As the Baltic process went on in the background, public ratification proceedings unfolded across the member states of the alliance. Albright, Talbott, Asmus, and their colleagues at the NSC monitored them closely because all sixteen NATO allies needed to check that box in a timely fashion if new members were to join in 1999.[95] Albright received a bold-face briefing from Rosner on August 28, 1997, warning that there were "**major concerns**" potentially endangering that ratification, namely, "costs, Russia, and NATO dilution."[96] The latter phrase was a shorthand for the question posed by some senators as to whether brawny, hairy-chested NATO really needed to take on a lot of little guys. Some critics, Asmus learned, were making headway with the argument that it was "not worth risking the arms control agenda with Moscow because of the Baltic issue."[97]

There were also frictions surrounding the NATO-Russia council set up by the Founding Act, also known as the Permanent Joint Council (PJC). Alliance staff members involved in practical implementation felt it quickly turned into a politically driven exercise with little substance. Russians apparently sensed the same, and their media gave it little attention. The first ministerial-level meeting of the PJC, held in September, did not earn any time on Russian TV news. And the US embassy in Moscow reported on September 29, 1997, that "Russian officialdom has been mum."[98]

The lack of coverage or official comment could have been because interest in NATO expansion was much higher among Russian political elites than among the public at large—as Berger advised Clinton, "new polling data shows NATO is just not a grass-roots issue in Russia"—but the embassy suspected something else was going on.[99] Official Moscow seemed less and less willing to provide a veneer of public approbation of NATO enlargement. Solana admitted he had expected "'teething' problems at the start," but as he reported to allies on December 10, 1997, the PJC's issues were worse than expected. Solana disliked, for example, the fact that Russia was trying "to place items on the PJC agenda for consultation or cooperation which test the parameters of the Founding Act." He considered it essential not to "permit Russia to have a *droit de regard* over Alliance activities."[100]

Tensions flared between Albright and Primakov over whether the United States had committed to refrain from placing either foreign troops or permanent military installations in new member states. On the troops, the Clinton administration felt it had already made sufficiently clear NATO would not station substantial forces—but that was of course different from saying no forces, and Primakov should be smart enough to understand that. On the installations, Albright stood her ground, saying on December 17, 1997 that NATO "would not consult on future infrastructure including in the territories of the three invitees."[101]

If the Russian reaction to Madrid was proving difficult to manage, however, at least the incoming members were working hard with the alliance on their assigned tasks. Poland's foreign minister, Bronisław Geremek, offered moving words: "For over two hundred years, when foreign leaders put their signatures under documents concerning Poland, disasters were sure to follow." But in 1997, Poland was master of its own destiny. He continued: "I wish to stress that we are not trying to draw a new line between the West and the East." Rather, Poland "would prefer to live in a Europe with no arms and no alliances." Unfortunately, "we do live in a world where military power remains the ultimate guarantor of security."[102]

The Clinton administration would employ such statements to win over skeptical senators in 1997 and 1998. At a time when his administration's focus was shifting from persuading allies abroad to persuading senators at home, the president did not want to give the Senate any unrelated reasons to oppose him. He knew that if his relationship with Lewinsky became public, he would find it hard to implement any of his policy objectives—with NATO expansion one of the many goals that would come under attack. Asmus later concluded that supporters of expansion "were lucky that the President's impeachment hearings" did not begin sooner than they did because "ratifying enlargement against that backdrop" might have been "impossible."[103]

For that and many other reasons, Clinton tried to lessen the risk of revelation of his conduct with Lewinsky, especially after somehow learning during his trip to the Madrid NATO summit that Lewinsky knew Tripp. As soon as possible after his return, Clinton requested that Lewinsky come to the White House. When she appeared on July 14, 1997, he asked if she "had confided anything about their relationship" in Tripp. She lied and said no. Clinton then kept Lewinsky waiting for an hour while, she later recalled, he spoke with his attorneys in the Jones case. After that, he told Lewinsky to track Tripp down and ask her to get in touch with one of those attorneys. Clinton called later to see if Tripp would be doing so. After Lewinsky answered no, she noted that the president got "in a sour mood."[104] The president subsequently asked the White House chief of staff, Erskine Bowles, to find Lewinsky a job in the Old Executive Office Building, next door to the White House, presumably to get her away from Tripp.[105] But Tripp heard from a White House contact that Clinton's staff resisted the idea of Lewinsky's return, and told her so.

After hearing this latest twist, Lewinsky contacted Clinton to say it had all become too much and she wanted out. She would now rather have a job in New York, near her mother.[106] The president agreed to help and asked his well-connected friend Vernon Jordan to begin helping her find a job, which he started doing in the autumn of 1997.[107]

None of them knew that Tripp was by this time making recordings of Lewinsky for Goldberg, who had extensive contacts among Clinton's opponents. Through Goldberg, the recordings ended up in the hands of conservative activists George Conway, Ann Coulter, and Jim Moody, who passed them on to Paula Jones's lawyers.[108] Lewinsky was blindsided by a subpoena from the Jones team on December 19, 1997.[109] After a series of meetings and calls with Clinton and Jordan, the three eventually decided that Lewinsky should produce an affidavit stating she "never had a sexual relationship with the President."[110] Such an affidavit, they apparently hoped, would decrease her usefulness to the Jones lawyers and obviate the need for her to testify. Lewinsky took an active role in drafting the exact language.[111] She wrote that the president had "always behaved appropriately in my presence."[112] It was a false statement from any objective standpoint, meaning she was committing the crime of producing a false affidavit. But she apparently felt the wording was accurate enough from her point of view—since she later testified to a belief that she and the president were in a mutual love affair—to sign under it on January 7, 1998. Two days later, with Jordan's help, she received and accepted a job offer at the New York office of Revlon. Jordan told Clinton's secretary, "mission accomplished."[113] They were unaware that Tripp's tapes were circulating ever more widely, including to the staff of independent counsel Kenneth Starr.[114]

Prom Night

As Lewinsky was drafting her affidavit in January 1998, across town at the State Department Albright was reviewing her priorities for the year, assembled into a list for her by Assistant Secretary Marc Grossman. Ratification of NATO enlargement topped the list. Since liberal and conservative opponents might make common cause to defeat it, Grossman advised his boss to use her personal relations with senators—particularly with Jesse Helms, Republican of North Carolina, who admired the secretary as a refugee from both Hitler and Stalin—to ensure that did not happen. She should fight not just for current invitees but also for future members: priorities two and three on Grossman's list were getting "the Balts to work together to be ready to be candidates for NATO," and "Southeast Europe," particularly Romania and Bulgaria.[115]

Another issue on the horizon was a fight over exactly how much enlargement would cost, and who would pay. Publicly available estimates for the overall cost varied dramatically, from a low of $1.3 billion to a high of $125 billion.[116] When the Clinton administration suggested that, whatever the costs, Europeans would pay more than 90 percent of them, the result was a "howl across the Atlantic," as one January 1998 news article put it. The French president countered that he would not pay one centime.[117] NATO officials announced that the alliance could keep the overall total to the lower end of that range, around $1.5 billion—but would reportedly need to repurpose older equipment and infrastructure on the new members' territory to do so, precisely what Moscow feared.[118]

Critics stuck by their belief that such an estimate was artificially low and tailored to avoid endangering enlargement's ratification.[119] In an internal assessment of the controversy in early 1998, NSC experts "endorsed an estimate of $1.5 billion "over ten years," but with the caveat that the alliance would indeed have to rely on existing "facilities and infrastructure within new members' territory." The Russians would resist, but reuse of this infrastructure was sensible, since the NSC believed it was in "better than expected" condition. And, such reuse would enable the United States to keep its annual share down to $37 million.[120]

This lower number was much easier to sell to senators, but the plan to use Warsaw Pact infrastructure incurred Russian anger, as expected. Yeltsin also complained to Clinton about the United States taking advantage of a different kind of infrastructure: "you are using some of the people of the special services of the . . . former Warsaw Pact and are using them against Russia." Even worse, Yeltsin suspected Americans were actively recruiting intelligence officers in former Soviet republics, and "this also is a blow against Russia." He suggested that they instead "get our special services to see how they can help each other." Clinton proposed they both try to reduce the number of people involved in their intelligence services overall, which Yeltsin said he was willing to do, but on an equitable basis.[121]

Amid this wrangling, Clinton's affair with Lewinsky suddenly became public knowledge. The revelation emerged in the wake of the scheduling of Clinton's sworn testimony as a defendant in the Jones case for January 17, 1998. Starr was still investigating the president because of the unrelated Whitewater scandal, but lawyers working for him had heard Tripp's tapes and realized they could potentially use the president's upcoming Jones testimony to cast doubt on his honesty more generally. Their idea was that the president would deny his relationship with Lewinsky while under oath, and they could immediately undermine him by releasing evidence to the contrary to the media. But they needed proof that Lewinsky's recorded claim of a love affair with Clinton was, in the words of one of Starr's subordinates, "not a figment of a young impressionable girl's mind."[122] Starr's attorneys decided to force Lewinsky to wear a wire in advance of Clinton's January 17, 1998, testimony, have her contact the president, and record him—and then broadcast the proof of his dishonesty to the world after his expected false testimony.

The challenge was how to force Lewinsky to comply. Starr first had to get permission from the attorney general to expand his remit, which he received on January 16, the day before the president was scheduled to give his testimony. Then Tripp met Lewinsky for lunch that day, showing up with surprise guests: a team of FBI agents and attorneys.[123] The team confronted Lewinsky with her false affidavit and said it would cost her twenty-seven years in jail, but that if she came with them voluntarily they might be able to help her. Their claim that she would spend twenty-seven years in jail was an exaggeration. One of the Starr attorneys, Bruce Udolf, later confessed that if they had in fact brought such a charge, it

would likely have represented "the first time in the history of that jurisdiction where someone was indicted for such an offense," and would almost certainly not lead to such a sentence. They assumed, however, that
Lewinsky would not know that.[124] Then they took her not to an office or
conference room but to a hotel bedroom.[125] Once Tripp left, Lewinsky
spent most of the next eleven hours facing ever more male strangers, as
Starr sent reinforcements after initial efforts to intimidate her failed.

The Starr team's internal code name for the events of January 16 was,
reportedly, "Prom Night."[126] It was an early indication of the kind of sexually suggestive language that members of Starr's team would later use in
their report on these events as well; one of the strongest advocates of using
such suggestive terms was, according to the *New York Times*, an on-again,
off-again member of the team, Brett Kavanaugh.[127] The Starr report was
still in the future on that night, however, and the question of whether
the tactics would work still hung in the balance.

At times composed and at other times hysterical with fear, Lewinsky
consistently refused to cooperate. She insisted on having her mother join
her. It took her mother hours to get there from New York. After arriving,
in the hearing of Steve Binhak, another of Starr's agents, the mother told
her daughter, "'you're going to tell these people everything they need to
know, and we're going to be done with this.'" Lewinsky refused, saying,
"'I am not going to be the person who brings down the president of the
United States.'"[128] Faced with that impasse, Lewinsky's mother decided
to call her ex-husband, from whom she had been divorced for a decade.
Shocked by what was happening to his daughter, he contacted a friend who
was an attorney. The friend agreed to help. He let the FBI agents and
lawyers know that nothing should happen until he spoke to his new client
and learned more.[129]

Lewinsky departed the hotel with her mother shortly thereafter. She
had, in the course of the ordeal, reportedly tried and failed to reach the
president to warn him, but she did not make any further attempts once
her mother and the lawyer became involved. Unaware of "Prom Night,"
the next day the president, as Starr had expected, denied having sexual relations with Lewinsky in his sworn deposition to the Jones legal team.[130]
The Drudge Report website—which by then had also gotten information
about Tripp's tapes—broke the story to the American public.[131] Now the
clock began ticking. Allegations of Clinton's improper conduct were in the
open, but hard evidence that he had lied under oath was not, since Lewinsky had not worn a wire as Starr wanted. How much more could the

Clinton administration accomplish before Starr obtained the other evidence in her possession?

The revelation dominated the news for many months and increased the Clinton administration's need for wins to offset it. As Albright put it, "'98 was the Monica year."[132] Clinton's cabinet members tried to focus on their various tasks at hand, but "the uproar was impossible to block out." The practical consequences, such as reduced briefing time with Clinton, simply could not be ignored. Previously, before any press conference with a foreign leader, it had been the job of Albright and other experts to prepare the president for the media. But after the revelation, according to Albright, "we had to leave the room early so the president could also review the investigation-related subjects about which he was sure to be asked." The scandal may have even forced the rescheduling of an event aimed at promoting the Baltics' interest in NATO, for fear that all of the press questions would be about Lewinsky. Coming on top of unrelated but distressing events abroad such as North Korea's launch of a rocket over Japan, a financial crisis in Asia, and a war between Ethiopia and Eritrea, the scandal contributed to Albright's sense of 1998 as the year everything "seemed to go wrong."[133]

The lack of proof that Clinton had lied under oath, however, allowed the president to deny accusations and rally supporters to his defense. Some members of the NATO enlargement ratification team sensed, after the initial shock wore off, that they had caught a break. The Lewinsky revelation had seemed potentially catastrophic at first. As Rosner later put it, there were no automatic lines around issues; nothing walled foreign policy off from domestic scandal.[134] Neither he, nor Albright, thought that ratification was in any way inevitable—and now the Lewinsky revelation handed Republicans who had always hated Clinton fresh ammunition on the very topic where he was most vulnerable: the question of character. Given that Rosner was, as the administration's "ratification ambassador," engaged in an all-out effort to get at least sixty-seven senators to stand up for the president's wishes, he feared that senators would become loath—perhaps to the point of saying, *I'll be damned*—to hand Clinton a win by ratifying NATO expansion. But as Asmus and Rosner quickly realized, the lack of hard evidence undermined Clinton's opponents.[135] What they could not know was that Lewinsky had such evidence in the form of her stained blue dress. For the rest of spring 1998, Asmus and Rosner were, without realizing it, in a race against the lawyers negotiating a cooperation deal between Lewinsky and Starr in hopes of obtaining that evidence.

For as long as those lawyers could not reach agreement, the president maintained his ability to pursue his policy agenda for 1998. He even began receiving sympathy. Congress gave him a thunderous ovation when he appeared to deliver his State of the Union address on January 27, 1998. The president felt secure enough to omit any mention of Lewinsky in the speech.[136] He also received support from abroad. After the address, Kohl called to compliment him on how well the speech had been received and to express "renewed confidence in the common sense of the American people." Clinton appreciated the praise, saying, "if we can hold off the stampede and get fair treatment, we will be just fine."[137]

Lewinsky's silence, however, did not mean that everyone else was also keeping silent. A grand jury compelled testimony from an array of individuals, including Jordan, and much of it quickly leaked. These leaks, and the headlines they created, had to be counterbalanced—and Senate ratification of expansion, as an achievable big win, became even more important. Rosner was able to report good news on that front. On February 2, 1998, Canada became the first country to ratify accession protocols. A host of other allies were on track to do the same, creating useful precedents for the Senate. Even better, Rosner believed that he had successfully persuaded the two-thirds of US senators needed to ratify enlargement. He wanted to keep persuading more, however, in the hope of achieving an even bigger win.

The controversy over Clinton's conduct with Lewinsky was not the only reason Rosner felt he needed a safety margin. The NSC became aware of a new risk: an effort by Senator Warner "to legislate a delay in when the second round of enlargement might occur."[138] Warner had remained upset about expansion after the SNOG session, and he worried that the fiftieth anniversary of the alliance would inspire a "stampede" to invite more members. He felt that rather than add them as a way of celebration, there should be more serious consideration of potential members' merits.[139] He sought to yank the alliance's collective foot off of the gas pedal with legislation, and he was not alone in this effort. In a bipartisan *New York Times* op-ed on February 4, 1998, former senator Nunn and Brent Scowcroft, Bush's national security advisor, advised mandating a delay. Scowcroft had of course contributed to the Bush administration's successful efforts to open the door to NATO's expansion eastward in 1990, but now he thought his successors were going too far. In his and Nunn's opinion, "what is called for is a definite, if not permanent, pause" in enlargement. They quoted John Maynard Keynes's remarks about the errors made after World War I: "the fatal miscalculation of how to deal with a demoralized former adversary" represented "the error we must not repeat."[140] But if the Senate delayed or blocked later rounds, that would undermine the Talbott Principle. Both the State Department and the NSC opposed any such mandated pause because it would demolish "the credibility of [the] open door commitment," the promise made to would-be members that NATO was coming for them soon.

To counter such opposition, a private advocacy group began bringing senators together with representatives of the potential new member states "in a relaxed social environment." They kept the NSC informed about what they were doing. The prime movers of this group included well-connected figures such as Julie Finley, Bruce Jackson, Steve Hadley, Robert Zoellick, and Peter Rodman.[141] Within the Senate, Biden and Richard Lugar also organized dinners in advance of key hearings and invited both Asmus and Grossman, giving senators the chance to hear pro-expansion views in the form of a casual, convivial conversation. Grossman recalls being very grateful to Biden and Lugar, as their social gatherings helped to create trust between advocates of enlargement and senators.[142]

The final act in the ratification drama began when Clinton formally transmitted the accession protocols to the Senate.[143] Commentary abounded on both sides, but supporters of enlargement felt confident they had the upper hand for a number of reasons. Czech, Polish, and Hungarian representatives, working hand in hand with their allies in the United States, had made passionate, persuasive cases to senators for admission. Albright had effectively lobbied a number of senators on both sides of the aisle, not least Helms. Asmus and Grossman made good use of their contacts from Biden and Lugar's private events. Broad segments of the US population, such as business leaders and voters of Central and Eastern European ancestry, had supported expansion; an elected body such as the Senate could hardly ignore such support. And last but not least, Lewinsky had not yet given up the evidence in her possession.

The Senate's Foreign Relations Committee approved the package, moving it forward to the full Senate. Final floor debate opened on April 27, 1998.[144] Clinton and his advisors skillfully worked every possible connection, and their efforts bore fruit. They rejoiced when the Warner amendment was rejected, 59 to 41.[145] They and their allies were also able to block what Rosner viewed as another serious threat: one by Senator John Ashcroft, Republican of Missouri, limiting the alliance's out-of-area missions.[146] The Senate also rejected, 83 to 17, an amendment to require NATO members to join the European Union first. Finally, by 80 to 19, the Senate approved the expansion of NATO.[147] The vote cut across party lines; 35 Democrats joined 45 Republicans in support of it, while 10 Democrats and 9 Republicans opposed it.[148]

If the political constellation was unusual, it was nonetheless a big win. Despite an array of foreign and domestic political risks, Clinton and his ratification team had gotten enlargement through both the alliance and the Senate, and in a way that made clear the first round was only the beginning. There would be no mandated pause, no restrictions on out-of-area activities, and no binding limitations on new member states' territories.

This result was yet another disappointment for the unhappy Kennan. Ever since the collapse of the USSR, he had opposed any measure that precluded "'possibilities for arriving at solutions'" other than conflict with Moscow, and he viewed expansion as the worst of such measures.[149] In contrast, the countries invited to join NATO were thrilled at their success and at the new horizons coming into view. They felt increasingly confident they would take part in what would be only the beginning of multiple rounds of enlargement.

Their representatives began working with the Clinton administration and the alliance to clear all practical and legal hurdles to becoming full members by the time of the fiftieth anniversary in April 1999. But they were still not out of the woods because there was more presidential scandal to come. At the end of July 1998, months of legal haggling between Lewinsky and Starr finally yielded a deal. The young woman received immunity and, in exchange, on July 29 relinquished her stained blue dress. Two days later, a laboratory confirmed a positive test result for human semen. The lab requested a blood sample to check for a DNA match with "'any known subject'" of investigation.[150]

Clinton soon found himself fighting off impeachment, suddenly unsure of his ability to stay in power. Economic collapse in Russia and fighting in Kosovo would create more upheaval. These disparate events were all grinding, slowly but massively, toward a collision in 1999 that would carve out the political landscape of the twenty-first century. In Russia, the collision would also claim Yeltsin and thrust into power a former KGB officer for whom it was only the beginning as well.

CHAPTER TEN

Carving Out the Future

B Y SUMMER 1998, the Clinton administration had successfully managed the process of convincing both its NATO allies and the US Senate to proceed with a maximally flexible vision of enlargement. Harder to manage, however, were the political consequences. Just as a glacier sweeps across a landscape slowly, yet alters broad swathes of terrain profoundly, so too did NATO's expansion eastward force elements of the post–Cold War political landscape to shift and settle, leaving behind landmarks for the twenty-first century. Between summer 1998 and December 1999, enlargement combined with five other major developments to carve out the contours of the future. These events were the financial collapse in Russia and the succession contest that followed; the impeachment of President Bill Clinton; the bloodshed in Kosovo, just as the alliance was adding new members; the rise of Vladimir Putin through the Kremlin ranks; and the decision by Russian president Boris Yeltsin to resign abruptly and make Putin his successor. This carving process did not define every last aspect of Western relations with Russia in the new century, but it narrowed the parameters of the possible post–Cold War order, setting up a future of stalemate.

"Who Will Be Our Partner in Russia?"

Clinton made a prescient forecast during his second term: "if Russia is not stable, the rest of the world will know misery."[1] In 1998, however, stability for Russia was in short supply, and misery was abundant. That year,

Russia's GDP dropped by 4.6 percent, thanks not least to a major financial crisis starting on August 17.[2] The upheaval created yet more uncertainty and volatility in Russia, restarted the battle over who would succeed
Yeltsin, and decreased the ability and willingness of Russian elites to tolerate other challenges.

Among the factors causing the crash was a budget deficit of 8 to
9 percent of GDP from 1993 to 1998. Further complications arose in the
wake of the 1996 IMF aid package, which had provided Yeltsin with a $10
billion loan program over three years and helped to ensure his reelection
even though he did not commit to any significant reform. Foreign investors saw this loan as a sign that the IMF would bail Moscow out no matter
what it did. To the markets, as one analyst put it, "the signal was clear:
Russia was too big and too nuclear to fail." Private investors kept the Russian government afloat for a time, as large international portfolios poured
money into the country's domestic treasuries. In 1997, private portfolio
inflows amounted to $46 billion, or 10 percent of GDP. The real yields
on Russian domestic treasuries reached 100 percent, costing the Russian
treasury enormous amounts. The situation was unsustainable, but it allowed purchasers of domestic Russian treasury bonds to get rich as long
as they got out before a crash.[3] On top of this problem, an Asian financial
crisis in 1997 had spillover effects that made matters worse.[4] Assistant Secretary of State Marc Grossman noticed that the desperation created by
the combined woes made Russians less willing to tolerate anything seen
as a further threat—such as NATO enlargement.[5]

Domestic decisions in 1997–98 had contributed to the crash as well.
Yeltsin had proved unable or unwilling to cut the stubborn budget deficit
at home, given the likely political consequences of doing so. Prime Minister Viktor Chernomyrdin had even decided to increase that deficit. On
October 28, 1997, the Russian stock market had fallen 19 percent in one
day, a sign of what was to come, but few policy changes resulted.[6] In
March 1998, Yeltsin decided he had to at least reshuffle his government,
so he replaced Chernomyrdin with a thirty-five-year-old reformer, Sergey Kiriyenko, but it made little difference.[7]

Amid impending economic disaster, Russia attended the May 15, 1998
economic summit in Birmingham, England, as a member state, turning
the body into the G8.[8] Clinton greeted Yeltsin warmly there but was increasingly concerned about his hold on power. As the US president confided to German chancellor Helmut Kohl, "there is a lot of rumbling in
Russia against Yeltsin," and "there is only so much we can do" to help.[9]

Clinton was right to worry. On Friday, July 10, Yeltsin called the Oval Office in a state of enormous agitation. The IMF had told him it was considering more disbursements and would let him know in three weeks—but "three weeks is too long for us." He told Clinton that "if we do not get a decision soon," meaning during the upcoming week, "it would mean the end of reform and basically the end of Russia." Given that the "consequences would be catastrophic and drastic" not just for his country but for "the global financial system as well," it was in American interest as well to act with alacrity. Clinton promised to contact the IMF that weekend. He mentioned pointedly that he had just vetoed a bill that, due to Moscow's links to the Iranian missile program, imposed sanctions on Russia. A rethinking of Russian dealings with Iran, he hinted, would help the United States to do more for Moscow in the future. Yeltsin swore he would look at "each and every point where we can enforce compliance and reduce or restrict cooperation between Russian and Iranian companies."[10]

Clinton delivered on his promise in return. On that Monday, July 13, the IMF announced it would act, and a week later it confirmed financial support of $11.2 billion; the *New York Times* reported the total as $17.1 billion; added aid from the World Bank and Japan apparently brought that total to $22.6 billion.[11] Whatever the exact amount, it did little good. Since the IMF funding was not accompanied by sufficiently credible fiscal measures, the funds quickly floated out of Russia. A basic axiom was in effect: if money is put into a country in crisis without believable policy to accompany it, and the removal of cash from a country is legal—as was the case in Russia—then money will be taken out of that country, and it was. Hence, when a rebellious Russian parliament blocked Yeltsin's efforts to make legislative reforms that the IMF wanted as part of this funding, the rebellion spooked the IMF. After a disbursement of $4.8 billion, the IMF (in the words of one expert) "dropped Russia like a hot brick."[12] Clinton's advisors concluded that "despite the landmark agreement with the IMF and an ambitious economic reform program," Yeltsin's government faced "daily challenges to its survival."[13]

Playing to nationalist sentiment at a desperate hour, Yeltsin spoke at the reburial of Czar Nicholas II, Czarina Alexandra, and their children in St. Petersburg on July 17, 1998, calling it an "'act of human justice.'"[14] Markets and investors were unimpressed, and workers across Russia remained unpaid and angry. The NSC noted that, as ever, "the infamous oligarchs continue to put their personal interests above the common good."[15] Overwhelmed by multiple crises, Yeltsin decided that yet another reshuffle of his advisors was needed. Among other appointments, he bypassed scores of high-ranking secret police officers and promoted a relative unknown to the top of the federal security service (FSB): forty-five-year-old Putin.[16]

After returning from his KGB outpost in a collapsing East Germany to his hometown in a collapsing Soviet Union, Putin had found employment with Anatoly Sobchak, one of his former law professors from Leningrad State University. Sobchak was active in city politics and on his way to becoming mayor of what would once again be named St. Petersburg. Putin became his indispensable aide, serving among other things as translator during Sobchak's conversations with Kohl. The German's "deep knowledge of Russian history" impressed Putin, who was pleased to hear Kohl say "that he couldn't imagine a Europe without Russia." Putin also discovered, as historian Stephen Kotkin later put it, "that Leningrad's self-styled democrats could get almost nothing done and that he could embezzle money both to help address the city's challenges and to enrich himself and his cronies."[17] He also developed a talent, according to an investigation by a *Financial Times* journalist, for managing relations between the elected authorities, the remnants of the KGB, and the local crime bosses, in a way that would later serve as a model for Russian governance.[18]

Where Putin distinguished himself above all was in his deep loyalty to the mayor. Even after Sobchak was voted out of office in 1996 and came into legal peril due to alleged corruption, his former subordinate protected him, reportedly organizing a swift exit for the ex-mayor to France in November 1997 by private jet. Such fealty impressed Yeltsin's deputy chief of staff, Aleksei Kudrin, who had worked for the mayor as well and knew Putin.[19] Through Kudrin and other contacts, Putin got a foothold in the Yeltsin administration and moved to Moscow.[20]

Now, in summer 1998, the upheaval in Russia created an opportunity for Putin but a conundrum for Clinton. The president had previously agreed to visit Moscow on September 1, but wondered whether he should go at such a difficult time. The banking crisis also meant that practical implementation of NATO expansion came at a particularly terrible moment for Moscow. Yet despite the existential threats facing Yeltsin, Clinton's advisors felt the president should go and maintain a hard line, to ensure that expansion remained open-ended. The consequence of keeping the first group of NATO invitees small must not, they argued, be a Russian belief that the United States had de facto drawn a new line at the border between Poland and Kaliningrad (where Putin's wife hailed from) and ceded everything east of it to Moscow's sphere of influence. The alliance had served notice that NATO's door would stay open, and Clinton should not budge. Budging would promote fighting among would-be allies, competing for a suddenly limited number of spaces in NATO. Under no circumstances, National Security Advisor Sandy Berger warned Clinton on July 22, 1998, should he say that "Baltic membership is off the table," or that the conventional forces treaty might place "constraints" on the amount of equipment in NATO's new territories. That the Russian economy was going under gave no reason to abandon these positions.[21] In short, the alliance's expansion limited what the United States was willing to do for Yeltsin politically, even in the desperate hours of the 1998 financial crisis.

Another problem intersected with both Yeltsin's and NATO's futures: the aggressive moves in Kosovo by the Serbian leader Slobodan Milošević. Fighting between Serbian-controlled forces and Kosovar Albanians had caused, according to NATO's estimates, the deaths of 1,500 people and the displacement of hundreds of thousands from their homes. Clinton invested a surprisingly large share of his personal time in 1998 and 1999 strategizing ways to stop Serbian security forces, consulting widely for advice. The president of Romania, Emil Constantinescu, proposed a solution that, in his view, should have long since been implemented in the Balkans as a whole: "We should have given every 14-year-old a computer, which links them to the world so that they would never want to pick up a gun, which separates them from the world."[22] Since it was too late for that in Kosovo, more dramatic measures seemed necessary. Clinton despised the fact that Milošević was "engaged in a systematic campaign of violence and repression," as he put it to Kohl on August 7, 1998. The Serb apparently thought "NATO will only act with a Security Council resolution" and, given that "Russia will block it," he was in the clear.

Milošević was right that a resolution represented a challenging proposition for Yeltsin. If the Russian president instructed his UN ambassador to appease hard-liners in Moscow by vetoing the intervention in a Security Council resolution, he would alienate the Western countries whose financial help he desperately needed. But if he abstained from a Security Council vote, letting intervention go ahead, the apparent capitulation to NATO would weaken Yeltsin at home, where nationalists would accuse him of selling out fellow Slavs. Clinton concluded that it would be better to spare Yeltsin from having to go on the record at all. As the US president advised Kohl, "if we go to the UN, we will put Yeltsin in the worst possible position." Moreover, "we need to make clear that NATO can and will act without a Security Council resolution if necessary."[23] A major element of the political landscape of the twenty-first century was shifting into position: increasing American willingness to intervene abroad, either within NATO or by itself, without securing UN approval.[24]

In the midst of all of these debates, Russia hit bottom. On August 17, the government and the Bank of Russia announced an end to the "rigid daily limits on ruble exchange rate fluctuations in the form of the buying and selling rates of the US dollars."[25] The ruble's value dropped precipitously, and the consequences were far-reaching. Half of Russia's banks went bankrupt. Middle-income Russians lost an estimated two-thirds of their savings, and inflation surged.[26] Visiting Moscow at this time, Deputy Secretary Strobe Talbott was shocked at what he found. Currency markets had simply closed after the ruble's crash "and did not reopen." Stocks were plunging, and "lines for basic goods and at banks are being reported in various cities."[27] Rumors circulated that Yeltsin had either resigned or died, and Talbott worried that there might be a "coup d'état."[28]

The NSC reported on how a "smoldering domestic banking crisis that intensifies each day as the oligarchs press for a bailout" was visibly taking a toll on Yeltsin—but Clinton's strategy for his September visit to Moscow did not change. In addition to the hard line on the Baltics, Berger also advised the president to make Yeltsin see the necessity of recent US bombings in Afghanistan and Sudan, about which the Russian was complaining publicly. These had been, in Berger's view, necessary attacks on a terrorist named Osama bin Laden—a figure who would also do much to shape the early twenty-first century. "Conclusive evidence" had shown him to be the mastermind behind the August 7, 1998 bombings of US embassies in Kenya and Tanzania that had left 224 dead, including twelve Americans, and more than 4,500 injured. Because "American lives were at stake" and there had been "no other choice," Clinton should insist Yeltsin "state publicly that he now understands the rationale for our actions."[29]

Just before leaving for Moscow, Clinton tried to take a summer vacation, but Yeltsin called him on Martha's Vineyard on August 25 with a new issue. The Russian parliament was pressuring him to resign; he was resisting and had decided to fire Prime Minister Kiriyenko instead—but that meant he needed a new prime minister. Yeltsin wanted Clinton's advice because he wanted to bring back his old prime minister, Chernomyrdin, who knew Vice President Al Gore well from shared work on a US-Russian intergovernmental commission. According to Berger, there were rumors that "Yeltsin signed a letter of resignation, but will not date it until Chernomyrdin is confirmed as prime minister."[30]

Yeltsin told Clinton he hoped Chernomyrdin and Gore could resume their "work jointly in a constructive way." The subtext, apparently, was that Yeltsin was indeed potentially willing to resign; given that the American vice president was preparing his own run for the Oval Office, the Russian president seemingly wanted to work with Clinton to set up cooperation between their preferred successors. Clinton would not be drawn out on details and said only, "I know the pressure must be enormous with so much at stake for Russia."[31]

But this latest crisis led Clinton to consult, yet again, with Kohl on August 30 about what he could realistically hope to achieve by visiting Moscow. As the president put it, "the real problem is that the Russians are taking their own money out of the country. All the money the IMF put into Russia" recently was "gone now." Clinton felt that "somehow" they had to "get the money flowing in instead of flowing out." For his part, the German advised impressing upon Yeltsin that the situation in Kosovo was intolerable. Milošević's aggression had left a hundred thousand people "hiding in the woods," and Kohl was "not willing to have Germany take in another 150,000 refugees," as he had done during earlier Yugoslav crises, because it was an election year. "Being attacked while campaigning because we took in over 300,000 from Bosnia-Herzegovina," he told Clinton, was not helping his reelection chances. The chancellor stood by his decision to admit those refugees but insisted, "we can't do this every couple of years."[32]

In the end, Clinton got on the plane for his September 1–2 summit with Yeltsin, although with much trepidation. Talbott recalled that the flight to Moscow was the first time he heard the president utter the phrase "'if we lose Russia.'" Once there, Clinton tried to deliver his various stern messages on NATO's future and bin Laden. Yeltsin was more interested in strategizing with Clinton about how to outmaneuver his parliament, which opposed Chernomyrdin's return.[33] The Russian president seemed willing to disband parliament and force new elections, even though that would add yet another political crisis. Clinton departed without a clear picture of how Yeltsin proposed to manage any of this. As he reported to Kohl on September 9, he did not glean "any better information" as to who might be the next Russian prime minister—or president.

The Duma soon forced Yeltsin's hand. It rejected Chernomyrdin's reappointment as prime minister on September 7. For a couple days, the future leadership of Russia hung in the balance; the White House learned that some of Yeltsin's advisors urged him to proceed with his preferred candidate anyway and force the Duma to dissolve.[34] But on September 9, Yeltsin let Clinton know that his desired succession plan "was not to be." Instead, he gave in to parliamentary pressure and appointed Foreign Minister Yevgeny Primakov, who had strong support in the Duma.[35] Yeltsin soured on Primakov, however, as it quickly became apparent that the new prime minister now wanted the top office for himself.[36]

To add to the complexity, another capital also witnessed transitions in high offices on September 27, 1998. In Germany, Helmut Kohl lost to his Social-Democratic challenger, Gerhard Schröder, ending sixteen years in office. The defeated leader guessed that his loss resulted from too much focus on integrating Europe and creating a common currency.[37] But, as he told Clinton, "life goes on, as it always has. I have been through eight battles of this kind, and I lost one. I'll just have to live with it." Clinton assured Kohl that "no one in the last 50 years has been more important to the future of Europe than you have. You should be very proud of that." Saying he would "be your friend forever," the president closed by assuring Kohl, "you are always welcome here."[38]

Clinton's first extended contact with Schröder after the election, on October 9, made apparent there was a sea change. Whereas Kohl had prioritized expanding the EU, one of Schröder's first remarks to Clinton suggested that the new chancellor might not. As he told Clinton, "we hope to maintain momentum but expectations do seem quite excessive." It would have to be clear that "some candidate countries will take longer to enter the Union than others." Schröder had his doubts about Primakov as well and wondered how long the United States thought the new prime minister would last. Thomas Pickering, a former US ambassador to Moscow who was taking part in this conversation, offered a guess that there would be "stability for the next 6–8 months." Primakov had "as little economic capability as anyone you could imagine," he suggested, and was ill-suited for the current crisis. But he conceded that the United States had expected "by now there would have been 20 to 40 million Russians in the streets"; instead, there were fewer than a million. The low numbers showed that Russia was "a resilient society. They are always fooling us."

Schröder remained deeply worried, saying that even if Primakov had an understanding of economic issues, it would be of no use to him and his aides. Russians, in his opinion, had a much bigger challenge: "they don't have a state." That was "the real problem" and "why all economic progress has failed." Under his leadership, Germany would henceforth offer only "project-oriented assistance" because it was "the only way to ensure that assistance funds will not get eaten up or end up in numbered accounts in Cyprus, Switzerland, and elsewhere." He thought there was now only one truly important question about Moscow, with no answer in sight: "who will be our partner in Russia?"[39]

Another question lacking a good answer was what to do about the on-going violence in Kosovo. Clinton pressed Yeltsin on the matter in writing, saying that Milošević's forces had continued "senseless slaughtering" and that the West was running out of "diplomatic options."[40] But when he got the Russian on the phone, on October 5, 1998, it was a disaster. According to Talbott, Yeltsin at one point "ranted for twelve minutes, pausing neither for interpretation into English nor for Clinton's reply." He condemned Washington's "aggressive talk" of "irreversible use of force by NATO in Yugoslavia." When Clinton refused to yield, Yeltsin hung up on him.[41] The boisterous bonhomie of past years, whether real or strategic, was gone. The president had known in advance how Yeltsin might react, but he valued the Russian's feelings less highly than maintaining NATO's freedom of action. It was yet another harbinger of what the twenty-first century would bring.

Foreign ministers from leading NATO countries converged on October 8, 1998 for a crisis meeting at London's Heathrow Airport. The alliance soon issued its "activation orders" (ACTORDs), meaning attacks could begin in ninety-six hours.[42] At the last minute, diplomatic initiatives achieved a breakthrough and enabled the OSCE to go in, leading to the postponement of airstrikes.[43] Clinton was relieved at the outcome. Although he had been pushing for a strong response, the postponement meant he would not have to defend military action to Congress right away. As he put it to British prime minister Tony Blair, "this is a terrible time for me to deal with it with this Congress of mine."[44]

Impeachment

It was a terrible time because his relationship with Monica Lewinsky was back in the headlines. After Lewinsky had turned over her dress on July 29, 1998 and a lab test commissioned by independent counsel Kenneth Starr had found semen on it, Starr's lawyers had begun heated negotiations over obtaining a presidential blood sample to check for a DNA match. Clinton's attorneys kept pushing back, saying they would only provide a sample if Starr would make available semen from the dress for "'a later, outside comparative test of the same type.'" Starr finally agreed, and they struck a deal. The White House physician drew and delivered the requested blood, and the lab ran a series of high-accuracy DNA tests. On the morning of August 17, 1998, the lab confirmed that the odds Clinton was the source of the stain were 7.87 trillion to 1.[45]

There seemed little point in a comparative test. The president decided to address the American people on television that day. He confessed to the affair and expressed his regret for misleading many people, "including even my wife." But he also defended himself, saying "even presidents have private lives." It was time, he said, to "stop the pursuit of personal destruction" because there was "important work to do" and "real security matters to face." He asked Americans to "turn away from the spectacle" and "repair the fabric of our national discourse."[46] Starr was unmoved, considering the president's dishonesty to Paula Jones's legal team under oath to be more significant. To document that dishonesty, he decided to disseminate Lewinsky's evidence and testimony in a sexually explicit account of her physical relationship with the president.[47] Starr delivered his graphic report to the Republican-led Congress on September 9, 1998, not long before the midterm elections of that autumn.[48] Congress, in turn, released the report to an astonished public.

Among other reactions, the novelist Philip Roth memorialized this stunning sequence of events in his novel *The Human Stain*. Through the words of his characters, Roth depicted summer and fall 1998 as the time "when the nausea returned, when the joking didn't stop, when the speculation and the theorizing and the hyperbole didn't stop," all thanks to "the brazenness of Bill Clinton." One of Roth's characters dreamed "of a mammoth banner," draped "from one end of the White House to the other and bearing the legend A HUMAN BEING LIVES HERE."[49] Roth's words were both a condemnation of Clinton's failings and a lament for the coarsening of public political discourse, the latter yet another harbinger of the twenty-first century.[50]

Following the revelations, the House of Representatives decided on October 8, 1998 to commence presidential impeachment proceedings for only the second time in US history, accusing the president of providing false testimony and obstructing justice. Not everyone was convinced, as shown by midterm election results on November 3. Voters stuck with the president's party despite his misconduct. Republicans lost four House seats and did not gain any in the Senate. The show of public support failed, however, to deter House Republicans from proceeding with impeachment.

To prevent Jones's team from airing yet more details of his personal life during that process, Clinton settled her case on November 13, agreeing to pay her $850,000.[51]

The House was due to open formal debate on impeachment on December 16. On that day, Clinton launched airstrikes against Iraq to enforce compliance with UN weapons inspections. He insisted in a televised address that the timing of the attack was unrelated to impeachment, saying that he could not have delayed "even a matter of days." His opponents cried foul. Gerald Solomon, a Republican congressman from New York, remarked, "'it is obvious that he is doing this for political reasons, and I and others are outraged.'"[52] The House of Representatives impeached Clinton three days later. As 1999 began, the Senate held the fate of the president in its hands for only the second time in US history.

Suddenly, everyone had to recalibrate to a nearly unprecedented risk. While NATO expansion was popular and well underway, it nonetheless seemed safest to get new members firmly on board as soon as possible, before the political landscape became unpredictably transformed.[53] In this swiftly changing political context, however, one aspect of enlargement's implementation gained new importance: the Czech Republic, Hungary, and Poland were not capable of fully integrating themselves within NATO structures and command from day one as members. They had come a long way while going through major democratic and economic transitions—in particular, Czech chemical warfare units, Hungarian military engineers, and Polish special forces had reached a high standard—but there were justifiable questions about their military readiness overall.[54]

This issue was not technically a problem for joining. NATO's founding treaty listed only general requirements for a new member, namely that it be a European state unanimously acceptable to current allies and able to "contribute to the security of the North Atlantic area" overall. Once invited by existing allies, a country then officially joined by "depositing its instrument of accession with the Government of the United States of America," without needing to prove military readiness in any formal way. But as a political matter, this lack of readiness could potentially become a political weapon in the hands of Clinton's opponents.[55]

Over the course of 1998, Poland found itself required to reassure Secretary of Defense Bill Cohen that it would be able to meet its NATO obligations. Secretary Madeleine Albright, who worried about the Czech Republic and Hungary as well, advised all three states on the need to "avoid precipitating a debate over the invitees' readiness to join the alliance." Since Washington had worked hard to ensure they would not have second-class status, it was important that they not be seen as having second-class capabilities. The three countries assured her that "work would be accelerated" on improvements to those capabilities.[56]

Momentum was on the invitees' side, however. Their future allies were understanding of the challenges they were facing—and the alliance would hardly mark its fiftieth anniversary by turning them down, especially with Clinton needing a win. On January 29, 1999, NATO secretary general Javier Solana formally invited the new members to join the alliance more than a month in advance of the April Washington summit, specifically through a ceremony at Missouri's Truman Library on March 12, with Albright presiding. The goal was partly to finalize matters as soon as possible, and partly to have the invitees able to take part in the subsequent 1999 anniversary summit as full allies, meaning to share fully at that event in decisions about a new "Alliance Strategic Concept"—and further new members.[57]

While Washington was trying to manage enlargement during its season of nausea, Russia continued to experience its own upheaval. On February 10, 1999, the US ambassador to Russia reported that Boris Berezovsky, a Yeltsin ally, had warned Washington that a full-fledged "'war'" between Yeltsin and Primakov over the Russian presidency was underway.[58] Berezovsky held a token government post, but his real importance lay in his immense wealth and membership in an informal group of Yeltsin advisors known as the Family—which included some actual family, such as Yeltsin's daughter Tatyana and her soon-to-be third husband, Valentin Yumashev.[59]

They all felt under siege because Russia's chief prosecutor, Yuri Skuratov, was looking into presidential corruption at a dangerous time.[60] Among other issues, a Swiss company holding the contract for lavish Kremlin renovations was allegedly giving the Family kickbacks. Swiss investigators raided the company's Lugano office on January 22, 1999, risking revelation of the relevant files.[61] In Kotkin's words, the Family members urgently needed someone who "would protect the Family's interests, and maybe those of Russia as well."[62] Skuratov could not be allowed to continue investigating, nor could Primakov be allowed to oust Yeltsin at this critical moment; family members might then face arrest.[63] When behind-the-scenes efforts to halt the prosecutor failed, a tape allegedly of Skuratov naked and in bed with two unclothed women—neither of whom was his wife—was broadcast nationwide by the government television network, its authenticity confirmed on the air by Putin.[64]

Primakov was harder to undermine, but the Family was determined. Yeltsin, according to Berezovsky, "had a nasty confrontation" with his prime minister, and the battle lines were drawn. To be sure, Berezovsky was hardly a disinterested, reliable observer, but the bottom line of his message to Washington, that Primakov "would be out of a job by May," nonetheless rang true. Berezovsky advised the embassy that Yeltsin would do his best to pull off a "'soft'" switch to a new prime minister. The tycoon advised Washington to support Yeltsin in the coming struggle because Primakov remained as "'red as a tomato.'"[65]

Showing a remarkable sense of timing, Putin apparently decided this was a good moment to display his loyalties. He had known Berezovsky since meeting him in Leningrad in 1991. The FSB head now decided to make a show of appearing at a birthday party for Berezovsky's wife. Upon arriving, he apparently announced to the host, "'I absolutely do not care what Primakov thinks of me.'"[66]

Berezovsky did not tell the US embassy about another burden weighing on Yeltsin, this one involving NATO. The alliance was once again the source of active contention between the Russian president and his Ukrainian counterpart, Leonid Kuchma. The two Slavic presidents were haggling over modernization of marine aviation equipment for the Russian Black Sea Fleet, docked in the Ukrainian port of Sevastopol.[67] As part of their negotiations, Yeltsin demanded that Kyiv sign a "document" setting out "limits of relations with NATO." The "orientation of Ukraine first and foremost toward Euro-Atlantic structures" was causing "growing anxiety in Russia," and the Russian president apparently wanted to prevent the nightmare of the Atlantic Alliance parking US Navy warships in the Black Sea Fleet's home port.[68] Kuchma was noncommittal in response. He also resisted Russian pressure to decline Ukraine's invitation to NATO's fiftieth-anniversary summit in April 1999.[69] Fighting between Moscow and Kyiv over relations with NATO and the West was clearly going to be yet another landmark of the twenty-first century, with consequences far beyond the border of either country.[70]

To assess what to do about Yeltsin's crises, Schröder visited Clinton on February 11, 1999, just before the Senate vote on whether to remove the US president from office. Clinton, who wanted to get business done while he could, thanked the German for coming on short notice. The two leaders agreed that "Russia is in dire straits," since "the health system has collapsed and life expectancy is dropping." One of the chancellor's advisors, Michael Steiner, conceded that not all of Moscow's problems were home-grown. Germany had made mistakes; "we rushed in" and "made money

quickly," but then left with the profits. As a result, the West had lost credibility. Clinton agreed, saying, "I am not sure everything I did over the last
six years was right" either. But in his view, Russia's problems rested ultimately in the way it had "privatized its economy without laws to protect
investors." It was "as if they had poured flesh without a skeletal frame to
hold it erect." The German agreed that Russia had transitioned directly
from being "too much state-controlled" to having "no state left." The upshot
for Schröder was plain: "he who banks on Yeltsin is dumb."

Upgrading his earlier negative view of Primakov, Schröder concluded
that the prime minister was "more than a transitional figure, he is a piece
of stability for the medium term." Of course, once Primakov "drives the
car into a wall, he thinks that we will pay—for stability." But Berlin and
Washington could do much worse than to deal with him as the next Russian president. Clinton agreed, saying, "I kind of like him; he's strong,
honest, sober, shows up to work every day. He's pretty good." Berger
interjected that Primakov had little chance of becoming president given
Yeltsin's fierce opposition. In the national security advisor's view, Primakov "is kidding himself" and, worse, "he is kidding us." Everyone agreed,
however, that the main Russian problem was "organized crime." As
Clinton put it, black marketeers were trading in chemical and biological
weapons, using "Colombian cartels" as "their investment bankers." But
the president emphasized that despite Yeltsin's agonies, avoiding limits on
NATO's freedom of action remained essential. The alliance must keep its
"door open to others." Schröder, hesitant, suggested they remain vague
as to "which countries are next in line."[71]

Whether Clinton would be the one transforming even the first invitees into allies still hung in the balance that day, but not for long. The
concluding vote to the Senate impeachment trial took place on February 12, 1999. In the end, senators voted on two counts, one of perjury and
one of obstruction of justice. Both were defeated, by votes of 55 to 45 and
50 to 50, respectively, well short of the two-thirds majority required to
convict.[72] Clinton survived, but so too did the bitterness generated by the
season of nausea.

New Members, New Missions

The new NATO members' obvious joy at the Truman Library ceremony
the next month provided a welcome break from the bitterness. The Czech,
Hungarian, and Polish foreign ministers joined Albright in Washington

and went onward together to Missouri on her plane. En route, Polish foreign minister Bronisław Geremek, a historian and close friend of Albright, called the trip the "'fulfillment of a dream'" and "'the most important event that has happened to Poland since the onset of Christianity.'" Albright told her advisor, Ron Asmus, that "'it doesn't get any better than this. We are making history.'"[73]

During the ceremony, the ministers signed the documents of accession on the same table Truman had used to sign the Marshall Plan.[74] This symbolic gesture showed that US aspirations for NATO's role were much more than military. Fireworks went off simultaneously in Budapest, Prague, and Warsaw. Afterward, Albright held the signed protocols "aloft like victory trophies," in the words of the *New York Times* reporter covering the event, Jane Perlez.[75] In a moving speech, the secretary praised the new members for their history of "putting their lives on the line for liberty," promised her new allies that "never again will your fates be tossed around like poker chips," and confirmed that they were "truly home." Together, they were "erasing without replacing the line drawn in Europe by Stalin's bloody boot." Since enlargement was not an event but "a process," their next challenge was to help more states become allies.[76]

A more immediate challenge was dealing with the new allies' military unpreparedness. Lower-level NATO staff charged with enlargement's practical implementation began tackling the problem that the new states simply could not yet operate with the alliance. A congressional assessment found that they needed not only to "modernize their equipment" but also to take the fundamental step of "buying communications gear that is interoperable with NATO's systems." In addition, "while the armed forces of all three new members are firmly in the hands of civilian defense ministries, a lack of civilian defense experts in the legislative branches has resulted in minimal parliamentary oversight." All three states had yet to move away "from the Warsaw Pact model of absolute reliance on top-down centralized authority."[77]

They would have to learn on the job, however, because NATO was once again ramping up for action in Kosovo. Clinton let Yeltsin know yet again in late February 1999 that the renewed violence had made military action necessary.[78] Together with her British and French colleagues Robin Cook and Hubert Védrine, Albright organized multilateral talks in Rambouillet, France, to produce a set of cease-fire accords that were delivered to Milošević in March.[79] It seemed unlikely that the Serb leader would agree to them, however, so to plan for that refusal, Clinton welcomed

Solana to the White House on March 15. Together with the secretaries
of defense and state, and in consultation with European leaders such as
Blair and Jacques Chirac, they decided on an open-ended NATO air
campaign against Milošević. Cohen wanted to avoid any pause in that
campaign because breaks would give Russia and China a chance to rush
to the UN Security Council to stop it—and might open up a debate
within the alliance itself. There were strong misgivings among European
leaders about the prospect that Kosovo might become a precedent, enabling NATO (or perhaps the United States alone) to intervene in future
non-Article-5 contingencies without a UNSC resolution, and Beijing and
Moscow could potentially play on those.

The secretary general further noted that Primakov, who was due to
visit Washington on March 24, "would certainly not react well to air
strikes" if they began before or during his visit. As a result, "the US needs
to be prepared to do damage control." Clinton acknowledged the point
but believed, as he later explained to Blair, that Primakov "still needs to
come here because he needs the money" and was trying to convince the
IMF to give him a better deal. The IMF was, not surprisingly, balking at
providing more funds. Clinton estimated to Blair that "all the money disappeared in 48 hours the last time."[80]

This renewed threat of NATO airstrikes drove Yeltsin to new heights
of rage. The Russian assailed Clinton by cable on March 23, objecting to
the "readiness of NATO to employ force." He warned, "if Kosovo ex-
plodes in flames, it could spread to the entire region."[81] Yeltsin and his
advisors were horrified not only that NATO would take the unprecedented step of bypassing the UN Security Council in order to bomb a
country but that it would do so for reasons unrelated to either Article 5 or
aggression against another state. Instead, unbelievably in his view, the
alliance was taking this dramatic step simply because of actions inside a
country's own borders. Coming at the same time as the implementation
of enlargement, it seemed to prove irrefutably that the claim NATO expansion would bring peace to Europe had been pure deceit. As one US
diplomat put it, "Yeltsin's critics warned him 'Belgrade today, Moscow
tomorrow!'"[82]

The Russian president's intervention was to no avail. It was obvious
to all that Moscow had little leverage, NATO spokesman Jamie Shea later
recalled, since the country needed Western investment, trade, and support.[83] Once Milošević refused to sign the cease-fire accords, the die was
cast. Airstrikes began on March 24, 1999. Primakov, who had by then de-

parted for his US visit, ordered his plane turned around in midflight, a maneuver that became known as "Primakov's loop."

Clinton tried to defuse Yeltsin's anger afterward, but his prospects for success were limited—and not just because of the situation in Kosovo. The Russian president had only just emerged from his latest hospital stay six days earlier. Yeltsin immediately found himself facing, as Berger put it on the day the airstrikes began, yet another "bare-knuckles political crisis" at home on top of the one in Kosovo, with "credible revelations of corruption" being "laid at his family's and entourage's doorstep" by Communists in the parliament. The Russian president suspected that Primakov was behind it all.[84] Trying to reason with the overwhelmed Yeltsin, Clinton told him that "Milošević has stonewalled" and "continued to move his forces into Kosovo," leaving the United States "no choice." Despite knowing that Yeltsin opposed what he was about to order, Clinton was "determined to do whatever I can to keep our disagreement on this from ruining everything else we have done and can do in the coming years." Yeltsin replied bitterly, "I'm afraid we shall not succeed in that." He pointedly reminded Clinton "how difficult it was for me to try and turn the heads of our people, the heads of the politicians towards the West, towards the United States." He had succeeded in that venture at great effort, and it was a tragedy "now to lose all that" because of the NATO intervention. Yeltsin allowed that "of course, we are going to talk to each other, you and me. But there will not be such great drive and such friendship that we had before. That will not be there again." For the future, he saw only "a very difficult, difficult road of contacts, if they prove to be possible" at all.[85] He would soon suspend Russian contact with the Permanent Joint NATO-Russia Council, established with so much fanfare less than two years earlier.[86]

Yeltsin even resorted to threats. "We have many steps to aim against your decision," he told Clinton, "maybe inadmissible steps." He had just "reached agreement with the State Duma with regards to START II." Parliamentarians were "supposed to ratify that Treaty," but he had agreed with them that would no longer happen "under the circumstances."[87] Yeltsin's implication was that the United States was sacrificing its own nuclear safety for Kosovo. These threats highlighted what would gradually become a particularly tragic feature of the twenty-first-century world: the reversal of the large strides in arms control made during the 1990s and shredding of treaties from earlier decades by both Washington and Moscow. The *New York Times* reported on April 9, 1999 that Russia had resumed "targeting NATO states with nuclear warheads." The foreign ministry half-heartedly denied the report, saying "'as far as we know,'" no such orders had gone out.[88]

It seemed to Russians that events in Kosovo were making the negative consequences of enlargement all too painfully obvious: it enabled America, in the name of NATO, to bomb Slavs at will.[89] A saying began making the rounds in Moscow: roughly, the difference between Serbia and Russia was that the latter possessed nuclear weapons and was therefore safe from American attack. If not for that, Russians might face the same fate as Serbs—or the same fate that the Chinese had faced in their embassy in Belgrade, hit accidentally by US bombardment on May 7, 1999.[90]

That same month, Yeltsin decided that given all the risks he was facing, he could no longer tolerate Primakov.[91] The president managed, as Berezovsky had predicted, to oust his prime minister in a "soft" transition. Yeltsin replaced him in the first instance with the relatively colorless Sergey Stepashin, but since he was not a substantive enough figure to become president, the succession question remained open.

Meanwhile, airstrikes against Serbia continued through April and May and into June, with Albright actively managing the process. *Time* magazine put the secretary on its cover with the caption "Albright at War."[92] She later recalled that Secretary of Defense Cohen "was crazed" that the SACEUR, Wesley Clark, talked with her repeatedly by phone during the attacks, which Cohen saw as "breaking the chain of command." But Albright and Clark felt that if Clark could talk to other foreign ministers, why should he not talk to his own?[93] They shared a goal of getting Milošević to pull back his troops and, as Berger put it, "embrace the Rambouillet settlement" as soon as possible, and they felt that all steps in service of that goal were admissible.[94] For his part, Clinton regretted that Clark was "having to spend half or more than half his time every day trying to schmooze the Allies" into agreeing on targets, and called for a more straightforward procedure.[95] The French in particular wanted to restrain the list of targets, foreshadowing later clashes with another administration over limits on US actions in another part of the world: Iraq. Maintaining cohesion among top-rank leadership was clearly proving to be a challenge.[96]

Republicans and some Democrats in the House of Representatives were unhappy as well; on April 28, they approved a measure blocking funding for US ground forces in the Balkans without congressional approval by a vote of 249 to 180. To avoid provoking them further, it was essential for Clinton to protect US troops and avoid casualties.[97] As he recounted to Blair, "the lowest point of my presidency" had been seeing an American soldier's "body being dragged through the streets of Somalia" in 1993. "It was a goddamned nightmare" that he did not want to relive. "We will look like assholes at the garden party if we don't make sure that everybody understands NATO means keeping our people alive."[98]

Yet again, Clinton tried to reconcile with Yeltsin, writing to him on April 3. The US president noted his happiness that the IMF was at least sending "a full mission to Moscow to continue negotiations." Clinton flattered Yeltsin personally as well, saying, "in troubled times such as now, your courage, common sense and foresight are an encouragement to me personally and to all who are trying to build a new, more peaceful world for the next century."[99] The flattery did not work. Yeltsin responded in a phone call that "the US and NATO have made a big mistake" and that "the anti-American and anti-NATO sentiment in Russia keeps growing like an avalanche."[100] The NSC reported that opinion polls showed that 93 percent of Russians disapproved of NATO's actions.[101] Russian representatives displayed their displeasure by declining their invitations to NATO's fiftieth-anniversary summit. One of the early reformers from the start of Yeltsin's tenure, Yegor Gaidar, now a private citizen, contacted Talbott with a lament: "'if only you knew what a disaster this war is for those of us in Russia who want for our country what you want.'"[102]

These events overshadowed NATO's fiftieth-anniversary event, even though it was the largest gathering of international leaders in the history of Washington, DC.[103] On April 23–25, 1999, the members of the alliance, along with a wide array of guest countries—forty-four states in all, including Ukraine—descended on DC.[104] They attended a ceremony in Mellon Hall, the very location where the twelve original alliance members had first signed the North Atlantic Treaty back on April 4, 1949.[105] The *Washington Post* reported that in the streets around the hall, "Natonian physics" had caused "the repulsion of most of the people from downtown Washington" as a security precaution. At last "we know what Washington will be like as the world is coming to an end," the *Post* editorialized: it will be "Orwellian, lined with barricades and patrolled by cops, soldiers and armored cars."[106]

Inside the hall, the "Natonians are almost all male, including, without exception, the heads of state," since "they are, after all, warriors" who were "actually fighting" a war as the summit was going on. Unfortunately, the war "is not going so terribly well." The conflict took top priority at the summit.[107] As Clinton explained to Blair, the goal was to "get from beginning to end with the NATO alliance intact." Since this was, in the president's view, "the first thing NATO has had to do in 50 years," it was not a given that it would succeed. The alliance had of course been involved in Bosnia, but Clinton felt that was different because "we had a lot of help on the ground from Croatian and Muslim forces; we didn't have to do as much as we do here." In Kosovo, he had to defeat ethnic cleansing, maintain alliance cohesion, and ideally keep ties with Russia as strong as possible. But that "might be too much to hope for."[108] Clinton's public remarks at the summit naturally focused on Kosovo as well: while Milošević's "forces burn and loot homes and murder innocent people," he said, NATO was delivering "food and shelter and hope."[109]

Yet the summit was also a victory for the Clinton administration's "robust open door" strategy. At the summit, allies formally welcomed the interest of no fewer than nine more countries in cooperating with the alliance, clearly with an eye toward membership: Albania, Bulgaria, Estonia, Latvia, Lithuania, Romania, Slovakia, Slovenia, and the former Yugoslav republic of Macedonia (FYROM).[110] The summit thereby signaled that an open-ended, iterative process of enlarging NATO was beginning, with no limits set on how far the alliance could extend in its next round or what it could do on its new territory. The upcoming expansion soon gained a nickname: the big bang. Albright called this strategy the "blueprint for NATO in the 21st Century."[111] By the year 2020, the alliance would expand to thirty members.

There was one concession, both to Russia and to the reality that future members would need more guidance on how to ready themselves, so as not to be as militarily unprepared as the class that had just joined in March. The alliance unveiled a new precursor step to membership: production of a so-called Membership Action Plan (MAP). Each future member would need to work out an individualized MAP, defined as a program of "activities to assist aspiring countries in their preparations for possible future membership."[112]

The MAP also modulated the pace of enlargement, thereby providing useful face-saving features for dealing with Russia. It meant that as the April 1999 summit fulfilled the Talbott Principle and put the Baltic nations in line for membership, the headlines were less likely to enrage Moscow. The news that the Baltics would receive MAPs was less insulting than news that they would receive membership.[113] In practical terms, the outcome would be the same, but it sounded better.

NATO reaches thirty members in 2020.

Notably, Ukraine was not among the nine indicated as aspiring members. There was still a sense that it was a bridge too far, not least because of tensions over Sevastopol. In addition, Western diplomats kept recounting horror stories about what it was like working with Kyiv, in sharp contrast to their positive experiences working with Baltic leaders, who had now returned from bitterness to enthusiasm in their dealings with Washington. At one point, Estonia sent half its cabinet to DC, effectively as a lobbying group. And Latvians, Lithuanians, and Estonians seemed able to fight major corruption in a way that Ukrainians unfortunately did not.[114] The alliance decided to give the Ukrainian leader, Kuchma, a summit-within-a-summit instead, holding a special meeting between all nineteen NATO members and Ukraine as a signal that NATO was not simply ceding the country to a new Russian sphere of influence.[115] The event could not conceal the fact that Ukraine had been taken off of the conveyor belt of future members.

With that conveyor belt now operational, NATO turned its focus to its short-term mission in Kosovo. The challenges there grew after the airstrike that hit the Chinese embassy in Belgrade in May 1999. Clinton immediately expressed sorrow in public, saying that the "injuries were completely inadvertent" and extending "deep regret to the people and leaders of China."[116] Moscow seized the opportunity. Chernomyrdin suddenly appeared in China, where he sympathized with Chinese leaders about NATO's "'act of aggression.'"[117]

Another challenge for Clinton was that Yeltsin was soon physically incapacitated again. As Berger advised the president on May 11, 1999, it was a reminder "of the fragility of his health and the fact that even a small return to alcohol can knock him seriously off balance." In addition, the Duma was now copying the US Congress and trying unsuccessfully to impeach Yeltsin. His aides were frantically trying to count—and, it was rumored, buy—votes to keep the top man in office. He ultimately survived, but his authority was waning rapidly.[118]

Despite this weakness, Yeltsin got Clinton to agree that American and Russian representatives should meet in some "third country" to find a way around "the dead-end in Kosovo and in Russian-American relations."[119] Chernomyrdin and Talbott, working with the Finnish president, Martti Ahtisaari—whose country was about to assume the EU presidency, giving his view added weight—agreed that NATO would be at the core of a new, joint Kosovo Force (KFOR).[120] Clinton negotiated personally with a frail Yeltsin by phone on June 8, 1999 over the exact timing of a Serbian withdrawal and an end to the bombing.[121] Although the process was fraught—not only because of tensions between the United States and Russia but also because of open arguments among Russian civilian and military leaders about how accommodating to be toward Washington—in the following days all of these negotiations revealed a light at the end of the tunnel.[122] Russian pressure helped to make the Serbians yield. NATO suspended its eleven-week air campaign on Thursday, June 10, as an international peacekeeping force made ready to begin work in the region.[123] The US deputy national security advisor, James Steinberg, later praised the way the administration conducted the intervention, saying "ethnic cleansing was not only reversed but reversed in a way that kept NATO together, prevented the destabilization of neighboring countries, and kept Russia engaged without sacrificing NATO's stated goals."[124]

Promoting Putin

An incident on June 11, 1999, during one of Talbott's many visits to Moscow, revealed the risks the Kosovo intervention still posed to US-Russian relations. The visit included a novelty: Talbott's first meeting with FSB head Putin. The deputy secretary was impressed by Putin's "ability to convey self-control and confidence in a low-key, soft-spoken manner."[125]

While they were speaking, Talbott's aide Victoria Nuland passed him a note reporting a rumor that Russian forces were unilaterally seizing parts of Kosovo, which was not foreseen in agreements between Washington and Moscow. The deputy secretary immediately asked the Russians what was going on. Putin replied in mild tones that he knew nothing—but in a way that seemed calculated to strain Talbott's credulity, which it did. Uneasy, the deputy secretary left Moscow immediately afterward by plane, only to learn in flight that a Russian unit from Bosnia was indeed heading for Pristina, the capital of Kosovo. Berger called the deputy secretary on the plane, telling him to turn his aircraft around and "'raise hell.'"[126]

Hell proved difficult to raise. Talbott "cooled his heels" at the US embassy for several hours, watching Russian armored columns making their way toward Kosovo on television.[127] The chatter among NATO allies was that Russians were trying to secure "a Russian sector," perhaps along the lines of the old Berlin model. It later became apparent that the forces were headed for the airport in Pristina.[128] What remained unclear was who had approved the deployment—an ailing Yeltsin, or perhaps military leaders feeling they had not gotten enough in the final days of negotiations?[129] Eventually, Talbott managed to organize an evening session at the foreign ministry, but it proved fruitless. He spent most of the night at the defense ministry, sometimes abruptly abandoned by his hosts. At one point near 3:00 a.m. he began wandering the halls in search of his absent negotiating partners but found only a drunken general. Finally, at 5:30 a.m., he departed the ministry in search of other interlocutors. On the afternoon of Saturday, June 12, Talbott managed to get back to Putin.

Talbott later reported that when he reappeared in Putin's office, the head of the FSB acted "as though nothing alarming or surprising had occurred in the twenty-four hours since I'd previously seen him."[130] Instead, Putin simply continued speaking in the same mild, taciturn manner, downplaying the events in Kosovo. He spoke in general terms about Russian hawks causing the intervention as part of a larger "'pre-election struggle'" but would give no details. And if Putin was pleased that the US president's top advisor on Russia had been taken down a few notches in their first encounter, he gave no recorded sign.

Clinton spoke with Yeltsin by phone on both Sunday, June 13, and Monday, June 14. Though the process was fraught, they agreed "to instruct our generals to meet and resolve the problem of command at the airport."[131] The generals did as ordered, but not without tense moments in which conflict between allied and Russian forces seemed possible.[132] General Clark had already ordered use of force to prevent the seizure of the airport, but the junior British officers charged with implementing the order, including the later pop star James Blunt, refused to carry it out.[133] British general Michael Jackson backed his men up, reportedly saying he was unwilling to start World War III. Clark and Jackson subsequently settled on a waiting strategy instead.[134] Clark reportedly contacted countries from which Russia needed overflight rights to resupply their forces—including potentially Bulgaria, Hungary, and Romania—to get those rights canceled or denied. The Russian troops' stay at the Pristina Airport became dry and hungry.[135] Blunt reported that "after a couple of days, the Russians there said, 'hang on, we have no food and no water. Can we share the airfield with you?'"[136] Potentially a disaster, this strategy became a successful example of how to absorb rather than exacerbate a problem.

Moscow reportedly kept trying to bully its former Warsaw Pact allies to release their airspace. With their eyes on new or future NATO memberships, they refused.[137] When Putin spoke to Berger by phone, the Russian used the same conciliatory tone he had used with Talbott, telling the national security advisor, "I do not think that the airport and everything connected to it will be a big issue." He added mildly, "we do have joint experience like this in Tuzla," a city where the Russians successfully pressured Bosnian Serbs to open the airport and allow delivery of humanitarian aid. Since they "managed to find an acceptable solution there," presumably they could do the same now.[138]

The United States and Russia were indeed able to do so. Just as in Bosnia, the Russians were once again on the ground with NATO in Kosovo.[139] Western relations with Moscow had survived the Pristina Airport crisis, but only just; the wounds inflicted were serious and left Russia bitter at seeing its weakness internationally exposed. Despite the patching up of differences, a shift in thinking had taken place in Washington as well. Pentagon policymakers who had been trying to see Russians as friends began to wonder, after Pristina, whether that would be so easy. New Central and Eastern European members of NATO said, in effect, we told you so.[140]

The American and Russian presidents subsequently met in person at the G8 summit in Cologne, Germany, on June 19–20, 1999. Clinton thanked Yeltsin for "not giving up on the relationship and making sure we passed this very tough test." In an odd move, Yeltsin then told Clinton that he had a gift for the US president: documents of unclear origin, which he said related to the Kennedy assassination. Clinton accepted the gift but tried to focus on business. He prompted Yeltsin to get discussions on START II ratification going again, as well as talk about START III; his efforts had little effect. At the end, the two men hugged in a show of cooperation, but both knew the friendship was waning.[141]

The problem, as Clinton pointed out to Schröder, was that "my time is running out, and so is Yeltsin's." The US president had a suggestion for the German: "Should we move up NATO enlargement and EU enlargement?"[142] It was a daring suggestion, to which Schröder did not respond with any enthusiasm; instead, he noted that there was "such a backlog" of countries trying to join the EU that it would be hard to add more "to the list."[143] Seeking a warmer reception for the idea, Clinton called his old friend Kohl, who advised the president to accomplish as much as he could while Yeltsin was still around. As the former chancellor put it, "everything you can nail down now" should be nailed down, because "you don't know how things are going to work out" with the next Russian president.[144]

Clinton agreed, saying he had told Yeltsin "we have to finish this nuclear work, because he can't afford to let his successor throw it all away."[145] The president hoped he could still get Yeltsin moving on START II, START III, and particularly the Comprehensive Test Ban Treaty. That treaty represented the culmination of a decades-long campaign to bar all signatory countries from detonating any nuclear devices whatsoever. When he had signed it on behalf of the United States in 1996, Clinton had praised it as "'the longest-sought, hardest-fought prize in arms control history.'"[146]

It would mark the culmination of a long run of success in arms control if it went into effect. As one US diplomat put it, in terms of superpower competition, "during the 1990s" the world had become "arguably the most secure against nuclear war than at any time since nuclear weapons were invented."[147] Clinton wanted to keep that trend going because vast arsenals remained. Despite the cuts and treaties of the past decade, Russia alone reportedly had enough plutonium in 1999 for 25,000 to 50,000 weapons.[148]

But Moscow was showing distressing resistance to both of those START accords and to CTBT. START II, which would have eliminated two-thirds of the US and Russian arsenals, would eventually be ratified but never truly go into effect. START III would not even progress to a signing.[149] CTBT was, if a CIA report from July 2, 1999 was true, under fire from Putin himself. According to a boldfaced, italicized report emphasizing his role, Putin's reasoning was as follows. He announced publicly that Moscow was moving forward with a new *"test plan,"* which the CIA took to mean for *"low-yield warheads."* In the CIA's view, Moscow believed that such weapons were necessary because of *"perceptions of a heightened threat from NATO,"* reductions in the *"capabilities of Russian conventional forces,"* and *"fears that a future conflict could be waged on Russian soil."* Putin and his colleagues therefore opposed CTBT because its strictures might make developing such weapons more difficult.[150] Following up on the same theme in the year 2000, the CIA added that Moscow was clearly trying to develop a class of "**'Clean' Very-Low-Yield Nuclear Weapons,**" creating "minimal long-term contamination" on the battlefield, in order to "blur the boundary between nuclear and conventional warfare" and thereby "head off a major conflict." Together with the US decision to withdraw from the ABM Treaty in 2002, the effects of all of these developments for early twenty-first-century arms control would be severely damaging. Looking back in 2015, former secretary of defense Bill Perry concluded that arms control ended up "'a casualty of NATO expansion'" and of fighting between the Kremlin and the Duma in the 1990s; "the downsides of early NATO membership for Eastern European nations were even worse than I had feared."[151]

Another troubling development was Moscow's decision, again apparently involving Putin, to reignite the conventional war in Chechnya. Skirmishes between Chechen fighters and Russian troops had resumed in the summer of 1999, but matters took a much graver turn in September.[152] That month, a series of bombings of residential apartment buildings in

Moscow and other cities killed 243 people and injured 1,700 more.[153] After Putin declared the bombings to be the work of Chechen-affiliated terrorists, Russia launched what came to be known as the Second Chechen War, which eventually culminated in direct rule of the region from Moscow.[154] By the end of the year, largely thanks to that war, Putin would be the most popular politician in the country.[155] But critics later identified evidence allegedly showing that the FSB itself—and possibly Putin—might have had a role in the apartment tragedy.[156] An American journalist in Moscow who had roomed with Talbott at Oxford, David Satter, wrote that "to grasp the reality of Russia, it is necessary to accept that Russian leaders really are capable of blowing up hundreds of their own people to preserve their hold on power."[157] He subsequently became the first US journalist since the Cold War to be expelled from Russia.[158]

In the course of that year, Putin also rose in Yeltsin's estimation; the Russian president decided to promote the younger man again on August 9, 1999, this time to replace Stepashin as prime minister.[159] Those who knew Putin were immediately wary. Nursultan Nazarbayev, still the leader of Kazakhstan, told Clinton during a visit to the Oval Office later that year that Putin "has nothing going for him besides the Chechen War." In the Kazakh's view, "he has no charisma, no foreign policy experience, no economic policy of his own. He just has the war—a fight with his own people."[160] Russian reformer Boris Nemtsov reportedly called Putin's appointment "'a very, very big mistake.'"[161]

That Putin was now prime minister was not in itself hugely significant, since by that point Russian prime ministers had become disposable items.[162] But on September 8, just before Clinton's departure to an Asia-Pacific Economic Cooperation summit in Auckland, New Zealand, the White House received a fateful call from Moscow. Yeltsin was sending Prime Minister Putin to New Zealand, and he wanted Clinton to understand why.[163]

Yeltsin recounted how he had taken "a lot of time to think who might be the next Russian president in the year 2000," but "unfortunately" none of the other candidates had worked out. After much searching, Yeltsin said, "I came across him, that is, Putin, and I explored his bio, his interests, his acquaintances, and so on and so forth." Yeltsin discerned that Putin was "a solid man who is kept well abreast of various subjects under his purview." The president also considered him "thorough and strong, very sociable," adding, "I am sure you will find him to be a highly qualified partner." The notion that Russian voters should pick his successor did not seem to concern him; Yeltsin was sure that Putin "will be supported as a candidate in the year 2000. We are working on it accordingly."[164] Who "we" were was not immediately clear, but after the call, Yeltsin's daughter Tatyana acknowledged to Talbott the behind-the-scenes role that she and the rest of the Family played in promoting Putin. She reportedly told him, "'it really was very hard, getting Putin into the job—one of the hardest things we ever pulled off.'" The Family had persevered, however, because its members were convinced Putin "'won't sell us out,'" and indeed he did not: he ultimately granted Yeltsin immunity from prosecution.[165]

Listening to the Russian president lay out his country's future on the phone, Clinton and his aides were aware of the significance of the moment. President George H. W. Bush had once been on the receiving end of a call from Yeltsin announcing the end of the Gorbachev era; Clinton and his advisors were now hearing something of similar magnitude. As Bush had done before him, Clinton stuck to cautious replies while the Russian was on the line, saying only that the information was "very helpful." He added that "we have had good contacts with Mr. Putin so far," and "I look forward to meeting with him in Auckland."[166]

Thus forewarned, Clinton traveled to Auckland on September 12, 1999, where he made a demonstrative show of Prime Minister Putin's new significance. According to a later account by Putin, when the president realized they were seated at different tables for a meal, Clinton walked to Putin's table and said to him, "'well, shall we go?'" Leaders of other states and guests, sensing the significance of the gesture, stood and applauded as the two men exited the hall together.[167]

Once they were alone with their aides, however, the atmosphere became chillier. Throughout Clinton's tenure, there had been "no leader who didn't want to be with him, spend time with him, engage with him, be associated with him," in Steinberg's words, because the US president was "unbelievably magnetic, especially for other leaders." Putin, however, was "indifferent" to Clinton's charms.[168] Albright noticed the same phenomenon: "when talking to Bill Clinton, Boris Yeltsin had been bombastic, enthusiastic, erratic, hot-tempered, and warm." He spoke to Clinton "as if everything were personal and could be solved by the two Presidents sitting alone." Putin, by contrast, "was clear-minded, cordial," but "cool."[169]

The American president decided, as an opening gambit, to express his hope of preserving the ABM Treaty, despite Republican support for a missile defense system that would threaten it. Putin expressed guarded support for the idea, saying, "my personal view may be closer to what you said than to the positions articulated by other people on the Russian side."[170] The prime minister added that Moscow had been "very close to ratifying START II," and he hoped it would do so in the end. Clinton next expressed sympathy over the apartment bombings. Putin seized the opportunity to declare not only that the "recent terrorist acts in Moscow" had originated in Chechnya but that "the perpetrators are the same as the ones who delivered the strikes against the United States." Lest there be any doubt what he meant, he told Clinton that "Usama Bin-Laden has declared his intention to move to Chechnya," where "his groups already have a presence." The only reason bin Laden had not appeared already was that "he is afraid we will apprehend him or take other actions."

To avoid being drawn into a murky discussion on bin Laden's responsibility for the apartment bombings, Clinton instead offered unsolicited campaign advice, saying, "you can try to show that there is no credible alternative to the path that you're on." He added, "if the opposition doesn't have a credible set of proposals, that will help you." Putin contradicted him: "unfortunately, that's not the case," because Russia "does not have an established political system. People don't read programs." Instead, they look only "at the faces of the leaders, regardless of what party they belong to, regardless of whether they have a program or not." Such behavior showed that "most of our population" was "not very sophisticated," but "that's the reality we need to deal with." The prime minister concluded cryptically, saying, "we have certain plans and are acting according to them." Now it was Clinton's turn to respond mildly, saying only, "I look forward to seeing how they unfold."[171]

Exit Yeltsin

The initial encounter with Putin, unsettling in itself, came at an increasingly unsettled time in US politics. Although Clinton had survived impeachment, he had become damaged goods, thanks to the public outrage his actions had inspired. He had to be careful about, among other things, how he promoted Vice President Gore's future. As he explained to Blair on October 13, 1999, thanks to the current "political culture," it "will hurt if it appears I'm trying to control the outcome of another election. I've got to be careful not to tell people how to vote."[172]

Given the public's bitterness, it was fortunate for both the president and the Atlantic Alliance that he had gotten NATO enlargement ratified when he did. The fate of the test ban treaty, presented to the Senate after impeachment, showed how much his persuasive powers with that body had declined. The treaty enjoyed overwhelming international support; nearly 200 countries would go on to sign it.[173] Yet the US Senate rejected it on October 13, 1999, by a vote of 51 to 48.[174] The *New York Times* described the rejection as "the first time the Senate had defeated a major international security pact since the Treaty of Versailles"—the fate Rosner had feared that NATO expansion would meet.[175] Steinberg called the failure "enormously damaging" and one of the "biggest disappointments" of the entire Clinton era.[176] Elsewhere, NATO expansion supporters breathed a sigh of relief, pleased not to be seeking their Senate ratification in the wake of impeachment.[177]

Clinton vented his fury about the Senate's attitude in his phone call with Blair that day. While "half of the Republicans are against this on its merit," for the rest "it's just politics. They are out to screw me because they don't want to help me and don't want to help Al." He found the Republican stance "stupid" and contradictory. All they wanted to do was oppose everything; "they won't pay UN dues and they don't want an aid budget." He had belatedly realized that many Republicans "are genuine isolationists" whose attitude was "'piss on our allies' and 'to hell with what they think; screw anybody who screws with us.'" The result, he went on, was that "it's just sick what a world we are living in here." As far as he could tell, what they really wanted was "a bunch of bombs and missiles and a defense system," but "then they just cut everybody's taxes. They want to put rich people behind gates so the starving can't get at them." In essence, "they basically want an upscale Brazil for America. It is awful, but I think we can beat them back."[178] In his anger, the president had hit on two further landmarks of twenty-first-century American politics: isolationism and inequality.

After losing that domestic battle, Clinton also had to endure a contentious rematch with Putin on November 2, 1999, at a Middle East summit held in Oslo, Norway.[179] The American used the opportunity to challenge the prime minister on the mounting casualties in Chechnya, saying, "this conflict may be playing well for you at home, but not internationally." He gave the prime minister more unsolicited advice: "in my experience, politics and reality eventually become aligned, and you need to keep this in mind." Putin thanked Clinton for having "raised our consciousness."[180]

Clinton also broached the still-outstanding issue of the treaty on conventional forces, hoping that an updated version could be signed as part of a scheduled OSCE summit in Istanbul roughly two weeks later on November 18.[181] Russia continued to exceed the treaty's limits on conventional forces, not least because of the presence of its forces in disputed regions of Georgia.[182] The US president admitted that Putin had been "straightforward about being over the CFE levels." As a result, "it's all been above board, and there have been no denials, and I want you to know I appreciate that." Still, the excess forces were blocking the CFE update, and "you need to decide if you want to get this Treaty done" in Istanbul. Putin replied, "we are exceeding our equipment levels due to the Chechnya operations, we notified that and we are not violating the CFE Treaty." Berger objected, saying, "how can you sign the treaty if Russia is out of compliance?" There had to be, at a minimum, some schedule for a drawdown. Putin demurred, saying, "it is not clear how quickly we can do this."[183]

Eventually, Moscow and Washington reached a compromise. The new treaty, like the old, placed limits on five categories of conventional weapons, but Russia was allowed to exceed those limits "temporarily." The definition of "temporarily" was left vague, however, giving Moscow a lot of wiggle room.[184] Meanwhile, Western negotiators successfully blocked Russia's effort to add treaty provisions "banning NATO stationed forces on the territories of new members." Instead, the alliance maintained its ability both to station forces and to ramp up "deployment levels above ceilings for crisis operations," with "no geographic constraints on aircraft and helicopters."[185]

But even though each side had gotten something it wanted, bitterness dominated. The Russian president revived himself enough to attend the CFE signing in Istanbul on November 18, 1999, going despite his frailty to deliver what he saw as an important message to Clinton. As Yeltsin explained later, "'Clinton permitted himself to put pressure on Russia'" because he had "'forgotten for a minute, for a second, for half a minute, forgotten that Russia has a full arsenal of nuclear weapons.'"[186] The Russian leader wanted to remind the American and the world that Moscow still mattered. In his memoirs, Yeltsin described how he personally edited his Istanbul speech, inserting "the toughest and sharpest formulations" possible. Once onstage, he could see that "the hall was scattered with shards of distrust and misunderstanding," which he could even feel "in my skin." But he felt that his harsh text "was right on target."[187] Yeltsin attacked the West for "'sermonizing'" about Chechnya and insisted "there will be no peace talks with bandits and killers."

These remarks did not sit well with Clinton. The US president discarded his prepared remarks and denounced the use of force in Chechnya as unworthy of Yeltsin's legacy. While Clinton was speaking, the Russian president angrily ripped off his translation headset.[188] Remembering the last time the two had sparred so publicly, Berger termed the event "Budapest on the Bosporus."[189] The difference between Budapest in 1994 and Istanbul in 1999, however, was that Clinton had no time to restore relations with Yeltsin afterward. His visit to Istanbul, he knew, was the last trip to Europe by an American president in the twentieth century, but he did not know that it was also his last meeting with Yeltsin as president.[190]

The two leaders had a brief encounter after the speeches that was a far cry from the joviality of their first, in Vancouver more than six years earlier.[191] Yeltsin was "unhinged," as Talbott put it, and made sweeping demands: "just give Europe to Russia. The US is not Europe. Europe should be the business of Europeans." Clinton tried to deflect the tirade, but Yeltsin kept pressing, saying, "give Europe to itself. Europe never felt as close to Russia as it does now." Clinton responded, "I don't think the Europeans would like this very much."

Abruptly, Yeltsin stood up and announced that "the meeting has gone on too long." In his view, they had spent too much time together: "we said 20 minutes and it has now been more than 35 minutes." Clinton would not let the Russian go, however, without asking who would win the upcoming election. Yeltsin replied curtly, "Putin, of course." Referring to himself in the third person, as his old nemesis Mikhail Gorbachev often did, he emphasized that there was no doubt that "he is the successor to Boris Yeltsin" and "he will win." The Russian president was confident that "you'll do business together."[192]

Returning home to Moscow, Yeltsin decided that the time for exit had come. According to his memoirs, he confided to Putin on December 14, 1999 that he would make the younger man acting president on the last day of the year, although Putin had to keep that information to himself until then.[193] Hearing the news, Putin reportedly responded, "it's a rather difficult fate." Yeltsin assured him that "'when I came here, I also had other plans. Life turned out that way. . . . You'll manage.'"[194]

A week after his conversation with Yeltsin, Putin took part in an unveiling ceremony for the restored plaque of former longtime KGB head (and later Soviet leader) Yuri Andropov, held on the anniversary of the founding of the Soviet secret police.[195] The symbolism was obvious. Andropov's formative experience had been the 1956 uprising in Hungary; he had watched in horror from the window of the Soviet embassy in Budapest as an uprising threatened to topple the Communist government and remove Hungary from the Warsaw Pact. Andropov never forgot watching the bodies of executed Hungarian secret police swaying from the streetlights. The experience marked the birth of what one US expert called "Andropov's—and the KGB's—'Hungarian complex,' the mortal fear of small, unofficial groups sparking movements to overthrow" their leaders.[196] The Andropov plaque had come down in August 1991 but was back, and Putin decided to give the restoration his public blessing.[197]

Putin also decided to move beyond his practice of using bland commentary with Talbott, who found himself in Moscow again with the prime minister just three days before Christmas 1999. At the press conference before their talks, Talbott recalled how badly his last visit with Putin had unfolded, since he had ended up turning his plane around midflight. Trying to make light of the memory in front of reporters, Talbott joked that this time "his flight was commercial so he didn't have that option." According to the US embassy, Putin responded "dryly," saying only that "he remembered the incident well."[198]

As the press was leaving, Talbott shifted tone, adding pointedly that he "remembered it well too." Once the journalists were gone, Putin let the mild facade fall. He complained bitterly that former Soviet states might find a way to use the updated CFE treaty to expel Moscow's forces, particularly from Georgia, adding that "'your friend Shevardnadze is a fool'" to want the Russians gone. The region, he predicted, would become so dangerous that "without Russian troops to accompany them," even "Georgian forces would not dare venture into certain regions of their own country." In the disputed territory of Abkhazia, "Chechen mercenaries" were already playing "soccer with the decapitated head of one of their captives," implying there was worse to come without Russian protection. When Talbott tried to shift to arms control and expressed hope for progress, Putin replied that he "'would like to share' Talbott's optimism," implying he did not.[199]

The reason behind Putin's increasing assertiveness became apparent to all on December 31, 1999. That morning, Yeltsin had recorded a brief video of his resignation, and it was broadcast nationwide at noon.[200] Even though Washington had known for months who the successor would be, the timing was still a surprise. The US ambassador in Moscow awakened Talbott at his home in Washington and told him to turn on a television. The two Americans, half a world apart, stayed on the phone as they watched.[201]

The echoes of Gorbachev's sad televised farewell were strong. Yeltsin's stiff, weak delivery intensified the melancholy of his words. Seated against the backdrop of an indifferently decorated Christmas tree, he revealed that he was "speaking to you for the last time as the president of Russia." He asked Russians for "forgiveness" and apologized to them that "many of our shared dreams did not come true." In the end, "what we thought would be easy turned out to be painfully difficult." Promising that a new generation of leaders would do everything "bigger and better," he disclosed that he had already signed a decree making Putin acting president. Finally, he bid farewell to his compatriots, expressing a last wish that they "be happy."[202]

After watching the broadcast in the Kremlin together with Putin, Yeltsin told his successor to "take care of Russia." He departed the Kremlin at 1:00 p.m. Russian time, feeling immensely relieved to have no obligations for the first time in decades, and told his driver to take him to his family. En route, his limousine's phone rang with a call from Clinton. Yeltsin declined the call from the president of the United States, telling him to call back later, at 5:00 p.m.[203] Clinton dutifully tried again roughly four hours later, and this time Yeltsin spoke to him.[204] The plan, Yeltsin explained, was to give Putin three months before the scheduled vote of March 2000 "to work as president" so "people will get used to him" and elect him in his own right as president. Yeltsin added that "this will be done without breaking away from democracy," and kept repeating he was "sure that he will be elected in the forthcoming elections; I am sure about that. I am also sure that he is a democrat."[205]

Meanwhile, the new leader of Russia made Clinton wait a further twenty-six hours. He finally found nine minutes for a call at 7:07 p.m. Moscow time on the evening of January 1, 2000. Clinton tried to put a good face on what was unfolding, saying, "I think you are off to a very good start."[206]

Yet another major landmark of the twenty-first century had begun moving into place: the gradual resumption of personal rule in Russia. Acting president Vladimir Putin had decided, on a December night in Moscow in 1999, to do whatever it took to defend Russian authority, his colleagues, and himself.

For Central and Eastern Europeans, who had suffered decades of brutality, war, and suppression, entering NATO on the cusp of the twenty-first century was the fulfillment of a dream of partnership with the West. Yet the transition from the old to the new century had long shadows over it. Looking back, Albright remarked that "a decade earlier, when the Berlin Wall had come down, there was dancing in the streets. Now the euphoria was gone."[207] A series of major political shifts had collided with alliance expansion to carve out the future and emplace landmarks—some impressive, some threatening—delineating the post–Cold War order. The Clinton administration's successful expansion strategy, building on precedents from the Bush era, had ensured maximum flexibility for NATO's future; taking advantage of it, after 1999 the alliance would eventually add eleven more states.[208] But the hammer blows of economic disintegration, unremitting illness, and fear of prosecution for corruption had forced Yeltsin to choose a successor; seeking to protect himself and his family, he turned to one who would reverse Russian democratization.[209] Meanwhile, the US president's personal dishonesty and the resulting impeachment had coarsened American political life; smelling blood, Clinton's most emboldened foes would continue to distend the zone of the politically permissible in both domestic and foreign policy. And the painful decline in US-Russian cooperation had started to reverse a long run of success in arms control; letting a decades-long trend lapse, Clinton and Yeltsin failed to conclude any major new arms control accords.[210] Nuclear targeting of US and European cities instead resumed under a man who, in December 1999, started a reign that would be measured in decades. For US relations with Russia, these events signaled, if not a refreezing back to Cold War conditions precluding all cooperation, then the onset of a killing frost.

Partnership Potential: Membership in international organizations in 1994,
based on a map issued by the German Foreign Office. Note the absence of a
clear political dividing line down the middle of Europe due to the overlapping nature of these organizations and Russia's membership in every

Legend:

- ☐ CSCE - Conference on Security and Cooperation in Europe
- ☐ NACC - North Atlantic Cooperation Council
- **ITALY** NATO - North Atlantic Treaty Organization
- ☐ PfP - Partnership for Peace as defined by signature date of the PfP Framework Document

0   200   400   600 Km.

0   100   200   300   400 Mi.

FINLAND

Baltic Sea

ESTONIA

LATVIA

LITHUANIA

BELARUS

RUSSIA

RUSSIA

UKRAINE

SLOVAKIA

KAZAKHSTAN

ROMANIA

REPUBLIC OF MOLDOVA

Black Sea

Caspian Sea

SERBIA

BULGARIA

GEORGIA

FYROM

ARMENIA

AZERBAIJAN

GREECE

TURKEY

IRAN

KYRGYZSTAN

TAJIKISTAN →

TURKMENISTAN →

CYPRUS

SYRIA

IRAQ

UZBEKISTAN →

organization except NATO. (FYROM is the Former Yugoslav Republic of Macedonia, which would later become North Macedonia. Slanted shading bars indicate that the CSCE had, in 1992, suspended the membership of the then–Federal Republic of Yugoslavia, that is, Montenegro and Serbia.)

Conclusion

The New Times

We need to wait for the new times all over again, because we
missed our chance in the nineties.

—SVETLANA ALEXIEVICH

AFTER HE RETIRED, STROBE TALBOTT told the *New York Times* some of
what he had learned about the conduct of foreign policy: "'If the leadership of a country has any view but the following, it's not going to be the
leadership of that country for very long. And that is: We do what we can
in our own interest.'"[1]

This statement demands a question in response: who defines the meaning of the word *interest*? Talbott's definition was clear: American interests
mandated extending full Article 5 guarantees at least to the Baltics, and
possibly beyond. His conviction on this point increasingly helped to convince President Bill Clinton—the person whose definition of *interest* mattered most—that not one inch of territory need be off-limits to alliance
troops or nuclear weapons. Clinton came to believe that it was in US interests to have the "broadest, deepest alliance" possible. Acting accordingly, he presided over the alliance's fiftieth anniversary in 1999 in a way
that ensured NATO could enlarge not just that year, but repeatedly and
without restrictions in the coming decades.[2]

The alliance thereby gained a border with Russia—where Polish territory met Russian around the Kaliningrad enclave—and opened its door

to many future members, including the Baltic states.[3] When Estonia subsequently joined, NATO's border moved again, to less than a hundred miles from President Vladimir Putin's hometown of St. Petersburg.[4] In 1989 the distance was roughly 1,200 miles. This result fulfilled the justified hopes of many states oppressed by the Soviet Union in the past and worried about aggression from Moscow in the future. Yet American and Russian choices, in a series of cumulative interactions, had also yielded a less desirable result: a post–Cold War order that looked much like its Cold War predecessor, but with a more easterly European dividing line.

With the narrative of these events complete, it is time to address the questions asked at the outset. Why did the United States decide to enlarge NATO after the Cold War, how did the American decision interact with contemporary Russian choices, and did that interaction yield the fateful decline in relations between the two countries? Were there feasible alternatives to the decisions that they made? What was the cost of expansion as it occurred, and how did it help to shape the era between the Cold War and COVID? Finally, how can knowledge of this history guide efforts to create a better future?

To answer the first question: The evidence shows that the "why" and the "how" evolved in tandem between 1989 and 1999, in what were effectively a series of three presidential turns of the ratchet—a tool that allows motion in one direction only. The first turn occurred in 1990. Asked after the fall of the Berlin Wall whether, to achieve German unification, he would compromise with Moscow over NATO's future, President George H. W. Bush responded, "to hell with that." The reason behind that attitude—his "why"—was his firm belief in the need to ensure that an expanded Atlantic Alliance served as the dominant security organization beyond the Cold War.

To achieve that goal, Bush opposed all options—including ones promoted by his West German allies for contingent enlargement—short of extending full Article 5 guarantees beyond the inner-German line of 1989. His efforts to perpetuate NATO's leading role were neither surprising nor unjustified, given the way the Cold War order, anchored by the alliance, had brought success for Washington. The president's defense of an existing American-led institution also had the power of precedent. International organizations, once entrenched, persist.[5] NATO remaining the dominant European security organization conformed to that pattern. What was surprising, however, was Bush's ability to publicize the results of his efforts as a "new world order," since it was not.

His strategy also raised the tricky question of what it would cost to remain unwavering on the need to expand Article 5 eastward while persuading the Soviet Union to permit Germany to unify. Bush astutely turned to German chancellor Helmut Kohl to meet that cost. Kohl had deep pockets and was willing to pay Moscow's price in order to unite his divided country. Together, Bush and Kohl achieved both German unity and NATO's enlargement of Article 5 territory beyond the Cold War border on October 3, 1990. This combined achievement was a major precedent; even better, Washington and Bonn got Moscow to enshrine both components in writing, specifically in the treaty that enabled German unification—thereby completing the first turn of the ratchet.

But the 1991 coup in the Soviet Union, followed by the USSR's unexpected collapse, created vast new uncertainties—not least about its nuclear arsenal. Making matters yet more complicated was the unfortunate timing of several major events. The emerging Russian state was most open to cooperation with America at a time—1991 to 1992—when the United States was fixated not just on the First Gulf War and a presidential election, but also on a change of White House occupants. As leaders in Washington were juggling all of those dramatic events, the window of opportunity for establishing a more cooperative post–Cold War order with Russia was gradually closing.[6]

Different actions while that window remained open could have had far-reaching consequences. Reconsideration of Bush-era policies, such as the lack of debt forgiveness for Russia, might have helped the nascent democracy in Moscow. But by mid-1993, when Clinton got most of his team in place, hyperinflation and corruption in Russia were already weakening democracy's prospects, and Yeltsin and the extremists in the parliament were heading for violent conflict. Meanwhile, Central and Eastern European states, newly freed from the Warsaw Pact, had made clear their desire for alliance membership—and when push came to shove, Clinton agreed with them, not least because he believed alliance expansion would stabilize all of post–Cold War Europe. That belief was his "why" for enlargement.

Once in office, Clinton nonetheless tried to maintain cooperation with Moscow by how he implemented NATO's enlargement: through an incremental partnership strategy, one that made Article 5 guarantees a possibility in the longer term for states that performed well as partners. Launched by his Pentagon—not least by the chairman of the JCS, General John Shalikashvili, whom the president tasked with selling the idea to Poland, the land of the general's birth—this strategic vision was not wildly popular, but it worked. Embodied in the Partnership for Peace, the strategy offered a compromise sufficiently acceptable to key players, including even to Poland (thanks in part to Shalikashvili's personal diplomacy). This Partnership also provided options for post-Soviet states—again, remarkably, with Moscow's assent—and could have been a long-term solution not just for the Baltic states but perhaps even for Ukraine, all while sustaining Russia's cooperation. Joint action with Moscow in Bosnia around this time additionally showed that real-world military cooperation and PfP served to enhance one another.

In short, PfP enabled simultaneous management of many post–Cold War contingencies across the unpredictable European chessboard. Presumably for that reason, Clinton initially valued the concept's merits highly. As he noted to NATO secretary general Javier Solana in 1996, PfP "has proven to be a bigger deal than we expected—with more countries, and more substantive cooperation. It has grown into something significant in its own right."[7]

It succeeded a little too well. Opponents of PfP within the administration pushed the president not to stop there. Skilled bureaucratic infighters framed withholding Article 5 as giving Moscow a veto. They argued instead for extending that article as soon as possible to deserving new democracies. Here the interaction with Russian choices was particularly important: Yeltsin's tragic use of violence against his opponents in Moscow and Chechnya, along with the alarming success of antireform nationalists, bolstered calls for a hedge against the potential renewal of Russian aggression. These calls, along with the relationships that Polish president Lech Wałęsa and Czech president Václav Havel had established with Clinton, increasingly made an impact on the American president, who also had to keep domestic political pressures in mind. He had narrowly won election in 1992, and if he wanted a second term he had to pay attention to the success of the pro-expansion Republican Party in the 1994 midterm vote. All of these considerations combined to tip the balance in Clinton's mind toward Article 5 guarantees for all. He foreclosed his own administration's option of incremental partnership and, as 1994 was ending, executed the second ratchet turn. From then on, his administration pursued one-size-fits-all, full-guarantee NATO enlargement. As an unfortunate corollary, Russians concluded that PfP had been a ruse, even though it had not.

The significance of this second turn became apparent over time. Clinton had, at the outset of his presidency, stated a goal of avoiding replication of the Cold War order—that is, avoiding drawing a new line across

Europe. He wanted instead to find some other solution for ensuring future transatlantic security. Using PfP, he could have worked toward the Vancouver-to-Vladivostok proposal from the Bush era: trying to create a real (as opposed to rhetorical) new world order, incorporating much of the Northern Hemisphere and all of its time zones. But once PfP was abandoned, a new dividing line became inevitable. The only question was how close to Russia's border that line would be drawn—in other words, where both sides would reach stalemate.

Hopes for lasting US-Russian security cooperation did not disappear immediately. Joint efforts on the ground in former Yugoslavia continued. But discord increased, contributing to the clash at Pristina Airport in June 1999 and the confrontation between Clinton and Yeltsin in Istanbul that November. These and earlier clashes between Washington and Moscow created scars, decreased trust, and reduced both sides' openness to cooperation. The effect was cumulative even before Yeltsin promoted Putin as his successor. The Russian foreign minister, Igor Ivanov, later recalled that by then a sediment of distrust had already accumulated.[8]

Critics both inside and outside the administration advised Clinton that the way in which Washington was expanding NATO was diluting the alliance, humiliating Moscow, and undermining arms control. These critiques did not slow the steady movement of policy toward maximalist positions.[9] The question inside the administration was no longer how to expand NATO but how far—and the answer was "to the Baltics." Strong hints from Nordic neighbors about the desirability of some kind of modulation could not resist expansion's momentum.

Clinton's decision to have the April 1999 Washington summit welcome Baltic interest in NATO represented the third turn of the ratchet: foreclosing other options, the alliance would reach within what Moscow considered to be the former Soviet Union itself. The United States could insist, correctly, that it had never recognized the Baltics' incorporation into the USSR—but that did not change the political import of the decision. Combined with Putin's installation as acting president in December of that year, this decision meant that the year 1999 closed with the settlement of a post–Cold War order that looked much like its predecessor: distrust between Moscow and Washington over a Europe divided into Article 5 and non–Article 5 portions, now with the dividing line farther East.

That outcome did not fulfill the hopes of 1989—meaning, among other things, the belief that the liberal international order had succeeded definitively, and that residents of *all* states between the Atlantic and the

Pacific, not just the Western ones, could now cooperate within it.[10] The root cause should be sought more in leaders' agency than in structural factors. Both American and Russian leaders repeatedly made choices yielding outcomes that not only fell short of those hopes, but were explicitly at odds with their stated intentions. Bush talked about a Europe whole, free, and at peace; Clinton repeatedly proclaimed his wish to avoid drawing a line. Yet with their actions, both in the end promoted a dividing line across Europe. Gorbachev wanted to save the Soviet Union; Yeltsin wanted to democratize Russia; and both, in different ways, wanted to partner on equal footing with the West. Yet in the longer term both failed as well.

Other Russians similarly saw their initial democratizing intent yield disappointing outcomes. Andrei Kozyrev, the former Russian foreign minister, wrote in his memoirs that the popular uprising against the August 1991 coup attempt had revealed the "democratic potential" inherent in Russia and "thus established an important historical precedent." For that reason, the popular triumph over reactionaries "was the highest moral and political point ever reached by the Russian people." It showed that his people did not want to go back to authoritarianism; they wanted their transformation to succeed, and to move forward to a better future. Because of such views, after Kozyrev's ouster in 1996 Talbott eulogized him as a true believer in the potential for that better future. In the American's words, Kozyrev was "a little bit like Gorbachev: scorned, flawed, a tad pathetic, but in a way heroic, and a long way from having been proved 'wrong' in any ultimate sense." Talbott added that if Russia ultimately succeeded in evolving into a lasting democracy, "Kozyrev will turn out to have been a prophet without honor in his own time and country."[11]

Residents of the former Warsaw Pact and Soviet states also experienced outcomes at odds with initial hopes. Although such states repeatedly said they did not want to end up in a gray zone, some did. The peoples of Belarus, Georgia, and Ukraine all struggled to define their relations with Russia and, at times, defend their borders. Former Warsaw Pact states experienced their own uncertainties. While they succeeded in joining NATO (and eventually the EU), they found that such memberships did not automatically lock in their democratic transformations—and, like the rest of the continent, they suffered rising tensions with Moscow.

In the twenty-first century, what increasingly became apparent was that the pressures of simultaneously democratizing and creating a market economy had produced fertile ground for latter-day, Soviet-trained

authoritarians such as Putin. Once securely in power, Putin began gradually throttling back the democratic transformation while resuming
old habits of competition with the West. American and Russian choices
had by then interacted in cumulative ways—worsened by the bad timing
of contemporary events—to steer the overall course of US-Russian relations onto a trajectory that fell well short of post–Cold War hopes.

Turning to the second question: Were there feasible alternatives to the
decisions that American and Russian leaders made, in particular alternatives for Washington that might have modulated the process of expansion,
aligned better with long-term US interests, and produced enlargement at
a lower political cost? To put it more pointedly: Given that Russia, once
it recovered from political and economic collapse, would almost certainly
remain a major player because of its size and nuclear arsenal, would it not
have been better to anticipate this problem in advance by giving Moscow
greater say over, and some secure berth in, a common security structure?
The answer is a qualified yes.

It is qualified because today's renewed tensions stem in large part from
Russia's own choices. As discussed above, Yeltsin's decision to use violence
in Chechnya in 1994 was tragic, particularly in the wake of the December 1993 electoral success by extremists. The combination of these events
alarmed neighbors and diminished prospects for successful Russian transformation away from its undemocratic past. Worse, the conflict in Chechnya, once renewed later in the 1990s, opened up a pathway to popularity
for Putin. Given what a damaging mistake Chechnya was, it is impossible to
know whether Moscow's responses to a different form of NATO enlargement would have been any less self-harming. And last but most definitely
not least, Central and Eastern European democracies had both a moral
and a sovereign right to make the choices they deemed best for their own
security, and they believed that meant joining NATO as full members as
soon as possible.

Yet it remains reasonable to speculate that, in the longer term, prioritizing a post–Cold War security order that included Russia could have
decreased tensions between the world's two nuclear superpowers—thereby
decreasing tensions for all of Europe—and kept both sides closer to the
goal of banishing conflict between them. For a while such an order existed, thanks to PfP. The Partnership simultaneously offered Russia an
acceptable berth—Yeltsin called the idea "brilliant"—while maintaining
the possibility of new allies joining NATO. Put differently, PfP enabled
Washington to avoid having to choose too soon between Russia, Central

and Eastern Europe, and post-Soviet republics such as the Baltics and Ukraine. Even if Russia had returned to personal rule and a threatening stance in the twenty-first century nonetheless, PfP could have kept Western options open by allowing movement toward full NATO expansion in response to those renewed threats. Lastly, though the Partnership was vastly less appealing to Central and Eastern Europeans than NATO membership, they understood that its inclusivity provided options for post-Soviet states that alliance expansion did not. PfP had the great advantage of reflecting Winston Churchill's advice: "in victory: magnanimity."[12]

The success of Churchill and other strategists after World War II in banishing conflict between former enemies had rested on that principle—helped by the need to make common cause against a new enemy. The post-1945 world would have looked very different if the United States had left the Europeans to fend for themselves. If the 1990s had seen something equivalent to the diplomacy displayed in the aftermath of World War II, it could have created a different future. NATO could have wrapped itself around that diplomacy by implementing a measured expansion, prioritizing nuclear disarmament, and working with Russia. As Michael McFaul, the former US ambassador to Moscow, has rightly written, "Russia was not destined to return to a confrontational relationship with the United States or the West." What happened did not have to happen.[13]

Among many other consequences, such a wraparound framework would have created opportunities for Americans, Europeans, and Russians to cooperate in dealing with China. Instead of rebooting Cold War–style confrontation, such a framework could have enabled widespread coordination in the face of challenges from the People's Republic. Clinton had already sensed the need to refocus US defense strategy on Asia, as he confided to senators during the SNOG session of June 1997. He thought, wrongly, that aggressive NATO expansion would free up US military resources in Europe for such a pivot in the longer term.

More public candor at the time from knowledgeable insiders about the options being foreclosed might have helped. Even as strong a supporter of NATO as then-senator Joseph Biden sensed that he lacked answers to key questions: Enlargement, yes, but at what cost to relations with former Soviet republics, and to nuclear disarmament? Biden asked an expert witness—former US ambassador to the Soviet Union Jack Matlock—questions to this effect at a Senate hearing on NATO expansion on October 30, 1997. Matlock responded that, despite the passing of the Cold War, "the most serious potential security threat to the American people" remained "weapons of mass destruction from Russian arsenals." Biden replied, "I agree with that concern." NATO expansion as proposed in 1997, Matlock continued, would not help to contain that threat and could even "undermine the effort." In reply, Biden concluded that "continuing the Partnership for Peace, which turned out to be much more robust and much more successful than I think anyone thought it would be at the outset, may arguably have been a better way to go."[14]

The Partnership might also have helped its greatest critics, the Central and Eastern European countries, toward a more permanent democratization. Social science researchers later established that it was not NATO membership that prompted these countries to complete civil and military reforms; it was the process of trying to join.[15] Congressional investigators and others warned that countries were entering NATO before establishing strong democratic institutions. If the Partnership had survived as originally implemented, potential allies would—admittedly through clenched teeth—have had to earn alliance status over a longer period, presumably making them more resistant to subsequent attacks on democracy.

And if NATO was too quick to expand, the EU was too slow. Alliance enlargement enabled the EU to postpone its own expansion and to urge new democracies to look to NATO instead. This postponement meant that European leaders were punching below their weight in the critical early days of democratization in the East. The EU also chose to rule out, privately, Russian membership, and to prioritize enlargement to Austria, Finland, and Sweden. In the decade after the remarkable events of 1989, only those three states—and no former Soviet Bloc ones—joined the union.[16]

But even without PfP, the Clinton administration still had other alternatives. The last Democratic president before Clinton, Jimmy Carter, wisely said on September 4, 1978, as he headed for the Camp David summit that earned him the Nobel Peace Prize: "compromises will be mandatory. Without them, no progress can be expected. Flexibility will be the essence of our hopes."[17] Even if Clinton had switched to full-guarantee NATO expansion when he did, there were still at least five ways that Washington could have tried to maintain better relations with Russia.

First, Russia's claim that it had permitted German unification in exchange for a guarantee against NATO expansion could have been discussed soberly, not dismissed out of hand. As German diplomats tried to point out, while Moscow's claim was wrong in substance, it had psychological weight. For a country that cares a great deal about how it is addressed, a more respectful rhetorical handling of this issue in the mid-1990s could have yielded benefits at little cost.[18]

A second concession—changing the name of the alliance, as Moscow requested, leaving all other aspects intact—could also have yielded benefits at limited cost. The Atlantic Alliance had long since moved past the Atlantic seaboard, defining the entire Mediterranean as a branch of that ocean to justify projecting naval power as far east as possible—and even gaining, in Turkey, an ally on the Black Sea.[19]

Third, after new allies joined in March 1999, the alliance could have paused instead of immediately commencing talks with nine countries while engaged in a controversial armed conflict in Kosovo. That conflict acquired a major legacy, thanks to the furor caused in Moscow by its combination with the 1999 start of what would eventually become the "big bang" expansion round of 2004. A pause between rounds would have made would-be members nervous, but Washington had managed other states' nerves before, and could have done so again.

Fourth, and more speculatively, the concerns voiced by Finnish and Swedish politicians could have received a wider airing. Earlier discussions about a Nordic security association, now to include the Baltic states, could have resumed; or there could have been bilateral treaties with the Baltics.[20] NATO instead became directly responsible for the area without creating strategic depth in the region. Even in 2016, after more than a decade of NATO membership, simulated war games conducted by the RAND think tank showed that Russian forces could take Baltic capitals in just hours. Obviously, there were other ways of fighting back against Moscow in such a scenario. As another analyst put it, NATO's "objective should be shrouding a Baltic high-end fight in incalculable risk for Russia," mainly by "maintaining uncertainty and strategic flexibility with air and naval assets." But the RAND report's summary was stark: an attack on the Baltics would leave NATO with "a limited number of options, all bad."[21]

Finally, NATO's long-standing practice of permitting different practical aspects of membership under a broader Article 5 umbrella—such as the Danish/Norwegian, French, Spanish, and eastern German variants—could have served as precedents for adding new allies less confrontationally. Through some of these varying deals, the alliance had already begun to live with restrictions on deployments of troops and nuclear weapons. While these were not ideal from Washington's point of view, it had accepted them and could have done so again. Central and Eastern European countries could, for example, have been treated like Scandinavian ones, since after the Soviet collapse they all shared a common trait: residency in a neighborhood near, but not controlled by, Russia.

Instead of these feasible alternatives, by 1999 the Clinton administration had secured an open road for extending the alliance eastward. To do so it had emulated the solution arrived at by Bush and Kohl: buying Moscow out. After Clinton and his advisors left office, they could only watch in alarm as Bush's son, George W. Bush, took the keys to the NATO car and gunned it down that open road. Among other stops, the younger Bush attended the alliance's summits in 2006 in Latvia, the first such event on former Soviet territory, and in 2008 in Bucharest, where he pushed hard for inclusion of Georgia and Ukraine.[22] For Putin, that Bucharest summit—coming on top of Bush's 2003 invasion of Iraq and his 2007 decision to erect ballistic missile defenses (in the form of ten ground-based interceptors in Poland and a radar facility in the Czech Republic), all around the time of "color revolutions" in post-Soviet states—proved to be the breaking point.[23]

Since the alliance frowns on allies joining NATO to pursue preexisting military disputes, Putin decided to escalate just such preexisting conflicts with Georgia in 2008 and Ukraine in 2014 in violent fashion.[24] The hope that such armed conflicts were gone for good had characterized much of the post–Cold War era.[25] Moscow's action signaled that the era was over. Putin also expanded Russia's conventional military budget, developed new missile defense and space capabilities, and began modernizing Russia's nuclear arsenal.[26] In response, the alliance's leaders suspended not only the NATO-Russia Council but "all practical cooperation between NATO and Russia."[27] Contrasting today's situation with other feasible outcomes to the process of reshaping order after the Cold War helps us to understand just how far short of better alternatives the current situation falls. As Russia expert Stephen Sestanovich presciently wrote in a 1993 op-ed in the *New York Times*, while real doubts could be raised about "all the many" alternatives being proposed for cooperation with Russia, "these doubts are nothing compared with the frustration and powerlessness we will feel once Russian democracy fails."[28]

What was the cost of expansion as it occurred, and how did it help to shape the era between the Cold War and COVID? Put differently, was George Kennan right? In hindsight, was expansion a bad idea?

Any serious response to the last question demands another: Bad for whom? The Central and Eastern European countries that pushed hard to join had a right to choose their alliances, and were rightly thrilled when they succeeded in joining NATO as full members, protected by Article 5 from the start. But Ukraine was left in the lurch, as were some other post-

Soviet republics. And the overriding challenge in post–Cold War Europe was to integrate Russia. Balancing all of these pressures was a daunting task for Washington, which is why it should have tried to avoid calling the question too soon.

Usually, however, "was NATO expansion bad?" means something else: "was it bad for the United States?" To answer, we must weigh the costs and benefits for America. Both Bush and Clinton knew the cost-benefit calculus. It led the former to pause after adding eastern Germany, once he realized the Soviet Union was collapsing; and the latter, at first, to take a partnership approach to expansion in the hope of maintaining the post–Cold War spirit of cooperation with Moscow. As Clinton consistently emphasized, the crucial issue was not whether to take on new allies "but when and how."[29] He saw the benefits of enlargement, but like Bush he worried about the effect on Moscow and pursued a valid compromise.

But the temptation to keep going, without adequately considering the consequences, ultimately proved irresistible. Partisans of unlimited expansion astutely realized they could drop "and how" from the president's words to create a powerful slogan: the question about NATO enlargement is "not whether but when." Yet what worked in rhetoric did not work in reality. It is not possible to separate the question of whether enlargement was a good idea from how it happened. Because of the costs, how Washington ultimately implemented expansion advanced American interests less in the long term than it might have done.

Another way to measure whether enlargement was a good idea is to examine its costs for other countries. Since NATO enlarged, Russia has not invaded any of the new post–Cold War allies. While correlation is not causation, it is hard to imagine that NATO membership was irrelevant to that outcome. But while allies have escaped large-scale physical attacks, they have suffered cyber infiltration and other forms of aggression from Moscow. In meaningful but hard-to-measure ways, Russia undermined European post–Cold War stability. It used a variety of means to promote erosion of democratic practices and norms in Central and Eastern Europe. Alliance membership has not prevented such backsliding.[30] The Hungarian activist who shot to prominence with his speech in 1989, Viktor Orbán, for example, has undone much of his country's democratization despite being in NATO, turning his country into the first EU member-state classified as a non-democratic autocracy. Poland and other states have similarly hollowed out many of their relatively new democratic laws and norms.[31]

Moreover, NATO has given the Article 5 guarantee to places at risk of having to invoke it. American tanks have reappeared in Europe in response, increasing the sense of confrontation. A cynical view would be that after its essential function was put into question by the end of the Cold War, NATO expanded itself into necessity again. A more nuanced view is that the alliance did not have to enlarge as it did, and did not have to expand inside the former Soviet Union. But if it wanted to do so, it should have paid more attention to what Moscow thought. As the historian Odd Arne Westad wrote in 2017, it is "clear that the West should have dealt with post–Cold War Russia better than it did," not least because "Russia would under all circumstances remain a crucial state in any international system because of its sheer size." Or, as Yeltsin put it to Talbott in 1996, "Russia will rise again."[32]

The costs for today have been significant. In 2016, Putin marked the twenty-fifth anniversary of the Soviet Union's collapse by conducting cyberattacks on US elections in support of presidential candidate Donald Trump, a man who saw little value in the Atlantic Alliance. Russian operatives in the Main Intelligence Directorate, or GRU, stole documents from the Democratic National Committee, the Democratic Congressional Campaign Committee, and the Hillary Clinton campaign and ensured their widespread distribution through Wikileaks and by fictitious online identities.[33] Once Trump won, the way that NATO, and thereby all of European security, remained centered on Washington as the ultimate Article 5 guarantor became problematic in unexpected ways. Claiming that the burden of NATO was not worth its cost, Trump raised the notion of US withdrawal. He brought back an anachronistic view of American security: that the United States should roll up the drawbridge and erect as many walls as possible. Among the many problems with Trump's threat were the consequences for Europe. The way the alliance has expanded, creating no significant auxiliary military entities or regional associations, means that European security remains centered on Washington. US withdrawal would create a massive security vacuum in Europe.[34]

These troubling events lead to the last question: How can an understanding of these events guide efforts to create a better future? The answer rests in three principles, the first being the need to make a virtue of necessity. Confrontation between the West and Russia is once again the order of the day. While that statement must inspire sorrow—reviving aspects of the Cold War is no cause for celebration—the necessity of dealing with renewed competition from Moscow provides a unifying mission that can help bridge fractures within the United States. During the divisive Trump era, Democrats and Republicans agreed on little, but at least some segment of the Republican Party was never comfortable with Trump's embrace of Putin. Even Senate Majority Leader Mitch McConnell, otherwise strongly supportive of Trump, bristled at being called "Moscow Mitch" for failing to challenge the president's treatment of Russia. A shared sense of mission in dealing with Moscow offers a path for rare domestic consensus—one that leads back to NATO.

The Atlantic Alliance, as an expression of deep American engagement in Europe, remains the best institution to take on this mission.[35] The guardrails in relations between the United States and Russia have largely disappeared, not least because the younger Bush, Trump, and Putin shredded nearly all remaining Cold War arms control accords. If NATO were to disappear as well, the consequences would be devastating.[36] Since the cost incurred by the manner of alliance expansion cannot be recovered, the best course is to make the best of the status quo. Given the risks posed by Russia and today's intense strains on the transatlantic relationship, it does not make sense to add to them by trying to undo the past. When a house is burning, it is inadvisable to start a home renovation—no matter how badly it was needed before the fire started. The focus needs to be on putting out the fire and keeping the structure stable.[37]

The second guiding principle is that a crisis is a terrible thing to waste. Washington should address Russian challenges by aggressively and unashamedly prioritizing transatlantic cooperation. The story presented here has illuminated the missed opportunities for cooperation with Russia after the Cold War. Washington should try to make sure it avoids another loss, namely that of the transatlantic cooperation achieved only at great effort after World War II—particularly with France and Germany as the key centers of power in Europe. If Madeleine Albright once branded America the indispensable nation, France and Germany are its indispensable partners, even more so in the wake of Brexit. Common sense dictates that in any conflict, conceptual or physical, a wise combatant should never fight without a reason, for long, or alone. If Washington has to face new forms of conflict with Moscow, it should seek renewed and reinforced transatlantic cooperation. During the Cold War, the shared need to deal with a major challenge concentrated minds and overcame differences. Ideally the same dynamic will apply again—and could also yield benefits for dealing with China.

Another issue requiring transatlantic focus is Ukraine. The large country at the gates of Europe is crucial to European stability, and the consequences of the lost opportunity to provide it with a berth in the 1990s linger. While simply pushing for its belated membership in NATO would only worsen current tensions, the West cannot ignore it either. Its conflict with Russia will not disappear, but Western efforts should focus on creating political rather than violent means of addressing the discord, in the interest of moving from an immediate conflict to a longer-term negotiated settlement of differences. Such an approach could also apply to relations between the West and Russia. A question asked by the historian Adam Tooze about China pertains here: "how rapidly can we move to détente, meaning long-term co-existence with a regime radically different from our own"?[38] Fortunately, the West has historic experience with reaching détente.[39]

That leads to the third guiding principle: an understanding of history can help us, if not to predict, then certainly to prepare for the future. The onset of a pandemic in 2020 at a time of political turmoil may have felt unprecedented, but of course it was not. The line of precursors reaches back to the ancient world, and there is insight on how to deal with such challenges in both historical and literary sources. In *Oedipus Rex*, Sophocles has Queen Jocasta speak the following words in a time of plague and strife: a sensible man should judge the new times by the past. The tragedy of the play was, of course, that the queen was more right than she knew. As her own and Oedipus's fates revealed—they had married without knowing they were mother and long-lost son, or that he had unwittingly murdered his father—ignorance of previous events, and of the significance of one's own actions, can have terrible consequences.

Knowledge of the past, by contrast, is profoundly empowering. Two modern-era leaders who understood that truth were French president François Mitterrand and his German counterpart, Chancellor Kohl. In 1995, German foreign office staffers published a map of Europe showing the institutional affiliations of all European and post-Soviet states as of the previous year. Today it is a startling document: as the reproduction in this book shows, there was no pronounced political dividing line down the middle. Between the overlapping areas of various international organizations, nearly every country had a berth. Places as distant as Kyrgyzstan and Uzbekistan, for example, became partners to NATO without requiring full membership—and with unexpected benefits. To facilitate exercises there after they joined the Partnership, the US Congress appropriated funds to upgrade their airfields so that NATO planes could use them. American aircraft later employed those upgraded airstrips to deploy special forces after the 9/11 attacks on the United States, showing the unexpected military as well as political benefits of inclusive partnership.[40]

The German Foreign Office's map from 1995 was a snapshot of how far the post–Cold War cooperative spirit had spread across a continent that had endured decades of hot and cold wars.[41] As he was dying of cancer that same year, the seventy-nine-year-old Mitterrand reflected, in one of his last conversations with Kohl, on the remarkable peace and success of their shared continent. Fifty years after the savage war that had divided their countries, France and Germany had found a lasting way to banish conflict between former enemies and become partners. Mitterrand saw one overriding lesson in those decades: "If we cannot comprehend" that there is "no other way" forward except cooperation, then Europeans were unworthy "of the grace and gift of these past fifty years."[42]

The fall of the Berlin Wall heralded new times of grace and gift—at long last, for more than Western Europe. Democracies and freedoms proliferated. But as the Belarusian writer and Nobel laureate Svetlana Alexievich remarked, we missed our chance in the 1990s to be fully worthy of that gift.[43] She lamented how the world was, after a period of optimism, instead reduced to waiting for the new times all over again.

It is in our interest to do more than just wait for them: we should do everything in our power to re-create such times, in order to renew our pursuit of the full measure of their grace.

Acknowledgments

This book represents the third in a loose trilogy of books on the shaping of the transatlantic world after the Cold War—although when I started writing, I did not realize I was embarking on a trilogy, and each of the three volumes can stand alone. It became apparent to me during my research, however, that I wanted to answer at least three detailed questions: How and why did the Berlin Wall collapse? How and why did Germany unify? How and why did NATO expand, and what did that expansion do to the newfound cooperation across the former Cold War divide? For the three events taken as a whole, an overarching question applied as well: What is their legacy for today's world? My books *The Collapse* and *1989* tackled the first and second events; now *Not One Inch* has taken on the third.

The passing of the post–Cold War moment of optimism only made these questions more compelling to me than ever. The events of 1989 and their immediate consequences revealed themselves as a rare time when a great deal went right—peacefully and quickly to boot. History does not frequently afford such opportunities. Understanding how that post–Cold War moment arose and what happened its hope and optimism grows ever more essential with time, I believe. I hope readers will agree.

While my gratitude to the people and institutions already thanked in the previous two volumes remains undiminished, in producing this current book I have accumulated many new debts. Sustained institutional support during various phases of this project came from, in alphabetical order, the Harvard University Center for European Studies, the Institute for Advanced Study in Princeton, the Johns Hopkins School of Advanced International Studies, and the University of Southern California's History Department and School of International Relations. I thank all of these institutions and universities. In particular, I am deeply grateful to the generous donors who funded my chair at Hopkins, Henry R. and Marie-Josée Kravis.

Additional funding and support came from the Transatlantic Academy of the German Marshall Fund. I would like to thank its former director, Stephen Szabo, along with Ted Reinert. I learned much from my fellow fellows Stefan Fröhlich, Harold James, Michael Kimmage, Hans Kundnani, Yascha Mounk, Heidi Tworek, and the late and much-missed Wade Jacoby.

Archivists and declassification experts in multiple countries helped me file many thousands of requests for documents and achieve a high rate of success in bringing those sources to light. In the United States, I thank the staffs of the George H. W. Bush and William J. Clinton Presidential Libraries, the US State Department, the US Defense Department, and, at the appellate level, the Interagency Security Classification Appeals Panel (ISCAP). Individuals who went above and beyond include Kelly Hendren, Keri Lewis, Rob Seibert, Meredith Wagner, and Van Zbinden. James Graham Wilson generously forwarded some relevant publications, and Ken Weisbrode sent copies of useful documents. I also give my heartfelt thanks to Barbara Wilkinson, the widow of Ron Asmus, for allowing me to see some declassified government documents in her late husband's collection. As ever, the National Security Archive remains an amazingly valuable resource; I am deeply grateful to Tom Blanton and Svetlana Savranskaya for years of support, documents, and conversations.

In Russia, I thank the staffs of both the Gorbachev Foundation and the Memorial Foundation. In Belgium, in the archives at NATO Headquarters, I benefited from the expert assistance of Ineke Deserno, Nicholas Nguyen, and Nicholas Roche. Also in Belgium, and in the Czech Republic as well, I thank Petr Luňák and Vít Smetana for their knowledgeable input on Czech membership in NATO. In Germany, I am grateful—among the many, many others acknowledged in previous books—to Tim Geiger and Michael Mayer for helping me navigate the German foreign ministry records (and additionally to Tim for help with the maps). In Poland, I thank Wiktor Babiński, Łukasz Kremky, and Fundacja Instytut Lecha Wałęsy for helping me, during the pandemic, to interview President Lech Wałęsa remotely. And around the world, I am grateful to all participants in events who granted interviews to me. They are listed in the bibliography, and they have my profound thanks. Of course, none of them bears responsibility for the views expressed in this book, which are solely my own.

A sabbatical with Caltech's Division of the Humanities and Social Sciences enabled a great deal of the writing. My time in California helped to inform my thinking in many ways, not least when I encountered Max Delbrück's book *Mind from Matter? An Essay in Evolutionary Epistemology* while there. This essay—which provides the framing epigraph for my introduction—emerged from lectures that Delbrück gave at Caltech and will now contribute to my own lectures on this topic as well; I am grateful to Caltech for enabling such dialogue across decades and disciplines. I thank Jed Buchwald and Diana Kormos-Buchwald for helping to make my visit there happen, Tracy Dennison for many insightful conversations about Russia, Jennifer Jahner for reading parts of an early draft, Nicolás Wey Gómez for his enthusiasm for my work, Cindy Weinstein for the generous use of her office, and David and Jane Tirrell for their hospitality. Special thanks to staff members Laurel Auchampaugh, Cecilia Lu, Fran Tise, John Wade, and Donna

Wrubelewski—and the unstoppable Caltech Library DocuServe and Circulation Staff, who never blanched at tracking down the most obscure of references: Dan Anguka, Ben Perez, and Bianca Rios.

Invitations to Russia and Germany at key moments in the research came from the Berlin Wall Foundation, the Willy Brandt Foundation, the Körber Foundation, and the US embassy in Moscow. Individuals at all of these institutions helped me advance the research, in particular Gabriele Woidelko, with whom I had many insightful conversations. Thanks are also due to Hannah Bergmann, Maria Lvova, Bruce McClintock, Thomas Paulsen, Bernd Rother, and Felicitas von Loë.

As the book moved toward publication, I was the beneficiary of wise advice from my agent Andrew Wylie, along with Hannah Townsend and Emma Smith of the Wylie Agency. More wise advice came from Graham Allison, Anders Åslund, Michael Mandelbaum, Joe Nye, and Bill Wohlforth. They were all kind enough to take time away from their own work to provide comments on selected parts of the manuscript.

When the pandemic cut me off from my office at a critical moment, my Hopkins colleague Chris Crosbie risked his own health to ensure that I got the materials I needed. Chris's professionalism and commitment are well known to all who have encountered him, and I feel deeply fortunate to have him on my side. Diane Bernabei, Megan Ophel, and Nathaniel Wong were also willing to help in any way needed, pandemic notwithstanding, as was Stephen Sears, a truly remarkable librarian. Travis Zahnow and A. Bradley Potter enabled me, through their excellent teaching support, to keep this work on track even while my classes were underway. I am also grateful to so many of my fellow professors at Hopkins that it is not feasible to thank them all individually here, so I hope they will accept my collective gratitude.

During the pandemic, Sergey Radchenko organized a global Zoom historians' seminar that turned the necessity of online meetings into a delight. I thank him for the seminar, insightful comments on draft chapters, and help with securing both documents and an interview with a former Russian foreign minister. Another participant in the "Sergey Seminar," Una Bergmane, provided useful suggestions on literature about the Baltics and tips on how to find Estonian documents online. Yet another participant, Vlad Zubok, generously made time in the midst of finishing his own pathbreaking book on Soviet collapse to share his wisdom and views.

Throughout, the faculty and staff of the Center for European Studies at Harvard provided unparalleled friendship and support. I am deeply grateful to Grzegorz Ekiert, Vassilis Coutifaris, Laura Falloon, Elizabeth Johnson, Gila Naderi, Anna Popiel, and above all Elaine Papoulias. Former students and research assistants from Harvard and the University of Southern California, Denis Fedin and Jacob Lokshin, proved to be wise beyond their years; the future is in good hands.

Once Yale University Press acquired the manuscript, I became the beneficiary of invaluable advice from my editor Bill Frucht. He greatly improved both the text and the argument on every page, showing humor and forbearance as he did so. Bill Nelson enhanced the book with his maps; Matthew White provided the index; Karen Olson and Mary Pasti kept everything on track; and Susan Ecklund, Nancy Bermack, and above all John Donohue did a terrific job with copyediting, proofreading, and production. My former teaching assistant Colleen Anderson graciously took time away from her own work to read through all of the copyedits, providing insightful commentary on nearly every page. I am also deeply grateful to Professor Steven Wilkinson, the Henry R. Luce Director of Yale's MacMillan Center, for inviting me to present the 2022 Henry Stimson Lectures on the main themes of this book.

As ever, I am indebted to friends and family, not least to our felines, Juno and Toby, who were my constant companions at the computer. They spent countless hours lying on my lap—and, once I made the (from their point of view) deeply distressing decision to switch to a standing desk, on my feet. Among my friends on the European side of the Atlantic, I particularly thank Peter Brinkmann, the Hadshiew-Tetu family, Hans-Hermann Hertle and Hilde Kroll, Ruth Kirchner and Andreas Hoffbauer, Axel Klausmeier, Thomas Kleine-Brockhoff, Christian Raskob, Dorothea and Ernst-Georg Richter, Siggi Schefke, and the Von Hammerstein family. On the US side, I thank Oluwasegun, Desiréia, and Simone Abegunrin, Aroussiak Baltaian, Neal Blatt, Bill Cameron, Michael Gervais, Shannon, Charlie, and Ella Hensley, Jane Leopold, Jennifer and Michael Lynn, Eleanor Maynard, Joan and Tanya Oosterhuis, Albert Shaumyan, Theresa Shibuya, Jennifer Siegel, Ray and Eileen Silva, Leslie, Wes, Annika, and Aneira Tamppari, Teresa Walsh, and Deborah Winkelman. Jan Otakar Fischer and John Logan Nichols deserve thanks for reading the whole book, with special thanks to Jan for his eagle-eyed proofreading of the maps. I am especially grateful to Charlotte, David, and Nick Ackert for years of generous hospitality and friendship—and many good bottles of wine. My extended family—Terry and Donna Crandall, Diane Licholat-Surati, Michael Licholat, Zachary Licholat-Surati, Tony Sarotte, and Mark Flynn—provided love and support from afar. Carmen Sarotte even read a draft from start to finish, thus going far beyond the call of familial duty.

For their editing of parts or all of the manuscript, I am deeply indebted to Frédéric Bozo, Kathy Conley, John Lewis Gaddis, Chris D. Miller, Norman Naimark, Serhii Plokhy, Andreas Rödder, and Robert Zoellick. They did not always agree with me, but they always made the text stronger. Their collective wisdom is as staggering as their generous spirit.

I am deeply saddened that my godfather, Albert Minicucci, a true gentleman, is no longer with us to celebrate this publication. My godmother, Dianne Minicucci, my brother, Steve Sarotte, and I keep him and my much-missed parents, Frank and Gail Sarotte, alive in our hearts and cherish each other even more.

This book is dedicated to my family-by-choice on the other side of the Atlantic: Marc, Sylvia, and Tim Jonni Scheffler, and Claus-Dieter and the late

Rita Wulf. Because of them, transatlantic relations are not just an abstract concept but a matter of personal significance to me. From the moment a student exchange agency brought us together nearly forty years ago, they have been my gateway to the world. I offer this book to them in loving memory of Rita, who, despite a childhood scarred by war and hatred, trusted in the power of cooperation and love beyond borders to forge new bonds and a better future.

Lastly, as ever, there are no limits to what I owe to Mark: θαυμαστὰ ἐκπλήττονται φιλίᾳ τε καὶ οἰκειότητι καὶ ἔρωτι . . .

Notes

ALL EMPHASES ARE PRESENT in the original texts, and all translations are my own, unless otherwise indicated. Minor errors, such as misspellings of common words, are corrected without comment. More significant errors are identified with [*sic*]. A large number of the citations below are from diplomatic cables and other official communications originally in ALL CAPS. For readability, I have usually converted them to upper- and lower-case letters, also without further comment. Names are generally given below in the language used in the original source (unless I am adding my own commentary in English), which may lead to intentional inconsistencies between their spellings in different places in this book (for example, spellings of proper nouns in the endnotes and bibliography may differ from spellings in the main text). Declassification request numbers are provided when known and useful as a means of retrieving the relevant source; bear in mind that a single source can be associated with multiple declassification numbers if it was requested multiple times. A declassification number prefaced by "my" refers to the number the relevant authority assigned to my request to declassify that source. I include this information because I frequently declassified documents in large batches of related files. As a result, the indication that an individually cited source was part of one of my batches signals there is more where that particular document came from; that is, my case number will lead interested future researchers not only to that individual source but also to a larger collection of related materials. For documents that I declassified individually and that are not associated with some larger batch of material, I have omitted my case number in the interest of keeping the notes to a manageable length because the information provided below can be used to find that individual source. Also in the interest of keeping the notes below the allotted word count, I have generally attempted to cite a source no more than once per paragraph, even if there are multiple items in that paragraph from that source (but if there was more than one source for paragraph, each source receives an individual listing). In cases where that practice did not yield the necessary specificity, however, the source is cited more than once per paragraph.

Additional Abbreviations in the Notes and Bibliography

Note: Some items listed below with abbreviated names are edited volumes of published documents. Fuller information about these volumes appears in the bibliography, where the abbreviation is repeated for identification. (Some minor abbreviations, used internally for archival classification, are not on the list below if they appear rarely in the notes.)

AAP-89, -90	*Akten zur Auswärtigen Politik der Bundesrepublik Deutschland 1989 or 1990* (West German foreign ministry documents, published roughly annually)
ADDR	*Die Außenpolitik der DDR 1989/1990* (published East German documents)
ADGD	Asmus declassified government documents (declassified by Ron Asmus for his book *Opening NATO's Door*)
AIW	Author's interview with, followed by last name of interview partner; date(s) and location(s) of interview(s) are listed in the bibliography
AN	Archives Nationales (France)
AP	Associated Press (US news service)
APBD-49–94	*Aussenpolitik der Bundesrepublik Deutschland: Dokumente von 1949 bis 1994* (published West German foreign ministry documents)
APP-UCSB	American Presidency Project, University of California, Santa Barbara (online government documents)
BDGD	Burns declassified government documents (published collection of documents declassified by William Burns for his book *The Back Channel*)
BPL	George H. W. Bush Presidential Library
BPL online	George H. W. Bush Presidential Library online archive of memcons and telcons, https://bush41library.tamu.edu /archives/memcons-telcons
BRD	Bundesrepublik Deutschland (German name for West Germany, later for united Germany)
BST timeline	Timeline edited by Mariana Budjeryn, Simon Saradzhyan, and William Tobey: "25 Years of Nuclear Security Cooperation by the US, Russia, and Other Newly Independent States," June 16, 2017, https://www.belfercenter.org/publication/25 -years-nuclear-security-cooperation-us-russia-and-other -newly-independent-states

BStU	Bundesbeauftragte(r) für die Unterlagen des Staatssicherheitsdienstes der ehemaligen Deutschen Demokratischen Republik (German name for the Stasi Archive, Germany)
BzL	*Berichte zur Lage 1989–1998* (published West German CDU documents)
CAB	Cabinet Office (UK)
CFPR	*The Clinton Foreign Policy Reader* (published US documents)
CFR	Council on Foreign Relations (US)
CL	William J. Clinton Presidential Library
CWIHPPC	Cold War International History Project Paris Conference
DA-90–91	*Deutsche Aussenpolitik 1990/91* (published German documents)
DBPO	*Documents on British Policy Overseas*, series III, vol. 7, *German Unification, 1989–1990* (published British documents)
DCI	Director of Central Intelligence (US)
DDR	Deutsche Demokratische Republik (German name for East Germany)
DE (unpub)	*Die Einheit* (published East and West German foreign ministry documents; note, there also exists an extended collection of declassified government documents edited out of the final publication for length reasons, but viewable at PA-AA; sources from it are cited as "DE unpub," short for *Die Einheit* unpublished collection)
DESE	*Deutsche Einheit Sonderedition* (published West German federal chancellery documents)
DFUA	*La diplomatie française face à l'unification allemande* (published French documents)
DS	Department of State (US)
DS-ERR	Department of State, Electronic Reading Room (online US documents)
DS-OIPS	Department of State, Office of Information Programs and Services (office releasing documents declassified by FOIA/MR)
EBB	Electronic Briefing Book (posted online by NSA, followed by identifying number of briefing book)
FAZ	*Frankfurter Allgemeine Zeitung* (German newspaper)
FCO	Foreign and Commonwealth Office (UK)
FOI, FOIA	Freedom of Information (UK), Freedom of Information Act (US)
GBOHP	George H. W. Bush Oral History Project, Miller Center, University of Virginia
GC	Georgia Conference (original documents distributed at conference, organized by NSA, "End of the Cold War in Europe, 1989," May 1–3, 1998, Musgrove, St. Simon's Island, Georgia)

GDE	*Geschichte der deutschen Einheit* (four-volume German history of unification)
GFA	Gorbachev Foundation Archive
HIA	Hoover Institution Archive, Stanford University
ISCAP	Interagency Security Classification Appeals Panel (US)
IWG	Interagency Working Group (US designation)
JAB	James A. Baker III
KADE	Kabinettausschuß Deutsche Einheit (West German Cabinet Committee on Germany Unity)
KASPA	Konrad Adenauer Stiftung Pressearchiv (Konrad Adenauer Foundation Press Archive, Germany)
LSS	*Last Superpower Summits* (NSA published documents)
MC	Miedzeszyn-Warsaw Conference (declassified government documents distributed at conference, organized by NSA, "Poland 1986–1989: The End of the System," October 20–24, 1999, Miedzeszyn-Warsaw, Poland)
MDB	*Mein Deutsches Tagebuch* (excerpts from Chernyaev's diary published in Germany)
Memcon	Memorandum of conversation
MfAA	Ministerium für Auswärtige Angelegenheiten (Ministry for Foreign Affairs, East Germany)
MfS	Ministerium für Staatssicherheit (Ministry for State Security, official name of the East German Stasi)
МГ	*Михаил Горбачев и германский вопрос* (published Soviet documents)
MGDF	*Michail Gorbatschow und die deutsche Frage* (annotated German translation of МГ)
MOD	Minister (or Ministry) of Defense
MR	Mandatory Review (US, part of document declassification process)
NIC	National Intelligence Council (US)
NSA	National Security Archive
Овв	*Отвечая на вызов времени* (published Soviet documents)
OD	*Open Door* (edited and published memoir accounts)
ÖDF	*Österreich und die deutsche Frage* (Austrian published documents)
PA-AA	Politisches Archiv, Auswärtiges Amt (Political Archive, Foreign Ministry of West Germany; after October 3, 1990, of united Germany)
PC	Prague Conference (original documents distributed at conference, organized by NSA, "The Democratic Revolution in Czechoslovakia," October 14–16, 1999, Prague)
PPPWC	*Public Papers of the President, William Clinton* (US published documents)

ППР (1 or 2)	*Переписка Президента Российской Федерации Бориса Николаевича Ельцина . . . 1996–1999, в двух томах* (published Russian documents, vol. 1 or 2)
PREM	Prime Minister's Office (UK)
PRO-NA	Public Records Office, National Archives (UK)
RHG	Robert-Havemann-Gesellschaft (Robert Havemann Foundation, archive of the former East German dissident movement)
SAPMO	Stiftung/Archiv der Parteien und Massenorganisationen der DDR (Archive of Former GDR Parties and Mass Organizations, East German documents)
SDC	State Department cable (US documents, followed by year-sender-number; unless otherwise indicated, from DS-OIPS)
SMML	Seeley Mudd Manuscript Library, Collection of Documents from James A. Baker III, Princeton University
SSSN	Scowcroft Special Separate Notes (BPL designation)
Telcon	Memorandum of telephone conversation (US; note, at times the more general term of Memcon is used to apply to telephone conversations as well)
TOIW	Transcript of interview with (for published interviews not conducted by the author)
TSM	Teimuraz Stepanov-Mamaladze Collection, HIA
WCPHP	William J. Clinton Presidential History Project, Miller Center, University of Virginia

Introduction

1. In a letter to Kohl on February 10, 1990, Baker repeated the words that he [Baker] had said to Gorbachev on February 9, 1990: "Would you prefer to see a unified Germany outside of NATO, independent and with no US forces or would you prefer a unified Germany to be tied to NATO, with assurances that NATO's jurisdiction would not shift one inch eastward from its present position?"; DESE 794. See also Weiner, *Folly and the Glory*, 170–71.

2. For more on the last concept, see Andrew Bell-Fialkoff, "A Brief History of Ethnic Cleansing," *Foreign Affairs*, Summer 1993, https://www.foreignaffairs.com/articles/1993-06-01/brief-history-ethnic-cleansing.

3. The defense secretary was Bill Perry; see chapter 5 for the context of his comment. On loss of potential options for Russia, see Haslam, "Russia's Seat," 130. For an insightful example of another through line for narrativizing the 1990s—the spread of neoliberalism—see Ther, *Europe*.

4. For the full text of the alliance's founding treaty, see the NATO website: https://www.nato.int/cps/en/natolive/official_texts_17120.htm. Estimate of a billion citizens covered by NATO comes from "Brussels Summit

Communiqué," June 14, 2021, https://www.nato.int/cps/en/natohq/news
_185000.htm. See also Hal Brands, "If NATO Expansion Was a Mistake,
Why Hasn't Putin Invaded?," *Bloomberg Opinion*, May 14, 2019, https://
www.bloomberg.com/opinion/articles/2019-05-14/nato-expansion-if-it
-was-a-mistake-why-hasn-t-putin-invaded; Nicholas Burns and Douglas
Lute, "NATO at Seventy: An Alliance in Crisis," Belfer Center for Science and International Affairs, February 2019, https://www.belfercenter.org
/publication/nato-seventy-alliance-crisis; and Michael Kofman, "Fixing
NATO Deterrence in the East," *War on the Rocks*, May 12, 2016, https://
warontherocks.com/2016/05/fixing-nato-deterrence-in-the-east-or-how-i
-learned-to-stop-worrying-and-love-natos-crushing-defeat-by-russia/.

5. These two quotations are discussed at length in chapters 2 and 7. French
   president François Mitterrand had promoted yet another alternative: a
   European confederation. See Bozo, "Failure"; Bozo, "'I Feel More Comfortable.'"

6. As Robert Legvold has written, the key test of any European security system is Ukraine; Legvold, *Return*, 99–100.

7. Delbrück won the Nobel Prize for Physiology or Medicine in 1969. Quota-
   tion from Delbrück, *Mind from Matter?*, 167. For similar thoughts from
   Niels Bohr, see Legvold, *Return*, 99; Rozental, *Niels Bohr*, 328. On post–Cold
   War strategic choices, see Bozo, "Failure," 393–94; Lašas, *European Union*, 1.

8. This issue is discussed further in the conclusion, but for a preview on the
   matter, see Poast and Chinchilla, "Good for Democracy?"; Vachudova,
   Europe Undivided, 134–36. On Eastern Europe, international organizations,
   and democratization more generally, see Applebaum, *Twilight*; Epstein,
   "NATO Enlargement"; Epstein, "When Legacies"; Gheciu, "Security Institutions"; Gibler and Sewell, "External Threat"; Ikenberry, *World*; Jacoby,
   Enlargement; Von Borzyskowski and Vabulas, "Credible Commitments?"

9. Pentagon complaint summarized in "Memorandum for Brent Scowcroft,
   from Condoleezza Rice, Preparing for the German Peace Conference," February 14, 1990, in my 2008-0655-MR, BPL; AIW Zoellick.

10. George Kennan, "A Fateful Error," *New York Times*, February 5, 1997; Tal-
    bott, *Russia Hand*, 232. On this point, see the exchange between Anatoliy
    Chubais, Chief of the Russian Presidential Administration, and Talbott, in
    which Talbott stated that the main argument against NATO expansion
    was "that Russia would be upset" and Chubais responded, "no, the main
    argument against enlargement was, and remains, that it will decrease secu-
    rity for everyone": Memcon, Chubais–Talbott, January 23, 1997, DS-ERR.

11. Baker, *Politics*, 84.

12. Nuclear warhead statistic from "Global Nuclear Arsenals Grow as States
    Continue to Modernize," Stockholm International Peace Research Insti-
    tute, June 14, 2021, https://www.sipri.org/media/press-release/2021/global
    -nuclear-arsenals-grow-states-continue-modernize-new-sipri-yearbook
    -out-now; "short-lived" description from Legvold, *Return*, 121.

13. See Robert Kuttner, "Was Putin Inevitable?," *American Prospect*, January 30, 2020, https://prospect.org/world/was-putin-inevitable/; Anika Binnendijk et al., "At the Vanguard," RAND RR-A311-1, 2020, October 2020, https://doi.org/10.7249/RRA311-1; Kofman, "Fixing NATO"; Bruce McClintock, Jeffrey W. Hornung, and Katherine Costello, "Russia's Global Interests and Actions," RAND PE-327-A, June 2021, https://doi.org/10.7249/PE327; Kori Schake et al., "Defense in Depth," *Foreign Affairs*, November 23, 2020, https://www.foreignaffairs.com/articles/united-states/2020-11-23/defense -depth; Ven Bruusgaard, "Russian Nuclear Strategy"; Alexander Vershbow and Daniel Fried, "How the West Should Deal with Russia," Atlantic Council, November 23, 2020, https://www.atlanticcouncil.org/in-depth-research -reports/report/russia-in-the-world/.

14. Adam Tooze, "Whose Century?," *London Review of Books*, July 30, 2020; see also McFaul, "Putin," 103; Stoner, *Russia*, 3, who argues that "a common argument among many analysts has been that Russia has a weak hand in international politics, but plays it well. This book argues instead that Russia's cards may not be as weak as we in the West have thought."

15. For Clinton and Yeltsin quotations, see Memcon, Clinton–Yeltsin, March 21, 1997, 8:30–9:45 p.m., DS-ERR, during which they also discuss whether the plot of the movie *Crimson Tide* could "actually happen." On Croce, see Vernon Bogdanor, "I Believe in Yesterday," *New Statesman*, December 17, 2009. For an interesting interpretation of Yeltsin's revelations to Baker as part of a conscious process of carrying out a "peaceful coup" to destroy the Soviet Union, and of trying to win over Baker and other Americans as a way "to ratify its outcome," see Baker and Glasser, *The Man*, 475; they attribute the insight to Dennis Ross.

16. Vershbow and Fried, "How the West."

17. "Talbott–Chirac Meeting in Paris," January 14, 1997, DS-ERR; Margaret MacMillan, "1989: The Year of Unfulfilled Hopes," *Wall Street Journal*, December 28, 2018; Carter and Perry, *Preventive Defense*, 64. For more on economic issues and neoliberalism, see Ther, *Europe*; on dark futures after 1989, see John Mearsheimer, "Why We Will Soon Miss the Cold War," *The Atlantic*, August 1990, https://www.mearsheimer.com/wp-content/uploads /2019/07/A0014.pdf.

18. My first scholarly article based on these sources appeared in 1993 (Sarotte, "Elite Intransigence"); subsequent relevant publications are listed in the bibliography.

19. In particular, the hard work of the NSA, and of Thomas Blanton and Svetlana Savranskaya, has resulted in declassification of huge numbers of valuable documents. Also important were the decisions of Ronald Asmus, Condoleezza Rice, and Philip Zelikow to provide full citations for classified documents in their respective memoir accounts of these events (Asmus, *Opening*; Zelikow and Rice, *Germany Unified*), which greatly aided declassification by the NSA, myself, and others. See also William Burr,

"Trapped in the Archives," *Foreign Affairs*, November 29, 2019, https://www.foreignaffairs.com/articles/2019-11-29/trapped-archives.

20. See my 2010 article based on these sources: Sarotte, "Not One Inch Eastward?"

21. I remain grateful to Jeffrey Engel and his unstoppable student Nick Reves for his help on this visit.

22. My initial assessments of these sources appeared in 2010 in Sarotte, "Perpetuating U.S. Preeminence," and in 2011 in Sarotte, "In Victory, Magnanimity."

23. For more on the Directive on the Public Disclosure of NATO Information, see https://www.nato.int/nato_static_fl2014/assets/pdf/pdf_archives/AC_324-D_2014_0010.pdf.

24. "Kremlin Chides US for Bypassing Russia When Declassifying Yeltsin-Clinton Dialogue," TASS, August 31, 2018, https://tass.com/politics/1019 409. The appeals that I filed to declassify Clinton Library documents, along with those from other collections, are a matter of public record; see the appeals log on the ISCAP National Archives and Records Administration website, https://www.archives.gov/declassification/iscap. (Note: at the time of writing, some documents covered by these appeals had not yet been declassified, and some of the appeals numbers are not yet posted to that public log). My most significant Clinton Library appellate cases are as follows (this list shows, first, my original Clinton Library mandatory review request case number, 2015-xxxx, followed by my matching ISCAP appeal number, 2016-xxx): -0755/-140; -0756/-141; -0768/-142; -0769/-143; -0770/-144; -0771/-145; -0772/-146; -0773/-147; -0774/-148; -0775/-149; -0776/-150; -0777/-151; -0778/-152; -0779/-153; -0780/-154; -0781/-155; -0782/-156; -0783/-157; -0788/-158; -0789/-159; -0791/-160; -0792/-161; -0793/-162; -0807/-163; -0808/-164; -0809/-165; -0810/-166; -0811/-167; -0812/-168; -0813/-169; -0814/-170; -0815/-171; -0816/-172. Additional Clinton Library requests that succeeded without an ISCAP appeal: M-2016-0215, -0216, -0217, -0218, -0219, -0220, -0222, -0223, -0224, -0225, -0226.

25. Gaddis, *Landscape*, 4.

26. Maxim Kórshunov, "Mikhail Gorbachev: I Am against All Walls," *Russia Beyond*, October 16, 2014, https://www.rbth.com/international/2014/10/16/mikhail_gorbachev_i_am_against_all_walls_40673.html.

27. Leading advocates of the view that NATO expansion either never came up, or came up only with regard to Germany, include James Goldgeier and Mark Kramer. Goldgeier, in his fall 2020 article "NATO Enlargement," 154, uncritically accepts how "Gorbachev himself said later that the conversations they held in 1990 were solely about Germany rather than all of Eastern Europe." According to Goldgeier, he and "Kramer combed through the documentary evidence" and "there was no promise or even a discussion about countries like Poland and Hungary." Quote from James Goldgeier, "Promises Made, Promises Broken?," *War on the Rocks*, July 12, 2016, https://warontherocks.com/2016/07/promises-made-promises-broken-what

-yeltsin-was-told-about-nato-in-1993-and-why-it-matters/. Kramer states that "the issue never came up during the negotiations on German unification"; Kramer, "Myth," 41. Philip Zelikow and Condoleezza Rice echo Goldgeier and Kramer, writing in 2019 that in February 1990 "the notion of Poland or Hungary or any member of the still-extant alliance joining NATO was not yet on the table"; Zelikow and Rice, *To Build*, 233. Similar statements—"the Russians never raised the question of Nato enlargement"— appear in Christopher Clark and Kristina Spohr, "Moscow's Account of Nato Expansion is a Case of False Memory Syndrome," *The Guardian*, May 24, 2015, https://www.theguardian.com/commentisfree/2015/may/24/russia-nato-expansion-memory-grievances; and Spohr, "Precluded or Precedent-Setting?," 18, 39, 52–53, which states that the "issue of NATO enlargement never came up as a separate topic." The evidence presented in this book renders these views untenable. See also NATO's own statement in "NATO Enlargement and Russia: Myths and Realities," https://www.nato.int/docu/review/2014/russia-ukraine-nato-crisis/nato-enlargement-russia/en/index.htm.

28. Gorbachev quotation is from his transcript of a conversation with Mitterrand; the Soviet leader was explaining to the French president what he had told Baker. "Из беседы М.С. Горбачева с Ф. Миттераном один на один," May 25, 1990, МГ, 458; see also MGDF 425.

29. Memcon, Bush–Thatcher, November 24, 1989, BPL online; "Prime Minister's Meeting with President Bush at Camp David on Friday 24 November" [1989], my FOI 0884-07, UK Cabinet Office. The British version adds that Bush said he was "troubled about supporting continuation of the Warsaw Pact. He agreed that the West should not take any initiative to break it up. But what if the pressure to leave came from inside? The West could not assign countries to stay in the Warsaw Pact against their will." Thatcher quotation on "keeping" the Warsaw Pact in her summary of the November 24 summit to her Cabinet: "Speaking Note for Cabinet on 30 November [1989]," PREM 19/2892, Thatcher Foundation (which offers a useful online collection, compiling sources from multiple countries). Description of the pact as a "fig leaf" from July 1990, when Thatcher and Bush once again discussed "the wisdom and/or desirability of keeping a ghost Warsaw Pact in existence. The Prime Minister suggested that it could be a fig leaf for Gorbachev. The President accepted that Gorbachev needed a bit of cover, at least for a year or two, but said his spirit rebelled against doing or saying anything to encourage the Pact's continued existence. The Prime Minister pointed to the risk that, if the Warsaw Pact formally dissolved itself, then people would question the need for NATO": "Prime Minister's Meeting with President Bush," July 6, 1990, PREM 19/3466, Thatcher Foundation.

30. On February 2–4, see the detailed analysis in chapter 2. On February 6, see Sarotte, "Perpetuating U.S. Preeminence," 116–17. On February 8, see "Memorandum for the President, from: James A. Baker, III," February 8, 1990, SDC 1990-SECTO-01009, SSSN USSR 91126-003, BPL; as Baker

told Bush, the Czech leaders' "main objective is to get Soviet troops out," and they "worry that NATO justifies the Pact," so were suggesting that the former leave as a way of getting rid of the latter; Baker insisted in reply that the two alliances were not equivalent and instead "made a strong case for NATO's continued role" in Europe. On February 20–27, see "Memorandum for the Secretary, Impressions from Hungary, Poland, Austria, and Yugoslavia," March 1, 1990, Hutchings Files, CF01502-005, BPL; see also Shifrinson, "Eastbound," 823. On the March 3 visit of the Czech foreign minister, see "Summary of Diplomatic Liaison Activities," SERPMP 2124, n.d., but from context circa July 1991, Barry Lowenkron files, FOIA 2000-0233-F, BPL. On March 12, see Sarotte, "Not One Inch Eastward?," 137. On March 17, see the record of that day's meeting of Warsaw Pact foreign ministers, during which Czechoslovakia, Hungary, and Poland opposed the Soviet foreign minister's efforts to block NATO moving eastward across the inner-German dividing line and on to East German territory; "Drahtbericht des Botschafters Blech, Moskau," March 21, 1990, DE 378n3; and "Vorlage des Ministerialdirektors Teltschik an Bundeskanzler Kohl," March 23, 1990, DESE 972, also note 5 on same page. On the March 21 visit of the Polish foreign minister, see "Vorlage des Ministerialdirektors Teltschik an Bundeskanzler Kohl," 972n7. On the summer and fall 1990 visits to NATO (June 29 by the Hungarian foreign minister, July 18 by the Hungarian prime minister, October 23 by the Romanian prime minister, November 15 by the Bulgarian foreign minister, with additional visits by deputies not listed here; note, the secretary general also made visits abroad, such as May 5 to Prague, July 17–19 to Moscow, September 5–8 again to Prague, September 13–15 to Warsaw, November 22–23 to Budapest), see "Summary of Diplomatic Liaison Activities"; Borkovec, *Naše cesta do NATO*, 8; and Kecskés, *View*, 21–22 and 22n5 (which is a truly remarkable and useful source on this topic, from a Hungarian research center). See also Stephan Kieninger, "Opening NATO," OD 58–59.

31. For Bush's discussions of potential NATO links to the Baltics, see Chapter 4. On the official "Antrag Ungarns auf Mitgliedschaft im EUR," see "Botschafter von Schubert, Straßburg (Europarat), an das Auswärtige Amt," November 16, 1989, AAP-89, 1558. Quotations about Warsaw Pact member states not wanting to destroy the pact too soon in "Aufzeichnung . . . Dreher," AAP-89, 1801.

32. Baker and Glasser, *The Man*, 526–28, and Carpendale's original letter in SMML; on Baker and Carpendale's relationship, see Baker, *Politics*, 11, 524, 648.

33. Michiko Kakutani, "A Political Insider with Bush Tells of the Outside," *New York Times*, October 6, 1995.

34. Churchill made this remark during a speech in the House of Commons, January 23, 1948; see https://www.oxfordreference.com/view/10.1093/acref /9780191843730.001.0001/q-oro-ed5-00002969. For Talbott's personal history of decision-making on NATO expansion as presented in negotiations

with Moscow (with an eye to winning Russian acceptance for enlargment), see Memcon, Chubais–Talbott, January 23, 1997, DS-ERR. In this memcon, Talbott ascribes expansion wholly to the way Clinton answered a series of "yes-or-no" strategic questions (that is, without addressing Bush's previous answers to similar questions).

35. This challenge was recognized at the time: "The Bolshevik Goetterdaemmerung," SDC 1991-Moscow-32811, November 15, 1991, CF01652-12, John A. Gordon Files, FOIA 2000-1202-F, BPL.

36. McFaul, "Putin," 134–35; see also Rid, *Active Measures*, 387–422; Vershbow and Fried, "How the West."

37. "Address by President of the Russian Federation: Vladimir Putin Addressed State Duma Deputies, Federation Council Members, Heads of Russian Regions and Civil Society Representatives in the Kremlin," March 18, 2014, http://en.kremlin.ru/events/president/news/20603. See also Vladimir Putin, "The Real Lessons of the 75th Anniversary of World War II," *National Interest*, June 18, 2020, https://nationalinterest.org/feature/vladimir-putin-real-lessons-75th-anniversary-world-war-ii-162982.

1. Two Dresden Nights

1. Putin et al., *First Person*, 78–79.

2. Putin et al., *First Person*, 69 (main opponent), 78 (documents); Belton, *Putin's People*, 27, 33, 40, 50–54; Sarotte, *Collapse*, 10, 30. On the Dresden events as part of a larger "Sturm auf die Dienststellungen," see the Stasi official online history, https://www.bstu.de/geschichten/die-stasi-im-jahr-1989/dezember-1989/; see also https://stasibesetzung.de/bezirk.

3. Quotation is in Putin et al., *First Person*, 79; Myers, *New Tsar*, 50–51; the witness was Siegfried Dannath, whom Myers interviewed.

4. Putin et al., *First Person*, 76 (destroyed, papers, furnace), 81 (hasty), 168 (hit); see also Belton, *Putin's People*, 44–45; Myers, *New Tsar*, 50–52.

5. Dalton quotation in Kaplan, *United States*, 120; Truman quotation in Kerri Lawrence, "National Archives Presents Rare Chance to View NATO Treaty," *National Archives News*, March 26, 2019, https://www.archives.gov/news/articles/national-archives-presents-rare-chance-to-view-nato-treaty; see also Hill, *No Place*, 16–18; Kaplan, *NATO 1948*, 218–19; Kaplan, *NATO Divided*, 15–17.

6. Paraphrased from Gaddis, *Strategies*, rev. ed., 9; Gaddis refers to this as "containment by integration."

7. Truman "accepted this [hard-line] instruction with an alacrity that unsettled even those providing it"; Gaddis, *Strategies*, rev. ed., 15–16.

8. Gaddis, *We Now Know*, 115; for more, see Applebaum, *Iron Curtain*.

9. Henrikson, "The Creation of the North Atlantic Alliance," in Reichart and Sturm, *American Defense Policy*, 300–302; Kay, *NATO*, 16–17; Ratti, *Not-So-Special*, 29–31; Sloan, *Defense of the West*, 21. For more information on the

Marshall Plan, see the George C. Marshall Foundation Collection, Lexington, VA.

10. See the text of the Vandenberg Resolution, https://www.nato.int/ebookshop/video/declassified/doc_files/Vandenberg%20resolution.pdf; description of Vandenburg in Kaplan, *NATO 1948*, 93–94; Sloan, *Defense of the West*, 22.

11. Gaddis, *Strategies*, rev. ed., 71–72; Sloan, *Defense of the West*, 21–22. Planning for another air bridge for Berlin was apparently kept current until 1990; see B130-13.525E, PA-AA.

12. Kennan quoted in Gaddis, *Strategies*, rev. ed., 72; on American narrowing of choices, see Logevall, "Critique of Containment," 474.

13. Olesen, "To Balance," 63; Henrikson, "Creation," 306–7. Subsequently, once becoming members, Spain also limited its military integration into the alliance, and France withdrew from the integrated military command in 1966. On customized membership conditions, see the historical summaries on the NATO website, including "Denmark and NATO," https://www.nato .int/cps/en/natohq/declassified_162357.htm?selectedLocale=en; "France and NATO," https://www.diplomatie.gouv.fr/en/french-foreign-policy/de fence-security/france-and-nato/; "Norway and NATO," https://www .nato.int/cps/en/natohq/declassified_162353.htm; and "Short History of NATO," https://www.nato.int/cps/ie/natohq/declassified_139339.htm; for context, see Grzymala-Busse, *Redeeming*; Hill, *No Place*; Jacoby, *Enlargement*; Kaplan, *NATO Divided*, 24–26; Kay, *NATO*, 43; Sayle, *Enduring Alliance*; Shapiro and Tooze, *Charter*, xi; Sloan, *Defense*; Solomon, *NATO*, 22.

14. See the text of the Washington Treaty on the NATO website, https://www .nato.int/cps/en/natolive/official_texts_17120.htm. See also Kaplan, *United States*, 41–43.

15. Grayson, *Strange Bedfellows*, 16–18; "SHAPE in France," https://shape.nato .int/page134353332. On Soviet divisions, see Shapiro and Tooze, *Charter*, ix; on the NAC, see Kecskés, *View*, 12.

16. Kaplan, *NATO before the Korean War*; Kaplan, *NATO Divided*, 9–10; Wells, *Fearing the Worst*.

17. The quip comes from Kaplan, *United States*, 8; see also Ratti, *Not-So-Special*, 41–47. For more on the Korean War, see Wells, *Fearing the Worst*. For more on the hard-line policy document, NSC-68, see Gaddis, *Strategies*.

18. Grayson, *Strange Bedfellows*, 17–19; "Short History of NATO"; Sloan, *Defense of the West*, 26–33. On Taft, see United States Senate, "Robert A. Taft: More than 'Mr. Republican,'" https://www.senate.gov/artandhistory/history /common/generic/People_Leaders_Taft.htm. On the US role in rebuilding Europe after World War II more generally, see Suri, *Liberty's Surest Guardian*.

19. "Short History of NATO"; Kay, *NATO*, 36.

20. On Greece and Turkey joining, see NATO's website: https://www.nato.int /docu/review/2012/Turkey-Greece/EN/index.htm.

21. Uelzmann, "Building Domestic Support," 147; European Defence Agency, "Our History," https://eda.europa.eu/our-history/our-history.html.

22. For NATO's own account of this history, see https://www.nato.int/docu /update/50-59/1954e.htm. For a brief history of the legal issues involved in the presence of foreign troops on German soil, see the German foreign ministry's information page, https://www.auswaertiges-amt.de/en/aussenpolitik /themen/internatrecht/-/231364; see also Michael Creswell, "France, German Rearmament, and the German Question," in Bozo and Wenkel, *France and the German Question*, 55–71.

23. The legal means was a revision and expansion of the Brussels Treaty of 1948 in October 1954 to include the FRG, which became a NATO member in May 1955; see DBPO, 313n2. On the military conflict between the two Germanies that ensued, see Nübel, *Dokumente*.

24. William Burr, ed., "U.S. Cold War Nuclear Target Lists Declassified for First Time," December 22, 2015, EBB-538, NSA, which notes that "the atomic bombing of East Berlin and its suburbs would very likely have produced fire storms, among other effects, with disastrous implications for West Berlin. Whether SAC conducted studies on the vulnerability of West Berlin to the effects of nuclear attacks on East Berlin or in other East German targets is unknown." For more on Berlin during the Cold War, see Hamilton, *Documents*.

25. For more on the fights over nuclear weapons in Europe, see Colbourn, "NATO as a Political Alliance"; Nuti et al., *Euromissile Crisis*.

26. Quotation from Gorbachev, *Memoirs*, 59; see also Baker, *Politics*, 79–80; Kotkin, *Armageddon Averted*; Sarotte, "Not One Inch Eastward?," 125; Taubman, *Gorbachev*. For more on the revolutions of 1989 in Eastern Europe from the British point of view, see Smith, *Documents*.

27. At the time Orbán was an admirer of Nagy, but thirty years later Orbán removed a statue of Nagy from a prominent place in Budapest; see Rainer, *Imre Nagy*; "Hungarians Remember Imre Nagy, Hero of '56, as Orbán Tightens Grip," *The Guardian*, June 16, 2019; Valerie Hopkins, "Hungary's Viktor Orban and the Rewriting of History," *Financial Times*, July 24, 2019; Henry Kamm, "Hungarian Who Led '56 Revolt Is Buried as Hero," *New York Times*, June 17, 1989.

28. Excerpt from Gorbachev-Németh conversation, March 3, 1989, GFA, translation in GC.

29. The accord was called the "Abkommen vom 20. Juni 1969 zwischen der Regierung der Deutschen Demokratischen Republik und der Regierung der Ungarischen Volksrepublik über den visafreien grenzüberschreitenden Verkehr nebst Protokoll," in BStU, MfS, Rechtsstelle 101, 70; "drift" quote in "Aus den Darlegungen Erich Honeckers," June 15, 1989, Politbüro-Sitzungen im Büro Krenz, DY 30/IV 2/2.039/74, SAPMO; "burial" quote in Grachev, *Gorbachev's Gamble*, 173; see also records of the July 7–8, 1989, Bucharest Warsaw Pact meeting, July 11, 1989, DY 30/J IV/2/2A/3229, SAPMO.

30. Engel, *When the World*, 26–29; Sarotte, *1989*, 24–25. On Bush's combination of competitiveness and prudence, see Zoellick, *America*, 420.

31. For an overview of Scowcroft's background, see Robert D. McFadden, "Brent Scowcroft, a Force on Foreign Policy for 40 Years, Dies at 95," *New York Times,* August 7, 2020; see also Sparrow, *Strategist.* On Baker, see his memoirs, *Politics.*

32. Gates, *From the Shadows,* 460. On Baker's team, Robert Zoellick was central, with Baker having "every piece of paper" sent to him go through Zoellick first; Baker, *Politics,* 34.

33. TOIW Robert Gates, July 23–24, 2000, GBOHP.

34. Memcon, Bush–Mitterrand, July 13, 1989, 4:00–4:35pm, BPL online.

35. Memcon, Baker–Shevardnadze (on plane to Jackson Hole, Wyoming), September 21, 1989, MR-2009-1030, BPL. On the efforts of the Bush administration to slow the pace of change in Poland, see Domber, "Skepticism and Stability," 54.

36. "Sowjetische Haltung zu Ungarn," August 18, 1989, 213–322 UNG, Ref. 214, ZA139.937E, PA-AA (Schmerzgrenze); "Mein Gespräch mit dem ungarischen AM Horn am 14.08.1989, 09.00–11.15 Uhr," Staatssekretär Dr. Sudhoff, August 18, 1989, ZA178.925E, PA-AA ("precarious position"). See also "Gespräch des Bundesministers Seiters mit Botschafter Horváth, Bonn, 19. September 1989," DESE 405; Hanns Jürgen Küsters, "Entscheidung für die deutsche Einheit," DESE 44. For more on Hungarian–West German relations, see Schmidt-Schweizer, *Die politisch-diplomatischen Beziehungen.*

37. Two largely identical German versions are available: "Vermerk des Bundesministers Genscher über das Gespräch des Bundeskanzlers Kohl mit Ministerpräsident Németh und Außenminister Horn, Schloß Gymnich, 25. August 1989," DESE 377–80; and "Vermerk über das Gespräch am 25. August 1989 von 10.30 Uhr bis 13.00 Uhr in Schloß Gymnich," ZA 178.925E, PA-AA.

38. Baker and Shevardnadze also discussed Hungarian and Polish indebtedness to Moscow; see Memcon, Baker–Shevardnadze, September 21, 1989. For comment on tears welling up, and more on Hungarian dependency on Moscow, see Kohl, *Erinnerungen 1982–1990,* 922; the historian who wrote on Hungarian debt was Spohr, *Post Wall,* 309.

39. "Gespräch des Außenminister Fischer mit dem ungarischen Außenminister Horn in Ost-Berlin," August 31, 1989, DE 75–79; "Drahtbericht des Leiters der Zentralabteilung, Jansen, z. Z. Budapest, an den Leiter des Ministerbüros, Elbe, persönlich, 7. September 1989," DE 81–82.

40. The French ambassador to Moscow reported that "Budapest n'avait pas reçu dans cette affaire un 'feu vert' de Moscou." See "Télégramme de Jean-Marie Mérillon, ambassadeur de France à Moscou, à Roland Dumas," September 21, 1989, DFUA 67.

41. Telcon, Bush–Thatcher, February 24, 1990, BPL online; "Drahtbericht des Leiters der Zentralabteilung, Jansen"; on the party conference, see Küsters, "Entscheidung," DESE 44–45.

42. Telcon, Bush–Kohl, September 5, 1989, BPL online, in which Kohl also gave Bush a confidential heads-up about Hungary's intentions; on Moscow not approving in advance, see "Télégramme de Jean-Marie Mérillon," September 21, 1989, 67.

43. Statistic of nearly 50,000 (to be precise, 49,338) citizens leaving between September 11 and November 13, 1989, in a note from November 16, 1989, in Hilfe für Deutsche aus der DDR und Ostberlin, ab November 1989 bis 30.04.90, B85-1993, PA-AA.

44. "Gespräch des Bundesministers Seiters mit Botschafter Horváth, Bonn, 19. September 1989," DESE 405.

45. "Bürgerinitiativen in der DDR," October 12, 1989, Ref. 210, Az.: 210–320.10, RL: VLR I Dr. Lambach, ZA140.684E, PA-AA.

46. Telegram, Kohl–Németh, September 12, 1989, DESE 404 (quotes); "9. Oktober 1989," BzL 13 (line of credit); "27. November 1989," BzL 55–56 (to his home).

47. The "Antrag Ungarns auf Mitgliedschaft im EUR," as well as the signals of intent to apply from Poland and Yugoslavia, discussed in "Botschafter von Schubert, Straßburg (Europarat), an das Auswärtige Amt," November 16, 1989, AAP-89, 1558–61.

48. "Aufzeichnung des Vortragenden Legationsrats I. Klasse Dreher," December 21, 1989, AAP-89, 1801, explains that all Soviet satellite states interested in reform knew "daß für die Sowjetunion der Bestand des Warschauer Paktes eine Existenzfrage ist. Ein Auseinanderbrechen des Warschauer Paktes würde die Stellung Gorbatschows vermutlich unhaltbar machen und damit den Reformprozeß in ganz Mittel- und Osteuropa einschließlich der SU im höchsten Maße gefährden; Ausbau und Absicherung der inneren Reformen hängen mithin von der Stabilität des östlichen Bündnisses ab." On "Rücksicht auf SU [Sowjetunion]" as a reason for not joining NATO, see AAP-90, 1717; on all parties in the Hungarian parliament nonetheless expressing a desire to leave the pact, see AAP-90, 786.

49. On the historic first visit by a Soviet foreign minister to NATO headquarters in Brussels and his warm reception, see "Botschafter von Ploetz, Brüssel (NATO), an das Auswärtige Amt," December 19, 1989, AAP-89, 1784, 1788; quotation from ambassador in "Botschafter Blech, Moskau, an das Auswärtige Amt," November 28, 1989, AAP-89, 1631; see also Kecskés, *View*, 21.

50. "GDR Crisis Contingencies," November 6, 1989, with handwritten cover note to Brent Scowcroft from Robert Blackwill, November 7, 1989, my 2008-0655-MR, BPL.

51. "Schreiben von Alexander Schalck an Egon Krenz, 6.11.1989, mit der Anlage 'Vermerk über ein informelles Gespräch des Genossen Alexander Schalck mit dem Bundesminister und Chef des Bundeskanzleramtes der BRD, Rudolf Seiters, und dem Mitglied des Vorstandes [sic] der CDU, Wolfgang Schäuble, am 06.11.1989,'" in Hertle, *Fall der Mauer*, 484.

52. An internal West German report prepared two weeks later estimated that 4 million people had visited the no-longer-divided city; "Auswirkungen des 9. November auf die Lage in und um Berlin," November 24, 1989, in ZA140.685E, PA-AA. For a fuller description, see Sarotte, *Collapse*.

53. TOIW Brent Scowcroft, November 12–13, 1999, GBOHP.

54. Gorbachev comment to the visiting president of the Bundestag, Rita Süssmuth, reported in "Botschafter Blech, Moskau, an das Auswärtige Amt," November 18, 1989, AAP-89, 1571–72.

55. "Handed over by the Soviet Ambassador at 2200 on 10 November," in file "Internal Situation in East Germany," Series "Germany," Part 1, PREM 19-2696_191.jpg, PRO-NA. See also "Letter from Mr. Powell (No. 10) to Mr. Wall," November 10, 1989, DBPO 103–4.

56. Sir R. Braithwaite (Moscow) to Mr. Hurd, November 11, 1989, DBPO 108.

57. The UK ambassador to East Berlin summarized Braithwaite's comments in "Mr. Broomfield (East Berlin) to Mr. Hurd," December 6, 1989, DBPO 152.

58. "Minute from Sir P. Wright to Mr Wall, Secret and Personal," November 10, 1989, DBPO 105.

59. See "Vorlage an Bundeskanzler Kohl," n.d., but from context after November 10, 1989, DESE 548–49. See also letter from Mr. Powell to Mr. Wall, November 14, 1989, DBPO 120–22.

60. Baker's wife's remarks, and Baker's comment about himself, in Marjorie Williams, "He Doesn't Waste a Lot of Time on Guilt," *Washington Post*, January 29, 1989. For the list of animals, see Baker, *Politics*, 217. On Bush and Baker's relationship, see Sarotte, "Not One Inch Eastward?," 126.

61. Baker quotations from Baker, *Politics*, 134, 213; Bush quotation is from telcon, Bush–Kohl, November 17, 1989, 7:55–8:15am, BPL online; the German record of this conversation is also available in DESE 538–40.

62. Kohl provided the number of 110 in "Gespräch des Bundeskanzlers Kohl mit Präsident Bush, Camp David, 24. Februar 1990," DESE 863.

63. Memcon, Genscher–Scowcroft, November 21, 1989, Hutchings Files, FRG Memcons and Telcons, CF01413-019, BPL; see also "Telegram aus Washington, Nr. 4743 vom 22.11.1989, 1337 OZ, An: Bonn AA," in ZA178.931E, PA-AA; "Gespräch des BM Genschers mit dem amerikanischen Außenminister Baker in Washington," November 21, 1989, AAP-89, 1590–94.

64. "Vorlage des Leiters des Planungsstabs, Citron, für Bundesminister Genscher," February 23, 1990, DE 301–303; the subtitle of the document is "Kein Bedarf für einen Friedensvertrag."

65. Memcon, Bush–Genscher, November 21, 1989, 10:10–10:45am, BPL online, in which Bush notes that "we have been criticized here for not jumping on top of the Wall and cheering"; "Gespräch des BM mit Scowcroft am 21.11.1989," ZA178.931E, PA-AA; and the copy of the latter document in DE unpub which contains the additional note on Yalta.

66. Telcon, Bush–Mulroney, November 17, 1989, 9:49–10:05am, BPL online.

67. Memcon, Bush–Mulroney, "Working Dinner with Canadian Prime Minister Brian Mulroney," November 29, 1989, BPL online.

68. As Philip Zelikow and Condoleezza Rice noted in their joint memoir, "Mulroney's warning seemed to suggest that the Soviets would take a tough line at Malta"; Zelikow and Rice, *Germany Unified*, 125.

69. The existence of the back channel is referred to at the start of "Vorlage des Ministerialdirektors Teltschik an Bundeskanzler Kohl," December 6, 1989, DESE 616.

70. They were presumably chosen to manage the Soviet side of the channel because Falin was a Germany expert and Portugalov and Teltschik knew each other. On Falin and Portugalov, see "SU und 'deutsche Frage,'" DESE 616–18, especially 616n1; see also Belton, *Putin's People*, 50–52; Teltschik, *329 Tage*, 42–43; Sarotte, *1989*, 70–72; Vladislav Zubok, "Gorbachev, German Reunification, and Soviet Demise," in Bozo, Rödder, and Sarotte, *German Reunification*, 91. Information about Falin is also available on the website of the Chancellor Willy Brandt Foundation, https://www.willy-brandt-biografie.de/wegbegleiter/e-g/falin-valentin/.

71. Belton, *Putin's People*, 53.

72. Teltschik, *329 Tage*, 43–44.

73. "SU und 'deutsche Frage,'" DESE 616–17. In his memoirs, Teltschik ascribes a slightly different authorship to the official part than he did in his written records from the time. Later, in Teltschik, *329 Tage*, 43, he says that the official part came from Chernyaev and Falin, and that he, Teltschik, assumed that meant it had Gorbachev's approval as well. In contrast, in a note to Kohl on December 6, 1989 (DESE 616), Teltschik states that he received the document with the clear message that it came from Gorbachev.

74. "SU und 'deutsche Frage,'" DESE 617–18.

75. "SU und 'deutsche Frage,'" DESE 618nn2–3.

76. "Conditio sine qua non" described in "SU und 'deutsche Frage,'" DESE 618. Falin later described how he had raised the issue of nuclear weapons in Germany with Gorbachev in 1990: see Falin, *Konflikte*, 198–99 (information about disapproval rate of 84 percent also there), and Falin, *Politische Erinnerungen*, 494–95; and also with the East German foreign minister, Rainer Eppelmann, in "8.5.1990 Gespräch zwischen DDR-Minister für Abrüstung und Verteidigung, Rainer Eppelmann, und Falin in Moskau. Bericht," May 14, 1990, ADDR 618 (where Falin also cites Genscher proposing "Deutschland solle so zur NATO gehören wie Frankreich"). See also Küsters, "Einführung," DESE 189. For context on nuclear weapons in Europe and Germany during the Cold War, see William Burr, "The U.S. Nuclear Presence in Western Europe, 1954–1962, Part I," July 21, 2020, EBB-714, NSA; Turner, *Germany*, 174.

77. Kohl, Diekmann, and Reuth, *Ich wollte Deutschlands Einheit*, 254.

78. Letter from Stephen Wall (FCO) to Charles Powell (No. 10), March 2, 1990, first attachment, "German Unification: Security Implications," March 1, 1990, paragraph 35, released by my FOI request, ref. IC 258 724.

79. The message added, as an afterthought, perhaps together with the GDR as well; see "SU und 'deutsche Frage,'" DESE 618.

80. On this question see Von Plato, *Vereinigung*, 113–15; see also Sarotte, *1989*, 71.

81. The West German intelligence service reportedly obtained a transcript of a conversation that Falin conducted in the Soviet embassy in East Berlin on November 24, 1989; see Dirk Banse and Michael Behrendt, "BND-Akte: So drängte Moskau die DDR-Führung zur deutschen Einheit," *WELTplus*, February 18, 2020, https://www.welt.de/politik/deutschland/plus205949935 /BND-Akte-So-draengte-Moskau-die-DDR-Fuehrung-zur-deutschen -Einheit.html.

82. While the authorship remains unclear, the more sensational part of the note may have been the work of multiple men. Since Falin coordinated the channel, and the text of the "unofficial" part duplicated advice he gave Gorbachev under his own name, it seems possible that Falin was at least one of the authors; at the time Portugalov identified the document as coming from Falin's department with the participation of Alexander Yakovlev, a Gorbachev ally and Politburo member. See "Vorlage des Ministerialdirektors Teltschik an Bundeskanzler Kohl," December 6, 1989, DESE 616. The Soviet ambassador in Bonn, Yuli Kvitzinsky, may also have had a hand in writing it; see Zubok, "Gorbachev, German Reunification, and Soviet Demise," 91. While not owning up to authorship of this note, in his 1993 memoirs Kvitzinsky lamented that Moscow had not pushed Bonn harder to force Germans to choose between unity or NATO after the Wall came down: Kwinzinskij, *Vor dem Sturm*, 22. See also Bozo and Wenkel, *France and the German Question*, 223; Stent, *Russia*, 59; and Teltschik, *329 Tage*, 44.

83. Teltschik, *329 Tage*, 45; Sarotte, *1989*, 72. Kohl may have doubted whether the note truly had top-level backing but realized that the implied ultimatum could justify dramatic action on his part.

84. AIW Blackwill; "Gespräch des Bundeskanzlers Kohls mit Außenminister Baker, Berlin (West)," December 12, 1989, DESE 639, in which Kohl reported on these developments retroactively to Baker, saying, "Wenn er den 10-Punkte-Plan nicht gemacht hätte, wären er selber und der amerikanische Außenminister eines Morgens aufgewacht und hätten festgestellt, daß Gorbatschow einen entsprechenden Vorschlag auf den Tisch gelegt hätte. Ein solcher Vorschlag hätte dann allerdings die Bedingung enthalten, daß die Bundesrepublik sich aus der NATO zurückziehen müsse. Man müsse sehen, daß derartiges doch in der Luft liege." Baker answered, "ähnliche Überlegungen habe Gorbatschow in der Tat schon im Gespräch mit den USA angestellt."

85. As Teltschik later told the British ambassador in Bonn, Kohl "felt a need to set out clear German views, to influence the thinking that was evidently taking place in Moscow"; see Sir C. Mallaby (Bonn) to Mr. Hurd, November 28, 1989, DBPO 140; see also Sarotte, *1989*, 70–72. For the speech itself, see "Zehn-Punkte-Programm zur Überwindung der Teilung Deutschlands und Europas: Rede von Bundeskanzler Kohl vor dem Deutschen Bundestag am 28. November 1989 (Auszüge)," APBD-49-94, 632–38.

86. "Schreiben des Bundeskanzlers Kohl mit Präsident Bush," November 28, 1989, DESE 567–73. The US ambassador in Bonn, Vernon Walters, later cabled the State Department that Kohl had "made clear to the Soviets and East Germans in advance what he intended to say," which is somewhat different than sending them a text of the speech; SDC 1994-Bonn-37206, November 28, 1989, F-2015-10823, DS-ERR (I thank Bernd Rother for a copy of this cable); on the Hitler comment and its context, see Sarotte, *1989*, 72–76.

87. "Из беседы М.С. Горбачева с Ф. Миттераном," December 6, 1989, МГ, 286–91. Later, Kohl sent Gorbachev a detailed letter on his motives for announcing his November 28 plan; "Bundeskanzler Kohl an den Generalsekretär des ZK der KPdSU, Gorbatschow," December 14, 1989, AAP-89, 1733–41; see also Bozo, "'I Feel More Comfortable.'"

88. On the critical period from late November to December 1989 under the French presidency of the EC, see Frédéric Bozo, "In Search of the Holy Grail," in Gehler and Loth, *Reshaping Europe*, 324–25.

89. Betts, "Three Faces," 33.

90. "Gespräch Mock-Hurd," December 20, 1989, ÖDF, 439–40. Austria had applied for EC membership on July 17, 1989: AAP-90, 67n3.

91. Memorandum for the Secretary of State, from Lawrence Eagleburger, "Impressions from Hungary, Poland, Austria and Yugoslavia," March 1, 1990, Robert L. Hutchings Files, Eastern European Coordination, CF01502-005, BPL. See also the similar comments in Memorandum for Brent Scowcroft, from Adrian Basora, "Impressions from Warsaw, Budapest, Vienna, and Belgrade," in the same file.

92. See the discussion of the four principles in Rödder, *Die Bundesrepublik Deutschland*, 149–51; Von Arnim, *Zeitnot*, 286.

93. "Kohl's Ten-Point Program—Silence on the Role of the Four Powers," SDC 1989-Bonn-37736, December 1, 1989, CWIHPPC, which added "nor did he share it with the leaders of the other major parties." See also "Vorlage des Ministerialdirektors Teltschik an Bundeskanzler Kohl, Bonn, 30. November, 1989, Betr.: Reaktionen aus den wichtigsten Hauptstädten auf Ihren 10-Punkte-Plan," DESE 574–77.

94. For more on Genscher's role in West German politics, see Kirchner, "Genscher and What Lies behind 'Genscherism,'" 159–77.

95. The chancellery also routinely managed most aspects of East German–West German relations, which it did not consider foreign relations. The US embassy in Bonn attempted to explain the division of labor between the chancellery and the foreign ministry in a memo, "Inner-German Decisionmaking," SDC 1989-Bonn-25528, August 11, 1989, received by NSC August 12, 1989, Robert Hutchings Files, FRG Cables, CF 01413-012, BPL; see also "Schreiben des Bundeskanzlers Kohl an Bundesminister Genscher," February 19, 1990, AAP-90, 190; and Telcon, Bush–Kohl, November 29, 1989, BPL online.

96. Baker explained to Genscher on December 3, 1989, that these ideas had been the US basis (Grundsatz) for the conduct of Malta; see "Vorlage des

Ministerialdirektors Teltschik an Bundeskanzler Kohl," December 7, 1989, DESE 622.

97. Memo for Brent Scowcroft, from Arnold Kanter and Robert Blackwill, "Possible Initiatives in the Context of Malta," November 24, 1989, sent to the author by BPL.

98. Scowcroft quotation in TOIW Brent Scowcroft, November 12–13, 1999, GBOHP. Bush's biographer Jeffrey Engel agreed, saying, "little that can be measured changed in Soviet-American relations as a result of the Malta talks." See Engel, *When the World*, 304.

99. Transcripts of the Malta summit are now available in various forms. Among others, BPL put US memcons online by date, and Gorbachev published Soviet versions in Oвв. Baker retained records in SMML, and this quotation comes from "Used by G.B. at initial session, 10AM to 11AM on board Soviet Cruise Ship MAXIM GORKI," December 2, 1989, folder 9, box 176, 12c/12, SMML; see also Sarotte, *1989*, 78.

100. "10:10am 12/3—2nd Extended Session (as yesterday—on board the Maxim Gorki)," copy sent to author by SMML.

101. Beschloss and Talbott, *At the Highest Levels*, 159–61.

102. There was a hitch, though: the appeal of the EC had succeeded a little too well. Now East Germans wanted in, but "17 million more [Germans] was too many." Kohl comments in "Gespräch des Bundeskanzlers Kohl mit Präsident Bush, Laeken bei Brüssel, 3. Dezember 1989," DESE 603; see also the US version in Bush–Kohl, December 3, 1989, BPL online. On a related topic, namely Bush pushing the G7 agenda at an earlier meeting to consider Eastern Europe, and the related creation of the European Bank for Reconstruction and Development, see Zoellick, *America*, 437.

103. For more on the NATO summit itself, see "Botschafter von Ploetz, Brüssel (NATO), an das Auswärtige Amt," December 4, 1989, AAP-89, 1672–76. For more on US–German cooperation, see Spohr, *Post Wall*, 5.

104. Scowcroft quotations from TOIW Brent Scowcroft, November 12–13, 1999, GBOHP; joint memoir quotation from Bush and Scowcroft, *World Transformed*, 199; Scowcroft's recollection about his jaw dropping, AIW Scowcroft.

105. "Gespräch des Bundeskanzlers Kohl mit Präsident Bush, Laeken bei Brüssel, 3. Dezember 1989," DESE 604; see also note 9 on same page.

106. "Dresdner Kohl-Besuch, Rede bei Kundgebung vor der Frauenkirche," December 19, 1989, copy available under the month of December in http://www.chronik-der-mauer.de/chronik/#anchoryear1989. "Stood in the crowd" in Putin et al., *First Person*, 76.

107. The chancellor's remarks "about the interests of others were treated with respectful silence, whereas his references to German unity . . . provoked ecstatic applause." Cable from East Berlin to FCO, Telno 488, December 20, 1989, ref. PREM-19-2696_006.jpg, PREM 19/2696 Part 1, PRO-NA.

108. Quotation from Kohl, *Erinnerungen 1982–1990*, 1020; on the way Kohl suddenly "warf das Konzept einer Vertragsgemeinschaft über Bord und strebte

die Wiedervereinigung in Form einer bundesstaatlichen Lösung so schnell wie möglich an," see Hanns Jürgen Küsters, "Helmut Kohl, der Mauerfall, und die Wiedervereinigung 1989/90," in Küsters, *Zerfall*, 231.

2. To Hell with That

1. The exact number and location of US nuclear weapons in NATO Europe in the 1990s is classified, but there apparently were about 8,000 in the 1960s; see William Burr, "The U.S. Nuclear Presence in Western Europe, 1954–1962, Part I," July 21, 2020, EBB-714, NSA; see also Turner, *Germany*, 174. On debates over nuclear weapons in Germany, see Trachtenberg, *Constructed Peace*, 399; on the "Wintex" war game of "'limited nuclear war,'" see Spohr, *Post Wall*, 1.

2. Scowcroft quotation in TOIW Brent Scowcroft, August 10–11, 2000, GBOHP; Zoellick quoted in Engel, *When the World*, 327.

3. For my previous work on these themes, see Sarotte, *1989*; Sarotte, "Broken Promise?"; Sarotte, "Perpetuating U.S. Preeminence"; and Kramer and Sarotte, "Correspondence"; see also Marten, "Reconsidering"; Shifrinson, "Deal or No Deal?"; Trachtenberg, "United States"; Westad, *Cold War*, 606–7. See also Klaus von Dohnanyi, "Russland im Visier," *Die Zeit*, June 18, 2019, https://www.zeit.de/2019/26/nato-osterweiterung-russland-horst-teltschik-william-burns/komplettansicht?print; and Horst Teltschik, "Die Legende vom gebrochenen Versprechen," *Die Zeit*, July 11, 2019, https://www.zeit.de/2019/29/nato-osterweiterung-versprechen-1990-usa-sowjetunion.

4. Baker, *Politics*, 32; AIW Blackwill; AIW Zoellick.

5. "Letter from Mr Powell (No. 10) to Mr Wall [PREM: Internal Situation in East Germany]," January 31, 1990, DBPO 235–36.

6. Memcon, Bush–Thatcher, November 24, 1989, BPL online.

7. An analysis of Soviet politics for Genscher on January 12, 1990 concluded that Moscow was undecided as to what to do next and had a "spectrum of political possibilities"; see "Vorlage des Referatsleiters 213, Neubert, für Bundesminister Genscher, Haltung der Sowjetunion zur deutschen Frage," January 12, 1990, DE 210.

8. Initially oblivious to the growing closeness between Washington and Bonn, in early 1990 he fruitlessly kept trying to organize more four-power sessions. See the multiple communications on this subject in December 1989 and January 1990 in B130-13.524E, PA-AA. Baker told the British in January 1990 that Washington had decided "the Four Power forum was not appropriate for talks about the whole of Germany": "Secretary of State's Visit to Washington: Meeting with Baker," in Sir A. Acland (Washington) to FCO, January 30, 1990, DBPO 232.

9. Quotations in "Vorlage des Referatsleiters 213, Neubert, für Bundesminister Genscher," January 12, 1990, DE 210, 213.

10. "The Direction of Change in the Warsaw Pact," National Intelligence Council, 21 NIC M-90-100002, April 1990 (the report notes that it is based on information available as of March 1, 1990), CWIHPPC.

11. While the concession did not affect either Poland or East Germany—Soviet troop presence there rested on agreements from 1945 and/or occupation rights—this concession created an opening for Hungary and Czechoslovakia; see "BM-Vorlage des RL 201, VLR I Dreher, Betr.: Sowjetische Streitkräfte in den nichtsowjetischen Warschauer-Pakt-Staaten, hier: Stationierungsgrundlagen und Perspektiven," Ref. 213, Bd. 151690, January 23, 1990, DE unpub, PA-AA; see also "Vorlage des Referatsleiters 201, Dreher, für Bundesminister Genscher," February 7, 1990, DE 239–42; "Agreement Concerning the Withdrawal of Soviet Troops Temporarily Stationed on the Territory of the Hungarian Republic, 11th March 1990," in Freedman, *Europe Transformed*, 510–12.

12. Kwizinskij, *Vor dem Sturm*, 24.

13. Baker discussion with Soviet finance minister, Memcon, March 14, 1990, folder 15, box 108, 8/8c, SMML; Zubok, "With His Back," 627–29.

14. On the subsidy, see "Gespräch des Bundeskanzlers Kohl mit Botschafter Kwizinskij," February 2, 1990, DESE 747n4; see also "Vorlage des Ministerialdirektors Teltschik an Bundeskanzler Kohl," January 29, 1990, DESE 722–24; Küsters, "Entscheidung," DESE 79–81. As Zubok put it, Shevardnadze had begun "to regard his Western partners, especially the American secretary of state James Baker, as crucial allies against [the] domestic forces of 'reaction' and 'dictatorship.'" He worried that, as an ethnic Georgian, he would become "a natural scapegoat for Soviet-Russian hardliners" in the face of crises such as a food shortage and wanted to prevent the crisis from worsening; Zubok, "With His Back," 627.

15. Hanns Jürgen Küsters, "Helmut Kohl, der Mauerfall, und die Wiedervereinigung 1989/90," in Küsters, *Zerfall*, 231–32; on canceling all foreign travel, see Zubok, "With His Back," 626.

16. Falin, *Politische Erinnerungen*, 466, argued "die Außenpolitik wurde zur geheiligten Zone Gorbatschows, in allen Erfolgen und Mißerfolgen trägt sie seine Handschrift." See also Küsters, "Entscheidung," in DESE 86–87.

17. Chernyaev's original notes are in GFA. They have been published in multiple versions. CNN reproduced images of the handwritten pages, with "GDR-FRG" at the top and a date that looks like "27.1.90," in *Confidential CNN Cold War Briefing Book*, self-published and distributed by CNN as a companion to its 1998 television series *Cold War*. Typed versions of the notes (with additional text added at an unclear later date and without acknowledgment of authorship) are available in "Обсуждение германского вопроса на узком совещании в кабинете Генерального секретаря ЦК КПСС," МГ, 307–11; and "Diskussion der deutschen Frage im Beraterstab von Generalsekretär Gorbačev," MGDF 286–90, both of which give the date as January 26, 1990; but in a later interview with Alexander von Plato, Chernyaev said that the correct date was January 25, 1990; Von Plato, *Vereinigung*,

188. The CNN book notes that its copy of Chernyaev's notes came directly from GFA, which informed CNN of the following: "these are the notes of Gorbachev's aide A. Chernyaev. They were written down right after the meeting. The meeting was not recorded in any other way." The archive added that "these notes have never been complete, even the original version. The author did not include his own speech, as well as the remarks made by Falin, Akhromeev, [and] Shakhnazarov." The German translation (MGDF 291) includes the almost identical note that "im Verlaufe der Erörterung äußerten sich auch ausführlich Falin, Šachnazarov, Fedorov, Achromeev und Černjaev. Die Aufzeichnung wurde unmittelbar nach der Sitzung angefertigt, bei der kein Stenogramm (und selbst kein Protokoll) geführt wurde. Die Aufzeichnung ist unvollständig." In other words, nothing of Falin's remarks appear; he presumably would have opposed what was under discussion, given what else he was saying and writing at the time. Chernyaev's omission of remarks by Falin and other hard-liners (as opposed to his and Gorbachev's pro-Western comments) presumably skew his notes in a more pro-Western direction. Falin's account of this meeting in his memoir, *Politische Erinnerungen*, 490, notes that it concluded not with resolution but with open questions: "Die Vereinigung Deutschlands soll die NATO nicht an unsere Grenze bringen. Wie ist das zu bewerkstelligen? Man muß darüber nachdenken. Die Sitzung des Krisenstabs endet in dem Tenor: Alles haben sich gründlich Gedanken zu machen." On this problem with the source, see Sarotte, "Führungsduo?"; for larger context, see Stent, *Russia*, 104–6.

18. Chernyaev notes, GFA; MGDF 286–91. See also "Vorlage des Ministerialdirektors Teltschik an Bundeskanzler Kohl," January 29, 1990, DESE 722–24; Küsters, "Entscheidung," DESE 86–87.

19. MGDF 287; as one of those moves, a Politburo commission started looking into troop withdrawals, although Gorbachev allowed that Soviet troops should anticipate staying as long as US troops remained in West Germany; Zubok, "With His Back," 634.

20. Chernyaev notes, GFA; see also MGDF 289. For more on Gorbachev's thoughts about German unification at this time, see "За Германию, единое отечество," МГ 325–26.

21. "Die 'Vereinigung der Deutschen' wird nicht 'in Zweifel gezogen,'" MDR. de, https://www.mdr.de/zeitreise/gorbatschow-deutsche-einheit-100.html; the West German foreign ministry took particular note of the timing of Gorbachev's remarks: "Der Zeitpunkt von Gorbatschows Äußerungen (Bildtermin vor Beginn des Gesprächs mit Modrow) macht deutlich, daß der Besuch des DDR-Ministerpräsidenten zwar den Anlaß gegeben, Ihren Inhalt jedoch nicht beeinflußt hat": "Aufzeichnung . . . Lambach," January 31, 1990, AAP-90, 89. See also "Botschaft von Michail Gorbatschow," November 24, 1989, in Nakath, Neugebauer, and Stephan, *"Im Kreml,"* 69–72.

22. "Vorlage des Referatsleiters 213, Neubert, für Bundesminister Genscher," January 31, 1990, DE 225. For more on Neubert, see AAP-1989, 1904;

Sarotte, "Führungsduo?" When Gorbachev, on February 2, 1990, invited Kohl to Moscow, the invitation seemed to validate Neubert's words; "Schreiben des Generalsekretärs Gorbatschow an Bundeskanzler Kohl," February 2, 1990, DESE 748–49.

23. Genscher quoted in "Botschafter von Ploetz, Brüssel (NATO), an das Auswärtige Amt," December 15, 1989, AAP-89, 1758.

24. Genscher did so at the FDP Drei-Königs-Treffen in early January 1990, according to Von Arnim, *Zeitnot*, 265. At the time, the internal assumption in the West German foreign ministry was as follows: "eine sowjetische Zustimmung zur Einbeziehung der DDR in den NATO-Verbund [ist] nicht vorstellbar." "Aufzeichnung des Staatssekretärs Sudhoff," January 11, 1990, AAP-90, 32.

25. "Rede in der Markt-Kirche in Halle," December 17, 1989, in Genscher, *Unterwegs*, 238.

26. "Rede des Bundesministers des Auswärtigen, Hans-Dietrich Genscher, zum Thema 'Zur deutschen Einheit im europäischen Rahmen,' bei einer Tagung der Evangelischen Akademie Tutzing, am 31. Januar 1990," reprinted in Kiessler and Elbe, *Ein runder Tisch*, 245–46; in English in Freedman, *Europe Transformed*, 436–45; on US reactions, see SDC 1990-Bonn-03400, February 1, 1990, EBB-613, NSA; Sarotte, *1989*, 104.

27. Bush and Scowcroft, *World Transformed*, 237. Thatcher was taken aback as well; see Letter from Mr. Powell (No. 10) to Mr Wall, January 31, 1990, DBPO 233; AIW Zoellick; Zelikow and Rice, *To Build*, 228.

28. "Memorandum for Brent Scowcroft," January 26, 1990, my 2008-0655-MR, BPL. On Bush's and his advisors' guesses at the motive, see "Notes from Jim Cicconi [notetaker] re: 7/3/90 pre-NATO Summit briefing at Kennebunkport," and "Briefing of Pres on NATO summit at Walker's Pt," folder 3, box 109, 8/8c, SMML. On the Hungarian desire to get all Soviet troops out as soon as possible, ideally before the end of 1990, see "Gespräch des Bundesministers Genscher mit dem ungarischen Außenminister Horn in Budapest," November 23, 1989, AAP-89, 1602.

29. SDC 1990-Bonn-14094, May 4, 1990, DS-ERR. For more on the Hungarian troop withdrawal, see "Agreement Concerning the Withdrawal of Soviet Troops," 510–12. For more on Soviet withdrawal from Czechoslovakia, see "Из беседы М.С. Горбачева с А. Дубчеком," May 21, 1990, МГ 446–47.

30. "55. Deutsch-französischen Konsultationen, Paris," April 26, 1990, DESE 1057. A few years later, Estonians reported something similar to the Clinton Administration, namely that former Soviet troops on their territory represented "a domestic security threat because they were smuggling all kinds of weapon[s], including a nuclear-tipped missile, and had close links to organized crime": "Estonian PM Laar's Meeting with Depsec Talbott and U/S Tarnoff," April 18, 1994, DS-ERR.

31. Genscher, *Erinnerungen*, 715.

32. Quotation from SDC 1990-State-036191, February 3, 1990, "Subject: Baker/ Genscher Meeting February 2," 2008-0620-MR, BPL; related papers in

folder 14, box 108, 8/8c, SMML; for the British reaction, see Sir A. Acland (Washington) to Mr. Hurd, February 5, 1990, on the subject of "Genscher's Visit to Washington: 2 February," DBPO 254–55. See also Al Kamen, "West German Meets Privately with Baker," *Washington Post*, February 3, 1990; Al Kamen and R. Jeffrey Smith, "Baker Carrying Crowded Agenda to Moscow Talks," *Washington Post*, February 4, 1990; Genscher, *Erinnerungen*, 716–19.

33. Thatcher had finally accepted that "the Americans and French are probably unlikely to agree" to any more four-power events. Letter from Mr. Powell (No. 10) to Mr. Wall, February 6, 1990, DBPO 264.

34. See Falin, *Politische Erinnerungen*, 491–92.

35. Their aides spoke about the six-power idea immediately in advance of their meeting: Genscher, *Erinnerungen*, 716–19; Zelikow and Rice, *Germany Unified*, 174–77. On the meeting itself see "JAB notes from 2/2/90 press briefing following 2½ hr meeting w/FRG FM Genscher, WDC," folder 14, box 108, 8/8c, SMML.

36. Genscher's summary of Bush's view in Genscher, *Erinnerungen*, 718–19. Genscher says he met on Friday, February 2, 1990, with Baker; was later received by Bush in the White House, at which time Bush blessed what he and Baker had discussed; and, lastly, flew back to West Germany the same day. Baker's appointment calendar in SMML confirms that he and Genscher began meeting at 5:15 p.m. and held a press conference together around 7:45 p.m. (from which there are also numerous press reports); but Bush had departed at 8:28 a.m. that morning for events in North Carolina and Tennessee, going onward to Camp David for the weekend without returning to the White House, so Genscher's recollection that Bush welcomed him to the White House after his talk with Baker on February 2, 1990, is inaccurate; it is not clear when the conversation with Bush to which Genscher refers took place. I am grateful to Zachary Roberts of BPL for providing Bush's schedule on February 2–3, 1990.

37. SDC 1990-State-036191, February 3, 1990.

38. "Gespräch des Ministerialdirektors Teltschik mit Botschafter Walters, Bonn, 4. Februar 1990," DESE 756–57, discussing "Zentraleuropa."

39. Hutchings, *American Diplomacy*, 114.

40. See the summary of Washington's skepticism toward Genscher in Küsters, "Entscheidung," DESE 91. On the concept of "Genscherism" as used in the debate over short-range nuclear forces, see Kirchner, "Genscher and What Lies behind 'Genscherism,'" 159–77.

41. Mr. Hurd to Sir C. Mallaby, Bonn, February 6, 1990, "Secretary of State's Call on Herr Genscher: German Unification," DBPO 261–62; see also Sarotte, "Perpetuating."

42. "Ministerbüro, Bonn, den 07.02.1990, Vermerk, Betr.: Gespräch BM mit britischem AM Hurd am 06. Februar 1990," in ZA 178.927E, PA-AA; see also Spohr, "Germany, America," 237n69.

43. The British foreign minister had a chance to convey this complaint personally to Kohl while in Bonn; see Letter from Mr. Wall to Mr. Powell (No. 10),

"Foreign Secretary's Call on Chancellor Kohl: 6 February," February 7, 1990, DBPO 270.

44. "Ministerbüro, Bonn, den 07.02.1990, Vermerk, Betr.: Gespräch BM mit britischem AM Hurd am 06. Februar 1990"; Mary E. Sarotte, "Diplomatie in der Grauzone," *Süddeutsche Zeitung*, November 7–8, 2009; and Sarotte, "Enlarging NATO, Expanding Confusion," *New York Times*, November 29, 2009.

45. On the scheduling of the meeting, which took place on February 2, 1990, for a visit a week later, see Teltschik, *329 Tage*, 124.

46. "Memorandum for the President, From: Brent Scowcroft, Subject: Trip Report: Wehrkunde Conference in Munich, FRG, Feb. 3–4, 1990," in my 2008-0655-MR, BPL.

47. "Trip Report: Wehrkunde Conference"; see also Küsters, "Entscheidung," DESE 90–92; Teltschik, *329 Tage*, 127.

48. AIW Zoellick. For a draft of a message to the German chancellor, see Memorandum for Brent Scowcroft, from Philip Zelikow, "Message to Kohl," February 8, 1990, my 2008-0655-MR, BPL.

49. "Trip Report."

50. "Rede von Hans-Dietrich Genscher vor der SIPRI-IPW-Konferenz in Potsdam," February 9, 1990, ADDR 457.

51. Quotation in "Deutsch-französische Direktorenkonsultation in Bonn," February 8, 1990, DE 253.

52. Von Arnim, *Zeitnot*, 265.

53. "DB Nr. 551 des Botschafters Blech (Verf.: v. Arnim), Moskau, an AA, Erörterung der dt. Frage im Plenum des ZK der KPdSU vom 05.02-07.02," DE unpub, PA-AA. On von Arnim's opposition to Genscher, see Gerhard A. Ritter, "Deutschland und Europa," in Brauckhoff and Schwaetzer, *Genschers Außenpolitik*, 224–25. Von Arnim's colleague in Moscow, the French ambassador, similarly informed Paris that Soviet leaders were still swinging between extremes concerning German unification, and in particular between "deux stratégies (celle du blocage—celle du marchandage)"; see "Télégramme de Jean-Marie Mérillon, ambassadeur de France à Moscou, à Roland Dumas," February 8, 1990, DFUA 209–12.

54. Teltschik contributed an introduction to von Arnim's memoirs, confirming their contacts: "Vorwort von Horst Teltschik," in von Arnim, *Zeitnot*, 7–10, quotations at 266–67; AIW Teltschik.

55. Von Arnim, *Zeitnot*, 268.

56. "Aufzeichnug des Ministerialdirigenten Hartmann," January 29, 1990, DESE 733–34.

57. Sir C. Mallaby (Bonn) to Mr Hurd, February 5, 1990, DBPO, 254.

58. "Vorlage des Ministerialdirektors Teltschik an Bundeskanzler Kohl," n.d., but from context between February 7 and 9, 1990, DESE 772.

59. AIW Ross; AIW Zoellick.

60. Sarotte, "How to Enlarge NATO," 7.

61. "The Beginning of the Big Game," Memorandum for Brent Scowcroft, from Robert Blackwill, February 7, 1990, my 2008-0655-MR, BPL. See also "Vorlage des Referatsleiters 201, Dreher, für Bundesminister Genscher," February 7, 1990, DE 242–43.

62. "Speech by NATO Secretary General Manfred Worner [*sic*], Hamburg, 8 February 1990," in Freedman, *Europe Transformed*, 466; Zelikow and Rice, *To Build*, 233–34.

63. Baker's February 1990 trip was only his second to the USSR, following a visit in May 1989; Baker, *Politics*, 72–83.

64. David Remnick, "Protesters Throng Moscow Streets to Demand Democracy," *Washington Post*, February 5, 1990. For more on the problems then facing Moscow, see Beissinger, *Nationalist Mobilization*; Kotkin, *Armageddon Averted*; Suny, *Revenge of the Past*. As mentioned in the introduction to this book, Baker had spoken to Czechoslovak leaders en route to Moscow and had heard how much Soviet authority was waning. It is worth quoting his summary of the conversation in more detail. Baker reported confidentially to Bush while on the road that the Czechoslovak leadership's main goal at the time was "to get the Soviets out." As his Czechoslovak hosts had put it to Baker, "the soviets came in a day in 1968 . . . so why does it take the Soviets so long to depart?" The Czechoslovaks "seem to worry that NATO justified the [Warsaw] pact, and they want nothing to do with that; to them, the alliances mean a divided Europe." In other words, the Czechoslovak leaders discussed NATO's future with Baker in similar terms to Genscher: in the interest of unifying Europe, the alliance should accept a reduced role because it would ease Moscow's retreat. Showing that he understood the connection between German unification and the future of Central and Eastern Europe just a day before his meeting with Gorbachev, Baker noted that "managing the unification of Germany within NATO could be very important for these central Europeans." SDC 1990-SECTO-01009, Memorandum for the President, from James Baker, "My Visit to Czechoslovakia," February 8, 1990, SSSN USSR 91126-003, BPL.

65. There was also some inconclusive mention of "a European referendum on the question of German unification." Memcon, Baker–Shevardnadze, Obsobuyak Guest House, February 9, 1990, 9:00–10:00am, EBB-613, NSA.

66. "JAB notes from 2/7-9/90 Ministerial Mtgs., w/ USSR FM Shevardnadze, Moscow USSR," note "GERMANY 2/8/90," in folder 14, box 108, 8/8c, SMML; see also copies in folder 13, box 176, 12/12b; and Baker, *Politics*, 202–6.

67. On this conversation, there are multiple published sources. Baker's summary appears in English under the German title "Schreiben des Außenministers Baker an Bundeskanzler Kohl, 10. Februar 1990," DESE 793–94. Gorbachev reproduces parts in both "Из беседы М.С. Горбачева с Дж. Бейкером, 9 февраля 1990 года," МГ, 332–38; and, broken into different sections, in "Из беседы с Джеймсом Бейкером Москва, 9 февраля 1990 года,"

Овв 250–54, 349–50, 377–80. Various other translations and excerpts exist as well, but these sources are among the most useful.

68. "Nuclear potential" quotation in Овв 378–80; Baker's question in both DESE 794 and МГ 338; "zone" and "we agree" quotations in МГ 338.

69. Gorbachev later described it as the moment that "cleared the way for a compromise" on Germany; Gorbachev, *Memoirs*, 529; see also Филитов, *Германия*, esp. chap. 8.

70. Von Arnim, *Zeitnot*, 286.

71. Gates, *From the Shadows*, 476–77 (on an earlier meeting in May 1989), 491–92 (on February 1990). See also Engel, *When the World*, 330–32; Shifrinson, "Deal or No Deal?," 24.

72. Memcon, Gates–Kryuchkov, KGB Headquarters (New Building), Dzerzhinskaya Square, Moscow, February 9, 1990, 1500–1715, EBB-691, NSA.

73. In Gates's view, "Gorbachev had better watch out"; Gates, *From the Shadows*, 491.

74. Baker, *Politics*, 206; Teltschik, *329 Tage*, 137.

75. "Schreiben des Außenministers Baker an Bundeskanzler Kohl," DESE 794.

76. Teltschik, *329 Tage*, 135–36.

77. See the note about the February 8, 1990 signing of an accord about foodstuffs in "Gespräch des Bundeskanzlers Kohl mit Botschafter Kwizinskij," February 2, 1990, DESE 747n4.

78. "Internalized" quotation in Zelikow and Rice, *Germany Unified*, 187; see also 423n62.

79. "Schreiben des Präsidenten Bush an Bundeskanzler Kohl, 9. Februar 1990," DESE 784–85; "Speech by NATO Secretary General Manfred Worner [*sic*], Hamburg," February 8, 1990, 466.

80. Von Arnim, *Zeitnot*, 287; on the venue, see Myers, *New Tsar*, 188.

81. "8. Februar 1990," BzL 95–96.

82. "Из беседы М.С. Горбачева с Г. Колем один на один," February 10, 1990, МГ 345; and "Gespräch des Bundeskanzlers Kohl mit Generalsekretär Gorbatschow, Moskau, 10. Februar 1990," DESE 799. See also the discussion in Teltschik, *329 Tage*, 137–43.

83. "Gespräch BM mit AM Schewardnadse am 10.02.1990 im Kreml (16.00 bis 18.30 Uhr)," February 11, 1990, ZA178.928E, PA-AA.

84. "Gespräch des Bundeskanzlers Kohl mit Generalsekretär Gorbatschow, Moskau, 10. Februar 1990," DESE 799–800; see also DE 226n8.

85. "Из беседы М.С. Горбачева с Г. Колем один на один," 10 February 1990, МГ 351. The phrase originated in a briefing paper from Falin, who added the condition that if Germany created a state, it would have to be "bloc-free." In his memoirs, Falin wrote that he had chosen that word carefully because he thought it sounded more acceptable than "neutral"; Falin, *Konflikte*, 159.

86. "Gespräch des Bundeskanzlers Kohl mit Generalsekretär Gorbatschow, Moskau, 10. Februar 1990," DESE 801–5.

87. Teltschik called the part of his book covering these events "Grünes Licht in Moskau"; Teltschik, *329 Tage*, 137–46.
88. "Gespräch des Bundeskanzlers Kohl mit Generalsekretär Gorbatschow, Moskau, 10. Februar 1990," DESE 807.
89. One later Russian leader would particularly regret the lack of written conclusions from February 10; Примаков, *Встречи*, 211.
90. "Delegationsgespräch des Bundeskanzlers Kohl mit Generalsekretär Gorbatschow," February 10, 1990, DESE 809.
91. Von Arnim, *Zeitnot*, 288.
92. Excerpts from television coverage of February 10 are online at https://www .youtube.com/watch?v=AWPecuWX7Pg; "Erklärung des Bundeskanzlers Kohl vor der Presse am 10. Februar 1990 in Moskau," DESE 812–13.
93. Genscher, *Erinnerungen*, 724; Teltschik, *329 Tage*, 142.
94. As they recalled in their joint memoir, "Since Kohl did not call President Bush immediately following his meetings, . . . it was a relief to hear Kohl's press conference comments"; Bush and Scowcroft, *World Transformed*, 241.
95. Falin, *Konflikte*, 162.
96. TSM Collection, HIA. These records exist in two forms: abbreviated notes, presumably taken during events, and a diary. The information above is drawn from the diary entry for February 12–13, 1990, 331–32, also published in translation in EBB-613, NSA; the NSA version gives it the date of February 12, 1990. See also Zubok, "With His Back," 631.
97. For example, in conversation with Thatcher; see "Gespräch des Bundesministers Genscher mit der britischen Premierministerin Thatcher in London," February 14, 1990, DE 268. See also Mr. Fall (Ottawa) to FCO, February 13, 1990, DBPO 288; and "Gespräch der Außenminister Genscher, Baker, Dumas und Hurd in Ottawa," February 11, 1990, DE 254–56.
98. Genscher statements in von Arnim, *Zeitnot*, 288–90.
99. Teltschik, *329 Tage*, 143.
100. GDE, vol. 4, 247.
101. Telegramm aus Moskau, Nr. 602 vom 11.02.1990, 1028 OZ, An: Bonn AA, and "Meeting between Mikhail Gorbachev and Helmut Kohl" (document in English in German archive), both in Reisen, Konsultationen BK, ZA151.638E, PA-AA; von Arnim, *Zeitnot*, 289.
102. See, for example, Dieter Kastrup's use of the TASS press announcement with skeptical Soviet negotiators in "Gespräch des Leiters der Politischen Abteilung, Kastrup, mit dem sowjetischen stellvertretenden Außenminister Adamischin in Genf," March 2, 1990, DE 324–25, also note 32 on the same pages.
103. These quotations, from the Gorbachev–Modrow telcon of February 12, 1990, appear in both MГ 362 and MGDF 339.
104. The original phrase in German was "betont unspektakulaer." Telegramm aus Moskau, Verfasser: Haller, No. 629 vom 13.02.1990, 1415 OZ, in Reisen, Konsultationen BK, ZA151.638E, PA-AA.

105. Letter from Mr. Powell (No. 10) to Mr. Wall, February 10, 1990, DBPO 282.

106. Quotation from recorded AIW Hurd, SMML. See also Hurd, *Memoirs*, 384, where he adds that "I never blamed him [Kohl] for driving ahead with unification as fast as he could. That was legitimate leadership; in his position Margaret Thatcher would have done the same. . . . The window was narrow, he scrambled through it, breaking a little glass on the way, but less than might have been expected."

107. Zelikow and Rice, *Germany Unified*, 190.

108. Baker, *Politics*, 208; for Baker's travel schedule, see https://history.state.gov /departmenthistory/travels/secretary/baker-james-addison.

109. Hutchings, *American Diplomacy*, 114.

110. "NATO-Ministerratstagung in Ottawa," February 13, 1990, DE 263; see also "Drahtbericht des Botschafters von Ploetz, Brüssel (NATO)," February 17, 1990, DE 271–76, on "zunehmende Zeichen der Verstimmung bei kleineren Bündnispartnern."

111. "Drahtbericht des Botschafters Knackstedt, Warschau," February 19, 1990, DE 276.

112. TSM Collection, Diary, February 13, 1990, HIA.

113. Baker, *Politics*, 209, 213.

114. Scowcroft and Baker quotations in Baker, *Politics*, 213.

115. The Bush–Kohl telcons of February 13, 1990, with calls starting at 1:49 and 3:01pm eastern US time, are available both in English, in the hard-copy document collection "End of the Cold War," NSA, and in German, DESE 826–28; see esp. 828. See also Sarotte, *1989*, 121–23, and the relevant dates of the TSM Collection, HIA.

116. Baker, *Politics*, 215.

117. The Canadian government later complained directly to the West German foreign ministry; see "Drahtbericht des Botschafters Behrends, Ottawa," February 23, 1990, DE 304.

118. Memcon, Bush–Mulroney, April 10, 1990, BPL online.

119. "To: Secretary Baker," March 20, 1995, and attachments, in folder 2, box 184, SMML; Baker, *Politics*, 11, 524, 648; see also Baker and Glasser, *The Man*, 526–28.

120. Quotations in Gates, *From the Shadows*, 456; see also Bush and Scowcroft, *World Transformed*, 243–35. On tension between Baker and Gates, see AIW Zoellick; on the relationship between Gates and Scowcroft, and how Gates "glued himself to my side," see TOIW Brent Scowcroft, August 10–11, 2000, GBOHP.

121. Robert Blackwill, "Six Power Conference," February 13, 1990, my 2008-0655-MR, BPL.

122. Memorandum for Brent Scowcroft, from Condoleezza Rice, "Preparing for the German Peace Conference," February 14, 1990, my 2008-0655-MR, BPL.

123. TOIW Richard B. Cheney, March 16–17, 2000, GBOHP.

124. "Proposed Agenda for Meeting with the President, Friday, February 16, 1990, 1:30pm," folder 7, box 115, 8/8e, SMML.

125. The quotation is Szabo's summary of what Zoellick said, in Szabo, *Diplomacy*, 59.

126. "Proposed Agenda for Meeting with the President, Friday, February 16, 1990, 1:30pm"; "Our Objectives for Chancellor Kohl's Visit," n.d., but appears to be an attachment to "Note for Bob Blackwill," from the Counselor [Robert Zoellick], Dept. of State, February 22, 1990, my 2008-0656-MR, BPL.

127. "Two Plus Four: Advantages, Possible Concerns and Rebuttal Points," February 21, 1990, EBB-613, NSA; Shifrinson, "Deal or No Deal?," 35.

128. Memorandum for Brent Scowcroft, from Condoleezza Rice, "German-Soviet Diplomacy," February 23, 1990, my 2008-0759-MR, BPL. Scowcroft noted by hand: "Good start but needs second half: effect in more detail of Germany's relationship with Fr/UK, rest of Allies, US, of such a deal."

129. "Our Objectives for Chancellor Kohl's Visit," n.d., but from context mid-February 1990, in 2008-0654-MR, BPL. This document adds the complaint that "we do not feel we've gotten complete briefings from the FRG's discussions with the Soviets. For example, we should not have to hear from the Soviets that the Chancellor would be traveling to Moscow."

130. "Note for Bob Blackwill," from the Counselor [Robert Zoellick], Dept. of State, February 22, 1990, and attachments, my 2008-0656-MR, BPL.

131. Memorandum for Brent Scowcroft, from Robert Blackwill, "State Department Papers on Two Plus Four Talks," February 23, 1990, MR-2008-0656-MR; see also my 2008-0654-MR, BPL.

132. "Konstituierende Sitzung der Arbeitsgruppe Außen- und Sicherheitspolitik des KADE, Bonn, 14. Feb. 1990," DESE 830–31; see also "Runderlass des Referatsleiters 200, von Jagow," February 21, 1990, DE 283–84n14, which refers to Stoltenberg's views appearing in a newspaper article called "Stoltenberg will ein Deutschland in der NATO," February 17, 1990, *FAZ*, and Genscher responding in a radio interview the same day; see also the report of the Cabinet committee meeting of February 14, 1990, in AAP-90, 157–63; see also Hanns Jürgen Küsters, "Helmut Kohl," in Küsters, *Zerfall*, 234; and Stent, *Russia*, 117–19.

133. See their joint statement, "Sicherheitspolitische Fragen eines künftigen geeinten Deutschlands—Erklärung des Bundesministers des Auswärtigen und des Bundesministers der Verteidigung," February 19, 1990, reprinted in *Die Bundesregierung Bulletin*, no. 28/90, February 21, 1990. See also the analysis of Genscher's victory over Stoltenberg in Telegram, "Sir A. Acland (Washington) to FCO," February 24, 1990, DBPO 307n6.

134. "No expansion" quote in "Runderlass des Referatsleiters 200, von Jagow," February 21, 1990, DE 283; quotation about Horn's comments in "Gespräch des Bundesministers Genscher mit dem italienischen Ministerpräsidenten Andreotti und Außenminister de Michelis in Rom," February 21, 1990, DE

289. On the reaction to Horn's remarks inside NATO—questioning whether it was serious—see Kecskés, *View from Brussels*, 15.

135. Memorandum for the Secretary, from Lawrence Eagleburger, "Impressions from Hungary, Poland, Austria and Yugoslavia," March 1, 1990, Robert L. Hutchings Files, Eastern European Collection, CF01502-005, BPL; the memo describes his trip of February 20–27, 1990, as mentioned in the introduction.

136. Initially, the White House wanted Genscher to come to Camp David as well, despite the discord with Kohl. Baker was tired of dealing with Bonn in duplicate and wanted to speak to the two of them together, but Kohl apparently would not allow Genscher to accompany him to Camp David. See Baker's views on this matter, handwritten on his copy of the "Proposed Agenda for Meeting with the President, Friday, February 16, 1990, 1:30 p.m."; see also Sarotte, *1989*, 126; and Hutchings, *American Diplomacy*, 121–22. For Kohl's account, see Kohl, *Erinnerungen 1982–1990*, 1080.

137. "Meetings with Chancellor Helmut Kohl, Date: February 24–25, 1990, Location: Camp David" (preparatory papers), n.d., but from context just before February 24, 1990, in my 2008-0618-MR, BPL. For more on the role of Congress in foreign policy, see Lindsay, *Congress*.

138. Both the British and the US versions of this memcon have been released, the former published—Letter from Mr. Powell (No. 10) to Mr. Wall, February 24, 1990, DBPO 312—and the latter online: Telcon, Bush–Thatcher, February 24, 1990, BPL online.

139. Telcon, Bush–Thatcher, February 24, 1990, BPL online. For more on Havel's February 22, 1990, speech to Congress, see the website of the Václav Havel Library Foundation, https://www.vhlf.org/havel-quotes/speech-to-the-u-s-congress/.

140. Telcon, Bush–Thatcher, February 24, 1990, BPL online.

141. Letter from Mr. Powell (No. 10) to Mr. Wall, February 24, 1990, DBPO 312.

142. The two leaders concluded by noting how much trouble Gorbachev was facing. Telcon, Bush–Thatcher, February 24, 1990, BPL online; Letter from Mr. Powell (No. 10) to Mr. Wall, February 24, 1990, DBPO 314.

143. Teltschik, *329 Tage*, 158.

144. The timing of the conversation is unclear; (1) Memcon, Bush–Wörner, February 24, 1990, 1:15–3:15pm, BPL online, gives a date and time that, if correct, would probably have conflicted with Kohl's visit to Camp David; and (2) Blackwill remembered that Wörner spoke with Bush in late January or early February, not February 24 (AIW Blackwill). The date of the memcon, though probably inaccurate, is used below, however, because it is in the printed record.

145. Memcon, Bush–Wörner, February 24, 1990, BPL online.

146. Memcon, Bush–Wörner, February 24, 1990, BPL online.

147. Memcon, Bush–Wörner, February 24, 1990, BPL online.

148. Teltschik, *329 Tage*, 158–59; AIW Blackwill.

149. Memcon, Bush–Kohl, February 24, 1990, 2:37–4:50pm, my 2008-0613-MR, BPL; the German version is available in DESE 860–73.

150. See DESE 863. On the history of Germans who fled Polish territory, see Ahonen, *After the Expulsion.*

151. This April 9, 1990, letter is in B 43 (Ref. 214), Bd. 156374, DE unpub. An overview in mid-March noted that the foreign ministry had answered 307 letters received between March 5 and 13 alone, criticizing Genscher for considering keeping the East German–Polish border after unification. The author of this report was surprised by the "Virulenz antipolnischer Gefühle" and the assumption that the opening of the Wall was "eine günstige Gelegenheit zur 'Arrondierung' Deutschlands nach Osten"; "Vorlage des Referatsleiters 214 i.V., Schrömbgens, für Bundesminister Genscher . . . Auswertung von Privatbriefen zur Westgrenze Polens," March 14, 1990, DE 364–65.

152. Memcon, Bush–Kohl, February 24, 1990, 2:37–4:50pm, my 2008-0613-MR, BPL. The team of people writing Baker's autobiography debated whether to publish this line, with "MDT"—presumably Margaret Tutweiler—thinking that "GB [George Bush] will have a prob[lem]" with it and suggesting a phone call; a handwritten note cleared the quotation, however: "4/26/[95] POTUS [President of the United States] has no problem w/this." Indeed, Bush not only published it himself, but also added an exclamation point not present in the original memcon; see Bush and Scowcroft, *World Transformed,* 253. See note from Baker to Carpendale, folder 6, box 184, Chapter 14 General Files, SMML.

153. DESE 869; see also Spohr, *Post Wall,* 231.

154. "The working relationship with Paris, as a consequence," Zoellick later recalled, "was not as established as with Bonn and London." See Zoellick's comments, reproduced in Dufourcq, *Retour,* 110–11. On the trial balloons, see the extended archival collection of documents in Bundesarchiv Koblenz associated with, but not published in, DESE (which I was granted permission to view, but not to cite specifically by name). Some of Kohl's preparatory papers, for example, included a West German willingness to prevent the forward movement of NATO's military structures and forces across the 1989 inner-German line as part of the overall process of unification.

155. Bozo, "The Sanctuary (Part 1)," 120.

156. Bush and Scowcroft, *World Transformed,* 252.

157. AIW Blackwill; Teltschik, *329 Tage,* 161.

158. On the president dismissing a "French-like German role in NATO," see Bush and Scowcroft, *World Transformed,* 255–56; AIW Blackwill; see also Teltschik, *329 Tage,* 162.

159. First Baker quotation from Memcon, Bush–Kohl, February 25, 1990, 9:22–10:30am EST, BPL; second from Letter from Baker to Genscher, February 28, 1990, quoted in AAP-90, 254n10; I thank Tim Geiger for the latter reference. Genscher had been repeating Baker's line about NATO's jurisdiction not extending to the GDR: see Memcon, Genscher–Mulroney,

February 13, 1990, AAP-90, 169. Since neither Genscher nor the West German ambassador to the United States had been invited to Camp David, he and his staff had to figure out afterward what Baker's letter and the summit press conference signified; see AAP-90, 207–10, 235, 254.

160. While Bush attempted to emphasize the spirit of cooperation at the press conference, it was Kohl's ongoing reluctance to make a clear public statement about the Polish border that caught the attention of the journalists: R. W. Apple Jr., "Upheaval in the East," *New York Times*, February 26, 1990. Bush and Scowcroft later wrote in their joint memoir that they were disappointed that Kohl ducked the Polish question in the press conference; see their *World Transformed*, 255–56.

161. In fact, it was such bad news that Blackwill advised against even raising it in a scheduled call with Gorbachev. They did not know who else would be listening on the phone line and, given the animosity Kryuchkov and others now felt toward him, that could be seen "as a calculated or insensitive attempt to embarrass Gorbachev." Memorandum for Brent Scowcroft, from Robert D. Blackwill, Subject: Call to Gorbachev, February 26, 1990, my 2008-0654-MR, BPL.

162. Baker, *Politics*, 231.

3. Crossing the Line

1. Gates, *From the Shadows*, 492–93. For the Soviet approach to the United States about loans, see Memcon, Baker–Pavlov, March 14, 1990, folder 15, box 108, 8/8c, SMML.

2. Gates, *From the Shadows*, 492; Cable, Fm Rome, telno 347, 160715Z MAY 90, "Following from Private Secretary, Secretary of State's Call on Chancellor Kohl: 15 May," May 16, 1990, 3–4, released to author via UK FOI, CAB Ref. IC 258 724. See also "Gespräch des Bundeskanzlers Kohl mit Außenminister Hurd, Bonn, 15. Mai 1990," DESE 1119–20.

3. Preparing for a meeting with Thatcher in spring 1990, Baker noted by hand that "Kohl prob. agrees" that "North Atlantic Treaty applies fully (FRG hasn't decided)." Baker then added, apparently to clarify the phrase "applies fully": "Arts. 5 + 6—guarantee defense of GDR territory." See "JAB Notes from 4/13/90 mtgs. w/POTUS & UK PM Thatcher, Pembroke, Bermuda," briefing paper, and "Thatcher Meeting—Key Points," April 11, 1990, folder 16, box 108, 8/8c, SMML.

4. "Two-Plus-Four Preparatory Paper," no author, n.d., but from context late February or early March 1990, my 2008-0763-MR, BPL; the no-compromise list is on page 2.

5. Memcon, Bush–Andreotti, March 6, 1990, BPL online.

6. Memorandum for Brent Scowcroft, Robert Gates, from Philip Zelikow, March 12, 1990, Subject: "The Two Plus Four Agenda," and attached matrix, my 2008-0832-MR, BPL.

7. The British, French, and West Germans wanted to cover more topics; Robert Zoellick resisted his allies on this point "but got no support" from the FRG's representative, presumably on Genscher's instructions. Memorandum for Brent Scowcroft, from Philip Zelikow, "Readout on March 13 Meeting between US, UK, French and FRG Representatives for March 14 Two Plus Four Discussion," March 13, 1990, my 2008-0755-MR, BPL.

8. "JAB Notes from 4/13/90 mtgs. w/POTUS & UK PM Thatcher, Pembroke, Bermuda," briefing paper, "Thatcher Meeting—Key Points," April 11, 1990, Baker Papers, folder 16, box 108, 8/8c, SMML.

9. Letter from Charles Powell (No. 10) to Stephen Wall (FCO), March 5, 1990, "German Unification: NATO and Security Aspects," released by my FOI to CAB, COFOI-05-846 (IR254728), IC258724. See also the Letter from Mr Hurd to Mrs Thatcher, March 13, 1990, DBPO 338–39. For Kohl's subsequent meeting with Margaret Thatcher, see "20. Deutsch-britische Konsultationen," London, March 30, 1990, DESE 996–1001.

10. Fax from British embassy, Washington, DC, to P. J. Weston, FCO, February 26, 1990, PREM 19/3000, PRO-NA; quotations are the British embassy's summary of Blackwill's remarks. In the same file, see also (1) an untitled cover note from Stephen Wall of the FCO, sending information about this fax to Charles Powell on March 5, 1990; and (2) note from Powell, further passing this news on to Thatcher (in "Secret and Personal, Prime Minister, Relations with President Bush: German Unification," March 5, 1990), in which he comments, "it is alarming that the White House should be so muddled." He advised the prime minister that "when you speak to the President on the telephone, you should explain your points in <u>very simple language</u> and <u>repeat them</u>." (The underlining is by hand, and almost certainly Thatcher's.) Powell added that Kohl had clearly bad-mouthed the United Kingdom and that "we have a major problem in our relations" with Germans.

11. Original: "Kohl est capable de tout": "Télégramme de Luc de La Barre de Nanteuil, ambassadeur de France à Londres, à Roland Dumas," London, March 13, 1990, DFUA 258.

12. This is the summary of Quai views in Bozo, *Mitterrand*, 177, see also 213.

13. "Fm White House," April 17, 1990 (original in English), Antenne Spéciale, Télétype Bleu, 5 AG 4 / EG 170, O 171642Z APR 90, Entretiens officiels, AN; note, there is underlining in the original but as it is not entirely clear where it originated, it is not reproduced above. On the relationship between Bush and Mitterrand, see TOIW Brent Scowcroft, November 12–13, 1999, GBOHP.

14. Hurd was concerned about what Genscher was doing and pressed him on it. According to Hurd, Genscher replied that, "in the last analysis," Article 5 (and Article 6) would apply to former East German territory, but he [Genscher] wanted to move carefully "when the Russians were still present"; Hurd added, especially if "by any mischance Gorbachev were overthrown

by the generals." See Mr Hurd to Sir C. Mallaby (Bonn), March 12, 1990, DBPO 332.

15. "Fm White House," April 17, 1990. For context, see Mary Elise Sarotte, "The Contest over NATO's Future," in Shapiro and Tooze, *Charter*, 212–28.

16. "Интервью М.С. Горбачева газете «Правда» 7 марта 1990 года," МГ 381; see also MGDF 354.

17. "Memorandum for the Secretary, Impressions from Hungary, Poland, Austria, and Yugoslavia," March 1, 1990, Hutchings Files, CF01502-005, BPL. See also Shifrinson, "Eastbound," 823.

18. Memorandum from Harvey Sicherman to S/P–Dennis Ross, and C–Robert Zoellick, March 12, 1990, folder 14, box 176, 12/12b, SMML; Sarotte, *1989*, 139.

19. For more on Mitterrand, Havel, and the failure of the so-called Prague endgame, see Bozo, "Failure," 408–11.

20. Memcon, Bush–Kohl, March 15, 1990, BPL online; see also "Telefongespräch des Bundeskanzlers Kohl mit Bush, 15. März 1990," DESE 952–55.

21. Memorandum from Harvey Sicherman to S/P–Dennis Ross, and C–Robert Zoellick, March 12, 1990.

22. Sicherman had cautioned that "we shall fail utterly if we cannot give Poland and the other nations a choice of more than a Russian domination or a German domination"; Memorandum from Harvey Sicherman to S/P– Dennis Ross, and C–Robert Zoellick, March 12, 1990; AIW Ross.

23. To the Secretary, from S/P–Dennis Ross, Subject, "Warsaw Scene Setter," n.d., but from context circa April/May 1990, my 2008-0718-MR, BPL. By April 10, 1990, senior diplomat Bill Burns, like Sicherman, was advising his superiors that they should be thinking about "East European security concerns" lest these states might engage in measures unappealing to Washington, such as a "pan-European collective security regime." See Information Memorandum, to the Deputy Secretary, from S/P Bill Burns, Acting, "Deepening US–East European Relations," April 10, 1990, BDGD.

24. See the account of their participation in "Außerordentliche Tagung des (Außen-) Ministerkomitees des Europarats am 23./24.03. in Lissabon," March 26, 1990, DE unpub, PA-AA.

25. Mitterrand quotations and discussion of confederation in Memcon, Bush– Mitterrand, April 19, 1990, BPL online; Scowcroft quotations in TOIW Brent Scowcroft, November 12–13, 1999, GBOHP; AIW Sikorski. On the phenomenon of Western European reluctance to embrace eastern Europeans, see Mälksoo, *Politics*.

26. Quoted in "Vorlage des Ministerialdirektors Teltschik an Bundeskanzler Kohl," March 23, 1990, DESE 972n7, which describes the visit of the Polish diplomat to NATO headquarters. That month, at a meeting of Warsaw Pact foreign ministers, Czechoslovakia, Hungary, and Poland criticized Shevardnadze for standing in the way of NATO expanding eastward on to

East German territory; "Drahtbericht des Botschafters Blech, Moskau, Sowjetische Haltung zur DDR-Volkskammerwahl am 18. März," March 21, 1990, DE 378n3.

27. On these visits, see the discussion in the introduction to this book; see also "Summary of Diplomatic Liaison Activities," SERPMP 2124, n.d., but from context circa July 1991, Barry Lowenkron files, FOIA 2000-0233-F, BPL; and Kecskés, *View*, 21–22.

28. "Gespräch des Ministerialdirektors Teltschik mit dem Berater der Abteilung für internationale Beziehungen des Zentralkomitees der KPdSU, Portugalow," March 28, 1990, DESE 982.

29. The West German embassy in Moscow reported that one of Falin's confidants had passed along this information: "Aus: Moskau, Nr. 1666 vom 26.04.1990, 1334 OZ, An: Bonn AA," B130-13.524E, PA-AA.

30. "Telefongespräch des Bundeskanzlers Kohl mit Bush," DESE 952.

31. "Gespräch des Ministerialdirektors Teltschik mit Botschafter Karski und dem stellvertretenden Abteilungsleiter Sulek," March 19, 1990, DESE 956n1; see also Rödder, *Deutschland einig Vaterland*, 223–25.

32. Kwizinskij, *Vor dem Sturm*, 39.

33. "Drahtbericht des Botschafters Blech, Moskau, Sowjetische Haltung zur DDR-Volkskammerwahl am 18. März," March 21, 1990, DE 377.

34. "19. März 1990," BzL 107 (good day), 118 (mistake, poker).

35. "Gespräch des Bundeskanzlers Kohl mit Botschafter Kwizinskij," March 22, 1990, DESE 966–70.

36. "Rede vor der Westeuropäischen Union (WEU) in Luxemburg," March 23, 1990, in Genscher, *Unterwegs*, 265–66; Spohr, *Post Wall*, 227–28.

37. "Schreiben des Bundeskanzlers Kohl an Bundesminister Genscher," March 23, 1990, DE 380–81. Shortly after this cease-and-desist letter from Kohl, Baker underlined advice to "note <u>importance of extending Articles 5 & 6 Security Guarantees to GDR</u>," and added by hand, "Don't want a freak in the system": "Point Genscher May Raise," April 4, 1990, folder 16, box 108, 8/8c, SMML.

38. For an overview of some of the practical steps needed to achieve unification, see "Information Memorandum," to C-Mr. Zoellick, from EUR-R.G.H. Seitz, "Four-Power Rights and Three-Power Responsibilities in Berlin," April 6, 1990, in my 2008-0658-MR, BPL.

39. Minute from Sir C. Mallaby (Bonn) to Mr Budd, Bonn, April 2, 1990, DBPO, 366; Zubok, "With His Back," 645.

40. Quotation in Minute from Mr Cooper (Policy Planning Staff) to Mr Weston, April 6, 1990, DBPO 372; on arms talks, see Lever, "Cold War," 509–10.

41. Falin expressed the idea of a referendum in "Записка В.М. Фалина М.С. Горбачеву," April 18, 1990, МГ 404–5; see also his later discussion of the same topic in Falin, *Konflikte*, 173. On the way that Gorbachev had few other alternatives, see Zubok, "With His Back," 635. On previous attempts to

drive a wedge between Americans and Europeans and "break NATO," see Miles, *Engaging*, 49. On the discourse about, and popularity of, Gorbachev in the West, see Wentker, *Die Deutschen*.

42. This aspect apparently occurred to Falin later in the year. In his memoirs, Falin recalled discussing the unpopularity of nuclear weapons in Germany with Gorbachev in July 1990, reprinting what appears to be the transcript of a conversation with the Soviet leader in which Falin stressed that "84 Prozent der Deutschen" supported "die Entnuklearisierung Deutschlands"; reprinted in both Falin, *Konflikte*, 198, and Falin, *Politische Erinnerungen*, 494. See also Hanns Jürgen Küsters, "Einführung," DESE 189; and Szabo, *Diplomacy*, 56, which states the following about the period immediately after the opening of the Wall: "Unification euphoria was still high in both Germanies, and public support for NATO was fragile and could have collapsed if it were seen as standing in the way of unification and the withdrawal of foreign troops. Many, both in West Germany and the West in general, were worried that a referendum on NATO might be called with negative results."

43. On plans to defend Western Europe during the Cold War and the concept of "ten divisions in ten days," see Tom Donnelly, "Rethinking NATO," *NATO Review*, June 1, 2008, https://www.nato.int/docu/review/articles /2003/06/01/rethinking-nato/index.html.

44. "Gespräch des Bundeskanzlers Kohl mit Präsident Bush in erweitertem Kreise Bonn, 30. Mai 1989," DESE 272.

45. The exact numbers of Soviet troops in Germany and their dependents was a matter of some controversy in 1989–90; see "Zum Vertrag zwischen der Bundesrepublik Deutschland und der UdSSR über die Bedingungen des befristeten Aufenthalts und die Modalitäten des planmäßigen Abzugs der sowjetischen Truppen aus dem Gebiet der Bundesrepublik Deutschland, Informationserlaß des Auswärtigen Amts vom 18.10.1990 (Auszug)," DA-90–91, 231–32, which estimated that there were 380,000 troops, making with family members a total of 600,000 Soviet citizens. Charles T. Powers, "Soviet Troops Begin Czech Pullout," *Los Angeles Times*, February 27, 1990, estimated a total of 590,000 Soviet troops in Eastern Europe, including 370,000 in East Germany. The West German foreign ministry estimated 388,000 in the GDR, 80,000 in Czechoslovakia, 55,000 in Hungary, and 40,000 in Poland: "Aufzeichnung . . . Dreher," January 23, 1990, AAP-90, 60. For more on the East German army, or Nationale Volksarmee, see Ehlert, *Armee*; Rüdiger Wenzke, "Die Nationale Volksarmee der DDR," https://www.bpb.de/politik/grundfragen/deutsche-verteidigungspolitik /223787/militaer-der-ddr; on their arsenals, see Turner, *Germany*, 174.

46. "Записка В.М. Фалина М.С. Горбачеву," April 18, 1990, МГ 400–403; see also MGDF, 370–71, 373. See also Falin, *Konflikte*, 179, where he explains that, with this April 18, 1990, document, he was trying to warn Gorbachev that NATO expansion to East German territory would be "lediglich eine Zwischenstation bei der Ausdehnung des Nordatlantikblocks nach Osten."

47. Chernyaev talks about how Falin was being left out of drafting key documents and becoming enraged as a result in his diary entry for May 5, 1990. Note: Chernyaev has published different parts of his diary at different times: a Russian version, *Совместный исход*; a German version, *Mein Deutsches Tagebuch (1972–1991)* [hereafter MDB]; and English excerpts, translated by NSA and posted online at www2.gwu.edu/~nsarchiv/NSAEBB/NSA EBB192. As these publications are not identical, the precise source of the quotations in each case is given in the notes below. In this case, the German version includes additional text not present in either the Russian or English translations (and identified as notes that he gave to Gorbachev at the time), so the citation is from the German-language MDB 257. Falin, *Konflikte*, 187, similarly states that, by about June 1990, he was no longer receiving key documents.

48. "Из докладной записки А.С. Черняева М.С. Горбачеву," May 4, 1990, МГ 424; see also MGDF 394. According to Braithwaite, *Across the Moscow River*, 144, Chernyaev had remarked to a British diplomat in February 1990 that "as long as the Russians kept their nuclear weapons they could look after themselves. What was more, Chernyaev had added with his characteristic grin, no one would bother to talk to the Russians in their current political and economic difficulties if they gave up their nuclear weapons as well."

49. Bush and Scowcroft, *World Transformed*, 286.

50. "Vorlage des Ministerialdirektors Teltschik an Bundeskanzler Kohl, Bonn, 3. Mai 1990," DESE 1076. According to the West German Foreign Office, US assistant secretary of state Ray Seitz remarked that talks with lower-level Soviet delegations over the details of unification were getting "z̲ä̲h̲ und s̲c̲h̲w̲i̲e̲r̲i̲g̲, ganz anders als im Februar," so the hope was that signals from above, such as from the summit, might help clear matters up; "Vermerk des RL 204, VLR I von Moltke, Betr.: Unterrichtung (Assistant Secretary Seitz bei D2 Kastrup am 21.05.) über . . . Außenministertreffen Baker–Schewardnadse vom 16.-19.05. in Moskau," May 22, 1990, DE unpub. In contrast, Kohl believed such a summit should not take place until after Gorbachev survived the upcoming contentious Party Congress; "Gespräch des Bundeskanzlers Kohl mit Außenminister Baker, Bonn, 4. Mai 1990," DESE 1079.

51. "Address by Secretary General Manfred Wörner to the Bremer Tabaks Collegium," NATO Online Library, May 17, 1990, https://www.nato.int /docu/speech/1990/s900517a_e.htm. The incorrect hyphen after "newly" is in the original text.

52. Hutchings recalled a real sense of camaraderie between the Americans and the West Germans. As he noted after one meeting: "Atmosphere. Couldn't have been better. Kohl particularly, but all the Germans, were effusive in their gratitude for US support. What a contrast to a year ago, when our mutual trust and confidence were slipping badly"; Hutchings, *American Diplomacy*, 130.

53. Memorandum for the President, from Lawrence S. Eagleburger, Acting Secretary of State, "Your Meeting with Chancellor Kohl, May 17, 1990," n.d., but from context on or just before May 17, 1990, my 2008-0797-MR, BPL.

54. Memcon, Bush–Kohl, May 17, 1990, BPL online; Sarotte, "'His East European Allies Say They Want to Be in NATO,'" in Bozo, Rödder, and Sarotte, *German Reunification*, 69–87.

55. "11. Juni 1990," BzL 144 (Poland in NATO, praise, destroy), 145 (catastrophic, possession).

56. SDC 1990-SECTO-07015, May 19, 1990.

57. "Из беседы М.С. Горбачева с А. Дубчеком," May 21, 1990, МГ 447; MGDF 414. On Kohl's unwillingness to hold talks about the border with Poland, see "Vermerk des Staatssekretärs Sudhoff für Bundesminister Genscher," May 25, 1990, DE 517.

58. "Из беседы М.С. Горбачева с Ф. Миттераном один на один," May 25, 1990, МГ 458–59, 464; MGDF 425, 430; see also EBB-613, NSA; Bozo, "'I Feel More Comfortable'"; and a separate discussion between Genscher and Meckel about Hungary trying to end its military integration in the Warsaw Pact: "Gespräch zwischen Bundesminister Genscher und Außenminister Meckel in Ost-Berlin," June 1, 1990, DE 524.

59. See pages 24–25 of "Rede des Präsidenten der Union der Sozialistischen Sowjetrepubliken, M. S. Gorbatschow, Moskau," June 7, 1990, MfAA, DE unpub; see also Nakath and Stephan, *Countdown*, 336–41.

60. SDC 1990-SECTO-07015, May 19, 1990.

61. Bush speech: "A Europe Whole and Free: Remarks to the Citizens in Mainz, President George Bush, May 31, 1989," https://usa.usembassy.de/etexts/ga6-890531.htm. Baker comments: "Из беседы М.С. Горбачева с Дж. Бейкером," May 18, 1990, МГ 438; "Gorby Kremlin 5/18/90," handwritten notes, folder 1, box 109, 8/8c, SMML.

62. "Из беседы М.С. Горбачева с Дж. Бейкером," May 18, 1990, МГ 442–44; "Gorby Kremlin 5/18/90."

63. Bozo, "'I Feel More Comfortable,'" 150; for more on the Conference on Security and Cooperation in Europe, see Morgan, *Final Act*. Zoellick later recalled realizing how useful the Helsinki principle was around this time (with the bonus that some conservatives had a fondness for the Helsinki process), so he dug up as much information as he could on it for use in negotiations; AIW Zoellick.

64. "Delegationsgespräch des Bundeskanzlers Kohl mit Präsident Bush, Washington, 17. Mai 1990," DESE 1130; see also "Schreiben des Bundeskanzlers Kohl an Staatspräsident Mitterrand, Bonn, 23. Mai 1990," DESE 1143–45.

65. Memcon, "Telephone Call from Chancellor Helmut Kohl of West Germany," May 30, 1990, BPL online; "Telefongespräch des Bundeskanzlers Kohl mit Präsident Bush, 30. Mai 1990," DESE 1161.

66. Sarotte, *1989*, 166–67.

67. "Из второй беседы М.С. Горбачева с Дж. Бушем," May 31, 1990, МГ 466–76; Baker's notes from the summit, in folder 1, box 109, 8/8c, SMML; Beschloss and Talbott, *At the Highest Levels*, 219–21; Gates, *From the Shadows*, 493; Zelikow and Rice, *Germany Unified*, 278.

68. Falin, *Konflikte*, 183.

69. "Из второй беседы М.С. Горбачева с Дж. Бушем," May 31, 1990, МГ 473–74. Bush, in a call to Kohl on June 1, 1990, called the "two anchors" concept "a screwy idea"; Telcon, Bush–Kohl, June 1, 1990, 2000-0429-F, BPL. The two also discussed the significance of Gorbachev's acceptance of the Helsinki principle; Telcon, Bush–Kohl, June 3, 1990, BPL online; see also "Fernschreiben des Präsidenten Bush an Bundeskanzler Kohl," June 4, 1990, DESE 1178.

70. Falin, *Konflikte*, 183.

71. "Из второй беседы М.С. Горбачева с Дж. Бушем," May 31, 1990, МГ 474–75; "The Washington/Camp David Summit," EBB-320 and EBB-707, NSA.

72. In an interview with the Miller Center, he added that "in all of the heads of state meetings I've been in, this was the most remarkable I have ever seen": TOIW Brent Scowcroft, November 12–13, 1999, GBOHP.

73. Bush and Scowcroft, *World Transformed*, 283.

74. Falin, *Konflikte*, 183.

75. Küsters, "Einführung," DESE 177.

76. Paraphrased from Colton, *Yeltsin*, 110; see also Aron, *Yeltsin*, 4–9, 132–34.

77. Talbott, *Russia Hand*, 20.

78. Aron, *Yeltsin*, 202–21; Colton, *Yeltsin*, 110, 132–50.

79. Colton, *Yeltsin*, 178–86. As Colton puts it, "the Gorbachev group's take on Yeltsin's Russianism was that it was a smoke screen" concealing his desire for power (184). Chernyaev confided to his diary that Yeltsin was on the right track when he turned his back on the party, however, and thought that Gorbachev should have done the same thing; see Chernyaev's diary entry for July 12, 1990, *Совместный исход*, 864.

80. Scowcroft quoted in Goldgeier and McFaul, *Power*, 22.

81. Marilyn Berger, "Boris N. Yeltsin, Reformer Who Broke Up the USSR, Dies at 76," *New York Times*, April 24, 2007. The German foreign ministry produced a study on Yeltsin in May 1990, evocatively describing him as follows: "In Jelzin scheinen sich großer persönlicher Mut und Dickschädeligkeit . . . zu verbinden. Er ist das, was die Russen eine 'breite Natur' nennen, in der Insichruhen mit Unberechenbarkeit, Kraftakte mit Schwächen zusammen die Ausstrahlung des Typs ausmachen, Macho, Underdog, und Schlitzohr in einem": AAP-90, 686.

82. Memorandum for the President, from Robert M. Gates, "Boris Yeltsin," June 6, 1990, and attachment, my 2008-0759-MR, BPL. The details of the plane accident and spinal surgery are murky and vary from source to source, but it appears to have happened in the late 1980s; Yeltsin, *Midnight Diaries*, xii; McCauley, *Bandits*, 117–18.

83. Gates thought that Gorbachev's time in power might be growing short, given that he "increasingly stands alone in lacking electoral legitimacy." Memorandum for the President, from Robert M. Gates, "Gorbachev—Moses, not Joshua," July 13, 1990, SSSN, 91126-0004, BPL; excerpts also reproduced in Gates, *From the Shadows*, 495–96. Zoellick later recalled that Baker also sensed that Gorbachev's star was waning but figured there was no rush to recognize Yeltsin because once Yeltsin made it to the top, he'd need the United States more than the reverse; AIW Zoellick.

84. Küsters, "Einführung," DESE 178.

85. And Kohl faced a new challenge: the foreign minister of East Germany, Markus Meckel, had begun calling for "a demilitarized zone consisting of the territory of the GDR, Czechoslovakia, Poland and Hungary." When US diplomats pressed Meckel about the consequences of his idea for NATO, Meckel was "vague about whether NATO security guarantees should apply to such a zone"; SDC 1990-STATE-190169, June 12, 1990, "Secretary's Meeting with GDR Foreign Minister, June 5, 1990," in 2008-0670-MR, BPL. Hungary was also talking openly about leaving the Warsaw Pact, a suggestion that reached Bush's ears, so the question of what would follow such a departure was becoming more urgent, and Meckel's suggestion was an unwelcome answer to it. Bush and Kohl discussed the Hungarian desire to leave the pact in Memcon, Bush–Kohl, June 8, 1990, BPL online; and Bush spoke directly with the Hungarian prime minister in Memcon, Antall–Bush, October 18, 1990, BPL online.

86. "Fernschreiben des Staatssekretärs Bertele an den Chef des Bundeskanzleramtes, Berlin (Ost), 25. Mai 1990," DESE 1146–47.

87. Zubok, "With His Back," 641; see also Sarotte, *1989*, 170.

88. Scowcroft and his subordinates wrote an initial draft press release, which he then edited in dialogue with Teltschik and his advisors. DESE contains a number of documents related to this topic, among them "Vorlage des Oberstleutnants i.G. Ludwigs und des vortragenden Legationsrats Westdickenberg an Ministerialdirektor Teltschik, Bonn, 25. Juni 1990," DESE 1256–61; "Schreiben des Ministerialdirektors Teltschik an Sicherheitsberater Scowcroft, Bonn, 28. Juni 1990," DESE 1276; "Entwurf NATO Gipfelerklärung," DESE 1276–80.

89. Sarotte, *1989*, 173–76; "Notes from Jim Cicconi [notetaker] re: 7/3/90 pre-NATO Summit briefing at Kennebunkport," and "Briefing of Pres on NATO summit at Walker's Pt," folder 3, box 109, 8/8c, SMML. Original: "JAB: we resisted sending decl. thru NATO bureaucracy=Woerner, others worry re this." See also Zelikow and Rice, *To Build*, 284–85.

90. "Notes from Jim Cicconi," July 3, 1990. Cheney also called for a "rethink" of what NATO's future "out-of-area" operations might be.

91. "Schreiben des Sicherheitsberaters Scowcroft an Ministerialdirektor Teltschik, 30. Juni 1990," DESE 1285; see also "Gesprächsunterlagen des Bundeskanzlers Kohl für das Gipfeltreffen der Staats- und Regierungschefs der Mitgliedstaaten der NATO, London, 5./6. Juli 1990," DESE 1309–23.

92. "Notes from Jim Cicconi," July 3, 1990.

93. "Fernschreiben des Präsidenten Bush an Bundeskanzler Kohl, 21. Juni 1990," DESE 1235; "Entwurf Gipfelerklärung," DESE 1237–41; see also Baker, *Politics*, 258; Sparrow, *Strategist*, 378–79.

94. "Champagne" quotation in "Fm Manfred Wörner 003 To White House for President, Brussels," June 25, 1990, my 2008-0657-MR, BPL; Wörner's worry in "Notes from Jim Cicconi," July 3, 1990. See also Thatcher's reaction in "Note from Bob Blackwill to Brent Scowcroft and Bob Gates," June 25, 1990, in my 2008-0657-MR, BPL.

95. "Drahtbericht des Botschafters Knackstedt, Warschau . . . Entschließung des Deutschen Bundestages vom 21. Juni 1990," June 22, 1990, DE 585n1; Zoellick also recalled multiple US efforts to reassure Poland; AIW Zoellick.

96. Baker notes from NATO summit, London, July 5–6, 1990, folder 3, box 109, 8/8c, SMML. Invitations to visit and to establish permanent diplomatic missions were, as the NSC wanted, extended not to the Warsaw Pact as a whole but to individual states. A copy of the final communiqué is available in various languages and locations, for example on the NATO website, "Declaration on a Transformed North Atlantic Alliance," July 5–6, 1990, https://www.nato.int/cps/ie/natohq/official_texts_23693.htm.

97. "Your July 6 Message to Ambassador Matlock," July 7, 1990, confirmation and repetition of Bush message as delivered by the embassy to Chernyaev for Gorbachev, in SSSN USSR 91128-002, BPL. See also Kieninger, "Opening NATO," OD 58.

98. Sarotte, *1989*, 176; "Vorlage Ministerialdirektors Teltschik an Bundeskanzler Kohl, Bonn, 4. Juli 1990, Betr.: Innere Lage in der Sowjetunion nach Beginn des 28. KPdSU-Parteitages," DESE 1297–99; see also Stent, *Russia*, 123–34.

99. "Rede von Michail Gorbatschow, Präsident der UdSSR, auf dem Gipfeltreffen der Warschauer Vertragsstaaten am 7. Juni 1990," in Nakath and Stephan, *Countdown*, 341; as he put it, "ich möchte daran erinnern, daß es gerade innerhalb des NATO-Blocks mindestens fünf/sechs verschiedene Arten der Mitgliedschaft gibt." Gorbachev also discussed these differing models of NATO membership with Thatcher; see "Из беседы М.С. Горбачева с М. Тэтчер," June 8, 1990, МГ 482. See also Jacoby, *Enlargement*.

100. On the practicalities of arranging this visit, see Klein, *Es begann*.

101. Kohl, *Erinnerungen 1990–1994*, 164; Teltschik, *329 Tage*, 318–19. The chancellor further prepared the ground by granting a generous exchange rate for Soviet forces in the wake of German-German monetary unification, and a promise to fulfill various East German supply treaties with the USSR; Küsters, "Kohl-Gorbachev," 198.

102. Falin, *Konflikte*, 198; Falin, *Politische Erinnerungen*, 494. On the timing of the call, see Küsters, "Einführung," DESE 189.

103. Gorbachev quoted in Falin, *Konflikte*, 199; also in Falin, *Politische Erinnerungen*, 494.

104. The description above of the July 15 talk comes from three firsthand accounts of this meeting: (1) the German transcript, "Gespräch des Bundeskanzlers Kohl mit Präsident Gorbatschow, Moskau, 15. Juli 1990," DESE 1340–48; (2) the Russian transcript, "Из беседы Горбачева с Г. Колем один на один," July 15, 1990, МГ 495–503; and (3) Chernyaev's Russian-language published diary entry for that date, in *Совместный исход*, 864–65; see also MDB, 269–70. Locations of specific quotations are given in the notes below.

105. Howls and selling victory quotation in "Gespräch des Bundeskanzlers Kohl mit Präsident Gorbatschow, 15. Juli 1990," DESE 1344; member of NATO and territory quotations, DESE 1346.

106. "Delegationsgespräch des Bundeskanzlers Kohl mit Präsident Gorbatschow, Moskau, 15. Juli 1990," DESE 1354.

107. Von Arnim, *Zeitnot*, 386.

108. "Gespräch des Bundeskanzlers Kohl mit Präsident Gorbatschow im erweiterten Kreis, Archys/Bezirk Stawropol, 16. Juli 1990," DESE 1361; "Из беседы М.С. Горбачева с Г. Колем," July 16, 1990, МГ 516. If Moscow's forces had stayed ten years after autumn 1990, they would still have been in Germany in the fall of 2000—after Vladimir Putin had become president.

109. See the diary entries in *Совместный исход*, 864–65; MDB, 269–70.

110. The West German foreign minister also seemed concerned that Gorbachev was still clutching at the straw of Bush's rhetorical flourish that Germany might choose not to join the Atlantic Alliance after unification; in the interest of clarity, Genscher stated explicitly that a united Germany would be part of NATO; "Gespräch des Bundeskanzlers Kohl mit Präsident Gorbatschow im erweiterten Kreis, Archys/Bezirk Stawropol, 16. Juli 1990," DESE 1357; "Из беседы М.С. Горбачева с Г. Колем," July 16, 1990, МГ 510.

111. In addition to the meeting transcripts cited above, see Kohl, *Erinnerungen 1990–1994*, 175–83. This figure would eventually be codified in an annex to the CFE treaty. See "Rede des Bundesministers des Auswärtigen, Genscher, vor dem VKSE-Plenum in Wien am 30. August 1990 (Auszüge)," APBD-49–94, 687; Falkenrath, *Shaping Europe's Military Order*, 74–75.

112. See, for example, the television coverage of "Im Brennpunkt," Video, July 17, 1990, KASPA. Gorbachev had hesitations about the written results of Arkhyz; in response to Genscher's call for a clear written statement that a united Germany would be in NATO, Gorbachev responded that he "wünscht, daß die NATO nicht ausdrücklich erwähnt wird." The reason for his preference was not entirely clear; perhaps he wanted to ensure that domestic enemies did not have written evidence of his concessions—or perhaps he wanted to keep open the possibility for changes later. This preference would, however, leave his successors empty-handed when they later looked for written accords on NATO; "Gespräch des Bundeskanzlers Kohl mit Präsident Gorbatschow im erweiterten Kreis, Archys/Bezirk Stawropol, 16. Juli 1990," DESE 1357; "Из беседы М.С. Горбачева с Г. Колем," July 16, 1990, МГ 510.

113. Telcon, Bush–Kohl, July 17, 1990, my 2008-0608-MR, BPL; "Stavrapallo" in Stent, *Russia*, 137.

114. As reported by the Austrian ambassador in Moscow; "Bericht: Erste Wertung des Kohl-Besuchs in Moskau, 17.7.1990," ÖDF 656–67. West German commentators also noted that Soviet media only reported on the event "'mit auffäligem Verzug'": see "Drahtbericht des Botschafters von Ploetz, Brüssel (NATO)," July 18, 1990, DE622n6; this document also contains a summary of what was agreed at Arkhyz, useful because, as discussed above, there was little in writing. After Arkhyz, there were also disputes between West and East German leaders about next steps. For example, at the two-plus-four meeting immediately afterward, East German foreign minister Markus Meckel called for a prohibition on *all* nuclear weapons and on foreign troops in *all* of united Germany (not just eastern Germany); "Presseerklärung des Außenministers Meckel, z. Z. Paris," July 17, 1990, DE 614–15; see also "Erklärung des Außeniministers der DDR auf dem 2+4-Ministertreffen am 17.7.90 in Paris" (preparatory paper), July 16, 1990, ZR 3269–94, MfAA, PA-AA. On differences between Meckel and his Western colleagues, see Ritter, *Der Preis*, 45–46.

115. "Rage" from Falin, *Konflikte*, 204. I thank Norman Naimark for the second and third Falin quotations, which come from Falin Collection, box 1, 29, HIA. Another advisor also thought that Gorbachev was behaving like an emperor; see Boldin, *Ten Years*.

116. Falin, *Konflikte*, 199; see also Stent, *Russia*, 135.

117. On the West Germans' realization that the conversations in Moscow and Arkhyz had not, contrary to their expectations, resolved all matters of importance, and that there were more than just details to sort out, see GDE, 4:593; see also AAP-90, 1068–80.

118. See the account of West German negotiator Martin Ney in Dufourcq, *Retour*, 255.

119. "Vermerk des Dg 20, MDg Hofstetter, Bonn, 22.08.1990, Sprechzettel, Betr.: Gespräch BM mit BM Waigel am 23.08.1990," DE unpub; "To: The Secretary, From: EUR–James F. Dobbins, Acting; Subject: August 23 One-Plus-Three Political Directors Meeting in London," n.d., my 2008-0705-MR, BPL. On Soviet negotiators openly trying to undermine these negotiations, as at least one Soviet diplomat confided in his West German counterparts, see "Vorlage des Leiters der Unterabteilung 20, Hofstetter, für Bundesminister Genscher . . . Verhandlungen in Moskau 24./25.08.1990," August 27, 1990, DE 672.

120. For discussion of some of the considerations going into scheduling, see "Telefongespräch des Bundesministers Genscher mit dem sowjetischen Außenminister Schewardnadse," August 7, 1990, DE 645; "Beschluß der Volkskammer," August 23, 1990, DESE 1498; see also Zelikow and Rice, *Germany Unified*, 351. Kohl was particularly eager to add East German voters for the national election because, in contrast to the chancellor's

success in the GDR election of March 1990, West German state elections in May 1990 had not gone well for the CDU: for details of the state elections, see AAP-90, 597n2.

121. For details of some of the demands directed at the West Germans, see "Aufzeichnung des Vier-Augen-Gesprächs zwischen Bundesminister Genscher (BM) und dem sojwetischen Außenminister Schewardnadse (SAM) am 17. August 1990 in Moskau," in Hilger, *Diplomatie*, 224–25.

122. For discussion of the tension between the Soviet foreign minister and the Soviet military already arising in April 1990, see "Gespräch des Ministerialdirektors Teltschik mit dem stellvertretenden Außenminister Kwizinskij, Bonn, 28. August 1990," DESE 1505; see also AAP-90, 1222. To Bush directly, Shevardnadze also described the pressure that he and Gorbachev faced from "conservative elements": Memcon, Bush–Shevardnadze, April 6, 1990, 11:50am–12:20pm EST, 2009-1024-MR, BPL (this was a smaller meeting, separate from the larger session with delegations at 10:00 a.m. the same day; at the time of writing, the earlier meeting was posted on BPL online, but the later one was not).

123. For a useful collection of primary documents on the US response to the invasion, see EBB-720, NSA. See also Engel, *When the World*, 376–94; Bozo, *History of the Iraq Crisis*, 25.

124. From August 1990 onward, Bush's communications with Gorbachev and Kohl would often prioritize Iraq rather than Europe. See, for example, "Telefongespräch des Bundeskanzlers Kohl mit Präsident Bush, 22. August 1990," DESE 1484–86.

125. Stent, *Russia*, 145. For documents on the Gulf War illicitly taken from the Gorbachev Foundation Archive, see Stroilov, *Behind the Desert Storm*.

126. Žantovský, *Havel*, 359.

127. Memorandum for Brent Scowcroft, from Robert L. Hutchings, "Military Exchanges with Eastern Europe," August 16, 1990, stamped "Nat Sec Advisor has seen," Hutchings files, CF01502-002, BPL. See also Liviu Horovitz, "The George H. W. Bush Administration's Policies vis-à-vis Central Europe," OD 78.

128. On Mitterrand's vision, which got as far as a conference in June 1991 before fading, see Bozo, "Failure."

129. Appendix to previously cited "Military Exchanges with Eastern Europe," August 16, 1990, "Draft: Military-to-Military Contacts with Eastern Europe," n.d. A related and more pressing question was how, exactly, East Germany would depart from the Warsaw Pact, which still existed in name. A solution was found whereby the GDR would ask the other states in the pact to end its membership; "Außenpolitische Sonderinformation des MfAA," September 11, 1990, DE 696n1.

130. Memorandum for Brent Scowcroft, from Robert Hutchings, August 27, 1990, "German Unification: New Problem at End-Game," my 2008-0816-MR, BPL.

131. According to Genscher; AIW Genscher, transcript and recording in SMML.
132. "German Unification: New Problem at End-Game," August 27, 1990. The language that the West Germans proposed was, according to Hutchings, as follows: Non-German forces "'shall not cross a line which shall correspond to the present intra-German border between the FRG and GDR except for movements . . . to and from Berlin.'" Hutchings followed up with another warning on September 5, 1990, that the issue was still not resolved: "we may well lose the fight over the passage [in the treaty] that would prohibit US, British, and French forces from 'crossing the line' into current GDR territory after unification." Memorandum for Brent Scowcroft, from Robert Hutchings, "Telephone Call from Chancellor Kohl of the Federal Republic of Germany, September 6, 1990," September 5, 1990 (preparatory document), my 2008-0690-MR, BPL.
133. "Two Plus Four: State of Play in Preparation for Ministerial Meeting in Moscow," September 6, 1990, PREM-19-3002_73.jpg, PRO-NA; Zelikow and Rice, *Germany Unified*, 357–63, especially 358.
134. Message from US ambassador in SDC 1990-Bonn-27370, "FRG-GDR Unification Treaty—Recommendation for High-Level Message to the FRG," n.d., but with handwritten date and time "8/29/90 1730" at top, in my 2008-0716-MR, BPL; Hutchings wrote by hand at the top, "Brent—This is among the problems I identified . . . Bob Zoellick called his FRG counterpart today and hopes for a shift in the German position. If none is forthcoming, we will recommend that the President send a privacy channel message to Kohl to try to set things right.—Bob Hutchings." Scowcroft noted by hand in reply, "Keep me posted. B." On Baker's August 16, 1990, letter to Genscher, and fear of this debate becoming public, see GDE, 4:591–92. See also "The right of precence [*sic*]: The Convention on the Presence of Foreign Forces in the Federal Republic of Germany of 1954" on the German foreign ministry website, https://www.auswaertiges-amt.de/en/aussenpolitik/themen/internatrecht/-/231364, which explains how the specific "rights and duties" of foreign NATO forces in Germany under the Convention on Presence had been set out in a Status of Forces Agreement (SOFA) of June 19, 1951, and a SOFA Supplementary Agreement (SA) of August 3, 1959. The foreign ministry website provides the legal details of how the issue was eventually resolved (also given in summary fashion in the main text): While the SOFA and SA did not extend over East German territory (in other words, East German territory was officially "excluded from the application of both"), the German government would decide "in each individual case whether to grant the armed forces of the sending states the right of temporary presence" on former East Germany territory, and that grant would be in accord with the provisions of the Cold War accords. The foreign ministry added that while the "open-ended Convention remains effective following the conclusion of the Two plus Four Treaty . . . [it] can

now be terminated by giving two year's notice," pursuant to a relevant "Exchange of Notes of 25 September 1990." For internal West German thinking, see AAP-90, 1023–25.

135. Washington sent "repeated demarches up to and including a letter from Jim Baker to Genscher" to Bonn, according to "For: The President, From: Brent Scowcroft, Subject: Telephone call from Chancellor Kohl, Federal Republic of Germany, Date: September 6, 1990," September 5, 1990 (preparatory paper, with appendix "Points to be Made for Telephone Call from Chancellor Kohl"), my 2008-0690-MR, BPL. The US ambassador in Bonn also informed Teltschik of American displeasure; see "Schreiben des Ministerialdirektors Teltschik an Staatssekretär Sudhoff, Bonn, 30. August 1990," DESE 1515.

136. SDC 1990-State-297622, "Secretary's Letter to Genscher: Bilateral Issue," September 5, 1990, my 2008-0716-MR, BPL; "Schreiben BM Genscher an amerik. AM Baker," August 31, 1990, DE unpub; GDE, 4:591–93. See also "Vorlage des Leiters der Rechtsabteilung, Oesterhelt, an Bundesminister Genscher . . . Stationierungsverhandlungen mit den westlichen Verbündeten," September 18, 1990, DE 722–25, esp. 722n1, which talks about how the united Germany sought "ein Kündigungsrecht" to the "Aufenthaltsvertrag" for Western forces. For fuller explanation of the final result—which included the right to cancel sought by the Germans—see "The right of precence [*sic*]" on the German foreign ministry website, cited above in note 134.

137. Quotations in "For: The President, From: Brent Scowcroft, Subject: Telephone Call from Chancellor Kohl," September 5, 1990. Considering that Washington had "asked nothing of Kohl for many months," Scowcroft recommended "that you seek his agreement" to undo these concessions to Moscow. In the appendix, Scowcroft also advised Bush to decline to attend the October 3 German unity celebration by saying the following to Kohl: "I appreciate the invitation, but my schedule is simply impossible at that time. I don't see how I could possibly make it, despite the historic nature of the event. But I will be celebrating with you in spirit." Hutchings's concern expressed in Memorandum for Brent Scowcroft, From: Robert L. Hutchings, "Subject: Telephone Call from Chancellor Kohl of the Federal Republic of Germany, September 6, 1990," September 5, 1990. See also Küsters, "Einführung," DESE 224.

138. Telcon, Bush–Kohl, September 6, 1990, BPL online.

139. Quotation in Telcon, Bush–Kohl, September 6, 1990, BPL online; see also Zelikow and Rice, *Germany Unified*, 351. For broader context, see Adomeit, *Imperial Overstretch*.

140. "DB Nr. 3551/3552 des Gesandten Heyken, Moskau, an AA, Betr.: dt-sowjetische Verhandlungen am 30./31.08.," September 1, 1990, B 63 (Ref. 421); Bd. 163593, DE unpub.

141. "Schreiben des Bundesministers Waigel an Bundeskanzler Kohl, Bonn, 6. September 1990," DESE 1525; see also AAP-90, 1233–34.

142. "Telefongespräch des Bundeskanzlers Kohl mit Präsident Gorbatschow, 7. September 1990," DESE 1529. The German notetaker recorded Gorbachev as saying, "es komme ihm [Gorbachev] vor, als sei er in eine Falle geraten." The Russian version, "Телефонный разговор М.С. Горбачева с Г. Колем, 7 сентября 1990 года," МГ 557–58, reports Gorbachev as saying "we," rather than "he," fell into a "political trap"; see also MGDF 516.

143. "Message from the President to Chancellor Kohl of West Germany via White House Privacy Channels," n.d., but from content circa September 8 or 9, 1990, in my 2008-0691-MR, BPL; see also "Vorlage des V.L. I Kaestner an Ministerialdirektor Teltschik," September 10, 1990, DESE 1538, describing how Scowcroft called on September 8, 1990, at 4:45pm from Helsinki to ask that a message about US worries be given to Teltschik. Scowcroft worried that what the Germans were doing "könnte Fragen nach der vollen NATO-Mitgliedschaft des vereinten Deutschlands aufwerfen."

144. Memcon, Bush–Gorbachev, September 9, 1990, BPL online.

145. As Zelikow and Rice later recalled, the West Germans made no "serious analysis" of how this funding "would help perestroika. That, for Kohl, was not the point." Instead, his primary motive was "political—the need to make powerful symbolic gestures"; Zelikow and Rice, *Germany Unified*, 326.

146. For more detailed analysis of these phone calls, see Sarotte, *1989*, 191–93. See also Adomeit, *Imperial Overstretch*; Küsters, "Einführung," DESE 226–27.

147. Letter from Mr Weston to Sir C. Mallaby (Bonn), Personal and Confidential, FCO, September 17, 1990, DBPO 467.

148. "FCO to Sir R. Braithwaite (Moscow) . . . for Weston and Secretary of State's Party," September 11, 1990, DBPO 464.

149. This status continues to this day; see Dufourcq, *Retour*, 254.

150. The French were not as concerned as the Americans and British, and served as mediators between them and the West Germans; see Bozo, *Mitterrand*, 292–93.

151. "Military Exchanges with Eastern Europe," August 16, 1990; Sarotte, *1989*, 174–75, 192.

152. Letter from Mr Weston to Sir C. Mallaby (Bonn), September 17, 1990, DBPO 468.

153. Zoellick quoted and paraphrased in Letter from Mr Weston, September 17, 1990, DBPO, 468.

154. "Gespräch BM Genscher mit AM Schewardnadse in Moskau am 11.09.90 (19–21.00h)," September 14, 1990, in Hilger, *Diplomatie*, 253–55. In the original, after the two agreed on the wording of the agreement, Genscher said, "er werde das in der Sitzung der AM [Außenminister] sagen." The Soviet foreign minister asked, "ob eine solche Erklärung notwendig sei (förmlich, zu Protokoll der Verhandlungen)?" Genscher "verneint dies, aber verweist darauf, daß er den gleichen Text benutzen werde, wenn er in der PK [Pressekonferenz] gefragt werde." See also "Sir R. Braithwaite (Moscow) to FCO," September 12, 1990, DBPO, 465.

155. Letter from Mr Weston, September 17, 1990, DBPO 468.

156. Kwizinskij, *Vor dem Sturm*, 61.

157. Genscher's worry summarized in Kwizinskij, *Vor dem Sturm*, 62.

158. AIW Genscher, recording in SMML. Original: "Wir können um Himmels willen nichts mehr riskieren, denn wir wissen nicht, was da in Moskau jetzt plötzlich für eine neue Diskussion aufbrechen würde."

159. Letter from Mr Weston, September 17, 1990, DBPO 469. On the events of that evening, see also Frank Elbe and Martin Ney comments in Dufourcq, *Retour*, 166–67, 253–54; Brinkmann, *NATO-Expansion*, 235–38; GDE 4:594–602; Zelikow and Rice, *Germany Unified*, 361–33.

160. The phrase about neither stationed nor deployed appears in Article 5, paragraph 3 of the final two-plus-four accord; the text about the German government interpreting the meaning of the word *deployed* appears in the agreed minute; the full text of the final accord is available in multiple places and languages; see, for example, the German copy in Presse- und Informationsamt der Bundesregierung, *Die Vereinigung Deutschlands*, 167–73. See also Raymond Seitz's later report on the success of the agreed minute to the NATO allies, "Drahtbericht des Gesandten Bächmann, Brüssel (NATO) . . . 2 + 4-Ministertreffen am 12.09.90 in Moskau," September 14, 1990, DE 717–22.

161. Comments by Robert Zoellick in Dufourcq, *Retour*, 114.

162. For examples of cutting the agreed minute off of the treaty, see the website of the German Historical Institute: http://ghdi.ghi-dc.org/sub_document.cfm?document_id=176; Dufourcq, *Retour*, 76.

163. See the photo of the original treaty with the two full, identical sets of signatures on the German foreign ministry website: https://archiv.diplo.de/arc-de/das-politische-archiv/-/1502282.

164. On the signing ceremony itself, including the unexpected practice (to Eastern eyes) of signers keeping the pens used, see the eyewitness account in Brinkmann, *NATO-Expansion*, 237. When I later asked James Baker about the Russian assertion that they had a commitment from the West not to expand NATO, Baker responded with words to the effect of, if they felt they had a commitment, why did they sign a formal treaty expanding NATO's boundary eastward in September 1990? AIW Baker.

165. "Из беседы М.С. Горбачева с Г-Д. Геншером," September 12, 1990, МГ 572. For more on other speeches at the final session, see "Sept. 12 Two-Plus-Four Ministerial in Moscow: Detailed Account," EBB-613, NSA.

166. "Из беседы с . . . Дж. Бейкером," September 13, 1990, in Горбачев, *Собрание сочинений*, vol. 22, 94–97; see also EBB-720, NSA; Hurd quotations from Hurd, *Memoirs*, 389.

167. Chernyaev diary entry for October 23, 1990, *Совместный исход*, 883–84; see also MDB 274–75.

168. Letter from Mr Weston, September 17, 1990, DBPO 470. See also "JAB's 1-on-1 mtg. w/FRG FM Kinkel @Dept. of State (First JAB-Kinkel mtg.),"

June 30, 1992, folder 5, box 111, series 8, SMML, on replacing Elbe with Chrobog or Kastrup.

169. For earlier Russian discussion about the question of attending October 3 in person, see "Докладная записка А.С. Черняева о предстоящем телефонном разговоре с Г. Колем и возможной поездке в Германию 3 октября," September 10, 1990, МГ 562, where Chernyaev suggested Gorbachev go even if Westerners did not, to get Germans on Moscow's side.

170. The US version, Letter from Kohl to Bush, October 3, 1990, is in my 2008-0783-MR, BPL.

171. The process of unification becoming official included a number of components—and loose ends. On former Soviet nuclear weapons in Germany, see Central Intelligence Agency, "German Military Forces in Eastern Germany after Unification," September 27, 1990, in my 2008-0642-MR, BPL, which noted partly in boldface that the Soviet-German stationing agreement "does not cover Soviet nuclear weapons in eastern Germany. **The Soviets have been withdrawing nuclear weapons from the area but probably will retain at least some nuclear weapons in eastern Germany until the last Soviet troops leave.**" Seeking to prevent such a gradual thinning out (of conventional weapons at least), the Germans tried to specify, in "Zum Vertrag zwischen der Bundesrepublik Deutschland und der UdSSR über die Bedingungen des befristeten Aufenthalts und die Modalitäten des planmäßigen Abzugs der sowjetischen Truppen aus dem Gebiet der Bundesrepublik Deutschland," APBD-49–94, 734, that Soviet forces would remove as complete units with their armaments, that is, "der Abzug erfolgt in ganzen Einheiten unter Mitnahme der gesamten Ausrüstung (also keine 'Ausdünnung')." On other aspects of Soviet troop withdrawal, see "Ortez des Referatsleiters 012, Bettzuege," October 18, 1990, DE 759–62; and three documents in DE unpub: (1) "Vermerk (Sachstand) des Referats 201, Betr.: Dt.-sowjet. Aufenthalts- und Abzugsvertrag," September 21, 1990; (2) "DE Nr. 23 des Dg 42, MDg Dieckmann an D2 Kastrup/LMB, Elbe, z.Z. New York (BM-Delegation), Betr.: dt.-sowjetisches Überleitungsabkommen," September 25, 1990; (3) "StS-Vorlage RL 201, VLR I Dreher, Betr.: Sowjetische Haltung zu offenen Punkten Aufenthalts- und Abzugsvertrag," October 4, 1990. On the status of foreign forces in Germany after unification, see the Auswärtiges Amt website, https://www.auswaertiges-amt.de/en/aussenpolitik/themen/internatrecht/-/231364. On Soviet requests for early payment, see "Vorlage des Ministerialdirektors Teltschik an Bundeskanzler Kohl, Bonn, 25. September 1990," DESE 1550. On the breakdown of German aid, see "Ortez Nr. 74 des Rl 012, VLR I Bettzuege Betr.: Deutsch-sowjetisches Überleitungsabkommen," October 8, 1990, DE unpub, PA-AA. On the surrender of four-power rights (a necessary precursor to unification becoming official), see "Erklärung der Vier Mächte über die Aussetzung ihrer Vorbehaltsrechte über Berlin und Deutschland als Ganzes in New York vom 1. Oktober 1990," APBD-49–94, 715; "Gespräch des D2 Kastrup

mit sowjetischem Botschafter Terechow (= Vermerk des VLR Pauls vom 21.09) Betr.: Erklärung der vier Mächte zur Suspendierung der Vier-Mächte-Rechte am 01.10. in New York," September 21, 1990, DE unpub.

172. "Schreiben des Präsidenten Gorbatschow an Bundeskanzler Kohl, 26. September 1990," DESE 1551. The Soviet Union would, in fact, be the last power to ratify the accord, which did not happen until March 4, 1991. On the topic of how many loose threads there were after September 12, 1990, see Teltschik, *329 Tage*, 7.

173. On Soviet ratifications in March and April 1991, see "Zeittafel," APBD-49–94, 119; see also Stent, *Russia*, 142–44, which details the fight over ratification, with Falin still trying to advance his views, and the Germans adding to the amount they were already paying Moscow.

174. On Shevardnadze's thinking just after the September struggle, see "Выступление Э.А. Шеварднадзе на заседании комитета по международным делам ВС СССР," September 20, 1990, МГ 575–81; on his resignation, see Stent, *Russia*, 143.

175. On these talks, see Action Memorandum for Brent Scowcroft, From: Arnold Kanter/Condoleezza Rice, Subject: Arms Control Talks in Moscow, September 14, 1990; on the same problem, Letter from Gorbachev to Bush, September 17, 1990, both in SSSN, USSR, 91128-003, BPL.

176. Gorbachev comments in Baker, *Politics*, 529; Scowcroft quotations in TOIW Brent Scowcroft, August 10–11, 2000, GBOHP.

177. Letter from Mr Weston, September 17, 1990, DBPO, 470; Ratti, *Not-So-Special*, 326–27.

178. US Department of State, Memorandum from S/P Harvey Sicherman, to S/P–Dennis Ross and C–Robert Zoellick, "A New Europe: Articulating the Common Interest," May 1, 1990, declassified by Sicherman; I thank him for a copy.

4. Oblivion and Opportunity

1. Opening Strauss quotation from "The Bolshevik Goetterdaemmerung: End of Empire and Russian Rebirth," SDC 1991-Moscow-32811, November 15, 1991, 2011-0145-MR, BPL. Strauss remark about himself quoted in McGarr, *Whole Damn Deal*, 431. According to McGarr, Strauss later described his thoughts on arriving in Moscow as follows: "What was I thinking? . . . This is one big, big problem and a big mess that you are ill equipped to deal with by background and training" (445). Strauss relied heavily on James Collins, a career diplomat and Russia expert, in doing his job (445). The pick of Strauss, despite his lack of expertise, had the obvious advantage of signaling to Yeltsin that Bush cared about Russia because he was sending a friend, but a disadvantage in that the post of US ambassador to Russia, previously occupied by Russian expert Jack Matlock, was now in the hands of someone who knew little about the country and was homesick. Matlock had turned the US embassy in the evenings into a salon for pro-reform Rus-

sians, but Strauss preferred to spend his evenings watching videos mailed to him from the United States by friends: "Treasury Secretary Nick Brady sent a three-hour tape of the Breeder's Cup races. Tom Brokaw sent episodes of the legal drama *Matlock*. Legendary producer Ray Stark at Columbia Pictures sent movies, as did Jack Valenti and Lew Wasserman. And Jim Lehrer sent the *MacNeil/Lehrer NewsHour*" (454). For more on Strauss, see the web page of the Robert S. Strauss Center, University of Texas at Austin, https://www.strausscenter.org/robert-s-strauss/. For more on the disintegration of the Soviet Union, see Zubok, *Collapse*.

2. Strauss quotations from "The Bolshevik Goetterdaemmerung." Cheney's and Baker's views summarized by Scowcroft in TOIW Brent Scowcroft, August 10–11, 2000. On Soviet economic collapse, see Miller, *Struggle*, 4–9.

3. Baker quotation from James Baker, "Soviet Points for Meeting with the President," December 10, 1991, folder 8, box 115, series 8, SMML; Scowcroft quotation from TOIW Brent Scowcroft, August 10–11, 2000.

4. Memcon, Bush–Havel, November 18, 1990, BPL online. Undeterred, Havel informed a US Defense Department delegation visiting Prague on April 24–26, 1991, that he saw "two possibilities in the next 10 years: NATO and the EC." Havel said this to a visiting Paul Wolfowitz; see Memcon, Havel–Wolfowitz, April 27, 1991, and "USDP Wolfowitz's Report on the Trip to Prague," n.d., but from context late April 1991, both in EBB-613, NSA.

5. Memcon, Bush–Wałęsa, March 20, 1991, BPL online; see also Stephen Flanagan, "NATO From Liaison to Enlargement," OD 93–110; Stephan Kieninger, "Opening NATO," OD 60.

6. László Póti, "Hungarian-Ukrainian-Russian Triangle," in Balmaceda, *On the Edge*, 128–30.

7. Antall paraphrased in Géza Jeszenszky, "NATO Enlargement," OD 121–22, which also notes that the foreign minister visited NATO in Brussels on June 28–29, 1990, and Antall had "most cordial talks with Wörner at NATO Headquarters on July 17–18, 1990." Póti, "Hungarian-Ukrainian-Russian Triangle," 132, insightfully notes that "the Hungarian government—although it desperately wanted to do so—did not opt for a more radical solution" than making public calls for the dismantling of the Warsaw Pact because, with "Soviet troops still stationed in most member countries," it did not want to provoke a backlash. As Antall complained to Bush in October 1990, there were still two full Soviet divisions in Hungary, "stationed near Budapest—not by accident," and they seemed in no hurry to leave, having "nowhere to go in the Soviet Union" because of a housing shortage. Antall also warned that "tension is high in Czechoslovakia and critical in Yugoslavia. War is possible." Memcon, Bush–Antall, October 18, 1990, BPL online.

8. The analysis of "Eastern Europe and NATO" is on page 3 of the attachment to "Revised NATO Strategy Paper for Discussion at Sub-Ungroup Meeting, October 24," from: EUR James F. Dobbins, Acting, October 22, 1990, EBB-613, NSA.

9. Gates, *From the Shadows*, 493–94; see also Shifrinson, "Eastbound," 819.

10. Memorandum for Robert Gates, From: Philip Zelikow, "Subject: Your Meeting of the European Strategy Steering Group on, Monday, October 29," October 26, 1990, 2000-0233-F, BPL.

11. From State/EUR–James F. Dobbins, Acting, to NSC–Mr. Gompert, "NATO Strategy and Review Paper for October 29 Discussion," October 25, 1990, EBB-613, NSA. See also "USDP Wolfowitz's Report on the Trip to Prague," n.d., from context circa April 1991, EBB-613, NSA; Stephen Flanagan, "NATO from Liaison to Enlargement," OD 98–105; Sayle, *Enduring*, 233, 332n101; Shifrinson, "Eastbound," 825.

12. Cheney's July 1990 comment in "Notes from Jim Cicconi [notetaker] re: 7/3/90 pre-NATO Summit briefing at Kennebunkport," and "Briefing of Pres on NATO summit at Walker's Pt," folder 3, box 109, 8/8c, SMML; Cheney's remark about associate status quoted in Solomon, *NATO*, 10. For more on Cheney, see Mann, *Great Rift*.

13. Bozo, "Failure."

14. As US diplomat William Hill later put it, by the end of 1991 it was clear that the United States "would remain a leading security presence in Europe" and that European security would be "subordinated to NATO"; Hill, *No Place*, 65.

15. Elizabeth Shogren, "Gunman Reportedly Wanted to Kill Gorbachev," *Los Angeles Times*, November 16, 1990.

16. The Hungarian president raised Moscow's proposed security agreements with Bush directly (Memcon, Bush–Göncz, May 23, 1991, BPL online), and Havel reported this development to a visiting Paul Wolfowitz (in Memcon, Havel–Wolfowitz, April 27, 1991, cited above). On the end of pact military activities and abrogation of the military structures of the pact, see Telcon, Bush–Havel, February 26, 1991, BPL online; "Agreement on the Cessation of the Military Provisions of the Warsaw Pact," February 25, 1991, in Mastny and Byrne, eds., *Cardboard Castle*, 682–83.

17. Marten, "Reconsidering," 140–41; Póti, "The Hungarian-Ukrainian-Russian Triangle," 133.

18. Jeszenszky, "NATO Enlargement," OD 122; Asmus, *Opening*, 10; Solomon, *NATO*, 8.

19. See the declaration, titled "Partnership with the Countries of Central and Eastern Europe: Statement Issued by the North Atlantic Council Meeting in Ministerial Session," June 6–7, 1991, https://www.nato.int/cps/ie/natohq/official_texts_23858.htm.

20. Memcon, Quayle–Wörner, July 1, 1991, 2000-0233-F, BPL.

21. Memcon, Bush–Mitterrand, March 14, 1991, BPL online. Mitterrand's guess of twenty was an accurate prediction; between June 1991 and June 1992, twenty new states would in fact appear in Europe as both Yugoslavia and the Soviet Union disintegrated; see also Hill, *No Place*, 68.

22. This sum represented "an enormous burden that slowed productive investment"; Szabo, *Germany*, 6. On top of that, Mitterrand notes that there were

still "nationalist movements in Germany which make it difficult for the Germans to renounce claims in Poland"; Memcon, Bush–Mitterrand, March 14, 1991, BPL online. The chancellor would later offer Moscow an additional $550 million in aid to move its withdrawal date from December to August 31, 1994; see the German federal government website, https://www.bundesregierung.de/breg-de/service/bulletin/besuch-des-bundeskanzlers-in-der-russischen-foederation-vom-14-bis-16-dezember-1992-791660; on Germans becoming cautious about how much they were spending, see Spohr, *Post Wall*, 480; see also Stent, *Russia*, 162.

23. Bozo, "Failure," 409.

24. Memcon, Bush–Mitterrand, March 14, 1991, BPL online.

25. See the discussion of Yugoslavian issues in Telcon, Bush–Kohl, June 24, 1991, BPL online. On the outbreak of war in former Yugoslavia, see Hill, *No Place*, 74–77.

26. Memcon, Bush–Mitterrand, March 14, 1991, BPL online.

27. Kohl made these comments to party colleagues in recounting discussions with Gorbachev and Lithuanian leader Kazimira Prunskienė: "21. Januar 1991," BzL 243. In a similar conversation a month later, he added that "wer also von der Auflösung der Sowjetunion träumt, muß alle nur denkbaren Konsequenzen mitträumen"; "22–23. Februar 1991," BzL 247.

28. Chernyaev diary entry for August 26, 1990, *Совместный исход*, 869; MDB 271; Plokhy, *Last Empire*, 37–40.

29. Bergmane, "'Is This the End of Perestroika?'"; Plokhy, *Last Empire*, 195–96.

30. Memcon, Baker–Shevardnadze, "On the Plane to Jackson Hole, Wyoming," September 21, 1989, 6:30–8:30pm, 2009-1030-MR, BPL; see also Bergmane, "'Is This the End of Perestroika?'"

31. Bush complained to Gorbachev about the violence "and deaths of at least twenty people in the Baltic states"; see Letter, Bush–Gorbachev, January 23, 1991, 2011-0857-MR (504), BPL. See also LSS xxxiii; Plokhy, *Last Empire*, 38.

32. Gorbachev said this to Matlock when the ambassador delivered Bush's complaint; see "From: Jack Matlock, For: General Scowcroft" (on Matlock's meeting with Gorbachev), January 24, 1991, 2011-0857-MR, BPL.

33. He signed on November 9, 1990, the one-year anniversary of the fall of the Wall; "Vertrag über gute Nachbarschaft, Partnerschaft und Zusammenarbeit zwischen der Bundesrepublik Deutschland und der Union der Sozialistischen Sowjetrepubliken vom 9. November 1990," APBD-49-94, 738–44. For an overview of all of the treaties signed, see "Sachstandsvermerk Ref. 213, Betr. Stand Vertragsverhandlungen D und SU," November 12, 1990, DE unpub. Chernyaev had to compose a letter in March 1991 asking for more aid from Germany after Gorbachev could not bring himself to ask for more on the phone with Kohl; the letter leaked and appeared in *Der Spiegel*. See Chernyaev diary entry for March 10, 1991, *Совместный исход*, 927; the *Spiegel* version was "Neue Milliarden aus Bonn?," part of the article "'Geld in die Müllgrube werfen,'" *Der Spiegel*, 23/1991, https://magazin.spiegel.de/EpubDelivery/spiegel/pdf/13487616.

34. Hill, *No Place*, 21–23.
35. On the accords resulting from that summit, see "Gemeinsame Erklärung der 22 Staaten der NATO und der Warschauer Vertragsorganisation in Paris vom 19. November 1990 (Auszug)," and "Die 'Charta von Paris für ein neues Europa,' vom 21. November 1990, Erklärung des Pariser KSZE-Treffens der Staats- und Regierungschefs," APBD-49–94, 755–71.
36. Daryl Kimball and Kingston Reif, "The Conventional Armed Forces in Europe (CFE) Treaty and the Adapted CFE Treaty at a Glance," Arms Control association, August 2017, https://www.armscontrol.org/factsheet/cfe. On CFE, see also Falkenrath, *Shaping*, xv–xvii.
37. This sentence is a paraphrase of Sloan, *Defense of the West*, 108.
38. According to Quentin Peel, "Moscow Report Tells How Thousands of Tanks Avoided CFE Count," *Financial Times*, January 10, 1991, reprinted in Mastny, *Helsinki Process*, 295–96; see also Falkenrath, *Shaping Europe's Military Order*, xv–xvii, 117–19; Zelikow and Rice, *To Build*, 479n74. Secretary of State Warren Christopher later advised President Bill Clinton that Russian military leaders saw CFE as "a bad treaty, a remnant of the Cold War 'imposed' on the old USSR in a moment of Gorbachev's weakness and even more unfair to the new Russia": Memo, Christopher to Clinton, "Your Meeting with Yeltsin in Halifax," June 12, 1995, DS-ERR. On Gorbachev's pushback against Bush administration efforts to end the Soviet Union's development of biological weapons, see Hoffman, *Dead Hand*, 361.
39. Letter, Bush–Gorbachev, October 20, 1990, LSS 762–63; on Gorbachev's support for UNSCR 675 (described on the US State Department website, https://2001-2009.state.gov/p/nea/rls/13456.htm) and his peace initiatives, see also "22–23. Februar 1991," BzL 247–67, and the various documents in EBB-745, NSA.
40. This sentence is a paraphrase from Engel, Lawrence, and Preston, *America in the World*, 335.
41. Engel, *When the World*, 467.
42. LSS xxxiii.
43. For the onset of the war, see the notes about Baker's calls to heads of government and other leaders in folder 9, box 109, series 8, SMML.
44. Bozo, *History of the Iraq Crisis*, 26–27; Bozo, "'We Don't Need You,'" 183–208; LSS xxxiii–xxxiv.
45. TOIW Richard B. Cheney, March 16–17, 2000, Dallas, Texas, GBOHP. The transporters meant the United States could avoid, in Cheney's words, "tearing up the tanks before we ever got to the launch point." In addition to the transporters, Washington had also requested access to former East German tanks, helicopters, and planes "for exercise purposes": AAP-90, 1574–75.
46. Bush and Mulroney comments at the "Opening Session of the London Economic Summit," July 15, 1991, 2:20–5:40pm, BPL online; on Bush's worry

about the biological weapons program, see AIW Zoellick; for context, see also Hoffman, *Dead Hand*.

47. Memcon, Bush–Gorbachev, July 17, 1991, London, BPL online.

48. See Chernyaev's diary entry for July 20, 1991, in *Совместный исход*, 963–65.

49. Chernyaev diary entry for March 20, 1991, in *Совместный исход*, 930.

50. Memorandum for John Helgerson, DDCI, from David Gompert/Ed A. Hewett, April 10, 1991, "The Gorbachev Succession," and Directorate of Intelligence, April 29, 1991, also entitled "The Gorbachev Succession," both in EBB-544, NSA.

51. Memcon, Quayle–Wörner, July 1, 1991, FOIA 2000-0233-F, BPL. Bush heard directly about the Soviet Union's dire straits when Primakov, visiting Washington in May 1991, asked for "large-scale assistance." Despite his worries about Gorbachev's longevity, Bush answered, "we are broke right now, more or less"; Memcon, Bush–Primakov, May 31, 1991, BPL online. See also Letter from Bush to Gorbachev, July 1991 (no exact day given), LSS 845–48; McFaul, *From Cold War*, 23–24.

52. Memcon, Bush–Göncz, May 23, 1991, BPL online. He added that Ukraine would be a particular problem; in Göncz's view, "absolute sovereignty" was probably "not possible for the Ukraine. In the end I think they will form some new confederation. It seems the only way out."

53. See Matlock's account from June 20, 1991, PC.

54. He had won 57 percent of the vote in a field with six candidates on June 12, 1990, and was inaugurated as Russian president on July 10, 1991. David Remnick, "Yeltsin Sworn in as Russian President," *New York Times*, July 11, 1991; Aron, *Yeltsin*, 740; LSS xxxiv.

55. In February 1991; see Aron, *Yeltsin*, 740.

56. Kozyrev, *Firebird*, 8–12. On the banning of the novel, and how the CIA took advantage of it, see Peter Finn and Petra Couvée, "During Cold War, CIA Used 'Doctor Zhivago' as a Tool to Undermine Soviet Union," *Washington Post*, April 5, 2014.

57. Memcon, Bush–Yeltsin, June 20, 1991, BPL online; Maureen Dowd, "Yeltsin Arrives in Washington with Conciliatory Words about Gorbachev," *New York Times*, June 19, 1991; Colton, *Yeltsin*, 189–90.

58. Memcon, Bush–Yeltsin, June 20, 1991, BPL online.

59. Marilyn Berger, "Boris N. Yeltsin, Reformer Who Broke Up the USSR, Dies at 76," *New York Times*, April 24, 2007; Craig Hlavaty, "When Boris Yeltsin Went Grocery Shopping in Clear Lake," *Houston Chronicle*, September 13, 2017.

60. Memcon, Bush–Yeltsin, June 20, 1991, BPL online.

61. "The Bolshevik Goetterdaemmerung," SDC 1991-Moscow-32811, November 15, 1991.

62. Memcon, Bush–Mulroney, August 19, 1991, FOIA 2000-1202-F, BPL online.

63. For news coverage of Yeltsin on the tank, see https://www.youtube.com /watch?v=LsF4co6txHM.

64. Colton, *Yeltsin*, 200.

65. Memcon, Bush–Mulroney, August 19, 1991, BPL online.

66. Memcon, Bush–Mulroney, August 19, 1991, BPL online; Ron Synovitz, "What Happened to the August 1991 Coup Plotters?," RadioFreeEurope/ RadioLiberty, August 19, 2016, https://www.rferl.org/a/what-happened-to -the-august-1991-coup-plotters/27933729.html.

67. Telcon, Bush–Yeltsin, August 21, 1991, 8:30–9:05am, BPL online.

68. As Matlock put it, Gorbachev's "trust in Kryuchkov's loyalty was as complete as it was misplaced"; Matlock, *Autopsy*, 665. For interesting transcripts of interviews with Matlock and other former US ambassadors to the Soviet Union/Russia, see EBB-769, NSA.

69. Kozyrev, *Firebird*, 34. Kozyrev felt it was a mistake to prevent protesters from entering its main buildings (in contrast to East Germany, where they gained entrance to Stasi buildings).

70. Arkady Ostrovsky, "Special Report Russia: Inside the Bear," *The Economist*, October 20, 2016.

71. Telcon, Bush–Yeltsin, August 21, 1991, 8:30–9:05 am, BPL online; Plokhy, *Last Empire*, 118–19.

72. Telcon, Bush–Yeltsin, August 21, 1991, 8:30–9:05 am, BPL online.

73. Kozyrev, *Firebird*, 26–27.

74. Kozyrev, *Firebird*, 36.

75. Telcon, Bush–Yeltsin, August 21, 1991, 8:30–9:05 am, BPL online.

76. TOIW Brent Scowcroft, November 12–13, 1999, GBOHP. See the detailed account of the coup in Plokhy, *Last Empire*, 95–109.

77. Telcon, Bush–Yeltsin, August 21, 1991, 9:20–9:31pm, BPL online; on Akhro- meyev, see "Gorbachev's Top Military Advisor Commits Suicide," AP, Au- gust 25, 1991, https://apnews.com/article/0942b9518f893f69b3560c69ceod e7c2; Plokhy, *Last Empire*, 148.

78. Quoted in Falin, *Politische Erinnerungen*, 477.

79. Bush finally spoke to him on August 21; see Telcon, Bush–Gorbachev, Au- gust 21, 1991, BPL online.

80. Plokhy, *Last Empire*, 143–45; Taubman, *Gorbachev*, 622.

81. Taubman, *Gorbachev*, 622; Colton, *Yeltsin*, 202–3.

82. This is the main argument of "Part III, A Countercoup," in Plokhy, *Last Empire*.

83. Bozo, "Failure," 412.

84. Colton, *Yeltsin*, 203.

85. BST timeline.

86. Memcon, Bush–Mulroney, August 19, 1991, BPL online.

87. Talbott cited in Plokhy, *Last Empire*, 15.

88. The context of this remark was as follows: Prime Minister Major suggested representatives of G7 nations meet to consider an aid package to help

Gorbachev get back on his feet in a letter to Bush; David Gompert and Ed Hewett of the NSC advised Scowcroft to head off such a meeting. See "From Prime Minister, to President Bush," August 22, 1991; and Memorandum for Brent Scowcroft, from David Gompert and Ed A. Hewett, "Message from John Major on the USSR," August 22, 1991, both in Burns Files, FOIA 2000-1202-F, BPL.

89. Memcon, Bush–Mulroney, August 19, 1991, BPL online.
90. Ashton B. Carter, "Statement before the Defense Policy Panel, House Armed Services Committee," December 13, 1991, Fax from Ashton Carter to General John Gordon on December 13, 1991, FOIA 2000-1202-F, BPL. A 2012 Harvard report raised the estimated number of Soviet nuclear weapons in late 1991 to 35,000, many aimed at US territory. See Graham Allison, "What Happened to Soviet Arsenals," Discussion Paper No. 2012-04, March 2012, Belfer Center for Science and International Affairs, Harvard University.
91. "30. August 1991," BzL 298–300; Budjeryn, "Power," 207.
92. Allison, "What Happened."
93. Thomas L. Neff, "A Grand Uranium Bargain," *New York Times*, October 24, 1991.
94. "The USSR Two Weeks after the Failed Coup," SDC 1991-Moscow-25359, September 6, 1991, FOIA 2000-0233-F, BPL.
95. Baker and Strauss quoted in McGarr, *Whole Damn Deal*, 450. Strauss had returned to the United States in late August 1991, but then traveled back to Moscow with Baker by plane in September; the two men reportedly had this exchange during the car ride from the airport into town. According to McGarr, the date of this exchange was September 10, which she describes as the day before Baker met with Gorbachev; this date is consistent with documents showing a meeting between Baker and Gorbachev on September 11 (see below).
96. "Из беседы с Джеймсом Бейкером, Москва," September 11, 1991, Овв 288–90.
97. See the documents setting up this September 12, 1991, dinner in folder 7, box 110, series 8, SMML.
98. Baker, *Politics*, 559.
99. Robert Zoellick informed the French of this development in a letter to Anne Lauvergeon, October 7, 1991, 5 AG 4/CDM 48, AN.
100. Goldgeier and McFaul, *Power*, 69.
101. "JAB Notes from 10/2/91 mtg. w/Gen. Scowcroft, Sec. Cheney, The White House," folder 8, box 110, series 8, SMML. See also Bush's comments to the visiting Danish prime minister, Poul Schlueter, in Memcon, Bush–Schlueter, October 16, 1991, BPL online.
102. SDC 1991-Moscow-28682, October 7, 1991, EBB-561, NSA.
103. AIW Kozyrev.
104. Hoffman, *Dead Hand*, 379–80; AIW Nunn.

105. Plokhy, *Last Empire*, 81.
106. It authorized the appropriation of $500 million from the Department of Defense budget for fiscal year 1992 for dismantling Soviet nuclear and chemical weapons and for humanitarian assistance: BST timeline. See also Hoffman, *Dead Hand*, 384–87; Statement by Senator Nunn, Congressional Record, Soviet Defense Conversion and Demilitarization, November 13, 1991, https://nsarchive2.gwu.edu//NSAEBB/NSAEBB447/1991-11-13%20 Statement%20by%20Senator%20Nunn,%20Congressional%20Rec ord,%20Soviet%20Defense%20Conversion%20and%20Demilitarization .PDF.
107. For more on the US strategy of inhibiting the spread of nuclear weapons, see Gavin, "Strategies of Inhibition."
108. Scowcroft quotation, and Scowcroft paraphrase of Cheney, in TOIW Brent Scowcroft, August 10–11, 2000, GBOHP; number of tactical weapons in Allison, "What Happened"; Allison, *Nuclear Terrorism*, 43–49. See also Amy F. Woolf, "Nonstrategic Nuclear Weapons," updated March 16, 2021, Congressional Research Service 7-5700, https://crsreports.congress.gov /product/pdf/RL/RL32572.
109. Quotations from Bush and Scowcroft, *World Transformed*, 541–44. Since quotations elsewhere in their joint memoir match the declassified fuller documents of other relevant conversations, it is a reasonable assumption that their quotations from this event are accurate as well. Scowcroft recalls that, among Bush's top advisors, he was the "least worried" about the breakup of the Soviet nuclear arsenal: "anything which would serve to dilute the size of an attack we might have to face was, in my view, a benefit well worth the deterioration of unified control over the weapons" (544). On US nuclear strategy after the end of the Cold War, see also Leffler, *Safeguarding*, 257–65.
110. Cheney's views quoted and summarized in Bush and Scowcroft, *World Transformed*, 541; see also Plokhy, *Last Empire*, 199.
111. That arsenal consisted of an estimated 2,883 tactical nuclear weapons, 44 strategic long-range bombers, 176 ICBMs, and at least 1,240 strategic nuclear warheads, probably many more: Sinovets and Budjeryn, "Interpreting," 2; see also Allison, "What Happened"; Budjeryn, "Power," 203.
112. Quoted in Baker, *Politics*, 560; see also Bush and Scowcroft, *World Transformed*, 540–42; and Plokhy, *Last Empire*, 262.
113. Bush signed it on July 31, 1991, in Moscow; see BST timeline.
114. On the "Chicken Kiev" speech, see Goldgeier and McFaul, *Power*, 28–29; Plokhy, *Last Empire*, 47–96; LSS xxxiv.
115. Memcon, Bush–Kravchuk, September 25, 1991, BPL online. Even though there was a question mark over the Ukrainian declaration of independence pending the referendum, that declaration was still a profound shock for Moscow. It was one thing for the Baltics but quite another for a large Slavic republic such as Ukraine to take such a step; Plokhy, *Last Empire*, 168–70. See also Budjeryn, "Power," 210–11.

116. Memcon, Bush–Kravchuk, September 25, 1991, BPL online; Plokhy, *Last Empire*, 206–7.

117. Bush and Scowcroft, *World Transformed*, 545; on Cheney, see Leffler, *Safeguarding*, 261–65.

118. Telcon, Scowcroft–Wörner, September 27, 1991, 2000-0233-F, BPL. Wörner also asked whether TASM (presumably the Tactical Air-to-Surface Missile) was canceled as well. Scowcroft responded in the affirmative, saying, "we are dropping TASM. It is a terrible program."

119. He also announced "the cancellation of the short-range attack missile," or SRAM, and terminated "the development of mobile basing modes for ICBMs," meaning "both the MIRVed Peacekeeper and the single warhead small ICBM." See "JAB notes from 9/27/91 mtgs. w/UK, France, Germany," on "POTUS Speech on Defense Strategy," Waldorf Astoria Hotel, New York, folder 7, box 110, series 8, SMML. See also Secretary of Defense, Memorandum for Chairman of the Joint Chiefs of Staff et al., "Reducing the United States Nuclear Arsenal," September 28, 1991, EBB-561, NSA, which stated that "pursuant to the President's direction to me, I direct accomplishment of the following as soon as possible," and then listed the specific arms control measures in detail.

120. For a summary of the consequences of that televised announcement, see Woolf, "Nonstrategic Nuclear Weapons."

121. Telcon, Bush–Gorbachev, September 27, 1991, BPL online. For more on the details of Bush's announcement, see Daryl Kimball and Kingston Reif, "The Presidential Nuclear Initiatives (PNIs) on Tactical Nuclear Weapons at a Glance," Arms Control Association, https://www.armscontrol.org/factsheets/pniglance.

122. Telcon, Bush–Yeltsin, September 27, 1991, BPL online. Bush also called Kohl, Major, Mitterrand, and Wörner the same day; all memcons, BPL online. For the televised announcement, see https://www.youtube.com/watch?v=v7h3Razthco. On further nuclear initiatives in Bush's 1992 State of the Union address, see Baker, *Politics*, 658–59.

123. Telcon, Bush–Gorbachev, October 5, 1991, BPL online; Hoffman, *Dead Hand*, 383–84; Kieninger, "Opening NATO," OD 61; Plokhy, *Last Empire*, 209–11.

124. Woolf, "Nonstrategic Nuclear Weapons," 13–14. Gorbachev was unable to get the Soviet minister of defense, Yevgeny Shaposhnikov, to agree to liquidating nuclear bombers, however, in part because the minister was a former aviator himself. Shaposhnikov did concede, as Chernyaev later recalled, that "our TU-160 [Soviet aircraft] are flying coffins" because "if, God willing, they manage to get to the coast of the United States or Canada, it would be only be to drop the bombs. Getting back—that's another question!" Chernyaev diary entry for October 6, 1991, in Совместный исход, 994; translation as published in EBB-345, NSA.

125. "Scene Setter for Meeting with President Gorbachev," n.d., but from context late October 1991, LSS 936–37.

126. Brent Scowcroft, "Meeting with SYG Manfred Wörner" (preparatory paper), October 11, 1991, CF01526, FOIA 2000-0233-F, Barry Lowenkron files, BPL. Quotations from the year 2000 in TOIW Brent Scowcroft, August 10–11, 2000, GBOHP.

127. Memcon, Bush–Havel, October 22, 1991, BPL online.

128. Brent Scowcroft, "Meeting with SYG Manfred Wörner," October 11, 1991. Instead, Scowcroft suggested enhancing liaison programs between NATO and former Warsaw Pact states.

129. Memcon, Bush–Wörner, October 11, 1991, BPL online.

130. The key aides developing this idea were Frank Elbe and Robert Zoellick; AIW Zoellick. See also Flanagan, "NATO from Liaison to Enlargement," OD 102; and Solomon, *NATO*, 13, which dates the conception of the idea to October 2, 1991.

131. "NATO Liaison: General Principles for Development," n.d. I thank Flanagan for a copy of this declassified document.

132. Bozo, *Mitterrand*, 382.

133. Memcon, Bush–Wörner, October 11, 1991, BPL online.

134. SDC 1991-USNATO-04913, October 26, 1991, Lowenkron files, 2000-233-F, BPL. For more on the NACC, see Baker, *Politics*, 584; Kieninger, "Opening NATO," OD 61–65; Solomon, *NATO*, 15; and the information on the NATO website, https://www.nato.int/cps/en/natolive/topics_69344.htm.

135. Population statistics in 1990–91: Ukraine, https://www.worldometers.info /world-population/ukraine-population/; Britain, https://countryeconomy .com/demography/population/uk?year=1991; France, https://www.population pyramid.net/france/1991/.

136. For more on Ukrainian history in the context of both Russian and European history, see Plokhy, *Gates*, in which Plokhy refers to Ukraine as the "gates of Europe," but the years 1991–92 might arguably have allowed for redefining European boundaries to include Ukraine rather than keeping it on the perimeter. See also Reiss, *Bridled Ambition*, 90–92.

137. "The Bolshevik Goetterdaemmerung," SDC 1991-Moscow-32811, November 15, 1991.

138. On Gorbachev's background, see Plokhy, *Last Empire*, 258.

139. Gorbachev said they did this "only because the Bolsheviks did not have a majority in the Rada": "Record of the Dinner Conversation between Gorbachev, Bush, Gonzalez, and King Juan Carlos of Spain," October 29, 1991, EBB-576, NSA.

140. Quotation from "Draft Options Paper, US Relations with Russia and Ukraine," n.d., but attached to Memorandum for Brent Scowcroft, From Nicholas Burns, "Your Meeting or Phone Discussions on November 25 with Secretaries Baker and Cheney and General Powell Concerning US Policy Toward Russia and Ukraine," November 22, 1991, Burns files, CF01498-007, FOIA 2000-1202-F, BPL.

141. "Our concern is the weapons," he told Yakovlev; see Memcon, Bush–Yakovlev, November 19, 1991, BPL online. The 25 percent statistic comes

from "Nuclear Weapons in the Non-Russian Republics and Baltic States," Defense Intelligence Brief, October 1991 [no specific date], EBB-691, NSA.

142. Memcon, Bush–Yakovlev, November 19, 1991. On Ukrainian-Russian hostility, see also Kostenko, *Ukraine's Nuclear Disarmament*, 24.

143. "The Bolshevik Goetterdaemmerung," SDC 1991-Moscow-32811, November 15, 1991.

144. Unofficial Translation of Letter, Yeltsin–Bush, no typed date but handwritten at top "Handed to Pres by Russian FM Kozyrev during 11-26-91 mtg," SSSN 91130-001, BPL.

145. Baker and Genscher quoted in Kieninger, "Opening NATO," OD 61–62; Frank T. Csongos, "Baker Sees Trans-Atlantic Community with Former Soviet Bloc," UPI, June 18, 1991, https://www.upi.com/Archives/1991/06/18 /Baker-sees-trans-Atlantic-community-with-former-Soviet-bloc /7164677217600/.

146. "Handed to Pres by Russian FM Kozyrev during 11-26-91 mtg."

147. Telcon, Bush–Yeltsin, November 30, 1991, BPL online; lower-case letters in original.

148. Telcon, Bush–Yeltsin, November 30, 1991, BPL online; Plokhy, *Last Empire*, 230 (ark), 292–93 (December 1 referendum), 387 (quitting the empire). For more on Russia's status within the Soviet Union, see Hosking, *Rulers and Victims*. For a different view which downplays the significance of Ukrainian independence on Soviet collapse, see Zubok, *Collapse*.

149. Telcon, Bush–Kravchuk, December 3, 1991, BPL online; see also Plokhy, *Last Empire*, 304.

150. William C. Potter, "Ukraine as a Nuclear Power," *Wall Street Journal*, December 4, 1991; on the US recognition of Ukraine, see US State Department, Office of the Historian, "A Guide to the United States' History of Recognition, Diplomatic, and Consular Relations, by Country, since 1776: Ukraine," https://history.state.gov/countries/ukraine. For more context, see Shields and Potter, *Dismantling*.

151. For more on the NPT, see Budjeryn, "Power," 203–37; Lever, "Cold War," 501–13.

152. Potter, "Ukraine as a Nuclear Power"; on US recognition of Ukraine, formally granted on December 25, 1991, see "A Guide to the United States' History of Recognition, Diplomatic, and Consular Relations, by Country, since 1776: Ukraine," https://history.state.gov/countries/ukraine.

153. For some key dates in this process, see LSS xxxiii–xxxiv.

154. Plokhy, *Last Empire*, 304–5.

155. BST timeline; the Belarusian spelling of the leader's first name is Stanislau.

156. Telcon, Bush–Yeltsin, December 8, 1991, BPL online; Kozyrev, *Firebird*, 45–53; Plokhy, *Last Empire*, 300–310.

157. Plokhy, *Last Empire*, 309–10. The Transcaucasian Federation had also helped to found the USSR in 1922, but Yeltsin and his two colleagues decided that, since that entity had ceased to exist, they could proceed on their own. For a timeline on the formation and collapse of the Soviet Union, see the BBC's

https://www.bbc.com/news/world-europe-17858981. Putin later criticized this sequence of events. See "Address by President of the Russian Federation," March 18, 2014, official website, http://en.kremlin.ru/events/president /news/20603, where Putin remarked, "we have to admit that by launching the sovereignty parade Russia itself aided in the collapse of the Soviet Union. And as this collapse was legalized, everyone forgot about Crimea and Sevastopol—the main base of the Black Sea Fleet. Millions of people went to bed in one country and awoke in different ones, overnight becoming ethnic minorities in former Union republics, while the Russian nation became one of the biggest, if not the biggest ethnic group in the world to be divided by borders."

158. Telcon, Bush–Yeltsin, December 8, 1991, BPL online.

159. Plokhy, *Last Empire*, 314–27; Telcon, Bush–Gorbachev, December 13, 1991, BPL online.

160. He added: "We will not have the position of President of the Commonwealth. We will all be equals. The all-union Soviet organs will be moved to Russia"; Telcon, Bush–Yeltsin, December 13, 1991, BPL online.

161. James Baker, "Soviet Points for Meeting with the President," December 10, 1991, folder 8, box 115, series 8, SMML; Scowcroft quotation in TOIW Brent Scowcroft, August 10–11, 2000, GBOHP.

162. This program was later renamed the Cooperative Threat Reduction (CTR), also known as the Nunn-Lugar program. For more on its history, dating back to a failed effort by Congressman Les Aspin to take $1 billion from the defense budget to provide aid to the USSR, followed by an autumn 1991 effort by Senators Nunn and Lugar to insert $500 million into a Senate-House reconciliation of the defense budget authorization bill (without Bush administration support), see Allison and Zelikow, *Essence*, 281–82; Goldgeier and Saunders, "Unconstrained," 144–56; Goldgeier and McFaul, *Power*, 51; BST timeline; and the Lugar Center's posting, http://www.thelugarcenter .org/blog-The-New-U-S-Russia-Nunn-Lugar-CTR-Agreement.

163. Baker quoted in Thomas L. Friedman, "Soviet Disarray: Baker Presents Steps to Aid Transition by Soviets," *New York Times*, December 13, 1991; see also BST timeline. For some of the thinking behind the aid conference, also at times called the donor conference, see the document reprinted in Zelikow and Rice, *To Build*, 411; on the "vision of American global engagement," see James Traub, "The Coming Crisis in International Affairs," *New York Times*, September 27, 2019.

164. Planning (and some initial deliveries) for what became Operation Provide Hope started immediately and, in February 1992, American C-141 and C-5A cargo planes began taking off from Rhein-Main in Germany bearing roughly $60 million worth of supplies left over from the Gulf War: food, medicine, and medical equipment. Thomas L. Friedman, "As Food Airlift Starts, Baker Hints US Might Agree to Role in a Ruble Fund," *New York Times*, February 11, 1992.

165. Goldgeier and McFaul, *Power*, 77–78.
166. BST timeline; Friedman, "Soviet Disarray."
167. Baker, *Politics*, 564.
168. "JAB Core Points Used during Trip to Moscow, Bishkek, Alma Ata, Minsk & Kiev, 12/15-18/91," and "Core Checklist for Republic Leaders," December 15, 1991, folder 10, box 110, series 8, SMML.
169. The United States would implement humanitarian assistance, but only if the countries would "provide us with a list of city and oblast official and voluntary organizations in your republic who can serve as the point of contact"; "Core Checklist for Republic Leaders," December 15, 1991.
170. "Security Issues Checklist," n.d., but from context December 1991, folder 10, box 110, series 8, SMML.
171. "Core Checklist for Republic Leaders," December 15, 1991.
172. Baker's conversation with Gorbachev highlighted to Baker the fact that a separate Ukrainian army would be 470,000 strong, larger by about 100,000 than the German military; "Record of Conversation between Gorbachev and Baker," December 16, 1991, LSS 989.
173. "The Secretary's Meeting with Russian Federation President Yeltsin; St. Catherine's Hall," December 16, 1991, R. Nicholas Burns files, 2000-1202-F, BPL; "JAB notes from 12/16/91 mtg. w/Russian Pres. Yeltsin @ The Kremlin, St. Catherine's Hall, Moscow, USSR," folder 10, box 110, series 8, SMML; "JAB notes from 1-on-1 mtg. w/B. Yeltsin during which command & control of nuclear weapons was discussed 12/16/91," folder 10, box 110, series 8, SMML; Baker, *Politics*, 571–73; on this meeting, see also Baker and Glasser, *The Man*, 475.
174. "The Secretary's Meeting with Russian Federation President Yeltsin, St. Catherine's Hall, December 16, 1991." Kozyrev later recalled that he preferred a loose confederation, preserving the union in some form; see Kozyrev, *Firebird*, 39.
175. "The Secretary's Meeting with Russian Federation President Yeltsin, St. Catherine's Hall, December 16, 1991"; on Shaposhnikov, see "Last Soviet Defense Minister Dies from Coronavirus," *Moscow Times*, December 9, 2020, https://www.themoscowtimes.com/2020/12/09/last-soviet-defense-minister-dies-from-coronavirus-reports-a72286. On the mid-December letter to Brussels, see Thomas Friedman, "Yeltsin Says Russia Seeks to Join NATO," *New York Times*, December 21, 1991; Trenin, *Post-Imperium*, 102.
176. "The Secretary's Meeting with Russian Federation President Yeltsin, St. Catherine's Hall, December 16, 1991."
177. "The Secretary's Meeting with Russian Federation President Yeltsin, St. Catherine's Hall, December 16, 1991."
178. "JAB notes from 1-on-1 mtg. w/B. Yeltsin during which command & control of nuclear weapons was discussed 12/16/91."
179. "The Secretary's Meeting with Russian Federation President Yeltsin, St. Catherine's Hall, December 16, 1991."

180. "JAB notes from 1-on-1 mtg. w/B. Yeltsin during which command & control of nuclear weapons was discussed 12/16/91."

181. "JAB notes from 12/18/91 mtg. w/Ukraine Pres. Kravchuk . . . in Kiev, Ukraine, ONE-ON-ONE POINTS," folder 10, box 110, series 8, SMML. Baker added that the Ukrainian leader's recent announcement that he was now the commander in chief was "unsettling." Such comments inspired uncertainty and could, in Baker's opinion, be destabilizing. See also SDC 1991-Frankfurt-15679, December 10, 1991, EBB-691, NSA, on US diplomats going to Kyiv, only to discover in a December 9, 1991, meeting that the Ukrainians "could not describe exactly how the central authority and [nuclear] chain of command would now work in practice" with Ukraine in physical possession of nuclear weapons but no longer part of a union with Moscow, which still had control over launches.

182. "NAC Ministerial 19 December: Restricted Session: US Secretary of State Baker's Intervention," December 19, 1991, in file named "UK/Soviet Relations, Internal Situation," PREM 19/3562, PRO-NA.

183. "JAB notes from 12/21/91 telephone conversation w/Kazakh Pres. Nazarbayev re: Commonwealth mtg. in Alma-Ata (Aboard aircraft from Brussels to Andrews AFB)," December 21, 1991, folder 10, box 110, series 8, SMML; see also Baker, *Politics*, 579, 584–86, 661–64.

184. Plokhy, *Last Empire*, 356–65.

185. "Readout on Alma Ata Meeting," December 21, 1991, in folder 10, box 110, series 8, SMML; see also BST timeline.

186. For more on the US-Kazakh relationship, see Budjeryn, *Inheriting*.

187. Quoted in Baker, *Politics*, 539.

188. Nazarbayev explained this story of his ill-fated December 8 trip to Moscow to Baker, who quoted the conversation in his memoirs; Baker, *Politics*, 579. According to Baker, the Kazakh leader complained further about Yeltsin's conduct that day: "'Why was he in such a hurry to cut this deal? I mean, if nothing else, it's like an off-the-top of the head deal. It's an off-the-cuff deal. It's totally unprepared.'" On how Nazarbayev insisted that Yeltsin hold a subsequent meeting in Kazakhstan, see the introduction to EBB-576, NSA. See also Reiss, *Bridled Ambition*, 139–41.

189. "JAB notes from 12/21/91 telephone conversation w/Kazakh Pres. Nazarbayev re: Commonwealth mtg. in Alma-Ata (Aboard aircraft from Brussels to Andrews AFB)," December 21, 1991, and "Readout on Alma Ata Meeting," December 21, 1991, both in folder 10, box 110, series 8, SMML. This arrangement sounded very much like the system that Yeltsin had confidentially described to Baker: the four nuclear republics would consult, but Russia alone would hold the briefcases that could actually initiate a launch.

190. Memcon, Bush–Yeltsin, December 23, 1991, BPL online; on the secret decree, see Sinovets and Budjeryn, "Interpreting," 6.

191. Telno 2831, Fm Moscow to Deskby, "Prime Minister's Message to Yeltsin: Call on Kozyrev," December 24, 1991, in file "UK/Soviet Relations, Inter-

nal Situation," December 24, 1991, PREM 19/3562, PRO-NA; AIW Maxi-mychev.

192. Plokhy, *Last Empire*, 372–78; Zubok, "With His Back," 627.

193. Telcon, Bush–Gorbachev, December 25, 1991, BPL online. Only later did Bush learn that Gorbachev had allowed Western television journalists from ABC and CNN to film their conversation; Plokhy, *Last Empire*, 371–74.

194. Genscher, *Erinnerungen*, 837.

195. Genscher emphasized in closing that Gorbachev had friends in Germany. Perhaps sensing that he might in fact be in safer hands with Germans than at home, later that night Gorbachev asked an aide to prevent transfer of a payment from a German publisher to Moscow. It seemed better to leave the money in Germany; Plokhy, *Last Empire*, 378.

196. Plokhy, *Last Empire*, 374. On the friendship between Johnson and Strauss, see McGarr, *Whole Damn Deal*, 454–55.

197. On the UN seat, see Letter from Yeltsin to Bush, "Delivered by Amb. Kompletkov, 12/20/91" handwritten at top, SSSN 91130-0013, BPL; and BST timeline.

198. Telno 2843, Fm Moscow to Deskby, "Gorbachev Goes: The End of an Era," December 25, 1991, in file "UK/Soviet Relations, Internal Situation," PREM 19/3562, PRO-NA.

199. Plokhy, *Last Empire*, 375–77.

200. Colton, *Yeltsin*, 207.

201. Plokhy, *Last Empire*, 385–87. Plokhy thought this sordid scene "exposed with brutal clarity the depth of distrust and sheer hatred" that had arisen between Yeltsin and Gorbachev. For more context on Soviet disintegration, see Zubok, *Collapse*.

202. See Connelly et al., "'General,'" 1434: "Practitioners began to find it difficult to imagine that the Cold War could ever be resolved in any way other than nuclear war, leaving them ill-prepared for the collapse of Soviet power."

203. BST timeline. For Yeltsin's thinking on arms control, see Allison, "What Happened"; and for Bush's thinking, see Kimball and Reif, "The Presidential Nuclear Initiatives (PNIs) on Tactical Nuclear Weapons at a Glance."

204. C-SPAN video of the event is available at https://www.c-span.org/video/?23944-1/international-aid-soviet-union; Baker's notes from this conference in folder 11, box 110, series 8, SMML. See also Bush's announcement of more nuclear initiatives in his State of the Union address, January 28, 1992, summarized in BST timeline, and in Baker, *Politics*, 658–59.

205. On the czarist era and its legacy, see Siegel, *For Peace and Money*, 211. Scowcroft quotations from TOIW Brent Scowcroft, August 10–11, 2000, GBOHP. Perle quoted in Goldgeier and McFaul, *Power*, 71 (see also 68–72 on the contest between Baker and Brady).

206. As shown, among other ways, by the first-ever meeting of the UN Security Council held at the summit level, meaning with the participation of heads of state and/or government, including President Bush; see SDC 1992-USUN N-00454, February 1, 1992.

207. On the UN summit, see "UN Security Council Summit Meeting," January 31, 1992, SDC 1992-USUN N-00454, February 1, 1992; "Note by President of the Security Council," January 31, 1992, https://www.securitycouncilreport.org/atf/cf/%7B65BFCF9B-6D27-4E9C-8CD3-CF6E4FF96FF9%7D/PKO%20S%2023500.pdf; see also "JAB notes from 1/29/92 phone call w/POTUS—following JAB meeting w/Russian Pres. Yeltsin @ Kremlin, Moscow, Russia," folder 11, box 110, series 8, SMML.

208. Memcon, Bush–Yeltsin, Camp David, February 1, 1992, EBB-447, NSA; Office of the Historian, Bureau of Public Affairs, US Dept. of State, "US-Russian Summits, 1992–2000," July 2000, https://1997-2001.state.gov/regions/nis/chron_summits_russia_us.html. Covering the various high-level meetings, the *New York Times* noted that the United States had 375 military installations abroad with 500,000 servicemen and women, a giant apparatus that it could now begin to draw down. Joel Brinkley, "Bush and Yeltsin Declare Formal End to Cold War," *New York Times*, February 2, 1992.

209. The question of a joint Mars shot, and other cooperative space ventures, was discussed in Memcon, Bush–Yeltsin, first expanded meeting, June 16, 1992, 2:30–4:10pm, EBB-447, NSA.

210. Åslund, "Russia's Collapse."

211. Spohr, *Post Wall*, 478, notes that in October 1992 Bush signed a law giving "$1 billion of bilateral assistance, tied to the purchase of American food," and raising the US contribution to an accompanying IMF package to $12 billion.

212. Goldgeier and McFaul, *Power*, 71.

213. SDC 1991-Paris-32917, December 6, 1991, DS-ERR; see also Matthijs, "Three Faces"; Sarotte, "Eurozone Crisis."

214. Memcon, Bush–Kohl, March 21, 1992, BPL online.

215. SDC 1992-Bonn-10767, April 22, 1992, FOIA 2000-0233-F, BPL.

216. On the May 27, 1992 attack, see John F. Burns, "Mortar Attack on Civilians Leaves 16 Dead in Bosnia," *New York Times*, May 28, 1992; on UN-PROFOR, see Hill, *No Place*, 75.

217. On March 10, 1992, see "Fact Sheet: The North Atlantic Cooperation Council," Bureau of European and Canadian Affairs, US Department of State, May 7, 1997, https://1997-2001.state.gov/regions/eur/nato_fsnacc.html, which also notes that Baker and Genscher had originally proposed the NACC on October 3, 1991, in a joint statement. See also "Aufnahme der GUS-Staaten in den Nordatlantischen Kooperationsrat: Erklärung der Außenminister des Nordatlantischen Kooperationsrates vom 10. März 1992 in Brüssel," APBD-49–94, 854–85.

218. Quotations from Congressman Gerald Solomon in his book *NATO*, 17. On the May 6, 1992, meeting, and related discussion of Zbigniew Brzezinski's February 1992 testimony to the Polish Senate on Polish membership in NATO, see Asmus, *Opening*, 17.

219. To complicate matters, there was now a parallel discussion about reviving the EU's moribund security arm, the Western European Union (WEU); Information Memorandum, EUR–Thomas M. T. Niles to E/C–Mr. Zoellick, "Security Implications of WEU Enlargement," n.d. on document itself, but stamped on top "THU 19MAR92 09:00," FOIA 2000-0233-F, BPL; and From EUR–Thomas M. T. Niles, to E/C–Mr. Zoellick, April 27, 1992, FOIA 2000-0233-F, BPL. For more on Niles, see Baker, *Politics*, 639; for more on the WEU, see Hill, *No Place*, 55.

220. "Security Implications of WEU Enlargement."

221. Inflation statistic from Conradi, *Who Lost Russia?*, 27. See also "Security Implications of WEU Enlargement"; Memorandum for the President, from Brent Scowcroft, "Overview for Your Upcoming Meetings with Boris Yeltsin," June 13, 1992, EBB-447, NSA.

222. In Flanagan's opinion, "even vigorous implementation of the NACC" would be unlikely to satisfy the security needs of Central and Eastern European states; Memorandum to S/P—Dennis Ross, E/C–Robert Zoellick, from S/P–Stephen Flanagan, "Developing Criteria for Future NATO Members: Now Is the Time," May 1, 1992, FOIA 2000-0233-F, BPL.

223. Patrick E. Tyler, "US Strategy Plan Calls for Insuring No Rivals Develop," *New York Times*, March 8, 1992. The newspaper obtained excerpts from the "Defense Policy Guidance"; see also Leffler, *Safeguarding*; Shifrinson, "Eastbound."

224. This assertion comes from Yuri Kostenko, Ukraine's minister of environmental protection and nuclear safety from 1992 to 1998; he wrote that, on December 7, 1992, the undersecretary of state for international security affairs, Frank Wisner, contacted Oleh Bilorus, the Ukrainian ambassador in Washington, and apparently urged Ukraine to seek NATO membership; Kostenko, *Ukraine's Nuclear Disarmament*, 140.

225. They would later write an influential pro-expansion *Foreign Affairs* article: Asmus, Kugler, and Larrabee, "Building a New NATO." See also Asmus, *Opening*, 33–34; Grayson, *Strange Bedfellows*, 35–45.

226. Kugler quoted in Keith Gessen, "The Quiet Americans behind the US-Russia Imbroglio," *New York Times*, May 8, 2018.

227. On Bush's tendency to caution, see Spohr, *Post Wall*, 3, 586–90.

228. SDC 1992-State-205400, June 4, 1992; see also Shifrinson, "Eastbound," 838.

229. On the language drafted for the presidential speech of July 5, 1992, and its non-use, see Asmus, *Opening*, 17.

230. This was as an appendix to START I, since the Soviet arsenal covered in that treaty was now in four countries, so the four signed the so-called Lisbon accord to recognize that change: Baker, *Politics*, 658–65; Bernauer and Ruloff, *Politics*, 116–17; Goldgeier and McFaul, *Power*, 54–58; Pifer, *Trilateral Process*. Yeltsin's big promises on arms control in other areas were failing at the time; Yeltsin had placed two generals in charge of dismantling

Russia's biological weapons program, but they "subverted Yeltsin's promise of full openness" and managed to continue the program; Hoffman, *Dead Hand*, 428.

231. Conradi, *Who Lost Russia?*, 34.

232. Baker's words in a conversation with Chris Patten on July 25, 1992, paraphrased in Telno 1972, Fm Hong Kong, To Immediate FCO, July 26, 1992, PREM 19/4496, PRO-NA. Baker added that he hoped to "take some of his key people with him (Zoellick, Ross and Margaret Tutweiler)" to help with the reelection campaign.

233. Baker, *Politics*, 671; Baker and Glasser, *The Man*, 493–94.

234. "Prime Minister's Telephone Conversation with President Bush: Friday, 6 November," November 6, 1992, PREM 19/4496, PRO-NA.

235. BST timeline, which mistakenly gives the name of the US president on January 3, 1993, as "President Clinton."

236. Fm White House, To Cabinet Office, November 8, 1992, PREM 19/4496, PRO-NA.

237. "The Bolshevik Goetterdaemmerung," SDC 1991-Moscow-32811, November 15, 1991.

238. Kennan wrote this in his diary at the end of January 1948; quoted in Gaddis, *Kennan*, 300.

5. Squaring the Triangle

1. Strategic questions paraphrased from Gaddis, *Strategies*, rev. ed., ix.

2. On the number of warheads, see Sinovets and Budjeryn, "Inheriting." On the significance of getting them out, see Letter, Talbott to Gore, October 6, 1993, DS-ERR, in which Talbott thanks Gore for "doing an unscheduled drop-by on the Ukrainian foreign minister in Tony Lake's office today—and then getting the President to do the same. You really did help to advance the cause. If we succeed in getting those nuclear weapons out of Ukraine, I'll try to arrange for one to be mounted on your wall as a trophy." Note: Czechoslovakia split into two states, the Czech Republic and Slovakia, shortly before Clinton's inauguration, on January 1, 1993.

3. The nineteenth-century German chancellor Otto von Bismarck used to advise that the "Politik der freien Hand" was well-suited for any country trying to master a precarious situation and retain its position of power; Gall, *Bismarck*, 741. For more on the triangular concept, see Balmaceda, *On the Edge*.

4. For more biographical information on the two presidents, see Branch, *Clinton Tapes*; Clinton, *My Life*; Drew, *On the Edge*; Engel, *When the World*; and Naftali, *George H. W. Bush*.

5. It was a spoof of a popular US comedy sitcom *The Beverly Hillbillies*. Carrey later posted the video on Facebook; https://www.facebook.com/jimcarrey online/videos/new-president-jim-carrey-as-bill-clintonthe-capital -hillbillies-a-parody-of-the-/10154794583868825/.

6. From Germany, Chancellor Helmut Kohl predicted that "Clinton wird rasch erkennen, daß die Kasse leer ist und daß die Möglichkeiten begrenzt sind"; "14./15. Januar 1993," BzL 414.

7. Kozyrev thought the incoming team wrongly saw President Boris Yeltsin and his aides not as reformers to be admired but merely as "strangers to bargain with in pursuit of the Clinton administration's immediate interests"; Kozyrev, *Firebird*, 202.

8. The inflation estimate comes from Treasury Secretary Lloyd Bentsen; as he put it, "it's bordering on hyperinflation": Memcon, Clinton–Kohl, March 26, 1993, my 2015-0776-M, CL.

9. "14./15. Januar 1993," BzL 413. See also David McClintick, "How Harvard Lost Russia," *Institutional Investor*, January 13, 2006, https://www.institutionalinvestor.com/article/b15onpp3q49x7w/how-harvard-lost-russia.

10. "14./15. Januar 1993," BzL 413.

11. See Rodric Braithwaite, "Yeltsin and the Style of Russian Politics," n.d., but handwritten on document January 12, 1993, M-2013-0449, CL. This British analysis informed later briefing papers for Clinton (see, for example, February 18, 1993, M-2013-0449, CL).

12. Paraphrased from a later commentary making much the same argument as Braithwaite; MccGwire, "NATO Expansion," 34.

13. Braithwaite, "Yeltsin and the Style of Russian Politics."

14. Confidential, Mr Lyne, from Rodric Braithwaite, 24 March, no year but from context 1993, "Prime Minister's Talk with Clinton," PREM 19/4499, PRO-NA.

15. Clinton quoted in Talbott, *Russia Hand*, 38.

16. "14./15. Januar 1993," BzL 415.

17. Steinberg quoted in Packer, *Our Man*, 291; the NSC staff member was Jenonne Walker; AIW Walker.

18. For more on Lake's life and relationship with Holbrooke, see Packer, *Our Man*, 42, 151.

19. Roderic Lyne, "Meetings with the US National Security Adviser [*sic*], 18/19 May," May 20, 1993, in UK/USA Relations, PREM 19/4499, PRO-NA. See also Radchenko, "'Nothing but Humiliation.'"

20. Clinton chose Aspin after "it became clear that Sam Nunn wouldn't accept the appointment"; see Clinton, *My Life*, 455.

21. Douglas Hurd to the Prime Minister, "Washington, 24–25 March," March 26, 1993, in UK/USA Relations, PREM 19/4499, PRO-NA. Hurd added that "once again there is an ease of discussion between ourselves and members of the Administration which is really the right definition of the special relationship (a phrase which the Americans use to please us but which following your custom we ought ourselves to use sparingly, if at all)."

22. Letter from Aspin to Major, February 25, 1993, in UK/USA Relations, PREM 19/4499, PRO-NA.

23. John Barry, "The Collapse of Les Aspin," *Newsweek*, December 26, 1993; Grayson, *Strange Bedfellows*, 80–82; Korb, "Who's in Charge Here?," 5. For

more on the consequences of the Black Hawk Down tragedy, see EBB-511, NSA.

24. Douglas Hurd to the Prime Minister, "Washington, 24–25 March," March 26, 1993.

25. Clinton quoted in Packer, *Our Man*, 393; TOIW Samuel Berger, March 24–25, 2005, WCPHP.

26. For more on Talbott, see Keith Gessen, "The Quiet Americans behind the US-Russia Imbroglio," *New York Times*, May 8, 2018.

27. Talbott, *Khrushchev Remembers;* Talbott, *Russia Hand.*

28. Telcon, Clinton–Yeltsin, January 23, 1993, 2015-0782-M, CL; see also the documents relating to Talbott's appointment in early 1993 in a particularly large and useful FOIA collection, F-2017-13804, DS-ERR, which also show that Talbott tried to add the Baltics to his area of responsibility as well; and Clinton, *My Life*, 504–5, where he talks about how he "became my own 'Russia hand'" because of the significance of the issues involved; Talbott, *Russia Hand*, 5–10.

29. Donilon quoted in Steven Erlanger, "Russia Vote Is a Testing Time for a Key Friend of Clinton's," *New York Times*, June 8, 1996; see also Goldgeier, *Not Whether*, 25. Talbott's biggest worry, as a result, was not at State but at the Treasury Department, where he feared Undersecretary Larry Summers might try to conduct his own economic diplomacy. "The trickiest matter," Talbott advised NSC staff, "is going to be . . . keep[ing] Summers on board and under control. That means stroking him when possible, bonking him (or having Tony [Lake] bonk him) when necessary": Memo, Strobe Talbott to Toby Gati and Nick Burns, "By Hand—Personal and Confidential," February 7, 1993, DS-ERR.

30. SDC 1993-USNATO-01043, March 4, 1993.

31. Scowcroft quotation in TOIW Brent Scowcroft, August 10–11, 2000, GBOHP. The result was that even someone as steeped in the issue as Ron Asmus could understandably persist in the belief that when the Bush team negotiated German unification, "no one in either Washington or Moscow was thinking about further NATO expansion in the spring and fall of 1990. Indeed, the issue had not yet been raised by Central and East Europeans." Such statements confirm the principle that institutional memory is short. Asmus, *Opening*, 6.

32. "Hearing of the House Foreign Affairs Committee," Subject "US Aid to the Republics of the Former Soviet Union," September 21, 1993; I thank Matthew Bunn for a copy of Ash Carter's testimony at this hearing. On number of troops and miles, see Talbott, *Russia Hand*, 26. See also William J. Broad, "Russia Has 'Doomsday' Machine, US Expert Says," *New York Times*, October 8, 1993; Wohlforth and Zubok, "Abiding Antagonism," 405–19. The program initiated by Senator Sam Nunn, with the help of Senator Richard Lugar, would eventually cause about 7,600 Soviet nuclear warheads to be deactivated; see "Former Sen. Richard Lugar, a GOP Foreign Policy Expert, Dies at 87," *Los Angeles Times*, April 28, 2019.

33. Perry remark according to his former subordinate, later Ambassador Laura Holgate: AIW Holgate.

34. The goal was "to work closely with you to resolve differences on Ukraine's ratification of START I and the NPT so that we can make progress on START II"; Telcon, Clinton–Yeltsin, January 23, 1993, my 2015-0782-M, CL. On Ukrainian ratification of START II and the NPT, see Sinovets and Budjeryn, "Interpreting."

35. On March 24, 1993, Clinton issued a presidential decision directive (PDD-3) designating ratification of START I and II as priority objectives of US foreign policy; from BST timeline. See also the "Cooperative Threat Reduction Timeline," Harvard Kennedy School Belfer Center for Science and International Affairs, https://www.russiamatters.org/facts/cooperative -threat-reduction-timeline. On the significance of START II, particularly to Perry, see Stent, *Limits*, 29.

36. Carter and Perry, *Preventive Defense*, 26.

37. Les Aspin diary entry, September 9, 1993, EBB-691, NSA. Perry tried whenever possible to travel to Russia, despite the logistical challenges involved. A simple hotel stay involved covering the walls in brown paper to block any cameras; setting up encrypted faxes, phones, and soundproof phone booths; pitching "a tent in the middle of the floor" to hide equipment; and donning a "sealed rubber 'oxygen mask' designed to muffle voices." Carter and Perry, *Preventive Defense*, 37.

38. The total of eighteen comes from Talbott, *Russia Hand*, 8.

39. Kohl kept Reagan's reasoning to himself. Memcon, Clinton–Kohl, March 26, 1993, 2015-0776-M, CL.

40. Memcon, Clinton–Kohl, March 26, 1993, 2015-0776-M, CL; see also Letter, Chernomyrdin–Major, March 4, 1993, PREM 19/4420, PRO-NA (I thank Sergey Radchenko for a copy of this document).

41. "29. März 1993," BzL 443; see also Kohl's take on the Clinton administration in "3. Mai 1993," BzL 449–50.

42. Clinton, *My Life*, 527.

43. SDC 1993-State-106512, April 9, 1993.

44. Yeltsin, *Midnight Diaries*, 134.

45. Talbott description of Yeltsin in Colton, *Yeltsin*, 7.

46. Memcon, Clinton–Yeltsin, April 3, 1993, 2015-0782-M, CL; Clinton, *My Life*, 506–8; Talbott, *Russia Hand*, 64–65.

47. Clinton, *My Life*, 20 (shooting incident), 45–46 (golf club incident).

48. Clinton quoted in Talbott, *Russia Hand*, 65; Todd S. Purdum, "Virginia Clinton Kelley, 70, President's Mother, Is Dead," *New York Times*, January 7, 1994.

49. Clinton said this in a discussion with British prime minister John Major: Memcon, Clinton–Major, November 29, 1995, SDC 1996-State-018217, January 31, 1996.

50. This sentence paraphrases Wright, *All Measures*, 10.

51. Memcon, Clinton–Major, November 29, 1995.

52. Discussed in briefing book for Clinton's trip to Moscow, January 12–15, 1994; "Strategic Deposturing/Detargeting," n.d., but from context December 1993, 2016-0134-M, CL.

53. Clinton quoted in Talbott, *Russia Hand*, 67.

54. Telcon, Clinton–Kohl, April 12, 1993, in my 2015-0776-M, CL.

55. Quotation from Memcon, Clinton–Kohl, July 2, 1993, my 2015-0776-M, CL; on the summit, see "US-Russian Summits, 1992–2000," US Department of State, https://1997-2001.state.gov/regions/nis/chron_summits_russia_us.html.

56. According to Pifer, *Trilateral Process*, 5, at the collapse of the Soviet Union, "Belarus had 81 mobile, single-warhead SS-25 ICBMs deployed on its territory, which operated out of two bases." For more on the subject of "loose nukes," see Allison *Nuclear Terrorism*.

57. Telcon, Clinton–Kravchuk, January 26, 1993, my 2016-0215-M/2016-0122-M, CL.

58. For more on Chernobyl, see Plokhy, *Chernobyl*; Reiss, *Bridled Ambition*, 129–30; Sinovets and Budjeryn, "Interpreting."

59. Plokhy, *Chernobyl*, 339. Roughly 1.5 percent of Russian territory was affected as well.

60. Moscow's mismanagement of Chernobyl contributed to support for Ukrainian independence by giving rebels against Russian control "a new cause to add to their previous agenda of political freedom, human rights, and the development of the Ukrainian language and culture"; Plokhy, *Chernobyl*, 299; see also Reiss, *Bridled Ambition*, 129–30.

61. Andrew E. Kramer, "In Russia, Days of Fake News and Real Radiation after Deadly Explosion," *New York Times*, August 12, 2019. On the risks of civilian nuclear power, see Perrow, *Normal Accidents*.

62. Statistics from Pekka Sutela, "The Underachiever: Ukraine's Economy since 1991," Carnegie Endowment for International Peace, March 9, 2012, https://carnegieendowment.org/2012/03/09/underachiever-ukraine-s-economy-since-1991-pub-47451; see also D'Anieri, *Economic Interdependence*.

63. This quotation is from a summary of Rada attitudes in summer 1992 in Bernauer and Ruloff, *Politics*, 117.

64. The prime minister of Spain, Felipe González, personally advised Clinton about these comments by the president of Ukraine; see the memcon of the working lunch, Clinton–González, December 6, 1993, 2015-0548-M, CL.

65. Foreign Ministry of Ukraine, "Possible Consequences of Alternative Approaches to Implementation of Ukraine's Nuclear Policy," February 2, 1993, EBB-691, NSA.

66. Reiss, *Bridled Ambition*, 126–27, notes that "the inescapable technological fact was that Ukraine never had operational command and control over the nuclear weapons. . . . The liquid fuel for the SS-19 ICBMs made these weapons systems difficult to service and dangerous to keep. The SS-24s were also troublesome for Ukraine to maintain."

67. The author of this statement, Yuri Kostenko, was Ukraine's minister of environmental protection and nuclear safety from 1992 to 1998; Kostenko, *Ukraine's Nuclear Disarmament*, 28.

68. Reiss, *Bridled Ambition*, 126–27.

69. Foreign Ministry of Ukraine, "Possible Consequences of Alternative Approaches to Implementation of Ukraine's Nuclear Policy," February 2, 1993, said that retaining the arsenal would require "substantial capital" and "undermine efforts aimed at conducting social and economic reforms"; see also Pifer, *Eagle*, 39–40. In other words, Ukrainian leaders had realized that although nuclear weapons caused revulsion, they also conferred leverage. John Mearsheimer made this argument in an influential *Foreign Affairs* article; Ukrainian parliamentarians apparently requested dozens of reprints shortly after it appeared; see Mearsheimer, "Case"; Sinovets and Budjeryn, "Interpreting," 15. On parliamentarians and denuclearization, see also report to Kravchuk, July 1, 1993, EBB-691, NSA. See also Letter from Kravchuk to Clinton, March 3, 1993, 2016-0128-M, CL, in which Kravchuk sought US credit assistance to purchase $200 million worth of American grain.

70. Quotation from Memorandum for the Secretary of Defense, from John A. Gordon, "Trip Report on Strobe Talbott's Mission to the Former Soviet Union," May 19, 1993, EBB-691, NSA. On Shaposhnikov, see Richard Boudreaux, "Military Chief of CIS Defects to Russian Post," *Los Angeles Times*, June 12, 1993, which notes that his departure was "a sign that the dream of a NATO-style joint defense structure among former Soviet republics is over."

71. Yeltsin comments from excerpt of Clinton–Yeltsin conversation in cable from the White House to Amembassy Moscow, July 16, 1993, posted under "doc. 46," EBB-691, NSA; "paranoids" in Talbott, *Russia Hand*, 79; Reiss, *Bridled Ambition*, 100. Such Russian moves provoked nationalists in Ukraine to call for retention of nuclear weapons as a possible deterrent to future such behavior. See Memorandum for Anthony Lake, from Rose Gottemoeller, May 1, 1993, Tab I, Memorandum to the President, "US Policy toward Ukraine," 2016-0128-M, CL, where she argues that "the main factor influencing Ukrainian views on this issue is not the attitude of the United States, but the Ukrainian conviction that Russia will eventually try to reassert control over Ukraine."

72. Les Aspin, diary entry for July 27, 1993, EBB-691, NSA.

73. Memorandum for Anthony Lake, from Rose Gottemoeller, "US Policy toward Ukraine: Talbott–Gati Trip Preparations" and appendices, May 6, 1993, 2016-0128-M, CL.

74. Memorandum for the Director for Russian and Ukrainian Affairs, NSC, "US Security Objectives vis-à-vis Russia and Ukraine," United States Arms Control and Disarmament Agency, March 3, 1993, 2016-0048-M, CL.

75. Letter from Clinton to Kravchuk, SDC 1993-State-246255, August 12, 1993, 2016-0128-M, CL.

76. "Note for the File: Meeting with US National Security Adviser [*sic*], 18 May: NATO," no year on document but, from cover note (R M J Lyne, "File Note") 1993, no author on document but presumably Lyne, in UK/USA Relations, PREM 19/4499.

77. For more on shared goals, see their "Declaration on Cooperation between the Czech and Slovak Federal Republic, the Republic of Poland and the Republic of Hungary in Striving for European Integration," February 15, 1991, http://www.visegradgroup.eu/documents/visegrad-declarations/vise grad-declaration-110412-2.

78. Talbott, *Russia Hand*, 95; see also Memorandum for Anthony Lake, from Charles Kupchan and Barry Lowenkron, "NACC Summit," July 16, 1993, my 2015-0755-M, CL.

79. András Simonyi, "NATO Enlargement: Like Free Solo Climbing," OD 161.

80. On the jockeying for bilateral meetings and the process of setting up the Clinton–Havel bilateral, see Memorandum for Anthony Lake, from Beth Sanner, "Holocaust Museum Opening," March 3, 1993, my 2015-0773-M, CL; see also Žantovský, *Havel*, 435–37.

81. SDC 1993-State-137029, May 5, 1993, summarizing meeting on April 20, 1993.

82. SDC 1993-State-137029.

83. SDC 1993-State-134465, May 4, 1993, summarizing meeting on April 21, 1993.

84. "Ambassador Strobe Talbott's Visit to Estonia," SDC 1993-Tallinn-00886, May 17, 1993; see also Talbott, *Russia Hand*, 93–94.

85. Memcon, Balladur–Clinton, June 26, 1993, on June 15, 1993 conversation, SDC 1993-State-192834.

86. Telno 957, Fm Washington To Immediate FCO, "The Clinton Administration: A Shaky Start," April 28, 1993, PREM 19/4496, PRO-NA.

87. Clinton, *My Life*, 466–67, 513–14.

88. "The Clinton Administration: A Shaky Start."

89. The first special counsel was Robert Fiske, later replaced by Kenneth Starr; see Susan Schmidt, "Judges Replace Fiske as Whitewater Counsel," *Washington Post*, August 6, 1994.

90. Joe Conason, "The Vast Right-Wing Conspiracy Is Back," *Salon*, October 5, 2009, https://www.salon.com/test/2009/10/05/clinton_obama_17/. Ruddy wrote a book entitled *The Strange Death of Vincent Foster* (New York: Free Press, 1997).

91. She had served Foster possibly his last meal, in the office shortly before he departed and killed himself; Jeff Leen and Gene Weingarten, "Linda's Trip," *Washington Post*, March 15, 1998.

92. TOIW Linda Tripp, *Slate*, September 12, 2018, https://slate.com/podcasts /slow-burn/s2/clinton/e5/tell-all.

93. Lake complained about the way that "Bosnia was taking all the attention in the press, and a great deal of the time of the American foreign policy ma-

chine," in Roderic Lyne, "Meetings with the US National Security Adviser [*sic*], 18/19 May," May 20, 1993, in UK/USA Relations, PREM 19/4499, PRO-NA.

94. Elaine Sciolino, "Clinton Urges Stronger US Stand on Enforcing Bosnia Flight Ban," *New York Times*, December 12, 1992.

95. It was established by UN Resolution 816; see "NATO Launches 'Deny Flight' Operation over Bosnia," UPI, April 12, 1993, https://www.upi.com /Archives/1993/04/12/NATO-launches-Deny-Flight-operation-over -Bosnia/6962734587200/. See also TOIW Madeleine K. Albright and associated "Briefing Materials," August 30, 2006, WCPHP. There was conflict with the British and the French at this time; see Paul Lewis, "US Rejects British-French Bosnia Peace Step," *New York Times*, March 31, 1993, which recounts how the Clinton administration "rejected a plan by Britain and France for a new Security Council resolution giving the international community's full support to the Bosnian peace plan of the two Balkan mediators, former Secretary of State Cyrus R. Vance and Lord Owen," also known as the Vance-Owen Plan.

96. See TOIW James Steinberg, April 1, 2008, WCPHP. Talbott made similar remarks to Christopher in 1994, noting that "the NSC is becoming too operational," not least because "we, State, have underperformed in long-range planning," leaving a "vacuum." Worse, "there's a general uneasiness out there, among people who wish us well, about whether we know what we're doing." This uneasiness existed inside the administration as well: "Sitting in meetings around the Department or over at the White House, I often find that the air is heavy with self-doubt." See "Sunday, August 21, 1994, Chris," DS-ERR.

97. Powell made these remarks in conversation with John Major; see "Prime Minister's Meeting with the Chairman of the Joint Chiefs of Staff: 24 May," from context May 24, 1993, in UK/USA Relations, PREM 19/4499, PRO-NA.

98. "Strengthening Outreach to the East," with handwritten note on top: "Shali speaking notes," n.d., but from context August 3, 1993, DS-OIPS. See also Asmus, *Opening*, 35; on picking Shalikashvili to succeed Powell, see Clinton, *My Life*, 539.

99. US Department of State, Office of the Spokesman, "Intervention by Secretary of State Warren Christopher before the North Atlantic Council Ministerial Meeting, Nafsika Hotel, Thursday, June 10, 1993," DS-OIPS. See also Asmus, *Opening*, 29.

100. "Talking Points," with handwritten note on top "used by S at NAC lunch," n.d., but from context, on or before June 10, 1993, DS-OIPS.

101. Memcon, Clinton–Yeltsin, July 10, 1993, my 2015-0782-M, CL. See also Pifer, *Trilateral Process*; Talbott, *Russia Hand*, 82–84.

102. Memorandum, to EUR–Stephen A. Oxman, from EUR/P Jon Gunderson, "NATO Expansion to the East," July 20, 1993, DS-OIPS. On US-promoted democratization generally, see Milne, *Worldmaking*.

103. SDC 1993-USNATO-003194, August 3, 1993. See also TOIW Robert Hunter, Association for Diplomatic Studies and Training: Foreign Affairs Oral Project, https://www.adst.org/OH%20TOCs/Hunter,%20Robert %20E.toc.pdf?_ga=2.218035477.2094530902.1590687336-1814181698 .1590687336.

104. "From T–Dr. Davis, to the Secretary, Expanding and Transforming NATO," August 12, 1993, DS-OIPS.

105. Kozyrev, *Firebird*, 214–17.

106. The comment that this took place over "dinner and drinks" comes from SDC 1993-Warsaw-12734, September 1, 1993; Yeltsin's statement is quoted verbatim in SDC 1993-Moscow-26972, August 26, 1993.

107. Kozyrev had been indicating that Russia would not accept Polish membership; see SDC 1993-Warsaw-12390, August 25, 1993; Andrei Kozyrev, "Russia and NATO Enlargement," OD 453–55.

108. SDC 1993-Warsaw-12734, September 1, 1993. See also Jane Perlez, "Yeltsin 'Understands' Polish Bid for a Role in NATO," *New York Times*, August 26, 1993.

109. SDC 1993-Warsaw-12734, September 1, 1993.

110. Memorandum for Anthony Lake, from Rose Gottemoeller, May 6, 1993, quotation from appendix entitled "US Policy toward Ukraine," 2016-0128-M, CL.

111. Clinton told this to the writer helping him to record an audio diary of his time in the White House: see Branch, *Clinton Tapes*, 168–69.

112. "Memorandum for the President," from Anthony Lake, "Subject: Your Trip to Germany, July 10–12," plus attachments (preparatory papers), July 2, 1994, CL.

113. Asmus, Kugler, and Larrabee, "Building a New NATO," 28. For background on the *Foreign Affairs* article and Asmus's work at the RAND Corporation, see Asmus, *Opening*, 32–34; for Asmus's obituary, see Emma Brown, "Ronald D. Asmus, Who Pushed for NATO Expansion, Dies at 53," *Washington Post*, May 3, 2011.

114. Anthony Lake, "From Containment to Enlargement," remarks at the School of Advanced International Studies, Johns Hopkins University, Washington, DC, September 21, 1993, https://www.mtholyoke.edu/acad/intrel/lakedoc .html.

115. Andrei Kozyrev, "Russia and NATO Enlargement," OD 454–56; see also Kozyrev, *Firebird*, 214–17. For US coverage of Primakov's views, see Steven Erlanger, "Russian Warns NATO on Expanding East," *New York Times*, November 26, 1993. On the kind of pro-American view espoused by Kozyrev losing ground in Moscow, see also SDC 1994-Moscow-27484, September 22, 1994, DS-ERR.

116. SDC 1993-USNATO-3568, September 3, 1993. A NATO spokesperson, Jamie Shea, began talking in September 1993 about opening up Spanish-style coordination arrangements to new members from Eastern Europe; Shea quoted in Solomon, *NATO*, 22.

117. Memorandum for Anthony Lake and Samuel R. Berger, from Daniel Fried, summarizing the September 14–22, 1993, trip of an interagency delegation headed by Principal Deputy Undersecretary of Defense Walt Slocombe, September 23, 1993, my 2015-0772-M, CL.

118. SDC 1993-Ankara-14464, September 10, 1993.

119. SDC 1993-State-03804, September 21, 1993.

120. The Russian president had previously "made gestures to his hosts during previous visits abroad that were quickly walked back by his government"; SDC 1993-Moscow-26972, August 26, 1993; Talbott, *Russia Hand*, 95–96.

121. Kozyrev also "cautioned against excluding Russia from any NATO expansion to include states of the former Soviet Bloc"; SDC 1993-Moscow-29067, September 13, 1993.

122. Memcon, Clinton–Yeltsin, September 7, 1993, my 2015-0782-M, CL.

123. Warnings that the "walk-back" was on the way appear in SDC 1993-Moscow-28101, September 3, 1993. See also Strobe Talbott, "Bill, Boris and NATO," OD 410–12.

124. SDC 1993-State-309943, October 9, 1993, EBB-621, NSA; a handwritten note on the side flags the reference to the two-plus-four accord: "ST [presumably Strobe Talbott]—I've marked the passage on 2 + 4 and NATO expansion." Word of the letter leaked to the *New York Times*; see Roger Cohen, "Yeltsin Opposes Expansion of NATO in Eastern Europe," *New York Times*, October 2, 1993; see also the discussion of Yeltsin's use of the two-plus-four in Solomon, *NATO*, 24. Contrast this Yeltsin letter and frequent renewed Russian assertions of this argument, discussed in this chapter, with Goldgeier, "NATO Enlargement," 155, claiming that "Yeltsin rarely mentioned the 1990 discussions."

125. On how Genscher still had influence over the Foreign Ministry after retirement through Kinkel, see Volker Rühe, "Opening NATO's Door," OD 222.

126. SDC 1993-State-309312, October 8, 1993. The most relevant part of the treaty to Wörner's remarks is Article 5, Paragraph 3; see also the agreed minute: "Die Zwei-plus-Vier Regelung," in Presse- und Informationsamt der Bundesregierung, *Vereinigung*, 171. The State Department summary of this conversation does not include a specific mention by Wörner of the agreed minute, but this document is not a full transcript of his remarks, and does confirm that he explicitly raised the issue of foreign forces (the subject of the agreed minute). For more on the nature of German territorial defense forces, about 50,000 strong, that could be present while former Soviet forces were still in Germany, see Memorandum from Philip Zelikow to Robert Zoellick, "Territorial Defense Forces in a United Germany," September 26, 1990, my 2008-0642-MR, BPL, who notes that German territorial defense forces "are something like our National Guard, except that they are always under federal—not state—control."

127. SDC 1993-State-309312, October 8, 1993.

128. Memorandum for Deputy Secretary Strobe Talbott, from Eric Edelman, "Phone Notes for Strobe on NATO Expansion," n.d., but "Sept./Oct. 93"

handwritten on document, DS-OIPS; see also Sarotte, "How to Expand NATO."

129. For more on Rühe's thinking, including an important speech in London on March 26, 1993, see Rühe, *Betr.: Bundeswehr*; Rühe, "Opening NATO's Door," OD 217–33; see also Goldgeier, *Not Whether*, 34; Stent, *Russia*, 216–17. I am also grateful to the former Polish diplomat Jerzy Margański for an email on this speech. On the way Rühe was leaning forward more strongly than the rest of the German government, see Memo to the Secretary from Robert L. Gallucci, "Your October 6 Lunch Meeting with Secretary Aspin and Mr. Lake," subsection "NATO Expansion: Eastern and Allied Views," October 5, 1993. I thank Svetlana Savranskaya for a copy of this document.

130. Memo to the Secretary of State, from T–Dr. Davis, with attachment titled "A Strategy for NATO's Expansion and Transformation" (quotation in attachment), September 7, 1993, https://assets.documentcloud.org/documents /4390816/Document-02-Strategy-for-NATO-s-Expansion-and.pdf.

131. Branch, *Clinton Tapes*, 167; Solomon, *NATO*, 31.

132. Weisser quoted in Goldgeier, *Not Whether*, 34. See quotations of similar remarks from Rühe in Solomon, *NATO*, 31; see also Stent, *Russia*, 216–17, which refers to Ulrich "Weise," probably a misprint for Weisser's last name.

133. Bonn's thinking described in previously cited attachment entitled "A Strategy for NATO's Expansion and Transformation," September 7, 1993.

134. Hill and Gaddy, *Mr. Putin*, 22–24.

135. Radchenko, "'Nothing but Humiliation,'" 778.

136. Yeltsin quotations in Telcon, Clinton–Kohl, September 21, 1993, my 2015-0782-M, CL; on Rutskoi as acting president, see Hill and Gaddy, *Mr. Putin*, 25. See also Marilyn Berger, "Boris N. Yeltsin, Reformer Who Broke Up the U.S.S.R., Dies at 76," *New York Times*, April 24, 2007.

137. Telcon, Clinton–Kohl, September 21, 1993, my 2015-0776-M, CL. The US and German leaders agreed that they should issue coordinated statements in support of Yeltsin. For more on US support for Yeltsin, see CFPR 45.

138. Mark Bowden, "The Legacy of Black Hawk Down," *Smithsonian Magazine*, January/February 2019, https://www.smithsonianmag.com/history/legacy -black-hawk-down-180971000/.

139. Excerpt from Holbrooke's Bosnia audio diary, reprinted in Packer, *Our Man*, 290–95. See also Perry, *My Journey*, 87.

140. Death and injury statistics from Hill and Gaddy, *Mr. Putin*, 25; on Rutskoi's imprisonment and release, see Radchenko, "'Nothing but Humiliation,'" 785–86.

141. Carter and Perry, *Preventive Defense*, 26.

142. Serge Schmemann, "Yeltsin Approves New Constitution Widening His Role," *New York Times*, November 9, 1993; Hill and Gaddy, *Mr. Putin*, 25–26.

143. "1./2. Oktober 1993," BzL 496; see also 496n9.

144. Serge Schmemann, "Russia's Military: A Shriveled and Volatile Legacy," *New York Times*, November 28, 1993.

145. Stent, *Russia*, 163.
146. Central Intelligence Agency, "German Military Forces in Eastern Germany after Unification," September 27, 1990, my 2008-0642-MR, BPL.
147. Kohl announced publicly that he and Yeltsin spoke every fourteen days in "Erklärung des Bundeskanzlers Helmut Kohl anläßlich einer gemeinsamen Pressekonferenz mit dem Präsidenten der Russischen Föderation, Boris Jelzin, am 11. Mai 1994 in Bonn," APBD-49–94, 1058.
148. "1./2. Oktober 1993," BzL 496.
149. Radchenko, "'Nothing but Humiliation,'" 14–15; Antall quotations from Letter, Antall–Clinton, October 8, 1993, in my 2015-0778-M, CL.
150. "Copenhagen European Council (Copenhagen, 21–22 June 1993)," https://www.cvce.eu/en/obj/copenhagen_european_council_copenhagen_21_22_june_1993-en-ccf5d553-55c1-4e3a-99eb-8d88b09cfb24.html.
151. "The President's Meeting with Chancellor Vranitzky," April 20, 1994, summary in SDC 1994-State-114595, April 30, 1994. See also similar comments from the Bush era: Memorandum for the Secretary of State, from Lawrence Eagleburger, "Impressions from Hungary, Poland, Austria and Yugoslavia," March 1, 1990, Robert L. Hutchings Files, Eastern European Coordination, CF01502-005, BPL; and "Gespräch Mock-Hurd," December 20, 1989, ÖDF, 439–42. See also Hill, *No Place*, 120.
152. "Your October 6 Lunch Meeting with Secretary Aspin and Mr. Lake," October 5, 1993 (preparatory paper); see also Lynn Davis's argument for calling the question as soon as possible: "NOTE TO: The Secretary," from Lynn Davis, October 15, 1993, DS-OIPS; Asmus, *Opening*, 49–52; Christopher, *In the Stream*, 129–30.
153. Memo to Peter Tarnoff from Stephen Oxman, "Your Deputies' Committee Meeting on the NATO Summit," September 14, 1993, DS-OIPS.
154. "OSD Option for Principals' Meeting, Partnership for Peace with General Link to Membership," n.d., but "10/18/93" handwritten on document, State Department copy, DS-OIPS; see also Talbott, *Russia Hand*, 97–98.
155. Goldgeier, *Not Whether*, 27.
156. For basic information about the Partnership, see https://www.nato.int/cps/en/natohq/topics_50349.htm.
157. Quotation in Perry, *My Journey*, 117; see also 125–28.
158. "John Malchase David Shalikashvili," JCS website, https://www.jcs.mil/About/The-Joint-Staff/Chairman/General-John-Malchase-David-Shalikashvili/.
159. SDC 1993-USNATO-04194, October 16, 1993; AIW Hunter; AIW Nye; AIW Spero; AIW Townsend. On Shalikashvili's role, see Solomon, *NATO*, 26–27. Contributors to development of the PfP concept included, among others, Charles Freeman, Robert Hunter, Clarence Juhl, Joseph Kruzel, Charles Kupchan, James McCarthy, and Jenonne Walker (this list is not comprehensive): see Jenonne Walker, "Enlarging NATO," OD 266–68; Kupchan, "Strategic Visions"; Robert Hunter, "Toward NATO Enlargement," OD 304–6; Sloan, *Defense of the West*, 113–15.

160. Asmus, *Opening*, 35, for an early discussion of the merits of letting such troops get "'NATO dirt under their fingernails.'"

161. SDC 1993-USNATO-04194, October 16, 1993; "OSD Option for Principals' Meeting"; AIW Hunter; AIW Nye; AIW Spero; AIW Townsend.

162. This flexibility was later spelled out in more detail in the process for becoming a partner, which was tailored for each individual country; see the current information on this process on the NATO website at https://www.nato.int/cps/en/natohq/topics_80925.htm and https://www.nato.int/cps/en/natohq/topics_49290.htm.

163. Solomon, *NATO*, 26–29; AIW Flanagan.

164. "OSD Option for Principals' Meeting."

165. Shalikashvili quoted in Goldgeier, *Not Whether*, 26. See also Sloan, *Defense of the West*, 113–14; see also discussion of how PfP should build on the NACC, which he helped to create, in Robert Zoellick, "Strobe Talbott on NATO: An Answer," *Washington Post*, January 5, 1994.

166. On visions of such an organization, see M. E. Sarotte, "The Contest over NATO's Future," in Shapiro and Tooze, *Charter*, 212–28.

167. SDC 1993-Moscow-31886, October 8, 1993.

168. Many of the points above come from the thinking of Aspin; see Solomon, *NATO*, 34–35; for more on the advantages of PfP, see Sloan, *Defense of the West*, 113; Treisman, *Return*, 317.

169. Albright quotations from Madeleine Albright, "Memorandum for the President, the Vice President, and the Secretary of State and the National Security Advisor, Subject: PfP and Central and Eastern Europe," January 26, 1994, DS-OIPS. Kissinger quoted in Solomon, *NATO Enlargement*, 48. See also SDC 1994-USNATO-1505, April 20, 1994, DS-ERR, which noted that the Poles were "skeptical about President Clinton's vision of a Europe where no dividing lines exist."

170. Note to the Secretary, from Strobe Talbott, October 17, 1993, in SDC 1993-State-317538, October 19, 1993. For Talbott's description of these events, see Talbott, *Russia Hand*, 99–101.

171. SDC 1993-State-317538; see also Talbott, *Russia Hand*, 78–80.

172. "Summary of Conclusions, Principals Committee Meeting on the NATO Summit, October 18, 1993," October 27, 1993; I thank Savranskaya for a copy of this document. The significance of Talbott's intervention was later leaked to the press; see Michael R. Gordon, "U.S. Opposes Move to Rapidly Expand NATO Membership," *New York Times*, January 2, 1994. For more on the October 18, 1993 principals' meeting and its aftermath, see Asmus, *Opening*, 51–57; Goldgeier, *Not Whether*, 39–44.

173. As Lake reported to the president, the principals "reached agreement on recommendations for handling NATO's engagement with new and aspiring democracies in Europe's east"; Memo from Lake to Clinton, October 19, 1993, stamped "The President has seen, 10.19.93," my 2015-0772-M, CL.

174. SDC 1993-State-319425, October 20, 1993.

175. Brzezinski paraphrased in Asmus, *Opening*, 56–57.

176. Brzezinski, "Premature Partnership," 67–82.

177. Kozyrev, *Firebird*, 218–22.

178. SDC 1993-Secto-17024, October 25, 1993.

179. Talbott, *Russia Hand*, 100–102.

180. SDC 1993-Secto-17027, October 25, 1993. The secretary let Clinton know that Yeltsin thought the proposal was "terrific"; "Night Note from Moscow, October 23, 1993," SDC 1993-Secto-17011, October 23, 1993 (also the source of the "bury Lenin" quotation). On Yeltsin's description of PfP as "brilliant," see Kay, *NATO*, 71; on the conversation overall, see James Goldgeier, "Promises Made, Promises Broken? What Yeltsin Was Told about NATO in 1993 and Why It Matters," *War on the Rocks*, July 12, 2016, https://warontherocks.com/2016/07/promises-made-promises-broken-what-yeltsin-was-told-about-nato-in-1993-and-why-it-matters/; Solomon, *NATO*, 53; Talbott, *Russia Hand*, 101–2.

181. SDC 1993-Secto-17027; Kozyrev, *Firebird*, 219–21; on Christopher's conversation with Yeltsin, see Asmus, *Opening*, 53–54.

182. "To the Secretary from Strobe Talbott," n.d., but from context December 31, 1993, 2014-0905-M, CL.

183. SDC 1993-USNATO-05209, December 9, 1993.

184. SDC 1994-Moscow-00594, January 10, 1994.

185. SDC 1993-USNATO-05209; for Chinese views on NATO expansion, see SDC 1997-Beijing-40078, November 13, 1997, DS-ERR.

186. Christopher, *In the Stream*, 130–31. Clinton told Kohl that he was "encouraged by the positive reaction" to PfP, particularly from NATO allies and Yeltsin. See Telcon, Clinton–Kohl, November 29, 1993, in my 2015-0776-M, CL.

187. Republicans attacked Clinton's approach to NATO expansion, and specifically PfP, to the point that the Russian defense minister said "he was concerned with the growing criticism of the 'Partnership for Peace' concept by politicians in Russia and the US Congress" to his American counterpart. The two men were speaking during "an inaugural phone call to MOD [Minister of Defense] Grachev on 05 January using the 'Partnership Line.'" During this call, the American expressed "hope that the 'Partnership Line' would be used frequently and could serve as a symbol of increasing contacts between our defense establishments"; "Memcon of 05 January SecDef Call to Russian MOD Grachev," 2014-0905-M, CL. See also Goldgeier, "NATO Enlargement," 170.

6. Rise and Fall

1. For discussion of both optimistic and pessimistic reasoning, see Sarotte, "How to Enlarge NATO," 25–26. For the Europe "whole and free" argument, see Asmus, *Opening*, 33. On the US habit of viewing other states' integration into US-designed institutions as essential, see Porter, "Why."

2. Clinton, *My Life*, 566–69 (mother's death), 576 (hardest year); Todd S. Purdum, "Virginia Clinton Kelley, 70, President's Mother, Is Dead," *New York Times*, January 7, 1994.

3. SDC 1993-Secto-17049, October 27, 1993.

4. Expression of Ukrainian interest in long-term credits: SDC 1994-State-002161, January 5, 1994. On the way that a nuclear-armed Ukraine would receive "nothing" from the West to help its economy if it did not denuclearize, see Pifer, *Eagle*, 75–76. On status of discussions about denuclearization, see SDC 1993-Frankf-16859, "US/Russian/Ukrainian Trilateral Talks on Deactivation," December 17, 1993.

5. SDC 1994-Kiev-00042, January 4, 1994.

6. SDC 1993-Budape-11648, October 29, 1993.

7. Wałęsa quoted in Jane Perlez, "The NATO Summit: 4 Countries in Audition for NATO," *New York Times*, January 11, 1994; Letter from Olechkowski to Christopher, December 22, 1993, DS-OIPS.

8. SDC 1993-State-386829, December 28, 1993.

9. SDC 1993-State-383575, December 23, 1993.

10. SDC 1994-State-000058, January 3, 1994.

11. The president asked Lake to find out how many US personnel were deployed overseas and their locations; Lake replied that the exact numbers were 326,630 permanently stationed overseas and 59,711 either afloat or deployed. Memorandum for the President, from Anthony Lake, "Overseas Troop Strength," January 10, 1994, my 2015-0772-M, CL.

12. Goldgeier, *Not Whether*, 78–82; Korb, "Who's in Charge Here?," 4–7; Solomon, *NATO*, 48–49.

13. Lugar quoted in Solomon, *NATO*, 49.

14. Albright explained that Clinton had chosen emissaries born in Eastern Europe to show his concern for the region; SDC 1994-Warsaw-00490, "Ambassador Albright's January 7 Dinner with Polish Foreign Minister Olechkowski," January 11, 1994; see also SDC 1993-Budape-11648, October 29, 1993; Republic of Poland, Minister of Foreign Affairs, Letter to Warren Christopher, December 22, 1993, DS-OIPS; Goldgeier, *Not Whether*, 52–53.

15. Madeleine Albright, "Memorandum for the President, the Vice President, and the Secretary of State and the National Security Advisor, Subject: PfP and Central and Eastern Europe," January 26, 1994, DS-OIPS.

16. AIW Koźmiński; AIW Margański. What his Polish hosts presumably did not dwell on was his father's later military history. After leaving Georgia, Dimitri Shalikashvili had fought in the Polish Army against German invaders in September 1939 and become a prisoner of war. He was later released and became a liaison officer for a Nazi-organized "Georgia Legion, a group of ethnic Georgians hoping to free their native land from Soviet domination," thereby siding "with the Nazis" on an "anti-Communist crusade to liberate his native land": Stephen Engelberg, "General's Father

Fought for Nazi Unit," *New York Times*, August 28, 1993; see also Melissa Healy, "Shalikashvili's Father Tied to Nazi Unit," *Los Angeles Times*, August 28, 1993.

17. SDC 1994-Warsaw-00308, January 7, 1994.

18. SDC 1994-Warsaw-00308.

19. SDC 1994-Warsaw-00350, January 10, 1994.

20. Memcon, Clinton–Claes/Dehaene, January 9, 1994, L-WJC/DOS-16-1, CL.

21. Kohl quotation in "11. April 1994," BzL 566–67. He was concerned about resistance to enlargement to not only eastern but also western and northern countries. As Kohl put it to party colleagues in spring 1994, "diese Erweiterung um Österreich, Schweden, Finnland und Norwegen ist ein ungeheuer wichtiger Vorgang." Kohl complained that Spain and Britain were particularly obstructive in blocking these new members, but Germany pushed back: "Wir haben in der Frage des Beitritts wirklich 'full power' gefahren, und die Verhandlungen wären nicht zu Ende gekommen, wenn wir nicht mit äußerster Entschiedenheit vorangegangen wären"; "14. März 1994," BzL, 559–60; see also 559n7.

22. In April 1994, NATO conducted combat efforts to stop the violence in Bosnia, named Operation Deny Flight, after previous European efforts to quell the conflict had not worked. On the operation, see Jonathan Masters, "The North Atlantic Treaty Organization," Council on Foreign Relations, last updated December 3, 2019, https://www.cfr.org/backgrounder/north -atlantic-treaty-organization-nato.

23. "Remarks to the North Atlantic Council, Brussels, Belgium, Jan. 10, 1994," CFPR 85. In an audio diary he was recording with the help of his biographer Taylor Branch, Clinton said he was lobbying "NATO officials in Belgium on a delicate timetable for adding new members from the Soviet empire—rapidly enough to ease their fears of being isolated or reabsorbed, slowly enough not to topple Yeltsin beneath Russia's ultranationalist revival"; Branch, *Clinton Tapes*, 106. For theoretical work on the point that the president was making—the importance of not drawing a line—see Kenneth Waltz, who argued that "the reasons for expanding NATO are weak. The reasons for opposing expansion are strong. It draws new lines of division in Europe, alienates those left out, and can find no logical stopping place west of Russia"; Waltz, "Structural Realism," 22. Waltz added that "the ability of the United States to extend the life of a moribund institution nicely illustrates how international institutions are created and maintained by stronger states to serve their perceived or misperceived interests" (20). On the maintenance of international institutions, see Robert Keohane and Stanley Hoffmann, who write that "international institutions—both organizations and regimes—are significant not because they exercise control over states (with few exceptions they do not) but because they are useful to states"; Robert O. Keohane and Stanley Hoffmann, "Conclusion: Structure, Strategy,

and Institutional Roles," in Keohane, Nye, and Hoffmann, *After the Cold War*, 383.

24. See the NATO "Declaration of Heads of State and Government," January 11, 1994, https://www.nato.int/cps/ie/natohq/official_texts_24470.htm ?mode=pressrelease; and "Partnership for Peace: Framework Document," January 10–11, 1994, https://www.nato.int/cps/ie/natohq/official_texts _24469.htm?mode=pressrelease; see also Goldgeier, *Not Whether*, 54–57.

25. On key milestones in PfP's evolution, see the NATO website, https://www .nato.int/cps/en/natolive/topics_50349.htm.

26. SDC 1994-State-011226, January 13, 1994. See also Richard Rupp, "Lithuania's Campaign for NATO Membership," *Lituanus*, Summer 2002, http:// www.lituanus.org/2002/02_2_04.htm.

27. "The President's Meeting with Czech Leaders," January 11, 1994, 5:30–7:00pm, DS-OIPS; SDC 1994-State-010751, January 12, 1994; SDC 1994-Bonn-00904, January 12, 1994.

28. SDC 1994-Secto-10020, January 16, 1994.

29. See records from a lunch with multiple Central and Eastern European leaders, January 12, 1994, L-WJC-DOS-16-1, CL. I thank Svetlana Savranskaya for a copy of this document.

30. "The President's Meeting with Czech Leaders," January 11, 1994.

31. Havel's biographer noted that Havel did the same to Yeltsin: he "wined and dined Boris Yeltsin in the Lesser Town Golden Thirteen Tavern until the latter couldn't tell the difference between the Warsaw Pact and NATO"; Žantovský, *Havel*, 483.

32. Wright, *All Measures*, 9, notes that one of Clinton's favorite books, called *Nonzero*, suggested that any bargaining process could yield multiple successful outcomes for different participants.

33. Description of, and quotation from, Clinton in Talbott, *Russia Hand*, 133.

34. Douglas Jehl, "All of Prague's Their Stage, and They Play It Like Troupers," *New York Times*, January 12, 1994. In his audio diary, Clinton recalled how moving it was to walk over the storied Charles Bridge with Havel and Albright; the latter had been forced to flee her native Prague during both World War II and the Cold War; Branch, *Clinton Tapes*, 107.

35. Purdum, "Virginia Clinton Kelley."

36. "The President's News Conference with Visegrad Leaders in Prague," January 12, 1994, APP-UCSB, https://www.presidency.ucsb.edu/documents /the-presidents-news-conference-with-visegrad-leaders-prague.

37. Lake quoted in Asmus, *Opening*, 66. The NSC staff member was Jenonne Walker; AIW Walker.

38. When he reported on the summit to the Bundestag in January 1994, he added that "'Germany's eastern border cannot be the border of NATO and the European Union'"; Rühe quoted in Asmus, *Opening*, 313n40. But Rühe notes that "the Clinton Administration did not fully turn in our direction until after the US mid-term elections in November 1994. Even in September 1994, at a meeting of NATO Defense Ministers in Seville, Spain, my

US counterpart Bill Perry warned me about moving too fast. Perry is a friend of mine and I hold him in high esteem. At the time he told me that President Clinton did not like what I was doing. His advice was 'Don't push too much. You will run into big problems'": Volker Rühe, "Opening NATO's Door," OD 229.

39. See R. W. Apple Jr., "Clinton in Europe: A Russian Tightrope," *New York Times*, January 15, 1994.

40. Kozyrev, *Firebird*, 255. Kozyrev thought it was "doublespeak—soft for foreign consumption and tough for domestic audiences," and lamented that Yeltsin was now engaging in the same doublespeak.

41. "Working Dinner with Russian President Yeltsin on Foreign Policy Issues," preparatory papers, December 31, 1993, 2016-0134-M CL.

42. Memcon, Clinton–Yeltsin, "One-on-One Meeting," January 13, 1994, 2016-0117-M, CL. Clinton understood the magnitude of the opportunity. While in Moscow, he held a public town hall, telling the audience that "the measure of your greatness . . . will be whether Russia, the big neighbor, can be the good neighbor"; Clinton quoted in Talbott, *Russia Hand*, 116.

43. Yeltsin quoted and paraphrased in SDC 1994-Moscow-01457, January 14, 1994. See also records from this summit in F-2017-13804, DS-ERR; and "Text of Moscow Declaration by President Clinton and Russian President Yeltsin, Moscow, Russia, January 14, 1994," https://fas.org/nuke/control/detarget/docs/940114-321186.htm.

44. The Ukrainian parliament had delivered approval of Ukrainian accession to the NPT as a nonnuclear state on November 16, 1994; Bernauer and Ruloff, *Politics*, 125. See also see Goldgeier and McFaul, *Power*, 170; Morozov, *Above*. For context on Ukraine's role in the Clinton–Yeltsin January summit, see Telcon, Clinton–Yeltsin, December 22, 1993, my 2015-0782-M, CL.

45. In the mid-1990s Ukraine was, in Talbott's words, "spiraling into chaos" and headed for the economic abyss; Talbott, *Russia Hand*, 79.

46. Pifer, *Trilateral Process*.

47. Goldgeier and McFaul, *Power*, 169–70; for the larger context, see Pifer, *Trilateral Process*.

48. Kravchuk quoted in SDC 1994-State-004615, January 6, 1994. The Trilateral Agreement had three "side letters," not for public consumption, addressing issues that had nearly derailed the accord: one confirming that Russia would compensate Ukraine for the nuclear fuel in the weapons it surrendered; another saying Ukraine would agree to complete transfer or deactivation of all weapons by certain dates; and a third noting that the United States would recognize these mutual commitments and also extend "substantial assistance." Memcon, "Trilateral Meeting with President Boris Yeltsin of Russia on Security Issues," January 14, 1994, EBB-691, NSA.

49. Summary of what would be due to new states from Memorandum for the President, from Anthony Lake, "Your Trip to Germany, July 10–12," July 2, 1994, M-2013-0471, CL; quotations from "Memcon of Clinton–Kohl January 31 Lunch," SDC 1994-State-037335, February 12, 1994.

50. Kohl was particularly pleased by Clinton's initiative because he was disappointed in the lack of interest on the part of his fellow European leaders in enlargement: "11. April 1994," BzL 566–67.
51. SDC 1994-State-037335.
52. Perry, *My Journey*, quotations at 92; see also 1–2, 52. Perry knew that if the attack were real, American leaders would have "only minutes to make . . . the most foreboding decision ever": whether to order "apocalyptic destruction." He imagined the consequences in Washington of such a launch, which might have started only "because of a false alarm (such as I had personally experienced)" (92).
53. SDC 1994-Moscow-06075, March 4, 1994; see also Stent, *Russia*, 214–15.
54. Kozyrev, *Firebird*, 264–65.
55. On the troop withdrawal issue, see correspondence with Estonian and Russian leaders in 2014-0656-M, CL.
56. As reported by the US embassy in Germany: SDC 1994-Bonn-11493, May 13, 1994.
57. Clinton discussed his happiness with the popularity of PfP in "Remarks to the French National Assembly, Paris, France, June 7, 1994," CFPR 87–89; on the Russian application for membership, see SDC 1994-USNATO-02433, June 21, 1994; see also SDC 1994-USNATO-02458, June 22, 1994.
58. SDC 1994-Moscow-009628, April 7, 1994; see also SDC 1994-Moscow-009022, April 1, 1994; SDC 1994-State-109220, April 26, 1994; SDC 1994-Secto-06026, April 30, 1994; Solomon, *NATO*, 58–60.
59. SDC 1994-USNATO-02458, June 22, 1994; see also SDC 1994-USNATO-02433, June 21, 1994.
60. Kozyrev quoted in Адамишин, *В разные годы*, 334. I thank Sergey Radchenko for the reference.
61. "11. April 1994," BzL, 577n13, which mistakenly has the date of the shoot-down as March 28, 1994. See the Atlantic Council and NATO accounts of February 1994 in, respectively, "NATO's First Combat Action Occurred 18 Years Ago Today over Bosnia," https://www.atlanticcouncil.org/blogs/natosource/natos-first-combat-action-occurred-18-years-ago-today-over-bosnia/; and "1994–1998: One Team, One Mission! NATO Begins Peace-keeping in Bosnia," https://shape.nato.int/page14672955.aspx.
62. On Wörner's illness, see "Manfred Wörner," NATO website, https://www.nato.int/cps/en/natohq/declassified_138041.htm.
63. Telcon, Clinton–Yeltsin, April 10, 1994, my 2015-0782-M, CL.
64. SDC 1994-Secto-10002, June 7, 1994. On similar Russian demands that NATO become a watered-down collective security organization, see Solomon, *NATO*, 59.
65. On the intersection between US domestic politics and NATO expansion, see Grayson, *Strange Bedfellows;* Johnston, *How NATO Adapts;* Kay, *NATO;* Solomon, *NATO.*
66. SDC 1994-State-166385, June 22, 1994. On the Korean crisis, see Carter and Perry, *Preventive Defense*, 123–33.

67. William J. Clinton, "Address to the Polish Parliament in Warsaw," July 7, 1994, APP-UCSB, https://www.presidency.ucsb.edu/documents/address -the-polish-parliament-warsaw.

68. Alexander Vershbow, "Present at the Transformation," OD 430–31; see also Asmus, *Opening*, 73.

69. Email from Alexander R. Vershbow to W. Anthony Lake, "NATO Expansion," July 15, 1994, 12:11pm, DS-OIPS. For Albright's original question— "Have we dealt with the realistic possibility that Moscow will qualify [for NATO membership] before the others do?"—see Madeleine Albright, "Memorandum for the President, the Vice President, and the Secretary of State and the National Security Advisor, Subject: PfP and Central and Eastern Europe," January 26, 1994, DS-OIPS.

70. Telcon, Clinton–Kuchma, July 21, 1994, my 2016-0217-M, CL Kuchma; see also Jane Perlez, "US and Ukraine Cooperate to Destroy Nuclear Arsenal," *New York Times*, December 9, 1994.

71. Telcon, Clinton–Kuchma, October 13, 1994, in my 2016-0217-M, CL.

72. "Telephone Call to Ukrainian President Leonid Kuchma" (preparatory paper), From: Anthony Lake, July 21, 1994, 9:45am, stamped "The President has seen 7/21," my 2016-0217-M, CL.

73. Branch, *Clinton Tapes*, 168.

74. Kohl and Yeltsin agreed to this bargain during the former's visit to Moscow (note: the title of the source, unusually for a German-language document, does not have any capital letters): "besuch des bundeskanzlers in der russischen foederation vom 14. bis 16. dezember 1992," https://www.bun desregierung.de/breg-de/service/bulletin/besuch-des-bundeskanzlers-in -der-russischen-foederation-vom-14-bis-16-dezember-1992-791660; see also Stent, *Russia*, 162–63.

75. "US Troops Leave Berlin," German Information Center, n.d., but from context September 1994, Zelikow Box 3, HIA. Stent, *Russia*, 164, says a total of 546,200 troops had left by then. On the planning for this event, see SDC 1994-Bonn-11493, May 13, 1994; "Erklärung des Bundeskanzlers Helmut Kohl anläßlich einer gemeinsamen Pressekonferenz mit dem Präsidenten der Russischen Föderation, Boris Jelzin, am 11. Mai 1994 in Bonn," APBD-49–94, 1060.

76. Stent, *Russia*, 163.

77. "Rede von Bundeskanzler Dr. Helmut Kohl beim Festakt aus Anlaß der Verabschiedung der russischen Truppen am 31. August 1994 im Schauspielhaus Berlin," APBD-49–94, 1087.

78. Quoted in Colton, *Yeltsin*, 312; Stent, *Russia*, 164; Treisman, *Return*, 58.

79. On the legal basis pertaining after the Soviet withdrawal in 1994, see the German foreign ministry website, https://www.auswaertiges-amt.de/en /aussenpolitik/themen/internatrecht/truppenstationierungsrecht-alt /231678.

80. Statistics from "US Troops Leave Berlin," which also notes that, as of September 1994, the United States had a total of 154,332 troops stationed in

Europe overall. See also "Erklärung des Bundeskanzlers Helmut Kohl anläßlich einer gemeinsamen Pressekonferenz mit dem Präsidenten der Russischen Föderation, Boris Jelzin, am 11. Mai 1994 in Bonn," APBD-49-94, 1060; the summary of "May 12 Kohl/Yeltsin Talks," in SDC 1993-Bonn-11493, May 13, 1994; and Stent, *Russia,* 164.

81. Statistics from "Bilateral Relations Paper for Codel Cohen to Wehrkunde: German Foreign Policy and US-German Relations," January 4, 1996, no cable number, DS-ERR. On the 1994 US withdrawal from Berlin, see Stent, *Russia,* 163; on US bases becoming small towns in their own right, see Ben Knight, "US Military in Germany," Deutsche Welle, June 16, 2020, https://www.dw.com/en/us-military-in-germany-what-you-need-to-know/a-49998340.

82. Talbott quoted in, and Holbrooke quotation from, Holbrooke, *To End,* 57, 59. For more on Holbrooke and Lake's relationship, see Parker, *Our Man,* 21–22 (on their meeting in Vietnam), 151 (on the affair).

83. As one author put it, "Holbrooke's brief tenure in Germany made him a true believer in enlargement"; Grayson, *Strange Bedfellows,* 47; see also Goldgeier, *Not Whether,* 69–71.

84. Asmus, *Opening,* 87.

85. "U.S.-German Relations and the Challenge of a New Europe: Vice President Gore, Speech via Satellite to the Conference on New Traditions, Berlin, Germany, Sept. 9, 1994," *U.S. Department of State Dispatch* 5, no. 37 (September 12, 1994): 597–99.

86. SDC 1994-Berlin-02794, September 10, 1994; see also Solomon, *NATO,* 65–66.

87. The first training exercise was "Exercise Cooperative Bridge 94"; see press release, September 12, 1994, NATO website, https://www.nato.int/cps/en/SID-432830E3-9D58B27B/natolive/news_24256.htm; Gore noted this upcoming exercise in his speech, "U.S.-German Relations and the Challenge of a New Europe," 597–99.

88. Wesley Clark, one of those who cleared the speech, later recalled being surprised that phrases he had crossed out twice kept reappearing; AIW Clark.

89. Asmus, *Opening,* 87–88.

90. AIW Townsend.

91. Clinton described this operation to Kohl in Memcon, Clinton–Kohl, September 15, 1994, in my 2015-0776-M, CL. On the Pentagon being "furious" about this sequence of events, see Asmus, *Opening,* 87-88; on British views, SDC 1994-London-14877, September 19, 1994.

92. Carter and Perry, *Preventive Defense,* 28.

93. Asmus, *Opening,* 87–88; Grayson, *Strange Bedfellows,* 93.

94. Memorandum for the Secretary from Strobe Talbott, Subject: "The Future of European Security," September 12, 1994, DS-OIPS.

95. "NATO Expansion: Concept and Strategy," September 17, 1994, part of preparatory papers distributed for IWG meeting, DS-OIPS.

96. SDC 1994-State-262133, September 28, 1994, provides a summary of views consistent with other accounts from the same meeting cited in this chapter.

97. Quotations from Michael Dobbs, "Wider Alliance Would Increase U.S. Commitments," *Washington Post*, July 5, 1995; AIW Clark; see also Goldgeier, *Not Whether*, 73–75. See also Marten, "Reconsidering," 155–56.

98. In addition, "while we are discussing START III, each side will take unilateral reductions beyond START II" and "unilateral steps toward START III"; "Expanded Session on Security Issues with President Yeltsin of the Russian Federation," September 27, 1994, 4:35–5:35pm, my 2015-0782-M, CL.

99. For more, see Hoffman, *Dead Hand*, 101–26.

100. "Second Clinton/Yeltsin One-on-One 1pm–2:30pm, Sept. 28, 1994," DS-OIPS; see also the summary of Yeltsin's visit in SDC 1994-State-266647, October 1, 1994.

101. According to Kozyrev, *Firebird*, 269.

102. Yeltsin quoted in SDC 1994-State-266647, October 1, 1994. See also Talbott on US policies toward the Baltics: the dismantling of early-warning Soviet radar in Latvia was "lubricated by $2.5 million from the US to help"; Talbott, *Russia Hand*, 126, 443n3.

103. AIW Clark.

104. Yeltsin quoted as making this remark to Talbott in SDC 1994-State-266647, October 1, 1994.

105. Branch, *Clinton Tapes*, 198.

106. SDC 1994-State-266972, October 2, 1994. As the US ambassador to France, Pamela Harriman, informed Washington, Chirac believed "France is somehow uniquely positioned to recruit others to Russia's, and, more especially, Yeltsin's cause"; SDC 1996-Paris-00761, January 12, 1996.

107. Memorandum for Anthony Lake from Alexander Vershbow, Subject: "NATO Expansion," October 4, 1994, my 2015-0755-M, CL, called "October 4 draft" below. Word of these developments apparently leaked to Wałęsa, who was thrilled. He wrote to Clinton to say Poles were "receiving information that the question of enlarging the Atlantic Alliance is becoming the subject of wider reflection" and "we are grateful for this"; Letter, Wałęsa–Clinton, September 23, 1994, my 2015-0813-M, CL.

108. "NATO Expansion: View of Richard Schifter," Addendum to Memorandum for Anthony Lake from Alexander Vershbow, Subject: "NATO Expansion," October 4, 1994.

109. "NATO Expansion: View of Richard Schifter."

110. Memorandum for the President from Anthony Lake, Subject: "NATO Expansion," October 13, 1994, stamped "The president has seen, 94 OCT 13 p1:28 [*sic*]," my 2015-0755-M, CL. Lake's final, October 13, 1994, version (the one viewed by the president) upgraded Ukraine's stance from the October 4, 1994, draft notably and in multiple places. The October 4 draft had proposed developing, "in parallel, an institutionalized relationship between

NATO and Russia (and something similar between NATO and Ukraine)." Lake's final version, in contrast, proposed "an institutionalized relationship between NATO and Russia" only, upgrading Ukraine to consideration for membership (in the new paragraph cited in the main text above). Lake also similarly edited out numerous other places in the draft that had spoken of Russia and Ukraine in parallel. For example, the "road map" for action in the October 4 draft listed the following next steps (emphasis added to highlight differences): "*With Russia/Ukraine:* continue dialogue on rationale for NATO expansion" and "*With CEEs:* outline way ahead; lay down precepts; review military implications (e.g. extent of integration NATO will require); . . . stress need for them to support positive parallel track *for Russia/Ukraine.*" In contrast, Lake's final "road map" upgraded both Ukraine and the Baltics: "*With Russia:* continue dialogue for rationale on NATO expansion," but "*With CEEs, Baltics, and Ukraine:* outline way ahead; lay down precepts; review military implications (e.g. extent of integration NATO will require—drawing on OSD/JCS briefing); . . . stress need for them to support parallel track *for Russia.*" Finally, Lake had the references to Holbrooke removed before forwarding his final October 13 version to the president.

111. For more on BALTBAT, see the Baltic Defence College website, https://www.baltdefcol.org/?id=1534; Poast and Urpelainen, *Organizing Democracy,* 125–28; Memorandum for the President from Anthony Lake, Subject: "NATO Expansion," October 13, 1994.

112. Memorandum for the President from Anthony Lake, Subject: "NATO Expansion," October 13, 1994.

113. Carl Hulse, "How Congress Passed an Assault Weapons Ban in 1994," *New York Times,* September 7, 2019.

114. Korb, "Who's in Charge Here?," 5.

115. Adam Clymer, "GOP Celebrates Its Sweep to Power," *New York Times,* November 10, 1994.

116. On Christopher's offer to resign, see Bart Barnes, "Former Secretary of State Warren Christopher, Who Negotiated Settlement to Iran Hostage Crisis, Dies at 85," *Washington Post,* March 19, 2011; on the reaction of Clinton's aides, see Albright, *Madam Secretary,* 217.

117. He made this remark in Memcon, Clinton–Schröder, September 9, 1999, in my 2015-0777-M, CL Schröder. For more on the Contract with America and the impact of the November 1994 midterm elections, see Goldgeier, *Not Whether,* 82; Korb, "Who's in Charge Here?," 4–7; Volker Rühe, "Opening NATO's Door," OD 225–26.

118. Quotations in Carter and Perry, *Preventive Defense,* 30. On the United States' ability to dictate the terms of its security commitments, see Beckley, "Myth."

119. Final Communiqué, NATO M-NAC-2(94)116, Ministerial Meeting of the North Atlantic Council, NATO Headquarters, Brussels, Belgium, Decem-

ber 1, 1994, https://www.nato.int/docu/comm/49-95/c941201a.htm; Carter and Perry, *Preventive Defense*, 30–31. The United States got this language inserted despite German policymakers' (though not Rühe's) concerns that it was "too early to go public with alliance discussion"; SDC 1994-Bonn-26966, November 3, 1994.

120. Christopher, *In the Stream*, 227.

121. SDC 1994-Kiev-321032, December 1, 1994.

122. SDC 1994-Secto-28010, December 4, 1994.

123. To their amazement, they were told that Washington had assured its allies the Russians had already seen and approved the communiqué; Kozyrev, *Firebird*, 281. On the Russian signature of the PfP Framework Document, see https://www.nato.int/cps/en/natohq/topics_82584.htm.

124. Andrei Kozyrev, "Russia and NATO Enlargement," OD 456. The SVR was a partial successor to the KGB, focusing on foreign intelligence; among other successor-components was the FSB, or Federal Security Service, which focused more on domestic issues.

125. Description of 1993 report and 1994 events in Kozyrev, *Firebird*, 246–47, 281, quotation at 246; Radchenko, "'Nothing but Humiliation,'" 785.

126. On conditions in Russia, see SDC 1994-Moscow-35565, December 9, 1994, BDGD. On the difficulties facing Yeltsin, see Hill, *No Place*, 139–41.

127. SDC 1994-Moscow-36374, December 16, 1994; see also letter from Yeltsin to Clinton of December 29, 1994, quoted in Talbott, *Russia Hand*, 444n11.

128. SDC 1994-USNATO-04586, December 2, 1994; Asmus, *Opening*, 93–94; Christopher, *In the Stream*, 228–30. On Russia's eventual signing of its "Individual Partnership Programme" in 1995, see the "Remarks by the Secretary General," May 31, 1995, https://www.nato.int/docu/speech/1995/s950531a.htm.

129. These hopes were soon dashed. As William Hill has written, one of the sadder stories of the past decades was "the rapid development and then equally rapid atrophy of the once ambitious OSCE"; Hill, *No Place*, 8. See also "Budapest Summit Marks Change from CSCE to OSCE," Organization for Security and Co-operation in Europe, December 5, 1994, https://www.osce.org/event/summit_1994.

130. Kuchma received an invitation to a state visit to Washington on November 21–23, 1994; at that event, Clinton announced that Ukraine had become the fourth-largest recipient of US assistance worldwide; SDC 1994-State-321161, December 2, 1994.

131. Memorandum for the President, from Warren Christopher, "Night Note," October 20, 1994, DS-OIPS.

132. SDC 1994-Moscow-32874, November 16, 1994, EBB-571, NSA.

133. SDC 1994-State-321301, December 2, 1994.

134. "Excerpt from Strobe Talbott's Letter to the Secretary," attachment to Memorandum for the President, from Warren Christopher, October 20, 1994, DS-OIPS; see also Solomon, *NATO*, 67–68.

135. SDC 1994-State-317979, November 29, 1994; on the NPT, see SDC 1995-State-125411, May 23, 1995; see also Larrabee, "Ukraine's Balancing Act," 143–65.

136. The delegation member was unnamed. SDC 1994-Kiev-10532, December 1, 1994.

137. See the text of the memorandum as transmitted to the United Nations on December 19, 1994, in https://www.securitycouncilreport.org/atf/cf /%7B65BFCF9B-6D27-4E9C-8CD3-CF6E4FF96FF9%7D/s_1994_1399 .pdf.

138. SDC 1994-Kiev-10648, December 5, 1994. For the argument that Ukraine could have gotten a better deal, see Kostenko, *Ukrainian Nuclear Disarmament*, 15–16. Ukraine first invoked the consultation mechanism established by the Budapest Memorandum after the influx of Russian troops without insignia into Crimea in 2014; Budjeryn, "Power," 225.

139. If he did so, that would be "effectively thrusting the CSCE, the host of the gathering, out of the picture"; Kozyrev, *Firebird*, 283.

140. Office of the Press Secretary, "Remarks by the President at Plenary Session of 1994 Summit of the Council [*sic*] on Security and Cooperation in Europe," Budapest Congress Center, Budapest, Hungary, December 5, 1994, 9:58am, https://clintonwhitehouse6.archives.gov/1994/12/1994-12-05 -president-remarks-at-csce-summit-in-budapest.html.

141. Kozyrev, *Firebird*, 283.

142. Dean E. Murphy, "Broader NATO May Bring 'Cold Peace,' Yeltsin Warns," *Los Angeles Times*, December 6, 1994; Carter and Perry, *Preventive Defense*, 31. Talbott recalled being worried that, with "cold peace," Yeltsin had found a "catchphrase" for the post–Cold War era; Talbott, *Russia Hand*, 134.

143. As recalled the following year by Talbott in Memorandum for the Secretary, from Strobe Talbott, "From Moscow to Halifax, and Beyond—US Policy toward Russia through 1996," May 17, 1995, EBB-447, NSA. He added that it also took Clinton's personal engagement "to pry the Russian troops out of the Baltics before the deadline."

144. Warhead numbers and percentage from "Remarks by the President at Plenary Session of 1994 Summit of the Council [*sic*] on Security and Cooperation in Europe."

145. Memcon, Clinton–Kohl, December 5, 1994, my 2015-0776-M, CL.

146. Murphy, "Broader NATO."

147. BzL 628n7; on Grachev, see Talbott, *Russia Hand*, 75.

148. Memcon, Clinton–Kohl, December 5, 1994. Presumably he meant "rubble and debris," but the translation of his remarks is as it appears above.

149. Talbott, *Russia Hand*, 141.

150. Telcon, Clinton–Kohl, December 13, 1994, my 2015-0776-M, CL; see also Clinton, *My Life*, 636–38.

151. SDC 1994-Moscow-36374, December 16, 1994; see also Goldgeier, *Not Whether*, 85–88.

152. Kozyrev, *Firebird*, 283.

153. Memo from Talbott to Christopher, Subject: "The Vice President's Trip to Russia," December 19, 1994, DS-OIPS; Talbott, *Russia Hand*, 140–41.

154. Kozyrev, *Firebird*, 285; for a chronology of events in Chechnya, see Александр Черкасов, "Война как способ предотвратить срыв мирных переговоров," https://www.ekhokavkaza.com/a/28170161.html, December 11, 2016; I thank Radchenko for an email on the Chechen sequence of events.

155. Talbott, *Russia Hand*, 141–51; on Yeltsin's decision to order the Chechen action on the advice of his aides, Burns, *Back Channel*, 95–97, which also notes (on 96) the following: "Tired and isolated, Yeltsin relied more and more on an inner circle of conservative power ministers and drinking companions, whose capacity for court politics exceeded their professional competence." See also Lieven, *Chechnya*.

156. Volker Rühe, "Opening NATO's Door," OD 232.

157. SDC 1995-Moscow-00883, January 11, 1995, BDGD. By the start of 1995, Perry determined that "Chechnya is a disaster for Yeltsin and is becoming a disaster for our relationship": see "Memorandum for the President," from the Secretary of Defense, January 28, 1995, my 2015-0810-M, CL.

158. Kozyrev, *Firebird*, 290.

159. AIW Gati.

160. Andrew Higgins, "The War That Continues to Shape Russia, 25 Years Later," *New York Times*, December 10, 2019; see also Gall and de Waal, *Chechnya*; Radchenko, "'Nothing But Humiliation,'" 796–97.

161. Kozyrev, *Firebird*, 285.

162. "Gore Debrief with Yeltsin One-on-One," n.d. but from context December 1994, DS-ERR, which notes that "they shake, but Yeltsin is a little reluctant, thinking he should have sought more." Yeltsin also asks, "when you come to the middle of 1995 and you need to send a signal to the Poles to tell them they are going to join, what will you do?" Gore responds by saying "that 1995 will be a year of study and briefing only." Clinton quotation from letter from Clinton to Yeltsin, White House Situation Room, Nodis 9500177, January 6, 1995, DS-OIPS.

163. SDC 1994-Moscow-36923, December 23, 1994.

164. This conclusion appears in "Meeting with the Vice President on Russia and NATO Expansion," Study in Residence (preparatory paper), December 21, 1994, "President has seen" handwritten at top, my 2015-0772-M, CL.

165. On the 1994 North Korean nuclear crisis, see Carter and Perry, *Preventive Defense*, 128–29; on a later missile crisis, see Perry, *My Journey*, 160–71. Perry's views summarized by Talbott, and quotations, in untitled note from Talbott to Christopher, January 2, 1995, DS-OIPS.

166. "Meeting with the Vice President on Russia and NATO Expansion"; see also Carter and Perry, *Preventive Defense*, 31–32.

167. Quoted in "Mtg./Pres. on NATO+Russia—12/21/94" (Nicholas Burns was the notetaker), DS-OIPS. See also Asmus, *Opening*, 97, which treats this meeting as a catch-up session, informing Perry of what was already US

policy; the evidence from the time presented above suggests, however, that the policy was less settled than Asmus's account conveys.

168. Carter and Perry, *Preventive Defense*, 32.

169. Clinton later discussed this timetable with Kohl; see Memcon, Clinton–Kohl, February 9, 1995, my 2015-0776-M, CL.

170. "Mtg./Pres. on NATO + Russia—12/21/94."

171. On the way denuclearization deprioritized Ukraine, see Kostenko, *Ukraine's Nuclear Disarmament*, 267.

172. Statement about Perry considering resigning in Perry, *My Journey*, 128–29; in that book Perry dates this meeting to 1996, but in his coauthored biography with Carter, Perry dates it to December 21, 1994. Based on the written record, "Mtg./Pres. on NATO + Russia—12/21/94," DS-OIPS, the coauthored date is accurate; Carter and Perry, *Preventive Defense*, 31.

173. Perry quoted in Solomon, *NATO*, 66. See also Goldgeier, *Not Whether*, 12–13.

174. Perry announced five principles in a speech in Norfolk, Virginia, in June 1996: commitment to democratic reform, commitment to a market economy, good neighborly relations, civilian control of the military, and military capability to operate effectively with the alliance. See the summary provided in Assistant Secretary for European and Canadian Affairs Marc Grossman, "Statement Submitted for the Record, as Prepared for a Hearing before the Senate Foreign Relations Committee (canceled)," October 1997, https://1997-2001.state.gov/regions/eur/971000grossman.html. See also Daniel S. Hamilton, "Piece of the Puzzle," OD 54–55n105.

175. Perry, *My Journey*, 129.

176. The first two quotations are from Carter and Perry, *Preventive Defense*, 32; the next two are from Perry, *My Journey*, 151–52. See also Grayson, *Strange Bedfellows*, 94–95; Talbott, *Russia Hand*, 146. Talbott's interpretation of the meeting differs from Perry's; Talbott suggests that the main result was to continue supporting PfP. Talbott's recollection of the short-term strategy, however, is not inconsistent with what Perry saw as the long-term strategy resulting from the meeting: to move forward with full Article 5 expansion, but quietly.

177. Kay, *NATO*, 92; Solomon, *NATO*, 70.

178. "Remarks in Cleveland, Ohio, at the White House Conference on Trade and Investment in Central and Eastern Europe," January 13, 1995, https://www.govinfo.gov/content/pkg/PPP-1995-book1/html/PPP-1995-book1-doc-pg41.htm; see also Goldgeier, *Not Whether*, 102.

179. Washington also issued a strategy for an upcoming "NATO Study/Presentation on Expansion"; SDC 1995-USNATO-00287, January 25, 1995.

180. SDC 1995-State-008688, January 12, 1995. Holbrooke advised Warsaw that 1994 was "the year in which NATO committed to expansion, and that Poland would be a likely beneficiary of that decision"; SDC 1995-Warsaw-01304, January 30, 1995.

181. AIW Carter.

182. Marten, "Reconsidering," 159–60, while noting that that Western "disregard for Russia's international interests would likely have soured" relations with Moscow, nonetheless argues that "PfP was a real policy alternative . . . that should be taken seriously."

183. Albright said this to Polish prime minister Pawlak: Memcon, Albright–Pawlak, October 22, 1994; I thank Savranskaya for this document.

7. A Terrible Responsibility

1. Memorandum for Anthony Lake, from Coit Blacker, Daniel Fried, and Alexander Vershbow, "Troika Meeting on European Security/NATO Enlargement," June 16, 1995, my 2015-0772-M, CL.

2. Memcon, Clinton–Major, November 29, 1995, SDC 1996-State-018217, January 31, 1996. Major responded that PfP "provides the halfway house for prospective members" and "has turned out better than many thought it would." Lake also raised the concept of a "veto" with Clinton during a discussion with Claes; in that conversation, Vice President Gore agreed that "we should never use the Russian elections as a reference date": Memcon, Clinton–Claes, SDC 1995-State-071477, March 7, 1995.

3. SDC 1995-State-002289, February 17, 1995.

4. "President's Dinner with President Yeltsin," SDC 1994-Moscow-01457, January 14, 1994.

5. Kozyrev quoted in "Secretary Christopher's Meeting with Andrei Kozyrev, Apr. 26," SDC 1995-State-106418, May 12, 1995.

6. SDC 1995-State-031006, February 7, 1995.

7. Wałęsa and Kissinger statements in SDC 1995-State-002289, February 17, 1995; suggestion that Kissinger's idea meant applying the two-plus-four treaty's prohibition on foreign troop stationing in Solomon, *NATO*, 48.

8. Memorandum for Anthony Lake, from Daniel Fried, "Presidential Message to Lech Walesa," February 3, 1995, my 2015-0813-M, CL.

9. Quotation from 1995 Congressional Research Service Report, quoted in Poast and Chinchilla, "Good for Democracy?," 475; see also Epstein, "NATO Enlargement"; Epstein, "When Legacies."

10. See the discussion in chapter 1 of differing terms of membership for various countries.

11. For more on this topic, see Sarotte, "How to Enlarge NATO," 7–41.

12. Holbrooke quoted by the US embassy in Warsaw, SDC 1995-Warsaw-002289, February 17, 1995.

13. Zieleniec quotation in Asmus, *Opening*, 148; see also 336n52; SDC 1995-USNATO-01259, March 29, 1995.

14. SDC 1995-Buchar-02061, February 27, 1995.

15. Memcon, Clinton–Horn, June 6, 1995, my 2015-0779-M, CL.

16. Gore remarks in Memcon, Clinton–Claes, March 7, 1995, reported in SDC 1995-State-071477, March 23, 1995.

17. SDC 1995-USNATO-00721, February 22, 1995.

18. Alessandra Smiley, "Clinton Visit to Ukraine Is Welcome," *New York Times*, May 11, 1995.

19. It took nine years after the collapse of the USSR for the leaders of Ukraine to agree to close Chernobyl; not until December 15, 2000, did the Ukrainian president announce the final decommissioning of the nuclear plant. The delay was due, as noted in Plokhy, *Chernobyl*, 334–42, to the economic crisis of the 1990s, the severity of which "not only paralleled but almost dwarfed the Great Depression of the 1930s" and meant that Kyiv could not go without the still-functioning parts of Chernobyl, "a power plant that produced up to 6 percent of the country's electrical energy." Put differently, "Kyiv would give up its nuclear arms but would not budge on Chernobyl." It also took more than a quarter of a century to build a sarcophagus over it.

20. Smiley, "Clinton Visit to Ukraine Is Welcome"; see also various papers constituting the briefing book for Clinton's trip to Moscow and Kyiv in May 1995, 2016-0135-M, CL.

21. Clinton quotations from "Expanded Plenary Meeting with President Kuchma and Ukrainian Delegation," May 11, 1995, my 2016-0217-M; handwritten note on memorandum for the President from Anthony Lake, "Subject: "Moving Toward NATO Expansion," with cover note of October 13, 1994, stamped "The President has seen 94 OCT 13," 2015-0755-M.

22. On the Ukrainian-Russian interactions, see Plokhy, *Gates*.

23. SDC 1995-Budape-02063, March 3, 1995.

24. Memorandum for the Secretary, from Strobe Talbott, "From Moscow to Halifax, and Beyond—US Policy toward Russia through 1996," May 17, 1995, EBB-447, NSA; AIW Blacker.

25. Tarasyuk quoted in Asmus, *Opening*, 339n90; see also SDC 1995-Kiev-01752, March 6, 1995.

26. Letter, Meri to Clinton, June 9, 1995, 2014-0656-M, CL.

27. Percentage reported in "24. April 1995," BzL 669.

28. As Lake reported to Clinton, "West European views [on NATO enlargement] are not yet crystallized"; Memorandum for the President, from Anthony Lake, "West European Attitudes toward NATO Enlargement," n.d., but from context circa July 17, 1995, in my 2015-0772-M, CL.

29. First quotation from "Secretary's Meeting with French Foreign Minister Alain Juppé, March 22, 1995, Paris," SDC 1995-Secto-05006, March 23, 1995; second quotation from SDC 1995-State-025603, February 1, 1995.

30. Gaddis, "History, Grand Strategy," 147; see also Reiter, "Why NATO Enlargement."

31. AIW Simons.

32. SDC 1995-State-049691, February 28, 1995, DS-ERR.

33. SDC 1995-Budape-02063, March 3, 1995.

34. Kozyrev made the end-of-the-honeymoon remark in the presence of Christopher, who relayed it to Clinton in Memorandum for the President, from

Warren Christopher, "Night Note, Thursday, Mar. 23, 1995," DS-OIPS; see also Asmus, *Opening*, 110–11.

35. "May 10: Moment of Truth," note from Talbott to Clinton, no year, but from context May 10, 1995, DS-OIPS.

36. Memorandum for the President, from Warren Christopher, "Night Note, Thursday, March 23, 1995"; Aron, *Yeltsin*, 667.

37. Kozyrev, *Firebird*, 285.

38. William E. Odom, "Chechnya, Freedom, and the Voice of Yeltsin Past," *Washington Post*, August 28, 1996.

39. This view proved durable, as Christopher made similar remarks repeatedly in different contexts: Christopher's "pretensions" note on untitled memo from Talbott to Christopher, January 2, 1995, M-2017-11330, DS-OIPS; "dark shadow" noted in Memcon, Clinton–Claes, March 7, 1995.

40. Juppé described the Chechen War as an affront to anyone who hoped for Russia's democratic reform to succeed; Juppé in SDC 1995-State-025603, February 1, 1995.

41. Christopher comment on untitled memo from Talbott to Christopher, January 2, 1995.

42. SDC 1995-State-096220, April 19, 1995.

43. Kozyrev and Hurd remarks quoted and summarized in SDC 1995-London-002522, February 16, 1995; see also Steven Erlanger, "Yeltsin Blames Army for Failures as He Defends War in Chechnya," *New York Times*, February 17, 1995.

44. For more on the treaty, see "The Conventional Armed Forces in Europe (CFE) Treaty and the Adapted CFE Treaty at a Glance," Arms Control Association, https://www.armscontrol.org/factsheet/cfe; Talbott, *Russia Hand*, 445–46n4. On the movement of equipment inside the Soviet Union, see Quentin Peel, "Moscow Report Tells How Thousands of Tanks Avoided CFE Count," *Financial Times*, January 10, 1991, reprinted in Mastny, *Helsinki Process*, 295–96; see also Falkenrath, *Shaping*, xv–xvii, 117–19; Zelikow and Rice, *To Build*, 479n74.

45. Memorandum for the Secretary, from Strobe Talbott, "From Moscow to Halifax, and Beyond—US Policy toward Russia through 1996," May 17, 1995, EBB-447, NSA. On efforts to revise the flank agreement, and in effect legalize the presence of Russian forces in Chechnya, see Hill, *No Place*, 108, 420–21n26; and Jim Nichol, "Conventional Forces in Europe Treaty," Congressional Research Service, September 15, 1995, https://fas.org/nuke/control/cfe/congress/22b2.htm.

46. Director of Central Intelligence, "Selected Items from the National Intelligence Daily," March 29, 1995, EBB-200, NSA.

47. CIA Office of Slavic and Eurasian Analysis, "The Eurasia Intelligence Weekly," March 15, 1996, EBB-200, NSA.

48. Talbott, *Russia Hand*, 206; see also Åslund, "Russia's Collapse."

49. Handelman, "Russian 'Mafiya,'" 83–84.

50. Burns, *Back Channel*, 89.
51. For more on the concept of "time of troubles," see Gaddy and Hill, *Mr. Putin*, 23.
52. TOIW James Steinberg, April 1, 2008, WCPHP.
53. TOIW James Steinberg, April 1, 2008, WCPHP.
54. "Secretary's Meeting with UK Foreign Secretary Hurd, January 16, 1995, Washington, DC," SDC 1995-State-016931, January 23, 1995.
55. TOIW James Steinberg, April 1, 2008, WCPHP.
56. Daniel S. Hamilton, "Piece of the Puzzle," OD 31.
57. Memcon, Clinton–Kok, February 28, 1995, SDC 1995-State-072302, March 24, 1995.
58. Hurd expressed this Russian preference to Christopher in "Secretary's Meeting with UK Foreign Secretary Hurd, January 16, 1995, Washington, DC," as part of discussions in preparation for Christopher's scheduled January 17 meeting with Kozyrev.
59. Claes summarized these French efforts to Clinton in Memcon, Clinton–Claes, March 7, 1995; on the concept of ordering from a menu of integration options, see Jacoby, *Enlargement*.
60. SDC 1995-London-000542, January 11, 1995.
61. In conversation with Claes and Clinton, Christopher asked whether "French elections will make any difference"; Memcon, Clinton–Claes, March 7, 1995.
62. Kozyrev asked about "opportunities for Russian defense industry collaboration with Western counterparts" at a meeting with Hurd in Stockholm on February 14, 1995, according to SDC 1995-London-002522, February 16, 1995; AIW Gottemoeller; AIW Ischinger.
63. Pavlo Fedykovych, "Antonov An-225: World's Biggest Unfinished Airplane Lies Hidden in Warehouse," CNN, September 4, 2018, https://www.cnn.com/travel/article/antonov-an-225-kiev-ukraine/index.html.
64. SDC 1995-London-002522, February 16, 1995.
65. Quotations from SDC 1995-State-052655, March 3, 1995; on the behavior of Russian visitors, see AIW Townsend.
66. On debate about the relevance of the ABM Treaty, see Dunbar Lockwood, "Administration Moves," 21; details on THAAD paraphrased from Jonathan Masters, "Ballistic Missile Defense," Council on Foreign Relations, August 15, 2014, https://www.cfr.org/backgrounder/ballistic-missile-defense#p4.
67. "Secretary Christopher's Meeting with Andrei Kozyrev, April 26," SDC 1994-State-106418, May 12, 1995.
68. Yuri Mamedov, Talbott's frequent interlocutor in Moscow, let the US embassy know this, as recounted in SDC 1995-Moscow-01059, January 13, 1995.
69. In April 1995 he had supervised the scrapping of an SS-19 Soviet missile and visited a housing complex that US aid was helping to build, so he knew

that such cooperation was possible: Carter and Perry, *Preventive Defense*, 5. See also "NATO Enlargement: Road Map for 1996," May 22, 1995, DS-OIPS.

70. Perry's term of "fictional spontaneity" in Carter and Perry, *Preventive Defense*, 30; SDC 1995-State-008688, January 12, 1995.

71. Claes remark in Memcon, Clinton–Claes, March 7, 1995; President Clinton agreed, saying, "that's the way to do it."

72. SDC 1995-State-008688, January 12, 1995.

73. SDC 1995-USNATO-00287, January 25, 1995.

74. Handwritten note by Christopher on untitled memo from Strobe Talbott to Warren Christopher, March 24, 1995, DS-OIPS.

75. "Mamedov-ST 1-on-1, Brussels, Jan 10, 1500–1800," n.d., year not given, but from context January 10, 1995, DS-OIPS. See also Asmus, *Opening*, 106–7.

76. "Memorandum for the Secretary," from Strobe Talbott, Subject: "Preparing for Geneva," January 12, 1995.

77. See the discussion of this comment in chapter 2.

78. Untitled memo from Strobe Talbott to Warren Christopher, March 24, 1995, DS-OIPS.

79. Gore comments during "Working Lunch with Prime Minister Jean-Luc Dehaene of Belgium," February 11, 1995, reproduced in SDC 1995-State-049057, February 28, 1995.

80. Republicans also suspected that Talbott was willing "to appease Russia"; Goldgeier, *Not Whether*, 65.

81. This information comes from a press release by Lee Hamilton on the congressional debate from January 1995; I am grateful to Chris Kojm for a copy. Christopher and Perry coauthored a February 1995 op-ed opposing the way the act "unilaterally and prematurely designates certain European states for NATO membership," rather than ensuring "each potential member is judged individually, according to its capacity to contribute to NATO's goals"; Warren Christopher and William J. Perry, "Foreign Policy, Hamstrung," *New York Times*, February 13, 1995.

82. Edwards and Samples, *Republican Revolution*, 224.

83. Goldgeier, *Not Whether*, 83.

84. Asmus, *Opening*, 312n27; Asmus says Morris conducted this poll without consulting the president.

85. Morris quoted in Goldgeier, *Not Whether*, 166–67.

86. Steil, *Marshall Plan*, 389.

87. Craig R. Whitney, "The D-Day Tour," *New York Times*, June 5, 1994.

88. Memcon, Clinton–Kohl, February 9, 1995, 10:50–11:30am, my 2015-0776-M, CL.

89. Memcon, Clinton–Kohl, February 9, 1995, 11:30am–12:30pm, SDC 1995-State-046609, February 24, 1995. Kohl added that Yeltsin "doesn't like it either. Nor does he like being portrayed as a dictator."

90. Memcon, Clinton–Kohl, February 9, 1995, 11:30am–12:30pm.

91. Memcon, Clinton–Kohl, February 9, 1995, 11:30am–12:30pm.

92. See the discussion of committing 20,000 troops to Bosnia in Allison and Zelikow, *Essence*, 273–75; see also SDC 1995-The Ha-03712, July 10, 1995, DS-ERR.

93. As a State Department cable issued over Talbott's name surmised, "Moscow has from the beginning seen the crisis in former Yugoslavia as a test of its great-power status," and "its claim to be a player depends in large part on its influence in Belgrade, and thus [it] has consistently protected the Milosevic government"; SDC 1995-State-174896, July 21, 1995, DS-ERR.

94. Memcon, Clinton–Kohl, February 9, 1995, 10:50–11:30am.

95. Memcon, Clinton-Kohl, February 9, 1995, 11:30am–12:30pm.

96. As Clinton explained to Mitterrand; quotation from Cable, Clinton–Mitterrand, March 19, 1995, my 2015-0808-M, CL. For Clinton's acceptance of Yeltsin's invitation to Moscow, see Letter, Clinton to Yeltsin, n.d. but from context spring 1995, F-2017-13804, DS-ERR.

97. Director of Central Intelligence, "National Intelligence Daily," April 11, 1995, EBB-702, NSA; Oleg Orlov and Sergey Kovalev, "A Brief Description of Events in the Village of Samaskhi," n.d., EBB-702, NSA.

98. See discussion of ways to "reinvigorate the Partnership for Peace" in Telcon, Clinton–Yeltsin, April 27, 1995, my 2015-0782-M, CL.

99. See the advice Talbott gave to Clinton about possible outcomes of the summit in "May 10: Moment of Truth," no year, but from context May 10, 1995, DS-OIPS.

100. "May Summit Objectives: Security Architecture/NATO March 30, 1995," cover note dated April 25, 1995, DS-OIPS.

101. Perry request reported by Talbott to Christopher in "Note to the Secretary," April 13, 1995, EBB-702, NSA.

102. See book of briefing papers for trip to Moscow, n.d., but before start of summit on May 9, 1995, 2016-0135-M, CL; quotation from Memorandum for the President, From: Anthony Lake, "Subject: Moscow Summit," n.d., but part of pre-summit briefing.

103. "May 10: Moment of Truth." Talbott thought Yeltsin had de facto told Clinton in Budapest, "'you can have either an undivided Europe or an expanded NATO, but not both.'" Now Clinton was supposed to undo that result.

104. In "Note to the Secretary," April 13, 1995, Talbott recounts Clinton's exact words (in quotation marks) to Christopher afterward.

105. "Summary of One-on-One Meeting between Presidents Clinton and Yeltsin," Memcon, Clinton–Yeltsin, May 10, 1995, M-2017-11528. Yeltsin added, "the hardest thing, Bill, is to persuade our militaries—both yours and ours—to accept the next step: START III." See also "12. Juni 1995," BzL 680.

106. Kokoshin, *Soviet Strategic Thought*, 199.

107. "Summary Report of One-on-One Meeting between Presidents Clinton and Yeltsin, May 10, 1995, 10:10am–1:19pm, St. Catherine's Hall, the Kremlin," my 2015-0782-M, CL; Radchenko, "'Nothing but Humiliation.'"

108. "Summary Report of One-on-One Meeting between Presidents Clinton and Yeltsin, May 10, 1995."
109. Clinton's words repeated in "Debrief for EU Reps of the President's Summits in Moscow and Kiev," SDC 1995-USEU B-05683, May 24, 1995.
110. "Summary Report of One-on-One Meeting between Presidents Clinton and Yeltsin, May 10, 1995."
111. See the timeline of events in Daalder, *Getting to Dayton*, xiii–xv.
112. To the Secretary of State, from DRL–John Shattuck, "Defense of the Safe Areas of Bosnia," July 19, 1995, DS-ERR. On the establishment of Srebrenica as a safe zone, see Bethany Allen-Ebrahimian, "The Hague Just Reminded Us Why Safe Zones May Not Be Safe," *Foreign Policy*, June 28, 2017, https://foreignpolicy.com/2017/06/28/the-hague-just-reminded-us-why-safe-zones-may-not-be-safe-syria-srebrenica-iran-russia/.
113. Refugee number reported in "4. Dezember 1995," BzL 708.
114. SDC 1995-State-206040, August 30, 1995, DS-ERR; Asmus, *Opening*, 127; and Packer, *Our Man*, 337–46.
115. Quotation from Talbott, *Russia Hand*, 171.
116. Spending statistics from Korb, "Who's in Charge Here?," 6; quotation from Talbott, *Russia Hand*, 171.
117. Quotations from TOIW James Steinberg, April 1, 2008, WCPHP.
118. Asmus, *Opening*, 127; Talbott, *Russia Hand*, 172; see also the history of this operation on the NATO website, https://www.nato.int/cps/en/natolive/news_21451.htm?selectedLocale=en.
119. Carter and Perry, *Preventive Defense*, 32.
120. Ischinger, *World in Danger*, 17; Sloan, *Defense of the West*, 137–38 (which notes that IFOR was replaced by SFOR, and then by an EU force in December 2004); see also the UN Press Release SC/6134, November 30, 1995, https://www.un.org/press/en/1995/19951130.sc6134.html.
121. Jenonne Walker, "Enlarging NATO," OD 266–67, 275; in addition, as Hamilton, "Piece of the Puzzle," OD 39, notes, IFOR "validated both the CJTFs and the PfP."
122. Telcon, Clinton–Kohl, July 25, 1995, my 2015-0776-M CL.
123. SDC 1996-USNATO-00056, January 6, 1996.
124. For the evolution of PfP, including deployment to Bosnia, see NATO website, https://www.nato.int/cps/en/natolive/topics_50349.htm. On Ukraine and IFOR, see SDC 1996-Kiev-00029, January 5, 1996.
125. IFOR thus proved a surprisingly successful way to promote NATO-Russian cooperation; see Hamilton, "Piece of the Puzzle," OD 39; see also Stent, *Russia*, 214.
126. Strobe Talbott, "Why NATO Should Grow," *New York Review of Books*, August 10, 1995. Talbott's article also named the January 1994 NATO summit as the moment when the alliance had decided to expand eastward, indicating his view that the announcement of PfP that month was the start of the full-guarantee enlargement process.
127. Talbott, "Why NATO Should Grow."

128. AIW McFaul.

129. A useful overview of the voluminous public discussion about NATO expansion at this time appears in Grayson, *Strange Bedfellows*.

130. Richard T. Davies, "Should NATO Grow? A Dissent," *New York Review of Books*, September 21, 1995.

131. SDC 1995-State-191416, containing text of letter, Clinton to Yeltsin, August 11, 1995, M-2010-0427, CL.

132. On the extension of the NPT, see Barbara Crossette, "Treaty Aimed at Halting Spread of Nuclear Weapons Extended," *New York Times*, May 12, 1995. For more on the 1995 extension, see William Burr, "Tracking the Nuclear Nonproliferation Treaty," EBB-701, NSA.

133. Defense Dept., CTR Program Office, "CTR Accomplishments during the Clinton Administration," October 31, 1995, EBB-447, NSA.

134. Michael Krepon, "The Long-Term Costs of NATO Expansion," *The National Interest*, January 29, 2020, https://nationalinterest.org/feature/long-term-costs-nato-expansion-118211; see also Lever, "Cold War."

135. Study on NATO Enlargement, Official Text, September 3, 1995, https://www.nato.int/cps/ie/natohq/official_texts_24733.htm. See also Memorandum for the President, from Anthony Lake, "The NATO Enlargement Study," October 2, 1995, marked "The President has seen 10-4-95," my 2015-0772-M, CL; Goldgeier, *Not Whether*, 93–96; Hill, *No Place*, 133–34.

136. Churkin quoted in SDC 1995-USNATO-03817, September 29, 1995. On Churkin, see "Vitaly Churkin, Russia's Combative 'Diplomatic Maestro,' at UN, Dead at 64," Radio Free Europe/Radio Liberty, February 20, 2017. Also in September 1995, Talbott advised Christopher that Russian leaders needed "doses of respect to cure their Rodney Dangerfield syndrome," that is, the sense that they got no respect. He added, "I know all this makes you sigh heavily . . . I can just hear you thinking to yourself: . . . there goes my trusty deputy, making the case not just for tolerance but for accommodation of the big babies in Moscow. I admit it: they're a real head case. But their capacity for doing harm . . . is immense": "Friday, September 15, 1995, Chris," DS-ERR.

137. Carter and Perry, *Preventive Defense*, 26; Talbott, *Russia Hand*, 177.

138. Telcon, Clinton–Yeltsin, September 27, 1995, my 2015-0782-M, CL. See also Kozyrev and Talbott's preparatory conversations before Hyde Park, "Talbott–Kozyrev One-on-Ones in Moscow, First session: October 17, 1995"; and "Memorandum to the President," from Warren Christopher, October 20, 1995, both DS-ERR.

139. Talbott remarks and Clinton quotations in Talbott, *Russia Hand*, 184–85. For an even more positive assessment of Yeltsin, see Colton, *Yeltsin*, 8–9.

140. Telcon, Clinton–Kohl, October 10, 1995, my 2015-0776-M, CL.

141. Memcon, Clinton–Yeltsin, October 23, 1995, my 2015-0782-M, CL.

142. On Grachev, see "Pavel Sergeyevich Grachev," n.d., but part of briefing papers for Hyde Park summit, October 23, 1995, 2016-0137-M, CL; SDC 1995-State-275658, November 29, 1995; Carter and Perry, *Preventive De-*

fense, 42; Perry, *My Journey*, 120–23. On Dayton generally, see Auswärtiges Amt, *Deutsche Aussenpolitik 1995*.

143. Statement of State Department optimism in "Secretary Christopher's Participation in the NAC and NACC Ministerials, Brussels, Belgium, Dec. 5–6, 1995" (I thank Svetlana Savranskaya for a copy of this document); Talbott quoted in Holbrooke, *To End*, 212.

144. On Yeltsin's October 26, 1995, heart attack, see Memorandum for the President, from Anthony Lake, "Get Well Message for Yeltsin," October 26, 1995, my 2015-0815-M, CL, which noted that Yeltsin had suffered an attack at 2:30 p.m. Moscow time that day.

145. The scandal dated to Claes's work as economics minister in the 1980s; Rick Atkinson, "Claes Resigns as NATO Secretary General," *Washington Post*, October 21, 1995.

146. Sam Roberts, "Ruud Lubbers, Former Dutch Prime Minister, Is Dead at 78," *New York Times*, February 15, 2018.

147. TOIW James Steinberg, April 1, 2008, WCPHP.

148. Kohl explained this to party colleagues; "9./10. Januar 1998," BzL 961.

149. TOIW James Steinberg, April 1, 2008, WCPHP.

150. TOIW James Steinberg, April 1, 2008, WCPHP.

151. Roberts, "Ruud Lubbers"; Rick Atkinson, "U.S. Blocks Lubbers from NATO Post," *Washington Post*, November 11, 1995.

152. On Solana taking office, see SDC 1995-USNATO-04793, December 5, 1995; Christopher quotation in SDC 1995-USNATO-04805, December 6, 1995. I thank Savranskaya for both documents.

153. SDC 1996-Secto-05005, March 17, 1996; Solana said this to Christopher in spring 1996, not late 1995, but it describes his approach in 1995 as well.

154. On Lewinsky's mother securing the internship, see Morton, *Monica's Story*, 53–54; see 1–52 for more details of Monica Lewinsky's childhood biography.

155. "Excerpts from Narrative Section of Starr Report," *Los Angeles Times*, September 12, 1998.

156. See Christopher's report on this session in Memorandum for the President, from Warren Christopher, "Night Note from Brussels," December 7, 1995, DS-OIPS.

157. SDC 1995-USNATO-04805, December 6, 1995.

158. SDC 1996-USNATO-00056, January 6, 1996.

159. French willingness to reengage discussed in Memorandum for the President, from Warren Christopher, "Night Note from Brussels," December 7, 1995, DS-OIPS.

160. Hunter quotations in SDC 1995-USNATO-05040, December 22, 1995.

161. Quotation from January 27, 1995, in SDC 1995-State-002289, February 17, 1995.

162. Steinberg later described it as follows: "There is a sort of chance that we have right now to lock in a foreign policy architecture for the 21st century." Steinberg quoted in Peter Baker, "Road May Be Refuge for Clinton," *Washington Post*, March 17, 1997.

163. Memcon, Clinton–Kok, February 28, 1995; as Talbott had put the same concept to German interlocutors in May 1994, "the West has a once-in-a-millennium chance to build an undivided Europe and we should not preempt possible alternatives": SDC 1994-State-125189, May 11, 1994, DS-ERR.

8. Cost per Inch

1. Approval rating statistic from Hill and Gaddy, *Mr. Putin*, 28.
2. In his memoirs, Kozyrev lamented Primakov's success in shielding the KGB from significant change as one of the new Russian state's major failings: "at no point in those years was a democratic civil control over the KGB ever established." Instead, a bureaucratic reorganization and name change divided the organization roughly into the internal and foreign services (called the FSB and the SVR, along with some other organizations), but the KGB's "essential character survived"; Kozyrev, *Firebird*, 332. On US awareness that "the relations of the Baltics and Ukraine to NATO and Russia raised special concerns," see SDC 1995-Helsin-4810, August 2, 1995, DS-ERR. On how, as Primakov told Albright, NATO expansion with "no nuclear weapons, no infrastructure" would be "palatable" to Russia, see "Secretary Albright's One-on-One With FM Primakov; Osobnyak, Moscow," February 20, 1997, DS-ERR.
3. SDC 1996-State-043241, March 4, 1996.
4. "One square inch" quotation in SDC 1997-USNATO-975, March 24, 1997, DS-ERR; SDC 1996-State-043241, describes, for example, a February 20, 1996, lunch with all of the named individuals (except Talbott), plus many more.
5. SDC 1996-Secto-05005, March 17, 1996.
6. SDC 1996-State-043241.
7. Christopher quotation of "unrealistic" in SDC 1996-State-043241; further quotations in SDC 1996-Secto-05005, March 17, 1996.
8. Steinberg comment made in meeting between Solana and Christopher: SDC 1996-Secto-05005, March 17, 1996.
9. SDC 1996-State-059734, March 27, 1996, describing lunch meeting of March 20, 1996; on the Baltics and NATO membership, see also Kasekamp, "Uncertain Journey."
10. Clinton had started complaining about this problem in 1993: Memcon, Clinton–Yeltsin, July 10, 1993, my 2015-0782-M, CL.
11. SDC 1996-State-030285, February 15, 1996; he also advised the Baltic states to bear in mind that "Russia had domestic reasons for keeping the Baltics edgy." On the topic of "Russian minorities" in the Baltics, and a similar German sense of a need to "push" the Baltics on the issue, see SDC 1994-State-179020, July 6, 1994, DS-ERR.
12. Memcon, Ahtisaari–Christopher, February 8, 1996, SDC 1996-Secto-03030, February 10, 1996. For discussion of the pros and cons of regional coopera-

tion in the Baltic areas, see Memcon, Clinton–Ahtisaari, March 20, 1997, in SDC 1997-State-062629, April 4, 1997; SDC 1996-State-186058, September 7, 1996; SDC 1997-Paris-5740, March 12, 1997, all DS-ERR; for concerns "of Nordic states" that they not automatically have "their futures linked to the future of the Baltics," see 1997-Paris-5146, March 6,1997, DS-ERR.

13. Kohl discussed French interest in NATO reintegration in "23. Februar 1996," BzL 721.

14. Memcon, Chirac–Clinton, February 1, 1996, my 2015-0775-M, CL.

15. Daniel S. Hamilton, "Piece of the Puzzle," OD 40–41.

16. On the resulting creation of the so-called Petersberg Tasks, see Hill, *No Place*, 144; on the WEU, see Treisman, *Return*, 317; on the WEU 1992 Bonn meeting that created the Petersberg Tasks, see Van Hooft, "Land Rush," 534–39.

17. Memcon, Chirac–Clinton, February 1, 1996, my 2015-0775-M, CL.

18. From Thomas M. T. Niles, EUR, to E/C—Mr. Zoellick, April 27, 1992, FOIA 2000-0233-F, BPL.

19. Yeltsin, *Midnight Diaries*, 135.

20. They reportedly spoke two to three times a month for the rest of 1996. See "Narrative Pt. IV," and "Narrative Pt. V," reprinted in the *Washington Post*, https://www.washingtonpost.com/wp-srv/politics/special/clinton/icreport /6narritiv.htm, and https://www.washingtonpost.com/wp-srv/politics/special /clinton/icreport/6narritv.htm; and "Excerpts from Narrative Section of Starr Report," reprinted in the *Los Angeles Times*, September 12, 1998, http:// articles.latimes.com/1998/sep/12/news/ss-23060. For Clinton's description of his relationship with Lewinsky, see Clinton, *My Life*, 773–811.

21. Stephen Sestanovich, Russia expert, quoted by Steven Erlanger, "Russia Vote Is a Testing Time for a Key Friend of Clinton's," *New York Times*, June 8, 1996.

22. Memorandum for the President, from Warren Christopher and Strobe Talbott, "Your Meeting with Yeltsin," n.d., DS-OIPS; Asmus, *Opening*, 145–46, quotes from this same document and dates it April 18, 1996.

23. Memcon, Clinton–Yeltsin, January 26, 1996, SDC 1996-State-019590, February 1, 1996, DS-OIPS.

24. Telcon, Clinton–Yeltsin, February 21, 1996, my 2015-0782-M, CL. On the announcement of the run for reelection, see Aron, *Yeltsin*, 741.

25. Åslund, "Russia's Collapse."

26. Quotation from Peter Beinart, "The US Needs to Face Up to Its Long History of Election Meddling," *The Atlantic*, July 22, 2018; examples of handouts from Colton, *Yeltsin*, 369; see also "POTUS Yeltsin One-on-One," April 21, 1996, my 2015-0782-M, CL; Michael R. Gordon, "Russia and IMF Agree on a Loan for $10.2 Billion," *New York Times*, February 23, 1996.

27. Colton, *Yeltsin*, 369.

28. SDC 1996-Bonn-01572, February 5, 1996. On the importance of providing Russia with "a place delayed rather than denied," see Haslam, "Russia's Seat," 130.

29. Perry, *My Journey*, 94.

30. Carter and Perry, *Preventive Defense*, 6–7.

31. For Kohl comments to Perry, see SDC 1996-Bonn-01572, February 5, 1996; for more on their significance, see SDC 1996-Bonn-01892, February 9, 1996.

32. Telcon, Clinton–Kohl, February 17, 1996 (Air Force One), my 2015-0776-M, CL.

33. For one of Yeltsin's many expressions of interest in joining the G7, see Letter, Yeltsin to Clinton, May 13, 1996, my 2015-0815-M, CL.

34. Telcon, Clinton–Kohl, February 17, 1996 (Air Force One), my 2015-0776-M, CL. Clinton also expressed worry about a possible Zyuganov win to Chirac; see Memcon, Clinton–Chirac, April 12, 1996, my 2015-0775-M, CL.

35. Telcon, Clinton–Kohl, February 28, 1996, my 2015-0776-M, CL.

36. Telcon, Clinton–Kohl, April 12, 1996, my 2015-0776-M, CL.

37. "26. Februar 1996," BzL, 719 (certain groups, Siberia, irrational, reactivate), 720 (Poland, lurch, partner), 721 (last detail).

38. SDC 1996-State-028159, February 13, 1996.

39. "Saturday, March 16, 1996, Chris," DS-OIPS; Talbott, *Russia Hand*, 194.

40. "Saturday, March 16, 1996, Chris"; Talbott, *Russia Hand*, 189–94. See also SDC 1996-State-054262, March 17, 1996, DS-ERR.

41. Memcon, Ahtisaari–Christopher, February 8, 1996, SDC 1996-Secto-03030, February 10, 1996.

42. Memorandum for the President, From: Warren Christopher, "Note on Helsinki Meetings with Primakov," February 12, 1996, DS-OIPS.

43. Stent, *Limits*, 22–23.

44. Hill and Gaddy, *Mr. Putin*, 23. Åslund, *Russia's Crony Capitalism*, 23–24, makes similar comments: "Before the presidential election in the summer of 1996, seven top oligarchs threw all their money and media power behind President Yeltsin and probably managed to turn the election to his advantage."

45. "Note on Helsinki Meetings with Primakov," February 12, 1996.

46. Memcon, Clinton–Kuchma, February 21, 1996, my 2016-0217-M, CL.

47. "The Secretary's Helsinki Meetings with Russian Foreign Minister Primakov, February 9–10," SDC 1996-State-029302, February 14, 1996. Kuchma wrote to Clinton on February 28, 1997, to complain that Russia still had "not fulfilled its obligations"; see Letter, Kuchma to Clinton, February 28, 1997, my 2016-0218-M/2016-0127-M, CL.

48. Quotation from "Presidential Decision Directive/NSC-47," March 21, 1996, 2010-0427-M, CL. For more on the CTBT, see "Comprehensive Test Ban Treaty at a Glance," Arms Control Association, https://www.arms control.org/factsheets/test-ban-treaty-at-a-glance; and "Comprehensive

Nuclear-Test-Ban Treaty," Nuclear Threat Initiative, https://www.nti.org /learn/treaties-and-regimes/comprehensive-nuclear-test-ban-treaty-ctbt/.

49. "POTUS Yeltsin One-on-One," April 21, 1996, my 2015-0782-M, CL. Clinton announced his support for CTBT in August 1995 but could not convince the Senate to ratify it; see Perry, *My Journey*, 113–14.

50. Primakov quoted in SDC 1996-Moscow-008810, April 1, 1996.

51. Primakov quoted in "Saturday, March 16, 1996, Chris," DS-OIPS; Perry quoted in Stent, *Limits*, 29. For more on START II, see "START II and Its Extension Protocol at a Glance," Arms Control Association, April 2019, https://www.armscontrol.org/factsheets/start2; Perry, *My Journey*, 111–12. The director of the US Arms Control and Disarmament Agency, John Holum, opposed Moscow's "START II–NATO linkage" categorically, telling Berger and Talbott that Russia was "grabbing everything at hand to pile in NATO's way." In Holum's view, the United States should under no circumstances "pay in the START II context for NATO's new members"; Memorandum to: Sandy Berger, Strobe Talbott, Leon Fuerth; From: John Holum, Director, US ACDA, Subject: "Denying A START II–NATO Linkage," January 15, 1997, 2016-0048-M, CL.

52. According to the US embassy in Bonn, Russian diplomats made this assertion "to German foreign minister Kinkel in Moscow, to the Wehrkunde Conference in Munich and elsewhere," and Bonn advised Washington of these developments in SDC 1996-Bonn-01800, February 8, 1996.

53. On the Gorbachev interview, see Hill and Gaddy, *Mr. Putin*, 36, 422n34.

54. The version of the Baker comment published in the United States, for example, was in Gorbachev, *Memoirs*, 529.

55. The way that "Gorbachev's memoirs" added fuel to the fire by citing "'the assurance that neither the jurisdiction nor the military forces of NATO will be extended to territories which lie east of the present NATO boundaries,'" particularly distressed the American embassy in Bonn; SDC 1996-Bonn-01800, February 8, 1996.

56. Baker quoted in SDC 1996-Bonn-01800, February 8, 1996; see also Michael Gordon, "The Anatomy of a Misunderstanding," *New York Times*, May 25, 1997.

57. SDC 1996-Bonn-01800, February 8, 1996.

58. SDC 1996-State-03296, February 23, 1996. (There is a typo in the original that makes it unclear whether the words "offensive forces" are a direct quotation. The all-caps original reads as follows, which I am rendering without added quotation marks to keep the citation exact: GENSCHER MADE A UNILATERAL STATEMENT THAT NATO "OFFENSIVE FORCES11 WOULD NOT BE MOVED EASTWARD. Presumably the typo "11" should be the second set of quotation marks, making the words "offensive forces" a quotation, but as the source is ambiguous, I have not reproduced those words as a direct quotation in the main text above.) According to Ron Asmus, the views expressed in this document became "the official US position in February 1996": Asmus, *Opening*, 307–8n7.

59. See the OSCE website for copies of both "Conference on Security and Co-operation in Europe Final Act," August 1, 1975, https://www.osce.org/files /f/documents/5/c/39501.pdf, and "Charter of Paris," November 19–21, 1990, https://www.osce.org/files/f/documents/0/6/39516.pdf.

60. SDC 1996-State-03296, February 23, 1996.

61. Quotation from Примаков, *Встречи*, 211.

62. SDC 1996-State-03296, February 23, 1996. Henry Kissinger had previously floated this idea; for details, see Solomon, *NATO*, 47–48. On the importance of the context of the original two-plus-four negotiations, see also Trachtenberg, "United States"; Shifrinson, "Deal."

63. Memorandum for the President, from Warren Christopher and Strobe Talbott, "Your Meeting with Yeltsin," n.d., but from context April 18, 1996, DS-OIPS. See also Asmus, *Opening*, 145–46, which quotes some sections of the same document.

64. SDC 1996-State-03296, February 23, 1996.

65. Memorandum to the Secretary of State, from EUR–Rudolf V. Perina, Acting, and S/NIS–John E. Herbst, Acting, Subject: "Primakov's Recent Statements on NATO Enlargement," March 15, 1996, DS-OIPS.

66. "Primakov's Recent Statements on NATO Enlargement," March 15, 1996.

67. SDC 1996-Secto-05022, March 23, 1996.

68. "MSMail, for Tony Lake and the Troika," from John R. Schmidt, Subject: "C-P-L Item: NATO Enlargement," June 6, 1996, my 2015-0770-M, CL; on the Norway model, see Asmus, Kugler, and Larrabee, "NATO Expansion," 14–15; Kaplan, *NATO Divided*, 25.

69. Their determination to resist noted in "Primakov's Recent Statements on NATO Enlargement," March 15, 1996.

70. Simon, *NATO and the Czech and Slovak Republics*, 163–64.

71. SDC 1996-Bratis-01048, June 17, 1996.

72. Solana quoted in SDC 1996-USNATO-00889, February 14, 1996 (which records a meeting between Hunter and Solana to discuss the latter's upcoming visit to Washington, February 19–22, 1996).

73. Quotations in Memcon, Clinton–Solana, February 20, 1996, 2015-0548-M, CL, with the exception of the "those things" quotation, which is in Talbott's account of the same meeting, in his *Russia Hand*, 217.

74. Memorandum for Anthony Lake, from John R. Schmidt, June 21, 1996, my 2015-0772-M, CL.

75. Statistic from Hamilton, "Piece of the Puzzle," OD 39–40; see also Carter and Perry, *Preventive Defense*, 38–44; Perry, *My Journey*, 125–26. The combination of PfP and IFOR was proving that Russians and NATO forces could function side by side. George Joulwan, the SACEUR at the time, later recalled working successfully with Russian military and civilian leaders (AIW Joulwan); he formed a successful working relationship in particular with Colonel General Leontiy Pavlovich Shevtsov, deputy to SACEUR for Russian forces; see a speech by Shevtsov, "Russian Participation in Bosnia-

Herzegovina," address to the Fourteenth International Workshop on Global Security, Prague, June 21–25, 1997, https://www.csdr.org/97Book/shevtsov -C.htm.

76. Hamilton, "Piece of the Puzzle," OD 39.

77. On the success of IFOR, see: To the Secretary, from EUR–John C. Kornblum, Acting; Subject: "Berlin NAC—Adaptation as Message," May 3, 1996, DS-OIPS.

78. Beinart, "The US Needs to Face Up to Its Long History of Election Meddling." See also Michael Kramer, "Rescuing Boris," *Time*, July 15, 1996; Scott Shane, "Russia Isn't the Only One Meddling in Elections," *New York Times*, February 17, 2018.

79. On learning of this connection, Lake's deputy, Samuel Berger, and Christopher tried to break it. They worried about the damage to Yeltsin if the connection became public, but they could not end it and were relieved when it did not become a major campaign issue. For more details, see Talbott, *Russia Hand*, 447n6; and Michael McFaul, "Yanks Brag, Press Bites," *The Weekly Standard*, July 22, 1996.

80. According to Steven Erlanger, "Russia Vote Is a Testing Time for a Key Friend of Clinton's," *New York Times*, June 8, 1996. On Deutch, see Russian complaints "about John Deutch's people running around all over the CIS persuading leaders of independent countries to do everything possible to block Russian efforts to reach agreements" in SDC 1996-Moscow-30108, October 25, 1996, DS-ERR.

81. Telcon, Clinton–Yeltsin, May 7, 1996, my 2015-0782-M, CL.

82. SDC 1996-State-113222, June 1, 1996, EBB-691, NSA.

83. For Clinton's remarks on CFE, see SDC 1996-State-113222, June 1, 1996, EBB-691, NSA. On the "flanks" compromise, see Jeffrey D. McCausland, "NATO and Russian Approaches to Adapting the CFE Treaty," *Arms Control Today*, https://www.armscontrol.org/act/1997-08/features/nato-russian -approaches-adapting-cfe-treaty. As noted in Sloan, *Defense of the West*, 108–9, the final ratification of the adapted CFE treaty was contentious. Russia ratified it in July 2004, but NATO countries "refused to complete their ratification process" until Russia fulfilled commitments made to Georgia and Moldova. Russia suspended compliance in 2007. See also Hill, *No Place*, 108, 130–31, 420–21n26.

84. Aron, *Yeltsin*, 741.

85. Letter, Yeltsin to Clinton, June 3, 1996, my 2015-0815-M, CL. See also the Russian version of the same letter, ППР2, 115–16. On the extension, see Daryl Kimball, "START II and Its Extension Protocol at a Glance," April 2019, https://www.armscontrol.org/factsheets/start2; Russia announced on June 14, 2002, that it would no longer be bound by START II commitments, ending efforts begun in 1993 to bring the treaty into force.

86. Memcon, Clinton–Wałęsa, June 3, 1996, DS-OIPS. Wałęsa added Yeltsin's power was unique. He told Clinton that Russia "is not like the United States

where an order is an order" because "orders are often just not realized." But Yeltsin could issue orders that people would carry out, and "this makes him dangerous in a situation of confrontation."

87. Aron, *Yeltsin*, 741.

88. Brudny, "In Pursuit," 255 (on July 3); see also "Yeltsin Had Heart Attack during Russian Elections," September 21, 1996, CNN, http://www.cnn.com /WORLD/9609/20/yeltsin.button.

89. On Yeltsin's second inauguration, see Talbott, *Russia Hand*, 212.

90. Beinart, "The US Needs to Face Up to Its Long History of Election Meddling."

91. Drafts of plan began circulating at the start of June 1996; see "From John R. Schmidt, for Tony Lake from the Troika," June 6, 1996, my 2015-0770-M, CL; Asmus, *Opening*, 165.

92. "NSC Staff Paper Handed to Secy Christopher by NSC (Tony Lake) on 6/7/96, NATO Enlargement Game Plan: June 96 to July 97," June 5, 1996, DS-OIPS. An open question was when, formally, to invite those new members, with the options being any time between December 1996 and summer 1997.

93. Volker Rühe, "Opening NATO's Door," OD 229.

94. Clinton's "shall not be the last" quotation in Memcon, Clinton–Brazauskas/ Meri/Ulmanis, June 26, 1996, 2014-0656-M, CL; Talbott's use of similar words a year earlier in SDC 1995-State-161570, July 6, 1995, DS-ERR; see also "Deputy Secretary's May 24 [1996] Meeting with Lithuanian Defmin"; Talbott comment about the third round of enlargement not being the last in SDC 1996-State-225177, October 29, 1996, all DS-ERR; other quotations from "NATO Enlargement Game Plan: June 96 to July 97," June 5, 1996.

95. Albright, *Madam Secretary*, 256.

96. Untitled note from Talbott to Christopher, July 9, 1996, DS-OIPS; TOIW James Steinberg, April 1, 2008, WCPHP.

97. Talbott quotations in, and Christopher comment handwritten on, untitled note from Talbott to Christopher, July 9, 1996, DS-OIPS; for an overview of some of what Russia wanted at this point, see Letter from Yeltsin to Clinton, September 17, 1996, ПП2, 117–18.

98. Untitled note from Talbott to Christopher, July 9, 1996.

99. Memorandum for Anthony Lake, From: Steve Pifer, stamped "Natl Sec Advisor NOTED," Subject: "Potential Decision Items for Nov./Dec.," October 28, 1996, 2016-0048-M, CL.

100. Untitled note from Talbott to Christopher, July 9, 1996. In 1994, Talbott had shared his thinking on this matter with Czech diplomats, saying that "a public admission that Russia will never be part of either NATO or Europe . . . would be the height of folly," not only because of "potential negative effects on Russia but because it might send the wrong signal to other countries from the former Soviet Union that might realistically join the

alliance": SDC 1994-State-159482, June 15, 1994, DS-ERR. See also similar British views in SDC 1994-London-16664, October 21, 1994, DS-ERR.

101. Untitled note from Talbott to Christopher, July 16, 1996, DS-OIPS, in which Talbott includes "the Primakov memcon, from our session Monday morning in his office." The Primakov quotation is in the memcon.

102. As the US embassy reported to Washington in early 1997, there was a growing sentiment that the "huge reservoir of good feeling in the Russian people towards the United States" had been drained by US actions since the collapse of the Soviet Union, particularly "broken promises to Gorbachev": SDC 1997-Moscow-01403, January 22, 1997. See also remarks on the Russian view that broken promises to Gorbachev during German unification created doubt about American trustworthiness on NATO in the mid-1990s, in: Memcon, Chubais–Talbott, and Memcon, Talbott–Primakov, both on January 23, 1997, and "Berger–Mamedov Meeting," February 5, 1997, all in DS-ERR.

103. Note from Talbott to Christopher, July 16, 1996. The US record of this conversation noted that Primakov laughed at his remark, calling it "good-natured laughter." On Ukraine's attitude, see Memcon, Gore–Kuchma, December 2, 1996, DS-ERR, in which Gore notes, "I understand Ukraine's unique moral concern over the possible deployment of nuclear weapons on the territory of neighboring states." See also SDC 1996-State-205479, October 2, 1996, DS-ERR.

104. Chirac quotations from Memcon, Chirac–Lake, Paris, November 1, 1996, my 2015-0755-M, CL (for more on Chirac's concern about humiliating Russia and Talbott's disagreement with Chirac's advice on how to handle that issue, see also "Talbott–Chirac Meeting in Paris," January 14, 1997, and "Talbott–Kinkel Meeting," January 15, 1997, both in DS-ERR); the rest of the quotations are in untitled note from Talbott to Christopher, August 28, 1996, M-2017-12008; for more on Talbott's problems with Chirac in particular, see Goldgeier and McFaul, *Power*, 204–5; see also Betts, "Three Faces."

105. Memorandum to the Secretary, from Strobe Talbott, July 25, 1996, DS-OIPS.

106. Note from Talbott to Christopher, July 16, 1996, DS-OIPS.

107. Letter, Clinton to Yeltsin, August 14, 1996, my 2015-0812-M, CL.

108. Kohl quotations in "9. September 1996," BzL 774. Christopher quotation in "A New Atlantic Community," speech on September 6, 1996, https://usa.usembassy.de/etexts/ga7-960906.htm. On the passage of the act, see "Transcript of the Remarks by President W. J. Clinton to People of Detroit," October 22, 1996, https://www.nato.int/docu/speech/1996/s961022a.htm; Goldgeier, *Not Whether*, 79; Solomon, *NATO*, 99–100.

109. Memcon, Clinton–Kohl, September 10, 1996, my 2015-0776-M, CL.

110. On the succession struggle, see SDC 1996-Moscow-033078, December 2, 1996, M-2012-0962, CL, in which US embassy chargé d'affaires John Tefft reported maneuvering by Lebed, Chernomyrdin, and Chubais.

111. Memcon, Clinton–Kohl, September 10, 1996.
112. Letter, Clinton to Chirac, Whitehouse 260250, September 26, 1996, DS-OIPS. See also Letter, Kohl to Clinton, October 23, 1996, my 2015-0810-M, CL.
113. "Remarks at a Reelection Rally, Detroit, Michigan, Oct. 22, 1996," CFPR 92–93. He also referred to the fiftieth-anniversary date in a letter to Yeltsin; see Letter, Clinton to Yeltsin, November 29, 1996, my 2015-0815-M, CL.
114. Memorandum for the President, from Anthony Lake, Subject: "Postponement of Yeltsin's Surgery," September 26, 1996, my 2015-0815, CL.
115. Note from Talbott to Christopher, September 13, 1996, DS-OIPS. See also "Paris ST-Mamedov Sept. 11-12, 96," DS-ERR.
116. Quotation from Talbott in his *Russia Hand*, 230.
117. Untitled note from Talbott to Christopher, September 26, 1996, forwarding "draft memcon, for your eyes only," with attachment titled "Monday, September 23, 1996, WC [Warren Christopher]–Primakov [memcon]," DS-OIPS. The Primakov quotation is in the memcon.
118. Primakov noted in March 1997 that, by continuing their dialogue, "the US side signified its acceptance that Russia affects NATO. If you deny that . . . there is no point in signing any document": quotation from Memcon, Albright–Primakov, March 15, 1997, DS-OIPS. "Steel claw" quotation from Memcon, Chubais–Talbott, January 23, 1997, DS-ERR.
119. Memcon, Primakov–Talbott, March 6, 1997, DS-OIPS.
120. SDC 1996-USNATO-03863, November 5, 1996.
121. Quotation is from a description of the event, which took place in Moscow in May 1997, in Asmus, *Opening*, 209. According to Asmus, the procedure was duplicated two days in a row.
122. Lawrence K. Altman, "Yeltsin Has 7-Hour Heart Surgery and Doctors Say It Was a Success," *New York Times*, November 6, 1996.
123. Memorandum for the Secretary, from INR [Intelligence and Research]–Toby T. Gati, Subject: "Yeltsin's Operation and Its Implications," November 5, 1996, M-2012-0962, CL.
124. SDC 1996-Moscow-033078, December 2, 1996, M-2012-0962.
125. "1992 Electoral College Results," National Archives, https://www.archives .gov/electoral-college/1992; Talbott, *Russia Hand*, 213.
126. Packer, *Our Man*, 395–96.
127. She guessed that the rival was most likely Holbrooke, but possibly former senator George Mitchell; Albright, *Madam Secretary*, 220.
128. Hillary Clinton's view is quoted in Albright, *Madam Secretary*, 222. Bill Clinton's view of Holbrooke is according to Talbott, who noted the remark in his diary, which is quoted in Packer, *Our Man*, 395.
129. Albright, *Madam Secretary*, 227–29.
130. Talbott quoted in Packer, *Our Man*, 392–93.
131. Jane Mayer, "Tony Lake Is Missing," *New Yorker*, March 31, 1997.
132. TOIW Madeleine Albright, August 30, 2006, WCPHP; on Berger's friendship with Talbott, see also Talbott, *Russia Hand*, 224.

133. Text of Solana letter sent to NATO foreign ministers, November 29, 1996, NATO Archive.
134. On the history of IFOR, see Kaplan, *NATO Divided*, 121. On how SFOR became the legal successor to IFOR on December 20, 1996, see UNSC Resolution 1088, December 12, 1996, https://www.nato.int/ifor/un/u961212b .htm; "History of the NATO-Led Stabilisation Force (SFOR) in Bosnia and Herzegovina," https://www.nato.int/sfor/docu/d981116a.htm; Burg and Shoup, *Ethnic Conflict*, 377–78.
135. "Press Communique M-NAC-2(96)165, held at NATO HQ Brussels," December 10, 1996, DS-OIPS.
136. Memcon, Clinton–Kohl, January 6, 1997, my 2015-0776-M, CL.
137. "10./11. Januar 1997," BzL 811; see also 811n8.
138. Kohl also felt strongly that he, Clinton, Chirac, and Major all needed to work on Yeltsin directly if they wanted to keep to the schedule of inviting new members in July; Memcon, Clinton–Kohl, January 6, 1997, my 2015-0776-M, CL.
139. Quotations from Memcon, Kohl–Talbott, January 15, 1997, DS-OIPS.
140. Memcon, Kohl–Talbott, January 15, 1997.
141. Memorandum for the President and Vice President, From Strobe Talbott and Leon Fuerth, "Next Steps with Russia," January 24, 1997, Attachment A to Memorandum for the President, from Samuel Berger, "Report on Talbott/Fuerth Mission and Berger-Levitte Talks," January 25, 1997, my 2015-0755-M, CL; the president added a check mark and wrote "looks better, thanks, BC" at the top of the Berger memo. See also Asmus, *Opening*, 205.
142. Memorandum for the President, from Samuel Berger, January 31, 1997, my 2015-0772-M, CL.
143. For an example of one of Yeltsin's direct requests to Clinton for guarantees that alliance military infrastructure would not advance eastward, see Letter, Yeltsin to Clinton, January 30, 1997, ППР2, 127–29. Primakov also made this case directly to Albright, telling her that new joiners should imitate "Norway and Denmark," which had "NATO guarantees but no NATO bases." Primakov allowed that foreign NATO troops might use the new territory for exercises for peacekeeping, but should not be "stationed permanently" there; Memcon, Albright–Primakov, March 15, 1997, DS-OIPS. On Denmark and Norway's special status, see Sayle, "A Nuclear Education."
144. Memcon, Primakov–Talbott, March 6, 1997, DS-OIPS. Primakov replied to Talbott: "I understand that you don't need or intend to move large forces into Central Europe" because "your Congress won't pay for it." View of Russian diplomats summarized in SDC 1997-USVIEN-01791, March 11, 1997.
145. "To: MKA, From: Strobe, Subject: The NATO-Russia Charter as Time-Released Medicine," March 14, 1997, DS-OIPS. On that day, NATO issued a press release that at least rhetorically addressed Moscow's complaints, saying that "In the current and foreseeable security environment, the Alliance will carry out its collective defense and other missions by ensuring the

necessary interoperability, integration and capability for reinforcement rather than by additional permanent stationing of substantial combat forces." Press release (97)27, March 14, 1997, https://www.nato.int/docu/pr /1997/p97-027e.htm.

146. For NSC suggestions, see Memorandum for Samuel R. Berger, from Ki Fort, February 27, 1997, my 2015-0772-M, CL. Clinton suggested a "permanent consultative mechanism" directly to Yeltsin; see Letter, Clinton to Yeltsin, February 18, 1997, my 2015-0815-M, CL.

147. On the way that "a reluctant Russia" was "pretty much without alternatives" by this point, see Legvold, *Russian Foreign Policy*, 5.

148. Clinton quoted in Goldgeier and McFaul, *Power*, 204–5.

149. Thomas Lippman, "US Talks Tough on Summit Issues; Albright, Berger Insist NATO Will Expand Whether Russia Likes It or Not," *Washington Post*, March 19, 1997.

150. As recounted by Albright, *Madam Secretary*, 256.

151. Memorandum to Secretary Albright, Deputy Secretary Talbott, APNSA Berger, and DAPNSA Steinberg, from Jeremy Rosner, February 26, 1997, DS-OIPS. For more on Rosner's role, see TOIW Samuel R. Berger, March 24–25, 2005, WCPHP; Jeremy Rosner, "Winning Congressional and Public Support for NATO Enlargement," OD 385–99; see also Goldgeier, *Not Whether*, 108–10.

152. Quotation from Ron Asmus, "To the Secretary, from RDA [Ron D. Asmus], Subject: "What to Watch Out for on Enlargement Issues," May 23, 1997, DS-OIPS.

153. Memorandum for the President, From: Samuel R. Berger, Subject: "Scope Paper: Your Meeting with President Yeltsin," March 17, 1997; on most reformist since 1992, Aron, *Yeltsin*, 742.

154. Yeltsin, *Midnight Diaries*, 87; Aron, *Yeltsin*, 668–70, which also notes that there were danger signals for the Russian economy, such as that 50 to 70 percent of trade was "transacted in cash."

155. Previously, foreigners were restricted to 15 percent participation. Locatelli, "Russian Oil Industry"; see also Aron, *Yeltsin*, 741.

156. Memorandum for the President, From: Madeleine Albright, Subject: "Meeting with President Yeltsin of Russia," March 19, 1997, 2016-0140-M, CL (note: this document is heavily underlined and marked up by the president). Clinton hoped that he could get Yeltsin's acceptance of NATO expansion in order to begin making that expansion a reality, but the US president would not do so at any cost. In the margin of this document he made a handwritten note of five "no's" he could not accept in Helsinki: "Ns [*sic*]—veto, delay, exclusion, 2nd class, subord," meaning no Russian veto, no more delay, no exclusion or second-class membership for any country, and no subordination of the alliance to other entities.

157. Memcon, Talbott–Primakov, March 6, 1997, DS-OIPS. See also discussion of the "bribe" concept in "Talbott/Chubais Memcon," n.d. but from context February 1997, DS-ERR.

158. On the "spectacular view," see Talbott, *Russia Hand*, 238.

159. On Yeltsin's illness in his second term, see Colton, *Yeltsin*, 380–82. Colton estimates that Yeltsin was hospitalized at least eight times between November 1996 and December 1999.

160. Clinton quoted in Branch, *Clinton Tapes*, 436; Albright, *Madam Secretary*, 257.

161. Memcon, Clinton–Yeltsin, March 21, 1997, 9:50–11:55am, my 2015-0782-M, CL. In a 2005 interview, Berger remembered the exchange as follows: Clinton said, "'Give it up on NATO enlargement. We're going ahead. . . . All you're doing, Boris, is creating a defeat for yourself. We're going forward.'" Then, "Yeltsin at the last moment said, 'But not the Baltics. You have to commit to me that you will not open up NATO to the Baltics.' And the President said, 'No, I will not make that commitment, and you should not define Russia in those terms. All you're doing is moving the line of the divide between East and West. You're moving the line farther to the east. You should define a different relationship with the West.' It was a dramatic moment. Yeltsin was obviously very troubled by Bosnia, by our intervention there, very troubled by NATO enlargement, but Clinton was very firm with him on that." TOIW Samuel R. Berger, March 24–25, 2005, WCPHP.

162. Clinton's rebuff to Yeltsin is summarized in Albright, *Madam Secretary*, 257.

163. Quotations about Crimea/Sevastopol in Memcon, Clinton–Yeltsin, March 21, 1997, 9:50–11:55am; "push Ol' Boris" quotation from preparatory session for Helsinki, quoted in Talbott, *Russia Hand*, 237; remainder of quotations from "Working Lunch with Russian President Yeltsin," Finnish President's Residence, March 21, 1997, 1:00–2:00pm, my 2015-0782-M, CL.

164. On the Paris Club, which Russia joined in 1997, see "Russia to Join Paris Club of Creditors," *New York Times*, September 17, 1997; on the G7, which Russia joined in 1998, making it the G8 (but was expelled in 2014 following its annexation of Crimea), see Alison Smale and Michael D. Shear, "Russia Is Ousted from Group of 8 by US and Allies," *New York Times*, March 24, 2014. WTO accession took until 2012; see https://www.wto.org /english/thewto_e/acc_e/a1_russie_e.htm. The OECD "postponed activities related to the accession process" for Russia in the wake of the invasion of Crimea in 2014; see https://www.oecd.org/russia/statement-by-the-oecd -regarding-the-status-of-the-accession-process-with-russia-and-co -operation-with-ukraine.htm. Quotation from "Working Lunch with Russian President Yeltsin," March 21, 1997. See also Goldgeier and McFaul, *Power*, 206–8.

165. "Afternoon Meeting with President Yeltsin," Finnish President's Residence, March 21, 1997, 4–4:50pm, my 2015-0782-M, CL.

166. On Yeltsin's resistance to Baltic membership, see Poast and Urpelainen, *Organizing Democracy*, 149.

167. Clinton's remarks summarized in in Branch, *Clinton Tapes*, 436–37. Asmus's account of this summit omits Summers's role, saying instead, "Yeltsin appeared to simply give up"; Asmus, *Opening*, 203.

168. "Press Conference of President Clinton and President Yeltsin," March 21, 1997, F-2013-08489, DS-ERR. The name was apparently meant to echo the Helsinki "Final Act." On how Russia wanted a legally binding treaty that would "put them on a par with the new NATO members" and the treaty that had founded NATO, see "Berger–Levitte Lunch," January 24, 1997, DS-ERR.

169. Memcon, Clinton–Yeltsin, March 21, 1997, 8:15–9:30pm, my 2015-0782-M, CL, has the following note at the end: "As the dinner breaks up, Mr. Talbott tells Mr. Ryurikov [identified as Yeltsin's Foreign Policy Assistant] that President Yeltsin had spoken in error at the press conference when he said that there had been an agreement with the President that NATO would not use Soviet-built infrastructure on the territory of new members states of NATO. Ryurikov acknowledges that there had not been such an agreement."

170. For some of the contentious details, see SDC 1997-State-069524, April 15, 1997; and SDC 1997-State-86892, May 9, 1997, both DS-ERR. See also "MKA Pre-Brief, ST [Strobe Talbott] 4/25/97, A Menu of Scenarios for Your May Day in Moscow: The Good, the Bad, and the Ugly," DS-OIPS.

171. Memorandum for Samuel Berger, from John R. Schmidt, Subject: "Inviting Partners to Madrid," April 15, 1997, my 2015-0772-M, CL. On the reason why the Russian ceremony would take place in Paris (to assuage Chirac, who had unsuccessfully called for a smaller "five-power" summit), see SDC 1997-Paris-005301, March 7, 1997, and SDC 1997-Paris-05742, March 12, 1997, both DS-ERR.

172. Memcon, Clinton–Solana, May 19, 1997, 2015-0548-M, CL.

173. For more on the new council, see "Basic Document of the Euro-Atlantic Partnership Council," May 30, 1997, in https://www.nato.int/cps/ie/natohq /official_texts_25471.htm?mode=pressrelease; on the NACC becoming moribund, see Hamilton, "Piece of the Puzzle," OD 45; on the EAPC, see Hill, *No Place*, 149.

174. Memorandum for the President, from Samuel Berger, Subject: "The NATO-Russia 'Founding Act,'" May 15, 1997, Stamped "The President has seen, 5-19-97," 2015-0772-M, CL; see also section IV, "Political-Military Matters," in "Founding Act," available at http://www.nato.int/cps/en/natohq /official_texts_25468.htm.

175. Michael MccGwire criticized this document, among other reasons, for removing hope for a nuclear-free zone in former Warsaw Pact territory: MccGwire, "NATO Expansion," 23. On vague Western language about NATO's options and its (negative) effects on relations with Russia, see also Treisman, *Return*, 318–19.

176. SDC 1997-State-097231, May 23, 1997, EBB-447, NSA.

177. Memorandum for the President, from Samuel Berger, Subject: "The NATO-Russia 'Founding Act,'" May 15, 1997, my 2015-0772-M, CL. To Primakov directly, Albright challenged a Russian press report quoting Primakov as saying that the final document was "legally binding," saying, "this

is a mischaracterization. The document, as Primakov knows, is politically binding." She added that Yeltsin claimed that it gave Russia a veto, which was also incorrect. The American record of their conversation notes that, in reply, "Primakov admitted that Yeltsin had spoken of a Russian veto. That was a mistake. He had explained this to the Russian president, but Yeltsin had misunderstood." Memcon, Albright–Primakov, Laurent Restaurant, Paris, May 26, 1997, SDC, 1997-State-110688, June 12, 1997.

178. It is unclear whether Clinton received advance word of that ruling, or if it inspired his behavior with Lewinsky the weekend before, but the news had a noticeable impact on his behavior in Paris, according to Talbott, *Russia Hand*, 247.

179. "Narrative Pt. VII," reprinted in the *Washington Post*, https://www.wash ingtonpost.com/wp-srv/politics/special/clinton/icreport/6narritvii.htm; and "Excerpts from Narrative Section of Starr Report," reprinted in the *Los Angeles Times*, September 12, 1998, http://articles.latimes.com/1998/sep /12/news/ss-23060.

180. When Lewinsky told her about the stained blue dress, Tripp advised her not to launder it; Roxanne Roberts, "Linda Tripp Wanted to Make History; Instead, It Nearly Destroyed Her," *Washington Post*, April 9, 2020.

181. Description of Yeltsin's behavior, and quotation, in Talbott, *Russia Hand*, 246; see also "Yeltsin Signs Founding Act, Says Missiles Will Not Target NATO," *Radio Free Europe/Radio Liberty Newsline*, May 27, 1997, https:// www.rferl.org/a/1141416.html.

182. Asmus, *Opening*, 210–11, recalled that "no one knew what it meant. Albright and Primakov, who were sitting next to each other, were talking intensely, but the Russian Foreign Minister did not seem to have a clue either." Observers could not tell whether Yeltsin, in making this gesture, was disoriented, dishonest, or disobeyed later. Although the US press spokesman, Michael McCurry, did receive a number of questions, he could only refer journalists to the Russian delegation; see "Press Briefing by Mike McCurry," Talleyrand Hotel, Paris, France, May 27, 1997, https://clintonwhitehouse2 .archives.gov/WH/New/Europe/19970527-3161.html. See also Colton, *Yeltsin*, 381, which chalks the statement up to illness.

183. Memcon, Clinton–Yeltsin, May 27, 1997, American Ambassador's Residence, my 2015-0782-M, CL.

184. Andrei Kozyrev, "Russia and NATO Enlargement," OD 457.

185. Michael R. Gordon, "Russia and Ukraine Finally Reach Accord on Black Sea Fleet," *New York Times*, May 29, 1997. On the difficulties in getting Yeltsin to Kiev, see discussion during the "Limousine ride of Vice President Gore with Ukrainian President Leonid Kuchma," May 14, 1997, DS-ERR.

186. "Ukraine and Russian Federation, Treaty on Friendship, Cooperation, and Partnership," Kyiv, May 31, 1997, entry into force April 1, 1999. On October 2, 2014, Ukraine registered the treaty with the Secretariat of the United Nations; see the UN website, https://treaties.un.org/doc/Publication/UN

TS/No%20Volume/52240/Part/I-52240-080000002803e6fae.pdf; and Soro-kowski, "Treaty," 319–29; Aron, *Yeltsin*, 742.

187. Talbott, *Russia Hand*, 247.

188. Memcon, US-EU Summit, Restricted Meeting, SDC 1997-State-112007, May 28, 1997.

9. Only the Beginning

1. George Kennan, "A Fateful Error," *New York Times*, February 5, 1997; Talbott, *Russia Hand*, 232.

2. Gaddis, *Strategies*, rev. ed., 70–77; for a nuanced analysis of Kennan's thought, see Logevall, "Critique of Containment," 474–79.

3. Gorbachev–Reagan, Final Meeting (US record), October 12, 1986, EBB-203, NSA.

4. Perry wrote in 2015 that "as it turned out, we never did build the SDI sys-tem.... When I think of the persistent history of the forlorn idea of de-fense against a nuclear attack, I am [reminded of] ... Einstein's grim and painfully realistic observation that 'the unleashed power of the atom has changed everything save our modes of thinking'"; Perry, *My Journey*, 68. See also his 2020 book: "Ten years later [after SDI was announced in 1983], after spending tens of billions of dollars on X-ray lasers, directed-energy weapons, particle-beam weapons, space-based kinetic interceptors, and 'Brilliant Pebbles,' the Pentagon was forced to conclude that none of these concepts would work. The idea of a massive defense against hundreds of incoming warheads was dead"; Perry and Collina, *Button*, 154.

5. Gaddis, *Kennan*, 667–68.

6. Kennan, "A Fateful Error," *New York Times*, February 5, 1997. According to Talbott, Clinton was sufficiently concerned about Kennan's article op-posing expansion to grill Talbott about its argument. Talbott responded that "Kennan had opposed the formation of NATO in the first place" so "it was no great surprise that he opposed its enlargement," which seemed to satisfy the president: Talbott, *Russia Hand*, 232.

7. TOIW James Steinberg, April 1, 2008, WCPHP.

8. Memcon, Clinton–Prodi, May 6, 1998, my 2015-0755-M, CL.

9. "26. Mai 1997," BzL 867 (barriers, written off); "9. Februar 1998," BzL 968 (reparations).

10. "30. Juni 1997," BzL 883.

11. Talbott recounted that Kohl said these words to him in Talbott, *Russia Hand*, 227.

12. On the protests against Kohl, see SDC 1997-Bonn-007047, June 12, 1997, my 2015-0771-M CL; on the difficulties of setting up currency union, see Sarotte, "Eurozone Crisis."

13. Memcon, Clinton–Kohl, May 22, 1997, my 2015-0776-M, CL.

14. Quotation from Memcon, Albright–Primakov, June 19, 1997, DS-OIPS; on using limits as a brake on enlargement, see Talbott, *Russia Hand*, 450n20.

For more on CFE adaptation, see "The Conventional Armed Forces in Europe (CFE) Treaty and the Adapted CFE Treaty at a Glance," Arms Control Association, https://www.armscontrol.org/factsheet/cfe.

15. MccGwire, "NATO Expansion," 23, 37. A further complication with updating CFE was, in Ukraine's view, the way in which "the agreement as written gave the Russians a legal basis to position troops and equipment on Ukrainian soil": SDC 1997-State-071333, April 17, 1997, DS-ERR.

16. This is the description of their view in Asmus, *Opening*, 205.

17. Talbott, *Russia Hand*, 450n20; Talbott's interest in the Baltics dated back to the very start of his time in office, as he had tried (unsuccessfully) to have the three Baltic states added to his portfolio as early as January 1993; see Memo, Strobe Talbott to Peter Tarnoff, "ISCA plus the Baltics," January 23, 1993, DS-ERR.

18. SDC 1995-Budape-02063, March 3, 1995.

19. Quotation from Memcon, Chirac–Clinton, June 20, 1997, my 2015-0775-M, CL, in which Clinton and Chirac discuss the problem that Yeltsin is not coming to Madrid.

20. Quotation from Memorandum for the President, from Madeleine Albright, "Night Note," May 30, 1997, DS-OIPS; Memorandum for the President, from Samuel Berger, "Deciding Which Countries to Support for NATO Membership at the Madrid Summit," June 9, 1997, my 2015-0772-M, CL, which was a draft but was consistent with other forms of similar advice given to the president at the time.

21. Madeleine Albright, "Harvard University Commencement Address," June 5, 1997, Archives of Women's Political Communication, https://awpc .cattcenter.iastate.edu/2017/03/21/harvard-university-commencement -address-june-5-1997/; quotation about Colin Powell from TOIW Madeleine Albright, August 30, 2006, WCPHP; Albright, *Madam Secretary*, 252–54. An expert on the Marshall Plan, Benn Steil, argued that Albright made the goals of NATO expansion remarkably similar to those of the Marshall Plan: "to integrate new democracies, eliminate old hatreds, provide confidence in economic recovery, and deter conflict"; Steil, *Marshall Plan*, 392.

22. Talbott, *Russia Hand*, 228–29.

23. Albright, *Madam Secretary*, 258.

24. Letter from Solana to Albright, June 17, 1997, NATO Archive.

25. Clinton's words summarized in Branch, *Clinton Tapes*, 456.

26. Talbott quotation in "Deputy Secretary Briefs Baltic Ambassadors," June 12, 1997, DS-ERR, where he added, "since 1994, we have known that enlargement should not exclude any emerging democracy, including for reasons based on history of geography." Talbott "cautioned," however, against "public statements anticipating NATO's next round in 1999," explaining such statements could "hurt US arguments in favor of continued enlargement" in "Acting Secretary Talbott's Meeting with Estonian Foreign Minister Ilves," July 31, 1997, DS-ERR. Asmus indicated that he understood adding the Baltics to be his overall goal in "Note to ST [Strobe Talbott] from RDA [Ron D.

Asmus], Subject: The Hanseatic Strategy," July 20, 1997, DS-OIPS. Asmus later wrote that Talbott's support for the Baltics conflicted with public (mis)perceptions that, as a Russia expert, Talbott always prioritized Moscow. Asmus was struck by "the contrast between the public caricature of Talbott's thinking and what he advocated in reality"; Asmus, *Opening*, 230. On the draft US/Baltic charter under development at this time, see SDC 1997-Tallinn-02159, June 23, 1997. See also Goldgeier, *Not Whether*, 115.

27. Albright quoted in Asmus, *Opening*, xxxi.

28. Coauthored with Robert Nurick; see Asmus and Nurick, "NATO Enlargement," 121.

29. Estonian president Lennart Meri complained that the act had "sacrificed" his country to "NATO-Russian accommodation": SDC 1997-State-110550, June 12, 1997; Asmus, *Opening*, 233–34.

30 Donald G. McNeil Jr., "Estonia's President: Un-Soviet and Unconventional," *New York Times*, April 7, 2001; see also Wolff, "Stalin's Postwar Border-Making Tactics."

31. Meri remark of May 28, 1997, quoted in SDC 1997-State-110550, June 12, 1997. Asmus, *Opening*, 234, termed this "the low point of our relations with the Baltics."

32. SDC 1997-State-110550, June 12, 1997; for more context, see Stent, *Limits*.

33. Memorandum for the President, from Samuel Berger, "Subject: Costs of NATO Enlargement," May 30, 1997, stamped "the president has seen, 6-2-97," my 2015-0772-M, CL. See also an earlier estimate prepared at Jesse Helms's request: Letter, US General Accounting Office to Senator Jesse Helms, June 28, 1995, https://www.gao.gov/assets/90/84671.pdf.

34. Memcon, Clinton–Kwaśniewski, Warsaw, July 10, 1997, my 2015-0781-M, CL.

35. The Cambridge Dictionary defines "to snog" as a "UK informal" verb meaning "to kiss and hold a person in a sexual way": https://dictionary.cambridge.org/us/dictionary/english/snog. On the SNOG sessions, see "Meeting with Senate NATO Russia Observer Group (SNOG), Date: June 11, 1997" (preparatory paper), June 10, 1997, from Samuel Berger, stamped "the president has seen 6/11/97," my 2015-0772-M, CL. On British diplomats' reaction, see AIW Rosner.

36. Talbott later briefed NATO ambassadors on the SNOG session using these words, as recorded in SDC 1997-State-11475, June 14, 1997 (it was apparently "intense" even without all SNOG members attending—available records suggest not all members did).

37. Memcon, Blair–Clinton, May 29, 1997, SDC 1997-State-113437, June 17, 1997, DS-OIPS.

38. The president was thereby following Berger's recommendation as expressed in "Meeting with Senate NATO Russia Observer Group (SNOG), Date: June 11, 1997," June 10, 1997. Asmus recalled that a key development on the way was when the Deputies Committee decided to support extending

invitations to only three states on May 19, 1997; see Asmus, *Opening*, 218. Albright also advised Solana on Clinton's preference for three: Memcon Albright–Solana, Sintra, Portugal, May 29, 1997, SDC 1997-State-112472, June 14, 1997.

39. "Notes by Jeremy Rosner, Senior Advisor to the President and Secretary of State for NATO Enlargement Ratification, from meeting at the White House of President Clinton with members of Senate NATO Observer Group," handwritten date of June 12, 1997, but from context June 11, 1997; I thank Jeremy Rosner for a copy of this document.

40. Quotations from "Notes by Jeremy Rosner . . . from meeting at the White House of President Clinton with members of Senate NATO Observer Group"; Warner's views in Asmus, *Opening*, 264. On the subject of diluting or ruining NATO, see Goldgeier, *Not Whether*, 12–13.

41. Quotations from "Notes by Jeremy Rosner . . . from meeting at the White House of President Clinton with members of Senate NATO Observer Group"; see also the JCS's advice that three "would be more practicable and easier for the alliance to absorb," in SDC 1997-State-11475, June 14, 1997.

42. "Statement on Enlargement of the North Atlantic Treaty Organization," June 12, 1997, Public Papers of the Presidents of the United States, William Clinton, Year 1997, Book 1, https://www.govinfo.gov/app/collection/ppp /president-42_Clinton,%20William%20J./1997/01%21A%21January%201 %20to%20June%2030%2C%201997; comment to Blair in Memcon, Blair–Clinton, May 29, 1997.

43. Jacoby, citing Celeste Wallander, compared NATO to a soccer team that could hold tryouts but could not cut anyone from the team once selected; Jacoby, *Enlargement*, xiii; Wallander, "NATO's Price." See also James Goldgeier and Garret Martin, "NATO's Never-Ending Struggle for Relevance," *War on the Rocks*, September 3, 2020, https://warontherocks.com /2020/09/natos-never-ending-struggle-for-relevance/.

44. He said this to Tony Blair; see Memcon, Blair–Clinton, May 29, 1997.

45. Talbott advised using this wording in SDC 1997-State-11475, June 14, 1997.

46. SDC 1997-State-114913, June 18, 1997.

47. Védrine quoted in SDC 1997-Paris-13923, June 19, 1997.

48. On Védrine, see Asmus, *Opening*, 224–25. This development coincided with the failure of a request by Chirac to share NATO command posts in Europe with Europeans, most notably Allied Forces Southern Europe (AFSOUTH); for more on that topic, see "Berger–Levitte Meeting on AFSOUTH," January 24, 1997, DS-ERR. I thank Frédéric Bozo for an email discussion on this topic; for more on AFSOUTH, see https://jfcnaples .nato.int/page6322744.aspx.

49. Asmus, *Opening*, 221.

50. Letter, Secretary Cohen to Minister Rühe, n.d. on document but dated July 1997 by archive, my 2015-0810-M, CL. The program was the NATO Alliance Ground Surveillance Program.

51. Ronald Steel, "Instead of NATO," *New York Review of Books*, January 15, 1998, https://www.nybooks.com/articles/1998/01/15/instead-of-nato/.

52. According to the association's vice president, Joel Johnson, paraphrased in Goldgeier, *Not Whether*, 135.

53. The spokesman was Barry French; quoted in Goldgeier, *Not Whether*, 135. The US ambassador was Jenonne Walker; her account of the fight between defense contractors is in Jenonne Walker, "Enlarging NATO," OD 273–74. See also a similar account in SDC 1997-Bonn-12846, October 14, 1997, DS-ERR.

54. Steel, "Instead of NATO."

55. On the sense inside the administration that time for debate was over, and the way that the "time of 'architecture' is over; the time of action is here," see "Beyond Architecture to Action," SDC 1996-USNATO-00056, January 6, 1996.

56. Albright, *Madam Secretary*, 254.

57. Steel, "Instead of NATO." See also Gaddis, "History, Grand Strategy," 145–51; John Kornblum and Michael Mandelbaum, "Was It a Good Idea? The Debate Continues," *The American Interest*, May 2008, https://www.the-american-interest.com/2008/05/01/nato-expansion-a-decade-on/; Yost, *NATO Transformed*, xii.

58. The writers also argued that it was not NATO but the EU that should enlarge, because that would do less injury to negotiations with Moscow over disarmament. "Open Letter to President Clinton," June 26, 1997, https://www.bu.edu/globalbeat/nato/postpone062697.html.

59. On the nuclear activity at Novaya Zemlya, see Director of Central Intelligence George J. Tenet, Memorandum for [Redacted], Subject: "[Redacted] Results of Special Panel Meeting on Novaya Zemlya Test Site," October 28, 1997; quotation from CIA Intelligence Report, Office of Russian and European Analysis, "Russia: Developing Nuclear Warheads at Novaya Zemlya?," July 2, 1999, both in EBB-200, NSA. The latter document discusses Vladimir Putin as having a role in the testing. See also "MKA–ISI One-on-One," September 20, 1999, DS-ERR, in which Albright and Ivanov discuss how "Putin is getting more immersed in arms control."

60. "Remarks by Stan Resor," Arms Control Association, June 26, 1997, https://www.armscontrol.org/act/1997-06/arms-control-today/opposition-nato-expansion.

61. There was a crucial difference, they felt, between then and now: the two-plus-four accord was ratified by signatories (including the US Senate on October 10, 1990, by a vote of 98 to 0; see https://www.congress.gov/treaty-document/101st-congress/20) and was a legally binding treaty; the 1997 Paris accord was not.

62. Letter, Solana to Kinkel, June 13, 1997, NATO Archive. The secretary general had told Yevgeny Primakov that "the Founding Act should in no way be understood to limit the possibility of establishing multinational

forces headquarters and multinational integrated units, including on the territory of new members."

63. The president sought to confirm this preference with Kohl days before the summit, and the German replied, "I think we can pursue it that way, but we simply need to give a message opening up a perspective for Romania and Slovenia": Telcon, Clinton–Kohl, July 3, 1997, my 2015-0776-M, CL. They also agreed they should not make too much of Baltic membership at present; instead, they needed "to find a way to keep them happy." On Solana's poll of member-state views, see SDC 1997-USNATO-02139, June 20, 1997; and Asmus, *Opening*, 224–25, which notes the results of Solana's informal poll as follows: seven countries preferred three new members; six preferred five; two preferred more than five. See also SDC 1997-State-120928, June 26, 1997.

64. Malcolm Rifkind, "NATO Enlargement 20 Years On," OD 511.

65. Asmus, *Opening*, 214.

66. Asmus, *Opening*, 214. The French appeared to be interested in adding Slovenia as well; I thank Bozo for this point.

67. Quotation, and account of Tripp pushing Lewinsky to exert more pressure on Clinton, in Melinda Henneberger, "The Testing of the President," *New York Times*, October 3, 1998. Excerpts from Lewinsky's July 3, 1997, letter are in "Narrative Part VIII," *Washington Post*, https://www.washingtonpost.com/wp-srv/politics/special/clinton/icreport/6narritviii.htm.

68. Quotation from "Narrative Part VIII."

69. Clinton request to see Lewinsky on July 4, and White House visitors log showing 8:51 a.m. arrival that day by Lewinsky, in "Narrative Part VIII."

70. Quotations in "Narrative Part VIII."

71. David Streitfeld and Howard Kurtz, "Literary Agent Was behind Secret Tapes," *Washington Post*, January 24, 1998; TOIW Lucianne Goldberg and TOIW Linda Tripp, both in *Slate*, September 18, 2018, https://slate.com/news-and-politics/2018/09/slow-burn-season-2-episode-5-transcript.html.

72. Quotations from TOIW Lucianne Goldberg in *Slate*, September 18, 2018, https://slate.com/news-and-politics/2018/09/slow-burn-season-2-episode-5-transcript.html.

73. Roxanne Roberts, "Linda Tripp Wanted to Make History," *Washington Post*, April 9, 2020.

74. Memcon, Clinton–Solana, July 7, 1995, 2015-0548-M, CL.

75. Asmus, *Opening*, 243.

76. Albright, *Madam Secretary*, 261.

77. "Madrid Declaration," July 8, 1997, https://www.nato.int/docu/pr/1997/p97-081e.htm. At the December 1997 ministerial, Solana emphasized the importance of repeating that the door stayed open; see his letter to this effect to the Canadian Foreign Minister, Lloyd Axworthy, on the upcoming December 16, 1997, NAC Restricted Session, December 10, 1997 (copy of letter sent to all ministers), NATO Archive.

78. "Madrid Declaration," July 8, 1997; AIW Ischinger.

79. "Madrid Declaration," July 8, 1997.

80. Albright, *Madam Secretary,*" 267.

81. On the indefinite extension, see Burg and Shoup, *Ethnic Conflict,* 378.

82. Ukraine got a separate charter with NATO in Madrid. For discussions of this document in advance, see Memcon, Clinton–Kuchma, May 16, 1997; and on the meeting following the signing, see Memcon, Clinton–Kuchma, July 9, 1997, Madrid, both 2016-0127-M, CL. For the text, see "Charter on a Distinctive Partnership between the North Atlantic Treaty Organization and Ukraine," July 9, 1997, https://www.nato.int/cps/en/natohq/official _texts_25457.htm.

83. Letter from Solana to invitee states, July 17, 1997, NATO Archive; "Protocol to the North Atlantic Treaty on the Accession of the Czech Republic," December 16, 1997, https://www.nato.int/cps/en/natohq/official_texts _25432.htm. See also Stent, *Russia,* 228.

84. Albright, *Madam Secretary,* 261–63, quotation at 263.

85. Quotation from Alison Mitchell, "Clinton Cheers Exultant Poles, and Vice Versa," *New York Times,* July 11, 1997; see also Albright, *Madam Secretary,* 261–63.

86. Memcon, Clinton–Wałęsa, Warsaw, July 10, 1997, my 2015-0781-M, CL.

87. Memcon, Albright–Primakov, July 13, 1997, SDC 1997-State-135609, July 19, 1997.

88. Memcon, Albright–Brazauskas, July 13, 1997, SDC 1997-State-135599, July 19, 1997, in M-2017-11789.

89. Memcon, Albright–Landsbergis, July 13, 1997, SDC 1997-State-135605, July 19, 1997.

90. Memcon, Albright with Baltic foreign ministers, SDC 1997-State-135597, July 19, 1997.

91. "Note to ST [Strobe Talbott] from RDA [Ron D. Asmus], Subject: The Hanseatic Strategy," July 20, 1997, DS-OIPS.

92. AIW Sestanovich.

93. "Note to ST from RDA."

94. "Note to ST from RDA."

95. Memorandum for the President, from Samuel Berger, December 17, 1997, stamped "the president has seen, 12/30/97," my 2015-0755-M, CL.

96. "MKA [Madeline K. Albright] Meeting: Road Ahead on NATO+ Ratification," August 28, 1997, DS-OIPS; no author identified on the document itself, but the US State Department identified Rosner as the author in the course of declassification.

97. "Note to ST from RDA."

98. SDC 1997-Moscow-24590, September 29, 1997, DS-ERR; on Russian attitudes to the PJC, see Legvold, *Russian Foreign Policy,* 5.

99. Berger made this remark in a meeting with the British prime minister; Memcon, Blair–Clinton, May 29, 1997. Upon being told the problem in

Russia was the elites, not average citizens, Blair responded, "what a surprise—they are just being normal and caring more about the economy."

100. Solana Letter to Axworthy, December 10, 1997 (note: this was Axworthy's copy of a letter sent to numerous recipients).

101. SDC 1997-State-235583, December 17, 1997.

102. Excerpts from Geremek's speech in December 1997, in "19.6 Poland Joins NATO, December 1997," in Westad and Hanhimäki, *Cold War*, 646–47.

103. Asmus, *Opening*, 281; AIW Rosner.

104. "Narrative Part VIII."

105. Bowles assigned the task to his deputy, John Podesta; "Narrative Part VIII."

106. "Narrative Pt. VIII"; "Narrative Pt. IX," *Washington Post*, https://www.washingtonpost.com/wp-srv/politics/special/clinton/icreport/6narritix.htm.

107. "Narrative Pt. IX"; "Narrative Pt. X," *Washington Post*, https://www.washingtonpost.com/wp-srv/politics/special/clinton/icreport/6narritx.htm; "Narrative Pt. XII," *Washington Post*, https://www.washingtonpost.com/wp-srv/politics/special/clinton/icreport/6narritxii.htm.

108. TOIW Anne Coulter in *Slate*, September 18, 2018, https://slate.com/news-and-politics/2018/09/slow-burn-season-2-episode-5-transcript.html.

109. "Narrative Pt. XII."

110. "Affidavit of Jane Doe #, Monica Lewinsky Affidavit," https://www.cnn.com/ALLPOLITICS/1998/03/16/jones.clinton.docs/monica.lewinsky.affidavit; "Narrative Pt. XII"; "Narrative Pt. XIII," *Washington Post*, https://www.washingtonpost.com/wp-srv/politics/special/clinton/icreport/6narritxiii.htm.

111. "Narrative Pt. XII"; "Narrative Pt. XIII."

112. "Affidavit of Jane Doe #, Monica Lewinsky Affidavit."

113. "Narrative Pt. XIII."

114. TOIW Linda Tripp in *Slate*, September 18, 2018.

115. Memorandum to the Secretary of State, from EUR–Marc Grossman, Subject: "Thinking about 1998," January 6, 1998, DS-OIPS; Albright, *Madam Secretary*, 263–65.

116. Steel, "Instead of NATO"; see also Kathryn R. Schultz and Tomás Valásek, "Hidden Costs of NATO Expansion," Institute for Policy Studies, May 1, 1997, https://ips-dc.org/hidden_costs_of_nato_expansion/. Before joining the State Department, Asmus and RAND colleagues estimated that the overall cost of enlargement would be $42 billion over roughly a decade, with an annual US share of $420 million to $1.4 billion; see Asmus, Kugler, and Larrabee, "What Will NATO Enlargement Cost?," 7, 23–26. Steil later called this estimate "way too low," not least because, in 2016, RAND called for NATO to spend $2.7 billion per year to defend the Baltics; see Steil, *Marshall Plan*, 395; and David A. Shlapak and Michael W. Johnson, "Reinforcing Deterrence on NATO's Eastern Flank," RAND, RR-1253-A, 2016, https://www.rand.org/pubs/research_reports/RR1253.html.

117. Steel, "Instead of NATO"; on difficulties with the French generally, see Asmus, *Opening*, 224.

118. According to the Congressional Budget Office (CBO), "NATO's Senior Resource Board (SRB) estimated in 1997 that integrating Poland, Hungary, and the Czech Republic into NATO would increase the common budgets by about $1.5 billion over 10 years." See "Appendix: Cost Insights from the 1999 Round of NATO Enlargement," one of the attachments to "Cost Implications of Implementing the March 26, 2003, NATO Accession Protocols," April 28, 2003, report prepared for Senators Richard Lugar and Joseph Biden by the CBO, https://www.cbo.gov/sites/default/files/108th-congress-2003-2004/reports/04-28-natoenlargement.pdf.

119. Goldgeier, *Not Whether*, 132.

120. Quotations from Memorandum for Samuel R. Berger, From: Susan Braden and Nancy McEldowney, Subject: "Committee to Expand NATO Dinner IHO Polish, Czech and Hungarian Foreign Ministers, February 10, 1998, 7:00pm, Metropolitan Club," preparatory briefing, February 9, 1998, my 2015-0772-M, CL. In other words, the alliance would have to make greater use than planned of Warsaw Pact leftovers—precisely what Primakov and Yeltsin sought to prevent.

121. Telcon, Clinton–Yeltsin, April 6, 1998, my 2015-0782-M, CL.

122. Quotation from TOIW Bruce Udolf in *Slate*, August 14, 2018, https://slate.com/news-and-politics/2018/08/transcript-of-slow-burn-episode-1-of-season-2.html.

123. "Chronology," CNN, https://www.cnn.com/ALLPOLITICS/1998/resources/lewinsky/timeline/.

124. TOIW Bruce Udolf in *Slate*, August 14, 2018.

125. "Chronology," CNN; TOIW Bruce Udolf in *Slate*, August 14, 2018.

126. Ed Pilkington, "Interview Ken Starr," *Guardian*, September 15, 2018.

127. Adam Liptak, "Brett Kavanaugh Urged Graphic Questions in Clinton Inquiry," *New York Times*, August 20, 2018. Brett Kavanaugh worked for Starr in 1997 but was transitioning away by November; after January 16, however, he decided to return to working for Starr in 1998.

128. Quotations from TOIW Steve Binhak in *Slate*, August 14, 2018, https://slate.com/news-and-politics/2018/08/transcript-of-slow-burn-episode-1-of-season-2.html; on mother's arrival, see "Chronology," CNN.

129. "Chronology," CNN.

130. "Excerpts from a Deposition Given by Clinton in January," deposition date January 17, 1998, *New York Times*, https://archive.nytimes.com/www.nytimes.com/library/politics/072998clinton-testimony.html.

131. Annys Shin, "Twenty Years Ago the Drudge Report Broke the Clinton-Lewinsky Scandal," *Washington Post*, January 11, 2018.

132. TOIW Madeleine Albright, August 30, 2006, WCPHP.

133. Albright, *Madam Secretary*, 352.

134. On the constellation of interactions among a wide array of events in relations between states, see Manela, "International Society."

135. As Albright put it, after ratification "people suggested that the outcome was inevitable. It certainly didn't seem so at the time": Albright, *Madam Secretary*, 263; Asmus, *Opening*, 280–81; AIW Rosner. An advisor to then-Senator Joseph Biden, Michael Haltzel, similarly notes in a memoir account that the vote was anything but "inevitable" and "the decision could have gone either way: Michael Haltzel, "U.S. Congressional Engagement with Central and Eastern Europe since 1991," in Dębski and Hamilton, *Europe*, 127.

136. John M. Broder, "State of the Union," *New York Times*, January 28, 1998.

137. Telcon, Clinton–Kohl, February 4, 1998, my 2015-0776-M, CL. Note: there are two versions of this document in the file, one with these quotations and the handwritten note "DO NOT SEND TO STATE," and an abridged version (presumably for State).

138. Quotation from Memorandum for Samuel R. Berger, From: Susan Braden and Nancy McEldowney, Subject: "Committee to Expand NATO," February 10, 1998; Canadian approval date on Polish foreign ministry, "Poland's Road to NATO," https://www.gov.pl/web/national-defence/poland-in-nato-20-years.

139. Warner quotation from Eric Schmitt, "Senate Approves Expansion of NATO," *New York Times*, May 1, 1998.

140. Samuel Nunn and Brent Scowcroft, "NATO: A Debate Recast," *New York Times*, February 4, 1998.

141. Quotations from Memorandum for Samuel R. Berger, From: Susan Braden and Nancy McEldowney, Subject: "Committee to Expand NATO," February 10, 1998. On February 19, 1998, Albright called the United States the indispensable nation in response to a question about Iraq, but aspiring NATO members presumably agreed with the sentiment. TOIW Secretary of State Madeleine K. Albright, *The Today Show*, February 19, 1998, State Department Archive, https://1997-2001.state.gov/statements/1998/980219a.html.

142. AIW Grossman.

143. "Remarks at a Ceremony Transmitting to the United States Senate the Protocol of Access to NATO for Poland, Hungary and the Czech Republic, Washington DC, February 11, 1998," CFPR 98–100. Asmus, *Opening*, 280, says that the president, to mark the event, appeared in front of a full-size photo replica of the Berlin Wall.

144. Congressional Record—Senate, Monday, April 27, 1998, https://www.govinfo.gov/content/pkg/GPO-CRECB-1998-pt5/pdf/GPO-CRECB-1998-pt5-5-2.pdf; Asmus, *Opening*, 282–88, esp. 285.

145. Schmitt, "Senate Approves Expansion of NATO."

146. Albright, *Madam Secretary*, 265; Goldgeier, *Not Whether*, 149; AIW Rosner.

147. Schmitt, "Senate Approves." Only ninety-nine senators took part in the final vote as Jon Kyl, Republican from Arizona, departed before the last vote to catch a flight; see Jeremy Rosner, "Winning Congressional and Public Support for NATO Enlargement," OD 394.

148. Voting "nay" were Ashcroft (R-MO), Bryan (D-NV), Bumpers (D-AR), Conrad (D-ND), Craig (R-ID), Dorgan (D-ND), Harkin (D-IA), Hutchin-

son (R-AR), Inhofe (R-OK), Jeffords (R-VT), Kempthorne (R-ID), Leahy (D-VT), Moynihan (D-NY), Reid (D-NV), Smith (R-NH), Specter (R-PA), Warner (R-VA), Wellstone (D-MN), and Wyden (D-OR); Kyl (R-AZ) did not vote. See https://www.senate.gov/legislative/LIS/roll_call_lists/roll _call_vote_cfm.cfm?congress=105&session=2&vote=00117#position; see also Schmitt, "Senate Approves."

149. Kennan quoted in Logevall, "Critique of Containment," 496. The quotation is from 1995 but is consistent with the sentiments he expressed in 1997–98 as well.

150. "Evidence: The DNA Test," *Washington Post*, September 22, 1998.

10. Carving Out the Future

1. Clinton made this remark to German chancellor Gerhard Schröder in Memcon, Clinton–Schröder, February 11, 1999, my 2015-0777-M, CL.

2. Åslund, "Russia's Collapse."

3. Quotation and IMF information from Åslund, "Russia's Collapse"; Åslund, *Russia's Crony Capitalism*, 22 (budget deficit), 71 (private portfolio inflows, yields, out before crash).

4. Michael E. Gordon and David E. Sanger, "Rescuing Russia," *New York Times*, July 17, 1998.

5. AIW Grossman.

6. Åslund, *Russia's Crony Capitalism*, 71.

7. "Profile: Sergei Kiriyenko," BBC News, August 24, 1998, http://news.bbc .co.uk/2/hi/special_report/1998/08/98/russia_crisis/157120.stm.

8. "Crowds Cheer G8 Leaders," BBC News, May 15, 1998, http://news.bbc.co .uk/2/hi/special_report/1998/05/98/g8/94439.stm.

9. Telcon, Clinton–Kohl, July 8, 1998, my 2015-0776-M, CL.

10. Telcon, Clinton–Yeltsin, July 10, 1998, my 2015-0782-M, CL.

11. Confirming $11.2 billion a week later: "Press Release: IMF Approves Augmentation of Russia Extended Arrangement and Credit," International Monetary Fund, July 20, 1998, https://www.imf.org/en/News/Articles/2015 /09/14/01/49/pr9831. Åslund, *Russia's Crony Capitalism*, 72, gives the amount provided by the IMF, the World Bank, and Japan as totaling $22.6 billion; on $17.1 billion, see Michael E. Gordon and David E. Sanger, "Rescuing Russia," *New York Times*, July 17, 1998; see also Miller, *Putinomics*, 1.

12. Quotation from Åslund, *Russia's Crony Capitalism*, 72.

13. "Framing Our Goals for the Upcoming Moscow Summit," n.d., but from context July 1998, my 2015-0815-M, CL.

14. Quoted in Aron, *Yeltsin*, 742.

15. "Framing Our Goals for the Upcoming Moscow Summit."

16. Kotkin, "Resistible Rise"; Myers, *New Tsar*, 123–25.

17. Kotkin, "Resistible Rise"; Putin comments about Kohl in Putin et al., *First Person*, 196; see also Dawisha, *Putin's Kleptocracy*; Plokhy, *Last Empire*, 161.

18. Belton, *Putin's People*, 83–87.

19. Kotkin, "Resistible Rise"; Miller, *Putinomics*, 9. Miller dates Sobchak's escape to October 1997, but Putin et al., *First Person*, 117, and media reports put it in November; see Celestine Bohlen, "A. A. Sobchak Dead at 62," *New York Times*, February 21, 2000; "Mayor of St. Petersburg Dies," AP, February 20, 2000, https://apnews.com/5efb84841d03f03afac138a9371f7b0d. Putin later denied having anything to do with the escape, saying that some of "his [Sobchak's] friends—I think they were from Finland" had simply "sent an airplane": Putin et al., *First Person*, 116–17. Note: the name of Putin's contact is also sometimes transliterated as Alexei Kudrin.

20. Kotkin, "Resistible Rise." Miller, *Putinomics*, 14, has Putin "beginning his rapid ascent in Moscow" in October 1997, whereas Hill and Gaddy, *Mr. Putin*, 38, and Putin et al., *First Person*, 128, date the beginning of his work in Moscow to August 1996; see also Belton, *Putin's People*, 111–13.

21. Memorandum for the President, from Samuel Berger and Gene Sperling, "Framing Our Goals for the Upcoming Moscow Summit," July 22, 1998, stamped "The president has seen, 7-22-98," my 2015-0815-M, CL. On Putin's wife hailing from Kaliningrad, see Putin et al., *First Person*, 56.

22. Memcon, Clinton–Constantinescu, SDC 1998-State-134141, July 23, 1998; description of conflict and NATO statistics about Kosovo from "NATO's Role in Relation to the Conflict in Kosovo," July 15, 1999, https://www.nato.int/kosovo/history.htm#B.

23. Quotations from Telcon, Clinton–Kohl, August 7, 1998, 2015-0776-M, CL; see also TOIW Madeleine Albright, August 30, 2006, WCPHP; and Resolution 1199 (1998), United Nations Security Council, September 23, 1998, http://unscr.com/en/resolutions/doc/1199.

24. As Marten put it, "Washington's refusals to seek UNSC legitimation for its actions . . . expanded over time. In 1998, the USA and UK conducted several airstrike operations in Iraq without seeking UN approval" and "in 2003, the biggest blow to UNSC authority occurred, when a US-led coalition invaded and occupied Iraq without UNSC authorization"; Marten, "NATO Enlargement," 413–14. The practice of maintaining maximum flexibility for the United States has parallels in its nuclear strategy; see Gavin, "Blasts."

25. "Joint Statement by the Government of the Russian Federation and the Central Bank of the Russian Federation on the Exchange Rate Policy," August 17, 1998, https://web.archive.org/web/20150131090423/http://www.cbr.ru/eng/press/JOINT.htm; Åslund, "Russia's Collapse"; see also Andrew Kramer, "The Euro in 2010 Feels Like the Ruble in 1998," *New York Times*, May 12, 2010.

26. Åslund, *Russia's Crony Capitalism*, 72.

27. Talbott's report from Moscow summarized in "Telephone Call with Prime Minister Blair," from Samuel Berger, no addressee but from context to the president, August 27, 1998, M-2013-0472, CL.

28. Talbott, *Russia Hand*, 278.

29. Memorandum for the President, from Samuel Berger and Gene Sperling, Subject: "Telephone Call to Russian President Yeltsin," August 24, 1998,

M-2009-1291, CL; on the bombings, see "East African Embassy Bombings," FBI History, https://www.fbi.gov/history/famous-cases/east-african-embassy-bombings.

30. The US national security advisor noted this rumor about Yeltsin's potential resignation letter in "Telephone Call with Prime Minister Blair," from Samuel Berger, August 27, 1998; see also Myers, *New Tsar,* 128.

31. Quotation from Telcon, Clinton–Yeltsin, August 25, 1998, my 2015-0782-M, CL; Talbott, *Russia Hand,* 278. For documents on cooperation between Chernomyrdin and Gore in the 1990s, see the large collection in F-2017-13804, DS-ERR.

32. Memcon, Clinton–Kohl, August 30, 1998, my 2015-0776-M, CL.

33. Clinton quoted in Talbott, *Russia Hand,* 286. On the summit, see also the State Department's "US-Russian Summits, 1992–2000," https://1997-2001.state.gov/regions/nis/chron_summits_russia_us.html. For more on paying the price of the loss of the gains made in relations with Russia, see "Discussion: European Security Next Steps," May 6, 1998, and "Berger Convenes Meeting—MKA Introduces Overview," n.d. but from context January 1999, both DS-ERR.

34. Clinton advised Kohl that he had learned of this idea in Telcon, Clinton–Kohl, September 9, 1998, my 2015-0776-M, CL.

35. Primakov's deputy, Igor Ivanov, became foreign minister: Telcon, Clinton–Yeltsin, September 12, 1998, my 2015-0782-M, CL.

36. The US embassy soon reported that Primakov was trying to "secure his claim to Yeltsin's post": SDC 1999-Moscow-002993, February 10, 1999; see also "Toria" [Nuland], January 28, 1999, both M-2012-0962, CL.

37. As he put it to party colleagues as they analyzed their defeat, "Ich selbst habe mehr an Preis bezahlt als jeder andere: Ich habe in meinem Wahlkreis erlebt, wie durch die Gruppe der Eurogegner mit gigantischen Mitteln die Verhetzung von Haushalt zu Haushalt gemacht wurde"; "28. September 1998," BzL 1075.

38. Telcon, Clinton–Kohl, September 30, 1998, my 2015-0776-M, CL. Clinton subsequently sent Kohl a handwritten letter on November 3, 1998, saying, "Dear Helmut, Today I am in the Oval Office waiting for election results, and enjoying the quiet. I wanted to write to thank you . . . for being such a good friend to me. Your wise counsel, support, and faith in me in my darkest days mean more than you will ever know. We look forward to having you here for the Medal of Freedom ceremony. And they want you back at Filomena's! Sincerely, Bill." Letter, Clinton–Kohl, my 2015-0810-M, CL.

39. Memcon, Clinton–Schröder, October 9, 1998. my 2015-0777-M CL. To the last question, Clinton responded, "a good question and I don't have a full answer." The only certainty, in Schröder's words, was that it was "not going to be Yeltsin."

40. Letter from Clinton to Yeltsin, October 5, 1998, ППР2, 177–78.

41. Telcon, Clinton–Yeltsin, October 5, 1998, SDC 1998-State-189900, October 14, 1998. On Yeltsin hanging up on Clinton, apparently for the first time

(and apparently not noted in the transcript given to the State Department), see Talbott, *Russia Hand*, 300.

42. "Statement to the Press by the Secretary General Following Decision on the ACTORD," October 13, 1998, NATO HQ, https://www.nato.int/docu /speech/1998/s981013a.htm; Albright, *Madam Secretary*, 392.

43. See NATO's timeline of events at https://www.nato.int/docu/update/1998 /9810e.htm; and "NATO's Role in Relation to the Conflict in Kosovo," https://www.nato.int/kosovo/history.htm.

44. Telcon, Clinton–Blair, October 6, 1998, M-2012-0600, CL.

45. "Evidence," *Washington Post*, September 22, 1998, https://www.washington post.com/wp-srv/politics/special/clinton/stories/evibloodo92298.htm.

46. "President Bill Clinton," CNN, August 17, 1998, https://www.cnn.com /ALLPOLITICS/1998/08/17/speech/transcript.html.

47. Adam Liptak, "Brett Kavanaugh Urged Graphic Questions in Clinton Inquiry," *New York Times*, August 20, 2018.

48. "Chronology: Key Moments In The Clinton-Lewinsky Saga," CNN, 1998, https://www.cnn.com/ALLPOLITICS/1998/resources/lewinsky/timeline/.

49. Roth, *Human Stain*, 3.

50. Packer reached a similar conclusion in *Our Man*, 399–400: "Pax Americana began to decay at its very height. If you ask me when the long decline began, I might point to 1998."

51. Peter Baker, "Clinton Settles Paula Jones Lawsuit for $850,000," *Washington Post*, November 14, 1998.

52. "Transcript: President Clinton Explains Iraq Strike," CNN, December 16, 1998, https://www.cnn.com/ALLPOLITICS/stories/1998/12/16/transcripts /clinton.html; Francis X. Clines and Steven Lee Myers, "Attack on Iraq," *New York Times*, December 17, 1998.

53. Clinton hosted Czech president Václav Havel at a state dinner to show support; on the dinner, see APP-UCSB, https://www.presidency.ucsb.edu /documents/remarks-the-state-dinner-honoring-president-vaclav-havel -the-czech-republic.

54. On the lack of military readiness, see Barany, *Future*, 26. I thank Petr Luňák and Vít Smetana for discussion of this topic.

55. See the relevant article on new members, Article 10: "The North Atlantic Treaty," April 4, 1949, https://www.nato.int/cps/en/natolive/official_texts _17120.htm.

56. Quotations from SDC 1998-State-235400, December 23, 1998; to Cohen, Polish leaders said that Poland "would meet all its NATO obligations": SDC 1998-State-127191, July 14, 1998. The lack of invitee preparedness is described in Barany, *Future*, 26–29; see also Poast and Chinchilla, "Good for Democracy?," 475.

57. As Albright put it, "early accession would avoid leaving the impression that the three could only rubber-stamp alliance decisions taken at the summit. Early March was a compromise date." SDC 1998-State-235400, December 23, 1998.

58. The embassy reported that Berezovsky had used this phrase on February 5 with the US ambassador: SDC 1998-Moscow-002993, February 10, 1999, M-2012-0962, CL; see also Yeltsin, *Midnight Diaries*, 217–19.

59. James Hansam, "Yeltsin's Daughter," *Evening Standard*, April 4, 2002; Kotkin, "Resistible Rise"; Myers, *New Tsar*, 140–41.

60. Michael Wines, "After Sex-Tape Attack on Prosecutor," *New York Times*, March 20, 1999; Hill, *No Place*, 140.

61. Celestine Bohlen, "Yeltsin's Inner Circle," *New York Times*, March 24, 1999; see also Belton, *Putin's People*, 123–25.

62. Kotkin, "Resistible Rise."

63. Baker and Glasser, *Kremlin Rising*, 50–52.

64. Celestine Bohlen, "Scandal Over Top Russian Prosecutor," *New York Times*, March 18, 1999; Wines, "After Sex-Tape Attack"; see also Belton, *Putin's People*, 130–31.

65. SDC 1998-Moscow-002993, February 10, 1999. Talbott noted that he found Berezovsky "a poor source of information and an unreliable channel through which to accomplish any business," but Berezovsky's prediction proved accurate: Primakov was ousted in May 1999. See Talbott, *Russia Hand*, 208, 278.

66. Baker and Glasser, *Kremlin Rising*, 52.

67. Letter from Yeltsin to Kuchma, February 16, 1999, ППР2, 338–39.

68. Letter from Yeltsin to Kuchma, February 22, 1999, ППР2, 339–40.

69. Letter from Kuchma to Yeltsin, March 9, 1999, ППР2, 341–42.

70. On the impact of this fighting on US politics, particularly the first Trump impeachment, see Plokhy and Sarotte, "Shoals of Ukraine"; see also declassified State Department documents related to Ukraine and the impeachment, FOIA F-2019-06332, https://docs.house.gov/meetings/JU/JU00/20191211/110331/HMKP-116-JU00-20191211-SD1313.pdf.

71. Memcon, Clinton–Schröder, February 11, 1999, my 2015-0777-M, CL.

72. "How the Senators Voted on Impeachment," CNN, February 12, 1999, https://www.cnn.com/ALLPOLITICS/stories/1999/02/12/senate.vote/.

73. Geremek and Albright quoted in Asmus, *Opening*, xxvii.

74. The Truman Library has a video on its website: "NATO Accession Ceremony," March 12, 1999, https://www.trumanlibrary.gov/movingimage-records/vt2000-108-nato-accession-ceremony. See also M. E. Sarotte, "The Convincing Call from Central Europe: Let US into NATO," *Foreign Affairs*, March 12, 2019.

75. Jane Perlez, "Expanding the Alliance," *New York Times*, March 13, 1999; see also Albright, *Madam Secretary*, 265–66.

76. See the video available at "NATO Accession Ceremony," March 12, 1999; see also Asmus, *Opening*, xxvii–xxviii.

77. These problems persisted until the congressional report was published in October 2000; "Integrating New Allies into NATO," CBO Paper, Congressional Budget Office, October 2000, https://www.cbo.gov/sites/default/files/106th-congress-1999-2000/reports/nato.pdf.

78. Letter, Clinton to Yeltsin, n.d., but from context late February, probably February 20, 1999, M-2009-1290, CL; on Russian interest in trying to find some kind of solution in the Permanent Joint Council, see SDC 1999-State-035179, February 25, 1999.

79. Albright, *Madam Secretary*, 400–402.

80. Memcon, Clinton–Solana, March 15, 1999, 2015-0548-M, CL; Memcon, Clinton–Blair, March 21, 1999, M-2012-0600, CL.

81. See document starting with the words "Dear Bill," with handwritten note "Advance Draft [of translation], March 23, 1999, Yeltsin-Clinton Letter," 2014-0473-M, CL.

82. Quotation in Hill, *No Place*, 169. In Russia, one analyst said, the impending Kosovo strikes drove opponents of the United States into a "frenzy"; Legvold, *Russian Foreign Policy*, 5–6; see also Goldgeier and McFaul, *Power*, 264–65, and Kieninger, "The 1999 Kosovo War."

83. AIW Shea.

84. "Phone Call with President Yeltsin," from Samuel Berger, March 24, 1999 (preparatory paper), 2014-0546-M, CL.

85. Memcon, Clinton–Yeltsin, my 2015-0782-M, CL, document dated March 24, 1998, but from context must be from 1999.

86. Legvold, *Russian Foreign Policy*, 5. On the establishment of the PJC, see Wade Boese, "NATO Unveils 'Strategic Concept' at 50th Anniversary Summit," Arms Control Association, https://www.armscontrol.org/act /1999-04/press-releases/nato-unveils-strategic-concept-50th-anniversary -summit.

87. Telcon, Clinton–Yeltsin, my 2015-0782-M, CL, document dated March 24, 1998, but from context must be from 1999; for Talbott's account of this call, see Talbott, *Russia Hand*, 305–6.

88. Quotations from Celestine Bohlen, "Crisis in the Balkans," *New York Times*, April 10, 1999; see also M-2013-0472, CL.

89. Gates, *Exercise*, 266.

90. Trenin, *Post-Imperium*, 105.

91. Primakov had gotten to be too popular, as noted in Daniel William, "'Primakov Phenomenon' Gains Momentum in Russia," *Washington Post*, August 6, 1999.

92. Albright, *Madam Secretary*, 413.

93. Quotations in TOIW Madeleine Albright, August 30, 2006, WCPHP. For more on Clark's view, see Clark, *Waging*.

94. Memorandum to the President, from Samuel Berger, Subject: "Message to President Yeltsin," n.d., but approx. April 1–3, 1999, 2014-0546-M, CL.

95. Telcon, Clinton–Blair, April 1, 1999, 3:54–4:04pm, M-2012-0600, CL.

96. Sloan, *Defense of the West*, 143; I thank Frédéric Bozo for discussion on this point.

97. Charles Babington and Juliet Eilperin, "House Votes to Require Assent for Ground Troops," *Washington Post*, April 29, 1999. At the time there were

223 Republicans, 211 Democrats, and 1 Independent in the House of Representatives; see https://history.house.gov/Congressional-Overview /Profiles/106th/ for details.

98. Memcon, Clinton–Blair, April 10, 1999, M-2012-0600, CL.

99. Yielding on their insistence on maximum freedom of action for NATO, US negotiators agreed to a partial rewrite of the CFE treaty on March 31, 1999, to provide more flexibility. It was presumably partial compensation for Kosovo; Clinton emphasized the concession in the same letter to Yeltsin that is the source of the quotations above: Letter, Clinton–Yeltsin, April 3, 1999, 2014-0546-M, CL.

100. Telcon, Clinton–Yeltsin, April 19, 1999, 2015-0782-M-2, CL.

101. "Phone Call with President Yeltsin," from Samuel Berger, April 19, 1999, 2014-0546-M, CL.

102. Gaidar quoted in Talbott, *Russia Hand*, 307.

103. On "largest gathering," see Albright's speech, "Remarks on Accession," video as part of the "NATO Accession Ceremony," March 12, 1999, text in the State Deptartment Archive, "Secretary of State Madeleine K. Albright and Foreign Ministers of the Czech Republic, Hungary, and Poland, Remarks on Accession to the North Atlantic Treaty Organization, Truman Presidential Library, Independence, Missouri, March 12, 1999," https://1997 -2001.state.gov/www/statements/1999/990312.html; see also "The Reader's Guide to the NATO Summit in Washington," April 23–25, 1999, https:// www.nato.int/docu/rdr-gde/rdrgde-e.pdf.

104. The number of participants given in Albright's "Remarks on Accession," March 12, 1999; see also Philip P. Pan, "For Visitors, the Capital Is Copacetic," *Washington Post*, April 24, 1999; and "Reader's Guide to the NATO Summit in Washington." On Kuchma's attendance in the summit, "for which he was roundly criticized" by "the Ukrainian left and from Moscow," see Memorandum for the President, from Samuel Berger, Subject: "Message to Ukrainian President Kuchma," June 29, 1999, my 2016-0218-M, CL.

105. A video of the event, including insert of historic footage from April 1949, is at https://www.c-span.org/video/?122737-1/nato-summit-50th-anniversary -event.

106. Joel Achenbach, "At the Bottom of the Summit: The World's at Our Doorstep," *Washington Post*, April 24, 1999.

107. Achenbach, "At the Bottom of the Summit"; Talbott, *Russia Hand*, 306.

108. The first three quotations are from Telcon, Clinton–Blair, April 29, 1999, M-2012-0600, CL; the last quotation is from Telcon, Clinton–Blair, May 4, 1999, M-2012-0600, CL.

109. "Speech by the President of the United States," April 23, 1999, https://www .nato.int/docu/speech/1999/s990423b.htm.

110. For discussion about naming all nine, see SDC 1999-Bonn-00914, February 19, 1999; see also SDC 1999-State-038293, March 2, 1999; both DS-ERR. All but two of these countries would enter NATO in 2004; Albania and Macedonia would join in 2009 and 2020, respectively, the latter

after a name change to North Macedonia; see "Reader's Guide to the NATO Summit in Washington." On subsequent enlargement, see Moller, "Twenty Years After."

111. Albright's "Remarks on Accession," March 12, 1999.

112. See the MAP as announced at the April 1999 summit at https://www.nato .int/docu/pr/1999/p99-066e.htm; see also "Reader's Guide to the NATO Summit in Washington."

113. For more on the Baltics and MAP, see Poast and Urpelainen, *Organizing Democracy*, 149–50.

114. On half of the Estonian cabinet visiting Washington at once, and Baltic eagerness, see Asmus, *Opening*, 353n18.

115. NATO and Ukraine signed the "Charter on a Distinctive Partnership": see "NATO and Ukraine," in "Reader's Guide to the NATO Summit in Washington," April 23–25, 1999, 97–98.

116. Quotations are from Clinton's summary of his own words to Blair after his public remarks: Telcon, Clinton–Blair, May 8, 1999, M-2012-0600, CL.

117. Chernomyrdin quoted in Albright, *Madam Secretary*, 421.

118. Memorandum for the President, from Samuel Berger, Subject: "Message to President Yeltsin on Kosovo," May 17, 1999, 2014-0546-M, CL; on buying votes, see Myers, *New Tsar*, 147.

119. Letter, Yeltsin to Clinton, April 8, 1999, ППР2, 198–99.

120. "Memorandum to Sec. Albright, APNSA Berger, OVP Fuerth, from Strobe Talbott, Trip Report No. 2 (from Moscow)," May 21, 1999 (Moscow time), May 20, 1999 (Washington, DC time), DS-OIPS; William Drozdiak, "Russia's Concession Led to Breakthrough," *Washington Post*, June 6, 1999. See also description of Albright's meetings in Petersberg (outside Bonn) and near Cologne on June 7 and 8, 1999, both in SDC 1999-State-120246, June 26, 1999.

121. Telcon, Clinton–Yeltsin, June 8, 1999, 2014-0546-M CL.

122. Telcon, Clinton–Yeltsin, June 10, 1999, 2014-0546-M, CL. Milošević was removed from power in 2000, arrested, and extradited to a war crimes tribunal in The Hague, where he died in prison in 2006; see Packer, *Our Man*, 411. See also Kieninger, "The 1999 Kosovo War."

123. For a detailed chronology, see "Balkans Special Report," *Washington Post*, June 13, 1999, https://www.washingtonpost.com/wp-srv/inatl/longterm /balkans/poststories2.htm.

124. Steinberg, "Perfect Polemic."

125. Talbott, *Russia Hand*, 335. For more on Putin's time in office, see EBB-731, NSA.

126. On the movement of Russian forces, see Robert G. Kaiser and David Hoffman, "Secret Russian Troop Deployment Thwarted," *Washington Post*, June 25, 1999; Talbott, *Russia Hand*, 336–37.

127. Talbott, *Russia Hand*, 336–37.

128. SDC 1999-State-120192, June 19, 1999.

129. Kaiser and Hoffman, "Secret Russian Troop Deployment Thwarted."

130. Talbott, *Russia Hand*, 344.
131. Telcon, Clinton–Yeltsin, June 13, 1999, and quotation from Telcon, Clinton–Yeltsin, June 14, 1999, both in my 2015-0782-M, CL.
132. Goldgeier and McFaul, *Power*, 263.
133. "Sources: Top NATO commanders clashed over Russians' actions in Kosovo," CNN, August 2, 1999, http://www.cnn.com/WORLD/europe /9908/02/jackson.clark; "Singer James Blunt 'Prevented World War III,'" BBC News, November 14, 2010, https://www.bbc.com/news/uk-politics -11753050; see also Keith Gessen, "The Quiet Americans behind the US-Russia Imbroglio," *New York Times*, May 8, 2018.
134. Mark Tran, "'I'm Not Going to Start Third World War for You,'" *Guardian*, August 2, 1999; Goldgeier and McFaul, *Power*, 262–64.
135. Kaiser and Hoffman, "Secret Russian Troop Deployment Thwarted"; Goldgeier and McFaul, *Power*, 262–64; AIW Clark.
136. Blunt quoted in "Singer James Blunt 'Prevented World War III'"; see also Gessen, "Quiet Americans"; Tran, "'I'm Not Going to Start Third World War for You.'"
137. Goldgeier and McFaul, *Power*, 263.
138. "Putino61599.doc," Memcon (draft), Berger–Putin, June 15, 1999, 2017-0222-M, CL. On Tuzla, see Radchenko, "'Nothing but Humiliation,'" 792.
139. In the end they were able to do so under a "Helsinki Agreement," signed June 18, 1999. See Lavoie, "Kosovo Force (KFOR): Military Quiz," October 1999, https://www.nato.int/KFOR/chronicle/1999/chronicle_199902 /p16.htm, which also noted that under the Helsinki Agreement of June 18, 1999, Russia agreed to deploy up to 3,600 troops in Kosovo (and subsequently deployed battalions in Multinational Brigades East, North, and South). This publication also noted the kindness of the staff of the KFOR Public Information Center in Pristina, who took in a sick kitten found on the office doorstep and got it medical attention; when word circulated to the locals, the kitten became a mascot and a public relations success for KFOR.
140. AIW Townsend.
141. Memcon, Clinton–Yeltsin, June 20, 1999, Cologne, Germany, my 2015-0782-M, CL. The transcript noted that the meeting ended when "Presidents Clinton and Yeltsin come around the table and hug."
142. Memcon, Clinton–Schröder, June 18, 1999, M-2013-0472, CL.
143. What Schröder said about the idea of moving up NATO expansion is redacted. See Memcon, Clinton–Schröder, June 18, 1999. According to the State Department, it was "taboo to mention the 'Balkans' and 'EU Accession' in the same breath" to the EU commission: SDC 1999-USEU B-04241, July 7, 1999, DS-ERR.
144. Telcon, Clinton–Kohl, June 21, 1999, M-2013-0472, CL.
145. Telcon, Clinton–Kohl, June 21, 1999.
146. Clinton quoted in James M. Lindsay, "TWE Remembers: The Comprehensive Test Ban Treaty," Council on Foreign Relations, September 24, 2011, https://www.cfr.org/blog/twe-remembers-comprehensive-test-ban

-treaty. For more on CTBT, see https://www.nti.org/learn/treaties-and -regimes/comprehensive-nuclear-test-ban-treaty-ctbt/; and https://www.un .org/disarmament/wmd/nuclear/ctbt/.

147. The quotation is from US diplomat William Hill in his book *No Place*, 174; presumably Hill was discounting the Indian and Pakistani nuclear tests of 1998. For more on the "global uproar" over those tests, see Michael Krepon, "Looking Back: The 1998 Indian and Pakistani Nuclear Tests," Arms Control Association, https://www.armscontrol.org/act/2008-06/looking -back-1998-indian-pakistani-nuclear-tests.

148. Carter and Perry, *Preventive Defense*, 77.

149. On the ratification of START II, see also Memcon, Clinton–Putin, April 15, 2000, 2017-0222-M, CL; Perry, *My Journey*, 152; Stent, *Limits*, 29.

150. Office of Russian and European Analysis, Central Intelligence Agency, Intelligence Report, "Russia: Developing New Nuclear Warheads at Novaya Zemlya?," July 2, 1999, EBB-200, NSA.

151. Perry quotation from Perry, *My Journey*, 152. Quotations from the CIA's analysis in the year 2000 in Intelligence Report Memorandum, Office of Transnational Issues, Central Intelligence Agency, "Evidence of Russian Development of New Subkiloton Nuclear Warheads," August 30, 2000, EBB-200, NSA.

152. "Chechnya Profile—Timeline," BBC News, January 17, 2018, https://www .bbc.com/news/world-europe-18190473.

153. Statistics from Steven Lee Myers, "Russia Closes File on Three 1999 Bombings," *New York Times*, May 1, 2003; Mike Eckel, "Two Decades On, Smoldering Questions about the Russian President's Vault to Power," Radio Free Europe/Radio Liberty, August 7, 2019, https://www.rferl.org/a/putin-russia -president-1999-chechnya-apartment-bombings/30097551.html.

154. Yeltsin justified his and Putin's decisions in Letter, Yeltsin–Clinton, October 18, 1999, my 2015-0815-M CL; see also Myers, "Russia Closes File"; Myers, *New Tsar*, 154–61.

155. Talbott, *Russia Hand*, 357–61, 364 (most popular politician).

156. Myers, "Russia Closes File"; Clover, *Black Wind*, 250–52; see also Belton, *Putin's People*, 158–60.

157. Satter, *Less You Know*, xiv. See also Talbott's efforts to find Satter a job within the Clinton administration in 1993 in "Wed. March 23, 1993 Galit/ Toria," and "24 March 1993," both in F-2017-13804, DS-ERR. For a documentary on the bombings by a Russian journalist, in Russian with English subtitles, see https://www.youtube.com/watch?v=_arwGPwLXRw.

158. Luke Harding, "Russia Expels US Journalist David Satter without Explanation," *Guardian*, January 14, 2014; Satter, *Less You Know*, 2. Åslund, *Russia's Crony Capitalism*, 47, similarly finds it "likely" the FSB carried out the bombings.

159. Belton, *Putin's People*, 137, on how Stepashin was a weak interim candidate; and Yeltsin, *Midnight Diaries*, 218, 329–30. On how Putin was still relatively unknown at the time, see also Frye, *Weak Strongman*, 22-23.

160. Memcon, Clinton–Nazarbayev, December 21, 1999, SDC 2000-State-014531.
161. Talbott, *Russia Hand*, 355.
162. Myers, *New Tsar*, 149–53.
163. Telcon, Clinton–Yeltsin, September 8, 1999, my 2015-0782-M, CL.
164. Telcon, Clinton–Yeltsin, September 8, 1999.
165. Yeltsin's daughter quoted in Talbott, *Russia Hand*, 7 (hardest things), 355 (won't sell us out); on the grant of immunity, see Belton, *Putin's People*, 175; see also Kotkin, "Resistible Rise."
166. Telcon, Clinton–Yeltsin, September 8, 1999; on awareness of the significance of the moment, see AIW Weiss.
167. Clinton quoted in Putin et al., *First Person*, 195.
168. TOIW James Steinberg, April 1, 2008, WCPHP.
169. Albright, *Madam Secretary*, 444. Clinton was also "very skeptical about Putin from the first meeting," as Steinberg recalled. TOIW James Steinberg, April 1, 2008, WCPHP.
170. Memcon, Clinton–Putin, September 12, 1999, 2017-0222-M, CL. For more on Yeltsin's views of missile defense, see Letter from Yeltsin to Clinton, October 30, 1999, ППР2, 208–10; on the ABM Treaty, see also Talbott, *Russia Hand*, 379–80.
171. Memcon, Clinton–Putin, September 12, 1999.
172. Memcon, Clinton–Blair, October 13, 1999, M-2012-0600, CL.
173. Lindsay, "TWE Remembers."
174. Daryl G. Kimball, "Learning from the 1999 Vote on the Nuclear Test Ban Treaty," Arms Control Association, https://www.armscontrol.org/act/2009 -10/learning-1999-vote-nuclear-test-ban-treaty.
175. Eric Schmitt, "Defeat of a Treaty," *New York Times*, October 14, 1999.
176. TOIW James Steinberg, April 1, 2008, WCPHP; see also Perry, *My Journey*, 114.
177. Asmus, *Opening*, 281.
178. Memcon, Clinton–Blair, October 13, 1999, M-2012-0600, CL.
179. John King, "Clinton, Putin Exchange Complaints in Oslo Meeting," CNN, November 2, 1999, edition.cnn.com/WORLD/europe/9911/02/clinton .putin/.
180. Memcon, Clinton–Putin, November 2, 1999, 2017-0222-M, CL.
181. This was one of the three big summits in 1999: NATO, US-EU, and OSCE.
182. Georgia and Moldova hoped to use the adaptation of the CFE treaty to get Russian troops out of their territory: Hill, *No Place*, 158–59; Wade Boese, "Georgian Conflict Clouds Future Arms Pacts," Arms Control Association, https://www.armscontrol.org/act/2008-09/news/georgian-conflict-clouds -future-arms-pacts.
183. Memcon, Clinton–Putin, November 2, 1999, 2017-0222-M, CL. See also "Mamedov on Chechnya and CFE," October 15, 1999, DS-ERR.
184. On the adapted CFE treaty, see Nuclear Threat Initiative, https://www.nti .org/learn/treaties-and-regimes/treaty-conventional-armed-forces

-europe-cfe/; "Agreement on Adaptation of the Treaty on Conventional Armed Forces in Europe," Organization for Security and Co-operation in Europe, November 19, 1999, https://www.osce.org/library/14108.

185. "OSCE Summit," n.d., but from context early November 1999, 2016-0145-M, CL.

186. Yeltsin quoted in Michael Laris, "In China, Yeltsin Lashes Out at Clinton," *Washington Post*, December 10, 1999.

187. Yeltsin, *Midnight Diaries*, 348.

188. "No peace talks" quotation in Breffni O'Rourke, "OSCE: Summit Hears Clinton, Yeltsin Comment on Chechnya," November 9, 1999, Radio Free Europe/Radio Liberty, https://www.rferl.org/a/1092699.html; "sermonizing" quotation and ripping off headset in Talbott, *Russia Hand*, 361; see also Stent, *Limits*, 45. The Russian delegation also kept a condemnation of Moscow's actions in Chechnya out of the final summit resolution; instead, it noted only that "issues related to the current situation in Chechnya in the Russian Federation were referred to by a number of participants." "1999 OSCE Review Conference, Vienna, 20 September to 1 October 1999; Istanbul, 8 to 10 November 1999, Final Report," Organization for Security and Co-operation in Europe, November 10, 1999, https://www.osce.org/files/f/documents/6/7/40962.pdf, 75; Yeltsin, *Midnight Diaries*, 348.

189. Berger paraphrased in Talbott, *Russia Hand*, 361.

190. On the last trip to Europe by a US president in the twentieth century, see Memorandum for the President, from Samuel Berger, Subject "Your Trip to Greece, Turkey, the OSCE Summit, Italy, Bulgaria, and Kosovo, Nov. 14–23," November 12, 1999, 2016-0145-M, CL.

191. On how much changed between their first and last official meetings, see Yeltsin, *Midnight Diaries*, 135.

192. Memcon, Clinton–Yeltsin, November 19, 1999, my 2015-0782-M, CL; Talbott, *Russia Hand*, 363.

193. Yeltsin, *Midnight Diaries*, 5–7; see also Myers, *New Tsar*, 166–67.

194. Quotations in Putin et al., *First Person*, 204.

195. Vladimir Kara-Murza, "Putin's Dark Cult of the Secret Police," *Washington Post*, December 28, 2017; Weiner, *Folly*, 127–28.

196. Benjamin Nathans, "The Real Power of Putin," *New York Review of Books*, September 29, 2016.

197. Russian democracy activist Vladimir Kara-Murza later recalled that event as the moment he and his colleagues realized that under Putin, much else from the past would also come back. See Kara-Murza, "Putin's Dark Cult"; TOIW Vladimir Kara-Murza, Center for a New American Security, July 10, 2020, https://www.cnas.org/publications/podcast/vladimir-putin-and-the-future-of-russian-politics-with-michael-mcfaul-and-vladimir-kara-murza.

198. Memcon, Talbott–Putin, December 29, 1999, SDC 1999-State-244337.

199. Memcon, Talbott–Putin, December 29, 1999.

200. Yeltsin, *Midnight Diaries*, 1–5.

201. Talbott, *Russia Hand*, 370–71.
202. A video of Yeltsin's resignation with English subtitles is available at https://www.youtube.com/watch?v=vTsqy18Mbvs; Yeltsin, *Midnight Diaries*, 386–87; see also Talbott, *Russia Hand*, 371.
203. Yeltsin, *Midnight Diaries*, 14.
204. Telcon, Clinton–Yeltsin, December 31, 1999, my 2015-0782-M, CL. The telcon notes the time of this call as 9:02–9:22 p.m., not a.m., US time. But Clinton was celebrating the last night of the millennium with 360 guests at a White House dinner at 9:02 p.m., which would have been 5:02 a.m. in Moscow, so 9:02 a.m. Washington, 5:02 p.m. Moscow time, is more likely, and the "p.m." is probably a typo.
205. Telcon, Clinton–Yeltsin, December 31, 1999.
206. Memcon, Clinton–Putin, January 1, 2000, 2017-0222-M, CL.
207. Albright, *Madam Secretary*, 446. See also Goldgeier and McFaul, *Power*, 287: "by the end of the Clinton administration, the deal making on bilateral security issues was over. The early pattern of security cooperation was a distant memory."
208. Nicholas Burns and Douglas Lute, "NATO at Seventy: An Alliance in Crisis," Belfer Center for Science and International Affairs, February 2019, https://www.belfercenter.org/publication/nato-seventy-alliance-crisis.
209. Kotkin, "Resistible Rise."
210. This lack of any major new arms control package was particularly notable given that, as mentioned in Yeltsin, *Midnight Diaries*, 134–35, "no other president came to Moscow so many times. (And as Bill said, probably none will do so in the future.) No other US president engaged in such intensive discussions with the leaders of our country or provided us with such large-scale aid, both economic and political." On the lack of a major arms control accord, see Goldgeier and McFaul, *Power*, 303; see also Lüthi, *Cold Wars*, 578–81.

Conclusion

1. Keith Gessen, "The Quiet Americans behind the U.S.-Russia Imbroglio," *New York Times*, May 8, 2018, https://www.nytimes.com/2018/05/08/magazine/the-quiet-americans-behind-the-us-russia-imbroglio.html.
2. Quotation from "Notes by Jeremy Rosner, Senior Advisor to the President and Secretary of State for NATO Enlargement Ratification, from meeting at the White House of President Clinton with members of Senate NATO Observer Group," handwritten date of June 12, 1997, but from context June 11, 1997; I thank Jeremy Rosner for a copy of this document. On Talbott's view that no democracy should be excluded from NATO, regardless of geography, see "Deputy Secretary Briefs Baltic Ambassadors," June 12, 1997, DS-ERR. On how the United States as a consequence of that view "extended the boundaries of its political and military defense perimeter very far," see Posen, *Restraint*, xii; see also Stent, *Russia*, 228.

3. On Kaliningrad, see Frühling and Lasconjarias, "NATO," 104–5; Robbie Gramer, "This Interactive Map Shows the High Stakes Missile Stand-Off between Russia and NATO in Europe," *Foreign Policy*, January 12, 2017, https://foreignpolicy.com/2017/01/12/nato-russia-missile-defense-stand -off-deterrence-anti-access-area-denial/.

4. George Friedman, "Georgia and the Balance of Power," *New York Review of Books*, September 25, 2008.

5. The persistence and role of international organizations, and their interactions with major states, are the subject of extensive scrutiny by political scientists. To cite just one example from the vast literature, see Keohane, Nye, and Hoffmann, *After the Cold War*, 19, 382–83. The editors write, "it is hardly surprising that in a period of rapid and unanticipated change governments were more likely to attempt to use what was available than to try to redesign international institutions to meet their own standards of perfection" (382).

6. For more on the end of the Cold War as a missed opportunity, see Ther, *Europe*, 288–90.

7. Memcon, Clinton–Solana, February 20, 1996, 2015-0548-M, CL; see also Treisman, *The Return*, 317.

8. AIW Ivanov. On Russia seeing PfP as a ruse, see SDC 1996-State-29911, February 14, 1996, DS-ERR, where German diplomats informed Washington that the Russians "did not want a repeat of 1994 when an offer of membership in Partnership for Peace was made in May only to be followed by the Alliance's decision to enlarge in December."

9. On the subject of "victory disease" and kicking Russia too much while it was down, see Betts, "Three Faces," 34. On maximalist positions, see Sestanovich, *Maximalist*.

10. On the optimism of 1989, see Fukuyama, *The End*. For more on the history of the liberal international order, see Ikenberry, *World*.

11. Kozyrev quotation from *Firebird*, 36; Talbott quotation from Saturday, March 16, 1996, Chris," DS-OIPS. Talbott added: *"This I believe very strongly:* just because he was canned does not mean that what he stood for and what he was trying to accomplish has been defeated in Russia."

12. For the Churchill quotation, see https://www.oxfordreference.com/view/10 .1093/acref/9780191843730.001.0001/q-oro-ed5-00002969.

13. McFaul, "Putin," 97. I thank Graham Allison for discussion of the wraparound concept.

14. Quotations were part of the exchange between Biden and former ambassador Jack Matlock at a hearing on October 30, 1997, one of the days of the "Hearings before the Committee on Foreign Relations, United States Senate, 105th Congress, First Session," October 7, 9, 22, 28, 30, and November 5, 1997, https://www.govinfo.gov/content/pkg/CHRG-105shrg46832 /html/CHRG-105shrg46832.htm; see also Goldgeier, *Not Whether*, 169.

15. For more on the social science research, see Poast and Chinchilla, "Good for Democracy?," 487: "The huge reward of NATO's security guarantee

after membership" creates "a strong incentive for prospective members to reform in order to join the alliance." On de-democratization in former Warsaw Pact countries, see the Freedom House website, which by 2021 had downgraded Hungary to a "transitional or hybrid regime," with Poland only a "semi-consolidated democracy"; https://freedomhouse.org/countries /nations-transit/scores. On Polish willingness to work within PfP, see SDC 1994-State-83196, March 30, 1994, DS-ERR, in which the Polish defense minister "emphasized Warsaw's determination to give substance to the PfP idea. Even without full NATO membership . . . Poland would hasten its efforts to meet Euro-Atlantic standards, because it wanted to be ready to be a 'lego block' for NATO's use as soon as possible."

16. "Conclusions of the Presidency," European Council in Copenhagen, June 21–22, 1993, https://www.consilium.europa.eu/ueDocs/cms_Data/docs /pressData/en/ec/72921.pdf; see also the EU's timeline of expansion, https://ec.europa.eu/neighbourhood-enlargement/policy/from-6-to-27 -members_en. For Ahtisaari's discussion of the way NATO expansion would allow the EU to postpone its own enlargement, see SDC 1995-Helsin-4809, August 2, 1995, DS-ERR. For discussion of the lack of coordination between the EU and NATO, see SDC 1997-State-24131, February 8, 1997, DS-ERR.

17. Carter quoted in Brzezinski, *Power and Principle*, 234.

18. On the way that Yeltsin was serious about cooperation with the West in the early 1990s, creating new possibilities in contrast to centuries of antagonism, see Aron, *Yeltsin*, 702.

19. Henrikson, "Creation," 307.

20. On earlier thinking about a Nordic Defense Pact, see Henrikson, "Creation," 307.

21. David A. Shlapak and Michael Johnson, "Reinforcing Deterrence on NATO's Eastern Flank: Wargaming the Defense of the Baltics," RAND, RR-1253-A, 2016, https://www.rand.org/pubs/research_reports/RR1253.html; Michael Kofman, "Fixing NATO Deterrence in the East or: How I Learned to Stop Worrying and Love NATO's Crushing Defeat by Russia," *War on the Rocks*, May 12, 2016, https://warontherocks.com/2016/05/fixing-nato-deterrence -in-the-east-or-how-i-learned-to-stop-worrying-and-love-natos-crushing -defeat-by-russia/. See also Jonathan Masters, Backgrounder, "The North Atlantic Treaty Organization," Council on Foreign Relations, last updated December 3, 2019, https://www.cfr.org/backgrounder/north-atlantic-treaty -organization-nato.

22. On the 2006 summit, see "President Bush Discusses NATO Alliance during Visit to Latvia," November 28, 2006, https://georgewbush-whitehouse .archives.gov/news/releases/2006/11/20061128-13.html. On the 2008 Bucharest summit, see the NATO press release of April 3, 2008, "NATO Decisions on Open-Door Policy," https://www.nato.int/docu/update/2008/04 -april/e0403h.html, which states that "at the Bucharest Summit, NATO Al-

lies welcomed Ukraine's and Georgia's Euro-Atlantic aspirations for membership and agreed that these countries will become members of NATO"; and Matt Spetalnick, "Bush Vows to Press for Ukraine, Georgia in NATO," Reuters, April 1, 2008, https://www.reuters.com/article/us-nato-ukraine -bush/bush-vows-to-press-for-ukraine-georgia-in-nato-idUSL014170 6220080401. For more on the NATO Liaison Office in Georgia, see https:// www.nato.int/cps/en/natolive/topics_81066.htm. See also Frye, *Weak Strongman*, 162, which notes the following about the 2008 summit: "After much internal debate, NATO pledged that Ukraine and Georgia 'will become members,' but did not offer a Membership Action Plan with any details or start date. The open-ended commitment was the worst of all worlds. It encouraged Moscow's suspicions that NATO wanted to surround Russia, disappointed governments in Ukraine and Georgia that wanted NATO to move more quickly, and caused resentment among alliance members" who were "divided on the issue"; and Marten, "NATO Enlargement," 409.

23. Trenin, *Post-Imperium*, 107–8; Alexander Vershbow and Daniel Fried, "How the West Should Deal with Russia," Atlantic Council, November 23, 2020, https://www.atlanticcouncil.org/in-depth-research-reports/report/russia -in-the-world/. President Barack Obama later changed course and did not put the above-described systems into Poland and the Czech Republic, instead installing the first land-based defensive missile launcher in Romania (for operation by NATO). See Peter Baker, "White House Scraps Bush's Approach to Missile Shield," *New York Times*, September 17, 2009; Ryan Browne, "US Launches Long-Awaited European Missile Defense Shield," CNN, May 12, 2016, https://www.cnn.com/2016/05/11/politics/nato-missile -defense-romania-poland. At the time of writing, a delay-plagued ground-based missile defense system was being built in Poland as well; see Anthony Capaccio, "The Pentagon's New Poland-Based Missile Defense System Is Now Four Years Behind Schedule," *Bloomberg*, February 12, 2020.

24. Particularly relevant is Article 8, intended "to place caveats on the foreign policies of its members in terms of when they can call on the alliance for help"; see Nikolas K. Gvosdev, "There's More to NATO Than Article Five," *The National Interest*, August 2, 2016, https://nationalinterest.org/feature /theres-more-nato-article-five-17222; see also Asmus, *Little War*, 5, who argues that Putin's 2008 intervention in Georgia "was aimed not only at Georgia but at Washington, NATO, and the West more generally."

25. As Ther has insightfully written, the minimal requirement for the post–Cold War order "was peace, based on secure borders"; Ther, *Europe*, 326.

26. McFaul, "Putin," 103.

27. "NATO–Russia Council," March 23, 2020, https://www.nato.int/cps/en /natohq/topics_50091.htm.

28. Stephen Sestanovich, "US Power, Less than Super," *New York Times*, March 23, 1993. As Ivanov noted in 2021, the crisis in US-Russian relations was not good for anyone; AIW Ivanov.

29. "President's News Conference with Visegrad Leaders in Prague," January 12, 1994, APP-UCSB, https://www.presidency.ucsb.edu/documents/the -presidents-news-conference-with-visegrad-leaders-prague. On the importance of considering the "how" of a strategy, see Brands, *What Good*, 199, which argues that, in analyzing strategic choices, "it is important to emphasize the 'how' as well as the 'what' . . . conception and implementation are both vital aspects of grand strategy, and neither one is worth much without the other."

30. Poast and Chinchilla, "Good for Democracy?," 471–90; see also Reiter, "Why," 41–67; Steil, *Marshall Plan*, 395–96.

31. On Hungary becoming the first autocracy in the EU, see R. Daniel Keleman, "Hungary Just Became a Coronoavirus Autocracy," *Washington Post*, April 2, 2020; and Keleman, "European Union's Authoritarian Equilibrium." For more on de-democratization in Central and Eastern Europe, see Applebaum, *Twilight;* Tsveta Petrova and Senem Aydın-Düzgit, "Democracy Support without Democracy," Carnegie Endowment for International Peace, January 5, 2021, https://carnegieendowment.org/2021/01/05 /democracy-support-without-democracy-cases-of-poland-and-turkey-pub -83485.

32. Westad, *Cold War*, 623; Yeltsin comment to Talbott on April 11, 1996, quoted in SDC 1996-Moscow-10123, April 12, 1996, DS-ERR (Yeltsin added, "we actually have better relations with some other countries than with the US now. This isn't the way it ought to be"); see also Kathryn Stoner, "US Was Wrong," *New York Times*, December 22, 2016; and for context, Stoner, *Russia Resurrected*.

33. This sentence paraphrased from McFaul, "Putin," 134–35; see also Hal Brands and Peter Feaver, "Trump's Transatlantic Crisis," *Commentary*, September 2018.

34. On NATO not being worth its cost, see Peter Baker, "Trump Says NATO Allies Don't Pay," *New York Times*, May 26, 2017. Also, according Julian E. Barnes and Helene Cooper, "Trump Discussed Pulling U.S. from NATO," *New York Times*, January 14, 2019, "in the days around a tumultuous NATO summit meeting" in July 2018, Trump "suggested a move tantamount to destroying NATO: the withdrawal of the United States." On the problem of Europeans being unable to provide for their own security if the United States withdrew, see the aptly titled Meijer and Brooks, "Illusions of Autonomy: Why Europe Cannot Provide for Its Security If the United States Pulls Back."

35. For more on this view, see Brooks and Wohlforth, *Why*, x.

36. On the shredding of arms control agreements, see David E. Sanger and William J. Broad, "A Cold War Arms Treaty Is Unraveling," *New York Times*, December 9, 2018; see also Perry, *My Journey*, xv.

37. On the stabilizing effects of NATO, see Richard Haass, "Assessing the Value of the NATO Alliance," testimony to the Committee on Foreign Relations, US Senate, 115th Cong., 2nd Sess., September 5, 2018.

38. Adam Tooze, "Whose Century?," *London Review of Books*, July 30, 2020.

39. For my own work on the détente era, see Sarotte, *Dealing*.

40. AIW Spero.

41. Map 5, APBD-49–94, 1150–51. On the significance of strategies of connection and affiliation, see Slaughter, *Chessboard*.

42. Mitterrand died of prostate cancer on January 8, 1996. As Kohl paraphrased Mitterrand's 1995 comments in "3./4. Februar 1995," BzL 649, "Wenn wir jetzt im Rückblick auf die 50 Nachkriegsjahre—er [Mitterrand] sieht das fast ausschließlich aus seiner persönlichen Situation—nicht begreifen, daß es überhaupt keinen anderen Weg gibt als den europäischen Weg und daß für diesen Weg die deutsch-französische Kooperation entscheidend ist, dann werden wir diese 50 Jahre, die Gnade und Geschenk sind, zu Unrecht empfangen haben. Das ist auch meine feste Überzeugung."

43. Interview with Svetlana Alexievich, *BBC Newshour*, December 31, 2015, https://www.bbc.co.uk/programmes/p03cwn66.

Bibliography

Interviews

Albright, Madeleine, December 21, 2020, by phone.

Allison, Graham, October 12, 2016, Cambridge, MA.

Applebaum, Anne, April 19, 2018, Cambridge, MA.

Asmus, Ron, March 16, 2008, Brussels.

Baker, James A., III, February 11, 2009, Houston.

Bindenagel, J. D., June 28, 2008, by phone and email; May 15, 2019, Berlin; August 2, 2019, by email.

Bitterlich, Joachim, June 1, 2012, June 17, 2013, and May 14, 2019, Berlin.

Blacker, Coit (Chip), September 26, 2018, by phone.

Blackwill, Robert, January 9, 2009, by phone.

Brinkmann, Peter, June 24 and December 13, 2013, Berlin.

Bunn, Matthew, December 20, 2017, Cambridge, MA.

Burns, Nicholas, December 19, 2016, and December 19, 2017, Cambridge, MA.

Burns, William, November 16, 2018, Washington, DC.

Carter, Ashton, December 20, 2017, Cambridge, MA.

Clark, Wesley, May 22, 2018, by phone.

Cooper, Robert, March 20, 2009, Brussels.

Culora, Thomas, October 19, 2018, by phone.

Dow, Jacqueline, March 22, 2017, NATO Headquarters, Brussels.

Edelman, Eric, May 3, 2018, Washington, DC.

Ehmke, Horst, May 21, 1996, by phone.

Elbe, Frank, June 10 and 11, 2009, by phone.

Falin, Valentin, May 17, 1996, Tostedt, Germany.

Fischer, Joschka, April 17, 2007, Princeton, NJ.

Flanagan, Stephen, September 10, 2020, by Zoom.

Fried, Daniel, June 14, 2018, by phone.

Gati, Charles, October 11, 2018, Washington, DC.

509

Genscher, Hans-Dietrich, June 2, 2009, Wachtberg-Pech, Germany.

Gottemoeller, Rose, February 4, 2021, by phone.

Grinin, Vladimir, December 19, 2013, Berlin.

Groenen, Eddy, March 22, 2017, NATO Headquarters, Brussels.

Grossman, Marc, May 18, 2018, by phone.

Holgate, Laura, May 10, 2017, Washington, DC.

Horváth, István, August–September 2013, by email.

Howard, Michelle, October 14, 2020, by Zoom.

Hunter, Robert, July 2, 2018, by phone.

Hurd, Douglas, March 17, 2009, London.

Ilves, Toomas Hendrik, April 5, 2021, by Zoom.

Ischinger, Wolfgang, May 10, 2017, Washington, DC; November 5, 2019, Berlin.

Ivanov, Igor, February 3, 2021, with Sergey Radchenko, by email.

Jäger, Harald, June 8, 2012, Werneuchen, with Hans-Hermann Hertle; July 2, 2013, by phone.

Joulwan, George, May 21, 2018, by phone.

Kastrup, Dieter, August 2013, by email.

Kiessler, Richard, March 20, 2009, Brussels.

Kojm, Chris, May 31, 2019, by phone.

Kokoshin, Andrei, March 21, 2016, Moscow.

Kornblum, John, April 4, 2008, by phone.

Koźmiński, Jerzy, February 11, 2021, by Zoom.

Kozyrev, Andrei, December 1, 2016, and December 6, 2018, Washington, DC.

Krenz, Egon, September–October 2013, by email.

Lake, Anthony, June 12, 2019, Washington, DC.

Lauter, Gerhard, June 21, 2013, Leipzig.

Lute, Douglas, April 30, 2018, by phone.

Mandelbaum, Michael, November 25, 2020, by phone.

Margański, Jerzy, July 2019, by email.

Matlock, Jack, April 18, 2007, Princeton, NJ.

Maximychev, Igor, July–September 2013, by email; March 21, 2016, Moscow.

McFaul, Michael, May 16, 2018, Cambridge, MA.

Meckel, Markus, June 1, 2012, and June 17, 2013, Berlin.

Momper, Walter, June 17, 2013, Berlin.

Munro, Colin, August–September 2013, by email.

Munter, Cameron, July 9, 2018, by phone.

Napper, Larry, February 22, 2016, College Station, TX.

Nuland, Victoria, January 9, 2009, and July 9, 2018, by phone.

Nunn, Samuel, May 2, 2019, Cambridge, MA.

Nurick, Robert, June 28, 2018, by phone.

Nye, Joseph, September 26, 2016, Cambridge, MA.

Perry, William, June 8, 2017, Stanford, CA.

Pifer, Steven, May 14, 2018, by phone.

Poppe, Ulrike, June 25, 2013, Berlin.

Powell, Charles, March 29, 2009, London.

Powell, Jonathan, October 20, 2008, London.

Radomski, Aram, June 20, 2013, Berlin.

Ruehle, Michael, March 22, 2017, NATO Headquarters, Brussels.

Rühe, Volker, May 17, 2019, by phone.

Ruiz Palmer, Diego, March 22, 2017, NATO Headquarters, Brussels.

Rosner, Jeremy, December 18, 2020, by Zoom.

Ross, Dennis, November 17, 2008, Washington, DC.

Rumer, Eugene, November 29, 2018, Washington, DC.

Scharioth, Klaus, April 30, 2018, by phone.

Schefke, Siegbert (Siggi), June 21 and December 12, 2013, Leipzig; April 1, 2014, Cambridge, MA.

Scherbakova, Irina, July 12, 2005, Moscow.

Schwabe, Uwe, December 12–13, 2013, Leipzig.

Schwarz, Ulrich, June 25, 2013, Berlin.

Scowcroft, Brent, September 19, 2008, Washington, DC.

Sello, Tom, August 30, 2006, and June 20, 2013, Berlin.

Sestanovich, Stephen, December 10, 2019, by phone.

Shea, Jamie, March 22, 2017, NATO Headquarters, Brussels.

Sherwood-Randall, Elizabeth, November 28–29, 2017, Cambridge, MA.

Sicherman, Harvey, December 12, 2008, by phone.

Sievers, Hans-Jürgen, August 19, 2013, by phone; December 13, 2013, Leipzig.

Sikorski, Radek, April 19, 2018, Cambridge, MA.

Simons, Thomas, December 7, 2017, Cambridge, MA.

Slotkin, Elissa, April 25, 2017, Cambridge, MA.

Solana, Javier, March 9, 2021, by Zoom.

Spero, Joshua, November 15, 2018, by phone.

Steinberg, James, November 27, 2018, by phone.

Talbott, Nelson (Strobe), June 11, 2018, by phone.

Tarasyuk, Borys, December 5–6, 2018, Cambridge, MA.

Teltschik, Horst, June 12, 2008, by phone; June 25, 2013, and November 7, 2019, Berlin.

Townsend, James, May 3, 2018, Washington, DC.

Védrine, Hubert, June 18, 2009, by email.

Vershbow, Alexander, July 15, 2005, Moscow; June 7, 2018, by phone.

Wałęsa, Lech, January 13, 2021, with Wiktor Babiński, by email and Zoom.

Walker, Jenonne, March 30, 2021, by email and Zoom.

Weiss, Andrew, June 19, 2018, by phone; October 25, 2018, Washington, DC.

Wolf, Markus, June 6, 1996, Berlin.

Wonneberger, Christoph, December 12, 2013, Leipzig.

Zelikow, Philip, July 27, 2008, by email and phone.

Zoellick, Robert, March 16, 2008, Brussels; June 20, 2019, by phone.

Primary Sources from Archives
and Personal Collections of Participants

Note: Frequently cited sources have an abbreviation, listed both in the opening section of the notes in alphabetical order, and in square brackets following the full source listing below.

Belgium

BRUSSELS

NATO Headquarters, Archives

Estonia

Rahvusarhiiv (consulted online during pandemic), https://www.ra.ee/dgs/explorer
.php

Germany

BERLIN

Bundesarchiv, Stiftung/Archiv der Parteien und Massenorganisationen der DDR
[SAPMO]
Ministerium für Staatssicherheit [MfS], Bundesbeauftragte(r) für die Unterlagen
des Staatssicherheitsdienstes der ehemaligen Deutschen Demokratischen Re-
publik [BStU]
Politisches Archiv, Auswärtiges Amt [PA-AA]
Robert-Havemann-Gesellschaft [RHG]

BONN/SANKT AUGUSTIN

Konrad Adenauer Stiftung, Archiv für Christlich-Demokratische Politik

DRESDEN

Sächsisches Hauptstaatsarchiv

HAMBURG

ARD-NDR Videoarchiv

KOBLENZ

Bundesarchiv

LEIPZIG

Archiv Bürgerbewegung Leipzig
Sächsisches Staatsarchiv

Poland

WARSAW

KARTA [Solidarity and opposition materials]

Russia

MOSCOW

Архив "Горбачев-Фонда" [GFA]

United Kingdom

LONDON

Foreign and Commonwealth Office [FCO] materials, released under FOI
King's College Liddell Hart Military Archive
Public Records Office/National Archives [PRO-NA], various collections, most
    notably CAB and PREM, some released under the 2005 Freedom of Infor-
    mation law [FOI]

United States

COLLEGE STATION, TX

George H. W. Bush Presidential Library [BPL]

LEXINGTON, VA

George C. Marshall Foundation Collection (consulted online during pandemic),
    https://www.marshallfoundation.org/

LITTLE ROCK, AR

William J. Clinton Presidential Library [CL]

PRINCETON, NJ

James A. Baker III Archive Collection, Seeley Mudd Manuscript Library, Prince-
    ton University [SMML]

SIMI VALLEY, CA

Ronald Reagan Presidential Library

STANFORD, CA

Hoover Institution Archive [HIA]

WASHINGTON, DC, AND ENVIRONS

Central Intelligence Agency, materials released and posted/published under the US Freedom of Information Act [FOIA]
Department of Defense, materials released to author under FOIA
Department of State, materials released to author under FOIA
National Archives and Records Administration
National Security Archive [NSA]

Primary Sources, Collected and Made Available at Scholarly Conferences

Columbus, Ohio, Conference: "US-Soviet Military Relationships at the End of the Cold War, 1988–91," October 15–17, 1999. Columbus: Mershon Center, The Ohio State University.
Miedzeszyn-Warsaw Conference: "Poland 1986–1989: The End of the System," October 20–24, 1989. Miedzeszyn-Warsaw, Poland: Cosponsored by the Institute of Political Studies at the Polish Academy of Sciences and the National Security Archive. [MC]
Paris Conference: "Europe and the End of the Cold War," June 15–17, 2006. Paris: Organized by the Cold War International History Project. [CWIHPPC]
Prague Conference: "The Democratic Revolution in Czechoslovakia," October 14–16, 1989. Prague: Organized by the National Security Archive, the Czechoslovak Documentation Center, and the Institute of Contemporary History, Academy of Sciences of the Czech Republic. [PC]
Princeton Conference: Greenstein, Fred I., and William C. Wohlforth, eds. *Cold War Endgame: Report of a Conference.* Center of International Studies Monograph Series No. 10. Princeton, NJ: Center of International Studies, 1997.
Princeton, Wilson School Conference: "Briefing Book for Cold War Endgame," March 29–30, 1996. Princeton, NJ: Sponsored by the Woodrow Wilson School and the James A. Baker III Institute for Public Policy, compiled by the National Security Archive.
St. Simon's Island, Georgia, Conference: "End of the Cold War in Europe, 1989," May 1–3, 1998. Musgrove, St. Simon's Island, Georgia: Organized by the National Security Archive. [GC]

Primary Sources, Selected Published Collections

Note: Frequently cited sources have an abbreviation listed both in the opening section of the notes and in square brackets below. Alphabetization of foreign words in this section (and the ones below) follows this rule: names and titles in languages other than English are alphabetized by first letter without discounting the foreign-language equivalents of "a" or "the" and without taking accents (such as umlauts) into account. Due to word count restrictions, it was not possible to cite all primary source collections consulted in the writing of this book; below are the collections most extensively cited and/or cited in the notes.

Auswärtiges Amt, ed. *Aussenpolitik der Bundesrepublik Deutschland: Dokumente von 1949 bis 1994.* Cologne: Verlag Wissenschaft und Politik, 1995. [APBD-49–94]
———. *Deutsche Aussenpolitik 1990/91: Auf dem Weg zu einer europäischen Friedensordnung eine Dokumentation.* Bonn: Auswärtiges Amt, April 1991. [DA-90–91]
———. *Deutsche Aussenpolitik 1995: Auf dem Weg zu einer Friedensregelung für Bosnien und Herzegowina; 53 Telegramme aus Dayton, Eine Dokumentation.* Bonn: Auswärtiges Amt, 1998.
Borodziej, Włodzimierz, ed. *Polska wobec zjednoczenia Niemiec 1989–1991: Dokumenty dyplomatyczne.* Warszawa: Scholar, 2006.
Bozóki, András, ed. *The Roundtable Talks of 1989: The Genesis of Hungarian Democracy, Analysis and Documents.* Budapest: CEU Press, 2002.
Buchstab, Günter, Hans-Otto Kleinmann, and Helmut Kohl, eds. *Berichte zur Lage 1989–1998.* Düsseldorf: Droste, 2012. [BzL]
Dierikx, Marc, and Sacha Zala, eds. *When the Wall Came Down: The Perception of German Reunification in International Diplomatic Documents, 1989–1990.* Bern: Diplomatic Documents of Switzerland, 2019.
Ehlert, Hans, ed. *Armee ohne Zukunft: Das Ende der NVA und die deutsche Einheit, Zeitzeugenberichte und Dokumente.* Berlin: Links, 2002.
Engel, Jeffrey A., Mark Atwood Lawrence, and Andrew Preston, eds. *America in the World: A History in Documents from the War with Spain to the War on Terror.* Princeton, NJ: Princeton University Press, 2014.
Freedman, Lawrence, ed. *Europe Transformed: Documents on the End of the Cold War; Key Treaties, Agreements, Statements and Speeches.* New York: St. Martin's Press, 1990.
Galkin, Aleksandr, and Anatolij Tschernjajew, eds. *Michail Gorbatschow und die deutsche Frage: Sowjetische Dokumente 1986–1991.* Translated and edited by Helmut Altrichter, Joachim Glaubitz, Andreas Hilger, Horst Möller, and Jürgen Zarusky. Munich: Oldenbourg, 2011. [MGDF]
Gehler, Michael, and Maximilian Graf, eds. *Österreich und die deutsche Frage 1987–1990: Vom Honecker-Besuch in Bonn bis zur Einheit.* Göttingen: Vandenhoeck & Ruprecht, 2018. [ÖDF]

Geiger, Tim, et al., eds. *Akten zur Auswärtigen Politik der Bundesrepublik Deutschland 1990.* Berlin: De Gruyter, 2021. [AAP-90]

Gorbatschow, Michail S., ed. *Gipfelgespräche: Geheime Protokolle aus meiner Amtszeit.* Berlin: Rowohlt, 1993.

———. *Годы трудных решений.* Москва: Альфа-Принт, 1993.

———. *Отвечая на вызов времени.* Москва: Весь Мир, 2010.

———. *Собрание сочинений.* Москва: Весь Мир, 2013.

Горбачев, Михаил, Александр Галкин, and Анатолий Черняев, eds. *Михаил Горбачев и германский вопрос: Сборник документов 1986–1991.* Москва: Весь Мир, 2006. [МГ]

Hamilton, Keith, Patrick Salmon and Stephen Twigge, eds. *Documents on British Policy Overseas.* Series III, vol. 6, *Berlin in the Cold War, 1948–1990.* London: Routledge, 2009.

Hilger, Andreas, ed. *Diplomatie für die deutsche Einheit: Dokumente des Auswärtigen Amts zu den deutsch-sowjetischen Beziehungen 1989/90.* Munich: Oldenbourg, 2011.

Jacobsen, Hans-Adolf, ed. *Bonn-Warschau 1945–1991.* Cologne: Verlag Wissenschaft und Politik, 1992.

James, Harold, and Marla Stone, eds. *When the Wall Came Down: Reactions to German Unification.* New York: Routledge, 1992.

Kaiser, Karl, ed. *Deutschlands Vereinigung: Die internationalen Aspekte.* Bergisch-Gladbach: Lübbe Verlag, 1991.

Karner, Stefan, Mark Kramer, Peter Ruggenthaler, and Manfred Wilke, eds. *Der Kreml und die deutsche Wiedervereinigung.* Berlin: Metropol Verlag, 2015.

———, eds. *Der Kreml und die Wende 1989.* Innsbruck: Studienverlag, 2014.

Kecskés, Gusztáv D., ed. *A View from Brussels: Secret NATO Reports about the East European Transition, 1988–1991.* Budapest: Cold War History Research Centre, 2019.

Küchenmeister, Daniel, and Gerd-Rüdiger Stephan, eds. *Honecker Gorbatschow Vieraugengespräche.* Berlin: Dietz Verlag, 1993.

Küsters, Hanns Jürgen, and Daniel Hoffman, eds. *Dokumente zur Deutschlandpolitik: Deutsche Einheit, Sonderedition aus den Akten des Bundeskanzleramtes 1989/90.* Munich: Oldenbourg Verlag, 1998. [DESE]

Lehmann, Ines, ed. *Die Außenpolitik der DDR 1989/1990: Eine dokumentierte Rekonstruktion.* Baden-Baden: Nomos, 2010. [ADDR]

Mastny, Vojtech, ed. *The Helsinki Process and the Reintegration of Europe 1986–1991: Analysis and Documentation.* New York: New York University Press, 1992.

Mastny, Vojtech, and Malcolm Byrne, eds. *A Cardboard Castle? An Inside History of the Warsaw Pact.* New York: CEU Press, 2005.

Möller, Horst, et al. *Die Einheit: Das Auswärtige Amt, das DDR Außenministerium und der Zwei-plus-Vier Prozess.* Göttingen: Vandenhoeck & Ruprecht, 2015. [DE]

Nakath, Detlef, Gero Neugebauer, and Gerd-Rüdiger Stephan, eds. *"Im Kreml brennt noch Licht": Spitzenkontakte zwischen SED/PDS und KPdSU 1989–1991.* Berlin: Dietz, 1998.

Nakath, Detlef, and Gerd-Rüdiger Stephan, eds. *Countdown zur deutschen Einheit: Eine dokumentierte Geschichte der deutsch-deutschen Beziehungen 1987–1990.* Berlin: Dietz, 1996.

Nübel, Christoph, ed. *Dokumente zur deutschen Militärgeschichte 1945–1990: Bundesrepublik und DDR im Ost-West Konflikt.* Berlin: Links, 2019.

Office of the Deputy Assistant Secretary for Defense for Nuclear Matters, US Department of Defense. *Nuclear Matters Handbook 2020.* https://fas.org/man /eprint/nmhb2020.pdf.

Pautsch, Ilse Dorothee, et al., eds. *Akten zur Auswärtigen Politik der Bundesrepublik Deutschland 1989.* Berlin: De Gruyter, 2020. [AAP-89]

Переписка Президента Российской Федерации Бориса Николаевича Ельцина ... 1996–1999, в двух томах. Москва: научное издательство "большая русская энциклопедия," 2011. [ППР]

Presse- und Informationsamt der Bundesregierung. *Die Vereinigung Deutschlands im Jahre 1990: Verträge und Erklärungen.* Bonn: Presse- und Informationsamt der Bundesregierung, 1991.

Public Papers of the President, William J. Clinton. Washington, DC: Office of the Federal Register, 1993–97.

Rubinstein, Alvin Z., Albina Shayevich, and Boris Zlotnikov, eds. *The Clinton Foreign Policy Reader: Presidential Speeches with Commentary.* London: M. E. Sharpe, 2000. [CFPR]

Salmon, Patrick, Keith Hamilton, and Stephen Twigge, eds. *Documents on British Policy Overseas.* Series III, vol. 7, *German Unification, 1989–1990.* London: Routledge, 2009. [DBPO]

Savranskaya, Svetlana, Thomas Blanton, and Anna Melyakova, eds. *The Last Superpower Summits: Gorbachev, Reagan, and Bush Conversations That Ended the Cold War.* Budapest: Central European University Press, 2016. [LSS]

Savranskaya, Svetlana, Thomas Blanton, and Vladislav Zubok, eds. *Masterpieces of History: The Peaceful End of the Cold War in Europe, 1989.* Budapest: Central European University Press, 2010.

Schmidt-Schweizer, Andreas, ed. *Die politisch-diplomatischen Beziehungen in der Wendezeit, 1987–1990.* Berlin: DeGruyter, 2018.

Smith, Richard, ed. *Documents on British Policy Overseas.* Series III, vol. 12, *Britain and the Revolutions in Eastern Europe, 1989.* London: Routledge, 2019.

Stroilov, Pavel, ed. *Behind the Desert Storm.* Chicago: Price World Publishing, 2011.

Vaïsse, Maurice, and Christian Wenkel, eds. *La diplomatie française face à l'unification allemande.* Paris: Tallandier, 2011. [DFUA]

Van Eekelen, Willem Frederik. *Debating European Security, 1948–1998.* Brussels: Centre for European Policy Studies, 1998.

Von Münch, Ingo, ed. *Dokumente des geteilten Deutschland.* 2 vols. Stuttgart: Kröner, 1976.

Von Plato, Alexander. *Die Vereinigung Deutschlands—ein weltpolitisches Machtspiel: Bush, Kohl, Gorbatschow und die geheimen Moskauer Protokolle.* Berlin: Links, 2002.

Westad, Odd Arne, and Jussi Hanhimäki, eds. *The Cold War: A History in Documents and Eyewitness Accounts.* Oxford: Oxford University Press, 2003.

Selected Substantial Accounts by Participants in Events, Including Major Published Interviews

Note: Frequently cited sources have an abbreviation listed both in the opening section of the notes and in square brackets below. Due to word count restrictions, it was not possible to cite all such accounts consulted; below are the memoir-style accounts most extensively consulted and/or cited in the notes.

Адамишин, Анатолий. *В разные годы: Внешнеполитические очерки.* Москва: Весь Мир, 2016.

Albright, Madeleine. *Madam Secretary: A Memoir.* New York: HarperPerennial, 2003.

Allison, Graham. *Nuclear Terrorism: The Ultimate Preventable Catastrophe.* New York: Times Books, 2004.

Allison, Graham, and Philip Zelikow. *Essence of Decision: Explaining the Cuban Missile Crisis.* 2nd ed. New York: Longman, 1999.

Asmus, Ronald D. "Europe's Eastern Promise: Rethinking NATO and EU Enlargement." *Foreign Affairs* 87, no. 1 (January/February 2008): 95–106.

———. *A Little War That Shook the World: Georgia, Russia and the Future of the West.* New York: Palgrave Macmillan, 2010.

———. *Opening NATO's Door: How the Alliance Remade Itself for a New Era.* New York: Columbia University Press, 2002, and associated collection of declassified government documents [ADGD].

Asmus, Ronald D., J. F. Brown, and Keith Crane. *Soviet Foreign Policy and the Revolutions of 1989 in Eastern Europe.* Santa Monica, CA: RAND, 1991.

Asmus, Ronald D., Richard L. Kugler, and F. Stephen Larrabee. "Building a New NATO." *Foreign Affairs* 72, no. 4 (September/October 1993): 28–40.

———. "NATO Expansion: The Next Steps." *Survival* 37, no. 1 (Spring 1995): 7–33.

———. "What Will NATO Enlargement Cost?" *Survival* 38, no. 3 (Autumn 1996): 5–26.

Asmus, Ronald D., and Robert C. Nurick. "NATO Enlargement and the Baltic States." *Survival* 38, no. 2 (Summer 1996): 121–42.

Baker, James A., with Thomas A. DeFrank. *The Politics of Diplomacy: Revolution, War and Peace, 1989–1992.* New York: G. P. Putnam's Sons, 1995.

Boldin, Valery. *Ten Years That Shook the World: The Gorbachev Era as Witnessed by His Chief of Staff.* New York: HarperCollins, 1994.

Braithwaite, Rodric. *Across the Moscow River: The World Turned Upside Down.* New Haven, CT: Yale University Press, 2002.

———. *Armageddon and Paranoia: The Nuclear Confrontation.* London: Pantheon Books, 2017.

Brandt, Willy. *My Life in Politics.* New York: Viking, 1991.

———. "*. . . was zusammengehört.*" Bonn: Dietz, 1993.

Brinkmann, Peter. *Die NATO-Expansion: Deutsche Einheit und Ost-Erweiterung.* Berlin: edition ost, 2015.

———. *Schlagzeilenjagd.* Bergisch Gladbach: Bastei Lübbe, 1993.

Brzezinski, Zbigniew. *The Grand Failure: The Birth and Death of Communism in the Twentieth Century.* New York: Charles Scribner's Sons, 1989.

———. *Power and Principle: Memoirs of a National Security Adviser, 1977–1981.* New York: Farrar, Straus, Giroux, 1983.

———. "The Premature Partnership." *Foreign Affairs* 73, no. 2 (March/April 1994): 67–82.

———. *Second Chance: Three Presidents and the Crisis of American Superpower.* New York: Basic Books, 2007.

Brzezinski, Zbigniew, David Ignatius, and Brent Scowcroft. *America and the World: Conversations on the Future of American Foreign Policy.* New York: Basic Books, 2008.

Burns, William J. *The Back Channel: A Memoir of American Diplomacy and the Case for Its Renewal.* New York: Random House, 2019 [see also the book's online appendix, the published collection of Burns's declassified government documents, or BDGD, https://carnegieendowment.org/publications/interactive /back-channel].

Bush, George H. W., and Brent Scowcroft. *A World Transformed.* New York: Knopf, 1998.

Carter, Ashton B., and William J. Perry. *Preventive Defense: A New Security Strategy for America.* Washington, DC: Brookings Institution Press, 1999.

Chernyaev, Anatoly. Diary, donated to the National Security Archive, translated and published online, www2.gwu.edu/~nsarchiv/NSAEBB/NSAEBB192 [cited as Chernyaev Diary, NSA].

———. *Mein Deutsches Tagebuch (1972–1991).* Klitzschen: Elbe-Dnjepr-Verlag, 2005. [MDB]

———. *My Six Years with Gorbachev.* Translated and edited by Robert English and Elizabeth Tucker. University Park: University of Pennsylvania Press, 2000.

———. *Совместный исход. Дневник двух эпох. 1972–1991 годы.* Москва: РОССПЭН, 2008.

Chollet, Derek, and James M. Goldgeier. *America between the Wars: From 11/9 to 9/11; The Misunderstood Years between the Fall of the Berlin Wall and the Start of the War on Terror.* New York: PublicAffairs, 2008.

Christopher, Warren. *In the Stream of History: Shaping Foreign Policy for a New Era.* Stanford, CA: Stanford University Press, 1998.

Clark, Wesley K. *Waging Modern War: Bosnia, Kosovo, and the Future of Conflict.* New York: PublicAffairs, 2001.

Clinton, William. *My Life.* New York: Vintage Books, 2005.

Daalder, Ivo. *Getting to Dayton: The Making of America's Bosnia Policy.* Washington, DC: Brookings Institution Press, 2000.

Diekmann, Kai, and Ralf Georg Reuth, eds. *Die längste Nacht, der grösste Tag: Deutschland am 9. November 1989.* Munich: Piper, 2009.

Dufourcq, Nicolas, ed. *Retour sur la fin de la guerre froide et la réunification allemande: Témoignages pour l'histoire.* Paris: Odile Jacob, 2020 [published interviews with participants in events].

Falin, Valentin. *Konflikte im Kreml: Zur Vorgeschichte der deutschen Einheit und Auflösung der Sowjetunion.* Munich: Blessing Verlag, 1997.

———. *Politische Erinnerungen.* Munich: Knaur, 1995.

Flanagan, Stephen J. "NATO and Central and Eastern Europe: From Liaison to Security Partnership." *Washington Quarterly* 15, no. 2 (1992): 141–51.

Gates, Robert M. *Exercise of Power: American Failures, Successes and a New Path Forward in the Post–Cold War World.* New York: Knopf, 2020.

———. *From the Shadows: The Ultimate Insider's Story of Five Presidents and How They Won the Cold War.* New York: Touchstone, 1996.

Genscher, Hans-Dietrich. *Erinnerungen.* Berlin: Siedler, 1995. Abridged English translation: *Rebuilding a House Divided.* New York: Broadway Books, 1998.

———. *Unterwegs zur Einheit: Reden und Dokumente aus bewegter Zeit.* Berlin: Siedler, 1991.

German Embassy London, ed. "Witness Seminar: Berlin in the Cold War, 1948–1990; German Unification, 1989–1990." Unpublished document, distributed by the Foreign and Commonwealth Office, London, 2009.

Goldgeier, James M. *The Future of NATO: Council Special Report No. 51.* New York: Council on Foreign Relations, 2010.

———. "NATO Enlargement and the Problem of Value Complexity." *Journal of Cold War Studies* 22, no. 4 (Fall 2020): 146–74.

———. "NATO Expansion: Anatomy of a Decision." *Washington Quarterly* 21, no. 1 (Winter 1998): 85–102.

———. *Not Whether but When: The US Decision to Enlarge NATO.* Washington, DC: Brookings Institution Press, 1999.

Goldgeier, James M., and Michael McFaul. *Power and Purpose: US Policy toward Russia after the Cold War.* Washington, DC: Brookings Institution Press, 2003.

Goldgeier, James M., and Elizabeth N. Saunders. "The Unconstrained Presidency." *Foreign Affairs* 97, no. 5 (September/October 2018): 144–56.

Gorbachev, Mikhail. *Alles zu seiner Zeit.* Hamburg: Hoffmann und Campe, 2013.

———. *Memoirs.* New York: Doubleday, 1995.

———. *Toward a Better World.* London: Hutchinson, 1987.

Gorbachev, Mikhail, Vadim Sagladin, and Anatoli Tschernjajew. *Das Neue Denken.* Munich: Goldmann Verlag, July 1997.

Grachev, Andrei. *Gorbachev's Gamble: Soviet Foreign Policy and the End of the Cold War.* London: Polity Press, 2008.

Hamilton, Daniel S., and Kristina Spohr, eds. *Exiting the Cold War, Entering a New World.* Washington, DC: Foreign Policy Institute, 2019.

———. *Open Door: NATO and Euro-Atlantic Security after the Cold War.* Washington, DC: Foreign Policy Institute, 2019.

Holbrooke, Richard. *To End a War.* New York: Random House, 1998.

Horn, Gyula. *Freiheit die ich meine: Erinnerungen des ungarischen Außenministers, der den Eisernen Vorhang öffnete.* Translated by Angelika and Péter Máté. Hamburg: Hoffmann und Campe Verlag, 1991.

Horváth, István. *Die Sonne ging in Ungarn auf: Erinnerungen an eine besondere Freundschaft.* Munich: Universitas, 2000.

Hurd, Douglas. *Memoirs.* London: Little, Brown, 2003.

Hutchings, Robert L. *American Diplomacy and the End of the Cold War: An Insider's Account of US Policy in Europe, 1989–1992.* Washington, DC: Wilson Center Press, 1997.

Ischinger, Wolfgang. *World in Danger: Germany and Europe in an Uncertain Time.* Washington, DC: Brookings Institution Press, 2021.

Kennan, George. *At a Century's Ending: Reflections, 1982–1995.* New York: Norton, 1996.

Kiessler, Richard, and Frank Elbe. *Ein runder Tisch mit scharfen Ecken: Der diplomatische Weg zur deutschen Einheit.* Baden-Baden: Nomos Verlagsgesellschaft, 1993.

Kissinger, Henry. *Diplomacy.* New York: Simon and Schuster, 1994.

Klein, Hans. *Es begann im Kaukasus: Der entscheidende Schritt in die Einheit Deutschlands.* Berlin: Ullstein, 1991.

Kohl, Helmut. *Erinnerungen 1982–1990.* Munich: Droemer, 2005.

———. *Erinnerungen 1990–1994.* Munich: Droemer, 2007.

Kohl, Helmut, Kai Diekmann, and Ralf Georg Reuth. *Ich wollte Deutschlands Einheit.* Berlin: Ullstein, 1996.

Kokoshin, Andrei. *Soviet Strategic Thought, 1917–91.* Cambridge, MA: MIT Press, 1999.

Kostenko, Yuri. *Ukraine's Nuclear Disarmament: A History.* Edited by Svitlana Krasynska. Translated by Lidia Wolanskyj, Svitlana Krasynska, and Olena Jennings. Cambridge, MA: Harvard University Press, 2020.

Kotschemassow, Wjatscheslaw. *Meine letzte Mission.* Berlin: Dietz, 1994.

Kozyrev, Andrei. *The Firebird, a Memoir: The Elusive Fate of Russian Democracy.* Pittsburgh: University of Pittsburgh Press, 2019.

Krenz, Egon. *Herbst '89.* Berlin: Verlag Neues Leben, 1999.

———. *Wenn Mauern fallen.* Vienna: Neff, 1990.

Kupchan, Charles. "Strategic Visions." *World Policy Journal* 11, no. 3 (1994): 112–22.

Kwizinskij, J. A. *Vor dem Sturm: Erinnerungen eines Diplomaten.* Berlin: Siedler, 1993.

Major, John. *The Autobiography.* New York: HarperCollins, 2000.

Matlock, Jack F., Jr. *Autopsy on an Empire: The American Ambassador's Account of the Collapse of the Soviet Union.* New York: Random House, 1995.

———. *Reagan and Gorbachev: How the Cold War Ended.* New York: Random House, 2004.

Maximytschew, Igor, and Hans-Hermann Hertle. *Der Fall der Mauer: Vorgeschichte und Hintergründe, eine russisch-deutsche Trilogie.* 2 vols. Berlin: Freie Universität, Zentralinstitut für Sozialwissenschaftliche Forschung, 1994.

McFaul, Michael. *From Cold War to Hot Peace: The Inside Story of Russia and America*. New York: Houghton Mifflin Harcourt, 2018.

———. "Putin, Putinism, and the Domestic Determinants of Russian Foreign Policy." *International Security* 45, no. 2 (Fall 2020): 95–139.

Meckel, Markus. *Selbstbewußt in die deutsche Einheit: Rückblicke und Reflexion*. Berlin: Berlin Verlag, 2001.

Mitterrand, François. *De l'Allemagne, de la France*. Paris: Odile Jacob, 1996.

———. *Ma part de vérité: De la rupture à l'unité*. Paris: Fayard, 1969.

Modrow, Hans, ed. *Das Große Haus: Insider berichten aus dem ZK der SED*. Berlin: edition ost, 1994.

Momper, Walter. *Grenzfall: Berlin im Brennpunkt deutscher Geschichte*. Munich: Bertelsmann, 1991.

Morozov, Kostiantyn P. *Above and Beyond: From Soviet General to Ukrainian State Builder*. Cambridge, MA: Harvard University Press, 2000.

Palazchenko, Pavel. *My Years with Gorbachev and Shevardnadze: The Memoir of a Soviet Interpreter*. University Park: Pennsylvania State University Press, 1997.

Perry, William J. *My Journey at the Nuclear Brink*. Stanford, CA: Stanford University Press, 2015.

Perry, William J., and Tom Z. Collina. *The Button: The New Nuclear Arms Race and Presidential Power from Truman to Trump*. Dallas, TX: BenBella Books, 2020.

Pifer, Steven. *The Eagle and the Trident: US-Ukraine Relations in Turbulent Times*. Washington, DC: Brookings Institution Press, 2017.

———. *The Trilateral Process: The United States, Ukraine, Russia and Nuclear Weapons*. Washington, DC: Brookings Institution Press, 2011.

Primakow, Jewgenij. *Im Schatten der Macht: Politik für Russland*. Translated by Feodor B. Pokjakov. Munich: Herbig, 2001.

———. *Встречи на перекрестках*. Москва: Центрполиграф, 2015.

Putin, Vladimir, with Nataliya Gevorkyan, Natalya Timakova, and Andrei Kolesnikov. *First Person: An Astonishingly Frank Self-Portrait by Russia's President Putin*. Translated by Catherine A. Fitzpatrick. New York: PublicAffairs, 2000.

Rühe, Volker. *Betr.: Bundeswehr: Sicherheitspolitik und Streitkräfte im Wandel*. Berlin: Verlag E. S. Mitter & Sohn, 1993.

———. "Shaping Euro-Atlantic Policies: A Grand Strategy for a New Era." *Survival* 35, no. 2 (Summer 1993): 129–37.

Sagladin, Vadim. *Und Jetzt Welt-Innen Politik: Die Außenpolitik der Perestroika*. Rosenheim: Horizonte, 1990.

Schabowski, Günter, and Frank Sieren. *Wir haben fast alles falsch gemacht: Die letzten Tage der DDR*. 2nd ed. Berlin: Ullstein, 2009.

Schachnasarow, Georg. *Preis der Freiheit: Eine Bilanz von Gorbatschows Berater*. Bonn: Bouvier Verlag, 1996.

Schäuble, Wolfgang. *Der Vertrag: Wie ich über die deutsche Einheit verhandelte*. Munich: Knaur, 1991.

Shevardnadze, Eduard. *The Future Belongs to Freedom.* London: Sinclair-Stevenson, 1991.

Shultz, George P., Sidney D. Drell, Henry A. Kissinger, and Sam Nunn. *Nuclear Security: The Problems and the Road Ahead.* Stanford, CA: Hoover Institution Press, 2014.

Solomon, Gerald B. *The NATO Enlargement Debate, 1990–1997.* Westport, CT: Praeger, 1998.

Stavridis, James. *The Accidental Admiral: A Sailor Takes Command at NATO.* Annapolis, MD: Naval Institute Press, 2014.

Steinberg, James B. "A Perfect Polemic: Blind to Reality on Kosovo." *Foreign Affairs* 78, no. 6 (November/December 1999): 128–33.

Talbott, Strobe. *Deadly Gambits.* New York: Knopf, 1982.

———, ed. and trans. *Khrushchev Remembers: The Last Testament.* New York: Little, Brown, 1974.

———. *The Russia Hand: A Memoir of Presidential Diplomacy.* New York: Random House, 2003.

Teltschik, Horst. *329 Tage: Innenansichten der Einigung.* Berlin: Siedler, 1991.

———. *Russisches Roulette: Vom Kalten Krieg zum Kalten Frieden.* Munich: Beck, 2019.

Védrine, Hubert. *Les mondes de François Mitterrand.* Paris: Fayard, 1996.

Von Arnim, Joachim. *Zeitnot: Moskau, Deutschland und der weltpolitische Umbruch.* 2nd ed. Bonn: Bouvier, 2013.

Walters, Vernon A. *Die Vereinigung war voraussehbar.* Berlin: Siedler, 1994.

Wolf, Markus. *Die Troika.* Berlin: Aufbau-Verlag, 1989.

———. *Im Eigenen Auftrag: Bekenntnisse und Einsichten.* Munich: Schneekluth, 1991.

———. *Spionagechef im geheimen Krieg: Erinnerungen.* Munich: List, 1997.

Wolf, Markus, and Anne McElvoy. *Man without a Face: The Autobiography of Communism's Greatest Spymaster.* New York: Random House, 1997.

Yeltsin, Boris. *Midnight Diaries.* New York: PublicAffairs, 2000.

Zelikow, Philip, and Condoleezza Rice. *Germany Unified and Europe Transformed: A Study in Statecraft.* Cambridge, MA: Harvard University Press, 1995.

———. *To Build a Better World: Choices to End the Cold War and Create a Global Commonwealth.* New York: Twelve Books, 2019.

Zoellick, Robert. *America in the World: A History of US Diplomacy and Foreign Policy.* New York: Twelve Books, 2020.

Secondary Literature

Note: Frequently cited sources have an abbreviation listed both in the opening section of the notes and in square brackets below. Due to word count restrictions, it was not possible to cite every secondary work consulted; this list includes only titles extensively consulted and/or cited in the notes.

Adomeit, Hannes. *Imperial Overstretch: Germany in Soviet Policy from Stalin to Gorbachev*. Baden-Baden: Nomos, 1998.

Ahonen, Pertti. *After the Expulsion: West Germany and Eastern Europe 1945–1990*. Oxford: Oxford University Press, 2004.

Applebaum, Anne. *Iron Curtain: The Crushing of Eastern Europe, 1944–1956*. New York: Doubleday, 2012.

———. *Twilight of Democracy: The Seductive Lure of Authoritarianism*. New York: Doubleday, 2020.

Aron, Leon. *Yeltsin: A Revolutionary Life*. New York: St. Martin's Press, 2000.

Åslund, Anders. "Russia's Collapse." *Foreign Affairs* 78, no. 5 (September/October 1999): 64–77.

———. *Russia's Crony Capitalism: The Path from Market Economy to Kleptocracy*. New Haven, CT: Yale University Press, 2019.

Baker, Peter, and Susan Glasser. *Kremlin Rising: Vladimir Putin's Russia and the End of Revolution*. New York: Scribner, 2005.

———. *The Man Who Ran Washington: The Life and Times of James A. Baker III*. New York: Doubleday, 2020.

Balmaceda, Margarita, ed. *On the Edge: Ukrainian–Central European–Russian Security Triangle*. Budapest: Central European University Press, 2000.

Barany, Zoltan. *The Future of NATO Expansion: Four Case Studies*. Cambridge: Cambridge University Press, 2003.

Beckley, Michael. "The Myth of Entangling Alliances." *International Security* 39, no. 4 (Spring 2015): 7–48.

Beissinger, Mark R. *Nationalist Mobilization and the Collapse of the Soviet State*. Cambridge: Cambridge University Press, 2002.

Bell, David. *François Mitterrand*. Cambridge: Polity Press, 2005.

Belton, Catherine. *Putin's People: How the KGB Took Back Russia and Then Took on the West*. New York: Farrar, Straus and Giroux, 2020.

Bergmane, Una. "'Is This the End of Perestroika?' International Reactions to the Soviet Use of Force in the Baltic Republics in January 1991." *Journal of Cold War Studies* 22, no. 2 (Spring 2020): 26–57.

Bernauer, Thomas, and Dieter Ruloff, eds. *The Politics of Positive Incentives in Arms Control*. Columbia: University of South Carolina Press, 1999.

Beschloss, Michael, and Strobe Talbott. *At the Highest Levels: The Inside Story of the Cold War*. Boston: Little, Brown, 1993.

Betts, Richard. "The Three Faces of NATO." *The National Interest*, no. 100 (March/April 2009): 31–38.

Borkovec, Zdeněk. *Naše cesta do NATO*. Praha: Ministerstvo obrany České republiky, 2019.

Bozo, Frédéric. "The Failure of a Grand Design: Mitterrand's European Confederation, 1989–1991." *Contemporary European History* 17, no. 3 (2008): 391–412.

———. *A History of the Iraq Crisis: France, the United States, and Iraq, 1991–2003*. Washington, DC: Wilson Center Press, 2016.

————. "'I Feel More Comfortable with You': France, the Soviet Union, and German Reunification." *Journal of Cold War Studies* 17, no. 3 (Summer 2015): 116–58.

————. *Mitterrand, German Unification, and the End of the Cold War.* Translated by Susan Emanuel. London: Berghahn Books, 2009.

————. *Mitterrand, la fin de la guerre froide et l'unification allemande: De Yalta à Maastricht.* Paris: Odile Jacob, 2005.

————. "Mitterrand's France, the End of the Cold War, and German Unification: A Reappraisal." *Cold War History* 7, no. 4 (2007): 455–78.

————. "The Sanctuary and the Glacis: France, the Federal Republic of Germany, and Nuclear Weapons in the 1980s (Part 1)." *Journal of Cold War Studies* 22, no. 3 (Summer 2020): 119–79.

————. "The Sanctuary and the Glacis: France, the Federal Republic of Germany, and Nuclear Weapons in the 1980s (Part 2)." *Journal of Cold War Studies* 22, no. 4 (Fall 2020): 175–228.

————. "'We Don't Need You': France, the United States, and Iraq, 1991–2003." *Diplomatic History* 41, no. 1 (2017): 183–208.

————. "'Winners' and 'Losers': France, the United States, and the End of the Cold War." *Diplomatic History* 33, no. 5 (2009): 927–56.

Bozo, Frédéric, Marie-Pierre Rey, N. Piers Ludlow, and Leopoldo Nuti, eds. *Europe and the End of the Cold War.* London: Routledge, 2008.

Bozo, Frédéric, Andreas Rödder, and M. E. Sarotte, eds. *German Reunification: A Multinational History.* London: Routledge, 2017.

Bozo, Frédéric, and Christian Wenkel, eds. *France and the German Question.* New York: Berghahn Books, 2019.

Branch, Taylor. *The Clinton Tapes: Conversations with a President, 1993–2001.* New York: Simon and Schuster, 2009.

Brands, Hal. *Making the Unipolar Moment: US Foreign Policy and the Rise of the Post–Cold War Order.* Ithaca, NY: Cornell University Press, 2016.

————. *What Good Is Grand Strategy? Power and Purpose in American Statecraft from Harry S. Truman to George W. Bush.* Ithaca, NY: Cornell University Press, 2014.

Brauckhoff, Kerstin, and Irmgard Schwaetzer, eds. *Hans-Dietrich Genschers Außenpolitik.* Wiesbaden: Springer, 2015.

Brinkmann, Peter. *Die NATO-Expansion: Deutsche Einheit und Ost-Erweiterung.* Berlin: edition ost, 2015.

Brooks, Stephen G., and William Wohlforth. "From Old Thinking to New Thinking." *International Security* 26, no. 4 (Spring 2002): 93–111.

————. "Power, Globalization, and the End of the Cold War." *International Security* 25, no. 3 (Winter 2000–2001): 5–53.

————. *Why the Sole Superpower Should Not Pull Back from the World.* Oxford: Oxford University Press, 2016.

Brudny, Yitzhak M. "In Pursuit of the Russian Presidency: Why and How Yeltsin Won the 1996 Presidential Election." *Communist and Post-Communist Studies* 30, no. 3 (1997): 255–75.

Budjeryn, Mariana. *Inheriting the Bomb: Soviet Collapse and the Nuclear Disarmament of Ukraine.* Baltimore: Johns Hopkins University Press, forthcoming.

———. "The Power of the NPT: International Norms and Ukraine's Nuclear Disarmament." *The Nonproliferation Review* 22, no. 2 (2015): 203–37.

Burg, Steven L., and Paul S. Shoup. *Ethnic Conflict and International Intervention.* New ed. London: Routledge, 2000.

Clover, Charles. *Black Wind White Snow: The Rise of Russia's New Nationalism.* New Haven, CT: Yale University Press, 2016.

Cohen, Stephen F. *Failed Crusade: America and the Tragedy of Post-Communist Russia.* New York: Norton, 2001.

———. *Soviet Fates and Lost Alternatives: From Stalinism to the New Cold War.* New York: Columbia University Press, 2009.

Colbourn, Susan. "NATO as a Political Alliance: Continuities and Legacies in the Enlargement Debates of the 1990s." *International Politics* 57, no. 3 (June 2020): 491–508.

Colton, Timothy J. *Yeltsin: A Life.* New York: Basic Books, 2008.

Connelly, Matthew, et al. "'General, I Have Fought Just as Many Nuclear Wars as You Have': Forecasts, Future Scenarios, and the Politics of Armageddon." *The American Historical Review* 117, no. 5 (December 2012): 1431–60.

Conradi, Peter. *Who Lost Russia? How the World Entered a New Cold War.* London: Oneworld, 2017.

D'Anieri, Paul. *Economic Interdependence in Ukrainian-Russian Relations.* Albany: State University of New York Press, 1999.

Dawisha, Karen. *Putin's Kleptocracy: Who Owns Russia?* New York: Simon and Schuster, 2015.

Dębski, Sławomir, and Daniel S. Hamilton, eds. *Europe Whole and Free: Vision and Reality.* Warsaw: Polish Institute of International Affairs, 2019.

Delbrück, Max. *Mind from Matter? An Essay on Evolutionary Epistemology.* Edited by Gunther S. Stent et al. Palo Alto, CA: Blackwell Scientific Publications, 1986.

Domber, Gregory F. *Empowering Revolution: America, Poland, and the End of the Cold War.* Chapel Hill: University of North Carolina Press, 2014.

———. "Skepticism and Stability: Reevaluating US Policy during Poland's Democratic Transformation in 1989." *Journal of Cold War Studies* 13, no. 3 (2011): 52–82.

Drew, Elizabeth. *On the Edge: The Clinton Presidency.* New York: Simon and Schuster, 1994.

Edwards, Chris, and John Samples, eds. *The Republican Revolution.* Washington, DC: Cato Institute, 2005.

Ekiert, Grzegorz. *The State against Society: Political Crises and Their Aftermath in East Central Europe.* Princeton, NJ: Princeton University Press, 1996.

Engel, Jeffrey A. *When the World Seemed New: George H. W. Bush and the Surprisingly Peaceful End of the Cold War.* New York: Houghton Mifflin Harcourt, 2017.

Epstein, Rachel A. "NATO Enlargement and the Spread of Democracy: Evidence and Expectations." *Security Studies* 14, no. 1 (2005): 63–105.

———. "When Legacies Meet Policies: NATO and the Refashioning of Polish Military Tradition." *East European Politics and Societies* 20, no. 2 (2006): 254–85.

Falkenrath, Richard A. *Shaping Europe's Military Order: The Origins and Consequences of the CFE Treaty.* Cambridge, MA: MIT Press, 1995.

Филитов, А. М. *Германия в советском внешнеполитическом планировании 1941–1990.* Москва: Наука, 2009.

Frühling, Stephan, and Guillaume Lasconjarias. "NATO, A2/AD and the Kaliningrad Challenge." *Survival* 58, no. 2 (2016): 95–116.

Frye, Timothy. *Weak Strongman: The Limits of Power in Putin's Russia.* Princeton, NJ: Princeton University Press, 2021.

Fukuyama, Francis. *The End of History and the Last Man.* New York: Penguin, 1992.

Gaddis, John Lewis. *The Cold War.* New York: Penguin, 2006.

———. *George F. Kennan: An American Life.* Paperback ed. New York: Penguin, 2011.

———. "History, Grand Strategy and NATO Enlargement." *Survival* 40, no. 1 (Spring 1998): 145–51.

———. "History, Theory and Common Ground." *International Security* 22, no. 1 (Summer 1997): 84.

———. *The Landscape of History: How Historians Map the Past.* Oxford: Oxford University Press, 2002.

———. *Strategies of Containment: A Critical Appraisal of Postwar American National Security Policy.* Oxford: Oxford University Press, 1982; also rev. ed., 2005.

———. *We Now Know: Rethinking Cold War History.* Oxford: Clarendon Press, 1997.

Gall, Carlotta, and Thomas de Waal. *Chechnya: Calamity in the Caucasus.* New York: New York University Press, 1998.

Gall, Lothar. *Bismarck.* Berlin: Ullstein, 1980.

Gans, John. *White House Warriors: How the National Security Council Transformed the American Way of War.* New York: Liveright, 2019.

Garton Ash, Timothy. *In Europe's Name: Germany and the Divided Continent.* New York: Vintage Books, 1993.

Gati, Charles. *The Bloc That Failed.* Bloomington: Indiana University Press, 1990.

———. *Failed Illusions: Moscow, Washington, Budapest and the 1956 Hungarian Revolt.* Stanford, CA: Stanford University Press, 2006.

Gavin, Francis J. "Blasts from the Past: Proliferation Lessons from the 1960s." *International Security* 29, no. 3 (Winter 2004/2005): 100–135.

———. *Nuclear Statecraft: History and Strategy in America's Atomic Age.* Ithaca, NY: Cornell University Press, 2012.

———. "Strategies of Inhibition: US Grand Strategy, the Nuclear Revolution, and Nonproliferation." *International Security* 40, no. 1 (Summer 2015): 9–46.

Gehler, Michael and Wilfried Loth, eds. *Reshaping Europe: Towards a Political, Economic, and Monetary Union, 1984–1989.* Baden-Baden: Nomos, 2020.

George, Alexander. "The 'Operational Code': A Neglected Approach to the Study of Political Decision-Making." *International Studies Quarterly* 12 (June 1969): 190–222.

Gheciu, Alexandra. "Security Institutions as Agents of Socialization? NATO and the 'New Europe.'" *International Organization* 59 (Fall 2005): 973–1012.

Gibler, Douglas M., and Jamil A. Sewell. "External Threat and Democracy: The Role of NATO." *Journal of Peace Research* 43, no. 4 (July 2006): 413–31.

Glaurdić, Josip. *The Hour of Europe: Western Powers and the Breakup of Yugoslavia.* New Haven, CT: Yale University Press, 2011.

Grayson, George W. *Strange Bedfellows: NATO Marches East.* Lanham, MD: University Press of America, 1999.

Grzymala-Busse, Anna M. *Redeeming the Communist Past: The Regeneration of Communist Parties in East Central Europe.* Cambridge: Cambridge University Press, 2002.

Handelman, Stephen. "The Russian 'Mafiya.'" *Foreign Affairs* 73, no. 2 (March/April 1994): 83–96.

Hanhimäki, Jussi M., Benedikt Schoenborn, and Barbara Zanchetta. *Transatlantic Relations since 1945: An Introduction.* New York: Routledge, 2012.

Harrison, Hope. *After the Wall: Memory and the Making of the New Germany, 1989 to the Present.* Cambridge: Cambridge University Press, 2019.

———. *Driving the Soviets Up the Wall.* Princeton, NJ: Princeton University Press, 2003.

Haslam, Jonathan. *Russia's Cold War.* New Haven, CT: Yale University Press, 2011.

———. "Russia's Seat at the Table: A Place Denied or a Place Delayed?" *International Affairs* 74, no. 1 (1998): 119–30.

Herrmann, Richard K., and Richard Ned Lebow, eds. *Ending the Cold War.* New York: Palgrave Macmillan, 2004.

Hertle, Hans-Hermann. *Chronik des Mauerfalls: Die dramatischen Ereignisse um den 9. November 1989.* 12th ed. Berlin: Links, 2009.

———. *Der Fall der Mauer: Die unbeabsichtigte Selbstauflösung des SED-Staates.* Opladen: Westdeutscher Verlag, 1996.

Hill, Fiona, and Clifford G. Gaddy. *Mr. Putin: Operative in the Kremlin.* New ed. Washington, DC: Brookings Institution Press, 2015.

Hill, William H. *No Place for Russia: European Security Institutions since 1989.* New York: Columbia University Press, 2018.

Hitchcock, William I. *The Bitter Road to Freedom: A New History of the Liberation of Europe.* New York: Free Press, 2008.

Hoffman, David E. *The Dead Hand: The Untold Story of the Cold War Arms Race and Its Dangerous Legacy.* New York: Doubleday, 2009.

Horovitz, Liviu, and Elias Götz. "The Overlooked Importance of Economics: Why the Bush Administration Wanted NATO Enlargement." *Journal of Strategic Studies* 43, nos. 6–7 (December 2020): 847–68.

Hosking, Geoffrey. *Rulers and Victims: The Russians in the Soviet Union.* Cambridge, MA: Harvard University Press, 2006.

Hymans, Jacques. *Achieving Nuclear Ambitions: Scientists, Politicians, and Proliferation.* Cambridge: Cambridge University Press, 2012.

Ikenberry, G. John. *A World Safe for Democracy: Liberal Internationalism and the Crises of Global Order.* New Haven, CT: Yale University Press, 2020.

Jacoby, Wade. *The Enlargement of the European Union and NATO: Ordering from the Menu in Central Europe.* Cambridge: Cambridge University Press, 2006.

Johnston, Seth. *How NATO Adapts: Strategy and Organization in the Atlantic Alliance since 1950.* Baltimore: Johns Hopkins University Press, 2017.

Kaplan, Lawrence S. *NATO before the Korean War: April 1949–June 1950.* Kent, OH: Kent State University Press, 2013.

———. *NATO Divided, NATO United: The Evolution of the Alliance.* Westport, CT: Praeger, 2004.

———. *NATO 1948: The Birth of the Transatlantic Alliance.* Lanham, MD: Rowman and Littlefield, 2007.

———. *The United States and NATO: The Formative Years.* Lexington: University Press of Kentucky, 1984.

Kasekamp, Andres. "An Uncertain Journey to the Promised Land: The Baltic States' Road to NATO Membership." *Journal of Strategic Studies* 43, nos. 6–7 (December 2020): 869–97.

Kay, Sean. *NATO and the Future of European Security.* Oxford: Rowman and Littlefield, 1998.

Keleman, R. Daniel. "The European Union's Authoritarian Equilibrium." *Journal of European Public Policy* 27, no. 3 (2020): 481–99.

Keohane, Robert O., and Lisa L. Martin. "The Promise of Institutionalist Theory." *International Security* 20, no. 1 (Summer 1995): 39–51.

Keohane, Robert O., Joseph S. Nye, and Stanley Hoffmann, eds. *After the Cold War: International Institutions and State Strategies in Europe, 1989–1991.* Cambridge, MA: Harvard University Press, 1993.

Kieninger, Stephan. "The 1999 Kosovo War and the Crisis in US-Russian Relations." *International History Review* (December 20, 2020, online), https://doi.org/10.1080/07075332.2020.1848899.

Kirchner, Emil J. "Genscher and What Lies behind 'Genscherism.'" *West European Politics* 13 (April 1990): 159–77.

Korb, Lawrence J. "Who's in Charge Here? National Security and the Contract with America." *The Brookings Review* 13, no. 4 (Fall 1995): 4–7.

Korte, Karl-Rudolf. *Deutschlandpolitik in Helmut Kohls Kanzlerschaft: Regierungsstil und Entscheidungen 1982–1989. Geschichte der deutschen Einheit* [GDE], vol. 1. Stuttgart: Deutsche Verlags-Anstalt, 1998.

Kotkin, Stephen. *Armageddon Averted: The Soviet Collapse, 1970–2000.* New York: Oxford University Press, 2001.

———. "The Resistible Rise of Vladimir Putin." *Foreign Affairs* 94, no. 2 (March/April 2015): 140–53.

Kramer, Mark. "The Myth of a No-NATO-Enlargement Pledge to Russia." *Washington Quarterly* 32, no. 2 (April 2009): 39–61.

Kramer, Mark, and M. E. Sarotte. "Correspondence: No Such Promise." *Foreign Affairs* 93, no. 6 (November/December 2014): 208–9.

Kramer, Mark, and Joshua R. Itzkowitz Shifrinson. "Correspondence: NATO Enlargement—Was There a Promise?" *International Security* 42, no. 1 (Summer 2017): 189–92.

Kramer, Mark, and Vít Smetana, eds. *Imposing, Maintaining, and Tearing Open the Iron Curtain: The Cold War and East-Central Europe, 1945–1989.* Lanham, MD: Lexington Books, 2013.

Krasner, Stephen. *Sovereignty: Organized Hypocrisy.* Princeton, NJ: Princeton University Press, 1999.

Küsters, Hanns Jürgen. *Der Integrationsfriede: Viermächte-Verhandlungen über die Friedensregelung mit Deutschland 1945–1990.* Munich: Oldenbourg, 2000.

———, ed. *Der Zerfall des Sowjetimperiums und Deutschlands Wiedervereinigung.* Köln: Böhlau Verlag, 2016.

———. "The Kohl-Gorbachev Meetings in Moscow and in the Caucasus, 1990." *Cold War History* 2, no. 2 (January 2002): 195–235.

Larrabee, F. Stephen. "Ukraine's Balancing Act." *Survival* 38, no. 2 (1996): 143–65.

Lašas, Ainius. *European Union and NATO Expansion: Central and Eastern Europe.* New York: Palgrave Macmillan, 2010.

Leffler, Melvyn P. *Safeguarding Democratic Capitalism.* Princeton, NJ: Princeton University Press, 2017.

Legvold, Robert. *Return to Cold War.* Malden, MA: Polity Press, 2016.

———, ed. *Russian Foreign Policy in the Twenty-First Century and the Shadow of the Past.* New York: Columbia University, 2007.

Lever, Paul. "The Cold War: The Golden Age of Arms Control." *Cold War History* 14, no. 4 (2014): 501–13.

Lieven, Anatol. *Chechnya: Tombstone of Russian Power.* New Haven, CT: Yale University Press, 1999.

Lindsay, James M. *Congress and the Politics of US Foreign Policy.* Baltimore: Johns Hopkins University Press, 1994.

Locatelli, Catherine. "The Russian Oil Industry between Public and Private Governance." *Energy Policy* 34, no. 9 (2006): 1075–85.

Lockwood, Dunbar. "Administration Moves Unilaterally to Begin Testing THAAD System." *Arms Control Today* 25, no. 1 (January/February 1995): 21.

Logevall, Fredrik. "A Critique of Containment." *Diplomatic History* 28, no. 4 (September 2004): 473–99.

Lüthi, Lorenz. *Cold Wars: Asia, the Middle East, Europe.* Cambridge: Cambridge University Press, 2020.

Mälksoo, Maria. *The Politics of Becoming European: A Study of Polish and Baltic Post–Cold War Security Imaginaries.* London: Routledge, 2010.

Manela, Erez. "International Society as a Historical Subject." *Diplomatic History* 44, no. 2 (2020): 184–209.

Mann, James. *The Great Rift: Dick Cheney, Colin Powell, and the Broken Friendship That Defined an Era*. New York: Henry Holt, 2019.

Marten, Kimberly. "NATO Enlargement: Evaluating Its Consequences in Russia." *International Politics* 57, no. 3 (June 2020): 401–26.

———. "Reconsidering NATO Expansion: A Counterfactual Analysis of Russia and the West in the 1990s." *European Journal of International Security* 3, no. 2 (November 2017): 135–61.

Matthijs, Matthias. "The Three Faces of German Leadership." *Survival* 58, no. 2 (2016): 135–54.

McCauley, Martin. *Bandits, Gangsters and the Mafia: Russia, the Baltic States and the CIS since 1991*. London: Routledge, 2016.

MccGwire, Michael. "NATO Expansion: 'A Policy Error of Historic Importance.'" *Review of International Studies* 24 (1998): 23–42.

McGarr, Kathryn J. *The Whole Damn Deal: Robert Strauss and the Art of Politics*. New York: PublicAffairs, 2011.

Mearsheimer, John. "The Case for a Ukrainian Nuclear Deterrent." *Foreign Affairs* 72, no. 3 (Summer 1993): 50–66.

———. "The False Promise of International Institutions." *International Security* 19, no. 3 (Winter 1994/95): 5–49.

———. *The Great Delusion: Liberal Dreams and International Realities*. New Haven, CT: Yale University Press, 2018.

Meijer, Hugo, and Stephen G. Brooks. "Illusions of Autonomy: Why Europe Cannot Provide for Its Security If the United States Pulls Back." *International Security* 45, no. 4 (Spring 2021): 7–43.

Miles, Simon. *Engaging the Evil Empire: Washington, Moscow, and the Beginning of the End of the Cold War*. Ithaca, NY: Cornell University Press, 2020.

Miller, Chris. *Putinomics: Power and Money in Resurgent Russia*. Chapel Hill: University of North Carolina Press, 2018.

———. *The Struggle to Save the Soviet Economy*. Chapel Hill: University of North Carolina Press, 2016.

Milne, David. *Worldmaking: The Art and Science of American Diplomacy*. New York: Farrar Strauss, 2015.

Moller, Sara Bjerg. "Twenty Years After: Assessing the Consequences of Enlargement for the NATO Military Alliance." *International Politics* 57, no. 3 (June 2020): 509–29.

Moravcsik, Andrew. *The Choice for Europe: Social Purpose and State Power from Messina to Maastricht*. Ithaca, NY: Cornell University Press, 1998.

Morgan, Michael Cotey. *The Final Act: The Helsinki Accords and the Transformation of the Cold War*. Princeton, NJ: Princeton University Press, 2018.

Morton, Andrew. *Monica's Story*. New York: St. Martin's Press, 1999.

Myers, Steven Lee. *The New Tsar: The Rise and Reign of Vladimir Putin*. New York: Vintage Books, 2015.

Naftali, Timothy. *George H. W. Bush*. New York: Times Books, 2007.

Naimark, Norman M. *The Russians in Germany: A History of the Soviet Zone of Occupation, 1945–1949*. Cambridge, MA: Harvard University Press, 1995.

Njølstad, Olav, ed. *The Last Decade of the Cold War: From Conflict Escalation to Conflict Transformation*. London: Frank Cass, 2004.

Nuti, Leopoldo, ed. *The Crisis of Détente in Europe: From Helsinki to Gorbachev, 1975–1985*. New York: Routledge, 2009.

Nuti, Leopoldo, Frédéric Bozo, Marie-Pierre Rey, and Bernd Rother, eds. *The Euromissile Crisis and the End of the Cold War*. Washington, DC: Woodrow Wilson Center Press, 2015.

O'Hanlon, Michael. *Beyond NATO: A New Security Architecture for Eastern Europe*. Washington, DC: Brookings Institution Press, 2017.

Olesen, Mikkel Runge. "To Balance or Not to Balance: How Denmark Almost Stayed Out of NATO." *Journal of Cold War Studies* 20, no. 2 (Spring 2018): 63–98.

Oplatka, Andreas. *Der erste Riß in der Mauer*. Vienna: Paul Zsolnay Verlag, 2009.

Ostermann, Christian F. *Between Containment and Rollback: The United States and the Cold War in Germany*. Stanford, CA: Stanford University Press, 2021.

Packer, George. *Our Man: Richard Holbrooke and the End of the American Century*. New York: Knopf, 2019.

Paczkowski, Andrzej. *The Spring Will Be Ours: Poland and Poles from the Occupation to Freedom*. Translated by Jane Cave. University Park: Pennsylvania State University Press, 2003.

Patel, Kiran Klaus, and Kenneth Weisbrode, eds. *European Integration and the Atlantic Community in the 1980s*. New York: Cambridge University Press, 2013.

Perrow, Charles. *Normal Accidents: Living with High-Risk Technologies*. Princeton, NJ: Princeton University Press, 1999.

Plokhy, Serhii. *Chernobyl: The History of a Nuclear Catastrophe*. New York: Basic Books, 2018.

———. *The Gates of Europe: A History of Ukraine*. New York: Basic Books, 2015.

———. *The Last Empire: The Final Days of the Soviet Union*. New York: Basic Books, 2014.

Plokhy, Serhii, and M. E. Sarotte. "The Shoals of Ukraine: Where American Illusions and Great-Power Politics Collide." *Foreign Affairs* 99, no. 1 (January/ February 2020): 81–95.

Poast, Paul, and Alexandra Chinchilla. "Good for Democracy? Evidence from the 2004 NATO Expansion." *International Politics* 57, no. 3 (June 2020): 471–90.

Poast, Paul, and Johannes Urpelainen. *Organizing Democracy: How International Organizations Assist New Democracies*. Chicago: University of Chicago Press, 2018.

Podvig, Pavel, ed. *Russian Strategic Nuclear Forces*. Cambridge, MA: MIT Press, 2004.

Porter, Patrick. "Why America's Grand Strategy Has Not Changed: Power, Habit, and the U.S. Foreign Policy Establishment." *International Security* 42, no. 4 (Spring 2018): 9–46.

Posen, Barry R. *Restraint: A New Foundation for U.S. Grand Strategy*. Ithaca, NY: Cornell University Press, 2014.

Radchenko, Sergey. *The First Fiddle*. Cambridge: Cambridge University Press, forthcoming.

———. "'Nothing but Humiliation for Russia': Moscow and NATO's Eastern Enlargement, 1993–1995." *Journal of Strategic Studies* 43, nos. 6–7 (December 2020): 769–815.

Radchenko, Sergey, Timothy Andrew Sayle, and Christian Ostermann. "Introduction to the Special Issue, NATO Past and Present." *Journal of Strategic Studies* 43, nos. 6–7 (December 2020): 763–68.

Rainer, János. *Imre Nagy: A Biography*. London: I. B. Tauris, 2008.

Ratti, Luca. *A Not-So-Special Relationship: The US, the UK, and German Unification, 1945–1990*. Edinburgh: Edinburgh University Press, 2017.

Reichart, John F., and Steven R. Sturm, eds. *American Defense Policy*. 5th ed. Baltimore: Johns Hopkins University Press, 1982.

Reiss, Mitchell. *Bridled Ambition: Why Countries Constrain Their Nuclear Capabilities*. Washington, DC: Wilson Center Press, 1995.

Reiter, Dan. "Why NATO Enlargement Does Not Spread Democracy." *International Security* 5, no. 4 (Spring 2001): 41–67.

Rid, Thomas. *Active Measures: The Secret History of Disinformation and Political Warfare*. New York: Farrar, Straus and Giroux, 2020.

Ritter, Gerhard A. *Der Preis der deutschen Einheit: Die Wiedervereinigung und die Krise des Sozialstaats*. Munich: Beck, 2006.

Rödder, Andreas. "'Breakthrough in the Caucasus'? German Reunification as a Challenge to Contemporary Historiography." *German Historical Institute London Bulletin* 24, no. 2 (November 2002): 7–34.

———. *Deutschland Einig Vaterland*. Munich: Beck, 2009.

———. *Die Bundesrepublik Deutschland 1969–1990*. Munich: Oldenbourg, 2004.

———. *Geschichte der deutschen Wiedervereinigung*. Munich: Beck, 2011.

———. "Zeitgeschichte als Herausforderung: Die deutsche Einheit." *Historische Zeitschrift* 270 (2000): 669–87.

Roth, Philip. *The Human Stain*. New York: Houghton Mifflin, 2000.

Rozental, S., ed. *Niels Bohr: His Life and Work as Seen by Friends and Colleagues*. New York: Wiley, 1967.

Sagan, Scott. *The Limits of Safety: Organizations, Accidents and Nuclear Weapons*. Princeton, NJ: Princeton University Press, 1993.

Sarotte, Mary Elise. "A Broken Promise? What the West Really Told Moscow about NATO Expansion." *Foreign Affairs* 93, no. 5 (September/October 2014): 90–97.

———. "China's Fear of Contagion: Tiananmen Square and the Power of the European Example." *International Security* 37 (Fall 2012): 156–82.

———. *The Collapse: The Accidental Opening of the Berlin Wall*. New York: Basic Books, 2014.

———. *Dealing with the Devil: East Germany, Détente, and Ostpolitik, 1969–1973*. Chapel Hill: University of North Carolina Press, 2001.

———. "Deciding to Be Mars." *Policy Review* 172 (April–May 2012): 71–83.

———. "Die US-Außenpolitik und das Ende der deutschen Teilung: Eine Fall-studie zur Demokratisierung." *Jahrbuch für Historische Kommunismusfor-schung* (2009): 251–68.

———. "Eine Föderalismusdebatte anderer Art." *Internationale Politik*, April 2005: 106–15.

———. "Elite Intransigence and the End of the Berlin Wall." *German Politics* 2 (August 1993): 270–87.

———. "Eurozone Crisis as Historical Legacy." *Foreign Affairs*, September 29, 2010. https://www.foreignaffairs.com/articles/western-europe/2010-09-29 /eurozone-crisis-historical-legacy.

———. "Führungsduo? Spannungen zwischen der USA und der Bundesrepublik im Jahr 1990 bei der Herstellung der deutschen Einheit." In *Dreißig Jahre Zwei-plus-Vier-Vertrag: Die internationale Gründungsgeschichte der Berliner Re-publik*, edited by Tim Geiger, Jürgen Lillteicher, and Hermann Wentker. Berlin: DeGruyter, forthcoming.

———. *German Military Reform and European Security*. Oxford: Oxford Univer-sity Press, 2001.

———. "How Did Political Leaders Experience the Fall of the Berlin Wall on November 9, 1989?" *Passport: The Newsletter of the Society for Historians of American Foreign Relations* 41 (April 2010): 18–21.

———. "How to Enlarge NATO: The Debate inside the Clinton Adminis-tration, 1993–95." *International Security* 44, no. 1 (July–September 2019): 7–41.

———. "In Victory, Magnanimity: US Foreign Policy, 1989–1991, and the Leg-acy of Prefabricated Multilateralism." *International Politics* 48 (August 2011): 482–95.

———. *1989: The Struggle to Create Post–Cold War Europe*. Princeton, NJ: Prince-ton University Press, 2009.

———. "Not One Inch Eastward? Bush, Baker, Kohl, Genscher, Gorbachev and the Origin of Russian Resentment toward NATO Enlargement in Febru-ary 1990." *Diplomatic History* 34 (January 2010): 119–40.

———. "Perpetuating US Preeminence: The 1990 Deals to 'Bribe the Soviets Out' and Move NATO In." *International Security* 35 (July 2010): 110–37.

———. "A Small Town in (East) Germany: The Erfurt Meeting of 1970 and the Dynamics of Cold War Détente." *Diplomatic History* 25, no. 1 (Winter 2001): 85–104.

———. "Spying Not Only on Strangers: Documenting Stasi Involvement in Cold War German-German Negotiations." *Intelligence and National Security* 11 (October 1996): 765–79. Also published in translation as "Nicht nur Fremde ausspioniert." *Deutschland Archiv* 3 (May/June 1997): 407–11.

———. "Under Cover of Boredom: Review Article of Recent Publications on the East German Ministry for State Security, or Stasi." *Intelligence and National Security* 12 (October 1997): 196–210.

———. "Vor 25 Jahren: Verhandlungen über den Grundlagenvertrag; Zum internationalen Kontext der deutsch-deutschen Gespräche." *Deutschland Archiv* 6 (November/December 1997): 901–11.

———. "The Worst Allies, Except for All the Others: US-European Relations in the Age of George W. Bush." *International Politics* 45 (May 2008): 310–24.

Satter, David. *The Less You Know, the Better You Sleep: Russia's Road to Terror and Dictatorship under Yeltsin and Putin.* New Haven, CT: Yale University Press, 2016.

Sayle, Timothy Andrews. *Enduring Alliance: A History of NATO and the Postwar Global Order.* Ithaca, NY: Cornell University Press, 2019.

———. "A Nuclear Education: The Origins of NATO's Nuclear Planning Group." *Journal of Strategic Studies* 43, nos. 6–7 (December 2020): 920–56.

Sestanovich, Stephen. *Maximalist: America in the World from Truman to Obama.* New York: Knopf, 2014.

———. "What Has Moscow Done? Rebuilding U.S.-Russian Relations." *Foreign Affairs*, November/December 2008. https://www.foreignaffairs.com/articles /russia-fsu/2008-11-01/what-has-moscow-done.

Shapiro, Ian, and Adam Tooze, eds. *Charter of the North Atlantic Treaty Organization.* New Haven, CT: Yale University Press, 2018.

Shields, John M., and William C. Potter, eds. *Dismantling the Cold War: US and NIS Perspectives on the Nunn-Lugar Cooperative Threat Reduction Program.* Cambridge, MA: MIT Press, 1997.

Shifrinson, Joshua R. Itzkowitz. "Deal or No Deal? The End of the Cold War and the U.S. Offer to Limit NATO Expansion." *International Security* 40, no. 4 (Spring 2016): 7–44.

———. "Eastbound and Down: The United States, NATO Enlargement, and Suppressing the Soviet and Western European Alternatives, 1990–1992." *Journal of Strategic Studies* 43, nos. 6–7 (December 2020): 816–46.

———. *Rising Titans, Falling Giants: How Great Powers Exploit Power Shifts.* Ithaca, NY: Cornell University Press, 2018.

Siegel, Jennifer. *For Peace and Money: French and British Finance in the Service of Tsars and Commissars.* Oxford: Oxford University Press, 2014.

Simms, Brendan. *Unfinest Hour: Britain and the Destruction of Bosnia.* London: Allen Lane, 2001.

Simon, Jeffrey. *NATO and the Czech and Slovak Republics: A Comparative Study in Civil-Military Relations.* Lanham, MD: Rowman & Littlefield, 2004.

Sinovets, Polina, and Marian Budjeryn. "Interpreting the Bomb: Ownership and Deterrence in Ukraine's Nuclear Discourse." Woodrow Wilson International Center for Scholars, Nuclear Proliferation International History Project, Working Paper No. 12, December 2017.

Slaughter, Anne-Marie. *The Chessboard and the Web: Strategies of Connection in a Networked World.* New Haven, CT: Yale University Press, 2017.

Sloan, Stanley. *Defense of the West: NATO, the European Union, and the Transatlantic Bargain.* Manchester: Manchester University Press, 2016.

Sorokowski, Andrew D. "Treaty on Friendship, Cooperation and Partnership between Ukraine and the Russian Federation." *Harvard Ukrainian Studies* 20 (1996): 319–29.

Sparrow, Bartholomew H. "Realism's Practitioner: Brent Scowcroft and the Making of the New World Order, 1989–1993." *Diplomatic History* 34, no. 1 (2010): 141–75.

———. *The Strategist: Brent Scowcroft and the Call of National Security.* New York: PublicAffairs, 2015.

Spohr, Kristina. "Germany, America and the Shaping of Post–Cold War Europe: A Story of German International Emancipation through Political Unification, 1989–90." *Cold War History* 15, no. 2 (2015): 221–43.

———. *Post Wall, Post Square: Rebuilding the World after 1989.* London: William Collins, 2019.

———. "Precluded or Precedent-Setting? The 'NATO Enlargement Question' in the Triangular Bonn-Washington-Moscow Diplomacy of 1990–1991." *Journal of Cold War Studies* 14, no. 4 (Fall 2012): 4–54.

Steil, Benn. *The Marshall Plan: Dawn of the Cold War.* New York: Simon and Schuster, 2018.

Stent, Angela. *The Limits of Partnership: U.S.-Russian Relations in the Twenty-First Century.* Princeton, NJ: Princeton University Press, 2014.

———. *Putin's World: Russia against the West and with the Rest.* New York: Twelve Books, 2019.

———. *Russia and Germany Reborn: Unification, the Soviet Collapse, and the New Europe.* Princeton, NJ: Princeton University Press, 1999.

Stoner, Kathryn. *Russia Resurrected: Its Power and Purpose in a New Global Order.* Oxford: Oxford University Press, 2021.

Suny, Ronald Grigor. *The Revenge of the Past: Nationalism, Revolution, and the Collapse of the Soviet Union.* Stanford, CA: Stanford University Press, 1993.

Suri, Jeremi. *Liberty's Surest Guardians: American Nation-Building from the Founders to Obama.* New York: Free Press, 2011.

Szabo, Stephen. *The Diplomacy of German Unification.* New York: St. Martin's Press, 1992.

———. *Germany, Russia and the Rise of Geo-Economics.* London: Bloomsbury Academic, 2015.

Taubman, William. *Gorbachev: His Life and Times.* New York: Norton, 2017.

Ther, Philipp. *Europe since 1989: A History.* Translated by Charlotte Hughes-Kreutzmüller. Princeton, NJ: Princeton University Press, 2016.

Trachtenberg, Marc. *A Constructed Peace: The Making of the European Settlement 1945–1963.* Princeton, NJ: Princeton University Press, 1999.

———. "The United States and the NATO Non-extension Assurance of 1990." *International Security* 45, no. 3 (Winter 2020/21): 162–203.

Treisman, Daniel. *The Return: Russia's Journey from Gorbachev to Medvedev.* New York: Free Press, 2011.

Trenin, Dmitri. *Post-Imperium: A Eurasian Story.* Washington, DC: Carnegie Endowment for International Peace, 2011.

Turner, Henry Ashby, Jr. *Germany from Partition to Unification.* 2nd ed. New Haven, CT: Yale University Press, 1992.

Uelzmann, Jan. "Building Domestic Support for West Germany's Integration into NATO, 1953–1955." *Journal of Cold War Studies* 22, no. 2 (Spring 2020): 133–62.

Vachudova, Milada Anna. *Europe Undivided: Democracy, Leverage, and Integration after Communism.* Oxford: Oxford University Press, 2005.

Van Hooft, Paul. "Land Rush: American Grand Strategy, NATO Enlargement, and European Fragmentation." *International Politics* 57, no. 3 (June 2020): 530–53.

Ven Bruusgaard, Kristin. "Russian Nuclear Strategy and Conventional Inferiority." *Journal of Strategic Studies,* October 14, 2020. https://doi.org/10.1080/01402390.2020.1818070.

Von Borzyskowski, Inken, and Felicity Vabulas. "Credible Commitments? Explaining IGO Suspensions to Sanction Political Backsliding." *International Studies Quarterly* 63, no. 1 (2019): 139–52.

Wallander, Celeste. "NATO's Price: Shape Up or Ship Out." *Foreign Affairs* 81, no. 6 (November/December 2002): 2–8.

Waltz, Kenneth N. "Structural Realism after the Cold War." *International Security* 25, no. 1 (Summer 2000): 5–41.

Weidenfeld, Werner, Peter M. Wagner, and Elke Bruck. *Außenpolitik für die deutsche Einheit: Die Entscheidungsjahre 1989/90. Geschichte der deutschen Einheit* [GDE], vol. 4. Stuttgart: Deutsche Verlags-Anstalt, 1998.

Weiner, Tim. *The Folly and the Glory: America, Russia, and Political Warfare 1945–2020.* New York: Henry Holt, 2020.

Weisbrode, Kenneth. *The Atlanticists: The Story of American Diplomacy.* Minneapolis: Nortia, 2017.

Wells, Samuel F. *Fearing the Worst: How Korea Transformed the Cold War.* New York: Columbia University Press, 2019.

———. *The Helsinki Process and the Future of Europe.* Washington, DC: Wilson Center Press, 1990.

Wentker, Hermann. *Die Deutschen und Gorbatschow: Der Gorbatschow-Diskurs im doppelten Deutschland.* Berlin: Metropol, 2020.

Westad, Odd Arne. *The Cold War: A World History.* New York: Basic Books, 2017.

Wirsching, Andreas. *Abschied vom Provisorium 1982–1990: Geschichte der Bundesrepublik Deutschland.* Stuttgart: Deutsche Verlags-Anstalt, 2006.

Wohlforth, William. *The Elusive Balance: Power and Perceptions during the Cold War.* Ithaca, NY: Cornell University Press, 1993.

Wohlforth, William, and Vladislav M. Zubok. "An Abiding Antagonism: Realism, Idealism and the Mirage of Western-Russian Partnership after the Cold War." *International Politics* 54, no. 4 (May 2017): 405–19.

Wolff, David. "Stalin's Postwar Border-Making Tactics." *Cahiers du monde russe* 52, no. 2–3 (2011): 273–91. https://journals.openedition.org/monderusse/9334.

Wright, Robert. *Nonzero: The Logic of Human Destiny.* New York: Vintage Books, 2000.

Wright, Thomas J. *All Measures Short of War: The Contest for the Twenty-First Century and the Future of American Power.* New Haven, CT: Yale University Press, 2017.

Yost, David S. *NATO Transformed: The Alliance's New Roles in International Security.* Washington, DC: United States Institute of Peace Press, 1998.

Žantovský, Michael. *Havel: A Life.* New York: Grove Press, 2014.

Zubok, Vladislav. *Collapse: The Fall of the Soviet Union.* New Haven, CT: Yale University Press, 2021.

———. *A Failed Empire: The Soviet Union in the Cold War from Stalin to Gorbachev.* Chapel Hill: University of North Carolina Press, 2007.

———. "With His Back against the Wall: Gorbachev, Soviet Demise, and German Reunification." *Cold War History* 14, no. 4 (2014): 619–45.

Index

Page numbers in *italics* indicate maps.

AFRICAN CARIBBEANS

A REFERENCE GUIDE

Edited by
Alan West-Durán

GREENWOOD PRESS
Westport, Connecticut · London

Library of Congress Cataloging-in-Publication Data

African Caribbeans: a reference guide / edited by Alan West-Durán.
   p. cm.
  Includes bibliographical references and index.
  ISBN 0-313-31240-0 (alk. paper)
  1. Blacks—West Indies. 2. Blacks—Suriname. 3. Blacks—French Guiana.
4. West Indies—History. 5. Suriname—History. 6. French Guiana—History.
7. Caribbean Area. I. West, Alan, 1953–
F1629.B55 B53   2003
972.9'00496—dc21   2002069603

British Library Cataloguing in Publication Data is available.

Library of Congress Catalog Card Number: 2002069603
ISBN: 0–313–31240–0

First published in 2003

Greenwood Press, 88 Post Road West, Westport, CT 06881
An imprint of Greenwood Publishing Group, Inc.
www.greenwood.com

Printed in the United States of America

The paper used in this book complies with the
Permanent Paper Standard issued by the National
Information Standards Organization (Z39.48-1984).

10 9 8 7 6 5 4 3 2 1

For Aimée Césaire, for the beauty and violence of his images
For C.L.R. James, for his roving intellect and thirst for justice
For Fernando Ortiz, for his curiosity, warmth and vision
But especially for Marcia Gail Cooke, to make amends, and in
thanks for her true sense of friendship

Contents

Acknowledgments

Many people were helpful in making this book possible, starting with Antonio Benítez Rojo for his recommendation, and Félix Matos Rodríguez for helping me find many of the contributors. In this regard I must also thank Angel Quintero Rivera. Special thanks to Harry Hoetink and Luc Alofs, who were extremely helpful on the chapters that dealt with the Dutch-speaking Caribbean, and Malik Sekou for invaluable assistance on the U.S. Virgin Islands chapter. However great my gratitude, the responsibility for the ideas and content expressed are entirely my own.

My deepest gratitude is to my collaborators and co-authors of this volume, who taught me so much about Afro-Caribbean history, culture, politics, and even sports. The only truism about the Caribbean's complexity and richness, is that the more you know about the area, the more you need and want to explore it. This inexhaustible journey was made much more manageable or even joyful by the co-authors.

Finally, the greatest of thanks to Ester Shapiro Rok for being an editor, critic, inspiration, and true companion in life. Mucho aché.

Caribbean Chronology

1492:	First voyage of Christopher Columbus
1508–1515:	First importation of Africans to the Caribbean
1509–1510:	First sugar mills on Hispaniola
1515:	First Caribbean exports of sugar to Spain
1518:	Charles V, king of Spain, grants permission for 4,000 African slaves to be imported to Antilles
1542:	*Encomienda* system and Indian slavery abolished (under New Laws of the Indies) by the Spanish Crown
1609–1620:	Dutch and English begin colonization attempts in Eastern Antilles
1625:	The Dutch, French, British begin to take control of Spain's previous colonial possessions in the region. British in Barbados and St. Kitts.
1630–1640:	French settle Martinique and Guadeloupe. Dutch in Curaçao, Saba, St. Martin, St. Eustatius. The British settle Antigua, Montserrat, St. Lucia.
1647:	First sugar shipments from Barbados to Great Britain
1649:	Slave revolt in Barbados, involving dozens
1651:	British colonists settle Suriname
1655:	British captured Jamaica from Spanish
1666–1667:	Anglo-Dutch War. Dutch gain Suriname in exchange for Manhattan Island.
1670s:	First Maroons (in Suriname)
1685:	French promulgate Code Noir (Black Code), system of laws to regulate slave system
1697:	Spain cedes western Hispaniola (later Haiti) to France

1733–1734:	Slave revolt involving hundreds in St. John, Virgin Islands
1734:	First Maroon War in Jamaica
1735–1736:	Slave revolt involving thousands in Antigua
1760–1762:	Maroon treaties with Dutch authorities in Suriname
1791–1804:	Haitian slave insurrection and independence
1789:	French Revolution
1790s:	Slave revolts on many islands: Curaçao, Guadeloupe, Martinique, Tobago, St. Lucia, Grenada, Dominica, Tortola and Guyana
1795:	Second Maroon War in Jamaica. Black Carib War in St. Vincent, and subsequent deportation to Honduras, Belize, etc.
1797:	British take over Trinidad and Tobago from the Spanish
1804:	Denmark abolishes slave trade
1808:	Great Britain and the United States outlaw slave trade
1810–1826:	Latin American wars for independence
1813:	Sweden abolishes slave trade
1818:	France and Holland abolish slave trade
1822–1844:	Haiti occupies Dominican Republic
1823:	Slave revolt in Guyana involving thousands. Grenada grants citizenship to free non-whites.
1831–1832:	Baptist War in Jamaica
1834–1838:	British emancipation in their Caribbean colonies
1848:	French emancipation in their Caribbean colonies
1863:	Dutch emancipation in their Caribbean colonies
1865:	Morant Bay revolt in Jamaica.
1868–1878:	Ten Years' War in Cuba (for independence and abolition)
1873:	Puerto Rico abolishes slavery
1886:	Cuban abolition of slavery
1895–1898:	Spanish-Cuban-American War
1902:	Cuba becomes Independent. Riots in Jamaica and Trinidad.
1912:	Uprising of blacks quelled in Cuba (4,000–6,000 killed)
1915–1934:	Revolt in Haiti. United States occupies Haiti.
1916–1924:	United States occupies Dominican Republic.
1917:	Puerto Ricans become U.S. citizens. Danish Virgin Islands are bought by the United States.
1930s:	Major labor unrest in Jamaica, Trinidad, Barbados, St. Vincent, Belize, Antigua, Guyana, St. Kitts, Bahamas
1937:	Massacre of at least 20,000 Haitians by Dominican president Rafael Leonidas Trujillo
1940s:	Universal suffrage in the British Caribbean; French islands become overseas departments.

1954:	Dutch territories and Suriname made legally autonomous and equal to the Netherlands
1958:	Formation of West Indies Federation (ten British islands); dissolved in 1962.
1959:	Cuban Revolution; Fidel Castro takes power.
1961:	Racial violence in Guyana. Trujillo assassinated. United States invades Cuba.
1962:	Cuban Missile Crisis; independence of Trinidad and Tobago and Jamaica
1965:	United States invades Dominican Republic
1966:	Barbados and Guyana gain independence
1968:	Caribbean Free Trade area formed
1970:	Black Power movement in Trinidad
1972–1980:	Michael Manley government in Jamaica
1973:	The Bahamas gains independence
1974:	Grenada independence. Riots in Suriname. Caribbean Community and Common Market (CARICOM) formed.
1975:	Suriname independence
1976:	Cuba sends troops to fight in Angola
1977:	St. Lucia gains independence
1978:	Dominica becomes independent
1979:	New Jewel Movement under Maurice Bishop in Grenada. St. Vincent and the Grenadines independent.
1980:	Mariel Boat Lift Crisis; 135,000 Cubans leave the island.
1981:	Antigua and Barbuda, Belize become independent
1983:	Bishop killed, and United States invades Grenada. St. Kitts-Nevis become independent.
1986:	*Status aparte* for Aruba within Kingdom of the Netherlands
1986–1992:	Maroon guerrilla war in Suriname
1989–1990:	Collapse of Soviet Union; Cuba's Special Period (1989–1994).
1990:	Afro-Muslim revolt in Trinidad
1992:	Derek Walcott from St. Lucia wins Nobel Prize for literature
1993 and 1998:	Puerto Rico has plebiscites on status issue
1994:	United States intervenes in Haiti
1995:	Suriname becomes 14th member state of CARICOM
1999:	Panama Canal passes over to Panamanian sovereignty
2000:	*Status aparte* for St. Maarten within Kingdom of the Netherlands. Aristide elected president in Haiti.
2001:	Political violence in Jamaica; more than 30 killed
2002:	At 23rd CARICOM summit in Guyana violence erupted, with 2 dead. Haiti admitted as 15th member state of CARICOM.

INTRODUCTION

The Caribbean is one of the richest treasures on the planet. Indeed, with its multiplicity of languages, music, thinkers, culinary traditions, religions, and cultures, it was a miniature version of globalization before the term became popular. At first sight the Caribbean seems bewildering: it has large islands like Cuba, with a population as large as that of New York City, and tiny ones like Saba, with fewer people than a Chicago neighborhood. Some nations, such as Suriname, have lush vegetation, with tropical rain forests; others are arid and harsh, like Bonaire. Geographically, the Caribbean ranges widely from the northern tip of South America (Venezuela) and parts, but not all, of Colombia, to Central America to New Orleans and Miami. (Some would include parts of New York City.) Its inhabitants speak not only Spanish, English, French, and Dutch, but also Creoles such as Sranan Tongo, Papiamentu, Haitian Creole, and Garífuna; some still speak Hindi, Chinese, or Arabic. Politically the Caribbean is also diverse, with colonies like Anguilla, a lone Communist regime (Cuba), "freely associated states" like Puerto Rico, independent republics like Jamaica, overseas departments such as Martinique, and a colony with a parliamentary democracy but without political parties as in the Cayman Islands. Every major religion is found in the Caribbean basin: Catholicism, Protestantism (including Baptists and Evangelicals), Judaism, Islam, Hinduism, Buddhism, plus a host of homegrown ones such as Vodou, Santería, Palo, Winti, Obeah, Orisha, Kali Mai, Rastafarianism, and Spiritual Baptist. Ethnically and racially the Caribbean seems like a microcosm of the planet: Amerindian, African, European, Asian, Middle Eastern, and Mediterranean cultures all converged here, though clearly not as equals.

So how to understand this complexity, how do we find common threads to grasp Caribbean reality? The most significant thread is its "African" presence, even in countries where African-Caribbeans are no longer a majority but instead have been surpassed in number by East Asians, as in Suriname or Guyana and possibly soon in Trinidad. Africans shaped by the powerful forces of Caribbean history that encompassed forced removal and enslavement, colonialism, racism, emancipation and varieties of sovereignty. "African" is in quotation marks to highlight two possible dangers: oversimplification and essentialism. The first of the two has been all too common: lumping together over forty countries of the sub-Sahara into an amorphous grouping called Africa, a rich mosaic of cultures and religions with hundreds of languages, is uncritical generalization, at best. The second pitfall (essentialism) tries to assign unchanging traits to Africa: a certain outlook on life, kinship structures, social organization, and culture. This overlooks the changes and dynamism of African societies, and equally affects how we look at Afro-Caribbean history, because within a Caribbean context that Africanness becomes transformed (transcultured) when it comes in contact with other Africans, Amerindians, Europeans, and later with East Asians.

The vibrant cultures of Africa survived and thrived in the Caribbean in spite of ominous attempts to eradicate their culture, wipe out ancestral memory, and violently force their assimilation into colonial regimes that were vast work camps of unfree labor. The African diaspora has left an indelible presence in the Caribbean, be it through music, language, religion, cuisine, sports, literature, storytelling and popular sayings, family, personal hygiene, attire, healing and folk medicine, and ways in which people socially interact.

The total population of the Caribbean (see Appendix for list of countries) is about 37 million and about 90 percent of the population inhabit landed areas that are independent states. Eighty percent of the population live in four of the islands: Cuba, Haiti, the Dominican Republic, and Puerto Rico. If broken down into broad linguistic blocks, the region would look as follows: Spanish speaking (60%), French speaking (22%), English speaking (16%), and Dutch speaking (2%). In terms of racial/ethnic mix it is overwhelmingly black or Afro-Creole, that is, of African mixed with European, Asian, or other (73%), with 4 percent East Asian, 22 percent white, and 1 percent other. Ninety percent of the white population is found on the Spanish-speaking islands, more than half in Cuba alone. If Cuba and Puerto Rico were excluded, the black and Afro-Creole population would be over 85 percent (and whites 7%). These are approximations, of course, because the definition of white in the Caribbean is more elastic than in the United States. And statistics do not tell the whole story: Cuba, which appears to be the whitest of all the Caribbean islands, is profoundly Afro-Cuban in many ways, be it through music, religion, or its social mores.

AFRICANS TO THE CARIBBEAN:
DIASPORA, RESISTANCE, FREEDOM

The trans-atlantic slave trade shipped approximately 11.6 million Africans to the Caribbean, Latin America/Brazil, and the United States. Only 10 million arrived, which means that one out of seven slaves did not survive the horrifying trip of the Middle Passage. In this period (1519–1867) almost half of all the slaves went to Brazil and Cuba. There were noticeable patterns to the trade: in the sixteenth century, it was dominated exclusively by Spain and Portugal, but in the seventeenth century the British and French began to contest Spanish dominance; by the eighteenth century, Britain accounted for a third of the trade (with Spain, Portugal, and France roughly equal), and in the nineteenth century Spain and Portugal (again, Brazil and Cuba) accounted for 90 percent of the slave trade. The nineteenth-century figures are due to several factors: England, France, Holland, and Denmark had ended their slave trades by 1815, and Britain, then the most influential European country on a world scale, abolished slavery from 1834 to 1838. Despite the British example, France did not act until 1848, Holland until 1863. Cuba (1886) and Brazil (1888) were the last two nations to abolish slavery in the Western Hemisphere.

In terms of the ethnic origins of the Africans forcefully brought to the Americas, they vary by region and time period. Over 90 percent of Africans came from what we call West Central Africa and West Africa (see Appendix). Although many scholars have spoken of a certain philosophical, social, and religious commonality to the West African region, the truth is that there is a staggering wealth and diversity of languages, cultures, and religions that make any generalizations treacherous.

CARIBBEAN TRANSCULTURATIONS

When Africans came to the New World as slaves, they interacted with other African slaves as well as with Europeans, and in some cases with Amerindians (especially in the early colonial stages). These contacts with other Africans that spoke different languages and with other cultures transformed them irrevocably. Immersed as well in plantation life, slaves very quickly began to fashion, albeit under highly coercive circumstances, a new culture. Through accommodation, resistance, and creativity African-Caribbeans began to shape their lives in ways that are still evolving, but were no longer "purely African."

This process of transculturation, as Fernando Ortiz (1881–1969) who wrote extensively on Afro-Cuban culture, called it, has an intricate and sometimes disturbing history. Transculturation here is meant as

[the] constant interaction, transmutation between two or more cultural components [say Spain and Yoruba-Nigeria], whose unconscious end is the creation of a third cultural whole [Cuban]—that is, culture—new and independent, although its bases, its roots rest on preceding elements. The reciprocal influence here is determining. No element is superimposed on the other; on the contrary, each one becomes a third entity. None remains immutable. All change and grow in a "give and take" which engenders a new texture. (Morejón 1993, in Pérez and Stubbs, 229)

A good musical example of transculturation would be the *danzón,* a musical and dance form from nineteenth-century Cuba. Its origins date from the British country dance, later imported into France where it became the *contredanse* played on piano, flute, and violin. The French brought it to St. Domingue (Haiti), but during the Haitian Revolution (1791–1804), many French and their slaves (known as "French blacks") immigrated to nearby Santiago de Cuba. The "French blacks"—and Cuban ones as well—added their rhythms as well as percussion, güiro (scrapers), and maracas. Not surprisingly, Spanish colonial authorities, and their supporters in the local elites, viewed the *danzón* as vulgar and low class (meaning black), and a dangerous example of cultural nationalism, which was true. Spain prohibited *danzones*, especially during and after the bloody Ten Years' War (1868–1878) for independence.

Later incorporating *sones* and even Chinese melodies and rhythms, the *danzón* finally evolved into the *danzón-mambo* and the cha-cha-cha. So an English melody and rhythm, by way of France, Spain, Haiti, and China is refashioned in the Caribbean (twice) to produce something quintessentially Cuban. Not all examples of transculturation are that "successful," but even the sweet, mellifluous *danzón* is the product of slavery and its abolition, a bloody revolution that killed possibly 200,000 and brought great suffering to many more.

Transculturation (some prefer the term "creolization") was by no means smooth. As a long historical process it was first marked by deculturation and forced assimilation, as when slaves were systematically stripped of their humanity and Africanness. This was enacted at many different levels: the type of food eaten or clothing worn, the changing of names, prohibition of religious practices or drumming, separation of family members, a grinding work schedule, not to mention the constant threat of violence, sexual abuse, and psychic humiliation. Employing young, that is, nonadult, slaves had a double purpose: to enlist youthful and strong laborers, but also to have workers who were easier to mold because they were not as well-steeped in a community, nor did they have a vast cultural memory that could be passed on to their slave brethren.

Slowly, over centuries, these power relationships changed, as did the transculturation of Caribbean societies. Many see this transculturation as having a mostly racial meaning, and as a way of denying racism, of defining the Caribbean as racial democracies. Transculturation as a racial term, however, does not imply that race mixing does away with racism. On the contrary, as one scholar notes, "intimacy does not mean equality" (Brereton, 1979, 181). But it does mean that both race and identity, as definitions and lived relations, change over time and are embedded within historically specific power relationships. Transculturation goes far beyond race to include language (Creoles), music, Carnival, religious syncretisms, cuisine, literature, and healing methods. Transculturation, or creolization, is usually used to speak of African and European encounters or confrontations, but in the Caribbean, its first instances are inter-African transculturation, or in some cases Afro-indigenous, as with the Garífuna peoples, or the historical examples of Aruba, Guyana, French Guiana, and Suriname.

THE COMPLEXITIES AND LEGACIES OF SLAVERY

Slavery has been described as a "total system," but it was by no means monolithic or homogenous. The colonial-slave systems produced several black societies within each country. The vast majority of blacks in most, but not all, cases were field slaves. In addition, there were domestic slaves, an artisan class of urban blacks (some free, some not), as well as what is known as a free colored and black class, which was mostly urban. Clearly, urban blacks had greater access to education and social opportunities than did field slaves. Some urban blacks who were enslaved contracted their work out to other employers and were paid for it, allowing many to purchase their freedom, which was vastly more difficult for those enslaved on sugar estates. On some islands this free non-white population was a noticeable portion of the population (Cuba, Trinidad, and Curaçao). In Puerto Rico, free non-whites vastly outnumbered slaves (but not whites)—this was the only island where this occurred.

The rhythm of development and duration of the plantation systems differed greatly as well. For example, the slavery-plantation lasted two centuries in Barbados, but barely fifty years in Trinidad and Tobago. Trinidad had slavery before 1783, but its proportional weight and importance to the society were not as great and were radically altered between 1783 and 1833. Puerto Rico and Cuba present interesting histories as well: while both had begun importing African slaves in the sixteenth century neither developed a large-scale plantation system until the nineteenth century, whereas Barbados, Suriname, Jamaica, St. Domingue, and Martinique had them fully developed by the seventeenth and eighteenth centuries. Countries with a large-scale plantation system usually had a much tinier population of free non-whites, higher mortality rates among the enslaved, and a much harsher social and disciplinary environment, since under these regimes blacks outnumbered whites 10 to 1.

Depending on the colonial power that enslaved them, blacks were faced with policies and laws (often disobeyed) that differed widely in terms of religious indoctrination, language acquisition, and educational possibilities, as well as in terms of attitudes toward miscegenation, or race mixing. For example, scholars have tried to explain this miscegenation and its socio-cultural impact in the Spanish-speaking Caribbean by the lack of Creole languages and the existence of large sectors of the population that are brown or mixed race. The supposed ease of race mixing was attributed to the following: that Spain (and Portugal) already had slaves (or free blacks) living within their territories before the conquest of the New World, thus creating a more lax attitude toward race mixing: Catholicism's zeal in converting those of "pagan faith"; and the importance of the Spanish and Portuguese languages not only as evangelizing tools but also as a method of creating loyal subjects to the Spanish Crown. While all these reasons contain some degree of truth, they do not tell the whole story, and more importantly, they should never be interpreted to mean that Spanish slavery was any less harsh than English or Dutch or French slavery. Different, yes, more benign, no. But it does help us understand why the word "mulatto," for a person of Euro-African heritage, might be used with a more negative connotation in places like Haiti (as well as in the French-, English-, and Dutch-speaking Caribbean), where mulattoes are a tiny elite in an overwhelmingly black populace, than in Cuba and Puerto Rico, which are often self-described as mulatto nations. And it also partially explains why Garveyism—with its appeal to racial exclusivity and repatriation to Africa—never found a mass appeal in the Spanish-speaking Caribbean. Despite these differences, all of the Caribbean practices some form of "shadism," an evaluation of people that minutely registers traits such as skin color, hair, and facial features in order to construct social hierarchies.

Often historians paint the history of Caribbean slavery as relentlessly bleak. No doubt, it is difficult to overstate the brutality, dehumanization, racism, and homicidal nature of the enslavement of millions. As African-Bahamian artist Stan Burnside reminds us, "Calling the kidnapping, rape, forced labor and murder of Africans a 'slave trade' is an insult to our intelligence. This is equivalent to saying 'Rape is sex'" (www.guanima.com/STAN.HTML). But there was resistance as well, and it ranged from armed insurrection and destruction of plantations to maroonage, that is, escaping from plantations for short periods or living in free settlements with other runaways. It also consisted of less collective measures such as feigning sickness, sabotaging machinery, working at a slower pace, feigning stupidity, poisoning masters, burning crops, self-inducing abortions, suicide, self-mutilation, or acts of small maroonage (disappearing for a few days, then returning). Slaves also displayed resistance by finding ways to earn money (by selling produce or animals or contracting their labor to another master) and buying their freedom. There are literally hundreds of instances of slave rebellions between 1520 and 1850, ranging from Maroon wars to the Demerara Revolt and the "Baptist War," (where thousands took arms) to smaller revolts involving only dozens of slaves.

The Maroons (free runaway slaves) offer the most heartening example, having been able to establish large or small communities of free slaves who had escaped their masters or waged successful guerrilla wars against planters and colonial armies or militias. Some communities lasted months, years, or decades, others hundreds of years. The only existing Caribbean Maroon societies are found in Suriname (50,000), French Guiana (7,000), and Jamaica (at least 6,000). Although they are not large within the overall Caribbean population, their influence and importance is far greater than their numbers would indicate.

Maroon societies that lasted decades or more took advantage of terrain, such as rain forests, like in Suriname, or inaccessible mountain ranges, as in Jamaica. However, there were maritime Maroons who would escape to other islands where their freedom was granted—especially if they became Catholics—as was the case of slaves from St. Croix fleeing to Puerto Rico or Curaçaoan slaves escaping to Venezuela.

The black Carib, or Garífuna, offer an interesting and different transculturation process: Africans mixing with Amerindians (Arawak and Carib), somewhat similar to the black Seminoles of the United States. Shipwrecked Africans made their way to St. Vincent and Dominica in the Eastern Caribbean in the mid–seventeenth century, and mixed in with the Arawak-Carib populations. Soon, escaped slaves from Barbados, St. Lucia, Antigua, Martinique, and Guadeloupe swelled their ranks. Although they looked black, they adopted many indigenous customs, including the Arawak language, and resisted British colonization, sometimes militarily. After several violent encounters, and 150 years of resistance, the Garífuna surrendered and were deported to Central America. Their language, is still predominantly Arawak but they have retained many African traits in their religious beliefs, oral traditions, dance, and drum styles. There are 120,000 Garífuna in Central America, mostly in Honduras, and more than 50,000 living abroad in the United States and the United Kingdom. In 2001, the United Nations designated the Garífuna a World Heritage culture.

Caribbean scholars often must tread a fine line between emphasizing the unquestionable importance of slavery in Caribbean history while avoiding making it seem like the sole defining trait of the region. Some, for example, have tried to theoretically define the Caribbean through its plantation system, and have provided useful insights about the nature of societies engendered by the plantation that are still pertinent today; for example, such societies, they have contended, tend to exhibit highly centralized decision-making, stratification along racial and ethnic lines, and weak communal structures.

Many countries, however, eluded the plantation grip: Belize, Curaçao, the Dominican Republic, Dominica, and St. Vincent, to name a few. But again, numbers can be deceptive. For example, in Puerto Rico, where the slave population never exceeded 15 percent of the population—and this only for about twenty years—slavery's legacy was devastatingly expressed by the mixed race Segundo Ruiz Belvis (and other abolitionists such as José Julián Acosta and Francisco Mariano Quiñones):

What has slavery not corrupted in the societies of the Americas? In the realm of the material it has degraded work, a principle so crucial to realizing human potential; in the economic order, by converting men into property it has provoked the depreciation of all other property; in the civil order, by violating a slave's personhood, by negating even the consolation of a family. It has created a corruption at the very core of privileged families; in the administrative order it has made omnipotent power necessary, indispensable, because wherever the rule of law has been sacrilegiously overturned, order cannot be created except out of the fear of those who suffer and the violence of those who rule; in the political order it has enthroned a state of affairs in which the energy of an individual is extinguished and the virility of character is almost impossible, because these great moral qualities need to breathe the air of freedom in order to live. As for the social order, slavery has created a kind of aristocracy whose only tradition is skin color and whose power stems from wealth; and in the religious and moral order it has plunged that society into a passive existence without ideals and reduced it to a state of affairs based on injustice and iniquity. (Ruiz Belvis 1985, in Quiñones, 49–50; translation by A. West-Durán)

Ruiz Belvis, Acosta, and Quiñones' critique outlines how slavery permeated every sector of society—in the degradation of work, the triumph of force over law, the personal humiliation, the existence of racism, and the destruction of an individual's character—and how slavery corrupted religion, morality, and politics. If this was true in Puerto Rico, how much more so in Haiti, where nine of ten people were slaves?

HAITI: THE FIRST BLACK REPUBLIC OF THE AMERICAS

Few Caribbean islands have captured the imagination as has Haiti. At the time of the American Revolution in 1776, Haiti was called St. Domingue. It was the richest island in the area, accounting for three-fourths of the world's sugar production and half of the slaves in the Caribbean. Though it is half the size of Maryland, St. Domingue generated more income than all of the thirteen colonies of the United States. Although St. Domingue had experienced uprisings previously (in the 1750s), the August 22, 1791, insurrection led by Boukman, a Jamaican-born Vodou (an Afro-Haitian religion) priest, was the beginning of a relentless and violent confrontation that culminated in independence thirteen years later. In the first two months 10,000 slaves and 2,000 whites were killed, and hundreds of sugar and coffee plantations were destroyed. The French were expelled; then the British invaded, but they were also kicked out. The French re-occupied the country (1802–1804) and were expelled again. The final toll was horrifying: more than 100,000 blacks and mulattoes killed (a quarter of the population), plus tens of thousands of French and British troops, most of whom died of tropical diseases.

Jean-Jacques Dessalines, the fierce general of the ex-slaves, ripped out the white stripe of the French flag, captured admirably in Madsen Mompremier's 1995 painting. The new flag would be red and blue, later changed to red and black. The new nation quickly defined itself as a "black republic," which according to scholars is the first time the word "black" was used ideologically. Whites who had favored abolition and had fought with black generals Toussaint L'Ouverture, Jean-Jacques Dessalines, or Henri Christophe were considered citizens, and, therefore, black. The nation's name changed to Haiti, an indigenous (Taíno) word that meant "land of high mountains." Whites were prohibited from owning property.

After the United States, Haiti was the first independent country of the Western Hemisphere. Its independence was achieved by black slaves overthrowing a European colonial power and subsequently resisting invasion by other European armies. It had sent a clear message throughout Latin America and the Caribbean, and its example was a source of pride for blacks throughout the hemisphere. Haiti's influence and that of the French Revolution in 1789, was profound: in the 1790s, there were major slave rebellions in Guyana, Curaçao, Jamaica, Guadeloupe, Martinique, Tobago, Tortola, St. Lucia, Grenada, and Dominica.

Aside from Haiti's example, events like the Demerara Slave Revolt (Guyana), the Baptist War (Jamaica), and the Ten Years' War (Cuba) indicate that abolition was not merely a "gift" from the metropolitan powers to a "passive" slave population, but was also an accomplishment brought about by the determination and agency of African-Caribbeans.

The demise of sugar production in Haiti was followed by its production in Cuba, which imported 80 percent of its slaves in the nineteenth century. Soon after Haiti's independence most European powers abolished the slave trade, but not slavery. And in 1810, the Latin American independence struggles against Spain began in earnest. For white and Creole elites, then, the issue would become either how to ensure that independence did not enthrone the non-white masses (indigenous, black, mestizo, Afro-Creole) in power, or, in the case of the Caribbean countries under French, British, Dutch, and Danish control, how to separate abolition from issues of independence. In every instance, the non-Spanish Caribbean abolished slavery but delayed independence until after 1950.

For white and Creole elites Haiti became a counterexample: these elites used the bitter and violent events of Haitian independence to claim that abolition and independence were anti-white. Emigration from Haiti was prohibited, and many countries simply refused to recognize its government, furthering its isolation. Pro-slavery elites in Cuba, Puerto Rico, and Brazil used these arguments to divide and confuse both abolitionists and pro-independence forces throughout the nineteenth century. They and other countries fostered European immigration to "whiten" their populations.

Haiti's unfortunate history of being misgoverned by militarized elites abusing an impoverished peasantry, with blacks and mulattoes divided along rivalries of class and color, means it is still manipulated as a counterexample even early in the twenty-first century by governing elites in the Caribbean and the U.S. The arguments used are that the country cannot govern itself and that it is prone to violence, disease (AIDS), and superstition ("voodoo"). The racist overtones of these arguments were (and are) evident not only in the Caribbean, but also in the U.S. immigration policy toward Haitians, especially when contrasted with its attitude toward Cubans.

Haiti has been focused on here because of its ideological and racial importance for Caribbean identity and history, both in the nineteenth and twentieth centuries and currently. Haiti is also a benchmark for scholars who study African influences in the region, keeping in mind that these retentions are neither "pure" nor static, but part of a living and evolving Afro-Caribbean reality.

THE NINETEENTH CENTURY: "FREEDOM WITHOUT RIGHTS"

The nineteenth-century Caribbean was a contradictory ensemble of differing labor regimes, most still unfree. Although the British colonies were the first to abolish slavery (1834–1838), others acted later, and Cuba did not finally do away with slavery until 1886. But the plantocracy (rule by the plantation owners) and the white elites knew the days of slavery were numbered, and they either slowed down the abolition process or tried to secure methods that would limit the freedom of their respective labor forces.

Whether through apprenticeship systems, limiting access to land, debt peonage, sharecropping, or the persecution of squatters, landowners tried to keep their former slaves from leaving the estates. Various measures were introduced to limit access to land: increasing its cost, creating minimum acreages for purchasing land, or making credit difficult to obtain. In many cases the plantocracy was successful, but in some countries like Jamaica, Trinidad, Suriname, and Guyana large tracts of unused land made it difficult to control these workers. Not surprisingly, these same four countries were the largest importers of indentured servants, mostly from India. Over half a million Indian laborers came to the Caribbean from 1845 to 1917. In Suriname, Guyana, and Trinidad they make up from a third to half the population; in Guadeloupe, almost a fifth.

In the nineteenth century, most blacks in the Caribbean, despite having won formal freedom, were still disadvantaged in terms of employment, education, and social mobility. The vast majority were illiterate, and became members of a growing rural village workforce. Some have described the nineteenth century as the era of the formation of a peasant class, although Cuba, Puerto Rico, the Dominican Republic, and Haiti had a numerous peasant class well before British (1834) and French (1848) emancipation.

Education was in pitiful shape, with high black illiteracy. In 1898 Puerto Rico had an 80 percent illiteracy, affecting its black and brown population disproportionately. In the French, English, and Dutch Caribbean the figures were comparable or worse.

A similar situation existed in politics: it was not until the 1930s that a majority of the population in the British Caribbean could vote. Before then, barely 6 percent of the population could do so. The major Caribbean exceptions were Cuba, the Dominican Republic, Haiti (all independent), and Puerto Rico.

Still, important voices were heard in the nineteenth century, such as de Vastey (Haiti); Jean Baptiste Phillipe, J.J. Thomas (Trinidad); Paul Bogle (Jamaica); Edward Wilmot Blyden (St. Thomas); R.E. Betances, E.M. Hostos (Puerto Rico); and Antonio Maceo, José Martí (Cuba). However, few black and free colored thinkers of the time favored complete independence, despite nationalist sentiments.

One exception was Ramón Emeterio Betances (1827–1898), a mixed-race physician who was considered white by Puerto Rican society, but instead chose to emphasize his black heritage. Betances was not only an abolitionist, but also the leader of an armed uprising to overthrow Spanish colonialism. An ardent revolutionary, he was a staunch defender of Haiti, strongly denouncing those who used racist arguments to criticize the country, and a tireless supporter of the Cuban independence cause. His famous slogan "The Antilles for the Antilleans" is one of the earliest attempts to create a pan-Caribbean unity with which to resist colonial and imperial powers. Betances was an influence on the racial and nationalist thought of Maceo and Martí, two Cuban revolutionary leaders who fought Spanish colonialism and racism.

E.W. Blyden (1832–1912), a writer from the Virgin Islands, then under Danish rule, was from a free black middle-class family. He went to the United States in 1850 seeking a college education, but was denied entry because he was black. Blyden immigrated to Liberia, where he spent the rest of his life, shuttling back and forth between Sierra Leone and Liberia during his last thirty years. Blyden's writings about being black, the fate of Africa, and the importance for blacks of receiving a non-Eurocentric education or practicing non-Christian religions were an important precursor to pan-Africanism, a political cultural movement that promotes the unity of African and Afro-diasporic peoples, and the work of Marcus Garvey.

Other African-Caribbeans were important in eighteenth and nineteenth century U.S. history. Prince Hall, born in Barbados, was one of the founders of the first African masonic lodge of Massachusetts (1776) and played a crucial role in the demise of the Massachusetts slave trade. John B. Russwurm (1799–1851), a Jamaican, was a pioneer in African-American journalism, being the publisher along with Samuel Cornish of *Freedom's Journal* (1827), the first black-owned and black-printed newspaper in the United States. In Russwurm's graduation speech from college, he urged U.S. blacks to move to Haiti. Denmark Vesey, born in St. Thomas, was the leader of one of the largest slave conspiracies ever (see U.S. Virgin Islands chapter).

THE TWENTIETH CENTURY: INDEPENDENCE AND NEW IDENTITIES

Nationalism was an early force in the Spanish-speaking Caribbean and by 1900 all the islands had pried loose of Spanish domination. However, Puerto Rico became and still is a U.S. colony. Currently, except for Suriname (1975), none of the Dutch and French Caribbean islands are independent countries. The British case is varied: Jamaica and Trinidad became independent in 1962, Barbados and Guyana in 1966, and most of the smaller islands in the seventies and eighties. But there are still five islands that are British possessions: Anguilla, Montserrat, the Cayman Islands, the British Virgin Islands, and Turks and Caicos (see Appendix).

But an intense cultural nationalism is still evident today, from Puerto Rico's rejection of English, to the use of Papiamentu in Aruba, Bonaire, and Curaçao. The French Antilles is a paradigmatic case. Since 1946 they have been a *département* (a province) or state of France and have had to balance political and economic assimilation with cultural non-assimilation. They have high standards of living, especially compared with the rest of the Caribbean, and they also have an excellent health and social welfare system. But the traditional economy has collapsed (three-quarters of income derives from French assistance), unemployment rates are over 30 percent, and close to half the population has immigrated. Because of this, the cultural milieu has staunchly defended the speaking of Creole as an affirmation of its Caribbean identity, under the banner of assimilation into the French system or Créolité. These cultural activists also favor independence, an option not favored by the vast majorities. The preservation of cultural dignity in the absence of political and economic sovereignty is an issue for all the states in the region, not just those that are not independent.

Many Caribbean islands broke away from King Sugar in the twentieth century: Curaçao, Aruba, and Trinidad and Tobago by producing or refining oil; Guyana, Suriname, and Jamaica by mining bauxite; others, like Puerto Rico, through manufacturing. But almost all have developed tourism as a major industry, some to the virtual exclusion of almost any other economic activity. And some islands have become major areas of finance; offshore banking is found, for example, in the Bahamas, the Cayman Islands, Aruba, and Curaçao.

Paradoxically, some of the islands that have achieved independence, Haiti, Guyana, and Suriname, are by far the poorest, while the islands with the highest per capita income are the Cayman Islands, the British Virgin Islands, and Aruba. There is one exception: the Bahamas, an independent nation, but with a long-standing offshore banking industry. The dependent territories of the region,[1] although composing 14 percent of the region's population, account for 56 percent of its income. This has kept many of the islands from seeking total independence, feeling more secure under the financial largesse of Europe (Britain, France, Holland) or the United States.

The twentieth century brought the growth of trade unions, political parties, and greater political participation. The British-ruled Caribbean witnessed major labor upheavals in the 1930s that affected Belize, St. Kitts, Antigua, St. Lucia, Trinidad, Jamaica, Barbados, the Bahamas, St. Vincent, and Guyana. The labor leaders and subsequent political parties that were formed in that period would eventually lead many of these countries to independence. Cuba also experienced labor and social unrest in the thirties, as did Haiti. Puerto Rico's independence movement had violent confrontations with colonial authorities in the thirties, leading to intense political repression of separatists. The Dominican Republic, after U.S. occupation, underwent a long and brutal dictatorship under Rafael Leónidas Trujillo (1930–1961).

In the 1940s and 1950s, in the British, French, and Dutch Caribbean, anticolonial sentiments, channeled through trade unions and political parties, grew strong, reflecting the worldwide decolonization process also raging in Asia and Africa. Charismatic and authoritarian leaders arose to lead these movements: Alexander Bustamante and Norman Manley in Jamaica, Eric Gairy in Grenada, Eric Williams in Trinidad, Grantley Adams in Barbados, Cheddi Jagan and Forbes Burnham in Guyana, Luis Muñoz Marín in Puerto Rico, V.C. Bird in Antigua, Aimé Césaire in Martinique, Robert Bradshaw (St. Kitts-Nevis-Anguilla), and Claude Walthey in St. Maarten. In some cases these rulers were openly and viciously dictatorial, as was François Duvalier in Haiti and Trujillo in the Dominican Republic.

Fidel Castro, a charismatic and authoritarian leader, led his July 26 Movement to power in 1959, unleashing the region's most radical revolution, and at the height of the Cold War, no less. The Cuban Revolution and the growing importance of one aspect of Frantz Fanon's ideological legacy brought the use of revolutionary violence to achieve decolonization. Fanon's focus was not only on violence but to create the psychological, political, and racial tools with which to fight colonialism, racism, and oppression. However, none of the former British colonies became independent through violent means or through protracted wars of national liberation. To date, the French-speaking islands maintain their overseas department status and try to decolonize through political and economic assimilation, and the Dutch non-independent islands maintain close ties to Holland (despite Aruba's and St. Maarten's *status aparte*). Puerto Rico, despite sporadic and unsuccessful urban guerrilla movements, remains a U.S. colony.

The other experiments with revolutionary change were attempted through elections (the Manley government in Jamaica, 1972–1980), coups (Suriname in 1982, Grenada in 1979), or dictatorial confiscation of the political and economic system (Guyana, 1970–1985). The outcomes for Suriname and Guyana were dismal failures, ending in political corruption, mismanagement, civil strife, and economic disaster, leaving them as the two poorest countries of the region after Haiti. Jamaica's case was more complex: while Manley's attempt at "democratic socialism" successfully made changes in housing, education, and health that benefited the poor, the World Bank, the International Monetary Fund, and U.S. hostility created an economic situation that resulted in his opponent power (Edward Seaga) undoing much of what Manley's PNP worked for. Since then, the PNP, though rhetorically progressive and for the people, has adapted to the "realities of globalization."

Grenada's case was the most interesting, if not the most heart-wrenching. After twenty-eight years of misrule by Eric Gairy, the New Jewel Movement (NJM), led by Maurice Bishop (1944–1983), ousted Gairy in March 1979. They initiated a literacy campaign and economic and political reform, and drew close to Cuba's Castro, who offered to build a new airport for the island. Internal divisions within the NJM devoured the revolution, including Maurice Bishop. With the country in chaos, the United States intervened militarily in October 1983.

The defeat of Manley, and the invasion of Grenada, was followed by the Sandinista defeat at the polls in Nicaragua (1990). The collapse of the Soviet bloc (1989–1991) seriously weakened Cuba economically. As the Caribbean headed into the nineties, "revolutionary alternatives" seemed dim or almost suicidal. As stated before, the region's richest countries are those still under colonial rule, making many in the region associate nationalism and independence with poverty. Sovereignty is still an issue, as the struggle over the island of Vieques between Puerto Rico and the U.S. military indicates.

Except for a few exceptions, most Caribbean countries have experienced continuous economic growth, a high human development index, and low rates of inflation for the last two decades. Still, a quarter, maybe a third, of the population lives under the poverty line, unemployment rates are high (20%), public external debt is high (but proportionately decreasing), and wages are low compared with costs of living; there is unequal distribution of the land, even though many own land; most countries depend on one product (sugar, bananas, tourism, bauxite, oil); and health and education, while certainly better than in most developing nations, are still inadequate. Still, growth is not necessarily development, and many countries, comparatively speaking, have slipped in the Human Development Index rankings (Cuba, Haiti, Dominican Republic, Jamaica, Guyana, and Suriname), nations that make up 80 percent of the region's population.

The influence of the United States in the twentieth-century Caribbean has been immense, and now eclipses that of all the European powers put together. This influence ranges from overt military intervention, to political arm-twisting and financial pressures through multinational corporations, the World Bank, and the International Monetary Fund, to the pervasive presence of shopping malls, personal computers, and Hollywood movies. The United States is also a magnet for the jobless as well as those seeking a university education.

CARIBBEAN MIGRATIONS

The Caribbean's diasporic dilemmas have current dimensions by way of multiple migrations. The peoples of the area are among the most mobile and "transnational." And the migrations are not only from South to North (United States, Canada, United Kingdom, France, Holland). There are Dominicans and Cubans in Puerto Rico, Haitians in the Bahamas, Barbadians in Panama, Puerto Ricans in St. Croix, Dominicans in Aruba, Kittitians in St. Eustatius, Grenadians in Trinidad, Guyanese in Jamaica, to name the best-known patterns.

From 1950 to 1989 some five and a half million people (one out of every seven inhabitants) left the region. The great bulk of those migrants came from four countries: Haiti, Cuba, Jamaica, and Puerto Rico, but the proportional figures for many of the countries are striking, if not alarming. For example, there are half as many Surinamese living in Holland as in Suriname; the figures for Martinicans, Guadeloupeans, and Jamaicans are similar, but slightly lower. Ten percent of the population of Cuba, the Dominican Republic, and Haiti live abroad; for the Netherlands Antilles (including Aruba) it is 30 percent (Grosfoguel 1997, 598).

Many circumstances affect these migrations: for Puerto Ricans and Martinicans, their ability to immigrate is facilitated by having citizenship of their respective metropolitan powers (the United States for the former, France for the latter). A similar case would hold true for the Netherlands Antilles and Holland. Cuba's case is unique, since the Cold War made Cuban emigrés "desirable," because they were fleeing a Communist regime. Others, despite legally established numbers for immigration, must cross borders illegally.

The importance of these immigrants has considerable impact through remittances back home. Entire families are supported by a family member working abroad, often at two or three jobs. These remittances equal 71 percent of all exports in the Dominican Republic, 32 percent of Haiti's, 29 percent of Jamaica's, and 17 percent of Barbados' (Girvan 2001, 15). In Cuba, the remittances are double the amount earned from tourism. The immigrant's contributions are not only appreciated back home; they are also transforming their host cities: New York, Miami, London, Washington, D.C., and New Orleans are becoming increasingly "Afro-Caribbeanized." By 1998, a third of New York's black population was of the English-speaking West Indies, and if we add Haitians the figure would be notably higher. In fact, many prominent African Americans are also of Caribbean descent: Malcolm X, Harry Belafonte, Colin Powell, Stokely Carmichael, Shirley Chisholm, Audre Lorde, Kareem Abdul Jabbar, Michelle Wallace, Sonny Rollins, and Lani Guinier.

THE CARIBBEAN INTELLECTUAL TRADITION

The Caribbean has a rich intellectual tradition. Because the region has been a crossroads for the entire planet, its thinkers have had roving intellects. Among those Afro-Caribbean scholar-activists are the likes of C.L.R. James, Frantz Fanon, Walter Rodney, Rex Nettleford, Marcus Garvey, Carl Stone, Eric Williams, Aimé Césaire, Edouard Glissant, José Luis González, Edward Kamau Braithwaite, René Depestre, Jean Casimir, and Jean Price-Mars. Some, like James, were revolutionaries in addition to writing on everything from Toussaint L'Ouverture to Black Power and cricket; others became ministers (Nettleford), mayors (Césaire), or prime ministers (Williams), but all have contributed to understanding the region's history, culture, and society, offering more complex views of race and blackness. Of course, white scholars, such as Fernando Ortiz, Lydia Cabrera, Alejo Carpentier, Manuel Moreno Fraginals, Antonio Benítez Rojo, Juan Bosch, Pedro Henríquez Ureña, Tomás Blanco, Antonio S. Pedreira, and Fernando Picó, have also contributed greatly to this process.

The overpowering presence of the United States in the Caribbean helped motivate anti-imperialist thought, with military interventions occurring in the Dominican Republic (1916–1924), Haiti (1915–1934), Cuba (several times between 1906 and 1922), and Puerto Rico, not to mention Panama and Nicaragua. This anti-imperialism clearly fed nationalist sentiments and an exploration of national culture, which meant reexamining the Caribbean's African roots. But each island proceeded in a different fashion: Haiti reaffirmed its Africanness through scholars such as Jean Price-Mars and negritude, whereas Puerto Rico exalted a Hispanic (that is, white) nationalism to oppose U.S. influence, even if figures like Palés Matos and Fortunato Vizcarrondo were exponents of Afro-Antillean poetry in the thirties. In Cuba, the Afro-Cubanism movement provided the groundwork for reexamining the country's religious, cultural, and musical roots, though its adherents were not exempt from appropriation, stereotyping, and Europeanization (whitening).

While C.L.R. James and others have emphasized class, Aimé Césaire emphasized race and culture, particularly in his withering attack on domination, exploitation, and racism published as *Discourse on Colonialism* (1950). All were seeking decolonization, not only in a political sense, but in an intellectual sense as well, as they came to acknowledge that Eurocentric methods were inadequate to understand the Caribbean. The years during which James, Fanon, Williams, Nettleford, Césaire, and Walter Rodney, the Guyanese historian and political leader, where working marked a period in which Caribbean intellectuals were also activists, politicians, diplomats, and so on. Now scholars from the region tend to be more specialized and "professionalized," and though they are still active as public figures, scholars are less inclined to run for office or be full-time members of political parties.

DEFINING AND REDEFINING BLACKNESS

In spite of its current woes, political, economic, racial, or otherwise, it is always tempting to compare the Caribbean (favorably, of course) to the United States in terms of racial harmony. No doubt, the Caribbean has much to teach the world about living in societies of great ethnic, racial, and cultural diversity. But it is still a region living with a legacy of slavery, racism, and discrimination.

In defining its own Afro-Caribbean reality, the region has seen its blackness from different perspectives. We could broadly define them as Afrocentric, Pan-Africanist, or Transculturated-Creolized (Henry, 2000, 47–114). The first, drawing inspiration from Blyden, was characteristic of Marcus Garvey; it centered on black self-help, was opposed to miscegenation, (race mixing), but more importantly, espoused a nationalist position that at one time encouraged African-Caribbean and African-American immigration back to Mother Africa. Not many heeded Garvey's call for repatriation. Most African-Caribbeans no longer interpret "back to Africa" literally, but instead symbolically, including Rastafarians. Many African-Caribbeans resonated to reclaiming their African heritage, feeling: "'I have no voice, I have no history, I have come from a place to which I cannot go back and which I have never seen. I used to speak a language which I can no longer speak. I had ancestors whom I cannot find, they worshipped gods whose names I do not know'" (Hall 2001, 35). Going back was a symbolic way for blacks to reengage that experience with their own language, their own interpretation of history, their own view of freedom and redemption (Hall, 36–37). Unfortunately, the country that could forward the cause of black nationalism, Haiti, underwent a cruel manipulation of this nationalism under François Duvalier and his son (1957–1971; 1971–1986) that has made racially based ideologies in the region highly suspect.

However, the ideological legacy of Garvey, Césaire, Damas, and others helped create a climate for also revaluing and studying Afro-Caribbean cultures, and particularly its religions, be it Santería, Palo, and Abakuá (Cuba); Vodou (Haiti); Winti (Suriname); Shango/Orisha (Trinidad); Kumina, Myal, Obeah (Jamaica).

Most thinkers on race and/or blackness in the Caribbean, whether Pan-Africanist or Creolist (the two are not mutually exclusive) use images of racial and cultural mixing, emphasizing the region's plurality, hybridity, and transculturation. Even when speaking of blackness or the African dimension of the Caribbean experience, thinkers as diverse as James, Fanon, Glissant, and Wilson Harris emphasize that the Africanness or blackness has been and is being constantly transformed and historically grounded.

Pan-Africanists like James, Rodney, George Padmore (also Marxists) and Fanon (influenced by Marx) all recognized that the fate of Africa and its decolonization were not unrelated to similar concerns in the Caribbean. Their writings and activism have been crucial for an understanding of the Caribbean within both a national-regional context and an international one. If slavery was a triangular phenomenom (Africa-the Americas-Europe), with world repercussions, the Afro-Caribbean realm also has a world scope, central to what has been called the Black Atlantic. This Black Atlantic would include Latin jazz, Yoruba influences in Afro-Cuban religions, Bahamian storytelling traditions, Curaçaoan funeral practices, hip-hop influences in Puerto Rico's rap scene, Trinidadian cuisine, Fanon's crucial contributions to the independence of Algeria, Bob Marley's invitation to sing at Zimbabwe's independence celebration, Cuba's military prominence in ending apartheid in South Africa, and Wifredo Lam illustrating books by Aimé Césaire.

However, it is the Creolists/transculturists, like Nettleford, Braithwaite, Glissant, Ortiz, and Harris, who have made the most eloquent case for Afro-Caribbean hybridity. Black Caribbean reality is neither purely African nor European (nor East Asian, Chinese, etc., for that matter). Echoing Fanon's "culture abhors simplification," Caribbean scholars and artists have devoted much ink and creative energy to exploring its complexity. Metaphors have been culinary (*callaloo, ajiaco,* stew), metallurgical (crucible, melting pot, forge) spatial (crossroads, four-storied house, limbo, repeating island, open gnostic space), natural-ecological (trees, roots, rhizomes, mangrove), poetic (cross-cultural poetics or spirit), as well as related to racial or cultural mixing (creolization, *mestizaje,* hybridity). While all these thinkers are interested in examining the region's past, history is not seen as inalterable, nor its meaning fixed. This prophetic vision of the past would be congruent with Jamaican born cultural studies scholar Stuart Hall's definition: "[I]dentity is not to be found in the past, but in the future to be constructed." Hall's words are a warning that identity and race are socially and historically shaped: what might be considered white, black, or mixed-race in Puerto Rico might not be true in Trinidad, Martinique, Haiti, or the United States.

West Indians in the U.S. are also redefining blackness in New York and other American cities. Since English-speaking West Indians come from societies where people of African ancestry (black and brown) are an overwhelming majority (85 percent or more; Trinidad and Guyana are the exceptions), blackness is normal in a way that whiteness is normal in the U.S. (Vickerman 2001, 241) West Indians downplay race in favor of ethnicity (West Indian) or nationality (Jamaican,

Guyanese, etc.) and it is only when they immigrate to the U.S. do they realize the consequences of having black skin. And because of the "shadism" previously mentioned, even the West Indian notion of blackness differs substantially from that of the U.S. For example, in the West Indies "blacks" might refer to not only someone of African ancestry, but also be poor, dark-skinned, have certain facial features and be uneducated. Someone just as dark, but highly educated, well mannered, and powerful (or well-connected) might not be considered black. By Caribbeanizing U.S. race definitions, these West Indian immigrants (as well as their Hispanic Caribbean brethren) will alter the more monolithic Black-White model that has traditionally operated in America.

However, with this in mind, and even acknowledging the greater fluidity of racial definitions and race relations in the Caribbean, "whiteness" is still the "norm" in the region. It is a complex norm because many things can "whiten" in the Caribbean: money, class status, the car you drive, education, where you live, who your parents and grandparents are. So despite claims that the islands make ("Out of many, one people"), racism is still pervasive. One example will suffice: in 1999 the government of Jamaica had to crack down on the importation of bleach creams that were causing skin disorders on the island (Meeks 2000, 210 n. 23).

AFRICAN-CARIBBEAN WOMEN

The region's intellectual milieu was traditionally dominated by males, but that has changed in the past decades. Not all women scholars concentrate on gender issues—included in this group are the late Elsa Goveia, Maureen Warner Lewis, and Olive Lewin—but many do, such as Rhoda Reddock, Christine Barrow, Patricia Muhammed (Indo-Trinidadian), Verene Shepherd, Olive Senior, Erna Brodber, Lucille Mathurin Mair, Barbara Bailey, Barbara T. Christian, Dany Bebel-Gisler, and Maryse Condé, not to mention some of the contributors to this volume.

Women scholars who were interested in gender issues began studying women under slavery; research revealed that women were much more active resisting slavery and had greater economic autonomy during slavery and post-emancipation—working plots of land and selling their produce or peddling wares—than was previously thought. In the post-slavery English-speaking Caribbean many peasant women became landowners, which differed in the French-speaking and Spanish-speaking islands because of patriarchal inheritance laws. Men have also typically migrated to advance economically, which in rural settings has left women in charge, who have tended to advance socially through education. For a period that lasted from 1840 to 1920 women's participation in the labor force increased dramatically, then decreased sharply until the 1970s.

Since then the recent and huge growth in services and manufacturing free-trade zones has resulted in women being employed at greater rates than men:

they have become a key component to the globalization of the Caribbean economy. However, they are paid far less than men for the same work, labor under harsh conditions, and have met stiff resistance to unionizing.

African-Caribbean women and their family life has traditionally received much attention, since a third or more of households were headed by women and two-thirds of children were born out of wedlock. It engendered a matriarchal stereotype of the superwoman, making ends meet, raising children abandoned by deserting fathers; of "sexual promiscuity" and "social deviance." At first these behaviors were seen as pathological and explained as holdovers from slavery and oppression, then viewed as Afro-Caribbean flexibility and adaptability to poverty, unemployment, and uncertainty. More recently women have focused on issues of family and gender ideology (rejecting Eurocentric nuclear family models), culture, and history to gain a more complete picture of both private and public dimensions of women's lives (Barrow 2001, 418–426).

Until recently, the most complex and nuanced views of African-Caribbean women—with a few exceptions—were not offered by social scientists, but by writers, poets, singers, and playwrights. In the last thirty years, it has been writers like Erna Brodber or the Sistren Theater Collective (Jamaica), Guadeloupe's Simone Schwarz-Bart, or Nancy Morejón's poetry that have explored the sexuality, spirituality, power, and oppression of African-Caribbean women.[2]

CARIBBEAN CREATIVITY: WRITERS, ARTISTS, MUSICIANS

The Afro-Caribbean transculturated heritage has infused the region with a unique creativity. Few parts of the world can match the verve and imagination of Caribbean music, literature, dance, and the visual arts. Though not exclusively, it was mostly writers who spearheaded the negritude or Afro-Antillean movements of the twenties and thirties. From the biting syncopations of Nicolás Guillén to the violent landscapes of Aimé Césaire, from the mythologically infused novels of Wilson Harris to the raucous (and sometimes raunchy) tales of Ana Lydia Vega, Caribbean literature has a quality, insight, and imagination that is world-class. Not surprisingly, four writers from the region have won the Nobel Prize for literature in the last four decades.[3]

What is true for its literature is doubly so for its music: from Mario Bauzá to Boukman Eksperyans to Buju Banton, from Tito Puente to the Mighty Sparrow (Slinger Francisco), from mambo to Marley and Guerra to Guédon, the Caribbean has spawned infinite rhythms and music. Rumba and reggae, calypso and *kaseko*, *compas* and merengue, *son, bomba, plena*, and salsa are all Afro-Caribbean creations, some more African (*bomba*, rumba, *gwoka*), others more creolized (*son*, calypso, salsa), but African-derived. What is important is that this music has often played a key role in defining the national culture of a country: *danzón* and *son* for Cuba, calypso for Trinidad, reggae for Jamaica, or merengue for the Dominican Republic.[4] All of these musics have profound African roots.

Would our image of the Caribbean be complete without the paintings of Wifredo Lam (Cuba); Wilson Bigaud (Haiti); LeRoy Clarke (Trinidad); Claude Fiddler (St. Vincent); Stanley Greaves (Guyana); Albert Huie, David Boxer (Jamaica); and David Gall (Barbados)? Gall's cautionary words remind us of the temptation to simplify in defining the region: "To look for a Caribbean style through superficial examination of forms would be to limit us to stereotypes and partial truths.... If the United States is overshadowed by white founding fathers and grand notions of democracy, Caribbean people are mobilized by death and rebirth, the Middle Passage and triumph over the attempts to belittle our humanity. This is a central characteristic of the Caribbean experience" (Gall in Lewis 1995, 100).

CONCLUSION

On the positive side, the black majorities are now in government, industry, the professions, in all sectors of society, even if whites, proportionately speaking, still wield considerable economic (and political) power. And while women are still underrepresented in politics, they have made significant advances. Some black women have become heads of state, like Eugenia Charles and Maria Liberia Peters. For the most part—Cuba, Puerto Rico, and the Dominican Republic are the exceptions—the white monopoly on public power has been broken. However, Afro-Caribbean cultural creativity and transculturation have not been translated to the economic, legal, and political sphere, where colonial and Eurocentric modes are dominant.

The region is still heavily and intimately interwoven with the world economy, not always to its own benefit. Tourism is one example: while it is an important source of foreign exchange and employment, its income flows are highly volatile and its ultimate success in the hands of foreigners. In the post–September 11 climate, Caribbean tourism is suffering greatly, with possible devastating consequences for Caribbean economies. Tourism can also be a distorting element on Afro-Caribbean culture, engendering a "folkloric" or "exoticizing" veneer, whether for white or "Afrocentric" travelers. Recent "stagings" of Afro-Cuban religious rituals (*Santería*) in Cuba are not an encouraging sign. Still, it is difficult to imagine a drastic reorientation of this industry in the near future, since the attraction of sun, sea, and sex is too tempting for travelers, and equally lucrative for locals. The issue is not whether Afro-Caribbean nations and peoples should withdraw and protect itself from the world. That not only is impossible, but also flies in the face of the region's history as a global crossroads. The issue is more one of how the Caribbean can use its connectedness to the world politically and economically in a way that is similar to how it has creatively done so in the realm of culture, music, and religion.

Marcus Garvey's legacy remains as an important reminder of what has been achieved and what remains to be done. The region has finally come to assert the beauty and authenticity of its African cultural heritage, and harnessed that culture to modernity. But it has yet to access a true power through its creativity and imagination, and it still lacks a truly Afro-Caribbean vision of economic development, politics, and civil society (Nettleford 1994, 162). To borrow an image from sports that reinforces Garvey's message, we have great players but we still don't fully own the team, or make up the rules.

As African-Caribbean populations negotiate new social, cultural, and economic realities in the twenty-first century, they will redefine their black identity. In some countries—Suriname, Trinidad, Guyana, Guadeloupe—that redefinition will include dealing with their East Asian ethnic groups, a politico-cultural "douglarization" (a mix between an African and East Asian), if you will. Cuba, Puerto Rico, and the Dominican Republic have used racial mixing to present themselves as racial democracies, or to "whiten" the population overall. Except for Cuba, they not only need to recognize and own up to their Afro-Caribbeanness, but also, in the case of all three, they need to address racial discrimination, particularly in the workplace and the media. The French Antilles, without totally forgetting negritude, are defining their blackness or Creoleness multiracially (almost non-racially) as they try to determine how "French" or "Antillean" they want to be. The Dutch-speaking Caribbean is equally complex since some islands have majority African-Caribbean populations while in others blacks are a minority. Aruba, St. Maarten, and the Cayman Islands have sizeable foreign-born populations, mostly from the last thirty years, which will alter their cultural/racial mix substantially. Some of the islands speak Papiamentu, others English; some are more "Latinized" given their proximity to Venezuela.

All this is to say that Caribbean blackness is in flux. Some nations will retain a strong Afro-Caribbean core (Jamaica, Barbados, Haiti, most of the English-speaking Caribbean); others, while retaining that core, will modify it by interacting with East Asians (Trinidad, Guyana, Suriname, Guadeloupe to a lesser extent). Others will reinforce a mixed-race-creolized identity (Cuba, Martinique, Curaçao, the Dominican Republic, Puerto Rico). And finally, there will be a group of nations that because of demographic volatility will have their Afro-Caribbeanness shifting constantly (Aruba, St. Maarten, Cayman Islands, Belize, and French Guiana to a lesser extent).

All, in their different ways, will exemplify the transcultured Caribbean self, always evolving, that was evoked by poet Luis Palés Matos. His definition, however, needs substantial modification: an Antillean is someone who dresses like a European, has the manners (and moves) of an Afro-Creole who speaks Creole, possesses a Chinese culinary instinct, is imbued with the spirituality of a person from northern India, and has the creativity, irreverence, and tolerance of an African. Given the dazzling cross-cultural transformations of the Caribbean, many of the terms of this definition could be switched around, except one: the core is and will long remain, African. This ever-changing African-Caribbean core looks backwards and forward: it has been able to vanquish the ghost of violence of their forbears, and has the serenity, transparency, and spirit to embrace the unknown.

SCOPE OF THIS STUDY

In this volume, our efforts to include islands and countries are meant to be as representative or emblematic as possible. We have included the four major language groups: Spanish, English, French, and Dutch. Population-wise the countries included make up 92 percent of the region's population. Politically, all types of systems have been included: independent republics, colonies, non-independent microstates, and a Communist regime. Ethnically and racially we have included countries where blacks are an overwhelming majority, such as Haiti, Barbados, and Jamaica; countries where they are about half the population (Suriname, Trinidad); and countries where they are a minority, like Aruba and St. Maarten. The same is true for historical uniqueness, be it in terms of whether the society was defined (or not) by the plantation system, differing circumstances of abolition, immigration patterns both to and from each country, varying paths to independence, revolutionary periods, and plurality of post-independence experiences. A maximum of cultural, societal diversity has also been reflected in the chapters, ranging from Afro-Caribbean religious practices to music, Carnival, literature, and the arts, as well as family structure, gender relations, and notions of time.

This introductory reference guide is complemented by a chronology, glossary, and appendix.

NOTES

1. The dependent territories are under: (a) the United States—Puerto Rico and the U.S. Virgin Islands (St. Thomas, St. Croix, St. John); (b) Great Britain—Montserrat, the Cayman Islands, Anguilla, Turks and Caicos, the British Virgin Islands; (c) Holland—Aruba, St. Maarten, the Netherlands Antilles (Curaçao, Bonaire, Saba, and St. Eustatius); (d) France—Martinique, Guadeloupe, and French Guiana.

2. Even a partial list gives the magnitude and importance of the region's African-Caribbean women writers: Maryse Condé, Simone Schwarz-Bart, Myriam Warner-Vieyra, Dany Bebel-Gisler (Guadeloupe); Erna Brodber, Olive Senior, Velma Pollard, Sylvia Winter, Louise Bennett, Pat Powell, Una Marson, Lorna Goodison (Jamaica); Zee Edgell (Belize); Beryl Gilroy (Guyana); Jamaica Kincaid (Antigua); Edwidge Danticat (Haiti); Astrid Roemer, Thea Doelwijt (Suriname); Ana Lydia Vega, Mayra Santos Febre (Puerto Rico); Nancy Morejón, Georgina Herrera (Cuba); Merle Hodge, Valerie Belgrave, Marlene Nourbese-Philip (Trinidad and Tobago); Nydia Ecury (Aruba).

3. The writers are almost too numerous to mention: Derek Walcott (St. Lucia); Earl Lovelace (Trinidad); Nicolás Guillén (Cuba); José Alcántar Almánzar, Norberto James, Pedro Mir (Dominican Republic); Andrew Salkey, John Hearne, Roger Mais, V.S. Reid (Jamaica); Caryl Phillips (St. Kitts); Aimé Césaire, Edouard Glissant, Raphael Confiant, Patrick Chamoiseau (Martinique); León Damas (French Guiana); Jacques Stephene Alexis, Jacques Roumain, René Depestre (Haiti); Frank Martinus Arion (Curaçao); Edgar Cairo (Suriname); Austin Clarke, Edward Kamau Braithwaite, Frank Collymore, George Lamming (Barbados); Fred D'Aguiar, Martin Carter, Wilson Harris, Jan Carew (Guyana).

4. Composers or singers are equally numerous. Among the most prominent are Bob Marley, Buju Banton, Toots Hibbert (Jamaica); Henri Guédon, the group Kassav (Martinique); Rafael Hernández, Willie Colón, Rafael Cortijo (Puerto Rico), Juan Luis Guerra, Luis Alberti (Dominican Republic); the group Boukman Eksperyans, Nemours Jean-Baptiste (Haiti); Arsenio Rodríguez, Chucho Valdés, Ignacio Piñero, Israel "Cachao" López, Mario Bauzá (Cuba); Mighty Sparrow, Brother Resistance, Black Stalin (Trinidad and Tobago); Lieve Hugo (Suriname); Joseph Spencer (Bahamas); Andy Palacio (Belize).

REFERENCES

Barrow, Christine (2001). "Men, Women, and Family in the Caribbean: A Review." In Barrow, C., and R. Reddock (eds.), *Caribbean Sociology: Introductory Readings*, Kingston, Jamaica: Ian Randle, pp. 418–426.

Brereton, Bridget (1979). *Race Relations in Colonial Trinidad 1870–1900*. Cambridge, UK, Cambridge University Press.

Girvan, Norman (2001). "Reinterpreting the Caribbean." in Meeks, Brian, and Folke Lindahl (eds.), *New Caribbean Thought: A Reader*. Mona, Jamaica: University of West Indies Press, pp. 3–23.

Glissant, Edouard (1989). *Caribbean Discourse: Selected Essays*. Charlottesville, VA: University Press of Virginia.

Grosfoguel, Ramón (1997). "Colonial Caribbean Migrations to France, the Netherlands, Great Britain and the United States." In *Ethnic and Racial Studies* 20, no. 3 (July): pp. 594–612.

Hall, Stuart (2001). "Negotiating Caribbean Identities." In Meeks, Brian, and Folke Lindahl (eds.), *New Caribbean Thought: A Reader*. Mona, Jamaica: University of West Indies Press, pp. 24–39.

Henry, Paget (2000). *Caliban's Reason: Introducing Afro-Caribbean Philosophy*. New York: Routledge.

Knight, F., and C. Palmer (eds.) (1989). *The Modern Caribbean*. Chapel Hill: University of North Carolina Press.

Lewis, Samella S. (1995). *Caribbean Visions: Contemporary Paintings and Sculpture*. Alexandria, Virginia: Art Services International.

Meeks, Brian (2000). *Narratives of Resistance: Jamaica, Trinidad, the Caribbean*. Mona, Jamaica: University of the West Indies.

Meeks, Brian, and Folke Lindahl (eds.) (2001). *New Caribbean Thought: A Reader*. Mona, Jamaica: University of West Indies Press.

Mintz, Sidney, and Richard Price (1992/1976). *The Birth of African-American Culture: An Anthropological Perspective*. Boston: Beacon Press.

Morejón, Nancy (1993/1982). "Race and Nation." In Pérez Sarduy, P., and J. Stubbs (eds.), *Afro-Cuba: An Anthology of Cuban Writing on Race, Politics, and Culture*. Melbourne, Australia: Ocean Press.

Nettleford, Rex (1994). *Inward Stretch, Outward Reach, A Voice from the Caribbean*. Basingstroke, UK: Macmillan.

Nicholls, David (1996). *From Dessalines to Duvalier: Race, Color, and National Independence in Haiti*. Rev. ed. New Brunswick, NJ: Rutgers University Press.

Ortiz, Fernando (1995/1940). *Cuban Counterpoint: Tobacco and Sugar*. Durham, NC: Duke University Press.

Ruiz Belvis, Segundo et al. (1985/1870). "Proyecto para la abolición de la esclavitud en Puerto Rico." As quoted in Díaz Quiñones, introduction to Tomás Blanco, *El prejuicio racial en Puerto Rico*. Río Piedras, Puerto Rico: Ediciones Huracán.

Scarano, Francisco A. (1989). "Labor and Society in the Nineteenth Century." In Knight and Palmer (eds.), *The Modern Caribbean*.

Vickerman, Milton (2001). "Tweaking a Monolith: The West Indian Immigrant Encounter with 'Blackness.'" In Nancy Foner (ed.), *Islands in the City, West Indian Migration to New York*. Berkeley, CA: University of California Press.

1

Anguilla

Pedro L.V. Welch

FROM AMERINDIANS TO EUROPEAN SETTLEMENT

The island of Anguilla is the northernmost of the islands that make up the Lesser Antilles chain. It is situated about 125 miles directly east of the Virgin Islands and almost 200 miles east of Puerto Rico. It is just 16 miles long and 3 miles wide, making it one of the smaller territories in the English-speaking Caribbean. Over 90 percent of its population of about 10,000 is of African descent. The earliest inhabitants of Anguilla were the Arawaks who left their "signature" in hundreds of petroglyphs and other artifacts, found scattered over more than twenty-one sites. The island is considered one of the driest in the Caribbean and it has rather thin soil, thus precluding large-scale agriculture. However, the marine environment abounds in several species of fish and other marine species. This afforded the Arawaks and their successors, the Caribs, enough of a food supply for them to establish viable settlements.

The present name, Anguilla, was apparently given by a French explorer, Captain Rene Laudonniere, who visited the island in 1564. He named the island L'Anguille, which is the French word for "eel," referring to the island's eel-like shape.[1] The Amerindian name for the island has also survived: *Malliouhara,* whose meaning has been lost. The Arawak name is being revived by a cadre of young Anguillans who are proud of their Amerindian heritage and anxious to blur the image of the European past.

In the first one hundred years or so after its "discovery" by Columbus, Anguilla was visited by the ships of various European nations. However, it was not until 1650 that the first permanent European settlement began with the arrival of English settlers on the island. These pioneers established small homesteads and planted corn and tobacco on their small holdings. The early years were plagued with difficulties such as attacks by Caribs and by the Spanish, who viewed the English settlement as a threat to their monopoly over the Indies. In any case, such attacks were not sustained and the English consolidated their hold on the territory.

English control over Anguilla received legal sanction under a grant made by the Crown to the earl of Carlisle. Under this arrangement, Anguilla was linked administratively to St. Christopher (St. Kitts). The political arrangements that linked Anguilla to its larger sister island did not permit the development of a representative form of government in the first years of settlement, and it was not until well into the eighteenth century that a legislative council was formed to act in an advisory capacity to the deputy governor. The subordinate role played by this council to the central government in St. Kitts prefigured a growing insularity that was to have its greatest manifestation centuries later.

The relatively harsh conditions on an island with limited land did not attract large numbers of settlers. By the end of the eighteenth century, the white population had reached about 400. Some persons had migrated to seek their fortune in the nearby islands of St. Kitts, St. Martin, Barbuda, and Nevis. Others had migrated to what would later become the United States. There were also some 2,000 slaves, the descendants of Africans who were imported to work on the small sugar and cotton holdings.

THE ERA OF SUGAR

Like all other English-speaking Caribbean territories, Anguilla was shaped by the "sugar revolution." The term seems more applicable to Barbados, for nowhere else in the Caribbean were the social and economic changes wrought by the development of the sugar industry so profound. However, in a small territory such as Anguilla, the impact of the demographic changes due to the influx of African slaves and the ratio of those slaves to the white population was intense.

Economically, the impact of sugar was rather muted. In particular, the sparse land resources, the relatively low annual rainfall, and the absence of rivers to drive sugar mills meant that costs of production were high and yields low. True, the constant blowing of the trade winds provided some motive force for the windmills, erected to grind the cane, as in Barbados. However, in this latter case, windmills were supplemented by animal-drawn mills, whereas in Anguilla, the lack of fodder made this option less viable. "Anguilla's thin soil and inadequate rainfall affected the quantity and quality of the sugar produced by slave-labour from Africa and for most of the time, therefore, sugar production was unprofitable" (Petty 1984, 6).

Anguilla, therefore, never developed a plantation system with large estates on the scale of those in other "sugar" islands such as Antigua and Barbados or even, in terms of comparable size, on the scale of those in Nevis. Indeed, by the late 1700s there were no more than twenty sugar estates on the island. Notwith-standing this, sugar and rum competed vigorously with cotton as the main ex-port staples. In 1788, for example, the value of sugar exports was some £3,337 compared with some £9,716 for cotton. Rum exports were valued at just over £2,000 (Petty 1991, 6). But the sugar industry was sufficiently established for Anguilla to be considered a society shaped by sugarcane.

By 1825, the population totaled about 3,080 persons of whom 78 percent were slaves, with 10 percent "free coloreds." This free colored group emerged out of sexual contact between whites and blacks, engendered by the relative shortage of white females and the almost total control that white males exerted over the persons of the entire population, free and enslaved. As elsewhere in the Carib-bean, the emergence of a mulatto cohort posed a dilemma to the maintenance of social distance between the enslaver and the enslaved. Some white parents manumitted their mixed-blood offspring and, where possible, settled property on them. Within the context of a numerically small society, the effect of these developments on the racial divide was bound to be striking.

On the small cotton and sugar estates, slaves found themselves subjected to the will of a small European elite. Laws were passed to prohibit slaves from grow-ing or selling cotton and other crops or commodities such as indigo, ginger, cof-fee, and cocoa. Competition with their owners in the production of these crops had implications for the maintenance of a social system built on notions of African inferiority. Despite the obvious racism that characterized slave systems throughout the region, the unsuitable conditions in Anguilla forced modifica-tions in the nature of their slave system. Anguillan slaves were permitted "room-to-manouevre," options *not* widely practiced elsewhere in the Caribbean. "Since sugar, tobacco, and cotton . . . produced poor yields on Anguilla, slaveholding be-came more a burden than a source of wealth. Intelligent slaves were encouraged to learn 'professions.' Thus, long before the British declared emancipation in their West Indies colonies, white planters on Anguilla permitted their slaves to work as ' . . . coopers, sailors and masons as well as field labourers, going as far as St. Bartholomew, Trinidad, St. Croix and sending their earnings to pay for the privilege of purchasing their own or their relatives' freedom" (Brisk 1969, 11).

The dependency of some planters on their slaves' hiring out their own ser-vices and time led to interesting developments. First, slaves had some autonomy in selecting hirers. Second, hirers might be unsure as to the extent of their dis-ciplinary control, thus permitting slaves to take liberties that might be un-thinkable in other contexts. Third, slaves might play off hirer against owner in seeking even more autonomy. Against this background, it is not surprising that planters "adopted the custom, very early in the nineteenth century of granting conditional freedom" (Brisk 1969, 11) to many of their slaves.

In Anguilla a high degree of miscegenation, mitigation in the severity of the slave system due to the economic conditions that prevailed, an insular intro-spection built on years of benign neglect by the colonial authorities, and an independence arising from the economic choices available to the mass of the population created among Anguillans a "sense of separate identity" (Goveia 1969, 55) and a "special creole identity" (Brisk 1969, 11). These traits will inform Anguilla's development over time.

POST-EMANCIPATION ADJUSTMENTS AND CONTINUITIES, 1838–1938

The post-emancipation history of Anguilla represents a struggle against great adversity. It is a testimony to the hardy, independent spirit that evolved in the preceding years when Anguillans found whatever options could be explored and used these to maintain a viable community. By the 1860s, sugar had all but disappeared and locals turned to boat-building, fishing, harvesting salt, and trading to provide the necessary hard currency to buy imports. When these options failed, they resorted to migration, working as temporary laborers in the nearby islands or immigrating to the United States, via the U.S. Virgin Islands. Remittances from this migration helped the island community to survive.

The first of the Anguillans to leave were the remnants of the European elite, and they went to places as distant as Rochester, NY, Los Angeles, Bogotá, Calcutta, Canada, and England. By the 1880s, a chaplain aboard a British warship that visited the island reported that there were only about 100 whites in a population of over 3,200. He also reported that life was austere, with few amenities to relieve boredom. There was no local newspaper, no printing press, no icehouse, no hotel or drinking saloon. These could be found on St. Kitts.

There were a few periods when life appeared more promising. In the 1860s, deposits of phosphate rock were identified on a small island dependency, Sombrero Island. However, within a short time, these deposits were exhausted. Then, during World War I, when the prices of most primary commodities rose in response to increasing demand, cotton production proved to be an important source of income for islanders. This boom did not last long.

Anguilla suffered from repeated droughts from 1870 to the 1920s. A survey stated the conditions on the island: "A famine of 1890 brought on by prolonged drought, repeated failure of the crops, lack of seed, death of cattle, sheep and goats for want of food and water ... left the islanders so poor they crept into the woods and gathered berries and herbs for food. Only timely charitable relief from St. Kitts—which provided vital foods and medicines to more than 2000 Anguillans—avoided mass starvation and epidemics" (Brisk 1969, 12). After this experience, Anguillans took to the sea, true to the reputation which islanders have as skilled shipwrights, sailors, and navigators (Petty 1991).

However, Anguillans were not totally overwhelmed by the events that fate dealt them. Their renowned resilience had been learned through extensive education in the school of shifting social and economic circumstances. Culturally, the people exhibited a penchant for adaptation and a syncretist spirit, making the best of the European and African worlds. Storytelling became an art, combining the skill of the African griot (West African professional singer, musician and storyteller) with the more formal cadence of European genres. Most Anguillans are familiar with the jumbie (spirits) stories that tell of ghosts and the walking dead.

Traditions developed that modified African motifs in a Caribbean environment. For example, a vision of a black baby on a grave was a sign that someone important was about to die. Superimposed over these beliefs was the influence of the Christian church, which provided an escape in times of adversity. The Methodist and Anglican (Church of England) churches consolidated their hold in this period. Later, the arrival of the Seventh-Day Adventist Church and other U.S.-based churches would diversify religious options on the island.

The growing impact of the Anglican Church in the period between 1838 and 1938 can be traced to the influence of the visit of Bishop Parry of Barbados to the island in 1825. Parry's visit brought donations to establish and build a church. Thus by the late 1840s, the religious influence of the church was matched by its impact on the architectural and educational landscape; an influence strengthened over the ensuing years by the appointment of qualified clergy. As for the Methodists, their apogee came in 1867 when Reverend David Schouter arrived in the island to oversee pastoral work there. His vigorous proselytism and the construction of two Methodist chapels in short order marked a new phase in their work.

If social life was austere, political developments offered little hope for relief to the islanders. Most of the changes taking place during the period were made without regard to the needs and aspirations of the Anguillan people. Similar to the first hundred years of settlement, Anguillan political decision-making was subordinated to the dictates of the St. Kitts legislature. In the mid–nineteenth century the Anguilla Council was re-designated the vestry. It was subject to the approval of the chief administrator in St. Kitts in matters of revenue legislation. New changes in the 1870s further alienated Anguillans from the legislative process and evoked an angry response from the vestry, which petitioned the Colonial Office as follows: "The interest of Anguilla, its resources and capabilities of development are not understood … by the legislative body of St. Christopher [St. Kitts] who are utter strangers to us, ignorant of the community, careless of their wants. … This legislative dependence on St. Kitts can in no sense be called a legislative union, it has operated and continues to operate most injuriously against us, and is mutually disliked" (Brisk 1969, p. 14).

The tone of the petition was clearly hostile to the prospect of any union with St. Kitts. However, the Colonial Office totally disregarded this appeal, and in the future continued to subjugate the interests of Anguillans to London's imperial will.

In 1882, the Anguillan vestry was abolished and local government had, to all intents and purposes, disappeared. In the same year, the British government, St. Kitts, Anguilla, and Nevis were united in a single administrative unit called a presidency. Even the naming of this unit did not include Anguilla's name until 1951.

In 1938, in the aftermath of labor unrest that swept the British Caribbean, a commission headed by Lord Moyne visited the region. The committee identified the sharp resentment that Anguillans felt at what they considered unequal treatment by the administration in St. Kitts. In particular, it reported that Anguillan workers were being discriminated against by employers in St. Kitts. This resentment would continue to fester, having implications for the political future of the colony.

ROAD TO REVOLT: 1938–1967

By the late 1930s, economic conditions were hardly better than they had been in the period immediately after emancipation in 1838. Unemployment, underemployment, and limited economic opportunity marked the lives of most Anguillans. The political developments to take place in the region over the next thirty years would show the mettle of its people.

In 1937, the Colonial Office decided to permit some limited change in the franchise by allowing three of the members of the legislative council that governed the St. Kitts-Nevis-Anguilla unit to be elected. Before this change, all of the members were nominated by the colonial authorities. The first three councilmen to be elected were all from St. Kitts, "merchants hardly concerned with the problems of small farmers in Anguilla and Nevis" (Brisk 1969, 15). This bureaucratic neglect further deepened the suspicion that characterized Anguillans' opinions of central administration in St. Kitts. Over the next decade as a labor movement emerged in the larger island and as political reform threatened to place power in the hands of the descendants of ex-slaves, Anguillans might have expected some interest in their affairs. However, the approach of the St. Kitts labor movement to Anguillan concerns was introspective, insular, and myopic.

The election of Robert Bradshaw's (1916–1978) Trade and Labor Union to political power in St. Kitts, in 1952, was a watershed in the history of the St. Kitts-Nevis-Anguilla unit. The elections of 1952 were preceded by a new constitution granting adult suffrage and this helped to deepen political awareness among the voting population. Bradshaw could hardly ignore the calls of Anguillans for greater attention to questions of infrastructural development. But he did, as his party pandered to the interests of the sugar workers who formed the bulk of his support in St. Kitts. A petition sent by Anguillans to the governor of the Windward Islands in November 1958 illustrates well their reaction to his leadership. The petition states the following: "the present political leadership in St. Kitts . . . left much to be desired. The methods employed by the St. Kitts political leaders in trying to secure better conditions for the masses was mainly "the method of hate, abuse, reprisals and spite." This the petitoners argued, "went hand in hand with the promulgation of lawlessness as a way of life." The framers of the petition went on to say that "St. Kitts [was] of no use whatsoever to Anguilla's welfare. Her enforced association with Anguilla [was] a perpetual assault to Anguilla's development, a threat and a menace to Anguilla's self respect."[2]

Significantly, the petition came at a time when the British West Indies Federation (BWIF) was making its first steps toward regional self-determination. Under United Nation pressure to decolonize, the British government preferred granting independence to a federation of islands. Whatever hopes this regional grouping might have had of welding together separate island polities into a West Indian nation, events in St. Kitts and Anguilla were a portent of the larger struggles that would tear the federation apart within a few short years.

By 1962, the federation had collapsed, with Jamaica and Trinidad and Tobago opting for independence. Barbados attempted to form a federation with the smaller units (the Federation of the Little Eight) but this soon foundered and Barbados became independent in 1966. The remaining territories entered into a political arrangement with Great Britain, which offered them "associated statehood." Associated statehood is a political system in which British Caribbean colonies accepted a political association with England that is short of independence. The country had full internal self-government, while the mother country was responsible for defense and foreign relations. The Constitutional Conference to determine the future of the St. Kitts-Nevis-Anguilla nexus took place in 1966. The political discussions it engendered led directly to the rebellion of 1967, in which Anguillans took a decisive step to rid themselves of the Kittitian yoke.

REBELLION AND AFTERMATH

The first tangible sign of the trouble came at, of all things, a beauty pageant. Held on February 4, 1967, the pageant was organized to celebrate "Statehood Day." It was expected that the pageant, time-tabled for Anguilla, would select a "Miss Associated State" from contestants drawn from the three islands. The symbolism of the pageant was lost on no one, certainly not on the Anguillans who organized a demonstration that shut down the local power station. The police force, staffed by Kittitians, arrested three men whom they had identified as ringleaders. The arrest was aborted by the intervention of some islanders.

Ronald Webster (1926–) took part in the demonstration and has been inextricably linked with the fortunes of Anguilla since the mid-1960s. Born in Anguilla in 1926, he came from austere surroundings: his father was a fisherman and operated a small shop to augment his meager income. At age ten he left for the Dutch island of St. Maarten, searching for work: the rest is a rags-to-riches story.

Mentored by a wealthy Dutchman, Webster studied and subsequently inherited property valued at U.S. $1.5 million when both his benefactor and his wife died. In 1960, he returned to Anguilla and became a political activist and entrepreneur, seeking to invest some of his financial resources in the infrastructural development of Anguilla. He approached Robert Bradshaw with some of his plans for the improvement of Anguilla, but was rebuffed, contributing to his frustration and future feelings that negotiations with St. Kitts would become all but impossible.

Peter Adams is another key historical figure, having been the official spokesman for the Anguillans as its representative to the St. Kitts Assembly. Adams represented a voice of moderation in the political relations between St. Kitts and Anguilla. However, his moderation was doomed to failure, given the growing polarization between the two islands.

As the new political events intensified, and political debate on associate statehood grew, sharp divisions between Adams and Webster—both of Afro-Caribbean origin—became more pronounced. Adams thought that compromises could be worked out with St. Kitts, but Webster thought that the country's future required a referendum, elections in Anguilla, and a new political arrangement. In light of future events, Webster seems to have read correctly the mood of his countrymen.

The growing confrontation with St. Kitts escalated in March 1967, when a mysterious fire destroyed the Government House. Other acts of violence soon followed. The police headquarters and the residences of Kittitian supporters came under fire, clear signals of Anguillan intent. Then the entire police force was evicted from the island, stripped of their arms and ammunition. Anguillans had taken charge of their own destiny, eager to obtain a full political separation. A committee of fifteen headed by a prominent Anguillan, Walter Hodge, was established to coordinate defense arrangements and to develop new institutions of governance. Peter Adams and Ronald Webster sat on this committee.

The Anguilla rebellion was in a precarious situation. Bradshaw declared a state of emergency and froze all Anguillan assets. In addition, the St. Kitts government sought to obtain arms and support from the British and from neighboring Caribbean territories. Trying to forestall military intervention, a delegation of Anguillans journeyed to St. Kitts to present a memorandum making it clear that the islanders wished to separate from St. Kitts and to be placed under direct British administration. Anguillans intended to hold elections at the earliest opportunity and appoint their own local administration.

The response of the Bradshaw administration was predictable. The Kittitians called for an immediate return to the *status quo ante* and for all arms and ammunition to be turned over to the government. The Aguillans' defense was to go on the offensive: on June 10, 1967, a small group of Anguillans landed in St. Kitts, in order to capture Bradshaw and his deputy and to take hostages as bargaining chips. The mission failed.

Following the abortive invasion by the Anguillans, the Kittitian authorities sought military assistance from Britain and from the Caribbean nations of Barbados, Trinidad and Tobago, Jamaica, and Guyana (Webster 1987). It was declined and instead they supported diplomatic initiatives to deal with the impasse. A mission from the Caribbean Community and Common Market (CARICOM) made up of English-speaking states tried to broker a negotiation between St. Kitts and Anguilla, but ultimately failed when it was rejected by the St. Kitts government.

Following the breakdown of negotiations, the Anguillans forged ahead with plans for elections and a referendum. On July 11, 1967, a 1,813-to-5 referendum vote ratified the decision to secede and establish an interim government. Afterwards, a delegation of elected Anguillan representatives traveled to Barbados at the request of the governments of Barbados, Jamaica, Trinidad and Tobago, and Guyana. The delegation was led by Peter Adams and later by Ronald Webster. Further differences between Webster and Adams led to Adams' ouster as president of the Anguilla Council, and Webster was installed in his place.

The island's new administration finally agreed to an interim arrangement with Britain. In return for a promise by the leaders to hold off on further political changes, the British government agreed to free up some financial aid. Britain miscalculated, believing this would end Anguilla's drive for secession. But between 1967 and 1969, during negotiations, the Anguillans, led by Webster, were quietly reforming the political landscape. On February 21, 1969, Webster was nominated unopposed and subsequently declared president of Anguilla. British authorities were upset and thought that the island "upstarts" must be reined in.

A British emissary arrived, and immediately showed his contempt for the islanders by refusing to meet with President Webster. Hundreds of people surrounded the house where the emissary had lodged, noisily showing their displeasure. Another display of insensitivity and colonial arrogance by the emissary made Webster order his immediate departure.

On March 19, 1969, the British responded to this rejection of their "beneficence" by sending an invasion force of some 400 paratroopers and policemen to occupy the island. It drew the immediate condemnation of world opinion. Opponents of the invasion pointed to the contrast between Britain's action against Anguilla and its treatment of Ian Smith's unilateral declaration of independence in Rhodesia, now Zimbabwe. Smith had installed a white minority, racist government in Rhodesia, similar to South Africa's apartheid regime. Stung by accusations of hypocrisy, the British subsequently took a more cautious approach in handling Anguillan affairs.

In post-occupation negotiations, the British recognized the members of the Anguilla Council of 1968 as legitimate representatives of the island's people, and agreed to a process of continuing consultation. However, Webster's leadership was not recognized, a factor that would destabilize the British administration of the island and force further accommodation over time.

Under British occupation, Atlin Harrigan, editor of the local newspaper, *The Beacon*, attempted to wrest control from Webster. Harrigan's political stardom quickly faded, and Webster continued as the major political player. In 1971, Anguillan hopes received a boost when the Anguilla Act appointed a commissioner and established the formal separation of Anguilla from the St. Kitts-Nevis-Anguilla nexus.

Anguilla's political connection with St. Kitts was further severed in 1980: an act of the British Parliament declared that Anguilla would "cease to form part" of the three-island state. This was an important step in fulfilling Anguilla's long-standing wish for full self-determination.

CONCLUSION

Whither Anguilla? Like many other small-island developing states, Anguilla faces several economic problems, even if it has a higher standard of living and a lower unemployment rate than most independent islands of the English-speaking Caribbean. Low rainfall patterns and slight agricultural resources restrict agrarian development. In addition, lack of accessibility to external markets and the impact of migration act as brakes on industrial development. However, in recent times, tourism has proven to have the potential to generate an increase in income levels and form the basis toward sustainable development. Visitor arrivals totaled 93,000 in 1992, and have averaged about 111,000 in the five years from 1995 to 2000. Tourism's share of gross national product is in excess of 65 percent. British aid continues to fund infrastructural development, leaving Anguillans to make up for any deficiency with their own creative, resilient spirit.

This spirit is also evident in the cultural adaptations taking place in the island. Rastafarianism has taken root, and while most Anguillan youth belong to mainstream churches (Anglicanism is the leading faith), some are willing to exchange these "trappings of the colonialist past" for a religious experience that extols African values and culture. Reggae music is widespread and popular, perhaps also hinting at a repudiation of the Eurocentric past.

In addition to these changes, the Anguillan cultural renaissance is embodied by Carnival, which, like those held elsewhere in the Caribbean, promotes the use of indigenous music and themes. Certainly, the local calypso competition, held during Carnival, though not on the scale of those in Trinidad or Barbados, is a hopeful sign of Anguillan cultural and racial pride. Carnival takes on a uniquely Anguillan stamp by linking the revelry of the costumed street parades and parties with a series of boat races and other waterfront activities.

Anguilla is still predominantly rural, and "jollification," a ritual performed during a cultural festival, reaffirms the island's Afro-Anguillan roots. Dressed in work clothes, Anguillans symbolically plant fields and commemorate the communal spirit of harvest through songs and spirituals. Jollification reminds us that in a competitive global environment, an island microstate is not merely a beach (with hotels), but a community with a creative spirit rooted in history.

NOTES

1. A good source for tracing the history of Anguilla is found in *Review 1981–1985* published by the Anguilla Archaeological Society, Anguilla, 1986.

2. See *Report of the Commission of Inquiry*, pp. 76–83.

REFERENCES

Brisk, William. T. (1969). *The Dilemma of a Ministate: Anguilla*. Columbia, SC: University of South Carolina.

Goveia, Elsa (1969). *Slave Society in the British Leeward Islands at the End of the Eighteenth Century*. New Haven: Yale University Press.

Manchester, Kathleen (1971). *Historic Heritage of St. Kitts, Nevis, Anguilla*. Trinidad: Syncreators Ltd.

Petty, Colville L. (1984). *Anguilla: Where There's a Will There's a Way*. Anguilla (self-published).

———(1991). *A Handbook History of Anguilla*. Anguilla: Anguilla Printers.

Webster, Ronald (1987). *Scrapbook of Anguilla's Revolution*. Anguilla: Seabreakers.

2

The Bahamas

D. Gail Saunders

INTRODUCTION

A part of the African diaspora, the Bahamas' population was small and the colony, a relatively insignificant part of the British Empire. The Bahamas' total land area is about 5,353 square miles with a population of 17,862 in 1834; 47,565 in 1891; 84,841 in 1953; and 304,000 in 2000. It is an archipelago that begins east of the southern coast of Florida, stretching close to the nothern coasts of Cuba, Haiti, and the Dominican Republic.

The Bahamas did not produce sugar on a commercial scale but attempted cotton cultivation. An important legacy of slavery in the Bahamas was racism. The majority of Caribbean people were of African descent but were considered morally inferior to Europeans by the local and metropolitan whites. This racist belief persisted into post-emancipation years and dominated Caribbean societies into the twentieth century. In the Bahamas, racial discrimination was more severe than in Barbados and most of the British West Indies plantation colonies. The Bahamas, like Barbados, had a fairly large white population representing 10 percent or more of the population. The absence of sugar, the brief plantation experience, its long and historical ties with the Southern United States, all made for more polarized racial relations. The institution of slavery left an indelible mark on Caribbean societies. Post-emancipation society was divided into three major tiers or classes. At the top of the social pyramid was the white upper class, in an intermediate position was the colored and black middle class, and at the bottom, the black majority, comprising the former slaves, liberated Africans, and their descendants.

The white upper class had a firm grip over the economy and the political and administrative machinery. They despised the black majority and barely tolerated the people of color who "knew their place," many of whom had gained some "respectability" by emancipation. The society generally remained divided by color and class until the late 1960s. During the Prohibition years (1919–1933) and the introduction of large-scale tourism in the late 1940s, the color line grew more rigid and Jim Crow (racial segregation of public places) attitudes and the system of segregation were practiced in hotels and exclusive clubs to please tourists.

Bahamians, like many other West Indians, suffered from inferiority complexes and feelings of low self-esteem and generally lacked confidence. It is only in recent times that Bahamians—through education and teaching and the dissemination of history, and through the recognition of aspects of their culture, especially the festival known as "Junkanoo"—have begun to come to grips with their national identity.

EARLY SLAVERY

The early settlers of the Bahamas were mainly white, but some blacks accompanied the Eleutherian Adventurers in 1648. They settled in Eleuthera, forming the first permanent settlement since the decimation of the Lucayans (Arawak Taínos), the indigenous people of the Bahamas. A substantial number of black slaves were among the population beginning in the 1670s. By the 1740s, the black population, which included both slaves and free blacks, numbered about 1,000—almost half of the population—and had increased considerably. By 1773 the total population was 4,293, with blacks slightly outnumbering the white population.

ENTER THE LOYALISTS

Before the arrival of the American Loyalists (those who sided with the British in the American War of Independence) in the 1780s, the inhabitants of the Bahamas were engaged mainly in a seafaring way of life, including fishing, wrecking, and turtling. They also gathered salt for local consumption and grew subsistence crops. There was no staple. Poverty typified the Bahamian Islands, and its chief town, Nassau, on New Providence Island, was a shabby port overgrown with bush and contained no impressive buildings.

The arrival of the Loyalists and their slaves made a significant impact on the Bahamian economic, political, and social life during the slavery period. The Loyalists, who brought with them relatively large numbers of slaves, increased the black population, placing it in the majority. The plantation system was introduced and attempts made to establish cotton as the staple crop. However, by 1800, due to the exhausted state of the soil, injudicious planting, poor management, and the attack of the chenille bug, cotton cultivation collapsed and most planters, facing ruin, either left the Bahamas or resorted to the cultivation of the old subsistence crops, such as guinea corn, peas, and yams. Some also turned to seafaring activities and salt-raking.

Despite the short-lived plantation system, slavery in the Bahamas was no less brutal than in the sugar colonies to the south. However, the less arduous labor of Bahamian slaves led to healthier slaves and also to high rates of natural increase. Bahamian slaves worked from dawn to dusk and received severe punishments, including whipping and being put in stocks or the workhouse, for small offenses. As in America and elsewhere in the Caribbean, the enslaved in the Bahamas resisted through individual and collective violence and through passive resistance. This included refusal to work, general inefficiency, deliberate laziness, running away, and suicide.

As in the British Caribbean, the Bahamas experienced both day-to-day resistance and collective violence. The most serious revolt was on Exuma in 1829; it was led by a Creole slave, Pompey, whose generation won the right for slaves to work for themselves for half of each day. (They and their descendants also claimed the land on which they lived after slavery had ended.) Evidence shows that masters punished their slaves as they wished and punishments in the Bahamas could be very brutal and end in death for the slaves at the hands of the owners, as the case of Poor Black Kate demonstrated in 1826.

Poor Black Kate was a domestic slave owned by Henry and Helen Moss. She was accused of theft and disobedience, of refusing to mend her clothes, and of not performing her work. She was confined to the stocks for 17 days, beaten repeatedly, and had red pepper rubbed into her eyes to prevent her from sleeping. Upon release, she was flogged and sent to do field work, where she died soon after of a fever. Her owners were tried and found guilty of a misdemeanor, and Henry Moss, after serving only months in jail, returned as a member of the House of Assembly and remained as a Justice of the Peace. Poor Black Kate's travails were used by British abolitionists, who published an 1828 pamphlet on the cruelty that led to Kate's death.

Without a profitable staple crop to replace cotton, and with a surplus of labor, the operation of labor tenancy and sharecropping was found to be a more satisfactory and profitable arrangement for the proprietors than directing the operation of their estates themselves. Sharecroppers usually grew guinea corn, peas, beans, potatoes, and yams during slavery. In post-emancipation years they grew pineapples also. It was an amicable solution for both the landlords and the tenants. The latter gained access to the land, while the proprietors retained the services of the ex-slaves.

The self-hire system whereby "slaveowners allowed their slaves to seek their own employment in return for a mutually agreed sum" also emerged in the Bahamas in the late eighteenth century (Johnsons 1996, 33). The collapse of cotton, the absence of an export staple to replace it, and agricultural stagnation led to the underutilization of the slave population. While some slave owners on the Out Islands employed their slaves in cultivating foodstuffs and raising livestock for the Nassau Market, others transferred their underutilized slaves to Nassau, which offered greater opportunities for skilled and unskilled labor to be sold, hired out, or permitted to work on the self-hire system at a variety of tasks. This practice had evolved before the arrival of the American Loyalists. By the closing years of slavery "slaves on the self-hire system dominated the urban scene" (Johnson 1996, 37). Scholars contend that the self-hire system was advantageous to both owners and slaves. Owners could look forward to cash payments and not have to supervise or supply food, clothing, or shelter (Johnson 1996). Slaves recognized the system as giving them an opportunity to "exercise extensive control over their lives" (Johnson 1996, 42).

ABOLITION, EMANCIPATION, AND THE APPRENTICESHIP PERIOD

The abolition of slavery in the Bahamas went into effect, as it did in all the British Caribbean colonies, on August 1, 1834. The Emancipation Act provided for an apprenticeship or transition period between slavery and full freedom. All children under six were to be completely free. Older slaves were to serve a term of apprenticeship, being required to work forty and a half hours each week for their former owners who would maintain them. Full emancipation was scheduled to take effect in August 1840.

A special body of magistrates, appointed in Britain, were sent out to see that the provisions of the apprenticeship were enforced. Apprentices could purchase their freedom. Compensation money totaling £20 million was granted to former slave owners based on the market value of the slave.

The apprenticeship system, which was set up under the Abolition Act and which aimed to provide an easy transition from slavery to freedom, to guarantee to the planters a labor supply, and to help slaves in their new responsibilities as free citizens, generally failed.

The British government agreed to full emancipation on August 1, 1838, instead of 1840, in its colonies. Slaves did own land but restricted regulations on the sale of Crown lands in "the immediate post-emancipation years severely restricted the ownership of land by the ex-slaves" (Johnson 1996, 90). Actual emancipation passed quietly in the Bahamas, there being no noisy rejoicing, except that many former apprentices celebrated in churches and there was lively singing.

The transition out of chattel slavery was generally smooth. Immediate post-emancipation years were a time of hope and optimism for the newly freed in the Bahamas, and in the Caribbean generally. However, the change proved more legal than real. The formerly enslaved lost the protection of their former owners, and the conditions of work, land tenure, and material welfare worsened. The former slave owners tightened their control over both the political system and the mercantile economy and the former slaves experienced continuing oppression and deprivation.

LIBERATED AFRICANS

The black population was expanded by the settlement of liberated Africans in the Bahamas. By the abolition of the Slave Trade Act of 1807, foreign trading vessels captured by the British were landed on the nearest British colony and the crew of these slave vessels was tried in the Nassau Vice-Admiralty Court, whereupon the "condemned" re-captives or liberated were declared the responsibility of the Crown of Customs (Chief-Customs Officer). Between 1808 and 1860 approximately 6,000 liberated Africans were settled in the Bahamas, mainly at New Providence. The majority of liberated Africans were apprenticed to "masters" and "mistresses" and performed similar tasks as the slaves, under similar conditions: "fishing, wrecking, cutting wood, raking salt and agricultural and domestic tasks" (Johnson 1996, 75). As has been argued, a peasantry developed during slavery in the Bahamas. The liberated Africans "formed the nucleus of that peasantry"; they were a part of the free black community, enjoying some independence and "a measure of prosperity" (Johnson 1996, 60–61).

Liberated Africans were taken to Head Quarters (later called Carmichael), Adelaide, and Gambier (settlements for liberated Africans), located some distance out of Nassau, and were established between 1825 and 1834. As the demand for the cheap and reliable labor of the indentured Africans continued, black settlements were established in the suburbs of Nassau. Other free black villages included Bain Town, Gambier, Delaporte, and Fox Hill/Sandilands Village.

Liberated Africans reinforced the African elements in African Bahamian society. Perhaps the most distinctive African-Bahamian institution that originated in Grant's Town was the Friendly Society. Formed by liberated Africans and former slave apprentices in about 1835, it was a self-help organization designed to promote African solidarity and to provide benefits for the sick, aged, widows, and orphans, and it offered a dignified burial for each of its members. The Grant's Town society became the model for a proliferation of similar societies and later "lodges," a colorful feature still a part of African Bahamian life.

AFRICAN CONTINUITIES

Liberated Africans also gave added vigor to the cultural forms and practices with African roots. These included John Canoe (later called "Junkanoo") a dance celebrated by slaves in the Bahamas on their three holiday days at Christmas. Essentially African traditions were present in the music of the majority of Bahamians, although, like the Caribbean generally, music had undergone a creolization process, blending African and European forms begun during slavery. Music, derived from the antebellum slave songs of the United States and from the hymns contained in the early Wesleyan and Baptist hymnals, was important in the lives of African Bahamians. Religious songs or spirituals were characterized almost exclusively by unaccompanied singing, and secular music was associated "with festive recreation and dance activities" incorporating the use of musical instruments. Religious songs or spirituals were important at social gatherings and wakes, and while they were heavily influenced by African music, they came almost exclusively by way of the United States. Secular music on the other hand, with its strong emphasis on drumming and dancing, emanated more directly from Africa.

Dance was also African derived, like the "Fire Dance," the "Jumping Dance," and the "Ring-play" (usually performed by children). All three are known as ring dances, in which the participants stood in a circle around one or more dancers. There is some sort of rhythmic accompaniment—singing, chanting, clapping, drumming, or a combination of these. To begin, a solo dancer would perform in the center of the ring and after a short time choose another person, usually of the opposite sex, as a replacement, and the succeeding dancer would do likewise until each person had danced in the ring.

The telling of traditional folktales with roots in Europe and Africa was a popular form of leisure among the black laboring population. For example, the B'Anansi West African spider trickster, a symbol of passive resistance, popular among Jamaican folktales, was also present in Bahamian folktales. Some African-inspired cooking survived into the early twentieth century, like *accara*, *foo-foo*, *agedi*, and *my-my*. An African game called "Warri" is still played in the Bahamas today.

African Bahamians kept their native languages alive into the early twentieth century. Most blacks, however, spoke Bahamian Creole, a dialect that resembled the Black English spoken on the U.S. mainland in the eighteenth century.

LAND TENURE AND LABOR SYSTEMS

Land was important to Bahamians and particularly to former slaves who used it as a vital source of food through peasant farming. However, large areas of the Bahamas were unsettled and uncultivated and the post-emancipation years showed a lack of interest by the Crown. By the last decade of the nineteenth century, the system of land tenure was chaotic. The Crown only granted or leased land to those who could afford to develop it. Formerly enslaved people usually could not, so most people owned no land.

Many peasants, mainly black, worked the land and built their houses on a small portion of it and could be considered squatters, having no legal tenure. Others, such as the former slaves of Lord John Rolle in Exuma, farmed on "commonages," that is, land held by the inhabitants in common, or on "generation lands," that is, land transmitted through the family, often informally, with dubious titles.

A small percentage of black Bahamians actually had legal title to the land that they claimed. On New Providence, where there was always a greater degree of wealth and sophistication, titles were better kept since the facilities, services, and professional personnel were available. The majority of people, who still lived on the Out Islands until the early 1950s, were without efficient services. Labor tenancy and sharecropping, which evolved during slavery and during the apprenticeship years, respectively, were, by the late nineteenth century, a very significant feature of the rural economy in the Bahamas. Usually governed by informal, and later by signed, contracts, labor tenancy allowed the African apprentices and slaves to work on their own plot of land for themselves for part of the week and to work the other part of the week for their masters, who supplied them with food and clothing.

Sharecropping, which emerged during the apprenticeship years, allowed the enslaved people to remain on the plantations and work the land allotted to them in order to support their families. One-third of the produce was given to the landowners; the remainder belonged to the laborer.

Land tenure was further complicated by the folk concept of "generation land," passed on from generation to generation. If such generation property or family land was left by will, the lands could not be touched, but in some cases there were no heirs and legally the lands should have reverted to the Crown. However, reverting to the Crown required legal proceedings that were rarely undertaken. In many cases there was no legal heir, so illegitimate or "outside children" and other more distant relatives occupied the land and questions of who owned generation property remained unsolved into modern time. Conflicts developed between poor islanders (almost exclusively black), who relied on customs and usage and rarely had written titles, and lawyers (until the mid-1960s, mostly white), eager to establish precise boundaries and formal title and uninterrupted possession on behalf of individual clients.

The Quieting of Titles Act of 1959 was enacted because of the difficulty in procuring sound title to real estate. For the first time, rules were laid down whereby unimpeachable freehold title to Bahamian land could be established. A large amount of land was sold between 1959 and 1967, much of it to foreigners. The Immovable Property (Acquisition by Foreign Persons) Act in 1983 required all who obtained acquisitions to obtain approval and a permit from a foreign investment board, as well as to be subject to duties and fees. The 1983 act was repealed in 1994 in favor of the International Land Holding Act, which decreed that non-Bahamians could acquire houses or parcels of land of fewer than five acres simply by registering the transaction and paying the requisite fees, as long as the acquisitions were for their own residential purposes. There are still disputes over the quieting of land, however, and many uncertainties exist in the present title practices in the Bahamas.

Ordinary peasant farming conducted on a sharecropping basis was often affected by the Truck System, as in the pineapple and sponging industries. The Truck System ensured that labor was tied to the Nassau merchant. The merchant provided advances in cash or provisions to the laborers to maintain themselves and their families. Interest rates were high on cash allowances. When advances in cash and kind were subtracted from the sale of pineapples produced or sponge collected, the laborer often ended up in debt to the landlord. This caused extreme poverty among the majority of laborers and sponge fishermen and there was hardly any circulation of money in the Out Islands (islands outside of New Providence, where Nassau is).

PROTEST DURING THE TWENTIETH CENTURY

Garveyism and the Pan-African movement had an impact on the British Caribbean, including the Bahamas. A number of black and colored Bahamians were ardent admirers of Marcus Garvey and a branch of the Universal Negro Improvement Association (UNIA), was established in Nassau in the 1920s. There were strong links between the UNIA in Nassau and those branches in Miami and New York that had been prompted by Bahamian migration to Florida and to New York in the late nineteenth and early twentieth centuries.

Garvey made a brief visit to Nassau in 1928 and undoubtedly had an impact on black and colored Bahamians. Racial consciousness grew and was helped by continued immigration of Bahamians to the southern United States and the arrival of several professional black West Indians in Nassau. The return of some black Bahamians who had been educated abroad, including Dr. Claudius R. Walker, also advanced racial pride.

By 1942, although lacking political organization, there was a growing racial consciousness among black leaders and also among some sectors of labor. Racial tension was an underlying cause of the 1942 riot in Nassau although it has been described as a wage dispute. A spontaneous outburst by a group of disgruntled black laborers—without black leadership emerging—highlighted the narrow socioeconomic and political policies of the day. Bahamians, like black Americans, suffered severe discrimination, at least until the 1960s.

In addition to the 1942 Nassau riot, discontent was made evident in black businessman and activist Milo Butler's demonstration on the commemoration of Emancipation Day in 1938 and in the mass appeal of the Progressive Liberal Party (PLP), the first political party, established in 1953. However, extreme conservatism and the lack of political and social unity among blacks meant that little headway was made in breaking down the barriers of racial discrimination in the Bahamas. The rapidly developing tourist industry was used as an excuse to maintain segregation in public places.

Etienne Dupuch, a colored proprietor and editor of *The Tribune*, presented a resolution (which was debated and voted on) in the House of Assembly in 1956 against racial discrimination in public places in the Bahamas. He also called for a commission of inquiry to investigate ending discrimination in schools, restaurants, cinemas, or any public space. While the House of Assembly accepted the first part of Dupuch's resolution, which condemned discrimination in "public" places on grounds of race and color, it rejected Dupuch's request for a commission of inquiry. The 1956 resolution demonstrated a new determination by blacks although discrimination in public places took time to

Former Prime Minister Lynden O. Pindling (left) and Sir Milo Butler (right) "on the march" or "Black Tuesday" when Pindling threw the mace out of the House of Assembly to protest the Boundaries Commission. Courtesy of the Department of Archives.

end, and racial discrimination generally persisted in the Bahamas until well into the 1970s.

Two years after the antidiscrimination resolution, in 1958, a sixteen-day general strike led by black lawyer and labor leader Randol Fawkes and supported by Lynden Pindling, then parliamentary leader of the PLP, closed hotels and most essential services throughout the Bahamas. It stirred the usually complacent Colonial Office into action. Lennox Boyd, the secretary of state for the colonies visited Nassau to investigate the causes of the strike, as well as issues related to an archaic constitution. Boyd's intervention was an important milestone. Significant electoral reforms were incorporated in the General Assembly Election Act of 1959. Male suffrage was introduced for those over 21. In order to bring constituencies into line with the movement of population, four additional seats in New Providence were created.

The gains made in 1958 created optimism and hope for the black majority. A new constitution in 1964 introduced the ministerial system, granted internal self-government, and led finally to independence in 1973.

In 1967, after massive demonstrations on Black Tuesday—protesting how voting districts were being designed—and the symbolic throwing of the mace out of the House of Assembly, Pindling and the PLP, in a "Quiet Revolution" and in a period of sustained prosperity, defeated the United Bahamian Party, dominated by the Nassau mercantile elite. Majority rule had been achieved.

THE ROLE OF WOMEN

The traditional role of Bahamian women as housewives and homemakers did not change dramatically during the early twentieth century. African Bahamian women from the nineteenth century participated in marketing, selling produce, straw, and fruit. In the 1920s a group from the African settlement of Fox Hill set up stalls in the central square and by the thirties and forties, some fruit and vegetable vendors in the public market also began selling straw goods.

Politically, Bahamian women, both white and black, were slow to mobilize. Beginning in the late 1920s, black and colored middle-class ladies participated in charitable work. Some colored middle-class women studied nursing and teaching abroad as early as the 1930s. It was not until the 1950s, however, that women—all of them black—began to voice their concerns about politics. The Women's Suffrage Movement, founded by Mary Ingraham, Georgina Symonette, and Eugenia Lockhart (all black) in the early- to mid-1950s, aimed to obtain the vote for women. With the help of Dr. Doris Johnson, the first Bahamian woman to obtain a doctorate, who mobilized the organization, women succeeded in obtaining the vote in 1961. They voted for the first time in 1962.

Dr. Doris Johnson was the first woman to be a cabinet minister (1968) and the first to be appointed president of the Senate. Women in recent years have made enormous strides in the political arena, especially since 1987, when Janet Bostwick became the first woman to be elected to the House of Assembly. In the 1997 election, there were six women, all black, who were elected to the House of Assembly. In 2000, there were three women cabinet ministers, mainly black, and many black women have excelled in most professions, dominating in education as teachers and administrators, as well as holding top civic service posts.

HAITIAN MIGRATION

A serious problem facing the Bahamas is the massive, mostly illegal, immigration of Haitians. Many earlier Haitian immigrants were assimilated into Bahamian society at the end of the eighteenth century. However, since the 1950s, and increasingly so since the 1970s, as Haiti's economy declined and political oppression increased, Bahamian prosperity lured many Haitian nationals to make their homes in the Bahamas, many illegally. Haitians comprise between 30 to 40 percent of the population. Although Bahamians agree that Haitians work in jobs that Bahamians generally despise performing, Haitians' competition in the retail trade and their use of the health, social welfare, and educational systems has caused Bahamian resentment. There is a definite prejudice, more class oriented than racial, between Bahamians and Haitians. The Haitian retention of African-based beliefs and customs, its music, folklore, and gambling habits, has had some effect on the Bahamas. Paradoxically, many children born of Haitian parents have become Bahamianized to a large extent. Although they usually live traditionally in all-Haitian communities, it seems that some Haitians desire to distance themselves from their Haitian roots and culture. Many have intermarried with Bahamians and are integrating into the society. Some have converted from Roman Catholicism to the more fundamentalist churches (Baptist and Pentecostal).

EDUCATIONAL AND CULTURAL DEVELOPMENTS AND SPORTS

Majority rule and independence stimulated the growth in national and racial pride. Bahamianization of the public service and the private sector, in both Nassau and Freeport and in the Family Islands, followed. In religion, the nonconformist churches, especially the black Baptist and the Pentecostal churches gained in membership, recognition, and prestige.

Since the 1960s, the government has made a concerted effort to improve the educational conditions and provide secondary education for the black majority of the population (previously denied to them) and to provide scholarships for Bahamians studying abroad. Education received more funding and the number of government secondary schools increased dramatically between the late 1960s into the 1990s. By the 1980s there was a core of trained professionals in a variety of fields including education, medicine, law, and accountancy.

Culturally, since 1967, there have been developments in music, dance, festivals, literature, painting, crafts, and architectural preservation, which have helped define a Bahamian identity. The Department of Archives (1971) preserves documentary material and island architectural heritage, as does the newly established Antiquities, Monuments, and Museums Corporation (1998).

There is a growing literary milieu, as Bahamian authors and artists have struggled to establish themselves, and their identity, despite lack of recognition by other Caribbean countries. Many in and out of the region have erroneously seen the Bahamas as an offshoot of the United States and as a tourism Mecca with sun, sand, sea, and sex, and as a society devoid of serious writers.

In theater and the performing arts, Meta Davis Cumberbatch, a Trinidadian/Bahamian, pioneered a national festival of arts and crafts at the Dundas Civic Center and has left an enduring legacy. Her protégés, Clement Bethel, Hubert Farrington, and Winston Saunders, have had an important impact on the music, dance, and drama of the Bahamas. Bethel's students, including Cleophas Adderley, founder and director of the National Youth Choir, have also profoundly influenced music and cultural development in the Bahamas.

Clement Bethel, writer, composer, pianist, and director of culture for many years, collected, transcribed, and also arranged many old Bahamian songs and managed to marry classical and traditional folk music. His folk musical, *Sammy Swain*, probably the largest single body of work containing original folk Bahamian music, melds African/Bahamian folkways through music and dance.

Secular music in the Bahamas, historically called *goombay* music, from the West African word "gumbay" for large drum, relies heavily on the goatskin drum. Modern calypso music is strongly influenced by African traditions. A popular manifestation of this is the rake and scrape band, which has roots in slavery and which used whatever was available: today bands combine the carpenter's saw, goatskin drums, and accordion. Although bands have electronic instruments, they draw heavily on the traditional rake and scrape music. Noted early performers include folk singer Joseph Spence and calypsonian (Blind) Blake Higgs. Ronnie Butler and Eddie Minnis are contemporary musicians who sing of Bahamian customs and problems.

Bahamian theater has been an area of national self-expression. In the 1950s it was dominated by expatriates, but it was steadily Bahamianized and popularized. The first Bahamian opera, *Our Boys*, libretto by Winston Saunders and Philip Burrows and music by Cleophas Adderley, was a nationalistic piece based on an actual incident, the sinking of a ship by Cubans. The final chorus, "Pride in Our Native Land," in breadth, scope, and feeling resembles the Bahamian national anthem.

Drama has been influenced by several authors including Jeanne Thompson, whose Bahamian soap opera "The Fergusons of Farm Road" riveted Bahamians to their radios in the 1960s, and Winston Saunders. Saunders, who is also an actor and a director, wrote *You Can Lead a Horse to Water* (1983), a powerful piece about the black Bahamian family in crisis. Ian Strachan's powerful play *God's Angry Babies* (1997) also portrays a young black Bahamian male's journey toward adult manhood.

The development of dance has generally lagged behind the other performing arts in the Bahamas: it was not until 1992 that Saunders established the National Dance Company, headed by Robert Bain and Shirley Hall Bass.

Some key writers of prose include Dr. Cleveland Eneas Sr., novelists Anthony Dahl, Ian Strachan, Nicolette Bethel, and Patricia Glinton-Meicholas who wrote the satirical *How to Be a True, True Bahamian* (1994). Of the many black poets, the most accomplished are Patrick Rahming, Susan Wallace, Robert Johnson, and Obediah Smith.

Perhaps the most expressive and prolific of all artists and writers in post-independence years have been the painters. Bahamian painting, truly nationalistic, has come from all sectors of the community and shares common themes and inspirations. Out of many, there are four black painters who represent "the Bahamian School." Amos Ferguson (1922–), who uses ordinary house paint and brushes on plywood and cardboard, is comparable to the naive painters of Haiti and is inspired by themes from folklife and the Bible.

Maxwell Taylor (1938–), strongly influenced by Black Power artists in New York, is uncompromising in his commitment to social realism and the portrayal of ordinary, poor and oppressed Bahamians. Antonius Roberts (1958–), a Nassauvian, is deeply influenced by the African-derived Bahamian Junkanoo as are Stanley and Jackson Burnside, contemporary artists.

TRADITIONAL CUSTOMS AND CULTURE

Traditional customs and culture have experienced some weakening, but Bahamian crafts such as boat-building, quilting, straw weaving, and woodcarving, which were exhibited on the Washington National Mall in 1994, show that much has been retained and preserved.

The strong belief in the supernatural forces of Obeah (not very widespread today), the practice of herbal medicine, the musical forms of anthems and rhyming spirituals that were so popular during the sponging era have all survived, but in weakened form.

Death rituals, wakes, and observation of other death-related rites, as well as "Rushin'" meetings, were still common in the 1950s and 1960s, and are still practiced in some communities today. A Rushin' meeting usually takes place in a Baptist (sometimes Pentecostal) church during the singing of anthems and spiritual songs. The congregation dances in a one step forward, one step back movement.

Customary dances, including the "Fire Dance," "Jumping Dance," and "Ring Play" were kept alive, even if by local dancers in local nightclubs in the fifties, for the benefit of the tourists, and in folk operas such as *Sammy Swain*.

JUNKANOO

The largest and most important Bahamian festival (particularly in Nassau) is Junkanoo. Despite the various bans on all public gatherings, especially after the 1942 riot, there was a resurgence of Junkanoo, proving its spirit could not be crushed. It was increasingly touted as a tourist attraction and organized, offering prize money. Perhaps the important change in Bahamian Junkanoo after the 1950s, however, "was its adoption by the government once majority rule was achieved and acceptance by the people as the quintessential expression of the new nationalistic ethos" (Craton & Saunders Vol. II, 486–490).

A festival of West African origins, it was celebrated in some form in the Bahamas from the early nineteenth century when slaves took advantage of the traditional three-day holiday at Christmas to let off steam and to assert their independence. Modern Junkanoo is more sophisticated and more organized by government agencies. Costumes are made primarily from bright colored-paper fringe and there are large fiercely competitive groups vying for first place. Music is essential to the festival: cowbells, horns, whistles, and *goombay* drums (and usually a brass section). However, despite the enormous changes in Junkanoo

Junkanoo circa 1950s. Courtesy of the Department of
Archives.

throughout the years, the roots of the musical tradition remain Bahamian. Previously a black working-class festival, Junkanoo is now universally accepted and
practiced regardless of class and color. The spirit of Junkanoo is truly the soul of
the Bahamian people.

CONCLUSION

The unprecedented growth of tourism and the success of its financial sector
has made the Bahamas one of the wealthier countries in the Caribbean. How-

ever, drug trafficking has become a major recent concern, having also contributed to violent crime; many of those involved are young black males.

While the political elites are black, the economic elites are mainly white, although many blacks have become upwardly mobile. Racial discrimination in the Bahamas is subtle. Some clubs will cater primarily to whites, but public spaces like schools, churches, and workplaces have been desegregated. Socially, blacks and whites are coinciding, and intermarriage is increasing, but still uncommon. Bahamian blacks are more comfortable marrying foreign rather than local whites. And despite the pervasive influence of the United States, psychologically and materially, the African heritage in the Bahamas is still strong, contributing to a black national identity that is especially prominent in its culture.

REFERENCES

Craton, Michael, and Gail Saunders (1998/1992). *Islanders in the stream: A History of the Bahamian People.* Vol. 1 and Vol. 2. Athens: University of Georgia Press, p. 229.

Higman, Barry W. (1984). *Slave Populations of the British Caribbean, 1807–1834.* Baltimore: Johns Hopkins University Press, p. 380.

Hughes, Colin (1981). *Race and Politics in the Bahamas.* St. Lucia: University of Queensland.

Johnson, Howard (1996). *The Bahamas from Slavery to Servitude, 1783–1933.* Gainesville: University Press of Florida, pp. 33–46.

Johnson, Whittington B. (2000). *Race Relations in the Bahamas, 1784–1834.* Fayetteville: University of Arkansas Press.

Saunders, Gail (1985). *Slavery in the Bahamas, 1648–1838.* Nassau Bahamas: Nassau, Guardian, pp. 160–162, 173.

——— (1994). *Bahamian Society after Emancipation.* Kingston, Jamaica: Ian Randle Publishers.

——— (1997). "The Peoples and Cultures of the Bahamas." Washington, D.C. Smithsonian Folkway Records Notes for CD. *The Bahamas: Island of Song,* pp. 1–10.

3

Barbados

Pedro L.V. Welch

The island of Barbados is located southward of the Greater Antilles, to the east of the Caribbean chain. It has a total surface area of 166 square miles and over 90 percent of its 270,000 people are of African descent. Barbados was a pioneer colony in the development of the plantation system in the Caribbean region, developing early as a slave society. A historian aptly sums it up: "Here indeed is the 'sugar revolution.' But where else? No other English or French island was so early conquered by sugar, and in few was the victory so swift or complete. Nowhere was a colony so peopled *before* sugar; and no other island disposed of so many landless unemployed *after* sugar. Part of the historical importance of Barbados is to force us to ask why other colonies were so different" (Davies 1974, 180).

The experiences of the white population in managing a slave society and in institutionalizing their hold on economic and political power established the colony as an exporter of precedent in the development of slave systems elsewhere in the Caribbean and North America. The 1661 Barbadian slave code was applied "almost clause by clause" to Jamaica in 1684, and to Antigua in 1702. "Barbados, therefore, showed the rest of the English Caribbean not only how to manage profitable sugar plantations, but also how to legally control their slaves" (Beckles 1990, 31). Barbados' socioeconomic development offers an extraordinary window to greater understanding of the colonial experience of other territories in the region.

SETTLEMENT AND EARLY DEVELOPMENT

The island of Barbados was mentioned in Spanish documents of 1511 and 1518. It had been settled by Amerindians as early as A.D. 350 but this population

Modernized "slave hut." Many Barbadians have modernized the old slave huts, which is, perhaps, a symbol of the transition from slavery to freedom. Courtesy of Pedro L.V. Welch.

appeared to have migrated by the time English settlers landed on the island in 1627. The British settlers were acting on behalf of a London syndicate, headed by a prominent mercantile family, the Courteens.[1] Its easternmost location, far from Hispanic settlement, and to the south of the routes taken by Spanish convoys, probably explains why the colony was not settled by the Spanish.

In the early years of settlement, a few Amerindian laborers were imported to assist with the planting of tobacco, cotton, and tropical subsistence crops. However, the bulk of the labor in this period was provided by white indentured servants, drawn primarily from Ireland, Scotland, and England where the agro-industrial revolution was rapidly developing (Beckles 1987, 34–35). Between 1627 and 1654, the white population had grown to over 30,000 persons and the prosperity of the island had become evident enough for one writer to comment that it was "one of the Richest Spotes of ground in the world" (Whistler 1959, in Connell, 145).

More astounding was the pace of development over the next thirty years, as sugar created a significant social and economic transformation. The sugar industry, established in the 1640s, consolidated the plantation system and its slave labor base, altering the demographic complexion of the island. By the mid-1650s, the costs of indentured servants had risen relative to the reduced costs of slaves, and the resulting shift to a predominantly African labor base would have profound implications for the socioeconomic and political future of the colony. In this period, the African slave component increased until it was twice that of the indentured servants (see Connell; Poyer, 1–21; Dunn; and Sheridan, 124–147).

By the 1680s, Barbados occupied the premier place, in terms of population size and density, in the English Caribbean. In 1680, there were over 23,000 whites and 38,000 slaves (Dunn 1973, 3–30). The white population had declined in part because they were forced to leave by the growing plantation control over land resources. Some whites were attracted by the prospects offered in other English Caribbean colonies and North America. However, it was the profits accruing from the sugar industry that marked the accomplishments of the island elite and underlay the colony's status as the most important "jewel in [His] Majesty's Crown" (Sheridan 1974, 124). The importance of Barbados in the English transatlantic trading system and in the region was undeniable.

Barbados' importance in the English New World trading system can be gleaned from its major port at Bridgetown, whose population was greater than or matched that of Kingston, Jamaica, Boston, Philadelphia, and New York until the 1770s. Travelers who visited the island in the late seventeenth and eighteenth centuries acknowledged Bridgetown as a metropolis of the Caribbean.

In the late seventeenth century Bridgetown occupied the premier place in English trade with the Caribbean colonies. Statistics show that the export trade of Bridgetown accounted for 60 percent of the value of English exports to the British Caribbean in 1697. In that same year, Barbados exported goods to England valued at some £196,532. Only Virginia and Maryland exceeded Barbados' trade with an export trade valued at £227,759 (Galenson 1980, 5, 6). Even though Bridgetown's percentage share declined in the period up to 1705, its share of British exports to the Caribbean averaged over 40 percent. The percentage of Caribbean exports to England was similar, with a 54 percent share in 1697 and an average of 45 percent in the period up to 1705.

Leaving aside trade and economic activity, the major defining element of Barbadian society from 1650 to the 1830s was the impact of the plantation system and slavery. Plantation slavery permeated every aspect of the society, from its laws to its social norms. The system operated on a basic premise: absolute social distinctions between its two groups, slave owners and slaves. On the rural plantation, rigorous supervision was applied to the slaves' lives, creating a division of labor that classified even children and infants into work gangs. The organization of labor, its structure and discipline, was designed to involve slaves in their own subordination by the creation of a class of slave supervisors (drivers, or rangers, who were black), but all aspects of the plantation system were fashioned to reinforce a racial divide with whites at the apex of the social pyramid.

As slave owners became more confident over time, modifications in the nature of power relationships occurred. Slaves who fit in with the masters' social ideals gained concessions, and ameliorative mechanisms were utilized to provide an illusion of tractability in the slave system, such as instituting markets and allowing slave festivals (Beckles 1988, 6–8). The slave owners' objective was to ensure smooth production and efficient labor control. However, the core social division between slaves and owners was never in question.

The emergence of a free colored population was a major feature of Barbados' formative years. As whites cohabited with slaves, the offspring resulting from such unions posed a dilemma to the racial-social divide between the enslavers and the enslaved. Often, white fathers manumitted (set free) African lovers and settled property on them. In some cases, sons and daughters were manumitted, sometimes with grants of cash and property. Some of these free coloreds acquired property holdings that rivaled the value of those held by some whites, adding layers to the social, cultural, and economic matrix that was beginning to define Barbadian society.

SLAVE SOCIETY AND THE ECONOMY, 1750–1816

By the late eighteenth century, the Barbadian economy and society had coalesced into features that would predominate up to the 1830s. The economy was dependent on the export of sugar and its by-products. The consolidation of the plantation system had led to further entrenchment of a European elite as masters of the sociopolitical structures that had emerged. The planters with the largest holdings and the big merchants held political sway to the extent that, over time, they possessed enough control over the public purse to challenge the political superintendence of the governors. Certainly, "by the end of the eighteenth century they (whites) were confident in the quality of Barbadian life" (Beckles 1990, 43).

If life for the white elite revolved around activities that mirrored their "superior" status, there were other whites referred to variously as "red legs," "ecky beckies," and "poor whites" for whom life was a daily struggle for survival. True, their European ancestry gave them privileges denied the slaves and free coloreds. However, many found themselves dependent on the latter for handouts.

Despite the misery of certain poor whites, their condition paled in comparison to the treatment of Afro-Barbadian slaves: "the field people on sugar plantations, are more treated like beasts of burden than like human creatures ... and suffer every hardship which can be supposed to attend oppressive toil, coarse and scanty fare, bad lodging, want of covering in the wet season, and a degree of feverity which frequently borders on, and too often amounts to, inhumanity" (Dickson 1970, 6). After being overworked and mistreated for years or decades, the "unproductive" slaves were often discarded: "In Barbados, I am sorry to say, there are some owners, who when their slaves become incapable of labor, from age, ill usage, or disease, especially leprosy; inhumanly expose them to every extreme of wretchedness ... they are often seen in the streets, in the very last stages of human misery, naked, famished, diseased, and forlorn ... " (Dickson 1970, 34).

In Barbados, the free colored population was heavily concentrated in Bridgetown, thus constituting a large group in a highly visible area of urban society. By 1800, more than 50 percent of this group lived there; the statistics were quite different for other Caribbean societies, however. For example, in St. Domingue (Haiti), only about 15 percent of the free colored population lived in towns by 1791. In 1829 the free colored presence in Bridgetown was more than 60 percent.

These statistics take on even more significance since they do not include free coloreds resident in the other urban seaport towns at Oistins and Speights (after 1840, Speightstown). The high visibility of free coloreds in Bridgetown drew many comments from visitors in the eighteenth and nineteenth centuries.

Free coloreds were engaged in a wide range of activities: as merchants, haberdashers, tavern- and innkeepers, hucksters, tailors, shoemakers, jewelers, artisans. They were excluded, however, from the civil and political bureaucracy and from the social gatherings of the white elite. Despite this limitation, the urban record documents a view of the freedman and freedwoman that reveals they loomed large in a slave society that, paradoxically, was predicated on ensuring his or her invisibility.

Women such as Mary Bellah Green, Betsy Lemon, Hannah Lewis, Sussanah Ostrehan, and Rachael Pringle Polgreen and men such as Joseph Rachel and London Bourne had large property holdings in the town. More importantly, some of these individuals engaged in pro-emancipationist activity, while at the same time conforming to the social norms imposed by whites. This duality epitomizes the reality of the urban experience: on the one hand, the harsh reality of a slave master-imposed social order; on the other, an increasing tension that derived from the interaction of a free African population with former masters/mistresses, and with slaves. The experiences of these free coloreds provide great insight into the dynamics of slave society.

Free coloreds operated in a social environment that subordinated their "freedom" to the dictates of the plantation economy. Moreover, these restrictions were compounded by the factor of racial inferiority. Free coloreds were forced into what were considered economically unattractive and socially undesirable areas by white males and some white females. This explains why the "hotel" and tavern services in urban Barbados by the late eighteenth century were almost exclusively in the hands of free coloreds, many who were women.

Typically, most of the businesses owned by free coloreds were in small shopkeeping, huckstering, and tavern or "hotel" keeping. With the operation of lodging houses, the particular service orientation implied a "staff" that was predominantly female. Paradoxically, however, the very forces that deprived them of the respectability enjoyed by their white counterparts also opened up avenues for wealth. Visitors to Barbados between the 1790s and 1820s commented that "white women were valued for domestic formality and respectability [and] "colored" women for exciting socio-sexual companionship" (Beckles 1992, 1–2). Free colored women quickly recognized the advantages that this offered and utilized this to their financial benefit. In several cases, free colored women used their relationships with rich whites to access the local capital market and expand their property holdings.

Two examples of the free colored woman's success in accessing capital markets are provided by Frances Collier and Sara Massiah, who in 1801, with the help of white benefactors, borrowed £2,464 and £1,000, respectively, for the purchase of land and buildings to establish taverns. These women triumphed over the forces that sought their perpetual subjugation, proof that they were mastering the economic and social parameters of their existence.

Their success and display of material wealth aroused the jealousy of some whites. While whites did not always attempt to restrict their social inferiors from owning property, they could and did harass the colored population in various ways such as forfeiting property on default of payment for minor debts. In some cases, they questioned the "freed" person's manumission status or the legitimacy of the property holding.

Like their female counterparts, some free colored men managed to outshine their white competitors. Both Joseph Rachel and London Bourne acquired enough property to become merchants. Moreover, they often loaned money to whites who were down on their luck. None of these successes, however, could remove the taint of racial inferiority from the free coloreds, male or female.

The success of their free colored kin could hardly fail to impress itself on the slave population. By 1780, the slave population had reached about 82,000 or 80 percent of the total population. This population share and size remained fairly constant into the first half of the nineteenth century. By the latter period, the population was largely Creole as success in slave breeding offset earlier population declines due to an excess of deaths over births. The reality of life for the slave population was mixed. In some cases, enslavers understood the value of caring for their plantation "stock." In other cases, slaves were entirely subject to the whims and fancies of their owners. Whether slaves were attached to urban or rural holdings also impacted on their quality of life.

Slaves who were fortunate enough to live in the houses of the well-to-do were probably well protected from the elements. Personal attendants and valets slept, for the most part, in the bedchambers of their mistresses or masters. There is little information on whether urban slaves slept on beds or on the floor, but their conditions were likely to have been superior to those of the typical field slave.

Those slaves who belonged to less prosperous households or engaged in the self-hire system were housed in less comfortable surroundings. In general, owners rented huts on behalf of the hired-out slave. At times, a slave might be given a special allowance out of the sums realized from his hire; in which case, he was responsible for his own accommodations (Higman 1995, 246, 255–256). Since the property rights of slaves were not recognized under the law, slaves who rented huts on their own had to find a white patron, whose name would appear in the parochial rate books, followed by the name of the slave(s). In other circumstances, the owner, lessee, or the slave would erect huts on lands owned by town residents.

As for food, visitors' reports indicate that the slaves of the poor were likely to be underfed and undernourished. Many urban enslavers only owned the land their residences were on and could not, therefore, supplement their slaves' meager fare.

Thus, in times of famine and drought, urban slaves, denied access to provision grounds, were at a disadvantage compared with their rural counterparts. Yet, there was wide variation in the conditions under which rural or urban slaves operated.

Slave recreational activity undoubtedly contributed to the emergence of Creole society in Barbados. Three visitors to the island record fascinating scenes of slaves at play. One visitor in particular was struck by a music that might permit a spectator with "only a slight aid from fancy," to imagine himself transported "to the savage wilds of Africa." Here are his words: "They assemble in crowds, upon the open green, or in any square or corner of the town, and forming a ring in the centre of the throng, dance to their beloved music, and the singing of their favorite African yell. Both music and dance are of a savage nature" (Pinckard 1806, 264–265).

He describes instruments as well: a "species of drum, a kind of rattle, and their ever-delighting Banjar (Banjo)." This description suggests a victory over the authorities' attempts to limit African musical expression. Legislation passed in 1688 limited the movement of slaves on Saturday nights, Sundays, and other holidays. It also prohibited their "Using, or Keeping of Drums, Horns or other Loud instruments" (Hall 1764, 112–118). Whatever the intent of the law, Pinckard's slave performers were expressing their African heritage within full view of a white man.

Another aspect of the slaves' recreational activities was storytelling. In his ignorance of an African storytelling tradition, Bayley dismisses the "nancy story" as "nothing more or less than a tale of ghosts and goblins, which pass with the negroes by the appellation of Jumbees" (Bayley 1833, 76, 77). The "nancy story" was no doubt a survival of the African folk hero/trickster "Ananse" (or Anancy). In Jamaica some slaves identified the Anancy character with a cruel master, but not likely so in Barbados. More plausible is that the adaptation and retention of the Anancy figure represents the triumph of the African spirit in the face of brutal attempts to expunge it, an Afro-Barbadian psychological victory in the constant battle for the mind and personality of the slave.

Without idealizing the slave personality, these scenes outline part of a wide spectrum of the slaves' life without slighting the reality of exploitation and racism that kept them tied as "property" to their enslavers. That slaves did not accept many strictures imposed by whites is testimony to their resilient spirits.

1816–1916: ABOLITION AND ADJUSTMENT

Barbados was socially stable up to 1816. Slaves had rebelled several times before then. However, each rebellion had been met with such savagery that slaves soon saw the futility of open confrontation. More often they chose accommodationist responses, opting for violent resistance when it could succeed. The 1816 rebellion shocked planters, who had been lulled into a false sense of security by the apparent docility of the slaves. The "Bussa rebellion," named after its principal leader, flared up as part of an ongoing discussion on abolition, a central preoccupation in Britain and the rest of the Caribbean. Indeed, an official report on the rebellion suggested that slaves had responded to rumors that British authorities had granted their freedom, but that planters in the Caribbean were holding up the process (Beckles 1998, 22–24).

The abolitionist movement in Britain had gained momentum in this period. The British slave trade was abolished in 1807, and thereafter, the British political directorate led an international effort to end the slave trade of other nations. As the abolitionists gained strength in their parliamentary fight, the emphasis shifted toward the abolition of slavery itself. The first step in this new battle was the passage, in 1815, of the Registry Bill.

The bill required the registration of slaves as a way of identifying and hopefully curtailing the high mortality that accompanied the expansion of slavery in the region. The discussion of the bill prompted Barbadian slaves to misinterpret its terms, leading to the 1816 rebellion, also known as the Easter Rebellion. Bussa, the reputed slave leader of the 1816 rebellion, represents, for Barbadians of African descent, the personification of a spirit of resistance, exploding the myth that Barbadian slaves were naturally docile, fitting the "Quashie" stereotype of the slave who lived in search of his master's/mistress's "pat on the back" (a dissimulating cheerfulness and strategy for survival that was servile).

There has been considerable debate on Bussa's origins, whether he was African born or a Creole from Barbados. The debate continued when Bussa was being considered as one of ten national heroes of Barbados. Further controversy ensued over the naming of a statue to commemorate the emancipation of the slaves. The sculptor had named the statue *Emancipation*. However, local pan-Africanists were furious, and rejected this as an amorphous denial of the African contribution to the abolition of slavery. They promptly renamed the statue *The Bussa Statue*, to widespread popular approval. Now even official pronouncements identify it as *The Bussa Statue*.

The next step toward abolition involved the 1823 recommendations for the amelioration of slavery by Lord Bathurst, the secretary of state for the colonies. These recommendations excited negative comment by white planters who viewed them as the death knell of their authority. The discussion made its way into the slave ranks and was marked by agitation, reports of planned rebellions, and the blaming of missionary activity by whites for inciting slaves. If matters were not resolved quickly, the enslaved would take matters into their own hands. Free coloreds, too, were petitioning the British authorities for the granting of full civil rights. Abolition was declared for all British Caribbean colonies in 1834.

Abolition of slavery did not end discrimination. Ex-slaves found themselves hamstrung by legislation that left them out of the formal political process. Voting rights were tied to the value of property holdings, and few ex-slaves earned enough or owned enough to enter the political race as candidates or to qualify as voters. Moreover, plantations owned over 84 percent of the arable land, leaving laborers limited access to owning property. The plantation owners used this advantage and their control of the legislative process to pass the Masters and

Servants Act in 1840, which remained in force until 1937. The act made it a crime for laborers to leave plantation employment in search of improved conditions.

Because of the problems that black workers faced, they explored all possible options. One was migration to other Caribbean territories, and to North and Central America. Thousands of Barbadians migrated to Panama to work on the Panama Canal and remitted sums of money to those left behind. In some cases, this money was used to buy land from plantations forced out of business by falling sugar prices.

By the early twentieth century, educational opportunities increased and living standards improved. With the outbreak of World War I, several Barbadians found additional opportunities and expanded their intellectual horizons in Europe. By the end of the war, there was a new spirit of activism with leaders such as Clennel Wickham (1895–1938) and Marcus Garvey, who began confronting white privilege. Garvey was not a Barbadian but his message of pride in the African heritage of Caribbean peoples had universal appeal. Wickham was editor of a local newspaper, the *Barbados Herald*, and used its pages to launch a blistering attack on the inequitable distribution of political and economic power in the island. Local and metropolitan officials alike were subject to the flogging of his pen.

SELF-ACTUALIZATION TO INDEPENDENCE, 1916–1966

From 1918 to the 1930s Barbadian workers were still disenfranchised and marginalized. Wages had barely increased since the 1840s, averaging about 30 cents per day for males by the 1930s. At that time, a pound of cheese cost 54 cents and rent could reach 4 cents per day for some small properties: these were desperation wages. Population went from 156,000 in 1921 to over 189,000 by 1937. With a tiny land area of 166 square miles, it is not surprising that there was high unemployment and underemployment. The worldwide depression further deepened the economic woes of the masses and social unrest exploded into the 1937 riots that left 14 strikers dead and 47 wounded.

After the riots, the Moyne Commission was sent to investigate the social and economic problems facing the island. It found that low wages, poor living standards, and lack of adequate housing, education, and nutrition were largely to blame. It also found that an absence of progressive legislation and labor organization alienated the black masses from the political process. Its recommendations prompted social reform initiatives. Indeed, the workers' agitation resulted in the extension of the franchise, the legalization of trade unions, and the improvement of workplace conditions.

By 1946, political reforms had reached their apogee with the appointment of the first black government in Barbados. Headed by Grantley Adams (1898–1971), the path of reform continued and expanded. Adams's power base rested on the support of the Barbados Workers' Union (BWU), of which he was a founder-member. The political power of the white planter-merchant establishment had been broken and, thereafter, white aspirants only entered the electoral race in alliance with mass-based political parties. However, the white commercial elite has continued to hold on to economic power.

In 1958, Adams became the prime minister of the short-lived British West Indies Federation. However, there were spirited challenges to Adam's leadership both at home and abroad led by a dynamic young lawyer, Errol Barrow (1920–1987), of the opposition Democratic Labour Party (DLP). The federation broke up and Adams was defeated at the polls, both in 1961. The future belonged to Barrow, who led the island to independence in 1966, and his DLP.

Independence highlighted the problems of a small-island developing state, shorn of its colonial protections. Barrow's foreign policy stated the island would be "friends of all, satellites of none" (Hanniff 1987, 92). Rhetoric aside, Barbadian pragmatism recognized the geopolitics of a region with a powerful northern neighbor, the United States. The island could express solidarity and support for the Cuban Revolution under Castro and proclaim sympathy for the non-aligned movement, but the political directorate knew how to tone down its rhetoric, deferring to United States interests. The non-aligned movement grouped together Third World countries who chose not to favor either the United States or the USSR during the Cold War.

Exposure to North American culture via television, radio, tourism, and migration meant that there would be a greater affinity over time with the United States than with Britain. Thus, music and other cultural manifestations of Barbadian life reflect a mixture of Caribbean, European, African, and North American influences, with the latter influence beginning to predominate. The success of the decision-makers in keeping the economy afloat during this period is testimony to the development of considerable negotiating skills and to a careful steering of national policy. Economically, the post-independence government tried to diversify the economy, mirroring the strategy of Puerto Rico in the late 1940s to early 1950s, emphasizing import substitution. In sum, this has been the basis for sustainable development from 1966 to the present.

FROM INDEPENDENCE TO THE PRESENT: YEARS OF CONSOLIDATION

By the mid-1970s, disaffection with Barrow shifted voter alliances and in 1976 the Barbados Labour Party (BLP) won the elections under the leadership of J.M.G.M (Tom) Adams, son of the first premier, now Sir Grantley Adams. The BLP followed similar economic policies as their predecessors, but emphasized economic diversification by developing an offshore financial sector, to be handled by a well-educated workforce. (Literacy in Barbados is about 98 percent). These BLP programs came to an abrupt halt with the untimely death of Adams. Subsequent elections brought Errol Barrow and the DLP to govern again.

The period between independence and the present has been a period of consolidation and growth. Culturally, there has been a reassertion of African contributions to Barbadian life. The impact of the Black Power revolution of the early 1960s, and the emergence of the Rastafarian movement as an alternative to Eurocentric religions, is visible in local artisans' work, as well as in entertainment. While centuries of European domination are reflected in the traditional Anglican church service or the occasional classical music performance, reggae and calypso music are the popular idioms of musical choice. Indeed, the tension between the old European imposed order and the newer modes is the subject of a vigorous debate, in part carried out by a new breed of historians at the University of the West Indies at Cave Hill, Barbados.

Economically, the island, like other small-island developing states, has been battered by the sweeping changes of the international market. Globalization and trade liberalization are everyday words in the national debate. During the period 1987–1991, a series of financial crises threatened to derail economic progress. After the death of Barrow (1987), the DLP under Erskine Sandiford attempted to halt the decline of the Barbadian economy by turning to the International Monetary Fund. However, thousands of public employees were fired and others faced 8 percent wage cuts, leading to widespread disaffection. Barbados' economy recovered and was highly praised by international financial institutions. However, the DLP was voted out and Owen Arthur (BLP) has ruled since 1994.

Economic growth has continued under the BLP and a series of imaginative poverty alleviation programs have captured the public imagination. Nevertheless, a social structure bequeathed by centuries of slavery has left big business in the hands of a white commercial elite, although blacks hold political power. Both major parties claim that the next major political initiative is the "economic enfranchisement" of the black masses by expanding access to local finance for business development.

Although economic matters are not always foremost in the Barbadian mindset, they are actively reacting to changes. While fully aware of the lingering wounds of the colonial past, Barbadians have fashioned a creative Creole lifestyle capable of handling the strains of modernity, as well as celebrating life. "Crop Over," which lets loose thousands of revelers, is a national festival with historic origins in the slave era, and is a re-creation of a party held on the plantations to celebrate the harvesting of the sugar crop. A moment of emotional and social release for slaves, it has been resurrected as Barbados's indigenous carnival.

"Crop Over" sponsors the local calypso competition. Calypsonians or "Kaisomen" vie with each other in composing songs that range from social commentary to raunchy innuendo. In true calypsonian tradition the singer-composers adopt colorful names such as "Red Plastic Bag," "Invader," "Serenader," and "The Mighty Gabby," one of the Caribbean's finest calypsonians. Some songs penned by these bards have attained international recognition, rivaling those from Trinidad, calypso's birthplace. The two islands have a healthy calypso rivalry that gives connoisseurs much room for discussing each island's musical merits.

More recently, there has also been a culinary revolution of sorts. While European and North American fare dominates in the local hotels, local foods such as "cou cou and flying fish," "black pudding and souse," and "sea egg" have become a badge of Barbadian identity. "Cou cou" is made of maize flour and okra. It is generally served with a flying fish sauce and is considered to be the quintessential Barbadian dish. Its name supposedly derives from a West African dish, "fou fou." The popularity of these dishes reflects an assertion of the Barbadian persona.

The National Cultural Foundation (NCF) has helped foster the arts. Lectures by noted Barbadian novelist George Lamming (1927–), author of *In the Castle of my Skin*, are frequent. Austin (Tom) Clarke (1934–) and his autobiography *Growing Up Stupid Under the Union Jack* is required reading at many universities. Together with the renowned poet, historian, and critic Edward (Kamau) Brathwaite (1930–) and Frank Collymore (1893–1980), the poet and founder and director of *BIM* magazine for more than thirty years, they have given Barbados international literary acclaim.

Faced with the vulnerabilities of living in a global market, Barbados has spoken loudly through its human talent, be it literary, musical, intellectual, or physical. As for the latter, no other country has produced so many world-class cricketers, such as Gary Sobers, Frank Worrell, Everton Weekes, and Clyde Walcott. Despite North American and European influence, Barbados has developed its own ethos: rich, layered, creolized, truly Barbadian in all its flavors.

NOTE

1. For details on the early history of Barbados, see Connell; Dunn; Poyer (pp. 1–21); Sheridan (pp. 124–147); and F.C. Innes, (1970) "The Pre-Sugar Era of Europe in an Settlement Barbados," *Journal of Caribbean History* 1: pp. 1–22.

REFERENCES

Bayley, F.W. (1833), *Four Years Residence in the West Indies*. London: William Kidd Publishers.

Beckles, Hilary McD (1985). "Plantation Production and White Photo-Slavery." *The Americas*, Vol. 41, No. 3, pp. 21–45.

———(1987). *Black Rebellion in Barbados*. Bridgetown, Barbados: Carib Research and Publications.

———(1988). *Afro-Caribbean Women and Resistance to Slavery in Barbados*. London: Karnak House.

———(1990). *A History of Barbados: From Amerindian Settlement to Nation State*. London: Cambridge University Press.

———(1992). "White Women and Slavery in the Caribbean." *Seminar Paper No. 2*, University of the West Indies, Cave Hill, Barbados, pp. 1–18.

———(1998). *Rewriting History: Bussa*. Bridgetown, Barbados: University of the West Indies and Barbados Museum and Historical Society.

Connell, Neville (1959). *A Short History of Barbados*. Bridgetown: The Barbados Museum and Historical Society.

Davies, K.G. (1974). *The North Atlantic World in the Seventeenth Century*. Minneapolis: University of Minnesota Press.

Dickson, William (1970/1789). *Letters on Slavery*. Westport, CT: Negro Universities Press.

Dunn, Richard (1973). *Sugar and Slaves*. London: W.W. Norton and Company.

Galenson, David W. (1980). *Traders, Planters and Slaves*. London: Cambridge University Press.

Hall, Richard (1764). *Acts Passed in the Island of Barbados from 1643–1762.* "An Act for the Better Governing of Slaves. Act. No. 82," London.

Hanniff, Yusuf. (1987). *Speeches by Errol Barrow*. London: Hansib Publishing Ltd.

Higman, B.W. (1995). *Slave Populations of the British Caribbean, 1807–1834*. Kingston, Jamaica: Press University of the West Indies.

Hoyos, F.A. (1984). *Barbados: A History from Amerindians to Independence*. London: Macmillan Publishers.

Pinckard, George (1806). *Notes on the West Indies: written during the expedition under the command of the late General Sir Ralph Abercromby; including observations on the island of Barbados. . . .* London: Longman, Hurst, Rees and Orme.

Poyer, John (1971/1808). *The History of Barbados*. London: Frank Cass and Co.

Sheridan, Richard (1974). *Sugar and Slavery*. London: Caribbean Universities Press.

Welch, Pedro L.V., and Richard Goodridge (2000). *"Red" and Black Over White: Free Coloured Women in Pre-Emancipation Barbados*. Bridgetown, Barbados: Carib Research and Publications.

Whistler, Henry. "Journal of a West India Expedition." Quoted in Connell, *A Short History of Barbados*, p. 145.

4

The Cayman Islands

Pedro L.V. Welch

EARLY HISTORY: 1503–1733

The Cayman Islands is a name given to a grouping of three small islands, Grand Cayman, Cayman Brac, and Little Cayman, located in the northern Caribbean. The two smaller islands are 80 miles northeast of Grand Cayman. With a current population of 37,000, the islands are located roughly 150 miles to the south of Cuba, and about 180 miles west of Jamaica. Christopher Columbus came across them in 1503, during his last voyage to the New World. First named Las Tortugas because the local beaches were inhabited by a species of marine turtles, the islands underwent several name changes. Eventually they were known as the *Caymanas*, because of the presence of alligators.

The Carib name of *Caymana* (meaning "crocodiles" or "alligators") has persisted in identifying this group of islands, but unlike other neighboring territories, the evidence for an Amerindian presence is particularly sparse. There is no indication that Columbus met any aboriginal inhabitants there, as was the case with Cuba, Hispaniola, and Jamaica, its nearest Caribbean neighbors. Apparently, the Amerindians treated the islands merely as a stopover on migratory treks to the larger, more endowed islands.

After initial European contact, the Caymans were left largely to themselves. The Spanish were engrossed in extracting what minerals and wealth they could find on the mainland of South and Central America. An occasional Spanish vessel stopped to take on a fresh water supply. Toward the end of the sixteenth century, the first English contact was made and, thereafter, the islands became more widely known as a place where boats could be revictualed with turtle meat. As the challenge to Spanish imperial monopoly grew bolder, others, too, began to frequent the island.

The occasional capture of a Spanish treasure ship on its way home from the "Indie" soon attracted the attention of a motley crowd of buccaneers, pirates, and freebooters. By 1660, the English had established themselves in Jamaica and treated the Caymans as natural appendages of the larger territory. However, apart from small settlements on Grand Cayman and Cayman Brac, most of the Cayman territory was left untouched. It was ideal for pirates:

Here there was fresh water, fish, turtle and fowl in plenty; here, too, were supplies of hard woods suitable for ship repairs. Conveniently hidden, because they were so few feet above sea level, the islands made excellent bases for buccaneer on the shipping of the main trade routes between Central America, Cuba, Jamaica and Florida. Here, quite naturally, they secreted their plundered gold and silver to make the Caymans treasure Islands. (Williams 1970, 13)

By the 1730s the scourge of the buccaneers had been largely tamed and set-tlement of Cayman Brac and Little Cayman joined that of Grand Cayman. Like other Caribbean territories of this period, the islands, too, witnessed the entry of African slaves. Slave holdings were small and most slaves were engaged in small-scale agriculture or in forestry. Some of the white population was drawn to the islands by the opportunities for a prosperous trade with Jamaica (Hannerz 1974, 24). In addition, there were some small estates engaged in cotton, cof-fee, and sugar cane cultivation as well as in the raising of livestock. "Like their Jamaican counterparts, these settlers were slave owners, and the Cayman Islands thus began as a slave society. Compared to the large plantations, however, they had only small numbers of slaves" (Hannerz 1974, 24).

CONSOLIDATION OF A SOCIETY, 1734–1834

While the first decade of settlements included some agricultural exploitation, much of the economic activity of the Cayman Islands revolved around the sea. There developed in the island communities a cadre of skilled sailors, which con-tinues to identify this island community.

The first land grants by the English Crown were made in the Caymans in 1734, and holdings were quickly disbursed, up to a thousand acres, granted to families named Campbell, Middleton, Bodden, Spofforth, Foster, and Cryymble. These are familiar names to most Caymanians, some of which live on in the descendants of the original settlers. By 1802, the population consisted of 930 persons, with 550 slaves. Among the 380 free persons were a number of free col-ored and free blacks. One historian mentions a location known as Boatswain's Bay, where "the majority ... were free people of color such as Henry Auguston, and Baret Ebanks" (Williams 1970, 35).

This illustrates one aspect of Caymanian society that will become prominent later: due to a relatively large ratio of Africans to whites and a relative shortage of white females, miscegenation was widespread. Moreover, because of the close physical proximity of master/mistress and enslaved, unlike the situation in plantation societies like Barbados, where the plantation Great Houses were located some distance away from slave villages, there was greater social interaction between enslaver and enslaved. This has led some to observe that slavery in the Cayman Islands was milder and more liberal than in other Caribbean countries.

The dynamics of slavery in the Cayman Islands differed in many ways from the countries in the region. At the time of emancipation in 1834, the maximum number of slaves, including Little Cayman was 985 and the estimated population was 2000 resulting in a ratio of about one non-slave to one slave. . . . This ratio makes the Caymans very unusual when compared with the major plantations in Jamaica and other Caribbean Islands where the ratio was about 10:1. From the information uncovered to date . . . there was less of a distinction between slaves and slave owners in the Cayman Islands. (Carlesso 2001)

Despite these observations, there are signs to the contrary, such as the case of William Eden, a slave owner who migrated from Jamaica and built a plantation house on a coastal site of Grand Cayman with many slaves under his control. There are other cases as well. Besides, a lower black to white ratio doesn't necessarily make slavery less harsh, just different.

On the one hand, there was the reality of a distinctive non-plantation slave culture. On the other, plantation slavery did impact on the islands' physical infrastructure and society.

Apart from sugar, life in the Cayman Islands during the period 1734–1834 also reflected the influence of a maritime economy. There was a brisk trade with Jamaica in island staples such as "turtle tack" and Sea Island cotton, as well as small-scale trade in mahogany. More than just maritime activity took place, though; the islands developed an economic mix based on subsistence agriculture and fishing. In addition, the Cayman islanders became quite adept in building small craft, which were employed in intra-Caribbean trade and in fishing.

While the islanders were concentrating on extracting exploitable resources, whether marine or land based, life also focused on issues of settlement and governance. The main settlement in the period up to the 1830s was on Grand Cayman. In 1833, Cayman Brac and Little Cayman received the first migrations of a more permanent settlement. Also in 1833, new legislative arrangements were enacted that placed the Caymans more firmly within Jamaican and British colonial governance.

Early in the settlement of the Caymans, there was a natural connection with the colonial authority in Jamaica. Indeed, in the frequent conflicts and complaints that arose over questions of jurisdiction, particularly over naval matters, appeals were made to the governor at Spanish Town (Jamaica). During the 1770s, for example, some Amerindians were kidnapped from the Mosquito Coast of Central America and sold as slaves in the Caymans. Amerindian chiefs petitioned the governor for the freedom of their people. Their request was granted, but the furor surrounding the matter led to an intense discussion on the nature of the relationship between the two colonial units, Jamaica, and the Caymans. The governor discussed the matter with the chief justice and also with the attorney general who advised submitting a memorandum to the colonial authorities in Britain recommending that the Caymans "should be expressly declared a dependency of Jamaica and not left for the future to uncertain conjectures and experiments" (Williams 1970, 25).

There was no official response to this suggestion, but it was understood that the Caymans came under Jamaica's immediate supervision. In this context, therefore, most civil duties were carried out by local magistrates who also performed marriages, christenings, and burials. Those who wished a more certified Christian ceremonial could always travel to Jamaica. Most Caymanians were related by marriage, a fact described as "a great cousinage of Boddens, Coes, Ebanks, Watlers, Fosters, and Edens" (Williams 1970, 33). This fact led the magistrates to encourage the transfer of serious civil and criminal cases to Jamaica, where they felt a more impartial justice might be obtained. Reform was not long in coming. In 1832, a legislative assembly was installed consisting of eight magistrates, nominated by the governor in Jamaica, and a number of representatives styled as vestrymen who were elected by adult male suffrage, a political feature that was in advance of its practice in other Caribbean islands. Thus, a formal statutory authority was established for the first time on the Caymans and closer Jamaican supervision was facilitated.

If "constitutional" reform characterized the period 1832–1833, the single most important event of the 1830s was the abolition of slavery. The single largest owner of slaves was Mary Bodden who possessed forty-five slaves or 5 percent of the island total. Legal uncertainties delayed the proclamation of abolition in the Caymans until 1835, almost a year after it went into effect in the other English-speaking Caribbean territories; but the apprenticeship period mandated under the Abolition Act of the British Parliament ended in 1837, a year before it ended in other British colonies. The Cayman Islands, therefore, have the distinction of being the earliest, after Haiti and Antigua, to legally abolish the enslavement of Africans in the Caribbean.

Former slave owners did not receive full compensation for loss of their slave property because of their failure to observe a legal technicality; thus, they faced a post-emancipation future without control over labor resources and without adequate financial resources. For the formerly enslaved, the economic outlook was equally bleak. However, there was some land outside of white ownership for ex-slaves to establish themselves as subsistence farmers, combining small-scale agriculture with fishing.

FROM EMANCIPATION TO IMMIGRATION, 1834–1934

The period from post-emancipation to 1934 was trying for the Caymanian people. While plantation slavery in some ways departed from the patterns identified elsewhere in the Caribbean, the racial adjustments were not being lived

Caymanian Population by Racial Origin (All Islands) 1881–1943

Year	Black	White	Colored
1881	972	864	1230
1891	992	1602	1705
1911	1031	2322	2211
1921	828	2431	1994
1943	1051	2086	3518

Source: Census of Jamaica and Its Dependencies, 1943.

out in utopian circumstances. A post-emancipation visitor described the houses of the former enslaved as "huts and hovels of the poorest description" (Hannerz 1974, 29). This description clearly reflected the social and economic status of persons of African descent. But a sluggish economy meant that poor whites were only marginally better off than their black counterparts.

One source of comfort for islanders in an economic depression was the Church. In 1839, Anglican Church presence waned as the bishop of Jamaica recalled the Reverend Charles Wilson. Wilson had worked hard to consolidate the position of the church in the Caymans. However, it seems that the islands occupied a low priority in the plans of the diocesan leadership. Thereafter, church property fell into disuse. The vacuum was filled by the Methodists who launched a vigorous missionary activity throughout the islands. As with the Anglicans, however, the work faltered due to a lack of official support in financing the mission; the next phase of church expansion and consolidation would be led by the Presbyterian Church (Williams 1970, 49).

The efforts of Presbyterians, and in particular the efforts of Reverend William Elmslie, resulted in membership of some 400 persons by the late 1850s. They focused on Grand Cayman, however, leaving an opening for other sects to infiltrate the other islands. The Baptists established themselves on Cayman Brac and Little Cayman. Other groups that evangelized in the Caymans included the Holiness Movement (later known as the Pilgrim or Wesleyan Holiness Church) and the Seventh-Day Adventists, who arrived in the late 1890s but did not gain momentum until the 1920s.

If religion became an overarching symbol of meaning in Caymanian lives, the small size of the islands and their population limited choice in conjugal relations. Thus interracial unions were reasonably common even if Caymanians maintained a keen sense of racial separateness and origin. The following table illustrates the impact of miscegenation on the population profile and helps in further defining the peculiar characteristics of Cayman culture.

By 1943, the "colored" group was the largest in the islands' ethnic makeup— larger than blacks and whites together. It reflected a population shifting rather quickly toward some kind of racial homogeneity albeit through mixing. Some observers say there has been a "compression of the social hierarchy," a key facet of "a relative cultural homogeneity" (Hannerz 1974, 30).

One of the important economic activities of this period, as in earlier ones, was the trade in turtle meat. Over the years, excess fishing led to the decimation of the turtle population. Faced with dwindling income and shrinking opportunities, Caymanians turned to immigration and seafaring, with considerable impact on families. This disruption in family life was described by one observer: "most of them were seamen, the brides usually remained on the island, raising their families and seeing their husbands only on the rare visits home. Women seem to accept separation from their husbands and marital infidelity as facts of life which they could not change" (Kohlman 1993, 93–94).

The first phase of immigration took Caymanians to the Bay Islands of Honduras and other areas of Central America. Understandably, some Caymanians migrated to Jamaica and to Cuba, islands with which the colonial links had been particularly strong. Later, in the first years of the twentieth century, there were opportunities in Florida to work on railroad construction. In addition, some Caymanians worked on the Panama Canal. In the second phase of migration, during the 1930s, several Caymanians traveled to the United States by way of their merchant marine contracts. Colonies of Cayman exiles emerged in parts such as Tampa, Florida, and Port Arthur, Texas. Some of these communities maintained their Caymanian culture through contacts with their kin at home. In many cases remittances from migrants maintained those who remained at home.

In the century after emancipation, life in the Caymans was a precarious balance between subsistence and moderate comfort. No one could imagine its future prosperity after World War II.

TOWARD POLITICAL MATURITY, 1934–1984

By World War II, the relative isolation of the Cayman Islands was disappearing. New modes of travel made the islands more accessible to travelers. In the postwar years, air service was begun with Florida and Jamaica. It did not last very long, but it motivated new plans to construct a modern airport. The plans came to fruition in 1953 with the opening of the Owen Roberts Airport, named after an aviator.

In addition to the expansion of links between the islands and the larger outside world, another aspect of the islands' development lay in the appointment of competent British administrators to oversee development. Sir Allen Cardinal was appointed in 1934 and during his term of office, which lasted until the mid-1940s, he oversaw the improvement of the local road network, the installation of a radio station, and the construction of new public buildings (from a very limited tax base), all paving the way for later development. Further improvements were made to the airport infrastructure and a modern hospital was constructed in the 1950s.

Caymanians did not uncritically accept the supervision of the British colonial authorities. From the 1960s to the 1970s, Cayman politics came of age and the islanders showed a spirit of independence that rejected tokenism. One aspect of the new developments in its political culture was the opening of the newspaper, *The Caymanian*, replacing an earlier publication, *The Trade Winds*, and it has chronicled the ebb and flow of local and international politics. The paper is a key element in the islands' politics.

A newfound political awareness came to light in 1960, when Ormond Panton (a "colored" Caymanian and, thus, in local genealogical terms, an outsider in the elite groupings) challenged the white and British island administrator. Panton's sin was that he had posted notices, allegedly demeaning the office of the chief judicial officer. Panton was arrested for breach of peace. He went to court and won, thus enhancing his political esteem among Caymanian non-whites.

Panton's political fortunes grew and he was elected to represent the islands at the conferences to establish the British West Indies Federation (BWIF). On his return to the Caymans, fortified no doubt by contact with other West Indies politicians, he teamed up with another legislator, Warren Conolly, to form the Cayman National Democratic Party (CND), putting the islands on a modern political footing. The CND was a catalyst for the formation of other political groups: a few months later, the Christian Democratic Party (CDP) was created.

The formation of the two political parties energized the political landscape, with intense discussion on the country's political future taking place, especially after Jamaica opted out of the BWIF. The question was clear: should the islands opt for incorporation into the political system of a newly independent Jamaica or should they stay as a Crown colony, remaining under the political tutelage of Great Britain? In the end, the latter option prevailed.

The major power player in the discussions was Roy McTaggart. McTaggart, scion of a Presbyterian family that had migrated to the Caymans in the 1860s, had been in the Legislative Assembly since 1916. He had diversified his business activities, investing in the local retail sector and in fishing and shipping interests. He was one of the most respected elders in local politics. In 1962, McTaggart joined the National Democratic Party (NDP) (as the CND came to be called) and was elected along with Panton and five others in the first elections fought along party lines in the Caymans.

The hope that the NDP would come to dominate the legislature was short-lived. Although the party won a majority in the elections, it found itself outmaneuvered by the British administrator, Jack Rose. Rose was vested with the power to make nominations to the Assembly and named three persons, which altered the balance of power in the Assembly. Disappointment was profound, negatively affecting the morale of party members. Disaffection took over and in the 1965 elections, the NDP was soundly beaten at the polls, winning only one seat.

Thereafter, two-party politics all but disappeared in the Caymans and the future would belong to loose coalitions of various interests coming together from time to time. Whatever the fortunes of the NDP, the impact on the political culture of the islands was irreversible. Henceforth, Caymanian politicians would take fuller charge of the destinies of their people.

Parallel to the political maturation of the islanders was the rapid tourist-driven economic growth, which led to an influx of outsiders, and affected several aspects of community life. Construction and real estate development was a sensitive issue. In order to control the development of land resources, the administrator sponsored the Land Development (Interim Control) Bill. It immediately drew condemnation from influential politicians and attracted attention across ethnic and economic boundaries because it was placing too many restrictions on local building styles. A protest march in 1970 protested aspects of the new legislation.

Three politicians were active in the protest, challenging the government: Annie Bodden, Berkley Bush, and Ira Walton. Bodden and Bush were members of the Assembly; Walton represented a more militant Afro-Cayman interest, centered in George Town. The heated debate alarmed the administrator, who requested the stationing of a British warship to guard the islands. Common sense prevailed and the administrator conceded in an assembly meeting. The bill was passed, but after protest the legislature repealed it and sent it to a committee which included members that had opposed it.

With political stability restored, the political directorship could turn their attention to more pressing issues. The 1960 report of the British government for the Cayman Islands showed that over 1,100 people were earning a living as seamen on American lines. At that time, there were only 300 hotel beds and less than 5,000 tourists visiting annually. By 1965, there were 532 beds and over 6,000 visitors. As tourism grew, the number of Caymanians working outside the islands decreased: as economic opportunities widened, Caymanians became more aware of homegrown possibilities for living and working.

Politicians and economic planners, too, tried to foment a path of sustainable economic growth. By 1975 tourism arrivals totaled some 54,000 and by 1984 that figure had almost tripled to 148,485 visitors. Much of the growth could be attributed to the Cayman Islands Tourist Board, through aggressive advertising and lobbying of legislators for increased financing of this important sector.

An additional economic boost came from the emergence of the islands as a major offshore financial center. By 1974, 5,948 businesses had been registered and this trend grew unabatedly throughout the 1980s. By 1984 the Cayman Islands were on the verge of an economic takeoff.

THE DRIVE FOR SUSTAINABILITY AFTER 1984

The history of the Cayman Islands portrays incredible success in overcoming the obstacles of small size in a competitively hostile global environment. Among small-island developing states, the Caymans are cited as an example to emulate. In the 1984–2000 period, the gains of the 1970s and early 1980s were consolidated and surpassed; this was in part attributable to a stable political culture and pragmatic economic planning.

In 1972 a new constitution was adopted, creating a legislative assembly of twelve members and dispensing with the anomaly of having members nominated by the governor after 1971. The administrator or commissioner was now referred to as the governor. By 1990, there were calls for a further democratization of the political process due to the rapid population growth; 34 percent of the population was made up of expatriates by 1992, in part due to the rapid economic expansion. In 1993 the number of elected representatives was increased to fifteen; and those the executive council raised by one, to eight, and are now ministers.

The virtual disappearance of party politics did not mean the end of factionalism. However, it did mean that there was a relative absence of the vicious political infighting so characteristic of other English-speaking Caribbean countries. Instead there was a loose grouping of persons known as the National Team, which won twelve of the fifteen seats in the 1992 general elections. The main feature of the political ideologies espoused by this grouping was that its adherents were vigorously opposed to the creation of the post of chief minister, which some felt was a prelude to independence (Ramos and Rivera 2001, 120). Moreover, there was the widespread view that the dependent status of the islands was an important factor in their political stability and, hence, their economic success. In fact, island prosperity has put a break on political nationalism: there is little interest in the Cayman Islands becoming independent.

Whatever one's view of how politics are practiced on the islands, the policymakers in the administration put together a legislation package that laid the foundation for sustainable growth. An economic report describes these policies as follows: "The combination of no foreign exchange regulations, no direct tax, flexible company laws, good communications, political stability and stringent secrecy laws have established the Caymans as one of the world's leading banking and financial centres. The islands are known as 'the Switzerland of the Caribbean.' By January 1997, 47 of the world's 50 largest banks had operations in Grand Cayman" (World of Information 1999, 181).

Tourism's healthy status is as striking as that of financial services. There were 166,082 tourists visiting the islands in 1986. By 1990 tourist arrivals had reached some 253,000, not counting the 360,000 cruise ship passengers making brief stops. By 2000, tourist arrivals had reached the 700,000 mark. The Caymans, over the period 1993–1997, averaged a per capita Gross National Product of some US$24,000, the third highest income in all of North and South America, after the United States and Bermuda. However, there has been a downside: the cost of living is high, housing prices can be exorbitant, and offshore banking has brought an increase in drug trafficking, with its attendant ills.

Caymanian life is not all saturated with economic matters. Tourism has sparked a renewed interest in the islands' heritage and culture. In 1990, a national museum opened its doors to the public, offering a rich display of Caymania, with over 4,000 items. The museum is located in the nineteenth-century Old Courts Building, and actively preserves the archival and museum heritage of the islands, with a deep awareness of the contributions of the African as well as the European past.

The Caymans share a common Afrocentric heritage with their other Caribbean brothers and sisters. Hence, usually in April, the Batabano festival is celebrated with all the colorful richness of a Caribbean carnival: costumed bands, the inevitable calypso and soca rhythms, jump ups (a type of carnival dance), and masquerading. Jamaica's influence is strong, especially through reggae and the occasional adherents of the Rastafarian faith.

Current Caymanian life is financially secure, some claim to the point of complacency. Though it is a country with a distinct Caribbean flavor, the ever present influence of the church acts as a conservative force, claiming that Caymanian norms are to be preserved at all costs. This can clash with British law and culture, which is liberal and accepting of alternative lifestyles, whereas islanders have a more puritan approach to life on some issues. Evidence of this clash was seen in 1998, when 900 gays, traveling on a Norwegian line, planned to stop off at Grand Cayman, and were barred entry. It is British authorities who have insisted on repealing archaic laws and aligning the islands' legal code with that of the "Mother Country." Resistance to change is also seen in preserving religious orthodoxy: only recently have Rastafarians been allowed entry into the Caymans.

CONCLUSION

For a society that has changed (and is changing) so quickly these clashes between "tradition" and "modernity" will keep cropping up. Added to this is the fact that up to a third of the residents are foreign born. With a history of slavery, and British colonial rule, the invasion of U.S. pop culture and money, and the strains that inevitably accompany a tourism economy, Caymanians can feel justifiably proud of their achievements. That they have managed to build and retain a quintessentially Caribbean culture is heartening.

REFERENCES

Carlesso-Ebanks, Sonia (2001). Personal communication with author 11-2-2001.

Drewett, Peter, et al. (2000). "Unoccupied Islands? The Cayman Islands." In Peter L. Drewett (ed.) *Prehistoric Settlements in the Caribbean: Fieldwork in Barbados, Tortola and the Cayman Islands.* Bridgetown, Barbados: Barbados Museum and Historical Society, pp. 5–7.

Goldberg, Richard (1976). "East End: A Caribbean Community under Stress." Unpublished Ph.D. thesis. University of Texas, Austin.

Hannau, Hans (1976). *The Cayman Islands.* New York: Hastings House Publishers.

Hannerz, Ulf (1974). *Caymanian Politics: Structure and Style in a Changing Island Society*. Sweden: University of Stockholm.

Kohlman, Aarona (1993). *Under Tin Roofs: Cayman in the 1920s*. Grand Cayman: Cayman Islands National Museum.

McLaughlin, Heather (1991). *Cayman Yesterdays: An Album of Child Memories*. Grand Cayman: Cayman Islands Memory Bank.

Ramos, Aarón, and Angel Rivera (2001). *Islands at the Crossroads: Politics in the Nonindependent Caribbean*. Kingston, Jamaica: Ian Randle Publishers.

Scudder, Sylvia, and Irvy Quitmyer (2000). "Environmental Archaeology at Great Cave, Cayman Brac: The Natural History of a Cave." In Drewett, Peter (ed.) *Prehistoric Settlements in the Caribbean*.

Williams, Neville (1970). *A History of the Cayman Islands*. Government of the Cayman Islands.

World of Information (1999). *The Americas Review*. Edison, NJ: Hunter Publishers.

5

Cuba

Tomás Fernández Robaina
Translated by Alan West-Durán

Cuba has been called the whitest and the blackest of the Caribbean islands. This contradictory assertion has a demographic and historical explanation: On the one hand, probably half the population is white. On the other, a huge majority of its black population came to the island in the nineteenth century from Africa, maintaining a strong ethnic and cultural identity. This identity was further affirmed by the presence of self-help societies (*cabildos*), a sizeable stratum of "free coloreds," and a long war for independence linked to abolition.

Cuba, the largest of the Caribbean islands, is about the size of Pennsylvania, and has a population of almost 11 million, accounting for almost a third of the population of the region. The population is officially listed at 15 percent black, 25 percent mixed race, and 60 percent white, but the definition of white in Cuba is more elastic than in the United States. Some claim this "whitening" is a distortion of reality and say the figures should be reversed. A former Spanish colony, Cuba has been independent for almost a century, and since 1959 it has lived under a one-party Communist state, the only one in the Caribbean region.

COLONIALISM AND SLAVERY UNDER THE SPANISH

Cuba was discovered on Columbus's first trip (1492), but it wasn't until 1512, under Diego Velázquez, that the ill-named colonization began, which initiated a policy of deculturation and annihilation of the native population, mostly Taínos (Arawak), and subsequently, the exploitation and deculturation of enslaved Africans.

The first blacks to arrive in Cuba did not come straight from Africa, but were slaves living in Spain, acculturated to Spanish ways; they spoke Spanish, and

Man on the Malecón, Havana. Photo © Héctor Delgado.

were called *Ladinos*. They were differentiated from the *Bozales*, or slaves from Africa who were non-Spanish-speaking. During the first decades, the number of African slaves was not great, but quickly that changed as the indigenous population was decimated (from overwork, harsh treatment, and deadliest of all, disease).

By 1520, Bartolomé de las Casas, a Dominican friar who had been in Cuba and Santo Domingo, petitioned the Spanish Crown to end Indian slavery. He was successful in championing Indian rights, but the European powers—in sixteenth-century Portugal and Spain—stepped up their importation of 300,000 Africans to the Americas.

The enslaved Africans brought to Cuba were from four main areas and were known in the island as the Congo (or Bantu), the Yoruba (or *Lucumí*), the *Araráš*, and the *Carabalíes*. The Congos were from what are today known as Congo-Brazzaville, the Republic of Congo, and Angola (and even Mozambique in East Africa). They were the first slaves brought to the island and have left their legacy in their music and religions, known as Regla de Palo Monte. The Yoruba were from what is now known as Nigeria and the Bight of Benin; most came in the nineteenth century, when Cuba imported over 550,000 slaves. Their religious and musical influence on Cuba has been profound, as has been their cultural resistance against slavery. It is the Yoruba who evolved a religion known as *Santería*, a syncretism of Yoruba practices and Catholicism. Third were the Africans brought from the former kingdom of Dahomey, now known as Benin

(Fon-Ewe cultures), the *Ararás*, who today live mostly in the province of Matanzas. Their religion bears similarities to the orisha worship of the Yoruba. And finally the *Carabalíes*, from the Niger delta–Cameroon area. Their religious world is unique and different from others, since they have kept alive a Calabar secret society known as the *abakuá*.

Cuba did not become a true plantation society until after Haitian independence (1791–1804). Although in the first half of the sixteenth century the vast majority of the population were slaves, in the seventeenth it was around a third, decreasing to about 25 percent by 1792. Even more significant was a "free colored" population that ranged from 15 percent to 25 percent of the total population. Several factors account for this: the lack of a full-blown plantation system before 1800, racial mixing, a high manumission rate, and the importance of the *cabildos*. The *cabildos* were self-help societies usually organized on ethnic lines that also had religious and cultural functions. If, say, a free Congo died and there wasn't money to bury him, the *cabildo* would collect the monies necessary; in many instances *cabildos* purchased the freedom of their brethren. The first mention of African *cabildos* in Cuba dates from 1568.

As the focus of the Spanish empire shifted toward Mexico and South America in the seventeenth and eighteenth centuries, Cuba became important militarily and as a port. Many of the goods, including gold and silver, to be shipped to Spain stopped in Havana where convoys protected them from British, French, and Dutch pirates or warships. Cuba's military role meant that slaves were just as often employed building fortifications than working on plantations.

Cuba was also unique in having a large urban black population, both slave and free, that had considerably more social and economic opportunities than their plantation brethren. They also openly or covertly subverted the legal barriers about purity of blood.

The British occupation of Havana (1762) spiked an increase in the importation of slaves, with an even more dramatic increase after the Haitian insurrection. Cuban blacks had admirably defended the city from the British, and the Spanish Crown granted slaves their freedom for such bravery.

By the late eighteenth century, Cuba was irreversibly on the road to a plantation system. The number of sugar mills is revealing: when the British invaded there were approximately 100 sugar mills; by 1825, 1,000. Already by 1810, the non-white population of Cuba was greater than the white population: the island's slave population increased almost sevenfold between 1792 and 1841! Interestingly, the free colored population tripled in that same period.

CUBA IN THE NINETEENTH CENTURY: PLANTATIONS AND RESISTANCE

Not all slaves could buy their freedom, nor did they passively accept their fate. Rebellions were both individual and collective. Collective responses were first tied to attempts to correct the abuses, but not to abolish slavery. Only later did they become linked to pro-independence movements. Many slaves became runaways, or *cimarrones*, the origin of the word for "Maroon" in English. The *cimarrones* would flee into areas with dense vegetation, or into the mountains, usually forming settlements of fifteen to twenty huts called *palenques*. These inaccessible *palenques* were protected by a barrier of camouflaged wooden stakes, to ward off troops and *rancheadores* (both people and dogs dedicated to tracking and punishing runaway slaves), who pursued them mercilessly. Punishment was severe, from torture, to severing of ears, to death. Many, but not all slaves thought that when they died their souls would return to Africa. When slave owners and *rancheadores* killed runaways or disobedient slaves, they would decapitate them, placing the head on a stake, said to prevent their resurrection and African journey home. Given their limitations, maroonage or sabotage (burning of plantations, killing owners and overseers), though important symbols of freedom, never attempted to end the slave system or seek independence from Spain.

One of the most important Maroon groups was from Poblado del Cobre in eastern Cuba and was composed of slaves who had worked in the copper mines. They revolted in 1731 and fifty years later had over a thousand people in scattered settlements in the area. They considered themselves slaves of the king, not of the mine owners. They petitioned the king and were declared free in 1800. Another Maroon community was in Bumba. Its captains, Cobas, Agustín, and Gallo, like those in other parts of the Caribbean, had been active since 1820; a decade later they negotiated a truce with the governor of Santiago in which their freedom was to be respected, as long as they agreed to hand over other Maroons. Neither side stuck to the agreement, and betrayal by a Maroon led to the execution of the Maroon leaders and the destruction of the *palenques*.

The most prominent conspiracies to foment rebellion were the ones inspired by José Antonio Aponte in 1812, and the one planned for 1843–1844, known as the La Escalera Conspiracy. Aponte was a black carpenter and *santero* (a person who practices *santería*) who planned an islandwide uprising to abolish slavery and promote independence. Some claim that Aponte also organized poor whites, making the movement even more dangerous. Aponte was inspired by Haiti's recent example and also by the Latin American independence wars that began in 1810. Discovered beforehand, the uprising was aborted; dozens were killed and hundreds detained and punished. Aponte was executed—he was decapitated and his head was placed in a cage in public view. Aponte's aborted insurrection spread panic among Cuban whites, who even coined the phrase, "worse than Aponte."

In 1843 and 1844, an even larger conspiracy was discovered by the Spanish. Colonial authorities then unleashed a wave of repression, killing over a thousand, including Plácido (Gabriel de Concepción Valdés), a mixed race and beloved poet, and arresting thousands more. Claudio Brindis de Salas, Sr. (1800–1872), a renowned musician and composer, and father of the stellar violinist of nineteenth-century Cuba (Claudio Brindis de Salas, Jr.), was tortured and deported. The system had been shaken, but it would take a great deal more to end it.

The 1857 census reveals that roughly 1 in 5 slaves lived in urban areas, with owners averaging about 3 slaves. In the countryside it was different—there the number of slaves was four times greater. More striking is that 1 percent of masters owned 25 percent of the slaves, averaging almost 200 per estate, but by 1861 it was clear that slavery was going to end. In twenty years the absolute and relative number of slaves had decreased sharply, from a high of 43 percent to 27 percent, a figure that would continue to drop until abolition in 1886.

TOWARD ABOLITION AND INDEPENDENCE: 1868–1898/1902

In 1868, landowner Carlos Manuel de Céspedes (1819–1874) freed his thirty slaves and initiated a decade-long war against Spain for independence. The insurrectionists called on the slaves to join them, but many slave owners who were sympathetic to independence were reluctant to embrace abolition, and did not free slaves under their areas of control. Many free blacks and colored joined their ranks, however, and became generals of the revolutionary army: José Maceo (1848–1896), Quintín Banderas Betancourt (1833–1906), Guillermo Moncada (1841–1895), and Flor Crombet (1851–1895). Some did not, especially the Maroons, seeing both white Creoles and the Spanish as cruel exploiters, and many Maroons were wiped out by both revolutionary and Spanish troops.

The Ten Years' War (1868–1878) shows an extraordinary and patriotic effort made by the black and brown populations, previously marginalized for reasons of race, class, and education. It marks a shift toward the centrality of blacks as active founders of the Cuban nation. One of the great figures of this war was Antonio Maceo (1845–1896), a general as revered by his troops as he was feared by the Spanish. Maceo, known as the Bronze Titan, was a bold leader, a top military strategist, and a lucid thinker. The Spanish accused Maceo of wanting to set up a black republic along Haitian lines, clearly meaning to scare whites from adopting either abolitionist or pro-independence views. Maceo never tired of repeating that a Cuban republic would consist of blacks, mulattoes, and whites. The Spanish, trying to divide the black masses, also passed a law freeing the offspring of slaves born after September 1868, slaves over the age of sixty, and slaves who fought in the Spanish army. Some, but not many, blacks took the offer.

Three factors led to the inability to spread the war to western Cuba: the internal divisions, the lack of resolve by landowners concerning abolition, and internal racism, eventually brought the war to an end. Since neither abolition nor independence was achieved, Maceo considered the Zanjón Treaty a truce, and he again took up arms a year later, unsuccessfully. However, Maceo's Baraguá Protest reminded colonial authorities that there would be no peace with slavery: abolition was declared in Puerto Rico (1873) and eventually in Cuba (1880–1886). The ten-year toll was horrendous: 50,000 Cuban dead, 200,000 Spanish casualties, and a $300 million loss to the economy.

But the Cuban planter class, foreseeing the end of slavery, as well as the decrease in the slave population during the final years of slavery, acted similarly to landowners in other Caribbean nations: it imported indentured labor from Asia. Over 125,000 Chinese came to Cuba between 1847 and 1874, along with several thousand Mayan laborers from Yucatán (Mexico).

One of the key figures of the post-emancipation period was Juan Gualberto Gómez (1854–1933), a director of several newspapers, and a champion of both independence and black causes. Gómez was a leader of the Directorate of Societies of Color, which sought to promote the educational, economic, social, and cultural advancement of blacks. Some accused Gómez of playing politics, but the black societies or clubs had members of all political stripes. While Gómez preached racial pride and advancement, these societies rejected Afro-Cuban religions and healing methods, and as a journalist Gómez was vocal in assuring that Cuba would not become another Haiti, using some dubious historical arguments. Despite not questioning the overall white supremacy of Cuban society, Gómez was jailed twice and deported for his independence views. Another black leader, Martín Morúa Delgado (1857–1910), would later become Gómez's rival.

In 1895, Cuba erupted in war again, with Maceo and Máximo Gómez as the prime military leaders, and José Martí as chief political figure. Although he was white, José Martí (1853–1895) had spoken eloquently on Cuban race issues, saying "A Cuban is more than being white, mulatto, or black." J.G. Gómez and Martí both agreed that the lack of racial unity had been the major obstacle to Cuban independence. In New York, exile Martí appointed J.G. Gómez as coordinator of the independence movement on the island.

The revolutionary army was anywhere from 50 percent to 80 percent black and/or mulatto. The Spanish tried to paint the war of independence as a "race war." The insurrectionists were dealt two great blows: Martí died soon after he took up arms (1895) and a year and a half later Maceo was also killed, after a ninety-day campaign from one end of the island to the other, winning twenty-seven battles, destroying fifty-nine towns, and capturing thousands of weapons, rounds of ammunition, and horses. It has been described as "the most audacious military feat of the 19th century" (Foner 1977, 221). Despite the setbacks, the rebels continued to advance, with many black generals instrumental in waging the Cuban independence war: Jesús Rabí, Agustín Cebreco, Quintín Banderas, Juan Eligio Ducasse, Prudencio Martínez, and Pedro Díaz. U.S. intervention brought the Spanish-Cuban-American War to a quick end in 1898.

EARLY REPUBLICAN YEARS TO MACHADO'S OVERTHROW, 1900–1933

Spain ceded Cuba and Puerto Rico to the United States as a result of the war. The U.S. military occupation lasted four years, and Cuba became independent in 1902. However, the United States imposed the Platt amendment, which barely passed in the Cuban legislature, allowing the United States to intervene if it felt its interests were threatened. Many Afro-Cubans opposed it, such as journalist Rafael Serra, who also continued to denounce racial injustice.

Many blacks had heroically fought for Cuba's independence, only to be treated again as blacks afterwards. Quintín Banderas offers a depressing example: after being honored with banquets and attempting, briefly, a foray into politics, he fell into poverty and was denied a government job as a janitor. Later, he petitioned President Estrada Palma for a pension and was ignored. Embittered, he joined the liberal revolt of 1906 and was assassinated in his sleep.

The political unrest prompted the first U.S. intervention from 1906 to 1909. Amazingly, it was under U.S. occupation that the Independent Group of Coloreds, a black movement led by Evaristo Estenoz and Pedro Ivonnet, was legalized. It became a political party, the Independent Party of Color (PIC), and ran in the 1908 elections. Though they never posed a threat in terms of winning elections, their strength was in their ability to influence the Liberals and Conservatives with crucial "swing votes," and to remind whites of all political persuasions that Martí's slogan "A homeland for all and the good of all" had become a country for the "good of a few." Not all blacks supported the PIC, and Martín Morúa Delgado, a black legislator, even passed an amendment to the constitution that made it illegal to organize political parties on exclusively racial lines. The PIC protested and lobbied for the amendment to be rescinded. After much frustration, on independence day of 1912, the "independientes," as they were known, launched a nonviolent armed protest to force the issue of the relegalization of their party. The government, the press, and most Cuban whites interpreted this as an incitement to "race war," and the ensuing violence by the police, military, and vigilantes over the next two months left between 4,000 and 6,000 blacks and mulattoes dead, including Estenoz and Ivonnet.

The myth of Cuban racial democracy had been shattered forever, more so because the deaths had been ordered and executed by Liberation Army veterans, who, fifteen years before, had fought shoulder to shoulder with their black brethren to overthrow the Spanish (Helg 1995, 226). To make matters worse, the soldiers who committed this genocidal act were honored with a banquet. Racist attitudes took two forms: the first was the belief that blacks and whites should be kept separate, and since the white race was "stronger," eventually blacks would disappear; the other, with similar premises, was the belief that blacks would eventually whiten, socially and racially, but also disappear "by absorption" into the white majority. This was buttressed by another whitening strategy: the encouragement of a huge influx of Spaniards immigrating to Cuba from 1880 to 1910, making up, by 1910, 15 percent of the population.

Despite the chilling effects of the massacre, black and mixed race Cubans kept politically active, with figures such as Lino D'Ou (1871–1939), who had fought under José Maceo in 1895. D'Ou was a journalist who wrote on issues of discrimination, addressing both blacks and whites. José Armando Pla, journalist and activist, called for a double-pronged strategy: blacks should form cohesive groups within each of the political parties, and outside politics in their own organizations, clubs, etc., to keep pressing for their demands.

Marcus Garvey (1887–1940) visited Cuba in 1921 and was received by Cuban president Mario García Menocal. Though Cuban blacks did not resonate to his back to Africa movement, they did respond positively to his calls for black pride and self-improvement. Tens of thousands of African-Caribbean workers (from Jamaica, St. Kitts, Haiti) enthusiastically welcomed his visit. Cuba had many UNIA chapters that were subsequently harassed and repressed under Gerardo Machado (1928–1930), ultimately leading to their demise. However, Garvey's message survived in the mission and practice of Cuba's Afro-Cuban clubs and associations.

Starting in 1925 Cuba underwent a dictatorship under Machado. Blacks did benefit from the Machado regime, with a significant few being appointed to government posts. In 1928, the Afro-Cuban societies of the island honored Machado for his "contributions to the colored race," even though his highly visible overtures favored only a black elite and middle class, and not the majority of Afro-Cubans. One of the most outspoken voices was that of Gustavo Urrutia (1881–1958), who emphasized the need not only for black education, but also for a sound economic base for Afro-Cubans to prosper. More importantly, Urrutia underlined the significance of Cuba's African religions and culture, viewing these religions as neither "backwards," "primitive," nor as "throwbacks to slavery" (Fernández Robaina, 1994, 124–133). Urrutia was a journalist for thirty years, widely known, and yet when Afro-Cuban themes are mentioned, it is Fernando Ortiz who is always mentioned first.

Interestingly, it was in the late twenties and early thirties that Cuba experienced an ever growing interest in things African, giving birth to Afro-Cubanism, which included poetry, music, ethnological research, and history (see Literature and the Arts). Although not exempt from condescension, stereotyping, or racial appropriation, Afro-Cubanism was an important movement in Cuba that finally recognized the centrality of Afro-Cuban culture to the nation's social, political, and cultural identity.

The main figure spearheading this recognition was a white Cuban, Fernando Ortiz (1881–1969), who dedicated himself to studying Cuban blacks, as did two of his disciples: Lydia Cabrera (1900–1991) and Rómulo Lachatañeré (1909–1952). Cabrera was a white short-story writer and cultural anthropologist who dedicated her life to Afro-Cuban folklore, religions, and languages. Lachatañeré was black and wrote extensively on Afro-Cuban religions. Ortiz, who coined the term "Afro-Cuban," wrote prolifically on Afro-Cuban music, religion, language, and history. In his most famous work, *Cuban Counterpoint: Tobacco and Sugar* (1940), using tobacco and sugar as organizing metaphors, Ortiz claims that Cuban history is the intricate story of its transculturations, a term he used to describe Cuba's unique mixture of races, music, cuisine, and religions. However, Ortiz, like his predecessor Martí, tended to downplay race (or deny its existence), subsuming it within a broader Cuban nationalism or culture. This blinded him to the persistent and more subtle forms of racism in Cuban society. Despite his limitations, Ortiz's importance cannot be overstated: first, he claimed that Cuba would not exist without its Afro-Cuban population and culture, and second, he established the study of Afro-Cuba as a discipline worthy of scholarly research.

The dictator Machado was overthrown in 1933, and soon after, the Platt amendment was abrogated (1934). Some blacks and mulattoes (middle and upper class) had benefited under the Machado regime; most had not. The Cuban Communist Party (CCP), founded in 1925, mostly through the unions it dominated, appealed to many Cuban blacks, not only on racial grounds but more so on class issues. The CCP was attempting to build a multiracial, revolutionary movement that included working-class whites (Cuban, Spanish, Polish emigrés), Chinese, West Indians (Haitians and Jamaicans mostly), and Cuban blacks and mulattoes.

Many Cuban blacks responded and by the late 1930s it was estimated that a third of the Communist Party was black, with the figures even higher in the forties. Many Cuban whites associated communism with blackness. The trade union movement had four prominent black leaders: Blas Roca, Jesús Menéndez (189?–1948), Salvador García Agüero, and Lázaro Peña. Menéndez was murdered for political reasons.

But most Afro-Cubans belonged to a myriad of black associations and groups, some quite exclusive like the Club Atenas, while others were more inclusive. They were organized along trade lines, or cultural interests (theater, dance, literature), and though some were avowedly apolitical and nonreligious, most were involved in politically mobilizing black constituencies.

These Afro-Cuban groups, along with the CCP, made several attempts to propose and pass antidiscrimination legislation, first when the new constitution of 1940 was being drafted, and later, under the administrations of Batista (1940–1944), Grau San Martín (1944–1948), and Prío Socarrás (1948–1952). The legislation usually foundered on how to enforce it—or punish those who had discriminated against Afro-Cubans.

Under the Fulgencio Batista dictatorship (1952–1958), the situation of blacks did not notably improve, although some were appointed to government posts and many were in the military, though not as high-ranking officers. Batista himself was mulatto, and was shunned by the white economic and political elites, but he was extremely successful in manipulating the established Afro-Cuban societies and groups to his favor. This led some racists to incorrectly label all blacks as supporters of Batista, which was patently untrue.

In 1955, Juan René Betancourt, an Afro-Cuban lawyer, published an important book called *Doctrina negra* (Black Doctrine). Betancourt argued that to overcome discrimination, blacks must have a solid economic base; he created an organization so that both blacks and whites could invest in black businesses and housing. Betancourt was a firm defender and promoter of the African roots of Cuban culture, but despite his advocacy of black self-help he was not a separatist or black nationalist; whites, he argued, have to take an active part in eliminating racism and discrimination. Not many blacks (and very few whites) responded to Betancourt's plea. In part this could be explained by the ingrained racism of Cuban society, but by the mid-fifties, increased governmental repression and the armed revolutionary struggle led by Fidel Castro's guerrilla army took center stage.

In barely three years, Castro's rag-tag insurrectionists overthrew the Batista regime, which had become increasingly violent, corrupt, and unresponsive to the people. Although a simplification, there was some truth to Cuba's image as whorehouse of the Caribbean (since it was a major tourist site), and many of the island's prostitutes were mulattoes or dark skinned.

Castro's revolution changed Cuba's economic, political, military, and cultural dependency on the United States. Radical reforms were made in land ownership, education, politics, and the economy. The revolutionary government nationalized many Cuban and U.S. businesses. The confrontation between the two countries, abetted by cold war ideologies, led the United States to back an invasion of Cuba (1961), which failed. Feeling it needed protection from U.S. military retaliation, Cuba brought in Soviet nuclear missiles, which led to a showdown during the Cuban Missile Crisis of 1962 that almost ended in nuclear annihilation. Cuba's nationalist, radical socialist, and anti-imperialist policies have kept it and the United States at loggerheads for more than four decades.

BLACKS AND THE REVOLUTION (1959–2001)

The 1959 revolutionary triumph augured a new era for Cuba, one which blacks and mixed race hoped would deal a blow to racism and discrimination. Indeed, many of the regime's early statements and actions were directed toward these ends: desegregating beaches, housing, clubs, schools, recreational facilities, and workplaces. Betancourt wrote two important articles on Cuban racism early in 1959. In March, no doubt inspired by Betancourt's analysis, Castro himself declared in a speech that one of the four principal aims of the revolution was ending racial discrimination.

Cuba was living through a rapid social transformation that also brought on confrontation with the United States; and, thus, the revolution's need for unity appealed to the country's nationalism, but at the same time, race was seen as a divisive issue. When Castro or other figures wanted to address race, they did so through class, especially as the regime declared itself Marxist-Leninist.

By 1962 the government claimed it had done away with race and sex discrimination, to the dismay of Betancourt and others. Because many blacks supported the new regime and were becoming socially and economically more important, the government decided on a measure that seemed popular at the time: the eradication of black societies and clubs. Since blacks and mulattoes were no longer facing discrimination from groups that had previously marginalized them, it made no sense to have their own organizations, so the logic ran. However, this measure undercut a base of support to lobby for non-whites in Cuba, as pointed out by some scholars, who also claimed (Moore 1988, 49–50) that racial discrimination could not be abolished by edict (Betancourt in Moore 1988, 17).

Despite these criticisms, blacks in Cuba have made important career gains in the professions, including education, the military, and health. Although blacks have a lower life expectancy than whites, the difference is much smaller in Cuba than in the United States. Still, at the governmental level, blacks are still underrepresented, and the higher you go in the political hierarchy, the whiter it becomes. Blacks are also not frequently seen on TV and in the movies, except for historical portrayals (period of slavery) or in stereotypical roles.

Cuba's foreign policy for many years was highly involved with African liberation struggles in Angola, Namibia, Mozambique, and South Africa. Cuba's commitment to the anti-apartheid forces was extraordinary; thousands of Cuban troops (mostly black) were sent to Angola (1975–1989) and eventually defeated the South African army, ending the apartheid regime, which led to Nelson Mandela's presidency. In the mid-seventies President Fidel Castro defined Cuba as an African-Latin nation, the first time any Cuban head of state had made such a declaration. Castro and Cuba were equally committed to Maurice Bishop and the New Jewel Movement regime that ruled Grenada under a revolutionary nationalist regime inspired by the Black Power movements of the sixties and seventies.

Despite the new prominence of Afro-Cuban cultural expressions in music, literature, and religion, books dealing with racism that were published in the mid- to late eighties by Pedro Seviat, Carlos Moore, and Tomás Fernández Robaina were virtually ignored on the island, even though they were discussed abroad.

With the fall of the Soviet bloc countries (1989–1991), Cuba's economy, which was highly dependent on these regimes, went into a downward spiral known as the "Special Period," where goods, food, and medicine were in short supply. The dire economic situation affected Afro-Cubans in particular, and thousands fled the island in makeshift rafts. Around the same time, thousands also took to the streets in the August 1994 Malecón Riots, which many white Cubans interpreted racially. Polls conducted in the mid-1990s revealed that 85 percent of all Cubans felt that prejudice was rampant and that 58 percent of whites considered blacks to be less intelligent, 69 percent believed that blacks did not have the same "values" or "decency" as whites, and 68 percent were opposed to interracial marriage (de la Fuente 2000, 322–323).

Starting in 1995, the economy began to recover, but dollarization and the emphasis on tourism have affected Afro-Cubans. Dollarization has increased social inequalities because Afro-Cuban families have fewer opportunities to acquire U.S. dollars. In tourism almost all the best positions go to whites, even though tourist brochures and advertising—either visually or verbally—entice male foreigners to engage in fleshy fun with mulatto and dark-skinned Cuban women.

Still, despite the persistence of racist attitudes and institutional barriers to black advancement, Cuba seems to be making an effort to recognize that racism is still a problem. The fifth Communist Party Congress (1997) spent considerable time on the issue, and the Politbureau is now a quarter Afro-Cuban, still not proportional to the general population, but a significant improvement over the past. The UNEAC (National Union of Cuban Writers and Artists) dedicated much discussion to issues of racism in 1998. Attempts have been made to form a black cultural organization and raise consciousness about racism and discrimination, but they have not coalesced, formally. Human rights and dissident groups also have many Afro-Cuban members and have made racial issues part of their demands.

In religious circles there is a renewed interest in orthodox African practices, as well as a growing Rastafarian presence. And some, coinciding with the prophetic comments by Juan René Betancourt, reject using the names of Catholic saints for the Yoruba orishas, claiming that Yemayá (the Afro-Cuban goddess of the seas) has nothing to do with the Virgin of Regla. This Afro-Cuban rejection of Eurocentrism works within a national framework, more fluid than before, motivating both blacks and whites to more deeply delve into their Cuban identity, seeing its blind spots, questioning its hidden assumptions.

AFRO-CUBAN RELIGIONS: SANTERÍA, PALO, ABAKUÁ-NAÑIGUISMO

Although nominally a Catholic country before 1959, Cuba has been home to different African-derived religions. The best known is La Regla de Ocha, also known as *Santería* (from the word "saint"), due to the mixture of Yoruba (Nigerian) *orishas* (deities) with Catholic saints. Santería rests on two fundamental concepts: *aché* and *ebbó*. *Aché* is the divine force of the universe, which the different orishas possess, given to them by Oloddumare, the central creative force or God. For humans to obtain this cosmic and life energy, *ebbós* or sacrifices must be made. *Ebbós* are also made to ward off sickness, loss, personal tragedy, or spells. *Santeros* are accomplished herbalists, treating their brethren for different ailments. Initiation involves a series of long and disciplined rituals that culminate in a ceremony where the person is mounted or possessed by his or her orisha. Most *santeros* are also practicing Catholics; for example, the orisha Ochún, the deity of love, marriage, and rivers, is the patron saint of Cuba, Our Lady of Charity. This combining of different religious elements was the way in which slaves could practice their African religions while publicly giving the impression they were Catholics.

Regla de Palo Monte or *Palo*, of Congo origins, is a religion whose followers also believe in a God, called *Nzambi* or *Sambia*. Like *santeros, paleros* also practice healing and magic, using an iron receptacle called an *nganga*, where sacred sticks (*palo* in Spanish) are placed. Palo also uses a series of signatures or drawings, done in chalk on black backgrounds. Along with Nzambi, paleros worship the spirits of the dead and nature spirits that dwell in trees, rivers, and the sea. Palo is a mixture of different Congo-derived religions, and it has also incorporated elements of Santería. One form, known as *kimbisa,* also has elements of spiritism and Catholicism.

The third major Afro-Cuban religion is *ñañiguismo* or *abakuá.* The abakuá secret society has often been compared to Masonic lodges: it is a mutual-aid society, a religious organization, and a brotherhood that exalts "manliness." It is an all-male society that traditionally was influential among dockworkers of Havana and Matanzas. As with Santería and Palo, there are initiation ceremonies with ritual drumming and dancing, sacrifices (some animal), chanting, and sacred drawings or signatures. Similar to *santeros* and *paleros, abakuás* can also be Catholics, spiritists. Some paleros and abakuás are also *santeros.* Because of rivalries and the occasional excesses of male behavior, their turbulent history gave them a reputation for violence that has often made them a target for repression. Perhaps the most visible element of *abakuá* culture in Cuba is the *íreme,* or *diablitos* (devil prankster), that parades on the streets on Three Kings Day.

All three religions have been accused of being purveyors of witchcraft, black magic, and criminality at different times, with public manifestations of their practices banned. However, currently all three Afro-Cuban religions have experienced growing numbers (including many whites) as well as social respect.

AFRO-CUBAN MUSIC: WORLD RENOWNED

The African influences in Cuban music are pervasive in almost all genres: *danzón,* ballads, boleros, rumba, *son,* mambo, cha-cha-cha, salsa, and *timba.* The *danzón,* which developed in the nineteenth century, grew out of European salon dances, but through Haitian and Cuban influences it became known as the national dance of the island. Its "originator," Miguel Faílde (1852–1921), a mixed race composer from Matanzas, was a nationalist, and colonial authorities considered the music too lowly (read "black") and a cultural threat. Eventually it became the symbol of Cuban music, until the 1920s. Its offspring include the *danzón-mambo,* and the cha-cha-cha.

The *danzón* was overtaken in the 1920s by the *son,* a popular genre with Afro-Cuban rhythms, melodies, and themes that is one of the musical roots of salsa. The *son* helped define a Cuban identity in the 1920s and 1930s, becoming a musical metaphor of national culture. Some of the great *son* composers were Ignacio Piñero (1888–1969), Miguel Matamoros (1894–1971), and Arsenio Rodríguez (1911–1971), but its popularity with current bands like Los Van Van, NG La Banda, and Adalberto Alvarez reveals that the *son*'s longevity is enduring. Three great Afro-Cuban women singers, all who left Cuba after 1959, have disseminated Cuban music internationally: La Lupe, Olga Guillot, and Celia Cruz. Cruz, known as the Queen of Salsa, has won several Grammies, and is one of Latin America's most revered singers.

Orguesta Aragón, Cuba. Photo © Héctor Delgado.

Both mambo and Latin jazz are also Cuban creations. Dámaso Pérez Prado (1916–1989) made the mambo famous in the fifties; it drew from Afro-Cuban rhythms and big band idioms. Afro-Cuban composers like Mario Bauzá (1911–1993) and Frank Grillo, or "Machito" (1909–1984), along with U.S. musicians like Dizzy Gillespie, fashioned what is now known as Latin jazz, using Afro-Cuban rhythms with jazz improvisations. It continues to be popular, with extraordinary exponents such as Chucho Valdez (1941–), pianist and composer-founder of the group Irakere. Composer-bassist Israel "Cachao" López (1918–) is a figure who spans several decades of Cuban music, and his prolific output of over 3,000 compositions includes *danzón*, mambo, *son*, cha-cha-cha, *descargas* (Latin jazz jam sessions), rumbas, and more.

Another important musical genre is the *rumba*, which grew out of the tenements of Matanzas and Havana. Although considered the most African of Cuban music, it also has influences from the Spanish rumba flamenca. It is a secular music with a call-and-response form and exclusive use of percussion. Because of its humble origins, it was often suppressed by the authorities, and as a result, drummers would use boxes or furniture drawers, fooling the police who were looking for conga drums.

If the *danzón* was a European creation with African touches, and the *son* an ideal mix of Euro-African musics and instruments, the rumba was definitely an African and working-class creation. Perhaps for this reason, after 1959 the Cuban Revolution tried to make the rumba Cuba's national music, and there was a governmental effort to present Cuba's culture as one of workers, Afro-Latin, egalitarian, collective, and socialist.

Cuba is also a country with a strong *bolero* (ballads, romantic or otherwise) tradition, which has a strong Spanish influence, but also became Afro-Cubanized: María Teresa Vera (1895–1965), Sindo Garay (1867–1968), Manuel Corona (1880–1950), and others were some of the great Afro-Cuban *boleristas* who became famous throughout all of Latin America. Afro-Cuban music also informs Cuba's classical tradition, and even white composers of popular music, such as Ernesto Lecuona (1895–1963), drew heavily on Afro-Cuban themes. Tania León (1943–) and Leo Brouwer (1935–) are Afro-Cuban classical composers. León was a former musical director of the Dance Theater of Harlem; Brouwer, a world-renowned guitarist.

LITERATURE AND THE ARTS

Cuba has had a rich literary tradition, starting in the sixteenth century. However, in the nineteenth century the mixed race poet Plácido (1809–1844) and the ex-slave Juan Francisco Manzano (1797–1854), who wrote an important autobiography, became key literary figures. However, they were overshadowed by white writers such as Cirilo Villaverde (1812–1894), Gertrudis Gómez de Avellaneda (1814–1873), and José Martí, but they often wrote about slavery or issues of race. Martí (1853–1895), who was a poet, journalist, essayist, writer, and activist is considered a founding father of the island, a mix of George Washington and Walt Whitman, the supreme poet-warrior.

Nicolás Guillén (1902–1989), a central figure of Afro-Cubanism, was one of the major poets of the twentieth century. Although he became famous for his Afro-Cuban poetry, which has often been put to music, Guillén's "mulatto poetry," always embedded its antiracism within a committed social message. Other writers, like Regino Pedroso (1896–1983), of Afro-Chinese descent, went from lyrical to socially committed black poetry to a more cosmic outlook. Gastón Baquero (1918–1997) was one of the island's most gifted poets and a member of the Orígenes group. Alejo Carpentier (1904–1980), whose magical realist novels encompassed historical, musical, and religious realms, and many of whose works were dedicated to Afro-Cuban culture, was white.

The Cuban Revolution brought about an enormous increase in cultural production, be it literary, cinematic, musical, or in the plastic arts. As a result, a series of Afro-Cuban writers came to the fore: Pedro Pérez Sarduy (1943–), Manuel Granados (1931–), Tomás González (1938–), and Alberto Pedro (1930–); many women also became established as writers as well, like Excilia Saldaña (1946–1999), Georgina Herrera (1936–), and Soleida Ríos (1950–). The best-known African-Cuban woman writer is Nancy Morejón (1944–), a poet, essayist, and translator. Víctor Fowler Calzada (1960–), a poet and outstanding literary critic, has lucid essays on feminism, gayness, and eroticism in Cuban literature.

In the visual arts, the two most accomplished artists from before 1950 were Alberto Peña (1894–1938), who drew socially charged black subjects, and Wifredo Lam (1900–1982), the Afro-Chinese artist, whose eerie paintings are known the world over for their haunting evocation of Afro-Cuban mythologies. More recent Afro-Cuban artists are Manuel Mendive (1944–), Ricardo Rodríguez Brey (1956–), Glexis Novoa (1964–), Tomás Esson (1963–), and Magda Campos Pons (1959–), a multimedia artist who combines painting, installations, and performance while exploring the personal dimensions of her Afro-Cuban identity living in the United States. Even white artists like José Bedia (1959–), a practicing *palero*, draws heavily on Afro-Cuban religions in his work.

Afro-Cuban writers and visual artists do not always concentrate on black themes or racial issues. However, they have recently raised issues on black representation, radically questioning the "exoticization" or "folklorization" of blackness through tourism or the trendy multiculturalism of U.S. and European museums. These issues were brought up in the sixties by ethnologist Rogelio Martínez Furé (1937–) and by historian Walterio Carbonell (1925–), whose "Critique: Birth of a National Culture" (1961) sharply contested the underlying whiteness and Eurocentrism of the Cuban elite's definition of national culture.

CONCLUSION

At different times in its history, Cuba's obsession with national unity has made it view discussing race as bordering on treason. But underneath, there is a disturbing paradox: singling out white racism can be viewed as unpatriotic, but making a derogatory remark about blacks is not viewed as "unpatriotic."

Nicolás Guillén, one of the island's great poets, stated that "Cuba's soul is mestizo, and it is from the soul, not the skin, that we derive our definite color. Someday it will be called 'Cuban color'" (in Perez Sarduy & Stubbs 1993, 235). Guillén's words on racial mixing must be understood as describing a "naturally evolving" historical process and not a program for forced whitening. And yet "whiteness" persists as an ideal norm, as do Eurocentric attitudes about family, race, and nation. A hundred years after independence, and after more than forty of socialist revolution, Cubans are finding that they need all the resources possible—state, civil society, and individuals—to make their soul and skin the same color, that is, truly Cuban.

REFERENCES

Barnet, Miguel (2001). *Afro-Cuban Religions*. Princeton, NJ: Markus Wiener/Ian Randle Publishers.

Carpentier, Alejo (2001). *Music in Cuba*. Minneapolis: University of Minnesota Press.

de la Fuente, Alejandro (2000). *A Nation for All: Race, Inequality, and Politics in Twentieth Century Cuba*. Chapel Hill: University of North Carolina Press.

Fernández Robaina, Tomás (1994). *El negro en Cuba, 1902–1958*. La Habana, Cuba: Editorial Ciencias Sociales.

Foner, Philip S. (1977). *Antonio Maceo the "Bronze Titan" of Cuba's Struggle for Independence*. New York: Monthly Review Press.

González Wippler, M. (1989). *Santería: The Religion*. New York: Crown Publishers.

Helg, Aline (1995). *Our Rightful Share: The Afro-Cuban Struggle for Equality, 1886–1912*. Chapel Hill: University of North Carolina Press.

Howard, Philip (1998). *Changing History: Afro-Cuban Cabildos and Societies of Color in Nineteenth Century Cuba*. Baton Rouge, LA: Louisiana State University Press.

López Valdés, Rafael (1985). *Componentes africanos en el etnos cubano*. La Habana, Cuba: Editorial Ciencias Sociales.

Moore, Carlos (1988). *Castro, the Blacks and Africa*. Los Angeles, CA: UCLA Center for Afro-American Studies.

Moreno Fraginals, Manuel (1976). *The Sugar Mill: The Socioeconomic Complex of Sugar in Cuba, 1760–1860*. New York: Monthly Review Press.

Ortiz, Fernando (1995/1940). *Cuban Counterpoint: Tobacco and Sugar*. Durham, NC: Duke University Press.

——— (1993/1950). *La africanía de la música folklórica de Cuba*. La Habana, Cuba: Editorial Letras Cubanas.

Paquette, Robert L. (1988). *Sugar Is Made with Blood: The Conspiracy of La Escalera and the Conflict between Empires over Slavery in Cuba*. Middleton, CT: Wesleyan University Press.

Pérez Sarduy, P., and J. Stubbs (1993). *AfroCuba, An Anthology of Cuban Writing on Race, Politics and Culture*. Melbourne, Australia: Ocean Press.

——— (2000). *AfroCuban Voices: On Race and Identity in Contemporary Cuba*. Gainesville, FL: University Press of Florida.

Scott, Rebecca J. (2000/1985). *Slave Emancipation in Cuba: The Transition to Free Labor, 1860–1899*. Pittsburgh, PA: University of Pittsburgh Press.

6

The Dominican Republic

Ramona Hernández and Nancy López

The Dominican Republic is located in the eastern part of the island of Hispaniola. The Republic of Haiti is found on the western side of the same island. After Cuba, Hispaniola is the second largest island of the Caribbean archipelago, with a current population of 7.3 milllion people, made up of 12 percent black, 73 percent mixed race (Afro-European or mulatto), and 15 percent white. The island of Hispaniola, the first European foothold in what came to be known as the New World, was known by its original inhabitants, the Taínos, as Haití or Babeque. On December 5, 1492, during his first voyage to the New World, Christopher Columbus found the island of Haití, and by the end of the same month, the Spaniard, along with his crew, took possession of the island, its wealth, and its people.

COLONIZATION AND BLACKNESS

Soon Hispaniola became a full-fledged Spanish colony. In the process of colonization, this tiny island, populated by peaceful and friendly people whose culture possessed values and norms that were diametrically opposed to those found in Spanish culture, saw a rapid deculturation, whereby aboriginal institutions were replaced by Spanish ones. As early as 1493, the Spaniards had fully accommodated themselves on the first settlement in the New World: Villa La Isabela. By 1535 when the Viceregal Court, supreme Spanish political and judicial authority in the New World, was moved from Hispaniola to Mexico, the institutional building process had already given way to an established colony boasting the first Spanish institutions erected in the New World: the city of Santo Domingo (1502), the San Nicolás de Barí Hospital (1503), a chamber of commerce (1503), and the Nuestra

Señora de Encarnación Cathedral (1521). Yet, also by 1535, the Taíno population had drastically declined, many of the blacks who had been brought as slaves to replace the Taínos as laborers had risen in the first rebellion of black slaves in the New World against their Spanish oppressors, and a new demographic configuration began to manifest itself. People of African descent would forever predominate over any other ethnic or racial group in Hispaniola.

LADINOS AND BOZALES

The exact date of arrival of the first blacks is unknown. Some believe that blacks were brought as early as 1496, to work on the construction of some of the first settlements in Hispaniola (Larrazábal Blanco 1998, 17–24). By 1501, a number of blacks brought by their owners directly from Spain, lived on the island. Similarly, by 1502, some of the 2,500 Spaniards who came to Hispaniola brought with them an unknown number of blacks. These blacks, many of whom were slaves (others were free) came as salaried workers, and having come from Spain, they were acculturated to Spanish mores. By this time, black male slaves were assigned to work in the gold mines found on the island. Quickly, these acculturated black slaves, called *Ladinos*, discovered that there was a drastic difference between working as a slave in Spain and working as a slave in Hispaniola, where the get-rich-quick mentality meant working long hours under harsh conditions, with insufficient food. By comparison, in Spain most slaves were seen as ornaments, working as domestic servants. Some have argued that during that time servitude in Spain was permeated by a paternalistic attitude on the part of the owners who were rich and belonged to the nobility, and that such an attitude characterized the social relationship between masters and their black slaves who worked as servants (Deive 1997, 20).

The tough working conditions black Ladino slaves faced in Hispaniola would prompt them to end their suffering. Soon black Ladino slaves began to run away from their masters. Secluding themselves in the high mountains, some runaways found refuge among some Taínos who had luckily escaped a premature death under the Spanish regime, while others ended up forming communities of their own. Slaves who ran away were called *cimarrones* by Spaniards. (*Cimarrones* was the origin of the English word "Maroon"). Cimarrones lived in *manieles* or *cumbes* (runaway settlements).

In 1503, a new governor arrived at Hispaniola, Fray Nicolás de Ovando. On arrival, Ovando asked the Spanish Crown to prohibit the sending of more black slaves to Hispaniola. The governor, a religious man, believed that black slaves were rebellious, vicious, and ungrateful. They looked for every opportunity to escape, corrupted Taínos by "teaching them bad habits," and once they escaped, it was not easy to capture them (Deive 1997, 20). As Ovando requested, the shipping of slaves to Hispaniola stopped. But slaves constantly escaped and the Taíno population was being decimated, leaving Hispaniola without enough people to be exploited. Thus, the concrete need for able bodies to perform the hard work and the Spaniards' insatiable ambition for wealth put an end to the prohibition on importing slaves to Hispaniola.

In 1505, the Crown authorized the sending of 17 slaves to work in the gold mines. Months later, governor Ovando himself requested another 20 black slaves to be assigned to multiple duties. Between 1505 and 1510, the Crown authorized the entrance of 250 slaves to Hispaniola. Contrary to the first groups brought prior to 1505, these slaves did not come from Spain, but directly from different parts of Africa. Slaves brought from Africa were called *Bozales*. Besides the authorized 250, an unknown number of slaves were systematically brought by Spaniards as contraband. This illicit trade rapidly spread throughout the New World to avoid strict commercial regulations, and high taxes imposed by the Spanish Crown.

The reason for importing slaves directly from Africa was twofold. First, black slaves had become scarce in Spain. Second, Spaniards who lived in Hispaniola believed that black Ladinos were inherently rebellious and malicious and that black Bozales were obedient and passive. The Spanish also believed that slaves from Africa were biologically capable of resisting hard work and were not "contaminated" by civilization. Early on, slaves were perceived as good or bad. At this point, at least among the authorities, there was no unilateral view among the Spaniards concerning slaves whose skin color was black. How slaves were perceived depended on whether they had been born in Spain or Africa. That perversely rigid distinction between evil and good slaves persisted for a while until the greed of both local and peninsular Spaniards overrode such subtleties. Gold production was dwindling and by 1511 was almost extinct. Gold reserves disappearing meant greater importation of slaves for working on sugar plantations (shift from gold to sugar). Equally important was the dramatic extinction of the aboriginal population, which declined from 300,000 in 1492 to 60,000 in 1511, and to 500 by 1548 (Cassá 1977, 58).

LIFE ON THE SUGAR PLANTATIONS AND ON THE FARMS

By 1527 the economy in Hispaniola had shifted from mining to sugar production and cattle raising. While cattle raising required land, it was labor-extensive; the production of sugar was labor-intensive, and technical skills were needed. Each economic activity would simultaneously generate distinct social relationships between masters and slaves, creating the basis for the subsequent development of different social behavior and attitudes among the slaves.

The first sugar mill began its operation in the city of Santo Domingo in 1520. Spain, wishing to participate in the lucrative sugar business, which at that time was controlled by the Portuguese, Venetians, and Dutch, invested heavily in Hispaniola's sugar development. To encourage its growth, the Crown eliminated all taxes associated with sugar, authorized the importation of a large number of black slaves, whether Ladinos or Bozales, made loans available to those Spaniards who wanted to get into the sugar business, and exonerated sugar mill owners from paying the required tithe to the Catholic Church. By 1527, twenty-five sugar mills were functioning at full capacity. Slaves assigned to the sugar plantations worked intensely, had little rest, were malnourished, and were exposed to constant supervision. Yet, it was difficult for the small white population to keep control over the large number of slaves who constantly escaped into the dense mountains, becoming *cimarrones* and forming *manieles* (runaway settlements).

The island's ideal climate facilitated cattle breeding, and the owners of the farms (*hatos*) were called *hateros*. Cattle raising was highly lucrative and compared with sugar, it required less capital investment and its products (particularly hides) were in high demand and easier to sell as contraband. As time went on, some ex-slaves and mulattoes would also become *hateros*, either by capturing wild animals or, in the case of the mulattoes, by inheriting the business from their white fathers.

The nature of cattle raising gave slaves greater mobility than plantation workers. It also meant that slaves in the *hatos* had access to more food (fruits and other foods), were not exposed to constant supervision, and were, therefore, less regulated. Because of this, it is believed that very few slaves who lived in the *hatos* escaped to the *manieles*.

THE RACIAL COMPOSITION OF HISPANIOLA

As sugar production increased so did the black population. This dynamic forever altered the racial composition of the island. Racial formation in the Dominican Republic was affected by the peculiar demographic composition of the colony: since its early years people of African ancestry became the overwhelming majority in a society with a small white minority. By 1546, while the white population amounted to some 5,000 people, the number of black slaves had already reached some 12,000 people. By 1587, when sugar production had already begun to decline, the number of slaves amounted to some 20,000, while the number of whites, mestizos, and mulattoes (the latter two were free) remained small. At the beginning of the seventeenth century, most of the people of Hispaniola were of mixed African and Spanish ancestry. By the end of the sixteenth century, already 69 percent of the people were either black, *pardo* (brown, dark gray), or mulatto, and over 70 percent of them were free (Larrazábal Blanco 1998, 183). For most of its colonial history, slaves were never more than 20 percent of the population, quite different from, say, Barbados, Jamaica, Haiti, or Suriname, where the figures were closer to 90 percent. By this time, seven classifications were used by the Spaniards to name the different racial mixtures found in the colony.

The mixing of blacks and whites and the reproduction of the dark population was intense and systematic. The demographic dynamics were provoked by an imbalance produced by the constant emigration of whites, the severe lack of white women, and the increasing importation of African slaves. The serious demographic disparity between whites and blacks, the need to expand the pool of people who were qualified to take bureaucratic and other white-collar jobs, but perhaps more importantly, the needy whites had to reassure themselves that they could count on the support of an overwhelmingly dark population to protect the colony from internal rebellion, and from marauding pirates ready to snatch goods and lands from Spain, forced the white colonial regime to discreetly close its eyes to the racial mixing of the groups.

THE ECONOMIC DECLINE OF HISPANIOLA AND ITS IMPACT ON RACIAL FORMATION

In the seventeenth century, the economy of Hispaniola was severely affected by a combination of factors including ill-conceived political decisions, natural disasters, plagues, and illnesses. In 1605, for instance, people residing in the towns of Puerto Plata, Yaguana, Monte Cristi, and Bayahá were ordered to move and relocate farther south under penalty of death. This drastic measure was enacted to stop the widespread contraband that reigned in these towns. The illicit dealings with people from Holland, England, and France generated tremendous capital flight from the Spanish colonies to the enemy countries. But contraband also generated relationships among the groups involved in the prohibited business and served as a direct channel for the penetration of religious and political beliefs that were completely at odds with the Spanish Crown and Spanish culture.

The devastations, as they are known, threw hundreds of families into poverty; they lost all their possessions, including land, homes, and livestock. Of the 110,000 heads of livestock, for instance, only 8,000 were able to be moved by their owners, and only 2,000 made it to their destination, with most of the animals dying on the way. The devastations affected the food supply, leading to a famine that shook the entire society. Between 1606 and 1609, for instance, more than a third of the population of Bayaguana starved to death while many of the young survivors violated the ordinance and left the town in search of food (Moya Pons 1984, 146).

Aside from the devastations, other factors submerged Hispaniola into general poverty. After 1620, its sugar industry could no longer compete with Mexico and Brazil, and it precipitously declined. Cattle raising was affected by low productivity and the lack of vessels to ship hides to Spain. High taxes imposed by the kingdom to support the permanent military presence further crippled the colony's economy, leaving people impoverished. And whoever escaped the scourge of history, politics, and economics was laid waste by epidemics and plagues that killed thousands.

THE COMPLEX AND EVOLVING RACIAL FORMATION

Some believe that the poverty and isolation to which Hispaniola was subjected during the seventeenth century slowly eroded the class/racial structure as it originally existed in the colony, where a rich white class oppressed an impoverished black population, slave or free (Bosch 1971, 109–123). Ironically, widespread hunger and isolation created the conditions for a more pluralistic society. Traditional norms prescribing the social behavior between masters and slaves, the landowners and the landless, the whites and blacks simply had to loosen up: survival was more important. A rigid white superiority-black inferiority racial scheme gave way to a redefined racial order, where both blackness and whiteness acquired a new variety of connotations and meanings, inherent to the new social realities.

The end result was a growing dark-skinned population that systematically began to participate in society at large, particularly in the most important institutions that regulated people's lives: the church, the military, and the government. It is precisely this dynamic that forced the Crown to allow mulattoes to become priests as early as 1707 in Santo Domingo. Such a ruling was only allowed in Santo Domingo, and not in any of the other Spanish colonies.

Although the Crown preferred to have these mulattoes in the lowest echelons of the ecclesiastical hierarchy, this was difficult to enforce. Social relations among blacks and whites had been transforming themselves for years: the all-white ruling elite's hegemony was continually eroded by non-whites.

Moreover, it is evident that in the early years of the colony a portion of the dark population, made up of mulattoes, mestizos, and free blacks, was already perceived by the Spanish authority as having a mind of its own and as people who resisted the imposition of regulations from above if it meant that such impositions went against their economic interest (Moya Pons 1984, 57). Seventeenth-century Dominican society underwent a process of ruralization as its economy shifted from the industrial production of sugar to one based mostly on farms (Bosch 1971, 47–61; Moya Pons 1984, 51–61, 99–111; Báez 1986, 67–80). The economic transformation necessarily entailed a transformation of the relations of productions (the manner in which things are produced in a given economic system like feudalism, slavery, capitalism), and in this case, the nature of the social relationship between masters and slaves of the *hatos* was necessarily more fluid and less rigid than on a sugar plantation. The racial landscape had different black strata: Ladino wage earners, Ladino slaves, and African-born slaves. Each of these three groups would be radically transformed by mixing with whites, Taínos, and among themselves.

Viewed from the outside, it is tempting to call all those of African ancestry black and not see how social status also affected racial perceptions. Indeed, during slavery, some blacks actively collaborated with their masters who paid them to identify runaway societies. Their status was predicated on seeing Maroons as "other," both socially and racially. Ironically, many runaway slaves saw blacks who collaborated with whites as members of their "race" and opted to hide farther into the mountains rather than attacking them.

Some historians have drawn at least two contrasting slave personalities: one servile and one rebellious, reflected in the *cimarrón*. One group tried to emulate whites, and acquiesced out of fear and a will to survive. The runaway, on the other hand, systematically resisted slavery, undermined the symbols of oppression, and insisted on shaping a culture of his or her own. The defiant attitude of the *cimarrones* and their countless ruses to strike back, which kept society on a permanent state of alert for centuries, had wide social repercussions. Masters, afraid their slaves would run away, were forced to soften their treatment of them, or did not dare punish them for "infractions" (Deive 1997, 122).

Matters grow more complex when ex-slaves or free colored are factored in: "there was no common interests and outlook between the slaves and the ex-slaves [for instance]; for the former accused the latter of being voluntary servants of whites, while ex-slaves, because of their freedom, felt that they were white, Spaniards ... [Moreover,] ... ex-slaves occupied an intermediate social position between the black who was born free and the one who remained slave. ... Because of these differences, there was no danger of rebellions that threatened the established social order" (Utrera 1975, 53).

THE FIRST DOMINICAN STATE: RACE AND IDEOLOGY

The Dominican state was created in 1844 when Dominicans separated from Haiti. Haiti, a black republic founded in 1804, ruled Dominicans from 1822 to 1844. The first political group that undermined the Haitian regime, La Trinitaria (Trinity), made up of nine young men who belonged to the middle class, had been formed in 1838. Led by a white Creole, Juan Pablo Duarte, the ideological architect of the group, he believed in the ideal of "independence pure and simple" and the inalienable right of Dominican national sovereignty. By 1844, the original independence movement had grown considerably. Besides the Trinitarios, whose leadership had been targeted and disbanded by the Haitian regime, the movement attracted members of diverse sectors of Dominican society, including members from the well-to-do landowning cattle-raising groups, the merchants, the clergy, members of the white, black, and mulatto middle class, and members of the landless proletariat who were white, free blacks, mulattoes, and black ex-slaves.

The group *los afrancesados* (the pro-French faction) also sought separation from Haiti. This group, however, under the leadership of Buenaventura Báez, proposed placing the new republic under the protection of France. More than intragroup rivalry, these divergences represented antagonistic ideologies whose effects would be felt afterwards in the development and consolidation of the new republic.

Hours after Dominican independence had been achieved, a small but incredibly significant event for Dominican identity took place: the Rebellion of Monte Grande. It was led by Santiago Basora, an African-born man who had been brought to the Spanish colony at a young age. The uprising was the result of distrust by ex-slaves concerning their future within the new republic since the head of the ruling group, Tomás de Bobadilla, an experienced official, had been a former slave owner. Ex-slaves were worried that "an association of the nascent republic with imperial Spain, which still enslaved blacks in Cuba and Puerto Rico, would have imperiled the freedom of many Dominicans" (Torres-Saillant 2000, 14).

The pro-Spanish faction had composed an anthem for the new republic whose opening words, "Rise up in arms, oh Spaniards!" clearly suggested that some separatist Dominicans perceived themselves as Spaniards rather than Dominicans. More reason for distrust.

But the pro-France devotees were also a cause of concern for ex-slaves. Placing the new republic under a French protectorate would have probably meant that colored Dominicans would be differentiated from whites. After all, France had not abolished slavery in its Antillean colonies yet.

Contrary to the Trinitarios who blindly trusted people who later turned against them, the ex-slaves in Monte Grande openly demanded concrete evidence that the new government had no ill intention toward them and that slavery was never going to return. Some suggest that these suspicions went beyond the ex-slaves involved in Monte Grande, extending to ex-slaves in all parts of the country as well (Franco 1984, 161).

President Bobadilla himself negotiated with Basora, the rebel leader of Monte Grande. The new government guaranteed the rebels that slavery had been permanently eliminated in the Dominican Republic. The government went beyond the verbal agreement and promulgated laws that transcended Dominican territory, indirectly undermining slavery in the whole region. "The very first decree promulgated by the Junta Central that first governed the country was the immediate abolition of slavery on March 1, 1844 ... [It] outlawed slave traffic of any kind as a capital crime, ruling that slaves from any provenance would instantly gain their freedom upon setting a foot on the territory of the Dominican Republic" (Torres-Saillant 1999a, 15).

The impact of the Rebellion of Monte Grande went beyond ensuring rights to Dominicans who were ex-slaves: it emphasized a politicized racial identity and challenged those who opposed it.

As in most countries in the Caribbean, nationalism has often trumped race in the Dominican Republic. Aside from the Haitian occupation, the country was reannexed by Spain (1861–1865), militarily occupied by the United States (1916–1924), and invaded by the United States in 1965. Dominican nationalism, thus, while clearly constructed with open or covert racial assumptions, is made up of a host of other factors as well.

Nineteenth- and twentieth-century immigrations also affected both the country's demographics and racial discourse. Cubans fleeing their independence war found relief in the Dominican Republic, as did Sephardic Jews from Curaçao and St. Thomas, Spaniards form the Canary Islands, and smaller groups of Syrians and Lebanese. Most, but not all, were able to assimilate into the white elites. But as sugar production expanded, there was a considerable influx of Haitians, and black workers from the islands: St. Kitts, Nevis, Antigua, St. Maarten,

St. Thomas, St. John, and Anguilla. These East Caribbean workers were usually brought for the cane harvest, but many stayed on; this immigration continued until 1930. Haitians and Eastern Caribbeans became part of the black and mulatto working classes.

TWENTIETH CENTURY: THE STATE AND THE CLASH OF RACIAL IDEOLOGIES

The Dominican Republic has been dominated by two rulers in the twentieth century: Rafael Leónidas Trujillo and Joaquín Balaguer. Both were active promoters of whitening the country.

During Trujillo's reign (1930–1961), popular manifestations of African cultural heritage among Dominicans were illegal. But people resisted such impositions by practicing religions and dancing to African-derived music, such as Vodou and *palos* (rhythmic drums). People's resistance brought on the state's reaction to blackness, enacting Law 391 in 1943. Law 391 made it illegal to participate in Vodou ceremonies, and those who did, could be incarcerated for up to a year, in addition to being fined 500 pesos (Deive 1992, 186).

The Trujillista state was committed to whitening the Dominican people. Some have claimed that the Dominican Republic contains the largest number of mulattoes in the world. Indeed, by the twentieth century, over 85 percent of the Dominican people exhibited an incredible variety of hues that ranged from black to light-skinned black. Only a small minority are light-skinned or white. But Dominican blackness went beyond skin color; physical attributes and culture were seen as overwhelmingly representing something other than white. To increase the number of whites, the Dominican state encouraged the immigration of people who were considered whites while a fee of 500 pesos was imposed on non-Caucasian or Indian migrants. The Dominican Republic was the first country in the world to welcome Jews fleeing Nazi persecution during World War II, not so much because they were against anti-Semitism, but because European Jews were phenotypically white to Trujillo.

But the racist state project went further. Traces of blackness among Dominicans were "eliminated" when the color of their skin became "Indian" on all of their official documentation (i.e., passport, national ID card). Dominican dolls dressed in typical attire, made for the export market, became light-skinned, blue or brownish eyed, and had long hair that was light or dark-silky. Trujillo also had economic plans concerning the borders between Haiti and the Dominican Republic, a zone highly populated by Haitian migrants. Some believe that Trujillo wanted to make the area into a prosperous industrialized zone, fully integrated to the rest of the country. But others differ in light of the most egregious racist act committed by the Dominican state: the horrendous 1937 massacre of over 12,000 Haitians (others claim 25,000). Though most resided in the border between the two nations, the Haitians were accused of trespassing and slaughtered.

In the case of Balaguer (1907–2002), Trujillo's successor, his pro-European and Negrophobic sentiments were systematically manifested in his public speeches and writings. In addition, during his governments (1966–1978; 1986–1990; 1990–1994; 1994–1996), the school system continued to use books in which the country's African ancestry was either trivialized or nonexistent. Balaguer associated the economic underdevelopment of the Dominican Republic with the country's proximity to Haiti. In his view, traces of what was perceived as African ancestry devalued a Dominican's physical appearance. Balaguer believed that by regulating Haitian immigration, African influences in Dominican society would eventually disappear (Balaguer 1984).

The assassination of Trujillo in 1961 marked an opening for ideas opposing the Negrophobic state. During the 1970s, intellectual circles in Dominican society produced groundbreaking writings on the black experience in the Dominican Republic. First published in the 1970s, Franklin Franco's work, *Los Negros, Los Mulatos y la Nación Dominicana* (Blacks, Mulattoes and the Dominican Nation), with fourteen editions, is perhaps the seminal work on the black experience in the Dominican Republic. The efforts of Franco and numerous other Dominicans have sought to uncover the missing chapters of Dominican history and insist that Afro-Dominicans and women be included in the official national curriculum.

Most recently, Dominicans demonstrated their challenge to the blatant Negrophobic state by casting their ballots for the "black" and reputedly "Haitian" candidate in recent presidential elections, Dr. Francisco Peña Gómez (1937–1998). Subject to a racist campaign that depicted him as a monkey, a Vodou practitioner, and as someone who wanted to annex the country to Haiti, Peña Gómez lost the presidency because of electoral fraud. Moreover, during the 1990s, certain sectors of Dominican society began to collaborate actively with Haitians residing in the Dominican Republic to demand from the state protection for thousands of Dominican-born children of Haitian parents who were routinely denied their citizenship rights, such as a birth certificate and an education.

In similar fashion, sectors of the Dominican and Haitian communities residing in the United States joined forces to condemn the Dominican government presided over by Dr. Leonel Fernández (president 1996–2000). The groups demanded a stop to the abuses commonly committed against Haitian citizens in the Dominican Republic and to the massive deportations to which Haitian citizens and Dominican children of Haitian parents were routinely subjected. Recently, the Dominican minister of education reiterated her commitment to allow any child residing in the Dominican Republic to attend public school, regardless of proof of citizenship.

The huge presence of Dominicans in the United States, close to or more than a million, has added new layers to their racial perception of themselves. Many Dominicans who thought they were white, or at least not black, found themselves, if they were dark-skinned, being called black—or defined as Hispanic, and often made to choose between the two. However, despite U.S. and Dominican differences on race, their U.S. immigrant experience has allowed Dominicans to see race from a different perspective, and both reaffirm blackness and Dominicanness in a new way (Torres-Saillant 1999a, 61–63).

CONCLUSION

Observers of race matters in the Dominican Republic have generally overlooked those sectors of Dominican society that have resisted and undermined racist projects, usually focusing on Dominican manifestations of pro-white, Eurocentric ideologies. If seen within the limited confines of the U.S. one-drop rule, resistance to racial oppression among groups who look "black" but who may not identify themselves as such, is not manifest. From a U.S. perspective, the distinctions and different classifications of blackness in the Dominican Republic camouflage overt racism against blacks, ultimately revealing a desire to only be white.

Racial formation in the Dominican Republic, nevertheless, has been characterized by historical complexities derived, in part, from the different social meanings applied to blackness throughout Dominican history. The perception of blackness among Dominicans becomes problematized when one factors in the Haitian occupation. In the process of forging an identity for their republic, Dominicans needed to construct an identity that radically differentiated them from that of Haiti, the old ruler and "mortal enemy." Such an identity resulted from different and competing ideologies of those times and from whether the destiny of the republic was in the hands of white Creoles—a colonial ruling class whose self-differentiation was racially defined to the core—so that Haiti was made synonymous with the denial of sovereignty, oppression, and, of course, blackness. This differentiation had linguistic, religious, and moral components as well: Haiti rejected Europe, spoke Creole, practiced Vodou and polygamy; Dominicans embraced their Hispanicness, spoke Spanish, were Catholics, and believed in marriage.

None of this denies the existence of racism in the Dominican Republic or the persistence of a mentality that perceives Dominicans as whites and obliterates any trace of their Afro-Dominican heritage. Given the island's complex racial history, factors other than plain anti-black racism need to be examined to understand how Dominicans interpret whiteness and blackness, especially in light of the fact that the overwhelming majority of the country is non-white. Increasingly, Dominicans are aware of how whiteness and blackness are social constructions, as in any society where these issues matter (Candelario 1999). But equally they are affirming their Afro-Dominican heritage with greater confidence but in a way that "defies racial extremism" (Torres-Saillant 1999a, 63). Given the country's political history, this will take place within a commitment to democratization; economic, social, and gender justice; and a more inclusive notion of identity, all uniquely Dominican.

REFERENCES IN ENGLISH

Austerlitz, Paul (1997). *Merengue: Dominican Music and Dominican Identity*. Philadelphia: Temple University Press.

Candelario, Ginetta E.B. (1999). "On Whiteness and Other Absurdities: Preliminary Thoughts on Dominican Racial Identity in the United States." In Brea, Espinal, and Valerio Holguín (eds.), *La República Dominican En El Umbral del Siglo XXI: Cultura, Política y Cambio Social*. Santo Domingo: Pontificia Universidad Católica Madre y Maestra.

Ferguson, James (1992). *Dominican Republic: Beyond the Lighthouse*. New York: Latin America Bureau/Monthly Review Press.

Georges, Eugenia (1990). *The Making of a Transnational Community: Migration, Development and Cultural Change in the Dominican Republic*. New York: Columbia University Press.

Moya Pons, Frank (1995). *The Dominican Republic: A National History*. Hispaniola Books. New York: CUNY-Dominican Studies Institute.

Torres-Saillant, Silvio (1999a). "Introduction to Dominican Blackness." Dominican Studies Working Paper Series #1. New York: CUNY-Dominican Studies Institute.

——— (2000). "Dominican Blackness and the Modern World." Unpublished manuscript.

REFERENCES IN SPANISH

Báez Evertsz, Franc (1986). *La formación del sistema agroexportador en el Caribe: República Dominicana y Cuba: 1515–1898*. Santo Domingo: Editora Universitaria.

Balaguer, Joaquín (1984). *La isla al revés: Haití y el destino dominicano*. 2d ed. Santo Domingo: Librería Dominicana, S.A.

Bosch, Juan (1971). *Composición social dominicana*. Santo Domingo: Editora Alfa y Omega.

Campillo Pérez, Julio Genaro (1994). *Documentos del primer gobierno dominicano: Junta Central Gubernativa, febrero–noviembre 1844*. Santo Domingo: Colección del Sesquicentenario de la Independencia Nacional.

Cassá, Roberto (1977). *Historia social y económica de la República Dominicana*. Vol. I. Santo Domingo: Editora Alfa y Omega.

——— (1992). *Historia social y económica de la República Dominicana*. Vol. 2. Santo Domingo: Editora Alfa y Omega.

Deive, Carlos (1992). *Vodu y magia en Santo Domingo*. 3d. ed. Santo Domingo: Fundación Cultural Dominicana.

——— (1997). "Herencia Africana en la Cultura Dominicana de Actual." In *Ensayos sobre Cultura Dominicana*. Santo Domingo: Editora Amigo de el Hogar.

Franco, Franklin J. (1984). *Los negros, los mulatos y la nación dominicana*. 7th ed. Santo Domingo: Editora Nacional.

Gimbernard, Jacinto (1971). *Historia de Santo Domingo*. Santo Domingo: Offset Sardá.

Gratereaux, Federico Enríquez (1988). "Negros de Mentira y Blancos de Verdad." Eme-Eme: *Estudios Dominicanos* 15, no. 81: pp. 73–80.

Guzmán, Daisy Josefina (1974). "Raza y lenguaje en el Cibao." Eme-Eme: *Estudios Dominicanos* 11: pp. 3–45.

Larrazábal Blanco, Carlos (1998). *Los Negros y la esclavitud en Santo Domingo*. 2d ed. Santo Domingo: Editora de Colores, S.A.

Malagón Barceló, Javier (ed.) (1974/1784). *Código Negro Carolino*. Santo Domingo: Ediciones Taller.

Moya Pons, Frank (1984). *Manual de Historia Dominicana*. 8th ed. Santiago, R.D.: Universidad Catolica Madre y Maestra.

——— (1992). *Manual de historia dominicana*. 9th ed. Santo Domingo: Caribbean Publishers.

Pichardo, Bernardo (1967). *Resumen de historia patria*. 5th ed. Colección Pensamiento Dominicano. Santo Domingo: Julio D. Postigo, C. por A.

Torres-Saillant, Silvio (1999b). *El retorno de las yolas: Ensayos sobre diáspora, democracia y dominicanidad*. Santo Domingo: Editora Manatí.

Utrera, Fray Cipriano de (1975). "La condición social del negro en la Època colonial." Eme-Eme: *Estudios Dominicanos* 3, no. 17: pp. 43–60.

7

French Guiana

Mickaëlla L. Pèrina

Located on the northeastern shoulder of South America, French Guiana is a sparsely populated country of 160,000. In February 2001, a surprising mission was organized by two magistrates on the Maroni River, which separates Suriname and French Guiana, a department of France. Their purpose was to meet with the "populations of the River" and clarify misunderstandings following 1996 and 1998 censuses. Initially designed to count French citizens along the Maroni River who did not have national identification documents, the results left many uncounted, causing great controversy. In fact, the two counts only included people born in France or with a parent born in France, thereby excluding all individuals unable to prove birth on French (or Guianese) soil or a direct family tie with a French citizen. According to French judicial executives, the census procedure was efficient and the controversy was essentially based on an unfortunate mix-up. By "evaluation of French citizens" the people of the River, in other words Amerindians and Maroons (also known as "Bush Negroes"), understood that the so-called regularization of illegal immigrants should have entailed the opportunity for citizens to obtain proper documentation. The controversy is based on unresolved prior difficulties related to the ongoing exchange of populations from both sides of the river.

That such a mission need take place at the beginning of the twenty-first century within a French department seems anachronistic, and yet highlights the specificity of Guiana's political status as a department within the French republic. Clearly Guiana was historically shaped by French colonialism, and it constitutes France's biggest department with a surface of 35,135 square miles, ten times the size of Puerto Rico.

Guiana's current population is very diverse and has resulted from constant efforts to bring in new migrants to compensate for a population too small to create a labor force for sustained economic development. However, not all migrants are the same, as the recent mission on the Maroni River illustrates. Lack of proper social integration and new migrations are now regarded as potential causes for social friction since now migrants represent more than 40 percent of the population.

Is Guianese identity at stake? How does Guiana reconcile these migrations with the political and economic challenges it faces? Is Guianese culture only a mirror of society or can it help create a new model for social harmony and development?

LAND OF MIGRATION OR HOSTILE LAND?

Amerindians were living in Guiana prior to colonization and today this precedence is a significant claim within the society, although they are considerably less numerous than other groups. It is by no means a homogenous group: they are divided into the Arawaks, Emerillon, Galibi, Wayana, and Wayapi, and are mostly established in small villages along the Maroni valley and river and the Oyapock, a river on the southeast coast that borders on Brazil. However, the ethnic groups have different relationships with non-Amerindian Guiana. While Arawaks have long intermarried with other groups and have formed part of Creole culture, Galibi feared and still fear assimilation to the point that in the early 1980s, they used first people's rights to argue for territorial rights, as well as for the right to remain Galibi. These claims are part of a long struggle to keep their independence that began with colonization and the decimation of their peoples. Their contact with previously unknown diseases reduced the original Amerindian population of 30,000 to 800 by 1946 when Guiana's colonial status changed to that of being a French department. After 1946 their population increased and was 4 percent of the population by 1981 (6,000).

It is difficult to assess if Amerindian numbers are still increasing, because estimates are no longer available: their statistical and judicial "invisibility" are part of French law, which sees it as discriminatory to distinguish citizens on the basis of their ethnicity. Some argue that their numbers are not expanding—and that the law papers over the ability to track their demise (and reverse it, hopefully)—since Amerindians are still highly vulnerable to disease and environmental destruction.

Similar difficulties apply to Afro-Guianese Maroons and their descendants, who originally settled in Guiana after escaping from Surinamese plantations at the end of the eighteenth century, as well as to recent Surinamese migrants of Maroon background. As Maroons they settled in the Maroni area and organized their life on both sides of the river, without considering the river as an official border between two colonies. They kept their distance from the French colonial order, refusing to work on Guianese plantations when contacted by the Guianese governor in 1782. Their integration within the French republic remains uncertain. They have kept their language, religion, customs, and architecture and have had episodic conflicts with the French administration as they go back and forth irregularly to both sides of the Maroni River, ignoring immigration laws. For them Guiana has long constituted a land of freedom where they could, and still can, make a living. However, a new generation of Maroons educated in Guianese schools and identifying with both Guiana and France need to be officially and legally integrated into society.

It is difficult to estimate the Maroon population because many do not have legal identification and the French administration has yet to define a strategy to integrate them. In 1946 estimates of Maroons were about 3,000 distributed in four ethnic groups: Djuka, Paramaca, Saramaka, and Boni. In 1981, they represented 8 percent of the population. They remain strongly attached to their lifestyle, culture, and values but do occasionally interact with other groups culturally and by intermarriage, especially with Afro-Creoles.

IMMIGRANT WAVES

While Guiana meant home for Amerindians and freedom for the Maroons, it meant enslavement and death for many Africans and even financial loss for some colonists. The ever encroaching jungle, tropical diseases, and natural disasters gave Guiana a reputation for being a hostile land. Since the commerce in slaves yielded little profit, the number of slaves was always limited (13,474 slaves in 1807). African slaves were initially sent to Guiana as labor and since for whites, blacks were reputed to excel at manual labor in harsh, tropical conditions, they were supposed to multiply, but when they did not, importation of slaves was restricted. However, slaves who survived and their children made Guiana their home after the abolition of slavery (1848) and became French citizens.

By the end of the nineteenth century, the Creole population was numerically weak and needed new members. From 1880 gold prospectors came from neighboring countries as well as from the Caribbean islands. Colonial administrators estimated a figure of 11,000 gold prospectors in 1921. The eruption of a volcano in Martinique (1902) also sent a group of Martinican settlers to Guiana.

Guiana always counted on Europeans, who constituted the second most important group during colonization (after Africans) and who now compose the third most numerous group of migrants. During colonization, Europeans were separated into a free population—essentially civil servants, military personnel, and businesspeople as well as industrial professionals—and a penal population was assigned to the St.-Laurent du Maroni penitentiaries.

LATE-TWENTIETH-CENTURY IMMIGRANT GROUPS

French Guiana has experienced enormous demographic and ethnic changes in the last forty years. Some local observers would rather speak of citizenship than of ethnicity regarding the new immigrant groups. To these observers, most immigrants, then, are foreigners. Immigrants from the French Caribbean represent "only" 41 percent of this recent immigration. Foreigners arrived in French Guiana in two waves: first, the Surinamese, Asian, and Hmong, responding to Guiana's political and economic plans of the 1960s, and second, Brazilians and Haitians who came in the eighties, uninvited.

In twenty years the immigrant population has increased fourfold. By 1980, the proportion of immigrants was close to 45 percent of the total population, increasing the diversity within the Creole community. Several factors motivated these migrations: the construction of the Kourou Space Center (perhaps the French equivalent to NASA), the Surinamese political crisis of the eighties, conflicts in Indochina, and Guiana's political and economic stability. To those immigrants Guiana was a land of freedom and economic opportunity, its inhospitable reputation a distant memory.

Most of the Brazilian immigrants are Amerindian and/or black, and come from the poor regions of Brazil close to Guiana. According to estimates their immigration has multiplied sixfold in twenty years, reaching a total of 5,300 individuals in 1985, making them the third largest immigrant group after Haitians and French Europeans.

The largest group, the Haitians, were estimated at 13,457 individuals by the end of the eighties. Although initially planned, their immigration has become "spontaneous," increasing rapidly.

This constant immigration has had tremendous effects on the society, influencing the demography, modifying the ethnic distribution of economic activities, shaping new identities, and causing some social unease.

THE LIFE OF COMMUNITIES VERSUS POLITICAL STRUCTURES AND ECONOMIC DEVELOPMENT

It would be hard to argue with those who say that "[t]he rhythm of France's history is what propels the great moments in Guianese history" (Mam-Lam-Fouck 1996, 13). But those moments always involved several sectors of society, and were dependent on their needs and will.

Although the slave trade lasted for almost two centuries, from 1652 to 1831, it never shaped space or society as much as it did in the sugar islands. In Guiana planters were not numerous—several hundred in the seventeenth and eighteenth centuries, slightly more than 2,000 in the nineteenth. Their limited production was far below that of other colonies and molded both their demand for slaves as well as their ability to pay for replenishing slave labor. In fact, the Guianese slave market was never as active as any of the other slave markets in the region, and the colony, ultimately, received only a fraction of the enslaved Africans brought to the Americas. In 1830 when the Guianese slave population was more numerous than ever (19,261 slaves), it was still far below what was considered necessary for the economic and demographic growth of a colony and new ways of populating had to be considered. Slaves did constitute over 80 percent of the population.

In 1848, on the eve of the abolition of slavery, the colonial population was almost 19,000 inhabitants, essentially organized on the coast, following the geographic pattern of the plantations. Planters and colonizers were concerned enough to consider populating Guiana with Europeans and France attempted twice to create white colonization, first in the eighteenth century and later in the 1850s.

In 1763 the first attempt, known as the Kourou expedition, was made when the French minister of the navy planned on introducing 15,000 Europeans to Guiana, which then only numbered 7,500 inhabitants. The new white colony was expected to supplant the former black colony and compensate for the French colonial loss of Canada and Louisiana. In addition, the new colony was also designed to provide a military base to defend French interests in the region and to produce goods for French consumption. Another effort lasted from 1850 to 1938. It made Guiana a penal colony, under a twofold strategy of exiling convicts and prisoners outside metropolitan territory while helping to populate the colony.

The end of slavery marked a new partitioning of the "colonial space" due both to the discovery and exploitation of gold and to the installation of the penal colonies. Starting in 1852 the arrival, installation, management, and employment of thousands of prisoners induced social transformations, especially in terms of communication, and provoked the development of new economic activity in the western part of the country. Similarly, the period of gold exploitation (1855–1945) resulted in an extension of the "colonial space" toward the south, modifying and disturbing Amerindian and Maroon territories and ecology.

Since landowners saw themselves as "victims" of abolition, colonists wanted the monopoly of the gold production. They created the General Gold Mining Co., which quickly splintered into various private companies created by former slave owners, businessmen, and Creoles. These companies then carved up the interior of the territory into concessions offered by the state, which had authority to grant research and exploitation permits. Ever since, these two contrasting spaces and economies have been interacting but have never merged. One world, forged by colonization and molded by exploitative strategies and the active intervention of the state, was one into which Creoles gradually integrated. The other world, areas inhabited by Amerindians and Maroons, was encroached upon by gold prospectors and had a weak State presence.

POLITICO-CULTURAL ASSIMILATION, SOCIAL EQUALITY, AND ECONOMIC DEVELOPMENT

In 1946, when Guiana became a French overseas department, along with Guadeloupe, Martinique, and Réunion Island, the French government seemed willing to consider the territory from a fresh perspective. Their new vision tried to avoid the "coast" versus "interior" outlook, and instead aimed to consider the new department as a whole. The desire for integration meant interaction with populations who previously had remained marginalized. Then, and now, it is a challenge for Guiana to integrate all segments of its population in a global project of economic development while simultaneously respecting Amerindian and Maroon culture and rights.

To the detriment of Guianese officials and the Guianese population, one could say departmental status did not initially provide room for specificity, distinctiveness, and considerations of ethnodiversity. True, the assumption of a singular and indivisible republic seems to contradict the idea of "exception." The very fact that Guiana was a French department, politically and juridically identical to any other French department, was surely an obstacle to the purported integration of Maroons and Amerindians who wanted their cultural specificity respected.

Nevertheless the evolution of Guiana's status, first to a *région* and now toward a specific political entity that is still being defined, opens doors for an effective policy of integration and recognition of distinct populations. The Région status was voted on in 1972, as France sought to further decentralize its political and administrative apparatus, which also applied to French Guiana, Martinique, and Guadeloupe. The challenge for political leaders is how to create paths of integration that will satisfy all parties, but still respect certain groups' rights not to completely assimilate, for fear of losing their culture, language, and land.

By the late seventies, benefits from departmentalization seemed obvious and plentiful: an increased standard of living, social security, education, health, and social welfare. There was a professional cadre of functionaries, with high Afro-Creole representation among them. But doubts expressed by the early sixties regarding the economic consequences of centralized decisions and limited local power had never disappeared. As in other overseas departments, public-sector high salaries had considerably expanded, but agriculture and industry had diminished. Large parts of the country were still underdeveloped. Although the French presence was not questioned, increasing political and cultural concerns made new relationships between France and Guiana a necessity.

Like previous legislation, the project of regionalization was not designed to distance Guiana from France but to reject cultural assimilation as well as administrative centralization, to acknowledge each department's specific "identity" within the framework of the Republic, and to promote more participation from local elected representatives in the management of local affairs. Regionalization and decentralization certainly complicated the delicate balance between autonomy and departmentalization that had organized Guianese political life since 1946. Regionalization made local management possible and local representatives responsible for social and economic changes. However, the equilibrium remains fragile, since the regional council functions sometimes overlap with general council ones. It is essential that new developments in status maintain political stability since it is a necessary although not sufficient condition for Guianese economic development. It is indeed a new challenge that the population of Guiana has to undertake by including and acknowledging all the contributions of its ethnically diverse population. No doubt, these challenges will be undertaken within the framework of the French republic both because there is a strong historical bond between Guiana and France and because Guiana is home for the Kourou Space Center.

Guiana's bond with France was, and still is, as strong as in other overseas departments (Martinique, Guadeloupe), perhaps even stronger. Indeed two Guianese historical figures are strongly identified with France, World War II, and the resistance to the Vichy regime (which collaborated with fascism) as well as the idea of an extended French community and departmentalization itself. The first figure is Felix Eboué (1884–1944), a Guianese native and descendant of African slaves who became a colonial administrator in what was then French Africa. As governor of Chad, he heroically helped keep France on the Allied side, by rallying to the Free French forces of General De Gaulle. The second is Gaston Monnerville, a Guianese native and lawyer, involved in Guianese politics. Monnerville, in the resistance to the Vichy regime, was nominated member of the French Temporary Consultative Assembly at the time of liberation (1945). On March 14, 1946, he was elected president of the French National Assembly, becoming the first (and only) Guianese and "person of color" to occupy this position. The two men believed in an idea of France that went beyond its borders, seeing its global reach more as a French community rather than a French empire. In his memoir, while remembering Eboué, Monnerville said: "Only France can make an Eboué!" (Monnerville, 1980).

This strong attachment to the idea of a greater France seems to have survived. In December of 2001, a French national party chose a Guianese as its candidate for the presidential election. Christiane Taubira Delanon, a "woman of color," founder and president of a Guianese political movement, Walwari, and a European deputy, is the official candidate for the Parti Radical de Gauche (Radical Party of the Left) for the presidential election. It matters little how successful her campaign turns out: her nomination, unprecedented in French history, sheds light on the way overseas political leaders rely on metropolitan political groups and vice versa. In her nomination acceptance speech she referred to both Monnerville and Eboué, along with Aimé Césaire and Léon Damas. Along with her references to two of the founders of the negritude movement, she added two figures of French Republicanism, all black.

The construction of the Kourou Space Center in 1965 can be regarded as a direct consequence of departmentalization and as a crucial factor in Guiana's development. Indeed, the center generated tremendous economic, demographic, and cultural changes on the coast, while simultaneously reinforcing the definition of Guiana as a part of France and the European Union. The center is surely the biggest company and largest employer in the country, attracting more than just European engineers and executive managers. Immigrants as well as laborers from all over Guiana work there. However, changes produced by the center's presence (rapid means of communication including roads, harbors, an airport, telecommunications, and media) in the coastal area magnify the neglect of the eastern part of the territory. The center has created an enclave of economic growth with a mostly European population (in the technical and administrative jobs), separate from other groups, mostly non-white low-paid workers.

Apart from the European population, new migrants, and especially Saramakan Maroons from Suriname, have settled in Kourou where a "Saramakan village" was quickly created and still exists. "Saramakas, who are considered by their bosses to be unusually conscientious workers, sweep the offices and clean out the toilets of French engineers, and do other low-paid local construction and maintenance work" (Price and Price 1989). But Saramakas take these jobs out of economic necessity and consider themselves as freedom fighters in the just tradition of the first Maroons. For most of them who came as "unofficial refugees" from the Suriname civil war (1986–1992), their current struggle for dignity and for the right to work and educate their children is part of a continuous history of their people's struggles. This proud legacy is not acknowledged by everyone: the rest of the population often regards them as freeloading beneficiaries of the French social system. These anti-Maroon attitudes, which derive from both ignorance and fear, are indicative that these issues have not been addressed by political or judicial authorities, as illustrated by the recent census episode where Maroons were not counted. Saramakas in Kourou, like most Maroons in Guiana, have not yet been integrated into Guianese society, although they have contributed significantly to its economy and culture.

CULTURAL DIVERSITY

Guiana's cultural life reflects the diverse background of its population, expressing its multiple roots that include Latin America, the Caribbean, and Europe. In metropolitan areas a mixed Creole culture dominates, highlighted by music and dances that reflect African, Asian, and Indian impact as well as eighteenth-century French influences. As in Martinique and Guadeloupe, zouk is currently the most popular music along with its corollary zouk-love; it is mainly associated with the Creole language although more "traditional music," like the Creole waltz, mazurka, and *biguine*, are still played and appreciated (see Martinique chapter).

Zouk expresses an ongoing process of creolization involving conservation of previous cultural forms and the addition of new frameworks. In Guiana's case this interaction has had its limits because the country has become so heterogeneous. While mixing and new cultural creativity continues, integration processes are not always reciprocal and even where they do exist they do not necessarily cover all areas of cultural expression. For example, while Maroon music, a music that recently protested oppression by the Surinamese military, has been brought into zouk and reggae, neither Creoles nor whites participate in Maroons' nightly

Mardi Gras 2000, Cayenne, French Guiana. Courtesy of
Mickaëlla L. Pèrina.

musical events. While Maroon music might not attract Creoles and whites, their
crafts and arts, along with Amerindian ones, are well known and generally appreciated by all local ethnic groups as well as foreigners.

Carnival, an event with a strong cultural presence in the French Caribbean,
exemplifies this creativity and diversity. Carnival is preceded by a long period
devoted to costume design and musical composition. Flushed with meaning, it
begins on the first Sunday after Epiphany, ending on Ash Wednesday evening.
Every year Vaval, the king of Carnival, resuscitates on the first day and dies on
the last (Lent); meanwhile, he rules over festivities, processions, and parades.

Carnival displays a true Guianese institution, the "Carnival universities." Several of them exist in the department; among the more fashionable are Nana,
Polina, and la Moina in Cayenne. They are dance halls that are open on Satur-

day nights only during the period of Carnival. Their existence is strongly associated with the "Touloulou," women wearing specific costumes that mask their identity completely. The Touloulou must remain anonymous during the entire Carnival, so they change their costume every night in order not to be recognized. This anonymity allows them to play various identities not normally approved of by society. Within the Carnival universities, only Touloulous can initiate dancing by inviting the men, and the rules—obeyed by everyone—firmly exclude men from initiating dancing. This space of "permissiveness," which is socially and culturally accepted during Carnival, is clearly a welcome relief to women, who can step outside the bounds of male privilege.

Although most of the Creoles and Europeans belong to the Roman Catholic Church, Guiana shows a diversity of religious practices primarily based on ethnicity. Maroons have kept their African-rooted religions (and some Creoles, too), and the Amerindians follow their own religious practices. Easter is also a festive moment, with highlights such as the "Bouillon Díawara," a traditional Easter dish.

Guianese literature has both a rooted and a cosmopolitan flavor. But given the culture of migration, it is difficult to say what makes a specific work Guianese. Is Guianese literature one written by a native and resident of Guiana, or by someone not born in the country who lives long enough in Guiana, or by someone living abroad but of Guianese descent or having been born in the country? There are no easy answers. For example, René Maran (1887–1960), whose novel *Batouala* won the prestigious Goncourt Book Prize in 1921, is usually considered a Martinican author. He was born in Martinique of Guianese parents. This question is pervasive in the long tradition of Guianese literature that includes works in both French and Creole.

Presumably the first literary work ever written in Creole, *Atipa* was written by Alfred Parépou in 1885 and portrayed nineteenth-century Guianese society while addressing political issues. Poetry has been the quintessential Guianese literary genre, best represented by the work of Léon-Gontran Damas (1912–1978). A poet and essayist, Damas participated with Césaire and Leopold Senghor in the creation of the negritude movement that celebrated the African roots of blacks around the globe. Damas voiced that Africanness in his abundant works such as *Nevralgies, Pigments, Black-Label* and *Retour de Guyane*. His poems express a rhythmic intensity by using short emphatic words, repetition of sounds, and visual metaphor.

Bertène Juminer (1927–) and Elie Stephenson (1944–) are both authors whose works attempt to raise social consciousness, avoid strict assimilation, and express the complexities of Afro-Euro-Guianese culture. Juminer was born in Guiana, of a Guianese father and a Guadeloupean mother, but grew up in Guadeloupe, where he retired. Juminer is also referred to as a Guadeloupean novelist and often appears in African literary anthologies since he lived and worked in Africa (Tunis and Dakar).

Stephenson was born in Guiana where he lives. While his poetry reflects on oppressor/oppressed relationships worldwide, his dramas are closely related to

Guianese Creole stories and local interactions between different communities. Stephenson, a nationalist who favors independence consciousness, keeps his distance from the Créolité (creolization) movement of Martinique, which is influential both in and out of the French-speaking Caribbean.

The Créolité debate, which embraces cultural, ethnic, and racial mixing, seems tailored for Guiana's plurality. But unlike Martinique and Guadeloupe, half the population is now foreign born. The population continues to grow dramatically, with new immigrant populations still arriving. The Afro-Creole culture that built the country is no longer the majority, though it is still the largest group. To some, the ethnoracial fragmentation of the country is not held in place by a true sense of national identity, making the different groups always look to the French to mediate these differences. And because of that, all expressions of specificity (Amerindian, Afro-Creole, Maroon, Haitian, Brazilian, Chinese, etc.) revert to a political question of the country's relationship to France (Jones and Stephenson 1995, 72–73).

CONCLUSION

After three centuries of colonization and more than half a century of departmentalization, Guiana entered the new millennium with more local autonomy and a degree of economic development, albeit uneven. However, with abundant land and natural resources, it is in a better position than Martinique and Guadeloupe to chart out its own economic development path. At the same time, Guiana has inherited unresolved problems from the past that might interfere with future choices.

Can Guiana develop while respecting and protecting specific ways of life and rights of its minorities (Amerindian and Maroon)? Can Guiana succeed in effectively integrating currently marginalized groups as well as future migrant populations? How will Guiana proceed to convert its social mosaic into a stable political entity with a growing and sustainable economy?

For the moment, these questions remain unanswered. Nevertheless, recent efforts to create a unique status for each department geared to its specific needs is certainly an opportunity for the Guianese to design new forms of economic development, social and regional integration, and political accountability.

REFERENCES

Anderson, Alan B. (1980). "Recent Acculturation of Bush Negroes in Suriname and French Guiana." *Anthropologica* 22, no. 1: pp. 61–84.

Bilby, Kenneth M. (1989). "War, Peace, and Music: the Guianas." *Hemisphere* 1, no. 3: pp. 10–13.

Burton, Richard D.E. (1992). "My mother who fathered me: a reading of Hoquet [hiccough] by Léon Damas." In Hawkins, Peter and Lavers (eds.), *Protée Noir: essais*

sur la littérature francophone de l'Afrique Noire et des Antilles. Paris: L'Harmattan, pp. 75–87.

Chanson, Philippe (1993). "From the Creole God to the God of Jesus: an Essay on the Concept of God in French Guiana." *Exchange* (Leiden/Utrecht), 22, no. 1: pp. 18–45.

French, Howard W. (1991). "Space Center or Not, Some Say It's Still a Jungle." *New York
Times* (April 26), p. A4.

Guibault, Jocelyne (1990). "On Interpreting Popular Music: Zouk in the West Indies." In
Lent, John A. (ed.), *Caribbean Popular Culture*. Bowling Green, OH: Bowling
Green State Press, pp. 79–97.

———(1993). *Zouk: World Music in the West Indies*. Chicago: Chicago University Press.

Jones, Bridget, "Prospect for literature in French Guiana." In Hawkins, Peter and Lavers
(eds.), *Protée Noir: essais sur la littérature francophone de l'Afrique Noire et des
Antilles*. Paris: L'Harmattan, pp. 75–87.

Jones, Bridget, and Elie Stephenson (1995). "Society, Culture and Politics in French
Guiana." In Burton, Richard D.E. and Freo Reno (eds.), *French and West Indian:
Martinique, Guadeloupe, and French Guiana Today*. Charlottesville, VA: Uni-
versity Press of Virginia, pp. 56–74.

Juminer, Bertène (1989). *The Bastards*. Charlottesville, VA: University Press of Virginia.
Translation & introduction by Keith Q. Warner.

Mam-Lam-Fouck, Serge (1996). *Histoire générale de la Guyane. Les grands problèmes
e guyanais: permanence et évolution*. Kouron, Guiana: Ibis Rouge Editions,
Presses Universitaires Créoles/GEREC.

Monnerville, Gaston (1980). *Temoignage, de la France éguinoxiale au palais du luxembourg*. Paris: Editions Plon.

Price, Richard (1983). *First Time: The Historical Vision of an Afro-American People*. Baltimore: Johns Hopkins University Press.

Price, Richard, and Sally Price (1989). "Working for the Man: A Saramakan Outlook of
Kourou." *New West Indian Guide* 63, nos 3 and 4: pp. 199–207.

Warner, Keith Q. (ed.) (1988). *Critical Perspectives on Léon-Gontran Damas*. Washington, DC: Three Continents Press.

Weinstein, Brian (1972). *Eboué*. New York: Oxford University Press.

8

Haiti

Anne M. François

INTRODUCTION

Haiti, the first black republic in the Western Hemisphere, is a country torn by a long history of invasions, enslavement, revolutions, and dictatorships. Situated at the entrance to the Gulf of Mexico in the Atlantic Ocean, the island of Haiti is one of two republics on the island of Hispaniola. The other is the Dominican Republic, a former Spanish colony distinct from Haiti with its Afro-Hispanic culture and language, as opposed to the black republic in the west, which evolved from a mixed Afro-Caribbean and French heritage. The Spanish-speaking Dominican Republic was occupied by Haiti from 1822 to 1844 under the Boyer government. It became a politically independent nation in 1844.

With its 10,200 square miles and 7.2 million people, Haiti is the third largest of the Greater Antilles, after Cuba and the Dominican Republic. Haiti has played an important if not contradictory historical and cultural role in Caribbean history, as political beacon, being the first black republic in the world. Its revolutionary heroes, Toussaint L'Ouverture, Jean-Jacques Dessalines, Henri Christophe, however flawed, are legendary figures for black scholars and intellectuals, and anyone interested in the history of slave revolts that succeeded in abolishing slavery. That slaves could overthrow a vicious system, and build a new republic in the Western Hemisphere, terrified the slave-owning nations of Europe, and the United States.

Great poets like Aimé Césaire, Léopold Sédar Senghor, and others, have been inspired by Haitian history. Vast literature on Haitian cultural, political, and social life exists. Next to Brazil and Cuba, Haiti is the one country in the Western Hemisphere where African cultures and religions have been retained with a high degree of "authenticity." Haitian music and many of its cultural expressions have deep roots in Africa. The importance of oral literature, the selective use of proverbs as moral tools, the narrative structure and content of oral literature, and how Vodou and its metamorphic gods and goddesses shape people's lives in Haiti have a direct lineage to African worldviews. But beyond that, Haiti's centrality is revealed by its fascinating history of freedom, involving some of the region's most unique figures.

HAITI UNTIL THE END OF THE FIFTEENTH CENTURY

Before Christopher Columbus's landing in December 1492, Haiti was divided into five kingdoms, each being governed by a chief or *cacique*. The original inhabitants, known as the Arawak or Taíno people, called their home island Haití, Quisqueya, or Boyo. They had come from South America to different Caribbean islands. They lived mainly from agriculture, hunting, and fishing. They practiced polygamy and believed in animism. The Caribs, originally from the jungles of Amazonia, later joined the Arawaks. When Columbus and the Spanish conquistadores invaded the island, they renamed it Hispaniola (Little Spain) because of its beauty. It was later called the Queen of the Antilles, because it was the most productive of all the European colonies.

INDIAN ENSLAVEMENT IN ST. DOMINGUE

Organized slavery started in Haiti as soon the Spanish stripped the Indians of their rights and properties. Despite fighting the invasion of their land and the looting of its gold, the aborigines were decimated by forced labor, diseases, and brutalities. By 1507, the initial aborigine population of 200,000 at the time of Columbus's arrival had been reduced to 60,000.[1] In 1503, Spain shipped a few African slaves to Haiti. They coexisted with the remaining Indian slaves. Soon after, a Spanish priest, Bartolomé de Las Casas, a controversial figure in the history of enslavement, denounced the Spanish oppression of the Indians and advised Charles V, the king of Spain, to give permission to import African slave labor instead. After eliminating the Indians and exhausting the island's gold mines, most of the conquistadores left Haiti to conquer other lands in South America. During that time, the Spanish constantly fought French, English, and Dutch pirates for control of Haiti's treasures.

AFRICAN ENSLAVEMENT IN ST. DOMINGUE

In 1629, French buccaneers and filibusters settled on the island of Tortuga, off the northwest coast of Haiti. In 1697, through the Ryswick treaty, France officially obtained from Spain possession of the western part of the island and renamed it St. Domingue. From that date to 1791, the colony prospered under French government officials who received orders from the French Crown. The tremendous economic development of St. Domingue, thanks to the exploitation of African slave labor, created enormous wealth for the colonizers who controlled St. Domingue's land. Reaping all the economic benefits, France established itself as a powerful hegemonic empire. St. Domingue's flourishing sugar, coffee, tobacco, and spice production supported the entire French economy.

From the second half of the seventeenth century to the end of the eighteenth, the French shipped half a million African slaves to St. Domingue. These men, women, and children from the African coast were from different cultures and geographical regions. They were mostly Bambara from Mali, Ibo from Nigeria, Fulani from Guinea. They spoke different languages. Fearing possible revolts from the slaves, the colonizers separated them from their families and their respective nations upon their arrival in St. Domingue. The uprooting from African soil caused profound social, psychological, and familial instability within the new plantation environment.

ST. DOMINGUE'S THREE CLASSES: WHITES, FREEDMEN, SLAVES

By the end of the seventeenth century, St. Domingue's population was estimated to be 287,806 inhabitants, with 20,438 whites, 5,897 freedmen, and 261,471 slaves (91%). Class hierarchy was strictly maintained. The first class was composed of three categories of whites. "Les grands blancs" (high-class whites) were rich land and slave owners. "Les petits blancs" (lower-class whites), unable to pay their voyage from France to St. Domingue, had a three-year contract that bonded them to their owners. The "Creoles" were whites born in the colony.

Those in the second major class were called *affranchis* or freedmen. This class was composed of blacks and mulattoes who obtained freedom either by paying for it or through the voluntary gesture of their masters. Mulattoes were children of African female slaves and white masters. Often a colonizer gave freedom to his mulatto children, who in turn could receive an education equal to that of whites. Mulattoes could own as many slaves and as much property as whites; however, they were never socially and politically equal to them. Despite the Code Noir's (Black Code) recognition of mulattoes (1685) as free men, the whites considered them an inferior class. Although this class resented rejection by the whites and had difficulties reconciling its mixed heritage, it managed to create its own distinct social space between whites and blacks.

The third class, the enslaved, was the lowest and the most discriminated against, despite the Code Noir laws that were supposedly established to protect them from the colonizer's abuses. Overall, the Code Noir stated that slaves should be held as properties of their masters. Under these conditions, whites, freedmen, and slaves maintained their distinct social status and despised each other.

HISTORICAL RESISTANCE AND MAROONAGE

Slaves resisted their dehumanization in the plantation system in different ways. Some openly revolted against their masters by fighting back. If unsuccessful, they eventually were punished or killed. Others used surreptitious methods like destruction of property or poison in their master's food. Women also resisted in their own ways. Some mothers committed infanticide in order to spare their offspring a life of slavery. Midwives helped pregnant women abort. Suicide was another means of resistance to slavery. The uprooted Africans thought that death would metaphorically take them back to Guinea (their spiritual homeland) where they would finally rest.

Slaves who gained total freedom on their own by deserting the plantations and taking refuge in the hills were known as Maroons. From 1519 to 1533, the Indian Cacique Henri escaped to the Bahoruco Mountains, where other Maroons joined him. Other famous Maroons chiefs besides the legendary Mackandal were Jean-François, Georges Biassou, and Dutty Boukman. The latter, a Vodou priest, inspired a slave revolt with the famous "Bois Caïman Ceremony" in 1791. (Haitian history textbooks state that before the insurrection, Boukman enacted a Vodou ritual, making a pact with rebel slaves by sacrificing a pig and drinking its blood.) Maroons, who categorically rejected slavery and fought for freedom, were central to the slave revolution that made Haiti independent from France.

Runaways either opted for long- or short-term maroonage (Debien 1973, 107–134). When they deserted the plantations, they faced hunger, cruel punishments, and the harsh natural conditions of the environment. For survival, they went down to the plantations at night to steal food and cattle, or satisfied their hunger with wild vegetables grown on the mountains. To defend themselves against the state police force, which continually hunted them down with trained bloodhounds, Maroons used weapons they had taken with them. What they accomplished "in terms of survival skills" was quite remarkable (Agorsah 1994, 14).

Maroonage caused tremendous economic loss for the plantation owner who relied on slave work to augment his wealth. In desperation, slave masters resorted to cruel methods such as hanging, or burying alive recaptured Maroons like Mackandal in 1757–58, to put an end to their escapes. A runaway slave's physical description would sometimes appear on the most-wanted list in newspapers such as *La Gazette de Saint Domingue*.[2]

HAITIAN REVOLUTION

In 1791, the repercussions of the French Revolution (1789) spread to Haiti, where bloody slave revolts erupted. France, at war with other European nations, abolished slavery in Haiti in August 1793. However, it intended to keep its prosperous colony, at a time when England, constantly battling France and Spain for colonial territory, occupied parts of Haiti. The Spanish army had in its ranks Toussaint L'Ouverture, one of the most influential leaders of the Haitian Revolution, who had been fighting the French since 1791. In 1794, Toussaint decided to turn against the Spanish because the new French republic had kept its promise to abolish slavery in St. Domingue. Toussaint successfully fought two of France's mortal enemies—the Spanish and the English—to reestablish order in the colony.

Although St. Domingue was relatively free of slavery by 1794, neocolonial rule replaced it under Toussaint's rule. Land cultivation was strictly organized. Toussaint found himself in a difficult situation: whites were allowed to keep their plantations, while former slaves were forced to work for wages. Slave status did not dramatically change, a situation that isolated Toussaint, a product of the French system (James 1963, 214). Still, Toussaint's goal was to liberate the black masses from slavery and guide them toward a careful and productive emancipation.

By 1801, Toussaint ruled the entire island. In 1802, Napoleon had him arrested and exiled to France, where he died in April 1803. Napoleon, who successfully reestablished slavery in Martinique and Guadeloupe, thought of reconquering Haiti by eliminating Toussaint. However, at the time of his arrest, Toussaint foretold the successful outcome of the Haitian Revolution. On January 1, 1804, Jean-Jacques Dessalines, an ex-slave and a general in Toussaint's army, whose famous battle command was "Koupé tet boulé kay" ("cut off heads and burn houses") defeated Napoleon's army, led the country to independence, and renamed it, using its original Amerindian name of Haiti.

HAITI AFTER INDEPENDENCE (1801–1915)

After independence, the young Haitian nation experienced political and economic instability. Isolated and shunned by the Western world, it cut off diplomatic relations with France, which refused to recognize its political sovereignty until 1826, but only after Haiti agreed to pay its former master 150 million French francs. Other Western nations were even slower to recognize Haiti's sovereignty, and the United States only did so in 1862. As the first independent black republic, Haiti seemed too dangerous to the rest of the slave-owning Americas. In addition, French colonizers fed the European imagination with racial fears, intentionally depicting slave rebellions with images of primitivism and savagery.

Recognizing the close link between race and land ownership, Dessalines, proclaimed emperor of Haiti in the 1805 Constitution, introduced a law banning any white person from owning land in Haiti. He granted Haitian citizenship to Polish and German soldiers who had deserted from Napoleon's army and had contributed to the liberation of Haiti. He called for the reform of property ownership but did not succeed. To boost the economy, he subjected the newly freed slaves to forced labor.

Henri Christophe, the second emperor, who reigned from 1806 to 1820, followed in Dessalines' footsteps. He exploited and forced the masses to build imposing monuments such as the famous massive citadel La Ferriere. Later rulers, Alexandre Petion and Jean-Pierre Boyer, concerned about land reform, tried to create "a stable republican government resting on peasant properties" but failed (Balch 1972, 8).

Since then, Haiti has known numerous peasant revolts over land injustices and abuses by governments in power. Though peasants are still the majority today, their numbers have dwindled due to erosion and deforestation of the land. Peasant collectives such as a *coumbite* unite men and women together in cultivating the land. Women play an important role in organizing and selling produce. They transport it to the open markets by public transportation, on a donkey's back, or on their heads. The market, an important social place, is definitely women's territory.

THE FIRST AMERICAN INVASION

From 1804 to 1915, Haiti was ruled by dictators, whose political agendas and ill management failed to protect it from foreign interventions, and instead brought on terror and corruption. In July 1915, an outbreak of violence in Port-au-Prince, the capital, along with the specter of German hegemony in Haiti, prompted the U.S. Marines to intervene. But the real reason for this brutal military intervention (1915–1934) was apparently to protect American economic interests (Balch 1972, 15).

After a 1916 treaty, the Americans took total control of the administration and legislation of the country, despite its status as an independent republic, and fierce opposition from the Haitian Senate. During the occupation, *la corvée*, an old system of forced labor, was reestablished, and Haitian laws banning land ownership by foreigners, on the books since 1805, were revoked. Haitians hated the racist and arrogant attitude of the American occupiers. For the first time since independence, they lost the freedom for which they had ferociously fought and strongly resented the occupation as an example of political and economic loss of sovereignty. The marines brutally repressed the peasant revolutionary movement, the Cacos (1919–1920), which opposed the invasion. Charlemagne Péralte, their leader, and 3,500 peasants were massacred (Bellegarde 1996, 7).

THE DUVALIER ERA

Haiti, like much of Central America, remained under the American sphere of influence during the Cold War period. The living conditions of the Haitian masses did not improve noticeably after the end of the American occupation (1934). The country produced numerous ephemeral presidents until 1957, when François Duvalier, a medical doctor, seized power. He gained national recognition from the rural population that he had treated for an epidemic skin disease devastating the country. In addition, he manipulated racial divisions between blacks and mulattoes.

Throughout Haitian history, the mulatto elite had largely dominated Haitian politics and was always resented by the black majority. The dark-skinned Duvalier, also known as Papa Doc, successfully projected himself as the redeemer of the rejected masses, but he was to become one of the most wretched dictators that the country had ever known. In 1961, he named himself president for life, and organized an especially dreaded paramilitary force, the Tontons Macoutes, which infiltrated and controlled every aspect of Haitian life.

Duvalierism was an obscure mix of negritude, terrorism, anticommunism, and vodouism. (Negritude is the revalorization and celebration of black culture and African civilization.) Duvalier's fourteen years of misrule and terror were all too typical of Haitian rulers, whether black or mulatto, who, once in power, failed the people through their egotism and total disregard for democracy, education, and the economic well-being of the population.

Compared with Papa Doc, his handpicked successor, Jean Claude Duvalier (Baby Doc), seemed a mere shadow of his father. He lacked the older man's education, political skill, and cunning. Nonetheless, under Baby Doc's government (1971–1986), the old guard of Duvalierism flourished with the same brutality, greed, and corruption. And, once again, as they had done under his father, people from different walks of life dreamed of leaving Haiti for political or economic reasons. Fearing persecution, hundreds of intellectuals and professionals went into exile to the United States, Canada, or West Africa. Hundreds of Haitian cane cutters (*braceros*) fled to the Dominican Republic, despite reported accounts in the press of Haitians' mistreatment by Dominicans. In addition, the son's marriage to Michele Bennett, a divorcée from a wealthy mulatto family, only made matters worse. The Haitian lower class could not relate to Bennett, despising her arrogance and lavish spending habits. Her union with Baby Doc revived old racial antagonisms. The black majority felt betrayed by Baby Doc who, unlike his father, allied himself with the mulattoes.

During the mid-eighties, it seemed that the Haitian people were in the throes of another revolution: numerous riots and strikes took place in major cities. Duvalierism was tottering. Pope John Paul II's words on his first visit to Haiti in 1984 were catalytic. The Haitian Church, usually silent, began to play a major role in awakening the population's consciousness. In February 1986, Haitians finally ousted Baby Doc, whose fortune was estimated at $800 million. No longer enjoying U.S. government support, he and his family went into exile in France. The jubilant population went on a violence spree and killed some Duvalier allies and Tontons Macoutes by means of *déchoukaj*, a Creole word that literally means uprooting, or erradicating the source of tyranny.

THE SECOND AMERICAN INVASION (1994)

After Baby Doc, the country was left with the devastating remnants of Duvalierism: a 48 percent illiteracy rate, malnutrition, the lowest standard of living in the hemisphere, social and political violence. A military junta replaced

Baby Doc for a short time; then several provisional governments were put in place including, for the first time in Haitian history, one with a female lawyer, Ertha Pascal-Trouillot, as acting president. In 1987, hundreds of Haitians who were attempting to vote for the first time to democratically elect a president were massacred.

Two years later, another attempt at democracy occurred. During the 1989 presidential campaign, Jean-Bertrand Aristide, an unknown Catholic priest, came onto the political scene. The masses saw him as the only alternative to the power-hungry Duvalierist candidates. Aristide was elected president of Haiti in November 1990. His Lavalas (which means "flooding river") Party had leftist leanings and espoused a humanist doctrine of helping the poor, popularized by Latin-American Catholic bishops and known as "liberation theology." But seven months after taking office he was ousted in a coup led by General Raoul Cédras, a die-hard Duvalierist, who sent the priest-president into exile in Caracas; later, Aristide went to the United States.

HAITI IN THE 1990s

Haiti has had a turbulent history of missed opportunities and repressive governments, and it might be argued that a sense of fatalism has overtaken the long-victimized masses. Is democracy possible in such a situation? The idea of democracy has proved to be elusive for a country with such a volatile history. After the Cédras coup, the situation in the country worsened at all levels. The country went through a period of moral crisis, political turmoil and economic disaster. The United States, along with the United Nations and the Organization of American States, imposed a total embargo on Haiti from 1991 to 1994. The loss of economic support led to a mass exodus to the United States. During that period, the United States Coast Guard intercepted at sea 41,342 Haitian "boat people." The Clinton administration, following the Bush policy on immigration, sent them back home or kept them in detention centers in Guantánamo Bay, Cuba. The U.S. immigration policy toward Haitians could be seen as racist (Farmer 1992, 209). Coming from a poor country and stigmatized as carriers of AIDS, Haitian refugees do not receive fair treatment especially compared with Cubans, the majority of whom are fleeing Cuba for economic and not political reasons. Anti-Haitian sentiment has not deterred them; probably half a million Haitians live in the United States. But the harsh treatment has led many to migrate to other Caribbean islands, such as the Bahamas.

In 1994, perhaps in an attempt to stop the tide of Haitian boat people, the Clinton administration returned Jean-Bertrand Aristide, the democratically elected president, to power by invading Haiti. More problems were created during the occupation (1994–1999) than before. The U.S. Marines, who suspected some Haitian officials' involvement in drug dealing, sought to eliminate the Haitian army, to which Aristide had agreed. Yet, they neglected to collect all the weapons. Weaponry, which was tightly controlled under the Duvalier regime, became more available to the Zenglendo, bands that terrorized, raped, and killed people. A sense of insecurity existed in the country, despite the presence of the marines and United Nations troops.

At the beginning of the twenty-first century, conditions remain very grim for the Haitian nation. During his presidency, René Préval, Aristide's successor (1996–2000), failed to deal with the political and internal affairs of the country. Drug trafficking, poverty, and violence still plague Haiti. The last presidential election that put Aristide back in power is considered a "shabby epilogue" (Contreras 2000, 2) by the U.S. media, since opposition leaders and the majority of Haitians boycotted the national elections. Aristide's second presidential term does not seem too promising, as it faces accusations of electoral fraud and government corruption.

LANGUAGE AND LITERATURE

Haiti's political fortunes have been offset by a remarkable and lively culture. Haitian art, music, and literature are among the finest in the hemisphere. Its writers, such as Jacques Roumain (1907–1944), Jacques Stephen Alexis (1922–1961), and Marie Chauvet-Vieux (1917–1975), are well known throughout the world. Others, not translated, are not well known in the United States. Haiti now has two official languages. In addition to French, the government declared Creole an official language in 1987. In the seventeenth century, Creole was developed between colonizers and slaves as a means of communication. It was more or less considered an inferior language due to its association with slavery. French, thought of as the language of reason and social mobility, became dominant. Haitian intellectuals who shun the Creole language have an ambiguous relationship with it. They strive to speak French well, which has become for them a sign of class. But this preference could also be a trap.[3] In order to still perceive themselves as Haitian, they become torn between the French and Creole culture, one of the core elements that define *Haïtianité*, or Haitianness. Every Haitian person speaks Creole. Only 10 percent of the population is fluent in French (Dejean 1983, 190), while 15 percent speak some French. The rest (75%) is illiterate and Creole is its only means of communication.

The oral culture is very much preserved. Folktales, proverbs, and songs are expressed in Creole. At night—especially in the countryside where there is no electricity—children and adults sit in circles saying riddles or telling the scary and funny tales of Compé Bouqui and Ti Malice. In order to capture the audience's attention, the storyteller usually opens with a call, "Krik," to which the audience answers, "Krak." This call/response format is repeated every time an oral poet performs. Proverbs containing words of wisdom are part of daily conversations. For example, many adults favor the following saying: "Male pa jam aveti ou" (One never knows when tragedy will strike).

Creole is now taught for the first six years in some selected primary institutions, although Haitian education is still based on the French system. At the end of secondary school, students take the Baccalaureate, the state examination, which gives them entry to the university system.

In the 1970s, a Creole language revival took place when theaters staged works by Felix Morisseau-Leroy (1913–1998), a Haitian novelist and playwright. He was the first to translate the Greek play Antigone into Creole in 1952. Almost two decades later, Frank Etienne published his first novel, *Dezafi* (1975), in Creole. The narrative, a political and social satire, achieved great local success. Etienne's famous play *Pélin-Tét* (1978), depicted the tribulations of an intellectual and worker's life in New York City, made him a nationally acclaimed writer. Etienne also writes in French.

Most Haitian writers write in French, very few in Creole or English, like Jacques Roumain (1907–1944), Jacques Stephen Alexis (1922–1961), and René Depestre (1926–). All three, though socially committed writers, went beyond social denunciation to create powerfully imaginative works that drew on Haitian folklore, religion, and history. Some writers from the post–Baby Doc generation, who discovered Creoleness as an expression of Caribbean life and culture, produced literary works in Creole. Haitian literature is still a literature concerned with the issues of racism, imperialism, and politics. Since its independence, Haiti has been fighting and struggling to establish itself as a modern state. This preoccupation is reflected in the literary production of every major literary or cultural movement.

Today, literary publication is very limited in Haiti; however, a minority of Haitian writers remains active, managing to produce literary works despite financial problems, political instability, and censorship. More so than ever, Haitian literature is anchored in exile and migration, with two out of three writers living and publishing outside Haiti, like award-winning poet Paul Laraque (1920–), who writes in French and Creole. In the sixties the Duvalier regime forced many writers and intellectuals into exile in France, Canada, West Africa, and the United States. For example, the Haitian writer Roger Dorsainville has produced mainly in Senegal, where he lived in exile for years. Today, the younger generation of writers, like Danny Laferriere and Anthony Phelps who live in Canada and Edwidge Danticat who lives in the United States, is breaking with "the tradition of literary nationalism with its root in the revolutionary fervor of 1804" (Arthur and Dash 1999, 214).

HAITIAN ARTS, RELIGION, AND CULTURE

Haiti is internationally known for what is termed its "naive painting," much as African art in general was classified as "primitive," although that did not prevent

Picasso from copying it. In the beginning of the twentieth century, the first generation of modern Haitian artists like Wilson Bigaud and Hector Hyppolite began to paint without formal artistic training, inspired mostly by their surroundings and by the pervasive influence of Vodou. Haitian pastoral art, depicting landscapes, scenes of everyday life, and Vodou mythical subjects in bold passionate colors, retained the interest of art dealers and collectors from all over the world.

A second generation of Haitian painters went to art schools in Port-au-Prince and Cap-Haïtien. They distinguished themselves from the previous generation by their skills, and today, Haitian painters work in a variety of styles from naturalistic to abstract to installation art, a combination of painting, sculpture, and sometimes video that uses the physical space of a work in a way in which the viewer walks about in this artistically shaped physical environment.

The 1998 exhibit "Sacred Arts of Haitian Voudou" at the Museum of Natural History in New York was a groundbreaking exhibit that brought together Haitian art and religion in order to portray a Haitian popular aesthetic and philosophy. The exhibit, which focused on Haitian paintings and altars, also helped viewers demystify stereotypes about Vodou, especially the depiction of zombies in Hollywood films.

Vodou is central to Haitian life. Inherited from West and central Africa, and transformed during slavery, Vodou is a religion that comprises African, Amerindian, and Roman Catholic spiritual practices as well as elements of Freemasonry. The majority of the Haitian population is Catholic (90%) and *vodouisant* (Vodou-inclined). The rest (10%) is Protestant. The Vodou priest (*oungan*), or priestess (*mambo*), the highest in rank, performs ritual ceremonies, such as members' initiations and healings, where believers are possessed by the *lwas*, (spirits or deities). The priests and priestesses also play an important social role in the community at home or abroad (Brown 1991, 344). Vodou adepts serve the *lwas*, which they believe intervene in their lives. They consult the spirits of ancestors for health, money, jobs, and lovers. They gather in temples for religious rituals and public ceremonies. The practice of Vodou preserves one of the most profoundly African components of Haitian culture. Vodou has survived in Haiti despite several campaigns by churches and governments aimed at eradicating it over the years. Given its low-class association, many people in Haiti consider Vodou a backward religion, deluding illiterate peasants into deeper ignorance and superstition.

Haitian music is a blend of African and Caribbean cultures and traditions. *Rara* folk music has vodou rhythms with upbeat drumming. Root or *Racine* music, which evolved from *rara*, has a ring of cultural resistance to it. In the mid-eighties, Boukman Eksperyans, a politically engaged musical band that took the name of the famous Maroon Boukman, made the music very popular. Its Creole lyrics, accompanied by the sound of *lambi* (the conch shell), a means of communication during slavery, were a powerful symbol of Haitian freedom struggles. The Haitian people also like *compas*, a rhythmic dance music that never goes out of style, made popular by Nemours Jean-Baptiste. Other Caribbean music like Afro-Cuban *son* and mambo, Dominican merengue, Jamaican reggae, and zouk have also influenced Haitian music.

Carnival is a religious and festive occasion held in the last days before Lent, when all social classes mix to dance to different types of Haitian music. For three days, in an outburst of sensuality, people wearing extravagant and colorful costumes parade and accompany bands of musicians performing on the streets. Carnival is a time of excess of scatological language as well as reversion of social roles and overt expression of sexuality. It is also a celebration of Vodou culture. The representation of Ogoun, a warrior *lwa*, reflects Haitian people's ties to their Africanness. During the time of slavery, these spirits were "a counterworld to white suppression" (Dayan 1995, 36). When slaves lost their identities and were possessed by spirits, they believed themselves invincible.

The culinary arts are important in Haiti. Every New Year's Day, Haitians, whether at home or abroad, prepare the *giromon* soup they love to eat. *Giromon* is similar to butternut squash. According to Haitian folk history, slave ancestors were forbidden to eat that specific soup. Therefore, the act of eating it on the first of January, which commemorates Haitian independence, is a reminder that the body hungers equally for freedom and food.

CONCLUSION

As the first black republic, Haiti has so far failed to fulfill its original dream of establishing itself as a strong, prosperous, democratic, and racially untroubled nation in the Western Hemisphere. The country has been beset by militarism, foreign intervention, and staggering levels of poverty, illiteracy, violence, disease, and exploitation. (Some workers make 28 cents an hour in sweatshops.) More than 10 percent of the population has immigrated abroad, where in cities like Miami, New York, Nassau, and Boston they have thrived. On the island, human rights groups, churches, and grassroots movements bravely work for change and social justice. Although it would be foolish to paint a rosy future in the short run, Haiti's people have shown a remarkable resilience, tremendous faith and spirituality, and immense cultural creativity in its two centuries as a nation.

NOTES

1. Thomas Madiou (1922), *Histoire d'Haïti*, vol. 1 (Port-au-Prince: Imprimerie d'Haïti), p. 13.

2. Jean Fouchard (1988), *Les Marrons de la Liberté* (Port-au-Prince: Imprimerie Henri Deschamps), p. 14.

3. Hurbon Laennec (1987), *Comprendre Haiti: Essai sur l'Etat, la Nation, la Culture* (Paris: L'Harmattan).

REFERENCES

Agorsah, Kofi E. (1994). *Maroon Heritage: Archeological, Ethnographical and Historical Perspectives*. Barbados: Canoe Press.

Arthur, Charles, and Michael Dash (eds.) (1999). *A Haiti Anthology: Libete*. Princeton, NJ: Markus Wiener Publishers.

Averill, Gage (1997). *A Day for the Hunter a Day for the Prey: Popular Music and Power in Haiti*. Chicago: University of Chicago Press.

Balch, Emily Greene (ed.) (1972/1927). *Occupied Haiti*. Reprint. New York: Garland Publishers.

Bellegarde, Dantes (1996). *L'Occupation Américaine d'Haiti*. 2d ed. Port-au-Prince: Editions Lumiére.

Brown, Karen McCarthy (1991). *Mama Lola: A Vodou Priestess in Brooklyn*. Berkeley: University of California Press.

Contreras, Joseph (2000). "Haiti: A Shabby Epilogue." *Newsweek* (November) p. 2.

Dash, J. Michael (2000). *Culture and Customs of Haiti*. Westport, CT: Greenwood Press.

Dayan, Joan (1995). *Haiti, History and the Gods*. Berkeley: University of California Press.

Debien, Gabriel (1973/1966). "Maroonage in the French Antilles." In Price, R. (ed.), *Maroon Societies: Rebel Slave Communities in the Americas*. Baltimore: Johns Hopkins University Press.

Dejean, Yves (1983). "Diglossia Revisited: French and Creole in Haiti." *Word* 34: 189–213.

Farmer, Paul (1992). *AIDS and Accusation: Haiti and the Geography of Blame*. Berkeley: University of California Press.

James, C.L.R. (1963/1938). *The Black Jacobins: Toussaint L'Ouverture and the Santo Domingo Revolution*. 2d ed. New York: Vintage Books.

Laguerre, Michel S. (1998). *Diasporic Citizenship: Haitian Americans in Transnational America*. New York: St. Martin's Press.

Nicholls, David (1996). *From Dessalines to Duvalier: Race, Colour, and National Independence in Haiti*. rev. ed. New Brunswick, NJ: Rutgers University Press.

Touillot, Michel Rolph (1990). *Haiti, State against Nation: The Origins and Legacy of Duvalierism*. New York: Monthly Review Press.

9

Jamaica

Alan West-Durán

An island of masters and Maroons, rebellions and Rastafarians, Jamaica's history is quintessentially Caribbean. A key possession during the British imperial heyday, and for almost two centuries a vast plantation, the island has witnessed insurrection, religious upheaval, and civil unrest on the one hand, but on the other, Jamaica has forged a complex, though fragile, democracy, given birth to one of the great Pan-Africanist thinkers, and become known the world over for its musical prowess.

Jamaica is the third largest of the islands of the Greater Antilles, after Cuba and Hispaniola. The island is 90 miles south of Cuba and the same distance west of Haiti, and Montego Bay is only 400 miles southeast of Miami. The island is about a fourth larger than the island of Puerto Rico, with a population of over two and a half million.

Since 1670, Jamaica has been a country with a majority black or Afro-Creole population, but recognition of the Afro-Antillean nature of the country was not widespread until the 1960s and 1970s. The 1991 census for the country lists blacks and Afro-Creole or "mixed black" as 96 percent of the population.

A former British colony, Jamaica's Afro-Creole spirit is evident in all dimensions of society: religion, music, food, literature, and a racial pride that is centuries old, starting with Maroons who resisted British rule, to followers of Marcus Garvey and, more recently, the Rastafarians.

PRE-COLUMBIAN JAMAICA AND SPANISH RULE (1494–1655)

Jamaica was inhabited by the Taínos of Arawak descent some 800 years before the arrival of Europeans. They called the island Yamaya or Xaymaca. About

60,000 Taínos lived on the island when Columbus landed during his second trip to the New World, on May 5, 1494, after hearing that there was gold there during his first trip. When no gold was found Columbus left after two months. In 1506, Jamaica became a military outpost for the Spanish, and by 1511 slavery —mostly Indian, but a growing African presence—was the leading source of labor. Most of the Taínos had died from overwork, malnutrition, disease, and ill-treatment by the mid–sixteenth century.

In 1611, the island's population of approximately 1,400 was roughly half European and half slave. Most slaves lived and worked alongside white settlers who owned land that produced yucca (cassava), plantains, and cocoa. The average settler had five slaves or less: Jamaica was still not the sugar-producing juggernaut it would become later.

THE BRITISH TAKEOVER UNTIL ABOLITION: 1655–1834

In 1655, several thousand British troops attacked the island. The Spanish, outgunned and outmanned, offered resistance, but clearly were on the defensive. To help their cause they freed the island's 1,500 slaves, hoping they would defend the island for Spain. Some actually joined the British, still others left with their Spanish masters, but many took to the hills where they became Maroons. The English offered British citizenship to all white settlers by 1662, and by 1670, the Treaty of Madrid officially ceded Jamaica to Great Britain.

Those *libertos* (freed slaves) who fled to the mountains, waged guerrilla warfare against the British, and were later engaged in what is known as the First Maroon War (1730–1740). Some of the Maroon leaders were Cudjoe, Accompong, Cuffee, Quao, and Nanny. Cudjoe was a formidable military leader, and his sister Nanny's mere name struck terror into the hearts of whites with her inspirational leadership. Of Ashanti origin and an "Obeah"[1] woman, many in her community revered her for her supernatural powers. She was subsequently granted 500 acres of land and also has a town named after her, Nanny Town, in the Blue Mountains. This queen mother/priestess/religious leader is rightly considered one of Jamaica's first national heroines.

In 1739 a treaty was signed between the British and the Maroons, who numbered about 1,000, under Cudjoe. The treaty apportioned land for the Maroons and granted their freedom, in exchange for the following: the Maroons promised to cease hostilities against white settlers and plantations, harbor no more new runaways, and help defeat any future slave insurrections. So even when defeated, the British exacted a heavy price—they would recognize the Maroons' freedom in exchange for ending maroonage, leaving slaves the following collective action: mass insurrection or rebellion combined with petitioning the Crown. Either option was extremely difficult.

Even before the British-Maroon treaty was signed, Jamaica had become a plantation economy. In 1730, out of a population of 82,183, slaves outnumbered whites 10 to 1. In 1675 the island had 70 sugar estates; by 1758 there were 455 plantations producing 24,000 tons of sugar, making Jamaica Britain's greatest source of sugar, surpassed only by St. Domingue (Haiti).

Most plantations employed hundreds of slaves with harsh working conditions (14- to 20-hour days), high mortality rates, disruption of families, and severely oppressive living conditions that meant an unbalanced diet, poor hygiene and health, little or no physical or social mobility, and severe physical punishment or death for infractions against the slave system.

Some have said that the plantation system was not a society but was more like a prison environment; others, that it was "an ill-organized system of exploitation" (Patterson 1969, 70). Despite the grim truth of these observations, Jamaica was probably the Caribbean island with the greatest (and largest) number of slave uprisings in its history: 1673, 1678, 1685, 1690, 1730–1740 (First Maroon War), 1742, 1745, 1760 (Tacky's Revolt), 1765, 1766, 1776, 1791–1792, 1795–1796 (Second Maroon War), 1806, 1808, 1815, 1822–1824, 1831–1832 (the "Baptist War"). Most of these incidents involved hundreds of slaves, a third of them involved thousands.

What accounts for this rebellious history? Some scholars have noted that several factors came together in Jamaica to produce this resistance to slavery: (1) slaves greatly outnumbered whites (10 to 1 in Jamaica's case); (2) there was a greater proportion of African-born to locally born slaves; (3) a great proportion of the imported slaves were of the same ethnic origin; (4) geographical conditions existed that favored guerrilla warfare; (5) a high incidence of absentee ownership existed; (6) the economy was dominated by large-scale monopolistic enterprises; and (7) there was weak cultural cohesiveness and high male-to-female ratios in the ruling population (Patterson 1972, 288). This rebellious spirit didn't die out when slavery was abolished in 1834; the Morant Bay Rebellion of 1865, Garveyism, the labor unrest of the 1930s, and the turbulent Manley years (1972–1980), prove that it continues to be central to Jamaican history.

One of the key features of Jamaica under slavery was the importance of absentee ownership. Although many landowners and proprietors of large estates were residents, the great majority of the largest plantations (and of slaves) were under absentee ownership. This trend grew more pronounced as abolition neared. Its effects were manifold and serious. The mentality of the absentee owner was to get rich quick and return to England, hardly an attitude that favored an interest in local affairs. It fostered an inefficiency in governance and difficulties in maintaining a local militia, education, religion, and morals, with many cases of ministers being accused of corruption and debauchery.

The Second Maroon War (1795–1796) pitted the Leeward Maroons of northwestern Jamaica against the colonial authorities. After a valiant fight the Maroons agreed to a truce, but instead were captured and shipped away to Nova Scotia and in 1800 the five hundred or so remaining Maroons were sent to Sierra Leone.

Between the white elite and the vast slave population, Jamaica had a tiny (2%–3%) sector of free blacks or colored. They were rejected on plantations since they were considered a "dangerous" example to the field slaves, and were equally spurned by urban whites, so they congregated on the outskirts of major towns like Kingston and Montego Bay. Despite the adjective of "free," they were limited to certain jobs, could not serve in the legislature or on juries, and were barred from testifying against whites. In 1831 they were allowed to vote, but needed to own property worth £100 pounds in order to do so.

By 1830 the pressure to abolish slavery was considerable. Britain had ended the slave trade in 1807, and sugar prices were dropping rapidly, ruining many sugar estates. Moravian, Baptist, and Methodist ministers, who were winning over many believers, included many who preached an abolitionist message. Moreover, many of the Baptist ministers were black ex-slaves from the United States who had come to Jamaica. Samuel Sharpe, a Jamaican independent Baptist minister and ex-slave, led a movement to demand freedom. His plan was to stage massive civil disobedience by having slaves not report to work after Christmas of 1831. Although it began peacefully, in many instances slaves began to burn down plantations. The violence escalated and it took the colonial regime several weeks to crush the rebellion. Between twenty and forty thousand slaves had participated in the uprising, with 207 killed. Later, another 376 convicted slaves were executed. The military costs were high, and damage to property was in the millions. Sharpe was executed in May of 1832, after announcing that he "would rather die upon yonder gallows than live in slavery" (Sherlock and Bennett 1998, 212–228). Despite the backlash by landowners and white elites, Britain abolished slavery for 311,000 African-Jamaicans in 1833.

Britain compensated slave-owners for £6 million, and set up an apprenticeship system with former slaves continuing to work for their old masters. Apprenticeship was so widely detested that it was ended in 1838. However, laws were passed to limit blacks from owning land and receiving an education, which was not free.

FROM EMANCIPATION TO LABOR UNREST: 1838–1938

Many slaves left the plantations and as elsewhere in the Caribbean, Jamaica imported indentured servants from abroad: Europeans (4,000), Africans (10,000), Chinese (6,000), and Indians (20,000). Though it took decades, these immigrants are now considered Jamaicans, but they do not constitute significant portions of the population as in Guyana, Trinidad, or Suriname.

The Church, under the leadership of William Knibb, sought to help ex-slaves by purchasing land and reselling it to blacks, who settled in free villages. By 1848, there were 2,000 free villages and by 1865, about one in every seven blacks owned land. Still, unemployment was high, and illiteracy was around 90 percent for Afro-Jamaicans. In the 1864 election less than one half of 1 percent of the black population was eligible to vote.

African-Jamaicans, in the words of one scholar, had "freedom without rights" (Bakan 1990, 68). In 1865 two leaders, Paul Bogle and George William Gordon, both members of the Assembly, led a protest-revolt that sought to redress the country's legal system, and more importantly, the issue of land, since the huge and black majority of Jamaica's peasants were landless. The events began at Morant Bay with the capturing of a police station by rebel forces, who then confronted the militia. Eighteen died and thirty-one were wounded. Several more people were killed in the following days. The government reacted quickly and brutally to end the rebellion, and even drew upon the Maroons. One thousand black homes were burned, over 500 were executed (among them Bogle and Gordon), and 600 were flogged. Although defeated, the rebellion provoked a British inquiry that took months. The governor was dismissed, the plantocracy's (rule by plantation owners) 200-year-old constitution was discarded, and the island became a Crown Colony. A new civil service system was set up, along with political, juridical, and educational reforms, but free elementary education would be introduced much later, in 1892.

Jamaica's sugar economy had collapsed and was replaced by a growing banana export industry. But many could not find work, prompting 146,000 Jamaicans to immigrate to the United States, Panama, Cuba, and other places in the Caribbean from 1888 to 1920.

In that period two key figures initiated a new consciousness of African-Jamaican identity and rights: Robert Love (1839?–1914) and Marcus Garvey (1887–1940). Love was born in the Bahamas and moved to Jamaica in 1889. An Anglican deacon and medical doctor, he actively campaigned for black participation in the political process, and also believed in self-determination, working-class rights, mass education, and preventive medicine. To some he was the first leader to publicly challenge the racist assumption that blackness and inferiority were synonymous. From the pages of the newspaper *The Jamaica Advocate*, he eloquently expressed his ideas, even publishing the proceedings of the First Pan-African Conference held in 1900.

Garvey was an influential and dynamic leader who promoted black self-improvement and racial pride, self-determination, African unity, and black repatriation to Africa. He formed the United Negro Improvement Association, or UNIA, in 1914. Garvey later immigrated to the United States, where the UNIA grew enormously as an organization for African Americans, with more than 1,200 chapters in 40 countries and 2 million members. Financial troubles landed Garvey in jail. He was deported back to Jamaica, but political and legal harassment forced him to leave in 1935, and he lived the rest of his life in England. Garvey's legacy has grown since his death: he was named Jamaica's first national hero in 1964. His work and thought have influenced the country's Rastafarians (see glossary, Religion section), African independence leaders such as Kwame Nkrumah, and black nationalists worldwide. His contributions to Afro-Jamaican racial pride and being the first Jamaican to found a political party and a workers' association are undeniable achievements. Many Jamaican women and feminists grew out of Garveyism or became active in that period: Amy Jacques Garvey (1896–), Amy Ashwood Garvey (1897–1969), Amy Bailey (1895–1990), the poet Una Marson (1905–1965), and Mary Morris Knibb (1886–1964), one of the first women elected to a public office.

In the 1930s, low wages, high unemployment, massive migration from the countryside to the major cities, and a worldwide economic depression created major social tensions. Only 6 percent of the population was eligible to vote. Labor disturbances in 1938 left 8 dead, 171 wounded, and 700 arrested. Major trade union activity began with Alexander Bustamante (1884–1977), who founded one of the country's main unions, and the Jamaican Labour Party (JLP) in 1943. His rival, and cousin, Norman Manley (1893–1969), created another union and political party, the PNP (People's National Party). Both parties and trade unions have been mainstays of the Jamaican political system for the last sixty-five years.

CONSTITUTIONAL DECOLONIZATION AND INDEPENDENCE: 1944–2001

Jamaica instituted universal suffrage in 1944, initiating a period of constitutional decolonization (1944–1962). Great Britain wanted to grant independence to a federation, not individual Caribbean countries. In 1958 the British Western Indian Federation (BWIF) was created, and included Jamaica, Trinidad and Tobago, Barbados, Grenada, St. Kitts-Nevis-Anguilla, Antigua and Barbuda, St. Lucia, St. Vincent and the Grenadines, Dominica, and Montserrat. The Bahamas and the British Virgin Islands were not included. Tensions within the federation and Jamaican concern that they would bear the economic brunt of some of the smaller islands caused Jamaica to withdraw in 1961, with the WIF being dissolved in 1962.

Jamaica became independent on August 6, 1962, and Bustamante was the country's first prime minister from 1962 to 1967. Despite their newfound confidence, Jamaicans were still reluctant to identify themselves as citizens of an Afro-Caribbean nation, understandable given the colonial and racial legacies of the country.

This unease became public when Walter Rodney (1942–1980), a Guyanese scholar-activist and Black Power advocate, was denied reentry into Jamaica (1968), despite his popularity with students and workers at the University of the West Indies at Mona. Students and the urban poor took to the streets, and the ensuing violence took two lives and caused much damage to businesses, vehicles, and government buildings. Many supported Rodney's expulsion, however, saying that Black Power was a foreign concept, appropriate for the United States or South Africa under apartheid, but not in Jamaica where the country's motto was "Out of many, one people."

But the country was changing: reggae, Rastafarians and Garvey's legacy were commanding more attention and support, radio stations were broadcasting in Jamaican Creole, neighboring Cuba was in the throes of revolution, Vietnam was at war, and many African countries were fighting wars of liberation (Angola, Namibia, Mozambique, South Africa).

In 1972 the PNP was voted into power under Michael Manley (1924–1997). Manley established programs for the poor (housing, health, and education) and initiated a plan of economic nationalism, levying taxes on bauxite for foreign companies. He advocated for democratic socialism and developed warm relations with Cuba. Fierce opposition, led by the JLP's Edward Seaga, soon developed into social unrest and political violence, and Jamaica became a flash point for the Cold War. Though politically popular, Manley and the PNP lost the 1980 elections— where more than 800 died in political violence—after they adopted International Monetary Fund–imposed economic measures that raised unemployment and drastically cut social services.

Seaga, the new prime minister, ruled until 1989, establishing a more pro-U.S. regime and a conservative, pro-market economic policy. Michael Manley and the PNP returned to power, but with a much less radical policy. Manley resigned for health reasons in 1992, and P.J. Patterson has been the prime minister since, being reelected in 1997.

In the nineties Jamaica was beset by a growing crime rate, unemployment (16%), drug use, strikes, high inflation, social inequality, and a large trade deficit. In 1995 the National Democratic Movement (NDM) was formed by disgruntled JLP members, breaking the two-party monopoly that had lasted for the previous fifty years, but armed confrontations among them has led to a serious increase in political violence. In the capital, garrison constituencies have emerged from public housing constructed in exchange for political loyalty. Over the years these constituencies formed armed groups that often clashed over politics, but with the recent increase in the drug trade, many in these armed gangs are used as foot soldiers by drug traffickers.

In 1999, when the government announced a 60 percent increase in fuel prices, rioting killed eight people and many businesses were burned or looted. During July 2001 more than twenty-five people were killed in these turf wars.

MUSIC

Say "Jamaican music" and most people think of Bob Marley and reggae. But the country's long-standing musical traditions, such as Kumina, Mandinga, and Buru drumming styles and/or songs, some maintained by existing Maroon communities, are centuries old. There are still about 6,000 Maroons on the island, numerically small but symbolically and culturally quite important. Genres from earlier in the twentieth century, like *mento*, similar to and competitive with calypso, though no longer popular, are sometimes reworked into dancehall or ragga tunes.

Even before the reggae explosion, Jamaica had a lively music scene, but it was a group of singer-composers such as Jimmy Cliff (1948–), Frederick "Toots" Hibbert of Toots and the Maytals (1948?–), Lee "Scratch" Perry (1936–), Bob Marley (1945–1981), Leroy Sibbles of the Heptones (1949–), Peter Tosh (1944–1987), and

Winston Rodney, aka Burning Spear (1948–), that catapulted Jamaican music into the international spotlight in the late sixties and mid-seventies.

What accounts for this explosion of creativity? Some point to the island's recent independence (1962), which was an obvious source of national pride that spurred artists to explore their roots, particularly the island's Afro-Caribbean traditions. This exploration and creativity also coincided with a renewed growth in Rastafarianism, a rediscovery of Garvey's legacy, African decolonization, Pan-Africanism, and the U.S. civil rights and Black Power movements, the latter having a Caribbean counterpart with the likes of Walter Rodney and Frantz Fanon.

Reggae artists like Marley came from either poor rural backgrounds or the slums of Kingston and other cities. Both musically and in their lyrics they gave voice to vast sectors of Jamaican society, predominantly black: those struggling to find work and educate themselves, but battered by racism and poverty, and staggering levels of social violence. Reggae has been able to create a special union of the social and spiritual (in the lyrics), with a laid-back, funky beat that is danceable, all imbued with a fun-loving, party-going vitality that encourages passion and togetherness.

Marley synthesized all these elements in his music, and his international fame made him the epitome of hipness, spirituality, and rebelliousness, a messenger of love who reminded us that peace without justice was hypocritical. Marley has become the Marcus Garvey of Afro-Caribbean music and black liberation.

While scholars have pointed out the U.S. influence of African-American music (blues, funk, soul) on Jamaica's, there is an indigenous tradition of religious singing (Baptist, Revivalist, Pentecostal) that has been "re-created" by African-Jamaicans. Musically speaking, Jamaica, like most Caribbean countries, has been able to take European (British, Scottish, Irish), African, and other influences (U.S., Latin, other Caribbean islands), and make it something uniquely their own.

But it works both ways: Jamaican sound systems and dub poetry/music can be seen as forerunners of rap and hip-hop, just as the latter have influenced dancehall, ragga, and deejays such as Shabba Ranks (1965–), Beenie Man (1973–), and Buju Banton (1973–). These mutual influences only confirm the underlying unity of all African-based music in the Western Hemisphere.

RELIGION

Although increasingly secular, Jamaica is still a profoundly religious country. Perhaps because of the world popularity of reggae music, there is a perception that most Jamaicans are Rastafarians, which is not true. Possibly 5 percent of the population are practicing Rastafarians (official figures put it at 1 percent), although clearly their influence is far greater than their numbers. According to the census, Jamaicans belong to the following faiths or churches: Church of God, a form of Pentacostalism (21%), Seventh-Day Adventists (9.1%), Baptists (8.8%), Pentecostals (7.6%), Anglican (5.5%), Catholic (4.1%), and other, mostly Protestant, denominations. A quarter of the population professes no religion and about 9 percent responded "other."

Missionary work did not begin in earnest in Jamaica until the late eighteenth century, and both Anglican and other Protestant churches were not very active in baptizing slaves. Slaves were controlled by the plantocracy, and whites made it clear to them that being baptized would not grant them freedom. For slaves, then, different African religions intertwined to create what in Jamaica are known as "Kumina" and "Myal."

Kumina is a Congo-based religion that believes in ancestral spirits that can possess the living. Ceremonies are conducted with drums and songs, and these rhythms and song styles are also called Kumina. Kumina is similar to the Petro rites of Vodou (Haiti), palo-mayombe (Cuba), and Macumba (Brazil).

Myal, which means "spirit," is used to refer to African-derived religious practices based on belief in a central God followed by a hierarchy of natural, divine, and ancestral spirits, and the practice of magic and healing, spirit possession, dancing, and drumming as part of ritual observance. Central to these practices are the beliefs that spiritual purity must actively engage mind, body, and soul and that spirits can bring both good and evil (i.e., there is no central figure of evil, like the devil) (Alleyne 1988, 76–106). Both Myal and Kumina, on the one hand, and Christianity, on the other, have exerted mutual influences on each other from the revivalist surge of the 1860s to the present.

The most active missionaries from 1780 to 1820 were U.S. Baptists like George Lisle (or Liele), an ex-slave from Virginia, and Moses Baker. These black religious figures had a galvanizing effect on the slave population, and they were met with hostility from white slave-owners. Most Native Baptist ministers, like Samuel Sharpe, believed in abolition, and led the 1831 insurrection (the "Baptist War").

Over time there was a growing division between mainstream (Anglican, Wesleyan, official Baptist, Moravian, etc.) churches and Native churches (Baptist, Myalist). In the 1860s there was a revivalist upsurge in Jamaica, and Myalists were then referred to as "Revivalists," but they were still strongly Afro-Christian, and mostly Protestant. Many of these Revivalists later joined Pentecostal churches. However, Jamaicans often have "dual membership," publicly belonging to a Baptist or Pentecostal church, but covertly being Revivalists-Myalists. Christian and African beliefs intertwine in the celebration of John Canoe (Jonkunnu or Junkanoo), with its intense drumming and bright costuming, celebrated between Christmas and New Year's.

In the 1930s, a new religion-social movement arose: Rastafarianism. Combining a belief in the divinity of Emperor Haile Selassie I (1882–1975), the sacredness of nature, and a Pan-African ethos derived from Garvey, the Rastafarians built a small but ever more influential movement, which gained international attention thanks to reggae superstar Bob Marley. Many have trivialized it by emphasizing its ritual use of marijuana and the sporting of dreadlocks, but Rastas are keen students of the Old Testament, believe in the divine nature of humans, are devoted to environmental issues, and believe in eating natural foods.

Perhaps it is because they are trenchant critics of racism, oppression, and corruption as well as because they believe sin is both personal and corporate that Rastas are considered "political," but they belong to no political party, and are suspicious of the status quo (left or right), using the insightful word *politricks* to describe the opportunism of mainstream politicians. Rastafarianism responded to deep-seated Jamaican grievances of poverty, injustice, racism, and spiritual indifference. Its promotion of racial self-pride, a non-Eurocentric religious outlook, and creation of a community grounded in nonmaterialistic values has resonated with many non-Rastafarians as well.

LANGUAGE

In Jamaica, as in other parts of the Caribbean, European and African languages came together (or collided) to produce a local vernacular that has been called "Jamaican Creole." Recently, it has been modified by certain Rastafarian idioms, known as "Dread Talk." Jamaican Creole has been extensively studied by linguists and there is even a dictionary, *Dictionary of Jamaican English* (1967).

During colonial times English was the norm and African languages (mostly Twi-Asante and Kikongo) were not encouraged. Thus slaves needed to learn English, but their masters showed no interest in speaking African languages. Slowly, the contact between different African languages and English led to a new language, but with English still dominant, though many words, sentence structure, and speech rhythms still showed African influences. Jamaican Creole was seen as inferior, substandard, and not a language, but instead a pidgin English, a dialect.

Poets like Claude McKay and Louise Bennett began using a Creole vernacular in their verses, and helped pave the way for greater acceptance of Jamaican Creole. Rastafarians made further contributions. Rastas use "I"-Talk, linking the pronoun "I" with the "eye" of vision and insight. So instead of "me" or "we," "I" or "I-an-I" is used. Rastas also try to convey sound and meaning more coherently: instead of the word "oppressor" they would use "downpressor," which more truthfully conveys the physical constraints of oppression.

Most Jamaicans express themselves in a continuum ranging from standard English to Creole, sometimes varying from one sentence to another, or depending on the situation (family gathering, school, business office, or hospital). Creole is a spoken language, but most Jamaicans write in a more standard English.

LITERATURE AND THE ARTS

Jamaica has a long and rich literary tradition. Among the first to achieve international prominence was Claude McKay (1889–1948), a gifted poet and novelist who wrote his first books in Creole; he later immigrated to the United States. and became one of the key figures of the Harlem Renaissance. Una Marson

(1905–1965) was not only a social activist and feminist but also a writer of highly charged poetry, like "Kinky Hair Blues," confronting white Eurocentric views of beauty. They were followed by novelists such as V.S. Reid (1913–1987), whose *New Day* (1949) re-created the Morant Bay Rebellion, Roger Mais (1905–1955), John Hearne (1926–1994), and Andrew Salkey (1928–1995).

Louise Bennett (1919–) is considered a national treasure and is a TV personality who performs her vernacular poetry in a vivid, witty, and dramatic way, drawing on folkore and local proverbs. Women writers have made major contributions with the likes of Velma Pollard (1937–), Olive Senior (1943–), Lorna Goodison (1947–), Erna Brodber (1937–), Michele Cliff (1946–), and Patricia Powell (1966–). Brodber's *Jane and Louisa Will Soon Come Home* (1980), at first unnoticed, is now considered a classic of Caribbean literature. The Sistren Theater Collective has been producing plays by working-class women since 1977 and has published Jamaican women's life stories as well.

In the seventies and eighties, dub poets emerged such as Mutabaruka, Linton Kwesi Johnson (1952–), Mikey Smith, and Jean "Binta" Breeze (1947–), one of the few women dub poets. These reggae-inspired voices were part of what is called "oraliterature," and they just as often recorded CDs as they published books.

Jamaica is a country with a strong intellectual-academic tradition, in part due to the University of the West Indies-Mona (1948) campus, a center for scholarship, research, and publication. Figures such as Rex Nettleford, a dancer, choreographer, and Pan-Caribbean thinker Carl Stone, and Barry Chevannes have written insightfully about the island's history and culture. Jamaican scholars resident in the United States have become well known, such as Sylvia Wynter, who is also the first black Jamaican woman to publish a novel, as well as Orlando Patterson, Franklin Knight, and Lewis R. Gordon.

Jamaican painters and sculptors have done much to shape a national and cultural identity. John Dunkley (1891–1947), Alvin Marriott (1902–1992), and Edna Manley (1900–1987) were among the first visual artists to explore local themes. Other painters have focused on natural landscapes or nature (Albert Huie), religious themes (Albert Artwell, E. Brown, Osmond Watson), social concerns (Carl Abrahams, Eugene Hyde, Barrington Watson), or issues of identity and racial consciousness (David Boxer, Albert Chong, Keith Morrison). Mallica "Kapo" Reynolds (1911–1989) was an intuitive painter-sculptor who was a Revivalist bishop; as a young artist he drew a black Christ that caused a stir. David Boxer (1946–), also a critic and the director of the National Gallery of Art, is both a painter and installation artist who focuses on themes of identity, conflict, and oppression, often from an autobiographical perspective.

CONCLUSION

Despite the social tensions and violence of the past decades, Jamaica maintains a commitment to a political democracy, with intense trade union activity, a lively if not confrontational press, and an active civil society. Economically, the country depends on bauxite, sugar, coffee, light manufacturing, rum, bananas, and, of course, tourism, which employs almost one out of every five Jamaicans. Although the country is urbanized, there are still hundreds of thousands of peasants eking out an existence on tiny plots of land. Inflation and unemployment (16%) are high, and that has prompted many Jamaicans to immigrate to the United States, Canada, and Great Britain. Over a million Jamaicans (or their offspring) are living outside the island, half a million in the United States alone. Official figures list illiteracy at 15 percent, but it is likely closer to 25 percent, high for the English-speaking Caribbean.

Jamaicans often speak of creolization, or the cultural and racial mixing of European and African traditions to form a uniquely Jamaican identity. Important though it is, in racial terms it promoted a middle-class "browning" of the country, given visual expression not only in its tourist literature, but also in its choice of beauty and carnival queens, where rarely has a black woman been chosen. This "browning" effect resurfaced during the eighties and nineties in attitudes toward dancehall (seen as lower class, black, violent), and the promotion of lighter-skinned "dancehall queens" (Edmondson 1999, 56–74).

Jamaica celebrated its fortieth anniversary as an independent country in 2002, beset by many of the same ills of many poor countries. Despite political violence, patronage, and elements of coercion, the political system features flexibility and democratic negotiation; despite social upheaval, it has stayed clear of coups, military dictatorships, or bloody revolutions; despite economic injustice, it has countered with a combative trade union movement that defends workers. Clearly the country is more self-assured now in its national and racial identity, more comfortable in being an African-Jamaican nation culturally and socially.

NOTE

1. "Obeah" is a loaded word and catchall term for magical practices. It pertains to a supernatural belief in spirits and the use of Obeah (charms, potions, herbs) to control those spirits for healing, casting spells, warding off evil, or seeking revenge. It is often contrasted with myalism (see Religion), which is seen as positive whereas Obeah has traditional negative connotations of "black magic." Obeah and Myal are closely linked to West African religious practices, and Obeah can be used for noble or ignoble purposes. During the slave and colonial era whites Eurocentrically viewed Obeah as "primitive" and "destructive," perhaps because it was used against them.

REFERENCES

Alleyne, Mervyn C. (1988). *Roots of Jamaican Culture*. London: Pluto Press.
Bakan, Abigail (1990). *Ideology and Class Conflict in Jamaica, the Politics of Rebellion*. Montreal, Canada: McGill University Press.

Barrow, Steve, and Peter Dalton (2001). *The Rough Guide to Reggae: The Definitive Guide to Jamaican Music from Ska, through Roots to Ragga*. London: Penguin Books.

Braithwaite, Edward K. (2000/1971). *The Development of Creole Society in Jamaica: 1770–1820*. Princeton, NJ: Ian Randle-Markus Wiener.

Edmondson, Belinda J. (ed.) (1999). *Caribbean Romances: The Politics of Regional Representation*. Charlottesville, VA: University Press of Virginia, pp. 56–74 (on Jamaican Carnival).

Lewin, Olive (2000). *Rock It Come Over: The Folk Music of Jamaica*. Jamaica: University of West Indies Press-Mona.

Mordecai, Martin, and Pamela Mordecai (2001). *Culture and Customs of Jamaica*. Westport, CT: Greenwood Press.

Murrell, Nathaniel Samuel, William Davis Spencer, and Adrian Anthony MacFarlane (eds.) (1998). *Chanting Down Babylon: The Rastafari Reader*. Kingston, Jamaica: Ian Randle Publishers.

Patterson, Orlando (1969). *The Sociology of Slavery: An Analysis of the Origins, Development and Structure of Negro Slave Society in Jamaica*. Cranbury, NJ: Associated University Press.

———(1979). "Slavery and Slave Revolts: A Sociohistorical Analysis of the First Maroon War, 1665–1740." In Price, Richard (ed.), *Maroon Societies: Rebel Slave Communities in the Americas*. Baltimore: Johns Hopkins University Press.

Shepherd, Verene (1999). *Women in Caribbean History*. Kingston, Jamaica: Ian Randle Publishers.

Sherlock, Philip, and Hazel Bennett (1998). *The Story of the Jamaican People*. Princeton, NJ: Ian Randle Publishers-Markus Wiener.

Zips, Werner (1999). *Black Rebels: African Caribbean Freedom Fighters in Jamaica*. Princeton, NJ: Ian Randle Publishers-Markus Wiener.

10

Martinique

Mickaëlla L. Pèrina

For centuries Martinique has been called *le pays des revenants*, the country where all return. This was first said in 1671 by Reverend P. Du Tertre, who emphasized the island's lingering charm on strangers, haunted by such regret after their departure that they always returned. The name has stuck for centuries, but as was later pointed out, beyond its enchanting natural power *le pays des revenants* might also be regarded as a place inhabited by *revenants* (also the word for "ghost" or "specter") in the sense that the "ancestors" never entirely left. Martinique is a place where people are always in contact with both foreign and "ancestral" (African) figures. This image can help us understand its complex history and society.

Located in the Lesser Antilles directly south of Dominica and north of St. Lucia, Martinique is a French overseas department of 392,000. It is both undeniably Caribbean and unquestionably French. More than three hundred years of French rule clearly have shaped the island's administrative, political, economic, and judicial structures, but Martinique's language, music, social mores, religions, and cuisine are marked by mostly African (or Afro-Caribbean), but also East Indian and Chinese, components.

The island of Martinique (421 square miles) was first inhabited by Arawak Indians who came around A.D. 200 from South America. About eight centuries later, the more warlike Caribs invaded the island. As a result, all the Arawak males were killed while the females were captured, leading to the first mixing of races in Martinique. The Caribs held firm control and defended the island tenaciously until the sixteenth century, when Europeans showed interest in it.

SUGAR AND FRENCH COLONIZATION

Since the very beginning of Martinique's colonization, colonists had unsuccessfully tried to establish sugar cane production, and cash in on "white gold."
In 1654, Dutch colonizers expelled from Brazil by the Portuguese arrived in
Martinique. They brought with them refining secrets along with a few black
slaves who were experienced in sugar production. Within fifteen years, 117 sugar
mills were created in Martinique generating a complete social and economic revolution.

Quickly, the production of sugar cane ushered in a new distribution of land
and an insatiable need for workers. At that time, about forty slaves were estimated necessary to work a 370 acre plantation, in order to produce a hundred
thousand pounds of sugar a year. In 1654 there were no more than a few hundred African slaves in Martinique, most of them taken away from the Spanish
by freebooters and sold to French colonists. In 1664 the Martinican population
consisted of 3,158 African slaves and 2,904 whites. After that the number of
slaves increased tremendously following the increase of sugar cane production.

By the end of the seventeenth century the colonial-slave system was consolidated. Martinique's increasing prosperity was based not only on sugar but also
on coffee, cocoa, and cotton. This triangular commerce (Africa-Caribbean-
Europe) took place within the framework of the "exclusive" system, whereby
French colonies only traded with France, clearly to the latter's benefit. Because
of their great wealth, the sugar islands were a contested area for European powers, especially between France and Great Britain, and Martinique was invaded
on numerous occasions, giving the country an international profile.

The end of the eighteenth century coincided with great political changes: the
American War of Independence, the insurrection in St. Domingue (Haiti), and
the French Revolution. Interestingly, Martinique benefited very little from the
French revolutionary period. At that time Martinique was first under revolutionary French administration (1789–1794), and after, under English authority,
during a counterrevolutionary period (1794–1802). When the English captured
the island in 1794, the French Revolution's decree abolishing slavery had not
yet arrived.

Unlike Guadeloupe, slavery was never abolished in Martinique during the
French Revolution. Similarly, during the Napoleonic regime (1804–1815) the
island was under French administration between two periods of English domination. In 1802 when Martinique was returned to France, coffee and tobacco production were decreasing and only sugar cane was yielding high returns. But trade
was interrupted and attempts were under way to find sugar substitutes. In 1812,
with the French Antilles once again under the British, Napoleon strongly encouraged sugar beet production in France. It would become a significant competitor of Martinican sugar.

Martinique's restitution to France in 1815 moved its politics back to a "domestic" realm, but the island's most important event of the nineteenth century

Statue of freed slave, St. Espirit, Martinique. Courtesy of
Mickaëlla L. Pèrina.

was the abolition of slavery (1848). In order to become law the decree had to be
brought to the colony by official commissioners. For the slaves, the wait was too
long and they revolted, sinking the island into chaos. To avoid more turmoil the
governor declared the immediate abolition of slavery; when the commissioners
arrived the colony no longer had slaves. Former slaves were not only free men
but also French citizens who could vote, which was significantly different from
other Caribbean post-emancipation scenarios.

While abolition changed society, auguring a new era, the old racial and social
hierarchies persisted. Quickly, former slaves faced resistance from both the central administration and colonists who feared their economic supremacy being
challenged. Economically, there was great inequality between landowners and

former slaves, and the former maintained the upper hand, and were compensated by the government for the loss of their slaves. Planters continued to control labor rules, paying dismal wages. In 1861 the "colonial pact" was abolished, allowing Martinique to trade with foreign countries.

The restitution of the French empire (1851) was a step back for former slaves. Universal suffrage was suppressed and governors regained the power to control municipalities. Former slaves faced economic and political inferiority for another twenty years.

The reestablishment of a republic in France (1870) was a new start for Martinique. Third Republic measures facilitated access for people of color to political leadership by reinstalling universal suffrage, colonial representation in French assemblies, and free and public primary education. The economy was still in the hands of wealthy whites, the *békés*. Blacks and *békés* became opposing forces.

An uprising known as the "Southern Insurrection" also occurred in 1870. For the first time former slaves, still working in the cane fields, united in revolt against the lack of improvement in their economic and social life. Though it lasted only a few days, more than forty plantations were destroyed.

In 1884 sugar stagnated and the crisis lasted up to the beginning of the twentieth century, causing numerous bankruptcies, which further concentrated the sugar plantations into the hands of a few powerful owners.

The first part of the twentieth century was shaped by workers' struggles and economic crisis. (The first general strike organized by agricultural workers was in 1900.) It was also a time of political violence caused by contested elections. In addition, the eruption of the Mount Pelée volcano near St.-Pierre, then the capital, killed three thousand, completely destroying the city; the capital was moved to Fort-de-France.

Political equality between citizens from the old colonies and metropolitan France was still a fundamental political issue. It was brought to the fore by World War I, when representatives petitioned France to serve in the military. Martinican soldiers were mobilized and participated in the war.

From 1920 on, workers' groups began to act in unified fashion. Socialism had become a popular working-class ideology, in part because of the war, but also due to the conncentration of wealth in the hands of a few and rum speculation. In 1923 massive demonstrations were organized during the sugar harvest, and in some cases cane fields were set ablaze at night, reviving past slave-revolt practices. By 1925 Martinican workers were effectively organized in a social movement, with political leaders and unions.

At the same time the General Council agitated for political integration with France, claiming that only the French legal system should apply to Martinique. Their demands were heard during the Third Republic (1870–1940) but were not considered during World War II by the Vichy regime in France that restored political supremacy to the white planters. The man who personified this period was an Admiral Georges Robert, whose impact on Martinicans was so great that islanders still refer to this period as "An tan Robé" (in Robert's time).

World War II was a time of famine, poverty, social inequality, and injustice, a time when allied warships blockaded the island. Rum and sugar could not be exported, nor could food be imported. Reacting to the deprivations of the war, Martinique and Guadeloupe voted massively in favor of the Communists when the French Fourth Republic was established (1946–1958).

FROM COLONY TO DÉPARTEMENT: 1946 TO THE PRESENT

In order to decolonize, Martinique requested departmentalization status from the parliament of the Antilles, supported by Aimé Césaire (the Communist mayor of Fort-de-France from 1946 to 2000). The French parliament also voted in March 1946 for the principle of assimilation, which was unanimously adopted. Officially this vote marked the end of French colonialism in the Caribbean.

The two decades preceding the departmentalization vote constituted a process of true assimilation. The search for greater democratization, political rights, and national sovereignty conflicts with the tenor of colonialism. But in the French Antilles that debate took place within a French political framework, not against it. Throughout the French Antilles and in French Guiana, effective political and social "progress" had been made in elective assemblies and daily citizenship practices. For this reason the Antilles "deserved" to be assimilated and their integration within France was considered a victory over colonialism.

However, by the late fifties the status regarded as a way out of colonialism appeared less satisfactory compared with independence or greater sovereignty. Politicians then began to question the relevance of assimilation and departmentalization. Many of them started requesting autonomy of decision-making, and a new nationalism against French citizenship resulted from this dissatisfaction.

This was a major threshold in Martinican history, certainly influenced by Césaire's resignation from the French Communist Party. Césaire had initially recommended departmentalization, but focused later on a struggle against Western imperialism, calling for greater autonomy and more local power. He criticized equally the communists for overlooking race and Martinican uniqueness.

However, the island was experiencing an economic boom and both elite and majority opinion were resolutely opposed to autonomy: the benefits from departmentalization, which also included social welfare, health care, and education, outweighed the risks. The French acknowledged the need to rethink departmental status and gave new power to prefects and general councils (1960). New laws did support local initiatives, but central administration power remained intact. Since 1960, the value and legitimacy of the departmental status has been constantly debated.

New decentralizing measures, called *région*, were introduced in 1972. Martinique became a *région* of France and gained new local powers. By the early 1990s the island had moved closer to becoming officially part of the European Union along with France. The seesawing between more local control and French centralizing tendencies has made the demands of the Martinican Movement for Independence (MIM) more credible than ever. Its leader, Alfred Marie-Jeanne, has been elected deputy and sits at the French National Assembly and also leads the Martinican regional council. A typical Martinican paradox, one could say: a former French colony in all its specificity that is currently an administrative part of France, a creolized culture located in the Caribbean in times of globalization. More recently, Martinique has initiated discussions on new administrative changes, and possible new forms of status.

FROM GROWING COLONY TO A CREOLIZED SOCIETY

Martinique's population results from various stages of settlement, migration, and slavery and its social stratification reflects the functions each group assumed when it first arrived on the island. At the top, there is a sort of aristocracy—initially based on land ownership and now more business-oriented—the *béké*. The *békés* constitute a homogeneous and dominant stratum of European descent and maintain their racial identity by a controlled inbreeding, while the rest of the population is mixed. They constitute an exception within the greater Caribbean. Their economic power is unquestionable within Martinique and elsewhere in the French Caribbean although they represent less than 1 percent of Martinique's population.

Within the plantation system, social and ethnic identification was fairly rigid: whites who owned land, resources, and people, and black slaves who owned nothing and did all the work. Today blacks and *békés* still constitute the two most powerful groups, the former in terms of numbers (over 90 percent of the population) and political power; the latter holds economic power. New immigrants modified this bipolar relationship, creating social, ethnic, and racial diversity, although *béké* inbreeding imposed and still imposes limits to this.

The people of African descent have limited economic power and constitute the majority of the social pyramid's lower level (Giraud 1979, 129), but their political commitment is very consistent. A key factor that still defines their current economic performance is that Africans' first function within the colony was that of being slave labor.

Martinican social stratification revolves around color and place of origin. A long list of words hints at the various shades of racial complexity, *nègre* (black), *chabine* (mixed race, but light), *câpre* (a mix of black with mulatto), *mulâtresse* (female mulatto). None of them is pejorative, but they express social as well as economic status. For instance, *mulâtres* (mulattoes) were historically the first mixed-breeds to reach the "middle" class, so the word still designates being both middle class and of mixed race. Education and reputation are also factors that define race and class in Martinique.

Between those two potent groups are two immigrant groups that contribute to Martinican social and ethnic diversity. East Indians were introduced in Martinique as contract workers during the nineteenth century when French authorities needed some form of indentured servants to limit the consequences of the abolition of slavery. Between 1854 and 1883, 25,509 East Indians (called *coolies* locally) were brought to Martinique but high mortality rates and repatriation caused their numbers to decrease to 3,764 by 1900.

During the nineteenth century, East Indians were marginalized because they were foreigners and were replacing black workers. Those who stayed on became French citizens only in 1904, but perception of their lowly status lingered long in public consciousness.

Chinese were also brought to the island as indentured workers; this was prompted by the ineffectiveness of East Indian immigration. Beginning in 1859, about 1,000 Chinese were introduced. They arrived in Fort-de-France at a time when Africans and East Indians were already waiting for plantation work, so few were employed. Planters also complained that Chinese workers were inclined to desert and rebel against plantation life. Though they didn't integrate well into plantation life, they integrated into Martinican society, becoming small shopkeepers and marrying interethnically. A later wave of Chinese who immigrated in the 1940s were less reluctant to intermarry. Though less than 1 percent of the population, the Chinese consider themselves truly Martinican. Whether they are of African descent, *békés*, East Indians, or Chinese, as in most of the Caribbean, Martinicans claim nationality before ethnoracial specificity.

WHEN CULTURE MEANS CREOLIZATION

Martinican culture is thoroughly creolized. Creolization is defined as a historical process in which original cultural elements are transformed by the addition of new ones. This process includes original retentions, clashes with other cultures, but ultimately new examples of cultural creativity. Every single dimension of Martinican culture shows pluralism, a diversity that expresses each of the population components as well as the creations of their interactions and modifications.

Literature is a good example of this ongoing process of connection, integration, memory, and invention. From the seventeenth to the nineteenth century, alongside a written literature by colonists that focused on sociology, economics, and anthropology, there was an oral literature expressed by slaves. At first, this oral literature referred exclusively to Africa, but its contact with European literary norms transformed not only its themes but its language (into Creole).

By the early 1900s, a literature written by people of African descent elaborated and progressively addressed the question of its specificity. René Maran, in his 1921 novel, *Batouala*, interrogated the authenticity of Martinican literature with regard to French literature and advocated for a more socially committed art. Some consider him to be a precursor of the negritude movement.

Maran's plea was answered by many twentieth-century Martinican writers. First by poets such as Aimé Césaire (1913–) and Edouard Glissant (1928–), then later by novelists. Césaire, ex-Communist and longtime mayor, is one of the fathers of negritude, and a close friend of Léopold Sédar Senghor. Negritude was a movement of writers and political activists that celebrated Africanness as an essential characteristic of black life, and expressed a pride in a common diasporic culture of not only suffering, but pride and creativity. In 1939 Césaire published *Notebook of a Return to My Native Land*, an extraordinary poem that both indicted Eurocentric domination and expressed hope in a black future.

Glissant's views based on Antillanité (or Caribbeanness) are a critique of Césaire's. Pointing to the Caribbean's mix of races, cultures, and languages, Glissant claims that looking at Africanness is too limiting since the region has European, indigenous, East Asian, and Chinese influences. The Caribbean's uniqueness, he argues demands a "cross-cultural poetics" with a global span across time, space, and history. If Césaire wants to plant an African tree with its well-defined roots deep in the soil, Glissant prefers a rhizome, a patchwork of roots near the surface that sprawls in all directions. The difference between them reveals a difference in how Martinican identity and race are viewed, even in the language used: Césaire has always written in French; Glissant praises and writes in Creole, but not exclusively so.

Writer Joseph Zobel (1915–) was influenced by these movements, but with a critical awareness. The author of *Sugar Cane Alley*—also a well-known film—Zobel believed in racial reconciliation based on social values. *Sugar Cane Alley* shows the Martinican underclass of the forties and fifties, portraying a young man's progression from peasant to intellectual.

From an antiracist humanist perspective, Frantz Fanon (1925–1961) also questioned negritude, proposing solutions that included but went beyond a racial analysis. The Martinican psychiatrist, political philosopher, essayist, and revolutionary wrote about the intellectual and political alienation of black people in a world dominated by white values. Fanon's conclusion for colonized people was that they should free themselves through armed struggle. Fanon joined the Algerian independence struggle against French colonialism. Author of *Black Skin, White Masks* and *The Wretched of the Earth*, Fanon is a key figure in Third World politics and thought. Fanon's global relevance might have obstructed his recognition as a Martinican thinker, but he is being "locally" reinterpreted in the light of the country's political status.

Building on Glissant's ideas of Antillanité, two novelists, Patrick Chamoiseau and Raphaël Confiant, and Jean Bernabé, a linguist, wrote *In Praise of Creoleness*. These Créolité thinkers further expound the island's cultural plurality (Indianness, Chineseness), making an impassioned defense of the Creole language, as well as an appeal for island independence—all criticisms of Césaire and negritude. They claim that Créolité transcends race and is a hybrid, cumulative, everchanging identity (Taylor 1998, 124–160). Critics claim that Créolité is indirectly slighting blackness and forgetting that racism still exists, not to mention its blatant sexism (Price and Price 1999, 139–144). Despite the sometimes high intellectual level of the debate, these are not arid academic discussions. At stake are issues of national identity, race, and political representation that affect cultural policy, immigration, language, economics, and politics, and how Martinicans view themselves.

Creolization also affects the language Martinicans speak. While some writers mix Creole and French languages, others write only in French, and still others only in Creole. To complicate matters further, most Martinicans cannot read or write in the Creole language, although they all understand and/or speak it. French is the language of education (and economic advancement) although since the early 1990s room has been made for learning Creole in optional language classes. Creole is heavily used in oral cultural forms, like music and drama. Debates over where and when to use Creole are heated, showing it is a sensitive political issue, as well as a way of letting others know how Martinican you are, instead of being French.

Martinican music shows a strong rhythmic component and is almost indissociable from singing—mostly in Creole—or dancing. Popular music in Martinique constitutes a mixture of African and European musical cultures. Sung dances are usually played on instruments such as piano, violin, flute, and clarinet accompanied by various drums and percussion. This music was first drum-based and built around call-and-response forms, but between the seventeenth and the nineteenth centuries, it integrated European dances modified by the addition of rhythmic variations and Creole language phrasing. Dances like the waltz, polka, and mazurka became creolized, and African rhythms were also modified. Both transformations produced new musical forms involving melodic-rhythmic transformations, with Creole lyrics and vocals.

In that respect, the *biguine*, a traditional Martinican form popular up to the seventies, expresses a compositional and instrumental alchemy that conjoins ragtime, jazz, French songs, and Afro-Cuban rhythms. Barrel and Hurard Coppet, Fernand Donatien, and Leona Gabriel were famous creators and interpreters of the Creole waltz, Creole mazurka, and *biguine*. Today Guy Vadeleux, Max Ransay, Max Cilla, Gertrude Seinin, and Céline Flériag, among others, keep those forms alive. These "traditional" musical forms, still played and danced to, have been overtaken by zouk.

Originating in carnival music forms, zouk emerged by developing new arrangements using modern instruments and mixing in various Caribbean musical traditions as well as English rock and American soul. A more romantic variant called zouk-love has contributed to even greater success. Kassav is indisputably the most famous zouk group but Martinican zouk artists and groups are numerous: Eric Virgal, Taxi Kréol, Léa Galva, Sylvie Thrébaut, and Célia Guitteaud. Usually new songs are released twice a year: for the "holiday" season (June to August) and Carnival.

Starting the Saturday before Mardi Gras and ending with Ash Wednesday, Carnival lasts five days and four nights. Traditionally Monday (lundi gras) is dedicated to burlesque weddings, Tuesday (mardi gras) to red devils. Ash Wednesday is black-and-white day, with colors of sorrow and with the death of

Vaval, the Carnival king, who is burned in effigy to symbolize the end of Carnival. Carnival is more than fun, music, and revelry: it also expresses social and political concerns.

Carnival recalls historical moments and social struggles. For instance, Maroons and their struggle for freedom are depicted and symbolized; also seen is "Marianne la po fi," a costume made with dry banana leaves, which also illustrates the social struggle between classes, and especially peasants' struggles against landowners. Carnival is an occasion to raise consciousness about Martinican culture, but it is also certainly a time of enjoyment, a time to exchange identities wearing costumes, but within a frame of permissiveness to express links between culture and politics.

SYNCRETIC RELIGIOUS PRACTICES

Though nominally an overwhelmingly Catholic country, everyday life is shaped by non-Western religious beliefs and traditions. While Christian practices happen to be public, non-Western beliefs often belong to the private sphere.

The separation between private and public religious practices resulted from how Martinique was settled. Clearly, Catholicism was first brought to the island under conquest and slavery. For centuries, non-Western traditions and beliefs were not considered religions, but instead were thought of as "magic," "superstitions," or "primitive diabolical habits." Progressively, as Christianity achieved official status, other beliefs were hidden in order for them to survive. During slavery the Catholic Church was the only legitimate symbolic-religious order: therefore, slaves converted to Catholicism as did immigrants after abolition. Today, although the official Martinican Catholic Church obeys Catholic rules and dogma, Catholic practices are plainly influenced by local culture, and often by beliefs they once combated.

Although Africans were persecuted under slavery and colonization for their beliefs and practices, they resisted and their practices and beliefs survived, though greatly modified. Their creolization started on plantations where they needed to disguise their beliefs to escape sanction. In Creole, the word *tchenbwa* designates practices and beliefs that originated in Africa, but subsequently became mixed with Christianity, with an additional overlay of nineteenth-century magical beliefs from European indentured servants. *Tchenbwa* is open to many influences and values, turning to prayers, using herbs, sacred powders, and animal sacrifice. Most Martinicans regarded Catholic practice and *tchenbwa* as overlapping: for otherworldly salvation they relied on Catholicism; for the problems of everyday life (jobs, sickness, loss, infidelity, obtaining lovers), people resorted to *tchenbwa*.

It is difficult to say how many people still believe and practice *tchenbwa*, because these beliefs are rarely acknowledged openly, and supposedly "modern" medicine has found many cures for ailments previously treated through *tchenbwa*. Given the rapid modernization of Martinique in the last fifty years, and particularly the advances in health care, it is probably safe to say these be-liefs are declining, but they have not disappeared completely.

Aside from *tchenbwa*, Martinican East Indian worship is another practice that originated on the plantations. Although East Indian immigrants came from var-ious religious origins (but mostly Hindu), they united on Martinican planta-tions and their religious observation became a means of group support and survival, of preserving their culture. Although their contracts stipulated that their religion must be respected, the Catholic Church struggled vigorously against East Indian practices, regarding their plurality of gods as evil.

However, East Indian worship is still alive in Martinique today, preserving a cult that is dedicated to a mother goddess, as well as other minor divinities. While integrating into Martinican society, East Indians interacted with the two other symbolic orders, Catholicism and *tchenbwa*. For Indians who wanted to remain in Martinique after their contract expired, conversion to Catholicism was a pre-requisite. East Indians did convert but never abandoned their traditional forms of worship. As a result, today they often practice both religions, considering them as clearly distinct and attributing separate functions to each. Interestingly, Mar-tinican East Indian religious practice acknowledges the principle of an afterlife, which distinguishes it from Hinduism, showing that it has become creolized.

Initially, black and colored Martinicans considered East Indian religions as similar to *tchenbwa*, even if East Indian beliefs seemed more structured and con-sistent than *tchenbwa*. Despite former discrepancies or misunderstandings, non–East Indians have manifested true interest in East Indian religions and par-ticipate in ceremonies where they ask for mercies. Recently, Martinican East In-dian priests made new connections with India, traveling there and bringing back new rites and divinities that have already modified their temples and will prob-ably affect their practices in the near future. It is too early to say how impor-tant these new influences will be and how they will be creolized with the black and Afro-Creole majority.

Martinique's rapid changes have brought other faiths as well: Jehovah's Wit-nesses, Seventh-Day Adventists, Mahikari, and Islam. These religions look neg-atively at *tchenbwa*. Rastafarianism was introduced in Martinique via Dominica in the late seventies and touched essentially young people who were rebelling against the dominant system of values. The Rasta community has never been numerous in Martinique but their followers adhere to nonviolence and other Rasta tenets of justice and racial pride.

CONCLUSION

Like other Caribbean islands, Martinique is a country with strong ethnic di-versity and a pluralistic cultural identity. But unlike them, it is a French over-seas department and region as well as a part of the European Union. Martinique faces several economic and political challenges. Nowadays, the French overseas-department standard of living is superior to the rest of the Caribbean, with some exceptions. But its prosperity depends mostly on French government subsidies that pay increased salaries to government employees, who absorb most of the budget. Tourism is the most important source of local wealth. Martinique must confront a huge gap between the standard of living and the reality of its economy. Since departmentalization, the traditional economy has literally vanished. Without French largesse, people would starve. And yet, unemployment is close to 30 percent, prompting many to immigrate to France. This double bind hinders those who favor political self-determination or independence: there seems to be no alternative to the present economic model.

Present-day Martinique is struggling to undue its past political and economic straitjackets, but has not yet come forth with a new path for its future. Part of the problem is the unfinished project of political creolization. While talk of pluralism, creolization, and hybrid identities is fine, there are hard political and economic questions that arise from Martinique's dual membership. Martinique is both part of France and Europe and *apart* because of it Caribbeanness, its West Indian uniqueness. Future decisions—that hopefully will consider the wisdom of its *revenants* and ancestors—will reveal if Martinique's dual membership was a thoughtful way to decolonize or, on the contrary, a new form of colonization.

REFERENCES

Alexis, Mylene (1998). "La Musique créole: enracinement et création." In Mylene, Atekis and Florence Pizzorn-Itic (eds.), *Tropiques métisses*. Paris. Editions de la réunion das musées nation aux.

Burton, Richard D.E., and Fred Reno (eds.) (1995). *French and West Indian: Martinique, Guadeloupe, and French Guiana Today*. Charlottesville, VA: University Press of Virginia.

Elizabeth, Léo (1972). "The French Antilles." In Cohen, David W., and Jack P. Greene (eds.), *Neither Slave Nor Free. The Freedmen of African Descent in the Slave Societies of the New World*. Baltimore: Johns Hopkins University Press, pp. 134–171.

Giraud, Michel (1979). *Races et classes a la Martinique, Les relations raciales entre enfants de differentes couleurs a l'école*, Paris: Anthropos.

Guibault, Jocelyne (1990). "On Interpreting Popular Music: Zouk in the West Indies." In Lent, John A. (ed.), *Caribbean Popular Culture*. Bowling Green, Ohio: Bowling Green State Popular Press, pp. 79–97.

———(1993). *Zouk: World Music in the West Indies*. Chicago: University of Chicago Press.

Hintjens, Helen M. (1992). "France's Love Children? The French Overseas Department." In Hintjens, Helen M. and Malyn D. D. Newitt (eds.), *The Political Economy of Small Tropical Islands: The Importance of Being Small*, Exeter: University of Exeter Press, pp. 64–75.

Horowitz, Michael M., and Morton Klass (1961). "The Martiniquan East Indian Cult of Maldevidan." *Social and Economic Studies* 10, no. 1, pp. 93–100.

Price, R., and S. Price (1999). "Shadowboxing in the Mangrove: The Politics of Identity in Postcolonial Martinique." In Edmondson, B. (ed.), *Caribbean Romances: The Politics of Regional Representation*. Charlottesville, VA: University Press of Virginia, pp. 123–162.

Taylor, Lucien (1998). "Créolité Bites. A Conversation with Patrick Chamoiseau, Raphaël Confiant and Jean Bernabé." *Transition* 7, no. 2, issue 74: pp. 124–160.

11

The Netherlands Antilles (Curaçao, Bonaire, St. Eustatius, Saba), Aruba, and St. Maarten

Alan West-Durán

Although grouped together because of their shared history under Dutch colonialism, the Netherlands Antilles, Aruba, and St. Maarten show a high degree of social, linguistic and cultural difference. Aruba, Bonaire, and Curaçao (also known as the "ABCs") are situated close to Venezuela and form the Dutch Windward Islands. St. Maarten, St. Eustatius (also known as "Statia"), and Saba are part of the Leeward Islands (known as the "SSS" or "Ss") and are over 600 miles northeast of the ABCs, just east of the Virgin Islands. Although the official language of all is Dutch, English is predominant in the Ss; in the ABCs, Papiamentu, a Creole language made up of Portuguese, Spanish, Dutch, and African languages predominates. The ABCs are larger islands and make up 90 percent of the total population. The Ss are in the hurricane zone and their climate is typically tropical: wet, resulting in abundant, lush vegetation. The ABCs are out of the hurricane zone, not as wet, with sparse, sometimes desertlike vegetation. The people of the Ss are predominantly Protestant; the ABCs are strongly Catholic, with small but long-established Jewish and Reform communities. All have significant tourism industries; the ABCs (mostly Curaçao and Aruba) have an oil industry, which made them in the past a magnet for workers not only from the rest of the Netherlands Antilles, but also from the other islands of the Caribbean. Ethnically and racially, the variety is equally wide; in Saba about half the population is of African descent; in Curaçao, closer to 85 percent are black or Afro-Creoles. Aruba has a large Euro-Arawak (indigenous) mix. St. Eustatius is overwhelmingly black and St. Maarten, which traditionally was black, is now becoming less so, with a large influx of nonlocals. And all the islands have immigrants from many European countries as well as from India, Lebanon, China, and the other Caribbean islands.

PRE-COLUMBIAN TIMES AND THE DUTCH TAKEOVER

The ABCs were inhabited by Caquetío Arawak Indians at the time of European conquest, whereas the Ss were uninhabited when the Spanish arrived, although the Arawaks had clearly inhabited the islands at one point. In 1515, the Spanish deported the Indian population of the ABC islands to Hispaniola, to work as slaves to replace the indigenous population of the island that was being wiped out from disease, overwork, and mistreatment.

Dutch imperial interests took over by the 1630s, drawn neither by the prospect of gold nor sugar, but salt. Holland had previously imported its salt from the Iberian Peninsula and the Venezuelan salt pans, but when the eighty-year independence war against Spain resumed in 1621, it had to look for salt elsewhere, finding significant salt pans in Bonaire, Curaçao, and St. Maarten. Salt mining is extremely labor intensive and tedious, so the Dutch began to import slaves.

The Netherlands Antilles, unlike Suriname, Holland's other major Caribbean colony, never developed a plantation system. However, Curaçao and St. Eustatius did become important importers of slaves for the region in the seventeenth century, selling most of them to the Spanish or English. Its sophisticated business techniques, maritime prowess, and commercial skills were a major component of the Atlantic slave trade.

THE WINDWARDS OR ABCs: CURAÇAO

The largest and most populated of the Netherlands Antilles, with a population of 170,000, Curaçao was first "discovered" by the Spanish in 1499. Because of the absence of precious metals, the Spanish called it an *isla inútil* (a useless island), a term they also applied to Aruba and Bonaire. Colonization started in 1625, when Curaçao and Aruba were appointed to the Spaniard Juan de Ampies. Later on they were placed under the control of the governor of Coro in Venezuela. Cattle was raised, but the Spanish did little to make the island economy prosper or to defend it from attacks.

The Dutch, however, were increasing their presence in the region after the outbreak of the war in 1621 and in 1634 they took over the island. They needed salt for the Dutch herring industry and an outpost for harassing Spanish shipping. Curaçao's salt pans and several excellent harbors made it perfect for both.

The first slaves were brought to Curaçao in 1648 and over the next 150 years 60,000 slaves were imported. The size, climate, and poor soil of the island made it unsuitable for plantation agriculture. Most slave owners owned fewer than 5 slaves, unlike, say, Suriname, where the average plantation employed over 100. Curaçao had only one plantation with over 150 slaves; Suriname had almost 60. The differences in harshness of Antillean and Surinamean slavery are much debated (1862 figures; Lamur 2000, 817). On its three largest plantations, Suriname employed more slaves than in 85 percent of Curaçao's plantations. Other factors have been mentioned to explain Curaçao's less severe system of slavery: the Protestant settlers stayed on the island for many generations (as opposed to Suriname's absentee owners), giving them an emotional attachment to the island; the slave owners were under closer government scrutiny (unlike being at the total mercy of masters), and Curaçao's landowners who owned slaves were not wildly prosperous, and so they had to "share" their misfortunes with their bondsmen and not mistreat their slaves (Hoetink 1972, 66).

For example, Curaçao had decided to build two hospitals to treat slaves in the seventeenth century, before similar facilities existed for soldiers and civilians. Labor conditions were more favorable for Curaçao's slaves, since they worked at cattle raising, corn, and sorghum, which had a six-month harvesting cycle. On sugar plantations the hours were longer, the work more grueling, the discipline more severe. Nutrition was also better: slaves in Curaçao ate corn, fruit, meat, and fish; in Suriname it was mostly plantains, yams, and some dried fish (a diet low in protein). Both nutrition and labor conditions affect fertility rates (both for men and women), and the larger the plantation the lower the fertility rates. The Netherlands Antilles had a natural increase in slave populations throughout most of its history (more births than deaths, similar to the United States); Suriname's slave population decreased, similar to huge plantation societies like Brazil, Cuba, and Jamaica (Lamur 2000, 816–818). For these reasons, then, historians claim that these factors made slavery in Curaçao and the Netherlands Antilles in general "benign," comparatively speaking. Different perhaps, but not "benign," and it did not keep slaves from rebelling, as will be seen.

But it was still a hierarchical society dominated by Sephardic Jews and European whites, mostly of Dutch descent, over the free colored, free blacks, and slaves. Given the slight enthusiasm for both converting slaves to Protestantism and teaching them Dutch, the slaves of Curaçao became Catholic and spoke what is now known as Papiamentu. Thus, the separation between whites and non-whites had several dimensions: social (proprietor and property; freeman and slave), racial (whites and non-whites), religious (Dutch Reform and Catholicism), and linguistic (Dutch and Papiamentu), although the white Creole minority also adopted Papiamentu as early as the seventeenth century.

Another salient feature of Curaçao was the importance of a group of free colored and free blacks. Given the economy of the island many slaves were not field slaves; instead, they worked as house servants, coachmen, gardeners, and artisans. Their manumission was more frequent than with field slaves, sometimes for personal or humanitarian reasons, but most often because in bad times freeing them relieved the masters of having to take care of these "less productive" slaves. Their numbers were sufficiently large that by mid–eighteenth century many complaints were voiced about their disruptive behavior, since they had formed opposing gangs and had engaged in violent confrontations in Willemstad, the capital. Laws were passed to limit their mobility and interaction. Although not slaves, the free colored were often poor and in periods of economic depression; their fate was often worse than that of slaves (Hoetink 1972, 67). A master, no matter how cruel, still had the responsibility of feeding, clothing, and housing his slaves.

In 1750 slaves on the West India Company estate of Hato, managed by Isaac Faesch, director of the island, rebelled. The rebellion was defeated but Faesch lost thirty-one men and twelve women and children, and there was great destruction of property; another slave owner lost sixteen people. When captured, many rebellious slaves committed suicide, knowing the vicious punishment that awaited them. Three years later thirty-four of the insurrectionists were put to death. In 1751 slaves turned on a master, Lamont, but this incident was also suppressed quickly (Hartog 1968, 120–121).

By 1789, Curaçao had a population of almost 20,000. Whites were 20 percent, slaves 66 percent and free colored 14 percent of the population. Whites and free colored constituted about a third of the population, which was quite high for the non-Spanish-speaking Caribbean, and these numbers might explain why whites were more concerned with the free colored than with the slaves, whose rebellions had once caught them unawares (and would again).

Another factor was the Catholicism of slaves and free blacks and coloreds. Not only was it strongly rooted by then, but also it was of a libertarian nature. During the seventeenth and eighteen centuries, Catholicism proved to be helpful in the oppression of slaves. After approximately 1660, Spanish priests from Venezuela were permitted to work on Curaçao. Roman Catholicism, however, mixed with African beliefs and their perspective as slaves, views that often put them at odds with the official church. For example, after a person's death, the Catholic custom of *la novena* (nine days) was observed but with Nanzi stories. Nanzi is a spider-trickster figure from African (Ashanti) folk wisdom, who was quite popular in Caribbean folktales. In addition, after 1750 the king of Spain had declared that slaves who sought refuge in a Spanish colony and were Catholics should be treated as free. But escaped slaves needed to present proof of baptism, no easy thing given the circumstances of their flight.

The dichotomy between the official church and slave religions was highlighted during the 1795 slave rebellion. The uprising began with a "water medicine" event that the slaves shared, administered by Mingeel Bulbaaij, one of their religious leaders. Two groups of slaves, one led by Tula and a second by Bastiaan, nicknamed Carpata, joined forces. Within a month a thousand slaves were in open rebellion. Just as the military was ready to launch its offensive against the slaves, a Franciscan priest, Jacobus Schinck, offered to mediate. He was unsuccessful and said "the blacks always behaved like an obedient flock and have accepted all I've proposed to them for their salvation. I can't understand why it hasn't happened now" (Lampe 1989, 92). Tula's parting words to Father Schinck were, "The only thing we want is our freedom" (Lampe 1989, 92). These two statements eloquently express the radically different worldviews of the Church and the Catholicism of the slaves.

The rebellion failed. Tula and Carpata were caught and handed over to the authorities by fellow slaves. Twenty-nine rebels were executed; the less serious offenders had their ears cropped, a standard if not cruel procedure of the times. Property and crop damage was heavy; planters were given a six-month reprieve on their mortgages.

Curaçao's society kept evolving toward a particular variant of a Caribbean nation: By 1816 the free colored were 32 percent of the population and slaves were under half. In 1833 there were more free colored than slaves. In less than fifty years the island had gone from being a society where slaves outnumbered whites and free colored 2 to 1 (also unusual compared with other islands) to almost the reverse: in 1833 whites and free blacks and colored outnumbered slaves 3 to 2. By abolition in 1863, slaves were a third of the population. Only Puerto Rico and Aruba had lower figures.

Post-emancipation brought an economic downturn that didn't end until the second decade of the twentieth century. By then 87 percent of the population was non-white, and only a tiny group had government positions or worked in professions. Most African-Curaçaoans had no fixed work and lived in desolation and hunger. Fortunately, oil was discovered in Lake Maracaibo of Venezuela (1914), making Curaçao a major refining center for the region. The petroleum giant Royal Dutch Shell employed thousands, attracting workers from the Netherlands Antilles, Suriname, and other islands in the Caribbean. By 1952 Shell employed some 11,000 people in Curaçao. These migrations shifted some of the religious and racial parameters of Curaçao. At the level of whiteness, the new influx of whites (mostly Dutch) created some friction with long-established local whites, who pejoratively referred to these newcomers as *makamba*, since they were very European in their ways and didn't speak Papiamentu. On the other hand, emigrants from the Caribbean, largely black, were Protestants. Historically, Protestantism was a white religion in Curaçao. These newcomers began to create a core feeling and definition about local culture and identity that would become important to the island's history.

Politically, things went more slowly. The Netherlands Antilles had to wait until 1936 before being given some type of self-governance and until 1948 before they had a parliament, called the "Staten," and until 1954 before autonomy was achieved. Three levels of power were created: the Dutch Crown, responsible for foreign relations, defense, and the supervision of finances of certain islands; a federal power, located in Curaçao, which handled police, social security, health, education, budget, and finances; and the local government of each island.

For fifteen years the Democratic Party (DP) led the country, but in 1969 a crisis revealed that Curaçao's prosperity was not endless. First, the petroleum-powered growth did not favor everyone equally, especially African-Curaçaoans. Second, the petroleum industry both reduced and automated its facility, which led to a sharp increase in unemployment. This provoked a protest movement begun by 5,000 striking workers and led by trade union leader Wilson Godett and teacher and journalist Stanley Brown. Unfortunately, events turned violent, with riots and looting. The Dutch marines were called in after 2 persons were killed, 80 were hurt, over 300 were arrested, and fires and looting caused $40 million in damages. Prime Minister Ciro Kroon resigned. The events marked a turning point in island politics: a new influence and power for the labor movement, an increased awareness and pride in African-Curaçaoan identity, and a declining influence of the "old white elite." Two new parties, left-leaning and with strong worker support, were created from those events, the Workers' Liberation Front 30 May (FOL) (1969) and Movement for a New Antilles (MAN) (1971).

Women have become more active in public life and the Netherlands Antilles has had two women prime ministers, Maria Liberia Peters (in the eighties) and Suzanne Camelia Römer (as of 1998–1999).

Starting in the 1970s, Curaçao's economy began to rely more on tourism and offshore banking facilities. The petroleum refining industry was unprofitable by 1985, due to economic factors outside of Curaçao. The government purchased it and is now leasing it to the Venezuelan state petroleum company until 2015, breathing new life into the island economy. By 1988 offshore banking accounted for almost a quarter of the economy's output, earning more foreign exchange than tourism. But Curaçao still has the highest unemployment of the Netherlands Antilles (13%).

ARUBA

Twenty miles north of Venezuela, and west of Curaçao and Bonaire, Aruba's history shows unique elements, despite a common Dutch colonial history, language (Papiamentu, though slightly different from Bonaire's and Curaçao's), and geographic proximity. The island was inhabited by Arawaks who had emigrated from Venezuela around 1,000 b.c. Though the Spaniards abducted the local Caquetío Arawaks to Hispaniola in the early 1500s, they brought some back to either work the land or help protect the Venezuelan coast. So, unlike most islands in the Caribbean colonized by European powers, Aruba's Amerindian population was not wiped out by the mid to late sixteenth century.

When the Dutch took over in 1636 the island was not settled by colonists. Instead it was used to breed cattle for trade and to supply food for Curaçao. Few slaves were brought to Aruba, mostly as house servants.

Aruba's uniqueness is reflected in its 1816 census: Slaves were only 19 percent of the population, but more than a third were mestizo. Of the free population, a third were Amerindian and a third were mestizo. Even today, a great majority of Arubans are of Euro-Arawak ancestry, with a 15 to 20 percent black population, mostly African-Caribbeans from the West Indies.

The discovery of gold in 1824 and later phosphates propelled economic activity during the nineteenth century, but Aruba's gold deposits were not huge. Until 1924 the economy was floundering, but the discovery of Venezuelan oil in nearby Lake Maracaibo brought rapid growth and modernization in the 1930s, with an oil refinery at San Nicolas, the second most important city after the capital Oranjestad. Aruba also experienced considerable emigration from other islands to work at San Nicolas. From the perspective of other Caribbean islands, Aruba was "wealthy."

Until recently, Aruba was part of the Netherlands Antilles and achieved greater autonomy in 1948 and 1954, like the rest of the members of the federation. However, many Arubans were resentful of the demands made on their resources by other members of the Netherlands Antilles that were poorer (Bonaire, Saba, Statia), and they were equally resentful of Curaçao's centralization of political power. Through its main political party, the MEP (People's Electoral Movement), led by Gilberto (Betico) Croes (1924–1986), they campaigned for Aruban independence since its inception (1971). The first black prime minister of the Netherlands Antilles was Ernesto Petronia, an Aruban.

In a March 1977 referendum, Arubans voted overwhelmingly (82%) to withdraw from the federation. After pressure from the MEP, the Dutch government brokered a negotiation that went into effect in January 1986. Independence was slated for 1996. In the meantime, Aruba would assume separate status (but not from Holland), but still form a cooperative union with the federation in economic and monetary affairs.

Aruba's separation proved initially disruptive and costly because it almost coincided with the closing of the San Nicolas oil refinery. In addition, discussions over how to divide up former assets between Aruba and the other five members of the Netherlands Antilles were destabilizing.

Aruba, fortunately, was able to rebound, its economy growing at an annual rate of 10 percent per year from 1987 to 1993. In late 1990 the oil refinery was partially reopened and further expanded in 1993, along with the creation of other oil-related industries. But it was tourism that led the surge. The island more than tripled its hotel rooms between 1986 and 1998, and received almost a million visitors in 1998.

By 1990, however, support for full independence seemed to be waning, and by 1994 any mention of full independence was dropped. For independence Arubans would have to vote in a future referendum, as well as have a two-thirds majority in the Staten, or parliament. Some scholars claim that the island is being recolonized: recent accords with the Dutch government have limited Aruban sovereignty in financial, political, and security matters. A case in point is drug trafficking, which has been linked to increased pro-independence views by Aruban elites, who previously were anti-separatists (Lampe 2001b, 110).

The recent economic boom has had an extraordinary impact on the Aruban population, which increased 36 percent in only six years to 91,364 (1997 figures). Probably close to 30 percent of the population is foreign-born. Recent immigrants include Colombians, Dominicans, and Venezuelans, who make up about half of the foreign-born, and also Peruvians, Filipinos, Jamaicans, and Surinameans. Marriage rates reflect these new changes: almost half of Aruban-born men take on a foreign spouse, even if many of these are "fake marriages," since by marrying an Aruban a foreigner can acquire Dutch nationality (Alofs 1991,

12). This massive migration has led to labor conflicts, ethnic tensions, housing shortages, and social resentment.

Understandably, this has prompted much debate on the island about who is an Aruban. A certain degree of cultural nationalism has flourished, some of it conservative, some of it open to many influences and creolization, but with a heartfelt concern for trying to retain a core of Arubanness. Currently, people from over forty countries live on the island. Aruba, like Curaçao, has had a long historical relationship with Venezuela—including with exiles during the Venezuelan independence struggle (1810–1830)—that dates back centuries. Today there are many cultural exchanges between the two and Venezuelan soap operas are popular in Aruba.

Culturally, the island still remains strongly rooted in the Caribbean but with Latin traits. The vast majority speak Papiamentu (71 percent speak it at home), although many are multilingual, speaking Spanish, English, and Dutch. Social and family traditions are Antillean, and the music is firmly entrenched in the region's rhythms (see Music).

Catholicism is the major religion (about 80 percent), although traditional healing and supernatural beliefs, called *brua*, are also adhered to. *Brua* probably owes as much to Amerindian as to African practices, but it is hard to gauge how widespread it is because socially it is held in low esteem (Alofs 1991, 13). Brua is also practiced on Bonaire and Curaçao.

For the Caribbean, Aruba has a high standard of living, low unemployment (7%), and low inflation. But its recent and rapid growth has brought on strains to Aruban society, some due to immigration, some not.

BONAIRE

With a current population of 14,000, Bonaire was originally inhabited by Arawaks when the Spanish arrived (1499). Also considered one of the "useless islands" by the Spanish, Bonaire subsequently was taken over by the Dutch in 1636. The West Indies Company wanted it for planting corn and mining salt, and it was not really considered a place to settle, in contrast to Curaçao. The island did not become a settlement colony until the nineteenth century.

Slaves were imported from Curaçao to work in the salt mines. In the eighteenth century Bonaire was also used as a penal colony for white, mestizo, and free black soldiers, who, as prisoners, also worked in the salt mines.

The first census dates from 1806 (945) and 1816 (1,135) show that roughly 62 percent of the population were free and 38 percent were slaves. Of the free population, however, whites were 12 percent, meaning that half the population consisted of mestizos and free blacks. More intriguing is the fact that in the 1806 census, the Amerindian category (284) was 30 percent of the population, but in the 1816 census the Amerindian category vanishes. Historians don't believe that Amerindians disappeared, but that they wound up in the free mestizo, slave mestizo, and free black categories. Even allowing for all these statistical manipulations, blacks probably made up 40 to 45 percent of the population, a much lower figure than in Curaçao, but significantly higher than in Aruba.

Interestingly, the oldest buildings on the island are slave huts on the salt pans. They are from 1820 and are built of freestanding stone with thatched roofs. The huts housed two people, but often many were crowded in. Unlike large slave-barrack buildings on plantations they were supposed to be temporary housing, since the slaves walked seventeen miles back home on the weekends (Gravette 2000, 120). Bonairans lived together in villages, and not spread out, like on the other islands. All economic activity was in the hands of the government and there was no real private ownership until 1863. After that a family would typically have two houses, one main house and another (usually no more than a shed), on their *kunnuku*, a little plot of land for crops, goats, and chickens. Most African-Bonairans lived in this village system.

After abolition Bonaire's economy went into a deep slump until the oil boom of Curaçao and Aruba of the 1920s, most living on subsistence plots. A third of the island immigrated from 1925 to 1949, sending back money to their families, the main source of income for them during this period. Tourism began in earnest in the 1950s, but it has been quite ecologically minded since the island's major attractions are its diving areas (over ninety sites) and marine life. Salt mining also continues and in 1975 the Bonaire Petroleum Corporation (BOPEC) was founded. Oil is not refined but merely transshipped (transferred from bigger to smaller tankers). Bonaire depends heavily on development aid from the Netherlands and the European Economic Community, as well as the "national contribution" from Curaçao. The government employs at least a quarter of the workforce; and 6 percent are unemployed.

Like Curaçao and Aruba, Bonaire also celebrates Carnival. Simadan, a traditional harvest festival for growers of sorghum, is also held. It includes a *wapa* dance symbolizing how a community has come together for a harvest, and then a parade with a basket of sorghum seeds to be blessed eventually by a priest. The *becu* flute is played during this festival.

Currently, the overwhelmingly black population is about 90 percent Catholic, and over 90 percent speak Papiamentu. Many Bonairans also speak Dutch, Spanish, and English.

PAPIAMENTU AND NETHERLANDS ANTILLEAN LITERATURE

In Curaçao (or *Korsou*), as well as in Aruba and Bonaire, people speak a Creole language called Papiamentu. The word comes from *papear*, which means "talk" in Portuguese. The language is a Portuguese-based Creole, although there is great influence of Spanish, Dutch, English, and words of African origin. It was the language forged by slaves under conditions of slavery and for centuries was considered "undeveloped," "childlike," "not suited for philosophy." It is spoken by over 80 percent of the populations of the ABCs; most local newspapers and TV and radio programming are in Papiamentu. The first newspaper in the language dates from 1870. Since 1979 primary schools are mandated by law to use Papiamentu in the first school year. Gradually, they switch to Dutch.

Many writers use Papiamentu, but most still use Dutch in order to reach a wider audience. Nicholas or "Cola" Debrot (1902–1980?), from Bonaire, was one of the first to write about racial creolization, in his novel *My Sister the Negress* (1935); Debrot was later governor of the Netherlands Antilles (1962–1970). Ornelio Martina (1930–), also a public figure, writes in Papiamentu as does Elis Juliana (1927–), who is also an ethnologist. There are prominent women writers such as Yolanda Corsen (1918–), Diane Lebacs (1947–), and Ilsa Winkel-Riseeuw (1930–), a prolific poet. But perhaps the best known is Frank Martinus Arion (1936–), who has written four novels (in Dutch) and as a trained linguist has written extensively about Papiamentu. Martinus has also undertaken studies of songs, rhymes, and limericks, often showing their African roots.

MUSIC OF THE NETHERLANDS ANTILLES AND ARUBA

One of the most significant types of Afro-Curaçaoan music is called *tambú*, which is derived from the Spanish word for drum, *tambor*. *Tambú* refers not only to the drum used, but also to a music or types of rhythm, as well as to a dance form. The *tambú* drum was originally single sided, but it is now a double-headed drum played with both hands. Originally, when this music was danced to, the couple danced apart, as in the rumba, but as the dance moved to the city in the early 1800s, it became more erotic and was associated with Afro-Curaçaoan anti-slavery protest. However, it is still popular and even Christmas music is set to *tambú* rhythms, albeit simplified.

Another popular Afro-Caribbean rhythm is *tumba*, which was popular in the fifties throughout the Netherlands Antilles. *Tumba* is still the most important musical style in yearly Carnival culture. Similar to the Cuban *guaracha* or son, tumba has a catchy and danceable rhythm. Other music and rhythms from the Caribbean are extremely popular as well: bolero, salsa, *son*, the Venezuelan *joropo*, as well as reggae and calypso.

Local folkloric instruments (not used in modern music) are *bentas* (a mouth-resonated bow), a cow-horn trumpet called the *cachu*, the *becu*, (a type of flute), and stamped tubes known as *bamba* that are used on the island of Bonaire. Bentas are played for zumbi (literally, ghosts) music, along with cowhorn, scrapers, a garden hoe head, and the tambú drum.

Carnival is held on all the islands, but the two most important are held on Curaçao and Aruba. Unlike Trinidad, it is fairly recent in their history: Aruba's began in 1954; Curaçao's began after 1915, stopped in 1954, and recommenced in 1971. There are masked parades, floats, jump ups, music and song competitions, children's parades, and the burning of the Rey Momo, the Mummer King, which marks the end of Carnival and the beginning of Lent.

THE LEEWARD ISLANDS: ST. MAARTEN

St. Maarten shares its island with St. Martin, a French possession, and is the most densely populated island in the Eastern Caribbean. The Netherlands or south side has a population of 40,000 and was first settled by the Dutch in 1631; the partitioning with the French was negotiated in 1648. The Dutch exploited the salt deposits and grew tobacco and imported slaves for this purpose. Later, by the 1750s, there were more than thirty-five not very large sugar plantations on the Dutch side alone, given the size of the island.

One of the key moments of St. Maarten's history is when its slaves achieved freedom fifteen years ahead of their Dutch colonial brethren. Since the French abolished slavery on the other half of the island in 1848, Dutch slaves went to the French side and began a collective strike to demand abolition. At that time, slaves were 83 percent of the population (Europeans were 17 percent). The Dutch planters and colonial authorities, ever pragmatic, did not want to be left without workers. Without formally abolishing slavery, they simply accepted the *de facto* freedom of the slaves. It illustrates dramatically that slave resistance and rebellions did have an impact on abolition. However, the Dutch did not abolish slavery in their other Caribbean possessions until 1863.

After abolition, freed slaves worked at cattle raising and fishing, and sugar went into decline. The last sugar plantation was closed in 1915. After that date many immigrated to Curaçao, Aruba, and Venzuela (to work in the oil industry), or to Martinique and Guadeloupe to work on sugar estates. Still others went to Puerto Rico, the Dominican Republic, and Haiti.

One of the key figures of black consciousness on the island was Thomas E. Duruo (1863–1949), a founder of Garvey's UNIA in the Dominican Republic and Pan-Africanist activist throughout the Caribbean. Others who followed in his footsteps were Carlos Cooks (1913–1966), who lived for many years in the United States and deeply influenced Malcolm X, and Joseph H. Lake (1925–1976), a journalist, a labor organizer, and a politician who was the main opposition to Claude Wathey and who dominated the political scene of the island for thirty-five years.

The tourist industry began in 1950 and by the 1970s the St. Maarten economy expanded enormously under the leadership of Wathey, who also favored island secession. However, the boom was accompanied by mismanagement, corruption, and drug trafficking. Protests forced Wathey to resign in 1991 and three years later he was convicted of perjury and forgery. As a result the Dutch limited the island's power on budget expenditures in 1992.

Despite these political setbacks, St. Maarten's economic and political position within the Netherlands Antilles system became increasingly important, particularly after Aruba's 1986 decision to leave the federation.

The bulk of the island's expansion has come from tourism. In 1998, for example, St. Maarten attracted over 1.3 million visitors, an extraordinary figure for such a tiny country, and even more remarkable in light of the island's being ravaged by two hurricanes in 1995, and another in 1998. With about a third of the island's total (Dutch and French) population being listed as unregistered immigrants, many were deported after the hurricanes of 1995. Unemployment stands at over 11 percent. The outflow of people from the island from 1900–1950 was followed by an influx of immigrants during the tourist boom; estimates now say that only 19 percent of St. Maarten's residents are locally born. English is the principal language, as well as French and Dutch.

ST. EUSTATIUS

An island that once had one of the busiest ports in the Caribbean, St. Eustatius is now a fairly tranquil island of 3,000 inhabitants. The Dutch arrived in 1636, but the island was disputed territory and changed hands twenty two times before the Netherlands assumed full control in 1816. By 1665, 72 percent of the population were slaves and it roughly stayed that way until abolition in 1863, (in 1850, 80 percent were slaves, 16 percent were Europeans, and 4 percent were free colored).

At its busiest moments in the 1770s, 3,000 ships were calling on its port each year with goods, produce, and slaves. From 1689 to 1795 Statia imported 29,000 slaves. Most worked in the warehouses, which stretched for a mile along the quay. The island had a population of 20,000 (75 percent were slaves), and many thriving businesses. During the U.S. War of Independence the island was a major source of smuggled goods for Washington's troops. St. Eustatius, unlike its British and French-controlled neighbors, was a duty-free port.

However, in 1776 a U.S. ship flying the Stars and Stripes, the *Andrew Doria*, sailed into Statia's port and fired a thirteen-gun salute, which governor Johannes de Graaff ordered be returned. This gesture was the first foreign recognition of the U.S. flag, and Statia earned the nickname America's Childhood Friend. The gesture turned out to be costly. In 1781, the British retaliated and launched a full naval attack on the island, pillaging and destroying the warehouses, exiling the island's merchants, and either keeping or auctioning off the goods, worth several million pounds, a formidable sum at the time. St. Eustatius never fully recovered from this blow.

In 1848, inspired by the events in St. Martin/St. Maarten, slaves in Statia gathered in numbers and publically voiced their desire for freedom outside the house of the director of the island. The authorities ordered the slaves to go back to work. They refused and the police and militia stepped in, with various deaths resulting on each side. Troops from Curaçao were sent to establish peace. The leaders were sentenced in Curaçao and sold in Puerto Rico.

Currently, most Statians are employed by the government. Unemployment is low and poverty is almost nonexistent given the social services and subsidies of the Dutch government. Around 70 percent of the mostly black population is local, with another 15 percent from the Netherlands Antilles and 12 percent from neighboring St. Kitts and Nevis. The island's economy also depends on fishing, small businesses, and tourism, but much less so than in Aruba, Curaçao, or St. Maarten. Oil is stored and reloaded for transshipment to different locations.

SABA

From the sea, Saba is an imposing presence, despite its tiny size (3 by 2 miles), with hills and mountains that almost reach 3,000 feet. The island is a volcano that has been extinct for 5,000 years. Home to 1,500 islanders, Saba's population is divided roughly in half between Sabans and a white population of Scottish, Irish, and Scandinavian settlers. About a third of the population is traceable to two surnames: Hassell and Johnson. In the eighteenth century Saba changed hands twelve times, between the French, Spanish, English, and Dutch, who finally took control in 1816. Saba's terrain was not suitable for a plantation economy, but slavery existed. However, the colonists who did own slaves usually worked alongside them, making Saba a much more integrated society than other Dutch-controlled islands.

There are actually very few Dutch or their descendants on the island. Although Dutch is the official language, recently the government allowed the education system to switch to English, since it is more widely spoken.

Economically, Saba lives from tourism and fishing. The government is also a large employer (unemployment is 5 percent). Many Sabans have gone to work in Aruba or Curaçao, either in the oil industry or tourism, or have immigrated to the Netherlands.

CONCLUSION

Despite certain resentment and anti-colonial feelings, the Netherlands Antilles has chosen to remain closely linked to Holland. In referenda held in the nineties, all the islands—Curaçao (75%), Bonaire (88%), Saba (91%), and St. Eustatius (86%)—voted for maintaining their federation. On St. Maarten, 59.4% preferred the status quo, but in referenda in 1999 and 2000, a majority opted for a separate status within the kingdom, following Aruba's example. The Netherlands Antilles have reached the point of disintegration in an economically insecure period. Aruba did not become independent in 1996 and keeps its *status aparte*, but is still closely linked to the Netherlands. The political system is in crisis as well: elections are frequent (about every two years), voter absenteeism is increasing, and there is fragmentation of interests, a lack of clear ideology between parties, and an uninformed electorate.

Many lower-class Curaçaoans, as well as people from the other islands have immigrated, with an estimated 90,000 from the six islands living in the Netherlands as of 1997, a large increase in merely a quarter of a century. This represents a third of the population of all the islands, but half of these immigrants living in Holland are unemployed. Many of those who immigrate are dark-skinned and face discrimination. Felix de Rooy (1952–), a Curaçaoan artist and filmmaker, and also the curator of the Negrophilia Collection in Amsterdam, captures the hardships of migrants in *Cry Surinam* (1992), a sculpture that critically plays with racial and religious stereotypes, as well as using artificial heat (Holland) and tropical heat (Suriname) to literally depict a cooked destiny.

Perhaps chastened by the post-independence experiences of Suriname, another former Dutch colony, Aruba and the Netherlands Antilles have reined in their political nationalism, limiting it to the cultural sphere (language, education, the arts). The Dutch have gone from offering cautious autonomy in the fifties to unilaterally pushing for independence in the late sixties and seventies (often against majority wishes), to grudgingly decentralizing and instituting greater autonomy in the eighties, to reasserting their role in the region in the nineties, under the rubric of security and combating drug trafficking and money-laundering. Initially, they wanted to eventually grant independence to a federation of the six islands, much like the British attempted to do in the late fifties with the West Indies Federation, but that has changed with Aruba's and St. Maarten's actions. The future status of the remaining islands is most uncertain.

Still buoyed by the oil-refining industry and a rapid increase in tourism, Aruba, St. Maarten, and the Netherlands Antilles boast one of the highest standards of living in the region, with high rates of literacy and good health care. However, unemployment rates are still high on the Antilles of Four (Saba, St. Eustatius, Curaçao, Bonaire), and the dependency on tourism is problematic (particularly for Aruba, Curaçao, and St. Maarten), since it is an industry that is highly unpredictable, as it relies on the wishes and whims of foreign visitors. This, without mentioning its attendant ills of gambling, sexual commerce, illicit drugs, and easy money. The idea of the Netherlands Antilles was perhaps a necessary fiction that is now unraveling. The islands have the following political options: keeping the status quo with perhaps more autonomy, assimilating (becoming a province of Holland), associating with a neighboring country (which for Curaçao and Bonaire would be Venezuela), or becoming independent. Independence is unpopular, association and assimilation seem to many as a loss of identity, and the status quo is seen as perpetuating the current political disarray and fragmentation. It is an uneasy future, one that seems to embrace the contradictory trends of greater self-determination within a colonial context.

REFERENCES

Alofs, Luc (1991). "Arubans." In *Encyclopedia of World Cultures*. Vol. 8. New York: Macmillan, pp. 11–14.

———(2001). "Aruba." In *Countries and Cultures*. Vol. 1. New York: Macmillan.

———(2001). "Netherlands Antilles." In *Countries and Cultures*. Vol. 3. New York: Macmillan.

Anderson, W.A., and R.R. Dynes (1975). *Social Movements, Violence, and Change: The May Movement in Curaçao*. Columbus, OH: Ohio State University Press.

Ansano, R., J. Clemencia, J. Cook, and E. Martis, (eds.) (1992). *Mundu Yama Sinta Mira: Womanhood in Curaçao*. Willemstad, Curaçao: Fundashon Publikashon.

Gastmann, Albert (1978). *Historical Dictionary of the French and Netherlands Antilles*. Metuchen, NJ: Scarecrow Press.

Goslinga, Cornelis Ch. (1979). *A Short History of the Netherlands Antilles and Suri-nam*. The Hague: Martinus Nijhoff.

Gravette, Andrew (2000). *Architectural Heritage of the Caribbean: An A–Z of Historic Buildings*. Princeton, NJ: Ian Randle-Markus Wiener.

Hartog, Johan (1968). *Curaçao: From Colonial Dependency to Autonomy*. Aruba, Nether-lands Antilles. De Wit.

———(1976). *History of St. Eustatius*. Aruba: De Wit.

Hoetink, Harry (1972). "Surinam and Curaçao." In Cohen, David W. and Jack P. Greene (eds.), *Neither Slave nor Free*. Baltimore: Johns Hopkins University Press.

Klomp, Ank (1986). *Politics on Bonaire*. Assen (Netherlands): Van Gorcum.

———(1990). "The Traditional Bonairan House: Its History and Its Chances for Survival." In Coomans, Henry E., Michael A. Newton, and Maritza Coomans-Eustatia (eds.), *Building Up the Future from the Past: Studies on the Architecture and Historic Monuments in the Dutch Caribbean*. Zutphen: De Walburg Pers.

Klooster, Wim (1994). "Subordinate but Proud: Curaçao's Free Blacks and Mulattoes in the Eighteenth Century." In *New West Indian Guide* 68, nos. 3 and 4: pp. 282–300.

Lampe, Armando (1989). "Iglesia y estado en la sociedad esclavista de Curazao" (Church and state in Curaçaoan slave society). In *Anales del Caribe*. La Habana, Cuba: Casa las Américas, pp. 75–124.

———(2001a). "Christianity and Slavery in the Dutch Caribbean." In Lampe, A. (ed.), *Christianity in the Caribbean: Essays on Church History*, Kingston, Jamaica: Uni-versity of the West Indies Press, pp. 126–153.

———(2001b). "The Recolonisation of Aruba." In Ramos, Aarón Gamaliel and Angel Israel Rivera (eds.), *Islands at the Crossroads, Politics in the Non-Independent Caribbean*. Kingston, Jamaica: Ian Randle Publishers, pp. 106–114.

Lamur, Humphrey E. (2000/1981). "Demographic Performance of Two Slave Populations of the Dutch-Speaking Caribbean." In Shepherd, Verene and Hilary McD Beck-les (eds.), *Caribbean Slavery in the Atlantic World*. Princeton, NJ: Ian Randle-Marcus Wiener, pp. 809–820.

Oostindie, Gert (1996). "Ethnicity, Nationalism and the Exodus: The Dutch Caribbean Predicament." In Oostindie (ed.), *Ethnicity in the Caribbean*. London: Macmil-lan, pp. 206–231.

Oostindie, Gert, and Peter Verton (1998). "Ki Sorto di Reino/What Kind of Kingdom? Antillean and Aruban Views and Expectations of the Kingdom of the Nether-lands." In *New West Indian Guide* 72, nos. 1 and 2, pp. 43–75.

Postma, Johannes Menne (1990). *The Dutch in the Atlantic Slave Trade, 1600–1815*. New York: Cambridge University Press.

Ramos, A.G., and A.I. Rivera (eds.) (2001). *Islands at the Crossroads: Politics in the Non-independent Caribbean*. Kingston, Jamaica: Ian Randle Publishers. (Chapter 6 on Curaçao and 7 on Aruba.)

Rowell, Charles H. (ed.) (1998). "Caribbean Literature from Suriname, the Netherlands Antilles, Aruba, and the Netherlands." In *Callaloo* 21, no. 3, pp. 441–724.

Schoenhals, Kai (1993). *Netherlands Antilles and Aruba*. World Bibliographical Series. Oxford: Clio Press.

Sedoc-Dahlberg, Betty (ed.) (1990). *The Dutch Caribbean: Prospects for Democracy*. New York: Gordon & Breach.

Sekou, Lasana M. (1996). *National Symbols of St. Martin*. St. Martin: House of Nehesi.

12

Puerto Rico

Alan West-Durán

INTRODUCTION

The smallest of the islands of the Greater Antilles, Puerto Rico is east of the Dominican Republic and west of the U.S. Virgin Islands. Three times the size of Rhode Island, Puerto Rico has a population of 3.8 million people, with another 2.8 million living in the United States.

As is true of its Caribbean neighbors, Puerto Rico's racial history is centuries old, sometimes troubled, always intricately layered, plagued by misunderstanding and denials, filled with insights, and just plain vexing. It has been called a racial democracy, the whitest of the Spanish-speaking islands, a country free of prejudice. Even its best minds have found race elusive, and often there is disagreement, but it is central to understanding the people of Puerto Rico.

In the 1930s, writer Tomás Blanco, comparing U.S. and Puerto Rican racial attitudes said "our racial prejudice is the innocent game of a child."[1] Elsewhere he wrote: "We have abundant black blood in us, and this should not make us feel ashamed; but, in honoring the truth, we cannot be classified as a black people."[2]

In 1974 Isabelo Zenón Cruz spoke of the hypocrisy of the expression *negro puertorriqueño*, where Puerto Rican has become an adjective. Why is a black Puerto Rican identified as black before he is considered Puerto Rican, he asks?

Mixed race writer José Luis González stated in 1979 that Puerto Rico was basically an African-Caribbean nation.

Who to believe, Blanco, Zenón or González? Perhaps all three, to a certain extent?

The racial complexities of Puerto Rico are great. A recent newspaper article alluded to this by listing a series of terms most commonly used: *blanco* (white), *blanquito* (upper-class or well-to-do white), *colorao* (white with reddish hair), *rubio* (blonde), *cano* (person with gray or whitening hair and light skin color), *jincho* (flour-colored white), *blanco con raja* (white with a streak of color), *jabao* (mixed race with light skin and chestnut or blond hair but with other physical features of blacks), *melao* (honey-colored), *trigueño* (wheat-colored, light brown), *moreno* (dark-skinned mulatto or black), *mulato, indio* (Indian, bronze-colored), *café con leche* (coffee with milk), *piel canela* (cinnamon-skinned), *grifo* (kinky-haired, black), *de color* (of color), *negro* (black), and *negrito* (a small or little black person). Many of these terms, depending on attitude and tone can be expressions of endearment, grudging acceptance, contempt, or condescension.[3]

What these writers address is a manifold racial history that is local and yet intersects with the racial dynamics of two imperial powers: Spain (1493–1898) and the United States (1898 to the present).

SPANISH COLONIZATION

Columbus arrived in Puerto Rico on November 19, 1493. The Taínos, the indigenous population of the island, numbered some 60,000. Although the Taínos had an organized political, economic, and religious system, neither their development nor their capacity to resist was comparable to other indigenous peoples of the Americas such as the Aztecs, Maya, or Incas. By 1530 the Taíno population was estimated at 1,148 but forty years later it had dwindled to 300, out of a total population of 11,300. The Taíno's legacy has been culinary and linguistic. Food unknown to the colonizers is still part of the Puerto Rican diet and the Spanish language has over three hundred words of Arawak origin, the language spoken by the Taínos.

The rapid decimation of the Taínos through overwork, mistreatment, and disease was offset by the importing of African slaves, which officially began in 1513. Spanish-speaking slaves brought from Spain were known as *Ladinos*; slaves directly imported from Africa were called *Bozales*. The Ladinos were initially favored because they were thought to be more docile. But with slave rebellions in 1514 and 1527, the Spanish government prohibited importation of Ladinos. By 1530 there were 1,523 slaves on the island, composing 50 percent of the population; in 1570 African slaves were 88 percent of Puerto Rico's 11,300 inhabitants. Over the next two centuries, these percentages became drastically lower, in contrast with other Caribbean islands colonized by other European powers, where slaves were imported by the tens of thousands. By 1673 slaves were 44 percent of the population and in 1765 the figure plummeted to 11 percent. Even more disturbing is the fact that in the period 1570–1673 Puerto Rico's population declined by 87 percent.

Several factors can explain this downturn: when gold deposits were exhausted in the Caribbean, Spain's colonizers sought riches in Mexico and Peru. The Caribbean became a military and provisioning center—first Santo Domingo and later Havana became strategic outposts, both to Puerto Rico's detriment. By the late sixteenth century, Spain's ships came under attack by British, French, and Dutch pirates. From 1570 to 1640 sugar production became costlier, and it was cheaper to produce sugar in Brazil, then under Spanish rule. As a result, most inhabitants dedicated themselves to cattle ranching and subsistence farming. Natural disasters and epidemics also exacted a heavy toll, at times wiping out entire towns or villages. Whites were particularly vulnerable to yellow fever and malaria, blacks to tuberculosis, smallpox, measles, and typhus.

In the eighteenth century the Caribbean was a prime battleground for inter-European imperial rivalry, beginning with the War of Spanish Succession (1702–1714). Great Britain, the Netherlands, and Austria declared war on Spain and France. During this period a mixed race shoemaker, Miguel Enríquez, acquired fame as a daring corsair, attacking British ships and reselling the captured booty. Enríquez's wealth and power made him a favorite to the elites, having a whitening effect on his social status, but by 1720, social, economic, and racial prejudice embroiled him in several legal disputes that eventually ended his extraordinary career.

Racial barriers in the Caribbean were often stretched or transgressed. Whites were at the top of the pyramid (first "pensinsulars," that is, from the Iberian peninsula, then *criollos* or the locally born). They were followed by Indians, *mestizos* (of mixed Indian and Spanish blood), free people of color (divided into *pardos* or light brown, *morenos* or dark brown, and *negros* or blacks), and finally, slaves.

By 1580 the indigenous population had been nearly exterminated, and by 1650 most mestizos had been absorbed into the ever growing category of free people of color. However, ethnically and culturally the concept of *indio* (Indian) would retain a certain currency: in the nineteenth and even the twentieth century some dark-skinned Puerto Ricans would refer to themselves as *indios* so as not to identify themselves as having African heritage.

Puerto Rico, unlike the non-Spanish-speaking Caribbean, developed its sugar plantation system late (1795–1850). From 1600 on, the island never had a slave population greater than 15 percent of the total population, and usually the figure hovered from 5 percent to 9 percent. In the French and British islands it averaged from 75 percent to 95 percent. From 1775 to 1873, the year slavery was abolished, the racial composition of Puerto Rican society was roughly as follows: whites (40 to 55%), free non-whites (40 to 50%), and slaves (5 to 15%).

These percentages reflect several realities: Puerto Rico experienced greater racial mixture than elsewhere in the Caribbean, its economy was not completely dominated by sugar, and both these factors uniquely shaped Puerto Rico as a non-plantation society. Even in the period when sugar gained ascendancy (1795–1850), many "free" laborers worked alongside slaves. And, finally, as was true in its Spanish-speaking counterparts, a Creole consciousness and nationalism created pro-independence movements by the 1820s. Unlike its non-Spanish-speaking neighbors, the abolition of slavery and independence were intertwined.

The free colored could travel freely on the island, gather publicly in groups, dance in the streets, and own stores. They could acquire land in whatever quantities, inherit property without restrictions, enter the crafts, acquire some education, and serve in the militia, albeit in segregated units. Serving in the militia allowed them to bear arms—normally prohibited to free colored or slaves—but those arms were primarily used against slaves. Despite this, there were many possibilites only enjoyed by whites: a university education, public offices or honors, or positions in the Church or as notaries. The free colored were still part of the "contaminated castes," according to the racial hierarchy under Spanish colonialism. However, bravery in battle or similar such deeds could ease any (or all) of these restrictions: slaves who fought bravely repelling the British attack on San Juan in 1797 were freed.

The importance of a free colored population might explain a painter like José Campeche (1751–1809), the son of an emancipated slave and a white father. Campeche's work depicts officials, the ruling elite, and religious themes with great nuance, detail, and use of color, and he is the only pre-twentieth-century Caribbean artist to have had a show at the Metropolitan Museum of Art.

THE NINETEENTH CENTURY: SUGAR AND SLAVES

With roughly half of the population white and a slave population of between 5 percent and 15 percent during Spanish control, can Puerto Rico be assumed to be a Caribbean exception, a country where slavery mattered little and whose culture and society is not Afro-Antillean? Many have argued that point, using the *jíbaro*, or rugged mountain peasant of the interior (presumed to be white, since the black populations supposedly only lived in the coastal areas), as the cultural and national symbol of the island.

A closer look reveals a different reality. Many *jíbaros* were (and are) of mixed blood. Roughly half the population was still black and mulatto in 1830, when the island had three times as many slaves than in 1790. Three historical events gave slavery in Puerto Rico greater importance than statistics would indicate: the independence of Haiti (1804), a nation of free blacks; the independence of the former Spanish colonies (1810–1826); and the outlawing of the slave trade by Britain (1807), Denmark (1807), France (1818), and Holland (1814). Haiti's role as the world's largest producer of sugar thus fell to Cuba and to Puerto Rico to a lesser degree.

From 1800 to 1850 sugar represented about half of the island's exports and by 1850 Puerto Rico produced as much sugar as Jamaica, Antigua, Martinique, and Barbados combined. Not surprisingly, from 1795 to 1848 historians have documented over twenty instances of slave conspiracies, rebellions, or insurrections. In 1826 local legislation was enacted to curtail this rebelliousness. Unlike the 1789 Spanish Slave Code, which the Spanish Crown crafted to protect certain rights of slaves (even if ignored), the 1826 regulations were meant to protect slave masters and their underlings. For example, machetes and other work tools had to be stored away every day, slaves were told when and where they could rest, and they were prohibited from visiting slaves from other plantations.

Even worse was the Edict against the African Race of 1848, which virtually erased any distinction between Africans who were free and those who were slaves. Africans who were found guilty of striking a white person lost their right hand. Threatening a white person could earn a five-year jail sentence. Fortunately, the edict was abolished six months later, but its psychological and social aftermath must have been a chilling reminder that whites were in control and could unleash a brutal, racialized repression any time they felt threatened.

ABOLITION AND BEYOND (1850–1898)

By the mid-1860s, slavery's days were numbered and the number of slaves was under 10 percent of the population. Yet abolitionists like the mixed-race Segundo Ruiz Belvis and whites like José Julián Acosta and Francisco Mariano Quiñones mention the ripple effect of slavery, of how it pervades a society even when most of its members are free, breeding corruption, degradation, violence, and injustice.[4]

On September 23, 1868, the Grito de Lares (Rallying Cry of Lares), a revolutionary insurrection, shook the island. Led by a mixed-race revolutionary doctor, Ramón Emeterio Betances (1827–1898), it was based on his Ten Commandments of Free Men. The document called for the abolition of slavery (and coerced labor); the right to reject all taxes; freedom of speech, press, and commerce; the right to assemble and bear arms; the inviolability of the citizen; and the right to elect their own authorities. Despite the insurrection's failure, it was a watershed in forging a national consciousness on the island, as well as instigating local and Spanish forces to formally abolish slavery by 1873. Spain and its pro-slavery island allies did not act solely out of altruism: the sugar industry was suffering (shifting to tobacco and coffee), and wage labor was becoming more profitable and productive. They were clearly trying to forestall a repeat of Cuba's bloody Ten Years' War (1868–1878) for abolition and independence.

Blacks and sectors of mixed parentage made important contributions to Puerto Rican society in the nineteenth century, be it in politics, education, business, or art. Aside from Ruiz Belvis and Betances, some of the best known are Ramón Baldorioty de Castro (1822–1889), an educator and politician, and founder of the Autonomist Party, Rafael Cordero (1790–1868), an extraordinary educator immortalized in a painting by Francisco Oller, and Francisco Gonzalo Marín (1863–1897), a poet and revolutionary who died fighting for Cuban independence. Oller (1833–1917), a realist, painted the canonical work *The Wake* (1893), a satirical look at local mores during the wake of a young child, beautifully executed in rich detail.

Music offered a crucial area of black-mulatto involvement and creativity. The 1862 census shows that the colored population made up 68 percent of all musicians: it was one of the few occupations where non-whites could attain some degree of acceptability and social mobility. Felipe Gutiérrez (1825–1900), Manuel G. Tavárez (1843–1883), and Juan Morel Campos (1857–1896) were three important composers of the nineteenth century. Gutiérrez composed religious music and operas and was choirmaster of the San Juan Cathedral for forty years. Tavárez was Morel's teacher and wrote prolifically, and his pupil, the island's most acclaimed and versatile nineteenth-century composer, wrote hundreds of *danzas*. Both are best remembered for their *danzas*, the island's national dance form, an elegant and sensual dance that combines European ballroom dance forms with African rhythms and percussion. Puerto Rico's national anthem, "La Borinqueña," is a *danza*.

PUERTO RICO IN THE TWENTIETH CENTURY

A key figure in Puerto Rican history was José Celso Barbosa (1857–1921), a prominent politician and physician. Under Spain Barbosa favored autonomy as did Baldorioty, but when the United States took over Puerto Rico, Barbosa became a statehood advocate, a member of the ruling Executive Council, and finally a senator. A poor, self-made black, he denied the existence of racial prejudice in Puerto Rico, because there were social racial barriers that black and brown had not crossed (Barbosa 1937). Despite his contradictory views, Barbosa always spoke of his African heritage with pride.

Barbosa reflects some of the racial dynamics of the first half of the twentieth century. First, like many Caribbean societies, Puerto Rico "defined blackness by negotiating degrees of whiteness" (Guerra 1998, 214). Although whiteness is still upheld as the norm, its definition is more inclusive than in the United States. Typically, in the Caribbean if you are not black you are white, whereas in North America it is the reverse. During Spanish rule it was possible—but not always—to be legally declared white through bureaucratic skill and/or money. This is not to deny racism or prejudice, but with roughly half the population being white and another 40 percent of mixed blood (which includes white blood), it is not difficult to see how "negotiating degrees of whiteness" could become a complex ensemble of social, racial, and cultural maneuverings. In Puerto Rico miscegenation was ultimately seen as a whitening of the black and brown population, and not the opposite. And by 1898, only twenty-five years had elapsed since the abolition of slavery: touting one's African ancestry was to evoke a past of humiliation and shame.

In 1898 Puerto Rico became a U.S. colony after the Spanish-Cuban-American War. Puerto Ricans were quickly introduced to U.S. racial attitudes, which they found harsh and polarized. Yet the size and dynamism of the U.S. economy provided jobs to many dark-skinned Puerto Ricans, either on the island or to immigrants. Under the United States, Puerto Rico's sugar economy rocketed, with absentee owners buying the land of many small local producers.

But the United States had not satisfactorily resolved issues of autonomy and citizenship, which was deeply resented by islanders. Finally, the United States unilaterally imposed citizenship on Puerto Ricans in the 1917 Jones Act. However, resentment did not recede since governors, the island's supreme authority, were still chosen by the United States and English was imposed as the official language in the school system. Successfully resisted, English only was eventually eliminated in 1930 and represents an important example of Puerto Rican linguistic and cultural sovereignty against U.S. colonialism.

Racial resentment flared up during World War I when Puerto Ricans who considered themselves white within the broader island definition of race were placed in segregated Negro units of the United States Army. To many this was an outrage and the U.S. solution was to create a "Puerto Rican white" category, viewed by many islanders as an unsatisfactory solution.

The burgeoning trade union movement featured many African-Puerto Ricans. The Socialist Party, created in 1915 as the political arm of the trade union movement, had a 40 percent non-white leadership, including figures such as Prudencio Rivera Martínez, Alfonso Torres, Andrés Arús Rivera, José Ferrer y Ferrer, and Nemesio Morales Cruz.

In this period Pedro Albizu Campos (1891–1965) became a major political figure. A Harvard-educated lawyer who turned revolutionary, he was jailed several times for actively trying to violently overthrow the island's colonial system. Albizu, in a famous speech, speaks proudly of his black (as well as Indian and Spanish) blood and vehemently criticizes the racial realities of the United States as being barbaric. However, he ultimately saw race as divisive to his political goals and subsumed race under the overarching concept of Puerto Rican culture and independence. Albizu shared a point in common with intellectuals of his time: in trying to counteract U.S. cultural and ideological influence in Puerto Rico, they fell back on an acritical and ahistorical Hispanophilia.

Two figures from the first half of the twentieth century who focused their energies on the island's African heritage were Arturo Alfonso Schomburg (1874–1938) and Luis Palés Matos (1898–1959). Schomburg moved to New York and actively collected literature and art about people of African descent. A prolific writer, Schomburg's growing collection was a resource for many, including members of the Harlem Renaissance. His purpose in collecting was to disprove the racist theories on black intellectual and creative abilities current at the time. His collection was purchased and donated to the New York Public Library in 1925. Now known as the Schomburg Center for Research in Black Culture, it houses the world's largest collection of African, Afro-Latin, and African-American cultural materials.

Luis Palés Matos, from Guayama, an area of strong African roots, was a poet. Although he wrote on many themes, it is his Afro-Antillean poetry that earned his fame. Intensely rhythmic, onomatopoeic, playful, and sensual, Palés's poetry explored the cultural, religious, historical, and sexual dimensions of Puerto Rico's African identity. For the first time a publicly known figure not only pointed out but celebrated African contributions to the island's language, music, food, sports, and social behavior. Despite Palés's achievements some (but not all) scholars view certain of his poems as stereotypical of blacks, both physically and culturally.

WHITENING AND RACIAL SELF-PERCEPTION

Despite social gains and new black voices, Puerto Rico still perceived itself as whitening. The 1899 census figures are as follows: 62 percent white, 32 percent mulatto, 6 percent black. By 1950, 80 percent of Puerto Ricans identified themselves as white. This shift cannot be explained by an influx of foreign-born white immigrants, since between 1900 and 1930 this figure decreased by over 40 percent. Perceptually, Puerto Ricans who saw themselves as mulattoes at one point became whites, and those who previously identified themselves as blacks became mulattoes. These perceptions have been questioned. One study lists the 1985 population of the island as 80 percent non-white (Knight 1990, 372). Another study from the late eighties of Puerto Ricans in New York yields a figure of 67 percent non-white (60% as tan, 7% as black) and 33 percent white (C. Rodríguez 1989, 61).

These contrastive perceptions reflect the radically different worlds of racial categorization used as reference points by U.S. observers compared with Puerto Rican viewpoints. In Puerto Rico under Spanish colonialism miscegenation was viewed as a whitening and not darkening process. Also, Puerto Ricans continued to resist the imposition of U.S. racial classifications. Indeed, many dark-skinned Puerto Ricans were often identified as African Americans, a classification that they rejected not only for racial reasons, but also out of nationalism and culture. Puerto Ricans are race conscious, but cultural belonging supersedes this, a common enough attitude throughout the Caribbean. Moreover, the uniqueness of the island's history often makes racial self-definition an expression of resistance to U.S. colonialism. Puerto Ricans in the United States, when asked what they are, respond that they are Puerto Ricans, not black or white. The dilemma has been stated as follows: "Within the U.S. perspective, Puerto Ricans, racially speaking, belonged to both groups; however, ethnically, they belonged to neither.... Puerto Ricans were White and Black; Puerto Ricans were neither white nor black. From the Puerto Rican perspective, Puerto Ricans were more than White and Black" (C. Rodríguez 1989, 51).

The shocking realization of moving between two worlds of race complexities is eloquently described in Piri Thomas's celebrated *Down These Mean Streets* (1967) or in Tato Laviera's poem "Negrito." Interestingly, many black and mulatto Puerto Rican writers born or raised from infancy in the United States have taken on issues of race in their literature: aside from Thomas and Laviera, there are Nicholasa Mohr, Ed Vega, Louis Reyes Rivera, Esmeralda Santiago, and Jack Agüeros.

However, in cities like New York the physical proximity of living with African Americans and other African-Caribbean peoples has also drawn Puerto Ricans into the orbit of other African-based cultures. In dress and language, many Puerto Ricans show influences of U.S. blacks and many identify with hip-hop culture. There are Puerto Rican rappers who sing in English and/or Spanish, like the late Big Pun, and many others who are graffiti artists. This intercultural effervescence is also reflected on the island, with rappers such as Vico C, Lisa M, Francheska, Ruben DJ, and Welmo.

MIGRATION AND THE MUÑOZ MARÍN ERA (1946–1964)

Puerto Ricans migrated to the United States during the entire twentieth century, but before 1946 about two-thirds of the 70,000 migrants returned. From 1947 to 1960, however, there was a net migration of 550,000 people, a quarter of the island's population. It was a period of profound economic and social transformation. Puerto Rico elected its first governor in 1948, Luis Muñoz Marín (1898–1980). Under his leadership the island undertook Operation Bootstrap, an economic program to industrialize the island, using tax incentives to draw U.S. manufacturing firms as investors. The program successfully industrialized Puerto Rico, but it caused the almost total decline of its agriculture. Unemployed rural workers flooded the cities, but Bootstrap could not absorb such a huge number of the jobless, many of whom were black and mulatto. As U.S. citizens, Puerto Ricans did not face the barriers to U.S. mainland migration experienced by other Caribbeans. With higher wages and greater opportunities for employment in the United States, and a reduction in airfares from San Juan to New York, over half a million chose the North. Teodoro Moscoso, Bootstrap's architect, later admitted that immigration was central to the program's strategy and that without that demographic safety valve the island would have erupted in revolution.

Muñoz Marín also sought a political solution for the island, charting a course between independence and statehood, but with a goal of greater autonomy. He called it the Estado Libre Asociado (the Freely Associated State), along with its own constitution (1952). Even though Puerto Rico is in many ways like a state within the U.S. federal system, it has its own constitution. Both remain operative to this day. In terms of civil rights and racial discrimination, U.S. federal laws apply in Puerto Rico.

One of Muñoz Marín's closest political companions was Ernesto Ramos Antonini (1898–1963), a black labor leader and politician. He helped draft the island's constitution, was Speaker of the House of Representatives from 1948 to 1963, and helped establish music schools and the first public conservatory. Ramos often brought up issues of race in public debate, but he was a rare exception.

Two African-Puerto Rican musical figures stand out in the Muñoz era: Rafael Hernández (1893–1965) was the island's greatest composer of popular music, be it a love song or a *plena* (an Afro-Puerto Rican musical and dance form that usually narrates spicy daily events). Hernández even sang at the White House. Songs like "Lamento Borincano" (Puerto Rican Lament) or "Cachita" are famous not only in the Caribbean but in all of Latin America. Ruth Fernández (1919–) is one of the island's most popular singers and media personalities, and she is also a former senator. Credited with having broken color barriers in certain venues of entertainment during the thirties and forties, her magnificent voice has sung from opera to romantic ballads, thrilling audiences for decades.

Despite federal antidiscrimination laws few cases have been brought forth. It has been mostly artistic, intellectual, scholarly, and sports figures who have highlighted racial issues on the island. Unlike the United States or parts of the Caribbean, Puerto Rico did not have a civil rights movement, a Black Power movement, or variants of back-to-Africa or Pan-Africanist adherents. Instead, a more Afrocentric pride has revealed itself in the shift from "high" culture to inclusive popular culture, particularly with music.

Since the 1960s there has been greater awareness and debate of racial issues, and increasing pride in being *Afroboricua* (Afro–Puerto Rican). One of the musical turning points of this consciousness was embodied in the work of bandleader Rafael Cortijo (1928–1982) and singer Ismael Rivera (1931–1987), who in the mid-fifties created some of the island's greatest music, based on the traditions of *bomba* and *plena*, both Afro–Puerto Rican musical traditions. Bomba is the most African of Puerto Rican musical-dance genres, consisting of drums, percussion, and singing, similar to Cuban rumba. Cortijo's sound became known internationally. Cortijo's music along with Afro-Cuban music formed the basis of what became known as salsa music. Salsa grew out of the urban experience of many Afro-Puerto Ricans and dealt with themes of poverty, racism, social violence, education, and drugs. Many Puerto Rican composers and musicians spearheaded the salsa boom of the late sixties to the early eighties: Willie Colón, Cheo Feliciano, Pete "El Conde" Rodríguez, Roberto Roena, Milton Cardona, Papo Lucca, El Gran Combo, songwriter Tite Curet Alonso, and more recently La India (Linda Cabellero) and Gilberto Santa Rosa. Latin jazz artists include David Sánchez, Hilton Ruiz, Giovanni Hidalgo, and Anthony Carrillo. Perhaps the best known is the Mambo King himself, Tito Puente (1923–2000), a New York–born Puerto Rican musician, composer, bandleader, and winner of three Grammy Awards. Puente was a pioneer of the mambo craze of the forties, the cha-cha-cha of the fifties, the salsa of the sixties, seventies, and beyond, and a mainstay of Latin jazz for over five decades.

At the time of Cortijo's rising popularity, a university-educated black and mixed-race middle class developed. And yet, in 1959 the Civil Rights Committee's report confirmed the presence of bigotry on the island, but issued no recommendations to remedy the injustices. In 1972 another government report openly discussed the same issues, but since it dealt with more subtle forms of racism, nothing came of it. Even when someone as famous as baseball player Roberto Clemente (1934–1972) discussed racial discrimination, it was easy to dodge the issue and attribute it to U.S. racial attitudes toward Puerto Ricans. Clemente once said: "I don't want to be put down because I'm Puerto Rican. I don't stand for disliking someone because of their color. If that is the case, then I don't want to be living. I am a double nigger ... because of my skin and my heritage."[5] Despite the obstacles, Clemente became the first Latin baseball player to be inducted into the Hall of Fame (1973). Many other African–Puerto Ricans have excelled in the majors, such as Orlando Cepeda and Vic Power, and in other sports such as boxing; for example, Chegüí Torres, a light-heavyweight champ, who has since become a distinguished newspaper columnist.

PUERTO RICO: NEW CONSCIOUSNESS AND CHANGE (1965 TO PRESENT)

Puerto Rico's economy became more capital intensive in the sixties and seventies. By then two-thirds of the population lived in urban areas. Unemployment grew, affecting the black and mixed-race populations the hardest. This unleashed social tensions: wildcat strikes (1968–1973), squatters movements (1966–1972 and 1979–1983), prison riots, political unrest, youth vagrancy, theft, violence, and increased drug abuse (Santiago-Valles 1995, 142–143). Muñoz Marín's party, the pro-commonwealth PPD (Popular Democratic Party), had lost much of its rural constituency and the new urban masses abandoned it for the PNP (New Progressive Party), whose slogan for the disenfranchised was "Statehood is for the poor!" (Santiago-Valles 1995, 145–146). Since 1968 the PNP has won five elections, the PPD three.

In the seventies the work of two authors, Isabelo Zenón Cruz and José Luis González (1926–1996), polemically raised issues of race. Zenón's exhaustive 1974 two-volume study, *Narciso descubre su trasero* (Narcissus Discovers His Back[side]), was pathbreaking in discussing hidden assumptions about race in popular culture. González's 1979 essay, the *Four-Storeyed Country*, has been widely discussed, bringing the discussion of the country's African roots to the fore. After Zenón and González, it was impossible to ignore racism and its insidious aftermath.

In the period from the seventies to the nineties, the middle-class stratum of color on the island fostered what has been called "culturalist expressions of black affirmation": music, books, art exhibits, scholarly research, and video documentaries. Black women such as Mayra Santos Febre (a distinguished writer), Ana Rivera, Rayda Cotto, Celia M. Romano, and Marie Ramos Rosado formed the Union of Afro–Puerto Rican Women. The Puerto Rican Council Against Racism, a watchdog group, was also formed. Still, even in 1988 Governor Hernández Colón said that the African contributions to Puerto Rican culture "were irrelevant, ... mere rhetoric" (Flores 1993, 95).

Racial discrimination is now indirectly expressed under concern about crime, with black and darker-skinned people of mixed race suffering the brunt of arrests, even though the police do not keep statistics on race. Under the guise of combating drugs, the National Guard has patrolled certain housing projects. The real issues of poverty, employment, and discrimination are not discussed, nor is the question of why there is a need for an underground economy of drugs, stolen goods (from watches to VCRs and computers), and firearms that is estimated at about a quarter of Gross National Product. Sometimes this racialization of crime is deflected onto the growing number of Dominican immigrants, many of whom are dark-skinned. They are additionally excoriated for allegedly taking jobs away from Puerto Ricans (Santiago-Valles 1995, 149–154).

African forms of religiosity are also becoming more prevalent. Though nominally a Catholic country, but now with many Protestants and Evangelicals, Puerto Ricans have also practiced Spiritism for over a hundred years. Despite its European origins, Spiritism's belief in communicating with live and dead spirits reveals an affinity with Santería and *Palo-mayombe*, religions that combine Catholic and African beliefs. Both religions have become increasingly popular on the island, especially (but not exclusively) among the urban poor. In fact, *espiritistas* are now incorporating elements of Santería into their practices. And even some Catholic holidays, such as the Santiago Apostol festival in the town of Loíza, a center of black culture, are highly Africanized.

CONCLUSION

Still a U.S. colony after more than a century, Puerto Rico has shown remarkable cultural and linguistic resilience to the American presence. Its economy, dependent on tourism and on a previous model of giving U.S. firms tax incentives to invest in the island, is in crisis. Manufacturing companies lured by lower wages, are going to other parts of the Caribbean or Mexico, because of NAFTA. Despite a high living standard, the island has high unemployment (20%), a public education system that is mediocre at best, high levels of substance abuse, and alarming crime rates.

The political and economic elites of the country are still mostly white or light-skinned mixed race. Puerto Rico's racial dynamics simultaneously show nuance and fluidity along with a degree of avoidance or denial. The major political and social issues still are expressed in terms of nation (political status) or class (economic opportunity) or education (social mobility). Making a statement of your blackness is often viewed as socially separatist, even unpatriotic. Despite pervasive and subtle forms of prejudice and discrimination, the country is ever more aware of and celebrating its African-Caribbean identity and culture.

NOTES

1. Tomás Blanco (1985/1942), *El prejuicio racial en Puerto Rico* (Río Piedras, Puerto Rico: Ediciones Huracán), p. 103.

2. Tomás Blanco (1975), "Elogio de la plena," in Eugenio Fernández Méndez, *Antología del Pensamiento Puertorriqueño, 1900–1970*, vol. 2 (Río Piedras, Puerto Rico: Editorial de la Universidad de Puerto Rico), p. 1004.

3. Jorge Duany (2000), "El censo, la raza y los puertorriqueños," *El Nuevo Día*, 18 de febrero.

4. For full quote see Arcadio Díaz Quiñones, in Tomás Blanco (1985/1942), *El prejuicio racial en Puerto Rico* (Río Piedras, Puerto Rico: Ediciones Huracán), pp. 49–50.

5. As quoted in Alan West (1993), *Roberto Clemente: Baseball Legend* (Brookfield, CT: Milbrook Press), p. 13.

REFERENCES

Barbosa, José Celso (1937). *Problema de razas*. San Juan, Puerto Rico: Imprenta Venezuela.

Dietz, James (1986). *An Economic History of Puerto Rico*. Princeton, NJ: Princeton University Press.

Fernández, Ronald, Serafín Méndez, and Gail Cueto (1998). *Puerto Rico Past and Present: An Encyclopedia*. Westport, CT: Greenwood Press.

Flores, Juan (1993). *Divided Borders: Essays on Puerto Rican Identity*. Houston: Arte Público Press.

González, José Luis (1993). *The Four-Storeyed Country*. Princeton, NJ: Markus Wiener Publishers.

Guerra, Lillian (1998). *Popular Expression and National Identity in Puerto Rico: The Struggle for Self, Community, and Nation*. Gainesville: University Press of Florida.

Knight, Franklin (1990). *The Caribbean: The Genesis of a Fragmented Nationalism*. 2d ed. New York: Oxford University Press.

Matthews, Thomas G. (1974). "The Question of Color in Puerto Rico." In Toplin, Robert Brent (ed.), *Slavery and Race Relations in Latin America*. Westport, CT: Greenwood Press, pp. 299–323.

Morales Carrión, Arturo (1983). *Puerto Rico: A Political and Cultural History*. New York: W.W. Norton.

Rodríguez, Clara E. (1989). *Puerto Ricans: Born in the U.S.A*. Boston: Unwin Hyman.

Santiago-Valles, Kelvin A. (1995). "Puerto Rico." In Minority Rights Group *No Longer Invisible: Afro-Latins Today*. London: Minority Rights Publications, pp. 139–161.

Wagenheim, Kal, and Olga Jiménez de Wagenheim (1994). *The Puerto Ricans: A Documentary History*. Rev. ed. Princeton, NJ: Markus Wiener Publishers.

Zeuón Cruz, Isabelo (1974–1975). *Narciso descubre su trasero*. 2 vols. Humacao, Puerto Rico: Editorial Furisi.

13

Suriname

Alan West-Durán

Suriname is located in the northern right shoulder of South America, between French Guiana and English-speaking Guyana. Large by Caribbean standards (it is twice the size of Hispaniola), 80 percent of the country is rain forest. Suriname has had a rich history, with a high degree of ethnic and racial diversity, and it is one of the Caribbean nations that has best preserved its African values and norms because of its Maroon and Afro-Creole communities. A former Dutch colony that became independent in 1975, Suriname has a population of 437,000 that is roughly 31 percent Creole (urban blacks and people of mixed race of African descent), 10 percent Maroon, 36 percent of East Indian descent (locally called Hindustani), about 17 percent Indonesian-descended Javanese, 3 percent Amerindian, 2 percent Chinese, and 1 percent European and others. Maroons are descendants of runaway slaves who live in autonomous communities and have retained mixed African customs, languages, oral traditions, religion, and art. By mixed African customs it is understood that different cultures from Africa (Ashanti, Fon, Congo, etc.) have been brought together (transcultured) to create a new, unique Afro-Surinamese culture. Suriname's ethnic-racial diversity is reflected in its linguistic pluralism as well. Although Dutch is the official language, many languages are spoken there: Surinamese Dutch, English, Surinamese-Javanese, Hindi or Sarnami (widely spoken), and Chinese (Hakka). There are also several Creole languages: Sranan-Tongo (the most widely spoken), Paramakan, Ndjuka, Aluku, and Kwinti (all with origins in African languages and English); Saramakan and Matawai are influenced by Portuguese.

PRE-COLUMBIAN TIMES AND THE EMERGENCE OF SLAVERY

Before European colonization and settlement, the Arawak, Carib, and Warrau (Awarao) Indians lived in small self-sufficient communities in Suriname. This northeastern coast of South America was called Guiana by the Amerindians, but a previous tribe that inhabited the area, the Surinas, is considered the source of the current name of Suriname.

The Spanish were the first to explore the area in 1499 and 1500. Various European expeditions went into the area as part of the ongoing but ultimately fruitless search for the land of El Dorado. The attempts to settle the area by different European powers failed because of stiff resistance from the Indians.

But in 1650, with Barbados becoming overcrowded, the British set out to colonize the area and established settlements with sugar planters and slaves. They were soon joined by Portuguese Jews, fleeing both Portugal and Brazil after Spain annexed them, imposing the Inquisition. Under the British, Suriname developed a successful export of sugar, but in 1667 the Dutch seized the country. The Treaty of Breda awarded the country of Suriname to Holland (in exchange for New Amsterdam, or New York) and the country remained under the Netherlands until independence, except for two brief periods of British rule (1795–1802 and 1804–1816) during the Napoleonic Wars.

SLAVERY AND COLONIAL RULE

Importation of slaves was under the aegis of the West India Company until the end of the eighteenth century, when the colony was placed under the Dutch Crown. Despite military and financial subsidies from the state, Dutch trade dominance was achieved through the West Indies Company's business savvy and sophistication: they offered lower interest rates on loans and for longer terms, better insurance terms, and lower freight rates. The French and English planters in the Caribbean used their ships.

Suriname imported over 325,000 slaves from 1667 to 1863, the year of abolition. Africans were brought from the Windward Coast (Liberia, Ivory Coast, Guinea-Bissau, Guinea, and Sierra Leone), the Gold Coast (Ghana), the Slave Coast (Togo, Nigeria, Benin), and Loango/Angola (Cameroon, Congo, Gabon, Angola). As elsewhere in the Caribbean, slavery was harsh in Suriname, with high rates of mortality. During the first hundred years of the colony, more than 75 percent of the slaves had been born in Africa, and a third had arrived within the last five years.

The presence of Maroon communities dates back more than three centuries. The first documented reference to Maroons is from the 1670s, when militias were organized to either recapture the former slaves or destroy their settlements. Punishment for recaptured slaves was ghastly: hamstringing, amputation of limbs, and a host of different tortures (hacking with axes, dismemberment with iron hooks, being burned at the stake), often leading to death.

But Suriname's Maroons offer one of the most extraordinary examples of resistance and defeat of the colonial powers in Latin American and Caribbean history. Rejecting full-scale and direct confrontation, and aided by climate and geography, slaves were able to escape into the dense rain forests of Suriname and establish their own communities as free peoples. However, it was not simply a matter of escaping to the bush and forgetting their previous life. A state of continuous warfare with colonial militias and slave-owners for decades led, eventually, to the creation of a 200-foot protective zone between plantations and Maroon territory. Finally, in 1760 and 1762, the Maroons were able to negotiate a peace treaty with Dutch colonial authorities that basically gave them autonomy over their own settlements and allowed for trade activities between the two previously warring camps. The Maroons pledged to return newly escaped slaves or other Maroons. A Scotsman, John Gabriel Stedman, published an important narrative with accompanying illustrations that is important to understanding the history of the country and the Maroons: *Narrative of a Five Years' Expedition against the Revolted Negroes of Surinam: 1772–1777* (1790).

At the height of the slave system in 1788, there were 591 plantations in Suriname, and of a total population of 55,000, 91 percent were slaves. In Paramaribo, the capital, almost one in every four inhabitants was white, while in rural areas whites were only 2 percent of the population. A huge influx of Dutch capital had created an artificial economic boom, especially in the production of coffee. But in 1773 the Amsterdam Exchange suffered a crisis and the rather easy credit available to Suriname began to evaporate, and many planters had to sell their property to metropolitan creditors. In forty years (1773–1813) the number of plantations dropped by a third.

The economic crisis caused the departure of many European families/owners of plantations, which went bankrupt. Companies in Holland bought and administered these companies and sent young, mostly unmarried, males to run the failed enterprises. They often had relationships with Surinamese free colored or black females. These relationships were known as "Surinamese marriages," which began with a "ceremony" and ended once the male partner returned to Europe. The offspring of these Surinamese marriages were cared for by their fathers and some studied in Holland. A small group of well-educated colored people was created, and they could work in higher government positions or the professions (law, teaching, medicine). These "respectable coloreds" over time became the Afro-Creole elites who would later run the country (Hoetink 1972, 61).

Under British rule (1804–1816) Suriname abolished the slave trade (1807), but not slavery. Illegal trafficking continued, but in vastly reduced numbers, and there was almost none after 1824. As a result, treatment of slaves grew less severe, because plantation owners could no longer depend on imported slaves. Still, by 1862, a year before abolition, Suriname had one-third fewer slaves than in 1788. In 1828, a society for the promotion of religious education among slaves and heathens was created: the hope was that by Christianizing the slaves they would form stronger matrimonial ties and increase their birthrates. To counteract the decrease in slave numbers, manumission became more difficult and in 1825 slaves were prohibited from buying their freedom, a prohibition that was lifted only in 1850.

After returning to Dutch rule, Suriname's economy did not recover, and large fires in Paramaribo in 1821 and 1832 only made matters worse. By 1844, the Dutch government had to make up the deficits in the colony's budget. On July 1, 1863, 33,000 slaves were emancipated, some thirty years after the British and fifteen after the French. Only Puerto Rico, Cuba, and Brazil abolished slavery later. Even then, there was a ten-year period where former slaves continued to work on a plantation of their choice, under state supervision.

POST-EMANCIPATION TO INDEPENDENCE

Since most ex-slaves had little interest in working on sugar estates, alternative sources of labor were sought: 37,000 indentured laborers were brought to Suriname from India between 1873 and 1917; another 33,000 were brought from Indonesia (Javanese) between 1893 and 1939. A smaller number of Chinese (5,000) were also brought in the nineteenth century.

European sugar beet production and the opening of the Suez Canal (1869) further weakened the competitiveness of Suriname's sugar. Attempts to grow other crops such as cotton, coffee, and cacao met with limited success. Gold became an important export from the 1870s to 1918, and rubber as well from the 1890s to the 1920s. By World War II they were eclipsed by bauxite, used to make aluminum, and it is still the country's principal export.

The Great Depression had a devastating effect on Suriname's economy. Many were unemployed and living in poverty. Social unrest led to riots in Paramaribo (1931), which were violently suppressed by the police. An Afro-Creole activist who had studied in Holland, Anton de Kom (1898–1945), returned to Suriname. A radical anti-colonialist, de Kom, whose views were increasingly popular, was arrested by the government in January 1933. When supporters gathered publicly to demand his release, the police opened fire, killing two and wounding others. De Kom was deported and protests ebbed. In Holland, de Kom kept active in union causes and tried to organize support for Surinamese and Indonesian independence. During the Nazi occupation of Holland he was arrested and imprisoned in several concentration camps. He died just days before the country was liberated in 1945. De Kom also wrote an influential history book, *We Slaves of Surinam* (1934), an impassioned indictment of Dutch colonialism and racism that was inspirational to Surinamese nationalists and radicals of the sixties.

Suriname in the 1930s still relied heavily on Dutch financial support, so Holland dictated the terms of how the budget was formed, often creating resentment as to whether its decisions had the true interests of Suriname in mind. The local government, ruled by the Koloniale Staten, had two-thirds of its members elected. The local parliament was an advisory group with little real power, and restrictions in the electoral laws meant that only 2 percent of the population could vote.

In 1942, Queen Wilhelmina of the Netherlands made a radio speech that envisioned a future where Dutch colonial possessions—Indonesia, Suriname, and the Netherlands Antilles[1]—would be free to handle their internal affairs. As a result, political mobilization began in earnest after World War II. The major parties were formed along ethnic lines in the mid- to late forties: Afro-Creoles (NPS), East Indians, known locally as "Hindustani" (VHP), and Indonesians (KTPI). Although originally not in favor of universal suffrage, the Creoles were pressured by the other parties to change their position. Suriname achieved autonomy in 1954. But since no ethnicity commanded an absolute majority, coalitions had to be negotiated. From 1955 to 1968 Afro-Creoles, led by Johan Adolf Pengel, under the principle of ethnic *verbroedering* (fraternization) ruled in conjunction with the Hindustani, led by Jaggernath Lachmon. Afro-Creoles still dominated the civil service and bureaucracy, holding about two-thirds of the jobs. Maroons formed their own party in 1968 (PBP), but due to their historically troubled relationship with Afro-Creoles, they have often not voted with Creole-led voting blocs.

INDEPENDENCE: MILITARY RULE AND REDEMOCRATIZATION

In 1973 the Dutch government and Suriname's prime minister, Henck Arron, an Afro-Creole and NPS leader, announced a timetable of late 1975 for the country's independence. The Hindustanis (and Indonesians) were concerned that this signaled an Afro-Creole domination of the country and wanted certain constitutional guarantees to ensure their role and power base within Suriname's political system. To make matters worse, the economy was in a recession and many feared that Suriname would not be able to sustain itself as an independent country. So in 1973, concerned about their future, thousands of Hindustanis immigrated to the Netherlands, later to be followed by Indonesians. Afro-Creoles have also immigrated and roughly one-third of the population of Suriname now lives in Holland.

After several deadlocks in the negotiations between Afro-Creoles and Hindustanis, Suriname became independent on November 25, 1975. But the previous political consensus had deteriorated, many strikes had further weakened the economy, and 40,000 well-educated Surinamese had immigrated so they could become Dutch citizens. Many Hindustanis still resent independence, seeing it as a Creole-inspired movement that was worked out with the Dutch, without proper consultation with the East Asian and Javanese populations.

The new nation's first years were marked by economic stagnation, social dissatisfaction, and political fragmentation, and the influx of Dutch aid brought on mismanagement and corruption of government funds. A new wave of immigrants, mostly Afro-Creole, went to Holland from 1975 to 1980. In early 1980 the military seized power, under the leadership of Desi Bouterse.

Bouterse, part Afro-Creole and part Amerindian, was initially popular in trying to create a multiethnic political unity as well as promising programs, jobs, and education for the poor. Initially, both the constitution and the rule of law were at least given verbal acknowledgment. But inexperience, ineptitude, and political miscalculation, as well as a growing repression, created dissatisfaction. By early 1982, after a second thwarted coup attempt, Bouterse declared martial law. In December 1982 the regime imprisoned scores of opposition leaders, and then executed fifteen of them, including Cyriel Daal, the head of the main trade union, as well as lawyers, academics, and three journalists. The Dutch government suspended aid, as did the United States and the rest of the European community.

The economy suffered a sharp downturn, and so Bouterse turned to Cuba and other socialist countries for help. In addition, both members of the military and businesspeople became involved in the drug trade. Bouterse, ever skillful, negotiated with the political parties to hold elections in 1987, and he lifted martial law in 1986.

But in that same year the ghosts of Suriname history were resurrected. A Maroon guerrilla group, the Surinamese Liberation Army (SLA), took up arms against the government. The insurrection demanded an end to military rule, elections, a free press, and respect for Maroon sovereignty. Incredibly, its leader was a former bodyguard of Bouterse, Ronnie Brunswijk, a Ndjuka Maroon. Soon, all the Maroon groups joined with the SLA, but when the government subsequently withheld financial payments to the Maroons, the Matawai Maroons withdrew.

Bouterse retaliated swiftly and destructively, raiding villages and killing noncombatants, causing 10,000 Maroons to seek refuge in neighboring French Guiana. The army also armed 1,000 Tucayana Amerindians to fight against the SLA. The 1987 elections defeated the pro-government National Democratic Party (NDP) party, but Bouterse still held military and considerable political control. By 1989 the government and the SLA began negotiations that ended in a 1992 treaty, where the rebels recognized the government's authority over the entire country. The government agreed to honor economic, political, and cultural rights of the Maroons, allowing them to also join the army.

Violence erupted again in 1994 when an unknown group seized a hydroelectric plant that was part of a U.S. subsidiary of Alcoa, a bauxite-aluminum consortium. They demanded the resignation of the government and a decentralization of power. A government commando freed the hostages. There were also violent clashes between police and demonstrators in Paramaribo over increased food prices. In 1996 violence was barely averted over the issue of foreign corporations' logging rights in the interior as opposed to the rights of Maroons and Amerindians who lived there, and environmentalists. After much pressure to do so, in 1999 President Jules Wijdenbosch dismissed Bouterse from his administration after the Dutch authorities initiated legal proceedings against Bouterse for illegal drug trafficking. He was indicted *in absentia*, sentenced to sixteen years in jail and fined $2.2 million.

Suriname has barely experienced a quarter century of independence and in that period has shown all the tribulations of its Latin American counterparts: one-product dependency (bauxite represents over 70 percent of export earnings), military rule, corruption, constitutional uncertainty, political instability, guerrilla insurgencies, ethnic and racial tensions.

Like many Caribbean nations, a lighter-skinned Afro-Creole elite has run the country since the late forties. Afro-Creoles are concentrated in Paramaribo, where they are three out of every five residents in the capital. Darker-skinned Creoles are referred to as *nengre*, and make up a majority of the Creole population. However, Creoles are only about a quarter of the population in the rest of the country, where the East Indians are almost half and Indonesians 20 percent. This racial and ethnic complexity is challenging politically and socially, since Suriname is a country with a strong tradition of patronage in its political system. When handled with vision, as Pengel and Lachmon did in the fifties and sixties, it can be effective and harmonious. But the strict partition on ethnic lines can lead to a pragmatism, fragmentation, and horse trading for votes that blunts real political debate and can induce political paralysis. The Dutch colonial authorities and Afro-Creole elites considered the East Indian and Indonesian population as foreign and exotic until the 1950s. In most of the Caribbean except Trinidad and Guyana (ex-British), the mixing of races and cultures known as creolization or transculturation usually occurred mostly between Europeans and Africans. But in Suriname the plurality was greater, with East Indians and Javanese being substantial minorities, and a significant Maroon population (over 10%). Although attitudes have changed, the pre-independence migration shows that this process of creolization or transculturation is far from smooth, and is still unfinished.

SRANAN TONGO: SURINAME'S CREOLE LANGUAGE

One of the central contributions of Creole society and culture is the *lingua franca* of Suriname: Sranan Tongo. It is a type of Creole language that uses English, Dutch, Portuguese, and African words. It is estimated that 80 to 90 percent of Surinamers speak Sranan Tongo, about half speak Dutch, 30 percent Hindi, and 15 percent Javanese. Most Surinamese are at least bilingual; some are tri- or quadrilingual.

Although Sranan began as an Afro-Portuguese language, its greatest influence is from English, which is surprising given Britain's brief control of the country. The British linguistic impact can be explained: when the Dutch formally took over from the British, who had been there from 1651 to 1667 (some until 1678), they basically left Sranan Tongo—then called "Creole"—intact. Dutch colonial rule severely limited contact between their settlers and the slaves; slaves were forbidden to learn Dutch and only used Creole. Similarly, the East Indian and Javanese indentured laborers brought to Suriname three centuries later learned Sranan Tongo because of their low economic status and their isolation in rural communities.

To advance socially in Suriname, Dutch was necessary and for many centuries Sranan Tongo was seen as inferior and lacking prestige. It was spoken mostly by slaves, immigrants, and blue-collar laborers. Johannes King (1830?–1898) is one of the first authors to write in Sranan Tongo, writing his diaries about Ndjuka and Matawai Maroon life, to which he was related. An illness led to a spiritual crisis and he eventually converted to the Moravian Brethren and became a self-styled missionary to the Maroons.

The person most responsible for advancing Creole as a national and literary language was J.G.A. Koenders, (1886–1957) who from 1946 to 1956 edited the journal *Foetoe-boi* (Servant), published in Dutch and Sranan Tongo. Wanting Surinamers to be self-assured and spiritually independent, Koenders published authors writing in Sranan Tongo and espoused an unabashed pride in blackness. Claiming that forgetting the past was tantamount to folly, Koenders quotes a folk saying: "You can hide your grandmother, but you can't keep her from coughing" (in Meel 1990, 276).

Other writers, such as Eddy Bruma (1925–), Trefossa, a pseudonym for Henny F. Ziel (1916–), Johanna Schouten-Elsenhout (1910–), Michael Slory (1935–), R. Dobru (1935–1983), and Edgar Cairo (1948–) also write in Sranan Tongo, as well as in Dutch; other writers write mostly in Dutch. Cairo's novels draw on both black Creole life in the capital and tales from slavery, as well as on Winti and the Anansi trickster tradition. Suriname also boasts significant women writers such as Bea Vianen (1935–), Thea Doelwijt (1938–), Trudy Guda (1940–), and Astrid Roemer (1947–). Roemer, who publishes in Dutch and lives in Holland, is the best known, having written four novels, the most ambitious being *Life-Long Poem* (1987), which intertwines many characters and ethnicities from many points of view. Roemer is an outspoken, sometimes controversial writer, but her summarization of Suriname's sociocultural complexity is as striking as it is true: "To Suriname I am married, the Netherlands are my lover, I have a homosexual relationship with Africa, and I tend to be adulterous towards all other cultures" (Meel 1990, 280).

MAROONS

There are six main groups of Maroons in Suriname: the Saramaka, Ndjuka, Matawai, Aluku (Boni), Paramaka, and Kwinti, constituting about 50,000 people in total. The Ndjuka and Saramaka, in roughly equal numbers, make up about 90 percent of the Maroon population. These populations are descendants of the Maroons who victoriously fought the Dutch slave owners in the eighteenth century.

They live in small forest villages of 100 to 200 residents, almost always near a river or lake. They grow rice, cassava, sweet potatoes, plantains, okra, maize, sugar cane, and tobacco and hunt for small game, as well as fish. They obtain tools, cloth, salt and other goods by trading with merchants from the coast or from the capital, Paramaribo. Many Maroons have immigrated to the coast and to Paramaribo during the last forty years in order to work, so there is much greater contact now between Maroons and non-Maroons.

There is a great deal of independence and freedom of movement in family life, since many men have two or three wives, sometimes in different villages. Children are usually raised by one adult, but that shifts: a child will spend the early years with the mother, then will be given to the father or an aunt and uncle, and perhaps to the grandparents further on.

Maroon artists and craftspeople are extremely talented and excel in textiles, architecture, and wood carving. The wood-carving work is among the most extraordinary in the world and includes food stirrers, beaters, door locks, carafes, grinding boards, combs, trays, door frames, stools, chests, and most notably, canoe paddles, masks, drums, and calabashes. Paddles are probably the best known, with intricate carving on the handle and colorful designs on the wide part. Calabashes are carved on the outside, with either abstract designs or flora and fauna of the region. Since museums collect the paddles and calabashes, they have become popular and now Maroon artists are producing carvings for tourism and export made in the form of briefcases and toy helicopters.

Despite almost two hundred fifty years of autonomy, the Maroons are still wary of Europeanized ways. They stress the importance of storytelling, what they called *fesi ten* (First Time) in the eighteenth century, that tells of the exploits of leaders such as Alabi and Ayako. "If we forget the deeds of our ancestors, how can we hope to avoid being returned to white folks' slavery?" says a Saramakan to an anthropologist (Price 1990, xii).

RELIGIONS AND WINTI

Suriname's major religions are Christianity, Hinduism, Islam, and Winti. About a quarter of the population, mostly Afro-Creole, is Catholic. Almost one in five Surinamers is Protestant. Hinduism is practiced by another quarter of the population, mostly by East Indians (although many are Muslim). Islam is also practiced by 20 percent of the population, mostly by the Javanese.

Winti, which means wind or spirit, is also a term used to describe a magical-religious complex of beliefs practiced by Surinam Maroons and Afro-Creoles. It is difficult to assess how many Creoles believe in Winti, but it does form part of their sociocultural life in both overt and subtle ways.

For centuries Winti was practiced clandestinely or in Maroon communities. There is a Supreme God known by different names by the different Maroon cultures as well as Gron Mama (Earth Mother), but the religion centers more on the harnessing of spirits and the practice of magic in order to affect a believer's soul. *Akra* (or *'kra*) is the term for "soul" and is derived from Twi (spoken by the Ashanti of West Africa). However, God is manifest everywhere, through spirits (winti), in the elements (air, fire, water, earth), as well as in animals and humans, mostly adults. Winti shares some commonalities with other Afro-Caribbean religions such as Santería, Vodou, and Candomblé: belief in many deities, spirit possession, ancestor worship, sacred drumming, a system of divination, feeding and making sacrifices to the deities, use of herbs for curing ailments and in the practice of magic. Winti is a holistic system that affirms a close relationship between humans, nature, and the divine; it is a form of therapy, a method for curing sicknesses, a religion with a cosmology, and a way of life (Roemer 1998, 49). Unlike its sister religions, however, Winti did not become syncretized with Catholicism or Protestantism, but instead with indigenous (Arawak) and African (Fon, Ashanti, Congo/Loango) beliefs.

During times of slavery, Winti was a means of communication between slaves of different ethnicities and a cultural resource with which to resist or rebel against the tyranny of plantation owners. In Maroon communities Winti could be practiced openly, as it still is today. One of the central elements of Winti worship is dancing, often performed in what Maroons call "plays," a communal event that includes singing, dancing, and drumming. Plays can be performed for social occasions, funerals, or the installation of new chiefs or officials. When related to winti and possession they are often called "obeah plays" (*obia pee*).

In the recent Maroon war led by the SLA (1986–1992), Winti played a prominent role. Some point out that the rebellion was the product of avenging spirits (*kunu*) from the past. Ronnie Brunswijk admits that at the beginning he was skeptical of Winti, and of the *obiamen* (medicine men) whose duty it is to heal and provide protective magic. But within a couple of years his Jungle Commando employed five *obiamen* on an almost permanent basis, proof that even within a context of modern warfare and politics, Winti still exercises a powerful influence in Surinamese society (Thoden Van Velzen 1990, 178). It is also practiced by many Afro-Creoles or Maroons who have immigrated to Holland.

FROM MAROON PLAY TO *ALEKE*: AFRO-SURINAMESE MUSIC

Maroon music and drumming has been one of the key sources to Suriname's music as well. *Kaseko*, the country's most popular music and dance form, has drawn on the rhythms of the Ndjuka and Saramakan Maroons. Like much else in the country, Suriname's *kaseko* comes from a welter of influences: *kawina* music (drums and vocals), military bands (with large bass drums called *skratji* and tubas), Trinidadian calypso, British Guianese song styles, Afro-Cuban dance music, and the use of banjo coupled with a snare drum called *boengoe-boengoe*. Types of music that developed later, such as reggae, soca, zouk, and dancehall have given it new inflections. Here is a musicologist describing modern *kaseko*:

Contemporary pieces are almost always divided into two or more contrasting sections, often in very different tempos. The snare drum, with its rolls and fills, plays a particularly prominent part, as does its companion, the *skratji*, with its rapid, off-center punches. Other hallmarks of contemporary *kaseko* are the bright, snappy brass arrangements; long stretches of instrumental vamping, with lots of jazzy horn solos; and especially, the characteristic transitional sections marked by dizzying stop-and-go breaks—staccato bursts of counterrhythm that temporarily play havoc with the otherwise rock-solid beat. Finally, most *kaseko* bands today mix in what they call 'bubbling,' meaning a blend of reggae, dancehall, and *kaseko*. (Bilby 1995, 225–226)

Singers also employ different languages from Dutch, to the Creole Sranan Tongo, English, Spanish, and Maroon languages (Ndjuka and Saramaka, mostly). Some of the best-known *kaseko* singers, composers, and/or bandleaders have been Lieve Hugo, known as the King of Kaseko, Max Njiman, Iwan Esseboom, and Stan Lokhin. A blend of *kawina* music with the more electrified *kaseko* has become popular and goes under the name of *kaskawi* (Bilby 1995, 223).

A newer muscial trend known as *aleke* is also Maroon-derived. The Ndjuka Maroon *lonsei* music was brought to coastal towns and the capital, where it changed when it came in contact with Creole rhythms, creating a hybrid Maroon-Creole form known as *aleke*. It is played by young people and the songs speak of many topical issues such as poverty, employment, and AIDS. After the Maroon insurrection and ensuing civil war (1986–1992), *aleke* songs often referred to government repression and a desire to return to a democratic system, with some degree of peace and harmony. Originally played on the traditional *apínti* drums, *aleke* bands were replaced by three conga-sized "aleke" drums, along with a bass drum and high-hat set known as *djas* (jazz). A new trend has been to blend *aleke* with *kaseko*, and this new *aleke-kaseko* fusion, seen in the likes of Yakki Famirie, led by composer-saxophonist Theo Swanenberg, has become extremely popular. *Aleke* bands are now popular in the Netherlands, and some Dutch cities hold *aleke* festivals (Bilby 1995, 226–230).

Though obviously a country with great ethnic and racial diversity, the core of Suriname's music has been African-based, whether from its own sources (Maroon, *kawina*) or from abroad (Jamaican reggae and dancehall, Martinican zouk, Afro-Cuban dance forms, American jazz). And through its music—both deeply, locally rooted and cosmopolitan—the country has managed to project an image of its identity and nationhood that is celebratory and yet conscious of its sometimes painful history.

CONCLUSION

Suriname is redemocratizing its political system, a healthy sign, but its pluralism is still divided along ethnic lines. Redemocratization, however, is not proceeding quickly enough for some: Holland stopped sending aid in 1999, claiming the political system was totally corrupt. Despite his outcast status, Bouterse, still a "fugitive" of Dutch justice, ran in the 2000 elections and received about one of every eight votes. Suriname's economy is still highly dependent on one product (bauxite), its currency is weak, and it has had a tendency to run high budget deficits. Prices for bauxite and its other exports have remained low. Unemployment and inflation are high. As a result, many continue to immigrate to the Netherlands. Suriname nationalism and its success as an independent country are seen by some as a mixed blessing, by others as a dismal failure. Many in the Netherlands Antilles use Suriname as an example as to why they should not become independent from Holland.

Suriname is one of the most complex societies in the Caribbean given its ethnic, racial, linguistic, and cultural plurality. But up until recently, the country has defined itself as Afro-Creole or African-Surinamese socially, politically, and culturally. However, its recent history since independence has exploded the myth that it was a calm, happy, multicultural country free of racial and ethnic tensions. And now with a majority of the population of East Asian–Javanese descent, this African-Surinamese identity will shift. The future creolization of the country will fashion an Afro (Creole-Maroon)-Hindustani-Indonesian transculturation that will redefine Suriname as we know it. The country's musicians seem to point the way in the direction of even greater pluralities in cultural mixing, but the sentiments echoed in Dobru's poem ("One Suriname/so many kinds of hair/so many colors of skin/so many languages/one people") still seem like a distant dream (Meel 1990, 267).

NOTE

1. The Netherlands Antilles includes Bonaire, Curaçao, St. Eustatius, and Saba. Formerly, it included Aruba and St. Maarten; both now have *status aparte*, but still with strong links to Holland (see chapter eleven).

REFERENCES

Bilby, Kenneth (1995). "Introducing the Popular Music of Suriname." In *Caribbean Currents: Caribbean Music from Rumba to Reggae*. Philadelphia: Temple University Press, pp. 221–231.

Brana-Shute, Gary (ed.) (1990). *Resistance and Rebellion in Suriname: Old and New*. Studies in Third World Societies. Williamsburg, VA: College of William & Mary.

Chin, Henk E., and Hans Buddingh' (1987). *Surinam: Politics, Economics and Society*. London: Frances Pinter Publishers.

Dew, Edward (1994). *The Trouble in Suriname, 1975–1993*. Westport, CT: Praeger,

Goslinga, Cornelis Ch. (1979). *A Short History of the Netherlands Antilles and Surinam*. The Hague: Martinus Nijhoff.

Herskovits, Mellville J. (1966). *The New World Negro*. Bloomington: Indiana University Press, pp. 267–319 (on Winti).

Hoefte, Rosemarijn (1990). *Suriname*. Oxford, England: Clio Press.

Hoetink, Harry (1972). "Surinam and Curaçao." In Cohen, David W. and Greene, Jack P. (eds.), *Neither Slave nor Free*. Baltimore: Johns Hopkins University Press,

Meel, Peter (1990). "A Reluctant Embrace: Suriname's Idle Quest for Independence." In Brana-Shute (1990), pp. 259–290.

Postma, Johannes Menne (1990). *The Dutch in the Atlantic Slave Trade, 1600–1815*. New York: Cambridge University Press.

Price, Richard (1990). *Alabi's World*. Baltimore, Maryland: Johns Hopkins University Press.

Price, Richard (ed.) (1996/1973). *Maroon Societies: Rebel Slave Communities in the Americas*. 3d ed. Baltimore: Johns Hopkins University Press.

Price, Richard, and Sally Price (1999). *Maroon Arts: Cultural Vitality in the African Diaspora*. Boston: Beacon Press.

Roemer, Astrid (1998). "Who's Afraid of the Winti Spirit?" In Baltutansky, Marie-Agnés and Sourieau, Kathleen M. (eds.), *Caribbean Creolization: Reflections on the Cultural Dynamics of Language, Literature, and Identity*. Gainesville: University Press of Florida, pp. 44–53.

Sedoc-Dahlberg, Betty (ed.) (1990). *The Dutch Caribbean: Prospects for Democracy*. New York: Gordon & Breach.

Thoden Van Velzen, H.U.E., and W. Van Wetering (1990). "The Maroon Insurgency: Anthropological Reflections on the Civil War in Suriname." In Brana-Shute (1990), pp. 159–188.

Voohoeve, Jan, and Ursy Lichtvel (eds.) (1975). *Creole Drum: An Anthology of Creole Literature in Surinam*. New Haven, CT: Yale University Press,

Wooding, Charles J. (1981). *Evolving Culture: A Cross-Cultural Study of Suriname, West Africa, and the Caribbean*. Washington, DC: University Press of America.

14

Trinidad and Tobago

Alan West-Durán

INTRODUCTION

Long described in the culinary terms of its tasty national dish, the *callaloo*,[1] Trinidad and Tobago is a microcosm of the Caribbean, even of the world. Ethnically, Amerindian, African, Asian, and European cultures are represented. The original inhabitants, who lasted well into the nineteenth century, were mostly of Arawak or Carib descent. Africans have been on the island since the sixteenth century and Europeans likewise. First were the Spanish, then the French, and finally the British. In the nineteenth century through the early twentieth, indentured servants came from northern India and China. There are also small Syrian and Portuguese communities in this nation of 1.2 million, located just off the northeastern coast of Venezuela.

African culture survives in many elements of Trinidadian life: music, food, speech, religion, and ways of socializing. The Spanish influence is clear in religion (Catholicism), folk songs, people who still speak the language, and the country's Christmas music, called *parang*. French influence is pronounced in the local Creole, or patois, as well as in the origins of Carnival and in the local architecture. The English presence is profound, being the official language, and both the legal system and the constitution are based on the British model. Cricket is a national passion. Indian influences are striking as well: in food, where roti is now considered a national dish; in religion (many are Hindu, some Muslim); in music (chutney). Divali, a Hindu religious festival, is a national holiday. And the small but influential Chinese community is felt in the island's cuisine, Carnival, and economy.

The Afro-Trinidadian population is estimated at 42 percent of the population, the Indo-Trinidadian at 39 percent, the white and Chinese at about 1 percent each, and about 17 percent is considered mixed. Most mixed would be Afro-Indo-Trinidadian (colloquially known as *douglas*), but there are many others as well: Afro-Chinese-Trinidadian, Indo-European Trinidadian, etc. Racial and ethnic terms can be extremely fluid. You find expressions such as Trinidad White (non-British, mostly of Spanish and French ancestry and born on the island), or consider that the Portuguese were not viewed as white in Trinidad, not because of skin color, but due to their profession (traditionally called "dirty shopkeepers," implying a non-white "unrespectability"). And those known as "Spanish" are considered "mixed," with an African or black identity that is "softened." This "softening" can happen through various means: straight hair or lighter skin, but also by surname, background, class position, behavior, or cultural traditions. The evershifting boundaries of ethnic/racial definition and identity of these mixed Trinidadians are an important reminder that the island's polyethnicity cannot be understood with the models or experiences of other countries.

SPANISH COLONIZATION (1498–1783)

Trinidad was inhabited by Ienian Arawaks when Columbus arrived in 1498, Tobago mostly by Caribs. Estimates vary, but about 30,000 Amerindians lived on the two islands, mostly dedicated to farming and fishing. A century later, the Amerindian population was half that amount. The Ienian Arawaks called the island land of the hummingbirds. Because the area where Columbus landed was surrounded by three mountain peaks, he called it Trinidad, or the Trinity.

The island was settled, but cacao, tobacco, and other products were grown instead of sugar. The lack of mineral wealth and Trinidad's geographical location did not make it a key possession for the Spanish empire. Slaves were imported to work on the cacao plantations, but for the most part the island remained unnoticed and undeveloped until the 1780s.

Centuries of Spanish control had not created either great prosperity or a thriving society. The Spanish Crown sought to encourage white immigrants (and their slaves), but they wanted the newcomers to be Catholics.

In 1783 Trinidad had a population of only 2,763 and three-quarters were Amerindian, about 22 percent were black or mixed race (half were free), and 3 percent were white. The Spanish Royal Cédula of 1783 would drastically alter the racial and social composition of Trinidad as French, French-speaking Creoles, free colored, and slaves came in numbers from St. Lucia, Grenada, Guadeloupe, Martinique, and Haiti. In just a year the population more than doubled and the slave population jumped from 11 percent to almost 40 percent, and thirteen years later slaves constituted 56 percent of Trinidad's inhabitants (free blacks and colored were another 25 percent). Amerindians had dwindled by half, but proportionately they were only 6 percent of the population. The Spanish became a minority, prompting the remark that although the Spanish ruled, the French governed.

FROM BRITISH TAKEOVER TO EMANCIPATION (1797–1838)

Quickly, Trinidad was transformed into a sugar plantation economy, but the turmoil unleashed by the French Revolution left the country vulnerable to British attack, which began in 1797, culminating in full control by 1802. Unlike Jamaica and Barbados, Great Britain's two great sugar producers, Trinidad posed a dilemma for the British. Its free black and colored population was quite significant both in absolute and proportional terms. Whereas in Jamaica and Barbados whites always outnumbered free blacks and colored (by anywhere from two or four to one), in Trinidad it was the reverse. For example, in 1825, free blacks and colored were four and a half times as numerous as whites. Many of the free blacks and colored owned property, and some owned slaves as well. All of this occurred while Britain was turning the island into a sugar plantation: in barely fifteen years (1795–1810) the amount of land devoted to sugar had tripled, and the amount of slaves had more than doubled.

Although subject to restrictions, free blacks and colored were treated better by the Spanish than they were in the French or British colonies. The British moved quickly to limit their rights: military officers were stripped of their ranks and put into segregated units now led by whites, they had to serve as guards as part of public service (even landowners), and they needed police permission to have a ball as well as being taxed $16 for holding the event. In addition, they had to show proof they were free if stopped by authorities. Blacks had a 9:30 P.M. curfew, and they had to carry a torch after dark.

British restrictions were met with outrage and resistance. Jean-Baptiste Philippe (1792/6?–1829), a doctor whose landowning family had emigrated from Grenada, petitioned Earl Bathurst, the British secretary for the colonies, in person. Philippe roundly criticized Governor Woodford and his policies against the free colored population. Philippe published his petition a year later as *Free Mulatto* (1824), and it is considered to be one of the first works of Trinidadian literature. Many positive changes occurred after Philippe's denunciation, but interestingly, his petition never openly called for abolition, perhaps because he, too, was a slave-owner.

While Philippe tried to work within and reform the colonial-slave system, other blacks did not. Jonas Mohammed Bath (1783–1838), a Mandingo slave who had purchased his freedom, established a society for buying the freedom of Mandingoes, who were Muslims. By the time of abolition, Trinidad's 140 Mandingoes were free. Bath also petitioned the island governor to repatriate the Mandingoes to Africa, but he was not successful, having died first. Some individual members did return, however; but most importantly the Mandingoes retained their Muslim names, religion (Islam), and language. There are other cases, such as U.S. blacks who fought for the British and other ex-soldiers of African birth who settled in certain areas, maintaining a distinct cultural difference.

But it it was Daaga (Donald Stewart) (1800–1837) who offered the most spectacular example of resistance. From Guinea, he was brought to the Caribbean as a slave and had fought with the British West India Regiment in Grenada and Dominica. When he came to Trinidad, he led an armed uprising, attacking the barracks of white officers with 250 men. The uprising failed, and he was shot before a firing squad, but not before defying his executioners by taking off his mask.

Philippe's influence, along with the growing sentiment for ending slavery in Britain, led to abolition in 1834, with a six-year apprenticeship (ex-slaves would still work for their former masters, but be paid a wage). However, as elsewhere in the British Caribbean, apprenticeship was loathed and was discontinued in 1838.

POST-EMANCIPATION TO INDEPENDENCE (1838–1962)

Although Trinidad had much land available to cultivate, few blacks or Creoles were willing to work on the sugar estates. Instead, indentured laborers were brought from India, and from 1845 to 1917 over 145,000 Indians came to Trinidad. Although they had five-year contracts, most stayed, altering the island's ethnic composition forever. The work they performed was brutal, the wages low, and the living conditions appalling.

In the second half of the nineteenth century Trinidad's social-ethnic structure acquired new layers. At the top were foreign-born whites (mostly British), then the locally born white Creoles (French, British, Spanish), followed by an Afro-Creole middle class (mostly mixed race, but blacks as well), then the working-class blacks and those of mixed race, and finally, the recent Indian (and Chinese) arrivals.

Initially, relations between Afro- and Indo-Trinidadians were cordial, but not exactly warm. But after 1880 the relationship became strained, as the competition for jobs became more intense. The opposition to new immigration was voiced by a new generation of colored and black politicians or leaders. Those who were in this middle class, or talented tenth, were teachers, lawyers, physicians, civil servants, druggists, printers, and journalists.

Post-emancipation Trinidad witnessed the emigration of "liberated Africans" freed by the British from slave ships of other European nations. In this manner almost 7,000 Africans (mostly Yorubas from Nigeria) arrived at the island between 1841 and 1861, and their religious and cultural impact on Trinidad would be significant (Wood 1968, 73–80).

M.M. Philip (1829–1888), who became mayor of Port of Spain in 1867, served as attorney general on several occasions and was the author of the first novel of the English-speaking Caribbean, *Emmanuel Appadocca* (1854). Another generation of public figures succeeded him, like Henry Albert Alcázar (1861–1930), Vincent Brown (1855–1904), and Edgar Maresse Smith (1860–1905).

J.J. Thomas (1841–1889), a self-taught schoolteacher deserves special mention. He wrote the first book on patois, *The Theory and Practice of Creole Gram-*

mar (1869), an important study on the island's vernacular that combines French, English, and African words. Later he published a response to a distinguished British historian, Anthony Froude, who had visited the West Indies and had written a vicious attack on black people of the area. Froude said that the Asian and African populations would not mix and he offered stereotypes of both to show why (Africans were spendthrifts, lazy, childlike, and promiscuous; Indians were thrifty, hardworking, calculating, and ascetic). Titled *Froudacity* (1889), a pun on the author's surname, Thomas's response was elegant and erudite, one of the West Indies' first essays that openly revealed the Eurocentric and racist views of the region.

There are two other important figures as well: Emmanuel Lazare (1864–1929) and C.P. David (1866–1923). David, who had been adopted by J.J. Thomas as a child, was the first black person to sit in the Legislative Council of Trinidad and Tobago; he was a militant voice for constitutional reform, which in his time did not allow for elected representatives. Like David, Lazare was a leader in political and legislative reform, an outspoken advocate for racial equality, and a true champion of the underdog. In 1897 the Trinidad Workingman's Association was created to unite black workers and colored professionals. It had some degree of success but was reshaped in 1934 by A.A. Cipriani (1875–1945), a white born of Corsican immigrants, into the Trinidad Labor Party.

Trinidad went through economic change during this period. Sugar production, while still supreme, was eclipsed by a boom in cocoa that lasted for fifty years (1870–1920), and then by the discovery of oil (1907–1909). Oil would subsequently transform the island, giving it a certain prosperity among Caribbean nations, even if that prosperity was not equally distributed.

World War I was a watershed for many African-Trinidadians, many of whom served in the Britsh army but were treated as second-class citizens. There was growing resentment of British colonial rule, labor unrest, and, despite the oil boom, economic stagnation in cocoa and sugar. Political reform was urgent, since only about 6 percent of the population could actually vote.

In the 1930s, the world economic depression hit Trinidad hard. Even with wages sinking, the oil industry continued to register handsome profits. Many oil workers resented policies that lowered wages and benefits while turning even greater profits, as well as the fact that whites had the cushier jobs while they were exposed to dangerous conditions: many did not have helmets, and they often had to work on slippery areas or inhale toxic fumes. Cipriani, now the ubiquitous mayor of Port of Spain, had lost his sway over the labor movement, and new leaders arose, such as A.C. Rienzi and Uriah "Buzz" Butler (1895–1977), a fiery mesmerizing orator who led the oil workers in a series of mass actions in 1937. Butler resisted arrest during a rally he was addressing, and when a riot broke out among oil workers, Butler fled. Later he turned himself in and spent two years in jail, but with the outbreak of World War II, the British kept him incarcerated until 1945. After the war Butler continued his involvement with trade unions and politics (and was one of the first to unite African-Trinidadian and Indo-Trinidadian workers), but soon he would be eclipsed by Eric Williams. Still, Butler's movement was a key element of Trinidadian nationalism that eventually led to independence, and June 19, the anniversary of the 1937 rebellion, is the island's Labor Day, and is referred to as Butler Day.

The 1930s also also saw a rise in Pan-Africanism, in part due to the influence of Marcus Garvey, but also due to the reaction to the West's lack of interest in helping Ethiopia when it was invaded by Mussolini's Italy in 1935. Black dockworkers refused to unload Italian ships, and support committees to aid Ethiopia were established. Pan-Africanism was not new to the island: H.S. Williams, a Trinidadian, was one of the organizers of the first Pan-African Congress in 1900. But it was George Padmore (1902–1959) and C.L.R. James (1901–1989) who helped shape it further in the thirties. Padmore was a revolutionary socialist who lived most of his life abroad and influenced many African students who later became heads of state. Padmore died in Ghana, a member of Kwame Nkrumah's government.

C.L.R. James was also a revolutionary activist, as well as a writer, essayist, and historian. One of the most fertile minds of the twentieth century, James's *Black Jacobins* (1938) is still an oft-quoted book on the history of Haiti, and his *Beyond the Boundary* (1962), is a classic study on cricket that reveals much about the race and class dimensions of colonial society in Trinidad and the West Indies. James lived for many years in the United States and also wrote on many U.S. topics such as Whitman, Melville, the Civil Rights movement, and Toni Morrison.

James's influence has been as great as Garvey's or Fanon's on many subsequent generations of intellectuals and activists, including Stokely Carmichael (1941–1998), who was born in Trinidad but immigrated to the United States, becoming a civil rights activist and author of the book *Black Power* (1967). Carmichael moved to Guinea and died there, after devoting his life to the Pan-African cause.

Trinidad and Tobago's oil production was central to the British and U.S. war effort. The United States built two bases during World War II and its influence on the island began to grow, prompting the famous calypso "Rum and Coca-Cola" that said: "Both mothers and daughters/Working for the Yankee dollar."

After the war, nationalist pressure began to mount. England, however, wanted to grant independence to the West Indies Federation, a ten-island federation created in 1958. When Jamaica withdrew in 1961, Trinidad and Tobago soon followed, becoming independent in 1962. The country had been guided to independence by another writer-activist, Eric Williams, its first prime minister.

TRINIDAD AS INDEPENDENT NATION (1962–2001)

Williams (1911–1981) was a brilliant scholar who wrote important books on Caribbean history, such as *Capitalism and Slavery* (1944); he was also a dominant force in Trinidad politics for over a quarter of a century, and ruled the country from 1962 to 1981. Founder of the People's National Movement (PNM) in 1955, Williams was a fiery orator and charismatic leader.

But his growing authoritarianism, the inability of the PNM to build a party that also incorporated the Indo-Trinidadian masses, and the persistence of poverty among most African-Trinidadians eroded his popularity. This became evident during the Black Power rebellion of 1970. Some were puzzled: why Black Power with a government that had black leaders? One historian remarked that "black men in power do not connote Black Power" (Millette 1995, 625–660). Clearly, many Afro-Trinidadians felt frustrated that those ruling in their name were not delivering on their promises of jobs, housing, and health care.

The protests and demonstrations lasted several months and ended with a state of emergency and the jailing of over seventy movement leaders. In the meantime, Indo-Trinidadian political clout was increasing, organized under its political party, the United National Congress (UNC), led by Basdeo Panday. Williams died in office in 1981.

But even after an oil boom in the seventies, Trinidad's economy faced difficulties again, particularly in 1982, after oil prices collapsed. By the late eighties 20 percent of the population lived under the poverty line (this percentage would double by 1997), and there had been an increase in crime and a huge increase in the prison population.

In 1990, a black Muslim group led by Yasim Abu Bakr (formerly Lennox Phillips) took over the parliament building and the state television station. They held Prime Minister A.N.R. Robinson and several cabinet ministers hostage. After tense negotiations they surrendered. Thirty people had been killed, another 500 injured. Again, Trinidad was being reminded of the frustrations of many black youths who felt their lives were senseless and out of control.

Since 1995, the UNC and its Indo-Trinidadian constituency have proved to be a central force in a coalition government with Basdeo Panday as prime minister. Many cabinet ministers are also Indo-Trinidadians. The Afro-Trinidadian dominance of the political system had been broken, even though Robinson is still the president.

RELIGIOUS BELIEFS AND PRACTICES

Because of almost three centuries of Spanish rule, the majority religion in Trinidad is Catholicism (34%), followed by Hinduism (26%), Anglicanism (14%), Islam (6%), Presbyterianism (4%), Pentecostalism (3%), Baptist (3%), and 10% other or no religion. As a whole, Trinidad's complex society is socially integrated, but with religion, matters are fairly segregated.

The one exception would be the Afro-Trinidadian religions such as Orisha and Spiritual Baptist. The latter, whose followers are known also as "Shouters," has believers who are more Protestant-oriented, others more Africanized. The

Shouters began in the early twentieth century, in the lower classes (mostly black). Their services were banned in Trinidad from 1917 to 1951. There is hymn singing (to receive the spirit), clapping (no drums), spirit possession (but only the Holy Spirit), rites of seclusion to become initiated (called "mourning"), and chalk markings on the floor, all reminiscent of West African religious traditions. There are compatibilities between the Spiritual Baptists and the Orisha religion, particularly in their vocal styles and repertoire (McDaniel 1998, 957).

Orisha is an incredibly syncretic and complex religion that is based on Yoruba religious beliefs, but it also has elements of Catholicism, Hinduism, Protestantism (Spiritual Baptist), and Jewish mysticism. Similar to Cuban Santería or Brazilian candomblé, it is a religion of spirits and belief in possession by those different spirits (or orishas) during ceremonies that include drumming, dancing, and ritual offerings. It also contains a strong healing component, supports a reverence for one's ancestors, and aims for its believers to harness the spirit of the orishas to help them in their day-to-day lives. The Orisha religion has grown more than tenfold since the 1960s. Many Orisha believers are also practicing Spiritual Baptists and Catholics. It is a constantly evolving religion, as seen by its incorporation of Hinduism and Jewish mysticism. Both the Orisha religion and Spiritual Baptists have an estimated 10,000 adherents each, but the figures are likely much higher, given the traditional prohibitions and secrecy that surround them.

CALYPSO, SOCA, AND CHUTNEY-SOCA

Trinidad has a rich musical tradition. Even before the popularity of calypso, the island had Afro-Caribbean rhythms like the *béle* (Trinidadian for belair, from the French *bel air*, or beautiful song) or the *kalenda*. The *béle* (also a drum) are dances stemming from the French-speaking islands of the Caribbean, as well as from St. Lucia, Grenada, and Carriacou. *Kalenda* is one of the oldest of the African dance styles and is associated with stick fighting, where a stick-wielding man would sing a boastful song before stepping into the ring (composed of a male chorus) and drummers. Otherwise, chantwells (singers) would sing the exploits of their fighter and insult the adversary: then, with long, light canes the two opponents would battle until blood was drawn. Like Brazilian *capoeira*, *kalenda* and stick fighting were both a martial art and a dance form.

Calypso grew out of the *béles*, the *kalenda*, French Creole songs, British ballads, Venezuelan music, and masquerade procession songs. Up until 1900 they were mostly sung in a French-influenced patois, but afterwards English was used. Calypso has had a long tradition of social commentary and satire, dealing with issues of racism, poverty, colonial subjection, and injustice. But equally it has been bawdy, mocking and sarcastic, and sometimes downright lewd (and sexist). Its popularity and its resistance to oppression, though, are undeniable: Britain censored calypsos in the thirties; currently, politicians use it in their campaigns; TV and radio use its alluring beat to sell products.

Some of the great early calypsonians were Attila the Hun (1892–1962), Lord Beginner, Roaring Lion (1909–), Mighty Destroyer, Lord Invader, Lord Melody, and Growling Tiger. Attila (Raymond Quevedo) not only was a master of the political calypso and fiercely denounced racial discrimination, but was also an elected member of Trinidad's Legislative Council, and remained there until he died. A newer generation of calypsonians followed: Lord Kitchener (1922–2000), Mighty Sparrow (1935–), Chalkdust, Black Stalin, Ras Shorty I, Cro Cro, and Calypso Rose, the first woman to be crowned Calypso Monarch, and she has been followed by Singing Sandra. But it was Mighty Sparrow who gave calypso an international status and popularity as social commentary, festive medium, and true poetic art form.

Calypso rhythms grew faster (and many lost their socially biting commentary) and became fused with soul and funk music and Indo-Trinidadian dance rhythms, becoming soca (or *sokha*). But not all soca is bereft of a critical edge with composers such as David Rudder (1961–) and Black Stalin. Calypso has also incorporated rap into its repertoire, becoming "rapso." Brother Resistance, a stellar soca-rapso star, sings trenchant songs on unemployment, hunger, and humiliation like "I Kyan Tek Dat."

It was a matter of time before a more Indianized soca (with chutney's *dholak* drums), often sung in Hindi, would create chutney-soca, a blazing fast and erotic Indo-Afro-Trinidadian dance form. Its popularity met with resistance from the Indo-Trinidadian community because chutney-soca has become part of Carnival, traditionally seen by Indo-Trinidadians as an Afro-Creole event. Traditionally, chutney had been performed in exclusively Indo-Trinidadian settings, and usually only among women. Some Indo-Trinidadians also fear that this musical "douglarization" implies Indo-Trinidadian assimilation into an Afro-Trinidadian identity.

These interethnic tensions go to the heart of the word *dougla*, a common word for a Trinidadian of mixed African and Indian ancestry. Trinidad's population is from 17 to 20 percent "mixed," and undoubtedly many of these are *dougla*. But it is a word with negative connotations, coming from the Hindi word for bastard. Most *dougla* do not use the word to describe themselves, or they deny their status by saying they are black or Indian. Fear of assimilation involves more than having reservations about ethnic intermarriage; it reveals beliefs that favor some types of segregation and conjures up some of the nineteenth-century attitudes expressed by Froude, and their pernicious and divisive legacy seems to have lasted until the twenty-first century.

CRICKET, CARNIVAL, AND CREATIVITY: TRINIDAD'S INGENUITY

Cricket was originally seen as quintessentially British, part of colonial society's three Cs: Cane, Church, and Cricket. It was an elite sport, played by the white planter class. When it was introduced to the West Indies it was clearly meant to be a symbol of high culture, civility, and morality and off limits to non-whites. But it became a popular sport among blacks and Afro-Creoles and eventually was a contested terrain where issues of race, class, and nationalism were expressed as West Indian players began to excel. Sir Learie Constantine (1901–1971) was not only one of the great players, but also the author of *Cricket and I* (1933), an important book that contributed to the struggle for civil rights, self-determination, and adult suffrage in Trinidad and the West Indies. The West Indies team defeated the British in England for the first time in 1950. Since then they have dominated the sport, and Trinidad has contributed many outstanding players, both African- and Indo-Trinidadian.

West Indian cricket has proved to be an example of how African-Caribbeans have both democratized, desegregated, and revolutionized a European sport, much like what has happened in the region's music. While conservative and radical tendencies have coexisted in cricket, the words of Vivian Richards, Antiguan star and former captain of the West Indian team, speak for many: "I believe very strongly in the black man asserting himself . . . I identify with black power, rastafarian and all the movements of black liberations. Once I was offered one million dollars to play cricket in South Africa, I could not go as long as the black majority in South Africa remained oppressed by the apartheid system . . . I would be letting down my own black people and I would destroy my sense of self-esteem. Cricket has always been politics and especially for us in the Caribbean" (Beckles 1994, 52–53).

Carnival is another example of how a European tradition has been transformed by African-Trinidadians. Established by French Creoles, only they and whites participated, usually by having masked balls. The free colored population also participated but under strict regulations. Slaves could not participate, but probably celebrated in secrecy. Emancipation brought ex-slaves out into the street and whites withdrew, hoping Carnival would die out. Instead, it became an Afro-European anti-slavery celebration with stick fighting assuming a prominent role. As authorities, fearing violence and disorder, became more repressive, riots erupted in 1881 and in 1884; as a result, both drums and the carrying of sticks were outlawed.

Ever creative, African-Trinidadians introduced bamboo bands and string orchestras from Venezuela, and from 1900 to 1930 they developed the calypso into a verbally sophisticated form, using words instead of sticks, "a reflection of the importance that many Trinidadians place on sharp wit and verbal dexterity, a useful metaphor for a country that often appears to rely on instinct and inspiration rather than long-term planning, coming through each crisis by the seat of its pants, yet with style into the bargain" (Mason 1998, 154). The wit and dexterity came in handy when British authorities censored calypso lyrics in the 1930s, for reasons of politics and obscenity.

A clear example of instinct, inspiration, and style is the steel drum, a unique Trinidadian creation, made in the late 1930s. The authorities despised them and outlawed their being played on the streets. With World War II and the banning of Carnival from 1942 to 1946, some hoped the steel drums would vanish. Instead, steel bands were formed by the hundreds and became popular the world over.

Another affirmation of Afro-Trinidadian roots came in the 1957 Carnival, when bandleader George Bailey (1935–1970) won Band of the Year award for "Back to Africa." Its significance was not just the theme, but that it was the first important band to portray Africans with richly colored, magnificent costumes instead of with the usual rags, tar, and dirt (Anthony 1997, 39).

Many have pointed out that Trinidad's Carnival is a national theater performed in the streets. This performativity has deep Afro-Caribbean roots (musically, verbally, socially, corporeally) and expresses the desires, fears, dreams, and aspirations of a whole society. If Carnival has been an Afro-Creole tradition, it is also changing, with a growing presence of Indo-Trinidadians. The popularity of chutney-soca has given many hope for a creative cultural "douglarization" that many say upholds the island's and Carnival's motto: "All o' we is one."

LITERATURE: CRITIQUE AND IDENTITY

Similar to Carnival and its musical output, Trinidad's literary and intellectual traditions are strong. Aside from C.L.R. James, there were other writers such as Alfred Mendes, C.A. Thomasos, and Ralph de Boissiere. Albert Gomes was a key writer-editor-publisher and although born of Portuguese parents he wrote an article, "Black Man," in 1931 that anticipated the Black Power rebellions of the sixties.

But it was Samuel Selvon (1923–1994), an Indo-Trinidadian novelist, who became well known for his *The Lonely Londoners* (1956), which was about black West Indian immigrants in Britain. Michael Anthony (1930–) and Earl Lovelace (1935–) are accomplished writers; Anthony has published eleven books of fiction and many historical works. Lovelace's novel *The Dragon Can't Dance* (1979) draws an intimate portrait of a poor neighborhood during Carnival, and his *Wine of Astonishment* (1982) chronicles a community of Spiritual Baptists during the time it was prohibited. Merle Hodge (1944–) wrote the acclaimed novel *Crick-Crack Monkey* (1970) and has long been involved in the struggle for women's rights in Trinidad.

One of the best-known writers from or associated with Trinidad is Derek Walcott (1930–). Walcott is from St. Lucia but lived and worked in Trinidad for many years, having been the founder and director of the Trinidad Theater Workshop from 1959 to 1976. A distinguished playwright, Walcott is best known for his exquisite, insightful poetry; he won the 1992 Nobel Prize for literature. Walcott also worked with Beryl McBurnie (1913–), one of the Caribbean's great dancers, who founded the Little Carib Theater in 1948. She did much to preserve Afro-Trinidadian dance traditions and was awarded the Trinity Cross, the nation's highest honor, in 1989.

CONCLUSION

Up to the 1960s, the Trinidadian economy centered around jobs that were divided up along racial lines: most Indo-Trinidadians lived in the countryside and labored on sugar estates or were farmers; most African-Trinidadians were in civil service, law, teaching, nursing, the police, and the army. Whites remained in control of the economy, as executives, managers, engineers. This changed after independence, when protests and social changes brought much greater economic and social mobility to the Indo-Trinidadian community, even if public patronage still gave African-Trinidadians an advantage in the political sphere. But this has changed since 1995; Indo-Trinidadians now control the government. But governing is difficult and social problems persist: unemployment is about 16 percent, there are many who are under the poverty line, and income inequality is pronounced. These social problems are acute among the Afro-Trinidadian lower and working classes.

Trinidad and Tobago is neither the multiracial paradise evoked by Carnival or tourist brochures, nor a completely fragmented society divided rigidly along racial, ethnic, and religious lines. The symbolic weight, still present in the *callaloo* or even the *pelau*,[2] used as a metaphor for the country's mixed ethnicities, is being outstripped by an increasingly complex reality. Not only the ingredients, but also the slow fire and sudden conflagrations of history are what give Trinidad its racial and cultural uniqueness, and make it a testing ground for how we look at citizenship, political power sharing, and cultural renewal in multiracial societies.

NOTES

1. *Callaloo* is a thick soup made of dasheen leaves, okra, pig's tail, crab, coconut milk, and green pepper. Afro-Trinidadians have also contributed *tooloom* and sugar cake (both made with coconut, molasses, and sugar), which provided energy during slavery.
2. *Pelau* is a rice dish with meat, vegetables, and fish that is similar to a paella.

REFERENCES

Anthony, Michael (1997). *Historical Dictionary of Trinidad and Tobago*. Lanham, MD: Scarecrow Press.

Beckles, Hilary (ed.) (1994). *An Area of Conquest: Popular Democracy and West Indies Cricket Supremacy*. Kingston, Jamaica: Ian Randle Publishers.

Brereton, Bridget (1981). *A History of Modern Trinidad: 1783–1962*. London: Heinemann.

Harney, Stefano (1996). *Nationalism and Identity: Culture and Imagination in the Caribbean Diaspora*. London: Zed Books.

James, C.L.R. (1992). *The C.L.R. James Reader*, ed. Anna Grimshaw. Oxford: Blackwell Publishers.

Manuel, Peter (1995). "Trinidad, Calypso, and Carnival." In Manuel, Bilby, Kenneth and Largey, Michael, *Caribbean Currents: Caribbean Music from Rumba to Reggae*. Philadelphia: Temple University Press, pp. 183–211.

Mason, Peter (1998). *Bacchanal! The Carnival Culture of Trinidad*. Latin America Bureau (London). Kingston, Jamaica: Ian Randle Publishers. Distributed by Temple University Press.

McDaniel, Lorna (1998). "Trinidad and Tobago." In Olsen, Dale A. and Daniel Sheehy (eds.), *The Garland Handbook of World Music, Volume 2*. New York: Garland Publishing, pp. 952–967.

Millette, James (1985/1970). *Society and Politics in Colonial Trinidad: 1783–1810*. London: Zed Books.

———(1995). "Guerrilla War in Trinidad 1970–1974." In Ryan, Selwyn and Taimoon Stewart (eds.), *The Black Power Revolution 1970: A Retrospective*. St. Augustine, Trinidad: Institute of Social and Economic Research.

Reddock, Rhoda (1994). *Women, Labour, and Politics in Trinidad and Tobago: A History*. London: Zed Books.

Ryan, Selwyn (1972). *Race and Nationalism in Trinidad and Tobago*. Toronto: University of Toronto Press.

Wood, Donald (1968). *Trinidad in Transition*. London: Oxford University Press.

Yelvington, Kevin A. (ed.) (1993). *Trinidad Ethnicity*. Knoxville: University of Tennessee Press.

15

The United States Virgin Islands

Jessica Suárez with Alan West-Durán

INTRODUCTION

Like its Caribbean neighbors, the United States Virgin Islands, by way of conquest, colonial imposition, purchase, slavery, interimperial rivalry, economic self-interest, and immigration, has become a political, economic, and cultural crossroads. For centuries, European countries vied for its resources, with the Dutch and British showing the most notable influence, followed by the Danish, French, and Spanish. The majority of its population is of West African origin and African-Caribbean immigrants from other islands in the eastern Caribbean. There are also immigrants from India, the Dominican Republic, Haiti, and the Middle East, as well as U.S. and Puerto Rican expatriates. All these presences have helped shape the Virgin Islands into an ever-changing and complex society, and they partly explain why native Virgin Islanders are no longer a majority in their homeland.

Though an African-Caribbean nation, the islands are formally part of the United States in its politics, legal system, and economy. The U.S. Virgin Islands comprises three islands with a total land mass of 133 square miles and a population of approximately 112,000. St. Croix is the largest island, with a population of 56,000, St. Thomas follows (52,000), and St. John is the smallest (3,500). Along with the British Virgin Islands they constitute the northernmost tip of the Lesser Antilles. St. Thomas and St. John, in close proximity to each other, are 50 miles east of the main island of Puerto Rico, and St. Croix is about 40 miles directly south from the other two Virgins. About 125 miles east begins a cluster of islands such as Anguilla, St. Martin/St. Maarten, Saba, St. Eustatius, St. Kitts-Nevis, Barbuda, and Antigua. These islands, along with Barbados, have played a significant role in Virgin Island history as a source of immigrant labor.

The racial makeup of the islands is approximately 80 percent black, 15 percent white, and 5 percent other. The native population is proportionately decreasing: although 74 percent of the total population is West Indian, 29 percent were born in the Virgin Islands and 45 percent were born elsewhere in the West Indies. The remaining 26 percent is made up of 13 percent from the United States mainland (mostly white), 5 percent from Puerto Rico, and 8 percent other, which includes Dominicans, Haitians, East Asians, Palestinians, and Jews.

Puerto Ricans and Dominicans are viewed differently; most Puerto Ricans are light skinned, while Dominicans are much darker. Virgin Islanders see the former sometimes as white at other times as black or nonwhite; Dominicans are referred to as black. The Indo-Caribbean population is considered black if they were born locally; otherwise they are classified as Asian or Indian (Sekou 2002b).

EARLY EUROPEAN INTERVENTION (1493–1733)

Christopher Columbus arrived in the Virgin Islands in 1493. The original indigenous peoples of the Virgin Islands were the Arawak Taínos and Caribs of whom there were probably 8,000 before the conquest. These peoples were decimated by the European arrivals in the sixteenth and seventeenth centuries.

While the islands were virtually deserted by the Spanish for over one hundred years after their "discovery," other Europeans began to inhabit the area in the 1600s. The islands were a haven for pirates, smugglers, and privateers. The harbor at Charlotte Amalie in St. Thomas is one of the world's finest. British and Dutch planters occupied St. Croix around 1625. The British drove out the Dutch, who went to St. Maarten and St. Eustatius, but the English were subsequently driven out by the Spanish, who would not tolerate a British presence so close to Puerto Rico.

The French expelled the Spanish and bought the island for the Knights of Malta in 1651. Despite spending lavish sums of money, drought and other factors made the French migrate to St. Domingue, and by 1713 they abandoned their claim to the island. In the meantime, Holland and Denmark began to commercially expand their interests in the area, particularly on St. Thomas, which by 1724 was a free port. The Danes operated through their Danish West India and Guinea Company, which was similar to their Dutch counterpart, the Dutch West Indies Company.

The growth of sugar and cotton plantations increased the need for slaves, and by 1686 St. Thomas's population was half slave; by 1720 almost nine out of ten inhabitants were slaves. Even tiny St. John had 109 plantations (most were not sugar) by 1733, when the islands were sold to the Danish West India Company. Most slaves brought to the Virgin Islands were from four areas: (1) "Mande-speaking Mandinga, Bambara and Kanga peoples who live in present-day Senegal, Gambia, and Mali; (2) the region of the Akan, Ewe, and Ga peoples in present-day Ghana, Togo, and Benin; (3) the southern part of Nigeria, home of the Ibo, Calabar, and Mokko peoples; and (4) the region of the Bacongo people around the lower Congo River and of the Loango people along the Atlantic coast north of the Congo estuary" (Lieth-Philipp 1993, 3).

DANISH OCCUPATION (1733–1917)

The Danish colonization of the Virgin Islands, which began in earnest in 1671, was fraught with trouble from the beginning. Prolonged drought and slave owner indifference to the feeding of their slaves caused many to become Maroons. As a result, harsh laws were passed to crack down on maroonage. Captured runaways would lose a leg or an ear; those who eluded capture for more than six months were executed. A slave or even freedmen who raised a hand to a white could lose their hand. In November of 1733, on St. John, a rebellion involving 150 slaves (out of 1,000) took over the island, killing many whites. The Danish government needed French troops from Martinique to quell the revolt, and it eventually took six months for the planter class to impose control. The revolt stopped the intensification of the plantation system in St. John and hastened the purchase of St. Croix from the French.

Eventually, the Danish replaced Company Rule with Crown Rule in 1754. At this time, a small number of white families owned nearly all of the land and property that was not already owned by the government. During this period the slave population of the three islands was about 90 percent of the population. However, in the case of the urban areas of St. Thomas and St. Croix, slaves were a majority. This urban environment, where many blacks worked in trades or as artisans, exhibited conditions of slavery less onerous than those on plantations.

Even more significant, by 1815 the free colored population roughly equaled that of whites, and by 1835 they outnumbered whites 3 to 1 on St. Thomas and St. Croix. In St. Thomas, one of every four people was free black or colored. One of those born to a middle-class family of free blacks was Edward Wilmot Blyden (1832–1912), of Ibo (Nigerian) descent. He went to the United States in 1850 seeking a college education, but he was denied entry because he was black. Blyden immigrated to Liberia, where he spent the rest of his life, shuttling back and forth between Sierra Leone and Liberia during his last thirty years. Blyden wrote about being black, the fate of Africa, and the importance for blacks to receive a non-Eurocentric education or practice non-Christian religions such as Islam. Feeling that whites would never accept black advancement, Blyden embraced his Africanness, was adamant about black self-improvement, and was vigilant in wanting to ensure the "purity" and moral integrity of their African values. He was also against racial mixing. Still, Blyden's cultivation of black pride, African cultural importance, and racial solidarity were decades ahead of the times. Blyden's writings were not only an inspiration for Caribbean pan-Africanists like Marcus Garvey, George Padmore, and C.L.R. James but also African leaders such as Leopold Senghor and Kwame Nkrumah.

Another important figure was Denmark Vesey (c.1767–1822), from St. Thomas (others claim he was born in Africa). Taken by his master to Haiti, then Charleston South Carolina, the polyglot and well-read Vesey bought his freedom, became a minister, and planned one of the largest slave uprisings (between 6,000 and 9,000 slaves were involved) in United States history. Denounced by fellow slaves, the rebellion was thwarted before hand. Vesey and thirty-four others were executed.

Maroonage or runaways remained a constant feature of the Virgin Islands. Although Maroons were never a huge percentage of the total slave population, they were significant because of the hope they gave to slaves and the apprehension they caused among the planter class. After clearing most of the wooded areas for plantations, Maroons took to the sea, going to Vieques, Culebra, and the main island of Puerto Rico. Even before the Danish took over there was a community of eighty Virgin Islanders east of San Juan who were free and owned land. In return, they functioned as an auxiliary militia. In 1750 a decree declared freedom for runaways who embraced Catholicism. The decree was more than religiously motivated: the runaways were a source of labor in an underpopulated country and they provided useful intelligence information about British, Danish, and Dutch military activity.

The Danish authorities passed strict laws about boat-building and usage, but ships were still pirated by slaves. Given the presence of a sizeable urban black and colored population, much of it free, field slaves also escaped into these anonymous urban environments. With British emancipation (1834–1838), the nearby British Virgin Islands was an irresistible magnet for runaways. The island of Tortola is a mere two miles from St. John.

By 1841, free elementary education was granted to all free and slave residents. A further step toward emancipation was taken with the 1847 decree to end slavery in the Danish Virgin Islands by 1859. However, this timeline was accelerated by an 1848 slave uprising in Frederiksted (St. Croix). John "Buddhoe" Gottlieb, Robert Moses, and Martin King led this revolt by sacking houses, sending whites fleeing to ships in the harbor. In only a day 8,000 slaves (about half of the entire slave population) had converged on Frederiksted. Some slaves were armed, most were not. Soon after, Governor-General von Scholten declared all slaves free. At the time of emancipation, half of St. Thomas's blacks were already free, while most blacks from St. Croix were still tied to estate serfdom (Lewis, 1972, 216). Unlike similar events in Barbados, Guyana, and Jamaica, the events were bloodless (although there was subsequent violence with rebel skirmishes and heavy-handed retaliation by the government).

Like the planter class in the rest of the Caribbean, the planter class in the Virgin Islands tried to keep their labor force on their estates through various coercive means. In the thirty years following abolition, the planters of St. Croix created the Labor Codes that tied the ex-slaves to the plantations and made it almost impossible for a cane worker to publicly complain without being imprisoned. However, some Virgin Islanders immigrated to Puerto Rico and Tortola. The planters then did what planters did elsewhere in the West Indies: they imported indentured laborers from India, but mostly from Barbados, St. Kitts, the Dutch Antilles, and Antigua.

In the 1870s drought and a reduction in sugar prices greatly affected the Crucian economy. Planters wanted to lower wages. Many immigrant workers wanted to return to their native lands, but regulations and high fees to emigrate kept them trapped on St. Croix. Native workers on St. Croix were similarly restricted. Violence erupted in 1878, in order to bring about full legal workplace freedom for the population. The rebellion, known as "Fireburn," resulted in between 90 and 250 killed and more than 400 imprisoned. Many of the leaders were immigrants, like Thomas Graydon (Barbados), Henry Adams (St. Eustatius), and Joseph Harrison (Jamaica). The best known was Mary Thomas, who had come from Antigua and was immortalized in legend and song as "Queen Mary." A national heroine today, Thomas's role points to a larger presence of women in the workforce, which is still true today.

As the post-emancipation years (1848–1917) saw sugar production become less profitable, or collapse, many black laborers immigrated to the other islands. Between 1835 and 1911 the population of the Virgin Islands dropped by a third. Racial segregation was still strong, particularly in education and the churches. Whites held both economic and political power. After "Fireburn," regulations were passed to constrain black conduct in public, like whistling or singing out loud. Finding the islands an economic burden, the Danish government sought to sell them. It began negotiations with the United States as far back as 1865, but it would take more than fifty years to conclude the sale (Rogozinski 2000, 215–216).

Despite flying the Danish flag and being under Danish law, the British were the most numerous of the planter class, and the Danes were a tiny majority. St. Thomas's growing commercial activity was with the United States. The Danes had never truly "Danified" the islands the way Britain, Spain, and France culturally "nationalized" their colonies. Post-emancipation society was said to be "economically American and linguistically English" (Lewis 1972, 32).

In the last years of Danish rule the islands were in dismal straits: unemployment was high, wages were low, and health conditions were appalling. A Danish doctor claimed that malnutrition between 1909 and 1913 was so severe that two-thirds of the children between one and five died (St. Croix). One of the figures who fought these and other injustices was David Hamilton Jackson (1884–1949). He was the founder of the first West Indian trade union, and as a journalist he was also the creator of the island's first uncensored paper, where he denounced the police brutality, labor abuses, and cultural desolation that beset the black majority.

UNITED STATES TERRITORIAL STATUS (1917–PRESENT)

In 1917, the United States purchased the Virgin Islands for $25 million in order to prevent Germany from gaining control over them during World War I. Still, it took ten years before islanders received U.S. citizenship (1927). As a part of the United States, Virgin Islanders could freely choose to go to the United States, and some 20,000 did between 1917 and 1930, mostly settling in Harlem. One prominent Virgin Islander was businessman Casper Holstein, who used his wealth to finance college scholarships for Virgin Islanders and lobby Congress in Washington for greater self-government for the islands.

The U.S. Navy governed the island until 1931, when a civilian governor was appointed by the United States. The successive Navy-appointed governors (1917–1931) were blatant white supremacists, and the islands were still living in abject poverty. In the early thirties the Virgin Islands was still rural, with over 80 percent of workers still involved in agriculture. But New Deal reforms enacted by the U.S. federal government (1933–1935) promoted homesteading, that is, the purchase of land and homes for the local population during the hard times of the Depression. Important progress was also made in infrastructure, health care, and hygiene.

The islands, still governed by a small white elite, "was a social system of alternating privilege and poverty based on a dual value pattern of class and color, not always readily distinguishable one from the other" (Lewis 1972, 101). A local schoolteacher, J. Antonio Jarvis (1901–1963) published *The Virgin Islands and Their People* (1944), in which he not only addressed these issues but also discussed with frankness lower-class beliefs, particularly Obeah (see Religion). The local Legislative Assembly passed a resolution condemning the book as immoral and stripped Jarvis of his teaching position. Clearly, local society was not yet ready to openly discuss race and class issues, since this would contradict the image it wanted to present of a multiracial, harmonious country.

The Virgin Islands took a major step toward self-government with the Organic Act of 1936. This act allowed for more governmental representation and local power. The right to vote was extended to all citizens meeting a literacy requirement (except for U.S. federal elections). However, this literacy stipulation rendered many locals unable to vote, since they were unable to meet the requirements. Furthermore, all of the rights of the U.S. Constitution were extended to the Virgin Islands except for indictment by a grand jury. Finally, any federal taxes collected in the Virgin Islands would be used in their local government. This act was again modified under the Revised Organic Act of 1954, which granted the Virgin Islands unincorporated territory status. Some claim that this status was granted in order to reassure certain members of Congress that the Virgin Islands would not become a state (Phillips 1991, 3).

The first black governor was appointed by President Truman. William Hastie ruled from 1946 to 1949. Hastie was a distinguished legal scholar from the United States but was married to a Virgin Islander. Two other nonlocal black governors were appointed, Archie Alexander (1954–1955), and Walter A. Gordon (1955–1958).

By 1971, the Virgin Islands had their first elected black governor, Dr. Melvin Evans, and by 1977 the United States realized that the "unincorporated status" of the islands was insufficient and that they needed greater autonomy and decision-making powers. Today, the Virgin Islands has only one nonvoting representative in Congress, and they cannot vote for the president or vice president of the United States. Therefore, the Virgin Islands is not nationally represented in the U.S. Congress.

The sixties are known as the "Development Decade" in the Virgin Islands. First, tourism boomed, going from 200,000 visitors in 1960 to 1.5 million in 1970, growing annually by a phenomenal 18 percent. By 1970, tourism employed almost one-half of the population and generated 60 percent of the islands' income (Boyer 1983, 278). Second, this decade brought about the introduction of heavy industry to the islands, specifically, oil refining in St. Croix. Third, like their fellow Caribbean island Puerto Rico, the Virgin Islands established tax incentives to attract mainland investment. Also of note during this decade was the large influx of Puerto Ricans, mostly to St. Croix, where they now constitute a significant minority of the population.

RACIAL TENSION AND UNREST

The Virgin Islands went through radical ethnic and economic changes in the 1960s. A historian said that "Virgin Islands social life can be seen as a series of concentric circles, both of social and ethnic groups, that surround but only marginally touch each other" (Lewis 1972, 166). Aside from the locals or natives, who are overwhelmingly black, there are the "continentals," mostly from the United States, almost all of them white. There is a small French population that has been on the island for centuries, a large Puerto Rican population, and an even larger West Indian population from the other islands.

Natives began to feel like they were becoming a minority, which is now demographically true. The tensions are not just among the white stratum and the black working majority. It is also between browns and blacks, "native" blacks and "immigrant" blacks, locals and tourists, and with Puerto Ricans, notwithstanding an official holiday that commemorates Puerto Rico Friendship Day (held on Columbus Day). On the minority status of the natives, aliens, Puerto Ricans, and continentals, "[i]t is evident that by the end of the 1960s the Virgin Islands had become a troubled homeland for aliens [Eastern Caribbeans] and the alienated [native Virgin islanders]" (Boyer 1983, 282).

There was a profound demographic shift from 1950 to 1970: emigrants from the Eastern Caribbean went from 3 percent to 30 percent of the population, continentals went from 6 percent to 14 percent, and there was a steady source of Puerto Rican immigrants. In twenty years native Virgin Islanders had gone from being 74 percent of the population to 37 percent, a startling change by any standards.

During the late 1960s, black militants organized a group at the College of the Virgin Islands. Led by Mario Moorhead, they called for the removal of all forms of white exploitation of blacks, unification of all black peoples in the Caribbean, and independence for the Virgin Islands.

In 1968, the Alien Interest Movement (AIM) was formed to protect and promote the interests of black Caribbean workers in the Virgin Islands. The issues addressed by the group included the grievance that natives did not want to take menial or poorly paying service jobs, especially in tourism, and so these usually fell to the aliens. The natives preferred government, civil service, professional, and administrative jobs, virtually excluding the immigrant population from these positions.

At this time, acting on reports that drew attention to possible social unrest, the Nixon administration appointed the island's first black governor, Melvin Evans. Evans was elected in 1970.

A sore issue between blacks and whites was the sale of beaches to individual property owners. These property owners were most frequently white, and this created resentment among the natives who were no longer able to use these areas. Moreover, crime issues were becoming increasingly "racialized." In 1970, with the black power movement gaining momentum and black-on-white crime increasing, many were concerned that the racial uprisings in the United States would be repeated locally. Much of this crime was also blamed on Rastafarianism, despite their small following, which was a way for Virgin Islanders to say that crime was "foreign."

The most dramatic example of these racial tensions culminated in the Fountain Valley Golf Course killings of 1972. At an exclusive resort, five blacks killed seven whites and one black person. The perpetrators claimed it was a revolutionary act to eliminate "the alien white ruling class" (Boyer 1983, 313). The media attention this received in the United States was extraordinary. The myth of the "tropical vacation paradise" had been shattered by this violent episode and set back the tourist industry on the island for five years.

Despite this history of tensions and politicians sometimes using them for their own gain, much has changed over thirty years, with a much greater degree of interethnic tolerance and cooperation. There have been many more interethnic marriages and some degree of social mobility that has defused some of the economic resentments of the past. African-Caribbean Islanders are proud of their roots (Sekou 2002b).

EDUCATION

Although the U.S. Virgin Islands now have high rates of literacy, educational opportunities are not equally distributed, and the quality is uneven. Furthermore, there was an increasing amount of violence in the public schools, overcrowding, and underpaid teachers. Schools were virtually segregated along racial, ethnic, and class lines. Blacks and Puerto Ricans made up the majority of the public school population, while whites and browns were largely found in the more prestigious private schools.

However, the local university, chartered in 1962, is an excellent liberal arts college. With more than 3,000 local and Caribbean students enrolled, it achieved university status in 1986 and was named one of the outstanding black colleges by the U.S. congress in that same year. The University of the Virgin Islands also publishes a respected and influential literary journal, "The Caribbean Writer," that aside from local authors and artists publishes authors from the Spanish-, French-, English-, and Dutch-speaking Caribbean.

Education is an important issue in the Virgin Islands: in a recent poll 60 percent stated that it was the highest priority of the government (a distant second was crime, at 15 percent) (Day 2002). Its importance is not only local but national; the Virgin Islands economy cannot absorb all its high school and college graduates. Many islanders must seek work in the United States, a highly competitive and increasingly technical marketplace that requires considerable preparation. Three high schools recently lost accreditation (the fourth is not accredited). Students are significantly below national averages in reading and math, budget limitations have hampered the hiring of substitute teachers, and a majority of teachers are not certified. Forty percent of adults on the island do not have a high school education (Moore 2002). Dropout rates have decreased by half since 2000, but overall public school enrollment has decreased by 15 percent in the last decade (Moore 2002).

Poverty affects educational achievement, and while recent events show that the economy has benefited many, others have been left behind. A recent study showed that 27 percent of the territory lived below the federal poverty line ($21,000 for a family of five), more than double the national rate of 12 percent (Day 2002). However, that does not factor in the higher cost of living in the Virgin Islands, 25 percent higher than on the mainland. Otherwise the figure would be close to forty percent of the population under the poverty line, with a proposed cut in welfare benefits that is ominous (Sekou 2002a). The brunt of that poverty is borne by black Virgin Islanders or their brethren from the Eastern Caribbean.

RELIGION

The Virgin Islands is an extremely religious society. Even in times of slavery, most of the enslaved were baptized (unusual for the West Indies), even though "[i]t is true that all of the churches compromised on the issue of slavery" (Lewis 1972, 265). Though baptism figures under colonial slavery were often exaggerated, the figures for the Danish West Indies are high: in 1835 they ranged from 84 percent in St. John to 99 percent in St. Croix. Even if the real figures were half the amount it would be extraordinary. The Moravians, Lutherans, Anglicans, Presbyterians, and Catholics were the main denominations, and their missionary work was quite successful. This might also explain the lack of Native Baptists, Revivalists, and other Afro-Christian syncretic religions that characterize Jamaica, Cuba, Trinidad, and other islands in the Caribbean.

Religious discrimination was virtually unknown throughout the islands; however, some denominations are predominantly black, like the Seventh-Day Adventists, Lutherans, and Methodists. Some churches are active in social causes: for instance, the Seventh-Day Adventists have offered much aid for the education of African-Caribbean immigrants since the 1960s. By 2000, the religious population was 42 percent Protestant (Moravian, Lutheran, Dutch Reform, Baptist), 34 percent Catholic, 17 percent Episcopalian, and 7 percent other (CIA Factbook webpage). Obeah, of West African origins, is a belief in spirits and the use of love potions, charms, and herbs to control those spirits (magic). Some say that it still persists, but it is difficult to ascertain how prevalent it is, since its low social prestige—with class and race connotations—make those who practice it not admit to it publicly. Others deny its existence altogether.

CULTURE

Little remains of the original Taíno-Arawak mixed with Carib culture in the present-day Virgin Islands. The islands are steeped in West Indian traditions and folklore, despite the huge American influence. There is a great cultural affinity with the Eastern Caribbean, which can be seen in the celebration of Carnival, the use of steel bands and calypso and the popularity of cricket and soccer (although baseball and basketball are more widely played), as well as certain foods and drink.

Carnival is an eagerly anticipated event throughout the islands. Each island has its own celebration, St. Croix in December, St. John on the Fourth of July, and St. Thomas in April. The Carnival tradition, influenced by Trinidad, began in 1912, organized by white and near-white elites. During World War I it was suspended and was not revived until 1952, in order to bolster tourism.

Today, Carnival includes music competitions, food fairs specializing in West Indian food, floats, and colorful costumes. "Moko Jumbie, the traditional symbol of Carnival, is the 'elevated spirit' on 10 to 20 foot stilts, dressed in bright colors that you see throughout the parade. The moko jumbie origins are deeply embedded in the traditions of West Africa" (Virgin Isles webpage).

Carnival has also been the site of tensions between continentals and natives. The former, despite their best intentions, have sometimes insensitively participated in Carnival, bringing in "Americanized" elements. In 1986 and 1987, violent incidents brought these tensions to the fore. At a time when native islanders were feeling that they were an embattled minority, Carnival appeared as one of those areas where local culture was threatened and had to assert itself.

The musical culture of the Virgin Islands is as diverse as its ethnicities: reggae, soca, calypso, merengue, and salsa are extremely popular, as are soul, pop, and hip-hop from the United States. The islands also have traditional musical genres, but they are not as popular as soca or merengue and are usually heard only in folkloric presentations. Traditional Scratch bands exist (also called fungi bands after a staple food of pasty cornmeal). Scratch bands usually feature a hollowed-out gourd that is scraped (or "scratched"), called a squash; a melodic instrument such as a violin, flute, or accordion; percussion (drums, triangle); and a guitar or banjo for rhythmic sustenance. For bass, either a bass guitar or a car exhaust tube blown with the lips, like a tuba, is used. *Cariso* and *quelbey* are popular song genres that comment on local topics and politics and are often spiced with sexual innuendo. *Cariso*, a forerunner of calypso, relied more on drumming and call-and-response and traditionally were only sung by women. *Bamboula*, which is like *cariso*, of Ashanti origin, is an extinct but reconstructed musical form, with two drums (one played with two sticks and the other with the hands), a lead singer, and a chorus. It is similar to the Puerto Rican bomba. The traditional folk dance of the Virgin Islands is the Quadrille, derived from European salon dancing and Afro-Caribbean influences. Dating from the eighteenth century, it is a figure dance with the partners dancing apart.

Some important visual artists who explore local themes or history are Ademola Olugebefola (1941–) and Roy Lawaetz (1942–). Olugebefola's work is cosmically oriented, revealing the interconnectedness of all elements that inhabit the universe. Lawaetz, born in St. Croix, has achieved world renown for his "Modular Triangular System." He paints only on triangular surfaces placed together to create nonrectangular or square forms, the latter considered by the artist as European forms. The triangular shapes are inspired by Taíno sacred Zemi figures, but visually and thematically he also draws on Afro-Caribbean lore. Despite this local creativity, according to the Arts Council, by the 1960s, the majority of those involved in the arts were continentals.

Although English is the official language, as in much of the Caribbean, the Virgin Islands evolved Creoles from European and African languages. On the islands of St. Thomas and St. John the Creole slaves and freedmen spoke a Dutch creole until about 1830, when English was introduced. On St. Croix the Creole was English, inflected because the landowners and businesses elites were Scottish and Irish; this Creole is similar to that spoken in Jamaica, Antigua, and Montserrat. Spanish is also widely spoken because of the large Puerto Rican presence on St. Croix.

THE STATUS OF WOMEN

During the time of slavery on the islands, "women vendors from the towns formed part of the aristocracy of servitude, enjoying latitude, mobility, flexibility in their working arrangements, and opportunities to handle on trust sums of cash that were sometimes substantial" (Hall 2000, 448). This flexibility within their environment made them key figures in helping other slaves escape. They were allowed the freedom to gather information about their surroundings that would be imperative to many escape attempts. Historically, women have been part of the workforce, and women were leaders in the labor unrest of 1878 and 1892.

In the last decades almost all women in the Virgin Islands work profession-ally, usually in clerical, service, and tourist industries. About two-thirds of women have children at home, making day care a necessity, but demand far out-strips supply.

Today, women in the Virgin Islands have created a number of organizations to benefit other women, including abuse assistance groups and the Women's Business Center, established in 1999 to promote and offer support to women in the business sector of the community.

Women have also excelled in other areas: Barbara T. Christian (1943–2000) was an outstanding scholar and teacher, pioneering studies on African-American women writers, and she became the first black scholar to become full professor in the University of California system (1986).

Despite these advances, issues of domestic violence, rape, and child sexual abuse are widespread and now publicly discussed. More than thirty women have been killed in the last decade because of domestic violence, and between 1999 and 2001 60 percent of sexual assault cases were against children between 6 and 17 years of age (Morris & Greaux 2001).

A recent initiative to revive the Commission on the Status of Women, cre-ated in 1966, has drawn cautious praise because of scant funding and the possi-bility that it might be window dressing.

CONCLUSION: POLITICS, CULTURAL IDENTITY, NATIVE MINORITY STATUS

The political environment in the Virgin Islands has been characterized by a struggle for greater autonomy. Despite the existence of several political parties—where almost all of the major candidates are local and black—they are usually more personality-driven, making the political distinctions between them almost indistinguishable and party labels virtually meaningless.

The independence movement has never been particularly strong. A 1993 ref-erendum produced 80 percent support for the current status and only 5 percent favoring independence. However, less than 30 percent voted, invalidating the re-sults. The House of Representatives is considering measures for enlarging the self-government of the islands.

The U.S. Virgin Islands has one of the highest standards of living of the Ca-ribbean and low unemployment (about 6 percent), not only making it an eco-nomic magnet for other Caribbean countries but also reinforcing a perception—not always accurate—in the region that associates independence with poverty and nonindependence with higher standards of living. However, its economy was in a recession for most of the 1980s.

The 1990s saw the island affected by natural disasters as well: major hurri-canes in 1989, 1995, 1996, and 1998 caused major damage in every case. Not surprisingly, the island has two holidays that address this threat: Hurricane Supplication Day in July and Thanksgiving Day in mid-October, which gives thanks for the end of the hurricane season.

Tourism has dominated the recent economy of the Virgin Islands, making up more than 70 percent of the gross domestic product and 70 percent of the total employment on the islands. The tourist industry usually brings in two million tourists per year to St. Thomas, St. John, and St. Croix (CIA Factbook webpage). But it is both boon and bane: on St. John three-quarters of the island is a national park, which has left St. Johnians feeling that there is little land for development and that the island belongs more to the U.S. National Park Service than to them. Meanwhile real estate prices are soaring.

Tourism has created its own problems, however. Many scholars have pointed out that anywhere from 60 to 80 percent of tourist dollars wind up back in the United States. Tourism also can bring about environmental degradation, since tourists consume water and electricity at far greater rates than locals and businesses that cater to visitors often dump their wastes in the ocean. The vulnerability of tourism was proven by a recent cruise line canceling its stops at St. Croix, at a cost of 40 million in revenue.

Also, tourism, whether it has a sexual purpose or not, reinforces racial and sexual stereotypes about the Caribbean. Most Caribbean sex workers, male or female, are usually dark skinned, and even if they are mixed parentage (lighter skinned), the women (or men) still embody the fantasy of the sexualized, "natural," other for white travelers. In this the Virgin Islands is no exception to the rest of the Caribbean, particularly since it has many (often illegal) immigrants from other islands of the region.

The U.S. Virgin Islands face dilemmas similar to those of other non-independent islands of the Caribbean: high standards of living and dependency on a metropolitan power, an opening up to the world and a loss of sovereignty (especially on immigration), cultural plurality (and imposition), and the loss of local culture. Some claim that while U.S. largesse feeds, clothes, and educates everyone, as a people Virgin Islanders are "disappearing." Virgin Islanders face a triple loyalty that is not always complementary: being native Virgin Islanders, West Indians, and citizens of the United States. The challenge is in how it handles this triple identity; if it can manage this triangulation less as a restraint and more as a resource for change and development, perhaps it can fashion a new sense of nationhood.

REFERENCES

Boyer, William W. (1983). *America's Virgin Islands: A History of Human Rights and Wrongs*. Durham: Carolina Academic Press.

Day, Jim (2002). "V.I. Polls Look at Public Policy Views, Poverty." In *St. Thomas Source*, June 4 (poll conducted by the University of the Virgin Islands).

de Albuquerque, Klaus. (1990). "'Is We Carnival': Cultural Traditions under Stress in the U.S. Virgin Islands." In Lent, John (ed.), *Caribbean Popular Culture*. Bowling Green, OH: Bowling Green State University Press.

Dookhan, Isaac (1974). *A History of the Virgin Islands of the U.S.* Epping: Caribbean Universities Press for the College of the Virgin Islands.

Gilmore, John (2000). *Faces of the Caribbean.* New York: Monthly Review Press.

Hall, Neville A.T. (1985). *Empire Without Dominion: Denmark and Her West Indian Colonies,* St. Croix, Virgin Islands: Bureau of Libraries, Museums, and Archeological Services.

———(1992). *Slave Society in the Danish West Indies: St. Thomas, St. John and St. Croix,* ed. B.W. Higman. Baltimore: Johns Hopkins University Press.

———(2000). "Slavery in Three West Indian Towns." In Shepherd, Verene and Hilary McD. Beckles (eds.), *Caribbean Slavery in the Atlantic World.* Kingston, Jamaica: Ian Randle Publishers.

Lewis, Gordon K. (1972). *The Virgin Islands: A Caribbean Lilliput.* Evanston, IL: Northwestern University Press.

Lieth-Philipp, Margaret (1993). "Music and Folklore in the U.S. Virgin Islands." Booklet accompanying CD, *Zoop, Zoop, Zoop: Traditional Music and Folkore of St. Croix, St. Thomas and St. John.* New York: New World Records 80427-2.

Moore, Richard (2002). "Challenge of Public Education is to Educate." In *St. Thomas Source,* May 12.

Morris, Molly and Jean P. Greaux (2001). "Domestic Violence, Rape Focus of Demonstration." In *St. Thomas Source,* March 24.

Olwig, Karen Fog (1985). *Cultural Adaptation and Resistance on St. John: Three Centuries of Afro-Caribbean Life.* Gainesville: University Press of Florida.

Phillips, Dion E. (1991). "The U.S. 'Special Relationship' with the Virgin Islands: Definition and Prospects for Independence." In Lipsowski, J. (ed.), *Caribbean Perspectives: Social Structure of a Region.* New Brunswick, NJ: Transaction Publishers.

Rogozinski, Jan (2000). *A Brief History of the Caribbean.* New York: Penguin.

Sekou, Malik (2002a). "Voters, You Must beware of the 'Monsters' that Stalk Us." In *The Virgin Island Daily News,* July 15 (editorial page).

———(2002b). Personal communication with authors.

Shepherd, Verene, B. Brereton, and B. Bailey (eds.) (1995). *Engendering History: Caribbean Women in Historical Perspective.* New York: St. Martin's Press.

Williams, Eric. (1984). *From Columbus to Castro: History of the Caribbean 1492–1969.* New York: Vintage Books.

http://www.cia.gov/cia/publications/factbook/geos/vq.h

http://www.virginisles.com

http://www.dailynews.vi/

http://new.onepaper.com/stthomasvi/

Appendix

Table 1.
Political Status of Caribbean Countries

Country	Political Status
Spanish-Speaking Caribbean	
Cuba	Independent (1902)
Dominican Republic	Independent (1844/1865)
Puerto Rico	U.S. Commonwealth (1952)*
French-Speaking Caribbean	
Haiti	Independent (1804)
Martinique	Overseas department of France (1946)
Guadeloupe	Overseas department of France (1946)
St. Martin	Administrative district of Guadeloupe (1946)
St. Barthélemy	Administrative district of Guadeloupe (1946)
French Guiana	Overseas department of France (1946)
Dutch-Speaking Caribbean	
Suriname	Independent (1975)
Curaçao	Member of Netherlands Antilles (1954)
Bonaire	Member of Netherlands Antilles (1954)
St. Eustatius	Member of Netherlands Antilles (1954)
Saba	Member of Netherlands Antilles (1954)
Aruba	Member of Kingdom of the Netherlands (1986)
St. Maarten	Member of Kingdom of the Netherlands (2000)

(continued)

Table 1.
(continued)

Country	Political Status
English-Speaking Caribbean	
Jamaica	Independent (1962)
Trinidad and Tobago	Independent (1962)
Barbados	Independent (1966)
Guyana	Independent (1966)
The Bahamas	Independent (1973)
Grenada	Independent (1974)
St. Lucia	Independent (1977)
Dominica	Independent (1978)
St. Vincent and The Grenadines	Independent (1979)
Antigua and Barbuda	Independent (1981)
Belize	Independent (1981)
St. Kitts and Nevis	Independent (1983)
Montserrat	British Associated Territory (1966)
British Virgin Islands	British Associated Territory (1967)
Cayman Islands	British Associated Territory (1972)
Turks and Caicos	British Associated Territory (1976)
Anguilla	British Associated Territory (1982)
U.S. Virgin Islands	U.S. Territory w/local self-gvt. (1968)

*Many in Puerto Rico argue that "freely associated state" is a euphemism for colony.

Table 2.
Trans-Atlantic Slave Trade (Total 11.569 Million)*

Region of Departure	Percentage of Trade
(I) West Central Africa (Angola, Congo, Gabon, Zaire)	38.4
(II) Bight of Biafra (Cameroon, Central African Republic, Equatorial Guinea, parts of Nigeria)	17.0
(III) Bight of Benin (Benin, Togo, parts of Nigeria)	18.0
(IV) Gold Coast (Ghana, Burkina Faso, Mali)	9.1
(V) Sierra Leone-Windward Coast (Liberia, Ivory Coast, Sierra Leone, Mali)	7.0
(VI) Senegambia (Guinea, Guinea-Bissau, The Gambia, Senegal)	5.0
(VII) Southeast Africa (Mozambique, Tanzania, Swaziland)	4.5

*Figures based on David Eltis, *The Transatlantic Slave Trade: A Database on CD-ROM* (1999), and taken from Appiah, K.A., and H.L. Gates (eds.), *Africana* (1999), p. 1867.

Afro-Caribbean Glossary

Animism: the belief that natural phenomena and objects like rocks and trees are alive and have souls. Afro-Caribbean religions are often incorrectly referred to as animistic.

Arawak-Taíno: name of people and language of Amerindian tribes who inhabited the Caribbean islands before European arrival (see also Caribs).

Béké: French Caribbean Creole expression that means whites, but it also implies belonging to the oldest and wealthiest families, a closed, elite circle.

Bozales: slaves who couldn't speak Spanish.

Burru or buru: Jamaican drums, style of drumming, and also a masquerade celebration by slaves and currently by Afro-Jamaicans (see also *Junkanoo*).

Callaloo: succulent national dish of Trinidad and Tobago, a thick soup with many types of ingredients, and a metaphor for the country's mix of African, European, East Asian, and Chinese races and cultures.

Caribs: the other major Amerindian group to inhabit the Caribbean and source for the word "Caribbean." They were often negatively compared with the "peace-loving" Arawak-Taínos as being warlike and "cannibalistic."

Caste system: racial hierarchy set up by Spaniards during their colonial system to maintain "purity of blood." Often it was ignored; not equivalent to castes in India.

Cimarrón: runaway slave, origin of the word "Maroon."

Creole: from the Spanish word "criollo." Can mean a person born in the New World, regardless of race; or in the case of the English-, French-, and Dutch-speaking Caribbean, a lighter skinned mixed-race person. Sometimes Afro-Creole is used.

Creole: languages spoken in the Caribbean mixing European, African, and other languages. There are French-, English-, Dutch-, Portuguese-, and Spanish-based creoles spoken.

Creolization: refers not only to racial mixing but to mixtures of languages, music, religions, and cultures unique to the Caribbean, like Carnival, Santería, or danzón (see also *Transculturation, Syncretic*).

Danzón/danza: Cuban musical and dance form that combines European and African elements, precursor of the cha-cha-cha. Called "danza" in Puerto Rico (see Introduction).

Département: French politico-juridical status equivalent to a state in the United States Guadeloupe, Martinique, and French Guiana are known as overseas departments. They participate in French national elections and can immigrate freely to France.

Dougla: racially mixed person from Trinidad, of African and East Asian descent.

Encomienda: system of land grants offered by the Spanish Crown that included Indian labor. When they were abolished in 1542, the importation of enslaved Africans increased.

Espíritos: literally, spirits, from the Spanish.

Garveyism: refers to the ideas of Marcus Garvey (1887–1940), of black self-help, racial pride, defense of African dignity and independence, and black repatriation to Africa.

Hateros: farmers in the Dominican Republic (from the word "hato," which means farm).

Jíbaro: refers to country or mountain dwellers in Puerto Rico, and symbolically to an emblem of national pride and culture.

Junkanoo or Jonkunnu: type of music and celebration with parades in the Bahamas during Christmas, played on goombay drums. In Jamaica known as "Jonkunnu."

Kumina: type of drum or drumming style. Congolese tribe and religious beliefs that are part of Afro-Jamaican culture.

Ladinos: term use to designate slaves who could speak Spanish.

Maroons: slaves who escaped from plantations or their masters and established settlements, living in freedom, usually with greater retention of African culture (see Suriname, French Guiana, and Jamaica chapters).

Mento: Jamaican musical form similar to the calypso.

Mestizaje: term used to refer to racial mixing in general, and more specifically an Amerindian-European mix.

Mestizo: mixed blood, usually European with Indian.

Miscegenation: racial mixing, through marriage or otherwise.

Mulatto: person of mixed European and African heritage. Term used in the nineteenth century, but it has fallen into disuse in the twentieth, except in the Spanish-speaking Caribbean. In Haiti, or the French-speaking Caribbean, it can refer to a person from the ruling elites, who see themselves as superior to the dark-skinned majorities. In the Dutch- and English-speaking Caribbean, mulatto has similar connotations (see also *Creole*).

Myal: Afro-Jamaican religious practice based on belief in spirit possession; the influence of Christianity on Myal led to Zion and other Afro-Christian religions practiced in Jamaica.

Negritude: cultural-literary movement led by French-speaking African and Caribbean writers that emphasized the centrality of African contributions to Caribbean culture. Culturally, it argued for a return to African roots.

Obeah: often pejorative catch-all term for Afro-Caribbean religious practices that use magic, usually contrasted with the more positive Myal (See note at end of Jamaica chapter).

Orisha: Yoruba religious deities (from Nigeria and Benin) who are also worshipped in Santería, Shango, and Brazilian candomblé. In Trinidad the Orisha religion is a Yoruba-based belief system that also includes elements of Catholicism, Spiritual Baptists, Hinduism, and Jewish mysticism (see also *Shango*).

Palo or Palo-Mayombe: Congo-based Afro-Cuban religion that works intensely with the spirits of the dead (a.k.a. Regla de Palo Monte).

Pan-Africanism: political-cultural movement that proclaims the unity of all African peoples around the globe, and specifically a unity for the defense of the political, economic, and cultural sovereignty of African nations. Pan-Africanism was especially strong during African independence struggles of the fifties, sixties, and seventies, even if it was over a century old.

Plantocracy: arbitrary, undemocratic, and racist rule of the Caribbean planter class, not only during the time of colonization and slavery but after emancipation as well.

Santería (aka Regla de Ocha): Afro-Cuban religion that combines Yoruba (African) cosmology and religion with elements of Catholicism, with saints and orishas being syncretized (see also *Orisha, Winti, Myal, Tchenbwa, Vodou*).

Shango: Afro-Trinidadian religion similar to Santería (see also *Orisha*).

Syncretic, syncretic religion(s): refers to complex interactions between African and European religious-cultural elements. It is not a mere mixture: sometimes the elements are superimposed but separate, at others they may blend together, still at others they seem in conflict. At one point one may dominate over the other. For example, in Santería, we say the orisha Changó is the equivalent of St. Barbara; but at different historical moments, or in diverse social contexts, this syncretism can favor a more Europeanized (St. Barbara) or Africanized (Changó) meaning (see also *Shango, Vodou, Techenbwa, Winti, Myal*).

Taínos: see *Arawak-Taíno*.

Tchenbwa: Afro-Martinican religion that combines African religious beliefs with elements of Christianity and that also uses magic (see also *Santería, Winti, Orisha, Myal, Vodou*).

Transculturation: term that refers to racial, linguistic, culinary, religious, and cultural mixing that combines two or more elements (African, indigenous, European) to create something new: Cuban, Jamaican, Haitian, Trinidadian (see also *Creolization*).

Vodou: West-African–based national religion of Haiti. Believes in loas, or deities, practices magic, and spirit possession. Commonly known as "voodoo" (sic) and erroneously associated with "black" magic and evil spells (see also *Santería, Orisha, Shango, Myal, Tchenbwa, Winti*).

Winti: literally means spirit and is used to describe a magico-religious complex of beliefs practiced by Surinamese Maroons and Afro-Creoles. They believe in spirit possession, making sacrifices, ancestor worship, and herbal healing (see also *Santería, Orisha, Shango, Myal, Tchenbwa, Vodou*).

Suggested Reading

GENERAL WORKS AND HISTORY

Barrow, Christine, and Rhoda Reddock (eds.) (2001). *Caribbean Sociology*: An Introductory Reader. Kingston, Jamaica: Ian Randle Publishers.

Haviser, Jay (ed.) (1999). *African Sites: Archaeology in the Caribbean*. Princeton, NJ: Markus Wiener Publications.

Knight, Franklin (1990). *The Caribbean: Genesis of a Fragmented Nationalism*. New York: Oxford University Press.

Knight, F., and C. Palmer (eds.) (1989). *The Modern Caribbean*. Chapel Hill: University of North Carolina Press.

Mintz, S., and S. Price (eds.) (1985). *Caribbean Contours*, Baltimore: Johns Hopkins University Press.

Rogozinksi, Jan (2000). *A Brief History of the Caribbean*. New York: Plume-Penguin.

Wilson, Samuel A. (ed.) (1997). *The Indigenous People of the Caribbean*. Gainesville: University Press of Florida.

CULTURE (LITERATURE, MUSIC, ART)

Béhague, Gerard (ed.) (1994). *Music and Black Ethnicity: The Caribbean and South America*. New Brunswick, NJ: Transaction Publishers, pp. 17–185 (on Caribbean).

Broughton, S., and M. Elingham (eds.) (2000). *World Music: The Rough Guide*. Vol. 2 *Latin and North America, Caribbean, India, Asia and Pacific*. London: Penguin Books, pp. 289–304 (French Antilles, Zouk), pp. 317–332 (Bahamas, Belize), pp. 386–457 (Cuba, Dominican Republic, Haiti, Jamaica), pp. 481–531 (Puerto Rico, Salsa, Trinidad).

Bulatansky, K.M., and M.A. Sourieau (1998). *Caribbean Creolization: Reflections on the Cultural Dynamics of Language, Literature, and Identity*. Gainesville: University Press of Florida.

Cham, Mbye (ed.) (1992). *Ex-Iles: Essays on Caribbean Cinema*. Trenton, NJ: Africa World Press.

Cudjoe, Selwyn R. (ed.) (1990). *Caribbean Women Writers*. Amherst: Calaloux Press, University of Massachusetts.

Ferracane, Kathleen K. (ed.) (1999). *Caribbean Panorama*. Río Piedras, Puerto Rico: University of Puerto Rico Press. (Anthology of poems, essays, and stories.)

Gravette, Andrew (2000). *Architectural Heritage of the Caribbean: An A–Z of Historic Buildings*. Princeton, NJ: Ian Randle Publishers-Markus Wiener.

Manuel, Peter, and K. Bilby (1995). *Caribbean Currents: Caribbean Music from Rumba to Reggae*. Philadelphia: Temple University Press.

Poupeye, Veerle (1998). *Caribbean Art*. New York: Thames and Hudson.

Price, Sally, and Richard Price (1999). *Maroon Arts: Cultural Vitality in the African Diaspora*. Boston, MA: Beacon Press.

West, Alan (1997). *Tropics of History: Cuba Imagined*. Westport, CT: Greenwood.

Williams, Claudette (2000). *The Politics of Color in Spanish Caribbean Literature*. Gainesville: University Press of Florida.

Wilson-Tagoe, Nana (1998). *Historical Thought and Literary Representation in West Indian Literature*. Gainesville: University Press of Florida.

KEY LITERARY WORKS

Braithwaite, Edward Kamau (1986/1973). *The Arrivants, A New World Trilogy*. Oxford, UK: Oxford University Press.

Brown, Stewart and Wickham, John (eds.) (1999). *The Oxford Book of Caribbean Short Stories*. Oxford, UK: Oxford University Press.

Carpentier, Alejo (1989/1949). *The Kingdom of This World*. New York: Farrar, Straus and Giroux.

Césaire, Aimé (1983). *The Collected Poetry*. Berkeley, CA, University of California Press.

Danticat, Edwidge (1994). *Breath, Eyes, Memory*. New York: Soho Press.

Donnell, Alison and Welsh, Sara Lawson (eds.) (1996). *The Routledge Reader in Caribbean Literature*. New York, Routledge. (Covers English-speaking Caribbean only).

Goodison, Lorna (1992). *Selected Poems*. Ann Arbor: University of Michigan Press.

Guillén, Nicolás (1972). *Man-Making Words: Selected Poems of Nicolás Guillén*. Amherst: University of Massachusetts Press.

Harris, Wilson (1985). *The Guyana Quartet*. London: Faber and Faber.

Hodge, Merle (1981/1970). *Crick Crack Monkey*. London: Heinemann.

James, C.L.R. (1992). *The C.L.R. James Reader*. Edited by Anna Grimshaw. Oxford, UK: Blackwell.

Lamming, George (1979/1953). *In the Castle of My Skin*. London: Longmann Drumbeat.

Lovelace, Earl (1998/1979). *The Dragon Can't Dance*. New York: Persea Books.

Phillips, Caryl (1992). *Cambridge*. New York: Vintage/Random House.

Rowell, Charles H. (ed.) (1998). "Caribbean Literature from Suriname, the Netherlands Antilles, Aruba, and the Netherlands." *Callaloo*, 21, no. 3, (special issue).

Schwarz-Bart, Simone (1982). *The Bridge of Beyond*. Portsmouth, NH: Heinemann.
Walcott, Derek (1986). *Collected Poems, 1948–1984*. New York: Farrar, Straus and Giroux.

AFRO-CARIBBEAN PEOPLES, CULTURES, RACE

Appiah, K.A., and H.L. Gates, (eds.) (1999). *Africana*. New York: Perseus.
Davis, Darién (ed.) (1995). *Slavery and Beyond: The African Impact on Latin America and the Caribbean*. Scholarly Resources.
Fanon, Frantz (1967/1952). *Black Skin, White Masks*. New York: Grove Press.
Lowenthal, D., and L. Comitas (eds.) (1973). *Consequences of Class and Color: West Indian Perspectives*. New York: Anchor/Doubleday.
Moreno Fraginals, Manuel (ed.) (1984). *Africa in Latin America*. New York: Holmes & Meier.
Oostindie, Gert (ed.) (1996). *Ethnicity in the Caribbean*. London: Macmillan.
Stephens, Thomas M. (1999). *Dictionary of Latin American Racial and Ethnic Terminology*. Gainesville: University Press of Florida.
Whitten, N.E., and A. Torres (eds.) (1998). *Blackness in Latin America and the Caribbean*. Vol. 2. Bloomington, IN: Indiana University Press.

SLAVERY, MAROONS, POST-EMANCIPATION

Beckles, Hilary Mc D, (1999). *Centering Woman: Gender Discourses in Caribbean Slave Society*. Princeton, NJ: Ian Randle-Markus Wiener.
Beckles, Hilary Mc D, and Verene Shepherd, (eds.) (2000). *Caribbean Slavery in the Atlantic World*. Princeton, NJ: Ian Randle-Markus Wiener.
Beckles, Hilary Mc D, and Verene Shepherd (eds.) (1993). *Caribbean Freedom: Economy and Society from Emancipation to the Present*. Princeton, NJ: Ian Randle-Markus Wiener.
Morrissey, Marietta (1989). *Slave Women in the New World: Gender Stratification in the Caribbean*. Lawrence, KS: University Press of Kansas.
Price, Richard (ed.) (1973). *Maroon Societies: Rebel Slave Communities in the Americas*. Baltimore: Johns Hopkins University Press.
Thomas, Hugh (1997). *The Slave Trade: The Story of the Atlantic Slave Trade: 1440–1870*. Simon & Schuster.

WOMEN

Barrow, Christine (1996). *Family in the Caribbean: Themes and Perspectives*. Princeton, NJ: Markus Wiener.
López Springfield, Consuelo (ed.) (1997). *Daughters of Caliban: Caribbean Women in the Twentieth Century*. Bloomington, IN: Indiana University Press.
Momsen, Janet (ed.) (1993). *Women and Change in the Caribbean*. Ian Randle Publishers. Bloomington, IN: Indiana University Press.
Navarro, Marysa, and Virginia Sánchez Korrol (1999). *Women in Latin America and the Caribbean*. Bloomington, IN: Indiana University Press. (This book has an excellent bibliography.)

Shepherd, V., B. Brereton, and B. Bailey (eds.) (1995). *Engendering History: Caribbean Women in Historical Perspective*. New York: St. Martin's Press.

RELIGION

Bastide, Roger (1971). *African Civilizations in the New World*. New York: Harper & Row.
Chevannes, Barry (ed.) (1995). *Rastafari and Other African-Caribbean Worldviews*. New Brunswick, NJ: Rutgers University Press.
Fernández Olmos, M., and L. Paravisini-Gebert (eds.) (1997). *Sacred Possessions: Vodou, Santería, Obeah and the Caribbean*. New Brunswick, NJ: Rutgers University Press.
Lampe, Armando (ed.) (2001). *Christianity in the Caribbean: Essays on Church History*. Norman: University of Oklahoma Press.
Simpson, G.E. (1987). *Black Religions in the New World*. New York: Columbia University Press.

POLITICS AND ECONOMICS

Clarke, Colin (ed.) (1991). *Society and Politics in the Caribbean*. New York: St. Martin's Press.
Domínguez, Jorge, Robert Pastor, and R. Delisle Worrell (eds.) (1993). *Democracy in the Caribbean*. Baltimore: Johns Hopkins University Press.
Marshall, Don D. (1998). *Caribbean Political Economy at the Crossroads*. London: Macmillan.
Payne, A., and Sutton, P. (eds.) (1993). *Modern Caribbean Politics*. Baltimore: Johns Hopkins University Press.
Ramos, A.G. and A.I. Rivera (eds.) (2001). *Islands at the Crossroads: Politics in the Non-Independent Caribbean*. Princeton, NJ: Ian Randle-Markus Wiener.
Ramsaran, Ramesh (ed.) (2001). *The Global Challenge: Survival Options for the Caribbean States*. Princeton, NJ: Ian Randle-Markus Wiener.
Watson, Hilbourne (ed.) (1994). *The Caribbean in the Global Political Economy*. Lynne Riener. CO: Boulder.

DEFINING THE CARIBBEAN: IDEAS AND THOUGHT

Benítez-Rojo, Antonio (1996). *The Repeating Island*. 2nd ed. Durham, NC: Duke University Press.
Coombs, Orde (ed.) (1974). *Is Massa Day Dead? Black Moods in the Caribbean*. New York: Doubleday.
Glissant, Edouard (1989). *Caribbean Discourse*. Charlottesville: University Press of Virginia.
Harris, Wilson (1995/1970). *History, Fable and Myth in the Caribbean and Guianas*. Wellesley, MA: Calaloux Publications.
Henry, Paget (2000). *Caliban's Reason: Introducing Afro-Caribbean Philosophy*. New York: Routledge.

Lewis, Gordon K. (1983). *Main Currents in Caribbean Thought: The Historical Evolution of Caribbean Society in Its Ideological Aspects, 1492–1900*. Baltimore: Johns Hopkins University Press.

Meeks, Brian and Folke Lindahl (eds.) (2001). *New Caribbean Thought*. Norman: University of Oklahoma Press.

Ortiz, Fernando (1995/1940). *Cuban Counterpoint: Tobacco and Sugar*. Chapel Hill, NC: Duke University Press.

TOURISM

Kempadoo, Kamala and Cynthia Mellon (eds.) (1998). *The Sex Trade in the Caribbean*. Boulder, University of Colorado/CAFRA/ILSA.

Pattullo, Polly (1996). *Last Resorts: The Cost of Tourism in the Caribbean*. Kingston, Jamaica, Ian Randle Publishers.

Taylor, Frank Fonda (1993). *To Hell with Paradise, A History of the Jamaican Tourist Industry*. Pittsburgh, PA: University of Pittsburgh Press.

IMMIGRATION

Foner, Nancy (ed.) (2001). *Islands in the City, West Indian Migration to New York*. Berkeley: University of California Press.

Georges, Eugenia (1990). *The Making of a Transnational Community: Migration, Development, and Cultural change in the Dominican Republic*. New York: Columbia University Press.

Grenier, Guillermo J. and Alex Stepick III (eds.) (1992). *Miami Now! Immigration, Ethnicity, and Social Change*. Gainesville: University of Florida Press. (On Cubans, Haitians, West Indians).

Herrera, María Cristina (1994). *Havana, USA, Cuban Exiles and Cuban Americans in South Florida, 1959–1994*. Berkeley: University of California Press.

Laguerre, Michel S. (1998). *Diasporic Citizenship, Haitian Americans in Transnational America*. New York: St. Martin's Press.

Torre, Carlos, Hugo Rodríguez Vecchini, and William Burgos (eds.) (1994). *The Commuter Nation: Perspectives on Puerto Rican Migration*. Río Piedras, Puerto Rico: Editorial de la Universidad de Puerto Rico.

Waters, Mary C. (1999). *Black Identities, West Indian Immigrant Dreams and American Realities*. Cambridge, MA: Harvard University Press.

USEFUL WEBSITES ON THE CARIBBEAN

General Caribbean (select Caribbean or regional resources; has many links to other web sites, including online newspapers, magazines, and journals)
http://lanic.utexas.edu/
Caribbean Studies Association (has many links to other sites)
http://www.caribscholars.org/default.html
http://www.unl.ac.uk/sals/carib/online.shtml

The Virtual Institute of Caribbean Studies (many links to other sites)
http://pw1.netcom.com/~hhenke/
Caribbean News
http://www.cananews.com/
Maroons
http://www.si.edu/maroon/educational_guide/10.htm
Caribbean Literature
http://www.scholars.nus.edu.sg/landow/post/caribbean/caribov.html
Vodou
http://www.amnh.org/exhibitions/vodou/learn.html
Reggae Website (has many links)
http://www.ireggae.com/reggae.htm
Afro-Cuban Web Site
http://www.afrocubaweb.com/
Cuban Music (discography from 1925 to 1960)
http://gislab.fiu.edu/SMC/discography.htm
Caribbean Sports (Cricket)
http://www.cricket.org/link_to_database/NATIONAL/WI/

Index

About the Editor and Contributors

TOMÁS FERNÁNDEZ ROBAINA was born in Havana, Cuba, in 1942. He works in the José Martí National Library in Havana. Fernández has written *Los negros en Cuba: 1902–1958* (Blacks in Cuba: 1902–1958; forthcoming in English) and *Bibliografía de temas afrocubanos* (1985). He was recently a Visiting Scholar at the Arthur Schomburg Center in New York. He has lectured widely on Afro-Cuban themes in the United States and Latin America.

ANNE M. FRANÇOIS, a native of Haiti, moved to the United States in the early eighties. She is a Ph.D. candidate in Francophone literature at New York University. Her studies have focused primarily on women writers from the French-speaking Antilles. She is currently teaching French and Francophone literature at Eastern University. She published a translated short story in *Calabash: A Journal of Caribbean Arts and Letters* (2000). A 1999 interview with the Guadeloupean writer Maryse Condé is forthcoming.

RAMONA HERNÁNDEZ, born in the Dominican Republic, is a sociologist who has taught at La Guardia Community College and the University of Massachusetts-Boston. Currently she is the Director of the CUNY Dominican Studies Institute. Hernández has published *Dominican New Yorkers: A Socioeconomic Profile* (1995) and co-authored *Dominican-Americans* (1998).

NANCY LÓPEZ is a sociologist born in the Dominican Republic who taught at the University of Massachusetts-Boston and is currently a professor at the University of New Mexico. Her research is focused on race/ethnicity, gender, and

Latino/Dominican community studies. She has published in many journals such as *Race, Ethnicity, and Education* (2002), *The Latino Studies Journal* (1998), and the CUNY Dominican Studies Institute Monograph Series (1997). López co-produced a documentary in Spanish called "Nobody Lives from Welfare: Dominican Women in New York" (1997). She has a forthcoming book, *Race(ing) the Gender Gap: Education and Second-Generation Dominicans, West Indians, and Haitians in New York City.*

MICKAËLLA L. PÈRINA was born in Martinique and is a research associate at the W.E.B. Du Bois Institute for Afro-American Research at Harvard University. She is the author of a book and several articles on the construction of political identity and political membership in the French-speaking Caribbean, including *Citoyenneté et sujetion aux Antilles francophones, post-esclavage et aspiration démocratique* (1997) and "From Slavery to Citizenship: The 'Origins' of a French Caribbean Modern Democracy?" (32nd Annual Conference, Association of Caribbean Historians, 2000). Currently, her research focuses on French Caribbean political identity and cultural creolization.

D. GAIL SAUNDERS is at present Director, Department of Archives, the Bahamas. She has co-authored and authored a number of books, including *Islanders in the Stream*, Vol. 1 (1992), Vol. 2 (1998), with Michael Craton; *Nassau Historical Landmarks* (2000), with Linda Huber; *Slavery in the Bahamas* (1985), and *Bahamian Society after Emancipation* (1993). She is the editor of the *Journal of The Bahamas Historical Society.*

JESSICA SUÁREZ received her Master's Degree in History from Northeastern University in Boston, Massachusetts.

PEDRO L.V. WELCH is assistant registrar at the University of the West Indies in Cave Hill, Barbados. He was a 1984 Commonwealth Fellow and a 1992 Johns Hopkins Fellow. He has written and published on the urban context of slavery, Sephardic Jews, and the role of free colored women in slave societies. He recently published *"Red" and Black Over White: Free Coloured Women in Pre-Emancipation Barbados* (2000) with Richard A. Goodridge.

ALAN WEST-DURÁN was born in Havana, Cuba, and raised in Puerto Rico. He is the author of two books of poems, *Dar nombres a la lluvia/Finding Voices in the Rain*, which won the Latino Literature Prize for Poetry (1996), and *El tejido de Asterión o las máscaras del logos* (2000). His books of essays, *Tropics of History: Cuba Imagined*, appeared in 1997 (Greenwood), and he co-edited the first scholarly CD-ROM on Caribbean literature: *Literature of the Spanish Caribbean to 1900* (1998), with Antonio Benítez-Rojo, which also includes his translation of the novel *Francisco*. He was a contributor to *Africana: The Ency-*

clopedia of the African and African American Experience (1999) and has translated many Caribbean authors: Alejo Carpentier, Rosario Ferré, Luis Rafael Sánchez, Nancy Morejón, and Dulce María Loynaz. West-Durán has published many articles on Caribbean and Latin American music, art, and literature. He is an Assistant Professor of Modern Languages at Northeastern University.